INDUSTRIAL MANAGEMENT AND ORGANISATIONAL BEHAVIOUR

Prof. K.K. Ahuja

B.Sc., B.E. (Hons.) (Mech.)
P.G.D.M.M., P.G.D.P.M.,
M.B.A., M.I.E., D.L.L.,
Course in Advance Personnel Management (Oxford) U.K.

KHANNA PUBLISHERS

Operational Office
4575/15, Onkar House, Ground Floor,
Darya Ganj, New Delhi 110 002
Phones : 011-23243042, 011-23243043 & Mob. 09811541460
email : contactus@khannapublishers.in

Published by :

Romesh Chander Khanna & Vineet Khanna
for **KHANNA PUBLISHERS**
2-B, Nath Market, Nai Sarak
Delhi- 110 006 (India)

Website : www.khannapublishers.in

Hologram & Description

To all readers of our books, from yourself if being defrauded by pirates to prevent, please make sure that there is an Hologram on the cover of our books with the below specifications. If you find any book without Hologram and Description, please mail us at **contactus@khannapublishers.in**

Thanking you

ISBN No. 978-81-7409-095-9

First Edition : 1998
Seventh Edition :
Fourth Reprint : 2012

***Price :* ₹ 399.00**

Preface

We are in the era of mind boggling change and cultural shock. Just when we thought the world's mightiest corporate giant in information technology "Microsoft" has lost the touch, the company has come back with a plan than dwarfs all that it has done so far. It now wants to dominate the net economy by creating what would in fact be an operating system for the web. There is nothing that escapes the broad sweep of leading corporates of their vision.

The changes in the corporate world are so fast that even Microsoft's dominance in the digital economy has been threatened by a range of developments—the rise of net.

Even in the brick and mortar companies, the scenario is not different. The FMCG giant, Hindustan Lever Ltd. (HLL) who already markets 75 percent of the items on your dry grocery list, in order to get larger share are going to deliver the product, at your home.

It is now the time to explore the new service profit chain, quite simply, the existing 40 year old industrial model for delivering customer service no longer works. Worse it contains a built-in cycle of failure that punishes customers, employees and share holders. In fact pressures are mounting, Competition for customer loyality is coming not just from regular competitors, but from e-business start ups. New productivity and services are being developed at a staggering pace. While manufacturing processes can often be duplicated, consumer's knowledge feelings and experiences with a brand often can not be. How do you build brand loyalty when the competition is only a mouse click away. Only the strong will survive. The brands are becoming more important than ever before, as consumers, faced with information overload, struggle to make purchasing.

In the light of the above, the managers everywhere have come to believe that they cannot increase productivity through technology and capital investment, or forcing to work longer hours or making its members slaves of their machines but can do so by motivating, creating teams and providing leadership.

One can achieve productivity by conserving and using to the fullest extent, the human resources by training and developing the existing employees and introducing effective promotion and transfer of existing employees. There is also a need for effectively organising the structure of functional relationship in such a way that each function can utilise its capability and produce its best work.

The book "*Industrial Management and Organisational Behaviour*" deals with human aspects of management as well as various other aspects of scientific management. The significance and importance of scientific management is being increasingly felt because of the over-growing industrial and social activities. There are no two opinions about it that unless these activities are systematically and timely organised and rationally managed, the modern society is going to face complexities and complications.

Industrial Engineering is an aspect of industrial management. Industrial engineering has permeated into virtually every walk of life. The usefulness of Industrial Management for the industrial health cannot be over-emphasised. Industrial engineering is concentrated mainly with the design improvement, installation of integrated system of Men, Materials and Equipments. It covers principles of work study, network techniques, optimisation, operational research, quality control, resources balancing, maintenance techniques and applications of computer.

The concepts, theories and analytical tools which comprise this book, are selected for the usefulness to the future executives. This book is certainly not intended to be the only way that industrial management and knowledge can be classified rather it is designed to help the students and executives by integrating the various systematic and scientific concepts of industrial management. I am sure that book is going to present a comprehensive guide to practising managers and students alike to help them in the management of industrial and human resources.

The book Industrial Management is divided into various areas of management grouped subjectwise *viz.* Nature and Principles of Management, Human Resource Management, Production Management, Industrial Engineering, Materials Management, Industrial Relations, Labour Laws, Operations Research, Marketing Management, Total Quality Management and Industrial Psychology.

The objective of the book is to help its readers by providing an insight into the concepts of various management functions, and for better diagnosis of the problems facilitating effective decision making.

The book will help in appreciation and understanding of some of the new techniques available for executives and students alike in the area of production, Industrial Management and other functional areas of the Management.

The book deals with the Human Resource Management, Manpower Development, PERT and CPM, Quality Control, Make and Buy Decisions, Plant Location, Plant Layout, Inventory Control and Break-even analysis, Linear Programming, Stores and Purchase Management, Orgnisation Structure, Computer and its application and other important aspects of industrial engineering, such as work study, Maintenance Management, Human engineering, Management Information System, Communication, Decision making, Motivation and Productivity etc. This is a comprehensive book, which will be of immense use to the students appearing for MBA, IIIE, Chartered Accountants, ICWA, Final Year Students of Elect./Mechanical/Aeronautical/ Electronics, Production Management and Industrial Engineering. The book has been written out of many years of experience as a student, teacher and Professional Manager of an industry. I am sure that the book will be able to meet the requirements of students, faculty members and the young executives. The book will act as a stimulus to their thinking process. I shall be happy to receive suggestions for the improvement of the book from my readers.

—Author.

About the Book

The book covers the following subject comprehensively :

- Nature and Principles of Management
- Human Resource Management
- Industrial Psychology
- Materials Management and Materials Handling
- Production Management
- Linear Programming and Operations Research
- Marketing Management
- Total Quality Management
- Industrial Relations and Social Welfare
- Some Important Areas of Management
  - Stress Management
  - Competitiveness of an Enterprise
  - Skills for success
  - Business Strategy and Strategic Thinking
  - Application of Transactional Analysis

Contents

About the Author

K.K. Ahuja

K.K. Ahuja is an established HRD professional in the industry who has carved a niche for himself in the area of Training and Development. He has addressed various training sessions for the senior executive of private sector, public sector and also keeps in touch with the young organisation of MBAs by sharing his ideas and thoughts with them. He has presented papers on Self Development and Assessment Centre in the International ARTDO conference.

He is presently the Executive Director at Gujarat Heavy Chemicals Ltd., Head of the Human Resources Department. He is innovative and experimental in nature and has used progressive techniques like Competency profiling, Self Development, Psychological Profiling and Assessment Centre Technology to develop the executives. Though difficult to codify and still harder to implement, he successfully implemented the concept of 'pay for performance' in GHCL.

Apart from his official duties, Ahuja has a passion for creative writing which is evident in his books on Management and HRD. He is a pacific writer and has written books on HRM, Orgnisation Behaviour, Industrial Relations and Training and Development.

K.K. Ahuja is a science graduate, Engineering from REC Nagpur, MBA fromFMS, Delhi University, and MS in PM and IR from Oxford university, U.K. Always firing on all his cylinder, he abounds in limitless energy and is a name to reckon with in the field of HRD.

Current Assignments
- Executive Director—HR, Gujarat Heavy Chemicals Limited
- Director, Dalmia Brothers, Pvt. Limited
- Director, Dalmia Power Limited.

Previous Assignments
- Sr. General Manager—HRD, Usha International
- General Manager—Personnel, Indian Drugs & Pharmaceuticals
- Professor, Delhi College of Engineering
- Management Trainee, Rallis India Limited.

Education
- B.Sc. Delhi University
- B.E. (Mechanical), REC Nagpur
- PG Diploma PM & PR, Faculty of Management Studies, Delhi University
- MBA, Faculty of Management Studies, Delhi University
- MS in PM & IR, Templeton College, Oxford University, London
- Diploma in Labour Law, Indian Institute of Law

Books Published on
- Managerial Excellence
- Human Resource Management
- Principles of Management
- Organisation Behaviour
- Training and Management Development
- Industrial Management and IR

Area of Interest
- Conducting Training Need Analysis
- Competency Profiling
- Designing Assessment Centers
- Designing and Conducting Training Programmes

- Designing and Using Psychological tools for the objective assessment of the managerial capabilities of individuals.
- Building Conducive Industrial Relation Climate
- Creating Learning Organisations.

Guest Faculty

- Indian Institute of Technology, Delhi
- FORE School of Management, Delhi
- Advisory Board Member—Lal Bahadur Shastri Institute of Management, Delhi
- Gurukul Kangri Vishwavidyalaya, Hardwar
- Graduate School of Business and Administration, Ghaziabad, UP.

Paper Presentation

- Performance Review, Institute of Chartered Accountants, Delhi, March '99
- Organisation Core Competencies *Vs* Person's Competency Profiling, 26th ARTDO Conference, Bali Indonasia, August '99
- Assessment Centre Technology—GHCL Experience, 27th ARTO Conference, Penang, Malaysia, September 2000.

Faculty Lecture

- Speaker — Symposium on HR Management—Nirma Institute of Management, November '98
- Speaker — Managerial Excellence in the 2000 Millennium, Top Rankers Management Consultants, July '99.
- Speaker — HRM Practices in Indian Industry—Contemporary Issues, Lal Bahadur Shastri Institute of Management, July '99
- Speaker — Changing Role of Employers' Organisations, FICCI, Sept. '99
- Chief Guest — National Seminar on 21st century Manager and Global Business Environment, Gurukul Kangri University, Hardwar, March '2000
- Speaker — Assessment Centre Technology, FORE School of Management, April '2000
- Speaker — Management Education and Corporate Expectations in India, Lal Bahadur Shastri Institute of Management August '2000
- Speaker — Organisation Cultural Transformation through effective leadership, Top Rankers Management Consultants, Sept. '2000

1

Evolution of Management

WORK OF LEADING MANAGEMENT SCIENTISTS

The principles of management can be traced back many centuries but there had been no continuous historical development of management theories over all these years. An attempt to study some of the contributions made in management thoughts has been discussed in this chapter.

Henry L. Gantt (1866 - 1919)

Taylor ideas were further strengthened and developed by Gantt and Gilbreth. Among the chief contributors of Gantt are :

(*i*) **Graphic Chart.** It helps in showing daily progress of production and thus facilitating production planning and control.

(*ii*) **Emphasis on the human element.** It emphasises the respect for human nature and the development of latent potential of workers. Its amounts to directing their development instead of driving them.

(*iii*) **Industrial democracy.** It amounts the organisation of industry in such a way that each individual has an equal opportunity to function at his highest capacity.

(*iv*) **Social responsibilities.** It emphasises that the business system must accept its social responsibility and devote itself primarily to service. Gantt also brought out that the resultant responsibility of management is to teach and train workers to become more skilled, for better work habbits and more dependability.

The Neo-classical theory. The theory emphasis human relations movement. Mary Parker deals with the human factor. Elton Mayo and Roeth's Berges pioneered the human relations movement. In this new ear they proceeded on the frame work of the classical thinkers but introduced many new elements, specially in the area of leadership, group psychology, human relations and organisational integration. The Neo-classical theory anticipated some of the recent trends as evident in the behavioural approaches.

Mary Parker Follett (1808 - 1933)

Marry area of contribution has been the psychological foundations of all human activity and the emotional reactions in the working of human groups. She contended that none can become a ful person unless he cecomes a member of a group. Follett major areas of contribution are :

(*i*) **Removal of conflicts.** There areas of removing conflicts are *viz.* Domination ; Compromise and Integration. It has been observed that integration as the best alternative of meeting the real needs of both the parties.

(*ii*) Partcipation of workers

(*iii*) Group--They regarded group more than a mere collection of individuals.

(*iv*) Leadership

(*v*) The law of situation

(*vi*) Management as a profession

(*vii*) Co-ordination

(*viii*) Authority.

Follett evolved ideas and theories which have stood the test of time and change which are stimulating the thinking of managers. According to Follett "Men can discover his true nature can reach greater heights, can relase his own creative powers, gains his true freedom only through powers of the group.

F.W. Taylor's Principles of Scientific Management (1880--1930)

Management has always faced with the problem of selecting various concepts from all these areas and integrating them in the process of decisions making regarding the major policies and day to day operations. During the 19th century, the efforts of managers had been to cope up with their environments and to organise and operate in those environments. During the first one third of the century the attempt was to rationalise the way work was done. The emphasis was to increase the productivity of the goods and services produced. After the World War II there was a considerable change in the working conditions of the working men. The working men began to demand that work environment should meet part of their socisa needs in addition to the basic needs. Then emerged the phael of human relations and the focus was on man's social needs the way of meeting them to increase productivity. But in late 1960's it became clear that knowledge on which the management is based is no longer adequate even for the basic areas there emerged needs for new knowledge particularly referred to productivity organisation structure, job design and management of people

Concepts of Management

Following are the nine important concepts high lighting the present concepts of management :

(*i*) Scientific management a key to productivitiy.

(*ii*) Decentralisation for quicker decisions and better control.

(*iii*) Personnel Management as a means of selecting people into organsation.

(*iv*) Manager's development programmes to train managers how to meet the needs of tomorrow.

(*v*) Management accounting--a foundation for managerial decision.

(*vi*) Marketing.

(*vii*) Long range planning.

(*viii*) Role of operational research in management decision making.

(*ix*) Financial Management for effective utilisation of money resources in the organisation.

Development of Management Science

Thus the process of development of management science can be studied under four heads.

(*a*) Taylor Scientific approach to management.

(*b*) Henry Fayol's human relations approach.

(*c*) Modern human relations approach.

(*d*) Behavioural science approach.

Fredric Taylor was a pioneer who propounded scientific principles of management as the result of his keen research in different areas of industrial activity. Before scientific management workers were completely dominated by their superiors and the relationship was based on social caste and autocracy. This was a stage when everything was determined on the basis of authority. This period came to an end when French Revolution gave the cry for fraternity, liberty and equality. In scientific management we take into account as may variables as possible and try to co-relate in rational manner.

Fredic Taylor was born in 1856 in a well to do family of Philadelphia although not a brilliant student, but had the quality of seriousness of purpose and hard work. At the Phillips Academy, he paid the price of serious impairment of vision because of too much study in kerosene light and was advised by doctors not to do anything involving close study. In 1874 he began as apprentice pattern making in a small workshop in Philadelphia. Attracted by the reputation of Midvale Steel he applied for a job in Midvale Steel Company. This job was for an ordinary labourer. Within a period of eight years he progressed through the stages of ordinary labourer to time keeper, machinist, gang boss, foreman, assistant engineer to chief engineer of the works. He completed his technical qualifications by taking a Master's degree in engineering at the Stevens Institute through evening study. Taylor not only had original ideas in the field of management but he had acquired a technical excellence in the field of engineering which itself would have brought him an enduring place in the history of engineering. Taylor left the Bethlehem Steel Company in 1901 and devoted the rest of his life to spread an understanding of his fundamental ideas.

Scientific Management is not any efficiency device, not a new scheme of paying men. It is not holding a stop watch on a man and writing things down about him, it is not time and motion study nor an analysis of the movements of men. In its essence, scientific management involves a complete mental revolution on the part of the work man engaged in any particular setablishment. It involves an equally complete mental revolution on the part of those on the management's side. This new technique of managing involved following two major elements *viz:* 1. Discovery by experiment the best way of performing and the proper time for every operation and every component unit of an operation in the light of the best material, tool, machine manipulation of tool or machine. 2. The division of labour as between management and workers. The great gains in productivity accurring from this technique of management came not from greater exertion on the part of workers but from elimination of wastages of worker's time, machine time through delays of misapplied efforts, failure in coordination of quantities and so forth etc.

Taylor was thoughtful and systematic in his approach and he advocated the replacement of rules of thumb with more carefully thoughtful guide-lines to action. The collection of data to-support decisions rather than reliance on casual judgements. Taylor had the following specific principles :

(*a*) The elimination of waste effort.

(*b*) Emphasis on fitting workers to particular tasks.

(*c*) Greater care in training workers to the specific requirements of their jobs.

(*d*) Greater specialization of work activities.

(*e*) The establishment of standards for performance.

Improvement of Various Operations

Managers can always improve various operations by a simple reflection in the way in which the work is being done and there is always a room for improvement. In association with Carl Barth, who was a better mathematician, Taylor developed a slide rule on which any foreman could calculate various variables for any job. It was apparent that many of the delays and interruptions in work were the consequences of faulty planning. *The main aim of scientific management was to maximise the production and efficiency of each worker and to design a system which would maximise the carrying of workers and employers.* The scientific management do not take into account the informal relationship existing in the organisation which have its own structure. This concept gave birth to **Human Relation Approach (1930--1950)**

Taylor advocated a philosophy of management under which management would undertake the basic resposibility of planning and control and prescribe the rules laws and formulas to gudie the actual operations by man and machines, so as to help employer to produce at lower costs giving more remuneration to workers. Taylor contended that workers should not be left to choose their own method of producing, and developing their skills on and their own. Management should evolve laws of standard work and rules for work measurement. Standardisation, Simplification, Time and Motion studies, functional Foremanship, Production Planning and Control, piece-Wage System of Payment on differential basis, were the main ideas enunciated by Taylor.

Criticism

Taylor's concept of Management attracted following criticism.

1. Taylor's emphasis on extreme specialisation is considered unrealistic. His advocacy of first class men with developed skills raised an expectation that each worker should be an extraordinarily talented. The standards of efficiency evolved as result of time and motion studies etc. were conceived to too high, beyond the calibre and capacity of an average workers.
2. Taylor ignored human elements. He thought man as a cog in the wheel. His emphasis on efficiency at all costs turned the workers into mere machine.
3. In Taylorism the workers are speeded up without fundamental improvements in factory layout, production methods, tool-design, training etc.
4. Worker's wages would not be increased in direct proportion to the additional productivity exhibited by the workers.

Gilbreths. Frank Gilbreth and his wife Lillian Gilbreth made memorable contribution to improvement of working methods. He contended that it would be essential to find out the best way to perform a particular job with marked efficiency and least exertion. He developed a unique technique of speed work. Speed-work however, did not refer to hurrying with the work but economising the time-sequence by eliminating unnecessary time-sequence and exhausting motions and methods of doing a work.

Best Method

The best method is that which implies least motions. Worker should not waste his energy and effort in moving his body unnecessarily. He advocated rythm in work with balanced movement of concerned members of the body while at job. His work analysis indicated 17 basic elements in working on any job. These elements were termed as 'therbligs'. To improve operational efficiency workers should be guided to develop balanced rhythmic motions. Gilbreth also introduced the use of micromotion study. In such studies, the operations were recorded on a film alongwith time values ascertained from a clock set up within the camera's focus. By this method he could analyse minute subdivisions of manufacturing activity. The present concept of scientific management is that the old methods are ineffective in giving proper direction or the utilisation of material and human resources for productive ends. Hence a new set of ideas are needed for orderly organisation of complex industrial activities.

Sequence of Scientific Method

Scientific method is comprised of following sequences :

(*i*) Identifying the problem and objectives.

(*ii*) Defining the objective and problems.

(*iii*) Collection of data on the problem and the objectives.

(*iv*) Analysis and interpretation of the data.

(*v*) Consideration of alternatives.

(*vi*) Formulate tentative conclusions about tackling the problem.

(*vii*) Taking up selected action on the basis of conclusion and testing the results.

(*viii*) Reviewing and evaluating the results and introducing any corrective action if necessary.

(*ix*) Framing 'laws and models' to serve as a guide to planning and execution.

Scientific management has been viewed as a systematic approach to conduct the enterprise on the basis of observation experimentation, rational conclusions or decisions rather than depanding on conventional methods based on trial and error.

Henry Fayol. A French industrialist, developed a general theory of management in all aspects of business of an undertaking. Fayol identified the following functions of management:

(*a*) Planning policies ; programmes and procedures.

(*b*) Organisation based on hierchy of authority.

(*c*) Commanding means directing the business in order to gain optimum return from all workers.

(*d*) Co-ordination, signifying harmony in activities of the organization and to facilitate its working.

(*e*) Control, meant to rectify the errors of the functionaries of organisation and to ensure that such errors do dot reoccur.

Six Catagories of Work

Fayol divided all the work carried out in business enterprises into six categories :

1. Technical activities (production, manufactures etc.).
2. Commercial activities (buying, selling, personnel and industrial relation).
3. Financial activities. (To have optimum use of capital).
4. Security Activities (Protection of property and persons).
5. Managerial activities (Planning, organising commanding directing co-ordination control, communication motivation and leadership).

According to Fayal the managerial activities consisted of drawing a plan of action, building up a dual structure-material and human to organise activities, unifying all activities and efforts through co-ordination and ensuring conformity of work to establish rules and express command.

Principles of Management

Fayol also laid down the following priciples of general management.

1. Division of labour
2. Authority and responsibility
3. Discipline
4. Unity of command
5. Unity of management
6. Subordination of industrial interest to the common good
7. Remuneration
8. Centralisation
9. Hierarchy
10. Order of team members.
11. Justice
12. Stability of tenure
13. Initiative
14. Sense of union.

1. **Division of Labour.** It is a law of nature. That is each man can develop special skills. The purpose of division of labour is to attain more and better returns from the same amount of effort.

2. **Authority and Responsibility.** Authority is the power to give orders and except obedience. It is derived from one's personal qualities such as intelligence, knowledge, moral attitudes, skills, and leadership and calls for both statutory and personal authority. Responsibility is inseparable from authority. It follows whenever authority is exercised, the man with authority carries responsibility for his decisions and actions.

3. **Discipline.** The agreement between an enterprise and its employees calls for obedience, deligence, energy, co-operative attitudes.

4. **Unity of Command.** Authority to give instructions to an employee must be limited to one man. If this rule is broken, authority will be weakened. An employee must know whom to give instructions, and he must not be confused by having to follow the instructions of several people who have authority.

5. **Unity of Management.** There should be only one plan and one manager directing all operations.

6. **Subordination to Industrial Interests to the Common Good.** In any undertaking the interests of single member, or of some of the members of the team, must not take precedence over the interests of the enterprise as a whole.

7. **Remuneration of the Team Members.** Fair rewards for work done must be offered to all members of the organisation.

8. **Centralisation.** Like division of labour, centralisation is one of the natural principle of organisation. In all organisations it is present to some degree. The question is : To what extent in a given enterprise will it be most advantageously adopted ?

9. **Hierarchy.** The line of command extends downward in order of rank from the top of the organisation through all levels of authority to the lowest employee. It is the channel throughwhich all official communications travel.

10. **Order.** Order in an organisation calls for "A place for everyone and everyone in his place". When the order of persons is clearly well established the function may be easily identified in relation to the whole.

11. **Justice (Equity).** The employees will put all their devotion and good intentions to work for the common effect if they are treated with friendliness and justice.

12. **Stability of tenure.** An organisation need employees who will stay with it. Such employees help the organisation to achieve stability.

13. **Initiative.** Providing opportunity to subordinates to exercise their initiative which gives them, satisfaction.

14. **Sense of Union (Espirit de corps).** Harmony and unity in the enterprise are source of strength. That is why modern management tries to bring the individual members of an organisation to work themselves as a team.

2

Management Science
Thoughts of Various Management School

Contribution of Management Authors

The contribution of various management authors to the principles of good organisation can be recognised as follows :

(*i*) The number of organisation units should be the minimum needed to cover the major enterprise functions.

(*ii*) All related functions should be combined within one unit.

(*iii*) The number of levels of authority should be kept to a minimum.

(*iv*) There should be room for initiative with the limit of his assigned authority.

(*v*) Functions should be assigned so as to minimise cross relations between organisational units.

(*vi*) No more employees should report to a superior than he can effectively direct and co-ordinate.

Robert Owen

Robert Owen was a scientific manager of his time and was greatly admired for giving human treatment to the workers. He worked throughout his life for building up of a spirit of co-operation between the workers and the management. He is noted for the development of--Personnel relations ; improved conditions of employment ; reform of working conditions.

Charles Babbage

Charles Babbage, the Cambridge professor of mathematics propounded that methods of science and mathematics could be applied to the operation of factories. He advocated that managers should take decisions through rigid investigation ; to divide work into physical and mental efforts ; to determine the cost for every process and to pay a bonus to the workers in proportion to their efficiency. His contributions of significance are :

(*i*) Cost accounting ;

(*ii*) The Babbage calculating machine and ;

(*iii*) His attempts to show the various disciplines as inter-related.

Max Webber

He provided the classical theory of organisation and management. He felt the bureaucracy was the most efficient form for complex organisation. His areas of emphasis are : (*i*) hierarchy of authority, (*ii*) a system of rules (*iii*) division of colour (*iv*) impersonality of relationship, (*v*) a system of work procedure and (*vi*) legal authority and power.

Elton Mayo (1880--1949)

A Harvard Sociologist and director of Hawthorne studies offered evidence that an organisation is not only a formal arrangement of men and functions, but also a social system which can be operated successfully only with the application of the principle of psychology and other behavioural sciences. Elton Mayo, recognised for the first time the importance of new aspect of the problems of industrial civilisation and this new aspect related to the complexity of the work situation. Mayo's initial interests were in fatigue, accident's and labour turnover. Mayo was the first to emphasise the understanding and realisation of the human factor in organisation. He calculated that of all the factors influencing employee behaviour the most powerful were these emanating from the workers' participation in social groups.

Chester I Barnard (1886--1961)

Barnard was a sociologist by choice had wide experience as President of New Jersey Bell Telephone Company and as Rockefeller Foundation. His major contribution was how to develop co-operation among individuals through the formal organisation. The formal organisation is a system of consciously co-ordinated activities or forces of two or more persons. Barnard defined that there are three universals in each system. (*i*) Willingness to co-operate (*ii*) common purpose and (*iii*) Communication. In a system there are non logical elements influencing the behaviour of the members of organisation. These elements constitute the informal organisation. Such organisation is the aggregate of the personnel contacts and interactions which are neither a part of nor government by, the formal organisation. But still informal organisations are indispensable is formal organisation. Bernard also highlighted the functions of the executive as : (*i*) providing a system of communication (*ii*) securing efforts (*iii*) formulating and defining purpose. His other areas of contribution are delegation of authority and decision making process.

Behavioral Science Approach

New thinking in Behavioral science started with the development of need hierarchy by Abraham Maslow followed by the workers of Fredric Herzberg, Douglas, Mc-Gregor ; Renis Likert ; Chris Argyris ; Oliver Sheldon Kurt Lewin ; Alvin Brown ; Henry Dennison ; Mooney and Reiley Lyndall ; Urwick ; R.M. Barnes ; Drucker, Breach and Lupton.

The essence of behavioral approach is the integration between he needs of employees and the goals of the organisation. Behavioral Science Movement is regarded as a further reinforcement of human relations movement. It covers much wider aspects in inter-personal roles and relationship. Some of the important aspects of behavioral since approach are :

- Employee motivation
- Leadership
- Employee development
- Organisation as a social system
- Communication

F. Herzberg

Herzberg maintained that the working conditions should at least be kept at satisfactory level for preventing dissatisfiers and satisfiers must be introduced with the work itself for obtaining a high level of performance.

Kurt Lewin

He is described as the further of Group Dynamics Kurt developed the field theory of organisation, the core idea of this theory is that the behaviour of a man is a function of the person and his field or environment--Lewin and his associates demonstrated through experiments that authoritarian leadership impairs initiative and breeds hostility while the democratic style is more effective in building morale and promoting active participation.

Rennis Likert

Likert conducted an extensive research at Institute of Social Science Michigan U.S.A. and based on the findings of research work the advocated four styles of management *viz.* : Exploitative ; Authoritative ; Benovelent Authoritative ; Consultative and Participative. Likert advocated participative style of leadership. He maintained that the use of supportive relationships; group decision making and high performance goals are must for achieving higher productivity. Likert put forward the supportive style of leadership as the new pattern of management. He concluded during the research that there are two distinct leadership orientations :

(*i*) Orientation towards employees with emphasis on interpersonal relations on the job.

(*ii*) Orientation towards production with emphasis on technical aspects of the job.

He concluded that employee orientation coupled with general rather than close supervision lead to higher productivity greater group cohesiveness, better morale, less auxiety and lower turn-over of employees.

Douglas McGregor (1906--1964)

McGregor is the father of Theory. He challenged the classical theory of management which he termed Theory X. Mc Gregor put forth theory Y as a modest beginning for a new theory with respect to the management of human resources. McGregor thesis is that the average employee has a high degree of imagination ; ingenuity and creativity and under conducive atmosphere the individual seek responsibility and if committed to objectives he will exercise self direction and self control. He advocated the task of management to be of creating opportunities ; encouraging growth ; removing obstacles ; providing guidance and releasing potential. To sum up, McGregor's contribution towards the solution of industrial problems of today is certainly significant.

Chris Argyris

According to Chris, as the individual grows from infancy to adulthood, he has a tendency to move from passivity to activity ; from dependence to independence ; from lack of awareness of self to awareness of self. Argyris suggested the redesign of jobs ; organisation structures and control systems and positive leadership styles for the effective motivation of employees. According to him managers must provide them with opportunities for a variety of experiences, give them responsibility and rely more on the employees, self direction and self control.

Abraham Maslow

Abraham Maslow an American Psychologist has given best known classification of human needs known as "Need Hierarchy". According to Maslow, human needs can be categorised as : Basical psychological needs, security or safety needs, social needs, Ego or Esteem needs and self fulfillment or self-actualisation needs. These needs are further divided into primary needs--Psychological and security needs and secondary needs--social, ego and self fulfillment needs. Maslow's work is that most employees experience a variety of needs motivating them to come to work and perform at a given level of effort.

Oliver Sheldon

Oliver recognised that a company should play an important role as a part of society rather than a means of earning. Better working conditions and efficient management are some of the important factors.

Henry Dennison

Dennison developed the concepts of motivation, leadership team work etc.

Alvin Brown

Alvin concentrated on an evaluation of the principles of delegation of authority.

Mooney and Reiley

They evolved the logical framework for the theory of organisation by presenting certain principles of organisation which occupy an important place in the modern theory of organisation and management.

Modern Management Theories

The modern ear is characterised by treads in management through (*i*) microanalysis of human behaviour in motivation, group dynamics leadership leading to many theories of organisation and (*ii*) the macro search for fusion of the many systems in business organisatioin--economic, social, technical, political and quantitative methods in decision making. The microanalysis of human behaviour has been discussed as Behaviour Scientists contribution under the neo classical theory. Modern Management era can be further classified as three steams *viz.* (*i*) Quantitative approach (*ii*) systems approach and (*iii*) contingency approach indicating further refinement, extension and synthesis of all the classical and neo-classical approaches to management. The contingency approach can be described as the Behavioral Approach has been discussed. While other two streams of management can be described as Systems Approach with its off short--Management Science of Operations Research.

Ludwig Von Bertauffy

Bertauffy, a biologist is credited with coining the General Systems Theory. His contentions were that it was possible to develop a theoretical framework for describing relationship in the real world and different disciplines with similarities could be developed into a general systems model. The similarities were : (*i*) Study of organisation (*ii*) State of equilibrium (*iii*) Openness of all systems and their influence on the environment and environment influence on the system.

According to system approach the organisation is a Unified, purposeful system composed of inter-related parts and also interrelated with its environment. Each unit must mesh/interact with the organisation as a whole, each manager must interact/communicate and deal with executives of other units and the organisation itself must also interact with other organisations and society as a whole.

Kenneth Building

Boulding emphasised the need for general systems theory to describe the relationships of the empirical world. Harvard Business Review pointed out that some executive viewed management as a social system, some as data processing system, some as system of fund flow. Based on this concept executive's task can be grouped into four basic elements *viz.* (*i*) Defining company as a system of interrelated parts (*ii*) Determining objective of each part (*iii*) creating formal subsystems and (*iv*) Integrating all the subsystems, the system and the enviroment. System approach focus on the independence and interrelatedness of the various subsystems from the stand point of the effectiveness of the larger system. For instance our body is also a system being a resultant of other sub-system live the nervous system, the circulatory system and the digestive system. In the real life we realise that even though systems are given boundaries so that we can analyse them. These can be no system that is completely isolated or independent of others. According to Koontz and O'Donnel there are no systems which are closed that is completely independent of others. Systems do play a key role within the area of managing itself. Systems include organisation systems, planning systems, control systems and so on. One can further identify within those many subsystems like systems of delegation, budgeting and feed back of information for control.

Management scientists who have significant contribution are Russel L. Ackoff ; E. Leonard Arnoff ; C. West Churchman ; Edward H ; Bowman; Robert B. Felter ; Elwood S. Buffa ; Jay W. Forrester ; and Samuel B. Richmond. The others who are worthy of mentioning for thier contribution *viz.* Norbert Wiener in USA and Stafford Beer in Britain. Since operation research is still in the early stages of application there are not many names who have made a significant contribution. John Diebold is probably the best known for his contribution in the field of computers and automation.

The pioneers on management have made several attempts to identify themselves with various schools of thought in management or have contributed to several schools of thought in management. Following are the major schools as analysed by Herald Koontz and George R. Terry :

(*i*) Management Process School
(*ii*) Empirical School
(*iii*) Human Behavior or Human Relations School
(*iv*) Social System School
(*v*) Decision Theory School
(*vi*) Mathematical or Quantitative Management School
(*vii*) System Management School
(*viii*) Contingency School

An attempt is made to summarise the important feature of the aforsaid schools of thought in the form of a flow process.

Schools of Management Thought

Management Process School	Emperial School	*Human Behaviour School*
Concept	**Concept**	**Concept**
The school provides a concept on framework which can be usefully utilised to identify the essentials of management.	Management is the study of the experiences of managers. It is also named as the management by customer school.	Management is the study of behaviour of people at work.
Scope	**Scope**	Scope
This approach is identified with-- Operational Approach ; Traditional Approach ; Universalist approach ; Classical approach.	Care method is the important tool of study for Emperial school of thought.	Depends on several behavioral science.
Contributors	**Contributors**	**Contributors**
Important contributors are Henri Fayol ; J.D. Mooney A.C. Reiley ; Lyndall Urwick ; Herald Koontz ; Newman : Summers ; and McFarland.	Earnest Dale.	Elton Mayo ; McGregor ; Keith Davis; Maslow ; McClelland ; Argyris; Herzberg and Rothlisberger.
Criticism	**Criticism**	**Criticism**
Since organisations function under dynamic conditions	Universal principles failed to stand the test of Emperial scrutiny.	Managers have to contribute under dynamic conditions and History does not exactly repeat itself.

Schools of Management Thought

Social System School	*Decision Theory School*
Concept	**Concept**
- Management as a Co-operative system and study of organisation as a collaborative system.	It is based on the rational approach to decision making.
Contributors	**Contributors**
Max Weber ; Mocreno ; Simon and Rensis Likert.	Chester Bernard ; James Merch ; Herbert Simon ; Foorester and Richard Cyert.
Criticism	**Criticism**
School of thought can not do justice to technological factors connected with psychological behavior of the people.	Decision making process can not be treated as an independent or separate function it is only one of the task of an executive.

Mathematical School or Quantitative Method School	*Systems Approach School*	*Contingency Approach School*
Concepts	**Concepts**	**Concepts**
- It offers a quantitative method of decision making.	- Management is a system or an organised whole	Effective management is always situational Practicing managers should take into account the relations of a situation.
- It is possible to quantity and express the various factors in the form of mathematical models.	- Overall effective ness of the system is more important than sub-systems.	

	- School of thought is more close to reality.	
Contributors	**Contributors**	**Contributors**
Taylor ; Gilbreth ; Gautt ; Joel Dean ; New mann ; Ackoff ; and Hicks	Kenneth ; Johnson ; Boulding ; Cast ; Rosen ; Zweing ; and C.W.Churchman.	Johan Woodward ; Fiedler ; Loisch ; and Lawerence
Scope	**Scope**	**Scope**
Operation Research ; Mathematical tools ; Simulation Model Building. PERT ; CPH Queuing Theory. Break Even analysis ;	System approach can be utilised by other approach including process approach ; decision theory ; and behavioral science.	It can be used in important such systems of management *viz.* Organisation Design ; Leadership ; Behaviour change.
Criticism	**Merit**	**Merit**
These techniques can not be substitute	for experience	knowledge
- Collaboration should be prompted among several groups.		
- System is an entity or interrelated subsystems.		

Contingency Theory : adapting organization to environment

"Organizations are open systems that need careful management to satisfy and balance internal needs and to adapt to environmental circumstances." Organizations, like organisms, can be conceived of as sets of interacting subsystems. These subsystems can be defined in many ways.

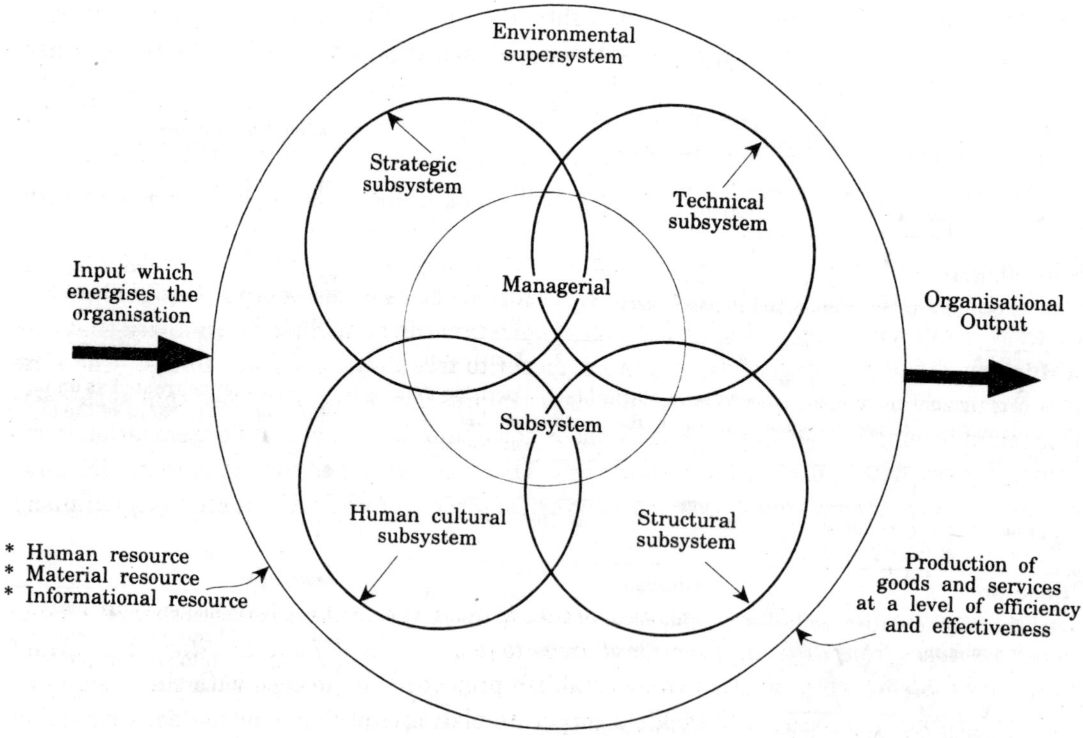

Fig. 2.1. Organisational sub-systems.

There is no one best way of organizing. The appropriate form depends on the kind of task or environment with which one is dealing. Management must be concerned, above all else, with achieving 'good fits'. Different approaches to management may be necessary do perform different tasks within the same organization, and quite different types or 'species' of organization are needed in different types of environment." Their study emphasized that successful adaptation of organization to environment depended on the ability of top manage—manner, and to adopt relevant courses of action. Both these studies thus demonstrated that in the process of organizing a lot of choices have to be made and were at one in suggesting that effective organization depends on achieving a balance or compatibility between strategy, structure, technology, the commitments and needs of people, and the external environment. Their research was built around two principal ideas. First, that different kinds of organizations are needed to deal with different market and technological conditions. Second, that organizations operating in uncertain and turbulent environments need to achieve a higher degree of internal differentiation, *e.g.* between departments, than those in environments that are less complex and more stable. *The Lawrence and Lorsch study redefined that contingency approach by showing that styles of organization may need to vary between organizational subunits because of the detailed characteristics of their sub envirnoments.* Production departments typically face task environments characterized by more clear-cut goals and shorter time horizons, and can adopt more formal or bureaucratic modes of interpersonal interaction than sales departments. The study showed that the degree of required differentiation in managerial and organizational styles between departments varied according to the nature of the industry and its environment and that an appropriate degree of integration is also needed to tie the differentiated parts together again. The study also yielded important insights on modes of integration, such as hierarchy, rules, and so on appeared to work quite well. But in more turbulent environments they need to be replaced by other modes, such as the use of multidisciplinary project teams and the appointment of personnel skills in the art of coordination and conflict resolution. The successful use of these integrative devices can be dependent on achieving an intermediate stance between the units being coordinated on the power, status, and competence of those involved ; and on the presence of a structure of rewards favouring integration. Lawrence and Lorsch gave a precision and refinement to the general idea that certain organisations need to be more organic than others, suggesting that the degree of organicism required varies from one organizational subunit to another. While some approaches to matrix organization can be so highly formalized that they operate as modified bureaucracies, others are closer to free-flowing organic forms. The term matrix organization was coined to capture a visual impression of organizations that systematically attempt to combine the kind of functional or departmental structure of organization found in a bureaucracy with a project-team structure. The fully developed matrix is team-driven in that priority is given to business, program, product, or project areas, with functional specialisms providing support.

Matrix organization provides a means of breaking down the barriers between specialists and allowing members from different functional areas to fuse their skills and abilities in an attack on common problems. Organizations may establish project teams to cope with the design and production of specific products, to tackle a corporate planning problem, or to deal with adhoc issues such as the reallocation of a plant or offices. While some organizations may establish few teams, others may be dominated be team activity. *Matrix organization typically increases the adaptabiliy of organizations in dealing with their environments, improves coordination between functional specialisation and makes good use of human resources.* The approach also diffuses influences and control allowing people at the middle and lower levels of an organisation to make contributions that might otherwise be denied.

3

Management

INTRODUCTION

An organisation, whether commercial, industrial, educational, charitable, governmental or any other comes into existence when a group of persons join together for the attainment of some objective or objectives. Whatever may be the nature and kind of the organisation, it cannot run successfully unless there is someone to manage its affairs. Management is an essential part of any group activity. It is the primary force within the group or organisation which tends to lead it towards the group goals. There is no doubt about is that persons working in an organisation need some system (which may be called management) to direct the activities of the organisation so that human and material resources may be effectively used to achieve the desired objective. It is the management which plants, organises coordinates and controls the affairs of the organisation. Management brings the human and material resources (*i.e.* machines, materials and money) together and motivates the people in the organisation in use of material resources for the achievement of the objectives of the organisation.

It is not difficult to realise the consequences of a situation in which an organisation has no management at all. If the people comprising the organisation are left to themselves, the result will be utter confusion and no piece of work will be done at the proper time and in the proper manner. As a matter of fact everybody will be managing his own activities and no body will be responsible to any one. Because of confusion in the organisation, there will be no question of achieving the desired objectives. Here, we feel the need of some agency to guide and control the activities of the people in the organisation. We may call that agency as 'management'. An organisation cannot survive without management. It is the management which makes the people realise the objectives of the organisation and directs their efforts towards their achievement. Used in this sense, management is taken to include the individuals who manage or look after the affairs of the organisation for the achievement of its objectives.

MANAGEMENT AND MANAGERS

Management

Management is a multi-purpose organ of an organisation that manages the work and the people or personnel (including managers) at work. It is a creative and innovative force striving to secure the maximum result by the use of available resources. Management provides new ideas and vision to the work group and integrates its efforts in such a manner as to account for better results. It ensurens smooth flow of work in the organisation by strengthening weak links, overcoming difficulties and establishing team spirit among the personnel. Therefore, management is an activating element of any organisation for getting done through its people by providing dynamic leadership.

Management is the life blood of an organisation. Management is an organ of business and the society responsible for making the resources productive. A business organisation must have a management to function. Management is what a manager does. According to Peter Drucker the only resources capable of enlargement can be human resources and all other resources stand under the laws of mechanics and physical resources even better utilised can never have an out-put greater than the sum of inputs and for these resources there has to be a minimum inevitable output shrinkage. Thus alone of all the resources available, men can grow and develop. An organisation without good management is a house built on sand.

Management is the primary force within an organisation which co-ordinates the activities of sub-systems related to environment. Management is basically a human activity. Wherever human life exists some forms of management is necessary to obtain and to prepare the resources needed for human survival. A house wife is a good manager if she utilised her resources effectively.

Management involves ability to communicate influence leadership qualities, ability to motivate people, ability to train and develop people beside other skills of management. Decision making is the essence of managers. The job of management is to provide dynamic leadership that combines the productive but passive resources into a fruitful organisation. Management adds a real plus value to the operation of any enterprise by enlisting a little extra-value amount of each person. It is like adding two plus two and getting five.

Manager

A manager is a human being who utilises the force in other human beings working under him for their benefit and for the benefit of the organisation by forecasting planning, organising, directing and controlling people and other resources.

The manager decides what is to be done and then motivate people to do it. Therefore manager requires information and data to decisions but quite often he will have to take decisions on incomplete data thereby take risks. The various kind of people in this world can be grouped as people who make things happen, and those who don't know what is happening. Managers should be the first kind. Managers should not sit and wait for the environmental conditions to be favourable. He should not wait for the future rather he would make the future. Manager should not adjust to obstacles rather he should overcome them. He should take creative action, thus becomes a creator and not the creature of the economy. Manager is a person who accomplished the objective of the organisation by directing the effort of others. The job of a manager is to create an environment conducive to the performance of people working under him to achieve the collective goal and the goals of individuals participating in the organisation. Thus job of management involves training, communicating coordinating, managing, organising, motivating and leading others.

A good manager should know, what he wants out of his subordinates and when he wants them to do it. Manager should also delegate responsibility to his subordinates with necessary authority to do their job.

One of the important function of a manager is to educate, train and develop people below him so that they develop in the job they are doing and is partly included in creating a right atmosphere for individual and team growth. Manager must create a climate which bri... satisfaction and discipline among the people.

Manager's job is like design, it consists of a creative phase and a communication phase Management can be divided into two task. 1. Deciding what to do. 2. Getting it done. The first task relates the setting of objectives, planning, decision making and the setting up of formal organisation and administration. The second task consists of communication, management control and the motivation and development of people.

Management as a Technique of Getting Things Done

Management is frequently defined as a technique of getting things done through the efforts of others. But this definition is incomplete and misleading. The conception of employees in an organisation as mere means to certain ends seems to be embodied in the concept of getting things done through others. There is no doubt that an organisation employs people because it need them for the efficient and effective utilisation of material resources to achieve its purpose. But, the people too have thier needs which they seek to fulfill through their work and work place. This aspect is completely ignored by the definition given above. People are not cog in the wheel; so they should not be treated as commodity and mere means to achieve certain ends. Needs and aspiration of the people working for the achievement of organisational goals should not be overlooked. People of the organisation must be satisfied so as to obtain sustained and consistent efforts towards organisational objectives. It is the duty of the management to keep the people in the organisation satisfied so that they may contribute without any hesitation for the achievement of the purpose of the organisation. So management is getting things done through other people by satisfying their needs, expectations and providing them opportunity for growth and also motivating them. It is certainly more than just getting things done through other people. A good manager is like an athletic coach who tries to help each member of his team to strengthen his good points and improve his weak points.

Management as a Process

Management is a process by means of which the goals of a particular human group are determined, classified and put into action. As shown in figures 3.2 and 3.3 for the effectuation of the goals, management plans, organises, directs and control the efforts of the people or personnel in the use of material resources. Management is that process by which managers create, direct, maintain and operate purposive organisation through systematic, co-ordinated and cooperative human efforts.* Though this is a good definition of the term 'management', but it does not indicate the exact nomenclature of the various phases of management process. Management, as a process has been represented graphically in Figs. 3.2 and 3.3. These figures show that the basic resources are subjected to certain fundamental functions in order to achieve the stated objectives. The functions performed by the order to achieve the stated objective. The functions performed by the management process are broadly classified as planning, organising, coordinating and controlling.

Henri Fayol also viewed management of a process and gave five phases of the management process. "To manage is to control.* In addition to these, staffing and directing are also the important phases of the management process. Planning, organising, staffing, directing and controlling are the functions which are performed while managing an organisation. It is important to note that management process starts with planning and ends with control. The order functions come in between the two functions. Management makes up the plans to translate the objectives of the organisation into reality. However planning is not sufficient unless the management is in a position to organise, direct and control the activities the group to execute these plans. Action takes place according to plans and it creates certain consequences, which are compared with the standard of performance already set by the management. This leads to taking corrective actions and changes in the original plan. This process is known as controlling.

Management is a creator and motor for development which should be self propelling and problem solving. It is the management task to enable human beings to perform and concentrate their strength to work. It is the task of the Management and its Managers to make private virtue rebound to public benefits.

Public undertaking are employing huge resources, highly trained people and scarce capital and thereby meeting the fundamental expectation of our society. The management in public sector undertakings is becoming more complex and essential. Public sector needs to organise for performance and should become result oriented. The managers of today have a greater role to play. The managers are human beings, likewise managers are also different in their approach towards planning, organising, directing and controlling. Let us all admit that in all countries and cultures, managers as people, young and old of whatever colour or culture or language, are to be found in many different types. These various types of managers can be grouped into the following important categories :

1. Pragmatic 2. Risk Takers 3. Bureaucratic 4. Technocrat 5. Elitist 6. Stylistic 7. Expert and Specialist 8. Professional.

The Pragmatic

Managers who believe in the law of the situation and will tackle problems with their brand of common sense. They are robust, not given to much dialogue but rather to command.

The Risk Takers

Five percent of managers are genuine innovators and we need more such managers as catalysts of change.

The Bureaucratic

Managers who are more interested in procedures than results. These are the managers who have never been accustomed to personal accountability, who can hide their error in the labyrinth of committees or in the skill of "bulk passing."

The Technocrat

Managers who have studied management theories too literally and have an undue confidence in the results of academic technings of management subjects. They wish for people and events to conform to theory and are somewhat inflexible. To them people do not seem to count so much as techniques and systems and such managers may not necessarily inherent democracy.

---

* Dalton E. Mc Far land : Principal and Practice of Management.

The Elitist

Those who have by inheretence, influence or education been lead to believe that it confers on them a divine right to manage or control others. In all cultures and families, some groups often have a better managerial application than others and by decisiveness, single mindedness shrewdness and other qualities acquired at an early age, they start thinking themselves as managerial Mafias.

The Stylistic

Managers by the nature of their professions, industries or trades, develop special characteristics which towards the end of this managerial era are becoming marked in many regions and cultures.

Expert and Specialist

Organisation have been built to accommodate specialists but they must not be exempted from frequent audit. In this period of fast change the expert knowledge is a limited knowledge and specialist and experts need to develop themselves in other areas also.

The Professional

The professional manager has been a strong emergence in the 1970's. Professional managers have no financial stake in the business except their careers on the basis of being hired in the market place. It is desirable for atleast 20% of a nation's managerial for to be mobile if they are to play a role of dynamic, wealth creating change agent role, giving validity and leadership to organisations and employees. The role of management in business organisation is to serve the present and future needs of the community, to create and generate wealth. Generation of wealth is of paramount importance in the sense that, without it the enterprise will not be able to achieve either its economic or societal aims.

To conclude, people are individually known as Mangers and collectively as Management. Management is a body of people who performs the managerial functions of planning coordinating, directing and controlling. Now let us discuss in detail the term manager and the role played by a manager in an organisation.

Management--A group Activity

Management term is often Jenote the persons who look after the enterprise. "Management of this plant is efficient" or Management is actually responsible for industrial unrest in this plan." It is clear from these that the reference is actually made to the people who are incharge of management of the organisation. These people are individually known as managers and collective as management. Used in this sense management may be defined as an agency or a body of persons which performs the managerial functions of planning, organising, controlling etc.

Factors of Management

The success in the performance of managerial functions is depending on various factors which require appropriate technical knowledge and skills, and secondly how the manager deals with human beings which demands an appropriate behaviour to motivate and inspire human beings. Fig. 3.1 shows how factors of management are related to other dimension of management.

This is also known as static model of management because manager's success is depending upon the objective of the individual and group. Following are certain important factors of management :

1. Philosophy
2. Objective
3. Functions
4. Policy
5. Human Facilities
6. Environmental Factors

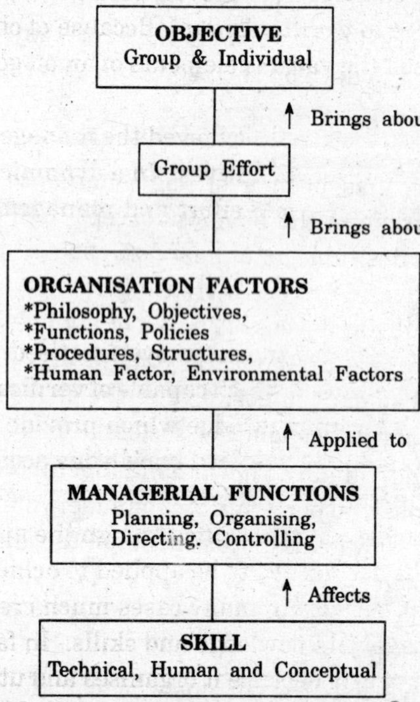

Fig. 3.1 Static Management

1. Philosophy

Philosophy relates to the basic guide that high light all actions of a manager.

2. Objective

It refers to the goals to be achieved. This refers to what enterprise must produce and distribute worthwhile goods or service.

3. Functions

It refers to the activities by whose performance the objective are achieved.

4. Policy

The term policy has assumed a greater significance in the sphere of human activities policy is a predetermined and accepted cours of thought that is defined and established as a guide to achieve the accepted goals and objectives.

5. Human Facilities

It emphasises that to achieve the objectives the performance of functions must be entrusted directly or indirectly to human beings. Thus it is important to specify, acquire and develop human skill to perform technical and managerial functions.

6. Environmental Factors

These factors emphasise that business is affected by physical, social and political, forces. Management must therefore give thought to provide technical, physical, social customers and political environment conductive to working group. Because of changing environment there is a continuous interaction between the various elements of an on going organisation as shown in Fig. 3.3.

The figure shows that as one objective is achieved the managerial process and group efforts are repeated continuously for additional objectives. In a dynamic management the objective is being attained it gives a feedback on group effort and management functions for succeeding objectives.

Management Science and Art

Management is a science. Science means a systematised body of knowledge acquired through observation and experimentation which capable of verification. A manager is a scientist as he requires a systematised body of knowledge which provide fundamental truth which he can utilise in job. Management is a systematised knowledge acquired through continuous and vigourous efforts on many managers and researchers.

Management is an art. It achieves the results through the application of skill. In management some knowledge and skills are needed to be applied to achieve the desired results. Art is very important in management because in many cases much creativeness and adroitness are necessary in applying the managerial knowledge and skills. In fact, management is one of the most creative arts. It is the art of arts because it organises and utilises the talent of the people. A manager is an artist because he uses the knowledge provided by the science of management in managing human and material resources.

The development of the science of management includes of knowledge about management principles and their applications. But at times, the application of a particular principle may not produce the desired result. The main reason for this is that management deals with complex human beings. It is very difficult to predict accurately the behaviour of people. This requires a continuous practice of the management principles. It is an art in itself. A manager who has developed the knowledge of the science of management needs an art to apply this knowledge. In simplest terms, a science teaches one the knowledge about certain subject and art teaches to do certain thing. The medical doctor acquires the knowledge in chemistry, biology and anatomy, but the intelligence in absorbing this apply acquired knowledge intelligently and his skill in perceiving how and when to use his knowledge is very important to make him an excellent practising physician. In the same manner, a manager to be successful in managing must acquire the knowledge and then learn to apply the knowledge so acquired.

Science and art are complementary fields of endeavour. They are two sides of the same coin. There must be a balance between these two. There is knowledge about management and it must be acquired in order to achieve highest competency in management. Likewise, there is skillful application of the knowledge of management and excellent accomplishment in this area must be achieved. A successful manager is both a scientist and an artist. As a scientist, he relies heavily on the existing knowledge and develops new knowledge and principles. As an artist, he applies the acquired knowledge to solve his problems of managing men, material, machines, methods and money.

Efficient Management

The establishment and the accomplishment of goals of any organisation is dependent upon the competency of management to a great extent. No organisation can desire to be successful without the utilisation of effective and efficient management. It is the management which determines the goals of group activity and then puts them into actions by organising the human and non-human resources. Management motivates the people in the organisation to the effective utilisation of material resource *i.e.* machines, materials, methods and money for the achievement of organisation goals.

Management provides effectiveness to efforts of the people. It keeps abrest of changing conditions and supplies foresight and imagination to the organisation. That is why management is often referred to as the brain of the enterprise. All the thinking is done by the management and all the policy decisions are taken by the management. For giving effect to its decision, management plans and coordinates various activities, which again requires thinking by the management.

Management brings order to endeavours. Management brings together the isolated efforts, factual information or beliefs and utilise these for the effectuation of certain definite goals. In fact, the task of making a better economic life possible and improving social standards and relations are the challenging jobs of the management. Beacuse of this, management has come to be recognised as the critical ingredient in a nation's growth and development. Both economic and social development are brought about by management. If we go through the economic history of India prior to her independence, we will come to know that there was no lack of material resources, but certainly there was lack of managerial ability and technical know-how. In essence, development of a country is highly related to quality of management of its resources.

Management plays a key role in national development because it provides direction of human and material resources. No amount of capital investment and import of technical know-how and equipments will succeed in furthering national development if such wealth producing resources are not managed properly. It is managerial know-how which utilises the available resources effectively towards the achievement of broad national goals.

In short, there is no substitute for management. To determine worthwhile goals, carefully select, procedure and utilise resources efficiently by means of applying planning, organising, coordinating and controlling require a high degree of judgement and foresight. Whosoever performs these activities is a manager and is a part of management. Management is a universal activity. Management of operations is a must whether it is a home, school, business or any other institution. Without effective management, better results cannot be achieved. It is significant to note that many aids have been offered to replace management from time to time, but actually they do not represent management. They can at best assist the management. Thus, management has no substitute and nothing can replace the management.

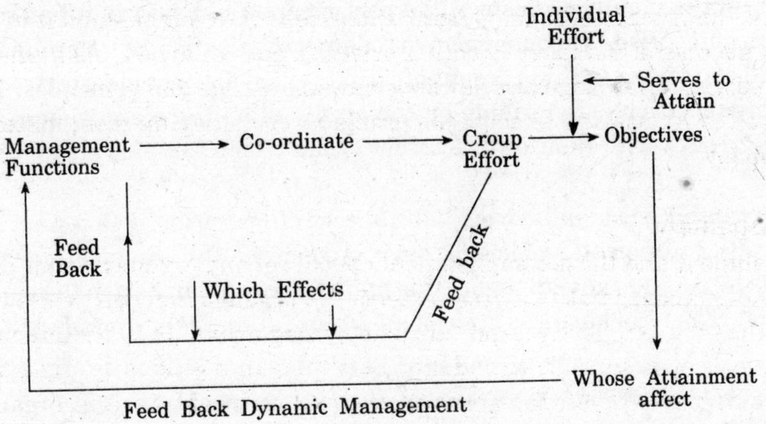

Fig. 3.2

Organisation Structure

It is a frame work which ties together technical and managerial experts and specialists in the organisation. The organisation structure provides lines of authority and responsibility to knit the members of the group into a more meaningful and effective team.

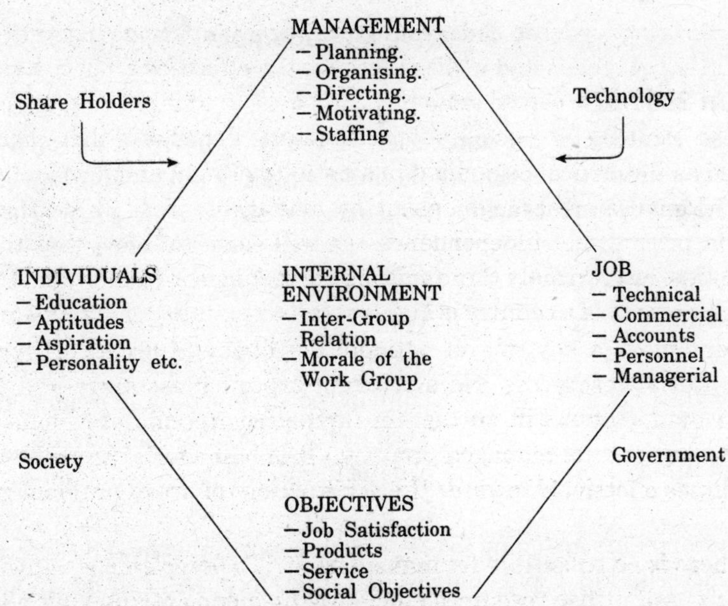

Fig. 3.3

Objective of Management

The following figure illustrates how management is concerned with achievement of objectives by creating an internal environment in the organisation through the people of the organisation by utilising the available resources, creating and doing the job effectively.

A manager is controlled only by the objective of performance. In other words the objective of a managerial unit is mainly consists of the performance and results it has to contribute to the success of the enterprise. The management of any organisation try to group the customers, shareholders and employees in three groups of people which also not identical to their own. The success of any organisation is determine by the ability of its top management to overlap the interest, of three groups with their own. Another group which can also play an important role is the suppliers.

In an heavy capital goods industries half its cost of operation if taken up in purchasing materials materials, equipment, and bought out components. The organisation transform these into usable goods by adding value to them. It is must for any organisation to keep good relation with its suppliers. The total business cycle of an organisation is shown in Fig. 3.2

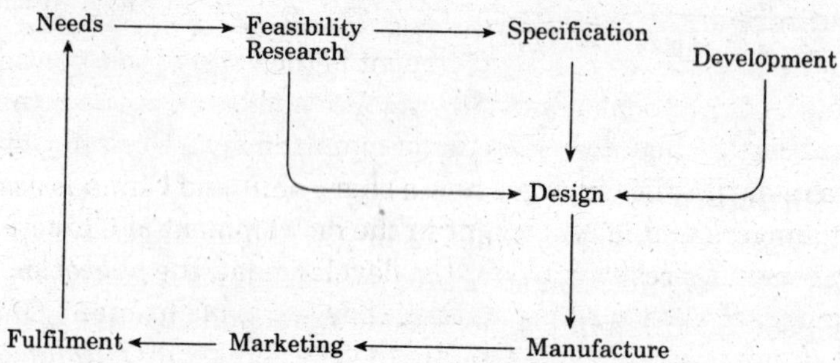

Dynamic Management

Management in 2001 AD

The business strategy of an enterprise is really a function of environmental factors. Therefore there is a need for developing an understanding of the environments, both external and internal. The environment factors that surround an enterprise can be classified as under:

External Environment	*Internal Environment*
- Economic	- Value systems
- Social	- Organisational design and structure
- Political	- Human resource including managers
- Regulatory	- Technocrats and other employees.
- Competition	- Financial resources

External environments are going to play a very important role. The external environments will also be characterised by rapid changes and, therefore, will call for an aptitute, ability on the part of managers to respond to any shift in the environment and management. The emergence of public sector undertaking as dominant economic units within the economy is likely to engender greater political and administrative attention in coming years. Public sector has emerged as key sector of economic power and in this process attract a great deal of attention. In the face of these developments the ancillary units and the small scale units will be able to survive perform and grow.

Social tension arising out of greater aspirations of people will continue to increase. Unless the radical changes are made within the organisational structure and systems as well as management processes, productivity will stagnate if not decline. A new culture with the social values will have to be evolved and practiced by the managers.

Internal Environments

The internal environments of the organisations will be characterised by greater emphasis on accountability for performance to the participating members, employment of sophisticated technologies, new production systems, participative organisational design, greater concern for the development and management of human resources. The management in future will be more information oriented and consequently computer based. Therefore the management process is highly situational and is related to interplay between environmental factors and stated objectives of the organisation.

According to Peter Drucker the management is the child of this century. A few years back the people were sceptical about management. But today, even the communist countries are quite definite and certain about the essence of management. Even in China where under Mao management was clearly taboo, there is now a sharp shift and China is asserting on the central importance of managers and management in the development of Chinese society and Chinese economy. Management is responsible for the development, the allocation and the productivity resources. Resources are not made by nature, they are made by man. Of all the resources, the two key resources, human being and capital are very important. *Human being as such is not a resource, he becomes resource only if trained developed and allocated to productive work. In developing countries more people are available than can be productively employed.* But there are very few productive human beings in these countries. Because, the people have not been developed in human resources. Thus a task of training, developing, managing and creating a right attitude is very important. There is a need that managers seriously work on managing work.

The second resource capital is perhaps even more crucial than that of the human resources. Capital can only be obtained by providing a surplus from today's production over today's cost. Capital formation may be the crucial factor in the continuing prosperity of the developed countries. There is no such thing as profit, the term itself is a misunderstanding. There are only costs of the past and the costs of the future. *The greatest cost of the future is the capital need to provide the jobs for tomorrow. There cannot be any job unless we can invest a substantial amount of capital.* One of the weaknesses of developing countries is thier desperate search for employment opportunities without creating an adequate capital formation for jobs of tomorrow. Manager must meet the future capital needs and would discover that it does not operate at a profit but operates at deficit. *Thus, of all the resources, we have money which need to be exploited the most. Money does not get tired, money does not charge overtime, money does not join unions, money does not needs vacations, money likes to work seven days a week and twenty four hours a day.* Harder you work with money, the-better money likes it. Thus, there is a need to work on making resources productive, specially on managing capital which is going to be scarce for the rest of the century and also to convert human being into a resource.

Management and Changing Environments

The new industrial overloads are the Trade union leaders who can by their influence and decisions can bring industries and even countries to a halt. The credibility of power of trade union leaders at present is also at stake. It must never be forgotten that trade unions and employers are backing together their respective members in order to :

- Preserve the right of association.
- Prevent exploitation by third parties.
- Bargain with the third parties.

The development of management and manager's individually or in the group, is part of the organic development of organisation.

The world, at time is very complex due to industrial and social systems, yet with the rationalisation brought about by science and technology, we are nearer to understanding each other. The role of business which management runs, is to service the present and future need of the community and to create wealth. Profit is paramount in the sense that without it, the enterprise would not have means to achieve either its economic or social aims.

Management and the Environment

An organisation must be sensitive to, the public policies and the present and future to which the enterprise has to respond. It is necessary to scan the environment influence in which business as well as the management operate. Management in its environmental analysis, (which is specifically concerned to identify the opportunities for societal involvement) will promote the interest, both of the community and the business.

The organisation, its share holders and customers share the same environment of interacting systems : ethical, social, cultural, political, economic and technical. Following are the five themes that need to be developed to understand environmental systems :

- The inter dependence of the world economy.
- The effect of instant communication.
- The fast changing values and value laden situations to which management must respond.
- The growing role of influencing groups on company's affairs.
- The growing complexity of the multiple environments a company encounters when it starts to operate transnationally.

Transnational Operations

When an enterprise moves its activities abroad, it has to take into account not only the domestic environments of each of the countries in which it operate but also some international variable also. More and more variable are involved and the enterprises are brought to the key dilemma of the transnational corporation reconciling the interest of the shareholders with those of the other stockholders in the home and host countries. Transnational business is now so large that many home and host country and the international community are unhappy that the control of them is in non-governmental hands. Hence setting up of U.N. centre on Transnational corporations and the demand for codes of conduct to which member agencies have readily responded. Common needs and opportunities constitute the driving forces impelling the developing country and transnational corporation towards each other. The transnational corporation entering a developing country is in fact an agent of change. Going into the situation with its eyes wide open, the company knows it will be expected to reconcile its goals with the planning priorities of the host government, with differing objectives of the company's own local employee's customers and suppliers local shareholders etc. The job of an international manager is to achieve a workable reconciliation of these interests in a new culture in which private enterprise is not necessarily taken for granted. Typically there is a dual economy, and the gap between the haves and have nots is immense and will be identified with the haves. The driving forces will be strengthened by enhancing the knowledge and improving communications about specific developing country needs on the one hand and the matching transnational resources on the other.

DYANMICS OF CHANGE

Elvin Toffler in his book "Future Shock" gave a good account of "How executives come to terms with the future ?". By future shocks he does not mean potential danger but a real sickness from which increasingly large number of individuals suffer. He emphasised on shattering stress and disorientation to which individuals will be subjected, in future. It will induce in individuals by subjecting them to too much change in too short a time. The coherent image of future can shower the executives with valuable insights of today.

Significance of Change

Alvion Toffler says that man's existence is 50,000 years old and if this period is divided into life times of approximately 62 years each, there have been about 800 life times. From the total 800 life times 650 life times man spent in caves. Only during 70 life times, man has been communicating effectively and passing information and knowledge from one life time to another. During the last six life times only, man has seen the printed world. It has been only during the last four life times that it has been possible to measure time with precision. During last two life times, man has learnt the use of electric motor. Majority of the material and comforts goods being used have been developed within the present life time. *This present life time is indeed very important as during this life time, man's relationship to resources has reversed itself. These statistics outline how fast the change has occured during the monumental 800th life time only.* In this life time boundaries have been burst, the network of social ties has been tightly woven. The automation, computerisation, space research and spaceships, nuclear advancement, communication, satellite, microwaves, application etc. have come during this life time only. We are now caught in what might be called time skip. It means there is a need for the man to appreciate the fast changing scientific, cultural and social environment. Culture shock what happens when a traveller suddenly finds himself in a place where Yes means No, where waiting outside the office of an executive is no cause for insult, where laughter signifies anger. Culture shock takes place when an individual working in one society suddenly finds himself in a strange, incomprehensible and new society. It cause a breakdown in communication, a misreading of reality and lack of capability to cope. Present cultural shocks are relatively going to be much less than the future shocks. Future shock can be defined as the premature arrival of the future.

Executives have to prepare themselves with increasing efforts to avoid disorientation and incompetence to deal rationally with their environment. *Future shock is a time phenomenon, a product of greatly accelerated rate of change is society. It is super imposition new culture on the old one. Change is hovering upon our heads and we have to prepare ourselves to cope with it.* It is important for executives to understand the technological innovation and also the changing environment. They should scan the technological changes constantly and should build useful models for effective applications. Executives may have work on computers and cope with fast changing technology as part of their configuration. The rate of increase in knowledge is tremendous, the rate at which man has been storing the useful knowledge about himself and the universe has been spiralling for ten thousand years. Today number of scientific journals and articles are doubled like industrial production. *Computer which came on the scene around 1950 with its fast memory storage is becoming a source of knowledge acquisition. Knowledge should change, knowledge is power and accelerating knowledge acquisition is a boom for the changing technology. Executives for survival must be able to avert the future shocks and must be more compatible and capable them ever before. Executive must search for new ways and means to anchor himself.* The old ways Religion, Nation, Community, Family and Profession are now shaking due to accelerated impact and Thrust. Therefore, in order to meet the above challenges, there is a need to understand transience.

Transience

Transience is the newness and temporariness in the individual life. Transience is the critical difference between men of the past or present or the future. It provides a link between sociological theories of change and the psychology of new human beings. If we integrate the two we can analyse the problems of fast or speedy change in a new way. Transience gave us the idea about individuals, institutions or organisations environment around us. It is the study of individuals' relationship to certain ideas or information flow in society. The five core elements forming the fabric of social experience are things, places, people, organisations and ideas of all situations. It is the individual's distinctive relationship to each of these components that structures the situation. Transience, therefore, is the rate at which our relationship turns over with time.

We all know that our relationships with the outer world are growing more and more transient and we have to lead a life in high transienct society. To understand the transience, it is important to grasp the idea of durational expectancy. The individuals' perception of time is closely linked with internal rhythms. *The durational expectancy is different in each society but deeply ingredient; for example, if a father tells his 14 years old son that he will have to wait two years represent a mere 4% of father's life time to death 13% of the boy's life time. It is not strange that to a boy delay seems nearly four times longer than father. Taking the other side two hours in the life of a four year old may be felt equivalent to 12 hours in the life of her 24 years old mother. Asking the child to wait for two hours may be equivalent to asking to mother to wait for 14 hours for a cup of coffee.* Most of the conflicts between generations, between parents and children, between husbands and wives are due to acceleration of the pace of life.

Change And Individual Personality

Each personality can be imagined as a unique configuration of thousands of such modules. No one personality is interchangeable with another, but certain modules are : If we are buying a commodity, we are not buying friendship or love or affection of the shopkeeper. In such interaction there is a limited liability on both sides. The interaction calls for certain expected forms of behaviour and communication. Both parties in the interaction consciously or otherwise understand the limitations. In such interaction, it is not important to interact with other modules of shopkeepers' personality. The difficulty or conflict or misunderstanding occurs when we attempt to connect up some modules which are not relevant in the interaction process. In big cities if an individual attempts to involve oneself with everyone, it may lead to self distribution or self emptiness. *Delhites or Bombayites must have more or less modular relationship with most of the people with whom they come in contact. The traditional man is highly sentimental and romantic in choosing friends or cultivating relations and frequently overlooks the consequences of such a relationship. The more intimately you are involved in a relationship, the greater will be the pressure on one another to fulfil the expectations of each other. In a modular relationship the demands are strictly bounded. Modular relationship entails no risks in the inter-personnel relationship process.* It has been observed that average urban individual comes in contact with more people in a week than a villager in a year and even in a life time. The urban individual may have a care group of people with whom his interaction are sustained over long periods of time but his interaction with thousands of people is so short lived that he may see them only once or twice.

The various relationships can be classified as :

(*a*) Longer duration relationships.

(*b*) Medium duration relationships.

(*c*) Short duration relationships.

Longer Duration Relationships

These are the ties with the members of the families. *The family links are exported to be long term if not life long and considerable guilt is attached to the person who breaks up such a relationship.* It does not mean that these relations are always cordial. It might result in divorce or family break up. Breaking up involves lot of emotional strain and dislocation.

Medium Duration Relationships

These are the relationships with friends, neighbours, job associates, co-members of club, etc. Friendship is supposed to survivor or almost continue as long as family ties. *Culture places high value on old friends and blame is attached in dropping a friend. Neighbourhood relations are expected to last as long as individual remains in the neighbourhood. Breaking up with a neighbour may involve other difficulties but it carries no great burden of guilt.* On-the-Job relationships, frequently overlap friendship and at times neighbourhood relationship.

Short Duration Relationships

These involve relationship with milkman, barber, servant, newspaperman, etc. *The turnover among these relations is relatively rapid and involves no guilt to the person who terminates such relationship.* The greater the mobility of an individual, greater the number of brief face to face encounters. Human contacts develop over a period of time more frequent is the mobility, shorter is the duration of relationship involved. *In some of the developing countries, the turnover among the executives is estimated as 30 to 40% per year. Any change in job entail certain amount of stress.* The individual may be required to modify the existing style of working or may improve old ways of coping and learning new ways of doing things. Even when the work involves a similar environment, the exective is always under pressure to form new relationships. *If the executive has formed a feeling that no job is permanent, the relationships formed are conditional, modular and 'Temporary' Certain executives make more job changes the others.* The executive who are geographically mobile are quite likely to be occupationally mobile as well. Prof. Sargeant in Britain estimated that a minimum population of ten lakhs people is needed to provide a professional worker with 20 interesting friends. He also observed that women who look for temporary work as strategy for finding friends such as Air hostesses. Hotel management are highly intelligent and adaptable as compared to other women.

Coping with Tomorrow

To cope up with the future changes the executives or manager have to change. They should change from one whole pattern to another. The only way to maintain the equilibrium during the future industrial revolutions will be to meet inventions with inventions, to design new personnel and social change regulations. *There is a need for neither personnel blind acceptance nor blind resistance but series of creative strategies for shaping, reflecting and accelerating the selective change. The executives have to learn new principles for coping and planning their life and developing themselves to cope with the changing process.* For meeting future shocks the executives must being at a personal level. We must know that much of our daily behaviour is, in fact, an attempt to ward off future shock. We must even understand our psychological and physiological reaction to change, turning out of the external environment to evaluate our inner environment. It is cool method of appraising and evaluating oneself. We should not forget that some level of change is vital for executive growth but frequent unplanned changes are damaging to his development. There is a need for personal strategy zones. We can cut down on change and stimulations and can consciously maintain longer term relationships with various elements of our physical environment. We may say 'No' to ourselves for too frequent purchasing of new garments, may continue with the existing vehicles, may reduce the need to break in ties with physical objects around us. In other words, there is a need for certain enduring relationship that are carefully maintained, despite all kinds of other changes. The problem is not to suppress change but to manage change. If we opt for rapid change in certain sectors of life, we can consciously attempt to build stability zones elsewhere. It is preferable to be with situational grouping, that is, people who happen to be passing through the similar life transitions at the same time such as Catch Thirty, Rooting and Understanding, etc. as suggested by Hal Scharlatt and Jack Macrae.

4

Functions of Management

Introduction

According to *Henri Fayol,* managerial activity consists of five elements or functions, namely, planning organising, command, co-ordinating and control. *L. Urwick* has divided management functions into six categories, *viz.*, forecasting, planning, organising, command, co-ordination and control. He has also recognised investigation (or research) and communication as the important functions of management. *R. C. Davis* recognized only three functions of management, namely, planning, organising and control. He thinks that command and co-ordination facilitate control and therefore, should be considered as part of it. *Koontz and O'Donnel* have classified management functions as planning, organising, staffing, directing and controlling.

From the above view points it is obvious that there is no universally accepted classification of management functions. The basic reason for this is that the relative importance of the functions of management varies from one organisation to another. That is why different authors, who were considering different organisations, gave a separate classification of management functions. It is very difficult to give a neat classification of the various functions given by different authors, however, for the purpose of analysis and interpretation, we have divided the functions of management into planning, organising, staffing, directing, and controlling. These functions of management are discussed below :

PLANNING

Planning is a mental process requiring the use of intellectual faculties, imagination, foresight, sound judgement, etc. It means deciding in advance what is to be done, how and where it is to be done, who will do it and how results are to be evaluated. In other words, planning is the determination of a course of action to achieve the desired results. According to *G. R. Terry,* planning is a deliberate, conscious research used to formulate the design and orderly sequence of actions through which it is expected to reach the objectives. Thus all planning involves anticipation of future course of events. It is the process of thinking before doing. Planning is to foresee which means both to assess the future and make provisions for it.

Planning is the basic function of management. Proper planning is a must for any business activity. The affairs of any organisation are most likely to be effected without a well thought out plan. Less important work may be done ahead of more important one or two or more pieces of the same kind of work may be done by different persons using different methods resulting in lack of uniformity. Some pieces of work may be unnecessarily repeated resulting in wastage of time, money and materials. Planning, therefore, is necessary to ensure proper utilisation of human and material resources to achieve the objectives of the enterprise.

The Nature of Planning

The nature of planning can be understood by four major aspects of planning ; contribution to objectives, primacy of planning, prevasiveness of planning and efficiency of plan. The purpose of any plan is to device certain predetermined objectives and purposes. Plans alone cannot make an enterprise successful. Planning seeks to achieve an objective through a consistent, coordinated efforts. It forecasts which actions will tend towards the ultimate objective and which tend away from it, which actions are likely to offset another and which are irrelevant.

Primacy of Planning

Although all the functions of management *i.e.* planning organising, directing and controlling are interlinked in a system of actions, but of all these, planning is unique since it establishes the necessary objectives for all group efforts. Organising without planning is impossible, planning helps the manager to know as to what kind of organization would be needed to achieve the pre-determined objectives, and to what course the subordinates are directed, and as to what kind of control is to applied. Unplanned actions can neither be organized, nor controlled effectively, and this result in chaos. Planning not only precedes all other managerial functions, but must also reflect itself in these functions, as all these must be planned if these are to effective.

Prevasiveness of Planning

Planning is a function of all managers in an enterprise irrespective of their position and authority. The channel and nature of planning may vary with the authority and responsibility of the manager depending upon the policies and the plans outlined by the superiors.

Planning at various levels may vary in its importance but everyone in an organization right from Chairman to the Supervisor must plan. Planning at senior manager level may be more important and applicable to a larger portion of an enterprise.

Efficiency of Plan

The efficiency of a plan is measured by the amount it contributes to purpose and objectives as offset by the cost and other unsought consequences required to formulate and operate it. A plan which contributes to the attainment of objectives at too higher costs cannot be considered efficient. A plan can be regarded as efficient if when put into action it brings about the attainment of objectives with minimum efforts and with maximum positive gains, greater than the costs.

Plans may also become inefficient in the attainment of objectives by jeopardizing group satisfaction.

Types of Plan

The failure to recognise the variety of plan results into difficulty in making planning effective. To build and equip a new factory is a plan but what is sometimes over looked is that a number of other cases of future actions are also plans thus we can see that plans are varied. They are also classified as missions, objectives, strategies, programmes and budgets.

Missions

Every kind of organised group operation has to be meaningful, with a purpose or a mission. In every social system, an enterprise has to function in some environment of society. The purpose of business generally is the production and distribution of goods and services. The purpose of Public Works Department is to build public buildings. The purpose of courts is to administer law and so on. To achieve the missions one must have plans. It is sometimes thought that the missions of business is to make profit. It is true that every kind of business must have profits but this has to be achieved keeping in view the environment in which business exist and that is possible to accomplish by giving in clear directions which need proper planning.

Objectives

Objective are the ends towards which an activity aims. They represent not only the end point of planning but the end towards which organising, directing and controlling are aimed. Thus, objectives are plans and they involve the same planning process as any other type of planning. A sales target for example cannot be guessed but it must be determined in the light of purpose and circumstances. Likewise a plan to accomplish a certain sales goal will have within it a project or departmental goal.

Strategies

For years the military used strategies, or a grand plan, made in the light of what is believed as adversary might. While the term 'strategies' still usually has a competitive implications, it has been increasingly used to reflect broad overall concept of an enterprise operation. Strategies therefore, most often denote a general programme of action and deployment of emphasis and resources to attain comprehensive objective. Anthony defines them as resulting from "the process of deciding on objective of the organization, on changes in these objectives, on the resources used to attain these objectives and on the policies that are to govern the acquisition, used and disposition of these resources. Chandler defines, *a strategy as the determination of the basic long-term goals and objectives of an enterprise, and the adoption of courses of action and the allocation of resources necessary to carry out the goals.*

Programmes

Programmes are a complex of goals, policies, procedure, rules, task assignment, steps to be taken, resources to be employed, and other element to carry out a given course of action. They are ordinarily supported by necessary capital and operating budget. Programmes may be major or minor one. A primary programme may call for many derivative programmes. All the programmes necessitate coordination and timings, since the failure of any part of net work of derivative plans means delay for the major programme with consequent unnecessary cost and loss of revenue. Thus one seldom find that a programme of any importance of any enterprise planning stand-by itself. It is usually a part of complex of programmes depending upon some and effecting others. This interdependence of plan makes planning very difficult. The results of poor or inadequate planning are seldom isolated, for planning is only as strong as its weakest link. Even a seemingly unimportant procedure or rule, if badly conceived may wreack an important programme. Coordinated planning requires extra ordinarily managerial skill. It truly requires the most rigorous application of system's thinking and actions.

Budget

A budget as a plan is a statement of expected results expressed in numerical terms. It may be referred to as a 'numberized' programme. As a matter of fact, the financial operating budget is often called a "profit plan". It may be expressed either in financial terms or in terms of man-hours, units of product, machine hours, and any other numberically measurable term. It may deal with operations. Expense budget reflect capital outlays while capital expenditure budget reflect flow of cash like cash budget.

Steps in Planning

The steps in planning discussed here are in connection with major programmes but essentially the same steps could follow in any thorough planning. As minor plans are usually simpler, earlier steps are easily accomplished but practical steps are of general application. Obviously valuable time to top executives should not be wasted in making a decision of lesser consequence, but on the contrary, it is also shocking if very little time is devoted to make a planning decision involving large investments.

Awareness of an opportunity is the real starting point for planning. It includes a preliminary look at possible future opportunities and the ability to see them clearly and completely. A knowledge of where we stand in the light of our strengths and weaknesses, an understanding of why we wish to solve uncertainties, and a vision of what we expect to gain is essential for planning. Setting realistic objective depends on this awareness, and thus planning requires realistic diagnosis of the opportunity situation.

Establishing Objectives

The first step in planning itself is to establish planning objectives for the entire enterprise and then for each subordinate unit. Objectives specifying the results expected indicate the end points, of what is to be done, where the primary emphasis is to be placed, and what is to be accomplished by the network of strategies, policies, procedures, rules, budget and programmes.

Enterprise objectives should give direction to the nature of all major plans which, by reflecting these objectives, define the objectives of major departments. Major department objectives, in turn, control the objectives of subordinate departments, and so on, down the line. The objectives of other departments will be better framed, however, if sub-division manager understand the overall enterprise objectives and the implied derivative goals and also if they are given an opportunity to contribute their ideas to the setting of their own goals.

Premising

A second logical step in planning is to establish and obtain agreement to utilise, and disseminate critical planning premises. These are forecast data of a factual nature, applicable to basic policies, and existing company plans. *Premises, then are planning assumptions, in other words, the expected environment of plans in operations.* This step leads to one of the major principles of planning, the more individuals charged with planning understand and agree to utilize consistent planning premises, the more coordinated enterprise planning will be.

Forecasting is important in premising. Apart from forecasting the basic economical data, forecasting of future, economic and social environments also effect the project, and are equally essential. A superior's plans effecting a subordinate manager's area of authority becomes premises for the latter's planning.

Because the future environment of plans is so complex, it would not be profitable or realistic to make assumptions about every detail of the future to those which are critical, or strategic, to a plan, that is, those which influence its operation most.

Lack of planning or coordination, by managers of different sets of premises, can be extremely costly. The use of consistent premises should therefore, be agreed upon. A single standard for the future is necessary for good planning, even through this standard includes several sets of premises with the instruction that different sets of plans be developed on each. Some companies, for sample ; customarily develop plans in prospect of both peace and war so that, regardless of what occurs, the company will be ready. Obviously, only one set of premise is desirable if coordination of its element is to be achieved.

Since agreement to utilize a given set of premises is important to coordinated planning, it becomes a major responsibility of managers, starting with those at the top, to make sure that subordinate managers understand the premises upon which they are expected to plan. It is not unusual for chief executives in well-managed companies to force top managers with differing views, through group deliberation, to arrive at a set of major premises that all can accept. But whether they are acceptable to all or not, no chief executive can afford to change a situation where his lieutenants are planning their portions of the company's future on substantially different premises.

The importance of premising is illutrated by the example where a company president, believing that all departments should develop their own budget and to find that the budgets did not fit, and he had a complex of inconsistent plans in his hands. Had he been aware of the importance of premises, he would never have asked for budgets without first giving his department heads their guidelines.

Determining Alternative Courses

The third step in planning is to search for and examine alternative courses of action. There is seldom a plan for which reasonable alternatives do not exist and quite often an alternative that is not obvious proves to be the best.

The more common problem is not finding alternatives, but reducing the number of alternatives so that the most promising may be analysed. Even with mathematical techniques and the computer, there is a limit to the number of alternatives that may be examined. It is, therefore, usually necessary for the planner to reduce by preliminary examination the number of alternatives to those promising the most fruitful possibilities or by mathematically eliminating, through the process of approximation, the least promising ones.

Evaluating Alternative Courses

Having sought out alternative courses and examined their strong and weak points, the fourth step is to evaluate them by weighing the various factors in the light of premises and goals.

One course may appear to be the most profitable but require a large cash outlay and a slow pay back : another may be less profitable but involve less risk ; still another may better suit the company's long range objectives. If the only objective were to maximize profits in a certain business, if the future were not uncertain, if cash position and capital availability were not a problem, and if most of the factors could be reduced to definite data, the evaluation should be relatively easy. But evaluation of planning is difficult with uncertainties, problems of capital shortage and intangible factors, and it is usually very difficult, even with relatively simple problems. A company may wish to enter a new product line primarily for purposes of prestige ; the forecast of expected results may show a clear financial loss, but the question is still open as to whether the loss is worth the gain.

Because the number of alternative courses in most situation are complex and the numerous variables and limitations are involved, evaluation can be also exceedingly complex. Due to the complexities the newer methodologies and applications of operations research and analysis, are helpful. Indeed, it is at this step in the planning process that operations research and mathematical computing techniques have their primary application to the field of management.

Selecting a Course of Action

The fifth planning step, selecting the course of action, is the point at which the plan is adopted to the real point of decision making. Occasionally an analysis and evaluation of alternative courses will disclose that two or more are advisable, and the manager may decide to follow several courses rather than the best course.

Formulation a Derivative Plans

At the point where a decision is made, planning is seldom complete, and a sixth step is to formulate derivative plan. There are almost invariably derivative plans required to support the basic plan.

Numberizing Plans by Budgeting

After decisions are made and plans are set the final step to give them meaning, as indicated above on types of plans, is to numberize them by convertising them to budgets. Each department or programme of a business or other enterprise can have its own budgets, usually of expenses and capital expenditure, which tie into the over-all budget. If planned well, budgets become a means of adding together the various plans and also important standards against which planning progress can be measured.

Principles of Effective Planning

A good and effective plan should conform to the following principles.

The Principle of Limiting Factor

A limiting factor is one which stands in the way of accomplishing a desired objective. If these factors are clearly recongnised, the planners will confine their search for alternative which will overcome the limiting factors. In choosing from among alternatives the more an individual can recognise and solve those factors which are limiting or critical to the attainment of desired goals, the more clearly he can select the most favourable alternatives. If we take any system or set of conditions or of circumstances existing at a given time, we recognise that it consists of element of parts of factors which together make up the whole system, set of conditions or circumstances.

Now if we approach this system or set of circumstance with a view to the accomplishments of a purpose, and only when the elements are parts. It becomes distinguished in two classes, those if absent or changed would accomplish the desired purpose, provided the others remain unchanged, and then others the first kind are called limiting factors, the second accomplishing factors.

The Commitment Principle

There should be some logic in selecting the right time and range in planning. As planning and forecasting which underlines it are costly, one should therefore not blame for longer period than is economically justifiable yet it is equally risky to plan for too short periods. The answer is to the right planning period, therefore lies in the 'commitment principle' that logical planning period. It encompasses a period of time in the future necessary to foresee through a series of actions, the fulfillment of commitments involved in a decision.

The most correct application of this principle is the setting of a planning periods long enough to anticipate the recovery of cost sink in a course of actions. But since things other than cost can be committed for various lengths of time, and because a commitment to spend after precedes an expenditure and may be unchangeable as sink costs seen inadequate to refer to the recovery of cost alone what the commitment principle implies is that long range planning for future decisions but rather implies is that long range planning for future impact of todays decisions. In other words decision is a commitment normally of funds, directions of action or reputation. And decision lies at the cost of planning.

The Flexibility Principle

The more the flexibility can be built into plans, the less the danger of losses incurred by unexpected events. But the cost of flexibility should be weighed against the risk involved in future commitments made.

The flexibility principle applies to the building into plan an ability to change directions. The ability to change a plan without undue costs or friction, to keep moving towards a goal despite changes in environments or even failure of plan has great value. Flexibility is critical when the commitment is great and cannot be discharged in a short time. But flexibility is possible only within limits. In the first place a decision cannot always be put off long enough to assure its rightness. In the second place, built-in flexibility of plan may be so expensive that the benefit of hedging may not be worth the cost. A third major limit be building flexibility into plans is the fact that there are often cases where flexibility either cannot be built into plan at all or can be only with such difficulty as to be impracticable.

The Principle of Navigational Change

The more planning decision commitment for the future, the more important it is to periodically check the events and results and redraw the plans as necessary to maintain a coarse towards the goals. Unlike the flexibility principle which applies to be adaptability built into plans themselves, this principle applies to the flexibility in the planning process. Built in flexibility does not automatically revise plans, the planner, like the navigator must continually check his course and redraw plan to meet a desired goal.

Principle of Open System Approach

It is essential for manager to take into account interactions with their total environment in every aspect of managing. Managing is not, nor could to be, a closed system approach to enterprise operation. This is nowhere more apparent than in theory and practice of planning.

Objectives must obviously be set in the light of the economic technological, social, political and ethical elements of an enterprise environment. Planning premises represent a clear recognition that plans cannot be constructed, nor decisions made, in the vacuum of an internal system. The interfaces and interactions of plans with every element of the conditions and influences surrounding an enterprise are indeed many and complex. While certain authors criticise the closed system approach of operational management theory.

Conditions of an Objective

Objective is a word that is used with many different meanings. Objective is understood as a conceived and wanted result event in future. A conceived and wanted result/event in future for the organisation as a whole is called a "Corporate Objective". An objective should fulfill the conditions so that it is operational or in the words can be used for planning and control. The conditions Dimensions ; Measurable ; Quantified ; Timed ; Responsibility . *The dimension of an Objective should be such that when* defined, no different interpretations are possible by different people. Different interpretations of same objective can lead to conflicting actions by the different managers. *The measuribility of an objective* means the possibility of identification of an objective on an undimensional or multi dimensional scale. Objective should be measurable so that it can be quantified for control. The *Quantification of an objective* is the identification of a defined situation/result/condition against a numerical value. Quantification is necessary to know whether the performed actions using relevant resources have led to a result which is identical with the objective or not. The timing of an objective is defining the time required to achieve that objective. This time is defined as the sum of times for necessary actions to be performed to achieve an objective. This time should be computed, keeping in view that many actions can be done concurrently. *The Responsibility Objective* are meant to be achieved and it is only the people in the organisations who have to achieve them by performing various actions. Therefore the responsibility for an objective has to be defined.

Management Value System and Objectives

The views and values of the management should get reflected in their objectives. There should be a complete harmony between the two. Such an harmony can be achieved when the objective are evolved from the views and values cherished by management. In this process of evolution the management may come to the conclusion that they are required to moderate their value system. In the absence of such an exercise which brings in this harmony, the managements can envelope the enterprise in a cloud of confusion where nobody knows whether the business is carried out to produce the product ; make profit ; create an ideal working place or develop a backward are. Such a situation should be avoided by establishing harmony between the objectives of an enterprise and the views and value system of the top management.

Need for an Objective

Objective is necessary to justify the existence and the struggle for existence of an organisation. Organisations like ships should know their destination so that they can decide on Equipment ; Manpower ; Material and finance which is required to be carried along with ; in other words, the resources to be deployed to achieve the objectives. Objectives are therefore, required in order to decide the actions to be performed and the resources required to perform these actions. In other words the starting point for planning are the objectives. The planning process takes off from the platform of objectives. The objectives are the reasons for the creation, existence and struggle of an organisation. These are required to understand the actions to be performed and resources to be deployed for them.

5

Management Development

Introduction

Management development regards to career planning for increasing the effectiveness of individuals and the needs of the organisation. Management development includes systematic review to identify the members of management who can be expected to increase their managerial effectiveness through training and special assignments. Organisation spend time on many developing managers because a manager alone, can achieve the objectives of the organisation. Organisation development is a way of improving the culture of the organisation so that it could be geared to excellence. The management development of executive talent is one approach to effective utilization of human potential. It is destructive and separate from management development since it involves only a few of the organisation's members. For the effectiveness of management development programme the managers need to be objective about his attitudes and overall performance if the total development effort is to have relevance and meaning to him, his employees and the organisatioin management development will only work under the situation when it has support from all levels of management. Following are certain pre-requisites for the effectiveness of a management development programme.

1. Support of the organisation's basic philosophy of management.
2. Commitment of the organisation to their lead down objectives.
3. Adequate resources like--time, money and manpower.
4. Personnel involvement of the chief executive.
5. Collaboration and team work between time and staff management. 6. Award system should reinforce the response directed towards the attainment of management and organisation development objectives.

Management development programme is the identification and development of qualified manager to assure a succession of management. Management and organisation development programmes aims bring about the following things in the organisation.

(*i*) To plan the career development of all managers according to the organisational managers ability.

(*ii*) To create an atmosphere in the organisation which encourages individual and group efforts towards organisational goals.

(*iii*) To maintain effective communication at various levels of the organisation.

Need for Management Development

The specific development needs of an executive can be determined by his appraisal which can be classified into following four areas.

(*i*) Need to increase knowledge and ability in his present position in order to improve current job performance.

(*ii*) Need to increase overall knowledge to prepare him to undertake greater responsibility within in his field.

(*iii*) Need to develop executive ability and understanding for a more general managerial position.

(*iv*) Need to develop personal characteristics, aptitude and attitudes to make him more acceptable.

Analysis Management Development Process

It is very difficult to measure the performance of managers but following are certain key factors contributing to evaluation.

- Learning aptitude.
- Oral and Written Communication Skills
- Human Relations.
- Awareness of Social Environment.
- Self objectivity.
- Resistance to change.
- Capacity for hard work.
- Quality of decision making.
- Analytical ability.
- Organising and Planning ability.

We know that the object of development is to bring about a change in the attitude, values and feelings. Individual personalities can be changed but it is quite difficult. The most efficient way of accomplishing a change is to modify the organisation itself. On the other hand it is not easier to improve a manager's output by modifying the organisational inputs, feedback and controls which effect his performance, but his transformation skills and his memory also need to be modified. In development programme the primary attention should be on the improvement of his memory as shown in Fig. 5.1. It is a fact that manager's who are exposed to off-the-job development often fails to transfer their learning on return to their own jobs, largely because the changes which they attempt to make in their behaviour are not supported by their own work group.

In order to find out whether a Development Programme is essential, it is important to find out whether the executive capacities of an executive and the organisational system need improvement. If in any organisation the desired output is generated then no action need to be taken. If the desired output is not generated in means that the problem exists and in order to overcome an analysis of following areas need to be reviewed :

1. Management skills only need improvement.
2. Both managerial skills and systems, elements need improvement.
3. Either managerial skills or systems can be improved.
4. Other systems elements alone need improvement.

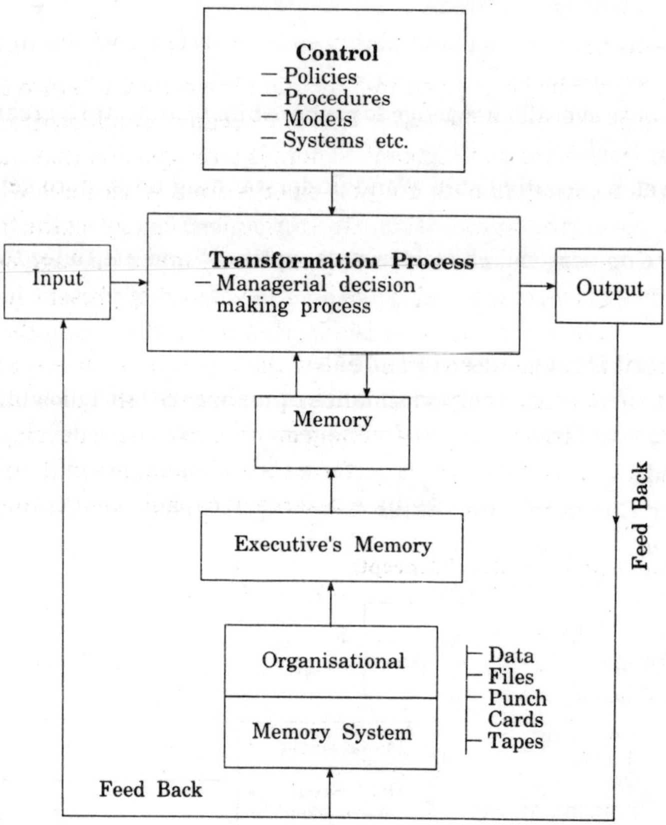

Fig. 5.1

Once we are sure that it is the management skills need improvement then a appropriate management development team can take care of this. If both managerial skills and systems elements need improvement we should analyse which one could be improved more easily. Depending upon the analysis we can either restructure other organisational elements or leave the responsibility with the management development team. Similar things hold true when either organisational elements need to be restructured or leave the responsibility with the management development team as shown in Fig. (5.2).

The analysis have shown that the object of a Managgement Development Programme is to highlight the following :

1. To sharpen the decision making process of executives.

2. Management development like other management activities is also a system with an object of improving the quality of the organisational outputs.

3. Quality of an organisational output is conditioned by inputs. (Men, Material Money, Datas, Information etc.)

Transformation (Decision making process) control (various guidelines given to an organisation) such as policies, procedures, objective and provide feed back (Two way communication system). If any of these elements is inadequate the output too will not be adequate.

Thus the managerial development efforts are to be effective in improving the quality of the output produced by the manager as a decision maker.

Executive Development

Tremendous emphasis has been given to Executive Development since the last world war and it has been named as the 'management revolution' because a sudden dramatic change took place in the area of management development. There is a recognition that qualified executives needed throughout the industry and do not just emerge from work force without consciously planned action on the part of the organisation. Good organisations select the talented employees and takes measures to develop them to have adequate inventory of management skill for use in the future. Management development also looks for developed of present in managers. Thus, everyone who is in a managerial position or is expected to be, the one in the future should be developed. All potential managers or anyone below the top man in the organisation who may be transferred or promoted to another job should be prepared for the promotion by the process of executive development. The objectives of management or executive development programme of any business concern are : to improve the performance of managers in their present positions ; and more importantly, to ensure an adequate reserve of capable well trained administrators for future needs.

Management Development (A System Concept)

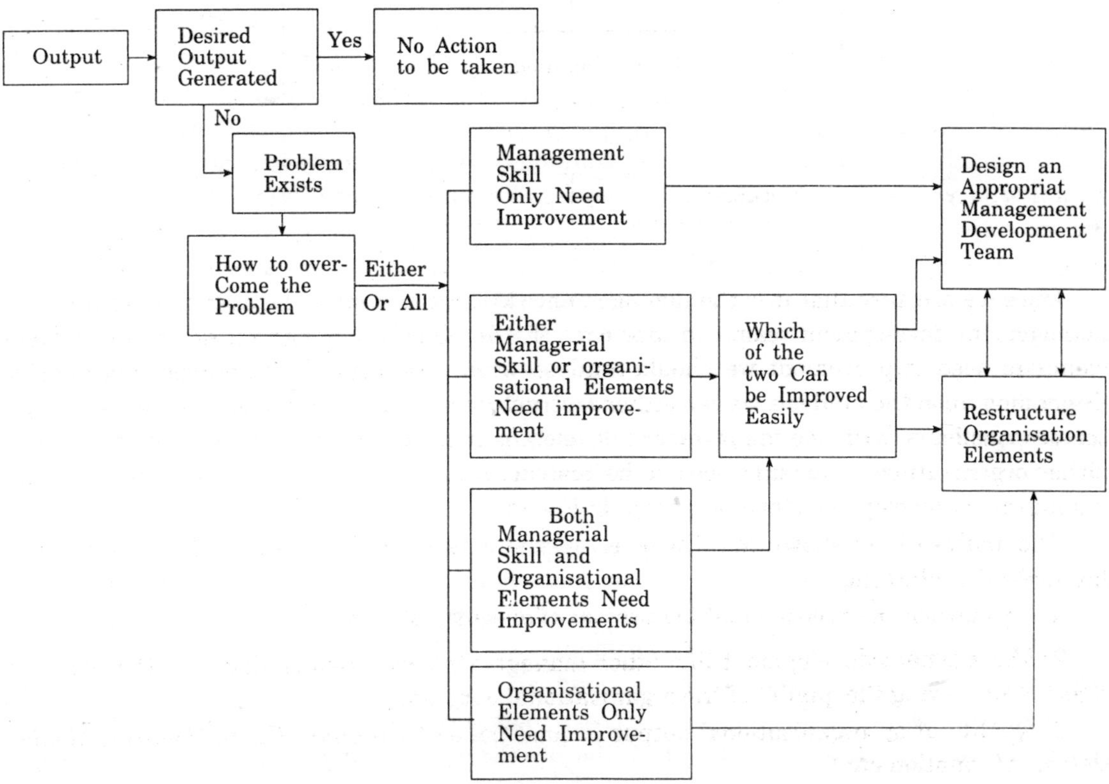

Fig. 5.2.

Executive development is a planned and systematic and continuous process of learning and growth designed to induce behavioural change in individuals by cultivating their mental abilities and inherent qualities through the acquisition, understanding and use of new knowledge, insights and skills as they are needed for the more effective performance of the work. This learning process involves the implication that there will be changed behaviour on the part of the individual given the adequate training and education. Managers develop not only by participating in formal courses of instruction drawn by the organisation but also through actual job experience in the organisation. It should be recognised that it is for the organisation to establish the developmental opportunities for its managers and potential managers. Self-development is an important concept in the whole programme of management development. The participants must have the motivation and the capacity to learn and develop. Development is more akin to education than it is to specific training in skills. Thus a manager cannot be developed only by taking a course, attending lectures and conferences job rotation assignments and the like. The process of learning on an executive's or future executive's part has to be accepted as discipline of self education. Management development implies development of people of different aptitudes, talents, aspirations, needs and motivation and because of the individual differences among them, they should be provided an effective organisational climate to develop themselves and to change their behaviours in managing the people and resources.

Training and Development

The process of training and development are often confused. Training means learning the basic skills and knowledge necessary for a particular job or a group of jobs. To put it in other words, training is the act of increasing the knowledge for doing a particular job. There is no choice before the employer whether to train or not, the only choice available is that of method. It is available to the employee in terms of job security and as an opportunity for future advancement. Actually, training is the follow up of selection which is the first stage in fitting of the individual into a particular job. In training the main objective is to attain a large degree of uniformity of conduct of different employees. Training is one of the areas of management where employer and employee have mutual interest. But development, on the other hand , means growth of the individual in all respects. An organisation works for the development of its executives or potential executive in order to enable them to be more effective in performing the various function of management. Any executive development programme aims at increasing the capacities of the individuals to achieve the desired objectives. Executive capacities simply his personal abilities and his potentialities. Desired objectives simply consideration for the goals of the organisation and individual. Increasing the capacities implies that change must occur in the executive and through him in his subordinates.

The initiative for development has to be taken by the individual himself. Unless he has the required potentialities for a good manager, and employee cannot be considered fit for development. No doubt, he can be given the necessary training to help him face the problems with the present job or to promote him for the higher job. Training is also necessary to prevent obsolescence of knowledge and skills of individuals.

Executive Development Programme seeks to develop the overall personality of the executives and not only the skill necessary to do the job efficiently. We have seen in an earlier chapter that job of executive is a very challenging one. So an executive development programme should be more concerned with the conceptual and human skill of the executives. As shown in Fig. 5.3, a comprehensive development programme uses various learning aids to increase the knowledge, decision-making ability, skill in dealing with people and maturity of executives.

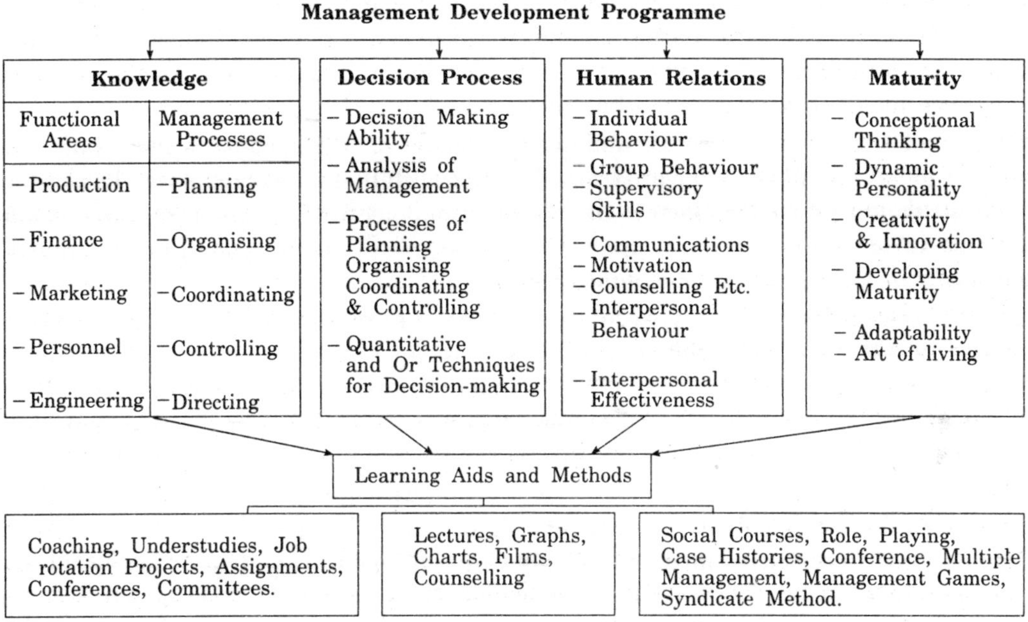

Fig. 5.3. Scope of Management Development Programme.

Need for Executive Development

The success of an organisation depends to a great extent on the quality of leadership provided by the managers. Now the assumption that a manager could acquire leadership skills and management abilities by serving long years as a worker has gone wrong. Every worker cannot be a good manager by his experience for a long time as a worker only. A manager's job requires certain abilities to lead and motive that people in the organisation for the achievement of some goals. Therefore, it is necessary for the organisation to continuously look for talented and education so that they may lead and motivate the people for the realisation of organisational objectives.

The necessity of executive development arises because of shortage of trained managers. This shortage is felt particularly during the large scale experience on the volume of activities of the organisation. It is very difficult to recruit and select the persons to man various managerial jobs from the labour markets. The organisation has to develop the talented employees and maintain an inventory of executive skills to meet the future demands.

There is an increasing realisation of the complexity of management job. The growth of the company form of organisation has brought separation of ownership from management of the organisation. This, coupled with the increasing recognition of the peculiar skills demanded of a manager, has contributed to the belief that management is an emerging profession because it is an established fact that it is a complex job, calling for certain skills, knowledge and attitudes which can be learnt only by systematic training and development. This is why there is an increasing tendency to recruit college or university graduates for future entry into executive ranks. After selecting the candidates the organisation tend to train and develop them systematically. But is should be noted that management is not a full-fledge profession, because of lack of recognised standard of competence and because the members have not created any accepted code of ethics. Nevertheless, management involves the learning of certain skills and knowledge. For this experience cannot be relied upon only because it will take a very long time to develop a person into a manager. It certainly calls for systematic training and development of the persons expected to perform managerial functions.

The rapid rate of technological and social changes in the modern society has made it imperative to have managers who are trained to cope with these developments. These changes have been brought by various factors like automation, electronic computers, intense market competitions from other countries, enlarge voice and role of labour, government controls and entrance of government in the field of business, etc.

Another reason for interest in executive development programmes is an increased recognition by business leaders of the social responsibilities because of changing social philosophy. The recognition of the need for new concepts of managerial tasks and leadership responsibilities arising out of social and technological changes has made the executive development absolute necessary.

Management obsolescence is another factor which calls for continuous executive development. Executive development is not a 'one-shot' affair ; it must continue throughout an executive's career. Otherwise, an acceptable executive of yesterday will not be acceptable to-day and an executive of to-day will not be good enough for the future. Therefore, in order to be dynamic and to change himself according to the needs, a manager must continually educate himself to successfully meet new challenges as they occur.

Thus better the management, better are the results of the organisation. Executive development therefore, is of paramount importance to have an effective and desired managerial manpower to meet the organisation's demands and to maintain and raise the level of managerial competence in the organisation.

EXECUTIVE DEVELOPMENT TECHNIQUES

A great variety of developmental techniques are used by different organisations to develop the executive manpower. But there are two principal methods which can be used to help people to acquire knowledge, skills and attitudes to become competent executives. One is through on-the-job experience and the other is through training and education courses away from the job. Actually, even in fiftees the emphasis was on one-the-job techniques, but now it is recognised that both off-the-job and on-the-job methods are important. Formal education through special courses, conferences, etc. is invaluable for learning new knowledge, new techniques and broader concepts. Yet real learning can only occur when the learner has an opportunity to practise and apply his knowledge acquired through formal courses.

On-the-job development is most powerful ; yet it is not totally proper to place sole reliance upon on-the-job methods. Under on-the-job development, a manager by the very nature of his position, serves as a guide for his subordinates. Such a guide or teacher may not be qualified to carry this important task. He may lack the skill, interest or patience of educating the subordinates. He may himself possess faulty notions about the process of management and imposition of such ideas on the subordinates will weaken the organisation. Therefore, on-the-job development must be properly balanced with class room (off-the-job) development.

A. On-the-job Methods

1. Coaching and Understudy.
2. Job Rotation.
3. Special Projects and Committee Assignments.

B. Off-the-job Methods

1. Special Courses.
2. Role Playing
3. Case Study.
4. Conference.
5. Multiple Management.
6. Management Games.
7. Syndicate Method.
8. Sensitivity Training.
9. Programmed Instruction.

The different methods outlined above are not mutually exclusive in nature. In practice, a typical programme of an executive development includes a number of methods in both categories because no single method is suitable for all the situations at all places.

Coaching

On-the-job coaching is a procedure by which a superior teaches job knowledge and skills to a subordinate. He briefs the trainee about what is expected of the latter and suggests how it may be done. He also checks his performance and advises him to improve his mistakes. The objective of coaching is not only to teach the subordinate the necessary skills for doing his assignment but also to provide him with diversified knowledge so that he may grow and advance. Coaching should be distinguished from counseling, which involves discussion between a superior and the subordinate of areas concerned with the latter's hopes, fears, emotions and aspirations. It reaches into very personal and delicate matters. In many cases the superior has to play the role both of coach and counsellor.

Coaching emphasizes a managerial responsibility for teaching which must be accomplished alongwith other duties. A manager should recognise an obligation to take a keen interest in the training and development of those who work under him. He can delegate more to prepare the subordinates not only to handle routine problems but also to handle non-routine complex situations. He can give his subordinates an opportunity to participate in making decisions affecting the department. An effective coach should avoid criticising his subordinate's personality. He should concentrate upon his work only and should try to help him in achieving self development.

On the job coaching constitutes learning by doing. The advantage is increased motivation for the trainee and minimisation of the problems of transferring learning from theory to practice. The danger in this method is the possible neglect by the guide or supervisor. Thus as a development technique, it cannot stand alone. It is primarily a device for ensuring that individuals grow within the boundaries set by their jobs and their organisational units. The man cannot develop much beyond the limits of his own boss's abilities. Coaching works best when other techniques of periodical classroom instruction are used along with it.

Understudy

Under this system a certain person is specifically designated as the heir apparent and his future depends upon what happens to his superior. Thus an understudy is a person who is in training to assume the full duties and responsibilities of the position currently held by his superior, when the latter leaves his post due to promotion, retirement or transfer.

A department manager may pick one individual from his unit to become his understudy. He will then guide him to learn his job and grapple with the problems that confront the manager daily. An understudy can be developed to take over one day the superior's job in a number of ways. When the superior is handling his daily operating problems, he may discuss these with his understudy to get his ideas and give him experience of decision-making. He may also assign the understudy to investigate and make written recommendations upon long-term problems. The understudy may even be asked to directly supervise a number of people at work. This will give him an opportunity to try out his leadership skills.

The advantages of understudy method pertain to practical and realistic situation in which the training is conducted. It is practical and fairly quick way of training designated persons for greater management responsibilities. It emphasizes learning by doing. It relieves the boss of some of his workload by delegating some portion of his work to the understudy. To the organisation it ensures that it will not be placed at a serious disadvantages if an executive suddenly leaves his job. The udnerstudy will be in a position to hold that position.

The disadvantages of understudy method are also numerous. Since the understudy has been specifically designated, there is often the feeling that competition for promotion is over. This reduce the motivation for both the one designated and the other personnel. The understudy is not certain when the job will be vacated and he will move up. The designation of one man as an understudy is seen by the others as an act of favouratism. This may even cause jealousy and friction within the department. Moreover, this approach to training suffers from the same disadvantages as all on the job training techniques. Firstly, the understudy may be picked on the basis of his similarity in thinking and acting with those of his superior and then, the understudy will learn the ways of superior, who in turn learnt from his superior. Thus understudy will tend to perpetuate existing practices--the bad as well as the good. Therefore, outside contacts through other development techniques are essential for the development of the person and for the well-being of the organisation.

Job Rotation

The transferring of executives from one job to another job and from one department, to another department on a coordinated and planned basis is a popular means of development among the modern business concerns. The major objective of job rotation is that of broadening the background of the executive in the business. The trainee is rotated from job to job and hence acquires a general background.

In modern organisations a high proportion of the entry jobs for junior executives require a considerable degree of specialised knowledge and skill. But a man can never acquire the broad perspective and diversified skill needed for promotion unless he is deliberately taken out of his speciality and placed in different types of situations. In order to develop the generalists for the upper management levels, the organisation must take action to provide a variety of job experiences for those having the potential for major executive ranks. Job or position rotation is the only answer in such a situation.

Job rotation has many advantages. It serves to break down the feeling of superiority of one department over the others. When a number of executives have served in each other's department, they can also understand the reason why a certain function must be done in a particular way. Thus inter-departmental coöperation will be enhanced. Job rotation injects new ideas into the different departments of the organisation. Under this system, a man is not destined to end up in just one spot but is equipped to step into any one of the several executive posts in any of various functional divisions. The trainee will learn the nature and significance of management principles by transferring learning from one job another. Here, again, the training takes place in a practical situation. This technique can stimulate a more co-operative attitude by exposing a man to other fellow's problems and view points.

The system of job rotation has certain drawbacks also. Productive work may suffer due to disruption caused by changes and limitations of individuals to adjust to new job. So it is better to lengthen the interval of rotation and to rotate fewer personnel at a time. The executive can't gain specialised knowledge in one particular branch of work during a short span of time. Job rotation may undermine the morale and efficiency of the departments managed by these executives, especially if a whole parade of them goes through in a relatively brief time span, because rotation also involves upseting of house and family life in addition to compelling the subordinate personnel to readjust their behaviour conform to new leaders.

Special Projects and Committee Assignments

A special project is a highly useful training device under which a trainee may be assigned a project that is closely related to the work of his department. For instance, a trainee may be assigned to develop a system of cost control in the execution of an order. The trainee will study the problem and then make written recommendations upon it. This project would not only provide valuable experience in the problem to the trainee but would also have the other values of educating the trainee the importance of costs and to understand the organisational relationships with the accounting department. Thus the trainee would acquire knowledge of the assigned subject and would also learn to work with others possessing the different view points.

Committee assignments are very much related to project assignments. Under this method an *ad hoc* committee is constituted and is assigned a subject to discuss and make recommendations. The committee has assigned objectives and responsibilities related to the work of the organisation. It will make a study of the problem and present its suggestions to the departmental manager. Committee assignments can provide the necessary general background to the trainees because every member of the committee gets a chance to learn from the other. From this purpose, the members of the committee may belong to the different departments. Committee assignment in an important device of educating the executives to acquire general background and to change their behaviour towards the problem. Here it is necessary that the terms of reference to the committee should be clear and scope of committee investigations should be clearly laid down.

Special Courses

Formal training courses for the executives can be conducted in a number of ways and under a variety of conditions, by a business, organisation as a part of its executive development programme. Firstly, the organisation may develop the courses itself to be taught to the trainees. Now the questionnaires who will do the teaching in executive training courses ? The answer is that teaching may carried out by the instructors from within the organisation and or by the specialists from other outside institutions. For instance, the subjects dealing with the organisation, its structure, policies etc., may be taught by a senior line executive or a member of the training staff of the organisation. Professors from universities and other like institutions may be invited to teach courses in statistics, operations research, production planning, etc. These management techniques may also be taught by specialists within the organisation who are professionally qualified in these topics.

The second approach to the special course technique is to send the personnel to programmes established by colleges and universities. These programmes very quite widely in length, content and methods of administration. The organisation can sponsor some of its members of the staff for study in courses in business management, personnel management, marketing management, etc. in university, departments and colleges. The expenses are borne by the organisation. These courses constitute more of education than of training.

The third approach to the special course technique is for the business concern to work with a college or other institution in establishing a course or a series of courses to be taught by its faculty members. These courses also usually tend towards the education end. A big organisation which is employing thousands of employees can also start its own training school. In India, almost all the leading banks have their own staff training colleges. In such institutions the courses are devised by the college experts in consultation with the top management of the organisations.

The lecture method is employed in such courses for all levels of management. However, lecture method is not the only method depended upon. Lectures are also supplemented by group discussions, films, case studies, demonstrations and role playing.

Contents of the Course

In cases where the organisation itself designs the courses or where it collaborates with other institutions in this regard, the essential subject matter covered may include the following :

1. Nature and purpose of organisation

(*a*) Objectives.

(*b*) Policies and procedures.

(*c*) Products and services.

(*d*) Organisation structure of relationships.

(*e*) Financial picture.

(*f*) Union management relations.

2. Management principle and techniques

(*a*) Principles of management.
(*b*) Principles of organisation.
(*c*) Financial planning and management.
(*d*) Administrative practice.
(*e*) Production planning and control.
(*f*) Cost analysis and control.
(*g*) Personnel management.
(*h*) Statistical quality control.
(*i*) Operations research.
(*j*) Data processing.

3. Human relations

(*a*) Nature of human behaviour.
(*b*) Group dynamics.
(*c*) Leadership.
(*d*) Motivation.
(*e*) Morale.
(*f*) Participation programmes.
(*g*) Supervision.
(*h*) Welfare programmes.
(*i*) Communication.
(*j*) Discipline.
(*k*) Grievance procedure.

4. Technical knowledge and skills

Managers must have an adequate understanding of various skills to perform the management functions well. Though it is desired that manager should be a generalist, it is also essential that he should have some specialisation in one field.

5. Economic, Social and Political environments

(*a*) Economic system.
(*b*) Relations with local, state and central governments.
(*c*) Community relations.
(*d*) Business ethics.
(*e*) Social responsibilities.
(*f*) Legal framework for business.
(*g*) Political environments in the country.

Emphasis on any of these topics will vary with management level. Although foreman, departmental heads, plant managers and general managers are all members of management, the nature of their jobs differ substantially. There is no doubt that all the five subjects listed above are relevant for all levels of management. However, certain topics are more relevant for one level than another. For instance, a course in operation research for plant managers, sales managers and personnel managers may be a necessary, but it may not be necessary for a foreman. Similarly, a foreman is not directly involved in the economic, social and political environment of an organisation, so he need not be given detailed knowledge of these subjects. Thus not only the contents but also the degree of knowledge and skill vary according to the level of the executives involved.

Courses for first line supervisors will concentrate upon technical processes and human relations. They tend to be closely related to the supervisor's day-to-day job. But courses for top management must emphasize such subjects as organisation behaviour, human relations, financial management, policy formulation, administrative controls, the business and politics, labour relations and public relations because top executives control and manage the overall operation of the organisation and maintain relations both with the insiders and the outsiders. Courses for members of middle management should contain elements of both upper and lower level executive development programmes. They may be given the teaching in various management techniques like cost analysis and control, data processing etc., and human relations management.

Role Playing

Role playing technique is use for human relations and leadership training. Its purpose is to give trainees an opportunity to learn human relations skills through practice and to develop insight into one's own behaviour and its effect upon others. Thus its objective is very narrow *i.e.*, to increase the trainee's skill in dealing with others. It can be used in human relations training and sales training because both these involve dealing with other people.

Under this method, a conflict situation is artificially constructed and two or more trainees are assigned different parts to play. No dialogue is given before hand. The role players are provided with either a written or oral description of a situation and the role they are to play. After being allowed sufficient time to plan their actions, they must then act out their parts spontaneously before the class. For instance, a role playing situation may be a supervisor discussing a grievance with an employee or a salesman making a presentation to a purchasing agent.

Role playing has a number of advantages. It provides an opportunity for development human relations understanding and skill and to put into practice the knowledge they have acquired from text books, lectures, discussion, etc. It is learning by doing. The interview may be taped to provide the trainees a chance to listen to their performance and note their strengths and weaknesses. Thus knowledge or results is immediate, because the trainee as well as the listeners analysis the behaviour of the role players.

Case study

Case method is a means of simulating experience in the classroom. Under this method the trainees may be given a problem to discuss which is more or less related to the principles already taught. This method gives the trainee an opportunity to apply his knowledge to the solution of realistic problems. Cases may be used in either of two ways. Firstly, they can be used subsequent to the exposition of formal theory under which the trainees apply their knowledge of theory to specific situations. Secondly, the trainees may be assigned the cases for written analysis and oral class discussion without any prior explanation of pertinent concepts and theory. In this case the trainees are expected to derive useful generalisation and principles themselves. The approach places heavy demands upon the trainees and require that they should have a good deal of maturity and background in the subject matter concerned.

Case studies are extensively used in teaching law, personnel management, human relations, marketing management and business policy in various educational institutions. Students learn that there is no single answer to a particular problem. The answer of each trainee may differ. Case discussions will help them to appreciate each other's thinking. That is why case study is frequently used in supervisory and executive training in business.

The case study method provides for learning by doing. The success of this method depends to a great extent upon the qualities of the guide to conduct the discussion so as to keep the speakers always on the right track. Moreover, it is also necessary to prepare good case material based upon real experiences and problem situations to make it interesting to the trainees. Good cases can develop analytical thinking and fostering problem solving ability. Narrow mindedness is reduced because the students realise that others have also studied the same problem and come up with different patterns of analysis and solutions.

Conference Training

A conference is a group meeting conducted according to an organised plan in which the members seek to develop knowledge and understanding by obtaining a considerable amount of oral participation. It is an effective training device for persons in the positions of both conference member and conference leader. As a member, a person can learn from others by comparing his opinions with those of others. He learns to respect the viewpoint of others and to realise that there is more than one workable approach to a problem. As a conference leader, a man can develop his skill to motivate people through his direction of discussion. He learns the effects of closely controlling and dominating the discussion as compared to adopting a more permissive type of direction.

Conference method overcomes certain disadvantages of the lecture, because here the participants play very active roles. They are not passive. Learning is facilitated through building upon the ideas contributed by the conference members. In fact, people learn from each other. Interest of the participants tend to be high. The conference is ideally suited to learning apart problems and issues and examining them from different angles. It is the best method for reducing dogmatism employed in supervisory and executive development programmes.

Conferences may be of three types :

1. the directed or the guided conference :
2. the consultative conference :
3. the problem-sloving conference.

However, the directed conference is most commonly used for training purposes because the programme director his certain concepts which he wishes the trainees to absorb. This device depends for its success upon the active participation of the trainees. The size of the group must be limited to twenty to thirty persons. The people should sit facing one another around a conference table. They should have some knowledge of the subject to be discussed before coming to the conference. This can be obtained from assigned readings. The programme co-ordinator introduces the topic and invited viewpoints from the group on problem areas related to this topic. He must, by skillful use of questions, make sure that the group analyses the topic thoroughly. In the directed conference the leader may introduces new material by occasional brief periods of lecturing.

The conference method is also not free from drawbacks. The main drawbacks are as follow:

1. It is limited to a small group ; and

2. Progress is often slow because all those desiring to speak on a point are generally allowed to do so.

Sometimes irrelevant issues creep in and the main issue is lost in the process.

Multiple Management

Multiple management is the name given to the system whereby permanent advisory committees of executives study problems of the organisation and make recommendations to higher management. The final decisions rest with the higher management. Thus committees are the device for executives development. Another device is the establishment of a junior board of directors in a company for the training of the executives. The junior board is given power to discuss any problem which the senior board (constituted by the shareholders) could discuss. The greatest value of this additional board is the training of junior executives. Memberships on the junior board becomes a pre-requisite to the membership of the senior board.

The junior board discusses a wide variety of subjects which a senior board can discuss. All recommendations that are forwarded to the senior board must be unanimous. This will prevent the lower boards from dumping their problems upon the senior board. The senior board is under no compulsion to accept the recommendations of the junior board. The junior board and various committees serve in an advisory capacity only. Though the major objective is training and development of junior executives, the company is benefitted by their productive ideas.

As a management development technique, multiple management has several advantage. Firstly, it gives board members an opportunity to gain knowledge and experience in various aspects of business. Secondly, it helps identify those who have good executive talent. Thirdly, the junior executives gain practical experience in group decision-making and in team work. Through the group interaction process they learn to respect the views of their associates. Lastly, it is a relatively less expensive method of development and it permits a considerable number of executives to participate within a reasonable period of time.

Management Games

A variety of computer and non-computer management or business games have been devised and used with varying success in development programmes. A management game is a classroom exercise in which teams of students complete against each other to achieve common objectives. The game is designed to be a close representation of real-life conditions. The trainees are asked to make decisions about production, cost, research and development, inventories, sales etc. for a simulated organisation. Since they are often divided into teams as competing companies, experience is obtained in team-work.

Under this method, the students learn by analysing problems by using some institution and by making trial and error type of decisions. The error of an unsound decision could be disastrous in a real business situation. But in a game an executive learns from his mistakes and has a chance to record his losses without harmful consequences. In some games players can even get a second chance to do something all over again if their first decision is wrong. A management game has objective feedback of the consequences of business decisions. Feedback is prompt and this facilitates learning. The games have the limitation that the model upon which a game is built may be typical of a general kind of situation, yet it may not be realistic.

Syndicate Method

Training and development of executives who are already in positions of responsibility and are marked out for assuming a place at the top or near the top in business or public services has to provide for suitable opportunities for :

(*a*) Critical reflections on their own work and the manner of doing it ;

(*b*) Updating their knowledge of new concepts and advanced techniques in the field of management ;

(*c*) Further improving executive skills under suitably simulated conditions ; and

(*d*) Developing better insights and sounder judgement on their part in respect of human resources.

To provide such opportunities to executives who possess long practical experience presents considerable challenge in the selection of the teaching techniques. Teaching in the conventional manner does not have much appeal to them nor does it make much impact on them. As said earlier, the process of learning on the part of an experienced executive is essentially a self imposed or willingly accepted discipline of self-education. The syndicate method as a technique of teaching admirably meets this requirement.

Syndicate method is used in management development programmes for executives whose age ranges between 30-40, who have 9-12 years experience in some special area of management to be fit for taking up higher responsibilities. The participants are men of mature judgement and proved ability. They are known to the director of the programme before actually joining it.

There is a tendency to call any kind of group discussion in management courses a 'syndicate' and the impression has grown that syndicates are just groups that discuss. This is not true. It is true that on the face syndicate work, it appears as if it consists only of discussion but there is much more than the discussion. Syndicate is in fact a form of organisation for the performance of a specific task of management with the help of a team much as in real life. In judging the syndicate method and its usefulness as an educational device, one must take into account the quality and characteristics of the participants as well as the objects of the course in which the syndicate method is used. The object of the course, apart from increasing the participant's knowledge of up-to-date ideas and tools of management is to enable him to acquire a proper perspective on his job in relation to the activities in areas other than his own and give him concentrated practice in skills, techniques and procedures which he has to use in his day-to-day work increasing as he moves up in the ladder of management.

The syndicate method is intended to stimulate critical thinking than to provide spoon fed information or opinions. Even highly qualified experts find it difficult to set their lectures at the appropriate level when the audience consists of men whose experience in a given area ranges from 10 to 15 years.

In developing the men of long experience and practical wisdom the syndicate methods has certain basic advantages over other educational methods. It secures the highest involvement from the participants. It is something like the idea of the 'selfled groups'. The greatest value of it lies in the practice it gives the participant in communicating with and in understanding and managing colleagues and in constantly compelling him to adjust and re-adjust himself to what he thinks his colleagues think of him. If the course is a residential one, it has again many more advantages. The confidence and friendliness which a residential course ensures, the healthy competition which automatically sets in between the different syndicates as also within the syndicate itself among the participants themselves to make a better showing, the constant pressure of group opinion as well as the expertise and advice of the friendly directing staff--all these factors compel each participant to do his best. Such a structured and carefully guided and supervised process of 'self-education' is highly conductive to the all round development of the executive.

Sensitivity Training

The aim of sensitivity training is to improve the trainees' skills in dealing with people. In sensitivity training the executives spend about two work periods attending the lecturers on topics such as leadership and communication.

T-Group which is sometimes called as Sensitivity Training Development Group has a two fold function :

1. To help its members learn how groups actually work.
2. To give each member of the group a chance to discover how other people interprent and are affected by his own behaviour.

As the members of a T-Group discuss what they should talk about and how their discussion should be structured, conflict obviously arise. Members criticise freely the behaviour of each other thereby giving a feedback which may be positive or negative.

T-Group or sensitivity training is an important tool of growing importance in helping managers to win the cooperation of people working with them. There is no doubt that the T-Group is one of the significant educational innovation of the century. It has been experienced that about two-thirds of the participants undergone laboratory training have displayed change in behaviour of positive type.

Despite the rising popularity of T-Group the value of this training is vigorously disputed by some specialists in management development. Specialists are willing to concede that a trainee may learn a thing which may be helpful at time in his life but of little use to a corporate manager trying to cope up with his job. To support their point of view they say that there is no proof that managers who have been to laboratory do their jobs better than before.

Even managers who have undergone sensitivity training feel that even after learning a lot in the laboratory it is difficult to apply the learning in real business situations. When sensitivity training technique is applied to engineering managers who are in dark as far as this area concerned, normally they do better.

It is found that there is a fundamental conflict between the values taught at a laboratory and the value inherent in the structure of the business. Argyris concedes that laboratory education is only a partial attack on the problem of organisational effectiveness. But if effectiveness is to be permanently introduced one must also change the organisation structure, managerial controls and incentive systems. The serious criticism of laboratory training is that it is of little practical use and the other disadvantage is that trainee may be badly hurt by the emotional feeling. So there is not doubt that certain anxiety and stress are inevitable in T-Group.

To sum up, in sensitivity training a few trainees get hurt and a few remain unaffected and great majority feel that they have been changed for the better.

The top management in any organisation must determine before introducing sensitively training that there is an appropriate environment for this and as there is always a risk of being hurt at a laboratory. Attendance should be on voluntary basis.

It is equally important that individual undergoing sensitivity training should be thoroughly and impartialy briefed and should be encouraged to give the idea if he cannot withstand any more criticism. Thus the advantage of this process of training is that the participants develop greater understanding of the behaviour of others and sensitivity of their attitude. The effectiveness of the method would be reflected by an ultimate change on the part of the participants on their jobs.

Programmed Instruction

Programmed instruction has recently gained lot of importance both in education and in industry. Programmed instruction may include teaching machines, auto-instruction, automated instruction and programmed learning.

Cook and Mechner defined Programmed Instruction as the application of the science of learning to the task of training and education. Cook and Mechner characterised programmed instruction in the following elements :

1. Active response by the trainees.
2. Immediate feed-back for each response.
3. Pacing the instruction at the rate at which the trainees learn the material.
4. The instructions should be in steps so that stimuli produces gradual increament in learning the material.

The core feature of programmed instruction is participation by the trainee and immediate feed-back by him. The programmed instructions include elaborate teaching machines films sound tapes, programmed books, illustrations, printed material, diagrams. Whatever may be the method of programmed instructions it basically performs following two functions :

1. It provides information to the learner.
2. It provides feedback whether the response is correct or wrong.

The critical feature of programmed instruction is the programming itself. The instruction programme used in programmed instruction consists of series of items each of which deals with small segment of information, intended to provide some response by the trainee. The various items should be arranged in a sequence and each item is built upon the previous one. As the trainee progresses from item to item, he builds up step the total material of the whole programme. The items of one programme vary from another.

Programming is a time consuming process and requires people who are qualified to carry it out. Experience has shown that it takes around 60 minutes in developing one item and each programme constitute hundreds of items. Thus it is clear that to design programme it requires lot of time and efforts.

Hickey used the programmed instructions in training telephone relay adjusters, a job largely depends on manual skills. The programme required that the instructions be read to the trainees by the use of magnetic tape recording in combination with visual films. A comparison of the cost training really adjustors by the programmed instructions and by the original method was plotted. In Fig. 5.4 the area above each curve represents the cost of training in terms of lost production. The two curves show that there is saving by the programmed instruction method of training. The result of the study showed that the time to reach 65% of standard production was 40 days in programmed instruction while it was 60 days with original method.

Programmed instructions has been viewed as an aid to instructors to be used with other techniques of training.

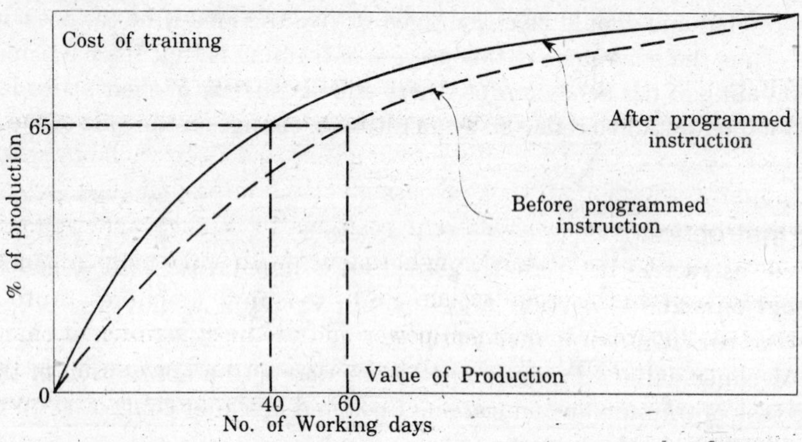

Fig. 5.4 Comparison of cost with and without Programmed Instruction.

Programmed instructions are used by most companies with enthusiasm because of many advantages but programmed instructions should be adopted as training method only if there is a reason to believe that it will bring improvement in learning and also the time and cost considerations are satisfactory.

At time it may by that the complete programme is not economically feasible but still it is possible to use some of the principles of programmed instruction to certain segments of training programmes such as in the preparation of manuals and related materials.

6

Effective Communication and Managerial Skills

COMMUNICATION

Communication is the number one problem of Management. Nothing happens in management until communication takes place. Success of a Manager depends more on his ability to communicate than any other skill. It is a process involving inter change of facts, view points and ideas between persons placed in different positions to achieve understanding through effective communication. Skill to work is brought in touch with will to work and both combined together lead to team work in the organisation.

Communication is our greatest source of power and the most significant characteristic of man-kind. Without communication, we would not have formed community, bring up our children, work together in organised way and pass down ideas, innovation and inventions from generation to generation.

Effective communication is a flash of lightening and often even more illumination. It enables us to see others and make ourselves seen and known. It is a distinctive human characteristic and sets one man apart from another. There is not much risk of over simplifying the statement that good managers are good communicators, poor managers are usually the opposite. If we analyse the genesis of crisis that arise in industry, leading to strained labour management relations generally it starts from gaps in communication. Communication gap results in crisis.

Communication is Important

In our life, we talk for 27 years covering 10,000 books of 400 pages each. We spent 80 to 90 per cent of our working times in communicating with others, of which 60 per cent is spent in talking and listening and 20 to 30 per cent in reading and writing.

The importance of communication starts from the fact that human beings demand information, knowledge news, gossip and rumour. After roti, kapra aur makaan, the most vital need is communication. *Moghul Emperor Akbar used a relay of drum beater all the way from Agra to Allahabad where he was then comping to convey him the news of the birth of his expected baby and also of its sex. He got the news of his son Salim in minutes instead of days.*

Communication Gains

Communication grows best in a climate of trust and confidence. Communication satisfies the need of self expression of the people who work and also those who take work from others. Effective communication leads to higher productivity and job satisfaction. With communication gains we come alive; we gain at work; at home and socially also, we gain.

At Work—As the job becomes more meaningful, interesting, rewarding and easier;

At Home—Family life becomes fuller, richer and happier;

Socially—Life takes a new dimension. One looks for new challenges. One interacts the new commers with more confidence and fits into scene better.

Communication Process

Communication process involves listening, speaking writing and non-verbal communication. Communication process starts with a minimum of two persons sender who sends the message; receiver, who receives it. Distortions or barriers in communication are in transmitting the message from mind to mouth in respect of sender: mouth to ear due to channel and media of communication; ear to mind in respect of receiver's perception and communication ability. In order to examine the communication process in an organisation. It is important to ask the following three questions :

(*a*) Does the organisation have functional channels of communication right down the shop floor without distortion.

(*b*) Does the ideas of employees travel upwards to the top.

(*c*) Does the information in the organisation travel horizontal.

If the communication process encourage secret atmosphere the result will be misunderstanding and attitude of cynicism down the line. An organisation in which this kind of an atmosphere pervails, will not only be full of inner tensions but will be isolated from reality and is likely to become inert in respect of fresh creative ideas. The golden rule of communication should be to communicate as much as you can and to every member in the organisation except those items of importance where as a deliberate matter of policy it may be necessary to hold information.

Barriers to Communication

There is a saying that reasonable men always agree when they understand what they are talking about. The various barriers to communication are—Tendency to evaluate; unclarified assumptions, hightened emotions; ability to communicate closed mind; inattentions; semantic status and position and resistance to change. Communication is a two edged sword. We have 2500 languages in the world not including dialects. Communication barriers are the road blocks. They have impaired the power of the world to solve human problems. Communication barriers create problems of misunderstanding and conflict between men who live together in the same community, who work together on the same job and even among men living in the different parts of the world who have never seen one another. The various barriers to communication are given in Figure 6.1.

COMMUNICATION BARRIERS

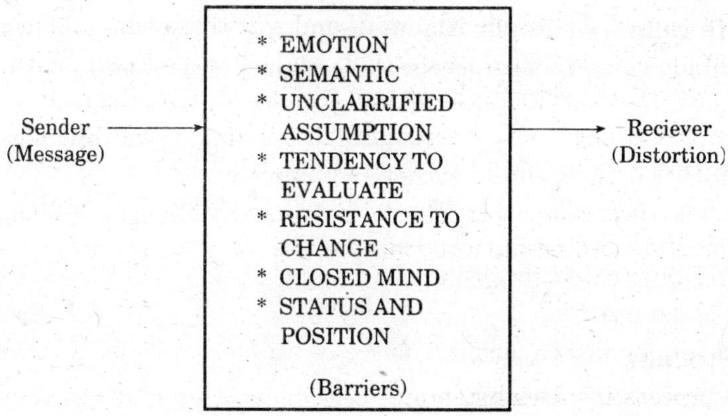

Fig. 6.1.

Tendency to Evaluate

Tendency to evaluate is a natural tendency among people to judge to evaluate and approve while communicating. A famous French Novelist had written that "We like every thing about the famous authors and we trace in them, things which we blame in others. "He narrates a very pleasant adventure. He had given the manuscript of the novel to a publisher. Because the author was going on a long trip, he had divided the manuscript into various actions each represented one instalment. As luck would have it, the printer distributed the chronology and sequence and printed materials from top to bottom, instead of from left to right as we should have. The novel had no head and tail, but nobody noticed. There was no criticism. Some intelligent brains even complimented him on the delicious style of imagination.

Unclarified Assumptions

We assume that others know it. Recently a message was received from an institute that some of their managers would be visiting IDPL, Rishikesh, for a study tour on a particular date. No indication was given regarding their detailed programme, particularly their boarding and lodging arrangements and period of stay. They assumed that all these arrangements will be made whereas IDPL authorities assumed that they are coming only for sight seeing. On their arrival, they informed, that they have come for two days and wanted boarding and lodging arrangements for 30 persons which was not possible as the Guest House was already full. The confusion occurred because of unclarified assumptions on both sides.

Hightened Emotions

Emotions are a part of personality of every human being. Those who have more emotions they are closer to their child ego. Those with controlled emotions are close to their adult ego. The persons with balanced emotion are matured people and it is easy to communicate with such people. When the atmosphere is tense and charged with high emotions, the matured executive remains cool and calm and so able to think and act rationally.

Ability to Communication

— To some it comes naturally.

— Others need training.

— Listening, reading and writing improve the communication ability.

Closed Mind

Idea that I know everything leads to a close mind. Attitude of a person that he knows everything makes him rigid and dogmatic. Example of closed mind can be the following conversation between two individuals Mr. X, and Mr. Y,

Mr. X met Mr. Y on the road side asked

Mr. X . . . What is the time ?

Mr. Y . . . Who don't you keep a watch ?

Mr. X . . . Look I just asked the time ?

Mr. Y . . . I have also not said anything ?

Mr. X . . . But who are you to say me anything ?

When the subordinate comes to executive with some personal issues or with some new ideas, the executive should listen to him with an open mind. In case of closed minded executive, the communication breaks. The subordinate loses the initiative to approach the Boss.

Inattentions

Attention is guided by self-interest. We are exposed to listeners, to events and stimulus, but we tend to notice only those that are significant for our own need. Inattention leads to break in communication. In other words inattention leads to psychological diversion and results in break communication.

Sementic

Symbols and words having variety of meanings and, therefore, the sender and the receiver have to choose one meaning from among the many. If both choose the same meaning, the communication will be affected, but this may not always be the case because of difference in formal education and specific situation of the people.

Status and Position

The negative attitude exhibited by the executives is a hurdle in the process of two way communication. This is normally due to nonlistening habit of the executive to their subordinates. It has been observed that executives devote for more attention to telling, informing and commanding than they do to listening, asking and interpreting. An executive may guard information for;

— Consideration of prestige, ego and strategy;

— Under rating and under-estimating the intelligence of subordinates.

— Deriving satisfaction in being the storehouse of information.

Resistance to Change

It is the general tendency of human beings to maintain status-quo. The resistance to change is an important obstacle to effective communication. The change should be brought about after the people are educated, trained, oriented for the change. This will be possible through the process of association, involvement, leadership, commitment, action and feed-back.

Communication Gap

The manager set the guidelines for the supervisors and the supervisors in turn make the frame of work for the policies and guidelines to workers, because of the various channel involved.

Cause of Communication Gap

Communication gap arises when an employee does not know :

— How important his work is;

— How far is he in queue;

— How well is he doing;

— How much additional skill to acquire; and

— What is expected of him.

Communication gap also arises due to lack of co-ordination between the various departments which leads to conflict and interdepartmental rivalries. Organisation of various functional areas is important, but strict demarcation between the various functions of organisation restricts the interaction resulting in tight compartments. Rules and Regulations are made for smooth functioning of the organisation but there should be enough flexibility to accommodate the changing conditions and emergencies.

Overcoming Communication Gap

Communication gap must be removed to ensure that workers produce good quality products and are motivated to produce more, ensuring higher productivity. Communication gap can be overcome by :

— Encourage feed back;

— Combat rumours, guesses and misconception;

— Encourage suggestion;

— Encourage two way communication;

— Issue clear-cut instructions.

— Encourage personal communication.

— Impersonal communication.

Types of Communication

Communication process involves following types of communications

(*a*) Listening,

(*b*) Speaking

(*c*) Writing communication,

(*d*) Non-verbal communication.

Guidelines for Listening

(*i*) Be interested and show genuine concern and lively curiosity encourage others to speak freely.

(*ii*) Tune into other person. Try to understand his/her view point.

(*iii*) Hold your fire. Avoid jumping to conclusions. Plan your response only after you are certain you have got the whole Message,

(*iv*) Look for the main ideas. Avoid being distracted by details.

(*v*) Monitor your own feelings and point of view. Each of us listens differently. Our convictions and emotions filter even distort-what we hear.

(*vi*) Give other person the benefit of doubt. We often enter conversations with our minds already made up, at least partially on the basis of past experience. Pre-judgement can shut out new messages.

(*vii*) Work at listening. Hearing is passive. Our nervous system does the work. Listening is active. It takes mental effort and attention.

(*viii*) Get feed back make certain you are really listening.

To summarise, Listing is the finest art, still to be mastered by men; To be a good listener, it requires :

(*a*) Work at listening,

(*b*) Weight what is being said

(*c*) Review from time to time.,

(*d*) Listen between the lines.

Speaking

Our attitude to what we have to say, to whom we have to say, where we have to say, when we have to say and how we have to say, makes all the difference. It is an acknowledged fact that 10 per cent of the impact of speech is for actual words, 40 per cent of the way the words are expressed and 50 per cent speaker's gesture and non-verbal communication.

To be a good speaker, we need to ask the following questions to ourselves :

- Are we clear in our mind what we want to say ?
- Are our choice of words and expressions clearly presented ?
- Is the topic, tone, volume, pitch, different from the words we use.
- Are we using too much jargon, high sounding words or too technical in style.

Way Points for an Effective Speech

If you are to make a speech, remember the following points :

- know your subject-collect ideas and material on it.
- Prepare an outline.
- Write out the opening and closing.
- Practice out loudly and don't try to memorise.
- Survey your audience before starting the speech.
- Use attention-getting opening.
- Close with brief summary.

A politician came to address a college audience. His speech was long and boring. In between there was lot of coughing from the audience. When he asked whether every one there had a bad cold ? One of the back bencher replied. "Those are not coughs, they are the time signals."

Writing

No business can exist without writing. It forms a small part of the life for many people. Trouble with writing is the poor diction. In writing, the language is the vital tool. The words can be used if we know language. An individual with normal intelligence learn ten thousand words till schooling; additional 3000 words during the University, extra 300 words during professional career. In most cases, not more than 20,000 words. But the working vocabulary, for most of us is between 1200 to 1300 words.

Effective Writing

Effective writing includes :

- Short sentence
- Writing with readers' experience in view
- Writing with use of variety
- Writing to express and not to impress.

Non-Verbal Communication

We communicate not only through words, but equally through tone of voice, expression, and body movements. We all have our body language. Though we may not speak, we still speak volumes. How we sit, stand and walk, conveys messages to others. How we smile makes a lot of difference. How we react to people, displays what we think. Eyes don't lie and for most people neither their face.

Grape-Vine

Grape-vine refers to an informal communication about company's matters outside the official net-work. It works with surprising speed and often much faster than official channels. It is usually inaccurate and mixed with private speculation and filtering and distortion occurs as message passes from one person to the next. An executive cannot eliminate Grape-vine even if he tries. He can rather make good use of this inevitable communication in following three ways :

(*a*) Grape-vine is a saying-the executive what he should know what his subordinate and others in an organisation believe in order to predict their behaviour.

(*b*) Executive can scotch false rumours. The best way to counter half truths and rumours, is to present correct fact and information well in time. But on executive should know exactly what is bothering people. Grape-vine being spontaneous has no-stable membership or form.

(*c*) Executive can spread information informally. One way to accomplish this purpose is to spread such information through the grape-vine.

If an employee is asked to resign, his associates are naturally curious about it. Management may not like to publically state the explanation perhaps insubordination incompetence or drunkenness, but may want other employees to know it to combat any rumour. In such situation, the actual reason for his removal can be revealed to active members in the grape-vine.

Effective Communication

Good communication is good business. In communication what counts is not what people are told but what they accept. Communication should be a continuing process. Once an atmosphere has been established, it is hard to shake it. Therefore, there is a need for creating a climate of trust and confidence; and for this, the following principles of effective communication should be considered :

THE 7 C's OF EFFECTIVE COMMUNICATION

1. **COMPLETENESS**
— Provide all necessary information
— Answer all questions when asked
— Give something extra - when desirable
2. **CONCISENESS**
— Eliminate wordy expressions
— Include only relevent material
— Avoid unnecessary repetition
3. **CONSIDERATION**
— Focus on 'YOU' rather then 'I' or 'ME'
— Show audience benefit or interest in the reciever
— Emphasise positive pleasant facts
4. **CONCRETENESS**
— Use specific facts and figures
— Put action in your verbs
— Choose vivid, image building words
5. **CLARITY**
— Choose precise, concrete and familiar words
— Construct effective sentences and paragraphs
6. **COURTESY**
— Be sincerely tactful, thoughtful and appreciative
— Use expressions that show respect
— Choose nondiscriminatory expressions
7. **CORRECTNESS**
— Use the right level of language
— Check the accuracy of figures, facts and words
— Maintain acceptable writing mechanics

(*a*) *Clarify your ideas* before communication. It is not good to open the tape if there is nothing in the tank. Don't start talking until you have begun thinking. Management communication normally fails because of inadequate planning.

(*b*) *Examine the purpose* of each communication. We must know the purpose of communication. What we really want to accomplish from the communication must be known.

(*c*) *Physical and human setting.* Communication is the basis for understanding, co-operation and action. At atmosphere of confidence is framed in the process of communication. An executive should create an atmosphere of confidence and openness. He should expose himself to people and encourage informal and cordial relation. He should encourage appreciation for a job well done. He should understand the problems of his subordinate and be sympathetic about them.

EFFECTIVE COMMUNICATION

Sender (Message) →

* DIRECT AND SIMPLE
* FEED BACK
* CONTROL GESTURES
* CONDUCTIVE ATMOSPHERE
* EFFECTIVE LISTENING
* CAREFUL TUNING
* ATMOSPHERE OF TRUST
* DON'T TALK, TALK, TALK
* DON"T IMPRESS

→ Reciever (Clear message)

Fig. 6.2

All these steps will improve the working relationship among the work force and will reduce the chance of miscommunication by exposing one self, appreciating others to communicate and creating a conductive atmosphere to communication.

Example

Effective communication where the physical and human setting are being involved is the dialogue between husband and wife on the dinner table. Husband while sitting on the dinner table, finds, that the table is very dirty and probably not cleaned since yesterday. Husband writes with his finger on the dust of the dining table "I love you". She immediately cleaned the table smilingly. This is a pleasant way of communication, where the husband has conveyed the meaning and also pleased his wife.

Criticism and passing blame does not help in any way. Sometime it is hard to digest but better to swallow and forget in the interest of good relations in the long run. It reminds me the words of Mother Teresa that the violence is not only through weapon but also without tongue, violence which is caused by our attitude is even a greater violence. We can exercise non-violence through our kindness, attitude and even by our smile in our day today life.

Mindful While You Communicate

Be mindful while you communicate. We should be particular of tone of voice, expression and apparent receptiveness while communicating. Communicate for tomorrow as well as today. Communication must be consistent with long range interest and goals. A promise one made must be followed through. It is easy to throw premises but we should not do promises unless we are sure to fulfill. An executive who invites requests for help or information and then disregards that is proving that he is not interested in people working with him.

Refusal to discuss is not the answer. Refusal may result in break in communication and an explosion at a later date. One Plant Manager paid no heed to the workers grumbling over the need for a Safety guard on their machine for years together. Ultimately this resulted in a walk out resulting in strike in the plant, because people read meaning even in silence.

Convey Something of Value to the Receiver

People on the job are most responsive to the Manager who takes their interest into account. Action must support your communication. To conclude, the effective communication is the life blood of an organisation and its main purpose is to effect change and to influence action. Communication is a flux which binds people together in an organisation.

Essentials of Communication

Following are essentials of communication :

1. To get better acquainted with yourself take 15 to 20 minutes in quiet each day to study yourself, your purpose, your relationship to your fellowmen and the Company.
2. What is said on the job, is the most important part of communication is business and industry. Intelligence, honesty, living with what is said, acting with cooperation as well as talking about it, are other essentials in developing good communication with in an organisation.
3. Over come your feeling, tendency to evaluate pass judgement, to agree or disagree with statements before finding out what they meant.
4. When talking think in terms of the total impression you create, and not just the words used and also consider every indication of the listeners.
5. When listening, look for what the speaker intends, not just what he says.
6. Ask more questions, to see whether your listeners have understood what you intended.
7. Where difficulties have arisen, try to keep the talk centered on the problem, rather than on personalities.
8. Recognise that during discussions, disagreement is normal and inevitable. Accept it, prepare for it, use it to obtain greater awareness of the various aspects of the problem at hand.
9. Do not abruptly disapprove someone's statement, and do not directly contradict. Disapprove indirectly, preserving the other individual's ego in the process.
10. Control your own natural ego and the desire to get the upper hand and to show up weaknesses in other fellow's point of view. Do reveal the weaknesses when they are important, but do it, in a way that leaves the other fellow's ego intact and take every honest opportunity to make the other person feel better or more important.
11. When talking, pause more often, to think about what you are about to-say.
12. Tone of voice is more important than we think. Consider what impressions you are conveying with your voice.

EFFECTIVE COMMUNICATION

Through effective communication, skill to work is brought in touch with will to work and both combined together lead to team spirit in the organisation. Advantages of effective communication are sense of motivation, clarity of thought, and orders, non-distorted information and consequent increase in production and morale of employees. In an organisation where mutual trust between the management and workers exist, it is easy to communicate effectively. Communication combines skill to work and will to work to create a team.

Written Communication

No business can exist without writing. Written words become a record of things planned, carried out and acknowledged. In writing also, the language is a vital tool. Words can be used effectively, if we have a good working vocabulary. It has been observed that an individual learns 10,000 words till his higher secondary. He learns additional 3,000 words during his University education, an additional 300 words during his professional career. Most of these words which can be maximum of 20,000, are hanging in the vocabulary but in no case one has a working vocabulary of more than 1,200 to 1,300 words. But above all, the ways of expressing thought and putting them on papers have no real substitute. There is a need to develop a better attitude towards reading and clear thinking. Following are certain guidelines for effective writing :

(*a*) Keep the sentences short.

(*b*) Prefer simple to the complex.

(*c*) Avoid unnecessary words.

(*d*) Write to express and not to impress.

(*e*) Use the concept of FOG-INDEX.

(*f*) Connect the writing with reader's experience.

(*g*) Use variety.

(*h*) Make your ideas clear, simple and direct.

FOG INDEX

Robert Gunning developed a yardstick by which readability can be measured. 'FOG-INDEX' indicates how to keep the sentences short and words simple. Following is the procedure for finding Fog-Index.

(*i*) Take a simple passage (100 words).

(*ii*) Divide the total number of words by number of sentences it contains.

(*iii*) Count the number of words that contain three syllabus or more, but do not count the words which are capitalised (name of the place, company, and so on).

Add the counts in steps '2' and '3' and multiply with 0.4. This gives Fog-Index figure. The good material normally have a Fog-Index of 10 to 12. The figures of 12 and above represent the danger point.

Effectiveness of Reporting

Reporting is an effective written communication and more often executive are required to write a report. Whenever a report is called for, there should be a sensible inspection of the time factors involved. An early planning is required to do the very best job of producing the report. After the report has been written, its effectiveness can be judged on the following points :

(*a*) **Purpose :** Is the purpose of writing report clear and the introduction and summary of report clearly spelled out ?

(*b*) **Leadership :** Is the report suitable for its intended readers ? Are the explanations adequate and assumptions explicit ?

(*c*) **Comprehensiveness :** Are all the points covered and nothing spelled out ?

(*d*) **Relevance :** Is the degree of relevance maintained throughout ?

(*e*) **Development :** Is the subject developed in a logical order ?
(*f*) **Summary :** Is it concise and informative ?
(*g*) **Conclusion :** Is it clear and well expressed ?
(*h*) **Style :** Does it read easily ?
(*i*) **Language :** Is it too academic or too technical ?

SPEECH

Our attitude to what we have to say, to whom we have to say, where we have to say, when we have to say, makes all the difference. It is an acknowledged fact that 10 per cent of the impact of speech is for actual words, 40 per cent of the way the words are expressed and 50 per cent speaker's gesture and non-verbal communication.

An interesting example to speech is of a politician who came to address a college audience. His speech was long and boring. In between there was lot of coughing from the audience. When he asked whether everyone there had a bad cold, there was a reply from the audience, "These are not cough signals but time signals".

Speech is a form of oral representation. While presenting the speech, following points must be taken care of :

(*a*) Objectives.
(*b*) Ordinance. Following information of ordinance must be kept in mind.
(*c*) Background information, knowledge of subject, attitude towards you and the organisation, knowledge of the performance.
(*d*) *Relevance.* The objectives and conclusions must be checked.
(*e*) *Language.* It should be clear, active, short sentences, short words, free from jargon.
(*f*) *Opening.* It should be short.
(*g*) *Closing.* Closing should be appropriate and after the problems and solutions have been clearly studied.
(*h*) *Time.* It should be handled in an appropriate short time.
(*i*) *Do not rush in presentation.* One should not hurry and should be positive in attitude and opening remarks. Relax with good breathing while delivering the presentation.

VISUAL AIDS

It should be used as far as possible, as usual sense is measured as 80% effective as an avenue of learning while hearing only 7% and other senses splitting up to the remaining 13%.

The visual aids help in creating a visual sense, better and fast presentation, can show a relationship among your ideas and can serve as a review device. Visual aids should be clear enough to stand alone, should be simple, legible, really interesting and should be kept to the minimum necessary.

Good Speaker

To be a good speaker, we need to ask the following questions to ourselves :

— Are we clear in our mind what we want to say ?

— Are our choice of words and expressions clearly presented ?
— Is the topic, tone, volume, pitch, different from the words we use ?
— Are we using too much jargon, slang, high sounding words or too technical in style ?

This is the other side of listening. The great amount of time is being spent over speech. Still the ability to express ourselves is a problem for many people. There are certain people who are unaware of this difficulty but there are larger number of people who are conscious of this difficulty. Words have a quality that must be made personal to the speaker. Without this personal treatment, the message will not have life.

Types of Speech

Words convey not only facts, ideas but above all feelings also. Following are the various types of speeches, and presentation commonly used in an industry.

(*i*) **Persuasive.** This involved more than the statement of the fact. It involves--emotions, feelings, prejudices, pre-conceived ideas. Speaker first sells his audience his competence and knowledge and then must sell the substance and its value to them.

(*ii*) **Explanatory.** In this type of speech or presentation, the object is not to sell anything. It is to give an overview and to increase understanding of something already known.

(*iii*) **Instructional.** This is used to teach or train others regarding new procedures, techniques and equipments. This requires greater participation with the audience to achieve the desired result.

(*iv*) **Reporting.** Here the object is to bring to the audience up-to-date information of something with which they are already familiar.

Preparation of the Speech. While preparing a speech following points must be taken into consideration :

Assembling. Collect all the information you have stored in your memory. Collect all material you obtain on the subject. Consult the expert regarding various aspects of your subject.

Arranging. Put your ideas on cards. Select the opening idea and the closing idea. Arrange the ideas between the opening and closing to create a smooth flow of thought and argument.

Assimilating. Take each card, keep it for a few days. Talk about each idea and try to express them at least half a dozen time before the actual speech. Write your speech. Have a trial run on a tape recorder and ask your friend to evaluate the same.

Deliver the speech. This will not be for the first time but should be 12th time in reality.

LISTENING

Art of listening has a far greater importance. An attentive listening is a compliment to a speaker. It is one of the most difficult aspects of communication. It has been observed that most of us are listening no better than 30 to 50 per cent efficiency. Listening is a hard work. It demands patience particularly when one is unloading the problems. Listening is not an in-born virtue, but a definite skill that can be acquired. The two main reasons of poor listening are speed and disattraction. Since our mind works 4-5 times the speed of the speech, there is always a danger of listener being side tracked. The extra time is mainly responsible for disattraction. In listening, one should not have pre-conceived ideas of self-importance, personal bias or prejudice.

Following procedure will help you to improve your listening :

Step I

To do preliminary practice by listening to Radio and Television to bring out the theme from the subject of discussions :

(*i*) Outline the statements that touch off your antagonism or sympathy;

(*ii*) Identify bias and propaganda appeals.

Step II

After the speaker has finished, write a single paragraph giving his main idea and theme and analyse why he has or has not made a convincing case. This process will help you, not only to be a good listener but a skillful speaker too.

Step III

Third step of improving the quality of listening is to control yourself that you will speak only after the previous speaker has finished his viewpoints. In order to have a clear concept of listening, we can take a small group of 3 people. *One of them 'A' will be sender and the other 'B' will be receiver and third 'C' will be the judge. To this group, we can give a controversial subject. 'A' will express his opinion about the subject to 'B'. Now 'B' will be asked to repeat the message of 'A' and then he will express his opinion about the subject, which now 'A' is required to reproduce. It has been observed, that 'A' or 'B' will never be able to reproduce the ideas of each other by more than 30%.*

One should listen between the lines, *i.e.*, listen to what is being said and also what is not being said. The increased efficiency in listening leads to greater enjoyment of life and also can help in overcoming major break-down and ill feelings being caused by bad listening. A great deal of practice and self-awareness is needed of an executive before he can incorporate an art of effective listening. Effective listening calls for apathy besides developing self-discipline. Executives are inclined to respond emotionally to what others say and normally tend to react in other ways. Better executives' listening, one has to remain objective and practice self discipline. Listening is a valuable leadership process and requires a great deal of executive's discretion.

Guidelines To Listening

Following guidelines for listening will help the executives to assume a positive, self confident role in making decisions and giving orders.

— Listening patiently to what the other person has to say even if you believe it is wrong or irrelevant.
— Indicate our acceptance by nodding or I see or please carry on indicating that the attention is being involved in the listening process.
— Try to understand his feelings and the intellectual context. This will involve attention.
— Restate the person's feeling, briefly but accurately and encourage the other person to continue talking. But during the encouragement do not lead him to your conclusions or decisions.
— Avoid direct questions and arguments about facts. Do not come into arguments such as "It is not true". "Why don't you state the facts". Executive may review evidence later but a review during the process is irrelevant.
— Listen to what is said.
— If the person is genuinely interested in the Executive's viewpoint, then the executive should be honest in his reply but limit the expression to what is being asked.
— Don't get emotionally involved and try to understand first and evaluate later.
— Be the speaker at ease. By your attitude, make the speaker relaxed and aware of a willing listener.
— Listen patiently. Hear the speaker even if you feel his approach is wrong.
— Study the objective. Avoid your emotional environment, feelings or point of view of the speakers.
— Remove distractions. Do not play with papers, pencils and eliminate extrenuous sound such as shutting the door or windows.
— Indicate Acceptance. A casual nod of the head indicates your attention and acknowledgement of what is being said.
— Respect pauses or silence. Silence is an embarrassment for most of us. We should not fall victim to speakers pauses and avoid jumping on it.
— Listen between the lines. One can think 4-5 times faster than normal speakers. This ability should be used by the listener in a constructive manner by anticipating the next point, identifying and evaluating the supporting evidence, recapitulating the ideas of the speaker. It is also required to have a strong feeling of empathy on the part of the listener.

NON-VERBAL COMMUNICATION

It pervades the other areas of listening, speaking and writing. It is conditioned by our health, emotions and moods. The philosophy of life and the attitude play an important role in non-verbal communication. This is also referred to as body language. Each one of us look at our non-verbal communication, because it makes a great difference to our lives. Non-verbal communication is something, which we do unconsciously. How one stands, walks, smiles, reacts has a meaning in conveying the impression and message to the other. Each one of us is practicing non-verbal communication since birth; still it is something of which we have no thought. Communication is the basis for understanding, co-operation and action. We communicate not through words but equally through tone of voice, expression, and body movements. We all have our own body language. Though we may not speak, we still speak volumes. How we sit, stand, walk, convey messages to others. How we smile makes a lot of difference. How we react to people, displays what we think. Eyes don't lie and for most people neither do their face. Other people read us to become more aware of ourselves.

We have various types of people but no two are alike. Different types of people are as:

— Confident type
— Indifferent type
— Forgetful type
— Wooden type
— Grumpy type.

Each of these persons communicate different messages through their gestures. It has been seen that same persons are able to communicate effectively in various interviews through the tone of voice, expression and body movements. Such people get selected because of their better eye to eye contact and confident look.

MANAGERIAL SKILLS

Management is the process of utilising material and human resources to achieve some predetermined objectives. Management is also taken as the agency to transform various inputs into desired outputs. Management transforms inputs into desired outputs by performing certain essential functions. The important functions with which the management is concerned involve planning, organising, controlling and coordinating. Thus management is the body of individuals entrusted with the performing of these functions to accomplish some goals. The persons comprising of management may be individually called as 'managers'. In other words, a manager is a person who performs the managerial functions of the organisation. He decides and identifies the goals of the organisation and then put them into action. While putting the organisational goals into action, a manager tries to reconcile the organisational goals and goals of the persons comprising it and then guides and coordinates the activities of persons working under him towards the achievement of common objectives.

The word 'manager' is used in a variety of ways by different people. To some the manager means top executive of an organisation. To others a manager is any person who supervises other employees. In this sense, a person supervising the managers will also be called, as a manager and he may even report to a manager. In practice, the organisation structure contains a number of echelons or levels and each level may possess the designation of manager. That means there may be top management, middle management (which may again, be upper-middle, middle-middle or lower-middle management) and lower management. Persons occupies different positions in different levels of management will be called as managers.

A manager performs the managerial functions of planning, organising, controlling, motivating etc. towards the achievement of organisational goals. Any person who performs these basic functions can be taken to be the member of management. Thus all supervisors from a foreman up through the managing director of a company are decided by managers. The job of a manager is to get things done with the help of other people. For this he has to plan and organise the activities and then motivate the people to put into actions his plans. He also acts as the controller because he always guides the activities of his subordinates and keeps them under his control. Planning involves looking ahead to future, setting goals and formulation of policies, procedures and methods for accomplishing these goals. Organising encompasses the breaking down of total work to be done into small parts and dividing them among different people. Organisation also involves determining authority and responsibility relationship, setting up patterns of communication etc., By motivation, we mean stimulating the people to do work for the achievement of goals. For this purpose, a manager has to direct and lead his subordinates. He also tries to integrate the personal goals of the employees with that of the organisation. Control function of a manager includes measurement of work done comparison of actual performance with determined standards and then taking corrective actions, when necessary, to ensure that plans are being implemented correctly.

Management is an art which involves the ability to communicate, provide leadership, motivate, train and develop the personnel besides other skills of management. Management's job can be divided into two tasks; namely, (1) Deciding what to do ; and (2) getting it done. The first task relates to the setting of objectives, planning, decision-making and setting up formal organisation. The second task consists of communication, leadership, motivation and control. A manager spends much of his time in communication and handling of people. His efforts are directed towards obtaining information and evaluation progress towards objectives set by him and then taking corrective action. As a matter of fact, a manager's job primarily consists of management of people. Though it is his duty to handle all the productive resources, but human factor is more important. A manager cannot convert all the raw materials into finished products himself but he has to take the help of others to do this. The greatest problem before any manager is how to manage the personnel to get the best possible results. The manager in the present age has to deal efficiently with the people who are to contribute for the achievement of organisational goals.

One of the important functions of a manager is to educate, train and develop people below him so that they may use their potentialities and abilities to perform the work allotted to them. He has also to help them in satisfying their needs and aspirations through incentives and other things. For getting best contribution from the people working under him, he must provide them with proper environments. A manager must create a climate which brings in an maintains satisfaction and discipline among the people.

Thus a manager's job is very much complex. It requires some qualities of head and heart and cannot be performed by everybody. Any person who is to be given a manager's job must have the capacities to meet the challenges of a manager's job. It should be further noted that a foreman is a manager like a top executive in the organisation, but contents of work and skills and knowledge he must utilise to do his work are different from those of a top executive. Thus, the nature of every manager's job differ. Skills needed by a manager are of three types : technical, human and conceptual skills. *Technical skill* refers to proficiency in handling methods, processes and techniques of a particular kind of business, *Human skill* refers to the ability to work effectively with others and build cooperative group relations to achieve organisational goals. *Conceptual skill* is the ability to see the organisation as a whole, to recognise interrelationships among different functions of the business and external forces and to guide effectively the organisational efforts. Conceptual skill is critical in top executive positions whereas technical skill is an essential ingredient of lower level management. However, human skill is important at all levels of managements. Though technical skill can be learnt easily, but other skills cannot be learnt unless and individuals has the potentialities and capacities and an inner urge to learn them.

Managerial Skills

The title 'Manager' is not like a medal awarded in recognition of past services. The job of a manager demands continually increasingly skills, whether, it be management of a business, an educational institution, a hospital or a club. A manager is said to be successful when he is able to make a smooth functioning steam of people with different skills required for the running of the organisation. Manager's most important function is to reconcile, to coordinate, to compromise and to appraise the various viewpoints and talents of the people working under him towards the organisational goals. A manager can perform this function well if he has got the required skills.

The work 'skill' is ordinarily applied to the understanding and control of a mechanical process of dexterity in the mutual shaping of a physical substance like clay, wood or iron. But it is a narrow view of the term skill. Skill may broadly be defined as the ability to transform experience and knowledge into action. It can also apply to mental activity used in directing the people at work. Here it is important to note that experience is valuable, but superiority in management demands more. A man may become a skilled mechanic through working at a bench, but a manager who is contented to learn by experience is on slippery grounds. It is wise to draw upon experience to avoid making mistakes in the future, but the manager must not let experience hobble him so that he never looks beyond what has happened before.

Now two situations are exactly the same. Most of the characteristics may be similar, but one new characteristic may turn the situation into a wholly new problem to which there may be no answer. In order to arrive at this answer, experience should be added to the results of knowledge acquired through study. It is expected of every manager that he has the required knowledge to manage his job. If a person lacks the required knowledge and skill in applying it, a name plate on his door will not make him a manager.

Being a manager requires mental, moral and physical strength. A manager must be careful, progressive and sagacious. He should also possess the qualities of dependability and reliability. He should keep up with the latest developments. He should have a philosophy and should know answer to "what do I wish to accomplish".

A person is not a manager in real terms if all he does is to keep the people in order and keep work moving. This is very low ceiling. His worth to the organisation includes his capacity to understand all kinds of people. Unless he understands them, he cannot direct them to the economic use of materials and energy. Therefore, a manager's chief requirement, given the technical skill to handle the personnel working under him, is to understand the people at work.

From the foregoing discussion, it is obvious that skills needed by a manager are of three types, namely—(*a*) technical, (*b*) human and (*c*) conceptual skills.

Technical Skills

Technical skills refer to an understand of and proficiency in handling methods, processes of a particular kind of activity. Of these three skills, technical skill is perhaps most popular because it has the most concrete and in the modern era of specialisation, it is the skill required of the greatest number of people. Most the vocational and on the job training programmes are largely concerned with developing the specialised technical skill. Technical skill is responsible for the great advances of modern industry. It is indispensable to efficient performance of technical jobs. Every manager should have some technical skill. The need for technical skill is more for the managers or executives at the lower or lower-middle level. As the manager moves up in the hierarchy, the need for technical skill becomes less important provided he has skilled subordinates and can help them to solve their problems.

Human Skill

Human skill means a manager's ability to work effectively as a group member and to build cooperative effort within the team he leads. Human skill is primarily concerned with working with people. This skill is demonstrated in the way the individual proceives his superiors, equals and subordinates, and in the way he behaves subsequently.

Developing Human Skill

The person with highly developed human skill is aware of his own attitudes, assumptions and beliefs about other individuals and groups, and is able to see the usefulness and limitations of these feelings. He is equally skillful in communicating to others. He works to create an atmosphere of approval and security in which subordinates feel free to express themselves without fear of censure and encourage them to participate in the planning and carrying out of the things which directly affect them. He is sufficiently sensitive to the needs and motivations of others in his organisation that he can judge the possible reactions to the outcomes of various courses of action he may undertake. Having this sensitivity, he is able and willing to take action in a way which takes these perceptions of others into account.

Real skill in working with others must become a natural and continuous activity, since it involves not only sensitivity at times of decision- making, but also in the day-to-day behaviour of the individual. Techniques cannot be randomly applied, nor can personality traits be put on or removed like shirt. Because everything which a manager says and does has an effect upon his associates, his human skill acquires more importance. Thus, to be effective, this skill must be naturally developed and unconsciously demonstrated in the individual's every action. Human skill in a vital part of everything a manager does.

Human skill, the ability to work with others, is needed at every level because every manager's task mainly consist of managing some people. But it seems to be most important at lower level of management, where the number of direct contacts between the manager and the subordinates is the greatest. As we go higher and higher in the echelons of management, the frequency of these personal contacts with the operative personnel decreases. But this does not mean that need for human skill becomes proportionately less. Top level and middle level managers require the human skill equally to deal with the outsiders, trade union leaders and the executives who have direct contact with the operative personnel.

Conceptual Skills

It involves the ability to see the organisation as a whole. It includes recognising how the various functions of the organisation depend on one another and how changes in any one part affect all the others, and it extends to visualising the relationship of the individual business to the industry, the community, and the political, social and economic forces of the nation as a whole. The success of any decision depends upon the conceptual, skill of the people who make the decision and those who put it into action. For example, changes in the marketing policy will have effect upon production personnel and finance functions. The people involved will also be affected. The attitudes of the top executives colour the whole character of the organisation's response the determine its personality which distinguishes it from others. Conceptual skill is also referred to as creative ability. The essential aspect of the managerial process is the sensing of the organisation as a whole and the total environments relevant to it.

Company's overall success is dependent upon its manager's conceptual skill in taking and carrying out policy decisions. This skill is the unifying and coordinating ingredient of the administrative process. The conceptual skill embodies both the technical and human aspects of the organisation.

The separation of managerial skills into three different skills is primarily an analytical distinction. In actual practice, these skills are so closely interrelated that it is difficult to determine where one ends and another starts. Moreover, it is not possible to say what type of and how much skill is required of a manager at a particular level in a particular situation. Many a times a manager takes the decisions which are based on the mixture of skills. For instance if a manager wants to take a decision whether to install a new machinery or not, he will be influenced by conceptual, human and technical skills. Conceptual skill will help him to take a broader view of the situation. He cannot understand the pros and cons of new machinery unless he possesses the necessary technical skill. He must also be sensitive to human relations in the organisation because of the introduction of new machinery. This sensitiveness is possible if the manager has the human skill. Conceptual skill becomes more important with the need for policy decisions and broad scale actions. The degree of conceptual skill increases as we go up in the hierarchy of management. But on the other hand, the degree of technical skill increases as go do in the level of management because lower-line managers are more concerned with the methods, processes and techniques of manufacturing or designing the product. The human skill is almost required equally at all levels in the organisation.

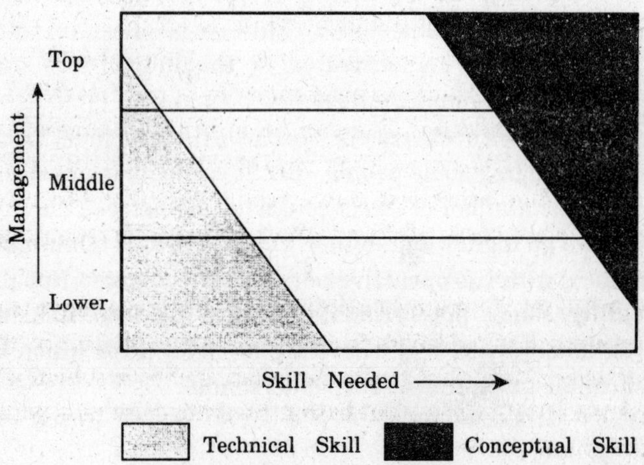

Managerial skills needed at various level of management.

The above diagram shows that the importance of technical skill is more at the lower of management, whereas at the top level the requirement of technical skill is less, but the requirement of conceptual skill is greatest. The human skill is required at every level more or less in equal degrees. The readers should note that the figure given above only illustrates the different skills required at different levels of management. The mixture of different skills in any manager at any time in the constant state of affairs. The degree of different skills varies generally as an individual advances is management hierarchy.

Developing Managerial Skills

There is no doubt that certain individuals naturally possess greater aptitude for certain skills. Such individuals can improve or develop their skills through practice and training without much difficult. Even those lacking the natural ability can acquire the skills and can improve their performance and effectiveness. Different individuals learn in different ways but skills are developed through practice and by relating one's knowledge to his personal experience.

Development of technical skill has received greater attention in industries and educational institutions alike. Technical skill involves grounding in techniques processes and specialisation coupled with principle and practice. But, now, human skill is also getting greater attention. Many executive development programmes have been initiated in the industry and universities, whereby opportunity is given to the young executive (or even would be executive) to develop his human skill of dealing with people. The art of dealing with people has acquired greater importance. That is why the courses on Personnel Management and Human Relations have become very popular.

Even though a manager seeking to upgrade his worth to the organisation attends a course in managerial skills—technical, human or conceptual (decision making), his development will be the results of his personal efforts. Therefore, a manager must develop his own skills, particularly human and conceptual rather than depend on other. To be effective, he must develop his own personal point of view towards human activities and decision-making process so that he may :

1. know his own limitations ;
2. have an attitude about his own experiences which enable him to re-evaluate and learn from them ; and
3. develop skill in successfully communicating his ideas to others.

Human skill becomes a part of manager's personality. It is not learnt by training, but by dealing with people in different situation. No doubt theoretical courses provide the background knowledge of the art of dealing with people, but this can be learnt and developed well by practicing it. The manager concerned should have an inner urge of developing this skill. Human skill cannot be imposed upon an individual because it is more concerned with the nature of the individual concerned. A manager is more successful in dealing with people when human skill becomes part of his personality.

Like human skill, conceptual skill must become a natural part of the manager is make up. Different methods are available for developing different people by virtue of their backgrounds, attitudes and experience. But in every case, that method should be chosen which will enable the manager to develop his own personal skill in visualising the enterprise as a whole and in coordinating and integrating its various parts.

To sum up, the relative importance of different skills varies with the level of managerial responsibility. At low levels, the principal need is for technical and human skills. At higher levels, managerial effectiveness depends largely on human and conceptual skills. At the top, conceptual skill becomes the most important of all the successful administration. These three skills emphasize that good managers are not born; they may be developed. It synthesizes many isolated traits considered common to successful managers.

7

Management Control

Introduction

Control is an important function of the management and it deals with the measurement and correction of the performance of subordinates in order to make sure that organisational objectives and the plans devised to attain them are accomplished. Control is the continuing process of measuring actual results of the operations of an organisation in relation to the results which were planned for that organisation, either as a whole or its various parts and of direction and action accordingly*. *Fayol* also recognised the importance of control decades ago when he said. "In an undertaking, control consist in verifying whether everything occurs in conformity with the plan adopted, the instructions issued and principles established,".

Controls are indicators of performance and set up to help measure progress against plan. These should be set up when plans are made but usually this is not done. The planner may not understand the importance of control being unfamiliar with the organization and work. The supervisor has to operate the controls and he should be able to set up, operate and adjust the controls according to needs. *Before setting up or designing controls is to have an assessment of the overall assignments and determine which activities are most important. The overall areas which are important and controls have to be set up are, Manpower, Materials, Quality of work, Quantity of work, Time, Space and Methods. Once the areas of control have been established the supervisor must find or set up standard for each activity in each area. Standards are the measuring devices for the activity.* A supervisor wishes to set up standards for production work. First he will like to review the past records and determine what has been accomplished in the past under conditions similar to present conditions.

A study of the present work load would be necessary to determine if the past performance has been high, low or average. Supervisor may examine all the data available to find what were the contributory factors to the highest performance in the past. *In every situation he will like to set standards which are a challenge to performance, at the sometime the objectives set as standards would be totally fair, attainable and above all reasonable from expectation from point of view. The supervisor, while devising standards finds two areas-tangible and intangible. It means areas of units produced, time used financial results etc., are all clearly measurable areas and can be shown accurately in reports. These are tangible areas . Human relations training, indiscipline etc. are intangible areas which affect the performance but are not measurable but has to be expressed in words.*

---

* Breach : The Principle and Practice of Management

It has been seen that it is possible to set up better controls over objects than over human activities. This is very important. The most valuable and effective part of an organization are its people and the standards which they set up for themselves and achieve ! These are induced, nursed and guided by management by incentives, motivation, training and counseling.

Performance Indicators

The supervisor needs certain indicators which tell him how well his team is doing in relation to standards as frequently as possible. These are like the instruments fixed on the dash board of a car. These enable the viewer to control, read, rent or reorganise the operations of the vehicle. Is is the case with the shop floor. The indication must express a relationship between the standard and performance. Following table will make it clear :

Possible Standard.	*Possible Indicators.*
Standard man hours for department.	Number of man-hours worked Vs. standard or allowed man-hours.
Materials list for job.	Materials used Vs. materials allowed.
Standard units produced	Actual production Vs. Standard Production.
Inspection Standards.	Acceptable units produced Vs. Standard waste permissible.
Standard time allowed for a job.	Actual time Vs. standard time for job.
Budgetary standards.	Actual Vs. budget.
Standard methods.	Variation on professional IVS standard methods.
Job description	Performance review Vs. Job requirements

The supervisor has to train himself to think in terms of percentages, ratio, units produced, unit costs and less specific standards and relationship which are expressed in words. There is no set proforma for setting up standards. It is up to the intelligence of the supervisor to device the controls. According to the situation and needs of the situation. By doing this he can prevent surprises and reduce disappointments, predict the future and diagnose trouble. On the other hand, if he is bogged down with paper work and is busy filling up report forms which may take too much of his productive time, his time preventing him to attend to more important parts of his job, he is probably the victim of too much of unnecessary controls.

Control Areas

These are different in nature and are measurable in terms of paper work and actual feed back through reports against assignments. The work, of specialised nature involving research collection of data, analysis and planning cannot be measured till the work is done and these measurements cannot be standards for future for the simple reason that managerial work is not strictly manual activity. In such cases, the concept of management by objectives on control come into existence.

Management by Objectives and Control

Objectives point direction for management activities in which supervisors are expected to move. So good management sets up reasonable, easily understandable and clear objectives for every key activity under their direction. These objectives can then be reduced to roughly measurable standards.

Suppose a supervisor feels that he is not using the available man-power to best advantage. His feeling is based on general observation and experience and there is no concrete evidence to support his belief. Then he begins to imagine what he would like to accomplish in following manners. To utilize manpower so that maximum output is achieved, quality is maintained and the skill and talents of employees as used to be maximum and advantage.

He now begins an investigation to determine the level of productivity which he is now getting. This he does by getting the following data.

— Total man hours Vs. total output.
— Total money invested per man Vs. total output.
— Individual quality records of employees.
— Total wages plus cost of fringe benefits Vs. total value of work produced.
— Wastage of time, money and material and so on.

He may find that people are busy as assigned tasks about 50% of the time (this is a modest estimate)). This may be the maximum application as per the national standards of efficiency.

Using a positive approach he tried to find reasons for low performance. The study turns up such interesting results such as :

(*a*) **People were not properly selected for their jobs.** The supervisor can hardly do anything about it except drawing up a job specification for the employees. He can advise the management about the standards required for future selection.

(*b*) **The people were not adequately trained and present work methods are ineffecient.** This requires training and revised planning. It would be a time consuming but a worthwhile job.

(*c*) **Equipment not properly utilised or no attempt to imbibe professional knowledge.** It may be that the right type of equipment was not purchased initially. It may need a new machine capable of 75% utilisation rather than present 25%. The long range benefit is worth having and the loss over a wasted machine can be considered as the cost of experience in faulty design and specification; similarly, people attain degrees/diplomas in professions only to seek appointments but stop keeping abreast the latest developments after securing appointments. Such people who continue to improve their knowledge should be encouraged and preferred over the deadwood.

(*d*) **Compensation in terms of money inadequate.** This has an adverse effect on morale, and it is difficult to measure. But it is a well known fact that money incentives cease to be motivating factor after a short span of time. Every organization, if engaged in business has to be economically viable. The salary received is not the only earned income. The employee should be aware of the total cost by way of wages, benefits like LTC, Medical, Reimbursement, gratuity, CPF, Leave with wages, and facilities like subsidised lunch, housing and transport. Unfortunately the cash income is tangible and the other things remain intangible. But the middle level manager whether in the Plant or services cadre can do little about it.

Control in Organisations

The control process in an organisation is more complicated than the corresponding process in the simple situation in several respects, however :

(*i*) Unlike the thermostat or body temperature, the standard that is used as a basis for assessing the significance of what is happening is not present. In the planing process, management decides what the organisation should be doing, and the control process compares actual accomplishment against these plans.

(*ii*) Like human hebaviour, but unlike the thermostat and body temperature regulating the system does not operate automatically. The important information in the organisation is often received through the manager's eyes, ears and others senses.

(*iii*) In an organisation the connection between the observed need for action and the behavior required to obtain the desired action is by means as clear cut as it is in the case of the simple control systems.

(*iv*) Control in an organisation requires co-ordination. An organisation consists of many parts, and the control system must ensure that the work of these parts is in harmony with one another. This need not exist at all in the case of the thermostat, and it existed only to a limited extent in the case of the various organs that influence body temperature.

(*v*) Control in an organisation does not come about solely or even primarily, as a result of actions taken by an external regulating device like the thermostat. Much control is self control; that is managers act the way they do, not primarily because they are given specific order by their superiors, but rather because their own judgement tells them the appropriate actions they should take.

Thus control in an organisation involves a variety of functions, some of which are not present in the simple situations that often come to mind when the word "control" is used. These include (*i*) Planning what the organisation should do; (*ii*) Co-ordinating the activities of the several parts of the organisation, (*iii*) Communicating information; (*iv*) Evaluating information and deciding what, if any action should be taken (*v*) Influencing people to change their behavior, and (*vi*) Processing information that is used in the other functions.

Therefore, control is that management activity whereby the managers compare actual performance against the planned one, find out the deviations, take corrective actions to remove the deviations, incorporate positive deviations in the plans and help assure the realisation of the plans. Thus control is very much related to planning. Planning be succeeded by control it is to be successful. But in a running concern planning and control go together because planning seeks to set consistent, integrated and articulated goals or programmes, while control seeks to comple events to conform to plans. The most notable feature of the process of control is that it is forward looking. A manager cannot control or do anything about the past but can avoid them in future by taking actions in the light of past experiences. In order to avoid heavy losses, control systems should be so designed that whenever there is a deviation from the plans, management gets the full information and takes the corrective action.

Managerial Control

Control is universal to nature. Human activities have always made use of control, consciously or not. In driving an automobile we must continuously compare the actual direction of the vehicle with its planned direction, if the actual performance falls short of plans we are in danger of hitting an object. Control is an essential feature of scientific management. Control is any process that guides activity toward some predetermined goal. The essence of the concept is in determining whether activity is achieving the desired results. In other words, the concept of control cannot exist without planning. The essentials of a control system involve—(*a*) A predermined goal, a plan, a policy, a standard, a norm, a criterion or a yard stick. (*b*) A means of measuring activity (*c*) A means of comparing activity and (*d*) A mechanism to correct the activity so as to achieve the desired result.

The core idea in control is to determine to some degree what should be the results or what is expected from a given action. Different names can be given to the predetermined criterion, sometime it is general qualitative plan such as improvement of morale or doing a good job or adjustment to society. The difficulty with the use of such qualitative statements is the lack of precision in what is meant. As quantitative means of expression contribute to precision therefore the evolution of managerial techniques in twentieth century lay more emphasis on the use of quantitative approaches. The effectiveness of a control system is in a large measure determined by the extent to which it has been incorporated into the daily routines and expectations of personnel affected by it. But an efficient and reasonable system of control may be ineffective if the people involved feel that it collects irrelevant data and its standards are unreasonable. In an effective control systems, reports must fit the needs of the upper levels of management and must also yield meaningful information to the lower levels. As a result of the human factor two systems of control may develop—the one designed by the specialists for top level and the informal one used by all levels.

According to Fayol in an undertaking control consists in verifying whether everything occurs in conformity with the plan adopted, the instructions issued and principles established. Its object is to point out weakness and errors in order to rectify them and prevent recurrence. It operates on every thing relating to people and actions.

The making of decisions is in a sense both the first and last step in continuing, never ending, dynamic managerial control process. The word control like many similar words of great significance can not be defined precisely. Its meaning is flexible. Its connotation in a particular case flows from the context of its use. The dictionary meaning of control is "to check, test, verify, regulate, to exercise a restrain, directing influence over; to dominate, to curb etc. The control means to be able to put any variable to its best possible use through pre-knowledge of its proper behaviour in relation tc the performance of a specified task and through full right of disposal over the amount of variable employed.

The need for control grows directly out of the delegation of authority and responsibility characteristics of modern large scale enterprise. Control, as the word is used above, may be applied at all levels of the organisation structure and to all phases of operations.

Control Process

The exercise of managerial control in all its manifestations, may itself be said to form a pattern, to be made up of standard elements. The elements in the basic process of control are described as an *objective* establishing what it is desired to accomplish, *procedure* specifying how, when and by whom the plan is to be executed, *criteria* as to what constitutes good performance and *appraisal* as to how well it was done. To secure effective control at all levels of organisational hierarchy, management must have :

(*i*) **Definite goals and objective**—these take many forms and cover every important aspect of operations such as :

(*a*) An over-all profit and financial position goal.

(*b*) The improvement of company position relative to the total industry sale.

(*c*) The improvement of employer-employee relations.

(*d*) The elimination of specified material wastes and operating inefficiencies.

(*e*) The strengthening of weak spots in the organisation plans or personnel.

(*f*) The reorganisation of financial structure.

Managerial control may also be expressed in the form of following questions and answers :

(*i*) What should be done ?

(*ii*) How should it be done ?

(*iii*) What should it cost ?

(*iv*) What did it cost.

(*v*) What are the differences between what it should cost and what it did cost ?

A process control mechanism thus acts to adjust operations to predetermined standards and does so on the basis of information it receives. Similarly information reaching, a manager gives him an opportunity for corrective action and it is his basis for control. Manager can not exercise control without such information. The objectives, plans and programmes are indispensible to the efficient management of a business but are not means of control. Control is checking to determine whether plans are being observed and suitable progress towards the objectives is being made and acting, if necessary, to correct any deviations. The another aspect of control is that control over some things must be relinquished as successively higher echelons of management are reached. Managers in the first echelon require certain information as their basis for controlling but in the next echelon the character of required information changes, some information is dropped, some is added. There is thus a kind of control spectrum.

Managers must control. Control is also quite evidently, an extremely important part of managing. In organisations, therefore, where the responsibility for control is not placed in the hands of managers, or not accepted by them difficulties are certain to arise. The management should be very careful while devising a control system. The essentials of an effective control systems are :

(*i*) **Appropriateness.** Manager should know clearly the objectives of the organisation before planning a control system.

(*ii*) **Responsibility for control.** The primary responsibility for the exercise of control invariably rests in the manager who is charged with the task of implimentation of managerial plans.

Prompt Reporting. An ideal control system should detect any report deviations as soon as, if not before, they occur so that manager can take timely corrective action.

Control by exception. Management must tail or its control techniques in such a way as the point out at exceptions at critical points because no useful purpose will be served if the control technique enables the management just to look at exceptions in general.

Objectivity. The measurement of performance should as far as possible, be objectives and specific. Effective control calls for objective, accurate and suitable standards.

Flexibility. Control system to be effective should be responsive to changing conditions. Management should so design the controls as to ensure flexibility if they are to remain workable and effective. Management can impart flexibility in control system through flexible plans.

Self control. A department that can succeed in having its own goals and control system can successfully handle within the department much of the detailed controls.

Human factor. A control system can work effectively only when it is very simple and easily understood by all concerned.

Characteristics of a control system. A sound control system control indicates that the process of control has certain basic characteristics as mentioned below :

(*i*) Control is a managerial function

(*ii*) Control is a continuous process

(*iii*) Control is a flexible and dynamic process

(*iv*) It is future oriented

(*v*) It is an act of direction and guidance

(*vi*) It is individual group and organisation oriented.

Delegation a key to control. Although control is to be exercised by means of prompt remedial action, the managers may not be able to discharge the controlling functions all by themselves by attending to all minute details.

It is enough if the action is taken within the authority delegated. It is in this context that the necessity of a proper delegation of authority by superiors to their subordinates is keenly felt while discharging the managerial functions of control. Senior managers can delegate the task of regulating the operational plans to the middle level managers as well as first live managers and with guideline to report only important issues requiring the attention of the senior managers.

Methods and Procedures for Managerial Control

The managerial control of a business enterprise is exercised through specific methods and procedures. The various control instruments are described below.

1. **Long term operating objective.** Long term planning requires the anticipation of changes and adjustments in products, markets, production methods and processes, plant location, personnel policies, organisation structure and financial structure. The long-term objective provide continuity and are stablising influence in setting up current month to month annual plans and budgets.

Long term Capital Planning. This type of forecasting requires consideration of need for plant investment, increase plant capacity, dividend policy, readjustment of capital structure and provisions of new capital from operations or creditors or stockholders. Long term capital planning must disclose both the needs for and the source of new capital.

Policy formulation. A policy is a general description of an altitude or course of action to be followed in dealing with a specified business event. Policies are made at all levels of management and should be carefully determined and expressed.

Standardisation

Standardisation serves the same function in the realm of physical control of operations as policy formulation for managerial direction and regulation.

Standardisation aim is to find and define the best productive conditions, materials and methods and to prescribe their utilisation in a constant undeviating manner.

Cost-Volume Relationships

The study of cost and volume relationships, is a most valuable field of study for understanding by management. The variation of cost with volume can be represented by the simple formula for a straight line *viz* $y = a + bx$ where x represents the number of units of volume ; b equals the change in cost per unit of volume ; a stands for total fixed cost and y is total cost.

The importance of studying and understanding cost-volume relationships for all types of costs and expenses, in all areas from the single cost centre to the multicost centre enterprise can both be overexpha-sised. The knowledge of cost-volume relationships is useful in :

(*a*) Setting normal productive department overhead rates.

(*b*) Basis for establishing service department rates used for allocating the operating costs of these departments to producing departmently.

(*c*) Basis for cost control through the flexible budget.

Cost-volume-profit relationship

This type of analysis are more particularly used as visual presentations and are described as a breakeven chart, a profit chart and a profit graph. These devices are very useful in visualising understanding and dramatising the effects on profits of proposed changes in selling prices, fixed costs, capacity and sales volume.

Cost Analysis. It is relationship of cost and price. Cost-price relationships are usually complex. The relationship may be light, remote or non existent. Cost price relationships also differ among businesses. In stablised industries costs are more determinative of price. Cost even when not significant in setting price is a basis for measuring profitability, therefore costs should be available, separately between fixed and variable items. Pricing is keyed to the future, therefore expected costs are more important than past costs or even current standard costs.

Techniques of Management Control

Techniques of management control refer to various methods which have been designed to help the managers to secure effective control. Some of the important methods used for the purpose of management control are :

(*i*) Budgets and budgetary control

(*ii*) Statistical data

(*iii*) Breakeven analysis

(*iv*) Ratio analysis

(*v*) Management audit

(*vi*) Interval control

(*vii*) Operation research

(*viii*) Management information system

(*ix*) Network analysis

(*x*) Logistice

(*xi*) Special reports etc.

Budgetary control.

It is an application of control in relation to budgets. Budgetary control is defined as a "tool of management" used to plan, carry out and control the operations of a business. It establishes predetermined objectives and provides the basis for measuring performance against these objectives. Budgeting is the function of expressing premises, plans and forecasts to operating levels. Budgetary control therefore should be construed as a company operating programme with not only momentary aspects but a complete plan of execution.

Budget

It is a plan which covers all phases of operation of the enterprise for a definite period of time into the future. The budgets reflect the estimates of sales, production, cost and profits for a future period of time. These estimates are based on past experiences, present business conditions as well as indicated future trends. Budgets are a means of control only in the respect that they report progress of actual performance against the program--information which enables managers to take action directed toward bringing actual results into conformity with the programme.

The average manufacturing company requires 28 major types of budgets to have complete budgetary control.

The purpose of these budgets is five fold :

(*i*) To clarify the programmes.
(*ii*) To coordinate activities of various branches.
(*iii*) To measure efficiency and simplify executive control.
(*iv*) To aid in financing the business and
(*v*) To provide informations to all concerned regarding company plan upon which these programs are predicted.

Advantages

Following are some of the advantages of budgetary control :

(*i*) It forces management to plan the most economical use of labour, material and capital. It is a valuable aid to management and provide managers with an overall view of enteprise.

(*ii*) It defines where one executive's responsibility begins and that of another ends. It helps in determining the responsibility centers for performance.

(*iii*) It provides for control of the expenditure of funds. It plans to utilise capital most effectively in accordance with budget plans.

(*iv*) It provides signal to management by means of variances. It provides information to management to decide whether it is necessary to take action in accordance with organisation alignments and the provisions stipulated in duty sheets.

(*v*) It establishes a goal at which to aim budgets and a means of measuring the accuracy of the aim. It also helps the enterprise to stablise production by optimum utilisation of resources.

(*vi*) It saves executive time and attention and he can concentrate his attention on budgeted performance only.

Weaknesses

Possible weaknesses in the budget plans could be one of the following :

(*i*) It could be a rigid budget allowing for no flexibility and hence will be out of date as soon as made.

(*ii*) Some executives has the itch to change the organisation so frequently that no one can keep pace with it and figures are made worthless for comparative purposes.

(*iii*) At times process of installation is so long that executives lose interest before the results are apparent.

(*iv*) Unless the plans are well communicated the plan becomes the personal property of the man who made it an therefore other will not have much interest in it.

Steps in Budgetary Control

The aim of budgetary control is to improve the final results of the business enterprise by facilitating control.

Budgetary control or Budgeting involves the following three important steps :

(*i*) Preparation of Budgets. It involves detailed planning of future operations in numerical and physical terms.

(*ii*) Comparisons of actual results. It calls for continuous comparison of actual results with the planned targets and

(*iii*) Continuous revision. It calls for continuous revision of budgets previously prepared in order to incorporate the altered business conditions reflecting changes in material supply, labour conditions, plant facilities, demand conditions etc.

Budgeting involves an exercise in three directions *viz* (*i*) planning, (*ii*) controlling and (*iii*) co-ordinating. The business budget serves as the principal financial means by which the manager can formalise and express a plan. Thus when once the budgets are established they serve as a control technique by setting predetermined criteria against which managers can compare actual results. The process of budgeting also serves as a tool for co-ordinating the activities of various functions and operating segments of an enterprise.

Information and Communication

Management involves the co-ordination of group. It requires communication among its members. Control however is so closely related to communication that it is difficult to distinguish between these functions. Information is a measure of one's freedom of choice when one selects a message. If there is no freedom of choice, there is no information.

Shannon and Weaver have distinguished three levels of communication problems :

(*i*) Technical problem of how accurately symbols can be transmitted.

(*ii*) The semantics problem of how precisely symbols can convey a desired meaning.

(*iii*) The effectiveness problem of how well the transmitted meaning affects conduct.

Feedback--an essential of control

Feedback is as old as the controls on windmills, the fly--ball governor on steam engine. However, the trend towards automation since World War II has made feedback more important. Feedback is the process of adjusting future actions based upon information about past performance. Feedback concept is common to ordinary control as well as to automatic control. Feedback involves inter-dependence of one part of a system with another. Thermostat is a classical illustration which is a control device of the closed loop variety which measures actual temperature in a room, compares it with the planned temperature, feeds this information back to source of heat and opens or closes a valve to make any necessary corrections as shown in Fig. 7.1

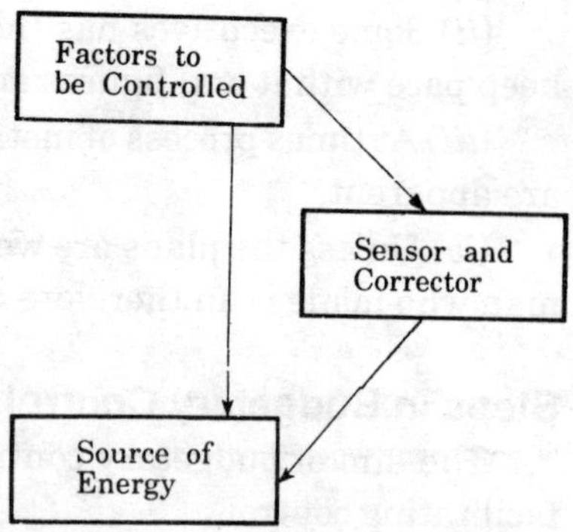

Fig. 7.1

Automatic Control

Automatic control substitutes instruments for simple mental and physical actions. Automatic controls are substitutes for human controls in many industries but costs determine the speed with which automatic controls are introduced. In the operation of airplanes and missiles automatic controls must be used because of space limitations and the need for quick action not within the capacity of human being.

Automation requires a change in management practices. Since the control system must be tailored to the situation, the manager must carefully plan the total operation. Automation places management in the position of machine designer. Automation is thus closely related to fundamental developments in management theory. Computers have also stimulated the development of mathematical and statistical applications to new problems computers have become important in two classes of operations. Firstly in the fields in which complicated formaulas required large amounts of human time for solutions. Secondly it includes those activities handling large mass of quantitative data but in routine and simple matter. In banking, insurance companies and financial sections of other business firms office automation means substitution of electronic data processing for manual operations. Automation has three more complicated meanings, reflecting new developments in management.

(*i*) It refers to an integrated view of manufacturing operations. It emphasises the relationships of machine with each other.

(*ii*) Automation is the increased use of automatic control devices using the closed loop feedback principle.

(*iii*) Automation is the use of electronic computers.

The other important techniques of managerial control are *viz.* Break-even Analysis, Programme Evaluation Review Techniques, Management Information System, Operation Research etc. which have been dealt in details in the subsequent chapters.

8

Motivation

WHAT IS MOTIVATION

Motivation is the action that impels or urges an individual to assume an attitude generally favourable towards his work leading him to perform satisfactorily. It concerns the study of urges, drives, impulse preferences aspirations etc. of people at work, who, if, satisfied tend to promote and maintain high morale. Motivation is a productivity factor in industry. Motivating a worker is to create a need and desire on the part of a worker to better his present performance. Motivation concerns itself with the will to work. Motivation means inspiring persons with a zeal to do work for the accomplishment of objectives of the organisation. Motivation is an important function which a manager has to perform for getting things done from the people. A successful manager know that the issuance of directions, however well conceived and worded, does not mean anything till they are followed. He makes appropriate use of motivation to enthuse the personnel to work.

The motivation is a key determinant of a person's behaviour. The salesman is always concerned with the needs and motives of his client. He often infer the motive underlying a given action but our understanding of human motivation is far from complete. Executives are being exposed increasingly to behavioural science. To understand behavioural science let us first understand what is "Behaviour". Webster defined behaviour as "Mode of conducting oneself", the way in which an organism acts, especially in response to a stimulus." Behavioural Science cannotes all the factors that go into man's fundamental personality, his needs, his emotions, his thinking, his ability to relate his thoughts and feelings. Behavioural scientist's main objective is the study of how and why people behave as they do. The study of behavioural scientist can be applied to economist. The political scientist, the human engineering social pschologist, industrial sociologist, labour economist educationist physicians anthropologists and managers come under the umbrella of behavioural scientist because all are concerned to varying degrees with human behaviour.

SYSTEMATIC STUDY OF BEHAVIOUR

Behavioural science is a systematic study of behaviour. The interest in human behaviour has been generated right from the day the man started interaction with other individuals. Human behaviour study is very old, but the systematic and scientific research on behaviour began in the mid-nineteenth century. The behavior is always the products of two things the nature of individuals and the situation in which individuals finds himself. The nature of the individual depends on heredity, the growing environment his culture and his earning. We know that individuals differ not only with respect to their appearances, but also in their sensitivities, intelligence, interests motivational attitude perception and personalities. Core disciplines in the behavioural sciences are psychology, sociology, anthropology.

Motivation the subordinates is one of the major concerns of the manager. Gone are the days of handicraft stage when it was possible to take the best from workers, who were but members of the same family. But in this age of factory production, the entreprenuers have to create an atmosphere within the workers who might be motivated for honest and sincere work. The will to work is something different from the power or capacity to work. A man might be possessing the physical, mental and technical capacity to work but these are of no consequences to his employer if he is not physically or physiologically willing to make use to his abilities for the ultimate good of the enterprise. It has once been remarked by the president of an American Corporation. "You can buy a man's time. You can buy a man's physical efforts at a given place, but you cannot by his enthusiasm, initiative or Loyality". Thus enthusiasm or willingness to work can be created by motivation. Motivation succeeds not only in having an order concepted but also in gaining a determination to see that it is fulfilled efficiently and effectively. So the manager must have keen appreciation of human behaviour if he has to provide the maximum motivation among his subordinates or associates. Some people are spurred only but intense outer pressures of rewards, others are highly self-motivated. Manager has to constantly provide for incentives or motivating forces in order to intensify their desire and willingness to apply their greater potentialities for the achievement of common objectives.

Definition. Thus motivation is an action that stimulates an individual to take a course of action which will result in attainment of some goal or satisfaction of certain material or psychological needs of the individual himself. We know that a man does not simply live as an economic man but likes to live as a social-economic-man. Major part of the time of a individual is spent more at work then at home.

STUDIES ON MOTIVATION

Industrial Revolution

The first systematic studies of human motivation occured in year 1800, during the industrial revolution when competition forced employers, to develop more efficient methods of producing high quality of products, quicker and at lower cost. At that time, money was used as the only motivating incentive. Frederick Taylor has noted in his "principles of scientific management" that all employees are fundamentally the same. They are uniformally motivated by a desire for money and other motives are either inconsequential or are non-existent.

It is an important function of the management to motivate the people working in the organisation to perform the work assigned to them effectively and efficiently. The management must understand the human behaviour if it has to provide maximum motivation to the personnel. Motivation is a hypothetical cause of human behaviour. There are many theories of motivation which try to bring not the needs which affect the human behaviour. But now it has come to be widely accepted that goals of individuals influence their efforts and that the behaviour of individuals select depends upon their assessment of the probability that behaviour will successfully lead to the goals. So the management must try to understand the goals of the individuals at different times in order to motivate them.

Financial Incentives

Though financial incentives are very important motivators, but they are not the only motivators. People are also motivated by non-financial incentives such as opportunity of advancement, authority to take decisions and freedom to do one's work. Therefore, the management must use both types of incentives to motivate the employees. Management should always remember that motivation is an important tool in its hands for achieving the full cooperation of the people in the organisation in the direction of organisational goals and should use this tool very carefully. It should constantly make use of the non-financial incentives, in addition to the financial incentives, to enthuse the personnel to work willingly and harmoniously for the attainment of organisational objectives. Motivation though defined in many ways still remains undefined because of its vary nature. It is more a realisation than discussion. As in the words of Young poet :

This does not come with houses or with gold
With palace with honour, or with theory X and Y
Its not in the words which market bought and sold
But the smooth hierarchy or needs
Droply and leave its seeker untired.

Hence realisation of needs *i.e.* need of organisation, need of people need of right type of atmosphere where people may work with their best efforts is paramount. The real realisation lies in administrative ecology in which the right type of men can live and breath and have their needs fulfilled. The right motivation springs from right sense of values. The right motivation does not come by attending various Institute of management or sitting at high salaried position.

It may be defined as any idea, need, emotion of organic state, that prompts a man to an action. A motive is inferred from the behaviour of a man. It cannot be observed directly. It may simply be assumed to exist as an internal factor that integrates a man's behaviour. As the motive is within the individual, it is necessary to study his needs, emotions, etc., in order to motivate him to do work. Motive influences the behaviour of a man. But there are also other factors which influence man's behaviour such as past experience, physical capabilities and environmental situation. Motive, however, should be distinguished from these factors. As a matter of fact, there is no best way of defining motive. According to some psychologists, motive also includes a conscious desire for something that is related to the goal selection function. This conscious desire may be called a 'want'. But there are other psychologists who do not share this view. They think that a desire or want is too subjective to be of value in a scientific sense. They believe that it would be desireable to take a man's verbal report of his inner feelings as one aspect of human behaviour that is influenced by the inferred motive.

Factor Influencing Motives

There is no universal theory that can explain the factors influencing movtives which control man's behaviour at any particular point of time. Generally different motives operate at different times among different people and influence their behaviour. That is why the concept of motivation has been variously identified as an unquestionable fact of human experience, as an indisputable fact of behaviour and a mere explanatory fiction. The common and unifying element in these diverse conceptions is that motivation is an agency or factor or force that helps to explain behaviour.*

Motivation may be defined as the complex of forces inspiring a person at work in an organisation to intensify his desire and willingness to use his potentialities for achievement of organisational objectives. It is something that moves a person into action and continues him in the course of action enthusiastically. The role of motivation is to develop and intensify the desire in every member of the organisation to work effectively and efficiently in his position. As said above, there are certain forces inside the person inspiring him to continue work, which may be called as drives, wishes, instincts or tension states. Thus, by motivation we mean mechanisms inside the person that sustain his continued activity as a human being.

Motivation has also been defined as the process or the reaction which takes place in the memory of the individuals. It may be viewed as a combination of forces (motives) maintaining human activity.

Productivity and Motivation

According to *March and Simon,* motivation is a function of perceived consequences of evoked alternatives and individual goals in terms of which alternatives are evaluated. March and Simon have established positive correlation between productivity and motivation by means of a theoretical model.

Following are the main generalisation in this model :

(*i*) Lower the individual satisfaction, greater the search for better ways of doing the job.
(*ii*) More the search for alternatives, greater the expected rewards.
(*iii*) Greater the expected rewards higher the satisfaction and level of aspiration.
(*iv*) Higher the level of aspiration, lower the satisfaction.

Thus, if the present level of satisfaction is low, the search is more and *vise versa.* Higher the expected rewards, higher will be the search. It will in turn lead to higher level of aspiration. When a person feels that he has to achieve higher satisfaction, he is naturally inclined in search for alternative programmes of action. Greater the expected value of rewards, greater is the search. If the expected value of rewards are materialised, satisfaction is achieved. The level of aspiration also goes up if the reward becomes higher so that individual is never satisfied. His level of satisfaction will be lower. Thus level of aspiration and satisfaction are negatively correlated.

If the level of aspiration raises at the same rate at the expected reward, the individual will continue to be motivated by this mild dissatisfaction. If the level of aspiration does not rise whereas the reward rises, the individual becomes complacent and his search activity declines. But on the other hand, the level of aspiration is too high that it is beyond the reach of the individual, the result will be frustration. March and Simon conclude from this analysis that high satisfaction does not necessarily stimulate productivity rather it is the dissatisfaction that stimulates productivity.

---

* Bodies, R.C. Theory of Motivation

Employees Wants

Wants are derived from needs. When needs are conditioned by environment, the result is a set of employee wants. Management can achieve operational motivation by appearling to wants. But the deeper foundations of its motivational programmes are always related to the needs. Needs are the cause of action, but wants are clues to the types of action likely to take place.

It should be seen that in trying to satisfy his wants, a person does not always try to choose the best action but only a satisfactory one.

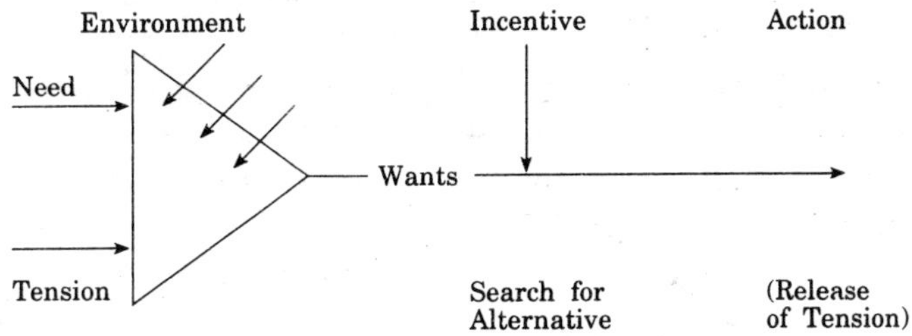

Fig. 8.1

Only in exceptional cases he tries to discover and choose the very best solution. In other words, he satisfies rather than maximises. It is important for managers to understand this point in developing incentives. Often, a simple straight forward workable incentive is more motivating than a complex one which actually gives the better reward because an employee sees the simple incentives and workable path toward the satisfactory goal.

The long run wants of a person at any given time are called his level of aspiration, which change to keep always ahead of actual achievement and spur him upward. The unsatisfied wants of a person are the starting point in any motivation model as shown in Fig. 8.2.

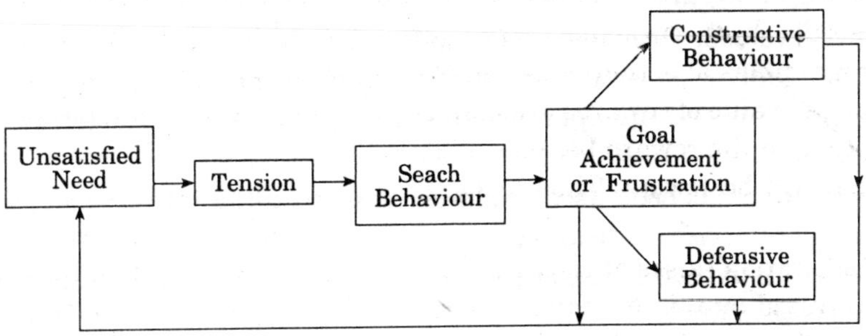

Fig. 8.2 Level of Aspiration

The above diagram indicates that an unsatisfied need results in tensions within the individual and motivates a search for ways to relieve the tension. If one is successful in achieving a goal, another need emerges. If, however, attempts as meet with frustration, one either engages in constructive behavior or resorts to defensive behavior. In either case the individual to the next unsatisfied need which emerges.

Theories and Models of Motivation

Motivation is important because in most cases people do must contribute towards the realisation of organisational goals as much as they can. Theories of motivation can be loosely divided into content theories and process theories. The former identify needs as important motivating forces and in so doing adopts a stimulus. Organism-Response model of behaviour. According to this model, if a desired behavioural response is to be obtained, the correct stimulus must first be applied. Operationalising this model within the work sitting necessitates making certain assumptions about human nature and expressing these in the form of individual wants, needs, desires or expectations. The job or organisation is then designed so as to satisfy the identified wants, needs in the belief that the desired behavioural response will be achieved.

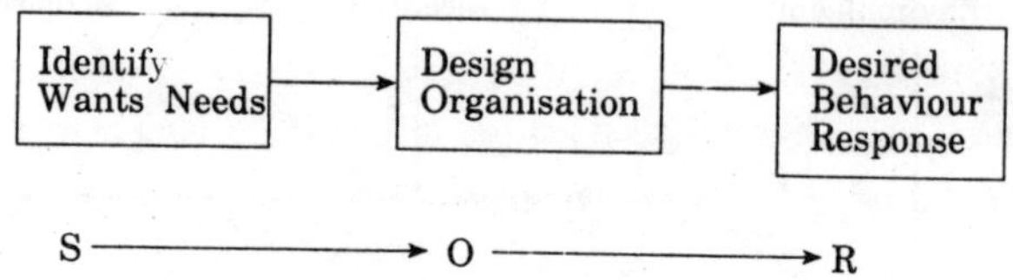

Fig. 8.3 (*S-O-R*) Model of Behaviour.

In contrast to content theories process theories, *e.g.* Expectancy theory and equity theory concentrate on the mental processes involved in motivation. The basic tenet of equity theory is that a person compares the ratio of his inputs to a job with what he gets out of that job, and should there be a discrepancy he will act to reduce it. Expectancy theory suggests that motivation is the product of the valency of the outcome of a certain action and the expectancy that the outcome will result from that action and the expectancy that the outcome will result from that action. Although both of the above mentioned process theories contain a degree of intuitive logic, they are notoriously difficult-if not impossible to operationalise, and have thus made no significant impact upon practicing managers.

Work Place Behaviour

Another approach to workplace behaviour is to be found in the social action perspective. This suggests that action is to be understood in terms of the meanings that different situations hold for the factors involved. Drawing on this approach Goldthrope suggested that the meaning a situation had for a individual would be reflected in his orientation to that situation, and that orientations to work provided the appropriate starting place for understanding behaviour at work.

The term motivation has been used in almost as many different ways as the term "Work". Psychologists who use it often disagree about the specific processes to which it applies. According top Warr: Motives are "reasons for action". Adopting this definition leads us to two questions with respect to work :

(*a*) Why do people work at all ?

(*b*) Why do people work hard and with a strong sense of commitment ?

Motivation to Work and Motivation at Work

These two phrases represent two conceptually distinct aspects of work motivation which will be called "the motivation to work" and "motivation at work". The former is concerned with why people work at all while, latter is concerned with why people work hard and with a strong sense of commitment at one particular job or one particular time. The understanding of the motivation to work is logically prior to an understanding of motivation at work.

According to Dale, "Work, Career and the Self" who supported the above contention.

"How the person reacts to the situation, what he sees as the necessary, possible and desirable limits of his action, in the situation, will be greatly affected by the reason for which he finds himself in that situation."

It is this contention that leads to the suggestion that an inadequate definition of motivation has contributed to an inadequate framework for understanding work motivation.

Motivation at Work

Motivation at work, is concerned with the individual's expenditure of effort and energy, and his sense of commitment at work. It is possible to view this in two rather different ways, A "narrower" view, which has been the concern of traditional motivation theory, focuses on the expenditure of effort and energy over a fixed and relatively short period of time, whereas a "wider definition" takes into account the longer term and includes absenteeism, lateness and labour turnover, which have traditionally been regarded as measures of job satisfaction rather than motivational work.

At individual's motivation at work will only be fully, understood in relation to his motivation to work. Thus, an individual's commitment behaviour at work will be influenced by the significance that work has for him, (or his motivation to work).

Goldthrope suggested that orientations to work would provide a useful starting point for the study of organisational behaviour, the concept of orientation has not gone uncriticised. The two major criticisms centre on (1) whether a worker's orientation is fixed by forces external to the work situation and (2) whether the orientation remains constant over time. But the traditional social action model shown in Figure (8.4) is likely to represent the crucial argument of both the major criticisms.

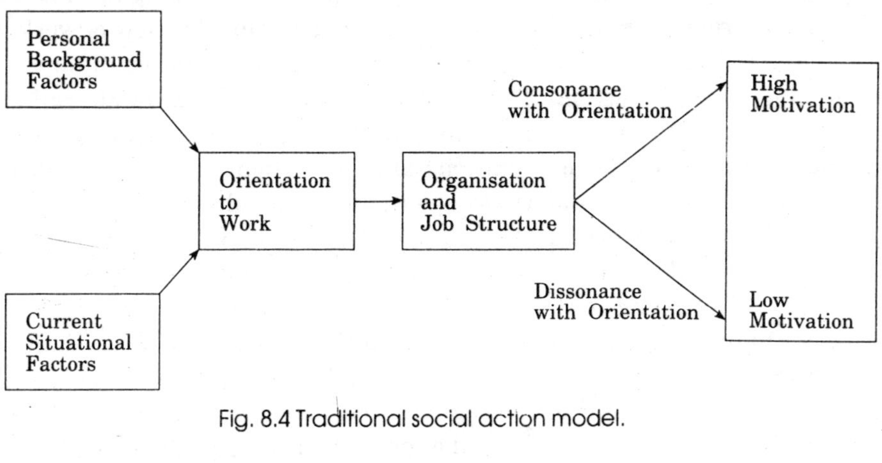

Fig. 8.4 Traditional social action model.

A Conceptual Confusion

A conceptual distinction has already been drawn between the motivation to work and motivation at work, and it has been suggested that an individual's motivation at work derives from his motivation to work, whilst his motivation to work derives from the view of work that he holds. This view of work will be the product of a number of factors *viz.* national culture, educational experiences family background and past and present work experience. It is now further contended that the individual's view of work will influence the basis of his attachment to work.

The attachment to work will influence behaviour at work and by formulating the relationships in this way the following model is developed :

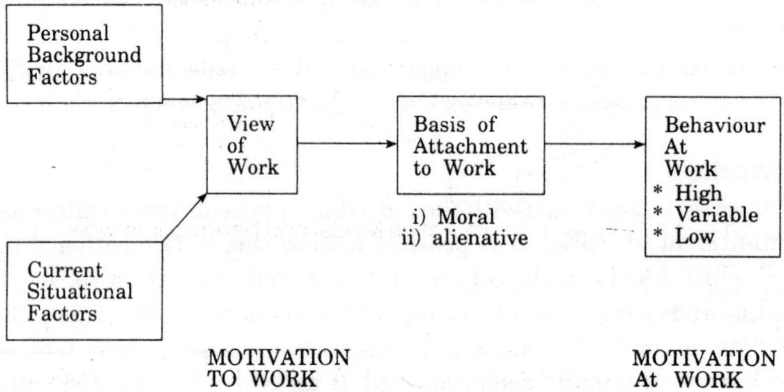

Fig. 8.5. Social Action Model.

Thus one of the first steps that must be taken in understanding workplace behaviour is to understand the basis on which the individual attaches himself to the place of work, which in turn necessitates the development of a profile of the possible bases on which the individual can attach himself to work. This model, then, differs from the traditional social action model by suggesting that the concept of orientation be replaced by the twin concepts of motivation to work and attachment to work.

The view of work held by an individual is one which produces in that individual a sense of moral attachment to work (*i.e.* positive orientation of high intensity). It could then be preidoted that this view of work is likely to be taken as a valid reason for working hard being punctual and not being absent from work without good cause. If, however, the view of work held by the individual produces and alienative attachment, then the prognosis is rather different. One could predict two possible courses of action. The individual either avoids work altogether or adapts to the situation he finds himself in by attaching his own personal meaning to work which is likely to emphasises other wants, expectations and aspirations and which will be likely to identify him as instrumentally or solidaristically oriented. An individual values social relationship at work, or in Goldthrope's terms a solidaristic orientation or, in Benett's terms, a relational orientation, may be less informative than knowing that his attachment to work is alienative rather than moral. By focussing on the solidaristic orientation, for instance, management may decide to redesign to redesign work so as to facilitate the satisfaction of sociability needs and thereby hope to increase motivation at work. Although the redesigned work situation may satisfy employee sociability needs there is no guarantee, however, that motivation at work will be increased. An alternative and more fruitful approach for management would be to focus on the individual's attachment to work with the aim of changing this attachment from being alienative to moral; from an "intense negative orientation' to a positive orientation of high intensity". Although redesigning work so as to facilitate more social interaction may be part of this policy but it is difficult to envisage it being the total policy.

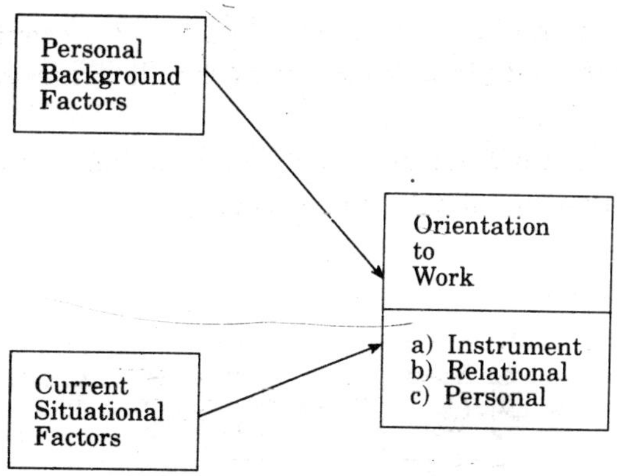

Fig. 8.6. Traditional Social Action Model and behaviour to work

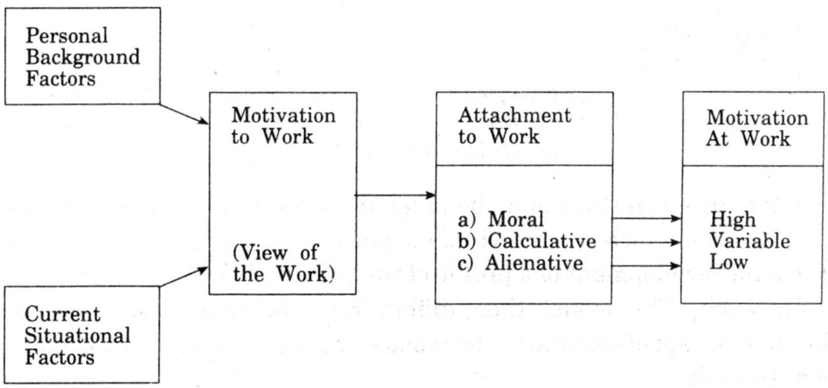

Fig. 8.7 Social Action Framework and Behaviour at work

To operationalising the model following three stage process should be adopted. (*i*) The first stage should be aquantitative analysis of relevant material relating to absenteeism, lateness, productivity, etc. The purpose of this quantitative analysis being the classification of individuals according to their motivation at work and from this classification the basis of their attachment to work can be inferred. (*ii*) The second stage should concern itself with exploring and identifying the meaning that work has for these individuals and by so doing classify the nature of their motivation to work. (*iii*) Finally, attempts should be made to identify factors that may be important in shaping individual's motivations to work, and through this their motivation at work.

The first stage of the analysis is carried out by constructing histograms from the available data on, absenteeism, late coming and productivity, and then grouping individuals into suitable units, such as quartiles or deciles. For instance, the upper decile on the absentee histogram can be taken as representing individuals who are alientatively attached to work, whilst the lower decile can be thought of as representing those morally attached to work.

Having grouped people on the basis of their attachment to work it is speculated that consistency will be found within groups and differences between groups in their motivation to work. However, if a meaningful classification of motivation to work is to be developed, it must be grounded in, and generated by, empirical study, and not simply reflect the mental constructs of behavioural theorists.

The third phase of analysis--identifying factors that shape individuals' motivation to work--is a matter of correlating personal background and current situational information with motivations to work. The collection of this date need not be a separate and distinct activity, but indeed a data bank is likely to be built up as a result of the activities in phased manner.

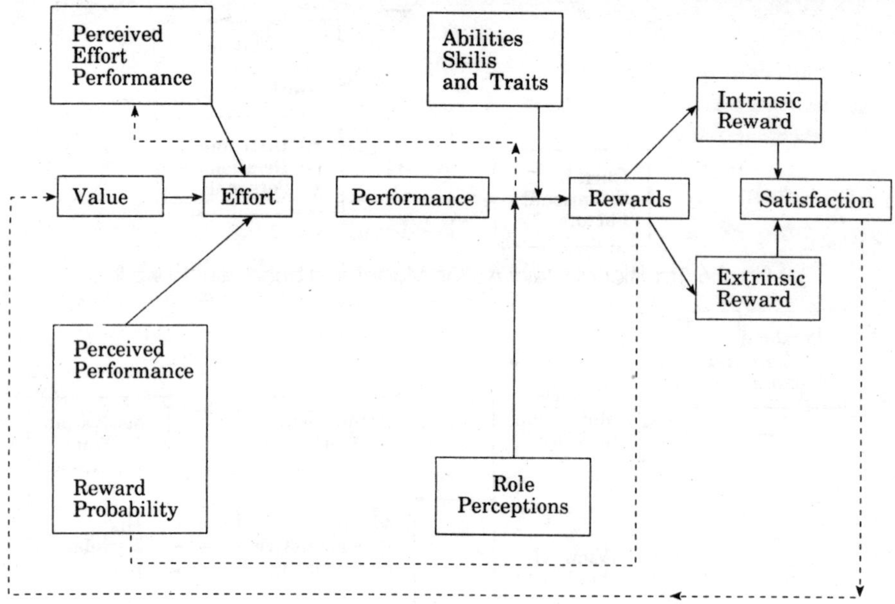

Fig. 8.8 Structure of Expectancies

From a management perspective, the model allows distinctions to be made between groups of workers who are highly motivated. It also offers the prospect of identifying factors which are important in shaping motivations to and thereby motivation at work. Once these factors have been identified the possibility arises of making practical and empirically based suggestions about motivation at work. These suggestions may be of two kinds. On the one hand, if motivation at work is found to be related to intra plant factors then organisation and job design become the relevant focus, while on the other hand. If motivation at work is found to be related to extra plant factors, then selection and recruitment becomes the relevant area of interest.

Expectancy Theory

Expectancy theory provide comprehensive frame work for dealing with complex industrial behaviour. In this theory, expectancies are defined as a special category of belief or the nature and dynamics of the environment and in this sense are to be regarded as important perception, judgement and decision taking by the individual.

Expectancies specify the relationships between what a person does and what outcomes he obtains in the organisational environment. Expectancy thereby explains how expectancies influence the voluntary behaviour of individuals in organisations forms. The theory states that the individual's decision to expend effort will depend upon three perceptions or beliefs about the effort receiving situations as given below :

(*i*) That there are available rewards for successful achievement resulting from the effort to be expanded, and that there rewards have value for the individual.

(*ii*) The achievement of success as a result of expanding the effort will in fact being forth there rewards.

(*iii*) The expenditure of effort will result in successful achievement. The achievement will depend not only upon the decision to expend effort but also upon the traits and skills or abilities of the individual and upon the role perceptions of the individual. The theory allows that rewards associated with performance may be either intrinsic or extrinsic. There are several other approaches to the study of motivation such as Be Strong Approach, McGregor's Theory X and theory Y, which are discussed below.

Be Strong Approach

Traditionally, management has resorted to be strong. This form of motivation in industry emphasizes authority and economic rewards. This rewards strategy consists of forcing people to work by threatening to punish or dismiss them or to cut there rewards, if they do not work. The assumption is that people would if they are driven by the fear of punishment. To prevent people from going away from the work, there must be close supervision, management must spell out every rule and give the workers the narrow range for discretion. This approach paid off fairly well in the early days of industrial revolution. It because needs for food, clothing and shelter were paramount. This approach is similar to the 'Carrot and Stick' approach.

In recent times, this approach has because less effective because people have began to expect more from their jobs rather than more money. Moreover, with the growth of unions, a rising standard of living and changing pattern of living has made this approach less effective as a motivational device. The basic aspiration of the 'be strong' approach that if a man does not do what he is told to do, he will be fired.

Be Good or Paternalistic Approach

This approach is a substitute for 'be strong' approach applied by many managements. The essence of this approach is conferring of various rewards on the organisation members in hope of increasing the productivity due to gratitude or loyalty to the organisation. High wages, rob security, subsidised education, recreation programmes, fair supervision and good working conditions are the instruments used for gaining the loyalty of the employees and thus promoting the efficiency. Increasing, effort are sought on a reciprocal basis management tries make to available to the subordinates the things they want and as a result expects the subordinates to display enthusiasm and loyalty.

Be good approach or paternalism may fail to achieve its purpose. Paternalism may create resentment rather than gratitude because some people do not like to feel dependent on others. They prefer to decide for themselves what they want. Paternalism incorporate some of the basic assumptions of 'Be Strong. People are expected to be docile in return for their gifts, and work is still regarded as a form of punishment that people undergo only in return for a reward. Moreover, many of the rewards must be enjoyed off the job. Little effort is spent on making the job itself more rewarding. Like be strong approach, paternalism also carries with it a negative threat if a worker does not do his job as ordered, his gifts will be taken away.

Effort Reward Approach

The third strategy tries to establish and relationship between efforts and rewards. The origin of this approach can be found in the scientific management of *F.W. Taylor*. Rewards in this approach are considered to be a function of efforts put into reach the standard set by the management. Individual wage incentives and promoting individuals on the basis of accomplishment are the manifestation of this approach. In order to practice this strategy, managers set up standards of performance, monitor the behaviour of employees to observe the extent to which these standards are attained or adhered to, and allocate rewards and penalties based on the observance of the performance.

This approach may also be called monistic approach because it assumes that people work for money. This theory seeks a single cause of behaviour. This theory accepts the notion of economic man who efforts carry more pay. The rewarding of correct behaviour should lead to the reinforcement of that behaviour. This theory can be described in a simple model as 'EFFORT-REWARD-EFFORT MODEL'. The model illustrates the greater efforts not only leads of greater pay but also the reward of greater pay stimulates greater effort. This strategy is not considered adequate because it touches only one aspect of human behaviour. This approach assumes that people work in an organisation with the only incentive of earning money; it forgets the necessity of providing on-the-job satisfaction to the employees. Moreover, this approach can be applied only where performance and results can be directly and quantitatively measured.

McGregor's Theory 'X' and Theory 'Y'

All the above mentioned approaches to motivation are based on the assumption of human nature included by Douglas McGregor in his Theory 'X'. The assumptions are :

(*i*) The average human being has an inherent dislike of work and will avoid it if he can.

(*ii*) Because of this human characteristic of dislike of work, most people must be directed and threatened with punishment to get them to put forth adequate efforts towards the achievement of organisational objectives.

(*iii*) The average human being prefers to be directed, wishes to avoid responsibility, has relatively little ambition and wants security above all.

According to McGregor, this is a traditional theory of what workers are like and what organisation must do to manage them. This gives us the conventional approach of management. According to theory 'X' the employees are passive and even resistant to organisational needs. They have to be persuaded and pushed into performance and this is the management's task. Management does the thinking, the employees obey the orders. But McGregor himself says that this approach does not represent the modern views on motivation. "The conventional approach of theory 'X' is based on mistaken notions of what is cause and what is effect". The assumptions contained in theory X do not reveal the true nature of human beings.

Theory 'Y'

McGregor himself states that the assumptions of theory 'X' do not portray the correct nature of human beings. He thinks that assumptions included in theory 'Y' are more valid precepts of human nature. The assumptions are :

(*a*) The expenditure of physical and mental effort in work is as natural as play or rest. The average human being does not inherently dislike work. Depending upon controllable conditions, work may be a source of satisfaction or a source of punishment.

(*b*) External control and threat of punishment are not the only means for bringing about efforts towards organisation objectives Man will exercise self-direction and self-control in the service of objective to which he is committed.

(*c*) Commitment to objective is a function of the rewards associated with their achievement. The most significant of such rewards *e.g.* the satisfaction of ego and self-actualisation needs, can be direct products of efforts directed towards organisation objectives.

(*d*) The average human being learns under proper conditions, not only to accept but to seek responsibility. Avoidance of responsibility, lack of ambition and emphasis on security are generally the consequences of experience, not inherent in human characteristics.

(*e*) The capacity to exercise a relatively high degree of imagination, ingenuity and creativity in the solution of organisational problems is widely, not narrowly, distributed in the population.

(*f*) Under the conditions of modern industrial life, the intellectual potentialities of the average human being are only partially utilised.

A study of the assumption of Theory 'Y' makes it clear that individual goals and organisational goals are not necessarily incompatible. These basic problem is that of securing the commitment of employees to organisational objectives. Employees' commitment is directly related to the satisfaction of employees' needs. Theory 'Y' therefore, places emphasis on the satisfaction of the needs of the employees. This theory does not rely heavily on the use of authority as an instrument of command and control. Employees exercise self-direction and self-control in the realisation of objectives to which they are committed.

In practice, a few industrial managements are tempted to adopt theory 'Y' fully, but many companies apply it self-consciously at certain points, particularly at the executive level just below top management. In that region, good human relations and a cooperative atmosphere likely to be specially valued by the chairman or president of the company.

In fact, in support of the assumptions as embodied in Theory 'Y' McGregor has cited a few innovative ideas wherein the workers have been given freedom to direct their own activities, to assume responsibility, and importantly to satisfy their egoistic needs. The concepts of job enlargement, participation and consultative management and management by objectives are quite consistent with Theory 'Y'.

Maslow's Theory of Motivation

Management can do its job effectively only through motivating people to work for the organisational objectives. But according to modern authors like Maslow, Herzberg and Vroom, it is difficult to understand motivation without considering what people want and expect from their work. Maslow's theory is considered an important theory of motivation because it highlights the needs of the people.

Human needs may be classified as (*i*) basic physiological or primary needs and (*ii*) social and psychological needs or secondary needs. Some of the psychological needs are food, water, sleep, air to breathe, sex, clothing and shelter. These needs arise out of the basic physiology of life and are important for the survival of a man. They are virtually universal among people, but they exist in different intensity. Needs are also influenced by the social environments. One man may require wheat to satisfy his hanger, other may require rice for the same purpose.

Secondary needs are related to mind or spirit rather than to the physiology of life. Many of these needs develop as one matures. Instances are belongingness, recognition, self-esteem, sense of duty, self-assertion. Actually, these are the needs which complicate the efforts of managers because secondary needs vary among people much more than primary physiological or basic needs.

Secondary needs develop a variety of motives in each person and are often hidden so that he himself cannot recognise them. Since these are not satisfied by the management, workers usually attribute their dissatisfaction to something more tangible, such as wage and bonus. It should also be noted that both primary and secondary needs may exist in a person at the same time so that it is difficult to differentiate among the various needs.

MASLOW's NEED PRIORITY MODEL

Maslow defines human effectiveness as a function of matching man's opportunity with the appropriate position in hierarchy of needs. Process of motivation begins with an assumption that behaviour, atleast in part, is directed towards the achievement of satisfaction of needs. Maslow proposed that human needs can be arranged in a particular order from the lower to the higher order. The need hierarchy is as follows :

Basic Physiological Needs

The needs that are taken as the starting point for motivation theory are the so called physiological needs. These needs relate to the survival and maintenance of human life. These needs include such things as food, clothing, shelter, air, water and other necessities of life.

Safety and Security Needs

After satisfying the physiological needs, people want the assurance of retaining a given economic level. They want job security, personal, bodily security, security of source of income, provision for old age, insurance against risk, etc.

Social Needs

Man is a social being. He is, therefore, interested in conversation, sociability, exchange of feeling and grievances, companionship, recognition, belongingness, etc.

Esteem and Status Needs

These needs embrace such things as self-confidence, independence, achievement, competence, knowledge, initiative and success. These needs are concerned with the prestige and respect of the individuals.

Self Fulfilment Needs

The final step under the need priority model is the need for self-fulfilment or a need to fulfil what a person considers to be his mission in life. It involves realising one's potentialities for continued self-development and for being creative in the broadest sense of the world. After his other needs are fulfilled, a man has the desire for personal achievement. He wants to do something which is challenging gives him enough dash and initiative to work. It is beneficial to him in particular and the society in general. The sense of achievement gives him satisfaction.

The above mentioned needs have a definite sequence of domination. Second need does not dominate until first need is reasonable satisfied and third need does not dominate until first two needs have been reasonably satisfied and so on. The other side of the needs hierararchy is that man is a wanting animal, he continues to want something or the other. He is never fully satisfied. If one needs is satisfied, the other arise. As said above, (according to Maslow), needs arise in a certain order of preference and not randomly. Thus if one's lower level needs (physiological and security needs) are unsatisfied, he can be motivated only by satisfying his lower level needs and not by satisfying his higher level needs. Another point to note is that once a need or a certain order of needs is satisfied, it ceases to be a motivating factor. Man lives for bread alone as long as it is not available. In the absence of air one can't live, it is plenty of air which ceases to be motivation.

Importance of Higher Order Needs

The physiological and security needs are finite but needs of higher order are sufficiently infinite and are likely to be dominant ones in person at higher levels in organisation. This has been proved by various studies. A study by Boris Blai supported this by showing that managers and professional in U.S.A. highly value self relization, while service and mutual workers value job security most highly*. Further a survey of 200 factory workers in India reported that they give top priority to job security, earnings and personal benefits--all lower order needs**. Studies have also revealed that those needs which are thought to be most important like social needs, egoistic needs and self-realisation, are also thought to be best satisfied. One study of two thousands and eight hundred managers in eleven countries reported that security, sense of belonging, esteem and self-realisation needs are progressively less satisfied according to the pattern of the need priority model.

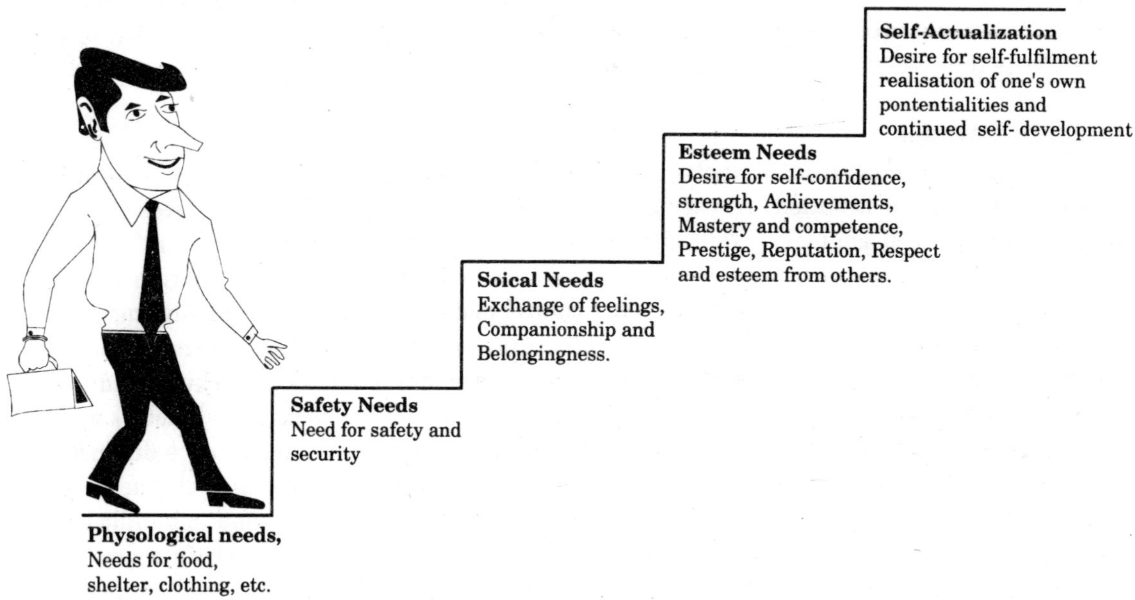

* Boris Blake : A job satisfaction predictor, Peronnel Journal, U.S.A. Oct., 1963

** Paras Nath Singh and Robert Wherry—Ranking of Job Factors by Factory Workers in India, Personnel Psychology, Spring, 1903.

*** Harie, Ghisheli, and Porter : Cultural Pattern in the Role of the Manager Industrial, Relations, Feb. 1963

Criticism of Need Priority Model

The need priority model may not apply at all times in all places. Surveys in continental European countries and Japan have shown that the model does not apply very well to their managers. Their degree of satisfaction in needs does not vary according to the need priority model. For example, Spain and Belgium felt that their esteem needs are better satisfied than their security and social needs. Apparently cultural differences are an important cause of these differences. Thus need hierarchy may not follow the sequence postulated by Maslow. Even if safety need is not satisfied the egoistic or social need may emerge. Proposition that one need is satisfied at one time is also of doubtful validity. The phenomenon of multiple motivation is of great practical importance in understanding the behaviour of man. Man's behaviour at many time is mostly guided by multiplicity of motives. However, one or two motive in any situation may be prepotent where other may be of secondary importance. Moreover at different levels of needs the motivation will be different. Money can act as a motivator only for physiological and social needs, not for satisfying higher level needs, employees are enthusiastically motivated by what they are seeking, more than by what they already have. They may react protectively to try to keep what they already have, but they move forward with enthusiasm only when they are seeking something else. In other words, man works for bread alone where there is no bread.

There are always some people in whom, for instance need for selfesteem seems to be more than that of love. There are also creative people in whom the drive for creativeness seems to be more important. In certain people the level of operation may be permanently lower. For instance a person who has experienced chronic unemployment, may continue to be satisfied for the rest of his life if only he can get enough food. Another cause of several reversal of the hierarchy is that when a need has been satisfied for a long time, this may be under evaluated.

Herzberg's Model

A significant development in motivation was distinction between motivational and maintenance factors in job situation. A research was made by Herzberg and his associates based on the interview of 200 engineers and accountants who worked for eleven different firms in Pittsburgh area. These men were asked to recall specific incidents in their experience which made them feel either particularly good or particularly bad about their jobs. The findings of the research were that good feeling in the group under test were keyed to the specific tasks that the men performed rather than to background factors such as money, security or working conditions and when they felt bad it was because of some disturbance in these background factors which had caused them to believe that they were being treated unfairly. This led to draw a distinction between what they called as 'motivators' and 'hygiene factors'. To this group of engineers and accountants the real motivators were opportunities to become more expect and to handle more demanding assignments. Hygienic factors served to prevent loss of money and efficiency. The hygienic factors provide no motivation to the employees, but the absence of these factors serve as dissatisfiers.

Some job conditions operate primarily to dissatisty employees when the conditions are absent, but their presence does not motivate employees in a strong way. Many of these factors traditionally are perceived by management as motivations, but the factors are really more potent as dissatisfiers. These potent dissatisfiers. These potent dissatisfiers are called maintenance factors in job because they are necessary to maintain a reasonable level of satisfaction among the employees. They are also known as dissatisfiers or 'hygienic factors' because they support employees' mental health. Another set of job conditions operates primarily to build strong motivation and higher job satisfaction, but their absence rarely proves strongly dissatisfiers. These conditions are 'Motivational Factor's. Herzberg's maintenance and motivational factors have been shown in the following Table :

HERZBERG'S MAINTENANCE AND MOTIVATIONAL FACTORS

Need Structure — Physiological or Primary Needs / Social, Psychological, Egoistic, or Secondary Needs

Maintanance or Hygienic Factors.	Motivational Factors Achievement.
Company Policy and Aministration.	
Technical Supervision.	Recognition.
Inter-personal reation with Supervision.	Advancement.
Inter-personal relations with Peers.	Work itself.
Inter-personal relations with Subordinates.	Possibility of growth.
Salary.	Responsibility.
Job Security.	
Personal life.	
Working Conditions.	
Status.	

Hygienic factors include such things like wages, fringe benefits, physical conditions and overall company policy and administration. The presence of the factors at a satisfactory level prevents job dissatisfaction, but they do not provide motivation to the employees. So they are not considered as motivational factors, Motivational factors, on the other hand and essential for increasing the productivity of the employees. They are also known as satisfiers and include such factors as recognition. Feeling of accomplishment and achievement, opportunity of advancement and potential for personal growth, responsibility and sense of job and individual importance, new experience and challenging work, etc.

Herzberg further stated that managers have hitherto been very much concerned with hygienic factors. As a result, they have not been able to obtain the desired behaviour from employees. In order to increase the motivation of employees, it is necessary to pay attention to the satisfier motivational factors.

Herzberg also said that today's motivators are tomorrow's hygienic factors because they stop influencing the behaviour of persons when they get them. When a person gets one thing then something else will motivate him and the need which has been fulfilled will have only motivate negative significance in determining their behaviour. It should also be noted that one's hygiene may be the motivators of another. For instance, it is likely that workers in underdeveloped societies will designate some of the maintenance factors as motivators because their primary needs have not been fulfilled and they continue to be motivated by these factors.

Comparison of Herzberg and Maslow Models

In fact, there is great similarity between Herzberg's and Maslow's Models. A close examination of Herzberg's model indicate that what he actually says is that some employees may have achieved a level of social and economic progress in the society and for them higher level needs of Maslow (Esteem and self-actualisation) are the primary motivators. However, they still must satisfy the lower level needs for the maintenance of their current state. Thus, we can say that money might still be a motivators for operative employees and for some managerial employees. Herzberg's model adds to the need hierarchy model because it draws a distinction between the two groups motivational and maintenance factors and points out that the motivational factors are often derived from the job itself.

Vroom's Model

One of the most recent models of motivation has been developed by Vroom. Vroom's model views motivation as a process governing choice. Thus, if a individual has a particular goal, some behaviour must be performed in order to achieve the goal. The individual weighs the likelihood that behaviours will achieve the desired goals and if certain behaviour is expected to be more successful than others, that type of behaviour is likely to be chosen.

The important contribution of Vroom's model is that is explains how the goals of individuals influence their efforts and that the behaviour individuals select depends upon their assessment of the probability that the behaviour will successfully lead to the goal. For instance, all people in an organisation may not place the same value of such job factors as promotion, high pay, job security and working conditions. In other words, they may rank them differently. Vroom is of the opinion that what is important is the perception and value the individual places upon certain goals. Let us assume that one individual places high value on salary increases and perceives superior performance as instrumental in reaching that goal. According to Vroom, this individual will strive towards superior performance in order to achieve the salary increases. On the other hand, another individual may value a promotion and perceive political behaviour as instrumental in achieving it. This individual is not likely to emphasize superior performance to achieve the goal.

In essence Vroom emphasizes the importance of individual perceptions and assessments of organisational behaviour. What is important here is that what the individual perceives as the consequence of a particular behaviour is far more important than what the manager believes the individual should perceive. Thus Vroom's model attempts to explain how individual goals influence individual efforts and like Maslow's and Herzberg's models, it reveals that behaviour is goal oriented.

The ability greater than Zero value performance is constantly increasing function of amount of motivation. In other words, the more motivated an individual to perform effectively, the more effective is performance. The is shown by a straight line in Fig. 8.9.

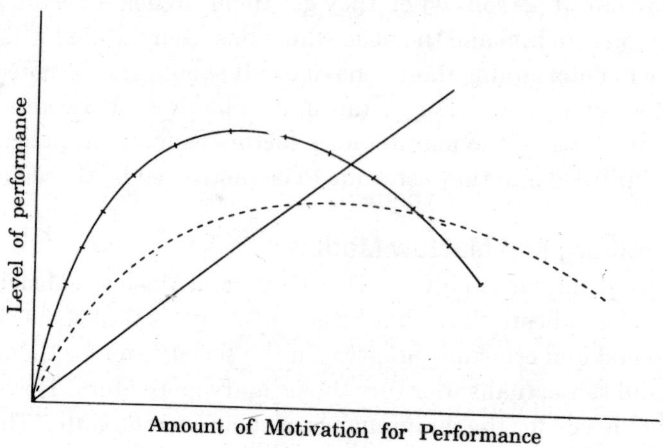

Fig 8.9 Hypothetical relationship between upper unit motivation and level of performance

The accelerated curve shown in dotted line in Fig. 8.9 implies the Law of diminishing returns that is succeeded movement in motivation result in smaller and smaller increments in performance. Function shown by broken lines is similar to the first except for reduction in performance under high level of motivation. The amount of motivation is difficult to be measured to precision. It could at best be done on manipulative basis.

Analysis of Various Studies on Motivation

The scientific study of human motivation is still relatively new; therefore, there is a single accepted theoretical framework for motivation. There are a number of competing conceptions, which have been studied by leading behavioural scientific such as Murry (1964), Vroom (1958) McClelland (1951), March and Simon (1958), Lawler and Porter (1967), Kurt Goldstein (1939), Erich Fromm (1941), Prescott Leacky (1944), Download Syngg and Arthur Combs (1949), Karen Horney (1950), David Reisman (1950), Carl Rogers (1951), Rollo May (1953), Abraham Maslow (1953), Gordon Allport (1955), Rensis Likert (1967), Blake and Mouton (1964), Mc-Gregor (1960), Livingston (1969), Bennis (1967), Fieller (1967), Reddin (1970), Litwin and Stringer (1968), Hunt and Larson (1974), and Frederic Herzberg (1957), Myers (1964), Hersey and Blachard (1972), Brown (1976) and can be classified as follow :

(*a*) Relationship between the intensity of motivation and level of performance most closely approximates the inverted 'U' function. As motivation increases in intensity, it first leads to an increase in efficiency of instrumental activity and then it decreases. ......Vroom

(*b*) Too little motivation leads to sluggishness and inertia, too much to disruption and defence against anxiety. ......McClelland

(*c*) The performance increases satisfaction through the intermediate effect of awards. Performance results from a state of dissatisfaction but dissatisfaction is not all that is required for human action since an employee may not perceive that productivity will satisfy his needs. ......March & Simon

(*d*) The Cognitive theories, Instincts and Drive theories are based on the concept of man as an essentially rational being. ......Murray.

(*e*) Motives, such as curiosity and exploration not only help us in understanding the primacy of love, affection and contact comfort, but is an important and powerful source of human motivation. It is a human tendency to maintain self consistency *i.e.* consistency of self image or self-concept is considered as the nucleus of personally. Personality is conceived as an organisation of ideas which are felt to be consistent with one another. Behaviour expresses the effort to maintain the integrity and unity of its Organisation. ......Prescott Lecky.

(*f*) The human subject will perform better on a task if their ego being involved in it. Similarly it has been observed that a person's evaluation of himself or his self-esteem, originates in his early affectional relationship and latter becomes a powerful motivating force. The desire to maintain or establish a positive evaluation of the self operates as a powerful motive. The expectation that individual is a worthwhile person, capable of being loved. Cared for at a time of need and holding a position or some security and dignity in the society of his fellow beings. Equally important is the self esteem in the eyes of the others, which makes people concerned about status, recognition, prestige and other symbols of social standing. ......Allport and Murrary.

(*g*) Barness set aside the category of self-actualisation and viewed man's safety needs as overlapping the other higher needs; *viz.* self-esteem of other sense of belonging, mutual relationship to the other etc. He related these need to the three dimensions--(*i*) Autonomy, (*ii*) Opportunity for interaction and (*iii*) influence, which define an organisation system.

(*h*) Renis Likert. Blake and Mouton, McGregor, Livingston gave normative overtone and suggested several commonalties, such as theory Y of McGregor, and task of supportive management and participative system of organisation as given by Rensis Likert. Blake and Mouton also suggested positive expectations to motivation which was also suggested positive approach on the part of management and the need for new concept of man, a new concept of power and also the organisation.

(*i*) Herzberg suggested two factor theory which separates those factors which merely reduce dissatisfaction in the work situation (Hygine or Maintenance) from those factors which seem to provide high motivation and satisfaction in the work (Motivators). Herzberg theory was designed to test the concept that man has two sets of needs; (*i*) his need as animal to avoid pain and (*ii*) his need to grow psychologically.

(*j*) Myers (1964) revealed that those persons who sought-opportunities for achievement and responsibility, who he characterised as "growth seekers" did fit in Herzberg's model while other people whom he called the maintenance seeker were generally concerned with environmental conditions.

(*k*) Factors which motivate people vary with the level of employees, their competence, individual personality and situation. The theory seek to identity the factors within an individual or in his environment that lead to high motivation. ......MeClland, Masol, Herzberg.

(*l*) Process theories attempt to identify the various interacting variables and their relationship in the process of motivation. This refers to Expectancy theory developed by Atkinson and Vroom. From suggested that person's motivation towards an action at any time would be determined by his anticipated values of all the outcomes of various actions multiplied by the strength of that person's expectancy that outcome would yield the desired goal.

The relevance of this analysis for understanding the process of motivation is that merely providing satisfaction of needs of employees would not necessarily lead to better performance it would be necessary to provide incentives and situational factors in such a way that their personal needs are integrated with the organisational goals.

New Strategies For Motivating Employees

Motivation is an internalised force. It is self generation, self controlling and self rewarding and not as subject to external control as traditional management and organisational practices would have it. As industry's problems of manpower utilisation have continues to grow, so has the need to better understanding the complexity of employee motivation. It has become crucial to find ways of realising the full potential of people at work.

Motivation is not simple or fixed human quality that can be turned on and off with some sort of key. But there exists no single technique, no universal approach to motivate all employees. Motivation has both short and long-range aspects. A hungry person has, short-range need, seeks fairly immediately satisfaction which directs behaviours toward a relevant goal. Eating a meal achieves that goal. The hunger need is thus satisfied and no longer operates as a motivational force. Other needs do not lose their potency after satisfaction, but persist and even increase in strength over time. The need for recognition may not diminish when some satisfaction has been achieved. Getting some recognition may simply what the appetite for more a need rarely exists in isolation. Several different needs can operate simultaneously and same may be in conflict with others. Different needs may exists at different levels of potency and the relative importance of motives within any person may fluctuate depending upon the individual's perception of people and circumstances surrounding him.

Motivation is identified with compliance. Employees who do what they are told are rewarded; these who do not, are punished eitherby with holding rewards or by disciplinary action. The most common kind of regard is economic-pay, promotions, fringe benefits. The view is still current that people work almost exclusively to get money. Thus it is believed if you pay people more they will work holder : or, conversely people will work harder so they can get more money.

Money Seldom Works as a Substitute

These problems of absenteeism and turnover bring into question traditional nations about the causes of these problems, one answer frequently given is that the workers involved are not motivated but fact is that such people are motivated not to come to work because other more powerful needs than work are fulfilled by not coming to work. Employees are avoiding what they see as an unsatisfying of meaningless job. They are attracted at the same time to what they perceive as more rewarding set of circumstances off the job. These more rewarding circumstances are not likely to be economic in nature. If an employee is away from work to fulfil some need, it is likely that such a need can only be satisfied through some forms of reward that are not monetary but are purely psychological like greater esteem, recognition, self respect. Additional money cannot "buy back the absent employee. He is trying to find a psychological reward he can get in his job, money seldom works as a substitute.

Research carried out but Frederick Herzberg of case Western Reserve University suggests that motivation in two dimensional : things which make people unhappy are not the same as there which make people happy. Herzberg's two factors of motivations he one set of conditions called hygiene factors. These conditions relate to the physical and psychological surroundings in which people work and include such factors as working conditions supervision, benefit plans and key, the other set of conditions is called the motivators. There include responsibility, advancement, recognition, variety and growth.

Chris Argyris of Harvard also looked at the impact of the organisation on the individual. He found that the usual organisational structure itself, along with its leadership and systems of control inhabited the growth of mature individuals. The typical organisation, Argyris said is primarily for men who are willing to remain child like. The structure is tight allowing little key way for choice or flexibility in adapting the rules to fit the circumstances. Workers are expected to do what they are told and leave the thinking to supervisors, where capacities they may privately question. The new employee soon learns that he is expected to be passive and submissive to do as he is told, to leave the thinking to others. Concentrating power and decision making in a relatively few hands at the tops Argyris claims inevitably factors apathy and inflexibility among the many hand further down. This is unhealthy for the men below and for the organisation as a whole.

Motivation and Job Design

The organisation will function at is best. Argyris believes, only if it meets the needs of both these it works and these who for it.

The tightly controlled environment which once seemed so logical has turned out to be self defeating. When decision making is dispersed appropriately through the ranks, when men encouraged to use their minds and participate in the choices that affect them, and when managers gain a better understanding of the real dynamics of motivation, then organisation will become more productive. A growing trend in industry by enlarging jobs, enriching job content and giving employees more control over their work. The simplification of a job easily learned or a dull repetitive operations, has not brought the advantages it was supposed to. Instead it has brought a sense of meaningless and burden to employees. It removed challenge and any sense of individual commitment to production. Here are approaches to job design which are beginning to be used either single or in combination.

Job Rotation

The employees is moved through a serious of related task or operations.

Job Enlargement

Task that normally would be done by several employees are combined in a sequence of tasks performed by a single employee.

Job Enrichment

The level of difficulty or complexity of the job is increased and the employee, assumes some responsibility for planning and controlling his job. Each of these approaches seeks to build greater meaning into jobs, to enhance employee motivation many companies are looking at the strategy of matching people and jobs. Some of the ways in which successful job matching is being accomplished are given as follows :

Job-Man Measurement

The needs of individuals and the potential of different jobs to satisfy needs should be measured.

Task-Progression

With the increasing need to provide expanded training opportunities for women and minority group employees, job performance levels must more precisely defined and linked sequentially in a pattern of job progression.

Team Building

It seeks to increases a group motivation. A group is just introduced to a process of self examination. Through the use of survey data, feedback, experience based learning, matched with the help of an outside team building specialist, group members become increasingly aware of their interdependency. Gradually the group acquires a capability for self diagnosis, self evaluation and self correction. Motivated people are people who share responsibility make decisions, take risks and seek growth and recognition through their own work and through their roganisation. Managers must take greater risks. They must be willing to strive for long range improvement, accepting perhaps some difficult intermediate periods.

Motivation and Job Satisfaction

Following factors must be taken into considerations for intrinsically motivating work and job satisfaction :

(*i*) Job should contain full module and meaningful work with clear functions.

(*ii*) Employee should be able to take decision and exercise some discretion.

(*iii*) Employee should receive some feed-back preferably from the work.

The term job satisfaction, attitudes and industrial morale are often used synonymously. An attitude may contribute to job satisfaction since the later comprises a number of attitudes. Similarly job satisfaction may also contribute to morale. Thus "Job satisfaction is the result of various attitudes the employee holds towards his job towards related factors and towards life in general". Job satisfaction refers to the feeling and the emotional aspects of individuals experience towards his jobs. Investigators used job satisfaction as independent variable and tries to correlate it with different facts of workers' behaviour such as production, absenteeism, accident and turnover. Also, many investigators used job satisfaction as a dependent variable and tried to establish its relationship with personal variables such as age, education, marital status, number of dependents, caste etc.

Measuring Job Satisfaction

Commonly used methods for studying job satisfaction of the workers are :

(1) Attitude scale and Questionnaires:, (2) Interviews;

(3) Direct observation; and, (4) Protective techniques.

One of the simplest and widely used techniques for identifying the job satisfaction of worker is the ranking of job factors in order of their relative overall importance by the interview or questionnaire method.

Factors in Job Satisfaction

The job satisfaction factors may be divided into two types :

(*a*) The characteristics of the individual, and

(*b*) The characteristics of the job.

Individual Characteristics Job Satisfaction

The money or adequate earnings is the first ranked incentive for Indian workers. These studies reveal that wages, security or service, opportunity for advancement, comfortable working conditions, suitable type of work, and sympathetic supervisor are some of the factors that are reported by Indian workers as the most desired factors in their job. Of these factors, it is seen that wages and job security stand out first and second respectively in the order of their importance. The workers give more importance to adequate earnings job security, opportunity, for advancement and comfortable working conditions and less to adequate personal benefits, hours of work and good and sympathetic supervisor.

The Indian worker is extremely had pressed for money, due to the ever-- rising cast of living keeps him away from adequate satisfaction of his basic needs of fold, clothing and shelter.

Money not only satisfies the basic physiological needs but the continued supply of money ensures the satisfaction of the higher order psychological needs. It secures of the individual food and protection, but more importantly, it symbolizes even emotional security. It also satisfies the social needs of the person especially when social life becomes institutionalized. Still higher-order needs of status can also be satisfied by money because, the money is often considered as an index of status.

Ganguli predicts, "At present and in the foreseeable future for Indian workers in general income (for wages) and security of service are going to be two most important incentives.

Studies on Job Satisfaction

The satisfaction and dissatisfaction employees derive from various sources in their job depends very much on the organisational structure, and this organizationals structure, in turn, to large extent depends very much upon the production technology of the organization. Job satisfaction is the result of various attitudes, and by definition, an attitude refers to a dynamic aspects of behaviour, and action potential and is conceptually quite different from an opinion. The critical incident technique, seems very useful in the study of job attitudes. The relative importance of job factors for Indian workers, fits well in the need hierarchy theory of Maslow. The workers rank adequate earnings and job security higher in importance and as these needs are satisfied he goes for a higher level in the need hierarchy such need for opportunity for advancement, comfortable working conditions, adequate persona benefits, and so on. Soon after needs are satisfied he strives for still higher-level needs such as prestige of company, self-expression, achievement and so on.

There is relationship between age and job satisfaction. Studies have been shown that younger workers are more satisfied than the older workers but the contrary results have been observed in case of old people near to retirement. In general the studies indicate that job satisfaction is high for younger employees immediately after the employment but drops sharply after a few years, and then it begins to increase as workers continue on their jobs.

Job Enrichment

The technique of job enrichment is applied as a motivational tool whose basis is "motivators" which satisfies higher order needs of the workers. Some of the key ingredient of job enrichment include more responsibility, control of employees over decision making, well defined job, opportunities to learn job, job variety, opportunity to utilise skills and abilities, job completion and opportunities to see concrete results of work namely contribution, achievement, short comings on the jobs.

There are five core dimensions that provide job enrichment namely :

(*i*) Task Variety,

(*ii*) Task Identity

(*iii*) Task significance,

(*iv*) Autonomy

(*v*) Feedback.

(*i*) Task Variety

Jobs that are high in variety are seen by employees as more challenging because of the range of skills involved.

***(ii)* Task Identity**

It allows employees to perform a complete module of work. The employees working on a small part of a task are unable to identify any product with their efforts. Therefore contains full sense of completion.

***(iii)* Task Significance**

This refers to amount of impact, that the work as on the other people has perceived by an employees. If an employee is engaged in the manufacturing of life saving drug. He perceive that he is doing something important.

***(iv)* Autonomy**

It is the job characteristic that gives an employee some control over his own affairs and it appears to be fundamental in building a sense of responsibility among employees.

***(v)* Feed-back**

It refers to information that tells workers how well they are performing. It comes from both the job and the management. It is desirable for a job to have all that above mentioned dimensions. If one of the dimensions is missing, employees is psychologically deprived and motivation tends to be reduced.

Motivator

The force of motivation lies in person who is motivator. Motivation is not merely higher pay or financial games. This may be a motivation in case of employees who are not getting wages or salaries which are sufficient to satisfy their physiological needs. Therefore, money is not the only motivating factor in case of all employees in all circumstances. Many people are motivated by the desire of self-realisation unique achievement etc. Based on the above organisational psychologists have classified employees into : Economic Man; Social Man; and self actualising Man.

Herzberg Study

The assumption of economic man is derived from the philosophy of Hedonism and the economic doctrines of Adam Smith. According to this, every man calculates the actions that would maximise his own self interest. Thus man is primarily motivated by economic incentives and rewards, etc. Thus the needs of higher order are generally found in employees at higher reveals in the organisation. In a study conducted by Herzberg, under which 200 engineers and accountants were asked what makes them feel "Good as well as Bad" in the organisation. The answers were :

"Feel Good"	"Feel Bad"
Achievement	Company policy. Technical supervision.
Recognition	Interpersonal relationship with supervisors.
Advancement in Work	Interpersonal relationship with peers. Interpersonal relationship with subordinates.
Possibility of growth Responsibility	Salary, Job security, Personal life, Working conditions, Status.

Herzberg classified factors under good feeling as motivational factors and factors under bad feeling as hygienic factors. According to him man is motivated by one of more of the six motivating forces and the other ten factors were described by him as maintenance factors. But we can say that a maintenance or hygienic factor of Herzberg may be motivating for some people, suppose a person is not getting enough money to afford his family or is temporarily employed, he will certainly be motivated by the desire to earn more money or job security, as the case may be. He will do everything service and to get the greatest economic gains and the organisation buys the obedience of employees strictly for economic rewards. But in the present age, the assumptions of economic man do not hold good. Man works not only for economic gains to satisfy his physiological needs but also to satisfy his social needs, to get recognition and to satisfy his egoistic needs. One must take into consideration certain basic factors, before employing the technique of motivation. These can be classified as :

(*i*) Motivator and

(*ii*) Person being motivated

Person being Motivated

The factor pertains to the person being motivated. The following factors must be considered in working out the motivation plan :

Personal background; Education; Age; Marital status; Financial status; Health; Political affiliations; Religious beliefs; Social relationship; Psychological make up; Union affiliation; Company experiences.

The above motivational approach reveals the fact that there must be a capacity or potential for motivation within a person. Finally motivation must be concerned with particular circumstances and environment.

Motivational Plan

Having discussed the various aspects of motivation, it will be appropriate to see how a motivational plan can be drawn, following are the various steps required in introducing a motivational plan :

(*i*) Sizing up the situation

(*ii*) Preparing a set of motivating tools

(*iii*) Selecting and supplying motivational plan

(*iv*) Follow up.

Guidelines to Motivation

Following are the certain guidelines in the performance of steps of motivation which are by no means, final :

(*i*) *Self-interests.* Undoubtedly motivation is largely dependent on self-interest. Self-interest is not an undesirable foundation so long it does not tend towards greediness. It is rather an intelligent act when a person realise that his own purpose are best served when he helps other in attainment of their purposes, conforming to the overall policy organisation.

(*ii*) *Attainability.* Motivational plan should set attainable goals. Attainability must be related to time as well as type of reward.

(*iii*) *Proportioning Rewards.* Good motivation is dependent on proper proportioning of rewards among persons and for the same person at different time.

(*iv*) *Human element.* People are carried away as much by integible concepts and appeals as by concrete goals. Some people think that emotion are the directions of human activity. In human relations, feelings, emotions, age, personality and ideas have to be taken care or lest they are offended and whole effort go wrong.

(*v*) *Individual Group, Relationship.* Motivation must be based on group as well as individual centered stimuli. Although to a large extent each one of us is an island upto himself, although the group pressure has a very dominating role on individual's action. No wage incentive policy or promotional policy can be successful if it is not acceptable to the group.

Motivational plan should also take into consideration the theory set forth by Victor H. Vroom (the nature of relationship between motivation and performance).

Managerial Motivation

Managerial motivation is normally weak in Indian Industries due to the following reasons:

(*i*) Remuneration in the form of salary and perquisites being not in line with the responsibilities of the manger.

(*ii*) The lack of involvement and sense of participation.

(*iii*) The inelasticities and rigidities of procedures.

(*iv*) The interference from Government, the operation of various strong controls etc., are stated to hamper the growth of dynamic managers.

There is no doubt that the manager in the private sectors enjoy much higher scale of pay and more generous perquisites but one has to recognise that government cannot afford such perquisites and governments executives should not try to compete with the private sector in the matter of pay and allowances of mangers. A welfare state with socio-economic-objective can hardly pay such remuneration because of its larger liabilities and limited resources. If the executives in public sector is not offered higher scales, the private sector will be able to draw upon the best talent in the country. But the analysis had shown that it is not true that best talent is going in the private sector. The experience have shown that certain private sector managers are prepared to come to the public sector at about half the pay they get there. This change is not only at the top level executives but at middle level managers also. Thus the financial incentive play an important part but still more important is the fact of recognition of merit and the prevalence of confidence in the impartiality of personnel management. There is always a limit to improve emoluments. The higher the executive placed the more he is concerned of prestige and position, a sense of pride and achievement and the consciousness of making a personal contribution to organisational development and prosperity. Organisational conditions are also becoming inhibitory rather than stimulating. Unless there is a realization from inside and there is an urge to work for motivating the managers is difficult. Following are the factors influencing executive motivation :

(*a*) Managerial unionism is increasingly evident today.

(*b*) Resistance to change is a reality even among the senior managers today.

(*c*) Important qualities of managerial motivation might be getting extinct today due to negative reinforcement such as calculated risk taking, sense of competition with a standard of excellence etc.

(*d*) Even among the top managers elements of defensive and frustration-investigated behaviour are manifest.

(*e*) Dissatisfaction about job content is increasing among managers.

(*f*) There is increasing evidence of role conflict and role ambiguity among middle mangers.

(*g*) Environmental threats and constraints are increasingly impinging on industry today. Centralization of control and decision-making appears to be widespread. There is evidence of role avoidance among the managers.

(*h*) Organization's appear to function in terms of obsolescence rather than innovation. As one senior manager said "A lot of lip services is paid by leaders of industry to management science, but in their own industries decisions are still entirely hunch-based." Generational conflict among managers has been reported, which finds expression in mutual, insecurity and defensive behaviour.

(*i*) The recruitment and career advancement of managers are largely determined by their family and social origin.

Non-Financial Incentives and Motivation

Financial incentives do not work for ever to motivate the people at work. The employees do not always run after money. They have other needs also. They want status, recognition and satisfaction of egoistic needs. In order to motivate the employees. The management can take the help of following non-financial incentives :

(*a*) *Competition.* Competition is a kind of non-financial incentive. If there is a healthy competition among the individual employees or groups of employees, it will lead them to achieve their personal or group goats.

(*b*) *Group Incentives.* Group incentives are more powerful to motivate the employees than the individual incentives. This has been provided in an experiment by Dr. Alexander Mintz, which is also known as "Bottleneck Experiment". It was observed that when the experiments worked selfishly, they caused traffic jams in the experiment. Dr. Mintz in his laboratory created a situation where four or five persons, each held a string with a cone tied to the other end. The cones were dropped into large glass bottle. The participants, when stood around the bottle in a circle tried to fish their cones out before the rising water touched the cones. Quick action was needed as also co-operation because only one cone could be pulled through the bottleneck at a time. If several tried to pull their cones out regardless of others there was a 'cone jam'. In one set of trials the people were offered individual rewards if they got their cones out dry. They produced traffic jams in three fourths of their trials. But in another experiment other groups were told at the start that it was a test of co-operation; there was no individual reward but only a group reward. There was not even a single traffic jam when a co-operative attitude was induced. Thus a group incentive was more effective to motivate the experimenters to work co-operatively.

(*c*) *Praise.* Praise satisfies one'a ego needs. Sometimes, praise is more effective than any other incentive. We have seen that in industry, at home or elsewhere, people respond better to praise. However, this incentive should be used with greater degree of care because praising an incompetent employee would create resentment among competent employees. Of course, occasionally a pat on the back of an incompetent employee can act as an incentive to him for improvement.

(*d*) *Knowledge of the Results.* Knowledge of the results leads to employees satisfaction. A worker likes to know the result of his performance. A worker gets satisfaction when his superior appreciates the work he has done. In modern industry the production workers have no contact with the customers so they can not get the reaction of their efforts from the consumers. However, they can be motivated to a greater extent if they are told the rating of their performance. They will work more to improve their performance.

(*e*) *Worker's Participation.* Employees participation in management provides an important incentive to the employees. It gives the employees psychological satisfaction that their voice is being heard because workers' participation in management provides for two way communication. This has been discussed in detail in the chapter on Worker's Participation in Management.

(*f*) *Suggestion system.* Suggestion system is an insentive which use satisfies may needs to the employees. Many organisations which use the suggestion system make use of cash awards for useful suggestions. They sometimes publish the worker's name with his photograph in the company's magazines. This motivates the employees to be in search for something which may be of greater use to the organization.

(*g*) *Opportunity for growth.* Opportunity for growth is another kind of incentive. If the employees are provided the opportunity for their advancement and growth and to develop their personality, they feel very much satisfied and become more committed to organisation goals because they feel very much motivated.

(*h*) *Security.* This is a very powerful incentive to Indian workers. Security is ranked second to money only.

Summary

Motivation deals with human behaviour in order to determine the factor that prompts an individual to do his best. In order to motivate the employees, management must first of all know what are the motivational factors influencing the behaviour of persons. Though it is simple but it is wrong to say that motivation is merely a relationship between effort and reward. The study of motivation is concerned with "How behaviour gets started, energized, sustained, directed, stopped and what kind of subjective reaction is present in the organism while all this is going on". There is need to study the relationship between motivation and performance and motivation and satisfaction because with both the managers are directly concerned.

The strength of motivation depends upon the equation :

$$\text{Motivation} = f\,(\text{Motive} \times \text{expectancy} \times \text{incentive}).$$

The strength of motive, is the position in the individual's hierarchy of motives. Expectancy is the probability that the act will obtain the goal. The value of incentive is the reward expected by obtaining the goal.

In the above mentioned equations, the expectancy and incentive are normally based on the past experience of the individual concerned. The individual motivational tensions are not merely biological but also psychological as well as economic in nature. It is often assumed that high motivation would automatically lead to high performance, provided the individual has some convenience to perform the job. This can be represented through another equation :

$$\text{Performance} = f\,(\text{Motivation} \times \text{Competence}).$$

This assumption however, is not valid under all situations.

9

Organisation Learning

A Learning Environment

The future lies in the job holder and not in the job. The era of lifetime corporate careers had its moments of historical dominance, but is now on its way to becoming extinct. Employment security, today, does not come from being employed, but from employability. The ultimate aim is self reliance or employability security. It promotes one's own growing reputation and the growing set of contacts makes employees in charge of their career. We have to get out of the fortes mentality. And it is the organisation which has to create conditions for building career reliance.

This is an era of competent employee — one who can perform not one role but a variety of roles with equal competence and proactivity. Organisations need to develop an enabling and facilitative work climate for the growth of such employees. Other resources for ongoing development of employees can be training aids, infrastructure facilities, in-house libraries, computer-based training, success story sharing and suggestion schemes with built-in rewards systems both for innovative suggestions and acquiring of relevant professional and skill-based qualifications.

Several mechanisms can be built into the system to ensure effective utilisation of feedback for culture building like appraisal system, open-house sessions feedback, exit interviews inputs and post training follow-up and action plans. The beauty of culture is that once it gets institutionalised, it creates it's own leaders, hence pro-active culture needs to be evolved.

Job rotation, job enlargement and job enrichment are very effective human resource techniques to equip the employees, with necessary skill-sets to enable them to take up higher responsibilities as they grow in the company. Cross-functional transfer, nomination to various task committees and projects have proved very effective to manage continuous discontinuities.

Skill-sets have to be upgraded on a continuous basis. This is only possible when the work climate provides the necessary impetus to one and all. Stipulations such as linkage of increament, promotion and rewards to acquistion of new skills, knowledge, achievement of annual targets, training of subordinates, elimination of non-value adding activities with thrust on paper-less office, doing away with department boundaries, abolishing traditional job descriptions and ensuring upward mobility based on competency and results achieved and not on seniority.

Today's market realities have made everyone insecure. No employer can promise how long he can be in business. He is not sure without he can avert take over of his business. There is no guarantee for life time employment with time bound upward mobility. Under these circumstances, loyalty and seniority have ceased to command premium.

The need of the hour is to create a culture of urgency with focus on employability. Change being permanent, changes have to be managed with imagination otherwise change will start managing us.

Competitive Advantage

Successful organisations are building competitive advantage through less controlling and more learning - that is, through continually creating and sharing new knowledge. In a world of increasing interdependence and rapid change, it is not longer possible to figure it out from the top. The implications of this change will have a significant impact on the existing practices of management in the organisation. But, organisation we can start by thinking about more basic concepts of leadership learning.

In the knowledge era, we will finally have to surrender the myth of leaders as isolated heroes commanding their organisations from the top alone. Top down directives, even when they are implemented, reinforce an environment of fear, distrust and internal competitiveness that reduces collaboration and co-operation. They foster compliance instead of commitment, yet only genuine commitment can bring about the courage, imagination, patience, and perseverance necessary in a knowledge creating organisation. *For these reasons, leadership in the future will be distributed among diverse individuals and teams who share responsibility for creating the organisations future. Building a group of leaders within an organisation requires recognising and developing--*

- Line Managers with significant bottom-line responsibility, such as business unit managers, who introduce and implement new ideas.

- Executive leaders, top-level manages who mentor local line leaders and become their "thinking partners", who steward cultural change through shifts in their own behaviour and that of top-level teams and who use their authority to invest a new knowledge infrastructures.

- Internal networkes, peiple, often with no formal authority, such as internal consultants or human resources professionals and front-line workers, who move about the organisation spreading and fostering commitment to new ideas and practices.

In knowledge-creating organisations, these three types of leaders absolutely rely on one another. None alone can create an environment that ensures continual innovation and diffusion of knowledge. The enduring institutional learning arises only from three interrelated activities:

"Research" - the disciplined pursuit of discovery and understanding that leads to generalizable theory and method;

"Capacity building" - the enhancement of people's capabilities and knowledge to achieve results in line with their deepest personal and professional aspirations; and

"Practice" - the acitivities that happens in organisations every day - people working together to achieve practical outcomes and building practical know-how in the process.

The knowledge creating process has become deeply fragmented. The three core activities are typically carried out by specialised, disconnected, often anagonistic institutions : universities, consulting firms and businesses.

We confront two critical challenges : how to address deep problems for which hierarchical leadership alone in insufficient and how to harness the intelligence and spirit of people at all levels of an organisation to continually build and share knowledge. Our responses may lead us, ironically, to a future based on more ancient - and more natural - ways of organising : communities of diverse and effective leader who empower their organisations to learn with head, heart, and hand.

Organisation Learning

Learning is at the heart of a company's ability to adapt to a rapidly changing environment. It is the key to being able both to identify opportunities that others might not see and to exploit those opportunities rapidly and fully. This means that in order to generate extraordinary value for shareholders, a company has to learn better than its competitors and apply that knowledge throughout its businesses faster and more widely than they do. The way we see it, anyone in the organisation who is not directly accountable for making a profit should be involved in creating and distributing knowledge that the company can use to make a profit. The wonderful thing about knowledge is that it is relatively inexpensieve to replicate if we can capture it. *Most activities or tasks are not one time events. But the philosophy should be fairly simple : Every time we do something again, we should do it better than the last time.*

There are a variety of ways we can learn how to do something better. We can learn from our own experiences. We can learn from our contractors, suppliers, partners, and customers. And we can learn from companies totally outside your business. All are crucial. *No matter where the knowledge comes from the key to reaping a big return is to leverage that knowledge by replicating it throughout the company so that each unit is not learning in isolation and reinventing the wheel again and again.*

A business has to have a clear purpose. If the purpose is not crystal clear, people in the business will not understand what kind of knowledge is critical and what they have to learn in order to improve performance. A clear purpose allows a company to focus its learning efforts in order to increase its competitive advantage.

What do we mean by purpose ? Our purpose is who we are and what makes us distinctive. It's what we as a company exist to achieve, and what we're willing and not willing to do to achieve it. But in our pursuit of exceptional performance and sustained growth, there are certain financial boundaries we should not cross and values we should not violate. The values concern ethics, health, safety, and the environment, the way we treat employees, and external relations with agencies connected with our business.

We needed to redefine exactly what we were trying to do. *The world never stands still, and a company has to keep moving on. That is the only way we can maintain control of our own destiny.* We all know that if people are highly motivated, understand exactly what they have to do to help create greater values, can see the results of their actions, and have a sense of ownership. They excel at building and using knowledge capital, which means assessing and applying knowledge that exists both inside and outside the company, we need to involve suppliers, customers, so that we all can work together to maximize value. We can't expect others to share their knowledge and resources with us fully, unless we have a strong relationship with them. The most important aspect of any relationship is understanding what your partners hope to get out of it and to work hard to help them achieve that goal. It is the key to transforming a contractual relationship into a genuine collaboration. We should deliver on our promises reliably and consistently. Our promises have to be realistic, and we need to move heaven and earth to keep them.

Building Relations

We never build a relationship between our organisation and a company or a government, we build it between individuals. Our people have to have real authority. We can't cut them off at the knees. They must be people who can deliver.

All relationship worth anything are open and flexible. In other words, we must invite people in, try to discuss the problem or opportunity, and say, "How do we solve it jointly ?" If I say, "Here is my solution. I'm having a great relationship with you if you agree, and I won't have a relationship with you if you disagree," then the relationship is not to mutual advantage.

We have to approach an opportunity - which should be the basis of every relationship - with humility. We have to recognise that others may actually know more than we do about something - that we can learn from them.

For people to learn how to deliver performance and to grow, the organisation has to make them feel that, individually and collectively, they could control the destiny of company's businesses. Of course, there are aspects of our business that are outside our control, but there are many others that we can control. To drive home that message, we should talk a lot about self-help, and should rigorously track and publicise the results that it produces. It is through self-help that we control the cost structure, get more bang for the investment buck, upgrade the quality of products and services, and improve relationships with suppliers and customers. It's about getting people to develop an intimate understanding of the structures of their businesses' margins and how they compare with those of their competitors. To get people to learn, we need to give them a challenge. Setting a target is crucial even if we don't actually know whether it's fully achievable -because in time of rapid change, we have to make decisions and get people to step outside the box. The process that an organisation employs to promote learning and drive the performers is to achieve higher and higher targets, and challenging them to achieve the same. The more unusual process involves breakthrough thinking.

The top management team must stimulate the organisation, not control it. Its role is to provide strategic directives, to encourage learning, and to make sure that there are mechanisms for transferring the lessons. The role of leaders at all levels is to demonstrate to people that they are capable of achieving more than they think they can achieve and that they should never be satisfied with where they are now.

The role of leaders at all levels it to demonstrate to people that they are capable of achieving more than they think they can. The executive leaders in any company do only a very few things. Ultimately, they have to make decisions on the organisational architecture and the way forward. They set policies, standards, and targets, and create processes to ensure that people achieve or adhere to them. It is while those processes are being carried out that learning should take place. What determines whether it does is the questions leaders ask and the way they approach what is going on. Leadership is all about catalysing learning as well as better performance. Leaders have to demonstrate that they are active participants in the learning organisation. You can't say "Go do it" without participating. In order to understand the process of Leadership in the organisation, let us understand basic concepts *viz.* "Leader"; Qualities of Leadership and Tools of Leadership.

10

Modern Management systems

Introduction

It is quite common in management profession to view growth and welfare with a management perspective. The application of management prospective to economic growth and human welfare is a revolutionary view. Growth and human welfare are not merely processes to be analysed. But are moral responsibilities to be assumed.

Management Culture

Management culture is a very important subject to be analysed. Management is either good or bad, extend to a greater extent the culture in which it is applied. There are always differences in management style and approaches. What is good in American management practice may be bad in Japan, India or in U.K. or the European consistent. What determines appropriate management for a particular society is a question to be answered. Every profession develops an implicit set of accepted principle, beliefs, standards for testing validity of cognition, criteria for judging good and bad, all of which put together sets the framework by which practitioners reach conclusions and make decisions. Thus professionals have a standard set of approaches. The term paradigm is applied to these implicit principles and standards. Within a single normal scientific tradition, there are certain modules which are implicitly accepted and recognised by the scientific community and without benefit of explicit articulation become the basis for accepting the validity or acceptability of scientific world.

MANAGEMENT AS A PROFESSION

Profession of management as it has developed through the years, derive from a whole, complex of antecedents, history, ideology, philosophy, particularly of the societies in which the leaders of the art have emerged in which their greatest successes have been demonstrated. *The vital functions of the community are distributed between two sectors, the Government and private sector. The Government maintains order, public health, public safety, education and investment in infrastructure. On the other hand private enterprises are bias towards picking out only those activities that offer the most attractive return. The Government policy and intervention, however, can correct the situation.* Business organisation are the example of all sectoral organisation.

Business is a well defined organisation. It is a discrete manageable unit. It has a specific object to produce and sell, to provide profit for both investors and managers.

Over the years, business has developed a professional corps of managers imbued with the enterprise philosophy and perspective, educated in the science and technology of profit seeking and trained in the arts required to control organisation, mobilise resources and wage the warfare of market competition. The business firm is an ideal unit of organisation, precisely because it has a narrow set of objectives, defined and measured compliment of resources, a technology of operation and a defined set of performance standards.

Social and Economic Organisations

Let us study some modes of social and economic organisations. The Chinese and Japanese. The Chinese hierarchy of organisation--the commune, the brigade and the production team. As an interesting system, the commune thus encompasses a system of villages with their market town and will encompass a population of about 25,000-30,000 people. Each commune will have number of rural brigade with about 200 families, corresponding to a village and each brigade would have about 8--10 production teams with about 20--25 families. Each belonging to a common neighbourhood and working together. The brigade is the basic unit of accounting and it is at this level that production and income accounts are consolidated. Brigade itself is a community with its resource endowment, *e.g.* agricultural and infrastructure facilities, community service units, schools, hospitals, clinics and other essential facilities.

The interesting aspect of Chinese system is precisely the identification of the unit of organisation, management and accounting with natural human community. The Japanese orientation rather than individual goal is equally strong but has its own modes. The Japanese society has always exercised a rigorous control over the import of foreign culture patterns. The Japanese systematically bought western science and technology by importing the literature, and launching a programme of translation and distribution. They based the adoption of new ideas and integrated them into the traditional structure and ideology of the society. Japanese society has values that are still rooted in its history and traditions. The main characteristics of Japanese system are :

1. A strong collective rather than individualistic character.
2. Village solidarity and communality remained the powerful cohesive force in the nation.
3. The integration of modern forms of production with the older traditional forms.
4. Closer links between large scale and small scale industries.

Thus the fundamental ideology and character of Japanese business were preserved. The human settlement can and should be the primary unit of management, of organisation and of accounting. There should be a scientific model of the human settlement that provides the analytical basis for the technology of its operation. Just as the economic theory of the business firm provides the scientific base for the technology of the enterprise, the theory of human settlement must necessarily be inter-disciplinary because of geographical base, a political or power system, a physical system, an organisational structure etc.

Modern Management Systems

Modern management regards systems as powerful management tools. The systems approach is found to be more effective in achieving organisational goals than adhoc and piecemeal decision-making. The systems approach, therefore, finds favour with management in almost all areas of activities of the organisation. There seems to be, however, hardly any application of the systems approach to the needs of the human and social sector of organisation. Manpower pianning, recruitment, training induction, wages, promotion policies industrial relations and grievance procedure, welfare programmes, retirement plans and so on, should be taken as in the total systems approach with a view to optimise the satisfaction of the physical social and psychological needs the people along with technical, commercial and administrative goals of the organisation.

The responsibility of bringing about such a change in the social climate in organisations rest on the top management as the culture of the organise action is highly initiative to top. The adoption of an open, outgoing style by the senior executives in their interaction at all levels of hierarchy both in their formal and informal relation, showing equal regard and concern for the dignity and self-respect of all persons regardless of their rank or emoluments, can lead to a more open and free climate of human relations to promote the happiness of its people. If those at the top are seen genuinely accept and act upon a certain organisational philosophy adopt a certain style of operation, the middle, junior managers, supervisor and workforce are apt to follow them and to respond to that style.

In the developing society the different hierarchical groups in the organisation stand apart, distant from one another, largely unconcerned with one another's interests, attitudes, problems and difficulties, such stratification and fragmentation, along with the affluence of a few, breed jealousy and bitterness among those less fortunately placed.

Some disparities in authority and rewards are perhaps unavoidable in any organisation, even if it is participatively managed once. This might not change the organisational climate too much if the degree of disparity is not too great and is itself open at least in some measure of participative decision making. Besides, such disparities a more free, open and authentic interaction among different groups, and individuals across the organisational hierarchy will generate better understanding and fellow-feeling to improve the quality on social interaction to enrich the lives of all those working in the organisation.

Social System in Organisation

An organisation exists to achieve certain specific objectives and has to be cost effective in the pursuit of these objectives. This applies not only to industrial and commercial organisations for whom profitability, growth are accepted as operational goals : but also for other types of organisations such as educational Institutions, Hospitals, Municipalities, Government departments and so on. The performance of an organisation is assessed in terms of the degree of achievement of its specified objectives and the cost incurred in achieving them.

For people who work in organisation, however, the objectives of the organisations are of primary, importance. Some degree of achievement of which is necessary for the achievement of their own personal or group objectives. The people's primary objectives are satisfaction of their own physical, social and psychological needs. These objectives, it is now generally recognised, are distinct from its thrust for cost-effectiveness. At the same time, satisfaction of people's objectives is, in no small measured dependant upon the achievement of the organisation's objectives : and reciprocally, achievement of the organisations objectives is end rendered difficult unless certain measure of satisfaction of its people's objectives is ensured.

While this interdependence of the organisation's objectives and the need of the people working in its is readily recognised the two operate constraints upon one another, rather than as two sectors of one broad objective. Those responsible for overall direction and control of organisations do, no doubt, give considerable and serious thought to the needs of their people. But this is because they recongnise that unless satisfied to some degree acceptable to the people, these needs become a constraint on the achievement of the organisation's objectives. The effort, therefore, is to look for that degree of need--satisfaction for employees at which their constraint effect will be neutralised at the lowest cost to the organisation. Reciprocally, hose who work in the lowest cost to the organisation, whether unskilled manual workers or top executives, do display a concern for its profitability stability and growth. But this again in because they recognise these as setting the limits for the satisfaction of their own goals. Their goals is to maximize their own need satisfaction to the limit of the constraints imposed by the extent of achievement of the organisation's goals.

In this kind of an organisational environment, some people or groups are better placed others to achieve higher degree of need satisfaction either because of high or strategic position in the organisation's hierarchy or of organised strength of numbers. This differential need-satisfaction as much as its actual level or perceived inadequacy, give rise to disrust, hostility, tensions, frustration and attitudes of confrontation among different groups within the organisation. The confrontation can be at several interfaces : Management and workers, white-collar and blue-collar workers, skilled and the unskilled workers, workers and supervisors and managers, managers and the organisation line and staff managers and many others.

Can an organisation not view the need-satisfaction of the people working in it not as a constraint on the achievement of it own objectives; but as a positive objective, of-a piece with its more conventional objectives like profitability, growth and cost-effectiveness ? In setting its operational goals and evaluating its performance, can one of the parameters not be the addition to the total happiness of the people working in it ? In evaluating the feasibility of a new project, should one of the tests applies not be wheather it will further enrich the quality of working like of the employees ? In many employees well-being be deemed irrelevant ? These are questions that management thinkers have raised in different forms and they continue to be vitally relevant to the theme of organisational effectiveness and human welfare.

Social Environment of the Organisation

The social environment outside the organisation does, no doubt, influence the human environment within it, because the external environment conditions the attitudes of people as individuals and groups and also sets limits to the degree to which their needs can be satisfied. It must be emphasised that it is the organisation's own philosophy, approach, style structure, systems and operation that prominently determine the quality of working life for all those who work in it. External conditions cannot absolve an organisations of its responsibility of positively striving to make its responsibility of positively striving to make its employees' working lives happier and more fulfiling.

Organisation a Complex of Subsystems

An organisation is a complex of a number and variety of subsystems. These subsystems have their assigned positions in the complex and assigned functions as well as relations to the work, to each other and to the organisation. These subsystems for instance, finance, materials, equipment, technology, energy etc. are operated by groups of people who bring different kinds the function roles and accountability for the people operating the subsystems are defined, what kind of relations the people of one subsystem have with those of another, the quality of interpersonal relations within the same functional group and the relation of each person and group to the whole organisation, to the happiness of the people working in it.

An organisation is also a hierarchy of several levels of functions and authority vested in different persons. It is perceived inequity from the standpoint of those at lower levels in the hierarchy notwithstanding, the hierarchical aspect of the structure and functions of organisations especially large organisations, may not be entire of avoidable.

The organisation develops and instals a system of rewards and penalties as the principal instrument for securing from employees satisfactory performance of the tasks and roles assigned to them. The rewards and punishment system is closely tied up with the functional subsystem people work in. A significant part of the organisational hierarchy and to a lesser degree with the frictions, tensions, frustrations, conflict and happiness in organisations have their roots in the reward and punishment system as perceived by the people to whom they apply. All these systems and subsystem are devised, set up and operated by the organisation primarily to achieve its techno-commercial or administrative goals. Maximisation of the satisfaction and happiness of the people working in the organisation, enriching the quality of their working life, is not a specific or positive goals that these systems and subsystems are designed to achieve. However, the way they are designed, the philosophy and approach underlying them and the way they operate largely determine what kind of climate the organisation will provide for people to work in the how satisfied and happy they will fell working in it.

Organisation Optimising Human Environment

A considerable amount of serious thought has been devoted to this area by management scientists in recent years and a number of concepts as well as operational techniques have been suggested for adoption by organisation. Their main thrust, however, has been to raise organisational effectiveness by minimising the frictions, frustration, alienation and conflict among those who work in the organisation. Their primary goals of the organisation itself. Optimising the human environment is viewed as a means and not human happiness as positive goals in itself. There is, of course, an assumption here that happiness of its people would be a goal in itself and not merely means to achieving the techno-commercial or administrative goals of the organisation. If we regard people's happiness as a positive concern of the society as a hole then various kinds of organisations in which members of the society spend a significant part of their waking and working lives, organisations which draw sustenance from society, cannot absolve themselves of the responsibility of promotions in a positive way the happiness of the people who work in them. People whose working lives are not happy cannot make a happy community.

The informal systems are the result of the likes and dislikes, aspirations, interests, social backgrounds, attitudes to life of the people : things which have no direct relationship to their jobs or positions in the organisations. Besides, the informal systems exercise a considerable influence on the way people work the way they actually perform their jobs regardless of what the formal systems enjoin the informal systems are the natural and spontaneous express on of their personalities as also their response to the restraints and rigorous imposed by the formal systems.

It is through the informal systems that people seek the satisfaction of some of their urges such as for companionship social esteem, leadership, self-expression etc. Which, in their perception the organisation does not provides for in positive way.

Organisation and Quality of Working Life

It is thus a variety of systems : functional, hierarchical, formal, informal, antagonistic and peripheral that interact to determine the quality of working life, the degree of need satisfaction and self-relisation experienced by employees. There is enough evidence all around us that in these respects the conditions prevailing in organisations today leave much to be desired. Organisational climate is, more often than not, characterised by distrust, apathy, frustration, alienation, jealousies and conflict. It is not only those who stand low in the organisational hierarchy or in their relative emoluments, that these conditions ; even those high up in these respects are not spared.

Challenge Before the Organisation

The challenge before the organisation is whether the social systems and their working in organisations be conceived in different way so as to contain and manage conflicts in order to optimise the achievement of the organisation's conventional goals, also to generate as an intrinsic value, a batter quality or working life in which all people working in orgnaisation can find opportunities for achieving greater fulfilment and happiness. The challenge, goes much beyond that of establishing an effective collective bargaining framework or that of establishing an effective collective bargaining framework or providing various kinds of the usual fringe benents, welfare facilities and safety devices out it encompasses the totality of the organisation, its philosophy, goals and the modalities of setting and achieving them.

The problem may be handled by concentrating and organisation's goals. The primary goals may be the techno-commercial or administrative effectiveness and viability of the organisation. But the positive goal of employees, the satisfaction and self-relisation of the maximising the optimisation of the quality of working life should be equally important goals.

If the employee's happiness and fulfilment are really to become an integral part of an organisation goals, the employees must have full opportunity of participating in the formulation of the goals and methodology of reaching them. People's happiness cannot be achieved through their physical need fulfilment. Organisational effectiveness will need a certain measure of discipline and conformity from the people who work in it. The need for restraints and discipline on the one hand and the freedom for individuals and groups to pursue their own goals of discipline and freedom have to be perceived by the people who are to live by them, as rational and equitable manner.

The goal of organisation are broken down into specific task to be accomplished by different groups and individuals. Each such group also needs to be involved in the formulation of its own task and the methodology of fulfiling it. Thus process of successive breaking up of larger goals or tasks into smaller and smaller ones to be performed by smaller and smaller groups is a common feature of the structure and functioning of organisations.

The urge of people to maximize their need-satisfaction and the limitation on the organisation to satisfy all needs of all people, does create situations of difference, the confrontations and even conflicts, beside the methods sought to be defined in a participative way. There will arise a honest differences on where the line between restraint and freedom should be drawn in a given situation. Such conflict may be over issues like wages and other material benefits, working conditions, disciplinary rules and procedures, promotions and so on. Such conflicts can, if properly understood have a diagnostic as well as a clinical aspect in asmuch as they bring to the surface problems which if not attended to can cause harm to organisation as well as to its people. In an open participative culture conflict need not take a win-lose form but can really be a problem centred and solution seeking approach.

Effective collective bargaining and grievance procedure and systems, therefore have to extend their coverage and scope because issues which in the past were considered outside the area of conflict are now increasingly coming within it. Beside workers, junior and middle managers, are also getting organised to pursue their collective interests but such pursuit occasionally brings them into conflict with the organisation.

11

Management and Socio-Economic Changes

Introduction

Our society is composed of different groups of people, the management of which is a critical factor in our social order. The management decisions in Government and Industrial organizations constitute a powerful social force which is vital to the effective operation of contemporary society. Management is the organ of society specifically charged with making resources productive and carrying the responsibility for organized economic advancement. Thus management may be termed as the specific economic organ of an industrial society. In the competitive economy, the quality and performance of management determine the success rather survival of a business.

Activities of management comprise planning, scheduling, organizing, directing, co-ordinating, monitoring, following up and controlling the different phases of work, effective, utilization of resources of man, material and money and ensuring successful completion of all the programmes and projects in time, achieving the pre-established target and accomplishing the corporate objectives.

Historical Development

The historical development of management in relation to socio-economic changes can be traced back to many centuries but it seems reasonable to divide the history into three successive periods :

1. The medieval period.
2. The period of Industrial Revolution.
3. The modern period of mass production or period of second Industrial Revolution which is synonymous with a break through in communication.

The Medieval Period

The medieval period was technologically an era of water wheels, bullock carts and handicrafts, and sociologically the feudal age of the land baron and the peasant. The agriculture was the pre-dominant activity. There was virtually no specialization and each family was almost self-sufficient in the production of food, clothing and the other necessities of life. The common people lived in poverty, superstitions ran wild, and the general level of health and sanitation were appalling. Inspite of low level of material well-being, human relations were apparently much more satisfying and in one sense better than they are to-day.

As the agricultural productivity increased, men were gradually utilized by feudal lords for specialized tasks and also by travelling merchants. Some of the travelling merchants won their freedom and eventually comprised a relatively rich middle class between the peasants and landlords. More peasants gradually freed themselves from feudal bondage, some deviated toward employment with merchants in the larger towns, and some started small crafts of their own. The economic activities were gradually built up as a result of self-employed crafts and flourishing trade.

The earliest industrial enterprises in the form of handicrafts were quite small having single craftsman with one or two apprentices. The craftsman was his own master, worked in his own home and was a respected member of the community. Craftsmen formed guilds to avoid exploitation by traders.

Industrial Revolution

The Industrial Revolution brought with it scientific progress, a sudden leap forward in technology and the beginning of capitalistic society. It also brought with it an increase in personal freedom and allowed the individual an opportunity to move up and down the social scale according to his capability, good fortune, and perhaps ruthlessness. In the long run, it also raised the standard of living of the people. Most marked was the change in the role of the individual. In the middle ages men had existed as members of social groups-family, the guild, or the feudal villages and they had lacked freedom and individuality. But with the Industrial Revolution they become free to succeed, or to fail, as a result of their own efforts. Along with individualism in commerce and industry, there was also a rise in individualism in commerce and industry, there was also a rise in individualism in the social and cultural areas. The old social groups were dissolved, the bonds between individuals within groups were broken, and the paternalism and security of feudal system were destroyed. Men became isolated psychologically, and the economically, and the universal credo became "Survival of the fittest". The cult of individualism reigned in art and science.

The invention of steam engine, rotary engine, lathe, boring mill, new methods of producing iron and steel etc. contributed greatly to large scale manufacturing of goods. Large scale manufacturing of course, required large supplies of labour and capital. Wealth created wealth, a new class of owner-managers dominated the scence--a ruthless, unscrupulous breed of men, lacking in compassion, feeling no social obligation and regarding the poor not as unfortunate but as lazy and immoral. During those early years of the revolution, the machine took its place as a factor of production which to the factory owner, was definitely more important and valuable than any other factor of production.

By the early 1800's the fatories started growing in size, requiring larger investment of capital. The individual factory owner could no longer raise the necessary capital alone, so investors began to pool their resources by buying joint ownership in joint stock companies. A new class of managers appeared which run the companies but did not own them. At the same time workers started banding together into unions for improving their working conditions and wages through collective bargaining.

Period of Mass Production

This period is also sometimes referred to as the period of Second Industrial Revolution and is synonymous with a break through in communication. Mass production meant that a component from one automobile, say, was inter-changeable with the same component from another automobile of the same kind. It involved the production of components of products in thousands and any one of the thousands of identical parts went into any of the thousands of units finished products. Mass production became not only a mechanical means of efficient production, but a social way of life. Mass production evolved the establishment of extremely large industrial complexes.

Two important points worth noting about modern period are :

(*a*) The research studies supported by the large scale production firms have shown that workers behave more as social creatures than as individuals.

(*b*) Workers have achieved power to bargain effectively for the material rewards of their work. In the industrial union they have found not only a collective power but also a social organization to knit them together, to provide a degree of status and security and comradeship.

The automatic control of process or break through in communication, is proving to be one of the outstanding technological advances of the modern period of industry. Not only the automatic control of production process (automation), but also automatic control in such areas as accounting, information, handling, transformation and many others. This has resulted in :

(*a*) Relieving the workers of the heavy and tedious manual tasks.

(*b*) General upgrading of the skills of workers with a higher premium on specialized skills.

(*c*) Reduction in working hours to both white collar and factory workers.

(*d*) Requirement of better training of professional managers in both the management science and in the social skills.

(*e*) Emergence of a new class of factory and office technicians.

Management occupies an important place in the economic development of the country. This is so because the management is responsible for the effective mobilization and utilization and utilization of the country's resources for a industrial development. To achieve this end, the role of management with a new sense of accountability and social responsibility needs to be recognised. To take a few examples the society expects from management to maintain the business in a sound financial position, to offer the best possible goods and services to the society, to provide its workers with fair terms of employment, to pay taxes honestly, and so on. But too often the society views the management's aims as selfish gain rather than advancement of this general welfare. This impression can be removed only if management is alive to its social obligations and helps the society to function in harmony as one organic whole.

The social responsibilities of management extend to consumers, suppliers, workers management associations as well as to the Government. Now consumers desire cheaper and better goods, suppliers expect a fair deal and workers desire a hand of active co-operation through schemes of participation. Management associations demand maintenance and development of professional standard and skills for the growth of managerial knowledge and Government desires a suitable socio-economic climate for the successful implementation of its welfare schemes. Management can contribute considerably in the attainment of these social objectives.

SOCIO-ECONOMIC CHANCES

These are the changes in the social structure and economic conditions of a country with the passage of time. How the society used and allocated the resources for the achievement and maintenance of growth and stability with the passage of time and how the social structure under went transformation in relation to economic changes, comprises of socio-economic changes.

The changes in the technique of production also revolutionized the organization of the entire society. In industries, where technique had been revolutionized, old organisation was no longer suitable and the size of the units increased as a result of the increased importance of capital. The increase in the size of production units had the far-reaching effect on socio-economic conditions of the country.

In India, beside social and cultural factors, political and economic dependence stood in the way to industrialization and socio-economic development. After independence, Indian Government is persuing a policy of progressive and planned industrial development, as a result there has been enormous economic growth and industrial development since 1951 when planning commenced.

It is heartening to note that India has overcome catastrophic situation and without lowering her sights and notwithstanding the temporary setback in the growth rate, continued its march towards the goals of an egalitarian society of which clear cut-lines are chalked out in the directive principles of the constitution. Here it also needs to be mentioned that over the period the broad goals set and seen at the beginning of the First Five Year Plan in the early fifties have been transformed into more detailed and down-to-earth goals in the recent years. There is now recognition of the fact with a consciousness exists among the weaker sections of the society and the inhabitants of backward regions to have a better deal at the hands of the other sections of the society under whose influence the economic and social institutions have in later years shown relative indifference tantamounting to an attitude of utter neglect. It would, in fact, not be wrong to say that even the Public Bodies and Institutions had in the past allowed the needs and case of these classes to go by default. Hence, a proper emphasis and perspective had to brought to this matter in the Fourth Plan an in the successive policy announcements of the Government. The simplistic goal of growth and development set out in the first plan get changed into the goal of growth with social justice after 1966. To quote from the plan documents, in the First Five Year Plan Document, it has been stated that the *"Central objective of planning in India at present stage is to initiate a process of development which will raise living standards and open out for the people new opportunities for a richer and more varied life,"* whereas in the Fourth Five Year Plan, it came to be stated that *'the basic goal is a rapid increase inthe standard of living of the people, though measures which also promote equality and social justice. Emphasis is placed on the common man, the weaker sections and less privileged."* Reference to removal of poverty and social justice became more direct and pointed after 1971 in every Government declaration. In the Fifth Plan Document, it has been said that, *"the existence of poverty is an incompatible with the vision of an advanced prosperous, democratic, egalitarian and just society implied in the concept of socialistic pattern of development. In fact, it holds a potential threat to the unity, integrity and independence of the country. Elimination of poverty must, therefore, should have the highest priority.*

Socio-economic Problems

The period 1966-1975 witnessed waves of crises one after another. During this decade, as years rolled by, the situation became more and more grim. The country had to face the aftermath of aggression by Pakistan in 1965 which was again repeated in 1971 during the liberation struggle of Bangla Desh. This subjected the country's economy to severe strains further enhanced by hardships resulting from three severe and consecutive droughts, shortages of foreign exchange and industrial inputs, shortage of power for agriculture and industry and problem posed by oil crisis. The impact of dislocation in international exchange parities and big balance of payment deficit which weakened the value of rupees in international market and the hyper inflationary conditions in the country as a result of external factors accumulated in the situation. Industrial disquiet on the big scale, and dis-approval shown by industrial enterpreneurs to Government's Policies initiated to lessen concentration of economic power and to provide stimulus to small and independent enterpreneurs, led to fall in production. This is just a passing mention of some of the economic difficulties faced by the country, ignoring the other internal non-economic ones which compounded the hazards for implementing the Five Year Plans the objectives of which, as said above, had been broad-based, more socially oriented and made more meaningful for the weaker sections of the society and if neglected could spell doom for the country.

Social Responsibilities

In the context of economic growth coupled with the need of social responsibilities of all sections of the society, a manager is not only judged by profits alone but also tested on the scale of his concern for social responsibilities. Therefore, every enterprise must be so conducted that it serves its own objectives as well as social purpose. It should be noted that social responsibility is not fixed but is always related to pressures at a particular point of time. Some of these are as follows :

(*a*) To reduce the concentration of economic power.

(*b*) To open all positions available to persons who have the requisite qualifications.

(*c*) To provide opportunities to all employees fro growth and advancement-through participation in management.

(*d*) To use modern science and technology in business for the development of nation.

(*e*) To create additional jobs each year for absorbing young persons.

(*f*) To help Government in increasing the rate of economic growth.

Action of manager affects the society. It is, therefore, his responsibility to use more productively the entire resources available with a business organization. The responsibilities of management can be divided into four groups as under :

1. The owners or shareholders of a company
2. The empolyees.
3. The customers.
4. The community at large.

Responsibility to the owners

It is the management's responsibility to effectively run the industry so that the owners (or shareholders) get a reasonable return on their investment.

Responsibility to the Employees

It is the management's responsibility to provide adequate monetary and psychological rewards as well as job security to the employees. In the Indian context, job security is more important in view of the large scale un-employment. Proper opportunities for growth and improving necessarily education or training are also the responsibility of the enterprise.

Responsibility to the Customers

It is the responsibility of the management to ensure that consumers are provided with adequate quality products at reasonable price duly supplemented with prompt courteous and dependable service.

Responsibility to the Community

Industry has responsibility to the community at large. Many factories are located in and around villages which supply the labour force. Indian companies used to make it a point to ensure that a philauthropic mission co-existed with the commercial agenda. Increasingly, however, the cult of shareholder value creation appears to the asking companies to focus relentlessly on maximising bottom line.

Changes Threatening Management

The objectives of the organisation are to be achieved through the medium of work which is the basic issue which concerns management to-day. With a view to optimising the various resources that contribute to work including the management itself, invariable these objective invole "changes". Any such change is found to influence the group of people called "Management". This influence will vary from group to group. The variation may lead to such a stage which is called threatening. *Managements have participated in bringing various kinds of changes in work processes. A clear testimony to this fact is in our own country where there is industrial growth and sophistication.* The very basic position of managers are affected by some of these changes and obvious problems arise when managers decide to implement these changes. The changes that affect the managers and appear to be threatening are in the :

— Organizational patterns.
— Hierarchical patterns.
— Authority.
— Responsibility structures.
— Managerial roles.
— Management knowledge.
— Managerial skills.
— Managerial attitudes.
— Management philosophy.

As the managers are human beings, they are resistant to changes because these changes affect them. For example, a situation that would be perceived by managers, as threatening is when a change is brought in through the workers' participation scheme. It involves changes in organizational and hierarchical patterns, authority and responsibility structures (which have now to be shared) and managerial roles, skills and attitudes.

Structural Change

A major change in the management system is workers' participation. Managements can make gross miscalculation if there is any complacency that joint committees and councils can be adjusted in the existing organizational system without the latter undergoing any change. However, there will be a tremendous problem of morale and leadership in the organization, if the legitimate role of the councils is not allowed to be played. Also there will be a generation of conflicting forces from the council *viz-a-viz* the executive system. Therefore, the managements must think of a well defined place for the councils in the corporate organism and spell out a definite role for them in the decision making process. Also it is necessary that the roles of the council be spelled out in promoting communication, involvement, participation and commitment, or even implementing in areas like employees welfare and safety.

Factors Affecting Socio-Economic and Political Changes

The factors affecting the socio-economic and political changes are government, shareholders, workers, society and consumers. These are discussed below :

Government

State intervention in the business is a necessary consequence as it control men, money, machine and market in one form or the other. Its main objects are :

1. To lay base for development of such industries which will lessen (ultimately eliminate) country's dependence on other countries.

2. To promote industrial growth in a way that regional disparities are reduced to minimum.

3. To give direction to economy along desired route to bring about qualitative change in social culture.

The management is greatly influenced by Government actions and policies. Socio-economic and political objectives act as guidelines for management's decision and approach for realisation of corporate goals. Government exercise control over organization and management mainly by the Companies Act 1956 supplemented by the Industries (Development and Regulation) Act 1951 and in some cases by the Issue of Capital Control Act 1947. Through the Companies Act the Government controls the capital structure, system of internal management, concentration of managerial control leading to inequalities of income and concentration of economic power.

Approval of managerial personnel by the Government is essential in the case of public companies and their subsidiaries, the basis of recruitment and promotions were based on the performance of individuals. But there was a systematic campaign against foreign collaboration and the materialistic sentiments of the public which used to limit the role of such organisation as being the foreign drain in India wealth.

(c) *Effectiveness in Public Sector.* Pandit Jawahar Lal Nehru, our first Prime Minister, was first to realize the importance of public sector to Indian economy. He could do it with foreign collaboration. Now we have realised its effectiveness in raising the productivity and adding to national economy. But it suffers from certain lacunas of commercial success and professional excellence as compared to private sector. However, these problems are now being overcome. Even the sick-industries of private sector taken over by the Government have started showing better results.

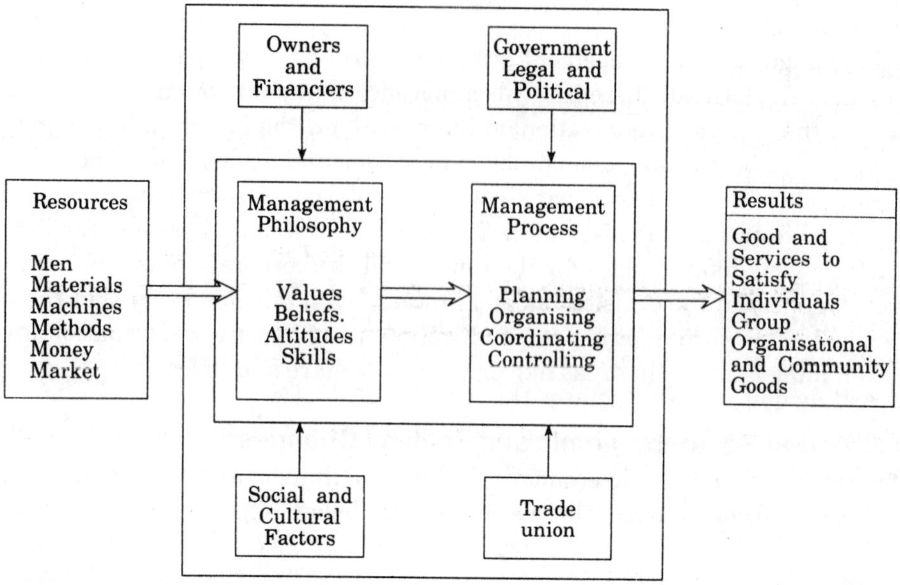

Fig. 11.1. Environment Factors and Management Process

2. Harmonising "work logic" and "workers logic"

In fact we have concentrated our efforts on organising the work according to the norms of technology. No sincere effort has been made to understand the motivation of our workers and to modify them and to harmonise with each other.

This resulted in a climate of labour unrest. The management has neither incalculated the right attitudes towards the workers nor technology is being adjusted to Indian Culture with the result, that a great deal of expenditure on development has failed to give adequate returns.

In fact, the results of aspect are most prominent in the public sector where there has been a neglect of the task to harmonise work logic with workers logic.

3. Understanding Socio-Economic Changes

The main cause of failure of the manager have been is not relating their understanding with the impact of socio-economic environmental changes and their relevance to managerial decision making. The managers have to be trained properly in understanding the significance of socio-economic changes. In most of the organisations, the managers have not been given enough chance to prepare themselves to tackle the broad areas of corporate policies and their effects on the environment rather they have been concentrating in a narrow areas. The other important thing is the nature of socio-political changes which have been surging like a pendulum between *status quo* and stagnation. In the context of socio-economic development of the country a manager's task would seem to be :

1. Constantly on a fire brigade mission of saving himself and his organisation from the whril wind of change. It will only be a problem of judgement of constantly shifting currents and under currents swirling in diverse directions.
2. Effective ensuring results according to predetermined objects.
3.

Harmonising "work logic" to "working logic", in the zeal of work according to norms of technology; a manager should not over-look the motivation of workers. He should rather modify them to harmonise with each other.

4. Adapting suitable technology whenever necessary.
5. Choosy in borrowing technology to suit Indian requirements and not compete blindly with developed countries.
6. Motivating and directing the energies of the human resources, controlling them in positive direction, and obtaining their willing cooperation and participation in the task of bringing socio-economic change.
7. Identifying with the local culture and practices.
8. Employing modern of inventory control and stock holding in place of age old practices.
9. Avoiding delays as it increases the costs.
10. Setting our production plans in a way that product does not create the problem of surplus in the market.

To conclude, the managers are the moulders of human interests and continuous thought. A very important characteristic which a manager must possess is the strength of personality. Another characteristic which appears essential is a scientific trend of mind because every manager faces with the problem of the kind that requires an analytical approach.

12

Stress Management

Stress

Stress is our body's physical mental and chemical reactions to circumstances that frighten, excite, confuse, endanger or irritate you. If controlled the stress is a friend that strengthen us for the next encounter. Today life's challenges are far more complex than they used to be, while life itself is altogethera harsher, less natural process than it used to be. Living in an age of immense and increasingly rapid change, we are subjected to greater, more insistent and inescapable pressures to adapt, keep up, and compete in short to survive than at any other time. Stress if handled poorly becomes an enemy which can cause diseases like High Blood Pressure, Ulcer; Asthma or overactive thyroid.

Impact of Stress

In America, the estimated annual cost to industry of combined absence from work, health charges, increased insurance, and diminished productivity, is thought to run close to Rs. 450 billion. In Britain, atleast 40 million working days are lost each year due to the effects of stress, and it is estimated that stress-related illness costs the medical and social services an average of 3.8 billion per year, accounting for a loss of 2-3 per cent in the gross national product. But stress is not only a problem for problem for people living in the fast track. Those who suffer excessive monotony, boredom, or frustration because of insufficient stimulus or challenge also become till frequently. This can be thought of as lack of arousal or as a result of anger or anxiety they feel at having little control over how they live and work.

Challenge and Stress

It is difficult to find the perfect balance between too much and too little challenge. Coping is made all the more difficult because we are often unconscious of the stress we are suffering. We have come adept at sublimating the effect of stress through motives such as ambition, perfectionist, and dedication to work. There is no single solution to the problem of stress. After all, what is stressful for one person is not necessarily stressful for everyone. As the ultimate responsibility for our well-being rests first and foremost with ourselves. In order to feel in control we must develop a healthy, stress proof lifestyle. We cannot separate our physical health from the well-being of our minds, both are closely inter-dependent. In turn, equilibrium of both mind and body is determined largely by the way we communicate and relate to other individuals. It is desirable to encourage awareness of this mind-body balance, and to foster more understanding of the relationship between ourselves and our surroundings. At a time when high technology is revolutionizing every aspect of the way we work, it has become more essential then ever to humanize our working environment and our professional relationships and to adopt more flexible attitudes to the structure of employment and our style of working.

Having the courage to examine long-held beliefs, to challenge-one can possible change attitudes toward one self and one's work, and relationships. Thereby one may in turn alter one's relationship to stress. Recognizing that we have a right to make mistakes, to refuse excessive demands, to say "no", to express our needs and feelings openly, to make time for ourself, and to cater for our wants as well as those of others.

Learn to Give Break to Oneself

Learning to give one self a break, in every sense of the world, takes practice, especially when we are the one who is driving self the hardest. Stress is the state of arousal with which the body responds to such demands. We cannot live without stress, since we face these challenges all the time. Our response to challenge is prompt, speedy, and efficiently. *Our personality, behaviour, and lifestyle all have important influences on our stress level. Much stress occurs through emotions such as aggression, impatience, anger, anxiety and fear.* All these kindle the body's stress responses. Eating an unhealthy diet, smoking, excessive drinking, and taking drugs can also contribute further to physical strain. Stress may be generated through work, at home, as a result of internal emotional conflict, through environment, financial insecurity as well as through major life events from childbirth to bereavement including phases like marriage or divorce.

Stress is what we Perceive

Above all, stress is what we perceive it to be. Some people may thrive on a particular situation while others may find to terrifying and highly stressful. Too little stimulus can be stressful as too much. *But stress only becomes harmful when we cannot control our responses to it. Recognizing this fact is the vital first step to reducing the harmful effects of stress in our life.* The body's answer to challenge or danger consists of a complex chain of bodily and biochemical changes involving the interaction of the brain, the nervous system, and a variety of different hormones.

Arousal Response

The heart and blood vessels play a major role in arousal responses and the arousal level can be gauged by measuring the heart rate which should be around 60-75 beats per minute. However for an health individual the resting heart rate maximum heart rate rapidly rising and leveling out at 190-120 beats per minute. The lower the heart resting rate, the more efficiently it can cope with extra demands.

The Production of Stress

Recent research into the interaction between mind and body show that we may place our body on stress "alert" quite unconsciously because of our psychological and emotional attitudes to stress. *Anticipatory emotions like impatience, anxiety, anger, and fear can produce the same nerve impulses and chemical reactions as being faced with a concrete challenge.*

So when faced with a stressful situation, we must either use up the energy created by the body to challenge or danger or learn how to "turn off" the response using a conscious relaxation exercise or technique. As the heart rate' blood pressure, oxygen consumption and muscle tension drop to their normal levels, and new blood flows to the muscles, the inner organs, and the skin, the body is relaxed. The initial stage of arousal remain the same whether we are faced with a major or minor challenges. But under extreme, prolonged, or persistent pressure the body continues to produce extra quantities of stress chemicals, triggering further processes to maintain energy. If arousal continues, the adrenal glands manufacture anti-inflammatory chemicals that simultaneously speed tissue repair while depressing the body's immune defence system. If all these changes continue, the body goes on trying to adapt under increasing strain and pressure. Eventually body breaks downs resulting in exhaustion, a variety of illness.

Stress and Personality

Personality is the most important influence of the way we respond to all events and situations. The values, attitudes, and behaviour patterns that make up our uniqueness as individuals ultimately make us more or less vulnerable to stress.

The origin of much personal stress lies within our perception or our concept of self. Low self esteem can lead to a number of stress-inducting problems : inability to adapt, willingness to place excessively high demands on ourself, and lack of assertiveness. It can also lead to poorself expression so that we harbour negative emotions such as anger, fear, aggression, and anxiety, rather than giving vent to them. Psychologists have identified two broad personalities one is more prone to stress than the other. The "Type A" is the notorious stress-prone personality whose typical behaviour and life-style constantly elicit physical arousal. *Type 'A' people are impatient, ambitious, competitive, aggressive, and hard working; they set high goals and demands of themselves and others; and they are particularly prone to stess-inducing anticipatory emotions such as anxiety.* While the other personality "Type B's which has a reverse profile. They are equable, calm, relaxed, not overtly amitious, and less at risk from stress and hear disease. In general our personality is made up one or other patterns of behaviour, or, in rare cases, a perfect balance of both. Virtually everything in life is potentially stressful to someone. Whether you allow a situation to affect you adversely depends largely on your appraisal and ability to control it. Unavoidable major life crises face us all some time or another; divorce, separation, bereavement, examination, financial struggles, and family conflict. Stress is more likely to occurs if we find ourself caught against our will in a certain way of little or if we cannot shape and amend our lifestyle to suit our needs.

Key Areas of Stress

There are certain areas of our lives where stress is likely to be a particular problem. These broad categories are changes in our lifestyle, challenges associated with performance (especially at work), emotions such as anxiety and fear, boredom, and the grief associated with bereavement or separation. It is worthwhile being aware of these areas, so that you can prepare ourself for crises centering on these problems. Following are some of the key points of stress :

Fear of Unknown. Inflexible attitudes, adherence to strict values and routines, fear of the unknown, can create undue stress, but when change challenges us to take risks and be adaptable. The better our health, the easier it will be to cope up the challenges.

Performance. We often thrive on stress connected with the challenges of physical performance or a test of our skills. This is healthy provided we remain confident and use up the energy and tension generated by extra demands.

Anxiety and Fear. Negative anticipatory emotions may prolong or amplify the arousal caused by actual events.

Boredom. Lack of stimulus or interest at work, unemployment, or retirement may create depression, apathy, and stress. Doubts as to whether you are needed or valued can lead to a poor self-image and a sense of alienation.

Grief. Bereavement or loss of a partner through divorce of separation can have a deep, prolonged psychological effect. If grief and anguish remain unresolved, suppressed or unrecognized they can trigger mental or physical breakdown.

The Social Readjustment Scale. Health and survival are based on the body's ability to maintain a balance of all the physical and mental processes. This state of equilibrium is called homeostasis. Bodily arousal is an integral part of the body's general adaptation system through which it adjust to change and tries to restore homeostasis. Too much change in our lives can overtax our adoptive resources causing illness. Personality is a decisive factor in how we react to environmental pressures-whether we are turned on or brought down by them.

Causes of Stress

The loneliness and isolation are often responsible both for domestic stress and mental illness. Dirt, smell, chemical pollution from petrol exhaust, and cigarette smoke can be equally stressful. By far the most pervasive stress factor is noise. Whether the mind blocks it or not, the body reacts to noise by arousing the sympathetic nervous system, bringing the stress response into play. The chemicals in many of our foods, drinks, and drugs contribute to stress. Caffeine and other stimulants in coffee, tea and cold drinks boost the output of stress hormones. The initial effect is to make us more alert : but it is not long before these substances cause feelings of irritability, while they can also cause sleeplessness. Nicotine in cigarettes directly stimulates the adrenal glands causing a full stress response. Alcohol in moderation helps the body and mind relax, but taken in excess it acts as depressant, damaging the liver, and impairing brain and sensory function. Many drugs and foods can exacerbate stress if taken to excess. Moderation is the best rule if you are in doubt about your diet.

Coping with Stress

Before we can cope with stress effectively, we must become aware our own stress responses. The effects of stress are inside and we often-fail to notice them. Both the mind and body have a tremendous capacity for adaptation. *The more readily we appear to adaptive to the pressure around us, the greater the temptation to drive ourselves barber beyond our capabilities. Stress distorts our perception, so that we do not notice what is happening, if we allow the process to continue the result can be fatigue, exhaustion, eventually, collapse.* The more stressed we are, the less chance we have of realizing it. So it is vital to make ourselves aware of our stress responses. We run the risk of health damage through personality responses to stress. "Type A" personality rarely pace long enough to ponder the effects stress is having on them. In fact, they thrive on stress, probably because their bodies manufacture greater quantities than normal of stress hormone associated with feelings of confidence. Perfectionists by nature, are driven by fear of falling short of their own expectations. They also tend to place the needs of others before their own and can find it hard to express their deepest feelings. Many people combine some of the qualities of both these personality types. They may accept stress-related symptoms as a normal and inevitable part of life-until health is affected. The principal way we can guard against becoming ill through too much stress is to recognize the early signals and known how far we can push ourselves without incurring the more serious symptoms.

Behavioural Signals of Stress

The human body is equipped to deal with stress but only up to a certain level. If your adaptive resources become over worked and exhausted your body ceases to function smoothly. Different organs can become stress targets. Symptoms may arise individually in various combinations. *Chronic stomach upsets, headaches, skin rashes, backpain, irregular breathing patterns, and sleepessness, are common early indications that we are pushing ourselves* too hard. Psychological symptoms tend to creep up on us more slowly and may be less easy to identify, behaviour is a prime indicator of tension. It is those who are close to us who may be the first to read these behavioural signals *viz.* erratic, uncharacteristic behaviour and mood swings. It is desirable to take all these signals seriously-ignoring them can make them get worse. The human body registers stress in a number of places, especially on the head and feet. Habitually touching the hair, ears, or nose, grinding of the teeth, and biting the lips are common signals, as are foot tapping and turning.

Mood Signals

Stress affects our mood in a variety of ways. Some mood changes take place on the surface, while others are deeper and more pervasive. Irritability and impatience are hyperactive states, relatively superficial manifestations of underlying anxiety and aggression. *Restlessness and frustration, if persistent, can be more serious, developing into full-blown hostility or anger. Aparthy and boredom are "flat" feelings, often associated with low stimulus.*

Behavioural Signals

Any behaviour which indicates that you are not acting our usual self may be a sign of adverse reaction to stress. *Nodding off during meeting or social gatherings, trying to do without sleep, losing your sense of humour, moving in a tense jerky way, and reacting nervously or irritably to everyday sounds are other signs.* Outbursts and overreactions can occur when we lose our perspective on problems that we would normally face.

Consistently acting and feeling our-of-character is a serious warning that we are losing our ability to cope with tension. Inability to feel or express any emotions or a sense of being indicates loss of contact with our surroundings and ourselves. The above indicators can help us in overcoming tensions in our day to day life.

Feeling leading to stress are :

1. Lack of definition of responsibility on the job.
2. Constant deal lines set by management with no consultation with the other.
3. Poor working conditions such as working in basement are.
4. No advancement on the job.
5. Multiple and conflicting role expectation.

Perspectives on Mental Illness

'Mental illness' is a comparatively new concept, although the sorts of behaviour to which it is commonly applied are as old as mankind. Today it is an accepted way of describing the behaviour so some of our fellow members of society. Most of us have some idea of what it means to say that someone is 'mentally ill'. We may even know people who are 'mentally ill'. The concept, then, is not unfamiliar to us. Yet when we begin to study further into the nature of 'mental illness', we discover that there are several ways of understanding and explaining it.

One common feature we do find is that the concepts of 'mental illness' and 'the mentally ill person' are usually applied to people who exhibit behaviour which the rest of us consider abnormal. Hearing voices, talking to oneself, having deep depressions, being unable to carry on normal conversations--these are some of the 'symptoms' we see as signs of mental illness.

The explanations of these behaviours are, however, numerous and various. We consider only a few example to illustrate how it is possible for a common phenomenon to be understood and explained in several different ways.

We know that in the Bible mandness was associated with out-of-the ordinary, or abnormal behaviour. The usual explanations offered for the condition referred to possession by evil spirits. It was generally assumed that the unfortunate madmen behaved the way they did because evil spirits had control of their bodies. It was understood that supernatural powers inflicted the condition primarily as a punishment for sin. Madness was seen as a curse of God. For example, we read in The Bible that when Saul, the King of Israel, rebelled against God's command, 'the spirit of the Lord departed from Saul and an evil spirit of the Lord tormented him'.

We also know that Hippocrates, in Ancient Greece, explained the sorts of behaviour we are referring to by reference to his 'Humoral Theory. He suggested that in the human body there were four humours of fluids which controlled our temperament, our emotions and moods. He considered that our behaviour was influenced by our moods and so in turn was controlled to a large extent by our bodily fluids. The fluids were known as *blood, phlegm, yellow bile and black bile* and in the normal healthy body these fluids were present in particular proportions. *But it was possible for excesses to develop, resulting in abnormal, unexpected behaviour.* For example, an excess of black bile was considered to cause excessive melancholy, or what today we might call a state of depression.

We have in these examples ways of understanding, ways of seeing and explaining particular forms of behaviour, which would not be acceptable today to the vast majority of us, but which were considered perfectly adequate in time. However, this is not to say the ways in which these conditions are seen and understood is merely a question of history. Rather, we are saying the variety of explanations can be viewed as a result of different basic assumptions about the nature of the world and life within it.

Today, just as in the past, the description and explanation of abnormal or odd behaviour can take a variety of forms. It is the case that most modern explanations are more likely to be scientific, although religious and supernatural explanations, in terms of possession by spirits, are still accepted by persons with particular religious convictions.

In modern Western culture scientific explanations, that is, explanations which are fundamentally testable in some way against empirical observations, are usually more acceptable to the majority of people. There are, however, a number of explanation both within and between such scientific approaches to understanding as biology psychology and sociology.

Generally speaking, biological approaches rest on the assumption that human behaviour can be explained to a large extent by reference to the genetic composition and chemical processes of the human body. Assumptions of this sort have led to a variety of investigations and subsequent explanations of mental illness in terms of heredity and physical defects.

Psychological theories of mental illness have been more common. Mental illness has been readily recognized as a problem of the mind and broad comparisons have been assumed between diseased bodies and diseased minds. *Psychology, as the human science which focuses its study on the human mind and its mental processes, has naturally produced a variety of explanations of mental abnormality.*

Within psychology, similar to most other disciplines, there are a variety of perspectives, each with its own bedrock assumptions about the psychological nature of the human being. Thus we find a variety of ways of seeing and understanding mental illness psychologically; but it is probable that the Fredian approach is the most well known and it provides us with an interesting example of a non-sociological, human scientific perspective.

Sociologist View on Mental Illness

The Freudian perspective on mental illness is found on the assumption that the normal, stable personality develops through a number of stages in which the innate pleasure drive or libido is directed on to different objects. The normal personality passes through an oral phase, an anal phase and a genital phase. During this last phase an individual's sexual drives, which were previously directed to the parent of the opposite sex, and transferred to an appropriate other person. For a variety of persons, mainly to do with inadequate familiar relationships and early childhood experiences, a person may regress to an earlier stage of development or become fixed in a particular stage. Such fixations can result in abnormal behaviour. *For Freudians, mental illness is seen largely as a pathological (that is, sick) condition of the personality brought about by experiences in early childhood which have hindered the normal development of the individual.*

For sociologists, mental illness has been as area of investigation for the several decades. *Ever since Emile Surkheim demonstrated at the turn of the century how such an apparently individually motivated act as suicide can be explained by social causes,* later sociologists have not hesitated to investigate and explain other aspects of behaviour which superficially have not appeared relevant to sociological consideration. Mental illness is one such typical area.

Following Durkheim's particular sociological tradition, some sociologists have sought the causes of mental illness in the structure of society. They, like Durkheim, have assumed that *what an individual does is very much a question of what his social environment what his society, structures him into doing. On the basis of this broad assumption, mental illness has been as a condition or attribute of the person like a disease or discbility, produced by the person's societal environment.* Consequently these sociologists have looked at the structure of various societies and particular parts of societies in order to discover what associations may exist between particular aspects of the social structure and mental illness.

What is important is that we recognize that this sort of sociological knowledge, this sort of generalization, is the product of a particular approach, a particular perspective. It is only arrived at because the investigators started our with certain assumptions about the nature of mental illness and what causes it. The production of this sort of explanation is an example of the use of the 'structuralist perspective' in sociology. In this particular case, social class a assumed to be a feature of the structure of society. Members of the same social class are assumed to have similar roles in the economic order of society, similar attitudes and educational backgrounds, and similar life-styles. *This broad economic and cultural similarity is assumed to differentiate large groups within the society and to produce different behaviours and conditions in the individual members of the groups.* In this case, it is assumed to produce difference in the incidence and type of mental illness.

Incidence of Mental Illness

Similar broad structuralist assumptions lie behind studies which seek to discover associations between the incidence of mental illness and ecological factors such as area of urban residence. Studies of this sort simply that the style of life and the general organization of different parts of a town or city can condition individuals into mental illness.

H. Warren Durham and Robert Fairs, for example, have shown that in Chicago the incidence of schizophrenia varies in different parts of the city (Phoenix. 1967). They found that areas near the centre of the city had extremely high rates compared with other areas. The highest rates for schizophrenia were in the area they called hobohemia--The area of rooming houses and foreign-born communities close to the city centre. They suggest that these areas are locations of social disorganization and as such constitute environments conducive to the development of schizophrenia. The implication clearly is that this particular form of mental illness as related to the ecological or spatial pattern of the city, which in turn produces different sorts of social organization and environment. *The condition of the person is assumed to be a result of the structural organization of urban, social and economic life, and in this way, this study presents-an example of the use of a structuralist sociological perspective.*

Meaning and Action Perspectives - Mental Illness

In contrast, the 'meaning and action perspectives' provide a rather different view of mental illness. Here, mental illness is not seen as a condition lying within the individual. Instead it is seen as a social status conferred on the person by other members of society. That is to say, instead of assuming that mental illness is something which persons can have 'within them', like a disease or incapacity which anyone can observe and recognize, it is seen as a state which is very much in the eyes of the beholder. A person is seen as mentally ill if other people say he is : the mentally ill person is one to whom that label has successfully been applied. Mental illness is seen as a label, a categorization, conferred on to particular individuals by other individuals.

This way of understanding mental illness is not founded on the assumption that society is an entity with a structure which determines, or at least very strongly influences, individuals and their behaviour. Rather, it derives from a stress on the individual actions and perceptions of persons. Members of society are seen as active agents who construct their social action on the basis of the meanings and interpretations they give to their environment. They do not simply transmit or reflect a given structure, but in fact create it by their interaction. The world has to be interpreted, has to be made sense of and has to be given meaning. 'Mental illness' and 'mental patients' are neither 'objects' nor 'conditions' which are assumed to be 'out there', to be discovered. Rather, the concern is with locating the processes by which people go about classifying others as 'mentally ill'.

Role of Society

Thomas Szasz (1973) has approached the study of mental illness from these basic assumptions and has attempted to show that there are some roles in society which have more power attached to them than most when it comes to the conferring of the label 'mentally ill' on the people. Although we may consider that we recognize a mentally ill person when we are with one, psychiatrists are generally accepted as being the 'experts' in diagnosing persons in need of treatment. Szasz points out that the psychiatrists has considerable power; on the basis of his observations and analysis of an individual's behaviour, he can declare that the person is sick, that he needs treatment and that he should be put into an institution. *The psychiatrist's diagnosis is likely to be accepted and acted upon by other members of society. In this way, the individual concerned becomes 'mentally ill' not simply because he does odd things, but also because the psychiatrist has put that particular label on him.* If others try to apply the level, it is less likely to stick.

Some studies, starting our from these assumptions, have shown how psychiatrists and others trained to identify the mentally ill person can disagree over the interpretation and meaning of the behaviours they observe. The possibility of disagreement shows how the differentiation of the 'mentally ill' from the 'normal' member of society can be largely contingent upon the circumstances of the social situation. An example of this work is the investigation by Thomas Scheff of the psychiatric screening procedures used in a Midwestern state in American to determine whether mental patients should be released. Scheff (1964) has shown how the diagnosis of a person as mentally ill, requiring involuntary confinement, can be affected by the financial, ideological and political position of the examining psychiatrists. He shows how these factors tend to predispose the court-appointed psychiatrists to assume that the subject is ill. The situation is defined as one in which the subject is presumed from the outset to be mentally ill and the psychiatrists then go on to interpret the behaviour and records of the patient on the basis of their prior definition of the situation. Scheff argues that without this prior definition of the records, behaviours and responses to the psychiatric tests can be interpreted differently.

Meaning and action perspectives also focus on the individuals conception of himself. That is, they assume that individuals have to interpret and give meaning to their own actions as well as those of others. It assumes that our self-image is largely a result of the interpretations of other people's reactions to what we say and do.

Sociological Analysis of Mental Illness

Thus we can see that the kinds of sociological analyses and explanations of mental illness produced by sociologists using meaning and action perspectives differ considerably from those produced by the sociologists using structuralist perspectives. The events and behaviour in the world that both are observing may be 'the same', but because they start from different bedrock assumptions about the nature of the social world and make use of different conceptual frameworks, they produce different sociological analysis.

The questions which shape their research strategies and the actual methods of investigation they use tend to differ because they start from different views of the nature of the social world. Sociologist making structuralist assumptions such as Hollingshed and Redlieh, or Dunham and Faris, tend to use questionnaires and survey methods. Qantifying their data into statistical tables to produce analysed involving a heavy reliance on mathematics. Interactionist, however, are more likely to use methods of direct observation. They try to see the world from the same points of view as the mental patients, doctors and official are studying. Their research approach often involves living with their subjects over a prolonged period of time and sharing their day-to-day experiences. Neither the structuralist nor the meaning and action, way of seeing investigating and explaining mental illness is necessarily more correct than the other. They simply represent different ways of seeing the world sociologically.

Overcoming Stress

The various techniques of reducing or overcoming stress has been discussed here.

Role of Yoga in Stress Relief

The evening is a time to be with the family. *Traditionally, the family has been viewed as a haven from stress, a buffer from the hardships, frustrations and injustices of the day. Although this view has been challenged in recent years, it is still commonly believed that the family is--and should be--a sort of life preserver in a sea of stress.*

Unfortunately, the family is not perfectly endowed to deal with stress; *In fact, the family itself can be one of the most devastating sources of stress. Primary family stresses--those that are generated within the family--include such milestones as marriage, divorce, childbirth and the death of parents or spouses. These events are so disruptive and intensely stressful that one or more of them can lead to stress-related illness or accidents.*

Other forms of family-related stress identified by researchers are result in specific points of distress. You have an aching back or shoulder, for instance, although you have not been lifting heavy objects or otherwise straining your back. Or perhaps you notice that your jaws are clenched shut, even when you think you are relaxed, or that your partner complains that you kept him or her awake at night by grinding your teeth. All these are signs of stress that the exercises in this chapter, which are targeted to your symptoms, can relieve or prevent.

One of the best ways to relax is through Yoga, which has been practiced for centuries as a means to achieve inner peace and relaxation. It is also the basis for most stretching exercises that relive muscular tension, which often results from stress, and speed recovery from muscle strains and overuse injuries.

A much newer relaxation method is called progressive relaxation, in which you tense and relax various muscle groups in succession from head to toe. Progressive relaxation has been shown to reduce some types of headache, backache and other symptoms of stress and is an effective, convenient method to clear your mind and release tension in your body as you prepare for bed. This chapter also shows you the proper posture for lying in bed, which can help relieve strain on the spine as well as prepare you for sleep.

Sleep

A sound sleep can restore you both mentally and physically. Yet according to national surveys, between 15 and 20 percent of the adult population routinely suffers from in somnia, a general term that refers to difficulty falling asleep or sleeping soundly. Chronic insomnia is often triggered by anxiety, but it may persist even after the source of stress is removed. If you have trouble getting to sleep, or if you do not regularly wake up feeling refreshed and alert, here are some suggestions :

— Establish a regular sleeping schedule, but do not try to force sleep. If you cannot fall asleep in 15 to 20 minutes, read until you feel drowsy. No matter when you fall asleep, always try to get up at the same time. Do not try to make up for lost sleep by napping or sleeping late on weekends.
— Do not drink coffee, tea, colas or any other caffeine-containing beverage within four hours of bedtime. Also, avoid alcohol and other drugs that will disrupt your sleep. And do not smoke before going to bed : Nicotine can have a stimulating effect.
— At best, sleeping pills should be used only for occasional insomnia, and you should never take them for more than three nights in a row.
— Do not take your troubles to bed. Clear you mind and release your body's tensions through progressive-relaxation exercises.

Lower Back-Pain Relief

About eight out of 10 people suffer from lower back pain at one time or another. Twenty-five million Americans endure chronic lower back pain, and some are permanently disabled as a result. Yet, in most cases, there is no discernible cause for all this misery.

Most lower back pain is preventable. More than 80 percent of all such pain is muscular in nature and is at least an indirect result of muscle weakness, inflexibility and tension. Obesity is also a common factor in lower back pain.

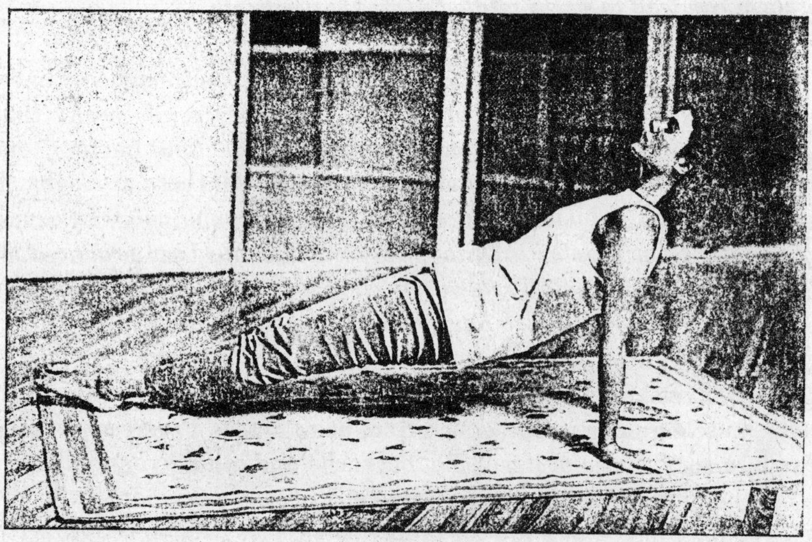

Fig. 12.1 Sit on the floor with your legs extended and your feet together. Support yourself on your hands and raise your pelvis, chest and head off the ground so that they all form a straight line down to your toes. Hold this position for at least 20 seconds.

Often, psychological stress that builds up for a long time manifests itself in muscle cramps in the back, particularly if you are predisposed to back pain for the reasons cited. Correct posture and sleeping positions may relieve lower back pain.

To prevent lower back pain, you should control your weight with a proper diet and aerobic exercise. You can also strengthen and stretch the appropriate muscles by performing the exercises.

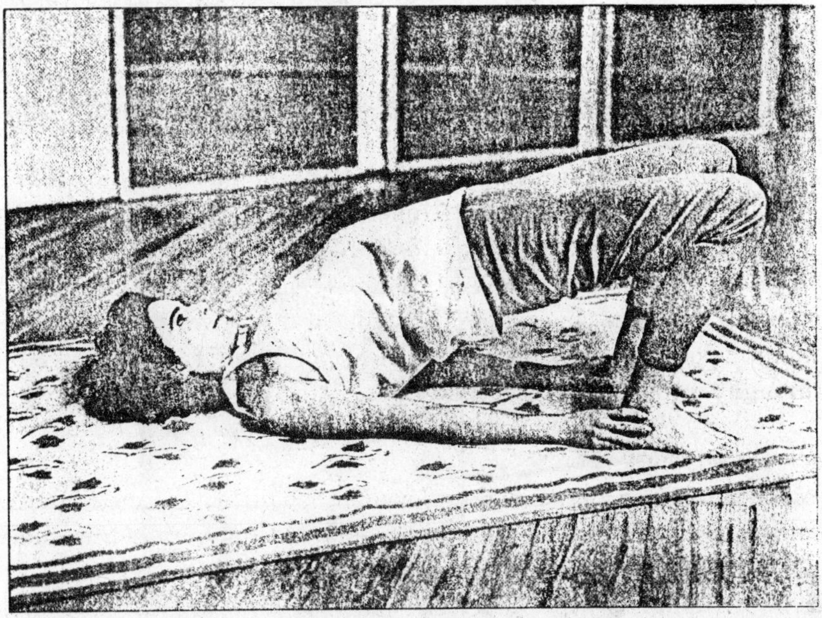

Fig. 12.2 Begin the Yoga camel by kneeling on the floor and sitting on your heels (*Inset opposite*). Place your hands on your heels, rise up on your knees, lift your chest toward the ceiling and press your hips forward (*opposite*). For an easier variation, lie on your back and place your feet flat on the floor so that your can grasp your heels. Press your hips toward the ceiling (*right*).

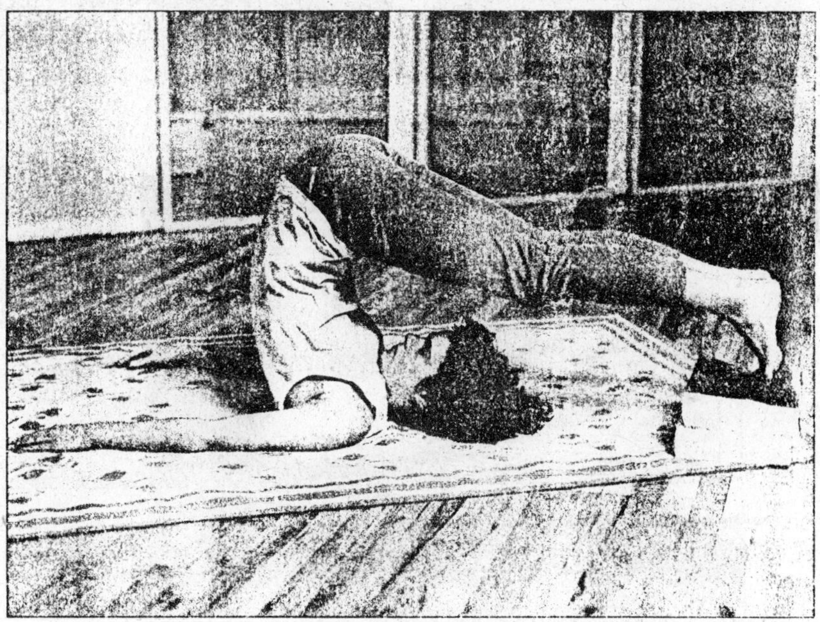

Fig. 12.3 To perform the plough safely, lie on your back with your arms at your side. Slowly swing your legs up over your head and place your toes on a pile of books. Be sure that your shoulders and arms, not your neck, support most of your body weight.

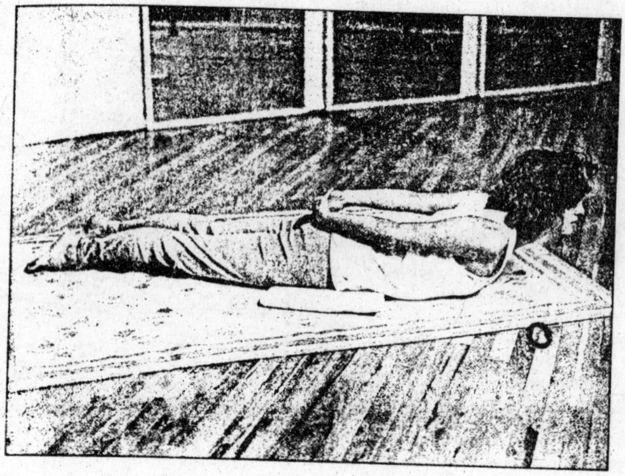

Fig. 12.4 Fold a towel under your hips and lie face down on the floor. Place your arms at your side and extend your toes. Bring your hands together behind your back and lift your chest and head.

Fig. 12.5 Bring your arms to your sides and make fists. Press your fists against the floor while lifting your head, chest and right leg, keeping your knee straight. Repeat for your left leg.

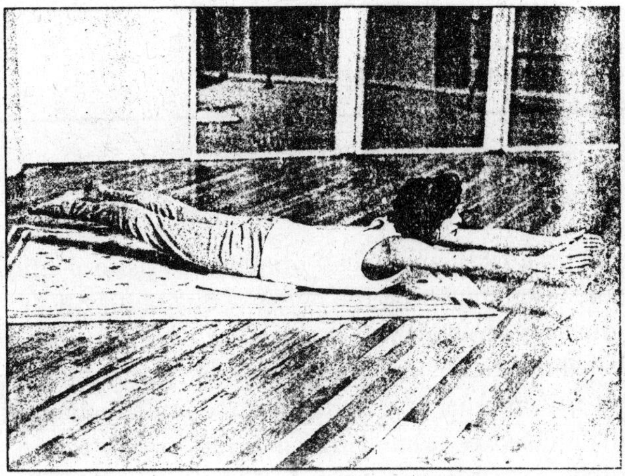

Fig. 12.6 Remain face down on the floor and extend your arms out in front of you. Lift your face, chest, arms and legs off the floor. Keep your arms parallel to the floor and your knees straight.

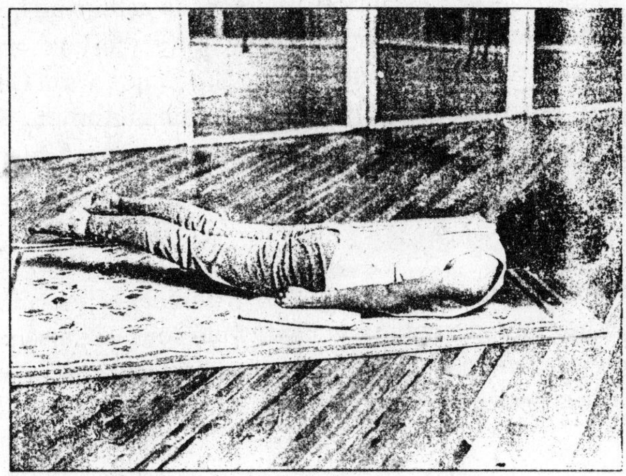

Fig. 12.7 For the locust position, repeat the exercise at left but lift both feet off the floor while pressing down with your fists. Make sure that your toes are extended and your knees are straight.

13

Organisation

Introduction

The existence of a sound organisation is an essential prerequisite of efficiency. A systematically planned flexible organisation matching the needs of business will save managerial time, permit concentration of the key problems, save costs and help in enhancing productivity. Organisation embraces the whole complex of relationship between managers and subordinate employees. The purpose of the organisation should be to enable managers and work force to carry out their responsibility efficiently, that is, what greatest concentration, effort and the least wastage of time and resources. According to Fedderic Hopper, organisation is a framework or responsibilities through and by means of which a concern may do it job. Brech refers to the organisation as a structure of responsibility and formal relationship existing amongst the personnel. The concept of an organisation is as old as mankind and has undergone tremendous changes with the growth of civilization.

Organisation is generally viewed as a group of persons formed to seek certain goals. An individual is unable to fulfil his needs and desires alone because he lacks strength, ability time and potential. So he seeks the co-operation of other persons in achieving his goals. This is not a new phenomenon; it is a universal truth. People have always formed organisations to pool their efforts for the achievement of their common goals. The Emperors of China used organisations a thousand year ago to construct great irrigation systems. And the first Pope created a universal church to serve a world religion. Modern society, however, has more organisations, thus fulfilling a greater variety of social and personal needs.*

Importance

An organisation comes into existence when there are a number of persons in communication and relationship to each other and are willing to contribute towards a common endeavour**. Thus to achieve a common purpose, people form groups and pool their effort by defining and dividing the various activities, responsibilities and authority. The important characteristics of an organisation are :

(*i*) Communication.
(*ii*) Co-operative Efforts.
(*iii*) Common Objective.
(*iv*) Rules and Regulations.

---

* Etzoni Amitai: Modern Organisation, Prentice Hall, Inc, Eaglewood Cliff.

** Barnard Chester I. The Functions of Executive. Harvard University Press, Cambridge.

Definition of An Organisation

The persons who form the organisation must be in a position to communicate with each other. They must also be willing to co-operate with each other for the achievement of their goals or objectives. The objectives must be common for which the organisation comes into existence. Lastly, rules and regulations lay down the formal structure of the organisation. They define the authority and responsibility relationship among various individuals in the organisation.

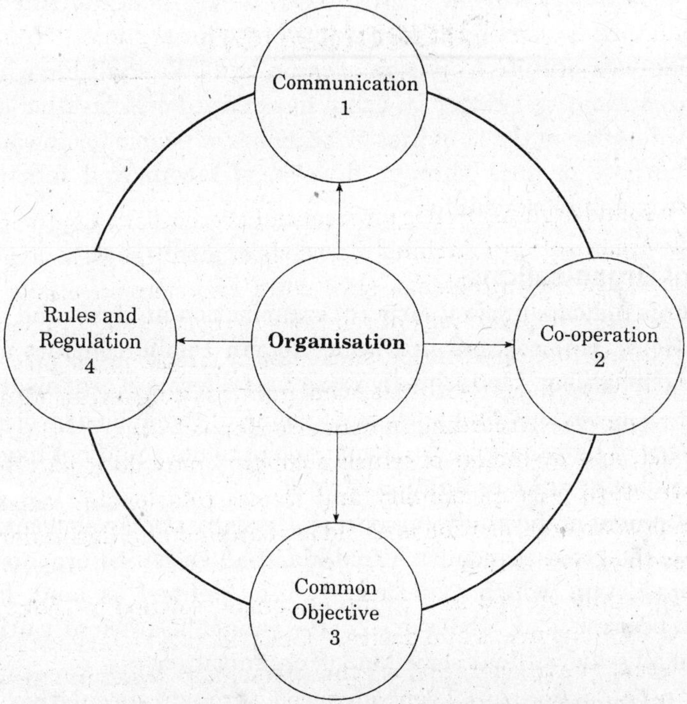

Fig. 13.1. Characteristics of organisation

Some people define organisation in a very narrow sense. Organisation is no more than the framework within which the responsibilities of management of an enterprise are discharged.* According to this definition organisation is recognised as a structure, which means it will be viewed as something static. But an organisation is a dynamic entity consisting of individuals, means, objectives and relationship among the individuals. In this sense "relationship" or formal organisation is only a part of the organisation.

Human organisations are organic in the sense that various parts are interdependent. Some of the basic pillars of the organisation are individual, groups and the work. Work place is one of the most important institutions for providing human satisfactions.

Organisation has also been known as a system of communications, a means of problem solving, and a means of facilitating decision-making. Organisations have been viewed as a social system and as systems of a group of interacting variable.

For practical purposes organisation can be simply defined as a process of :

1. Determining what must be done if a given aim is to be achieved;

---

* Breach E.F.L. :The Principles and Practice of Management.

2. Dividing the necessary activities into segments small enough to be performed by one person; and

3. Providing means of co-ordination so that there is no wested efforts and the members of the organisation do not come in each others way.

Organisation cannot be divorced from the idea of purpose. It is not an end in itself but a means to an end.

Organisation is necessary whenever two or more people must combine their efforts toward the same and even if task is short-lived such as moving a large stone. "You take that side, and I shall take this side" is a primitive division of work, and "We shall life when I count three" a primitive form of co-ordination. Edger H. Schin has defined organisation as "An organisation is the rational co-ordination of the activities of a number of people for the achievement of some common explicit purpose or goal, through division of labour and function and through a hierarchy of authority and responsibility".

Ancient Forms of Organisations

Historical records indicate ancient forms of organisation analysis and planning by priests in Mesopotamia, Court philosophers in China, Roman Public contract administrators and various military organisations. Undoubtedly many useful forms of organisation were developed over the centuries. It is obvious that such monuments of the ancient world as the Pyramids, the Hanging Gardens of Babylon and the Róman monuments could not have been constructed without division of labour and co-ordination of work.

With the development of the study of economics, organisation was treated more systematically. For example, the great economist Alfred Marshall classified organisation as one of the basic factors in production, which had formerly been defined as land, labour and capital. Marshall was right because land, labour and capital cannot be efficiently utilized in production except on a very small scale without some kind of organisation.

Knowledge of organisation has been advanced through speculative thinking, through controlled experiments, and through experience over long periods.

Modern Organisations

Modern organisations began in the early 1900s when F.W. Taylor developed concept of "Scientific Management" which called for the careful planning of the Human/Physical/Financial systems as well as for the co-ordination and control of it. Shortly thereafter, Henry Fayol Concluded that all work in industry can be divided into following six groupings :

(*a*) Technical (*b*) Commercial
(*c*) Financial (*d*) Security
(*e*) Accounting (*f*) Managerial.

Immediatley prior to World War II, Robert W. Porter, a management consultant, published a thesis entitled "Design for Industrial co-ordination." Porter focused attention on the fact that the work at every level of the organisation can be divided into three basic functions :

(*a*) Planning
(*b*) Implementing (doing)
(*c*) Inspecting (controlling).

By grouping all organisational tasks within these three functions at each level, the organisational design will be most conducive to the establishment of natural checks and balances. These are essential to the co-ordination of every system.

World War II and the expansion of corporate organisations in 1950s created unprecedented problems in organisational design with the result people involved in management and administration as teachers and practitioners have thought and written about organisation for many years. The distinguishing feature of Modern Organisation theory is the attempt to make the study of organisational behaviour more scientifically.

Ways of Looking at Organisation

Organisations of today are highly complex. Most managers think of an organisation in terms of its formal structure. If asked to describe it, they will talk about the work that they do. They may talk more abstractly about responsibilities and authority. They will think of the organisation as being composed of a number of levels, each of which is senior to the one below it. Many authors and many managers today thought of it as a formal structure. They sought to describe the principles, which should be used in designing its structure. Such principles as they thought were applicable to all types of formal organisations. The work of these classical writers is not, by itself sufficient for an understanding of organisation, it approach has important limitations. It is too concerned with formal structure not sufficiently with the individuals who make the structure. It is a static approach, paying attention to the many interactions that take place between different levels of the organisation. It emphasises without giving sufficient attention the diversity of problems but in different types of organisation.

People in Organisations

The classical writer think of organisation as a formal structure. Another way of thinking about it is terms of the people who are employed within it. Managers are usually sensitive to the fact that how their staff walk together which may affect how well the organisation works. Interest in how people behave in organisation dates from the famous Hawthorne studies into effects of fatigue on workers. The Human relations school provides a different approach to organisational problems from that of the classical writers, but it also has its limitations. Major limitation is that although we learnt a lot about people in organisations but still much that we do not understand about human behaviour.

System Approach to Organisation

It is now difficult to pick up a book a management or an organisation without using the word system. The word system like a long lineage in the physical science. It can be defined as a regularly interacting or interdependent group of items forming a unified whole. Under the heading of systems, it is useful to distinguish two main ways of looking at organisations. The first is one that has come to be adopted be many social scientists can be called the social systems, approach. It is concerned with inter-actions between the different aspects of the organisation-people, technology formal structure and environment. The second looks at the organisation in terms of the information that it needed for decision making and co-ordination, tracing the flow of information through decision centres. It can be called as the "information systems" approach and has its origins in operational research and Electronic Data Processing. The systems approach in all forms has also contributed to our study of how organisations work. All these ways of looking at organisations--the classical; the Human relations and the Systems Approach can be of help to the manager.

Causes of Organisations Malfunctions

According to behavioural scientists we have designed organisations which have ignored individual potential for competence, responsibility, constructive intent and productivity. We have created structure and jobs that at the lower levels alienate and frustrate the workers, lead them to reject responsible behaviour, not only with imunity but with a sense of justice; and tempt them to fight the organisation by lowering the quality of what they produce.

Incompetent Organisational Structure

Problems are equally severe at management levels, where incompetent organisational structures create organisation environments lacking in trust, openness and risk taking. The attitudes that flourish in such environments are conformity and defensiveness, which often find expressions in an organisational tendency to produce detailed information for unimportant problems and invalid information for important one. This tendency ensures ineffective problem solving, poor decision making and weak commitment to the decisions made. But the effects are so pervasive that people throughout the world are beginning to think which is natural and inevitable. Such acceptance makes organisational decay a self prepetuating process which reinforce the alienation of employees, the frustration of consumers, the anger of bureaucrats, the outrage of youth.

Behavioural science research and practice provide the most hopeful alternative. *The exciting conclusion that grows out of behavioural science research is that organisation can be made more humane and at the same time more effective. It is possible to design organisational systems where individual participants can give of themselves and not give themselves up.*

This does not mean that there are no basic conflicts between the individual and the organisation. There are, and probably will continue to be. But there can be new organisational structures, heightened competence in interpersonal relations among the managers, and increased group effectiveness. The problems of integrating individual needs and capacities with organisational requirements is still a major problem in organisations. If the reward and penalty systems emphasise punishment of mistakes, then the people who prefer the change and creativity will reduce ambiguity by staying within well-travelled pathways.

People have the capacity to go either way:toward growth or toward stagnation. The design of the system in which work can significant influence the way they go and how far. The more they slide toward stagnation, the higher, the probability of developing organisation illness. And in general the more they orient themselves toward growth, better it is for organisational health. Beyond a certain point, however, frustration may set in, because there must be limits to how much growth orientation system can permit and encourage.

The employees can be trusted to participate actively in the decision to determine at what point they can not have new challenges. It can be seen that one characteristics of a person who knows is free and autonomous in ability to define and accept limitations of his growth and growth of others.

Building an Organisation for the Future

The complex industrial organisation contains many problems that are difficult to deal with even they are identified. People complete with one another instead of working together in a common effort to get the job done. They tell their wives or husbands what is really bothering them on the job instead of discussing their problems with the colleagues with whom such problems must be solved. Managers are constantly being surprised by the sudden emergents of brewing problems. The studies were conducted on building an organisation for future and the following observations emerged as statement of philosophy.

(*i*) The individual employee is the company most important resource and major focus should be on providing him with things he needs.

(*ii*) Work should be challenging interesting and personally rewarding. A great deal of trust should be placed in each person, there should be minimum of controls, constraints etc. giving him feeling how to do his job.

A technical democracy should exist. There should be relatively less of distance between the employees and their supervisors at every echelon of management. Greater emphasis should be placed on quality and technical excellence and one long-term career opporunities and personal growth.

Adapting to Survive

Markets and environment do not stand still, and critical success factors must work toward a future goal. A company's ability to adapt to change is the key to its long term success. Strength in the market place is of direct concern to someone who is looking to build a career in a particular organisation. If a company is to be consistently successful in adapting to new circumstances, its power structure has to be in tune with the realities of a changing market place, a changing world economy and shifts in society. The secret of success lies in 3M's ability to nurture creativity : change is an essential part of the company's corporate philosophy. Does your organisation shrink from the prospect of change ? Or does it embraces change as a means of gaining competitive advantage ?

Signs of an Organisation heading for Problems

— Diminishing market share
— Low profit margins together with low volume
— Ageing products
— Consistent dissatisfaction of customers
— Quality/reliability problems
— Consistently late deliveries
— Heavy dependence on one or two customers/suppliers
— Long term fixed price contracts.
— Heavy borrowing requirement
— Production methods which are old fashioned
— Poor industrial relations
— High turnover of employees
— Management out of tune with commercial realities

— Top Heavy organisation
— Inflexible management
— Lack of communication between management and employees
— Inward looking management.

Sings of a forward looking Company

— Awareness of competition
— High investment in research and development
— Regular flow of new products
— Careful use of consumer research and test marketing
— Rapid response to complaints of customers
— The quality the customer wants.
— Concern for customer service.
— Pricing that is appropriate to the customer
— Enthusiastic employees
— Accessible management
— Flexible organisation
— Decentralised decision making
— Concentration on critical success factors
— Supportive financial controls.

14

Evolution of Industry

Introduction

Business Excellence can be activated if the organisation become a learning organisation. This demands the following :

— Visionary committed and involves leaders
— Clear understanding of company's critical business process and success factors
— Responsive Process
— Employee with relevant know-how and skills
— Continues Improvement - an integral part of policy and strategy
— Objective assessment of current and future performance.

World class companies are those which demonstrate consistent, measurable positive business results based on a philosophy of continuous improvement and capability to dead with constant change.

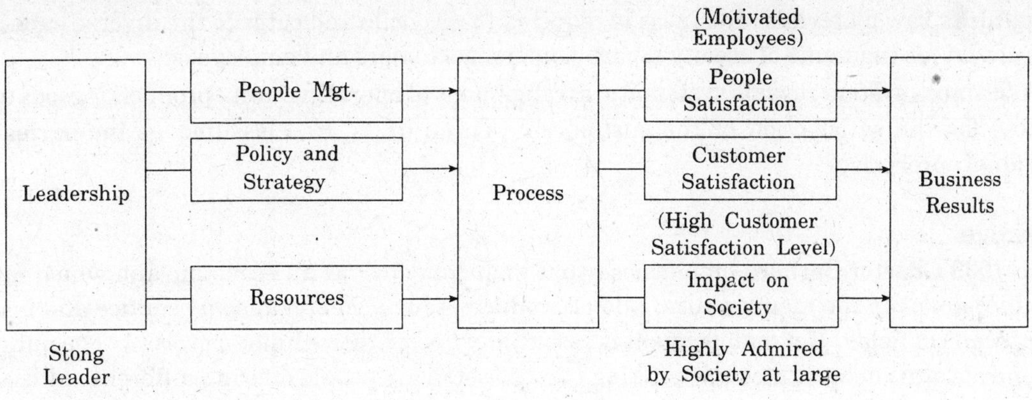

Industry

Industry is an inter-related system in which business firms use basic resources the guidance of management and the influence of environmental forces. Every business has a well defined structure, with an orderly arrangement of its various complex components. The business system is shown as follows :

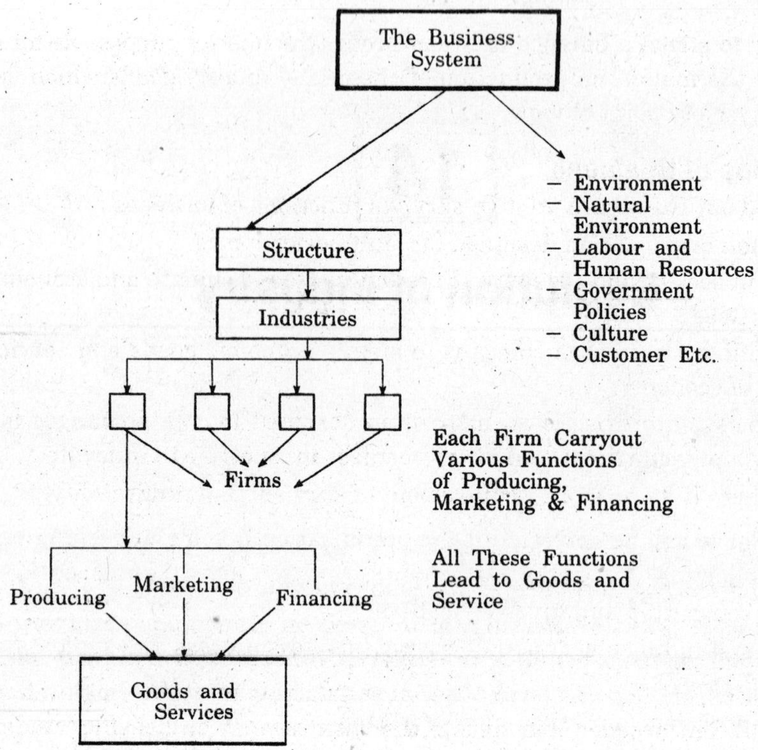

Fig. 14.1

A business firm can be defined as a concern, or an enterprise or a company which buy, sell and is owned by an individual or a group of persons and managed under a specific set of operating policies. Business is primarily meant create surpluses by putting together human ingenuity and nature's raw materials. Business is required to reconcile and cater to the diverse expectations of various segments of society--share holders, customers and employees.

A business system reveals systematic arrangement of operating units producing goods and services for the satisfaction of the customers. These units are classified as industries or individual enterprise.

Objective

In 1939 Chester Bernard emphasised that management has an economic aim which finds its achievement in the manufacture, sale of products, provision of transport service and many other technical fields. But management is essentially a cooperative human process. The pursuit of economic aims necessitates the working together of many people offering different skills and different levels of ability but all need to be coordinated in the pursuit of common task. Peter Drucker analysed the concepts of corporate type of business institution from three angles :

(*i*) it is an autonomous institution governed by rules of its own structure; determined by the desire of survival and growth.

(*ii*) it represents the society in which it functions to meet the promise, aspirations and belief of its members.

(*iii*) its policy to strike a balance between profit which is its purpose as an autonomous unit and the maximum production of cheap and quality goods which is its purpose from the society point of view.

Survival Functions of Business

He also pointed out that there are five survival functions of business :

(*i*) it is human organisation designed for joint performance.

(*ii*) it exists in society and economy. Forecasting, social climate and economic policy is a business need.

(*iii*) the specific purpose of business is to supply economic goods and services and thus creation of economy.

(*iv*) the business enterprise is an institution designed to create changes in a changing economy and technology, and every business must strive to innovate.

(*v*) finally there is an absolute requirement of survival and profitability.

Role of Business

Thus the business is supposed to play the following role.

(1) The creating of profit on the capital invested on plant and machinery etc., (2) The provision of employment for the people of the society, (3) The provision of the goods and services that the society needs. (4) The provision of social satisfaction for those employed and the basic value of work itself. The broader objectives of the business may be classified under three main heads.

(*i*) economic, (*ii*) social, (*iii*) human.

Economic

This is the first and foremost objective of a business organisation. According to Peter Drucker "the management is an economic organ and every decision of management has its first dimension as economic dimension".

Profits are the rewards for which a business enterprise is brought into being. No one will take risks unless he is assured of fair return on his investment. A business differs from government organsation which has no profit motive but which exist to serve the public, maintain law and order. Profit is meeting the costs of being and continuing to be in a business. Profit also serve three purposes (1) it ensures the supply of future capital for expansion, (2) it is an ultimate test of business performance and (3) it is an indicator of efficiency, the more efficient a business, greater the profit it earns.

Social

The limitations on profit motive arise from the fact that business does not exist in vacuum, it exists in a society. A business organisation may be compelled to maintain the quality of its products, the price and supply position etc., thereby putting certain ceiling on profit. A good business man keeps before him some social objectives such as good quality, reasonable price, fair labour practice etc. Business has to conform to certain social beliefs and promises. At present a business has to contribute to the well-being and uplift of the community in which it is situated. This is done by creating the welfare activities, hospitals, libraries, organising sports providing entertainment etc., etc.

According to H.R. Brown business should be conducted for the attainment of valued social goals like high standard of living, economic progress, economic stability, personal and national security. Business also helps in bringing international understanding.

Human

Business is an assemblage of not bricks and mortar but of human being who have to be organised for joint performance. Team spirit in business is best secured by recognition of worker as a human being, appreciation of dignity of labour and creation of healthy atmosphere for the relisation of his potentials, talents and aspirations. The human relation has been defined as the social industrial revolution which gives the employee a sense of usefulness and importance and makes his life more interesting by making the work more meaningful. One of the greatest need of present time is that the employees should be treated as respectable individuals, developed in their profession in order to take higher responsibility which helps the organisation and individual to achieve the objectives.

Evolution of Industry in India

During the Mughal period, India was known for her arts and handicrafts which was very popular vis-a-vis crafts of the contemporary Europe. At a time when the West was the birth place of modern industrial system, India was known for the wealth of her rulers and for the high artistic skill of her craftsmen in Europe. The trade of Indian cotton goods grew up at the beginning of 17th century as a subsidiary industry for meeting the requirements of the markets in South East Asian countries which supplied spices to the European markets. Very soon the Indian cotton goods became very popular in European markets. Similarly the Dutch, the French and the English, all began to buy a large quantity of cloth, silk etc. from India. With the fall of Mughal Empire, the British entered through East India Company and soon acquired the Bengal whose riches and geographical proved invaluable to them. Britishers moved gradually from Bengal to the whole of the country. Organisation of industries during this period can be classified into two heads, (*a*) rural industry and (*b*) urban industry. The rural industry or the cultural industries, was indeed the cottage industries serving the needs of local population. The cottage industries were manufacturing utility goods such as earthen-ware, cloths, baskets, etc. The aritisans applied their traditional occupation without being aware of the external environment and also without affecting the outside world. There was no specialisation and the economic organisation of the cottage industry was most primitive in character. On the other hand in urban industry which was the most organised and was meeting the needs of the foreign market. The major items of the urban market were silk, gold ornaments, silver ornaments, woollen garments etc. This industry was also manufacturing other luxury goods. The urban industry was organised by the middle men who advanced money to the craftman. From the middle of 17the century the import of silk, gold ornaments and woollen garments had expanded phenomenally in England. The urban industry flooded the British market with their products. But the supremacy of Indian handicraft could no longer be maintained because of technological, economical and political developments.

Industrial Revolution

The reasons for the decay of the indigenous industry was the industrial revolution in England which started during the second half of the 18the century and was at its full swing be the first quarter of 19th century. The innovation of steam, power and the automation of industry the process of manufacturing cheaper and faster and which subsequently effected the Indian trade persely. The major reasons affecting the market of Indian products were :

(*a*) Treating India as a colony.

(*b*) Prohibitory duties of Indian goods.

(*c*) High headedness of company agents.

(*d*) With the expansion of British cotton textile industry the East India Company started extending the areas of its operation. They started cultivation of cotton in India and improving the quality of the cotton. It was this period during which the specialisation in jute production was taken up in Bengal. The emphasis was on the export of raw materials, processing the same in their country and sending back to India and other countries as the finished products. Probably this was one of the best was of pumping money in their country.

(*e*) The disappearance of the courts of Nowabs and Rajas gave a heavy blow to the Indian handicrafts.

(*f*) The newly educated class due to the acceptance of their European standards turned their backs to the indigenous products.

By 1880, the decline of the handicraft was nearly complete and the masses engaged in the handicrafts had no means of livelihood.

Evolution of Modern Industry

The analysis of the forces helping the industrial evolution of India upto the First World War can be summarised as below :

(*a*) Destruction of capitalist urban handicraft and village artisan industry paved the way for the transformation of India into a single economic unit.

(*b*) Growth of the great merchantile centers which were the contribution of the british rule. The growth and development of towns contributed immensely to the growth of the leading industries of the country. Large number of cotton, textile, and leather industries started coming in Bombay, Ahmedabad, Hooghly and Kanpur.

(*c*) Introduction of English language among the educated class helped us in training a large number of younger Indians to the modern scientific techniques which came as a boom for acquiring the technical knowledges required for the industries.

(*d*) The abolition of the monopoly of the East India Company in 1833 provided a big opportunity to the English merchants to develop trade and industry in India.

(*e*) The improvement in the oceanic and inland transport system encouraged the establishment of various industries in the country by providing an infrastructure facilities for importing machines and skills from the foreign countries. Beside this the development of industries in India was not only slow bit it was lopsided in its character.

Second World War Period

The Second World War gave a big inducement to the development of industries in India. New companies were set up wherever opportunities were available. Many important industries started their production for the first time during the Second Would War. Industries like ferro alloys, non-ferrous metal, metal fabricating industries, economical industries like diesel engines, pump bicycle, machine tools, sewing machine etc. The consumer industries like textile, tea, ill processing machine, and chemical industries like soda, chlorine, etc. were set up. Besides this fast rate of growth there had been adverse affect on the industrial economy due to certain forces active in this period. Industrial development during this period did not take care of important factors such as location, scale of operation, centers of marketing, availability of raw materials etc. The regional imbalances was also not taken into consideration. The monopolistic conditions were created and powerful industrialists created big industrial houses which were able to control the prices of the products.

After Independence

Soon after independence the country assumed the role of total development. Our country is a classical example of developing country with all the problems of underdeveloped country. To meet the human aspiration of its masses the national goals and objectives were established to channelise the human, money and material resources.

The country's vast population of 850 million people the disparities between rich and poor, regional imbalances were the major problems of the country. Beside these the other problems which the country faced at that time were :

— Acute poverty removal
— Attainment of self reliance
— Expansion of employment opportunity for the people
— Removal of imbalances
— Development of professional skill in the country
— Reduction of foreign aid
— Wider public ownership to break down the concentration of economic power in a few hands.

The national goals were obviously the out flow of the range of problems which the country was facing. The achievement of the national objectives call for massive investment in education, transport, communication network, agricultural development, animal husbandry; and industrial development. This involved a three stage action programme.

The first stage was the direct activity of the government, both Central and State. These Government activities included the development of education, agricultural development, animal husbandry programmes, the construction of roads and bridges, major irrigation schemes, tribal and backward class welfare.

The second stage was the Indian private sector. It was evident that the private enterprise would made its investments solely on the basis of market estimations and profitability calculations. Such investments, of market estimations and profitability calculations. Such investments, therefore do not necessarily coincide with the prime national objectives. To ensure that the development and expansion of the private sector does not deviate from the National Goals to these goals, a system of Licensing and control to provide the directional impetus was introduced. The control can be brought through the following :

(*a*) Import controls which are intended to provide protection and shelter for the development of industry and to conserve foreign exchange;

(*b*) A system of industrial licensing under which investments exceeding Rs. 10 million are required to be formally licensed. The licensing procedures enable the government to channelise private investments in the desired directions and also ensure that there is neither over capacity or under capacity and that the investments are related to the availability of infrastructural inputs and;

(*c*) To prevent the concentration of economic power in the hands of a few individuals. To carry out this the Monopolies and Restrictive Trade Practices Act was introduced. The enactments of this sort are now fairly common even in countries having free enterprise system. In a country which is moving towards a socialist pattern of society, the need to curb the concentration of power in the hands of a few individuals in of utmost concern.

The third stage of activity was the growth and development of public enterprises. In its wider sense, public enterprises cover all the fields of infractural financial, industrial and commercial activity in which the government operates as an investor and enterpreneur. The public sector in India covers three broad areas :

(*a*) The departmental undertaking of the Central Government which include the massive railway system, the Post and Telegraph network and the network of Ordinance Factories producing defense equipments.

(*b*) The State Government Public Sector Enterprises which includes substantial investments in power generation and distribution, passenger road transport, agro-industries and local industries.

(*c*) The Central Public Sector Enterprise which cover a west area of industrial, commercial and trading activity.

It is the last group of activities which forms the hard core of public sector development in the country. It is this group of companies, today numbering 153 which comes within the purview of the Bureau of Public Enterprises and whose performance and activities are guided by the Parliamentary Committee on Public undertaking.

To analyse the hard core of the Indian public sector, its genesis and policy framework, its objectives its growth and development, its organisational and managerial problems, appraisal of its performance and the overall role which it has acquired.

The Policy Frame of Public Enterprise

Before independence which India achieved in 1947, the British colonial rulers had taken the first step towards creation of public enterprise in this country. The oldest public enterprise the Post and Telegraph system run by the government. The network of the Indian railways which was previously run by private companies were nationalised in the early and mid twenties of the present century. The All India Radio was created as a national undertaking in the Thirties. A group of departmental undertakings was set up for the manufacture of defence equipment described as the Ordnance Factories of India. As early as 1920 the Coal Fields Committee appointed by the then government of India recommended the State intervention in the business of cool mining. The observations of the committee made over 50 years ago, speak for themselves. "Coke is a national asset on which the manufacturing industries and the commercial expansion of the country depend. The State has the right, in the interests of the community, to step in the prevent the dissipation of the country's resources. Indian coal is not inexhaustible and scientific mining methods are needed for its conservation and economic extraction."

A large number of public sector industries from the generation of electric power to the production of steel were set up. Mysore Government earned for itself the name of progressive and modern State--its progress and modernity essentially reflected in the growth of public enterprises. In the two other States of the country, the ersthwile State of Hyderabad and Travancore Cochin, there were also a few State Undertakings set up by the State Governments the rest of the industrial economy, such as it was, at the time of Independence was in the hands of private enterprise. This included mainly the cotton textile industry, the jute industry, the agro based plantation industries of tea and coffee, and leather based industry and footwear manufacture. The policy framework for the growth of this public sector was specifically and categorically declared by the Government of India in the shape of two industrial Resolutions, the first one in 1948 and the second in 1956.

The Industrial Policy Resolution of 1948

The Industrial Policy Resolution of 1948 called for a dynamic national policy directed "to a continuous increase in production by all possible means, side by side with measures to secure its equitable distribution". For implementing that policy, the Resolution stressed the need for "the State to play a progressively active role in the development of industries". The resolution believed that development is possible when the State could contribute more quickly to increase national wealth by expanding its present activities where it is already operating and by concentrating on new units of production in other fields, rather than on acquiring and running existing units. It was, however indicated that "meanwhile, private enterprise properly directed and regulated, has a valuable role to play." The public and private sectors were thus given complementary roles in promoting industrial development. The manufacture of arms and ammunition, the production and control of atomic energy and the ownership and management or railways were to be the exclusive monopoly of the Central Government. Responsibility for setting up new undertakings was reserved to the state in the following six areas :

1. Coal.
2. Iron and Steel.
3. Aircraft manufacture.
4. Ship building.
5. Mineral Oils.
6. Manufacture of telephone, telegraph and wireless apparatus (excluding radio receiving sets).

The Industrial Policy Resolution of 1956

The need for further amplification of this policy and for extending the scope and coverage of the public sector arose due to subsequent development in the political and economic spheres. The Directive Principles of the State Policy enshrined in the Constitution adopted in January, 1950 very specifically indicated the socio-economic goals towards which the efforts of the State were to be oriented. In the light of these principles, planning for economic development assumed of these importance. A National Planning Commission was set up in March, 1950 and the nation's First Five Year Plan was finalised in 1950. While the first Plan was under implementation, the pursuit of a socialist pattern of society was accepted by Parliament as the principal objective of social and economic policy. With the completion of the First Five Year Plan, it became clear that there was urgent need for accelerating the pace of economic development through the expansion of heavy industries. Taking these changes and needs into account, the Government reformulated their industrial policy in April, 1956.

The Resolution of 1956 declared that "The adoption of the socialist pattern of society as the national objective, as well as the need for planned and rapid development, require that all industries of basic and strategic importance or in the nature of public utility services, should be in the public sector. Other industries which are essential and require investment on a scale which only the State in the present circumstances could provide have also to be in the public sector. The State has, therefore to assume direct responsibility for the future development of which was to be the exclusive responsibility of the State :

1. Arms and ammunition and allied items of defence equipment.
2. Atomic energy.
3. Iron and Steel.
4. Heavy castings and forgings of iron and steel.
5. Heavy castings and machinery required for iron and steel production for mining for machine tool manufacture and for such other basic industries as may be specified by the Central Government.
6. Heavy eletrical plant including large hydraulic and steam turbines.
7. Coal and lignite.
8. Mineral oils.
9. Mining of iron ore, manganese ore, chrome ore, gypsum, sulphur, gold and diamond.
10. Mining and processing of copper, lead, zinc tin and wolfram.
11. Minerals specified in the schedule to the Atomic Energy (Control of production and use) order 1953.
12. Aircraft.
13. Air transport.
14. Railway transport.
15. Ship-building.
16. Telephones and telephone cables telegraphy and wireless apparatus (excluding radio receiving sets).
17. Generation and distribution of electricity.

Schedule 'B' industries, which would be progressively state owned and in which the State would, therefore, generally take the initiative in establishing new undertakings, but in which, private enterprise would also be expected to supplement the effort of the State :

(*a*) All other minerals except minerals as defined in Section 3 of the Minerals Concession Rules, 1949.
(*b*) Aluminium and other non ferrous metals not included in Schedule 'A'.
(*c*) Machine Tools.
(*d*) Ferro alloys and tool steels.
(*e*) Basic and intermediate products required by chemical industries such as the manufacture of drugs, dyestuffs and plastics.

(*f*) Antibiotics and other essential drugs.
(*g*) Fertilizers.
(*h*) Synthetic rubber.
(*i*) Carbonisation of coal.
(*j*) Chemical pulp.
(*k*) Road transport.
(*l*) Sea transport.

All the remaining industries and their future development were generally left to the initiative and enterprise of the private sector.

The Resolution made it clear that the division of industries into separate categories does not simply that they are being placed in water-tight compartments. Inevitably, there will not only be an area of overlapping but also a great but of deviation between industries in the private and public sectors.

15

Business Strategy and Strategic Thinking

All companies have some form of formal planning procedure embedded in their management direction and control systems. These seemed to serve certain essential functions; in a decision-making sense, they :

1. *Formalized and calibrated strategic decisions already made.*
2. *Provided a systematic means for evaluating and fine-tuning annual budgets.*
3. *Formed a basis for protecting longer term investments and commitments that might otherwise have been driven out by budgetary pressures*
4. *Helped implement strategic changes once decided on* (for example, coordinating all elements of Exxon's decision to change its corporate name).

All these were important functions; however, formal planning systems rarely formulated a corporation's central strategy. Perhaps the most important contributions of formal corporate planning systems were in the "process" remain and include :

1. *a **network** of information that may not otherwise have been available.*
2. *periodically force operating managers to extend their time horizons and see their work in a **large framework.***
3. *require rigorous **communications about goals,** strategic issues, and resource allocations.*
4. *systematically **managers about the future** so they can better intitively calibrate their short-term or interim decisions.*
5. *often create an **attitude about** and a comfort factor concerning **the future**; that is, managers felt less uncertain about the future and consequently were more willing to make commitments that extended **beyond short-time horizons.***
6. *stimulate **longer term "special studies"** that could have high impact at key junctures for specific strategic decisions.*

In fact, in the companies observed, formal planning contributed most directly to significant change when it was set up as a "special study" on some important aspect of corporate strategy. It is difficult to describe what a real Business Strategy is. But it is always possible to define minimum conditions for getting a real business strategy which are given as under :

1. *To achieve profitable growth over an agreed time scale. The profit capsule which even in the best organised manufacturing based business, is unlikely to be much bigger than 15% on a CCA basis,* requires a very costly rocket propulsion unit to get it off the ground.

2. The *payload* for the rocket (which either makes the profit or the loss) has to be some kind of *portfolio of products* (or services). It follows, therefore, that *the first minimum condition is to have a coherent product portfolio which is actually managed* (not just allowed to emerge, or the accidental outcrop of a manufacturing capability). So you *have* to have *Product Portfolio Strategy* or *there is no way in which you can achieve a real Business Strategy.*

3. But you cannot have a *strategy* for a product portfolio without a *Market Strategy* which reasonably pin-points the *market*, its particular *segments* or its *geographic markets towards* which you propose to launch your portfolio and *for* which you need to design the products. So a *Market Strategy is a second minimum condition (though chronologically it comes first).*

4. And if, out of a *Market Strategy,* you design a coherent *Product Portfolio* Strategy, it's still no good without a means of delivering it physically to the chosen segments, markets, clients etc. and having someone to tell them the portfolio exists. So a *Sales / Distribution Strategy is the third minimum condition. It is more than crude "sales representation" - and involves coherent presentation of the whole chosen package of product / performance / delivery / technical / liaison servicing and price.*

5. But the rocket is still no good unless the Product Portfolio can actually be made or acquired. S *a Sourcing or Manufacturing Strategy is the fourth minimum condition of achieving a real Business Strategy.*

6. Yet if you have all four, and pile them one on the other, the rocket will *still* fall over on the launching pad unless the strategic components are firmly connected together. So the *strategies,* even if you have them, still only add up to (hopefully) the correct *flight plan. You need a crew (the Business Team) and mission control to manage the linkages, jettison the rocket modules at the right attitude, and make mid-flight corrections. That's you — and the way you do it (which is impossible if you don't even have the flight plan — or 4 strategies above) is the fifth but most crucial minimum condition. Unlike most strategy models, this one also has you in it.*

There are at least a components of these internal Management Linkages — bolting the Sourcing / Manufacturing Strategy to the Sales / Distribution Strategy; the latter to the Market Strategy; the Market Strategy to the Product Portfolio Strategy; and the Product Portfolio Payload to the Profit (or Loss) Capsule on top — and *all* them to each other.

So — with the *strategy* components and the *managerial* linkage components — we were *nine* crucial elements to fit together for successful blast-off :

Strategic Decision Behaviour

Strategic decision behaviour is the behaviour which is clustered around a specific decision. It is a language used by the Managers to talk about decision making using (*a*) politics (*b*) failure to learn/repeating mistake (*c*) reacting (*d*) risk/uncertainty/ambiguity/complexity. Decision behaviour is greater than decision plus behaviour process and context orientation. Strategic decisions involve finding out what the situation is, what are the resources and what managers should do with the resources. A manager is in fact concerned with these types of decisions and higher his level the more of these decisions are required to make. The strategy is basically a deliberate, general and intergrative plan. Strategy is a design to enable an organisation to reach its objective through the allocation and deployment of resources, beside, intelligence opposition found in the environment.

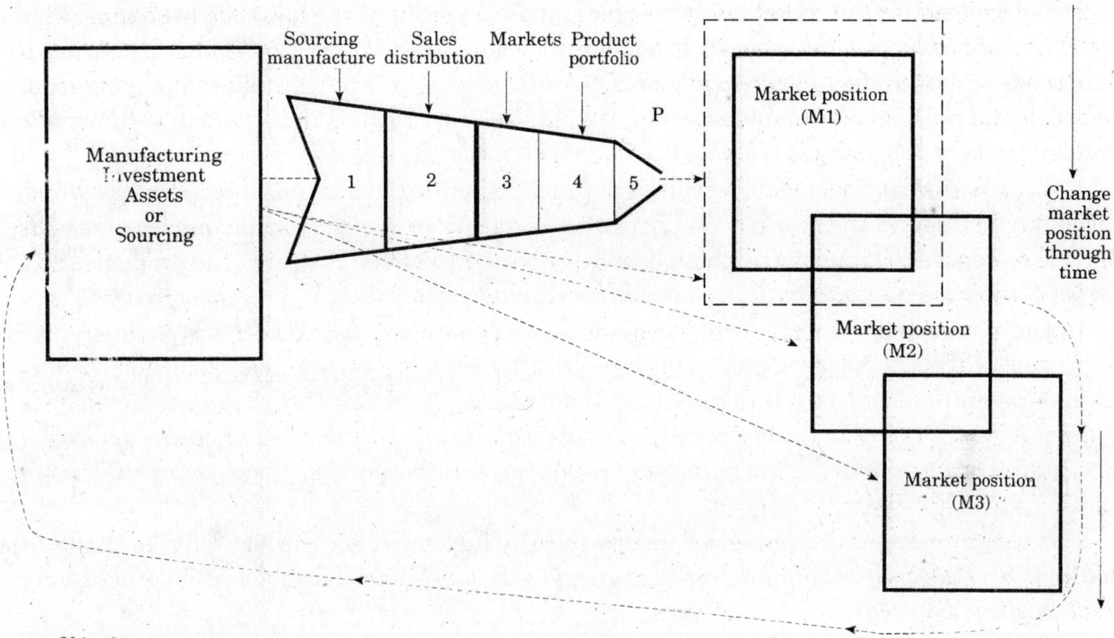

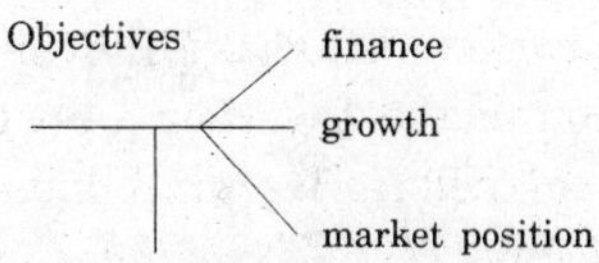

Business strategy

- manufacturing / sourcing strategy — 1
- sales / distribution strategy — 2
- markets strategy — 3
- product portfolio strategy — 4
- profits — 5

Characteristics of Strategic Decisions

(*a*) **Scale.** Relative to resources; Relative to market.

(*b*) **The Horizon.** Futurity; Consequences (multi business, multi functional)

(*c*) **External Environment.** Customers, Competitors, Political, Social, Legal.

(*d*) **Complexity.** Novelty, Uncertainty, Integration/Co-ordination.

A Practical Approach To Strategic Planning

A practical approach to strategic planning is given in Fig. 15.2. Strategic planning starts with the objective. The strategic formulative methodology must start with an objective and finish with some statement of strategies. Before an executive go for a strategy, he must force himself into options strategies that is to look out oneself to following three potential options :

(*i*) **External analysis.** Potential market, inflation, government policies, alternative potential, potential competitors.

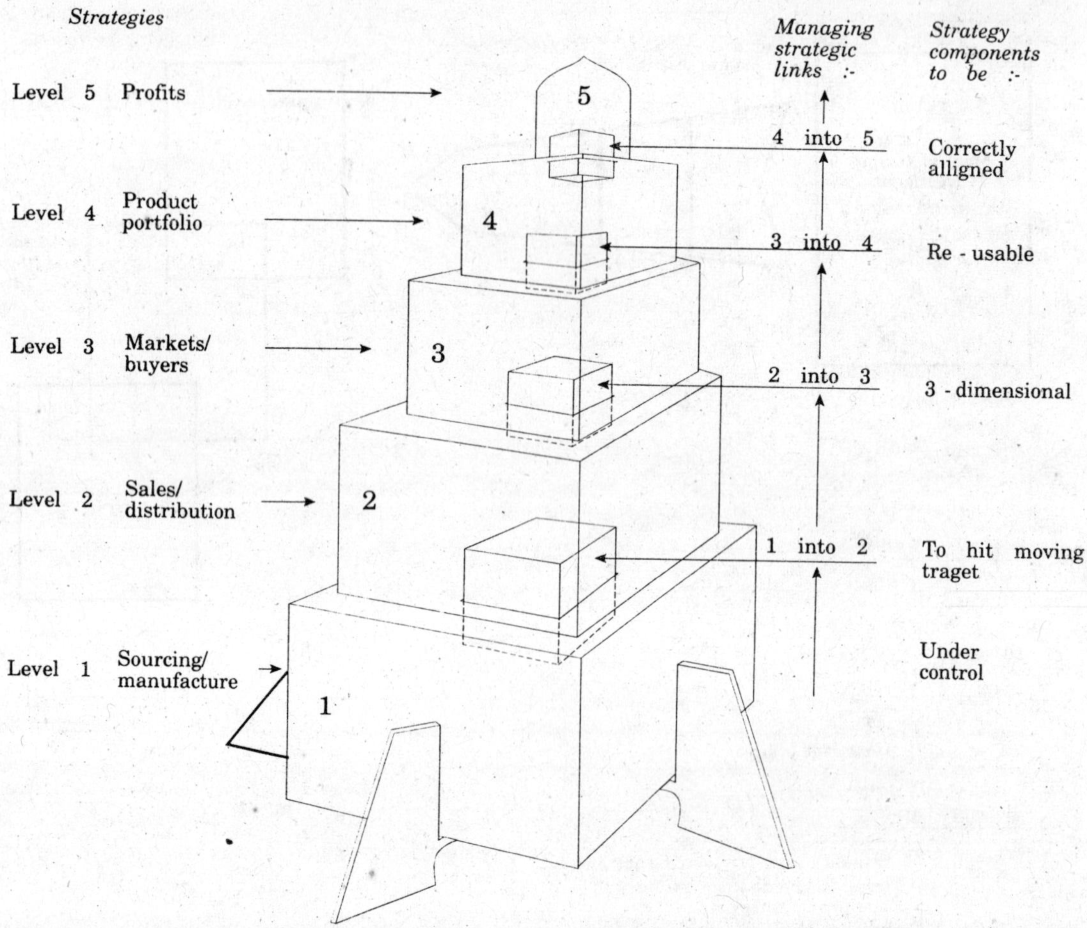

Finding and managing a business strategy.

(*ii*) **Internal analysis.** What are the resources ? What do we have ? What are our strengths and weaknesses ? Our position in technology, and in market.

(*iii*) **Resource analysis.** Skill, Capacity, Money resources.

Various studies on strategic planning approach revealed the following steps involved in strategic planning. Process methodology; Avoiding semantic confusion; Strategies as decision Rules; Opening strategic options; Analytical Components; Strategy and structure; Simplification and criteria of relevance and dynamics. An executive has to ensure so as to choose his strategies so that all strategies work. Executive should not concentrate on structure until as he has decided the strategies. The various strategic check list are shown in Fig. 15.3. Similarly figure 15.6 indicates the conceptual framework of Strategy Formulation and Strategic objectives Achieved. This gives us an idea regarding interdependent parameters such as organisation Structure; Management Process; Culture and Human Resource. The tactical decision on the

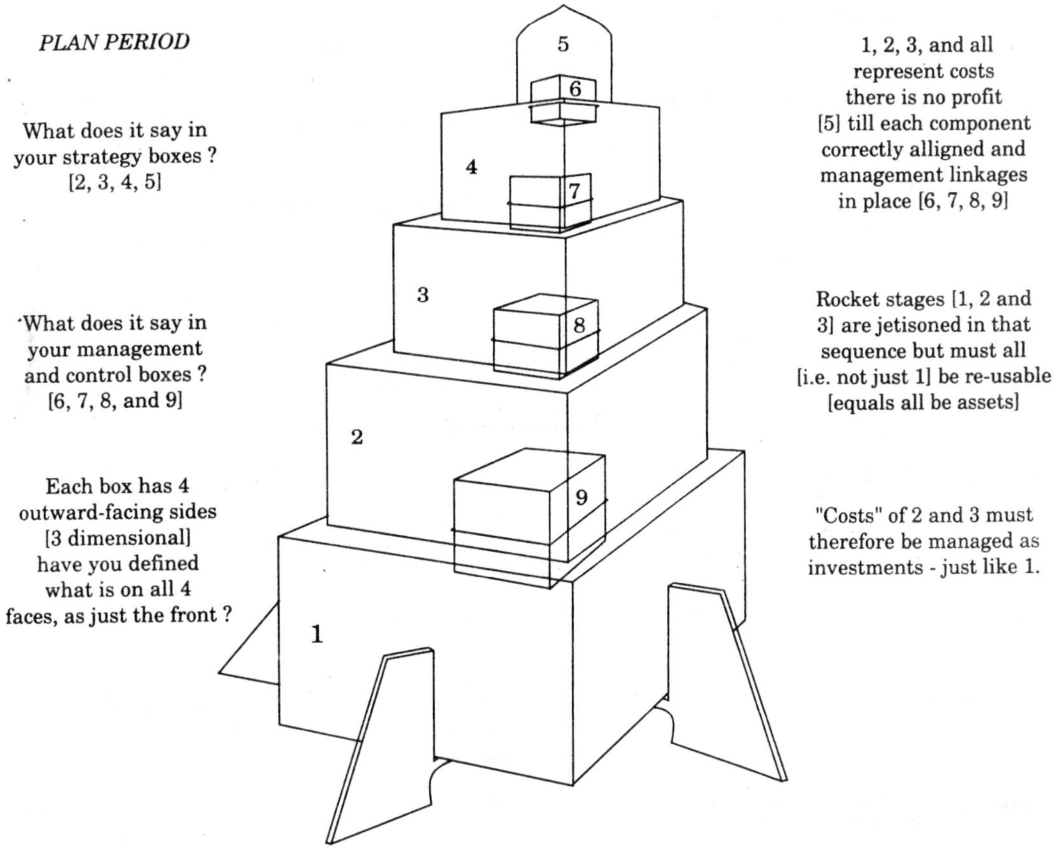

How to check whether you have a Business Strategy

other hand are routine decision. These are the decisions which an executive makes over and over again following the established rules, policies and procedure. These decisions do not require collecting new data nor it requires conferring with the people nor passing judgement. The strategic versus tactical decisions are given in Table 15.1. Similarly number of principle decisions in any organisation are given in Table 15.2. The principle deciding are classified decisions in the organisation hierarchy with its forces on context of decisions.

Table 15.1

	Strategic	*Tactical*
1. Importance	Great	Less
2. Level	Top level	Product/functional/operating
3. Time Horizons	Long horizons	Short duration
4. Regulatory	Continuous/irregular (continuous monitoring)	Periodic/link to budgeting cycle)
5. Nature of problems	Unstructured unique with uncertainty and risk : wide range of alternatives	More structured (Bonded and repetitive)
6. Information needed	Large amounts of external information on future	More internally generated and market research
7. Detail	Broad statements/Subjective judgements	More specific detailed information
8. Ease of evaluation	Hard (Proof in the future and difficult to disentangle)	Quickly evident more easily related to decision.

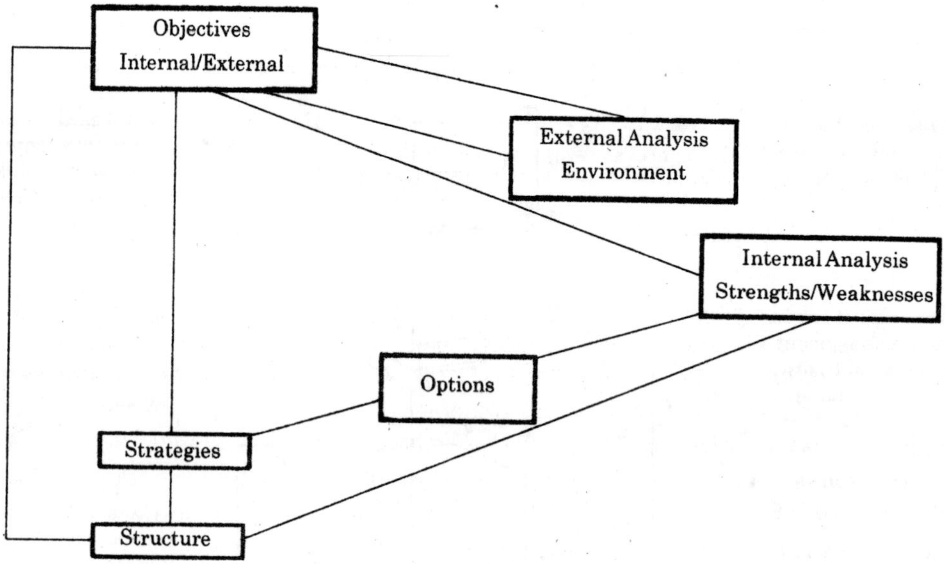

Fig. 15.1. Process of Strategy Development

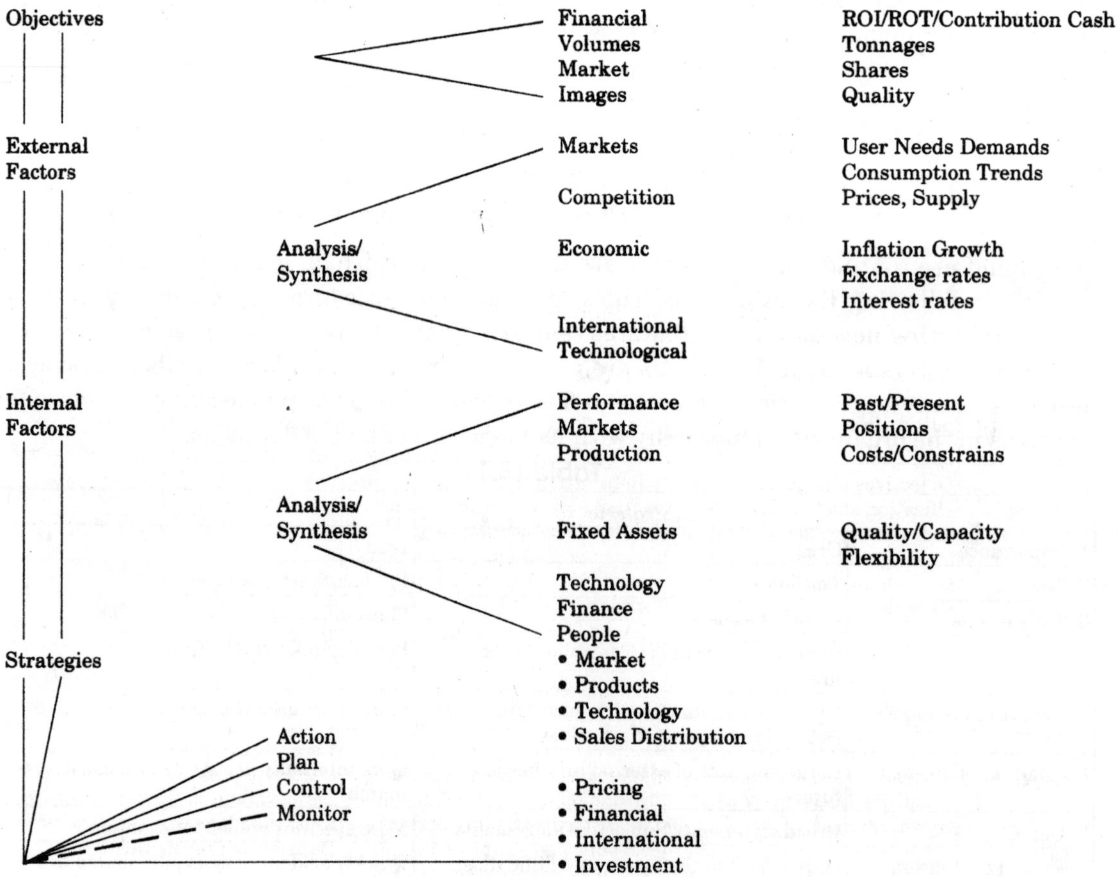

Fig. 15.2. Strategy Check-list

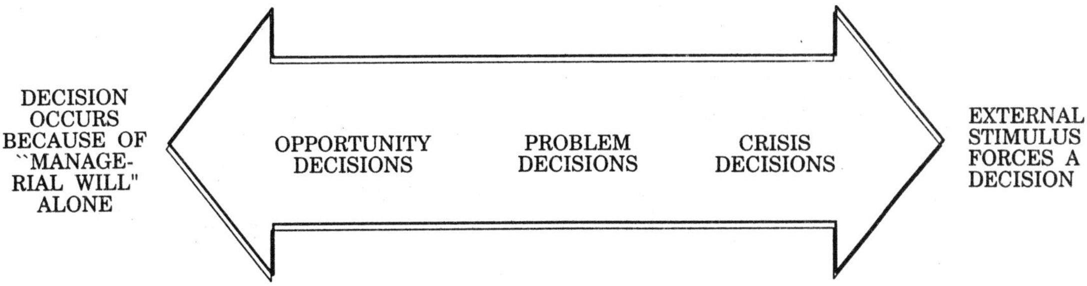

Fig. 15.3. The Decision Stimulus Adapted from Mintzberg. II, Raisinghani D and Thereat A, "The Structure of Unstructured Decision Processes"

Decision making lies deeply embedded in the process of Management. Decision making spreads over all at the managerial functions and cover all areas of the enterprise. Management and decision making go side by side whether knowing or unknowingly. Managers continue making decisions in their day-to-day life. The principles of decisions making requires that the task of decision making should be pushed down as far as possible in organisational hierarchy. The outstanding characteristics of a successful manager is his ability to make effective decision. Decision making is selection from among various alternative and it is of the core of planning. Decision making is a matter of planning, organisational objectives and methods that will be used to achieve. In fact, management is a always a decision making process, the decision occurs because of the managerial will alone. Similarly external stimulus forces a decision making process. Fig. 15.4 shows how decision stimulus affect the structure of unstructured decision process.

Table 15.2 Principal Decisions

Classified decision and its focus on the content of decision

	Strategic	*Administrative*	*Operating*
Problem	To select product-market mix which optimises firm's Return Investment Potential.	To structure firm's resources for optimum performance.	To optimize realization or Return on Investment Potential.
Nature of problem	Allocation of total resources among product-market opportunities.	Organisation acquisition and development of resources.	Budgeting of resources among principal functional areas. Scheduling resource application and conversion. Monitoring and control.
Key decisions	Objectives and goals Diversification strategy Expansion strategy Administrative strategy Finance strategy Growth method Timing of Growth.	Organisation : structure of information authority and responsibility flows. Structure of resource concession : work flows distribution system facilities location.	Operating objectives and goals
		Resource acquisition and development; financing facilities and equipment personnel raw materials.	Marketing policies and strategy control.
Key Characteristics	Decisions centralized Partial ignorance Decisions non-repetitive Decisions of self-regenerative.	Conflict between strategy and operations : Conflict between individual and institutional objectives. Strong coupling between economic and social variables Decisions triggered by strategic and/or operating problems.	Decentralized decisions. Risk and uncertainty. Repetitive decision Large volume of decisions Sub-optimization forced by complexity Decision self regenerative

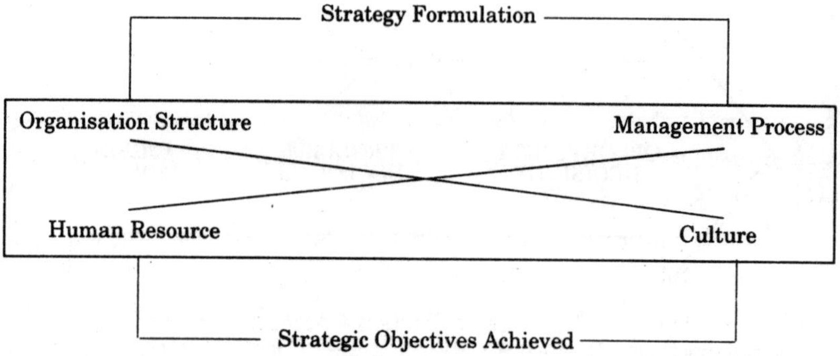

Fig. 15.4.

Impact of Strategies

In order to understand the impact of strategies, it is better to study how a new product is developed and introduced in the market. There are three routes to company growth *viz.* (*a*) growing sales of existing products (*b*) acquiring sales of other companies and (*c*) develop sales of new products. A new product is a new brand name and separate product line. The range of business development can be classified as follows :

1. Relaunch—Existing product/brand.
2. Line extension—existing product/brand.
3. New product/brand.

Various key issue of new product development are as follows :

(*i*) Strategy and objectives (*ii*) Innovation
(*iii*) Step by step programme (*iv*) Organisation
(*v*) Resources (*vi*) Commercialisation
(*vii*) Evaluation of Programme.

(*i*) **Strategy and Objectives.** Most of the company do not have a clear strategy. Similarly most of the people confuse objective and strategy. The determination of basic long term goals and objectives of an organisation is the adoption of important course of action.

(*ii*) **Innovation.** These should be an atompsphere for generating innovative ideas within the organisation. There are lost of senior executives who kill the innovative attitude of subordinates by knowingly/unknowingly using killer phrases as given under :

Killer phrases

(*i*) A good ideas but ..... (*ii*) Against company policy
(*iii*) All right in theory (*iv*) Be practical
(*v*) Don't start anything yet (*vi*) It needs more study
(*vii*) Who else has tried *i.e.* we have done it that way, let us discuss it.

(*iii*) **Step by step programme.** Establish a sequential system of new product development which take into account the objectives of the programme. Adequate screening programmes and procedure.

Strategies of product development

- New product strategy development
- Idea generation
- Screening and evaluation
- Business analysis

- Development
- Testing
- Commercialisation

(*iv*) **Organisation.** Organize the lost method of organising for new product development.

(*v*) **Resources.** Determine the level and type of resources one will need to execute one's new product programme. The basic business actions are :

1. Most existing business is over resourced.
2. Most new product development is under resourced.

Test Marketing. Ensure that test marketing is essential and that it is designed to measure the objectives you have established for.

Evaluation. Evaluate the proposals of new product development programmes and procedures.

The Development Dilema. New products are both costly and difficult. New products are essential to the long term survival.

The following tables indicate the various Products Launched during the last 5 years (1980-85); The business Growth from 1950's to 1980 and the range of Strategic Alternatives.

The studies have revealed that the various companies can be classified in the following categories :

(*i*) Single business companies

(*ii*) Dominant companies—Nearly 70 to 95% of the single business companies became Dominant Companies.

(*iii*) Related Companies—No single business companies exceed 70% of the sales of related companies and also no single business companies have similar market, distribution systems, production technology and scientific based research.

Related companies are electrons companies with similar production technology and same Distribution Systems with increasing markets. Unrelated.

Strategic Thinking

Competitiveness is born in the gap between company's resources and manager's goals. The essence of strategy formulation is coping with competition. In the fight for market share, competition is not manifested only in other players. Competition in an industry is rooted in its underlying economics and competitive forces. Customers, suppliers, potential entrants, and substitute products are all competitors that may be more or less prominent or active depending on the industry. The collective strength of these forces determines the ultimate profit potential of an industry.

Every industry has an underlying structure or a set of fundamental economic and technical characteristics that gives rise to competitive forces. The strategist, wanting to position one's company to cope best with its industry environment or to influence that environment in the company's favour must learn what makes the environment tich. Awareness of these forces can help a company stake out a position in its industry that is less vulnerable to attack. The balance of forces is partly a result of external factors and partly in company's control.

The corporate strategist need to assess the forces affecting competition in the industry and also identify the underlying causes. The strengths and weaknesses must be assessed from a strategic stand point. The corporate strategist can devise a plan of action that may include the following:

(*i*) Positioning the company so that its capabilities provide the best defense against the competitive force.

(*ii*) Influencing the balance of forces through strategic moves thereby improving the company's position.

(*iii*) Anticipating shifts in the factors underlying the forces and responding to them, with the hope of exploiting change by choosing a strategy appropriate for the competitive balance.

Corporate managers have directed a great deal of attention to defining business as a crucial step in strategic formulation.

The key to growth - even survival - is to stake out a position that is less vulnerable to attack from head-to-head opponents, whether established or new and less vulnerable to erosition from the direction of buyers, suppliers, and substitute goods. Establishing such a position can take many forms-solidifying relationships with favorable customer, differentiating the producing either substantively or psychologically through marketing, integrating forward or backward, establishing technological leadership.

Strategic Thinking

Strategic thinking involves both thinking and seeing into the future ; The strategic thinkers are called as "Visionaries". The strategic thinking is not strategic planning nor it is purely cerebral and purely thinking. To capturing strategic thinking involves that a company must have a picture of itself in the future. Strategic thinking means seeing the future strategically. Some of the concepts of Strategic Thinking are discussed as under.

1. Strategic thinking precedes strategic analysis.
2. It involves thinking creatively about the nature of the future the firm would like to face.
3. Though prediction may play some part here, it is only a residual part.
4. The best tool for strategic thinking is the awareness that it is necessary.

What *is* thinking strategically ?

1. Thinking strategically means seeing the future strategically
2. Understanding the past without being rooted in it
3. Not extrapolating but foreseeing discontinuities
4. Not relying on techniques but on informed creative institution

Seeing from above while digging in the dirt

Why do people speak of helicopter vision ?

A helicopter is an answer—don't trust answers

If you fight from helicopters, your foes will go underground

Strategic thinking may be likened to finding the diamond in the rough—the kernel of an idea

The problem

1. As managers we are trained to act...

2. In order to act, we need a plan
3. Plans require information :
   (*a*) About past performance
   (*b*) Trends...
4. Most of all they need
   (*a*) An idea, a vision, intent or whatever

They need the *thought*

Focus

Focus can improve a company's quality perception :

1. **The specialist effect** — Who you gonna call...?
2. **The leadership effect** — All those people can't be wrong
3. **The price effect** — Sometimes lower can be worse
4. **The name effect** — Adolf who ?

Points to ponder by chief . Executive Officers

1. The CEO has a disproportionate responsibility for strategic thought
2. Retreats are good, but you have to come back
3. Don't fight yesterday's battles
4. There are no answers to tomorrow
5. Strategic thought is the most important activity for which we receive no training

Driving Force

What driving force does your organization possess?

1. Searching for a reason to exist
2. Products
3. Your customers
4. Distribution-method driven
5. Capacity driven
6. Markest type
7. Natural resource driven
8. Technology driven

Questions about driving forces

1. Can a company have several driving forces ?
2. Isn't profit the only driving force ?
3. Shouldn't every company be customer driven ?
4. Aren't there reasons when you might want to change your strategic driving force ?

A model of the strategic thinking process

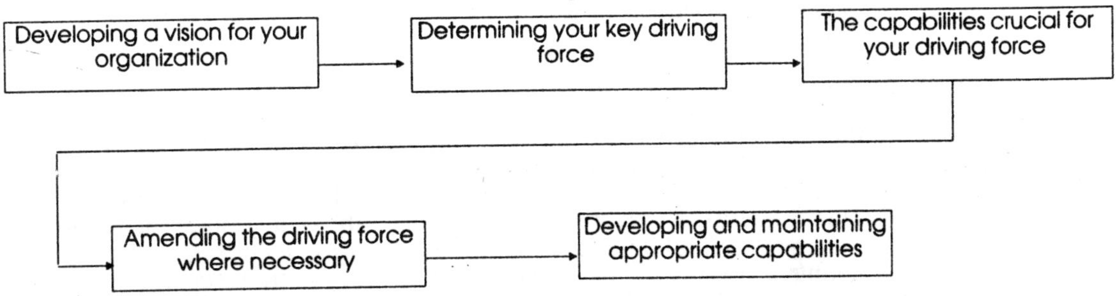

16

Organisational Planning

Definition

According to Peter Drucker, "Planning deals with what has to be done today to be ready for tomorrow." Perhaps there is no need for planning if the future is reasonably known to us. It is not the present decision by futurity of all such decisions that should be the primary concern of an effective executive. The executive involved in LRP exercise, should have the ability and willingness to take decisions. Long range planning involves establishing long range goals, working out strategies and policies to achieve these goals.

It is a management technique that co-ordinates all the people, functions and facilities of a company to develop and achieve the desired long range goals on a scientific basis. It helps to determine how to take advantage of the trends, how to minimize the negative effects of these trends which are unfavourable.

Once Abraham Lincoln was asked how long a man's legs ought to be, he replied enough to reach the greatness. The length of planning varies considerably from company to company. The time span of plan should cover, along with other things, the financial commitments, higher pay off etc.

Effective plans are more flexible to be adopted according to changing conditions to the organisation. Planning in general is the conscious determination of a course of action to achieve the preconceived objectives. Planning is the design of desired future and the effective ways of bringing it about. Better planning is the most talked about subject in business today. It is indispensible because of (1) Rapid growth, (2) New dimensions in size, (3) Intensification of competition and (4) increasing complexities and problems faced by industry. Planning pre-supposes a willingness to spend time, energy and money in the present for the results which will be realised in the future. These benefits are not assured but can only be anticipated on the basis of prior experiences. The reason for planning is not compulsion but opportunity. Planning system is best when it is broad based and includes not only plans.

Problems to Planning

Managers aim at achieving their objective through planning effort, but planning efforts usually encounter the following problems.

	Internal
1. Inflexibility	Policy and procedural inflexibility, External inflexibility, Capital inflexibility

2. Political climate
3. Organisational labour
4. Rapid change
5. Time and expense
6. Difficulty of accurate premising
7. Lack of flexibility

The awareness of planning problems can help us in overcoming frustrations and inefficiencies of planning.

Thus progressive planning requires an environment of change where some degree of freedom and willingness to assume the risks. Every manager should establish a climate for planning. This involves setting of goals, establishing significant planning premises, involving all managers in the planning process reviewing sub-plans and their performance, assuring appropriate staff assistance and information. So planning need to be forced at various levels of management and it just do not take place at its own.

Managing Plans

Plans are the foundation of management because the success and failure of a manager depends to a considerable extent upon his abilities to plan. (Refer Fig. 16.1).

Plans can not be executed but rather plans need to be managed. The managing of plans again require planning, organisation, directing and controlling. A good manager should plan his activities and should be aware of tools of planning and factors influencing planning. Thus a manager should plan with a view of planning process as shown in the figure.

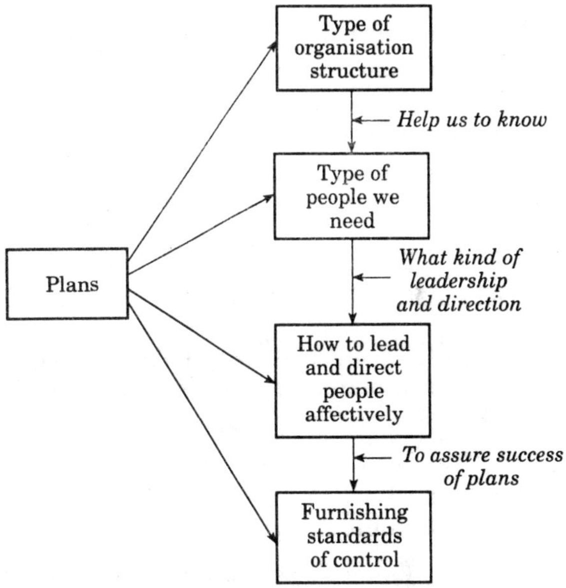

Fig. 16.1

Planning at Different Levels of Organisation

Management at all levels are involved in planning but managers higher levels in the organisation probably spend more of their time and efforts in planning than middle or lower level managers, the lower level managers tend to drive their plans from the plans of higher level managers. The General managers may spend majority of his planning activities on broad company objectives that are expected to be achieved in future.

The supervisor on the other hand is more concerned with immediate objectives of planning such as monthly production quota, immediate repair of machine etc.

Types of Plans: Plans can be classified as : (1) Standing plans, (2) Single use plans, (3) Strategic plans, (4) Administrative plans.

1. Standing Plans. These are the plans which are used again and again, these are repetitive in nature. Standing plans lead to the development of policies, procedures and rules. The single use plans produce programmes, projects and budgets.

(*a*) *Policies*— Policies are the statements that guide decision maker. It is the boundary within which decisions can be made. The first step is always the establishment of goals by the top management, and then various methods to achieve these goals are determined. Rules are specific statements of what should or should not be done.

(*b*) *Procedures*— It provides a more specific guide to action than a policy. A procedure should spell out series of steps should be taken while conducting an operation.

(*c*) *Rules*— There are the specific statements of what may or may not be done. The development and communication of rules are very important. Thus, as we move from policies procedures-rules, the limits become smaller and smaller.

Single Use Plans. The single purpose plans are used to accomplish the specific objectives of shorter duration. The examples of single purpose plans are :

1. Budgets. 2. Programmes. 3. Projects.

Budgets- The forecasting is the basis for establishing single use operating plans or budgets. The overall budget includes the following components.

1. Sales Budget 2. Advertising Budget 3. Production Budget
4. Raw Material Budget. 5. Personnel Budget 6. Cash Budget.
7. Profit Budget.

These budgets must be co-ordinated to integrate the organisational efforts.

Programmes and Projects. These are developed under the umbrella of organisational goals. A few examples of these programmes are expansion programmes, training programmes, management development programmes etc.

Strategic Plans

It is concerned with plans which are of vital importance to the organisation such as planning firm's product line. The strategic planning is indeed quite complicated in highly technical and complex organisations. The importance of strategic plans increases four fold when economic, technological and social environmental factors are fast changing. The strategic planning and organisational development are vital importance.

Administrative Plans

These are concerned with how a firm should optimise the use of its resources with in strategic objectives. Administrative plans are concerned with factors, with in the control of the organisation. Administrative planning is less subjective than strategic planning. A number of techniques are used in administrative planning such as PERT, CPM, Gantt-charts, Bar charts etc.

LONG RANGE PLANNING

The specific methodology of planning may vary from one company to another. However the important step which must be followed for drawings a successful plan is the planning to plan. We know that planning does not just happen, it must be planned. A suitable planning climate must be established and the organisation should be made planning conscious. Policy decisions must be made about who will do what planning, and step by step procedure must be worked out. On the other hand care should be taken to avoid overdoing this step. The standards must be determined to guide the planning programme otherwise there will be lack of co-ordination, unnecessary emphasis on less-important subjects, excessive planning cost, and confusion in drawings etc.

Characteristics of Long Range Planning

1. Plans should be directed toward the well defined objectives ; 2. Plans made by specialist should be co-ordinated and communicated in the organisation ; 3. Planning is a pre-requisite to the direct functions of the manager ; 4. Adoption of plans to current actions demands continual reshaping of plans and 5. Planning pervades the hierarchy of an organisation.

Long Range Planning. "Concept of planning means that the programme cannot be the brain child of only one man. In the first place, individual cannot possibly know enough. If the burden of long range planning is carried out by one man he will not be having the detailed knowledge of all the functions and it will cause failure in long range planning. Therefore one should consider: 1. Work should be directed by some one who is more or less in continuous contact with the different managers, 2. Long range planning should be confidential as its contents may be worth many hundreds or thousands of rupees to the competitors and therefore should be entrusted to only responsible and dedicated executives, 3. The planning head needs a particular kind of temperament. He should be the one who is not afraid of saying that this is right and that is wrong, 4. Long range planning presupposes a set of long range objectives. Long range planning should also have some basis of measuring the results through an effective management information and control system and 5. Long range planning should be both top down and down top, thus involving in the process all the people and assuming thereby the advantages from both the approaches.

It is to be emphasised that long range planning is essentially a Strategic Planning. Management control system relates to more or less a routing system to take care of decision making problems. Strategic planning on the other hand deals with a specific non-routine type of problems under a complete set of variables in order to take advantages of opportunity through forward planning. Long range planning system should have all the features of a strategic planning.

Planning Issues. The SOLD analysis is useful in developing some planning issues which in turn form the basis of a long range plan.

S = What are the strengths in present conditions ?
O = What are the opportunities in future ?
L = What are the limitations in the present conditions ?
D = What are the dangers likely to arise in future ?

The planning issues, relating to various departments of the organisation should be centralised in the planning department which will ensure solving of problems obtained from other departments. All planning issues may be further considered by top management by calling a meeting. The committee should be able to answer a clear outline of the following long term objectives :—

1. What we are ?
2. What we want to be ?

3. How we are to be there ?
4. What are our strengths and weaknesses ?
5. What are our limitations and how they are to be overcome ?
6. What are the future opportunities before us ?
7. What are the threats and danger in the way of our future operations and what strategies we are developing to overcome them ?
8. How we are going to make sure that there will be no divergence between goals and reality ?

Revising Long Range Plan. Long range planning should be a system by which it is revised and updated every year around the same time interpreting the changes that have occurred and that could not be foreseen earlier during the period between the last long range planning and the current one.

Suitable changes with specific reasons therefore would have to be made in the various contents of long range planning of namely objectives, forecasts etc. The objectives of the plan must be well defined. The purpose of the plan, the objectives to be sought in the planning process, the relation of planning goals to other goals and objectives in the enterprise must be clarified.

Methodology of Long Range Planning

Goals. Goals of long range planning should be realistic. The validity of goals for planning should be tested upon the basis of past experience of the company and its industry. Sometimes an immediate problem will serve as a local point for planning. If, for example, rate of return on shareholder's investment has been well below industry's average for the past five years, the prime goal for the company may be to achieve industry average or better. Long range company goals should be established for sales, profits, capital requirements, new and old product requirements etc. Therefore the gap between aspirations and projections on present plans and trends must be measured.

Exploiting Possible Strategies. This step is to develop strategies to fill the major gaps. The company must come fact to face with major questions of policy. For example, if there is a sales gap, to what extent will it be fulfilled by marketing old products or by further penetration of the old market. If this is not enough to what extent should the old product be modified by research ? Where can and should costs be reduced or increased ? Should new products be introduced or should we continue with the existing product line ? To begin with, tentative courses of action may be set forth for testing the planning process and the objective appraisal of company's strengths and weaknesses. Based upon the above investigations, the optimum strategy should be chosen from alternatives.

Subsidiary plans to fit strategy— A planning process is not complete until subsidiary plans are made to put into effect the strategies developed during the third stage. R & D progress should be supported, timed, and controlled to achieve the new products or other requirements needed to reach goals. These requirements for example may be, improving old products, reducing production costs, hiring new scientific skills, or increasing basis research. Marketing and promotional plans will include selling efforts, advertising programmes, re-organisation of sales territories, pricing etc.

Parallel Planning. An important feature of long range planning is parallel planning. It would be waste of time and resources to insist that production await engineering before beginning its derivative plans, or marketing await production and the organisation await all of them. It is true that what is decided in one area will have a determining impact on other area. But planning in all areas must proceed in parallel to the fullest extent practicable to save time. This can be accomplished by good communication in planning and keeping in touch with what is going on in other functional areas.

Integrated Plans. This step ensures the integration of long range and short range plans and to introduce the necessary control to be sure that operations take place in conformance with plans.

Essentials of Good Long Planning: 1. Objectives must be precisely set in terms of sales volume, the quality planning premises and product, 2. Objectives must be matched with resources available and likely to be available, 3. Different courses of action should be analysed and key factors of selection should be determined and 4. Setting up to acceptable performance standards which are feasible and flexible.

17

Productivity

Introduction

India is a developing country. Its vast population is to be provided food, clothing and housing. We are engaged in raising the standard of living of millions of our countrymen. Raising of standard of living means raising production to meet the growing demand of goods and services in all spheres.

Production can be increased by opening new industries or expanding the existing units. Jobs created by the new industries or expended industries will help the jobless to become employed. The second way is to buy and install new and automatic machines and process which will increase production and help to reduce price. These two methods are capital intensive and may not always be the best solution of the problem. The third way is to use existing machines, materials and labour of man so that more can be produced from the resources already available. Producing more from the costing resources is called 'Productivity'. Productivity is often confused with production. Productivity is simply the ratio of output in productive operations. Output can be translated into services and inputs over all forms of resources such as man-power, materials, machines, money etc. With a given extra input of resources, if production increases, the productivity, has increased. Production remaining the same, if the output of resources is reduced, then also productivity can be deemed to increase. Even when the output and input remaining steady, but the quality of the 'output' is improved, even then the productivity has increased, as the intrinsic value of the output will be more in this case. The productivity in terms is mathematical concept is described as under :

$$\text{Productivity} = \frac{\text{Output}}{\text{Input}}$$

Productivity means more goods in the market, more capital for investment, greater employment opportunities and lower prices. In the ultimate analysis, it is man who produces material wealth, he delivers the goods as we say. This man-power must however be motivated and directed. We may have a big reservoir of water, but that reservoir by itself has neither strength nor purpose. If however, we can divert this water, channel it and put it through a turbine, we get power. Similarly we may have the best of men in any industry and even then there may be a failure, simply because we may not know how to motivate the people to work in a dedicated manner.

Factors Increasing Will and Skill

Greater emphasis, is therefore, required to be laid on increasing the will and skill of the people. While the skill of the people can be increased through well designed training and executive development programmes but will of people still remain a force to be reckoned with. Even the highly skilled and experienced hand will not be able to give his best to the organisation in the form of his contribution unless he has a will to do. Let us analyse the various contributing factors that has influence on the will of the person to perform his job. These are :

(*a*) Industrial Psychology

(*b*) Perception

(*c*) Effective Communication

(*d*) Motivation

(*d*) Group and team work and dynamic leadership.

(*a*) **Industrial Psychology.** An individual is the smallest unit of society, organisation or a group. He is, however, the most important organ of any establishment. An individual, although by himself alone, may not be self-sufficient unit but one of the most important variable vis-a-vis other variables such as material, money and machine. An individual working in a group or in an organisation brings to his work place an imprint of his perception and personality. The discipline under which we study the individual and individual difference is known as psychology. Industrial psychology is the professional aspect of psychology *i.e.* the study of people at work.

(*b*) **Perception.** Every one wears his own rose coloured glasses *i.e.* does not always see what he wants to see. If people be have on the basis of the perceived than changing behaviour in a predetermined directions can be made easier by understanding their present perception of the world. People act as they perceive. Different people perceive differently and people's perception is determined by their needs. As people behave as they perceive therefore understanding their present perception to the predetermined action for changing the behaviour.

The individual's perception is more influenced by his social environments than by his physical environment. He perceives any situation or thing according to his frame of reference and attitude which develops from his socio-economic and cultural factors.

(*c*) **Effective Communication.** It is an important aspect concerning the management of human resources relates to the development of effective communication among the people in an organisation. A manager spends almost 75% of the time in communicating and at time as much as 95% in communicating to others and being communicated. It will not be an exaggeration, if we call the communication as the life line of an organization. It is, therefore, of utmost importance for us to study in depth of various aspects of communication.

Communication is the process of passing information from a person to another. The term communication has been derived from the Latin word 'Communis' which means common and thus if a person affects communication, he has established a common ground of understanding. Communication is the attempt to effect transfer between minds. This is essentially a two way process involving a sender and a receiver. The American Society of Training Directors defines good communication 'as the inter-change of thought or information to bring about mutual understanding or confidence to bring about good human relations'.

Principles of Communication. Koontz so donnel State the following principles of communication as useful guide for establishing good communication system.

(*i*) *Principle of Clarity.* The sender's communication must be in a commonly understood language.

(*ii*) *Principle of Attention.* The attention must be paid to the communication being received by the receiver.

(*iii*) *Principles of Integrity.* The communication must pass through the well defined channel.

(*iv*) *Principles of Strategic use of Informal organisation.* Informal organisation must be used constructively as a mean of communication.

(*d*) **Motivation.** It is a universally known that the human organism is not simply designed to survive very well in an environment that made little distinction between it and machine. Motivation of industrial personnel is not new. A man does not simply live as an economic man but likes to live a social-economic man. Major part of the time an individual spend at work rather than at home therefore it is important that his work place environment should be made meaningful and interesting. It is a known fact that mere issuance of instruction or direction does not mean that they will be implemented. Persons have, therefore, to be inspired, enthused to work harmoniously for achieving organizational goal. The effort of the organisational group is always to keep their members satisfied through different motivational techniques. The efforts of the group or the organisation and success of its leadership aimed at achieving the set goals, therefore, largely depends on the degree of contentment, they are able to cultivate amongst their members. The study of motivation is, therefore, very essential. There is a very strong relation between productivity and motivation. Its application to determine as to whether the plan has succeeded or not and to serve as the guide for future exercise.

The motivational plan should be able to serve legitimate self interest by legitimate means. It should be attainable, ensuring proportioning of reward. It should take into account human factors such as feelings, emotions, egos, personalities ideas to improve human relations and harmonize individual group relations.

Group Dynamics and Leadership

Men are known from times immemorial to form the groups for various purpose. Some of the commonly known reasons are desire to conforming, security, achieving a goal which is beyond the reach of an individual.

In order to deal with the complexity of the modern world and in particular to run the large business concerns organization are set up to achieve a common explicity goals. The organization works through various groups which are assigned the sub goals of the organizations. The management of an organization has, therefore, to work through groups and so the management must understand the significance of group dynamic. 'A group is an association of two or more persons who interact with each other in accomplishing a common objective'. 'Group dynamics' may be defined as the *social process by which people inter-act face to face in small groups.*

Group dynamics is an expression that describes the situation in which people acting together in a group accomplish certain things either positively or negatively, in a way that cannot be explained adequately in terms of the individual acting separately. The recognition of group dynamics, team spirit has an extensive history in military units and among athletic teams but its application in industry is fairly recent.

Role of Production Manager

The person who is given responsibility for the process of production is called Production Manager. Production manager should have both technical and managerial skills. Production manager needs to take two types of decisions : Problem relating to production system like operation and technology, planning and analysing.

Production manager must make decisions regarding lay out of equipments, techniques of material handling, location and size of the plant, motion and time study, process analysis and quality of the product. Once the production system has been designed and actuated the problems which production manager faces is the analysis and control of the production system. Routine, leading, scheduling, despatching expediting are the basic production planning and control activities. The role of the production manager in a production system as shown in Fig. 10.1. The production manager's role is that of a decision maker, after he has planned allocation of inputs , starts of creation of value through the production process. This is not the end but the beginning of production manager's activities. Once the production processes are started it must be controlled. The control involves observing results and checking that they confirm to the original plans. The checking is possible by feed-back mechanism, So the role of production manager in a production system is that of decision maker to plan and control the production processes. Production manger is one of the manager in the organisation.

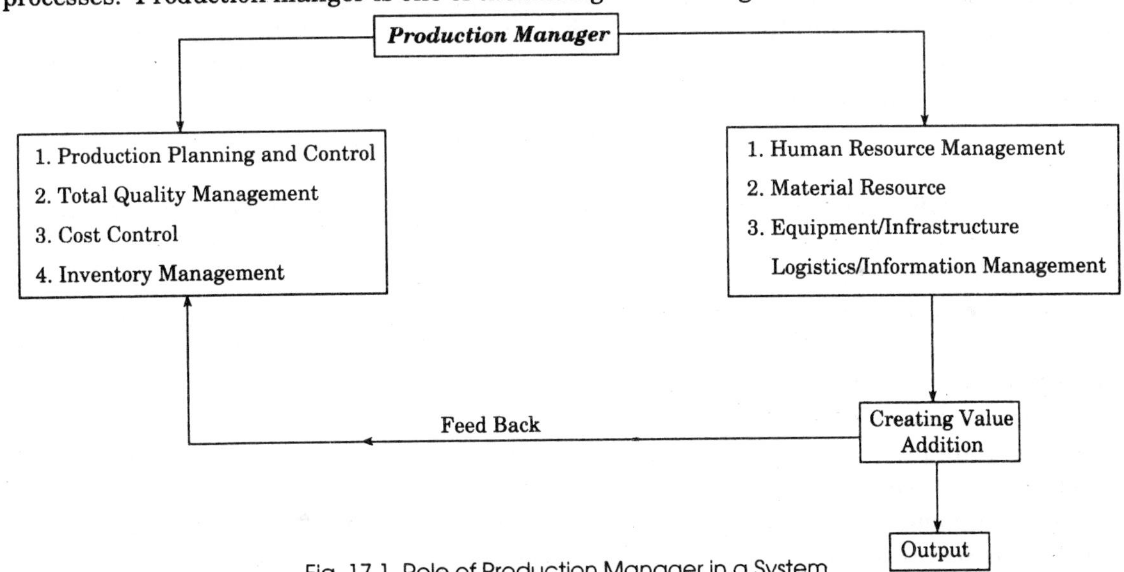

Fig. 17.1. Role of Production Manager in a System

Sub-system of the business organisation, similarly business organisation is also a sub-system in the environment of the business. The Production manager must perceive his role in all the three systems. To understand his role in a business environment he must examine first the Objective of Business Organisation. The first objective of any organisation is to survive and remain in business and to make reasonable profit. Many organisations do have the objectives of customer's service satisfaction and social objectives. The public sector enterprises have come to play a significant role in our economy. The objectives of public sector are :

—to check the monopolistic growth.

—to provide the basic services to private sector in the form of infrastructure.

—to create conditions for buyers market.

—to invest in low return and highly capital intensive industries.

Public sector thus has to act as a device and it plays the role of pace setter by function as to quality, design, price and ensure adequate quantity by supplementing the production in various short supply sectors. The first concern of production manager in any production activity is to provide input which include raw-materials, men machines etc. The inputs are then transformed to finished product thereby creating value. Generally to production of products alone is considered the area of interest of production manager but this can also be applied to the production of services also. The production system can be used in any activity which result in products and services such as restaurants, super bazars and automobile repair shops etc.

FUNCTIONS OF PRODUCTION MANAGER

The functions of Production manager, like any other manager involve the following six steps:

— Organising — Planning
— Directing Operations — Controlling Results
— Appraising Performance — Improving Effectiveness

The manager must organise his department to reach his goals effectively, he must plan his operations so that each activity will fit together in a pattern calculated to produce unfied and accurately directed action. He must control his action, and keep it aimeds at planned objectives. At the sometime, he must continuously appraise his results and his goals and further improve his performance by the feedback knowledge, experience, information and properly managed operations.

The management must use an 'Integrated precision management' approach to achieve the proper unification and cooperation of individual efforts and to synchronise the activities of machines, materials and manpower so as to realise company plan and objectives with the greatest possible effectiveness and at the lowest possible overall cost. The production manager can manage the six functions of management in the following manner :

Organising

The first task in developing an effective production planning and control group is to organise all the significant factors affecting the department's activities. The production planning and control function must have a solid framework which has purpose, direction and continuity in order to help maintain the basic structure of the department as operation changes take place over the years. Without this framework, the department would not be properly integrated with company objectives. The following, in brief, enumerates the organising activities :

(*a*) Obtain a statement of corporate objectives from top management.

(*b*) Prepare a statement of departmental objectives.

(*c*) Develop a policy manual for the production planning and control department.

(*d*) Draw up a department organisation chart.

(*e*) Evolve department job descriptions.

(*f*) Compile a system and procedures manual.

(*g*) Introduce a manpower rating and inventory system.

(*h*) Establish basic criteria for the management of developmental performance.

Planning

The role of planning is a multiple one. However, one of the basic purpose that it serves to relate the organisation to actual operations. Effective direction, control, appraisal and improvement of operations cannot be done, no matter how well the production department is organised, unless the activities are first planned. To try to operate without continuous planning on both - a short and a long range basis will lead to results which are far less than the optimum that is achievable. The following gives the elements or steps that are part of the overall concept of production, planning and control, hence they should be integrated with each other, as well as with the elements of other managerial skills.

(*a*) Prepare a statement of long and short term planning requirements.

(*b*) Develop operating plans (short and long term).

This might include some of the following:

(*i*) **Functions and activities**

— Sales forecasting and master planning.
— Routing, scheduling and despatching.
— Preparation of process orders.
— Internal transportation and materials handling.
— Marketing trends.
— Expansion and innovation of process.
— Inventory Control.
— Follow up.
— Receiving and warehousing.
— Shipping and traffic.

(*ii*) **Projects and programmes**

— Cost control and reduction.
— Value analysis and engineering,
— Scrap salvage and waste control.

(*c*) Make a departmental manpower forecasts (short term and long term).

(*d*) Set up a departmental time schedule for the operating plans.

(*e*) Establish cost and budgetary plans.

Direction

The production planning and control manager must direct the activities of his people within the framework of the total organisation, the manner in which it is done will determine the precision and effectiveness of the plans themselves, as well as the quality and value of the organisational planning.

Some of the basic elements that are essential to success in directing the activities are :

(*a*) Effective decision making.
(*b*) Effective communication and delegation.
(*c*) Effective motivation and supervision.
(*d*) Effective coordination and unification.

Controlling

Control serves to ensure that the activities will be carried out in accordance with the Plans. Without effective control of his operations, the manager may find that his planning and organising are in vain. Basic steps for control are :

(*a*) Measurement of progress and results.
(*b*) Comparison of results with plans.
(*c*) Taking corrective action, if called for.

Appraising Performance

Appraisal is primarily aimed at evaluating the results of operating plans on a continuous basis. In other words, the performance measured in the control phase of management is reviewed, then thoroughly analysed to establish the cause of any deviation, so that the proper changes can be made in either plans and practices. Appraisal and control, are of course, very closely allied and are often considered to be the part of the same management.

The appraisal of result consists of :

(*a*) The analysis of variances. (*b*) Performance evaluation.

Organisation of Production Department

The Production Department Organisation varies from industry to industry. It depends on the type of product, quantity of product manufactured, quality of product, number of people working etc. It also depends on the style of management. One typical organisation of Production Department is given below :

Organisation Structure

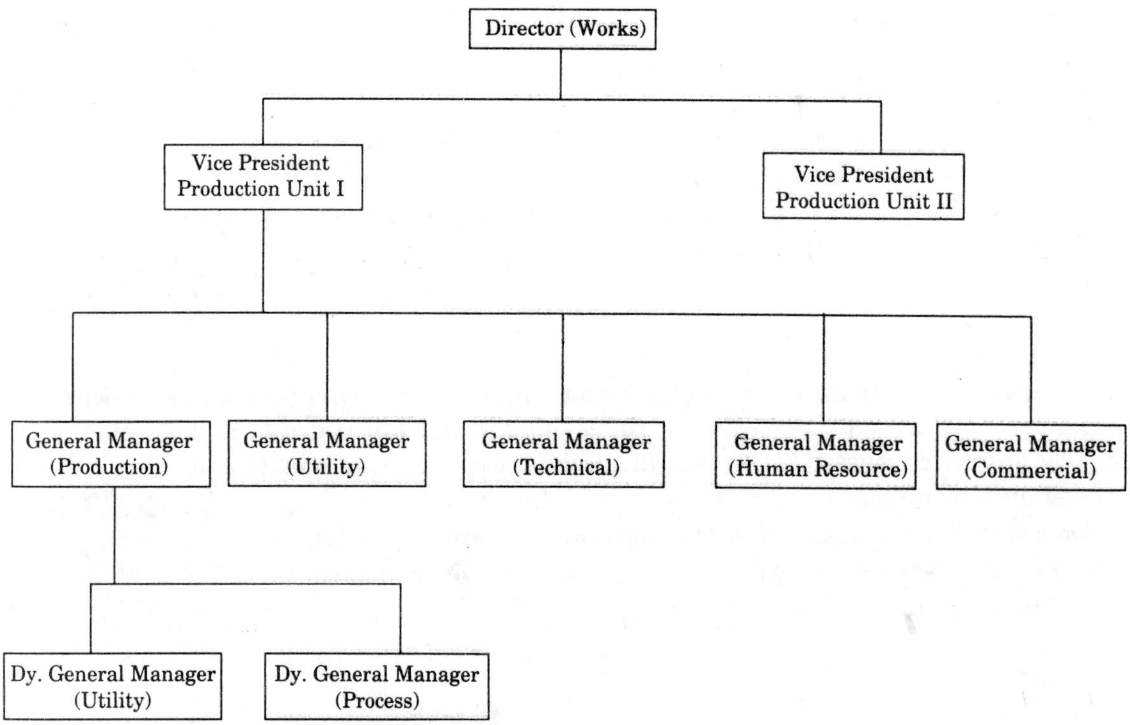

Factors of Production

The economics aspect of production can be analysed by studying the factors of production. The inputs are conventionally called "factors of production". Factors of production are essential elements which co-operate with one another in the production process. These are divided into four categories *viz* : Land ; Labour ; capital ; and entrepreneurship.

Land : It refers to all natural resources which are free gifts of nature and includes soil, rivers, waters, forests, mountains, mines, seas, climate, air, sun etc.

Labour : Human efforts or work done mentally or physically with the aim of earning income is known as labour. The compensation given by labourers in return for their work is called wages. The Land and Labour are the primary factors of production as their supplies are determined more or less outside the economic system.

Capital : See the inputs or man made goods which are used for further production of wealth are included in capital. An increase in the capital of an economy means an increase in the productive capacity of the economy.

18

Corporate Culture

Concepts

Culture is the collective mental programming of the employees in an organisation. It is not a characteristic of individuals; it encompasses a number of employees belonging to an organisation. The common characteristics by which its employees and the organisation itself can be identified, is called the Corporate Culture.

For an organisation to be successful in its existence, it is essential for the organisation to have a Culture which is in tandem with the business goals. Corporate culture depends basically on the organisation's history, technology, industry, custom and practice, leadership styles and the structure of the organisation. Over a period of time, as an oranisation practices certain identified practices irrespective of its hights and lows, certain definite and accepted principles would emerge which could be called as the **Corporate Culture Basics.**

Successful business cultures provide the motivation, incentives and sense of purpose which account for success in an oranisation. But all organisations are unique and therefore have unique cultures. However, if one examines the attributes of the majority of industrial organisations, there are a number of traits that are seen as desirable for effective oranisation culture *viz.*

- A high degree of conformity to rules and values. - Managing ambiguity ad paradox
- A high level of commitment and loyalty to the oragnisation's ends - knowing one's business
- The suppression of the individual in fovour of the organisation
- A clear and formal organisation structure which works in practice - simple and lean organisation.
- The ability to use and develop skills and experience of employees and utilise to the organisation's objectives.
- Constant search by everyone for better ways of improving organisational performance.
- Closeness to the customer and productivity through people.

Foundation of Corporate Culture

Foundation of corporate culture can be identified by the following eight primary values.

- *Purpose Principle* : Self worth can not be achieved in the absence of a sense of contribution to some higher purpose. The competitive leader will make the connection between 'our souls and our work'.
- *Excellence Principle* : Excellence is not described as an accomplishment, rather 'it is a spirit that dominates the life and soul of a person or a corporation.
- *Consensus principle : The future corporation will succeed by its ability to bring ideals together to stimulate the employees, and managers to think creatively.*
- *Unit Principle* : The employee experiences pleasure if the firm succeeds and suffers pain if it fails. This is the unity we should be seeking.
- *Performance Principle* : If the organisation is to be viewed as just, the senior managers must include themselves in the performances criteria for compensation.
- *Empiricism Principle* : Improving the quality of thought (skill improvement) in the firm will determine the long term viability of the business.
- *Intimacy Principle* : Intimacy as the ability to share oneself in a thorough and trusting manner which cannot exist without some measure of quality of spirit.
- *Integrity Principle* : The first and highest requirement of a new leader will be integrity, defined as honest consistent and responsible pursuit of a stated course of action.

Corporate Culture and Organisation Ideologies

Corporate Ideologies which are the symbols of cultural values and norms provide a rationale for organisational members' conduct towards one another and for the organisation as a whole in relation to the environment. Culturally defined frames set the context for mutual understanding. Thus culture matters because it helps to establish the premises for action.

As people are gradually socialised into an organisational culture they may be unaware of the powerful and pervasive influence it exerts. One of the reasons why cultural variables have been neglected in the past is that they are less obtrusive in the way they channelise behaviour and govern organisational performance than more explicit external factors such as organisational structure, control and reward systems and high level processes of decision making. The Great danger of course, is that people become so culture bound that they fail to recognise the extent to which culturally prescribed values and norms actually regulate their behavour. They become so habituated to certain patterns they come to regard them as part of the natural order of things.

Corporate Culture and Management Development

Differences in organisational cultures are likely to be reflected in the structures and systems of oganisational. *The creation of the right kind of 'culture', is the one which encourages outstanding contributions from employees. Culture is a central factor contributing to the success of 'excellent companies'. This view suggests that senior managers may be able to focus on culture as a key variable to influence organisational effectiveness.* Management development efforts cannot ignore the prevailing and desired culture. In fact, culture could be seen as a central factor in the overall process of management development. To aid the process of management development, it would seem useful to have an accurate picture of the existing culture.

The concept of organisational culture is particularly relevant to those involved in management development activities. It is a popular concept in the literature, but it does not provide a panacea for management and it needs to be viewed as a complex, multi-dimensional concept. Organisational culture includes many intangible variables, some of which are difficult to alter by conscious management. Nevertheless, it can provide a useful guiding framework for establishing management development needs and planning particular programmes in the organisation.

Study of Corporate Culture

Organisational culture can be assessed by interacting with executives/employees at different levels in the organisational hierarchy. Such assessment results are analysed on four basic types of culture *viz.* (*a*) power culture, (*b*) Role culture, (*c*) Task culture and *(dD) People (person) culture. Every organisation will have a mixture of all four of these pore type of culture. What makes each organisation unique is the combination and strength of types of cultures. The overall profile of surveys conducted in various organisations has revealed wealth of material concerning dominant beliefs that the organisation in the existing sulture treats the individual as if his/her time is at the disposal of persons higher in the hierarchy (Power), however, for desired culture, employees wanted that organisation should treat individuals as partners who are committed to working towards common objective (Task). Similarly they believed that presently the decisions are based on position in the hierarchy and the content of job description (Role), however, for the desired culture, the employees believed that decisions should be made by people with more knowledge/expertise about a particular problem (Task).*

Corporate Culture and Managerial Control

Organisations can be seen as structures of control. The essence of organisation is Management of Resources. Organisational culture may be a critical key which strategic managers might use to direct the course of their organisations. Culture is a management tool and its use is regarded as part of management theory. But what the leaders must do is to dispense the culture in ways that are perceived as helpful in achieving the goals of corporate leaders and culture should not be left to chance. Proper implementation of culture leads to internalisation of desired values and norms, whether or not conveyed through a formal indoctrination process. Such a property implemented culture could be used as a managerial strategy in promoting loyalty, enthusiasm, diligence and even devotion to enterprise.

Changing the Culture - Some Ideas

Where a change in the present culture is warranted by the internal and external forces which drive an organisation, what the leaders must do is to re-recognise the same, analyse its causes, the technology, the market and decide how far that culture is appropriate to the current situation. This is a step to change the culture itself, without destroying it. There are three levels at which this can take place.

Changing of Behaviour - Change in behaviour can be effected by appropriate training followed by the installation of some type of performance monitoring device such as an information system or performance review. It will cause people to work faster or slower to communicate better or works but definitely change will take place without any basic alternation to attitudes to work or values about work.

Changing Attitudes - Employee attitudes are based upon the perceived behaviour of the chief executive in determining culture. If the departmental head cares more for technical excellence of the product than sales turnover, then so will his subordinates. To change the attitudes of these people certainly requires some adjustment of their mental set up and may require structural readjustment to give greater prominence to some departments at the expense of others.

Changing Values - It has now been proved beyond doubt from the experience of many organisations that if you want to change the culture, you have to change the people at the top whose value system permeates the culture.

Critical Human Resource Management Initiatives

The Human Resource Manager must shed the role of a personnel administrator and evolve into a systems designer in order to create an environment which is conducive to bring in a cultural change in the organisation. Change can be managed in a smoother way with less resistance if certain HR initiatives are effectively employed in the organisation. This can be achieved by employing various approaches *viz* (*i*) through workshops and interactive for a various levels of employees that provide scope for open communication and feedback (*ii*) changing employee attitudes to work should be perceived as something enjoyable and challenging. (*iii*) by innovative learning mechanisms which make learning interesting, easy and kindle and even greater urge to improve one's knowledge, (*iv*) by institutionalising new methods by using catalytic agents of change within the organisation and (*v*) by creating employeeship which is a WE culture that is represented by responsibility, loyalty and initiative at the individual, team and corporate level. These initiatives would equip the company with flexibility, high speed and a quality of response making it an adaptive oranisation that will leave the competition way behind.

Corporate Culture In Action

In order to implement desired corporate culture in the organisation, the human resource strategies should be inline with the business strategies. As we all know, the playing field of business has compelled the organisation to undertake substantial changes in the organisation strategies, structure and processes. Linking HR strategies to the strategic business plan is vital to meet the changing organisational demands. The need of the time is that Human Resource Manager must play a strategic role as a change agent. The HR department of the organisation try to integrate training and management development activities in--line with the management culture. In one of the organisation where new work oriented culture was introduced, the oranisation has identified 18 values to be deployed in the organisation *viz* Openness, Equal opportunities, Empowerment and delegation, Harmony ad Cooperation, Preach what you say, Accepting mistakes, Displaying consistency in behaviour, Taking initiative, etc. Based on various workships, it has been decided to inculcate the following values out the aforesaid 18 during the year 1998 (*i*) Openness, Listening ability, (*ii*) Accepting mistakes (*iii*) Empowerment and delegation and (*iv*) Honouring commitment. The leadership of the organisation is sparing no efforts to see these values and imbibed deep in to the oranisation during 1998 itself.

19

Human Resources

Introduction

An entreprenuer must be good at Human Skill to achieve the organisational objectives. It is a key function determining his success, because it is perhaps, the oldest and most widely-researched subject in management. Yet, as technologies change, cultural diversities occur and people's expectations undergo fundamental shifts. And newer and newer dimensions emerge. For instance, professionals are gaining more say in the running of organisations. Even where governance is by people who own the majority stake, their own positions and the respect they command are contingent upon their competence rather than ownership.

The entry of multinationals has also brought in fundamental changes in the work culture, work ethics and remuneration patterns in India, all of which have a clear bearing on the career growth path of a individuals. Added to this are the rapid changes taking place on the technological front, flatterning hierarchies and making people come together more than ever.

Importance of Human Resources

Amidst all this change, the high ethical standards of an entreprenuer or the Chief Executive Officer, matter more now than ever. The dual ethical standards often maintained by people to differentiate between their highly ethical behaviour on the personal front-often the exact opposite when it comes to the way they conduct business are counter productive in the long run. The new authority is emerging and organisation are member led, officer driven, customer focused ; a team environment where the whole is greater than the sum of its parts ; a flat management structure where employees and managers are fully empowered and decisions are devolved close to the customer ; a culture of learning rather than blame ; a clear sense of direction and purpose. A firm commitment to delivering high quality public services through a combination of direct-provision and effective partnerships.

The industry is experiencing changes in societal, governmental, organisational and attitudinal areas. Rapid extension in the frontiers of knowledge, the continuing need for developing high-quality manpower, and the fear of managerial obsolescence, have necessitated executive development *i.e.* the utlimate reason for offering executive development within organisations is to improve a manager's attitudes, knowledge and skill to ensure the organisation's survival, growth, planned financial returns, and their ability to adept to changing circumstances.

Success of any Organisation is determined by the 'Team', its people, their caliber and their attitude to succeed and out perform. Employees are the only resource which is capable of self propulsion and value addition. Unlike any machinery that gets devaluated or depreciated with time and age, the human resource i.e., people, appreciates with age and experience. So they are very special but this is fruitful only if people are developed and kept satisfied. It is unlikely that any improvement can be made in terms of production, productivity, quality or customer service until people are developed.

Changing Business Environment and Role of Human Resource

The changing business environment, requiring companies to constantly innovate. Better awareness on the part of the consumers and other stockholders in the company makes the task of organisation managers more difficult. The Human Resource Manager has to continuously ask the following questions :

(*a*) How are our HRD Policies different from other leader organisations ?

(*b*) In what unique ways we can add value to our employees, provide motivation and develop internal customers to give their best.

(*c*) What are we doing today to ensure that our Personnel Policies are unique and best for the future ?

There is a need for bench marking and adopting outstanding practices and processes from organisations anywhere in the world in order to help the organisation to improve its performance. Benchmarking is an ongoing task at all levels of business in finding and implementing the world's best practices. It is classical Total Quality Management. The approach has proved to be effective not only in providing new ideas for change but also in building a commitment to change. One of the important objective of HRD Department is to build the organisation culture *viz.*

— Purpose of the Organisation for its existence
— Vision
— Values
— Processes and
— People

HRD department goals are based on the superordinate goals of the organisation. For culture building, the specific values of the organisation are identified that need to be inculcated in the employees. Some of the values are openness, empowerment and delegation, listening ability, ownership commitment and accepting mistakes. Regular training programmes are conducted to ensure that these values are imbibed and employees exhibit in their behaviour these values. This is the essence of helping employees through continuous change. HRD department can build a system of empowerment and ownership among the employees to develop a sense of commitment. *Employees are constantly motivated to involve themselves to produce best developmental activities and the organisation is sensitive to the employees feedback and shares with employees regularly the organisations future plans and programmes and other issues related to the management.*

Most of the organisations are undertaking HR Studies in-house or with the help of Consultants. The objectives of the study are to undertake the following :

— Position Analysis

— Position Evaluation
— Performance Contract
— Compensation Study
— Objective Study
— Human Resource Development

New Changes in HRD

Because of the fast changing technological, cultural, diversities, there is a need to achieve optimum utilisation of resources. HRD department is undergoing conceptual change and HRD can no longer remain a silent spectators as regards to Organisation policies, achievement of organisation mission, objectives and goals at all levels/ function of the organisation. HRD department is planing a leading role of change agent by way of introducing Quality Management. *Some of the concepts which were originated from Japan have become quite popular in India are now introduced through HRD namely.*

— Total Quality Management (TQM)
— Total Productive Maintenance (TPM)
— Just in Time (JIT)
— Quality Circles (QCs) etc.

TQM refers to an integrated organisation approach in satisfying customers (both external and internal) by meeting their expectations on a continuous basis ; by involving all the employees or Organisation, working on continuous improvement in all products/ processes, and adopting structured problem-solving methods. The main elements of TQM are :

— A quality policy and commitment to it
— Team work and positive culture
— Total employee involvement (TEI)
— Appropriate methods/process/technology which prevent the problems (built-in systems to eliminate quality problems rather than merely detect them, *i.e.* process control)
— Problem solving tools/procedures (quality system approach)
— Standardisation
— The design and implementation of a quality system
— Quality costs and measurement
— Education and training
— Customers and supplier integration—customer satisfaction
— Quality audits and reviews
— Continuous improvement

Total Employee Involvement (TEI)

TEI can be attained by company wide training and education in quality systems and practices. The introduction of small group activities, called quality circles, in Indian industries has also made employees participate in the quality improvement programme, resulting in an enhancement in quality. The implementation of TQM is an integrated approach, and for an organisation in pursuit of excellence with a long-term perspective, its implementation as an integrated approach along with JIT, TPM and TEI can be more rewarding. Of course, this involves certain changes in the employees at all levels.

The 5S concepts which emphasise workplace improvement -- *i.e.* housekeeping. An orderly environment brings the best atmosphere to work and arrive at the right decisions. The 5S are all Japanese works starting with 'S'.

SEIRI - Cleaning

SEITON - Arranging

SEISO - Sweeping

SEKETSU - Cleanliness/neatness

SHITSUKE - Discipline

Good housekeeping is directly linked to achieving discipline in production. It results in better compliance to schedules, fewer machine breakdowns, and prompt attention to problems. *The 5 S concept emphasises the good housekeeping of an organisation oriented towards good practices by all its employees.* It is based on the idea that every individual contribution to improving the workplace environment promotes an orderly mind to adapt right decisions in work.

Total Productive Maintenance (TPM)

TPM is directed at improving equipment. TPM aims at maximising equipment effectiveness with a total system of preventive maintenance covering at entire life of the equipment. Total Productive Maintenance involves everyone in all departments and at all levels. It motivates people for plant maintenance through small group and voluntary activities, bringing about the concept of autonomous maintenance.

Just in Time (JIT)

Just in time is the Japanese approach to material management and control. Just in time is more than a new way of handling material management, it represents a philosophy whose objective is to eliminate all sources of waste, including unnecessary inventory and scrap production. Just in Time is a quality and scrap control tool ; a streamlined plant configuration that raises process yield ; a production line balancing approach; and an employee involvement and motivational mechanisms. Just in Time is a structural approach in a manufacturing organisation focused on improving timeliness ; quality, productivity and flexibility initialising various resources, as well as work simplification and waste reduction.

Quality Circles (QC)

Quality circle is a small group activity to solve work-related problems, involving members performing the same task. They assemble voluntarily, put forward suggestions, and implement them. The management should facilitate this small group activity to function more effectively. In fact, the management's participation in the Quality Circle activities is a must with regard to:

- — Attaining QC perceptions
- — Assisting in the implementation of the QCs suggestions
- — Providing adequate resources for the continuous training of QC members, leaders, facilitators.
- — Organising periodical conventions
- — Awarding best circle shields and certifications (motivation)

— Nominating the members to seminars, worships etc.

— Organising social get together with the QC members.

HUMAN RESOURCE MANAGEMENT -CONCEPT AND DEFINITION

Human Resource Management, H.R.M., is concerned with the **"people"** dimension of management. Since every organisation is made up of people, acquiring their services, developing their skills, motivating them to give high levels of performance, and ensuring that they continue to maintain their commitment to the organisational objectives, Human Resource Management has a key role in the running of the organisation.

Generally speaking, management is the process of efficiently getting activities completed with and through other people. The management process includes the planning, organising, leading, and controlling activities that take place to accomplish objectives. To look at H.R.M more specifically, we suggest that it is a process consisting of four functions, acquisition, development, motivation, and maintenance, of human resources, In less academic terms, we might describe these four functions as getting people, preparing them, activating them, and keeping them.

In recent years there has been relative agreement among HRM specialists as to what constitutes the field of HRM. The model that provides the focus was developed by the American Society for Training and Development which identified nine human resource areas :

1. Training and development
2. Organisation and development
3. Organisation / Job design
4. Human resource planning
5. Selection and staffing

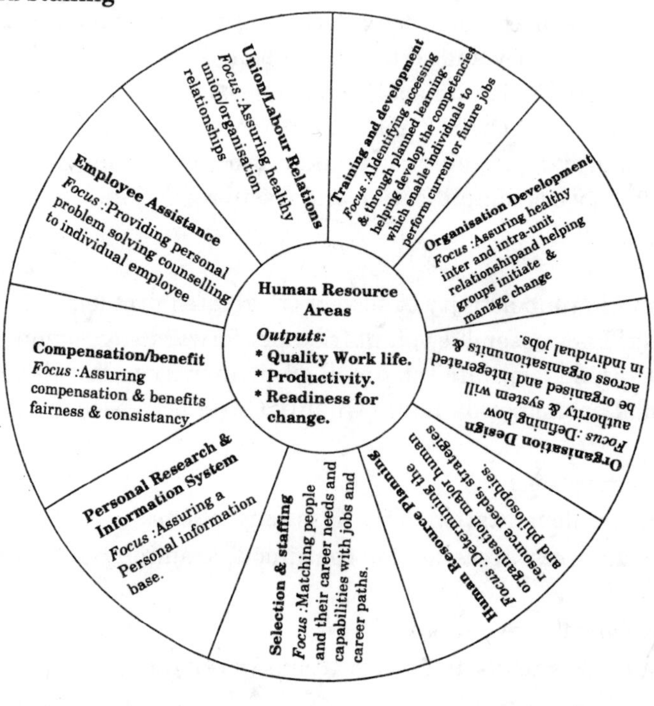

6. Personnel research and information systems
7. Compensation / Benefits
8. Employee assistance
9. Union / Labour relations

These nine areas have been termed as the spokes of the wheel in that each area impacts on the human resource outputs : quality of work life, productivity, and readiness for change. Hence Human Resource Management is a process consisting of the acquisition, development, motivation, and maintenance of human resources. It is the process of getting activities completed with and through other people.

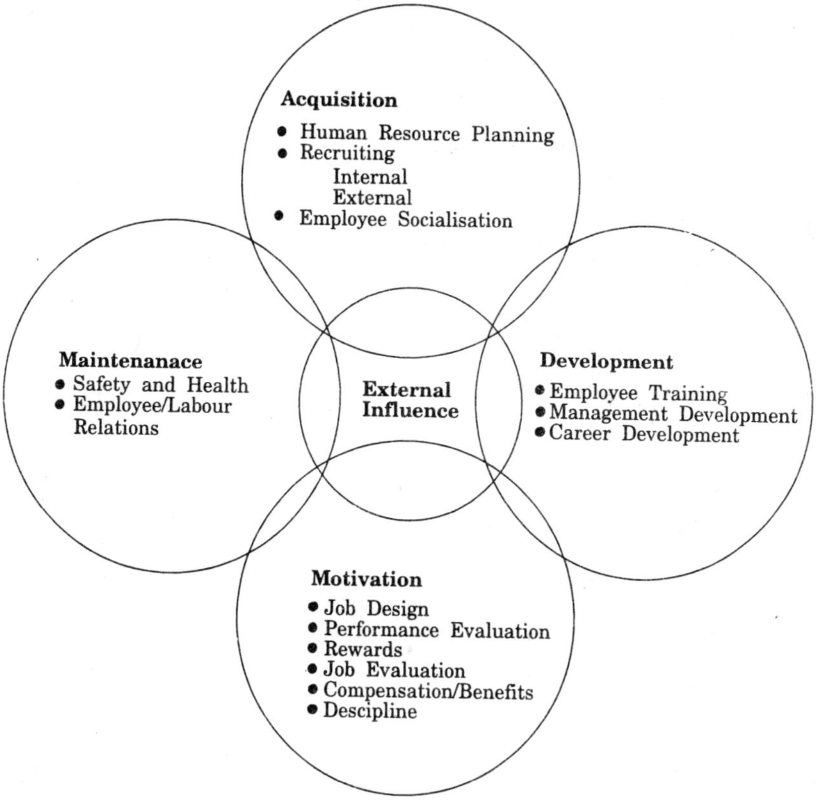

20

Human Resource Polymerisation

Business is a partnership of shareholders, employees, consumers, community and the Government. Each of these partners have different expectations from the business. The shareholders expect higher dividend ; the employees job security ; job satisfaction and growth ; the consumers better value for the money in terms of the quality and service ; the community the fulfillment of social obligation and price stability and the Government the economic growth and development of the country.

Human Resource

The challenge before the enterpreneur is to merge and balance the interest and expectations of various partners in the business and to ensure the productive utilisation if various resources. The managers have the responsibility of safeguarding the public and national interest besides meeting their obligation towards the organisation, employees, and consumers an all those who deal and transact with the society and the nation as a whole. Managers should endeavour to accomplish the modern methods of effective management and efficient administration.

We are aware of the various resources, *e.g.* Material, Machine, Men, Money, Energy and Management are all important in achieving the productivity of the organisation. It is the human asset, the centre of all resources which converts the various resources into the productive resource.

Organisations of today are producing products and services which were known in the past and thus giving a new life with more material comforts than ever before. All these comforts are possible through the effective utilisation of human resource which need to be ploymerised in an organisation to result in a cohesive and enormous force. The human Polymerisation needs individual, ideas and desire of organisational system. Polymerisation could be possible if an individual would establish a bond with other individuals, multiply and generate power to create, build and to produce. It is the human resource which has to harness all other resources effectively. It is only the human resource which appreciates with time whereas all other resources undergo the process of depreciation.

Human resource adds to value, while all other resources add to the cost. All the firms buy the same material and the machines but it is the people in the firm who build the organisation and make a different in the final product. A machine's maximum value reaches the day it starts producing. Man never reaches an ultimate value throughout his life time at work, but is able to change, grow and enrich his value. Success of an organisation mainly depends on the quality of its manpower and its performance. Any forward looking management will be greatly concerned with the problems of developing adequate talent for manning various positions in the organisation.

There is a need for effective manpower planning and development, motivation, effective personnel policies and dynamic leadership, resulting in an organisational climate which may adapt to the changing and dynamic environment.

The role of building a motivated management inventory is with the managers managing the Human Resource. Gone are the days of handicraft when it was possible to take the best efforts from workers who were the members of the same family. In the era of automation and computerisation, there is a need to create an atmosphere within the organisation so that the work -- force is motivated for honest and sincere efforts. The will to is something different from the power or capacity to work. One can buy man's time, his physical efforts, but not his enthusiasm, initiative or loyalty. Thus, enthusiasm or willingness to work can be created by motivation. Motivation means inspiring the person with a zeal to work for the accomplishment of the organisational objectives. Effective motivation succeeds not only in having an order accepted but also in gaining determination to see that it is fulfilled efficiently and effectively.

We all know that motivation gains momentum when it embraces leadership and direction that can elicit the full cooperation of the team which is so vital to the organisation. Basic concept behind motivation is to emphasize the importance of human resource and how this resource can utilise other resourses effectively. Because human performance is a product of ability and motivation and the business preformance being the product of human performance and physical factors, therefore, motivating the work force which is the product of situation and the attitude of the people need to be cultivated by the practicing managers so that they are able to get the best and consistent work out of their people towards productivity and resource utilisation.

Management is primarily a human activity. The various functions of a manager, may be in any discipline - Material, Finance, Production or Engineering - can be classified as Managerial Functions and Operative Functions. The Managerial functions in all the above disciplines are identical *i.e.*, Planning, Organising, Directing, Coordinating and Controlling but the operative functions vary, depending on the discipline. Therefore, for effective managerial functions, the professional art and science of working with and through the people is very important. Effective management is as good an asset as material, finance, machine etc. Effective management is the life blood of an organisation. Management adds a real plus value to the operation of any enterprise. It is like adding two plus two and getting five. Management is an activating resource which provides new ideas and vision to the work group for smooth flow of work by strengthening weak links and establishing team spirit amongst the personnel.

Human Resource Utilisation

Human resource utilisation cannot be put in a formula of output versus input as the individual highly complex and inter-personnel relationship still more complex besides the group dynamics and organisational ideology. Therefore, the need of the time and the challenge before the manager is to intensify the desire and willingness of subordinates in order to elicit the potentialities of their subordinates for the achievement of the organisational objectives. There is a need for the managers to equip themselves to understand the process of change and develop the ability for planning, organising, communicating, problem solving, managing conflict and tolerance. This will be possible only through the process of self-wareness and self-development. But self-development will demands the desire to improve, wisdom for selecting proper actions and time necessary to work toward the investment. The desire, therefore, must come from within, the wisdom must be developed and time must be planned. Self-development will not only provide a better executive life but also a richer and fuller social life.

Management is a composite and comprehensive discipline concerned with the introduction of effective means and methods for achieving organisational objectives. Present day management has no choice but to have a deep knowledge and understanding of the effective system and methods. Management must try to understand and help in solving the genuine problems of workmen arising in the course of their duty in order to effectively use their productive skills.

Polymerisation of Human Resource

Management has the responsibility for the development, allocation and productivity of human resources. Productivity is the first and foremost component of the management and its first responsibility cannot be achieved without its key resource. Human being as such is not a resource and becomes a resource only if trained, developed and allocated to productive work. This is the central task of Management. In a developing country like ours, we have far more people than can be productively employed but there are far less productive human beings. The central task before the management in a developing country is the planning, training, developing and managing of human resource. Initially it was thought that an individual's life time can be divided into two distinguished phases :

(*a*) Formative years.

(*b*) Working years.

Formative year provide the individual with a process of transfer by which he assimilates the knowledge and experience of his predecessors. During the working years, he is expected to confront reality, with the knowledge and wisdom he has obtained during the formative years. This concepts is no longer relevant because of the multi-directional social changes and of the accelerating pace at which it takes place. This is the moment when we must reconsider, rethink and reorder our concept concerning educational development. People of today possess rising aspirations and expectations. The modern communication system has also brought new ways of training, new relationships, new material potential and new social goals at all levels of society and in all parts of the world. In industrial set up of today, both employees and employers have accepted with the passage of time, provisions for health, insurance unemployment benefits, pensions, legal insurance, rights for humanity, job security, participation and joint decision making. directly related to and perhaps even an extension of the rising expectation is a growing concern for the inter-relationship of the individuals, groups, organisation and its systems. It is reflected in the concept that the individual makes an investment in the job. It represents concern for individual life beyond the working situation recognising the importance of issues beyond the job.

There is also a developing realisation that productivity is not the function or the responsibility of the management alone, but a concern for all, both within and beyond the work place. One of the most complex and challening factors is the increase in scope and significance of the transactional and cross cultural relationship and functioning. A problem which affects practically all cultures is the broad and permanent impact of technology on the society, the organisation and the individual. Managers are experiencing increasing pressure for greater creativity and resoucefulness by improved planning and effective leadership. To sum up, Human Resource is an asset which appreciates with time. A machine's maximum value is reached the day it is installed and starts producing. But human resource never reaches an ultimate value throughout the life time to work.

21

Human Resource Management

INTRODUCTION

Human Resource Management is a comparatively new and rapidly growing profession in India. Employees 'On the job' inter-personal relations is the primary concern of the personnel management. The main objective of an efficient personnel department should be supportive to the growth of an organisation. A manager achieves results through the people, by the people and for the people. According to this statement, every manager in the organisation is a personnel man and his objectives, aspirations, interests, fears, decisions, intelligence, creativity, innovation, loyalty, devotion, needs and the zeal to work in the organisation, determine the ultimate success or failure of an organisation. Motivating employees, cultivating the desired habits, development of internal drive, inspiration, encouragment among the people are the job of personnel executive. Personnel management is that part of the management which is concerned with the human constituents of an organisation. Personnel management is a science and art, which control labour and is also known by various names such as labour management, man-management, personnel administration industrial relations or industrial management.

Human Resource Management and Personnel Management

With the rapid industrialisation in the country, these has been a revolutionary change in the relationship between management and workers. The changes have been brought about due to labour legislation, the growing pressure of trade unionism and the new out-look and techniques of progressive management. All these dynamic changes have given a professional look to the personnel executive. In order to be effective, the executive should have an indepth information of various sophisticated techniques used in the field of labour and personnel management based on Indian conditions. Personnel Management calls for indepth study of various subjects like Manpower Planning, Recruitment, Training and Development, Incentives and Reward Systems, Labour Laws, Industrial Safety, Behavioural Science, Group Dynamics, Wage and Salary Administration, Management of Change, Impact of Environment on Personnel Policies, Grievance Handling, Participative Management, Problems in Labour Management Relations including disciplinary measures, Trade Unions, Collective Bargaining, Labour Legislation, Labour Welfare and Social Security etc. Realising the importance of man management, a leading industrialist of America remarked, "We do not manufacture automobiles, aeroplanes, refrigerators, radios, televisions but we manufacture men and they, in turn manufacture the goods". The aim of Personnel Management is to make the optimum use of personnel power of the employees and to get cooperation from one and all. Personnel Management is an approach, an established system, a technique and a philosophy of management.

SIGNIFICANCE

During the recent years, people working in our industries have received growing attention for their well being. It has been realised that there is a need to maintain harmony between the two principal factors of production, namely, capital and work--force. The efforts have been made to find a way out from the clash of interet characterised as present day personnel relations. The industrial harmony cannot be realised by sheer exercise of authority. It cannot be enforced from outside rather it must come voluntarily from within. To achieve this, there should be some real common interests among management and the workers.

Good industrial reactions are by far the greatest asset of an organisation. Labour in the unit of industrial production has an important place. Labour coordinates all other factors of production towards more production and lesser cost resulting in more profits. Personnel management is that part of management which is primarily concerned with the task of managing the personnel and human relationship within an organisation.

DEFINITIONS

There are number of definitions of Personnel Management. Some of the authorities on Personnel Management have defined it in the following manner :

"It is that phase of management which deals with the effective control and use of manpower as distinguished from other sources of power."

"Personnel Management is that part of Management process which is primarily concerned with the human constituents of an organisation." **

"Personnel function is concerned with the procurement, development, compensation, integration and maintenance of the personnel of an organisation for the purpose of contributing towards the accomplishment of an organisation in major goals and objectives."†

The Society of Personnel Adiminstration of America defines Personnel Adiminstration as the art of acquiring, developing and maintaining the competent workforce in order to achieve and accomplish the organisational goals with maximum efficiency and economy. The Indian Institute of Personnel Management defines personnel management as that part of Managementfunctions which is primarily concerned with human relationship in an organisation. Its objective is the maintenance of relationship which enables all those engaged in the undertaking to make maximum contribution to the effective working of the undertaking.

Personnel management is people center D. Effective management of human resources is one of the most crucial factors associated with the growth of an organisation. Its objective is the maintenance of better human relations in the organisation by development, application and evaluation of polices, procedures and programmes relating to the individuals in the organisation to optimise their contribution towards the realisation of organisational objectives. In other

---

* Dale Yoder
** E.F.L Brech
† Adwin B. Flippo.

words, personnel management is concerned with the basic function of management by getting better results with the collaboration of people. In this process it is mainly concerned with the collaboration of people. In this process it is mainly concerned with methods of recruitment, selection, training and placement of the personnel and their terms of employment, methods and standards of remuneration, working conditions, motivation, morale etc. It is also the duty of Personnel Manager to maintain and use effectively the facilities for joint consultation between the employer and the employees. It can be defined as *that part of management which is responsible for advising on all matters relating human relations in the organisation and in particular performs certain administrative functions relating to the employment, development and compensation of the personnel and the provision of working condition and welfare measures to maintain a good working force in the organisation.'*

Analysis

The analysis of various functions gives us an idea of the following characteristics of Personnel Management :

1. It is the management of human resources.
2. Labour is human; hence must get humanistic behaviour
3. Personnel Management is an approach, a point of view, a technique and a faculty of management. It is cooperation from one and all.
4. It is people centered.

GROWTH OF PERSONNEL MANAGEMENT

Nothing precisely can be said about the evolution of Personnel Management. The development of Personnel Management can be traced back to the end of last century. Before this, the development of this area was extremely slow. One can sub divide the evolution process of Personnel Management into following four periods :

(*a*) Before 19th century

(*b*) First quarter of 20th century.

(*c*) Second quarter of 20th century.

(*d*) Current era (after 1950).

Before 19th Century

It was Robbert Owen who can be regarded as the founder of Personnel Management. He wrote a book "A New View of Society" Where he has emphasised that there is a need for better labour relations, improvement in service conditions and cooperative labour movement. During this century, there has been enough emphasis on coordination and mutual welfare of labour management but there was no radical development due to lack of industrial development and growth.

First Quarter of 20th Century

During this period, the emphasis was laid on personnel management because of the various problems arising due to the formation and development of labour unions. During this period, thoughts of F.W. Taylor, the Father of Scientific Management, were greatly appreciated. This quarter is responsible for introduction of new systems and also the large increase in the number of industries and their sizes. This, in turn, gave rise to complexity of work resulting in large aspirations of the workforce because of the increase in production.

Second Quarter of 20th Century

During this period, revolutionary changes took place leading to hierarchy system with definite norms in the organisation for the selection of the workforce through different techniques like psychological tests, interviews, group discussions, etc. Norms were also designed for workers' training, and their welfare schemes. This period gave birth to the concept of human relations. It was in this period that Elton Mayo and his associates, initiates human relations in industry through various studies. The studies proved that human resources have a considerable influence on production. These studies changed the commodity concept of labour to social concept. Number of industrial disputes arose during this period and in order to handle the situation, the government and the producer came forward to recognise the labour unions. This gave rise to a new labour relation pattern. In the year 1931 the Labour Commission recommended the appointment of labour officer in the industries. Bombay Industrial Development Act made it compulsory to appoint Labour Welfare Officer whose responsibility is to ensure amicable labour relation and settle disputes. In 1944, the government of India called a Tripartite Labour Conference where representatives of Workers, Producers and Government participated. The objective of this conference was the implementation of labour rules, settlement of disputes and designing of advisory system for industrial cases. After independence, a lot of efforts has been made by the goverentment and number of laws have been enacted in order to protect labour cause in the Industry.

Current Era (After 1950)

After 1950, development of Personnel Management acquired a new profile of professional management. Personnel Management has now become an intra-disciplinary knowledge, where industrial psychology, behaviour science, labour laws, labour legislation have been introduced. Personnel Management is now considered as Science of Human Relations, Human Engineering, Organisational System and Design. The rapid growth of Personnel Management is because of the following reasons :

(*a*) Fast changes in technology.
(*b*) Industrial revolution.
(*c*) Positive findings of social sciences.
(*d*) Complexity of trade.
(*e*) Awakening in labour.
(*f*) Government attitude and policies.
(*g*) Cultural and social changes.
(*h*) Changes in the social value of labour.
(*i*) Changes in managerial views.
(*j*) Changes in organisational set up.

An Industrial Revolution of 1950 has brought about specialisation and growth in the size of the organisations, awakening in labour, resulting in the formation of various labour organisations and federation. Cultural and social changes are now very fast due to the changes in the educational background, changes in social values of labour and changes in the managerial viewpoint etc. In addition to the above changes, there are fast changes in the form of business organisations, cooperation of science and industry and the control and coordination in industrial set-ups. Now the subject of Personnel Management has acquired considerable authority and is fruitfully utilised for the welfare of personnel serving in the industry. This has acquired more dimensions, scope and significance in the wake of recent increase in industrial unrests.

Integraed Human Resource Management

Globalisation of the Indian economy has brought into focus the need for revitalised management in the corporate sector. The increasing intercompany competition calls for greater team efforts on part of the managers, with the sharing of responsibility and accountability among the team members becoming crucial. The focus has shifted from individual managerial excellence to managerial excellence.

In the case of team managerial excellence, the entire team contributes to the decision making after a thorough exchange of ideas; owns the decision and identifies itself with the interest of the company. These changes have made a tremendous Infact on Human Resource Management (HRM), which has acquired a new dimension. HRM encompasses a wider meaning which includes more responsibilities and accountability and plays a vital role in the company's success.

Success is the result of quality, which is the product of human effort. Thus, the human being is the 'core' and success is the corner stone. However, this assumption has led to ambiguities and vagueness among HR professionals, enhanced by less emphasis on education for team building. A 'Systematic Approach' and integrated Approach to Human Resources Management is given in the following diagrams :

To achieve the above, a need has been established to introduce an entire 'Human Resources Management' module. This model is an aid to improve the Career management system in the organisation. It integrates organisations grade and objective with the over all management. The objectives of the model are to :

- Establish and integrate all aspects of human resources management, within the framework of the company, with an aim to enhance overall performance.
- Increase organisational effectiveness and personnel motivation
- Ensure the consistency and applicability of all human resources management tools, procedures, and systems so that they are fully integrated
- Manage individual potential and organisation development programs through Competency analysis and Organisation needs analysis.
- Enhance company culture and values through effective communication and clear business understanding.

Economics through *compensation* as a major cost centre which has to be controlled within the overall cost structure of the organisation and a strong motivator of people who have to be rewarded according to their contributions and based on market conditions.

People through human resources development when it comes to recruitment, training & development and promotion of individuals as well as future organisation plans for career paths, manpower planning and succession planning.

With this model the Organisation get the following benefits.

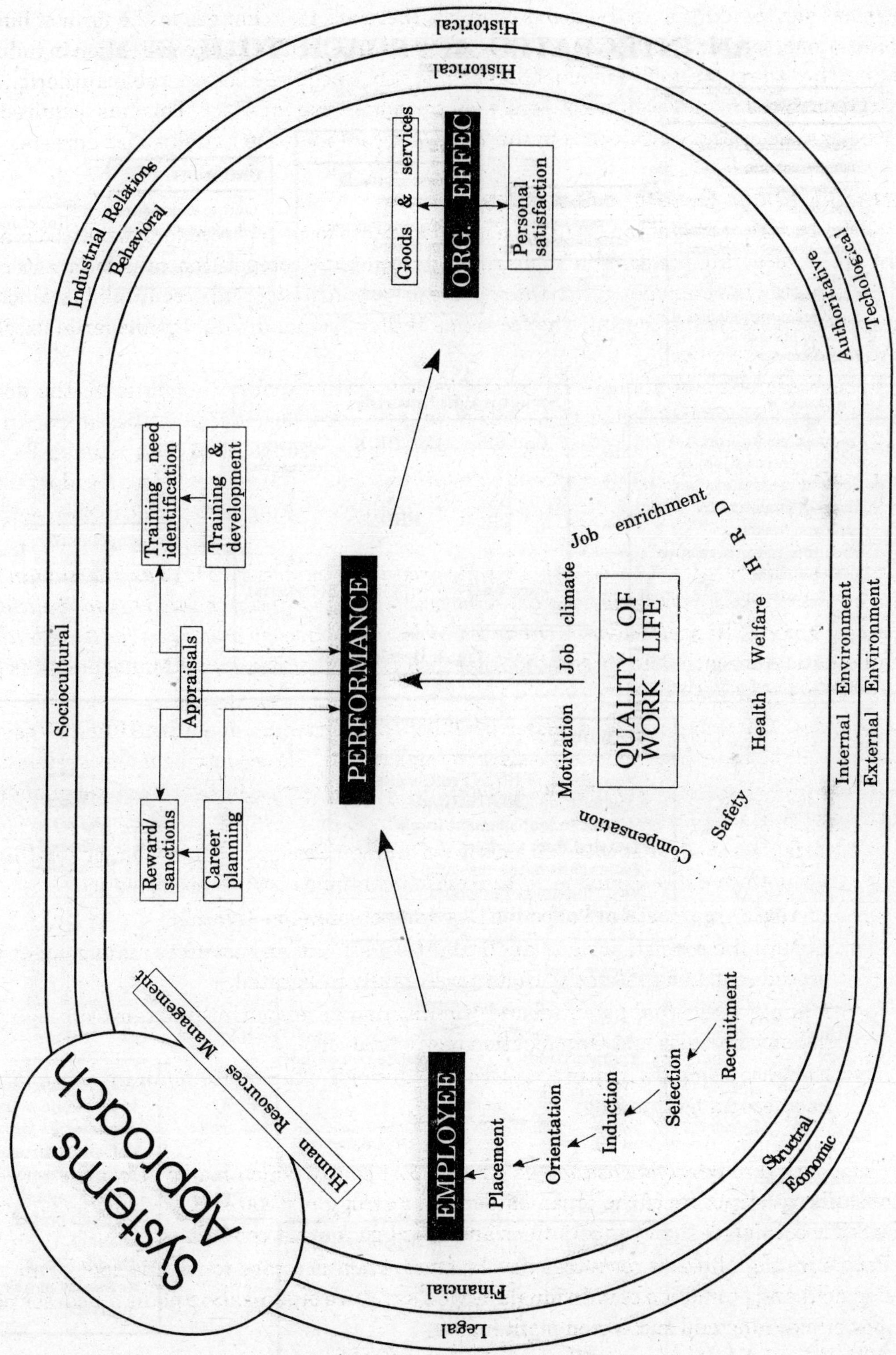
Systems Approach
Human Resources Management
EMPLOYEE
Placement
Orientation
Induction
Selection
Recruitment
PERFORMANCE
ORG. EFFEC
Goods & services
Personal satisfaction
Training need identification
Training & development
Appraisals
Reward/ sanctions
Career planning
QUALITY OF WORK LIFE
Motivation
Job climate
Job enrichment
H R D
Health
Welfare
Safety
Compensation
Internal Environment
External Environment
Sociocultural
Industrial Relations
Behavioral
Historical
Historical
Authoritative
Techological
Structural
Economic
Financial
Legal

AN INTEGRATED APPROACH TO H. R. M.

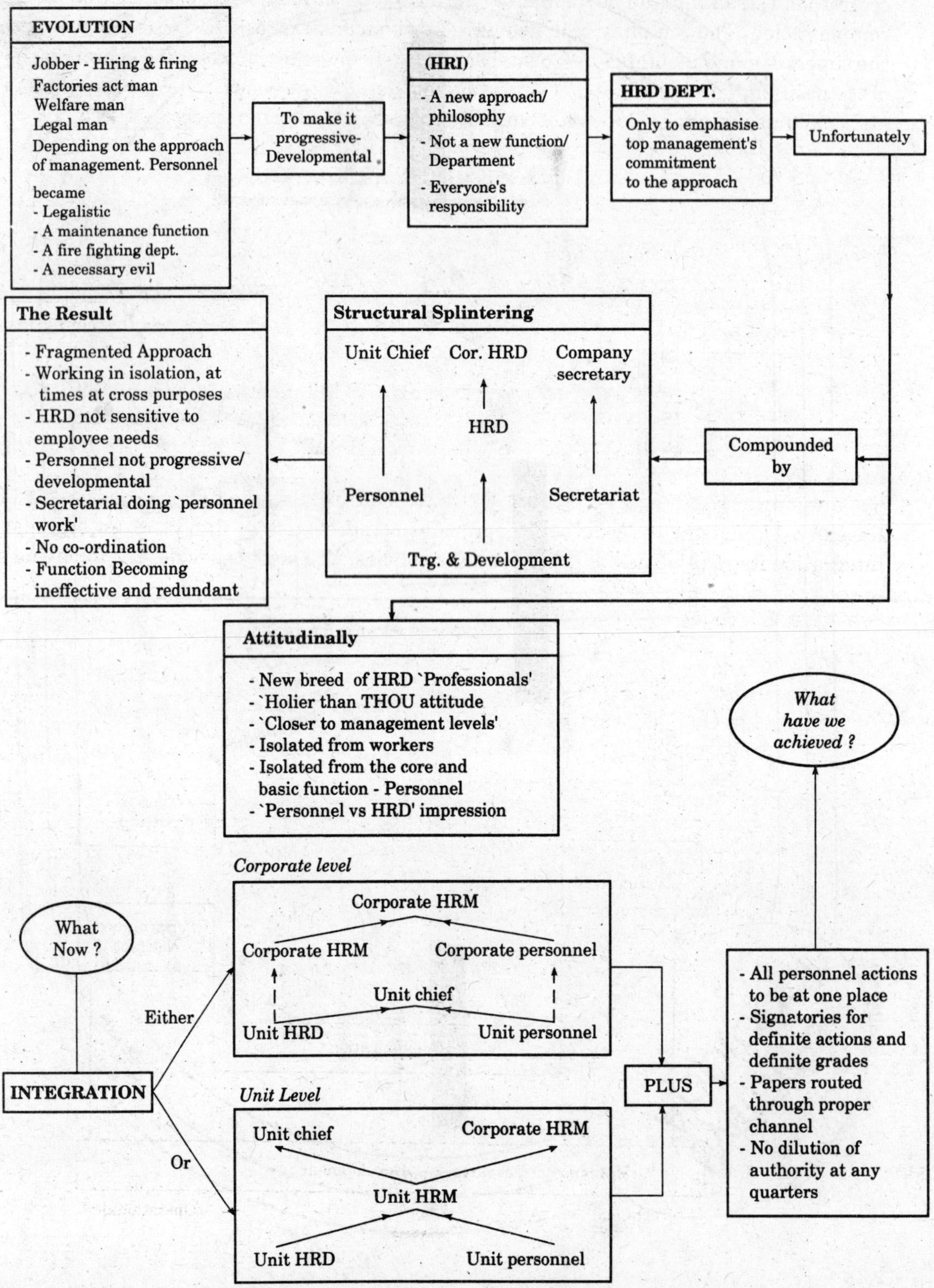

1. **Position Analysis** - Through the Position Analysis organisation will have a highly effective tool that can be used in all aspects of human resources management, including recruitment, training and development, performance management, organisation analysis and compensation. The company will also have key benchmark Position Descriptions approved by the supervisor and incumbent accurately and clearly indicate the scope and size of responsibility of the position. Thus organisation will be able to analysis the positions of the entire organisation and could use this to update rules and responsibilities, as given under :

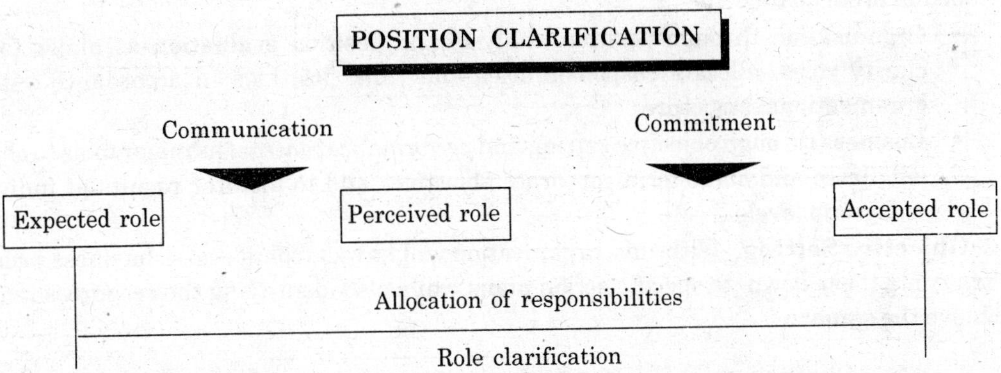

Corporate Resource Group (CRG), a global consulting organisation has designed an Human Resource Management Model which provides comprehensive support to an organisation in integrating its HR Policies with its business policies. The model provides the following support to an organisation :

Human resource management model

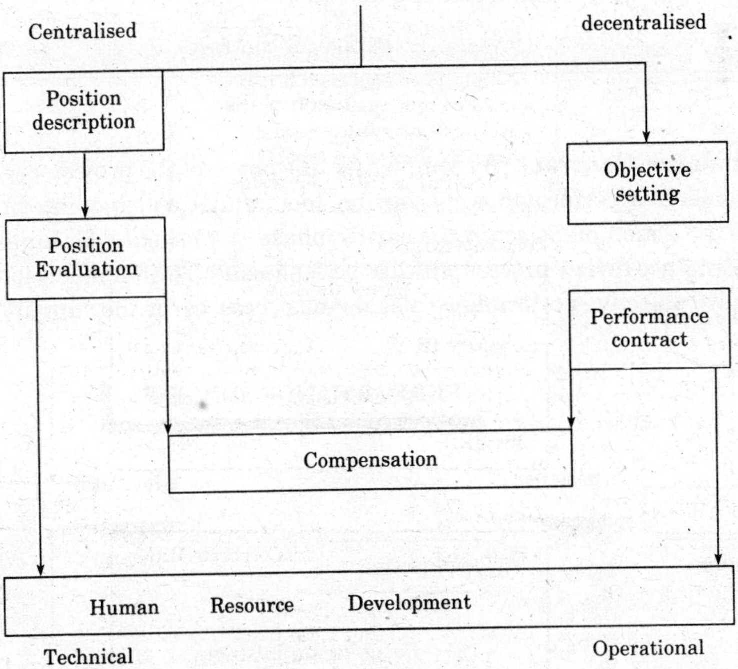

- Allocating responsibilities
- Ranking positions
- Targeting objectives
- Measuring results
- Rewarding individual and group contributions
- Monitoring people development over time

The Model integrates into an overall management concept linking Economics, Organisation and Personnel in a business strategy by performance and added value. This concept was developed in order to link :

- Organisation through position analysis and position evaluation as major tools to clarity roles, allocate responsibilities and rank positions in accordance with the organisational structure.
- Business through objective setting and *performance contract* as major tools to channel long-term and short-term corporate objectives and to monitor results at individual and group levels.

2. **Objective Setting.** With this, organisation will have a tool to assess business priorities and translate these down to specific action plans while also identifying the resources required to achieve the same.

OBJECTIVE SETTING

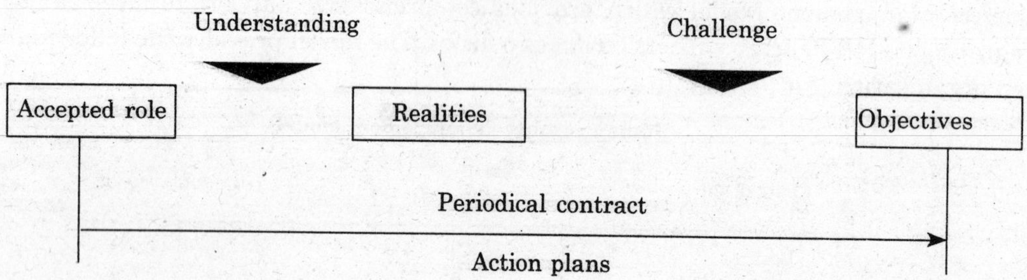

3. **Performance Contract.** By completing this phase of the project, organisation will have a clear and objective performance measuring tool, which will have a direct linkage to the objective and the action plans set in the earlier phase. A workshop for familiarising managers with the performance review process will also be conducted. The emphasis for the entire exercise would be to have objective performance measuring processes for the support function as well as for the line

PERFORMANCE REVIEW

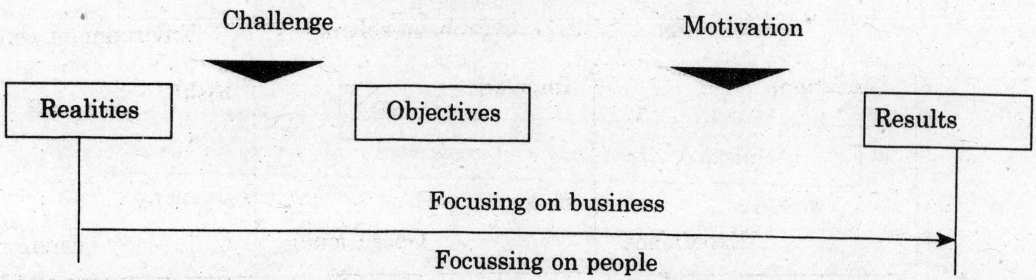

4. **Position Evaluation.** Organisation by the end of this exercise will have installed the CRG Position Evaluation System for use in establishing a salary grading structure based on a consistent, fair and equitable measurement of position responsibilities. A clear Grading Structure would emerge after this exercise. The relative impact, each position has on the organisation would be clear after the completion of this exercise .

POSITION EVALUATION

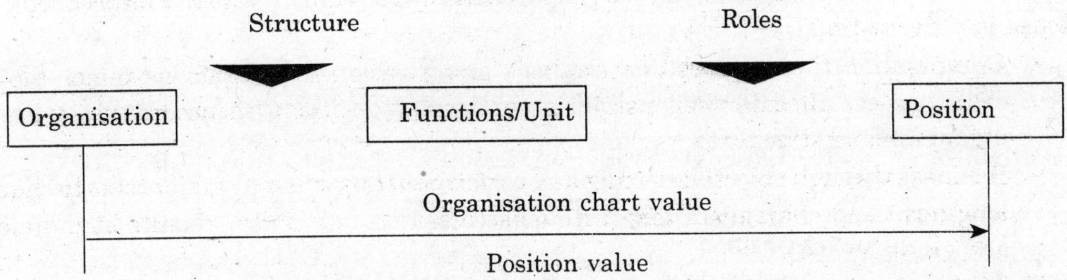

THE SEVEN FACTORS OF JOB EVALUATION

Size of Responsibility

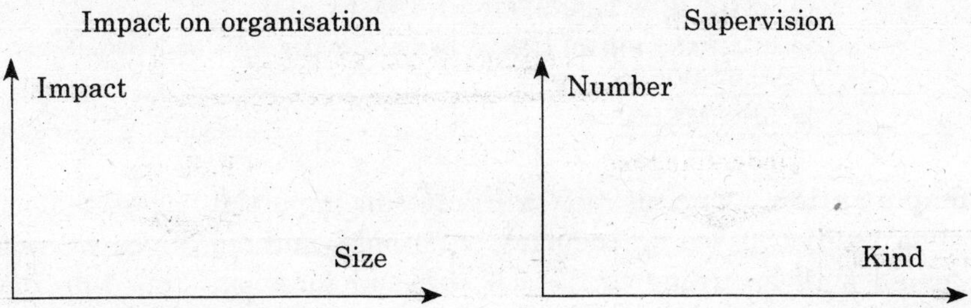

Scope of Responsibility

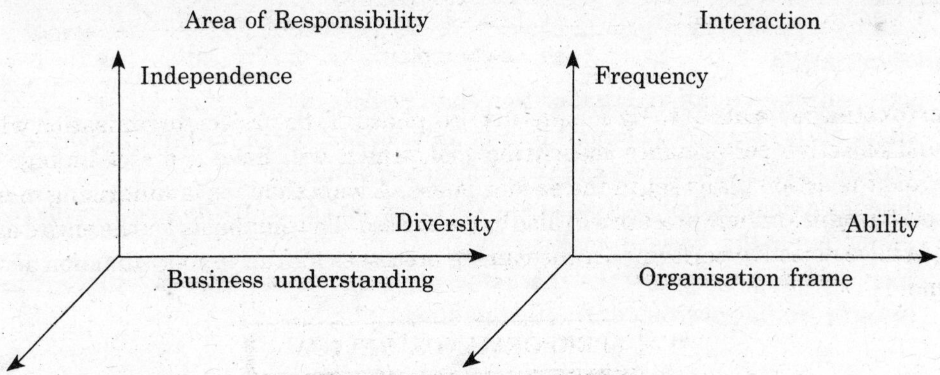

Job Complexity

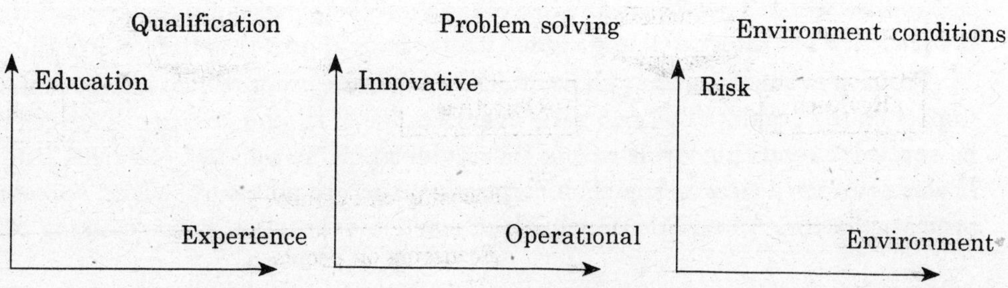

5. **Human Resources Development.** Organisation will have a module on the training requirements for the individuals within the organisation based on the present skill / competency levels available within the organisation and the projected and actual future requirements (fig)

COMPETENCIES

VALUES	MANAGEMENT	SKILLS	APTITUDES
1. INTEGRITY	1. PLANNING ORGANIZATION	1. AUTONOMY	1. RISK AWARENESS
2. PARTNERSHIP	2. DELEGATION CONTROL	2. WRITTEN COMMUNICATION	2. CREATIVITY
3. COMMITMENT	3. RESOURCES MANAGEMENT	3. VERBAL COMMUNICATION	3. INITIATIVE
4. ENTREPRENEURSHIP	4. HUMAN RESOURCES DEVELOPMENT	4. NEGOTIATING	4. VISION
5. PUBLIC BEHAVIOR	5. PROJECT MANAGEMENT	5. DECISION MAKING	
	6. ANALYSIS CONCEPT	6. CUSTOMER SERVICE	
	7. KNOW-HOW TRANSFER	7. TEAMWORK	
	8. COMPANY PRODUCTS AND SERVICES	8. LANGUAGE	
	9. KNOWLEDGE		

6. **Compensation.** Organisation will have an impartial assessment of the company's remuneration position based on company philosophy and objectives as well as the market position for all staff according to the job size and function. This will form the basis for establishing reference salaries and salary ranges for each grade, which are both internally consistent and externally competitive.

Position Evaluation

Through position evaluation, organisation shall be able to :

- Rank all benchmark positions in a definite order, based on their impact within the organisation and their overall scope of responsibilities:
- Provide a clear mapping of corporate structure for career paths, successions plans and promotion paths, decision making end
- Easy comparison against the market levels, w.r.t. those companies that are using the same or similar position evaluation methods.

The position process is sequential to the position description procedure. A position evaluation committee with personnel and line managers is set up to evaluate the positions. Afterwards, the positions are integrated and submitted for final approval to the CEO of the organisation.

Position evaluation ranks all positions in a definite order, which reflects and relates to their impact on the organisation and their overall scope of responsibilities. This ranking shall then be applied to reporting levels within the organisation, as well as to internal title classification. It also provides a clear mapping of corporate structure for career paths, succession plans and promotion steps. An additional benefit of position evaluation is the ranking of compensation when it comes to 'pay for position' and it also facilitates compensation comparisons with market levels for those companies using Hay's or Corporate Resource Group's method.

Consulting Organisation evaluates key benchmark positions and then covers the remaining positions through assimilation. Sound business management principles require integrating human resources development within overall organisation development plans as well as estimating know-how and skills requirements as part of the improvement of the operating system of the company.

People development programs shall be designed to fit within the framework of organisation development programs. This requires a definition of the position profiles needed in the present and future time period, identifying internal and external skills, which best fulfil actual and future requirements . Adequate growth and developmental opportunities will also be highlighted for the Support Functions.

The Model when followed, gives us an insight into the importance of each position facelessly and gives the relative organisation chart based on the relative worth of each job.

It gives us the competency gap between the position and the position holder. The gaps are addressed through appropriate training inputs. This helps us to address training only as per the organisational requirement. The whole process helps us to update the managerial skills of the organisation and integrate with the organisational objectives. The software for all the models can be obtained and after a certain level of executive viz. General Manager group the competency profiling and Competency mapping can be used for career profression ; Training and Management Development ; Management inventory etc. The software can help an organisation to strengthen its personnel policies and design scientific human resource activities to achieve organisational mission and objectives.

METHODOLOGY

Model can help us be carryout position description or Position Clarification, Position Evaluation and Organisational Analysis of Key positions of the organisation. The position description for key positions and position evaluation on seven factors of job evaluation can be finalised. The position evaluation of key benchmarking positions can be ranked in a definite order based on their impact within the organisation and their overall scope of responsibilities. The study will help the organisation towards finalising a clear mapping of organisational structure for career path, succession plans and promotion path. This will help the organisation to compare with respect to those companies that are using the same or similar position evaluation methods. *The position evaluation is ranking of compensation when it comes of 'pay for position.*

Model includes *career development and human resource development. It can undertake positions profile and persons profile, identify gap analysis to determine appropriate match between the two.* This also helps us to identify *training requirements based on present skill levels and projected future requirements.*

A brain-storming session are held with the top management team where core competencies and Corporate capabilities are discussed and deliberated. Competency profiling basically deals with comparing the competencies of positions and persons. *The competencies include identifying Attitude / Aptitude, Knowledge and Skill and as required by the Positions and persons manning the positions.* Steps in profiling include identifying competency, finalising competency skills, profiling positions and profiling persons.

Based on the deliberations, the core competencies can be identified.

Core Competencies

Attitude/Aptitude

- Commitment
- Customer Focus
- Entrepreneurship
- Integrity
- Quality Focus
- Teamwork
- Creativity
- Empathy
- Flexibility
- Openness
- Self Development
- Willingness to change

Functional Knowledge

- Production
- Human Resource
- Maintenance
- Finance

Knowledge

- Chemical Operations Management
- Cost/Benefit Undertaking
- Safety/Health/Environment
- Commercial Knowledge
- Project Management

Skill

- Communication
- Leadership
- Multi-Skilling
- Process Management
- Computer Literacy
- Logistics Management
- Negotiating Skills
- Relationship Building

Competency Directory

The 'Competency Directory' is prepared for various dimensions of competencies. Each dimension of competency is given a definition and also a definition is given for each profile from 2 to 5. After finalising the competency directory, the positions and the personnel are rated starting with level 3. If the definition justifies at level 3 then move to level 4. If the definition justifies at level 4, move to level 5. If this does not justify at level 3, come down to definition at level 2.

The Behavioral Iceberg

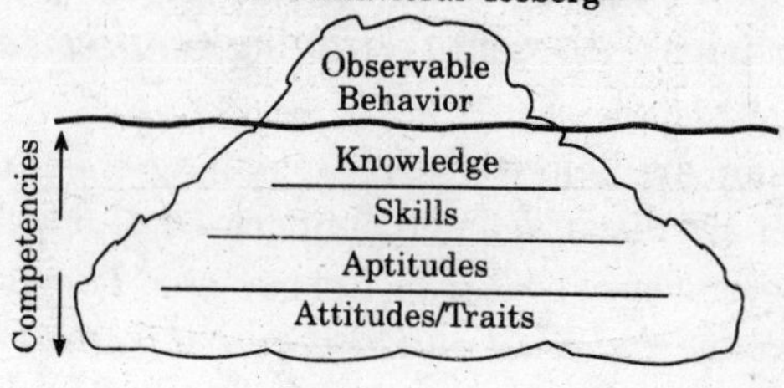

Types of Competencies

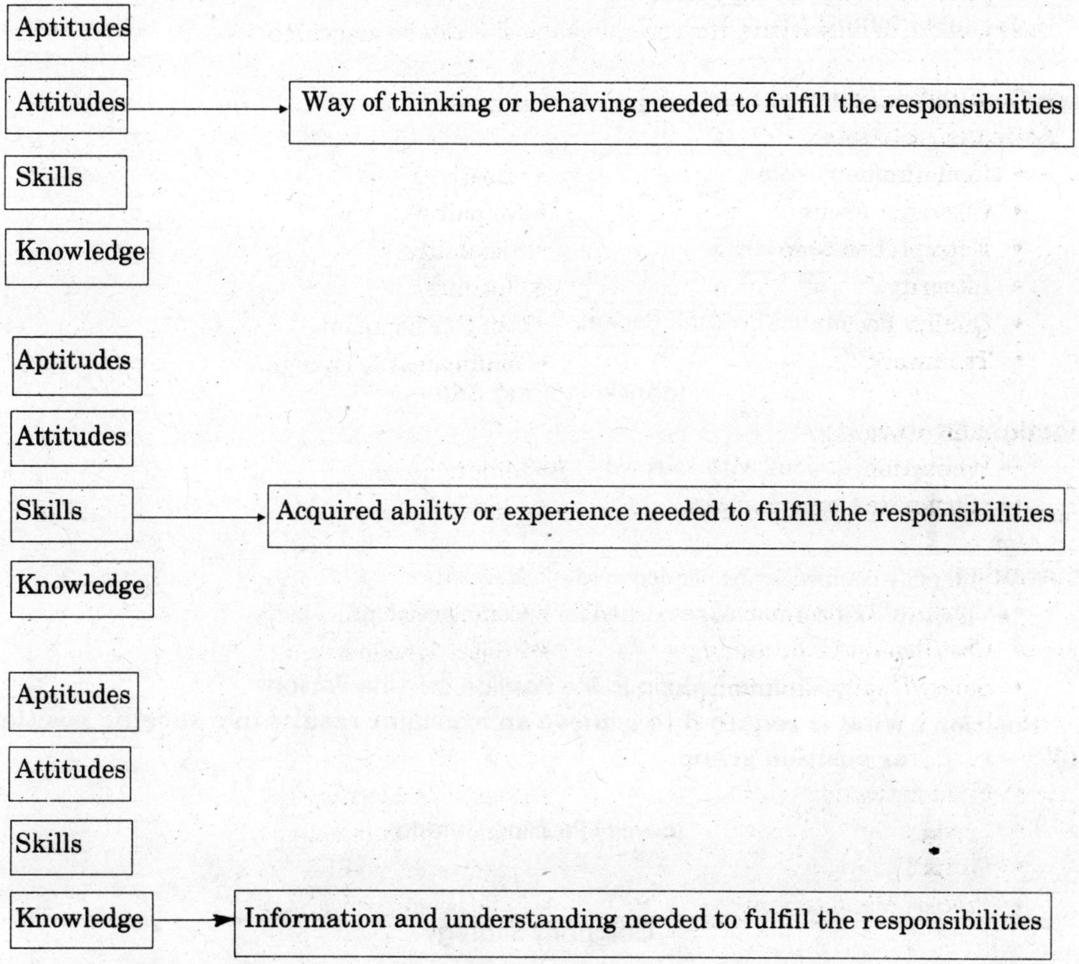

Competency Profiling

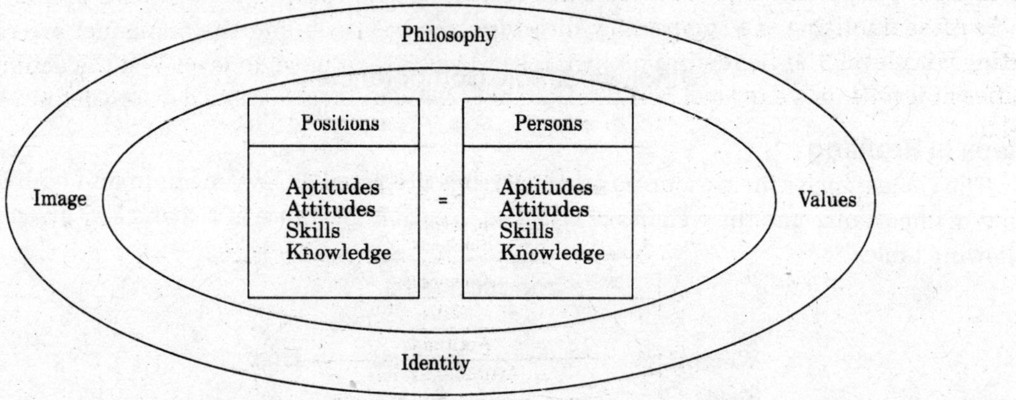

Steps on Profiling

1. Identify Profiling Criteria
2. Define Criteria Scales
3. Profile Position
4. Profile Persons
5. Match Position/Person

Identify Profiling Criteria

- Group discussions with selected executives
- Structured questionnaires

Aim :

- Identify competencies needed across organization
- Identify skills/knowledge needed for specific positions

Relate Criteria to the Position *and* the Person

Position : What is required to achieve an excellent results in a specific position or position group

Identify Profiling Criteria

↓

Company Strategy

↓

Core Competencies/Organizational Capabilities

↓

Individual/Role Competencies

Steps in Profiling

The competencies for various positions/persons are rated as low, medium and high on the basis of importance and the weightage attached to each importance is 1, 2 and 3 as given in the following table :

Importance

Weightage	Low	Medium	High
Score	1	2	3

Now the position and person holding the position are evaluated on the above mentioned competencies and the total score of the individual is worked out on competencies viz. Skills, Knowledge, Attitude and Aptitude.

While comparing the two scores, the competency gaps between the individual and positions are identified and while assessing the competency profile, we move to each dimension of competency and define the importance and the profiling independently first for the position and then for the person. Based on the data for position competencies and person competencies, the bar charts are drawn which help us to determine the ratio of overall competency to person, which should be around 80% - 85%. If there is too much of gap between the competencies of the positions and persons then it is an area of concern. As a part of Personnel Development Plan, the study gives us the gap analysis which help us to decide about the training inputs required. For Personnel Development the score of position is given as "X" and score of person is given as "O". Comparison of "X" and "O" indicate us the clear competency gaps viz. "Profiling and Developing Core Competencies" is given position with regard to person by (i) position ratio and (ii) position, and person profile gap analysis.

The model gives us an insight into the importance of each position facelessly and gives us the relevant organisation chart based on the relevant worth of each job. The model gives us the competency gap between the position and position holder. The gaps are addressed through appropriate training inputs. This help us to address training needs as per the organisational requirements. The whole process help us to update the managerial skills of the organisation and integrate with organisational objectives.

The Person Development - Person/Positon, Person Competencies, Person and Position, Profile and Gap Analysis are given in figure below. Similarly, the concepts given by Richard Payne during the training programme "Profiling and Developing Core Competencies" is also being discussed.

The Corporate Resources

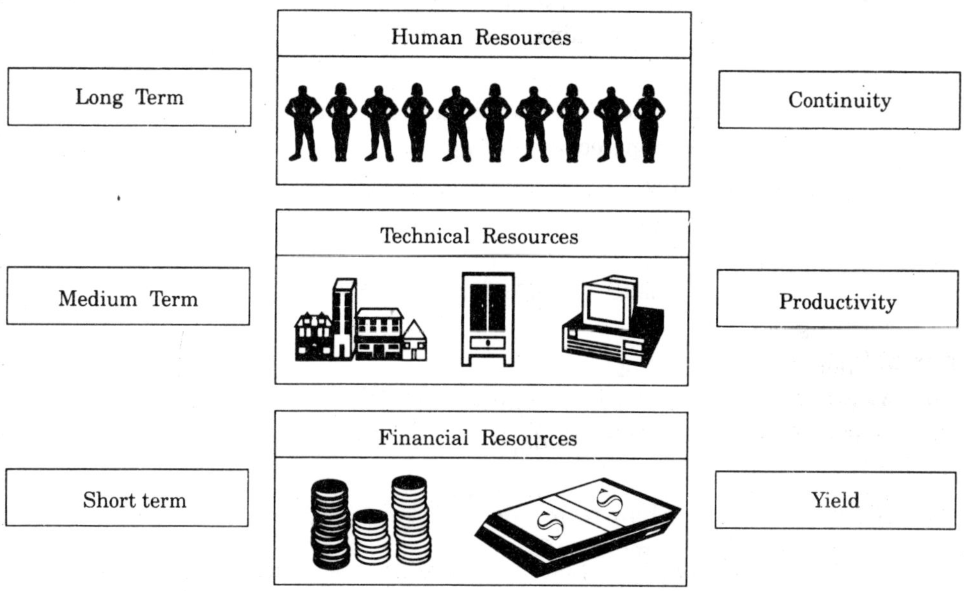

PROFILING AND DEVELOPING CORE COMPETENCIES

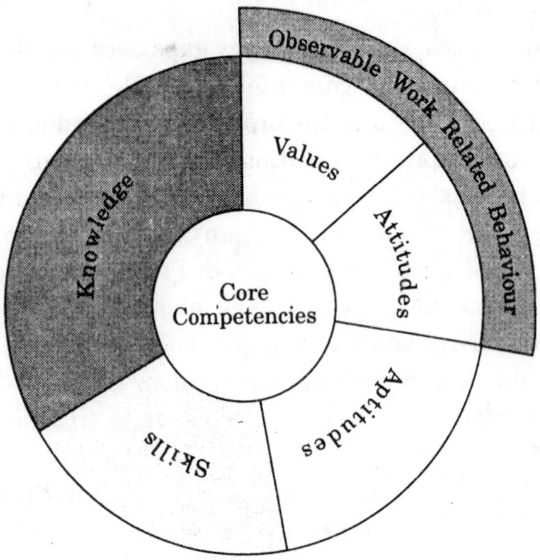

To identify the skills, knowledge, attitudes and aptitudes that the organisation requires (and has not yet tapped) to fulfill its vision and objectives

Workshop on Competency Profiling

- Develop Compectency profiling Criteria
- Profile Position Requirements
- Assesss and Employee's Aptitudes, Skills and Knowledge
- Match a Person's Competency against Position Requirement

Competency Profiling—A Critical Tool for Human Resources Management

- Purpose and Process of Competecy Profiling
- Develop Competency Scales
- Identify Core Competencies
- Workshop on writing Profiling Scales

Profiling Positions

- Workshop on Position Profiling
  - — Acquire the skills to develop profiling criteria
  - — Gain insight into current trends, practices and issues in human resources development.
  - — Have knowledge of how to profile employees and position, forecast recruitment, training and development needs.

Profiling Persons

- 10^0 to 180^0 to 360^0 Person Assessment
- Designing Profiling Tools
- Understanding effective approaches and techniques of Person Assessment

Maximising the Value of Competency Profiling

- Analysing Profiles for Individual Development
- Interpret results for Organisation Development
- Using results for Recruitment, Training and Development

22

Human Resource Planning

INTRODUCTION

Regaining Competitiveness

The new economic policy initiated in July 1991, is striving to transform India from a control-ridden, inward looking economy to a market-friendly, outward-looking progressive economy. It has unleashed a plethora of challenges to the Indian industry. Today's new world of business is characterised by (*a*) the power shift from the captains of industry to the customer, (*b*) the intensification of competition, and © the bewildering pace of change in the environment. To succeed and thrive in this liberalised era, Indian industry has no choice but to become globally competitive. It must seek to maximise the value delivered to its customers by offering products and services of superior quality at lower costs with minimum response/cycle time.

For most of the last 30 years, thoughtful strategic business planning and human resource planning (HRP) have been important predictors of organizational success. However, for most of this period these two disciplines were operating in almost total isolation of one another. Strategic planners typically viewed human resource management in general, and Human Resource Planning specifically, as functions peripheral to the immediate task of making money. Their efforts were classified as "personnel record keepers" by many who assumed that their sole function was to make sure that everyone received the right pay and took the correct number of vacation days. This limited view of the Human Resource function became self-confirming. Lack of recognition perpetuated Human Resource limited role and utility, although the fast changing business scene had already elevated human resources to a critical role in productivity and profits.

A number of factors have sped up the marriage between these important specialities. Internationalisation of American corporations, changing customer needs and rapid technological changes provided organisations a business climate that is dynamic and filled with uncertainty. In addition, the "quality imperative" gaining recent momentum has caused organisations to rethink the relationship of strategic planning and management development. The fast growing presence of foreign firms with U.S. workforce elevated the importance of Human Resource in these multi-cultural companies. Successful firms have found that "getting the right person in the right place" is overly simplistic: environments are too complex. To achieve and sustain a true competitive advantage, it is more important "to get the right person in the right place at the right time" and achieve sufficient flexibility to reconfigure staffing and competencies in much shorter cycle times.

The environmental factors above changed the way that theoreticians and top level managers view competitiveness. In earlier years, competitiveness was gained and held onto until other firms could either catch up or differentiate themselves in the consumer's eye. Presently, catching up does not take as long as it used to as firms have reduced product cycle time from weeks to hours.

Similarly, product substitutes enter the market on a continuous basis making long-term differentiation difficult. Moreover, decision-makers no longer see technological ability, pricing differentiation, and product perceptions as the sole forms of competitive advantage. Successful firms have come to the conclusion that some-one has to do the work. Technological knowledge is of little help if it isn't utilised and improved. Similarly, a pricing advantage is not one unless someone can produce it. In essence, many are finding that a true competitive advantage is internal to the organisation, not external as was once thought. A dynamic shift has occurred as strategic goals have merged with human resource planning goals involving staffing and development. Numerous organisational examples now document this shift for achieving competitive advantage in both private and public domains. These cases serve as models for other firms seeking similar results.

Business Strategy and Human Resource Management

HRP's major challenge of integrating business strategy and human resource practices probably achieves its greatest potential in the area of management development. The new paradigm of Management Development focuses on enhancing an organisation's effectiveness while simultaneously maintaining a competitive advantage. It is increasingly global in outlook and builds on a "seamless" organisational structure that minimises functional, unit, and international border lines. It is building organisational excellence through the continuous alignment of organisational members, business process and structures with vision values, strategies. The critical features of this newer perspective and approach: emphasis is on leadership and quality of management, rather than central authority and command : trust and partnership rather than bureaucratic control. Thus, this orientation defines the corporate specify global strategies and exerts functional control, establish standards and provide orientation. Programs are increasingly customised and systematically relative to individual needs. Notable in the development and assimilation of Management Development programs with strategic planning are such key issues as leadership, market/client thinking (which is often cross-cultural) adaptability, implementation strategies, and change management. The goal is to obtain the fullest use of human resource capabilities.

Developing positive human response to organisational change is therefore a critical success factor in the journey to competitiveness. Increasingly, the speed of implementing change in an organisation is emerging as the new competitive differentiator among organisations. With environmental change becoming pervasive and persistent, organisations would do well to institutionalise the capacity to adapt to change.

To address the business challenges of the open regime, the Human Resource function in an organisation must develop the capacity to :

- facilitate the strategy formulation process;
- translate the corporate strategy into a human resource strategy;
- design or redesign organisational structure and systems to serve the strategy;

- recruit and select employees to fit both the strategy and the desired culture;
- design performance management systems that motivate and energise the workforce;
- create work culture and emphasise organization's values;
- design systems for employee development and career management;
- actively support the line and staff management in problem solving, and accomplishing the desired organisational change.

To successfully meet this challenge, the Human Resource function must radically transform itself from its hitherto protective, score keeping role to a productive, leadership role.

The emerging role of the Human Resource professional can be delineated into four distinct stands as follows :

Business Partner

- providing inputs for corporate policy decisions
- aligning structure and systems to fit the strategy
- actively helping line managers in problem solving

Innovator

- reengineering those traditional Human Resource processes which are related to the personnel function
- creating better performance management and employee development systems

Integrator

- building a synergetic organisational culture
- creating a fit between individual aspirations and organisational objectives
- fostering a climate of trust and empathy for effective performance of cross functional teams

Change Agent

- Challenging the status quo and bringing new perspectives to the thinking of people in organisations
- catalysing change through effective communication of the vision of the organisation to employees.

New Competencies

The emerging role of the Human Resource professional calls for certain new competencies such as :

- Knowledge about the company and the industry; understanding the business direction of the company including how the company is positioned competitively in the market place.
- Change Management Skills: acquiring the content and process skills required to bring about the desired transformation in a company.

- Attitude of continual learning: staying current with state -of-the-art human resource practices and bench-marking against global standards.
- Cross-functional exposure: spending time with line managers to understand and appreciate their perspective of their department and the company as a whole.

Table A. The Evaluation of Change Thinking

S.No.	*Period*	*Focus*	*Objective*	*Change ingredients*
1.	1960s	Systems engineering	To enhance efficiency through the definition and standardisation of works practices	and the tight measurements of performance coupled with incentified bonus schemes
2.	1970s	Culture change	To introduce flexible working and so realise the potential in people	* Job/work design * teamworking * job enrichment/motivation * leadership training/ managerial GRID * interpersonal sensitivity training/T groups
3.	Late 1970s	Organisation redesign	To structure a flexible response to the changing business environment	* matrix management systems * centralisation *vs* devolution * strategic planning and review
4.	Late 1970s onwards	Introduction of psychometrics	To ensure that the right people are selected	developed and promoted
5.	1980s	Performance management	To motivate and reward people for measurable performance	* management by objectives * staff appraisal * reward systems * career management,
6.	1980s	Business internationalisation	to develop business on a world	* IT systems * telecommunications * planning conferences * strategic business units * portfolio management * the international manager * cross-cultural awareness mission and values
7.	1980s	Customer focus	To establish a customer/ market orientation to business growth	* just in time schemes * total quality management * market led planning * service/performance standards * customer care campaigns
8.	Mid 1980s	Management competences	To select and develop the people who will be high performers in the future business environment	* competency profiling * Best vs 'the rest' comparison * behavioural event interviewing * development/assessment centres * individual development planning * manager as a 'coach'
9.	Late 1980s	The flatter organisation	To shorten the lines of communication and the speed and quality of decision making	* broadened spans of controls * management by objectives/exception * devolution of responsibilities and authorities * organisation re-design * reduction of overheads/ bureaucracy
10.	Early 1990s	Process re-engineering	To focus on the critical management processes which deliver competitive advantages	* critical success factor analysis * task forces on process improvements * team/cross-team working * continuous improvement thinking

1. Pleassey introducing job redesign into the wiring line where the teams were asked to organise their work patterns and inspection procedures.
2. ICI investing in a major training programme across all management levels, aimed at questioning leadership approach and attitudes to people, and encouraging team and cross-team working and improvement planning.
3. Shell International devolving responsibility to the country operations and realigning the corporate Headquarter's roles.
4. Cable & Wireless carrying out management managerial strength audits of all their management levels.
5. Lloyds Bank introducing job accountability definition and training in appraisal skills.
6. Hiram Walker's start up of an apple juice factory in Eastern Europe.
7. Grant Thornton training programmes for all management and partner levels on client management skills.
8. Manchester Airport exercise, establishing the managerial competences needed from the top to the bottom of the organization to establish the transition from local authority control to international airport.
9. British Sugar Research Laboratories reducing management levels and defining the competencies, both scientific and managerial, needed to move from level to level.

23

Functions of Human Resource Management

Human Resource management requires constant alerts and awareness to human relation and its importance in day-to-day operations. Human Resource Management is of specialised nature and are mostly termed as staff functions. Human Resource Management are inherent in the process of management and are application to all managers in an organisation. Every manager in an organisation has to perform the personnel functions in one form or the other in order to get things done through others. The Human Resource Management functions can be classified as :

(*a*) Managerial.

(*b*) Operative.

The managerial functions are mainly concerned with planning, organising, directing and controlling of various activities of personnel department. The operative functions are those functions which are entrusted to the personnel department such as general supervision, employment, development, motivation, communication, compensation, integration and maintenance of personnel of the organisation. Personnel management deals with the managing of these functions efficiently and economically.

Managerial Functions

(*a*) **Personnel Planning**

Effective personnel planning should be responsive to organisational needs. Planning the activities of personnel department is not very different from the management planning, involving development of specific objectives and means of reaching these objectives.

Planning is deciding in advance what to do ; how to do ; where to do; and who is to do it. It bridges the gap between where we are to, where we want to go. For the personnel manager, planning means the determination in advance of personnel programme. The personnel management has to deal with many questions, for instance : how many and what type of people are required and how to motivate them. Planning involves the ability to think, to analyse and to search decisions or alternatives.

Characteristics of Effective Personnel Planning

Following are the three essential characteristics to effective personnel planning and control.

(*a*) To understand the organisation, its philosophy and scope.

(*b*) Appreciation of environmental constrains.

(*c*) Efficient and devoted people to achieve the objectives of the organisation within constraints.

The scope and techniques will vary from one organisation to another. But it is essential to understand the existing and continuously changing relationships and constraints. Constraints influencing personnel goals exist both inside and outside the organisation. Inside the organisation one of the important factors is the attitude of top management toward the organisation. The economic condition of the company and future business plans also affect personnel programme planning. The external environments like labour market, competition also affect personnel planning. The personnel goals can be classified as :

(*a*) Programme goals.
(*b*) Procedural goals.
(*c*) Professional goals.

(*a*) **Programme Goals.** Programme goals require a new activity which is likely to produce new results. Programme goals should be very specific and are not the same as department policy.

(*b*) **Procedural Goals.** It aims at improving the quality, time and cost effectiveness in he activity of the department. The possibilities for procedural goals are almost infinite.

(*c*) **Professional Goals.** The main growth and development process for employees are primarily professional goals. The goals for the Peronnnel Department are met when there is a broad-based participation in their formulation. The details of goals setting procedures in personnel department vary from organisation to organisation, depending upon the environmental factors.

The Human Resource department incurs cost to serve the entire organisation. As such it must earn the acceptance and support of the organisation if it is to be successful. The goal setting procedures should include the following steps :

(*a*) Evaluating past performance.
(*b*) Developing environmental inputs.
(*c*) Getting suggestions from different levels in the organisation including personnel staff.
(*d*) Evaluating recommended actions.
(*e*) Developing recommended objectives.
(*f*) Obtaining approval and support from higher management.

In developing personnel department objectives, it is important to undertake certain measures to overcome a number of problems. A few of the problems are :

(*a*) Top management uncrealistic expectation about personnel function.
(*b*) The setting of appropriate priorities and avoiding complex procedures.
(*c*) The capacity of the personnel department to pursue goals.
(*d*) Assessing accurately the relation of authority, influence esteem and goals.

(b) Organising

Organising means to create a structure or framework of authority and responsibility within which the functions of management will be discharged. It means to coordinate the efforts of a group to achieve certain aims and objectives with the help of other factors of production. The Personnel Manager has to organise certain personnel functions by designing the structure of relationship among jobs, personnel and physical factors to contribute towards organisational objectives.

(c) Directing

Direction is concerned with the initiation of organised action and stimulating the people to work. Direction involves the issuance of orders and the motivation of personnel to execute these orders. The personnel manager directs the activities of people of his department to get its functions performed. In other words, direction is meant to motivate and activate the people to follow the proper laid down path.

(d) Controlling

Control is concerned with the regulation of activities in accordance with the personnel plans, which, in turn, have been formulated on the basis of an analysis of the fundamental goals of the organisation. Thus control completes the cycle and leads us back to planning. It is the observation and comparison of results with the targets and correction and comparison of deviations that may occur. It assists to suggest directives and measures to rectify any mistake in the execution of plans. Controlling also helps the personnel manager to evaluate the performance of the personnel department in doing the various operative functions.

Operative Functions

The Personnel Department performs the following operative functions :

(a) Employment

The first operative function of personnel management is the employment of right kind and number of persons, necessary to achieve the objectives of the organisation. This involves recruitment, selection and placement of the personnel. Before these processes are performed, it is better to determine the manpower requirements, both in terms of number and quality of personnel. Recruitment and selection cover the various sources of supply of labour and the devices designed to select the right type of people for various jobs.

(b) Development

After placing the people on various jobs, the personnel management is concerned with giving them training to develop them to do their work efficiently. Proper development of personnel is essential to increase their skills and abilities to help them in the effective performance of their jobs. To achieve this, the personnel department will devise an appropriate training programme for developing the people at work.

(c) Compensation

This function is concerned with the determination of adequate and equitable remuneration of the people in the organisation for their contribution to the organisational goals. The personnel can be compensated both in terms of money as well as non-monetary units. Factors which much be borne in mind while fixing the compensation or remuneration of personnel are their basic needs, requirements of jobs, legal provisions regarding minimum wages, capacity of the organisation to pay, wage level of the competitors etc. For fixing the wave levels, the personnel management can make use of certain techniques like job evaluation, performance evaluation etc.

(d) Integration

This is an important function of personnel management to achieve a reasonable reconciliation of interests of the personnel with that of the organisation. The most important aspect related to integration is communication. The personnel manager must provide an efficient system of communication to ensure two way communication of personnel programmes and policies. Many a time industrial disputes develop because of poor communication ; therefore, the personnel manager should always keep in touch with the trade unions to understand their grievances and remove them so that harmony is maintained in the organisation.

(e) Working Condition

Merely appointing and training people is not sufficient; they must be provided with good working conditions so that they may like their work and workplace and maintain efficiency. Working conditions certainly influence the motivation and morale of the employees. This includes the measures to be taken for health, safety, welfare and ensure high morale of the employees to keep them interested in the work entrusted to them.

(f) Welfare Services

The personnel department provides for various welfare services which relate to the physical and social well-being of the employees. This may include provision for canteen, rest rooms, counselling, group insurance, education of the children of employees, and other recreational facilities.

24

Industrial Psychology

Concepts

Psychology is the study of human behaviour. The personnel problems are essentially the problems of industrial psychology and constitute a main subject of study. The first contact of an individual with the personnel department is at the time of employment. During this process the personnel department encounters with the problems of selection and placement growing out of individual differences. Many of the psychological studies in industry have been directed to tests, rating scales, interviews, and similar techniques and devices for use in vocational selection. In the areas of education and training some of the most fruitful applications of psychology directly stem from the laws of learning. It has been recognised that some of the greatest improvements in efficiency result from training not only the workers but also the foremen and other executives. Successful accident prevention, formation of safety and health habits, and development of efficient habits of work follow the principles of motivation and learning. The solution of problems of morale and commitment, grievances and misunderstanding, and various aspects of labour and management relations hinges upon adequate understanding of human motives, about which modern psychology can help. In order to understand the real application of psychology in personnel, we shall first study what is industrial psychology? What are its objects, functions and how does it help in the area of personnel management?

Definition

Industrial psychology is the study of people at work. It deals with their aptitudes and their qualifications for job. Industrial psychology is firstly the study of human behaviour and is concerned with the discovery of information relating to human behaviour. Secondly, it is concerned with the application of information about human behaviour to the various problems of human life. Industrial psychology is the professional aspect of psychology. In other words, it is the study of human relations, mental health of the personnel on the job and ways to help to maintain good mental health for those people who have become confused and upset. It is the study of boss and subordinates. The application of psychology to the problems of industry covers these areas ; namely, selection, placement, training and study of the behaviour of the people in the organisation, the design of man-machine system, etc.

In fact, each one of us play different roles in various aspects of human life in schools, at home, in colleges and in social and political circles. As we change hats from one role in our society to another we do not, in fact, become different individuals. Industrial psychology addresses itself to the study of behaviour in these various roles of life and to the application of pertinent information about human behaviour to the solution of human problems. The aim of Industrial Psychology is to give the worker greater physical and mental ease at his work. To achieve the aim of industrial psychology, the work of the psychologist in the industry can be described as follows :

(*a*) To investigate in an unbiased manner the ways in which psychological problems are handled at present.

(*b*) To develop new methods and to modify the methods which have been tried out and evaluated.

(*c*) To formulate certain principles which will help in the solution of new problems.

To sum up, the aim of industrial psychological is research rather than administration. The scope of industrial psychology is limited to material and social environmental to which an individual adapts himself while he is at work and by which his attitude is modified. As a matter of fact, industrial psychology is research. Since industrial psychology is the study of people at work and is concerned with the entire spectrum of human behaviour, its scope is the entire process of management's dealings with people at work. It is important to note that industrial psychology lays emphasis on scientific research aspects of people at work and omits many of the routine administrative details. Industrial psychology is a useful aid to the efficient management of people at work.

History

Industrial psychology address itself to the study of human behaviour in industrially related aspects of life. Psychology is the study of human behaviour and, it can be considered as embracing two major facets. In the first place, psychology is concerned with the discovery of information relating to human behaviour. The other phase is concerned with the application of information about human behaviour to the various practical problems of human life. This facet can be tought of as the professional aspect of psychology, in much the same way that physicians, engineers, and others are concerned with the application of knowledge about some field to the practical problems of the real world. Industrial psychology addresses itself to the study of human behaviour to the solution of human problems in this context. Industrial psychology is the existence of human problems in organisations, and its objective is to somehow provide the basis for resolving these problems or, more realistically, for minimizing them. The field of industrial psychology grew to its present maturity against the backdrop of these major changes in our economy.

This field of psychology has developed largely since the turn of the century. One of the first major books in the area was Hugo Musterberg's Psychology of Industrial Efficiency. The early industrial psychologists were concerned particularly with problems of personnel selection, but their interests also embraced other applied areas, such as advertising and selling, accidents, and employee rating processes. But by the 1930s the field of industrial psychology had been established as a reasonably distinct phase of psychology. Its major development and expansion, however, have occurred since then. In the intervening years the fields has developed in countries all over the world, with the primary development being in certain countries in Western Europe and in United States. The last four decades have seen various changes in emphasis with regard to the kinds of problems with which industrial psychologists have been concerned.

During the 1940s and 1950s considerable interest was generated in the human relations aspects of personnel management, with particular concern for group interaction, supervision and leadership processes, communications and job satisfaction. This increased emphasis on human relations in industry led to greater attention to human-relations training of supervisory and management personnel and to management development programmes. What is more, interest in the social aspects of human work has led logically to the crystallization of what is now referred to as organisational psychology; in this new discipline the dominant focus is on human motivation and efforts are made to understand effects of the organisational setting on motivation, job satisfaction, and work effectiveness.

Development of Organisational Psychology

The development of organisational psychology has entailed a growing interest in leadership styles, management philosophies. Organisational policies and structures, incentive systems, and other aspects of organisations as they relate to both human satisfactions and organisational effectiveness. Paralleling these developments during the past three decades or so has been the development of the field of human factors engineering (or ergonomics). The objective of this field is to design physical equipment and facilities tailored to human abilities and limitations. Although this field is an interdisciplinary one, psychologists have played an important role in it over the years ; the segment of this domain in which psychologists have made inputs in sometimes called engineering psychology. The efforts of industrial psychologists have been directed largely toward the study of the independent relationships between specific variables on one hand and various aspects of work-related behaviour on the other. Thus, there have been investigations dealing independently with such specific variables as individual differences, organisational characteristics, incentives, group structure, equipment design, and working conditions. According to Uhlaner, effective behaviour and work performance are not always the additive effects of whatever variables may be involved, as different variables interact in this process and may be complicated further with different types of jobs. Thus, for example, one type of incentive might be appropriate for some kinds of people and jobs but not for others.

Primary Role of Industrial Psychologists

The primary role of industrial psychologists in dealing with human problems in the industrial arena is to bring to bear knowledge and insight that can be used to resolve these problems. Because this is essentially a research function, the methods used in this process are central to the development of such knowledge and insight. Industrial psychologists become involved in a variety of activities, but in a sense their roles can be viewed as relating either to the science of psychology or to the profession of psychology. In this regard it should be emphasized that the profession of psychology needs to be rooted in psychological research. Thus even psychologists who are serving primarily in a professional role usually need to be well versed in research methodology. Psychology as a profession is concerned with the 'application' of knowledge to some practical problem. Thus industrial psychologists who perform such functions are serving as professional practitioners.

Psychologist's Role in Individual Evaluation

In the field of individual evaluation, the psychologist functions much like a clinical expert in assessing the potentialities of individual for specific positions, promotions, and so forth, or in counselling the individual himself. It is only in the field of individual evaluation that the psychologist in industry uses this psychological background extensively in dealing with individuals as individuals. In his other functions he deals with human behaviour in conceptual terms than on an individual basis.The findings, principles and techniques of industrial psychology may be applied with benefit to the following areas of the management :

(*a*) Selection and Placement

(*b*) Training and Executive Development

(*c*) Human Engineering

(*d*) Motivation

(*e*) Attitude and Morale

(*f*) Counselling

(*g*) Public Relation Research

(*h*) Organisational Behaviour

(*a*) **Selection and Placement.** To select the right person for the right job in the organisation, one should measure the candidate's aptitude, intelligence, skill, abilities, interests and temperament. Industrial psychology provides a valuable test for measuring these. The basic problem posed in the selection of people for jobs can be stated as follows :

(*i*) We must know what the job involves in terms of duties to be performed and in terms of skills and knowledge. This calls for the understanding of conditions under which it is carried out. After knowing and collecting all the relevant informations, they can be translated into personal attributes which must be possessed by an individual if he is to perform these duties efficiently.

(*ii*) After we have drawn up the specifications, the second part of the task is to screen the applications in order to decide whether they possess the attributes required in to the appropriate degree. This essential aspect of the selection problem involves careful consideration of human attributes, characteristics, or personal qualities. This demands a conceptual framework within which to deal with them.

What we require is an adequate set of categories to classify human attributes. Within each category there should be a series of levels so that the differing demands of jobs and assessment of individuals can be expressed in objective and communicable terms. Five aspects of the individual's personality, which are important.

(*b*) **Training and Executive Development.** After careful selection of executives using tests and interviews what is needed is training the executives so that they may perform better at their present jobs. In organising an executive development programme, the industrial psychology keeps a range of goal in mind to increase the effectiveness of the executive group.

Application : The industrial psychology may be applied with benefit to the following areas:

— Selection

— Training,

— Human Engineering, and

— Motivation.

In organising an executive development programme, the industrial psychology keeps a range of goal in mind to increase the effectiveness of the executive group. The technique of sensitivity programme when helps the executive to develop his areas of strength and weakness while working in group is a clear example.

(*c*) **Human Engineering.** It is designing and laying out equipment in order to get the greatest efficiency of man-machines system. The industrial psychologist working in human engineering provides data on which management can decide to improve the design, improve the product for the comfort of the users and to increase the sale and satisfaction of the customers.

(*d*) **Motivation.** The psychologists proceed on the assumption that human behaviour is caused and does not occur automatically. The cause of different types of human behaviour in industry and business are the needs or motives that drive an individual to behave in a particular way. Thus the problem of how to motivate the people has been made easy by the industrial psychology.

(*e*) **Attitude and Morale.** To keep high the morale of personnel is another significant problem of management. Industrial psychologist can go into the causes of low morale of the employees and can determine the factors influencing the relationship between the attitudes of employees and their performance. It explains the behaviour of people when they work in groups.

(*f*) **Counselling.** It is used to remove non adjustment problem while placing the right man for the right job. Counselling can be done when the individual registers himself with the employment exchange or where the man is in the job and because maladjusted. Industrial psychology helps the management in counseling employees to find solution to the problem of misplacement of employees.

(*g*) **Public Relations.** Industrial Psychology helps the management to develop effective and systematic public relation machinery in order to create a8 high image of the organisation. With the rapid expansion and growth of industrial undertakings the management is facing problems in effectively communicating its policies, procedures and practices to its employees, shareholders, consumers and general public.

(*h*) **Organisational Behaviour.** The managements in public, private and even in other sectors are realising the importance of team spirit in the organisation and redesigning their organisational structures and policies based on research findings on organisational behaviour.

25

Study of Individual

Study of Individual

Action is the beginning of everything in business. The core of all the activities in business is the human activity. We should not only judge the success of a business organisation mainly by statistics or the amount of money spent in expansion but also by the quality of human character that is evolved. In any human activity, nothing of any consequence happens until an individual wants to act. What individual can accomplish depends to greater extent on how much and why one wants to act. The individuals' Will to Work is something different from his Capacity to Work. One can buy man's time, his physical efforts but not his enthusiasm, initiative or loyalty. There is a saying you can lead a horse to water but you cannot make him drink. This proverb involves elements such as YOU, HORSE, LEAD, WATER. The element which is missing is the THIRST, or NEED or DESIRE. But in the context of man the terms 'need' and 'desire' are more difficult as human being is more complex than a horse. major problems in toady's Organisations are how to get maximum efforts and contribution of individuals. The conflict between individual needs and the achievement of organisational objectives has been of major concern to Managers. To understand the problems of an organisation a thorough study of the fundamental element-INDIVIDUAL is essential. An attempt has been made to study the characteristics of an individual such as personality, perception etc.

Individual personality is the dynamic organisation and it requires a continuous adjustment and development. According to Peter principle, every employee tends to rise to his level of incompetence. We also know according to distribution theory that majority of us are moderately competent and a few of us are competent and a few incompetent. An individual may be competent at a particular positon in the organisational hierarchy in terms of skill, potential and personality traits but may be incompetent for the next position in the hierarchy, as different organisational positions involve different skills, temperament, interest, efforts and traits. An employee may be competent as a Supervisor and reaches level of incompetence as an officer. There can be another case where an executive may be a competent executive as a departmental head and not as an organisational head. It is because of different job requirements and job specification that a man become competent or incompetent for a position.

The Peter's principle is shown in Fig. 25.1. Individual has to develop himself through the process of self development to match the changing needs of the organisation. If an individual wants to become a human resource he needs to develop himself through the process of self awareness and self development. Self development will demand the desire to improve, wisdom for selection of appropriate actions and time necessary to work for the improvement. The desire therefore must come from within, the wisdom must be develop and time must be planned. Self development not only provide a better executive life but also a richer and fuller social life. The study of an individual is required by the Manager not only for himself development but also for organizing Human Resource and Polymerizing the individuals in an organisation to result in a cohesive and enormous force. Human polymerization needs the individual, ideas and desire of organisational system. Polymerization could be possible if an individual establishes a bond with other individuals multiply and generate power to create, build and to produce. It is only the human resource which appreciates with time whereas all other resource indicate the process of depreciation.

Characteristics

Traits. Triats are the characteristics of an individual. Trait is a function of heredity learning similar situations. Traits are dimensions of behaviour in which individuals differ. Traits are present in almost all the people in varying degrees. Traits are learned tendencies to react to the environmental stimuli and are based on hereditary foundations. A trait is described as a dimension of personality which consist of a group of related and consistent characteristics of a person's typical adjustment. Every trait has three characteristics :

(*a*) Uniqueness
(*b*) Degree of likeableness
(*c*) Consistency

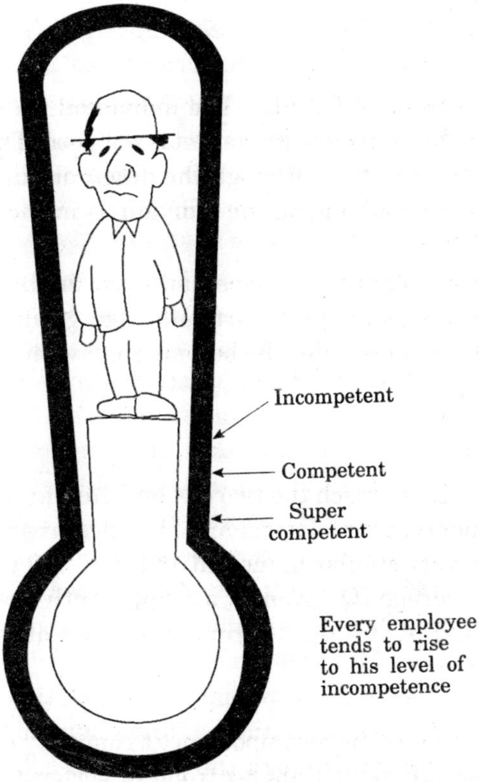

Fig. 25.1.

Beside the uniqueness of traits, the other important traits is likeableness. The traits liked by other include honesty generosity and trustworthiness, rudeness, cruelty and egocentreism. These traits result from social learning in a particular culture setting and are almost universal within a culture. The traits are liked or disliked because they contribute to social harmony and disharmony. The other characteristics of traits is consistency. It means that a person shall behave in the same way in similar situations. Traits are more variable in their limited tendencies while traits are generalised determining tendencies. Traits are often the result of integration of several specific habits. Traits are basically of two types *viz.*

(*a*) Expressive traits, and
(*b*) Performance traits.

Expressive Traits

The expressive traits are the group of traits consisting of regular habitual responses of individual. The expressive traits can be classified as :

(a) Physical traits
(b) Movement traits
(c) Perceptual traits
(d) Style traits
(e) Age
(f) Sex.

Physical Traits

Individual differences in physique are obvious and can be easily measured. Weight, and muscles are important in selection of men for certain types of jobs. But physique traits in themselves have failed to prove their value for the appraisal of personality.

Movement Traits

Individuals differ in posture, poise and movement with hands, legs and fingers. Co-ordination of fingers, legs and hands are important in many industrial jobs.

Perceptual Traits

Every individual perceivers the world and approaches his life problems differently. This factory is very important. We know that the world as we see is not necessarily the same as it really is. It is because what we hear is not what is really said. We buy what we like best and not what is best. It is because of perception that same job may appear a good job to one and staggy job to another.

Due to perception only 'facts' as they are seen by one viewer, may be different from the facts seen by another viewer. The tension or discomfort that one feels when he thinks he is missing something others cannot realise it.

Age

An individual behaves differently in different periods of his life. The individual over 45 years of age finds it very difficult to get new job when his employment market is not good. There is a feeling that older people cannot learn new things very fast although the difference in the ability to learn and the amount of intellegence is very small among the individuals in the age group of 50 to 60 years.

In selecting personnel as management trainees, engineer trainees and even for Indian Administrative Services. The age plays an important role. In a particular age group the individuals are more flexible and adaptable than the older people who become rigid with fixed ideas.

Sex

There is no psychological difference on the grounds on which the two can be differentiated. But some discrimination is due to the cultural influence, physiological and biological reasons. Because of jobs which they can perform, women are very similar in mental abilities. They are identical in mental abilities. They are identical in average IQ. Women are apparently better than men in memory work and in other routine jobs. But still the discrimination continues.

Performances Traits

Individual differences in performance traits are of considerable importance to industry even more than the expressing responses required a generally more complex trend in performance traits than the expressive traits. The performance traits can be of the following types :

(*a*) Intellectual abilities
(*b*) Special aptitudes and abilities
(*c*) Physical performance
(*d*) Non intellectual traits.

(*a*) **Intellectual Abilities**

A knowledge of mental abilities can be of importance in selecting personnel for various jobs. It has been observed that the turnover is excessive if employees' intelligence is too high or low. Similarly in other innovative jobs such as design, research and development, introducing new concepts and programmes, a high degree of mental abilities is indispensible for successful work. The differences between individuals is still greater as far as mental factors are concerned. In case of learning difficult material such as financial management, operational research, computer language, etc. the difference between the best and poorest is not more than 5 : 1.

The intelligence of an individual is the ability to learn and to understand instructins and ability to reason and make judgement. The understanding of these intellectual abilities of an individual is very important in selecting and placing the right man for the right job. The factors responsible for intellectual abilities are :

(*a*) *Numerical factor* : It refers to speed and accuracy in addition, subtraction, division and multiplication.

(*b*) *Verbal factor* : It refers to the vocabulary of an individual.

(*c*) *Perceptual factor* : It refers to bringing out a relationship between two objects.

(*d*) *Ability factors* : Mental abilities have been measured mainly by the use of I.Q. (Intelligence Quotient). It was Alfred Brief who designed the first practicable testing method. Brief was a physician who was concerned with the placing of children in schools. He devised a series of simple problems which he posed to the children who were presented to him for measuring intelligence.

He found that for each age group these was typical performance which represented the metal age for that group. He was able to set up a series of objective standards in terms of number of questions that should be answered correctly by the average child of five years, seven years, ten years and so on. When he tested a particular child, he was able to compare his performance with the average for his age. This was expressed in terms of an intelligence quotient which is no more than a simple arithmetical method or relating the child's age in years of his mental age.

$$\text{I.Q.} = \frac{\text{Mental age}}{\text{Chronological age}} \times 100$$

If the child is an average intelligence the I.Q. will be 100. If he is more intelligent than his age in years, the I.Q. will be above 100. If it is less, the I.Q. will be below 100. Any intelligence test which has been standardised for one group, may be of no use when applied to the members of another group. Normally there are two distinctions which must be borne in mind before applying any intelligence test. (*a*) Distinction should be made between the individuals living in the same community. (*b*) Distinction should be made between the intellectual environments.

There is always an inmate difference which shows in the different test scores the opportunity of acquring concepts, manipulating them and interchanging them with other individual.

(*b*) Special Aptitude

Aptitudes are the potentialities which the individuals have for learning a job quickly. Special aptitudes are important in industry, which, in other words, involve mechanical an titudes. The clerical aptitude is made up of verbal, numerical and perceptual speed factors. After testing the individual's aptitudes it becomes easy to select or reject him. The aptitudes and abilities are measured by observing this performance in that situation. During training and experience, aptitudes are relatively stable and constant. An individual's potentially for learning remains the same irrespective of his education.

(*c*) **Physical Performance**

It is rare that the individuals differ from one another by more than 25 per cent in bodily measurements. Although the difference may be little more in muscular control such as strength of grip, strength of legs, dexterity of fingers, eyes, hand co-ordination etc.

(*d*) **Non-Intellectual Traits**

Non-intellectual personality and inerest traits are important in the job of executives and supervisors. It is difficult to measure non-intellectual traits, such as honesty, integrity, initiative and ambition.

The non-intellectual traits are :

(*a*) Interests ; (*b*) Temperature ;

(*c*) Character ; (*d*) Schema ; and

(*e*) Motives.

(*a*) *Interest.* The individual normally has many interests in various areas. The top executives in any organisatoin do not have interests in common. The organisation should provide opportunities like job rotation and special training programme to satisfy the interests of executives. The successful persons in the same occupation have to a large extent, the same interests.

(*b*) *Temperament.* Temperament and other non-intellectual personality traits are distributed according to the normal distribution. Temperament is the degree to which one responds emotionally.

(*c*) *Schema.* It is the individual's belief, frame of reference role, perception, and attitude which the individual, possesses towards the management, the job, working conditions, pay, fringe benefits, incentive system, development programmes in the organisation. It depends upon individual's brief towards religion, government and the satisfaction derived from environment and from cultural influences of his community. The perception of individual depends upon his socio-economic condition and particular culture he lives to follow. The behaviour of an individual depends to a great extent upon his farme of references which he develops from the childhood experience and experiences are coloured by the social and ideological concepts of members of his family and community. The other important factors responsible for his behaviour are his religion, his education and his language. Because of these reasons there are marked differences among individuals so far as their beliefs, major orientations, role, perception, ideas and values are concerned.

(*d*) *Motives.* Motives are the inner drive of the individual. They represent goal directed behaviour of individual. Thus it is a cognitive factor which operates in determining one's behaviour towards goal. The study of difference kind of motives that are important in human help us to think the problem of motivation. Henry A. Murrary in 1930 along with his colleagues at the Harward Psychological Clinic invented a technique for assessing motivation which concertized the rich insight of Freud that human motives are most clearly expressed in free associative thought. This technique, the Thematic Appreception Test (TAT) require the individual to create imaginative stores in response to a series of pictures, the content of his fantasy is then analysed to reveal the underlying aims of his behaviour. Motivation does have an influence on the content of imaginative thought and that the influence of motivation is, encouragingly similar as one studies different kinds of motivating states. The measure of a motive should sensitively reflect the presence or absence of a motive. Psychologists have tried to vary the amount of motivation present in human beings in a number of ways some of ways are :

(*i*) To deprive the human subject of something in order to manipulate the strength of his hunger or thirst. It has sometimes been assumed that the perceptual and associative effects of prolonged starvation on conscientious object voluntarily depriving themselves amidst plenty would parallel the effects of starvation when food was simply scarce.

(*ii*) Psychologists have also applied strong persistent stimuli to the subjects in order to change their motivational state. Electric shock needle point showers have usually been the weapons of choice for producing such a stimulus. The effect of electric shock on conditioning and more leading has long been the subject of study but without any very tangible result, at least so far as the understanding of psychodynamics is concerned. Sometimes shock serve as information, sometimes as punishment, sometimes as a source of anxiety. The study revealed that electric shock is used not directly as a source of stimulation but indirectly as a source of anxiety, since anticipation of shock seems to produce many of the behavioural characteristics of anxiety.

(*iii*) The attempt to vary human motivation by the presentation of objects of different at activeness for example, barrier of children can be observed under the stimulus of "toys present" in the visual field as compared with barrier behaviour when no toys are present. This approach has not led to the development of any generalised measures of particular motives useful in assessing individual difference.

(*iv*) Attempts to manipulate human motives are also made directly by special instructions given to the subjects or by experiences that are experimentally induced. Sears and others suggested to induce ego involvement success and failure by various types of instructions and by manipulation of reported performance scores relative to levels of aspiration or norms reported for other competing individuals or groups. The frustration can be induced by such techniques as taking a bottle away from a baby, preventing Boy Scouts from seeing a movie they expected to see, keeping college students up all right etc. To date, human motives more or less successfully aroused in addition to the achievemnet motive more or less successfully aroused in addition to the achievement motive include *viz* : the affiliation motive aroused by exposing subjects to public sociometirc judgement the sexual motive aroused in male by nude female slide and by proximity to an attractive female and females by musical stimulations. The other major method of working with differences in motive strength is to go out and find these differences in nature, experimentally. That is, one finds two groups of subjects who differ in more conspicuous way and treats them as representing two different arousal states of motive. That is one can assume that academic achievers have higher achievement motivation than academic underachievers. But the difficulty with the group differences method is that groups may differ in more variables than the motive in questions ; overachievers differ from underachievers in other ways than in achievement motivation and these other differences may be picked up in the measure.

Motive As Latent Disposition

We conceive a motive as a latent disposition to strive for a particular goal-state or aim *e.g.* achievement, affiliation, power. The strength of a particular motive is assessed by Thematic apperception under neutral conditions. The term motivation can then be used to designate the around state of a person that exists when a motive has been engaged by the appropriate expectancy. If more than one of an individual's motives are engaged by expectancies that the same act will lead to several different goals, the total motivation for performance of that act will be the sum of the contributions made by the particular motives which have been engaged. An overdetermined action tendency *i.e.* one which will serve to satisfy more than one motive, is likely to be relatively strong.

The particular motives (Achievement, Affiliation, Power etc.) are conceived as latent dispositions to strive for certain goal states (aims) that are engaged in performance of an act when the cues of the situation arouse the expectancy that performance of an act is instrumental to attainment of the goal of the motive. The relationship of achievement motive (as measured by imaginative TAT stories) to performance is shown to the significantly positive when the expectancy that performance is instrumental to producing a feeling of pride in accomplishment is aroused and few if any other expectancies of goal-attainment are aroused. The experiments have provide that the task-relevant feedback for achievement-motivated subjects and 'feeling' feedback for affiliation motivated subjects would produce higher performance scores.

26

Organisation and the Individual

Individual in an Organisation

Major problems in today's organisations are how to maximise the efforts and contribution of individuals. The conflict between individual needs and organisational objectives has been of major concern to the managers and behavioural scientists. The management of an organisation should be concerned to develop personal characteristics and introduce operating effectivenss among its members. To understand the problems of an organisation a thorough study of an individual is essential. It is important to understand the behaviour of an individual, individual difference, characteristics of an individual such as personality, perception, attitude etc. Each one of us starts our life with a certain set characteristics. Every child which comes in this world is a unique personality.

Inheritance

An individual start life with certain set of characteristics. Each child right from his birth, is unique. Even identical twins upon closer observations may be found to be different. They physical traits such as height skin complexion, shape and size of nose, mouth, ears are largely hereditary. Similarly performance traits such as basic intelligence, muscle co-ordination, aptitude, dexterity, instintive drives, temperaments, interests are inherited. Alexander Thomas and Herbert G. Virch made a study on the behaviour of 231 children from infancy to teenage stage. The study outlined that there was marked difference in characteristics of new born children such as ability and persistence. The emergence of persistent attributes so early in life before outside influence can have much affect. It has been observed that all babies come equipped with certain instincts, reflexes and perceptual abilities.

Environment

Soon after the birth, person is affected by his environment. The inherited characteristics are modified by learning experiences to produce a complete personality. According to Locks "what a man become is entirely the results of experiences".

But many other behavioural scientists are of altogether different views that individual is conditioned by heredity in the womb and their lives are merely the application of his script. It has also been found that individual's who had not persuade any distinguished work for years together may produce work genious one day. The examples are Gregor Mendel who discovered the laws of heredity and Albert Einsten who has outlined one of the most momentous scientific researches on the area of relativity.

Heredity and Environment are so closely and inextricably linked that it is impossible to isolate the affect of any one in developing and moulding of individual. The inherited mental characteristics are modified by learning experiences to produce a complete personality. It is learning through experience combines with basic endowment to produce a complete personality. A person's habits knowledge, values and other personality characteristics are acquired through the learning process which involves stimulus--response patterns. By studying inherited human characteristics and human traits of perception, learning, emotions and complexes one can gain a better understanding of himself and appreciation of other person's actions. The understanding of himself and appreciation of other person's actions. The understanding of an individual's behaviour in an organisation can thus be understood with the knowledge of his individual personality characteristics. It is possible to ascertain the behaviour of an individual. We can find out whether an executive is rigid or indifferent from the score of an instrument. The instrument can be scored by finding out the sum of all positive and negative scores on various questionnaire given in the form of various situations.

Importance of Behavioural Information System

The primary value of a behaviour lines in its ability to make management aware of the sate of employee's perceptions, attitudes and preferences and how these may change overtime. In much the same way preventive maintenance and monitoring the condition of mechanical operations can minimise unexpected breakdowns and their associated costs. Monitoring the state of human elements can minimise unexpected cost of employees' dissatisfaction. The specific cost related to employee dissatisfaction is employee-turnover, absenteeism and counter productive behaviour.

Behavioural information system resolves this problem by gathering information, on employee's attitude and preferences before turnover occurs. This information allows management to be more effective to cope with the turnover problem, absenteeism and counter productive behaviour. The other value of behavioural information system is that it gives management the ability to logically and systematically analyse problems and suggest appropriate solutions. The first step towards better utiliation of the human elements is for management to understand how both the mechanical and human factors can effect employee's performance.

Relationship between Employee Attitudes and Job Performance

Employee attitudes are determined by—

(*a*) Their individual performances for certain types of jobs.

(*b*) The extent to which their perceptions of organisational and job characteristics are in agreement with their performance.

Generally the greater the extent of agreement, the more positive the employee's attitude towards his job. The existence of positive attitudes does

People are much the same yet altogether different. Man provides some 300 million sperm cells each packed with its sub-microscope load of heredity--controlling genes that transmit his own characteristics in particular and those of his race and human species in general. No two men in the world produce sperm with the same configuration of about 30,000 genes in each cell. The women ovum in turn also offers 30,000 genes ready for commingling with the sperms.

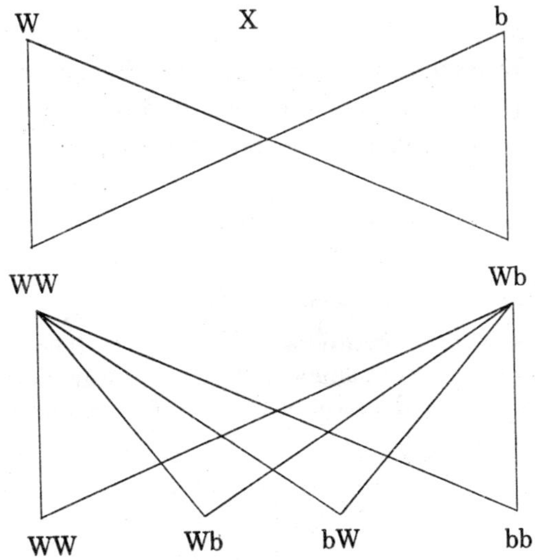

Fig. 26.1. Two parent White and Black
WW - White WB - White (dominant)
bW - Black (dominant) bb - Black
Thus it will be 1 : 2 : 1 (1 : 3) one pure white and two mixed
(dominant character) showing one pure black.

Sex : Sexual difference has a number of important consequences on later behaviour.

Boys : More unpredicatable, restless, noisy, take more risk, think independently and harder to educate.

Girls : More vulnerable to verify or diseases, more dependent, submissive and conforming and less adventurous. Sleep more, cryless and demand less attention.

Individual and Organisation

The relationship between individual and organisation is a psychological contract. It is a set of unwritten reciprocal expectation between the individual employees and the organisation. The contract is the essence of individual organisational linkage, because employment entails an implicit exchange of beliefs and expectations about what constitutes legitimate actions by either party. We not only share value, belief but also share situation. The psychological contract is given in Fig. 26.2.

Psychological Contract

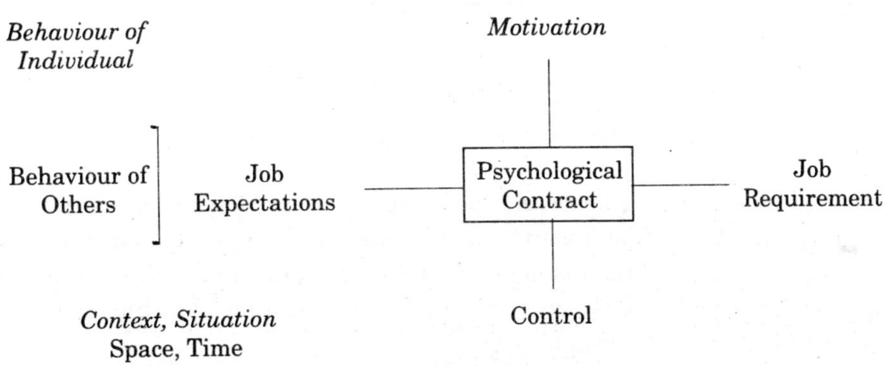

Fig.. 26.2

Motivation

Motivation arouses interest among people and thereby give direction and persistence to behaviour. For motivating people we have to understand the context as shown in Fig. 26.3.

CONTEXT AND MOTIVATION

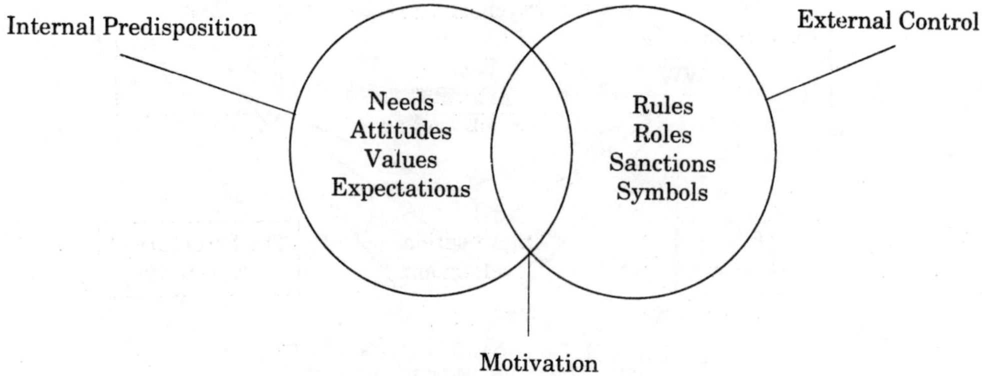

Fig. 26.3

In practice, people come with their knowledge (specialisation) and expectation. In earlier days people were highly identified with their job and were not ready to move from their specialised area to general management cadre. Similarly, people were reluctant to the idea of training but presently needs, jobs, value and beliefs are very closely inter-related. The job satisfaction motivation and performance can be understood from the Fig. 26.4. Expectation is the anticipation and reflection about behaviour, states and experience. Fig. 26.4. shows the relation between job expectation and job requirements. Job expectations are influenced by different life circle in the family development stage of the family.

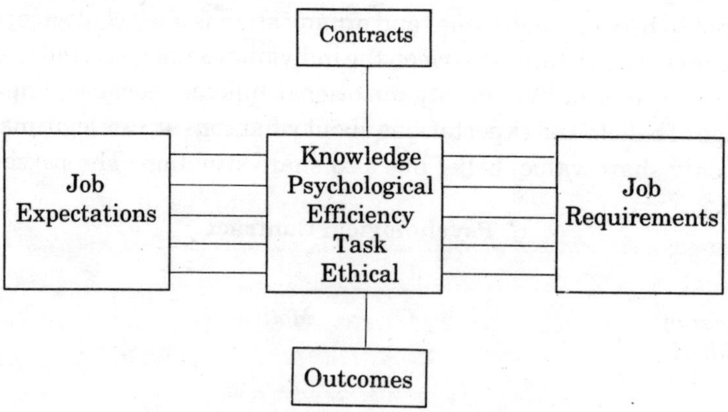

Job satisfaction, Motivation and Performance

Fig. 26.4.

Even in developed countries like Britain people are not very keen to move from one place to another because they do not find it worth. It is because of these reasons that there are more conflicts in the organisation and the managers find it difficult to handle the situation. In every organisation there are certain hidden contracts in the organisation. The hidden contracts are very complex and difficult to understand.

Job Expectation

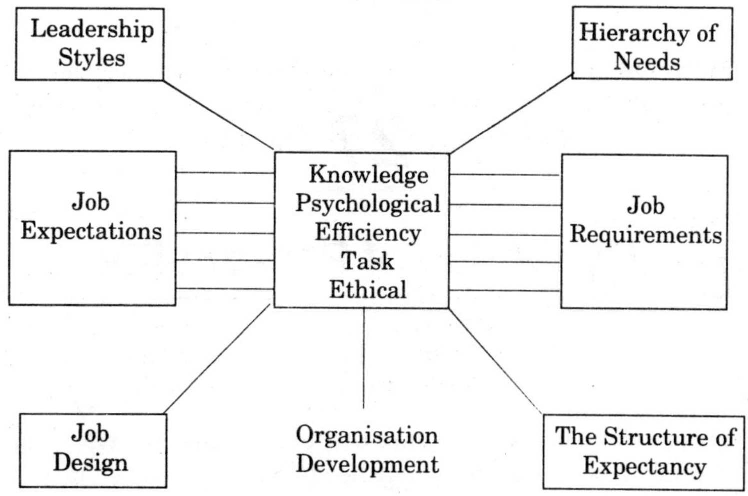

Fig. 26.5.

27

Dynamics of Personality

Introduction

Major problems in today's organisation are how to maximise the efforts and contribution of individuals. The conflict between individual needs and the achievement of organisational objectives has been of major concern to the managers and the behavioural scientists. We are striving hard to create and organisation in which individuals may optimise expressing and simultaneously the organizational objects may also be achieved.

The management of an organisation should be concerned with developing personal characteristics and introducing operating effectiveness among its members. These characteristics include organisational structure, managerial principles and practices, effective motivation and communication, the overall personnel growth and development and finally navigating the organisational changes in and outside the organisation.

Individuality

Each one of us performs different roles in our life, at home, in schools, in colleges, in social gatherings and at the work places etc. People change caps from one role to another but by doing so they do not become different individuals. It is need very important that the human behaviour in these specific roles and the application of pertinent information about human behaviour is available in solving the human behaviour problems. Information regarding behaviour can be derived from the various experiences and the insights into the behaviour of others which is again coloured by our own attitudes and values. Individually continuously strives to assert itself though key attribution of behaviour characteristics, such as :

(*a*) Intelligence
(*b*) Ability
(*c*) Creativity
(*d*) Flexibility
(*e*) Adaptability, and
(*f*) Capacity to change.

These characteristics are there in every individual to some degree. According to Locke, '*What a man becomes is entirely the result of experiences*', but many other thinkers of behavioural science are of the other extreme views. An individual is conditioned by heredity in the womb and their lives are merely the application of his script. Most of the scientists have compiled studies supporting one or the other view point, namely individual behavioural is largely determined by heredity or it is the product of environment in fact, without understanding of an individual's inner, hidden qualities it is difficult to assess the individual's potential. It has been found that the individuals who had not pursued any distinguished work for year's together may produce work of genious one day. The example to this is of Gregor Mendel who discovered the laws of heredity. Another classical example is of a young Austrian boy who was quite simple minded and never made success in anything but later on he became leading scientist known to the world as Albert Einstein who has outlined one of the most movementous scientific researches in the area of relativity.

The physical traits such as height, skin complexion, shape and size of nose, mouth, ears are largely hereditary. The basic intelligence, muscle, coordination instinctive desires are inherited. The individuals act differently because they think differently. The mental process of an individual provides him with different, thoughts, feelings, interpretations and responses to his environment. But the individual ability to learn and his other mental functions are inherited. But soon after, the birth, person is affected by his envirornment. These inherited mental characteristics are modified by learning experiences to produce a compete personality.

Individual difference in performance is a matter of concern both to the individuals and the management. Individuals with inadequate performance do not have the opportunity to achieve satisfaction in their work. Thus in the mutual interest of individuals and management in the organisation, placement of individuals on the job in which their individual potentialities can be effectively utilised in most desirable.

Individual difference can be grouped into broad classification in terms of personality. The area of human personality have been neglected in the past but are not recognised as having as effect on the day to day working of an organisation. The attention of management is consequently being drawn and the attempts are being made to handle the industrial situations. In its right, perspective personality is of great significance in all areas of complex society. We know that individuals behave in a similar fashion on under similar conditions. Thus behaviour is what others learn to recognise as their personality. They expect and can even predict certain kinds of behaviour from these people. Personality is a unitary mode of response to life situations. Personality is what man really is.

The term personality is derived from the latin word 'personal' which means 'mask'. The Greeks stage actors used a make to hide their identity on stage. Personality is the quality of the individual's total behaviour. The personality of an individual is the total picture of his organised behaviour.

Personality

It can be defined as the totality of man. It can also be defined as the most adequate conceptualization of person's behaviour. Personality is the unit that marks off any one member of the group as being different from other members of the same group. Personality is an organised whole which acts toward the fulfillment of purpose. *Personality is the sum total of all the tendencies that an individual has inherited and that he has acquired by experience. Personality can be defined as consistent behaviour patterns of an individual as perceived by others. It is the combination of body and mind which depends upon heredity and environment.* Personality is defined to encompass the characteristic traits and patterns of adjustment of the person in relationship with others and his environments. Personality is the dynamic organisation within the individual of those psychophysical systems that determine his characteristics, behaviour and thought.

Personality Pattern

Personality pattern is unique. Individuals are commonly described as belonging to certain types. One individual may be said to be the amibitious type, another may be conservative and still another may be aggressive type. Individually increases as children grow older. Individuality is apparent in the structural and behavioural differences of new born infants. Some new borns are active and prone to excessive crying. *The Individuality is a product of heredity and environment.* The natural process of sexual production guarantees novel genetic equipment for every mortal human beings. At the moment of conception the person's entire heredity endowment centered in 23 chromosomes from the mother and 23 chromosomes from the father. The total 46 chromosomes that appear in the nearly formed cell which will be responsible to develop into a new human beings contains approximately 30,000 genes or carries of individuals traits. The likelihood of duplication of this hereditary endowment is estimated as 1 in 300,000,000,000,000. Thus absolutely no possibility of similarity in heredity. In other words, no two human beings have even the potentially of developing alike, especially when do all these genetic differences we add the difference that will occur in the environment and experiences of each mortal person. The uniqueness of each individual's personality is derived from a combination of constitutional factors and environmental factors both of which vary from one individual to another individual. Even in case where hereditary endowment is similar (in case of identical twins) the chances of an identical environment of identical reactions and interactions are believed to be zero. The genes influence personality by affecting the quality of the nervous system, the biochemical balances of the body and structure of the body.

Formation of Personality

Personality is formed by interaction of mother, father and siblings with child. The new born child is like a partially programmed computer. Soon after the child start learning from the results of his own responses from other persons and from his social and cultural setting he uptodates his computer's programme, and cultural setting. Everyone is bombarded with a stream of stimuli; interprets them, makes new responses, reinterprets them and his whole cycle is repeated. An individual tends to continue with a response if in his views the response is rewarding. The frequently of stimuli plays an important role in developing stable patterns of reaction. The strength of reward also affects learning, geater the reward higher the learning.

A person who inherits a low grade intelligence even under the most favourable environment condition cannot much another individual who inherits a higher level of intellectual ability. Let us see the effect of different environmental influences within and outside home.

The childhood patterns persists in industry, and we need to know about our social isolation. For example, an individual who was an eldest child as a foreman in the organisation was treating his subordinates as he treated his younger brother and sister in childhood. He is unconsciouausly creating into the factory the attitude of domination which he acquired at home.

Growing up in Personality

From birth to maturity, growing up in personality is divided into ten stages, for convenience. Every individual passes through these stages but few individuals continue longer with some of these stages.

(*a*)

Stage of Dependence. Every individual starts his life completely dependent on others. A few individuals are never weaned out from this dependence and always have to learn on parents, friends or on some one else.

(*b*) **Stage of Comfort and Eating.** In this stage chief interest is bodily comfort and food. A few grow up and still feel and think that comfort is the most important thing in life.

(*c*) **Stage of Impulsiveness.** The parents praised the child when he took his first steps, but when he tried his walking by himself in the streets, his parents scolded him. The child is unable to make out the difference between the two activities and thus is a stage of impulsiveness. The individual did not understand the change from praise to punishment for walking. The child acts first and thinks later so do many adults who not have outgrown childish impulsiveness.

(*d*) **Show of Stage.** Show of stage is normal in childhood. But some adults do maintain this stage and feel proud in showing off.

(*e*) **Stage of Low Boiling Point.** Some individuals do not like being interrupted and they go through life with a low boiling point losing temper at little things.

(*f*) **Stage of Stubbornness.** Every child is too small and weak to win by his own strength, but he could be stubborn and thus corner his parents. If his parents handled him wrongly during this stage, it may become a permanent habit which he comes through life. Everytime he is told to do something before he actually does it.

(*g*) **Stage of Inferiority of Gullibility.** Some individuals never grow out of their early school stage of feeding interior and being gullible. They lack confidence in themselves and consult fortune teller or allow superstitions, to make their decision.

(*h*) **Gang Stage.** There are certain group of individual who form the gang unless they can be the 'chief' while others remain aloof and still want to be the chief. Some are still in the childhood gang stage. An adult who does not go out of his stage, form a clique in the office with his friends. They admire one another and would not pull on with other employees.

(*i*) **Interest in Opposite Sex.** During the college days another stage appears in which the gangs begin to break up, because many members develop more interests in the opposite sex than in their own sex. Some individuals do not come out of this stage. They marry because 'It was the thing to do' but keep their real companionship with a small gang of the same sex.

(*j*) **Mature and Independent.** Soon after the education, the stage for mature independence in gradually entered. Here one plansahead for a career, looks forward to have his own family, provides for old age, and helps his community by co-operating with large groups. One becomes responsible citizen and individual.

Structure of Personality

The personality consists of id, ego and upper ego. The id is a reservior of psychic energy and source of the human instincts. It provides the power that sustains a person's activities. The ego is a special part of the id which keeps the individual in touch with the outside world, and finds outlets for the expression of his instincts. The superego is a kind of moral censor which passes judgement on the individual's strivings according to the standards which he has acquired from this parents. It makes him full guilty when he goes against those standards, and proud of himself when he lives up to them.

In the id-personality the individual strives for the satisfaction of impulses. The id personality is guided by impulses on one's thinking and feelings.

The superego is the voice of conscience. A person dominated by his moral may be called a superego personality governed by analysis.

The ego characterise briefly by saying that is represents reason. An ego personality thinks logically, keeping his feeling under rational control and his actions are determined by commonsense.

According to Jung, the personality consists of six parts : the ego, the personal unconcious, the collective unconcious, the persona , the anima and the shadow. The ego is the consious mind made up conscious perceptions, memories, thoughts and feelings. The personal unconcious consists of experiences which have been forgotten but which can be recalled. The collective unconcious is a storehouse of ancestral memories. Persona is mask which often reflects the true nature of the personality. The anima is the feminine side of a man's personality. The shadow is the animal side of man's nature.

The personality looks not only backwards to its past but also forwards to a goal, which is the development of a unified whole, known as the self.

Functioning of Personality

This individual self has four basic basic functions, which should be present in every individual of the industry. These are, thought, feeling, sensation and intution. Thoughts seek to understand the problems, feeling apprehends it on the basis of a pleasant/unpleasant evaluation, sensation perceives things through the sense and intution perceives them through an inner awareness.

In addition to these four functions, the personality reveals two attitudes. They are introversion and extroversion. The intovert is influenced by what he finds with in himself. The extraverts takes his bearings from what lies outside himself.

Feelings of inferiority are rooted in the human condition. They are inevitable when man compares his insignificance with the immensity of the universe.

The inferiority complex is overcome by developing 'Social interest' and we should not be afraid of making mistakes, for there is no other way of learning how to work. Both making mistakes and learning how to work, however demands courage, and the 'Courage is the health of the soul'.

Individuals are motivated by two basic drives-the need of security and the need of satisfaction. One thing which in individual desires above everything else in the world is personal security from wants and to be able to provide adquately means for his family.

Next thing is the satisfaction of desires without which the individual would feel empty and lost. If employees in an organisation motivated by the need of security and the need of satisfaction, we can serve them best by helping them to feel secure and to satisfy their wants.

Elements of the Personality Pattern

The personality pattern is composed of a core called the concept of self and an integrated system of learned responses called traits. Freud referred the concept of self as the ego and sullivan used the term self system. James put self as the sum total of all that he can call him.

The attitude towards self is an organised configuration of perception of self, it is also at times referred as self schema. Allport puts self s something of which we are immediately aware. It is the warm, central, private region of our life. As such it plays a crucial part in our consciousness in our personality and in our organism. *It is a kind of core in our being.* In other words the self as it finally evolves is made up of all that goes into a person's experience of his individual existence.

28

Transactional Analysis

Concepts

Transactional Analysis offers a behavioural model of personality, the dynamics of self and its relationship to others. It helps the managers in understanding what is going on inside themselves. Transactional analysis refers to a total system that includes many related branches and ideas. The understanding of behaviour is fundamental to manager's success because his personal interactions have increased enormously.

In order to understand the dynamics of self there is a need to understand what is self. The ultimate purpose of life is to understand self. Self is the core of personality pattern which provides integration. In order to have a self study an individual, should know :

(*a*) Certain areas of an individual which he knows and others also know about that;

(*b*) Certain areas of an individual which he knows and others do not know;

(*c*) Certain areas of an individual which he does not know but others know;

(*d*) Certain areas of an individual which no body knows.

Transactional analysis helps an individual to know that portion of his self of which he is aware.

The earlier scientific studies on human behaviour carried out by Freud, made a pronounced impact in unearthing the mysteries of human behaviour. Soon after Freud the other behavioural scientists Jung, Adler, Sulivan made significant contribution either by interpreting or by developing behaviour. It was only in late fifties that modern Freud - "Eric Bune" came on the horizen and gave a new way of understanding interpreting and predicting behaviour Eric Berne's method is commonly known as Transactional Theory of Personality Berne's approach is based on the view that individual is an organic as well as a social unit. In an organic unit he has his internal system of environment to deal with, but as social unit it is necessary to relate with the external environment.

The internal organic system is made of bones, skin, glands, nervous system, etc., which are built in such a way that they maintain equilibrium or harmony within the organism. The symptoms of disharmony in the organism can be perceived as anger, fear, trouble, overweight, loss of weight. The object of the organisation is to generate optimum harmony within each individual and to give him maximum satisfaction as well as to make him more productive. The internal environment and consequently the behaviour of an individual can be best explained by the three different levels of consciousness.

EQUILIBRIUM BETWEEN EXTERNAL AND INTERNAL ENVIRONMENTS

Any social situation is full of conceivable types of transactions. Knowingly or unknowingly we are using child, parent and adult ego in most of our interactions such as talking to a child, romancing with the spouse, we use child ego state, while dispensing various strategies and long term planning we are using our adult ego state and while demanding some explanation or questioning even the wife on family budget we are using parent ego state. Shifts in ego state due to changes in either internal or external environments help to maintain organic balance, maintaining equilibrium under the various internal environments as shown in Fig 28.1.

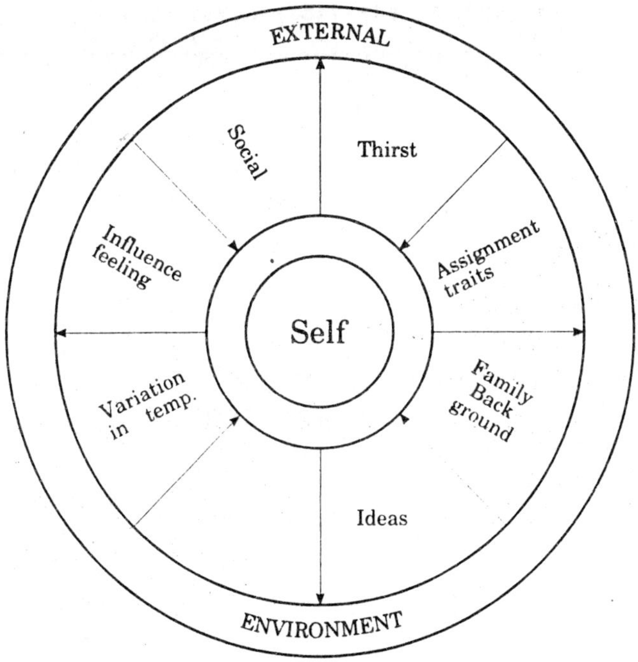

Fig. 28.1

Thus we have seen that in a given situation the resultant behaviour emanat as a fair combination of parental warning or permissions, child feelings, intuitions or guess works and adult reasoning, experience and objectivity. The Adult evaluates the feelings, messages and facts as well as external data and makes and objective and realistic decision where the driving force is the adult ego state.

The consistent impression about human nature is that man has multiple nature. There is always a conflict between good and evil, the lower and higher nature, the inner man and the outer man. Human being is striving hard to achieve goodness. Moses saw goodness as justice, Plato saw goodness as wisdom, Jesus saw goodness as love, yet they all agreed that virtue, however understood, was consistently undermined by something in human nature. Transactional Analysis is the method of examining transaction. Eric Berne, the orginator of Transactional Analysis has defined 'Transaction as the social intercourse of two or more people who encounter each other's. The transactional stimulus give indication acknowledging the presence of others. When a person communicates or does something which in some way relates to the stimulus that is called Transactional response. During the development of Transactional

Analysis, Berne observed that one can see people changing before one's eyes. There may be changes in gestures, movements, facial expressions and communication system and apprent changes in manner, appearance, words and gestures.

Studies have shown that there exists three types of egos in an individual ;

(*a*) A little professor (child ego)

(*b*) One's own parents (parent ego)

(*c*) A data processing computer (Adult ego)

The first two stages are recordings in the brain of actual experiences of internal and external events which occur during the first five years of life. The third stage is a data processing computer which grinds out decisions after assimilating information from three sources - parent, the child and the data which the adult has gathered or in the continuous process of gathering and updating This state is produced when the individuals playback the recorded data of events involving real people, real time, real place, real feelings.

In transactional analysis there are ego functions which are indicated as Parent, Adult and Child. The Transactional theory of Personality provides and inside view of the internal environment of a person.

ASSUMPTIONS IN TRANSACTIONAL ANALYSIS

Following are the underlying assumptions in Transactional Analysis :

The experience up to the age of five years are recorded in our mind and provides us the basic structure. The recorded experience are switched on whenever a situation demands.

Personality of a person can be understood with these three ego states :

Parent

Adult P — A — C are live three different voices.

Child

THE PARENT

The values and behaviour of parents are recorded and constitute the basic values of our personalities. Thus Parental aspect is very important. If the child hears and gets the same kind of values from his or her mother-father as the information is recorded, then it becomes a source. But if on one hand the child is asked to value the truth and on the other hand asked by his father sitting in the house to tell someone on the telephone that he is not there, then the recording to confused. The criminals normally, have so much of confused recording that they are unable to decide. This leads to the formation of negative attitude towards life.

Once certain values are formed, they can not be easily raised. But in later part of life one may block his Child and Parent and use his Adult state only. If an individual blocks his child ego then he is a hard task master with no feelings. If the children are brought up by maid servants and parents do not have time to attend them then they may not have strong values formation. The parent concept is called the "Taught Concept" of life. The child keeps updating his data of parent and child. For example, if the child is fed with fear of policeman by his parents but later in life he becomes the friend of Police Officer's son and gets an opportunity to understand his friend's father closely, he may find that what he had been thinking about a policemen is not the one he had observed. This will update his previous experience with more positive values. The child keeps verifying his information and only after verification the information becomes a source of data in our Adult. It is very difficult to overcome the feelings of a child *i.e.*, anger, love, fear and affection. But only through a developed adult that one can control and overcome those feelings. Assertive statements are due to Parent's ego. If the judgments are positive then it comes from Nurturing Parent otherwise it is from Punative Parent. If an individual supports his arguments with facts and figures then it is the Adult which he is using. Rejecting whatever told is in the Rebellious child. Feeling of nervousness is in the Adaptive child. Whenever a child is guided for small-small things and is never allowed to use his free child then it is a case of an Adaptive child. The general feelings of an Adaptive child are "I wish I could do this" "I hope this can be done". Free Jokes, free ideas and creative thinking are the characteristics of a Free child. The process of Adult formation goes through the following steps :

(*a*) His own experience

(*b*) Continuously updating parental injuction by varying.

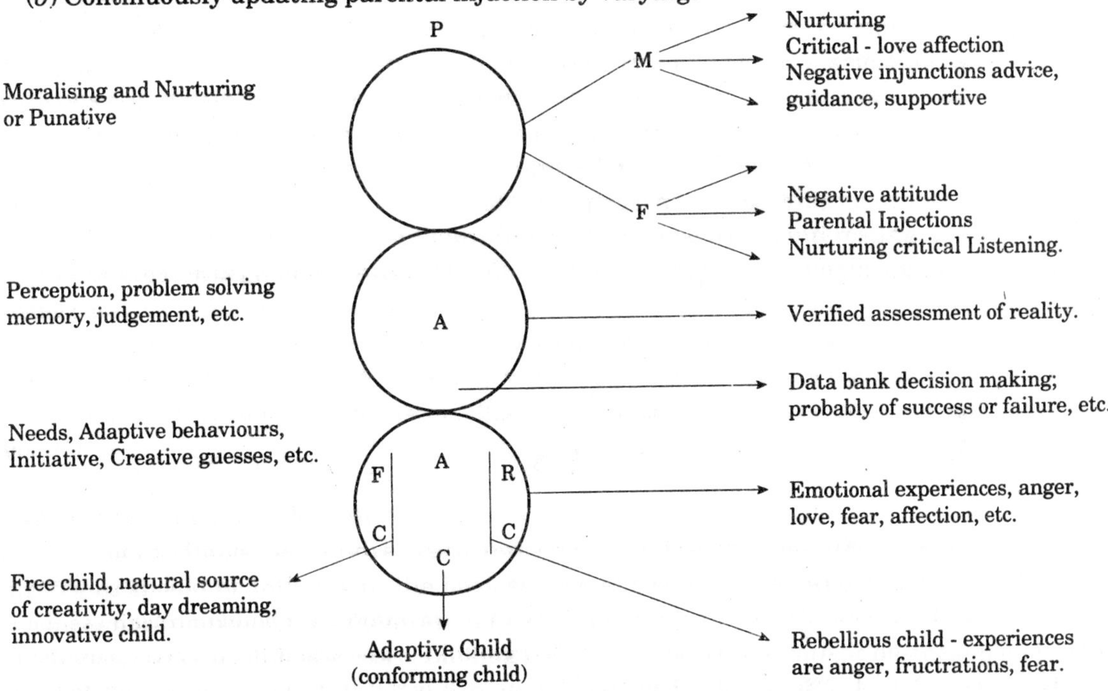

Fig. 28.2. Adaptive child (conforming child)

In India we do not allow the free child to develop and more often th parents cultivate a finger holding culture. From birth to 3 years of ago the child is guided and controlled by grand mother, grand father, aunties and uncles in addition to his parents. The child becomes so dependent that he acts as desired by elders. At the age of four, when he is sent to the school, the teacher emphasises, "You are too small and do not know anything what I am telling you is right". This process ultimately kills the child's initiative to explore new things and thus changes child from a Free child to an Adaptive child. It is the collection of recordings in the brain of imposed external events perceived by individuals in his early years of life. *i.e.*, before the social birth of the individual. The little child develops dependency and is unable to construct meaning with words and thus it is impossible for him to modify, correct or explain. In th parent the individual has collection of rules and laws that the child hears from his patents and learns in their living. Another characteristic of parents is the inconsistency of their action. Parents say one thing and do another. Parents teach children not to tell lies but they themselves tell lies. They tell their children that drinking is bad but they themselves doing. So one's parent is that body of data recorded and stored in one's brain, that comes from one's observations about the way one's parents (mother and father) behaves.

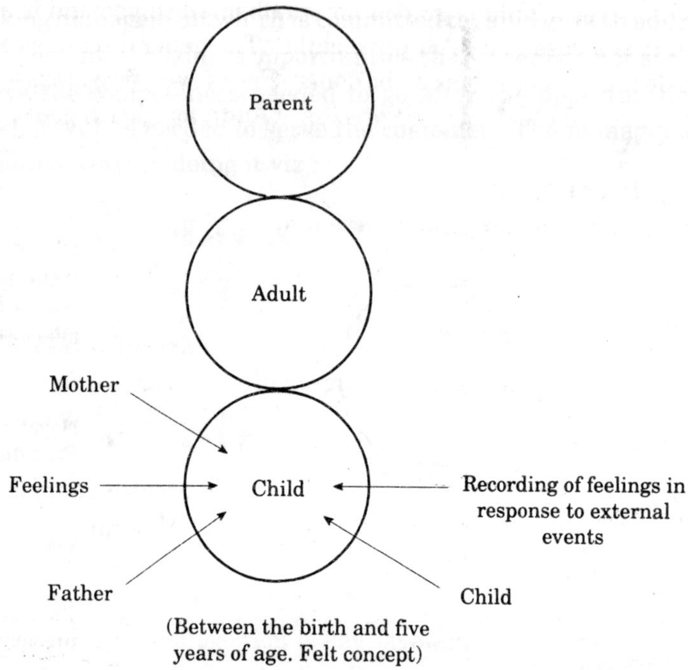

Fig. 28.3

THE CHILD

This is another recording being made simultaneously. This is the recording of internal events, the responses of the little persons to what he sees and hears. It is the hearing, feeling, and understanding of data which we define as the child. The child is dependent, incept, clumse, without understanding and ability to construct meanings. The child may have reservior of negative data about himself, like parent the child is a state into which, a person may be transferred any time during his current transactions. There can be many things that can happen to an individual which create the situation of childhood. The child is a vast store of creativity, curiosity, the desire to explore and know. In the child resides the carefree, happy child. The recordings of the Parents and the child are there till the child leaves the home for his first independent social experience, *i.e.*, school. Till the age of five years the child has already felt all types of emotions. The child ego in an individual is that body of data recorded and stored in one's brain when the individual was a child. The child includes feelings of frustration, inadequacy and helplessness that are an inevitable part of one's childhood. In addition, the child contains the early recordings of joy, curiosity, imagination, spontaneity and excitement born from new discoveries which were also part of one's childhood.

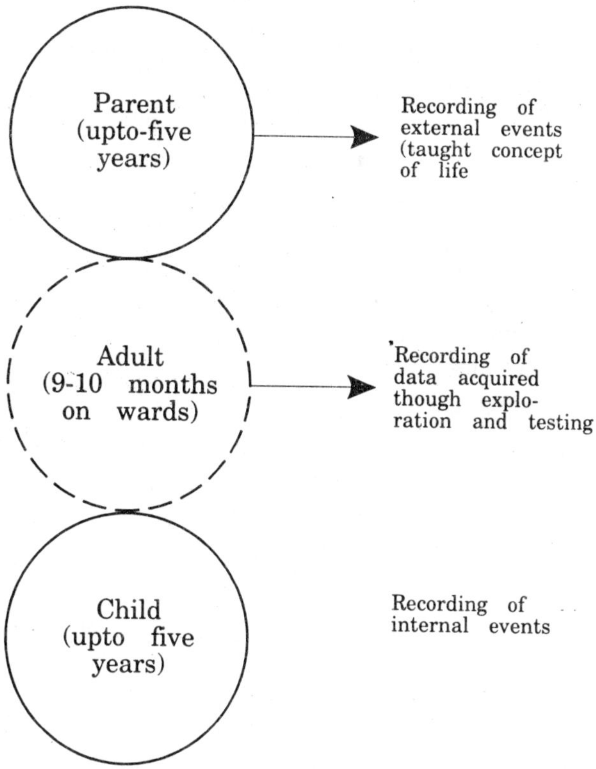

Fig. 28.4.

THE ADULT

Adult beginning starts the moment the child takes his first step out to walk. Till 10 months the child has only parent and child ego but child does have the ability either to choose his responses or to manipulate his stimulus. The child has no self direction, no ability to move out to face life. He takes whatever comes along his way. At the age of ten months he starts manipulating objects and begins to move out, concentrates on inspection and exploration to toys. Now the child has grown an awareness and original thought and thus begins self actualisation - Adult. There is a shift from the "taught concept" of life to "felt concept" of life in the child. The basic principle of Adult is to transform stimuli into pieces of information and then process the information on the basis of previous experience. The Adult starts testing parent data. If the parent directives are not grounded in reality, the child through his own Adult will give a sense of wholeness. The following figure will give the idea about the source of information of Adult.

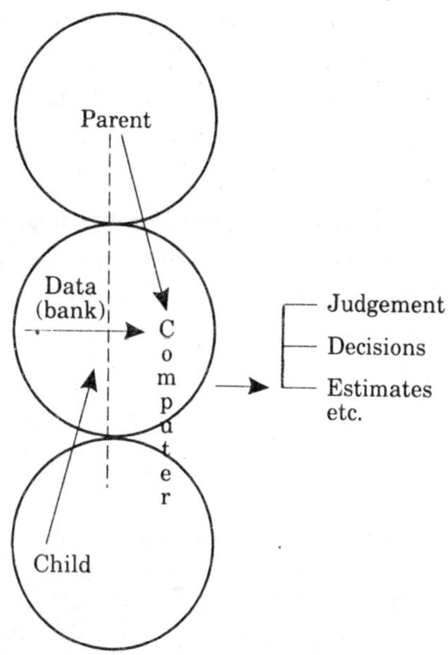

Fig. 28.5.

The adult updates the parent data to determine what is valid and what is not. Similarly, it also updates the child data to determine which feelings should be expressed.

The adult controls and keeps the emotional expression appropriate. The figure shows how the Adult within an individual refers to updated reality.

Unexamined data can underline our transactional failures and can cause more Adult decay. The Adult grows, improves and increases the efficiency through experience and training. Under stress and strain the Adult can be impaired to the point where emotions take over men. Every-one has got little child ego, parent ego, adult ego which is capable of making assessments about outside realities. Thus P - A - C are like three different voices.

When an individual experiences feelings or emotions, one's child is participating in that experience in some way or the other. The adult of an individual operates on facts based on what's true today. It is the voice which says things like "What's going on here?" One can become acquainted with one's own P - A - C by listening to these three different voices inside one self.

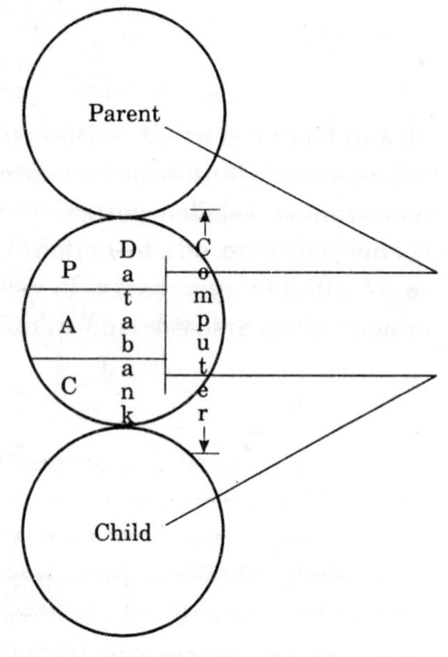

Fig. 28.6

TRANSACTIONS

Following are the various *forms of Transactions* :

(*a*) Complementary Transaction

(*b*) Crossed Transaction

(*c*) Ulterior Transaction

(*i*) Angular (*ii*) Duplex

(*d*) Gallows Transactions

(*a*) **Complementary Transaction**

When communication continues along parallel lines between individuals, the transactions are complementary. To understand complementary transaction, the following are a few examples :

I.

Supervisor (A - A) - Have you finished your job ?

Operator (A - A) - Yes sir, I finished it long back and it has already been delivered to the assembly section.

II.

Husband (C - P) - I cannot take this medicine, it is bitter in taste.

Wife (C - P) - You should take this medicine. It will give you sugar afterward.

III

The conversation between Mr. X and Mr. Y.

(Mr. X) - What is the time please ? (Question comes from Adult) (A - A)

(Mr. Y) - It is 10.45 A.M. (The response goes from the Adult) (A - A)

In this conversation Mr. X and Mr. Y are satisfied and communication is complete.

IV

(Mr. X) - I am feeling nervous. (C - P)

(Mr. Y) - Why are you feeling nervous ? (P - C)

This is also a complementary transaction

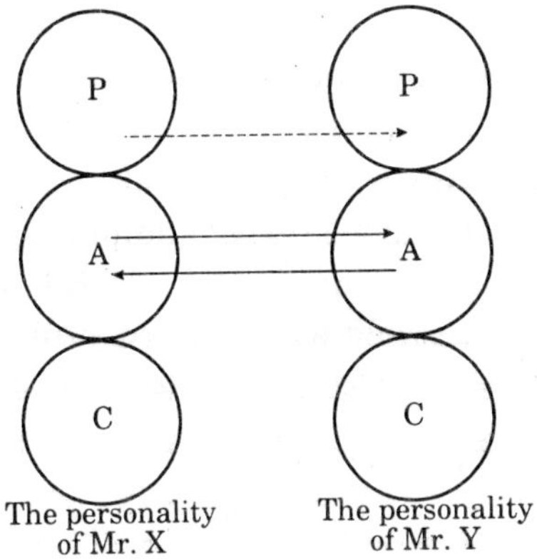

Fig. 28.7.

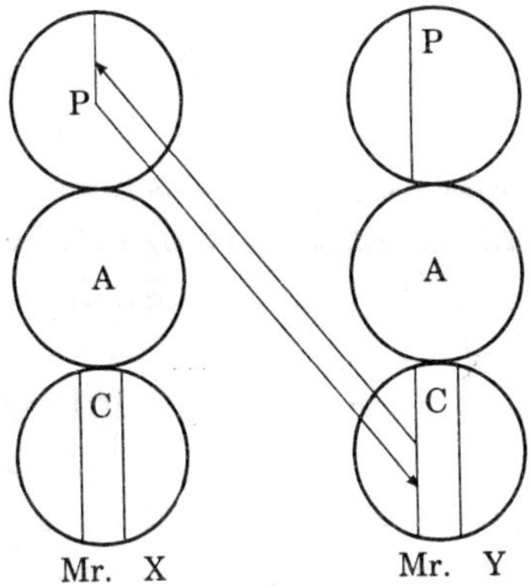

Fig. 28.8.

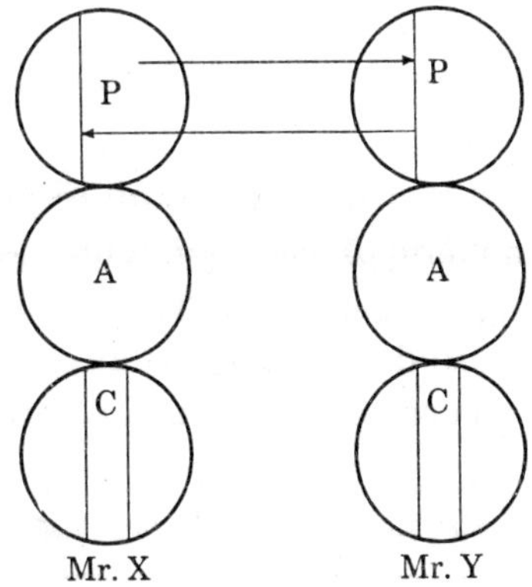

Fig. 28.9.

V

(Mr. X) - It is horrible, buses are always late. (P - P)

(Mr. Y) - You are talking about buses only, every thing here in this city is late.

VI

Girl 1. - Let us play, you become mummy and I will be a little child (C - C)

Girl 2. - No. I will be little child and you play the role of mummy. (C - C)

(*b*) **Crossed Transactions**

In this type of communication the vectors cross and communication ceases at that point of time. Crossed transactions in habit creativity, free thinking and social intersaction.

1.

Supervisor (A - A) How many pieces of job have you made by now ?

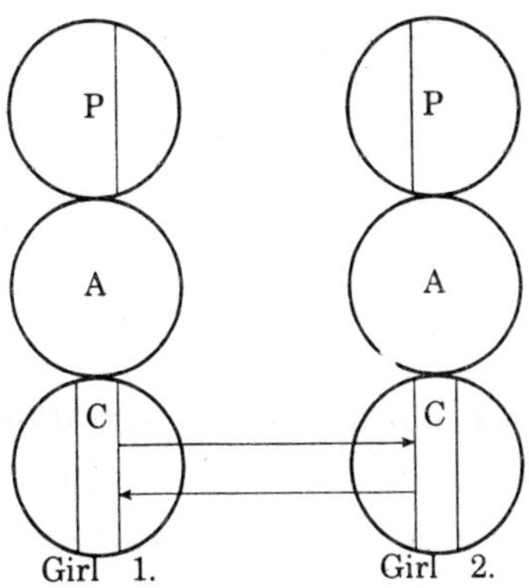

Fig. 28.10.

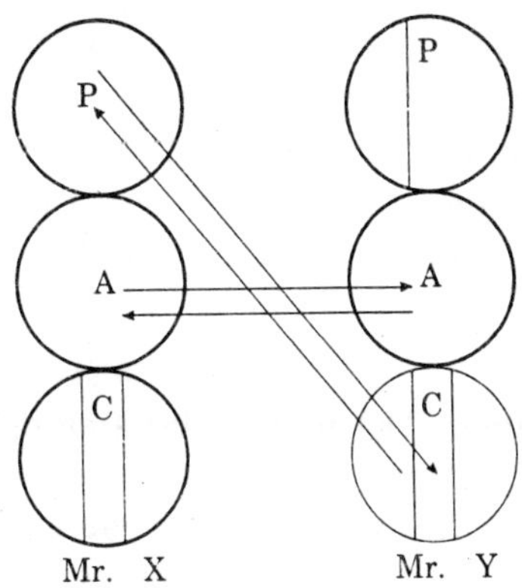

Fig. 28.11

Operation (P - C) Don't disturb me, when I complete it, I will let you know about it.

II

Mr. X - What is the time ? (A - A)

Mr. Y - Why don't you keep a watch (P - C)

Mr. X - Look I just asked the time. (P - C)

Mr. Y - I have also not said anything. (P - C)

Mr. X - But who are you to tell me anything ? (C - P)

Like this it will ultimately result into a quarrel. Once the transaction is crossed, the response may go from parent or may be from rebellious child. The experience has shown that if one remains on his adult he can make others also come back to his adult resulting into a compromise.

(*c*) **Ulterior Transactions**

This communication has double meaning. One at the surface level, there we have a clear adult message, whereas, there is a hidden message on the psychological level.

In this type of transaction one may be socially acceptable on the surface but at the interior level one may have different meaning.

One may shown his hospitality on the surface but may pull the leg of others in the form of Jokes. This transaction may be further divided into two types :

(*i*) Angular (*ii*) Duplex.

(*i*) *Angular*

1.

Mr. X says on the face to Mr. Y "You need not worry I am there help you", but Mr. X's interior motive may be to make Mr. Y dependent on him. Another example can be of a salesman who while giving rational information about the various products may also show his emotions to initiate buying.

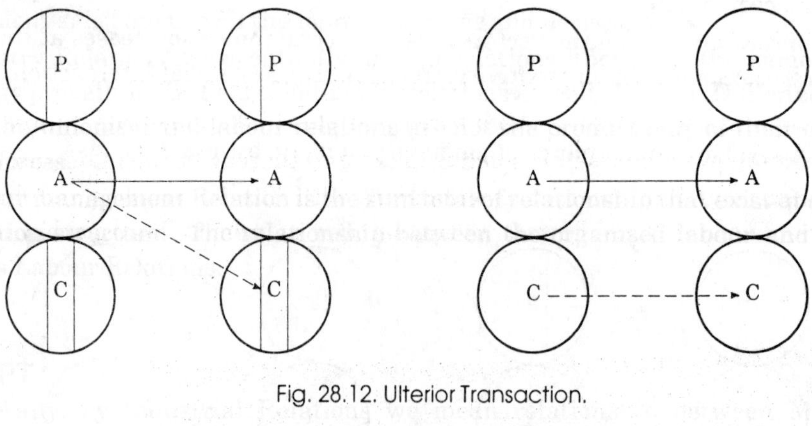

Fig. 28.12. Ulterior Transaction.

II

Salesman-(A - A) This washing powder is the best, but you cannot afford to buy it, its very costly.

House Wife-(A - A) That is the one I will take.

(*ii*) *Duplex*

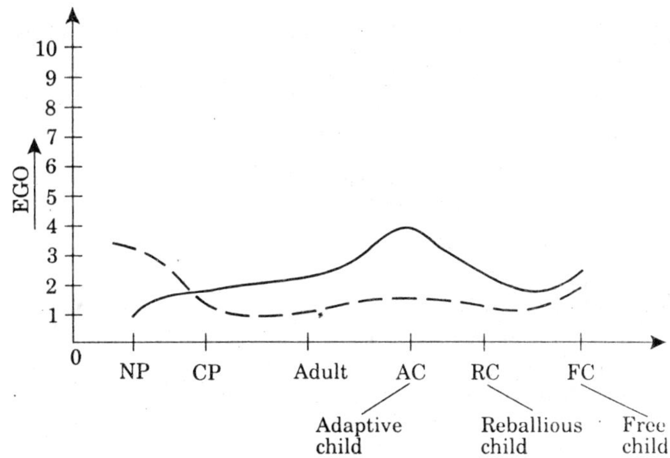

Fig. 28.13.

1.

Husband while sitting on the dining table may find that table is very dirty and probably not cleaned for days. If husband with his figure writes on the table "I love you", in this process he has used parent ego state to hint to her that you have not cleaned the table. The husband has sent the massage through his child ego state. Many a times it is not the works only which convey the meaning rather the face expressions postures, etc. convey much more meaning than the words. Following figures shown the 'Ego gram' in which the graph is drawn between various ego states on X-axis and relative predominance of various ego states on Y-axis. Adult to Adult transaction is on the social level asking for some information.

(*d*) **Gallows Transaction**

The inappropriate love or smile is the gallows transactions. A smile in response to a person's misfortune may serve as gallows transaction. The other examples to gallows transaction can be :

- a teacher getting amused at the stupid behaviour of her favourite student.
- a mother laughing on the falling of her three year old child and getting injured.
- a father beaming over the risk his son has taken and thereby losing in business.

Gallows transactions like other transactions are with ulterior motives and are common among the losers. The loser uses the gallows transactions to promote his psychological games.

29

Appplication of Transaction Analysis

Concepts

Transactional Analysis helps us to look back on Child-Parent Adult messages to integrate them so as to be emotionally stable and closer to reality. Parent is that body of data recorded and stored in one's brain, that comes from one's observations about the way one's Parent (mother and father) behaved.

Figure shows (P-P) as Parent in Parent. (A-P) Adult in Parent. (C-P) Child in Parent. An example of this can be of a pride who served a cake to her husband who asked her why she cut the ends. 'Well that's the way my mother always did it' she replied next time, mother-in-law was asked the same question 'why she cuts the ends of the cake', 'that is the way my mother did it' she replied and after some time when grandmother visited she too was asked, 'why she cuts the ends of the cake' she says that is the way only I could learn from my mother. The figure shows the outward expression of a Parent ego state. When a parent state is expressed, the person transacts with the ego states of others parent states. For example Mohan who has beaten with a rod by his father when he was a child, swore to himself that he would never hit a child as his father had done. However, when Mohan had his son, it seemed natural to him to strike the child when he misbehaved. He took a determined decision but the adult information from Mohan modified his super behaviour. People not only incorporate their parent behaviour but they also incorporate a set of parental message that are later heard in their heads like tapes. The parents establish an emotional claim which like atmosphere is warm or cold, mild or harsh, conducive or destructive to growth. The best thing a person can do for his child is to evaluate his own script and then decide whether it is worthwhile passing on the message to the other generation. If a child loses his parent by death and does not have a substitute parent, he will have a void in his parent ego state. The void in parent ego state may also be caused by parents excessive absence - physical or psychological. When a parent is absent for a long time, the child may turn to someone else whom he likes the most and constuct an ideal mother or father in his imagination. For example, Surrender who was youngest member of a large family. His father died when he was four years old. As an Adult he was competent and self-contended but suffered from periods of depression. In his own words 'I do not like to talk of my childhood and spend one week each year in deep depression before 3rd Feb., that was the day my father died. Ever since I have felt an unstability in my life, I went with my mother to live with my grand mother, where I had a lot of uncles. I used to hope against hope that they would accept me as part of their family but they never really noticed or gave me affection and love.

Integrated Adult

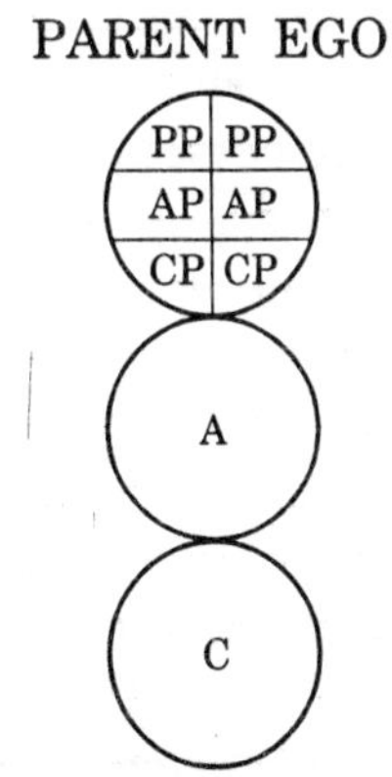

PP = Parent in the parent.
AP = Adult in parent.
CP = Child in parent.

Fig. 29.1.

Parent and child in conflict, the conflict being resolved by excluding parent, the new parent being incorporated and new parent, reparented are shown in Fig. 29.2. Many people see their parents through their coloured glasses or through psychological prism that distort the situation according to their perception. Parent ego State is a transmitter of cultural and family scripts. It is valuable for the survival of the home rays since it facilitate the automatic performance of parenting task feelings to the Adult ego state to deal with complex problems of existence. Awareness of one's parent gives more joy in one's behaviour which in turn can enhance one's chances to bring up one's children to be winners.

The adult updates the parent data to determine what is valid and what is not. Similarly it also updates the child data to determine which feelings should be expressed. The adjust controls and keeps the emotional expression appropriate. The Adult within an individual refers to updated releality data.

Un-examined datas can underline our transactional failures and can cause more Adult decay. The Adult grows, improves and increases efficiency through repeated use and training. Adult can be impaired under stress and strain to the point where emotions take over the man. Everyone has got little child ego, an adult ego which is capable of making assessments about realities. Thus, P-A-C are like three different voices. The adult of an individual operates on facts based on what's true today. It is the voice which says nothing like 'What's going on here' ? One can become acquainted with one's own P-A-C by listening to these three different voices inside one self. Adult ego state objectively deals with realities. It is not related to age but is influenced by education and experience. When Adjust is motivated the person can collect and organise the possible consequences of various alternatives and make conscious decision among the various alternatives and make conscious decision among the various alternatives. Adult helps us to minimise regretable actions and increases the probabilities of a person's success. Whenever there is an inner conflict between the Child and the Parent, the Adult ego state can interfere, rationalise, arbitrate, compromise and make new decisions for expression of the inner Child. The Adult Ego State as executive does not mean that person is always acting from Adult but means appropriate expression of all the states which contribute to make a total personality.

The Fig. 29.3 shows contaminated Adult awareness of parent and child. Adult realignment and decontamination, adult filtering behaviour, integrating process and true autonomy. An executive moving toward autonomy explains his capacity for wareness, spontaneity and intimacy. He is developing an integrated Adult filtering more and more child and material through his adult and learning new behavioural pattern as part of integrating process. An executive in the process of integration takes responsibility for everything he feels, thinks and believes. Integrated adult is a full developed of self-actualising executive.

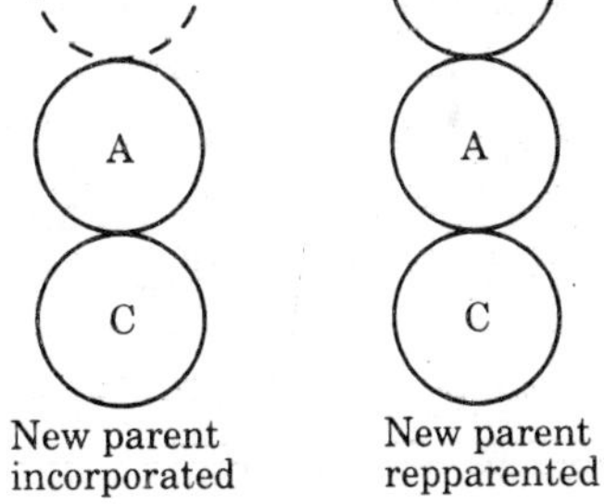

Fig. 29.2.

Adult as Executive of Personality

Adult as executive, adult rejecting parent programming, adult using child programming are shown in Fig. 29.3. An executive, whose adult is functioning as executive, learns to control gestures, so that these child like qualities emerge only at appropriate times and in appropriate situations. Executive has the potential to put his adult in executive control of his ego states. When the adult becomes the executive persons learn to receive more and more stimulus through his Adult. Executive stops, listens to himself and thinks before acting. He evaluates before action and takes full responsibility for his thoughts, feelings and behaviour.

Following are the two gestures for adult ego states :

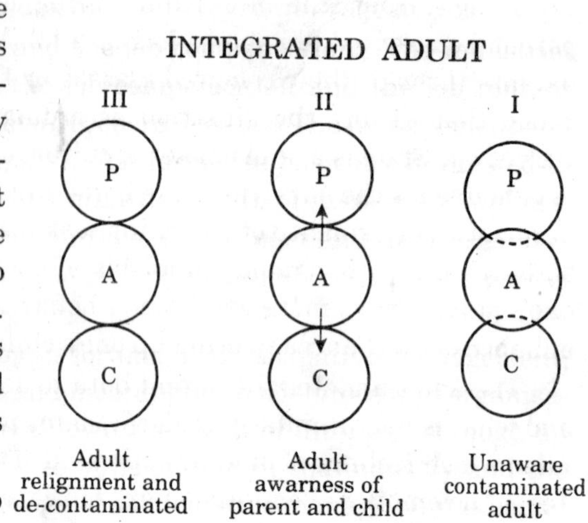

Fig. 29.3.

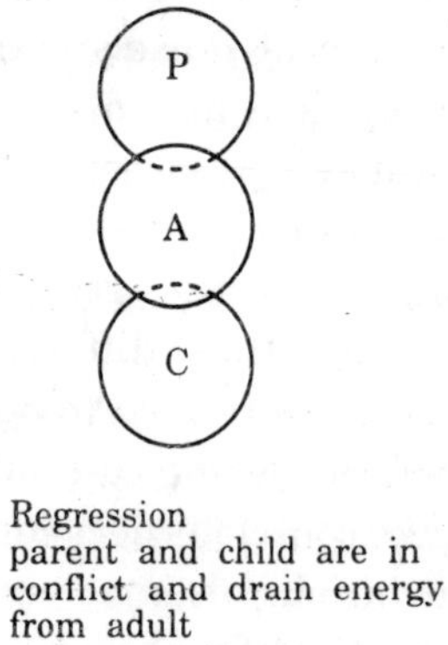

Fig. 29.3(*a*).

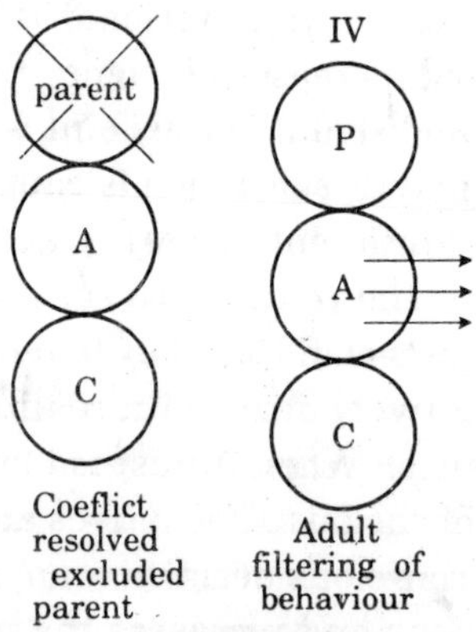

Fig. 29.3(*b*).

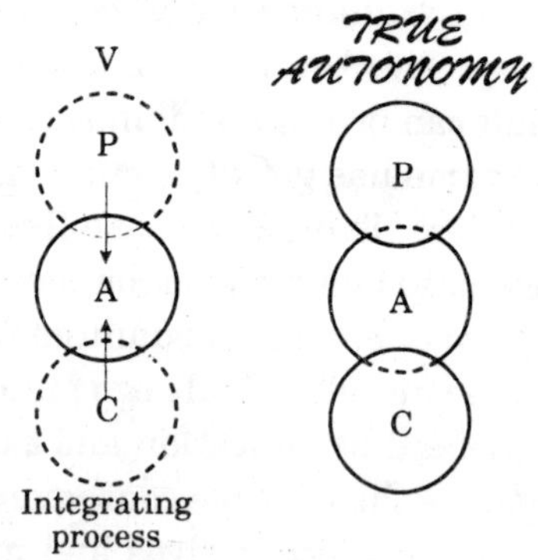

Fig. 29.3.(*c*).

(*a*) Find a quiet place, sit down and imagine yourself as old and on you death bed. Your life is passing before you. Close your eyes, project your life drama up to the resent moment. Take you time and consider the following questions.

(*i*) What memories bring you more pain ?

(*ii*) What experience, commitments and accomplishments have given meaning to your life?

(*iii*) Do you have any regrets ? If 'yes' what have you done ?

It is difficult experiment which requires lot of concentration and practice. This will give you an idea about your deeds, your inter-personnel relationship with others and the targets you have fixed for yourself the degree to which you have achieved your targets. Behaviour is something you want to change now whether you have spent more time or less time with anyone in particular, etc.

(*iv*) Taking PAC as the three ego states drawn as circles of different diameter. Now using circles of different size draw you ego state portrait as you perceive yourself most of the time.

ADULT AS EXECUTIVE
OF THE PERSONALITY

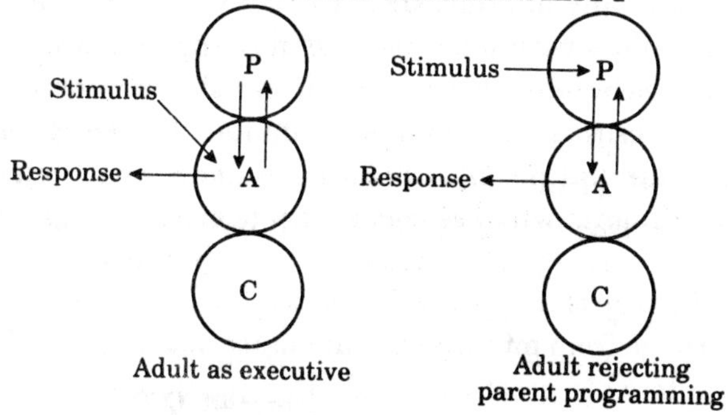

Fig. 29.3.(*d*).

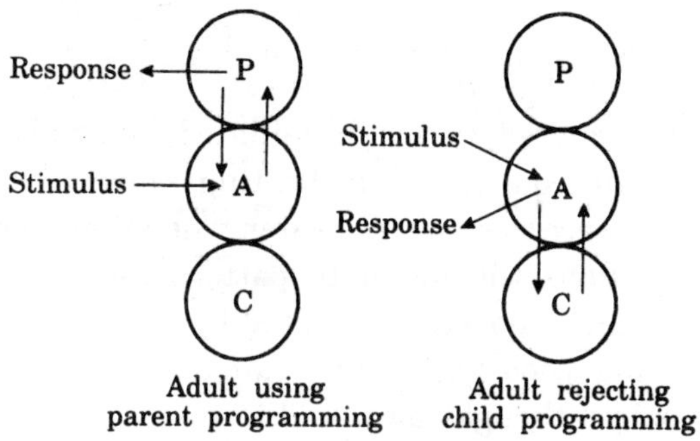

Fig. 29.3.(*e*).

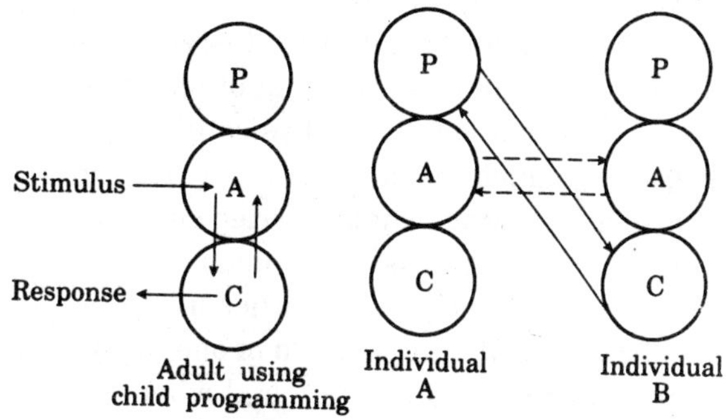

Fig. 29.3.(*f*).

Your portrait might be with the small P and small C and large size A or it may be small A from large P and small C. This will help you to identify you favourite ego states. Also imagine if you portrait will change when the situation changes at work, at home, at school, at social gathering, does your portrait change with certain people, boss, subordinate, spouse, children etc. Now ask one of your friends or spouse who knows you well to make a portrait of yours as they perceive you. NOw compare the two portraits. Do you notice any difference ? Does the new portrait satisfied you if not what needs to be changed ? These are the various questions which will give you an insight into your Adult ego state. Thus, this sort of probing will generate a feeling of self-concept and the need for changing transactions while interacting with others.

Strokes

Every one needs recognition. In the language of transactional analysis it is termed as stroking with means touch. The importance of touch it is known by the feeling of a child given in the Table below :

If you touch me soft and gentle
If you look at me and smile at me.
If you listen to my talk sometime before you talk.

I Will GROW, really GROW. (Child)

The child language of love is touch or stroking. Lack of storing has its consequences both on physiological as well as psychological well being of the child. Every person has the need to be touched and to be recognised by other people and every person has the need to do something with his time between birth and death. The strokes can be in symbolic form of recognition such as look, a word, a gesture or any act that says 'I know you are there.' A person's hunger for stroke determines what he does with his time. He may spend hours, days or even life time to get strokes or to avoid strokes by withdrawing. Even an infant needs touch to grow. The positive stroking enourages him to grow into a winner. Infants who are ignored, are encouraged to become losers. One's mental and physical health are likely to be related to the way he was touched and recognised. Infants who are constantly neglected or ignored get several mental and physical deterioration even to the point of death. Strokes stimulate an infant's body's chemistry. Positive strokes are there to develop emotionally healthy person with a sense of OK feeling. Positive stroke range from minimal maintenance of a hallow to intimacy. Some strokes are merely formal encounters *e.g.* greeting ritual. Besides strokes are complementary transactions, they are direct, appropriate and relevant to the situation. When strokes are positive they leave a feeling of good, alive, alert and being significant. Listening is one of the finest strokes one person can give to another. Listening does not necessarily mean agreeing. It simply means clarifying and understanding another person's feelings and point of view. It is lack of attention that bursts emotionally or physically when a person is ignored, teased, humiliated, laughed at, degraded, named, ridiculed, treated insignificantly and discounted. Child beating is an extreme form of discounting usually carried out by parents who were themselves beaten when they were children. This process continuous to plague generations till adequate pattern for parent behaviour is developed. A mother living in a joint family who was ill-treated by other family members, beat her infact child of one month old causing blood clots in his brain and was found telling 'No one likes me here and when I had my baby I thought he would love me. He kept crying I thought he did not love me, so I hit him.

Parents ignore and fail to stroke their children for many reasons. Most often because in their childhood they were themselves not touched and thus learnt to keep distance. Thus every individual has three basic hungers such as :

(*a*) Stroke hunger (*b*) Structure hunger and (*c*) Position Hunger.

1. Stroke Hunger

Spity in his studies discovered that inadequate handling in children cause dehydration and nervous tissue shrinking which leads to the concept of stroke hunger. It is a common experience that everyone needs and seeks recognition. In the language of transactional theory this recognition is called 'stroking'.

There are two types of strokes, the positive strokes and the negative strokes. The stroke that makes you feel you are OK is a positive stroke. Words of appreciation, encouragement and affection are called positive strokes. Strokes that make you feel not OK is a negative stroke. Criticising, hatred and scolding are negative strokes.

2. Structure Hunger

From the time of birth or the time of death each individual has the need to fill his time. This need for filling one's time is called structure hunger. Following are the ways to structure time:

(*a*) Withdrawing from threatening environment : Such a person may be physically present but mentally absent from people around him.

(*b*) Engaging in Rituals : Rituals are stereotyped series of transactions prescribed by society. Some are formal rituals like wedding ceremonies, death ceremonies, etc.

30

Life Positions

Concepts

The life positions deal with various areas such as how the mind operates.

The individual behaviour towards other individuals is largely based on specific assumptions which are made early in life by the adult ego state.

Thomas A Harries in his book I'm OK - You're OK brought out that there is a growing impatience among various classes of people. The increasing concern of impatience has attracted the attention of general public at large.

The concept of Transactional analysis emphasis the exchange of words and related behaviour between two people.

The transaction can be :

Adult to Adult, Adult to Child,

Parent to Parent, Parent to Child, Parent to Adult,

Child to Parent, etc.

The assumptions of one's self in relation to other are called life positions. They can be classified into one of the four categories as shown in Fig. 30.1.

I'm not OK You're OK : It is the life position held by many. It is based on one's early feelings about oneself, Individual feels a clear distinction between oneself and the people around him could do so many things that he could not. In this life position, the persons who always grumbles about one thing or the other are included. In this situation if the needs of the person, are satisfied through interactions with others, then he has the feeling of You're OK.

I'm OK You're not OK : This distrustful life position. It usually results when a person is too ignored or beaten by grown ups when he was small. These are the people with high rebellion child. This is the case of an aggressive person with an attitude that whatever he does, is right. In this life position the persons normally have rigid attitude with closed mind. This is the case of parent to child transaction.

• Life Positions - Assumption of one's self in relation to others - Gives an idea, how the mind of an individual operates.

• Gives idea regarding exchange of behaviour between two individuals.

I'm not OK and You're not OK - This is desperate life position. People in this position use too much of their energy getting nowhere with other people or with their own lives. The is the case of people who think that the whole world is hostile to them. These are the cases of

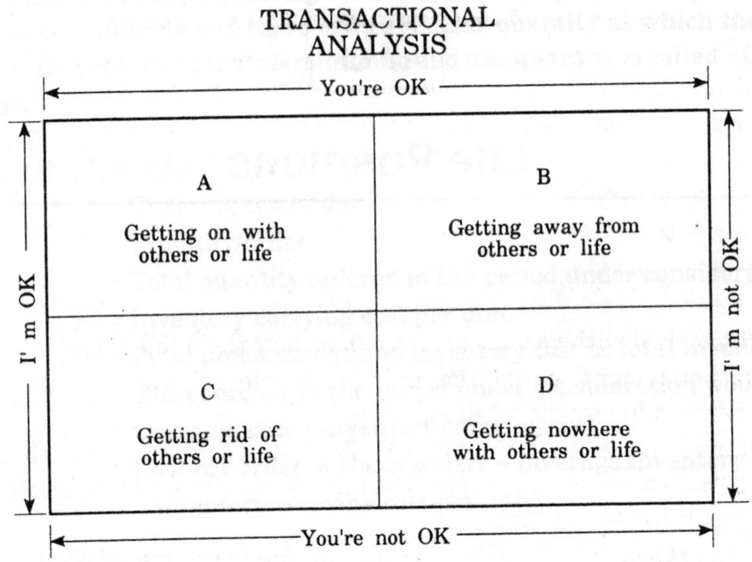

Fig. 30.1.

individuals who are neglected seriously by their parents and brought up by servants or maid servants. The criminal are in this situation because of distorted parent and child state. In this life position the interaction is between parent to parent. I'm OK you're OK -This is a rationally chosen life position. It is made after the individual has had a large number of OK experiences with others. In this life position the individuals operate an adult ego state. It is helpful to visualise these four life positions in the following ways :

How one sees oneself can be plotted on the 'Y axis with "I am OK" at one end, "I'm not OK" at the other end. Similarly, the way in which one see others can be plotted on the second axis 'X' with "You're OK" at one end "You're not OK" at the other end. If one of these is taken as vertical axis and the other as horizontal the life positions are formed.

One of these four positions dominates each person's life. Certain people decide as small children that the position, which seems to make sense is "I'm not OK and You're OK", with this idea dominating their lives they spend their time and energy "getting away from other and taking charge of their own lives. Individuals operating from this life position occassionally get on with others. Living in an "I'm not OK. You're OK" life position is not a pleasant experience. Even a small child discovers an antidote for the trouble. This antidote is stroking individuals who also live in "I'm not OK you're OK" life positions. People in their I'm OK You're OK life position use other adult ego state. Strokes are not only a critical antidote, for the destructive NOT OK feelings that are common to childhood, stroking is also essential for the physical survival of infants. Studies have revealed that infants who are not touched or stroked, soon become withdrawn and lifeless. If this process of physical deterioration continues the infact may even die. The need for stroking even remains in our grown up years. Stroking therefore, is also essential for our psychological well being as it is for our physical survival as an infant.

Exercise 1

To find out one's life position, one can draw a circle, setting out time one invests in various activities such as at home, at social functions, bars, hotels, studies, work etc. The sample diagram for successful people in your profession can also be drawn and then one can compare his diagram with the sample diagram. In this way one can find out if the amount of time one invests in various activities is proportional to the amount of time available with him and does his real interest lie where his time and energy are invented and who seems to be directing his drama of life and also if one is he satisfied with the time he invests in various setting ?

Exercise 2

Another way of having a look at life positions is to think of most important people currently in our life drama.

(*a*) Rank in terms of time, energy and real interest you invest in them.

(*b*) Now reverse the situation and think how much time, energy and real interest do they invest in you ?

(*c*) Do you feel they are furthering your life plans or not ?

Script

Each person has psychological script and succeed in a culture that has a script. The psychological script contains the on going programmes for the individuals life drama. It is associated with the message a child receives from his parents which can be constructive, destructive or non-productive. Life positions can be related to people in general. Scripts give the person a fairly realistic ideas about, what he can do ? What his potential and abilities are ? and what norms and resources are available in his society. A person with clear script can determine the course of his life and rewrite his drama in accordance with his own uniqueness. Following exercise will provide you with an idea about the self.

Exercise 3

(*a*) Go to some place where you have absolutely no disturbance and imagine you are looking at blank TV screen in your mind.

(*b*) Turn back yourself to your childhood and bring your mother and father on screen and try to recollect various incidents of your childhood.

Ask yourself what did you see at that time ? Keep your faces on what you did or failed to do. Repeat that with other parent figures and colleagues during your childhood and 'Ask Yourself.

(*i*) What do you learn about yourself ?

(*ii*) Could you get verbal message imaigning yourself to be a child ?

(*iii*) Could you recall your parents and other family members words that was said about your worth, abilities, morale, intelligence, health, future, etc.

(*iv*) Is your current appraisal related in any way to your parents opinion of you ?

(*v*) Could you recall non-verbal messages from parents through their actions such as pat on back, angry lap, affectionate kiss and pleasant or unpleasnat feelings ?

Exercise 4

You can do a role identification exercise by recalling the events during your last few days and how you related to different people.

(*a*) Did you find yourself playing the role of a builder or a victim, prosecutor or rescuer ?

(*b*) Did your role change when the setting changed ?

(*c*) Did you play one role more often than that of others ?

(*d*) Are the roles played similar to your values, myths and imaginations ?

Imagine your life drama being performed on a stage.

(*a*) Is it a comedy or tragedy or what ?

(*b*) Does your play have a script theme ?

(*c*) Is it success oriented or failure oriented, constructive, destructive or self productive or self deceptive.

Imagine yourself to be acting, watching your drama and then 'Ask yourself.

(*a*) Will you laugh, cry or go to sleep or what else ?

These exercises will give you an opportunity to look back in your Child and Parent messages and also will help you to integrate them with your present position and abilities.

Trading Stamps : Certain people learn in their childhood that the expression of their positive feelings and negative feelings get them into difficulty. So these people keep up their feeling for a definite situation. In other words, people trade stamps which are of two kinds.

(*a*) Dirty Stamps.

(*b*) Gold Stamps.

Dirty Stamps

It represents negative - Not OK feelings such as anger, depression, guilt, frustration, anxiety and fear.

Gold Stamps

It represents positive OK feelings such as joy, affection, excitement, enthusiasm and pleasure.

Racket

It is taught by parents or any one who brings up the child. If a child has not acquired I'm OK - You're OK life position then it means that some kind of bad-feeling racket is there given away by the parents. Rackets are cooked and manipulated ways, that people go about collecting their favourite brand of Trading Stamps. Whenever the parents respond with anger, confusion, depression anxiety, fear then there are chances that parents have taught racket feelings. Therefore to deal with Not OK feelings the Trading Stamps. Rackets and Games are commonly used.

Games

Games were popularised a few years ago by Dr. Eric Berne. Games are special transaction programmed by the child to deal with their Not OK feelings.

Following are the six popular reasons for playing games.

(*a*) Games help the child to keep up his appearance but in a dishonest way.

(*b*) Games help to keep an individual from facing responsibility, competition etc.

(*c*) Games help an individual to pass the time with people with whom he is very close.

(*d*) Games help an individual to give and get strokes.

(*e*) Games help to maintain the life position - 'I'm not OK'.

(*f*) Games help you to get close to the people without getting too close.

Employee comes to the work place as a total and complex person. Each individual has one's own unique P.A.C. An individual has feeling, his needs and talent on the job . A individual is a unique person with his own P.A.C., and handles the feelings of his customer or fellow employees in friendly I am OK - You are OK manner. Games are a means for handling feelings and satisfying stroke hunger. People play games in the places where they live. Individual in an organisation for psychological and monetary advantages. The games are vital to the psychological maintenance of life. Games, however, can seriously interfere with an individual, work group or an organisation in achieving its objectives. The intentionally played games tend to drive others away from several unwanted things. Intentionally played games create psychological pollution with high level of NOT OK feelings. As we are aware that in any individual healthy adjust is essential for working on his job, with other people and social set ups.

Most of us work in situations, in which team work is involved, and in these situations, intentionally played games isolate the player from others. The isolation creates break in communication and problem solving between individuals and groups. The following are the games notably played by people.

1. *"If it weren't for him."*

It is a hierarchy game which is normally used by individuals or groups to blame someone else may be the boss, the union or the teacher or the parents. The individual takes himself off the hook for working on a problem and places the responsibility on some one else. Following are the various statements which can be listed under this game.

Individual A I could really do a much better job if it were not for ....

Individual B You are probably right.

The interaction of two individuals A and B in this game is shown in Fig. 30.2.

(Individual A is again saved from trying to do something that is frightening to him).

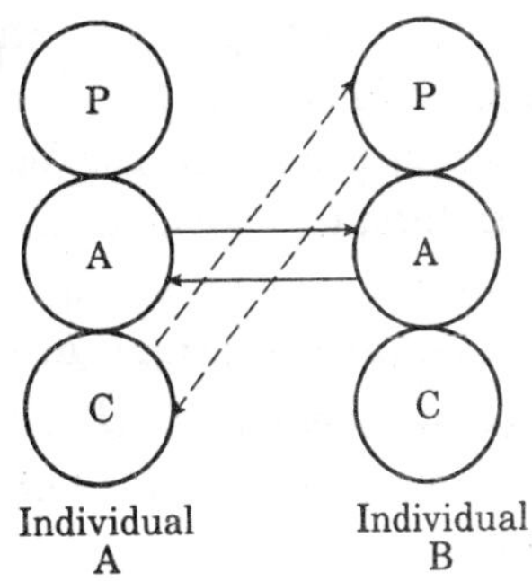

Fig. 30.2.

2. *"Why Don't You-Yes But"*

The another hierarchy game used by individuals or groups is "Why don't you ... yes, But."

This game is most commonly played between staff and line individuals and groups. Following are the various statements which can be listed under the game :

Individual A And that's my problem. Any suggestions.

Individual B Have you ever tried ....

Individual A Yes I have but ....

Individual B Why don't you try ....

(Individual A gets strokes and gives rejection stamps at the same time).

The interactions of (P-A-C) of two individuals in this game is shown in Fig. 30.3.

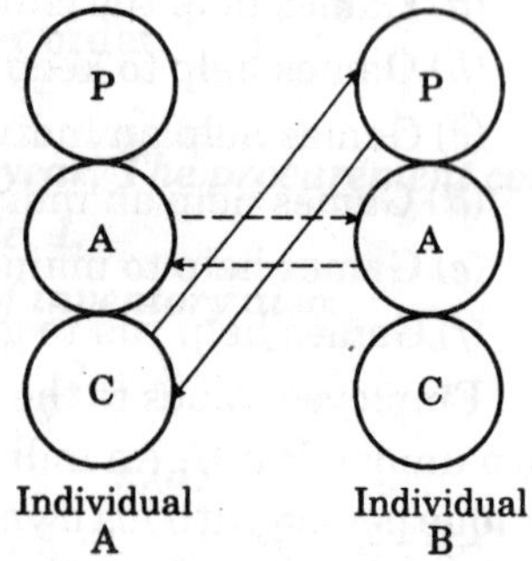

Fig 30.3.

3. *"I am only trying to help you"*

The another game which is used by players, commonly the experts, consultants and executives is 'I am only trying to help you'. Following are the various statements which can be listed under the game.

Individual A And that is my problem. Any suggestions ?

Individual B Why, Don't you ....

Individual A That's a good idea, but ....

Individual B Well, I was only trying to help you.

(Individual B gets rid of burst feelings caused by individual A's rejections.)

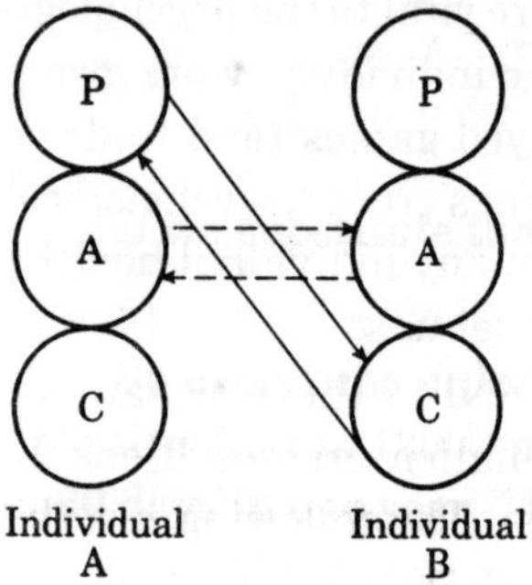

Fig 30.4.

The interaction of P-A-C of two individuals in this game is shown in Fig. 30.4.

4. *"Trapping game"*

This is a trapping game in which player attempts to catch another individual or group in some negative situation. If the player is able to trap another individual he earns a pay off which is usually a justification for taking some negative action. The interaction of P-A-C of two individuals in this game is shown in Fig. 30.5.

(This is a crooked way for individual A to give dirty anger stamps).

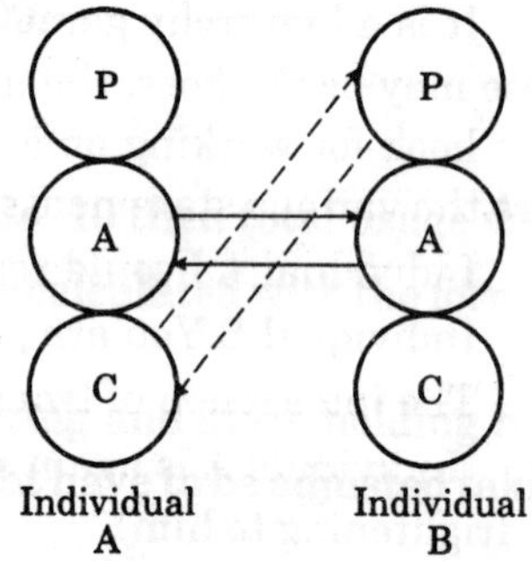

Fig 30.5.

The various interactions which can be listed under this game are :

Individual A Were you late today ?

Individual B I am afraid I was.

Individual A You have forced me to take action.

These negative actions can be used by players objectively without offending since other individual 'deserved what he got. These actions might be used as substitute for problem solving. Games should not be confused with problem solving as two things are different. However following are the similarities which is responsible for confusion.

(*a*) Games outcomes are more predictable and risky.

(*b*) It is easier to enlist colleagues in games than in problem solving.

(*c*) People involve their 'Not OK' feelings by playing games and thus overcoming their feelings.

Functional Disorder

Thus we know that each individual has a parent, adult and a child. The individuals differ from each other because of different degree of parent, adult and child and the recordings of

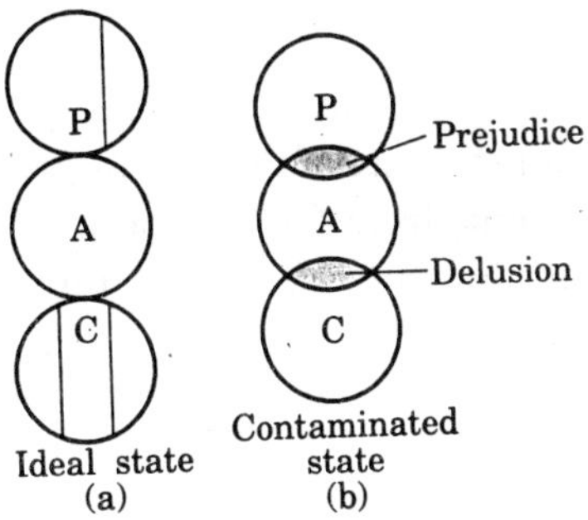

Fig. 30.6.

various unique experiences. In any individual the parent, adult and child should not overlap otherwise contamination may take place.

The contamination of adult by parent data leads to prejudice. The prejudice develops in early childhood when door of inquiry is shut on certain objects by the parent. The disadvantage with a prejudiced person is that it is difficult to reason with him. No amount of logical and convicing evidence on any subject can convince a prejudiced person. Fig. 30.6(*b*) is the contamination of the adult by the child in the form of feelings. This form of contamination is called delusion. The delusion is the grounded fear.

Exclusion

In addition to contamination the another important functional disorder is exclusion. Exclusion is the stereo-type predictable attitude which is maintained as long as the situation is threatening. In this situation the excluding parent can block out the child or the excluding child may block out the parent. This type of individuals are duty dominated.

Parent contaminated adult with a blocked out child are duty dominated. Such individuals are working late at the office and impatient with the family. This situation occurs when they are brought up by duty bound parents who switch off their child. The individuals found in this case that anytime he used his child ego he puts himself in trouble. Individuals with parent contaminated adult with blocked child has very little happiness recorded in the child. Such individual with his adult establish a value of being loving. Individual will not change the nature of his parents but can achieve the insights which makes him to live a satisfactory life in the present.

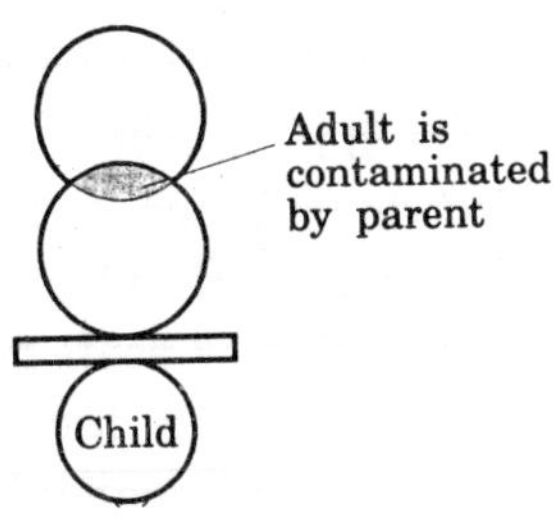

Fig. 30.7.

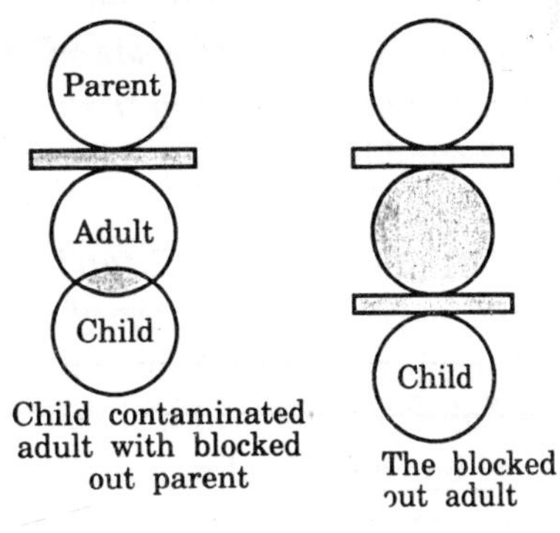

Fig. 30.8.

The other type of exclusion is presented by the child contaminated adult with Blocked-out parent. This situation arises when the individual's parents or guardians were so brutal that individuals had to block parent to preserve his life, such examples are in case of illtratement by step mothers. Such individuals do not learn to be loving because the individual has never been loved. In this situation the individual's behaviour is dominated by his child which with contaminated Adult manipulates other people to his own end. The treatment of such persons is difficult in the absence of functioning parent.

The Blocked Out Adult

In the situation the adult of the individual is not functioning and it's thus unware of reality. We have seen that people differ by virtue of different structured arrangements of Parent, Adult and Child. In every transaction the Adult takes data from the Parent, from Child and from reality before coming to a decision. Thus through the understanding of Parent, Adult and Child, one can understand and predict the behaviour of the individual.

31

Learning Process

Learning Process

The man had been anxious to learn more about the nature since the beginning of civilization. This process of learning has continued till today. He learnt in schools and colleges during education and training to have basic knowledge of subject and then he moved to the field of work. The process of learning is a never ending process.

The entire process of learning based on understanding and remembering. The research into the process of learning particularly in "remembering" and "forgetting" disclosed that the rate of forgetfulness was always greater. Study reveals that *shortly after the information was passed to the student he started forgetting* and retention became more and more difficult which is evident from the figure given below :

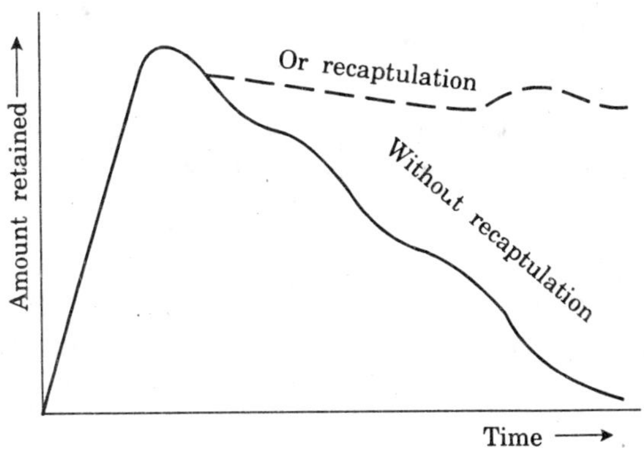

Fig. 31.1.

This problem of forgetfulness led the scientist to develop more effective methods for communicating the subject matter to the learner.

The use of most effective method of communication is an important factor of learning. Before developing lesson plans and courses review of the criteria for selecting the media is needed.

The term media is not restricted to the equipment but includes all forms of communication ranging from word to direct on-the-job experience.

To many audio-visual may be more meaningful than media but it will not give a complete description. The term media includes the human experience of learning through all of ones sensory channels.

Many channels of learning are available to the learners. No single avenue should be excluded if it will aid in learning. Seeing, hearing, smelling, tasting and feeling are the five sensory channels of learning. The learning must employ as many of these sensory channels as possible. To rely upon hearing also is like assuming we are blind : to rely upon sight alone is like assuming we are deaf. In our real life many a time all sensory channel function at the same time. We should persist in utilizing either one sensory medium at a time or at the best sense of sight and sound.

The "Senses of Learning" reveals that during general education sensory channel of seeing is utilized to the extent of 75% whereas hearing (13%), smelling (3%), and feeling (touching) is utilized 6% only. Similarly a student going through on-the-job training utilizes the sensory channel of feeling (touching) to the extent of 60%, hearing 10%, seeing 20%, smelling 5% and tasting 5%.

The same sensory channels which we use for learning also become inhibitive factors in learning. For example poorly constructed sight and sound presentations fail to motivate or teach. The learning environment may adversely affect the trainees' senses if it is too hot or too cold, stuffy, noisy or badly lighted. Therefore, the training programme should be devised such that it adequately considers and uses all human senses to advantages and neutralizes the inhibiting factors affecting these senses.

Instructional Methods

Considering the utilization of sensory channel in the process of learning, a few Instructional methods have been described.

1. **Direct Purposeful Experience**

There is a situation where only experience is useful for learning. For example, if one wishes to learn swimming, he has to jump in the pond and actual practice in pond will make him to learn swimming. Any other method like lecture or filmshow or demonstration will not e helpful.

This method is very effective but is least efficient for learning.

2. **Contrived Experience**

Sometimes situations are artificially created and practice of some job is done by the learner. For example, artificial war practices for defence service, fire fighting and civil defence practices for scouts and guides. Such method has been very effective for learning but efficiency has been quite low.

3. **Dramatised Experience**

Dramatising the subject matter of communication has been very effective media of communication. It leaves a prolonged effect on the minds of audience or a group of learners. It is capable of attracting the attention of audience to a greatest possible extent. Such method is quite effective but time consuming process.

4. **Demonstration**

A demonstration enables us to concentrate attention on a particular part of a total assembly or situation and present this clearly to the students with no obstruction of vision or distraction of attraction caused by the other parts of the assembly.

The student can handle it physically.

5. Study Trips

In study trips, students are taken to actual location site. They find more interest because a change in the routing environment and understand subject matter. It also has long effect on their mind and students remember the subject matter better. To example, study trips of historical places, industries and scientific research organisations.

6. Exhibits (Models)

A model is recognisable imitation of the original. They may or may not be working model and they are usually made in miniature form. Materials used are wood, metal, plastic etc.

Model is closest possible alternative to be shown to the students. It can be conveniently explained in lesser possible time. For example, model of a factory for teaching layout.

7. Educational Television

Television comes in many forms *viz* off-the-air, closed circuit programmes and video tape. Television is less flexible in terms of when one can view off-the-air and closed circuit programmes. Video tape overcomes this problem. Cost and complexity of T.V. are the greatest drawback to its widespread use.

A few formal training programmes can use off-the-air programmes for training. In industry, closed circuit T.V. and video tape systems are more important.

Closed circuit T.V. can be connected *via* cable to any number of locations. This allows simultaneous viewing of presentation by a large number of trainees. Films may also be shown on closed circuit T.V.

This method of communication is more effective than lecture on recording radio or still picture which uses only one sensory channel, but it is less efficient as it is time consuming as compared to other methods of communication like lecture and visual symbols.

8. Motion Pictures

Motion pictures are one of the most common among audio-visual aides.

Such method utilises seeing as well as hearing sensory channels. It is more effective since its impact in the minds of students remains for a longer time.

9. Visual Symbols and Verbal Symbols

1. The figure "Cone of Experience" explains that the methods of instruction shown in the bottom is most effective but at the same time it is least efficient. Similarly the methods of instruction shown at the top are most efficient and least effective.

The selection of appropriate media has significant importance in industrial training. More than one methods of instruction should be utilised in order to make the training programme more effective and intersting. However, the selection of medium of instruction should be mode. keeping in view the particular situation.

Learning and its Characteristics

Crux of any training programme is how adequately the trainees learn. Learning may be defined as the sum total of behavioural changes resulting from experience at training. Learning is said to have occurred if there is a change in the individual's behaviour prior to and subsequent to training programme. The purpose of training is to establish the relation between stimulus and the desired response. If we want to have a response we must design the stimulus by controlling the communication, materials, equipment etc., so that desired response in the form of job performance in achieved. The behavioural changes occurring as consequences of learning can be drawn in the form of a learning curve. Learning curve shows the level of achievement over the learning period. Fig. 31.2 shows the learning curves.

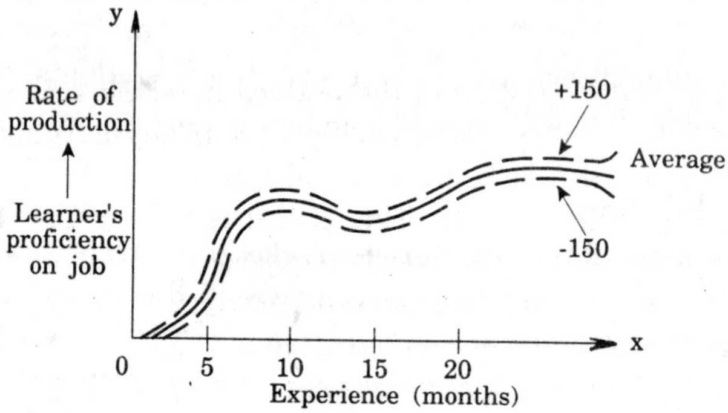

Fig. 31.2. Relation between Experience and Rate of Production.

The practical use of these curves is that of learning curve for an individual when compared makes it possible to comparing the curves for an individual with that for a group. This determine how individual is progressing during his training relative to others. If an individual falls too below the average it is necessary to give special attention or to transfer the individual to some other job.

The learning curve is plotted with rate of production per hour on Y-axis and experience in months on X-axis. In this learning curve the dotted lines indicate the standard deviation above and below the average production for varying accounts of experience. The experience has shown that individual difference tend to become smaller over the duration of training programmes. The relative degree of improvement in learning is greater in case of more difficult jobs than the easier ones.

Retention of learning

Everyone has a tendency to forget the learnt material over a period of time if the material is not used or not supplemented by additional learning. The extent of forgetting varies with type of information and the extent and the way it was learnt originally Fig. 31.3 shows two curves representing two different learning groups, one group who was given a formal guidance and other group learnt on their own.

Fig. 31.3 shows that virtually there is no difference during the re-learning period between two groups; performance during the re-learning period is different because level of difficulty of the related jobs differs.

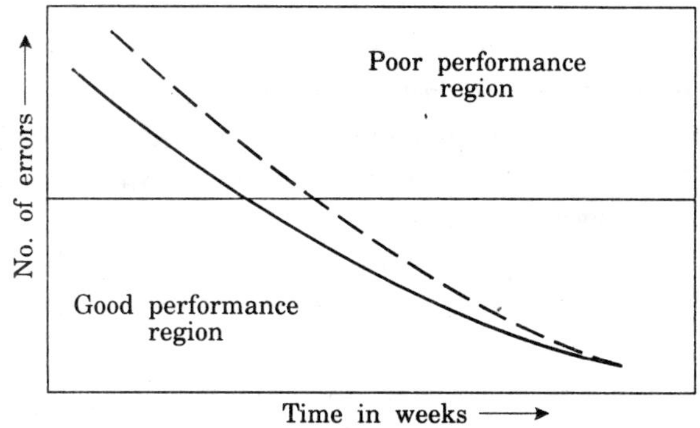

Fig. 31.3 Comparison of performance during original learning period and during re-learning period.

Learning Patterns

Mangers need some understanding of the pattern in which new skills are learnt by the trainees. The'learning curve' has been shown in Fig. 31.4. In any learning process, after a certain level of proficiency, a period of time arrives in which no improvement takes place in the trainee. This period is later followed by increase in skill incentives is required. Such motivation produces greater concentration effort, and a new attitude towards the job by which trainee can co-ordinate the elements of the job in a new way expressed as a whole.

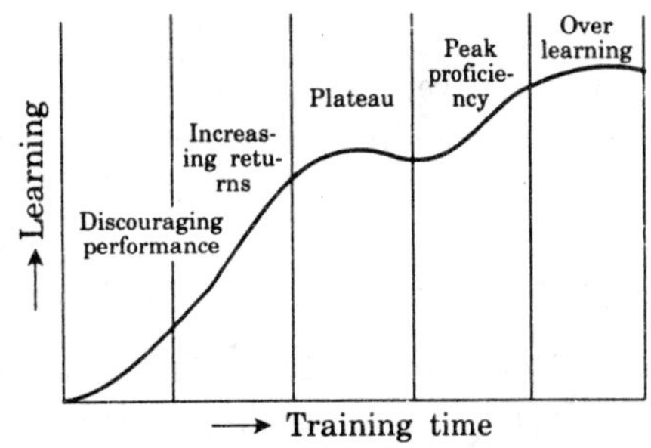

Fig 31.4. Learning curve showing proficiency.

Over learning

Once the trainee has achieved a peak skill, he should be asked to continuously repeat the training so that over-learning takes place because otherwise, he may forget the skills, if he is not using them in the near future. An experienced swimmer can refrain from swimming for six months or even six years and still he will be able to swim when he is required. This is largely the result of over-learning which reduces the likelihood of forgetting the skill. The rate of forgetting varies with the type of information, the extent to which to which it was originally learnt and the nature of individual. The re-learning of material takes much less time than the original learning.

Principles of learning

The learning principles which should be taken into account in designing a training programme can be summarized as follows :

1. The learner should be motivated to learn.

2. The responses should be meaningfully related to each other and to the motives which the learner brings with him into the situation.

3. The new responses should be reinforced by some reward or information that the response has been made correctly.

4. The new responses to be learnt should not be in conflict with old responses. If they do, the training should provide an opportunity for the responses to be unlearnt before the new responses are learnt.

5. The learner should be an active participant in the learning process.

6. The learning situation provides opportunities to practise the new responses and allows for 'plateau' periods of little improvement which often precede marked improvement. If the supervisor handles the situation intelligently. The period during which very little or no improvement takes place is known as *'plateau'*.

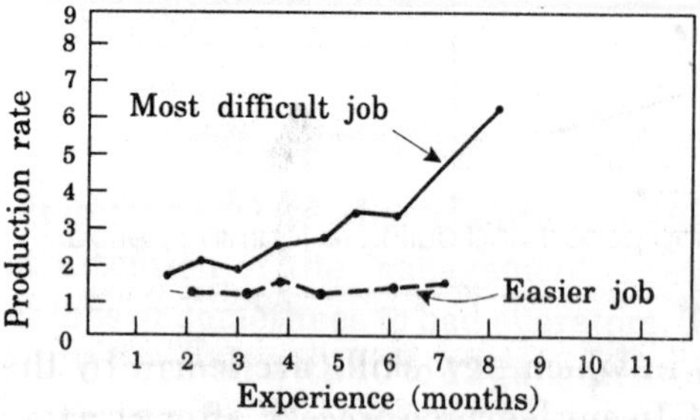

Fig. 31.5 Comparison of Learning levels of two related jobs that differ in difficulty level.

The plateaus in the learning curve can be eliminated by improved methods of instruction.

The learning curve shows that when the trainee first begins to learn a new skill, he is likely to find himself unusally clumsy. This can be very discouraging, particularly to a man who prides himself on his ability and so on. During this early stage, the learner needs the trainer's encouragements. The duration of the first stage will depend upon the complexity and newness of the skill being learnt. After this period, the typical learning rate is rapid. This is the stage of increasing returns, in which small additional amounts of practice by the trainee produce substantial increases in job proficiency. During this second period, the trainee's confidence and satisfaction rise.

Plateau

After more training time has elapsed, a plateau develops. New additional training time does not result in very significant increases in proficiency. At this stage the trainee begins to feel that there is nothing further to learn now in the place of his training. But this is only an illusion created by the 'plateau' in the trainee's learning curve. In order to push the curve of learning further up what is needed is that the trainee must be motivated to make reviewed and vigorous efforts. This is here the trainee's ability to learn on his own really put to test. Therefore, a trainee should not be taken away by this phenomenon and go ahead with renewed zeal.

The plateau in the training seems to be the result of two factors : (1) a loss of motivation because of the fact that further progress become more difficult, and (2) the trainee needs for substantial blocks of time to develop new and improved skills. At the beginning, the trainee may be forced to learn a new skill in segments, but a great deal of practice is required before a real break through takes place that permits these separate parts to become merged and the motions to be joined into a single coordinated sequence of actions. To break away the plateau and to establish high level of proficiency some sort of motivation in the form of financial and non-financial.

7. The new responses to be learnt should be broken up into learnable units and presented in the appropriately placed sequence.

8. Coaching should be available to help the learner develop new responses.

9. The learning situation should allow for individual differences in the speed of learning, the depth of learning and should be designed as per individual requirements.

Whole versus part learnings

This refers to the amount of the training content that are presented to the trainees. Whether the whole or the part training is superior depends upon the particular situation. Thus in the development of training programmes one should not blindly follow the practice of part or whole training but rather in p2articular practice that should be used that seems appropriate to specific situation *J.A. McGoel* and *A.L. Irion* in their book, "The Psychology of Human Learning" considered following factors which are important in one or more situations.

(*a*) For the more intelligent subject the whole method of learning should be used.

(*b*) The advantages of whole method increase with practice.

(*c*) The meaningful material favour the whole method.

(*d*) Part method of learning requires the need of connecting the separately learnt parts.

(*e*) Very short and very long passage call for the whole method of learning while in between favour the part learning.

Knowledge of results

There are two ways in which principle of knowledge of results can have an effect upon learning :

(*a*) It provides the basis for correcting one's errors.

(*b*) It makes the task more interesting and meaningful to the learner.

An operator would have trouble in learning to manipulate the controls of an equipment unless he knew how the equipment respond to control his actions.* *W. Stockbridge* and *B. Chambers* in 'Aiming Transfer of Training and Knowledge of Results' deal with rifle practice. The situation was one in which men fired rifles at moving targets in a simulated rifle range where 'Knowledge of Results' was furnished to the subjects.

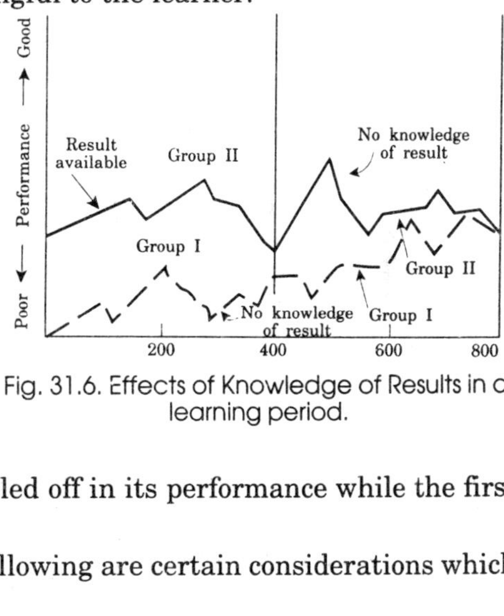

Fig. 31.6. Effects of Knowledge of Results in a learning period.

The subjects were divided into two equal groups on receiving the feedback while other not. After 400 runs none of two groups got the feedback of results. The figure shows that however the second group leveled off in its performance while the first group continued to improve.

In providing feedback of knowledge to trainees, following are certain considerations which should be kept in mind :

(*a*) Knowledge about the trainees' performance to be feedback should be specific rather than general.

(*b*) Trainees should not be overburdened with information. Only the necessary information should be presented that is appropriate for the proficiency of the trainees.

(*c*) Feedback about the trainees' performance should be immediate otherwise its impact is lost.

* R.B. Ammons 'KNOWLEDGE OF PERFORMANCE' Survey of Literature 'Some possible Application and suggested Experiments' USAF Air Development Centre Tech. Report, 1954.

Motivation

There is no about this that motivated individual learns much faster than an unmotivated one. In any aspect of life the motivation of people is central to any form of behaviour. Human motivation is charcterised by basic needs directed towards achieving certain desirable goals. A few of the determinants of motivation at work are hierarchies of needs, frustration, attitude, conflict, group relation, etc. These factors further interact in some manner with many other factors such as personal experience, emotions, likes, dislikes, fears, etc., to form the motivational base for each individual. In addition to this another very important factor is the set of values and beliefs of individual relating to his job.

32

Training

Training

Training has a long past but a recent history. It has travelled from Ashrama of Rishies, to Modern Five Star Culture. More emphasise has been placed upon training and development in industry in the past two decades only. The cause may be due to the changing nature of both modern employment and workers expectations of what it should provide. Training has been a part of Personnel Manangment but it has received a step motherly treatment as Personnel Managers are engaged mainly in industrial relationship and welfare problems. Training Departments have not attracted genuine people and the discipline has been mained by side tracked Managers. Training is the area where organization and the individual development can match and where personnel and organizational growth can occur simultaneously.

Strategy for Training. It may difficult to arrive at a consensus of strategy for training for following two reasons :

(*a*) Training is not always the best or most reasonable means to adopt to solve local problems, as changes in structure and organisation policy might effect the progress faster training.

(*b*) The training may manifest itself in quite different ways particularly some of the enterprise engage fresh talent from the Univarsities and put them under training in their own training institutes while other enterprises induct professionally qualified and trained people from the open market.

Training is a systematic development of attitude/Knowledge/skill and behaviour pattern required by an individual in order to perform adequately a given task or job. This is often integrated or associated with further education. The use of learning experience to integrated the concept of training and education is increasingly common. Consequently training as a process is seem to rest upon the application of a " system" model. In order to identify what the problems are and whether training might help to reduce them, it is necessary to find answers to a number of questions :

(*a*) What is the current level or kind performance. How does this compete with the level or kind desired.

(*b*) What changes are desirable. Can they be identified ? Are there changes in structure, policy, procedure practice or behaviour.

(*c*) Are the desired changes require training to affect them. Is there a place for training in change process.

On the making of training needs analysis it is possible to determine the gap between the present results and the desirable results if the learning process were to be improved. It is possible to establish training need by ascertained whether a gap between the expected and the actual exists. If there is one, and if training is considered to be the means by which it is most effectively and economically reduced, them the training need is determined.

The responsibility for determining training needs belongs in short to the line mangers. The research committee of the American Society of Training Directors lists 11 techniques for determining training needs; Observations; Management requests, Interviews, Group conferences, Job Analysis, Questionnaire surveys, Tests or Examination, Merit or performance rating. Personnel Records, Production reports, Long range organisational planning.

Training is a Management Tool

Training needs are the skills, knowledge and attitudes individual order to overcome problems as well as to avoid creating problem situations of however, the causes of problem situations are not people centered, training cannot be expected to resolve. The difficulty, when problem situations are people centered, when individuals have to change, learn new skills, replace incorrect habits with productive skills replace undesirable habits with productive habits, modify attitudes and acquire additional knowledge, training is one of the best management tools available. Training is considered as a solution to problems in case of following :

(*a*) When there is a possibility of surpassing standards by improving skills methods or attitudes.

(*b*) When there is difficulty in meeting standards because of present skills or methods or attitudes.

(*c*) When experienced employees are to be transferred, promoted or retired.

(*d*) When equipment and facilities dictate new skills or methods.

(*e*) When the results are contrary to desired direction beside managerial supervision and corrosive action.

Object of Training

The object of training is to maintain and improve the performance. Training relates to specific skills associated to job performance, it is therefore very difficult to train an uneducated person. Education enhances the whole person. The development on the other hand consists of developing attitudes and personality. It includes both training and education. Development is preparing for change of job and change in job. The relationship of training education and development is shown in Fig. 32.1.

An effective training programme must include the following :

(*a*) It should relate to business goals.

(*b*) It should start from where the trainee is.

(*c*) It accounts for individuality (different people learn at different speed)

(*d*) It should develop knowledge and skills.

(*e*) It should provide practices, ensure success (people learn by existing).

(f) It should recognize trainee's cost (if any individual volunteer for learning he learning he learns more than the one who is forced to learn).

(g) It should have supportive climate (Many organizaitons do not support training).

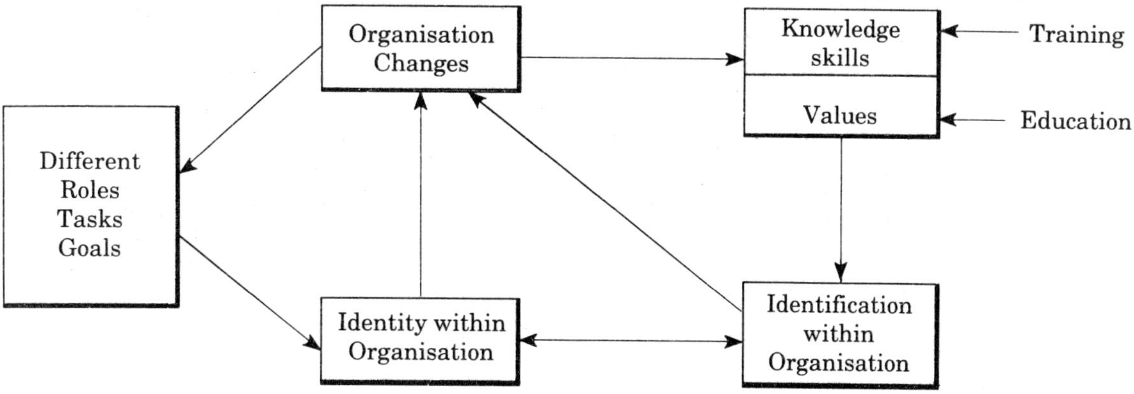

Fig. 32.1.

Training Style

Following are some of the training styles :

(*a*) Pre-courses briefing : It includes clarifying "Objectives", "Courses Content" and Purpose".

(*b*) Participative Learning

(*c*) Practice

(*d*) Co-coaching

(*e*) Freedom to adopt contents (flexibility to adopt to the 8need of the participants).

(*f*) Tutors' role : tutor role is of a catalyst. It is not a role of telling the people what to do accept but to give them idea.

(*g*) Feed back.

(*h*) Risk taking.

(*i*) Feeling and thinking.

The various aspects of training are :

(*a*) Training, tuitors.

(*b*) Selection of trainees, design of training.

(*c*) Co-operation with educational bodies.

(*d*) Report and accounts (statutory Annual Report)

(*e*) Award and celebrations.

Making Training Visible

In order to make training visible following points are very important :

(*a*) There should be a published training policy.

(*b*) There should be approved training calendar.

(*c*) There should be encourgement and feed back of successful training programmes in company newspapers.

(*d*) There should be broadcasts on training information.

(*e*) Exhibition : exhibiting and displaying of trainees photographs.

(*f*) Training and development activities as part of the organization.

Continuous Development

Continuous development is a process of preparing the people for change. It is taking charge of one's own learning and the self managing. Continuous development programme should normally be carried out jointly by line and Training Mangers. Following are key element of continuous development.

(*a*) Learning must be integrated with work.

(*b*) Learning should be owned by the learner.

(*c*) Learning preferably on the workplace (It is the duty of line Manger to encourage good learning).

(*d*) A partnership in learning (It should be a partnership between line Manger, individual and Personnel Department).

(*e*) Business plans should incorporate the learning plans (It should be on continuous basis).

The other critical aspects of continuous developments are :

(*a*) Preparing Organization.

(*b*) Preparing the people.

(*c*) Providing the opportunity.

For preparing the organization there is a need to have commitment of senior Manger. Every senior Executive has a public relation role. He need not be the best trainer but should able to express himself well. This can be achieved by suitable design of course with factors such as :

(*a*) Programme reflecting realities of job roles.

(*b*) Consultation with target growth.

(*c*) Pilot/evaluation.

(*d*) Linking and progression (training in one skill and any other should be inter-linked through various modules).

(*e*) Composite and specialist programme (inter-maxing of functional areas to higher value system).

(*f*) Parallel training (Learning during interaction).

The various elements of continuous development programmes are given in a diagram.

Training - A management activity. It is one of the most important activities of management. Industrial growth cannot take place without trained man power. The technological advancement is taking place at such a rapid speed that the knowledge and skill required by an individual become obsolete at a much faster rate. In order to cope up with the fast changes in requirement of skill and knowledge to the need for systematic training is now felt in almost all organisations. Having selected the most suitable persons for various jobs in the organisation through the application of scientific techniques, the next function of personnel management is to arrange for their training. All types of jobs in the organisation usually require some type of training for their efficient performance. Employees talent are not fully productive without a systematic training programme. Moreover, big organisations hire large number of young people every year who do not know how to perform jobs assigned to them in work organisations and they need to be trained by their employers. Even those who have learnt technical or professional concepts while at some college or institution, must receive some initial training in the form of orientation training regarding the policies, practices and ways of their employing organisations. The need for systematic training has increased because of the rapid technological changes which create new jobs and eliminate old ones. New jobs require some sort of special skills which may be developed in existing work force only by giving them necessary training.

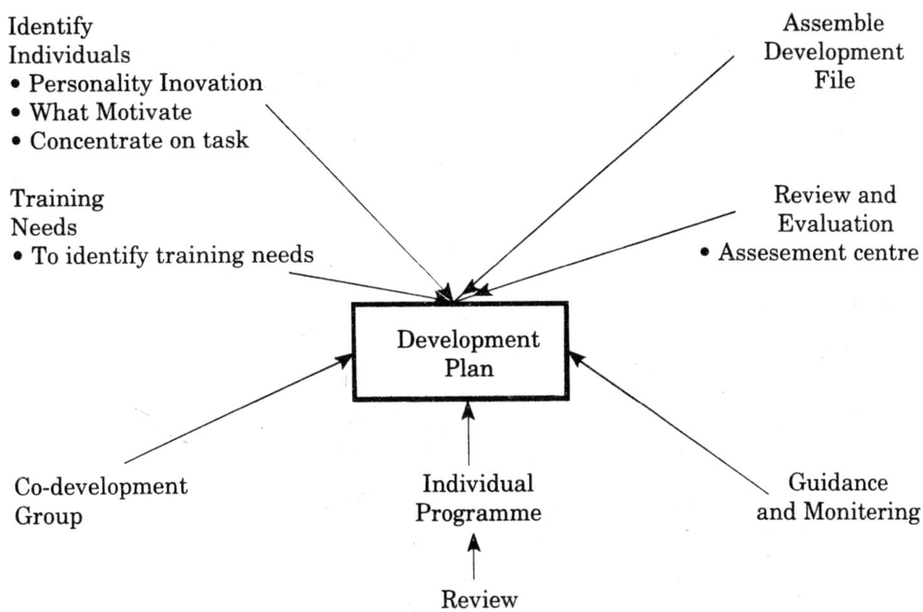

Fig. 32.2. Continuous Development Programme.

Training By Observing. The employee tries to train himself by trial and error or by observing others if no formal training programme exists in the organisation. But it is an established fact that the absence of a systematic training programme will result in higher training costs. The employee will take a much longer time in learning the skills. He may not be able to learn the best operating methods. Adequate training is equally desirable for the organinsation and the employee. Training is valuable to the employee in terms of better job security and greater opportunities for advancement.

Training is no more a luxury which can only be afforded by affluent nations. It is now considered a necessity which is required even buy the poorest of nations. In today's fast moving world a man's basic education and training is no longer sufficient to carry him through his job because jobs are growing faster than the men who hold them. This is primarily due to the increasing obsolescence of human knowledge by the ongoing revolution in science and technology. Apparently, a technologist, trained today shall find many gaps in his occupational knowledge which he must fill in through training if he is to grow in his position late. Whenever new persons are appointed they must be trained for an efficient performance of their jobs. Even if a person is a skilled one, he requires some training because many jobs in the Organisation consist of tasks which are unique and peculiar and many other jobs seen different in work situation from what is found at the place of learning.

Definition. Training is an organised procedure for increasing the knowledge and skill of people for a definite purpose. The purpose of training is to achieve a change in the behaviour of those being trained. In the industrial situations this means that the trainees will acquire new skills, technical knowledge, problem solving ability and attitudes. Any good training programme lays down the procedure by which people gain knowledge and skill to perform their job effectively and efficiently.

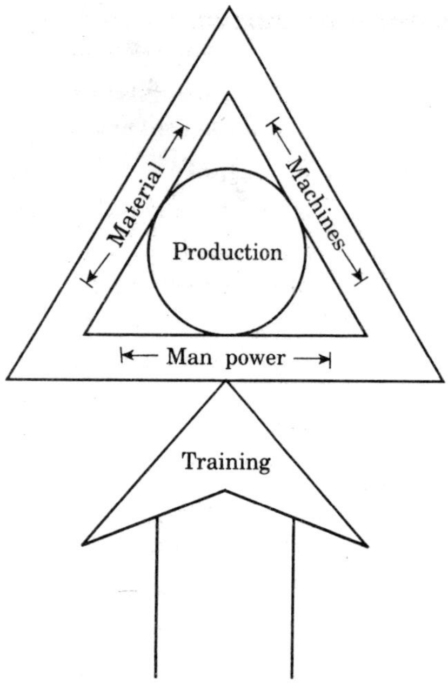

Fig. 32.3.

Distinguishing between education and training is not easy, the two overlap each other. Training is concerned with increasing knowledge and skill in doing a particular job and the major burden of training falls upon the employer. But education is at times narrowly used to mean the formal process of studying a syllabus of work which usually involves attendance of an educational institution. Training usually has a more immediate purpose than education. Actually, the distinction between training and education is not precise because in many cases both training and education occur at the same time. Some employee development programmes in industry which is quite wider in scope may be viewed as education. Particularly, where the emphasis is given on off-the-job training, the objective of the training is to increase the knowledge and understanding of the employees, regarding business and general environment.

Value of Training. Training enables the employees to get acquainted with jobs and increase their aptitudes, skills and knowledge. It helps the newly recruited employees to be productive in minimum amount of time. Even for the experienced workers, it is necessary to refresh and enable them to keep up with new methods, techniques, new machines and equipments for doing the work. Thus training is not a 'one step process', but it is a continuous or never edding process. It increases the knowledge and skill of new employees in performing their jobs and it serves as refresher course for the old employees.

Training job will never be finished as long as the organisation remains in business. Training does not disappear from any organisation merely because its presence is ignored.

Training when broadly conceived can help in orienting and indoctrinating a new employee; teaching him the specific knowledge, skills and attitudes he will need to perform on the job and provide him the opportunities for education and self-development.

The basic logic of training can be described as :

(*a*) Identifying the training needs or goals, involving a clear concept of the knowledge, skills or attitudes which the trainee is supposed to acquire during his training period.

(*b*)

Selecting a group of trainees. This involves the selection and preparation of employees who require training.

(*c*) Designing the training experiences in terms of the appropriate learning theory, taking into account the nature of what is to be learnt and who the trainees are.

(*d*) Preparation of the instructions and selecting the methods and techniques.

(*e*) Evaluating the outcomes of training with a scientifically designed evaluation scheme. The Evaluation programme should involve observation of the trainees back on the job for some period of time after training and should also determine whether changes observed are attributable to the training efforts.

Training is potentially one of the most useful tools available to management. A manager can make use of training to help him manage. But the importance of training is frequently overlooked because of certain difficulties and possible loss to be incurred as a result of any training programme. First of all, regular work is likely to be interrupted or delayed. The output of the trainee might be temporarily reduced. Also training might foster dependece upon others for solution to challenges which the employee should think for himself. Moreover, competent or well qualified trainers are not easily available. They may have to be developed from within the organisation. Nevertheless, the benefits to be obtained from training are many times more than to overall costs of training.

Any good manager should have goals in his mind for his operation in the organinsation. If these goals are to be translated into action then those working under him in the organisation. must share the responsibility for their fulfillment. Training helps the management in its obligation to communicate its purpose and policies to all levels of personnel so that they may co-operate in the achievement of organisational goals.

Training is a Service to Management. An important task before the management is to improve the overall competence of the organisation. Training focus upon interaction problem-solving, and information sharing and is a means of expeditiously pooling knowledge. As a matter of fact, those experiences and insights from training become the common property of the group which received training. The expertise obtained by group can be multiplied within the organistaion and can improve the competence of the organisation.

Training is an obvious way of imparting necessary skills among the personnel. It can also offer management an assessment of those within its labour force who might be well suited for new jobs and different responsibilities. If the training has a sufficient degree of openness, it will allow to disclose skills and abilities among the persons which might otherwise go unnoticed. A competent trainer can judiciously made appraisal of employees which will be useful for the management. Management can use such information in placing the employes correctly and in developing the talents of the promising employees for further use.

Training is a service to management; it is an adjucant of the management process. Under the umbrella of training, several useful functions of management can be performed. Training reduces the need for constant and close supervision; thus it helps in management by exception. A manager can delegate authority and responsibility to his subordinates, who will be reluctant to accept new assignments if they have not been given the proper training. In addition management can get better results and can put its plans into action surely with the help of trained workforce. Management can also increase the morale of the employees and motivate them to work for the achievement of organisational goals by installing a suitable system of training.

Management of an organisation should have goals in mind for the effective operation. If these goals are to be translated into action, then those within the organisation must share them and consciously try to fulfill their responsibility.

Training must be based upon the needs of an organisation. Training too often occurs in a vacuum. Trainers organise courses which seem to them to be interesting or an agenda is developed in terms of some preconceived notion of what constitute a body of useful information. It is possible that all problems cannot be obvercome by training, and it is important to screen out those organisational needs with which training can cope with and those which are beyond its competence.

The trainer needs professional expertise in order to fulfill his responsibility. If he is ill-informed about the training process or if he knows little about possible connections between training and management then he may indeed deserve the casual treatment that he frequently receives.

Where the objective of training is technical or at least designed around the development of a concrete technical skill, the evaluation task is easier. But if the purpose of the training is to influence or to modify attitudes and styles of behaviour, the more sophisticated techniques of evaluation are required.

Following are the main values of training :

(*i*) **Reduced Learning Time.** A systematic programme of training helps to reduce the learning time to reach at the acceptable level of performance. The employees need not learn by hit and trial or observing others and waste a long time if the formal training programme exists in the organisation. The qualified instructors will help the new employees to acquire the skill and knowledge to do particular jobs within a short interval of time.

(*ii*) **Better Performance.** Well trained employees usually show a greater increase in and a higher quality of work output than an untrained group. Training increases the skill of employees in the performance of a particular job. An increase in skill usually helps in increasing both quantity and quality of output. Training is also of great help to the existing employees. It helps them to increase their level of performance on their present job assignment.

(*iii*) **Reduced Supervision.** If the employees are given proper training, the responsibility of supervision is lessened. Training does not eliminate the need for supervision, but it reduces the end for detailed and constant supervision. A well trained employee is self reliant in his work because he knows what to do and how to do it. Under such situations, close supervision is ordinarily not mandatory.

(*iv*) **Standardisation.** With the help of training the best available methods of performing the work can be standardized and made available to all employees. Standardisation will make high levels of performance rule rather than the exception. Employees will work intelligently and made fewer mistakes when they possess the required know-how and have an understanding of their jobs and of the interdependence of one job on another.

(*v*) **Economy.** Trained personnel will be able to make better and economical use of materials and equipments. Wastage will also be low. In addition, the rate of accidents and damage to machinery and equipment will be kept to the minimum by the well trained employees. These will lead to lesser cost of production per unit.

(*vi*) **Increased Morale.** The morale of the employees is increased if they are given proper training. As a common objective of the organisation training programme will mould employees' attitudes to achieve support for organisation activities and to obtain better co-operation and greater loyalty with the help of training dissatisfaction, complaints, absenteeism and turnover can also be reduced among the employees. Thus training helps in building an efficient and co-operative work-force.

(*vii*) **Fill Manpower Needs.** When totally new skills are required by an organisation, it has to face great difficulties in the selection process. Training can be used in spotting out promising men and in removing defects in the selection process. It is better to select and train from within the organisation than to seek skilled employees from outside sources. Training may also quality them for promotion to more responsible jobs.

(*viii*) **Better Management.** A manager can make use of training to help him manage in a better way. To him training the employees can assist in improving his planning, organising, controlling and actuating. For instance, main-taining higher standards of quality, building a satisfactory organisation structure, delegating authority and stimulating employees, are all assisted by effective training.

(*ix*) **Organisational Stability and Flexibility.** Training increases the stability and flexibility of the organisation. Creation of a reservoir of trained replacements will increase the stability of the organisation in the sense that organisation will be able to sustain its effectiveness despite the loss of key personnel. Training can also be used to help the employees to gain multiple skills to enable their transfer to jobs where the demand is highest. It will bring about flexibility in the sense that organisation will be in a position to adjust to short run variation in the volume of work.

Training Needs. Training is a continuous process which is aimed at increasing the skill and knowledge of new as well as old employees to enables them to perform their jobs well. The process of training is shown in the diagram in Fig 32.4. Training involves learning about the job by the employee.

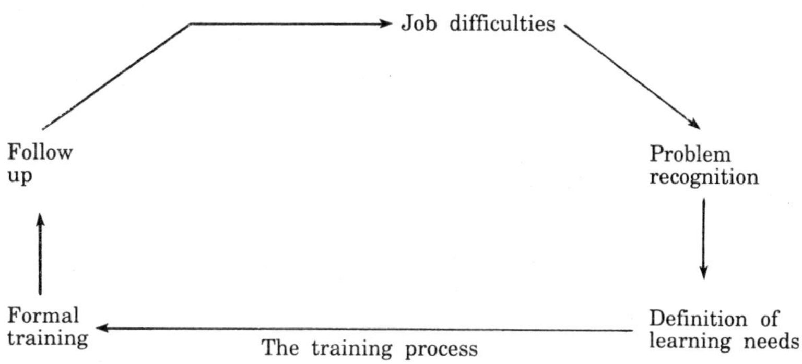

Fig. 32.4. The Training Process

But sometimes, a manager decides to set up a training programme because it is popular thing to do and because, other organisation are doing it. Such a tendency is not good in the long run. Training programme should be set up only after having clear-cut objectives in mind.

Training without objectives is useless and merely involves wastage of money. Training programme should be established only when it is felt that they can aid in solving specific problems. The rational way of deciding what kind of training activity to undertake is to make an analysis of the job and the qualities of the employees to identify trouble spots where training may help.

Training is not ultimate cure for all troubles. For instance, if the employees output is low this may be corrected by better skill training. But this problem may be because of faulty material, process equipment or engineering design. If it appears that general caliber of the employee is low, this problem may be solved by training. But in other cases, the training will not be of much use. Following are the steps for discovering training needs :

(*a*) **Analysis Jobs and Men.** If the men are less capable to perform the particular jobs they can be given training to increase their skills.

(*b*) **Identifying Production Problems.** If there is low productivity, poor quality, high cost, high rate of absenteeism and labour turnover and excessive grievances, indicipline, these will indicate the need for training.

(*c*) **Collecting Employee's and Managerial Opinions.** The training 8section may either by interviews or questionnaires obtain views of different people regarding necessary and desirable training programmes.

(*d*) **Anticipating Requirements of Different Jobs.** The line Mangers can forecast before and the manpower requirement on the basis of long-term plans regarding business expansion, new plants, new designs and new technology. Training may be given to the existing employees to enable them to meet the requirement of new jobs in the future.

Element of Training. Every training programme includes, trainees, trainers, a training programme and training material.

Preparation of the Trainee. The proper selection of trainees is of major importance if permanent and gainful results are to be obtained. A trainee should be trained for the kind of job he likes and is suitable to perform. In this respect, training is closely related to the selection of personnel. Careful screening of candidates for training raises the effectiveness of the training work.

While giving training to an employee, the first step is to place him at ease. It is generally seen that most are somewhat nervous when approaching an unfamiliar task. The instructor should not forget the newness of training programme to the trainee though he has repeated experience of this. The trainee must be given the proper background information before he starts learning the new job skills and knowledge.

In the case of supervisory training, it is better to include all supervisors and other employees considered suitable for promotion to such posts. Excluding some employees on the ground that they do not need the training or that they are already doing their work satisfactorily is a poor policy. Even outstanding persons benefit from well managed training programmes and their presence helps the less competent persons.

Trainer. The trainer is a key figure in an effective training programme. Qualified instructors may be obtained from inside or outside the organisation. He must be able to divide the job into logical parts, so that he may teach one part at a time without losing the perspective of the whole. He must have the skill to instruct and must be tolerant and patient. He must be able to appreciate the value of training work relation to the enterprise and an understanding of what the employees are in order to impart the skill and knowledge for which the programme is designed.

Training must be based upon the needs of an organisation and the trainer must have clear-cut idea about the requirements of the organisation. But too often training occurs in a vacuum. Trainers organise courses which seem to them to be interesting or an agenda is developed in terms of some preconceived notion of what constitutes of body of useful information. In many instances the trainer may hit an appropriate target, but he may also miss the need.

The trainer needs professional expertise in order to fulfil his responsibility. If he is ill informed about the training process or if he knows little about possible connection between training process or if he knows little about possible connection between training and management, then he may indeed receive the casual treatment. Therefore, it is 8desirable that the trainer must have at least minimum knowledge about the job for which he is going to instruct the trainees.

A well qualified trainer can present the operations involved in doing a particular job in various ways. In most of the cases, method of explanation is favoured. In addition an instructor may illustrate various points through the use of pictures and other teaching aids. When the job is essentially physical in nature the demonstration on the job is an excellent device. While demonstrating he operation, the trainer should stand beside the trainee rather than in front of him, so that the latter may adopt the better movements of the trainer.

The trainer should explain and demonstrate the operations step by step and should allow the trainees to repeat these operations. He should also encourage questions from the trainees in order to be sure that the trainee understands the job.

Training Period. The length of the training period depends upon the skill to be acquired, the trainee's learning capacity and the training capacity and the training media used. The use of effective visual material usually helps to reduce the training time.

To maintain interest and to secure maximum accomplishment, no single session should last longer than two hours. Now the question arises whether the training should be given during working hours which may effect production and the organisation will have to compensate for this time. Other alternative is to organise training after the working hours when the employees may not be able to make full use of the training programme during working hours will benefit the organisation as we would not forget that a trained employee will compensate in the form of increased productivity and high morale after the completion of training.

Training Methods. There are many methods or techniques for imparting training among trainees. The choice of any method will depend upon cost, time available, number of persons to be trained, depth of knowledge required, background of the trainees and many other factors. The following are the various methods of training :

(*a*) On-the. Job method.

(*b*) Vestibule training.

(*c*) Classroom method.

The last two methods are also known as Off-the-Job Training methods.

On-The-Job Training. This is considered to be the most effective method of training the operative personnel. That is why vast majority of training programmes organised are of on-the-job variety. Under this method, the worker is trained on the job and at his work place. This enables him to get training under the same working condition and with the same processes, materials and equipment that he will be using ultimately. The responsibility of the training is given to his immediate supervisor, who knows exactly what the trainee should learn to do or to some outside instructors, who is the training specialist in the field. Effectiveness of on-the-job training depends primarily upon qualified trainers. Without them, it is simply the old haphazard practice of putting new worker with old hands who may have neither the inclination nor the ability to teach the newcomers properly.

Another important on-the-job method is "Understudy", whereby a senior and experienced employee as his understudy. But this method takes a long time and the trainee loses his motivation because of uncertainty in his promotion position. "Rotation" is another method of training of the job. Its main objective is to broaden the background of trainee in various position of jobs. The trainee is periodically rotated from job to job instead of sticking to one job and hence acquires a general background.

On-the-job training techniques are most appropriate for teaching knowledge and skills that can be learnt in a relatively short time and where only one or a few employees need to be trained at the same time for the same job. But the success of the training depends almost entirely on the trainer. If he understands training principles and methods and if he takes an interest in proper training of new employees, chances are that it will be done properly.

On-the-job training has the chief advantage of strongly motivating the trainee to learn. It is not located in an artificial situation, either physically or psychologically. It permits the trainee to learn at the actual equipment and in the environment of the job. On-the-job training methods are relatively cheaper and less time consuming. If only a few persons are to be trained at one time, it is cheaper for the employer to resort to on-the-job training. It will take less time to learn on-the-job itself and production does not suffer. Another important fact about on-the-job training is that line supervisors take an important part in training their subordinates.

On-the-job training is the most efficient and effective method of training the employees because it is in complete according with the three basic laws of learning :

(*a*) The law of readiness; (*b*) The law of exercise; and

(*c*) The law of effect

When the person is confronted with a job which he is potentially able to do and is interested in learning how to do a job in order to hold it; the law of readliness is definitely satisfied. Such a situation presents as good an incentive for learning as would ever be found.

The second law of learning is that of exercise and it is satisfied when a person is trained on-the-job because he has the chance to immediately apply for what he has been trained to understand and to do.

The law of effect is likewise satisfied through on-the-job training. If the training is good and new employee is intelligently dealt with by his supervisor, he will satisfaction out of work and feel secured in his job and he will be better satisfied than he would have been left to learn by trial and error method.

Vestibule Training. The term vestibule training is used to impart training in a class room for semi-skilled jobs in the plant and the office. It is more suitable where a large number of employees need to be trained at the same time for same kind of work. Where this method is used, there should be well qualified instructor incharge of training programme. There the emphasis tends to be on learning rather than production. It is frequently used to train, clerks, machine operators, typists, etc.

Vestibule schools are adopted to some general type of training problem that is faced by on-the-job training. A vestibule school is run as a special endeavour of the personnel department. An attempt is made to duplicate, as nearly as possible, the actual material equipment and conditions found in the real work place. Now the question arises why we would have a vestibule school. The vestibule school may be started when the amount of training that has to be done exceeds the capacity of the line supervisor. Thus in vestibule training the workers are trained on specific jobs in a school run by the organisation. An attempt is made to create working conditions which are similar to the actual workshop conditions. The learning conditions are also carefully controlled.

Vestibule training is particularly suitable where it is not advisable to put the burden of training on line supervisors and where a special coaching is required. The staff of the vestibule consists of expert and specialist instructors. The trainees avoid confusion and pressure of the work situation and are thus able to concentrate on training. Their activities do not interfere with the regular processes of production. Moreover, trainees get an opportunity to become accustomed to work in routine and also to recover from their initial nervousness before going on the actual jobs.

Vestibule training has certain demerits also. The artificial training atmosphere may create the adjustment problems for the trainees when they return to the place of job. The vestibule training is relatively expensive because there is duplication of material, equipment and conditions found in a real work place.

Classroom Training. Classroom instrucations are most useful where concepts, attitudes, theories and problem-solving abilities are to be taught. It is associated more with knowledge than skill. For instance, there are certain aspects of nearly all jobs that can be learnt better in the classroom than on the job. Orientation about organisation and safety training can be accomplished most effectively in the classroom. The standard instructional method suitable for operational employees is a "formal lecture" by an instructor to the trainees. The lecturer is presumed to possess a considerable depth of knowledge of the subject at hand. He seeks to communicate his thought in such a manner as to interest the class so that they are able to retain what he has said. The trainees generally take notes as aid to learning.

The lecture method can be used for very large groups. Thus the cost per trainee is low. However, it has certain limitations also. The learners are passive. It violates the principle of learning and constitutes one-way communication. But students may be permitted to ask questions which will provide feedback from the students to lecture and can easily be combined with other techniques. Thus a teacher may conduct a class by the combined lecture discussion method. He may then lecture only to add new information that the group does not posses. Formal reading assignments may be given, demonstration may be presented and films may be shown along with the lecture.

The other classroom methods are Conferences, Case study and Role Playing. But these methods are not of much value for the operative employees. These can be employed to train and educate the employees preparing for various executive positions.

Apprentices Training. Apprenticeship training programmes tend towards more education than on-the-job training or vestibule schools the government have passed law which makes it obilgatory on every employer to provide apperenticeship training to young people. The usual apprenticeship programmes combine on-the-job training and experience with classroom instruction.

The advantages of apprenticeship training to the trainees are that they receive wages while learning and they acquire a valuable skills which help them to secure a job. In India also there are so many who earn when they learn. Apprenticeship scheme holds true both in private as well as public sector undertakings. This is also advantageous to the employers and some employers look upon apprentices as a source of cheap labour.

Apprenticeship training is desirable in industries which require a constant flow of new employees expected to become all round craftsmen. It is very much prevalent in printing trades, building construction and erafts like mechanics, electricians, welders etc.

Induction Training. After a candidate is finally selected, he is issued the appointment letter and requested to join to organisation upto some specified period. The induction function follows this step and generally considered to be a part of the hiring procedure. Induction is concerned with the problem of introducing or orienting a new employee to the organisation.

When a newly appointed employee reports for work, he must be helped to get acquainted and adjusted with the work environment and fellow employees. It is better to give him a friendly welcome when he joins the organisation, get him introduced to the organisation and help him to get a general idea about the rules and regulations, working a conditions, etc., if he has not already been introduced at the time of selection. It is the first step in a proper communication policy which seeks to build a two-way channel of information between management and employees. Induction may also be defined as the socialising process by which the organisation objectives are absorbed by the individual for the achievement of his personal goals.

Aims of Induction. Any big organisation should have a systematic induction or introduction process to achieve the following aims to :

(*i*) bring an agreement between the organisation goals and the personal goals of the person employed.

(*ii*) build the new employee's confidence in the organisation and in himself so that he may become an efficient employee.

(*iii*) promote a feeling of belonging and loyalty to the organisation among new comers.

(*iv*) ensure that new employees may not form false impression regarding the new place of work.

(*v*) give the new employees information and knowledge about the organisation--its structure, products, rules and regulations, etc.

(*vi*) give the new entrant the information that he needs such as locations of locker rooms, cafeteria and other facilities, time to break off, leave rules, etc.

(*vii*) foster a close relationship between the new workers and old workers and supervisors.

(*viii*) create a sense of security for the worker in his job by assuring him the idea that fairness to the worker is the inherent policy in the organisation.

(*ix*) avoid cost of replacing workers who separate during the early impressionable period because of lack of accurate information or incorrect business impressions.

The induction will be informal in case of small firms and may be formal of the duration of two to four weeks in case of big organisations. Orientation training course should not be too lengthy. It need not necessarily be given on the day when the new employee joins his work. But if a formal course is to be attended after two or three weeks on the job, the initial introduction and the immediately needed information may be given by the supervisor of the department.

A full introduction course should be handled by persons who are fully conversant with the course contents. The success of the induction course will depend upon the quality of trainers and their ability to draw out the interest of their listeners. The range of information that can be covered in such a course may be as follows :

(*i*) **Company's History.** A brief description of the early history and growth of the organisation and its future potentialities. This can be made more intersting when the company's history is built around personalities than around events.

(*ii*) **Product of the Company.** A brief story of the original products and its evolution to meet competition and consumer needs. Use of sales literature, exhibits and films can also help.

(*iii*) **Company Organisation.** Brief description of the organisation structure, relation of new employee's department with other departments and so on.

(*iv*) **Location of Departments.** Location and layout of the company's plants stores, departments, canteens, etc.

(*v*) **Personnel Policies.** Policies of the company regarding compensation, training, promotion, retirement, insurance etc.

(*vi*) **Employee's Activities.** Statements of the available programmes and activities carried on by workers, such as recreation, mutual benefit association, credit union, etc.

(*vii*) **Rules and Regulations.** Description of rules and regulations of the company regarding attendance, working hours, pay advances, sick leave, conduct, etc.

(*viii*) **Safety.** Safety measures taken by the company for the protection of the workers and their use by the workers.

(*ix*) **Standing Orders.** Grievance and disciplinary procedure and suggestion system in the company.

(*x*) **Counseling Service.** Information about the counseling service provided by the company to go into personal complaints of individuals and to help them about their problems.

(*xi*) **Job Routine.** Requirements of the particular job to which personally assigned as well as the job to which this may lead in the chain promotions.

(*xii*) **Special Training.** Information about take training programmes carried out by the company to help the employees learn new skills in doing their job.

Induction Training Practices. Different induction training practices may be used in industries such as :

(*a*) Induction guide or check-list may be prepared to provide supervisor with information on what induction steps have been taken and what are still to be covered. This is done by listing the necessary step to be taken in induction, by whom and when the instruction in to be given.

(*b*) The supervisor may take the new workers expected to work under him and induct them by introducing and counseling them by reassuring and reinforcing his confidence and by guarding against false impression.

(*c*) Follow up interview may be taken by the officers of the personnel department permitting the new worker to open up about shop supervisor or fellow workers without jeopardy. On the basis of this Interviews, personnel department can take action to improve the conditions reassure the workers, dispelfears, gain their confidence and promote their efficiency.

The best method of induction training is to explain with pictures, followed by printed materials. However, their use depends upon the size of plant, number of new workers to be inducted, etc. Motion pictures, visual aid, charts, printed materials, etc. can be used to explain company politics, processes and products of the company. Around of the plant and the departments should also be arranged to acquaint the new workers with the over all operations of the company.

Non-Managerial Job Training. It is important to find out the following points about the trainees.

(*i*) What kind of work must the employee handle ?

(*ii*) What must he do it ?

(*iii*) How can he be encouraged to react positively to what he is doing ?

After collecting information on the above questions one can draw the training requirements. Every non-managerial job requires (1) knowledge (2) skill and (3) attitude. The degree of knowledge skill and attitude required vary with constants of the job as follows :

S.No.	*Job requirements*	*Performance Required*
1.	Routine jobs, Repetitive in nature and adhere to producers	Knowledge--Basic but limited Skill--Manipulative Attitude--Working environment
2.	Moderately Individual and various alternatives are available	Knowledge--Cognitive Skill--Determinative
3.	Highly individual complex in nature wider choice judgement and technical expertise is needed.	Knowledge--Cognitive Skill--Analytical Attitude--Career opportunity

Procedure Training. Any training programme if systematically developed an introduced brings a desirable change in behaviour. The various steps involved in the training procedures are shown in Fig. 32.5 Managers normally assume that problems such as accidents, turnover, more errors, wastage and low productivity relate to inadequate training. But even after the training most of the problems continue to exist and only then the management realises that training efforts were premature. Formal training should be imparted only when the request for training comes from the concerned department and training analyst should test and obtain an objective measure as to whether employees could perform their jobs properly. A department requesting training should provide at least the following preliminary information.

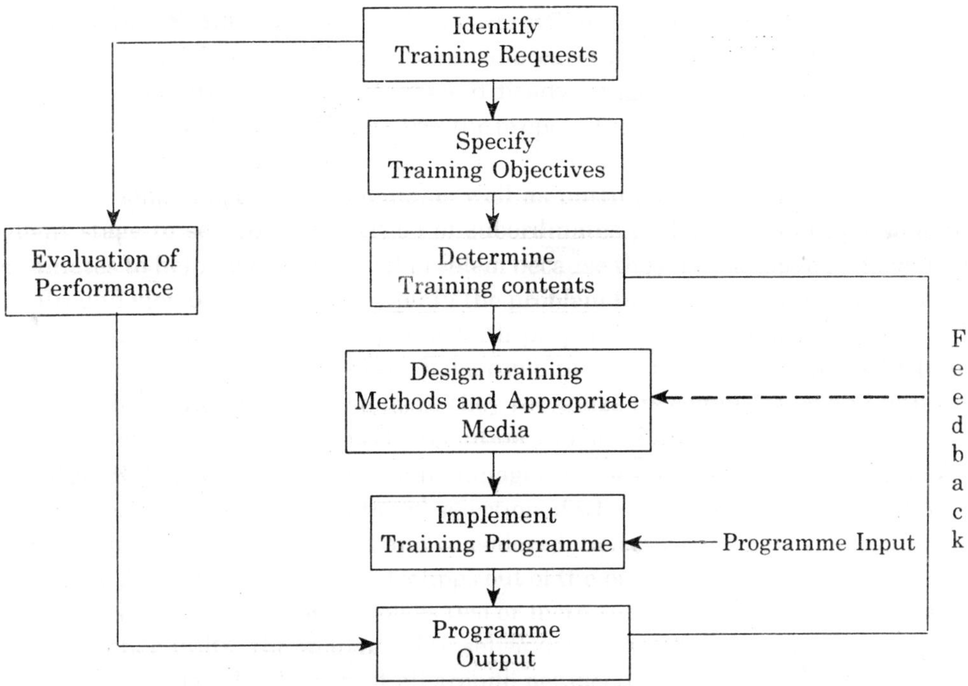

Fig. 3.5.

(*a*) When and how the problem was first recognised ?

(*b*) Whether attempts made to correct the problem ?

(*c*) What attempts were made and what were the results ?

(*d*) Illustrate examples to identify the specific problem.

(*e*) Estimate the amount saved if the problem ceased to exist.

These equations will help the training analyst to analyse the problem and training strategy. The analysis of any training problem begins with the statement of training needs. A need or performance deficiency is the difference between actual performance and desired performance. The actual performance of an individual can be illustrated as $PC + P$.

where PC = Present Capacities of the individual

P = Potential of the individual.

The desired performance of the same individual can be analysed in training and illustrated as $P_1C_1 + P_1$. Performance deficiency ($= P_1C_1 + P_1 - PC + P$).

If the performance deficiency is zero, then no training is required. Fig. 32.6 shows that training analysis is concerned with identifying the causes of performance deficiencies. Decision whether to train or not to train can be based on the extent to which the performance deficiency results from either acquisition or execution. Where the individual has the pre-requisite skills to perform the job properly and skill does not signify that execution type of problems exist and there is no need to train the individual. The ideal training situation is one in which the individual, has the skill and will to work and the job environment reinforces his performance. The following flow chart identify the performance deficiencies during training analysis.

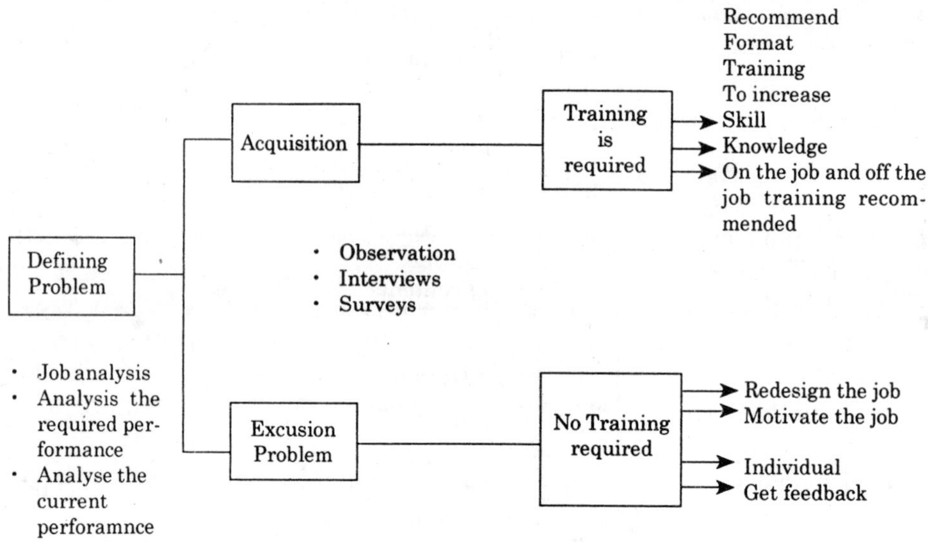

Fig. 32.6. Training Analysis

Soon after it has been decided that training is essential, the immediate starting point becomes the designing of an effective training programme. The two essential elements in preparing programmes are :

(*a*) Determination of training objectives. (*b*) Construction of performance measures.

Both these elements are examined in the model shown in Table 32.1.

The essential feature of the training design is to provide control points for measuring training effectiveness. The performance before training and after training can be compared and if discrepancies exists between the two the existing training system can be improved till the desired training objective are achieved. Next phase is the *development phase*. The training analyst is concerned with facilitating the desired change in the learner's behaviour so that terminal objectives of the design phase are fulfilled. The analyst selects strategies, methods and

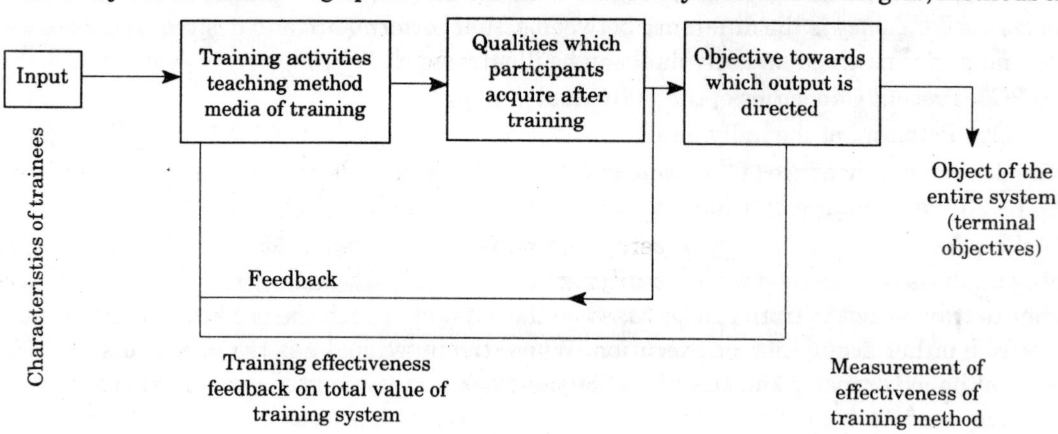

Fig. 32.7.

media which will fulfil these requirements and satisfy the objectives also. The strategies and methods can be grouped as follows :

Training Strategy	*Technique used*
Self Training Individual learn by themselves	Self instruction on the job, Programmed Instructions etc.
Tutorial Training	Individual get the guidance in one to one relationship with trainer
Group Training	Individual participates in training activities with others.

The desirability of using any one or a combination of these particular strategies and techniques depends upon the extent to which they satisfy, and specify the environmental constrains imposed by training analyst and the requesting department. The next phase is the administrative responsibility for organising training. To schedule training, arranging physical facilities such as classrooms, course materials etc. need not be overlooked as it determines the success or failure of even a well conceived, designed and developed training programme. The last but the most important phase is the *evaluation.* The evaluative methods will require the development of follow up studies which include questionnaires, surveys and affecting organisational climate. The success in implementing training depends upon the relationship between training staff and the requesting department. In order to meet the organisational training needs the training analysis should posses : intellectual skill, and ability to communicate and motivate.

Planning Training Programme. Training approach developed during World War II consists of the following steps : (*i*) Preparing the worker, (*ii*) Presenting the task, (*iii*) Trying the performance, and (*iv*) Following up on his job.

The training cycle that can be used in planning major training programmes as shown in Fig. 32.8.

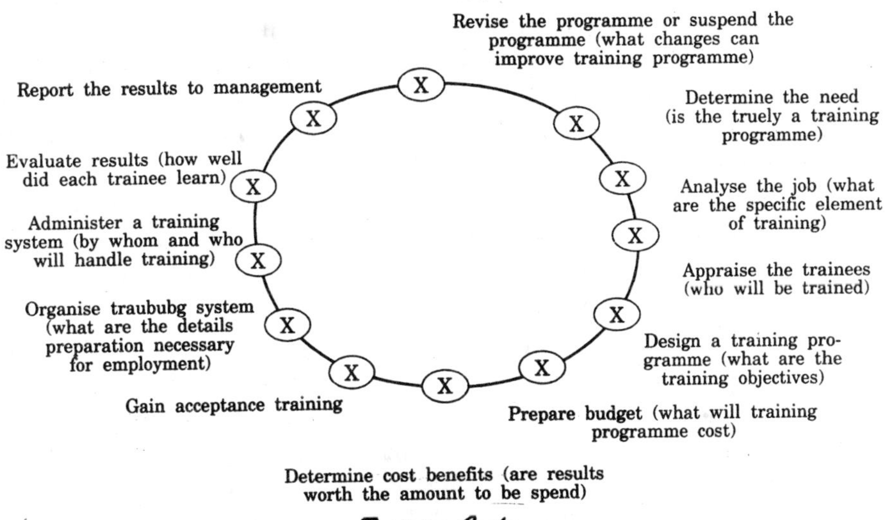

Training Cycle

Fig. 32.8

Essential of Training

The requirements of any training programme may be conveniently grouped into following heads which may be considered essential.

Knowledge. The first essential is that every person should be adequately knowledgeable about the men and material of the organisation concerned.

Attitudes. Knowledge, however, is not an end in itself but it must be directed to create right attitudes towards management's policies. In many training programmes the creation of the right attitudes is very essential for the development of people after the knowledge has been acquired.

Continuous Participation. Training is never ending process which never ceases in an organisaton. The continual process of direction, correction and improvement in performance, at every level of employment is one of the chief characteristics of training. Training must arouse active interest and willingness to co-operate.

Conformity with Objective. Training must be based on the requirement of a particular department or organization. Training programme must be in line with the policy and aims of the department which it serves.

Fulfilling Certain Needs of Employees. Training programme should be directed to fulfil certain basic needs of individuals in an organisation so that they can turn out to be better suited for the discharge of their present or future responsibilities.

Management Attitude. The favourable attitude of the top management to the day-to-day process for growth of the managerial cadres as well as operative level of employees is of paramount importance for the success of a training programme. Psychologically, the essentials of Training can be grouped as follows: Stimulus, Response, Motivation, Reward and Incentives.

Stimulus. The trainer must present clearly the stimulus to the trainee. His way of communication to the trainee must be scientifically designed. Unless the trainee understands what he is going to learn, the trainer must not expect the trainee to learn. The trainer or instructor can use different sense organs of the trainee for better communication. If he finds that trainees can understand the design complexity of the machinery more clearly through vision, he should be allowed to learn through vision. Similarly, if the trainee learns the operation of a machine more quickly by handling the machine than looking at the design and listening to the instructions, the instructors should select the former. Thus, selection of the medium of instruction is one of the important factors to which the instructors should pay due attention at the time of communication.

Response. The trainer must observe the responses of the trainees as a result of his stimuli. The responses of the trainees can be observed by asking questions or allowing him to do the job according to his direction. The instructor should allow the repetition of correct response and encourage the trainees to retain the improved behaviour.

Motivation. The trainee must be motivated to learn. Unless the trainee is interested and motivated in learning, even a good instructor cannot train him. Therefore, the attitude do learn should be developed by the instructors in the mind of the trainee. If the trainee does not develop this attitude, he will not learn though th instructions are clear to him capacity to learn is good.

Reward and Incentives. Reward and incentives act as a stimulus for the trainee to satisfy his need for social approval. For any effective training programme, the management must have a provision for reward for the trainees. The management should give sufficient information about the reward whether in the form of financial or non-financial benefits to the trainees who will come out successfully in the training programme.

Role of Training

At present, there is no systematic standardisation of the different training programmes in India. Each organisation has developed its own methods of training both the workers and supervisors. However management must consider a systematic training programme to improve will help management to standardise the job performance and as well as to selection and placement programme. As has been discussed earlier that for any training programme to be successful, the selection of trainer is of prime importance. The trainer should be picked up from the immediate supervisors in case of one should be equivalent to that of personal manager in the organisation. Thirdly, the need of training should be based on organisations needs. The last but not the least important point is the importance of human relations. Training in good human relations means training in good leadership and sound relationship among people.

Requirements of Effective Training

Training is a vital tool management, capable of making important contributions to the goals of the organisation. Starting with the identification of training needs and the requirements and problems of the organisation, training attempts to improve the performance by closing the distance between expectations and achievement. Training is a never ending process and an internal part of the business system, which aims at bringing about change in behaviour of people.

The effectiveness of an organisation's training programme depends upon the extent to which management is committed to support it, the proper assignment of responsibility to line managers and training in--charge for the training is planned, implemented and evaluated. Top management must provide a climate which is conductive to continued learning and growth.

Line managers have also a great responsibility for the training of their people. He must cooperate with the training specialists in determining the training needs and devising suitable training programme. They are also to help in conducting and evaluating the training activity. Lastly, their greatest contribution is to help the subordinates apply to their jobs what they have leant from training.

Evaluation of Training Programme

Evaluation is an essential feature of all programmes for the training of employees. The concept of evaluation is most commonly interpreated in determining the effectivess of a programme in relation to its objectives. We know that management invests in relation to its objectives. We know that management invests in training programmes of employees only with the expectation to see some tangible benefits derived therefrom. How to know the results of the training programme? The concept of evaluation of training becomes operational only when there is a real or tangible product to measure which will indicate how well a programme is received and how well the participants are doing.

Evaluation can be done for various purposes. The evaluator should be clear about why he has been asked to evaluate training. Evaluation of training programme may be done :

(*a*) To increase effectiveness of the training programme while it is going on.

(*b*) To increase the effectiveness of the programmes to be held next time.

(*c*) To help participants to get feedback for their improvement and efficient.

(*d*) To find out to what extent the training objectives are achieved.

Techniques to Evaluate the Training Effectiveness

Training officers may use a number or techniques to evaluate the effectiveness of training programme. One approach is to pass on a questionnaire to the trainees at the completion of the programme to obtain their opinions as to its worth. Their opinions could also be known by means of interviews. Another approach is to measure the knowledge as skill that employees possess at the beginning of training and again at the end of the training. This may be accomplished by giving them a test before and after the training.

The most immediate source of information required for evaluation of training is the participant himself. He can contribute pertinent data for the assessment of the potential value of a development programme for other participants, whose needs may be if similar nature. Techniques of data collection using the participant as the source include individual and group reaction sheet evaluation forms, questionnaires subsequently set by mail, structured interviews and techniques of assessment by means of critical incidents, observing group discussions, paper and pencil tests before and after the course, records or statistics of productivity, profiles and charts of career advancement of the participants and related assessment techniques. In evaluating the effectiveness of any programme whatever may be method used, the following criterias should always be kept in mind.

(*i*) Objectives (*ii*) Cost Benefit analysis. (*iii*) Flexibility. (*iv*) Results obtained, (*v*) Staff required (*vi*) Improvement possible.

The training and development managers must remain alert to the changing trends. A better way of measuring the effectiveness of training is to use various indices of performance and compare them after the course with the objectives set before the course. The output and quality of work of employees can be used for evaluation purpose. Before and after training figure on accident rates may show an improvement as a result of training, but it will take a longer period of time to produce sufficient evidence in this area. Analysis of absenteeism, employee turnover rates etc. may also reflect the benefits of training.

Though this may seem to be a furitful approach to the problem of evaluation, there is a basic flow in this approach. We have no way of knowing whether the training activity caused improvement in performance index or whether it was achieved as a result of combination of other factors. An improvement in various indices might have been caused by better production planning, better supervision, etc. In such a situation the evaluator may study the individuals who have got no formal training. The real purpose of training is to cause a change in employees behaviour on the job and ultimately to improve the effectiveness of the organisation.

A better way of measuring the effectiveness of training as to use various indices of performance and compare them after the course with the objectives set before the course.

33

Self Development

Self Development

Self Development is the most effective means of training because of the unsolicited commitment involved. Self Development is the core of development process. All the development is Self Development. Immediate question comes in mind is 'Why is it called self development and not self training.' Training is a process of increasing the skills and knowledge of employees to enable them to perform their job well while development is more akin to education.

The initiative for development has to be taken by the individual himself. Development is a process of becoming. It is toward the actualisation of potentialities. At each stage of development there are specific tasks such as skills, attitudes, understandings which are appropriate to that level of maturity and which society expects the individual to master. The development of individual is ensured when they are able to realise that in development themselves to meet organisational needs their own physiological and psychological needs are being fulfilled. The development process transform dependence to self direction ; impulsiveness to self discipline, ignorance to knowledge, competence to competence ; immorality to morality and self confine to concern for self and others. Self development has emerged as major concept in management development. *Self development is a process which helps the executive to define and use their own opportunities instead of being responsive to someone else.* The first step towards self development is to engage oneself in some degree of self analysis. The emphasis is on the following areas :

(*a*) Need for self development
(*b*) Self Analysis and Job Analysis
(*c*) How to achieve Self Development.

Need for Self Development

Many terms *have been used to describe the age in which we live. Some call it 'Space Age' other 'Atomic Age' or 'Computer Age' but one fact is clear that we are in the age of Development and Change.* In todays fast moving world our basic education and training is no longer sufficient to carry us through our jobs without continuous self development because jobs are growing faster than the man who holds them. The reasons why Self Development is required can be classified as Extrinsic Reasons and Intrinsic Reasons.

Extrinsic Reasons

- Inreasing role of knowledge
- Technological concepts
- Growth of system concepts
- Advances in knowledge which require a redesign of managerial competence.

The above extrinsic reasons are primarily due to the increasing 'OBSOLESCENCE OF HUMAN KNOWLEDGE' by the current ongoing revolution of knowledge. We are now caught in what might be called as 'Time Skip'. The pace of change has speeded up and may continue at an ever increasing rate. One has to keep oneself up-to-date for the very survival. Today each successive change renders the previous change obsolete.

But who is responsible for obsolence ? It is the individual, his superior, his employing organisation or his professional associates ? The major share is of the individual who has to take the necessary steps to keep himself up-to-date. The superiors, employers or professional associates play a leading role in this, but without individual efforts it is unlikely that others can help.

Intrinsic Reasons

— To be able to identify new areas and ventures for the organisation.

— To apply new concepts and acquire skills for solving problems.

Intrinsic reasons are primarily due to changing environment leading to cultural shocks which can be met by innovative techniques. In this life time houndaries have been burst and the network of social ties has been tightly woven. There is a need for each one of use to appreciate the fast changing scientific, cultural and social environment. Cultural shock are taking place and we are now finding overselves in a strange, incomprehensible new society. Present cultural shocks are relatively going to be much less than the future shocks.

Executive much search for new ways and means to anchor himself. This will only be possible if we keep pace with the time and continuously re-assess our training and development needs.

To cope up with future changes we have to change and maintain the equilibrium with knowledge revolution by meeting invention with invention. There is a need for neither blind acceptance nor blind resistance but series of creative strategies for shaping, reflecting and accelerating the selective changes. For meeting future shocks the executive must begin at personal level.

Self Analysis and Job Analysis

The need for self development can be identified only by finding the difference between the 'Present Capacities' and Potential to the 'Desired Capacities' and 'Potential'. The present capacities and potential can be assessed through the process of 'Self Analysis' while desired capacities and potential can be evaluated through Self and Job Analysis, Self Analysis means the way in which an individual views oneself--one way of doing this is to ask oneslef the questions 'If I were in business for myself, would I have given myself a Job.' In order to carryout self analysis, we have to understand what is 'Self' and then subject one self to various 'Self Analysis Tools' which give us an insight of our 'Self' and 'Self Behaviour'.

Transformation beginning with self

Management of change has always been a challenge both at the organizational level as well as at personal level. We often want others to change. All management development programmes on the subject of change, seem to produce little or no result, as they do not probe into the reasons whey people want others and not themselves to change. Following are some pointers for reflection on the subject.

Indian managers operate in the world of double or more realistically multiple standards. We always have one standard to measure our performance and another yardstick to measure other's performance. I am right and all other are wrong is the pet theme. People consider themselves as paragon of all virtues and find others deep in soakpit of follies.

We are very good diagnosticians for others. For us we need somebody else. Just exactly as the barber gets his haircut from another barber. One often comes across managers giving spell binding orations on the virtues of team building but unable to manage few of their subordinates or for that matter even their immediate family members.

We are unable to appreciate the magnitude of change occurring around us. Just imagine that on the 12th of August 1992, somebody made a statement to the effect that within one week communism would be dead. What would have been our reaction ? Incredulous ! But that was precisely what happened.

Now wise men, and we have plenty of them in this country, will perhaps say that there were enough signals. But that's post mortem and not a prediagnosis. Just look around us! The world has become unipolar. Internet has changed the complexion of commerce. E-mail s in. Hotmail is the hot thing going about. Yahoo does not mean the song of Shammi Kapoor but is the search engine. World has come first to our drawing room and now in our bedroom. So, we have to realize the bitter fact that the quo has left the status. There is no status quo.

Henry Ford made the following statement :

"Business people go down with their businesses because they like the old way so well, that they cannot bring themselves to change".

Do you find anything amusing in this statement ? Well! This quote is from the same man who once made another statement that he can have any other colour for the car so long as it is black ! The moral is that we need to have complete alignment within us between what we profess and what we actually do and believe in.

Why people do not change ? There could be several reasons. Perhaps there exists the fear of unknown. The present is familiar. Future is hazy. Very appropriately someone has remarked:

"It is not so much that we are afraid of change, or so in love with the old ways but it is the place in between we fear...It is like in between trapezes."

It is said of frogs that they are the most adaptable creatures in the world. If a frog is put in a pot of water and then gradually the pot is heated, what the frog should do ? It can easily jump to safety. But it does something totally different. It goes on increasing its body temperature to adjust itself with the boiling water till it boils down to death. We too have the tendency to boil ourselves to death rather than explore new solutions in the changed context. If you are not part of the solution then you are part of the problem. Such an attitude calls for a fundamental, transformational and not incremental change in the mindset.

What is Self

Man's greatest mystery is man himself. Self is the sum total of all that one call one's. In order to know one's self there should be three persons . (*a*) One is individual concerned, (*b*) Other is the individual requiring about oneself and (*c*) Obejectivity of one's evaluating oneself. The self is made of series of experiences. The concept of self is formed by the behaviour of others toward oneself. Man is object for others but subject for oneself.

Secretes, the great philosopher was once asked by one of his disciples 'why is it sir that you tell everybody who wants to become your disciple to look into this pond and tell you what he sees ? 'This is very simple, my friend', answered Socrates 'I am ready to accept all those who tell me that, they see the fish the swimming around or stones in the pond. But those who see only their own image mirrored in the water are in love with their ego. I have no use of them. For objective self evaluation egoism, pride, self devaluation and inferiority complex have to be ruthlessly cut out.

Self concept is really a social concept and other people are the standards against which emerging self is measured and defined. The self concept which we bring to the job is therefore the amalgamation of (*i*) Perception our parents gave us ; (*ii*) the role we have leaned to play with peers, and (*iii*) record of success and failures and (*iv*) our notions of what rewards we deserve.

Self Behaviour2

Self behaviour means actions, activities, verbal-non verbal communication of an individual. The effectiveness is not only the function of skill and abilities but how best it can be utilised in different situations in getting the work done from the people. It is indeed important for the executives to recognise the need for continual development and to incorporate the concept as integral part in his life. The individual will make efforts to project his image only through behaviour. The behaviour could have positive or negative response. The positive response develops self confidence in the development of that part of our personality. Negative responses disconfirms the understanding of oneself. At times one feeling inadequate and feeling of discomfort, anxiety, tension. These anxities and tensions results n anger, blame, feeling of retaliation and violence. *The self analysis and self assessment help us in overcoming the defensive mechanism.*

Self Analysis Tools

The self analysis tools can be termed as : Style analysis and Feedback from others.

Style analysis. The numerous self graded or computer graded style analysis programmes are available in the market. Each in some degree helps the individual to see himself clearly as other. The result is often an increased sensitivity to behaviour, to the needs of others and to the use of words, tone of voice and body language in order to create a desired impression.

Feedback from others. The questionnaire and instruments are available for sales person's subordinate staff ; managers ; customers to evaluate the individual effectivness as a communicator.

In order to provide an insight of oneself to battery of tests/instruments can be designed to help an individual to identify one's Personality, Attitude, Behaviour and Inter Personnel Skills.

The result of the instruments can be inferred depending on the score of the executive in the various instruments. The result from the instruments can help the participants to improve their own perception of self and others. The self assessment will help us to be more confident ; free from the feeling of insecurity, anxiety and inferiority feeling is one's day to day relations on the jobs. The various Instruments/Tests can measure the following :

(*a*) Measurement of Attitude

(*b*) Measurement of Personality

(*c*) Measurement of Behaviour

(*d*) Measurement of effective communication

(*e*) Measurement of various Transactions.

Measurement of Attitude

Attitude is state of mind or set of beliefs about life. We in our interaction meet with others around us as having a rigid or indifferent attitude to certain situations. Attitude develop in the process of need satisfaction. In coping with various problems in trying to satisfy one's needs, the individual develops attitudes. We develop favourable attitudes towards objects and people that satisfy our needs and develop unfavaourbale attitudes toward objects and persons that block the achievement of our goals. The attitude change can be ganged by analysing certain factors such as turnover rate, absenteeism and production level. The attitude of individual toward work, involvment in company intrinsic job satisfaction etc. can be measured through a set of questionnaire as given in Annexure I.

Self Analysis

S. No.	*Instrument / Test*	*Objects of the Instrument / Test*
1.	Measurement of Attitude	To find out the attitude
2.	Measurement of Personality	To measure the type of personality (*i*) Choleric (*ii*) Sanguine (*iii*) Melaucholic (*iv*) Phlegmatic
3.	Abrasive Personality	To measure whether the executive has abrasive personality or not
4.	Ascertain of individual behaviour	To measure executive behaviour (*i*) Rigid (*ii*) Indifferent (*iii*) Flexible
5.	Johri Window	To measure the exposure/Feedback score (*i*) Initiative (*ii*) Interpersonal Skills (*iii*) Communication Skills
6.	Transaction Analysis	Identify individual response to various situations. It represent the communication of individual. It measures the Ego State (*i*) Parent (*ii*) Adult (*iii*) Child - Rebellion - Adoptive - Creative

Measurement of Personality

Personality can be defined as the most adequate conceptualisation of peron's behaviour. Personality is the sum total of all the tendencies that an individual has inherited and that he has acquired by experience. Personality is the dynamic organisation within an individual of those psychological systems that determine his characteristics, behaviour and thought.

Measure of Behaviour

The individual behaviour is caused and it does not occur automatically by itself. It is the situation which stimulates him to behave in a particular way. Therefore, it is necessary to understand the cause of behaviour before any attempt to change or improve upon the behaviour is made. It is possible to ascertain the behaviour of an individual. We can find out whether our behaviour is rigid or indifferent from the Instrument.

Measurement of Effectiveness

In order to have an insight of personality, behaviour and attitude of one self the Johari Window is used. It is an important tool of interpersonnel effectivness and productivity improvement. It provides an excellent way to understanding the relationship between various individuals. It represents four quadrant representing four aspect of individual personality. We can measure the exposure and feed back score through an instrument. The exposure refers to how much an individual is alter to information. The exposure and feed back score are approximately same for an effective executive.

Transactional Analysis

Transactional Analysis helps us to gain both emotional and intellectual insight. T.A. is a rational approach to understand behaviour. It's principal can be applied wherever people deal with people. Through T.A. we can evaluate old decisions and behaviour and can change what we decide is desirable for us to change. By T.A. we can rely more on our capacities for analysis and making judgements. The object of T.A. is to help us to achieve Autonomy. The attainment of autonomy is manifested by release of recovery of these capacities 'Awareness', 'Spotaneity', and 'Intimacy'.

Awareness requires living in the here and now and not in the elsewhere, the past or the future. An aware person lives in the present moment with environment which is here.

'Spotaneity' means option, the freedom to choose and express one's feelings from the available (Parent feelings, Adult feeling, and Child feelings).

'Intimacy" means the spontaneous game free transaction. Intimacy is essentially a function of the natural child which expresses his affection and genuine feelings. So the day man will be able to transcend himself and perceive himself in the act to perceiving himself he will know himself. The instrument can find the Rebellions Child Adult Child, the Parent and the Adult ego of any individual. This helps us to know how an individual actually respond to different situations at different times.

How to Achieve Self Development

The executives are required to possess a wide range of knowledge, skills, competence and sound understanding of management processes. They are able to make the best use of their time and latents engeriges with and through people to achieve organisational objectives. They also need to demonstrate a full understanding of the business and of their key resources. The job analysis of the managers reveals that they need to provide quality of leadership, maturity, initiative and set high standards of ethical conduct. The job functions of the managers if brought on 'Skill Diagram' we find that 70% of the job relates to Human Relations Skills. A successful managers is one who is accepted by his team and emerge as the leader. All the above mentioned activities require 'Technical', 'Human Relation', 'Managerial and Conceptional' skills.

Therefore, to be effective manages have to have ability and motivation to achieve effectiveness. Effectiveness means getting best out of our people by winning and maintaining their whole hearted collaboration. The first element to effectiveness is the process of self development which start after individual has identified his adequacies and inadequacies and understanding of his behaviour 'At Work'. This requires an insight of one's own attitudes, assumptions and beliefs about other individuals, groups and understanding the usefulness and limitations of other's feelings. This can be achieved if one develops the sensitivity to understand the needs and motivation of others in the organisation. To be effective this skill must naturally be developed and unconciously demonstrated in the every action. Human skill is a vital part of every thing a manager does because the core of all activities in organisation are human oriented.

Effective Time Utilisation

Time is the most unique and also the most valuable asset. Unless a manager learns to manage this most unique resource, no other skill, experience, or knowledge will make him effective. If we assume the average life span on a man as 70 years then only 6 years are available for effective, constructive and creative work. The time available for other activities are 28 years for sleep ; 10 years for study and education ; 8 years for Recreation/Holiday, 6 years for Rest/Illness ; 5 years for Travelling/Commuting ; 4 years for eating ; 3 years for Getting Ready. The management of time at purposeful ends will spell the difference between success and failure, profit and loss, satisfaction and dissatisfaction. The importance of time management leads to following four factors.

1. Time should never be spend it should be invested.

2. Time that is invested in work and employment should be aimed at improving our productivity (accomplishing more in less hours)

3. The discretionary time available to us should be invested in :

(*a*) building friendships and cementing family ties.

(*b*) maintaining our health

(*c*) improving our skills and knowledge and contributing to the good of our home and community.

(*d*) relaxing in ways that refresh our body, mind and spirit.

Pre Requisites of Self Development

Self development includes a wide range of development activities and experiences. The correspondence courses distant education programmes, Part time courses in educational institutes, the membership in trade, technical and professional institutes offers another avenue for self development. Reading regularly the professional literature is a must for self development.

According to Peter Principal every employee tend to rise to his level of incompetence and an employee may be competent as an executive but may not be competent as Manager, because different positions require different skills. Potential and Capacities which can be developed through self evaluation followed by self development.

Self development demand the 'Desire to Improve', 'Wisdom for selecting proper action' and 'Time necessary for improvement'.

The desire must come from within the wisdom must be developed and time must be planned.

Will to Work

The next important component to self development is the 'Will to Work'. An executive may be possessing physical, mental and technical capacity to work, but these are of no consequence to the employer unless he wants to contribute effectively. We all know that we can buy a man's time, his physical efforts but cannot buy his enthusiasm, initiative and drive. To elicit one' zeal, drive and initiative we as an executive should able to motivate the people working with us and also self motivate them to a cause.

Overcoming Inferiority Feelings

Study of personality is not not only required for self awareness but required for self development. The improvement of personality hinges on executives study of oneself. Personality develop as we face the world, interact with people and undertake job responsibilities. Executive should overcome the feeling of inferiority which are inevitable when an executive compares his insignificance with the immensity of the universe. The inferiority complex can be overcome by developing social interaction at work. Executive should not be scared of making mistakes, as there is no other way of learning how to work.

Building Confidence

Confidence is the basic element to success in practically all walks of life. It is a stepping stone towards the process of self development. The lack of confidence is a characteristic which makes an executive different from other executives. To find out the causes of lack of confidence executive has to spend a few minute each day thinking about the past events of his life and relieving himself from the feelings of fear, depressed emotions and lack of confidence. This exercise will enable an executive to get an insight into the reasons leading to lack of confidence and thereby releasing the depressed emotions which lie at the root of lack of confidence and feeling of fear etc.

Admitting mistakes, however demands courage and courage is the health of soul. To be an effective executive we need persistence, self confidence, purposefulness and freedom from inferiority feelings. Persistence come from staying in the job, but changing one's attitude towards it. Persistence requires reappraisal of : 'One's job', 'Time' and 'New areas of interest' in the existing job.

Executive should reaffirm to one's self at frequent intervals quietly but forcefully to what ever change is desired. The instruments help the executive in self awareness and social awareness. It helps him to be assertive, recognise the other's point of view and to be sure to get one's point across. This exercise should be repeated till he can think about it without getting upset.

Setting Goals for Development

Self development is hard work and by definition it is our responsibility. Self development therefore involves personal change ; new abilities, different outlooks, new feelings. As a result of self development, we feel we are better person, or a better manager. It is due to these new qualities, rather than mere improvement of skills and abilities that we feel confident and matured. Self development is also understood as development for personal growth since it leads to development as a person rather than as a manager.

Role of Others in Self Development

As can be seen from the score on instrument 'Exposure/Feed back' given in Annexure IV as how much alert we are to information. In self development others have an importnat role to play. The others can help us by giving us feed back, by asking question, discussing and helping us to think and rethink. Others may support us then the process is difficult or they may challenge us and force us to reconsider our view point ideal/thoughts. These people could be our family members, friends or colleagues ; person with whom were are comfortable. Following are some of the people who can help us to improve our effectiveness in the job.

1. Boss
2. Professional Helpers
3. Internal Professional Adivsers
4. External Professional Adivsers and
5. Colleagues.

The executive normally has an explicit and certainly implicit managerial responsible for helping the development of subordinate. The responsibility is attributed but in practice avoidable. Professional helpers also carry formal responsibility which again can be explicit or implicit. Internal professional adviser cover personnel specialists, management development advisers, management trainers, and human resources specialists. This responsibility is not always met, especially where training and development are compartmentalized. These specialists can help in defusing the objective, philosophy and nature of desired management development and also in formulating formal schemes, policies and procedures necessary to support these objectives. Monitoring is the idea of an older manager choosing the younger manager for whom he will act as a coach ; counsellor or sponsor, is one that has long existed informally and accidentally. Colleagues can give help when they are more experienced or more skilled in direct coaching and counseling. They may not offer such help but may well respond to a request. Perhaps the most powerful aspect of learning relationship with colleagues revolves around the kind of feedback one offers another. Subordinates provide a great deal of knowledge when a manager moves into a new role.

Strengths of Personality Traits

Self development requires hard work, therefore certain personal qualities are required which provide the drive for such work. The various traits required for self development are 'Courage', 'Determination' and 'Freeness' from Stubborness and Complacency.

Keep Record of One's Activities

It is necessary that one must keep an account of the main events of the day, particularly those relating to our self development. Also keep record of innovative thoughts that suddenly come leading to self development. Keeping record is the master key to effective time management. Listing builds on the action and result orientation of executives and enables managers to produce above average performance.

Self Review

At the end of peak days we go over in imagination, and recall everything that has happened. Analyse your transactions and reassess your performance in the light of your behaviour. Although it sounds simple enough, this activity is surprisingly difficult, since it is very easy to let your mind waver off on something else. It is important that we review our action list for the day as many time as possible during the day. As a rule each such review need not take more than a minute or two and we can do it any where and everywhere.

Listening to One's Inner Self

Apart from our conscious thoughts and ideas we all have a sub-conscious mind. This is full of excellent ideas, knowledge and advice to us on what to do and what not to do. This is known as 'Institution'. In case we listen to our inner voice it would be of help to us in various situations involving difficult decisions and choice between alternatives. There are certain techniques for development of one's institution. These techniques are :

1. Forgetting the problem of sometime.
2. Carrying a record of certain ideas.
3. Checking one's motives.
4. Talking with oneself.
5. Listening to one's own feeling.

Positive Attitude

The instrument on finding one's attitude will provide us the feed back whether our attitude is positive or negative, In order to transform our attitude we simply need to change the direction in which we lean or move. No matter what attitude we adopt, the flow of life continues but in the moment we do have a choice about the direction in which we lean, within ourselves at each moment we can exercise the choice. At each moment we can reinforce our attitude to be in our favour. We can other lean with the direction that life is moving with a positive attitude or lean against the direction that life is moving with a negative attitude. When we go with the flow, life becomes more easier, when we resist the flow, life becomes more difficult. The positive attitude leans towards goals, visions, dreams and life plan objectives. By possessing positive attitude we can make new choice and create the future we want.

Concentrate on Future and Develop Your Own Method

The past is very much complete in the sense that there is nothing you can do now to turn back the clock. What happened yesterday is already history. The key to success is building a positive attitude no matter what blocks we have inherited from the past. The ideal would be to have a clear view ahead which draws from us our least resources energy while enjoying fully whatever we have immediately in hand. Time not only improves our effectiveness but also improve our quality of working life. As mentioned earlier listing is a great power and efficacy as an aid in managing one's time. Studies have revealed ability of such people to achieve a great deal more in less time than people who are not so effective. Everything needs to be listed including points for discussion with each key subordinates, on major telephone calls and at important meetings during the day.

Improving Communication

Communication is a process of change. In order to bring about self development, the communication necessarily has to be effective and purposive. How important the communication, is can be established from the fact that a normal human being communicates for 27 years which if recorded, might cover 10000 books of 400 pages each and 80 to 90% of our working time goes in communicating with others. (60% in talking or listening and 20 to 30% in reading or writing). The technique to improve communication is 'Self Knowledge'. To get better acquinted with oneself we should take 15-20 minutes in quiet each day to study oneself; one's purpose and relationship to other concerned employees and the Company. What is said on the job, is the most important part of communication in business and industry, intellectual honesty, living with what is said, acting co-operation, as well as talking about it are essentially in developing communication with an organisation.

Develop Listening

The art of listening is of far greater importance. It is one of the most difficult aspects of communication process and we listen to better than 30% efficiency. The increased efficiency in listening leads to greater enjoyment of life and also can help in overcoming major breakdowns, frustrations, ice feeling being cause by bad listening habbits. The guidelines for effective listening are :

- Listen with understanding
- Concentrate to exact information
- Listen the idea and not the facts or speaker.
- Emotions and prejudices should be away from listening

Phases of Development

The various important phases of development are :

- Early childhood
- Late childhood
- Adolescence
- Adulthood.

Early Childhood

Parents are the teacher of the child and should encourage the child to do many of the routine things for himself. Parents should pay special attention to child's language development and child's ability to express himself. Parents should pay special attention to the physical, intellectual, social, mental and emotional development of child.

Late Childhood

It is the period beginning with entrance to the primary school. It is the period between 6 to 12 years. The stage of development is a mirror of the whole life and reflects the past, the present and the future. During this period the habits are formed beside Physical development, Motor development, Emotional development, Social development, Mental development and Speech development. This period goes a long way in setting the pace for better adjustment during adolescence.

Emotional maturity is a matter of being caught rather than taught. The teacher should sublimate the various emotions such as fear, anger, jealously, ausicly, job and affection because emotional shocks can lead to deformity of personality. Teacher should create a climate where a child feels that he is loved, accepted and recognised. The teacher has a very important role in the intellecutal development of the child by teaching him how to criticise the right thing at the right time at the right place. He should explain the reasons of punishing the child and should behave in a sympathetic manner so that children show discipline from the core of their hearts and should be democratic rather than autocratic.

Adolescence

It is the period of rapid growth revolutionary changes of life—social, physical, emotional and mental.

Adolescence marks the culmination or maturation of the reproduction process. This period emerges from late childhood and merges with adulthood. Adolescence varies from individual to individual and from sex to sex. Adolescence period depends upon climatic conditions children of hot countries grow to adolescence quickly then those of cold countries. Adolescence is a period of stress and strain, day dreaming and adventure.

During the adolescent stage people find difficulty in adjusting with themselves, with the family and with the society at large. They experience difficulties in physical, mental, emotional, social and other adjustments.

Adolescence is an important period from the point of view of education. During this period sex education should be given in free, frank, scientific, judicious and impersonal manager, Realistic and straight forward answers regarding sex will help the adolescence to channelise their sex energy into various co-curricular activities such as outdoor games, declamation and debates. These are necessary for preparing them for adult life. During this period parents should inspire confidence in their children and teachers should treat them sympathetically. The morale and religious education should also be imparted beside spirit of brotherhood and humanitarianism being cultivated among adolescent by vocational guidance. Parents-Teachers associations in schools can counsel them in removing the misunderstanding and solving the problems of adolescence.

Adulthood

Halscharlatt and Jack Macrae in the book 'Passages' have given different passages indicating predictable crises in the Adult life.

This phase is the more important for an executive because most of the changes through which he undergoes is true during this period. He has classified the predictable crises of adulthood as follows :

(*a*) Pulling Uproots
(*b*) Trying Twenties
(*c*) Catch Thirty
(*d*) Rooting and Understanding
(*e*) Deadline Decade
(*f*) Renewal or Resignation.

(*a*) Pulling Uproots

This is a stage from 18-22 years in the Adulthood where a man is trying to get away from parents. During this time man wants to feel that his autonomy is being subjected to erosion. In Indian context, Pulling uproots occur at a later stage in life or in certain cases it does not occur at all. People who marry during this period often have prologued financial and emotional ties with the family and relatives parents them for becoming self sufficient. Pulling Uproots does not take place at this stage and crupt during a later stage when the penalties may be harder to bear. Pulling Uproots helps the individual to conduct, administer and direct himself. None of us wants to go too fast beyond the value system to become too much of an individual. The tasks during this period are to locate oneself in a peer group role, a sex role, an anticipated occupation, an ideology or world view.

(*b*) **Trying Twenties**

It confronts us with the questions of how to take hold in the adult world. It gives us an inner turmoils of 'Who am I ?' 'What is the truth ?' 'How do I achieve my aspirations ?' 'What is the best way to start ?' 'Who can help me ?' etc. It is the time of converting aspiration to reality. In this phase the tasks are enormous. This is the period of seeking a profession. The most pervasive theme of the twenties is 'Doing What We Should. One of the terrifying aspects of the Twenty is the inner conviction that the choices we make are irrevocable. It is not true as the change in the profession of choice is quite possible. It is this passage in which the inter personnel relationship and the strength of will power is understood. There is also a feeling that I am different from my parents.

(*c*) **Catch Thirty**

This is a period of being impatient. This is a period of outgrowth of career and choices of the twenties. Some inner aspects which were left out at striving to be taken into account. Important new choice must be made and commitments altered. The work involves great change, turmoil and often cries. This is the period during which executives will look for variety in their jobs. It is the time of job rotation in the job families or even to different jobs. During this passage the supervisors look forward to officers job and officers look for a broader spectrum, wider scope jobs. This is the time when there is greater possibility of disturbance in the married life, if the partner's aspiration are not taken care of. The single person desires to find a partner and the educated woman earlier contented with the families and the children venture out to find satisfaction in their profession and almost everyone who is married for nearly 7 years feels some sort of unknown discontentment. This is the passage of making one's own critical life steering decision. There is an urge to broaden oneself professionally with desire to outgrow the personal choices and making like richer.

Stage of Development

Early Childhood (0-6 yrs.)	*Middle Childhood (6-12 yrs.)*	*Adolescence (12-18 yrs)*	*Early Adulthood (18-30 yrs.)*	*Middle age (30-60 yrs)*	*Retired life (over 60 yrs.)*
Developing concept of self.	Acquiring wider knowledge and un--understanding of physical and social life.	Developing a sense of identity and self confidence.	Finding meaning in one's life	Establishing adequate financial security	Adjusting to decreasing physical strength.
Learning to be a member of family groups	Developing conscience and values.	Developing more mature relations with age mates.	Attending a family and looking after the needs of the children	Extending interest.	Meeting social obligations.
Learning Physical and social realities.	Learning to read and write and other intellectual skills	Preparing for an Occupation		Helping the children to become responsible and good citizens	Adjusting to the deaths of colleagues and friends.
Learning personal care	Learning to give and take and share responsibility	Acquiring values and social responsibility	Managing the house.		Maintaining concern beyond self.
		Developing concern beyond self.			

(*d*) Rooting and Extending

It is in the early thirties that man begins to settle down in the full sense. Life becomes less professional, more rational and orderly. Accomplishments are expected during this passage. This is the period when most of the executives begin putting down roots. Executives make major investments during this time and become serious about their career path. This is the passage which involves settling process and covering dream into concrete goals. During this period, couples reduce social life outside the family and in turn focus on raising their children. The family ties become stronger during this period.

(*e*) Deadline Decade

This is the phase half way through the career of a person. It is the time when one begins to see the point of termination. He starts to squeeze the activities. There is loss of youth faltering of physical power and fading purpose, likelihood of stereotype roles. This is the period between 40 to 50 years and is called the deadline decade. It is the time of both danger and opportunity. During this period, executives should re-examine their performances and re-evaluate how to plan their resources from now on. The women sense this inner crossroads earlier than men do. This is the time when executives want to become part of top management. There is more need of recognition. The executives become more vulnerable to criticism. Executives during this passage start feeling stale, restless, burdended and unappreciated. They start worrying about their health. During this phase executives respond with burst of caution in the rise for career position, a feeling that it is my last chance to pull away from the pack. It is during this period that certain executives start believing that his work performance is the only criteria of his worth and they play a narrow role of organisational man. To handle executives at this age group, the trainer may try to convince the executive that the role he is playing is an appropriate for him. He is good at it and to think about still higher position is not a wise aspiration for him, as they may involve lot of adjustment and he may even have to overcome obsolescence by self development. This is the time when there is a need for screening among the executives and finding out the top executives who can rise to occasion to shoulder still higher position. It could be that majority of them might have already reached to the level of incompetence (Peter Principle) and promoting incompetents to higher positions may not be in the interst of the organisation's growth and success.

(*f*) Renewal of Resignation

Equilibrium is regained. New stability is achieved which may be less satisfying. During this phase, parents will become children, children will become strangers, career will become just a job and each of these events will be felt as abandonment. Executives will have to renew all performance, around which they will be able to build a more authentic life structure. Personal happiness takes a sharp turn upward as partners can now accept the facts. This is the period when executive starts feeling that 'I cannot expect anyone to fully understand me'. At the age of fifty, there is a new warm mellowing. Partners now each other. This is the phase where renewal is coming to approve oneself ethically and morally to act independent of others beliefs, standards and agenda. One starts becoming aware of one's own style and can play it or around it. Executives at time feel that they have reached the peak of inefficiency and would be better to get back into something where he is declared successful and is best suited.

34

Human Relations

HUMAN SKILLS

Productive Human Resource

Productivity is the key word to success and progress in every sector of a business organisation in offices, plants, service points, dealer outlets, and so on. The concept of productivity applies to Human Resources and operational systems. Productivity 'People' -- People is an organisation at various levels and those connected with it from externally is something very critical and vital for the organisation and business. It is one of the key factors in the short-term and long-term success of the organisation. *There is a simple story which is relevant to the concept of productivity. A loaded truck got stuck while passing under a Railway bridge. No one could figure out how to get it out. An intelligence executive passing that way suggested that letting the air out of the tyres and pushing it would be the ideal solution to pass the truck under the bridge. The solution was down below at the wheels. By being productive, people can achieve better result for their efforts, low* costs, reduced time, and also derive the satisfaction and sense of achievement that comes with doing a job well. Productivity begins in mind -- It is an Attitude. You must therefore possess the right attitude towards work, a desire to improve and to do a job better, without first thinking of the reward.

The primary concern of Productivity is with the most precious resource -- the 'Human Being. *Human Resource Productivity affects the total productivity because ultimately it is the human factor which govern and organise all other factors. Productivity of the human resource deals with human behaviour in organisation environments and also with the study of factors that motivate men, individually and in a group. For acceptance of productivity techniques a climate should be created so that there is a positive attitude among the employees and supervisors for improving the productivity.*

Productivity is the ratio of output to input, however, the values for output or input are 'man determined' and hence productivity is very much dependent on our sense of values and attitudes. In order to improve Human resource productivity there is a need to study the relations between individuals and the groups -- an important phase of human relations.

HUMAN RELATIONS

When dealing with people, let us remember that we are not dealing with creatures of logic. We are dealing with creatures of emotions, creatures busting with prejudices, and motivated by pride and vanity.

I will pay more for the ability to deal with people than for any ability under the sun.

John D. Rockfeller

The Human Relation is the study of human behaviour at work. Good Human Relation practice is a key which unlock many business problems.The term human relations applies broadly to the interaction of people. Study of Human Relations is important and it explain why one man works harder than other? Why one employee quit his job much sooner than another? Why one group of employee restricts there output and another worked energetically ?

Role of Human Resource

Human resource is the only resource which appreciate and has to be handled with care.

In today's environment 'Human Relations' play a very important role in the success of any business enterprise. The knowledge and proper understanding of the human relations is extremely necessary for every executive irrespective of level and discipline.

A successful executive is usually a *socially* intelligent executive. He realizes the importance of getting alongwith people and knows how to do it. He also develops the requisite emotional qualities and hones his *communication* behaviours. An executive, however, required to get along with four groups of people :

- Superiors,
- Peers
- Subordinates and
- Clients.

Concept

Human relation is the integration of people in to work situation that motivates them to work together productively, co-operatively to provide economic, psychological and social satisfaction. Human relation in the context of a marketing Organisation is the development of marketing and satisfaction of group efforts.The subject of Human relations deals with *human emotions, impulses and deep feelings which arise out of one's* needs and drives such as the instinct of security, possession and emotions like love, hate, anger, fear, pride, curiosity etc.

In order to provide an insight of Human Relations Concept following are some of the ancodes, symbolisms and stories on the subject.

Human Relations Adds Value

A human relations teacher wrote on the board 1 + 1 = 2, 2 + 2 = 4, 3 + 3 = 6. He made a dozen simple additions. Finally he wrote 13 + 13 = 27. The entire class shouted. 'Teacher, wrong, wrong.' He caught on that point. 'Twelve times I was write. None of you appreciated me. I went wrong only once, you together have critised me immediately and that too, full throat'.

Everybody is Somebody

You have to treat your people as individuals. People are not machines nor merely some units of productive capacity. Every human has a feeling of self-importance and an ego. Even your scavenger feels that he is somebody in the organisation. Please bear in mind this psychological factor, especially when you deal with people at the lower level.

Do not Run Down People

"Two things are bad for the heart. Running upstairs and running down people". Benjamin Franklin adds : *"To be humble to superiors is duty, to equals, courtesy ; to inferiors, nobleness."*

Involve Everyone

Involve even the smallest man in your biggest project. Sometimes small things really create stumbling blocks. The INSAT-II, the ambitious baby of our satellite project flopped staking hundred cores of rupees and turning million to desperation. All was caused by a trivial snap of the small things system of its antenna.

Built up Gradually

Human relations are built up gradually like a castle brick upon brick. We have to nurture it tenderly. Slip of single harsh word can destroy it like a sand castle crumbling down by a single stroke, something like a cow that give a bucketfull of milk and titled it with a single kick.

Consistent Behaviour

A leader must have a steady mood. Your men must be able to predict what your mood will be today as well as tomorrow. A wide fluctuation in your mood and temper embarrase your people. This kind of inconsistent behaviour will not help to win confidence and co-operation of your people. They will be reluctant to deal with you.

Study Your People

The important precondition before you handle your people is to analytically study their characteristics and attitudes from a close distance. You are in fact a salesman selling some intangible products of human relations. If you study the interest of your customer the selling goes easier.

Empathy

Empathy is one's ability to project oneself imaginatively into another person's position. Empathy is the foundation for working effectively with people.

Respect Social Sentiments

People do not like sudden changes. *Personality is already moulded in early ages. You cannot change one's personality abruptly. Same is the case with social customs, traditions, values and manners.* You should conform to them and respect the social sentiments of your men. When you ask for a social change remember many individuals are involved.

Encourage Suggestions

A plant gives you beautiful flowers only if you water it. If your man has a suggestion, pay attention to it. What he wants from a suggestion is recognition, a credit for his efforts. Such things should not be delayed. He will feel that you are indifferent to him. His enthusiasm gets killed. Recognition delayed is recognition denied.

People Skills Are Survival Skills

Your success as a manager depends on your ability to get the job done — your skills to accomplish organisational objectives through others. When problem arise that interfere with the produtivity or morale of the work group — whether people problems or opeative problems -- a manager must step in and cam up with the answers. Following are the steps to improve one's chances of solving problems successfully.

— *Separate the person from the problem.* Let the person vent frustration or anger before you try to identify the real issue 'keep the conversation centered on fixing the problem'.

— *List to the issues.* Suppress the urge to dismiss the complaints, interrupt, or defend your position.

— *Get all the Facts.* Understand all the issues and those who are involved. Interview others if appropriate before responding or making decisions.

— *Explore Alternatives.* Often solutions proposed by those involved will meet with less resistance than those imposed from the outside.

An effective executive is usually a *socially intelligent executive. He realizes the importance of getting along with people and know how to do it.* He also develops the requisite emotional qualities and hones his *communication* behaviors.

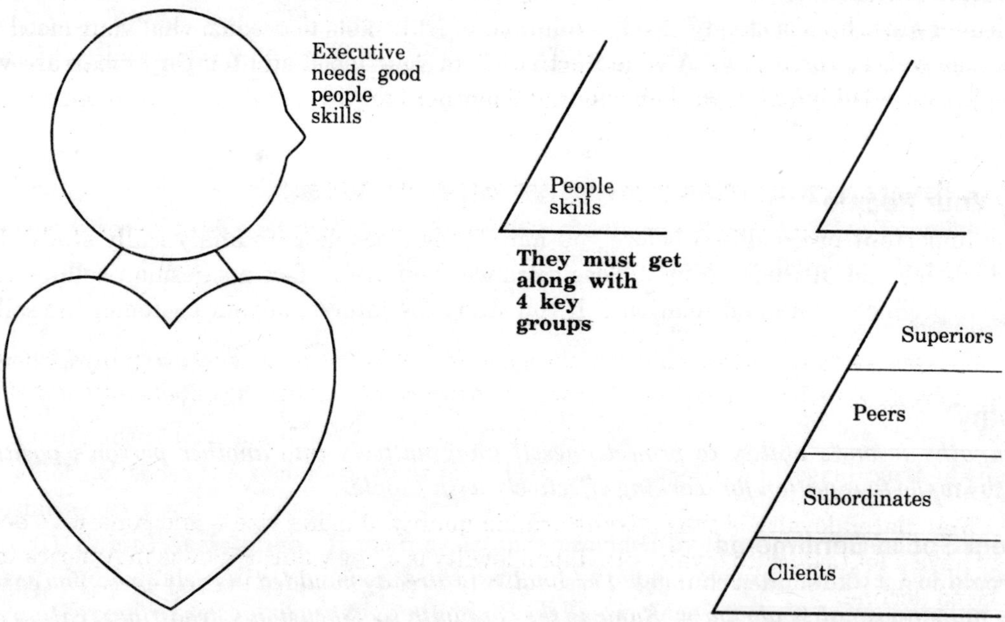

An effective executive, however, must get along with all manner of people, specifically, to four groups of people : Superiors, Peers, Subordinates and Customers.

Superiors

The person who can't get along with the boss is seldom going to last in an executive role.

Getting along with the boss entails being able to listen, exchange information, resolve differences, act in accordance with agreed policy, and back as necessary -- all while making the boss look as good as possible.

The idea, after all is that *both boss and subordinate are pursuing the same goals. When it becomes necessary to disagree and fight for another point of view, then an effective subordinate will do so, but with fact, confining the discussion to facts, options and consequences.*

Peers

An executive must win the acceptance of his peers if he is to function as a team player. Getting along with peers -- or anyone -- begins with the realization that this is the wise thing to do. Effective executives minimize conflict and do not alienate others unnecessarily. They listen and hear the ideas of others. They present their own ideas cogently, and with concern for the feelings of their listener.

Subordinates

An executive must gain the respect and following of his subordinates. Doing this requires realization that there is no one leadership style that will work in all settings and there is no leader without a follower.

Customers

An effective executive begin with the realizaton that*good clients are hard to find, and harder to keep.*An effective executive see the client as an ally — someone who will likely return if the product or service is as good as promised. Executives know that if they make themselves invaluable to the client, they may win that client for life.

FOUR HUMAN QUALITIES EXECUTIVE MUST POSSESS

To get along with superiors, peers subordinates and client an executive must possess and develop four crucial human qualities.

Empathy

We also want to share our ideas and experiences with them. Executive thus evoke more than mere good feelings. They also attract much *information,* thereby enhancing their effectiveness.

Loyalty

Well placed loyalty is thus a transforming quality. Japan's rise -- and America's decline -- may have a lot to do with loyalty. In Japan loyalty is a key value, whereas in America it seems to be on decline.

Social Dominance

An executive may dominate in many ways : by virtue of practical intelligence, by powers of emphaty, by poise or grace, by reputation, by sheer physical presence by being able to satisfy the needs of another.

Tact

Tact is the manifestation of judgement and empathy. It is social intelligence in operation. It is a ready and refined sense of what is fitting and proper in dealing with others, so as to win goodwill, or at the very least, to avoid giving offense.

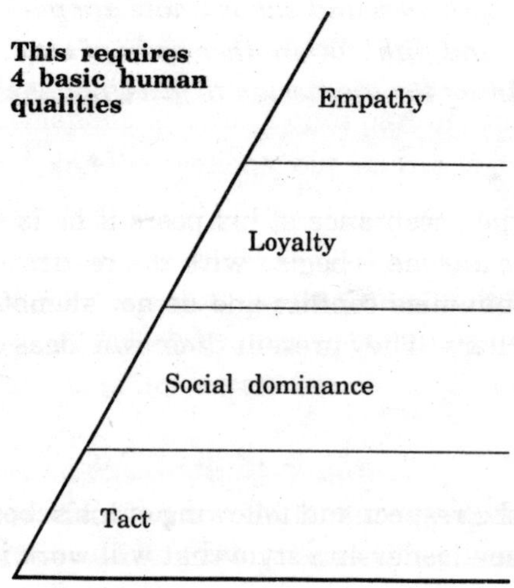

Communication Behaviour

An executive will rise or fall according to his communication skills, for at least three quarters of his time involves *communicating* and much of the rest contemplating how to communicate most effectively.An executive must master four fundamental communications skills.

Listening

Listening is more than remaining silent while looking attentive. Listening is making the *effort* to hear. It is paying attention. It is both hearing words and sensing meaning. It is discovering the feeling of what they are trying to convey.

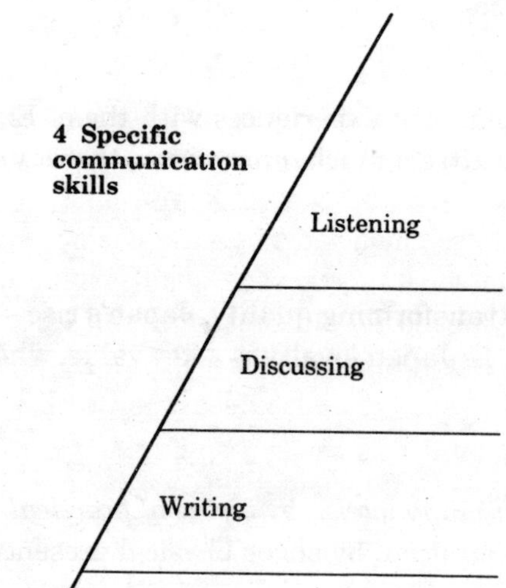

Discussing

Discussing should be conducted more like the game of tennis than the game of gold. In golf, you go on attempting to hit your own ball ; in tennis, you wait for your opponent to return your shots. And executives thus treat vircutally all discussions - including debates, and out-and-out arguments -- as *conversations.*

Writing

Writing is thinking. The writing part is easy. The thinking part is hard. People don't write badly because their vocabularies are limited, or because they can't string words together ; *they write unclearly because their minds are not clear.*

Advocating

The purpose of advocacy is persuasion. The advocate wants to instill an idea, or change an idea in order to bring about a change in thinking or behaviour. Advocacy is not the same as dominance. To advocate is thus to reach of the heart and mind, usually in that order. The tool of the advocate are words and tact. Thus the executive who lacks tact is seldom going to be an effective advocate.

HOW TO GET THE MOST FROM OTHERS

We don't operate in vacuum. In any organIsation other people play a vital role in our life and we can't succeed unless we can manage our relationship. One of the key to productive relationships is learning how to create situations that benefit conducive interpersonal relations. To achieve this iT requires sensitivity to the needs and wants as well as skill in creating a team that's pulling in the same direction. The techniques on getting the most from other people are:

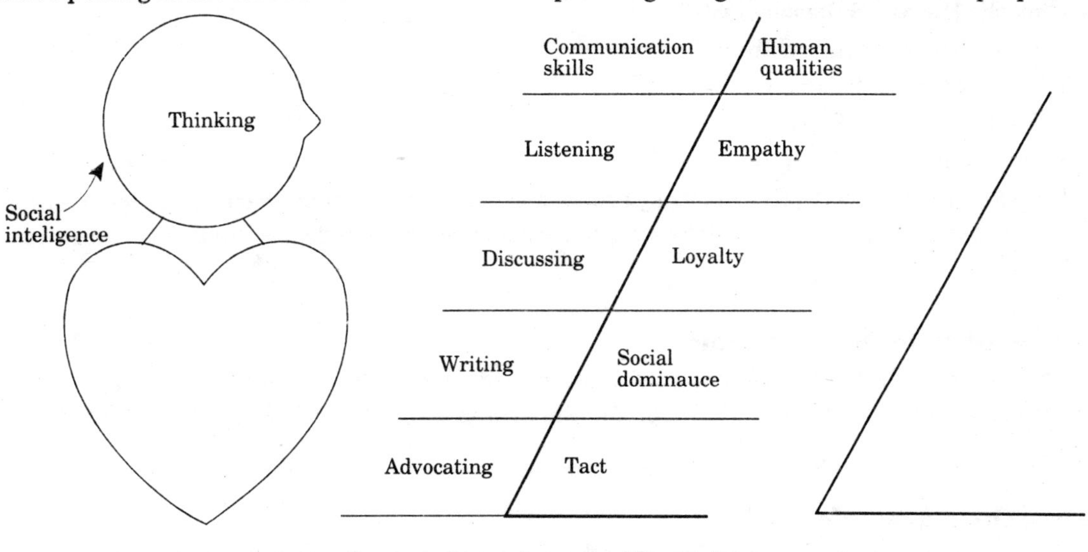

So, overall, good people skills require ;
Social intellegence (A good understanding of people and how to get along with them) Communication Skills : Listening/Discussing/Writing/Advocating
Human Qualities : Emphaty/Loyalty/Social Dominance/Tact.

Motivation

Even the best people won't perform up to their capabilities without a motivating environment. People don't change their behaviour unless it makes a difference to them to do so. We have to recognise that we can't change a person's mental state, but what we can change is the external behaviour and we can change that by manipulating the consequences. Creating a climate the motivates is an important part of an executive. People in such climate radiate self respect. They always know what's going on in their organisation, what is expected of them, and how they are doing. They never feel isolated because both their achievements and their problems are acknowledged continually.

Must of Motivation

To influence for the common good you need an understanding of motivational chemistry. To provide the right climate and opportunities for motivation and job satisfaction the executive must do the following :

- Feel a sense of personal achievement in the job individual is doing and must believe that he is making a worthwhile contribution to the objectives of the group of section.
- Feel that the job itself is challenging, is demanding the best of the indiviual.
- Have control over those aspects of the job which have been delegated to him.
- Feel that he as an individual, is developing, that he is advancing in experience and ability.

IMPROVING HUMAN RELATION SKILLS

Action is the beginning of every thing happening in business and core of all Actions is 'Human Activity'. Nothing of any consequence happens until Human Being wants to Act.

Individuals are hired/selected based on their technical skills but their success on the job is based on the Human Relations skills.

We have already studied the following :

What is--Human Relation

- Human Relation Skills
- Insight of Human Relations

In order to be more effective in our interpersonal relations we must learn the following task of Human Relations which have been explained with various anecodes, symbolisms and stories on the subject.

A. Senstive to One's Attitude

Fosdisk once remarked : 'Nothing left loose ever does anything creative. No steam or gas ever drives anything until it is confined. No life ever grows until it is focused, dedicated and disciplined.

Setting Good Example

The men who has to control others must have learned how to control himself. If he cannot control what is under his hat he cannot control what is under his roof. Setting a good example is one of the best ways of winning people.

Arm Yourself with a Smile

Arm yourself with a smile. You can disarm even your enemy. Life becomes too deadly desire without a sense of Humour. A leader with sense of humour is more warmly acceptable to his flowers. If a man cannot laugh, then who else can do it for he is the only creature endowed with the power of laughter.

Control Your Anger

Man is the product of his environment. Therefore, it is but natural that you are in the mood of anger sometimes. Even God has been angry several times. Enormous damage occurs on the feeble structure of human relations during such temperamental moments. Till you calm down, please do one thing : Do not talk to anybody. Do nothing.

Self Confidence

Self confidence is nothing but the awareness of one's own worth and will-power. The biographies of eminent people indicate that they were in possession of this gift. Persons with self confidence do not give up in the face of disaster. What is more important is that doubts and fears should not hold you back. Self confidence ignites the fuel that does the propulsion.

Determination

Having declared a patient hopeless, his grief stricken relatives and friends called for the priest. After administering the last rites they enquired of him sympathetically 'Is there anyone you would like to see for the last time ?' He nodded affirmatively. They eagerly hastened 'Who is he ? What is his phone number ?' The patient whispered, 'Another doctor'.

B. Sensitive to the Motivation of Others

Absence of Friction

Absence of friction in your team is your goal, nevertheless, abrasiveness may possibly emerge. When your role as arbitrator does not make any impact, do not give up the effort.

Greet Your People

Every morning your man waits to greet you. It is a good practice. To return a greeting indifferently is like throwing a splash of cold water on him. The few seconds, you spend on greeting. Your people is very important for the day. Do it warmly with a smile. If you do not know how to smile, you have to learn it.

Address Your People by Name

You have to identify your man by name and not by designation or physical appearance. Add a bit of courtesy when you address a person. If possible, call him by his pet name.

Develop Emotional Bondage with Your People

Words cannot bear the weight of certain emotions. Every loving touch is a communication of esteem and care. It tells silently aloud. 'You are precious to me. I care for you'. When you keep your hand on the shoulder of your subordinate for five seconds, it renders an emotional bondage between you and your man for five years.

He is Somebody to You

Create occasions to introduce your man to your visitors. This is the opportunity to tell tall of your man and all his plus points to a third person. Many are modestly inflated as a result of your compliments. This strategy reinforces his feeling that he is somebody to you and you are for him. The more of such occasions help adhere him more emotionally to you.

Count on Your People

When he goes on leave tell him 'Dear so and so, I do not know how I will manage in your absence.' When he comes back, tell him again that you had a hectic time during his absence. The very feeling that you count on him keeps him related and self important. This is one of the essential tactics of a successful leader.

Respect One's Opinions and Convictions

The right to express one's opinions and convictions is to be respected however small one may be. Thousands of men wasted away their days in prison for the sake of their opinions.

Social Calls--Cementing Effect

Visit to the families of your men occasionally. It strengthens your relations. You do not have to wait for a ceremony to take place in that family and a formal invitation thereof. Such casual compliments instal a sense of confidence in him and his family.

Be Benevolent

Social calls have a cementing effect on human relations. Visit the hospital sometime when your man is a patient there. A feeling that his leader is concerned about his health relieves this tension to a great deal. Tell him that you are anxious about his speedy recovery. Others appreciate your action as benevolent.

C. Recognise One's Feelings And Sentiments

Consider the fact that you are also a salaried employee of the organisation like anybody else. Your man knows well that you are his superior. It is your inferiority complex that makes you throw your weight around. Do not present that you are the Almighty because you are not.

Gentleness And Courtesy Pays

Mix some politeness in your instructions. Rather than ordering. 'Do it right now', tell him, 'let us do it without delay. It is required urgently'. As against commanding, 'get going better say 'let us go'. A request has more power in it than a command. Gentleness and courtesy do not weaken your authority whereas it strengthens.

Generosity Fetch High Dividends

The word 'Place' turns an order into a request. America spends millions of dollars extra every year in postal charges to *Add* the word *Please* in their telegrams and satellite cables. They are pleased to bear this extra expense because it make the other person feel important.

Admit Your Mistake

To error is human. To accept error is greatness. But unfortunately, it is the tendency of every human being to prove that his point is right. When you go wrong, admit to your people your errors without any reservation. It is the mark of a great man.

Courtesy Pays

President Lincoln was strolling with his friend when a passing old Negro bowed and tipped his hat. Lincoln stopped and returned that gesture more gracefully. His friend asked him 'Why did you tip your hat to that old darcky?' The President explained 'Because I did not allow anyone else to be more courteous than me.

D. Ability in Successful Communication

Communication besides being simple, has to be equally clear. Ambiguous communications keep the receiver between horns.

Avoid Misunderstanding

We are expert in misunderstanding things. When you give an instruction, better get confirmed that your man understood the message. Ask your man to repeat your instructions. If there is any doubt, you have to patiently repeat your instructions.

Listen Others

Some people are adamant in not listening to others. They want only to talk. They prevent others to utter anything. You please listen, no matter how much disagree with others' points. You are making a new friend by letting the other person talk to you. Everybody likes a good listener. Listening is not only a courtesy but a tact too.

It is a Joy to Be Heard

'One of the joys of life is to know that I have been heard and understood correctly and to know that someone cares enough to try to understand what I have said. I also get a great deal of satisfaction from seeing the same type of enjoyment and the part of the speaker when he knows that I have understood him correctly.'

Listen with Your Eyes

You cannot presume that difficulties vanish when you ignore them. Neglected, they are more likely to reach a boiling point and explode. Impart a sense of care and protection to your people by attending to their difficulties. At least listen to them. Listen with your ears. Listen through your eyes. Listen with your heart.

E. To Work Effectively As a Member of Group and Leaders of a Group

Keep Trying

Two frogs fell into a bucket of cream. Each time they tried to come up they slipped. The lazy one drowned. The enterprising one kept trying with his front legs while the back legs were kicking and propelling. Suddenly, he found something hard. His continuous kicking the cream, hopped on the top of it and leaped frog out to safely.

Elevate General Morale of Your People

Build up loyalty of your people and mutual sincerity by taking up front line especially when your men are in real trouble. Maintain a keen personal interest in your men. One who ensures whether his followers are well before he eats is an exemplary leader. The captain is the last one to bale out of the wrecked ship.

Employee Oriented Leader

A leader needs a conceptual change in his approach to people. Paying close attention only to task activities disregarding the human values cannot render higher quality or quantity. Contrary to this situation, there is constant evidence that employee-oriented leaders generally achieve better results when compared to their solely task-oriented counterparts.

Accept Change

A real leader must match his conceptions and convictions to the changing conditions. Nothing is static in this modern age, situations change, men change, conditions change, environments change, technology changes and thus everything is in a continuous process of change.

Identify Hidden Talents

Your role as a leader is to identify the hidden talents and to develop the strength of individual working with you. The weakest among the lot needs your help and guidance. They should not be treated as botherations.

Maintain High Levels of Ethics and Morale

You are regarded by your men not by counting how much money you possess or even by your hierarchical position. They hold you in esteem because of your behaviour not only inside the organisation but outside too. A leader has to maintain a high level of ethics and morale in his personal life. If he wants to be respected.

F. Self Awareness And Social Awareness

You can't Please Everyone

If you attempt to please each and everybody, you will go mad. An old man had two wives, one young and the other old. He agreed with his young wife to pluck out all his grey hair so that he might look young. He pleased his old wife to pluck out all his black hair so that he might look old. So, between the young and the old, he became bald.

Respect Social Sentiments

People do not like sudden changes. Personality is already moulded in early ages. You cannot change one's personality abruptly. Same is the case with social customs, traditions, values and manners. You should confirm to them and respect the social sentiments of your men. When you ask for a social change remember many individuals are involved.

Get Feed Back

Get to know what they think about you. Such a feedback is vital. You may be needing some corrections. Unless you converse with them periodically, you will never get it out. Every body needs a periodical self analysis. Introduce self appraisal forms and conduct self review systematically so that you can remain an ideal and pragmatic leader.

Stir the Talent of Your Men

Letting talent of your men remain undeveloped is like the door remaining unopended for so long that the hinges get rusted. Put as many cubes of sugar, but unless you stir it, the tea does not become sweet. A leader has to stir the talents of his men. It is stirring that matters, not additional sugar. Training to a man is like manure to a plant.

Follow Winston Churchill

When young, Winston Churchill was once drowning in a swimming pool. A poor lad rescued him. Churchill said, 'I want to give you an award for saving my life'. The boy expressed his desire to be a known doctor. 'I shall be glad to pay your way through till you finish all your studies.' Churchill kept his word. The lad was Dr. Flemming, the man who discovered Pencelline (Antibiotic).

Be Judicious

Be judicious in distributing the total load. Some people are cooperative and obedient by nature. Some make it difficult for you even to approach them. If you allow the willing man to overwork and let the unwilling get out of his share, you are indirectly demotivating the hard worker. Your people will not hold you in esteem any longer. They will label you weak.

Don't Grudge

Always pointing a finger of accusation at your men will only irritate him. Do not grudge against a particular man and give them all dirty jobs. Many leaders go wrong and spoil their goodwill this way.

Good to Forget

Some people are slow in forgetting the lapses of others. It is good to forget anything bad about others. How can you get along in life unless you learn to forget. Aristotle once said : 'To understand all, is to forgive all'.

Do not Reprimand in the Presence of Others

You will have some reason to reprimand your man on some occasions because some people are likely to err repeatedly in their performance or behaviour. Do not do it in the presence of others. His prestige will be wounded and his ego hurt. Call him to your office and Counsel him.

Praise before Criticism

Outright criticism bristles up the people. What you have to do as a counsel is to soften the atmosphere by throwing some words of praise and appreciation. Look at the barber. He softens your face with lather before he uses his razor. When you apply this knack, your man will be willing to listen to you without bristling.

How to Evaluate your People Skills

One of the best ways to improve your people skills is to consider your own personality style, and address the kinds of faults that are intrinsic to each type.

The Dominant

If you are a dominant, then you probably get what you want a lot of the time. You could do even better, however, if you try to improve you listening skills and your sensitivity to the needs of others. You have an annoying tendency to be certain of your opinions, and to press your views on others. At worst you are rigid, overbearing, and not much of a friend. You probably have many possessions but few real friends. You probably say you don't care, you might even thing you don't care. But you do ! With a little effort, life could be much easier and infinitely more rewarding.

The Detached

People admire your ability to strike a middle course and to reach a practical compromise. If you have a problem, it probably stems from overconcern with strategies and plans. You might try to develop the warmer and more outgoing side of your personality. Overall, however, you'll probably work out a way to get what you want from people.

The Dependent

You are a sensitive and (usually) popular person, whose problems as an executive probably stem from your over concern with winning the acceptance and approval of others. You are so anxious to be accepted that you find it difficult to press for results. When you attempt to assert yourself. You run the risk of overdoing it and losing your temper. You possibly try for greater status and power, without quite realizing that those who have it envy your knack for making friends. Best to reconcile yourself to a role that uses your abundant qualities of empathy and loyalty.

Analysis

Take a look at your responses ; they are probably something of a mixture, but you should still be able to discern a pattern. Anyway, here's the point : you can temper your style, but you can't radically alter it. Therefore, you should come to terms with it. If you are naturally Dominant, then a job directing others will hold a lot of appeal, and be a good fit. But you should guard against your autocratic tendencies. If you are Detached, you will like to find a job that uses your intellectual and perhaps creative -- learnings. If you are fundamentally Dependent, you may want seriously to ask yourself whether you wish to try to go against the emotional grain by taking on a role that calls for you to assert yourself on a daily basis. Better, perhaps to be in a people role, where your good nature can be appreciated and appropriately rewarded.

The term 'Human Relations' and 'Industrial Relations' are not the same. The scope of the former is wider and includes the latter. A good human relations policy assumes proper and effective industrial relations policy. Human relations in industry broadly signifies the relationship that should exist between the human beings engaged in industry. In actual practice it means relationship that should be cultivated and practiced by the management, or a supervisor with his subordinates. The concept of human relations in industry is to ensure that fundamental rights or not taken away from the individual for the simple fact that he is gainfully employed. It is a device to ensure him a fair deal taking into consideration his needs for existence as a respectable citizen of the country.

Human relations are important in industry because they explain why one man works harder than another ? Why one employee quits his job ? Why one group of workers restricts the output and another works energetically ? Why one group goes on strike and another does not ? Motivation is the unifying concept for human relations. Individual effectivness depends to a considerable extent upon the physical and mental efforts and abilities of those who manage and perform the productive operations with human energies, skill and knowledge. The natural and physical resources are inert and of little value.

Goals of Human Relations

Oliver Sheldon rightly said industry is not a machine, it is a complex form of a human association. The true understanding of industry is to understand the toughts of those engaged in it. How best can we achieve and maintain a fair balance between the things of production, the machines, the building, the materials and the systems, etc. The term human relations applies broadly to the interaction of people. Much of this interaction is in work organisation where people are found together in some sort of formal structure to achieve an objective. Human relations is the study of human behaviour at work and efforts to better action production desired goods. Human relations means relationship that should exist and be cultivated and practised by management. Human relations is an applied art and science. Human relations is integration of people into work situation that motivate them to work together productively, co-operatively to provide economic, psychological and social satisfaction.

Human relations has three goals :

1. To get people to produce ;
2. To co-operate through mutual interest ;
3. To gain satisfaction from their relationship.

Human relations is the development of producing and satisfying group efforts. It is a discipline in itself. Human relations stands for the development of an effective organisation. It is more than winning friends and influencing people. It is based on the recognition of human feelings and aspirations in the organisation. The goals of human relations are :

1. To gain better understanding of one's self.
2. To broaden and sharpen sensitivity to the feelings of others.
3. To develop respect for others.

In physical situation the basic philosophy is that elements of nature are uniform. The law of gravity operates uniformally all over the world and an atom of hydrogen is identical in Russia and America, but the same cannot be said for people.

35

Attitude

Concepts

Attitude is a bent of mind, predisposition of certain actions. It is a process by which the individuals learn as a result of experience to orient themselves towards objectives and goals. Attitude is associated with physical neutral state, verbal opinion, ideologies and above all integrated philosophy of life. Attitude is the detailed direction of human behaviour. Attitude is a stage of sensitiveness and proneness to act. *Attitudes can be defined as readiness to acts ; mental postures, guide for conduct ; feelings, desires, fears, convictions ; a state of readiness ; a set of organism as a whole ; a cumulative perception ; predisposition to form certain opinions; thinking one develops a kind of mental set ; a tendency to act for or against an object in the environment ; a residual experience ; a process of individual consciousness; a precondition of behaviour in various degree of readiness; frame of references that influence behaviour.*

GW Allport observes, 'There is a common thread running through these diverse definitions. Reflexes, unlike attitudes, are more specific, habits are more specific but invariably automatic. Instincts are innate and universal as against attitudes, which are acquired and personal. Sentiments are more permanent are hierarchical. Allport defines the attitude as a 'mental and neutral stage of readiness organised through experience exerting a dynamic influence upon the individual's response to all situations and objects with which it is related.'

According to Bernard, 'Social attitudes are individual attitudes directed towards social objects and individual attitudes inter-conditioned by collective or groups contacts.

Allport defines common attitudes as 'Those attitudes which are uniform owing to the operation of similar environmental and cultural conditions upon similarly constituted beings. Physical environment and culture provide cooperation in the production of common attitudes.'

Human Behaviour

Lapiere mentions four phases of totality of human behaviour :

1. Overt symbolic (speaking, writing etc.)
2. Overt non-symbolic (direct muscular act like closing a door, running, etc.)
3. Covert symbolic (thought),
4. Govert non-symbolic (feeling and emotions).

It is only the overt stage (symbolic or non-symbolic) that can be analysed. As regards the covert phases of behaviour, what any person is actually feeling and thinking cannot be measured an is still anybody's guess. It is in the light of this distinction that so much controversy as to the nature and measurability of genuine behaviour tendencies (attitudes) has risen. *For example in the quotation of Shakespear 'One might smile and smile and yet be a villain' it is not simply a case of double thinking but a case of double living as well.* Even within the sphere of covert behaviour the picture is not very rosy. Thus, overt symbolic behaviour (as in the case of opinion responses to verbalised social situations) is not identical with overt non-symbolic behaviour (the actual behaviour in an actual life situation).

The sum up, the concept of attitudes is a hypothetical postulate which implies broad-based behaviour tendency in individual towards a psychological object. Attitudes have to be analysed in the light of the broad-based pattern of real life situations to which they are related. Attitude cannot be directly observed, but only through inference, as real and substantial ingredients in human nature, it becomes impossible to account satisfactorily either for the consistency of an individual's behaviour or for the stability of any society.

Attitude can be measured through schedules and questionnaires termed as quantitative method. There are three principal sources of data which help in attitude research. These are :

1. Background information such as biographics, case histories, letters. etc.
2. Interview,
3. Questionnaires.

These methods are interdependent as information about life history can be gathered to some extent through interviews, questionnaires, etc. Attitudes are formed through experience which means that they are learnt. Once a person has developed a particular attitude, it may be difficult for him to determine how he acquired it. Once an attitude is formed whether based on rational considerations or strong emotional bias has little bearing on the effect or the attitudes on the person's thinking or behaviour.

Attitude Structure

All attitudes are not alike in their structure. The differ from one another in a number of characteristics. Attitudes develop in the process of need satisfaction. Individual develops favourable attitudes towards object and belief that satisfy his wants. The individual will develop unfavourable attitude towards objects and person that block the achievement of his goal.

The attitudes of the individual are not only developed by satisfaction of wants but also shared by information to which the individual is exposed. The information is frequently used to form attitudes which are in consonent with pre-existing relation attitudes. Many attitudes held by people lack validity, simply because they are not sufficiently will informed. No individual can help to collect all the first hand information and the essential affects about most of the objects. He has necessarily depend on the opinion of the exeperts. For a child, experts are his parents ; for a student, the teachers ; for the writers, the books ; for the religious persons, the pundit or priests ; for scientists, the findings of the other scientist in their field, etc. Individual is living in a complex world and is at the mercy of various experts and authorities for much of his cognitive content and his attitudes. Thus authorities of experts are sometimes unreliable. At times, the individual himself is unschooled in extracting substance or because of his perception he picks up a fact by himself and runs the risk of being fooled. Finally when he does not find facts either from authorities and experts or from his first hand information he may invent facts by himself and develop an irregular attitude.

Formation of Attitude

Many of the attitudes of the individual have their source and support in groups with which the individual comes in alliance. His attitudes tend to reflect the beliefs, values and the norms of his group, and to maintain his attitude the individual must have the support of like minded person. The group helps in the formation of attitudes. The son of an unskilled worker, aspiring for middle class status will tend to accept the middle class values and attitudes. His middle class outlook will embrace such diverse objects as sexual practice and political issues. The attitudes of the individual reflect personality.

The studies have revealed that the work situation apparently does not necessarily provide strong motivation to high level of job performance. Productivity and job satisfaction do not necessarily go together. In fact it is the circumstances in which job satisfaction is related to work performance and there other kinds of circumstance where there is no relation to job satisfaction and work performance H. Wilensky brought out certain variables which account for these differences, such variable are economic, technological social and cultural background, nature of leadership and nature of work incentives.

Measurement of Attitude

No doubt that the attitudes of people tend to be relatively stable but can always be modified at least to some extent. Certain difference in employee's attitudes is inevitable and that is responsible for effectiveness of individuals within an organisation. There are certain ways by which it is possible for supervisor and manager to get some inkling of attitudes of individuals such as interpreting the chance remarks of individuals, the behaviour of individuals in the work groups etc. A sensitive supervisor can always get a feeling with respect to the general reaction of his work group even though he cannot pinpoint such reactions specifically. The other way to find attitude change is the analysis of certain factors such as turnover rate, absenteeism and production level. Various methods have been developed for doing this, some of these consisting of questionnaires which are filled out by the employees.

There are two general types of questionnaires in common usage, one is 'attitude scale' and other 'opinion survey'.

Changing Human Values

Bringing about the desirable change in human values the attitudes and personality is the biggest challenge before the management expert of today. A study was conducted in India where the challenges before the training managers of today were analysed. Forty-two managers from different Public and Private Undertakings participated in the study and the observations from an unstructured questionnaires are as follows :

S. No.	*Area of challenge*	*Rating in percentage of executives*
1.	Changing the culture of organisation	67%
2.	Desirable change in human being	87%
3.	Making training as desirable function in the organisation	73%
4.	Problem of career growth	48%

Changing the attitude and developing a desirable attitude is the biggest challenge. The concept of attitude change is shown in Fig. 35.1. The strong attitude develops strong reactions and wrong information creates adverse reactions. Attitude is a pre-disposition and state of mind characterised when consistency and definite direction. The manifestation of attitude indicated values, feelings and behaviour is shown in Fig. 35.2. The component of the attitude is shown in Fig. 35.3. The figure shows that attitude is a product of environment, organisation systems and group pressure. Similarly, relationship between job, attitude and behaviour is shown in Fig. 35.4. Behaviour means action activities and communication and it just do not happen but it is caused. The self behaviour Human Behaviour and various forms of behaviour are shown in Fig. 35.5, 35.6 and 35.7 respectively. In the group the behaviour is governed by group pressure, irrespective of the attitude of individual and his culture. *The organisation also plays a very important role in changing the behaviour of an individual. Behaviour is the product of nature of individual and situation of the individual. Perception, attitude and defensive mechanism are the basis of behaviour.*

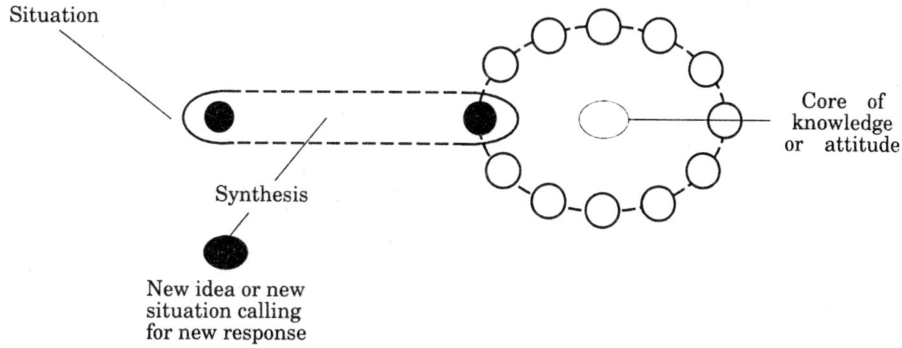

Attitude | Applies | Knowledge | To react to | Situation | To create | New ideas

- Strong attitude develops strong reactions
- Wrong knowledge/information creates adverse reactions

Fig. 35.1. Attitude change.

Attitude is-likes, dislikes and don't likes.
Self : I am a friendly person
Value : I value friendships
Feelings : I love people who are friendly
Attitude : I like people who are friendly
Behaviour : Friedly with others

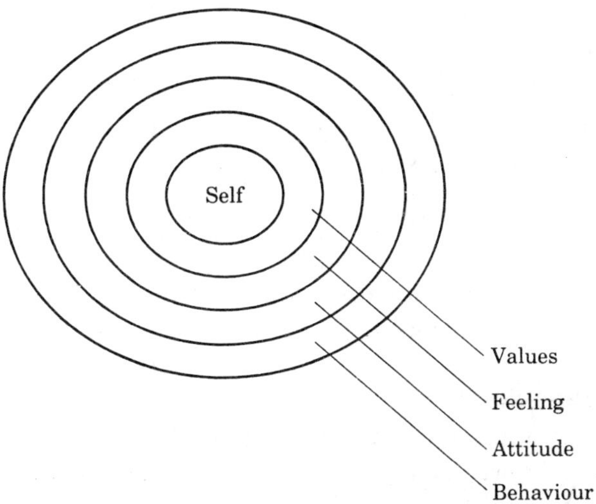

Fig. 35.2. Manifestation of attitude.

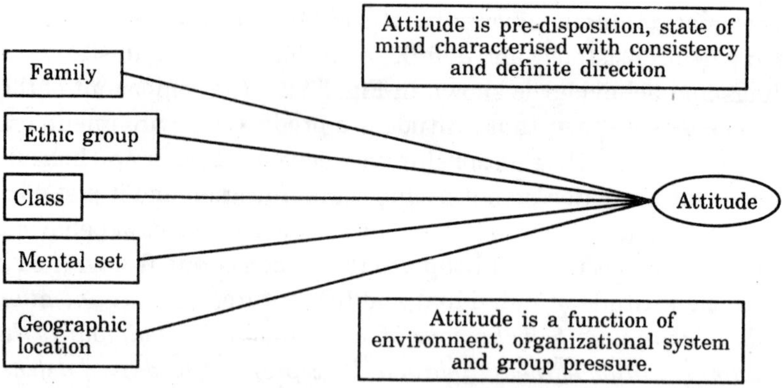

Fig. 35.3. Component of attitude

ATTITUDE

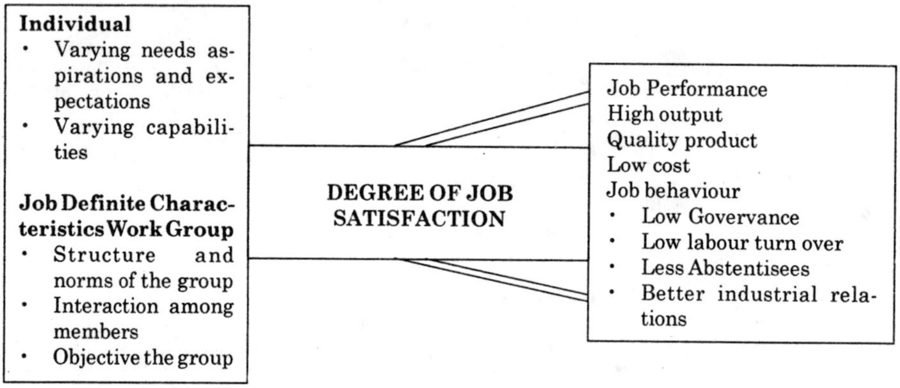

Fig. 35.4. Relationship between job, attitude and behaviour

Self Behaviour :

- **Behaviour means action, activities and communication.**
- **Behaviour just do not happen, it is caused.**
- **Behaviour response positive or negative.**
- **Positve response develops confidence.**
- **Negative response discomfort understanding or one's self.**

Fig. 35.5. Self behaviour

The organisation also plays a very important role in changing the behaviour of an individual. Behaviour is the product of nature of individual and situation of the individual. Perception, attitude and defensive mechanism are the basis of behaviour.

Relationship between Attitude and Behaviour

Human beings are basically keen to be motivated but if an individual does not like a thing, then even being motivated, he behaves indifferently in that situation. There is a positive relationship between attitude and behaviour which is around 66%. If we classify the Indian

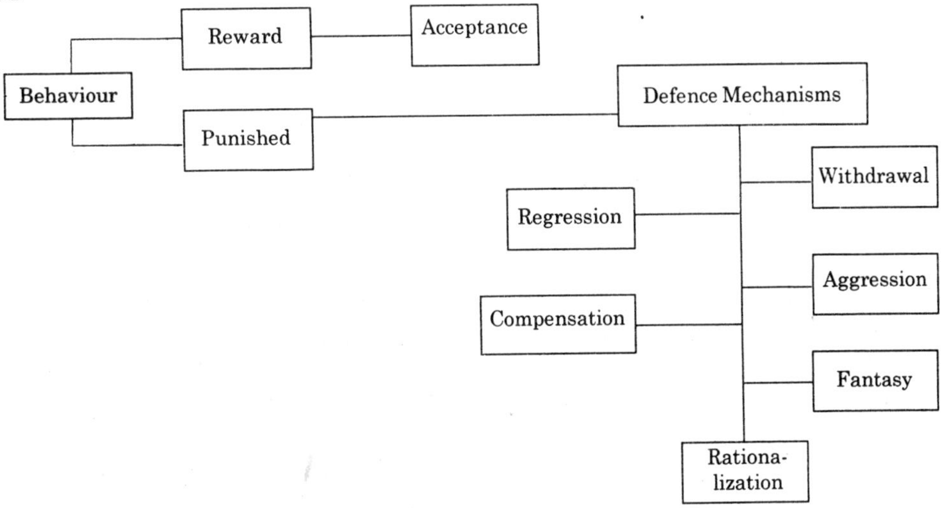

Behaviour is the product of nature of individual and situation of individual Perception attitude and defensive mechanism are basis of behaviour.

Fig. 35.6. Human behaviour

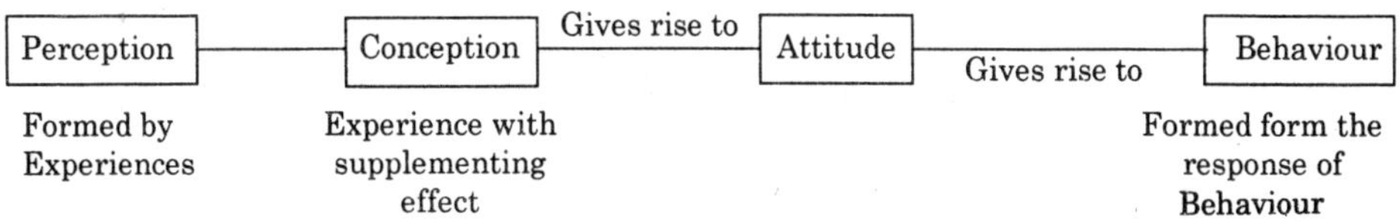

- Perception is a cognitive process.
- Conception also a cognitive process.
- Conception gives the power of constructive thoughts.
- Conception calls for vision and imagination and anticipating trends, preparing for eventualities and lead to creativity.

Fig. 35.7. Forms of Behaviour

managers, we find that their major time goes as a doer (68%), helping others (20%) and in planning (10%). If a doer manager moves out for one month, the total work load will come to a stand still and even the routine papers will not be moving. Doer manager does not have faith in his subordinates and wants to do everything by himself. Doer manager thinks himself as inevitable. The major function of a manager is to grow and to develop his subordinates and not to act as a doer alone. He must plan adequate time as planner as well as helper to others. A trainer must make an attempt to modify the attitude and give him an insight of his self rather changing the attitudes of an individual. For all changes, individual is the point from where we can start. With individual as central point an attempt has been made to study the various concepts of personality which executive might like to know and acquire. *The methods commonly used for changing the attitude or personality traits are Role playing. Case methods, Management games, Sensitivity, Training etc. The ultimate aim is to acquire autonomy and maturity.* The object of change in executive would be that they gain both emotional and intellectual insights by developing their Adult ego state and remain more near to the reality. An insight of personality by understanding transactional analysis will help the individual to establish and earn and authenticated communication between the intellectual and emotional components of personality. T.A. will help an individual to expose his emotions and intellect but not at the expense of other.

Individuals can be Changed

Individual can be changed and this change can be brought about, provided the trainer assume the role of a doctor. Individual is also capable and responsible of helping himself for the process of change as all development are self-development. In most f the organisations, the method of change is doctor-patient concept. In this process, the trainer will give a direction and provides a little help or approach in identifying his own problems.

Need for Self Examination

There is a basic need for self examination. The skill of a trainer is to put a man for self evaluation. A good training and development activity will create nothing more than self awareness in an executive. Johri window can give us an idea about the public area, self-blind area, private area and unknown area of self. This model is highly static in relation to time, and it keeps changing, depending upon the change in the private area, or unknown area of self descriptive area. In human beings, 75% of the behaviour is spontaneous like a burg of ice, 3/4 in water and 1/4 above water. In other words, 1/4 of individual behaviour is public and 3/4 of the behaviour is non-public.

An effective management development programme should only work on modifying the behaviour *viz* T group and FIRO-B, concentrate on this area. Transactional analysis operate on self, others, individual role and also on group Dynamics. It helps to learn about one's self. The sensitivity training is the other method of self-realisation and self-evaluation. Sensitivity training is initially a confusion if uncontrolled, unstructured, lacked in clarity but as the process goes on, initial reservation to open one's self fades away, resulting an atmosphere of understanding of each other. Thee is a need for creating a climate of psychological safety (You are not feeling threatened). It is a process of self-analysis through group dynamics. It enhance understanding and epathy at the end. A feeling 'I am for your and you are for me and here together.' A sense of intimacy, 'I see myself in your problem and you see yourself in my problem', There are some drawbacks in conducting sensitivity training. At times there could be some unpleasanteness or a process of break rather than of built but if the trainer conducts it efficiently, the possibility for the same can be avoided. Most of the good executives are good trainers, yet very few people make good counsellors or educators. A wise manager, of course, uses every opportunity to counsel, to encourage his subordinates to develop better insight. Counselling can not be restricted to any special time or place. It is a long range educational process.

The Cost of Changing Attitude

The current cost of poor attitude at the workplace is staggering. In a business there are many examples such as misunderstandings, overlooked problems, indifference toward customers of fellow employees, are to name few. Some of them are more subtle. They take the form of blocked creativity on the inability to solve even simple problems. *These attitudes are closely held and guarded by what we call the personality.* What does this mean ? There are deep traits that we are born with or pick up as children or young adults that cause us to react to situations or events in our lives with a standard response. This directly affects our attitude. This is not necessarily bad, but it can be very costly in business and in other areas of our lives. The business world, by and large, is aware that change is needed. Even this causes an attitude problem, for change is uncomfortable for a lot of people. The obvious answer is for people to shift to a more natural way to work and live-life. When people relate from this state, many things become automatic, such as communicating in ways that people understand. People look forward to change and feel more positive toward managers and fellow employees. The customers become their friends and the attitude is reciprocated with the result productivity and ingenuity increase. and so on. It is possible, but it involves working with people in such a way as to release the patterns that block this natural state of being. It is based on respect for other people, openness, and a willingness to give oneself into one's work rather than fighting with it. The interesting thing about this is not only the obvious benefit to the individual, but they begin to feel better themselves. Changing one's attitude can have a profound effect on an organisation and its employees.

Positive Attitude and Success

Success. No where the term 'Success' comes before 'Hard work' except Dictionary. The individual brings to the 'Work Place' various traits of his personality *viz.* : family background ; knowledge ; physical performance factors ; financial background ; social obligations, ethical/ value system. These parameters affect his productivity/performance 'On the job'. But there are same exceptions where individual having problems at home front get more engrossed at work. We should remember hammer shatter glass while forges steel. Most people break while some break records under stress.

Positive Attitude. Positive attitude of a person is responsible 85% time for one's success/promotion/recognition/salary increase. The positive attitude emphasis is on the following:

— 'Life is now'

— 'Time to do hat you want to do is now'

The positive attitude means : desire to achieve ; clarity in target/goals; commitment to action. Confidence to actual knowledge/training/experience and capacity to get along with others.

People take failure in an event as failure in life. Positive attitude help an individual to overcome one's failure. The positive attitude tells - Just Double up your failure rate and you will be successful. Believe in the law of correspondence - feel good and you will behave good. According to Secrets - *when you want success badly you will get it. Successful people are inner driven people. The people we have turned adversities into strength.* The dynamics of positive attitude ; negative attitude is given in the tables :

Develop Assertiveness

Dynamics of Negative Attitude

Activator Negative Attitude	*Personality (Attitude in Action)*	*Result*
Fear	Inconsiderate	Worry
Doubt	Pessimistic	Tension
Envy	Weak	Frustration
Anger	Rude	Failure
Conceit	Sour	Sickness
Self Pity	Irritable	Poverty
Suspicion		Fatigue

Indecision		Dissatisfaction
Criticism		Boredom
Inferiority Feelings		

Dynamic of Positive Attitude

Attitude Activator	*Personality (Attitude in Action)*	*Result*
Expectation		
Hope	Optimistic	Success
Anticipation	Courage	Recognition
Confidence	Enthusiasm	Elevation
Faith	Cheerful	Happiness
Patience	Considerate	Processional
Humility	Courteous	Growth
Love	Sincere	Admiration
Belief	Warm Relaxed	Friendship

Attitude Holds the Key To Success

As with every other aspect of life, any improvement in our communication effectiveness has to stem from a change in our attitudes. Most of our communication is rendered ineffective because the receiver does not understand the importance of and the need for responding positively to the message content of our communication. This can be avoided by : Being Task Oriented and Being Audience oriented.

TASK ORIENTATION means that, at no point in time should we forget the purpose behind our communication. Communication in business should always be aimed at realising a specific purpose. That purpose could be ensuring the co-operation of subordinates in a particular venture, diffusing tension at the workplace, giving instructions for operating anew type of machinery or simply creating goodwill for oneself. Whatever be the purpose, clarity in defining it will ensure minimisation of wasted communication efforts and maximisation of productivity.

AUDIENCE ORIENTATION means keeping your audience in mind at all points during the process of communication. Your ability to empathise with, be sensitive to and generally consider your audience's feelings is the best way to be effective in your communication. Your care for your audience should be reflected in the fact that you take all possible measures to get your message across in a manner that is meaningful to your audience. You take the trouble to find out what you audience's information, motivational and practical needs are and you satisfy each of those needs through your communication. Your intentions also matter. Your intent should be to benefit the audience as much as benefiting the organisation.

To overcome the anxiety that prevents behaving assertively. The other issues involved to develop assertiveness are to recognise the other's point of view but be sure to get your point across (say directly). The other view point is to express candidly how you feel. Be specific with a solution.

36

Self-Esteem and Assertiveness

Concepts

Self-esteem is essentially a measure of self worth and importance. Strong self esteem makes life enjoyable and future holds promises.

When self assessment is negative one feels worthless and in competent, life becomes dull and future appears hopeless. Self esteem determines whether we will function in ways that put our potential to the best or not. Self-esteem is shaped from our early years. During childhood if the feelings are respected, thoughts valued and abilities recognised the self esteem of the individual gets strengthened.

On the other hand if the childhood is neglected, thoughts of the child are belittled and abilities and creativity criticised the self esteem remains at low point of development. The self-esteem depends on how much success individual gets in various life situations and also on individual own reaction to various life situations and the support one gets from others. The way you stand for "your self," determine your self esteem. Self esteem is self assertion. Core of self respect remains even one may fail and feel disappointed and frustrated so long as the behaviour was assertive.

An individual with a strong self-esteem is able to relate to others in a friendly understanding manner, built healthy relationship and exhibit the following :

- Confident
- Goal oriented
- Appreciative

The individual who feels happy, confident and good about himself only can make others feel good. An individual with high self-esteem is warm, appreciative and shows genuine interest in and has regard for others. Thus a strong self-esteem is important and the wonderful and is something natural. Self-esteem can be strengthened with patience and perseverence at any point in life. Following are some tips for strengthening self-esteem :

(*i*) Give freely positive strokes

(*ii*) Accept positive strokes

(*iii*) Reject unconditional negative strokes

(*iv*) Listening

Give Positive Strokes

Building self-esteem calls for breaking this restraint completely. We need to be able to comfortably, spontaneously appreciate others whenever something is done well or better than usual. Appreciating hard working subordinate, giving positive strokes as parents are some of the example.

Accept Positive Strikes

Culturally we have been trained to feel uncomfortable while receiving positive strokes. Refusal to accept these valuable strokes is not a virtue. It is a drawback that discounts our feelings of self-worth and makes sure that our self-esteem stays weak.

Reject Unconditional Negative Stroke

Unconditional negative strokes are generalised all encompassing, negatively tonned statements. The penalties for accepting these negative strokes are high. When an unconditional negative strokes are given, we have the right to reject it. The unconditional negative strokes are garbage which mess up our self-esteem. They make us feel less worthy and we lower ourselves in our estimation. The negative strokes are statements which lack any factual basis, they can cause havoc to the self-esteem of the recipient. The recipient is often aware that the statement is not fully true but the individual ponders over it and wallows in self pity.

Listening

Listening is much more intricate and complicated than the physical process of hearing. Listening is an intellectual and emotional process that integrates physical, emotional and intellectual inputs in a search for meaning and understanding. Most communication education has focussed on skills of self-expression and persuasion quite recently.

Assertiveness

Assertion involved standing up for personal rights and expressing thoughts, feelings and beliefs in direct, honest and appropriate ways without violating another person's rights. Assertion involved respect - not deterence. Deference is present when people express themselves in ways that are self-effacing, appeasing, or overly apologetic. Two types of respect are involved in assertion; respect for one-self, that is, expressing one's needs and defending one's right as well as respect for other person's needs and rights.

In assertive behaviour, the nonverbals are congruent with verbal messages and add support, strength and emphasis to what is being said verbally. The voice is appropriate, eye contact is firm but not a stare-down; body gestures which denote strength are used. The speech, expression clear and emphasis on keywords. In aggressive behaviour the nonverbal behaviours are ones which dominate or demean the other person. These include eye contact that tries to stare down and dominate the other person, a striden voice that does not fit the situation, sarcastic tone of voice, and parental body gestures such as excessive finger pointing.

ASSERTIVE PERSONALITY

According to Webster's "assert" means "to state or affirm positively, assuredly, plainly, or strongly." One feels free to reveal oneself. One can communicate with people on all levels-with strangers, friends, family. One has an active orientation to life. One goes after what one wants and acts in a way one respects oneself. In early years, many mothers and fathers censor the child who decides to speak up for his rights and thus, hinder the child's assertion of self. Teachers reward the student who does not question the educational system and deal sternly with those who buck it. In most cases the church fosters the idea of humility and sacrifice rather than standing up for "Self". Many employees learns early in his career that if he "speaks up," he is not likely to receive a raise or promotion and may even lose his job. This attitude carries over to home and social life.

An individual may be conditioned to certain fears, *viz.,* fear of being disliked or rejected, anxiety, expression of anger, feeling tender. When you fear certain situations, you tend to avoid the circumstances that produce them, thus inhibiting assertive behaviour and placing your life beyond your active control. Many people have an erroneous concept of assertion, confusing it with aggression and telling themselves "aggression is always bad." They fail to distinguish between being liked and being respected. They mistake the essential difference between being selfish in the bad sense and selfish in the good sense. Some people lack assertion because they have not acquired the skill through experience and practice. By passed by others with no more talent, they remain in the same job for years because they don't understand the method of getting promotions. Others cannot withstand insults or humiliation because they don't know some of the responses with which to counter such behaviour.

The assertive trainer functions as a teacher, with the aim of helping the patient to understand what is wrong with his life-style and how to work to change attitude. Attaching little importance to the unconscious, assertive training stresses two factors :

(*i*) identification of the target behaviours that need changing, whether fear of closeness or lack of skills needed on the job.

(*ii*) the planning with the patient of a systematic program to achieve the life results he wants.

It is very difficult to say "No" for some executives it need to be learnt. There is no definite method of saying "No", but one should follow the principle of Bravity, Clarity, firmness and honesty. Following are the exercises which enable you. Learning to say "No"—Some Exercises.

Take each situation listed below and think of your answer to it or better still, write it out so that you don't fool yourself. For each example, assume that you want to say no, that it is appropriate to do so and only one problem exists : are you able to do it ?

Situation I : Co-worker asks to borrow some money for the office canteen coffee machine. Somehow he always does this and never repays the change. Co-worker says, "I have no silver. Would you lend me twenty cents for the machine?" How do you say no ?

Situation II : A friend had asked you to go with him sometime in the near future to select a new stereo system. You had assented. On the Sunday morning when you had been planning to catch up with house chores, he calls and says, "You promised to help me pick out stereo system. Can you come with me this morning ?" You really want to sort your book-shelves. How do you say no ?

Situation III : You nave been working on the organising committee for a local organization's upcoming fund raising event. You've already put in more time than anyone else. Now the president makes another demand, asking, Jagdish, you're such a terrific worker. Can I count on you to collect tickets at the door ?" How do you say no ?

Guidelines for saying "No"

There is no specific model which can be followed. However some of the examples from the real life situations are given as under.

In all these situations the response should be brief and direct.

Situation I : Co-worker and the coffee machine

Model : "No, sorry, you owe me for too many coffees already." "No, you never pay back."

Each reply is to the point, starts with no ambiguity and do not explain at great length.

Situation II : The Stereo System

Model : "No, I can't make it today. How about next Sunday". "I will go with you, but not today, I'm sorry."

The reply recognises the commitment but also the bad timing and interest to accompany on any other occasion of mutual understanding.

Situation III : The organisation and the hard worker.

Model : "No, you should give that job to someone who hasn't done one's share." as I have already done more than my share of service and some one should.

If times at work, an individual passively accepts all the assignments unwanted by others. When the boss says, that, can you take this on?" he does, even though the task has little relation to his particular job area. It has been observed that the wife resents her husband and often she disagrees with what he wants, she feels being a good wife means doing whatever he wants. We as a member of our society always make requests or place demands on others. You must be able to stand up for yourself by the simple process of saying "No." If you can't state this simple two-letter word when you want to say it, you begin to lose control of your life. This does not mean saying "No" to everything. You say yes when you want to give an affirmative response. If doing a favour for a friend or participating in a community event may inconvenience you, there is still nothing wrong with saying yes if you feel the matter is important enough to undergo discomfort for the sake of the friend or activity. Saying "Yes" becomes wrong when you want to say "No" and it is in your best interest to say "No," but instead, you end up with a feeble "OK, I'll do it." The inability to say no has following consequences.

It leads you into activities you don't respect yourself for doing. Various studies can lead us to the conclusion that with young, single women the greatest cause of unwanted concern stemming from their inability to say "No".

It distracts you from what you really want to accomplish. You become so burdened doing the things that you don't want to do nor you have time or energy for the things that are most important.

We allow other people to exploit us continuality, the resentments build up, and sometimes, after years of the "Yes routine" we lose our temper in an inappropriate outburst. If you perform all kinds of errands for others at great inconvenience to yourself and serve as the family patsy, eventually someone makes a trivial request and you explode. This stems not from the most recent incident, but from hundreds of small, happenings. What the yes-sayer doesn't realize is that this behaviour often creates lack of self-respect and ultimately resulting in lack of assertiveness.

Inhibitory Personality

The world contains many people who don't recognize their own strengths or who have learned to act in inferior ways because they believe themselves to be inferior. They find it impossible to express emotions like anger or tenderness; sometimes they don't even feel them. In psychological terms, we say these people have inhibitory personalities. They have a thousand reasons for not acting, ten thousand reasons to fend off closeness. Low on self-sufficiency, they live their lives by the rules and whims of others. They do not know who they are, what they feel, what they want. In contrast, people with excitory personalities do not fear their feelings. Frightened neither of closeness nor combat but they act out of strength. The excitory man knows who he is, what he wants. He is assertive.

Often a victim of unassertiveness does not recognize it as an emotional problem. Some of the statements of nonassertive people are:

"My boss will fire me if I ask for a raise" I'm bound to fail." Why do I try. People do suffer the sad and severe consequences due to their unassertiveness. Some of the traits under un assertive personality are lack of personal growth and success; undeveloped relationships; mental anguish, and psychomatic symptoms that range from "fatigue" and "migraines" to "ulceers" and "impotence". Assertiveness training helps us to change our attitude and have a control over our emotional feelings.

TYPES OF ASSERTION

Basic Assertion

Basic assertion refers to a simple expression of standing up for personal rights, beliefs, feelings or opinions. It does not involve other social skills, such as empathy, confrontation, persuasion etc. Examples of basic assertions are:

When being interrupted:

Excuse me, I'd like to finish what I'm saying.

When being asked an important question for which you are unprepared -I'd like to have a few minutes to think that over.

When returning an item to a store-

I'd like my money back on this saw.

When refusing a request-

No, this afternoon is not a good time for me to visit with you

When telling a parent you don't want advice

I' don't want anymore advice.

Basic assertion also involves expressing affection and appreciation towards other people:

I like you.

I care for you a lot.

Having a friend like you makes me feel happy.

You're someone special to me.

The following is a particularly touching example of assertively expressing affection:

A father overheard this five-year old child saying to a playmate : "Are you having a good time? When the playmate replied "Yes," the child continued "I am too. I'm so glad that I invited you to come over and play!"

Empathic Assertion

Often people want to do more than simply express their feelings or needs. They may also want to convey some sensitivity to the other persons. When this is the goal, the empathic assertion can be used.

Reasons for Acting Assertively

Assertion rather than non assertion. Losing other people's approval is usually a major issue for people who are often non assertive. In a way it's like believing 'I will only survive if I have other people's approval." However, non assertion does not guarantee approval. People may pity rather than approve of non assertion: often this pity eventually turns into irritation and finally disgust.

A major reason for acting assertively is that it increases one's own self-respect. Indeed, an unpublished study by July Demplewolff (1974) showed that group members' self-concepts significantly changed after assertion training. A second reasons is that assertion eventually results in greater self-confidence which can then reduce the need for others' approval. Third, while it is true that people will sometimes disapprove of assertion, usually other people respect for self and others, have the courage to take stands, and deal with conflict openly and fairly. Lastly, assertion-more frequently than nonassertion-results in individuals getting their needs satisfied and preferences respected.

Assertion rather than Aggression: A major fear of people who are frequently aggressive is that they will become more vulnerable and lose control over the other people. It's like believing "I can only survive if I'm invulnerable and able to control people." That aggression does not guarantee successful control over other people is usually overlooked. When people apparently acquiesce under aggression, often they simply have gone "underground" and subtly sabotage the aggressor's control. (This sabotage process is described more fully later in this chapter.)

A major reason for acting assertively is that it increases one's control over on self, which feels good. Second, assertion eventually results in greater feelings of self-confidence which reduces insecurity and vulnerability. Third and very importantly, assertion rather than aggression results, in closer, more emotionally satisfying relationships with others. Fourth, while it is true that assertion will mean that sometimes individuals will not achieve their objectives and "win" assertion maximizes the likelihood that both parties can at last partially achieve their goals and get their needs met.

There are many different ways of acting assertively. It is important that the trainer know the various types of assertion so that group members can be helped to find better alternatives when one type of assertion is inappropriate or does not meet a member's needs.

PRINCIPLES OF ASSERTIVENESS

Assertion is not a permanent state. As you change, life situations change, and you face new challenges and need new skills. Assertiveness is not aggression. It is not an actagainst others. It is appropriate standing up for yourself.

Basic principles of assertiveness are :

(*a*) Reveal as much of your personal self as is appropriate to the situation and relationship.

(*b*) Strive to express all feelings, whether angry or tender.

(*c*) Act in ways that increase your liking and respect for yourself.

(*d*) Examine your behaviour and determine areas where you would like to become more assertive.

(*e*) Realise you may be unassertive in one area and may be assertive in other area.

RIGHT TO BE ASSERTIVE

Some people are so distressfully concerned with an arbitrary range of "Rights" and "wrongs" and permit themselves so little freedom of movement that they exist in an emotional prison or confined capsule. You must recognise your rights and stand up for them. If you do not, other people define your role for you, and you stop being yourself.

Following are some of the questionnaire about "Rights" wherein some come in your way. Answer these questions in either (Yes/No). Tick mark the questionnaire which represent your way of thinking. 'Yes/No.'

1. Do I have the right to answer honestly when I am asked if I like something and I don't?
2. Do I have the right to refuse the car to my son on Saturday night?
3. Do I have the right to tell my spouse that he/she has gained too much weight, and I am repelled by it?
4. Do I have the right to tell my boss that I don't want to work overtime?
5. Do I have the right to go out and work part-time, and leave my children at a day-care centre?
6. Do I have the right to refuse to lend my new golf clubs to a friend?.
7. Do I have the right to refuse to entertain a friend of my spouse whom I dont' like?
8. Do I have the right to pamper myself?
9. Do I have the right to stand up for my rights?

SETTING ASSERTIVE GOALS

In formulating specific behaviour start from where you are now, learn or practice some of the assertive goals, then go on to the next step. Some of the Assertive Goals are:

(*a*) Be certain you understand the assertion concept.

(*b*) Recognize your rationalisations for not being assertive as rationalizations. Generally people fall into three categories:

(*i*) A low probability event as an excuse for nonassertion.

(*ii*) A higher probability event, but give it added meaning with "it would be terrible if this happened".

(*iii*) Creatively, make up rationalizations for their lack of assertion that have no validity at all.

3. Work out the areas where you have assertive problems. Are they in impersonal, social, or personal situations?
4. See what you fear: rejection, anger or tenderness. Formulate to yourself the very worst that can happen, and then examine this eventuality and its consequences as objectively as possible.
5. Look for the general behavioural areas where the difficulty comes about, and then try to formulate it in terms of very specific, concrete behaviours.

Assertive Behaviour-Concerns Standing up for one's Rights

- Knowing one's rights
- Doing something about it (rights)
- Doing this within the framework of 'striving' of *Emotional Freedom.*

The first concerns for doing of what you have to do in order to achieve success and involves the acquisition of work and social skills necessary for the purpose.

Pretensions-Concerns with one's goals and involves choice and decisions.

How to Identify

To identify as one's specific act was assertive or whether it increased one's self respect even slightly. If it did, it was assertive if not, it was unassertive. Self Esteem is based on Real Capacity; Achievement and Respect from others.

Self Esteem Needs are based on

— Desire for strength = Achievements
— Adequacy,-Confidence
— Independence and freedom. Desire for reputation or prestige
— Recognition,-Attention (strokes positive)
— Importance or approval
— It has been observed that satisfaction of selfesteem leads to:
— Self confidence
— Worthy, strength, compatibility;
— Adequacy of being useful and necessary.

Self Image/Self Esteem

Desire and fear are two greater motivators. They propel or compel us to action and make themselves visible through our thoughts and works. You are constantly talking either to others or yourself. You think in words and your life is affected either positive or negatively.

Negative 'self talk' locks up your mental resources and your attitudes and action.

Improving Self Image/Self Esteem

Positive self image result in better interpresonal relations; better quality of life, higher productivity and happiness.

Avoid negative 'self talk'- 'I am tried' 'I have a poor memory, and I forget etc. We all tend to forget why say this. Similarly if you will say I am tired you will really get tired. We release energy with our thoughts.

— Failure in an 'event' is not failure of life. *Take failure as challenge.*
— If you lower standards of operations then you reduce your quality of work.
— Never have the feeling of 'self pity'.
— Feeling of inferiority, weakness and helplessness resulting in discouragement.

Causes of Poor Self Image/Self Esteem

— Repeated failure, repeated negative strokes, unrealistic expectations of perfection, negative self talk, lack of discipline, negative or dishearting transactions from teachers/parent/superiors etc. victim of politics/ games played by others. Consequences of poor self esteem are:
— Discharmany, 'tension', 'stress' 'lack of confidence', 'low quality job', 'inferiority complex', 'negative attitude', 'poor interpersonal relations', 'closed mindness','anger', 'mistrust and feeling of being withdrawn'.

37

Morale

Morale

There may be as many ways of improving morale and motivation as there are managers multiplied by the numbers of employees they manage. Possibly it will be, always, left to a manager to find his ways to building up morale.

Morale signifies how people feel in relation to their surroundings, or in others words, their emotional reaction and adjustment to their environment. In the world of business and industry, morale is an employee's feelings in relation to his job.

Problem faced by managers in building up morale.

1. Employees are strongly influenced by their past experience on which managers have little control.

2. Employee responds join his own individual way to his physical enivonrment. Their reaction to a morale building programme is often unpredictable.

3. Managers may not have much control on employees off the job relationships with family, neighbours, clubs, temples, creditors, and on their health and personal habits which have significant influence on employees attitudes and actions on the job.

4. Causes of variations in human feelings being numerous, and contradictory, having no logical surface pattern. Varied personal programmes have been found most effective in maintaining good morale, however, even the best morale building programmes may become ineffective with time. Motivation factor may cease to be motivating when desires have been satisfied.

Individual approach to the problem or morale and motivation is more difficult and more expansive but it allows for personal adjustment to work situation.

Companies conduct at time attitude surveys to determine the level of morale. This morale does not necessarily mean greater efforts for higher productivity. Attitude surveys would, therefore, the meaningless unless relationship is established between high morale and high productivity.

It is acknowledged that high productivity can exist only where there is high morale, but the reverse is not true. Other things being equal, it is the production oriented high morale that will give high productivity. When both employees and managers gain a feeling of well being, working together on common production goals, we have production oriented high morale.

Management has a growing interest in employees attitudes and morale. This interest is reflected by the fact that many organisations conduct attitude and opinion surveys, provide human relation training to supervisors and managers, sponsor recreation programmes for employees and take other actions that are intended to create favourable attitudes among the employees and to increase their morale.

Nature of Morale

The term 'morale' is not very specific in the sense if conveys different meanings to different people. Like the word 'health' the word 'morale' by itself does not have any favourbale impact.

Employees with high morale like their jobs and may co-operate fully with the management towards the achievement of goals of the organisation. High morale makes way for effective work by the employees. It results from job satisfaction and generates job enthusiasm. High morale is indeed a manifestation of the employees 'strength, dependability, pride confidence and devotion. All these qualities of mind and character taken together create high morale among the employees. Low morale, on the other hand, indicates the presence of mental unrest. This mental tension not only hampers production but also leads to ill health of the working people. The other consequences of low morale are the following :

1. High rate of labour turnover,
2. High rate of absenteeism,
3. Excessive complaints and grievances
4. Friction among the employees,
5. Frustration, and
6. Antagonism towards management and regulations of the organisation.

These consequences are very much fatal to the industrial relations in the organisation. There will always be labour unrest in the organisation because of low morale of the employees. Whatever may be consequences of low morale, organisation has to suffer ultimately because quantity and quality of production both suffer. Thus, in order to avoid these evil consequences, every manager should work to maintain the high morale of the people working under him. For this he should have the constant knowledge of the opinions and attitudes of the employees towards their work and the organisation and should carefully understood the changes in their behaviour and appraise the factors responsible for change in the attitude of employees.

Factors Determining Morale

Morale indicators or factors determining morale are ingredients which the management must study in order to appraise the morale of the employees. Following are the important morale factors or determinants :

1. Personal Factors. These factors relate to age, training intelligence of employees, time spent by them on the job and interest in work taken by them. For instance, if an employee is not imparted proper training, he may have low morale because he always face difficulty in doing to work.

2. Factors Relating to Job

(*a*) *Types of Job.* Nature of job, skill required to do the job and fatigue associated with it determine the attitude of an employee towards this job.

(*b*) *Job Satisfaction.* If the job gives an employee an opportunity to prove this talents and develop his personality, he will certainly like the job and his enthusiasm to work will be higher.

(c) *Compatibility with Fellow Employees.* Man is a social being, he finds work more satisfying when he has the acceptance and companionship of his fellow employees. He should have confidence in fellow employees and faith in their loyalty confidence in fellow employees and feeling to togetherness generate high morale.

(d) *Nature of Supervision.* The nature of supervision can better tell the attitude of employees because a supervisor is in direct contact with the employees and can have greater influence on the day-to-day activities of the employees. Supervisor is the pivot around which many things revolve. He is the formal leader and the worker must have confidence in him and in his leadership. A supervisor, who is fair, helpful and social minded will create confidence among the employees and this will increase their morale.

(e) *Working Conditions.* Working conditions also influence the attitude of the employees towards their jobs and supervision. Thus if better working conditions are provided to the employees for enabling them to do the working assigned to them, morale will be high.

3. Other Factors

(a) *Objective of the Organisation.* Workers want to be a part of the organisation which has worth-while purpose in which they can believe. The commonness of the purpose will end them to work enthusiastically so that organisation may achieved the common purpose efficiently and effectively.

(b) *Rewards.* Employees expect adequate compensation for their services rendered to the organisation. Good system of waves and salaries and other incentives will help in increasing the morale of the employees. Advancements and promotions always have a stimulating effect on the employees.

(c) *Physical and Mental Factors.* There are certain off-the-job factors like trouble at home or ill health of any member of the family, which effect the morale of the employees. Emotions of the employees also influecne the morale. For instance, an employee may be satisfied with his home and social life, but may think that his job status is not there. In such a case, employee's job morale is relatively low because the job is below his expectations and gives him mental worries.

Improvement of Morale

Morale can be measured by checking the extent to which the organisation is achieving the result in respect of productivity, profit or other forms of goals achievement. But this is not reliable because morale may be higher yet productivity is lower and vice-versa because of other factors like absenteeism, labour turn over, fluctuation in output quality records, excessive waste and accidents etc.

38

Emotional Determinants of Personality

Introduction

Emotions are important personality determinants because they affect personal and social adjustments. Emotions colour the individual perception of himself and his environment and affect his behaviour. An individual who feels frustrated will be more hostile and impulsive than one who approach people and environmental obstacles with more self confidence.

Curiosity is a pleasant and valuable emotional stage. It enable the executive to discover new meanings and also broaden his interests and activities. *Emotions can add pleasure to a person's life motivate him toward action and improve one's social and personal adjustments.* The direct effect of the emotions on personality comes from social judgments based on how the person handles his emotions and also his ability to establish emotional relationship with others. The physical disturbances such as digestive disorders, insomina, headaches, high blood pressure, heart trouble, allergic reactions, skin disease and peptic ulcers are often related to emotional upset. With advancing age, the effects of the emotions on physical well being increases. The younger person is able to expend energy that has been mobilised for emotional response in work, play or strenuous exercise. The direct effect of the emotions or adjustment is their colouring of the person's interests, attitudes, likes and dislikes. *Therefore emotional stability is one of the most important characteristic of an employee. Therefore, for an effective employee, it is important to operate from his Adult go state while working on his job, with other people and ,social set ups.* How well the executive adjusts to life depends partly on which emotions predominant and how he expresses his dominant emotions. The dominant emotions are revealed in facial impression. The facial expression tells the story of executive's feeling about himself and his environment more than his actions. Deprivation of any emotion of love is especially damaging. *Love is deep, tender and rewarding. It includes not only the conditions of being loved but also the act of loving. Deprivation of love results in emotional starvation.* Freud pointed out that parental tenderness accelerates the child's sexual maturity. The overmothered executive become conservative and lacks in aggressiveness, self confidence and leadership qualities. An employee brought up in too much of love, lack in aggressiveness, confidence and approval. *A balance between deprivation and excess of love leads to better adjustment and greater happiness because such a balance permits the individual to learn to cope up with temporary deprivation of love successfully.*

Definition of Emotions

The human necessity to have adequate living conditions manifests itself as a requirements to create such conditions as is experienced as a feeling of need.

Whenever we find an experience is pleasant, we would prolong the same and appreciate its recurrence. But if an experience is valued negatively,

then it is felt as unpleasant, and it evokes the evident response. We know that affection is a mode of consciousness ; also that in each psychoses the rest of the two modes of cognition and cognition must be present in varying degrees. Thus each experience of mere pleasantness or unpleasentness, implies that there is some data of knowledge, through which the subject feels pleased or otherwise, and in relation to which, the subject would more or less definitely wish for some change, or none.

Affection merely indicates to the subject how he is adjusted to his environment. This awareness is not as definite or clear as is sensory experience of cold or pain, pressure or smell. The sensory experience seems to be mainly objective, and only partially subjective ; the affection experience is in contrast entirely subjective.

The most elementary experience of affection is a feeling. The typical feeling is pleasant or unpleasant, and is generally based upon the presence of some sense experiences. By and large all experiences are either pleasant or unpleasant. However, a large number of our daily experiences and routine impressions, do not have any noticeable degree of pleasantness or unpleasntness. Hence, it is suggested that in psychology, the term feeling be restricted only to those experience or psychoses, where affection is present to a noticeable degree.

Feeling

The simplest stimulus for a feeling is a sensation. We find that some odours and tastes are naturally pleasant, and others are unpleasant. The smell of roses, and the stage of sugar, both are pleasant. The bodily changes that accompany a feeling are generally covert. We cannot localise feeling in some parts of the body, as we can locate the sensations in the sense-organs. Usually, some changes of respiration, blood circulation, psychogalvanic response etc. occur during the experience of feeling.

Theory of Feelings

Wundt put forward a theory of feelings, and suggested that all varieties of feelings could be measured along three dimensions :

(*a*) Pleasantness, Unpleasanteness

(*b*) Tension-Relaxation ; and

(*c*) Excitement-Depression.

Any feeling would occupy some position on each of these dimensions *viz.*, pleasantness tension and excitement.

Thus, all sort of feelings could be referred to these three axes ; each having a pair of positive and negative actions, starting from a common origin, zero or neutral points. The tri-dimensional theory of feeling seems to adequately describe the majority of experiences of feeling. But experimental evidence is conflicting. Wundt concluded that pleasantness and Unpleasantness were the only true and independent feelings. The other two dimensions were neither independent nor elementary but complexes of kinaesthec and organic sensations.

Mitra regards 'feeling as the source of all our experience and is the essence of what we call mind'. Every mind is a store of energy, the nature of which is not at present known. Minds differ from one another in their potentialities. The original fundamental feeling o mind is the feeling of harmony. Pleasantness is the experience of this harmony. Unpleasantness is the experience when this harmony is disturbed. Actions produce changes in the external world and these again have been reverberations on the mind. And so the conflict continues. Thinking develops as a mode of defence and reaction.

Experience of Feeling

The experiences of feeling carry the attributes of quality, intensity and duration. Each feeling has a distinct quality ; it is pleasant or unpleasant. If any experience is in different, or affection is not present to a noticeable degree, then the experience is not a case of feeling. Very often it happens that two normally in different experiences can be compared, and the observer can easily say that one of them is more pleasant than the other. We can say with regard to each experience of feeling, that is carries a certain quality of affection. Its quality is also present in some noticeable intensity. A felt experience may be very pleasant, or fairly pleasing ; or it may be very unpleasant, or somewhat unpleasant. The interval of difference, near about the zero point, is often described negatively, as 'not unpleasant' or 'not quite pleasant.

Feelings are Reactive Attitudes

According to Woodworth 'feelings are reactive attitudes of the organism. Pleasantness and unpleasantness correspond to the attitude of acceptance and rejection ; excitement and depression, to the momentary level of muscular activity or readiness for activity ; tension and relaxation to the degree of muscular tension'. This hypothesis would deny an independent existence to the feelings, and reduce them to the status of being merely derived qualities of bodily processes, or dependent upon cognitive attitudes towards objects.

The more complex and intense experience of affection is found during emotions. The more common types of emotions are anger, fear, joy, sorrow, etc. In each caes, the occasion for emotions is a complex situation. The occasion is not merely a complex situation, that suddenly confronts the individual; but it is also appreciated in a more intimate manner by the person, as definitely related to him. When we cannot do anything, we feel unprepared to meet the emergency we are at a loss to deal with the situation, we cannot attend to any adequate way of response, then we feel strongly upset, and express our emotion in various ways. In other words, the emotional experience indicates the subject's appreciation of any situation which is intimately related to him, while he finds himself unprepared or in adequately prepared to deal with it; the subject is in a state of diffused attention, strongly upset and the emotion is expressed in varied behaviour.

Expression of Emotions

The expression of emotions is unrestricted during early childhood. But later on the cultural background of the individual modifies the manner of emotional expression along certain well-defined patterns. The said child weeps and cries for 'mamma', but the child in danger may scream for 'daddy'. And the child hurt during mischievous play may simply sob out its pain.

The face of a human being is often an index of his emotion. The forehead may be wrinkled or smooth. The cheeks may redden or grow pale, and they may be contracted inwards or they may be filled and bulging outwards. The eyebrows may be contracted or relaxed; the eyes may be sparkling or dull, they may also be tearful or smiling. The lips may curl in a sneer, relax in a smile, vibrate in laughter; may become tight in anger or pride; and feeble and fallen in fear and dejection. The teeth may be set with resolution, or chatter in fear. Most of these changes are visceral. The effect is also influenced by the tone of the voice, apart from its pitch, and symbolic meanings.

The conclusion is that the bodily processes are very important in reinforcing the emotion or facilitating the experience of emotions; but they need not be identified with the emotions.

Role of Emotions in Life

Emotions or feelings are special form of man's relations to objects and phenomena of reality conditioned by their correspondence or non-correspondence to his needs. In addition to perception and thinking, emotions are one of the forms of the world's reflection in the consciousness. But they have their own specificity. Reflecting the real relations of the worked, man experiences them as his own subjective relations to it. Emotions play a very important role in man's life. "Without human emotions there has never, been, nor can there be a human quest for truth", wrote V.L. Lenin with his characteristics emotionality. Gambling is emotional excitement connected with a desire to win at all costs and an urge to continue playing. It appears when the desire to win or win back becomes stronger than the voice of person, suppresses reason and renders thinking uncritical. Gambling is a manifestation of a weak will in a game, of unwillingness or in ability to control one's own emotions; it is a negative feeling and a negative quality of the personality. The happiness of man is feeling of satisfaction with his activity which is of benefit to others; it is a feeling of creativeness engendered in constructive work.

Psychologically the feeling of happiness is always experienced when the result of an activity coincides with the aim a person has set himself. The more important aim and the more difficult it is to achieve, the happier the person who achieve it.

The expression of feelings and experiences by man and animals are in many respects alike. this was pointed out by Charles Drawin. The biochemical changes, for example, the increase in blood of sugar caused by strong emotions are also very much alike. "Who would separate in the most complex unconditioned reflexs the physiologic, experience of the powerful emotions of hunger, sexual drive, range, etc.,?". Talented factors shed real tears on the stage and deeply experience the feeling of the characters they personate.

Life is Beauty

The beautiful is life. That being is beautiful in which we see life as we think it should be. The thing is beautiful which manifests life or reminds us about life. By beauty we imply such a combination of various materials, as well as sounds, colours and words, which imparts to the thing created, made by the human master, a form that affects the feelings and intelligence or pride or joy at man's creative ability. To perceive the beautiful, in other words, "to educate oneself the aesthetic sense, the sense of enjoying beauty by perceiving the beautiful and evaluating it by comparing it with the criteria of the beautiful borrowed from man's experience".

Stubbornness

Stubbornness is in expedient persistence. Little interest in the aim; it is more important for him to gain his object despite all reasons and circumstances which make his behaviour absurd. The most important thing is that the behaviour of a stubborn person is often based on a well disguised motive : "that's the way I want it".

Obstinacy

Obstinacy, as a trait of character, is sometimes the result of inertness of the nervous process typical of a particular person. But much more often it is due to upbringing, the habit of doing as one please. It is not so difficult to make a stubborn person persistent. To do this, he must merely be helped to find a Worthwhile aim. Courage, bravery, daring, fearlessness and cleanliness are high human qualities.

Fearlessness

A fearless person is not only the one who in a dangerous situation experiences no fear, but also he who experiences fear and acts as he deems it necessary just the same. Nobody will consider a person courageous if he foolishly, without the least understanding, rushes headlong into danger. But there are three very different forms of fearlessness. "A courageous person is the one who knows that there is danger ahead, but defies it just the same". *Bravery is connected with the emotional experience of fighting excitement and enterancement with danger.* One may be daring and brave in the pursuit of any aim, even in one's own interest. In a courageous person fear is displaced by a sense of duty.

Heroism

Heroism displays various aspects of the personality, some of them predominating in particular cases.. In addition the courage, daring or bravery, heroic deeds are the result of a person's worldly outlook, his high political consciousness, moral fibre, high principles, conviction of his rightness, patience, initiative, resourcefulness, determination, discipline, self-control, strong will. Heroism is a always active and is manifested in activity.

Temperaments

Hippocrates, the Greek physician who lived in 460-377 B.C., accounted for human temperaments and diseases by predominance of one of the following fluids in the organism. Persons of a sanguine temperament by predominance of blood secreted by the heart; phlegmatic temperament — by phlegm secreted by the brain; choleric temperament — by yellow bile secreted by the liver; and melanchoic temperament — by black bile secreted by the spleen.

A temperament is the most general characterisation of each individual person, the most fundamental characterisation of his nervous system, and temperament leaves a certain imprint on all the activity of each individual". Temperament manifests itself in the general make-up of the personality, although it does not in any way determine the social significance of person.

A person of any temperament way be clever or stupid, honest or dishonest, kind or malicious, talented or ungifted. According to well-known psychologist the myth of the social inferiority of personalities with a week type of nervous system reveal that those who get tired more easily, are more perceptive of the surrounding world and react more keenly to it. If the weak type did not have the advantage of greater sensitivity and faster reaction, it would long since have been extinguished by natural selection. However, persons with a weak type of nervous system really cannot be flyers.

Frustration

In any working situation an individual wants to be noticed, he wants to feel necessary and important to group's work he wants to be appreciated or recognised and if these expectations of any executive, are not fulfilled he feels frustrated, *One of man's strongest needs is the need for a sense of achievement, for the feeling that he is getting something done, that his work is of importance so he feels himself to be important to group's work. Frustration among employees may arise due to social, psychological and economic reasons.*

(*i*) **Alienation and Low Job Satisfaction.** Employees are alienated in the sense that they feel that they have no control over the work process and that the work is meaningless for them, and that the work is not important part of their lives and so they feel frustrated. Dissatisfaction or frustration at work will also depend upon the individual difference in intelligence level. An employee, whose level of intelligence is much higher than average, his frustration will be short lived than of those with average or below average intelligence level. Because the employee with high intelligence is capable, on the basis of his skill and intelligence, of finding out some way in removing the blocks which causes frustration.

(*ii*) **Lack of Motivation.** One of the central problems of any organisation is to motivate its members to work for the organisation's overall objectives. A situation has to be created so that the employee can satisfy their own needs while at the same time work towards the goal of the organisation. And when an employee is unable to satisfy his individual needs in a work situation then it may result in frustration and his frustration may cause obstruction in the occurrence of goal directed behaviour.

According to Frederick Herzberg, Bernead Mausner, Barbara Shyderman and so many other social psychologists, the "Satisfiers" are : achievement recognition of work itself, responsibility and advancement. The "dissatifiers" are : inter-personal relations, the technical ability of supervisor, company policy and administration, physical working conditions and the individual's personal life "off the Job". The satisfiers are job-centered and relate to the nature of the work itself and the rewards that flow from performance of that work. The dissatifiers are associated with the context of the work rather than the work itself. "Satisfiers" arise out of work and the presence of satisfiers leads to the motivator and lack of motivators may result in frustration.

(*iii*) **Difficulties of Communication Resulting Frustration.** Due to technological reasons working organisations have become large and with large hierarchical levels. The kind of structure create great difficulties of communication. Due to these communication difficulties, executives may feel frustrated in the sense that if the work is to be done immediately, in which certain consultations or certain points has to be cleared, then it becomes really difficult for the executive to communicate quickly and effectively. Another reason for frustration due to communication difficulties is culture. An individual's reaction to any communication is the consequence of how that communication is perceived and the perception of an individual is greatly affected by the culture to which he belongs. The level of satisfaction or frustration with different jobs will correspond very closely with the social status commonly associated with those jobs. Employees, when they find that there is not opportunity for recognition achievement and advancement in their jobs, they feel frustrated. Employees feel frustrated when they find that their jobs are not secured even they may put in hard and good work. Feeling of unsecurity also arises because of the insecurity of the organisation itself. Four example, an employee who is working in a new organisation that has been set up very recently and the future of it is unknown, will feel more unsecure than an employee who is working in an established organisation with good reputation.

Frustration is also caused by the individual relationship in their work group. Frustration may be greater in uncohesive group rather than cohesive groups. Cohesiveness refer to those qualities in group that are homogeneous, such as race, age, social status and attitudes relevant to the work situation. Groups containing both skilled and unskilled members can also be cohesive if their skills are complementary. *Economic reasons for frustration is the most important one because it is only through money that an individual can satisfy his primary needs.* If the pay that an employee receives is not sufficient to satisfy some of the basic needs then the executive gets frustrated. some other factors such as failure to complete a task or being insulted are also important causes of frustration. Frustration may be greater immediately after transfer when the contrast of the present status with former status is most evident but gradually this kind of frustration decreases. *The difficulty of the job in relation to skill and abilities is also responsible for frustration ;* (*a*) Frustration will be greater for employees who are below standard in production than for individuals who have already achieved the goal so standard production. (*b*) Frustration will be greater for individuals on difficult jobs than for individuals who are on easy jobs. (*c*) Frustration may increase with increasing efficienty when it is not suitably rewarded.

Jealousy Syndrome

In *Jealousy Syndrome anything better must be pulled down seems to be the prevalent motto.* There are two popular stories on this national malaise. The first story relates to two men who had a fight on who was taller of the two. It was agreed that their height will be measured, to resolve the conflict. But, when the height was measured, the stronger of the two made the weaker stand in a ditch. It was possible for him to have stood on a stool or a table when the height was measured. But he decided not to choose that alternative. He did not want to improve himself. He was interested in pulling down the other fellow.

The second story relates to export of crabs. The crates of crabs were exported to the US, one crate each by Korea, Japan and India. When the crate were opened in America, it was found that there were no crabs in the Korean and Japanese crates. But when the Indian crate was opened, it was found to have all the crabs. Now, let us hear the explanation for this from the storyteller. He said that there was a small opening in each crate to allow air to come in. The hole was big enough for one crab to escape. One crab from the Korean crate tried to escape, the other supported it from below. One by one all crabs escaped. The same thing happened to the Japanese crate. But when one crab from the Indian crate tired to escape, all others pulled in down. No crab could escape. *There is something in our psyche which makes us pull down those who are going up.* Envy in our society is of higher order.

The actual or threatened violation of self-esteem in later life in variable evoke some version of the pattern of restitutive measures occured in childhood. The "envy" phenomenon in our society in much simpler terms makes three important points :

(*a*) To a great extent, organisational behaviour is determined by experience of infancy. For all infants, the mother is the most important figure or resources within the family. On many occasions, when the mother is away, the infant fantasies that the mother is giving her breast to other, *i.e.*, other siblings or even the father, or else she is using it to nature herself. The former results in jealously and the later in envy. Some manager use this perception to justify their own lack of performance. Psychologically this is the equivalent of an infant biting its mothers breast.

(*b*) Sociologically, there are several factors which reinforce the nevy syndrome. One, with the joint family system gradually, breaking up, thus begins the alienation process. Moreover, at the child's level, for instance, education is measured in grades rather than in terms of knowledge acquired. This generates psychological pressure to beat the system in order to obtain good grades anyhow. Promotion and increament systems have to gain credibility in the eyes of an organisation's members as being talks related, with minimal subjective overtones. It such systems are established, managers can at least have the opportunity to manage envy by striving for better performances rather than feeding it with their fantasies.

(*c*) *The reward and punishment system in Indian organisations must be made more credible to reduce envy in our organisations.* A management consultant recently said that only one out of five promotions in professionally managed Indian Organisations are accepted by other managers having been given on merit. *The other four are considered to be given as rewards for sycophancy or because of good relationship maintained with the boss or some other considerations.* They are not perceived be rewards for merit and achievements at work. It is quite possible that such perceptions are just perceptions. But, perceptions do would the behaviour of manager. Such perceptions may lead to dysfunctional behaviour reducing the effectiveness of such organisations. An open system of rewards should be established in organisations. This openness may reduce the enviousness in Indian organisation to some extent.

39

Group Dynamics and Group Behaviour

Dynamics

The word dynamics means 'force'. The term group dynamics refers to the forces operating in groups. The investigation of group dynamics consist of a study of these forces and the conditions modifying them. The practical application of group dynamics consists of the utilisation of knowledge about these forces for the achievement of some purpose. Group dynamics is thought of as certain techniques to be used within groups.

Group

In order to fulfil social needs, people form small groups on the job itself. They behave as members of group and their membership as group helps to shape their work behaviour and attitudes towards the organisation and the job. There will be a significant change in the behaviour of a person who is acting as an individual and when allowed to act as a member of some group. Groups may exercise stronger control over their members than that of management. A question that comes to mind is why should we study work group dynamics in management. Following are some of the arguments :

(*a*) It is in the management's interest to understand what happens within the work groups because they are found throughout the organisation.

(*b*) Work groups strongly influence the overall behaviour and performance of members.

(*c*) Group membership can have both positive and negative consequences as far as the organisation is concerned. If managers are to avoid the negative consequences generated by work groups, then a thorough study of group dynamics is very essential.

The importance of group dynamics to a manager lies in the fact that people act differently as individuals than as members of a group. To quote Likert, 'An Organisation will function best when its personnel function not as individuals but as members of highly effective work groups with high performance goals'. A manager is simultaneously the leader of his own group and a participating member of the group.

Definition

Group dynamics may be defined as the social process by which people interact face to face in small groups. Thus it is concerned with the dynamic interaction of individuals in face to face relationship. The task goals of the group, originating from the basic organisation objectives, provide for their continued interaction. Group dynamics focuses on team work, wherein the small members groups are constantly in touch with each other and effectively contribute their ideas to accomplish a task. The group develops its goals clearly. The group has resources to accomplish its goals. The group furnishes very useful suggestions in goal achievement.

The group has a common objective. The group creates group leaders which can effectively co-ordinate the group efforts toward the achievement of their objectives. Lastly, it changes the formal role of participants. For instance, if a skilled workman is a member of the works committee and sits in a committee with his own supervisor as another member, his role as a committee member will be quite different from his role as a subordinate.

Importance of Groups

Groups serve various purposes not only for themselves but for the organisations as well. They provide norms for behaviour and thus teach new employees how to behave. Work often requires cooperation of more than one person to achieve its ends, and groups facilitate this co-operation. Groups provide personal relationship, at the work place. Groups provide understanding, companionship, supportive relations and friendship. Everyone needs the company of people at work to go for lunch, for tea breaks and to share experiences with each other. *Groups also provide an identity for the person at work place to achieve a feeling of belongingness from which he can derive esteem recognition and status.* Work groups also provide security to the individual members from external pressure from other groups such as unions or associations resist outside pressure on an individual.

Group Behaviour

Group behaviour has become a specialised subject. It is an entity of its own. It is not the sum total of the behaviour of the individuals making up the group. Group should be dealt as a unit rather than the components of the groups or the individuals independently. Most of us spend major portion of our time in work groups. The value and behaviour of an individual are related to the group to which he belongs.

Every member contributes something toward the accomplishment of the common goals. Fig. 39.1. has individuals 1, 2, 3, 4 and 5 working toward common goal. The contribution of each individual is indicated by a certain area. It is not at all essential that these contributions are necessarily equal but they are vital to the entire goals achievement and are inter-related in the process of integration of individual's efforts in smooth working of the group. The individual may lose some of his individual personality and characteristics while working in a group but after the transition has occurred the individual's personal wants are changed and becomes mainly thereafter of the group.

The group's cohesiveness and productivity is higher when the members are permitted to form or select their work groups. Under such conditions the job satisfaction of each member tends to increase.

Formal Groups

Formal groups can be divided into the following three groups :

(*a*) **Team Group.** Such form of groups are fairly autonomous, receiving little supervision and working within broad frame of reference.

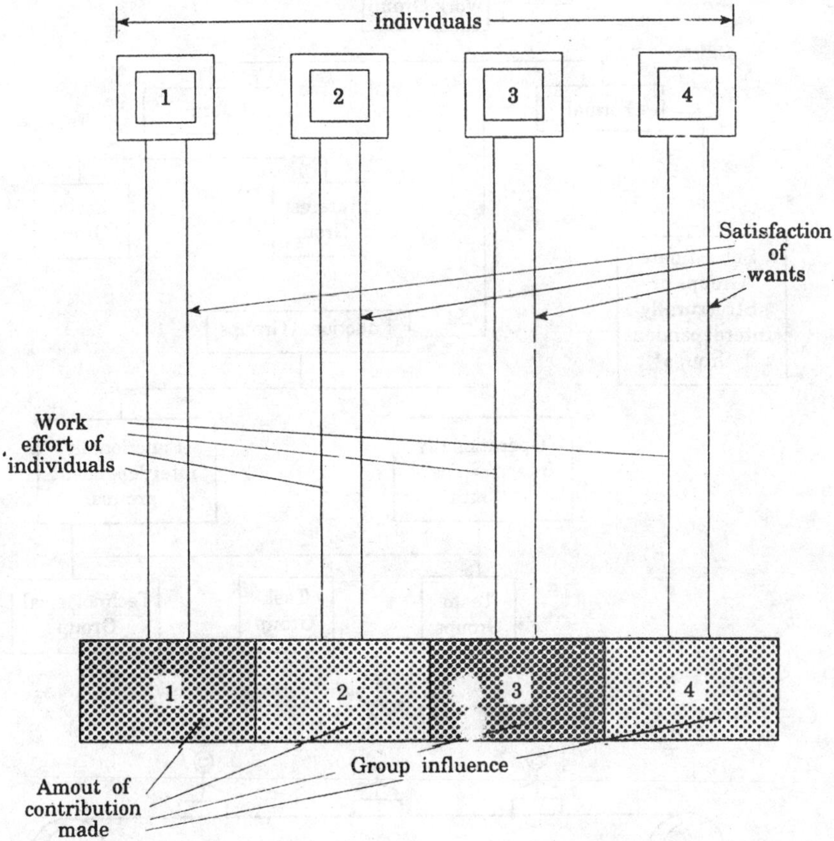

Fig. 39.1.

(*b*) **Task Group.** Here the group will have some flexibility over methods of work and rate of work.

(*c*) **Technological Group.** Here the work contents and methods are specified and assigned to the individual. The individual is given very little scope to the use of discretion.

Summary of the formal types of work group is shown in Fig. 39.2. The formal groups can also be classified by the type of interdependence :

(*a*) Operational interdependence.

(*b*) Functional interdependence.

(*c*) Structural interdependence.

1. Operational Interdependence. In this group members are dependent for completion of their task upon each other. A simple example of this is assembly line as shown in the figures given below :

2. Functional Interdependence. The members of the group are dependent upon others with complementary skills in order to achieve the group's objectives.

3. Structural Interdependence. It is resulting from organisation design, giving members common supervision and common work area.

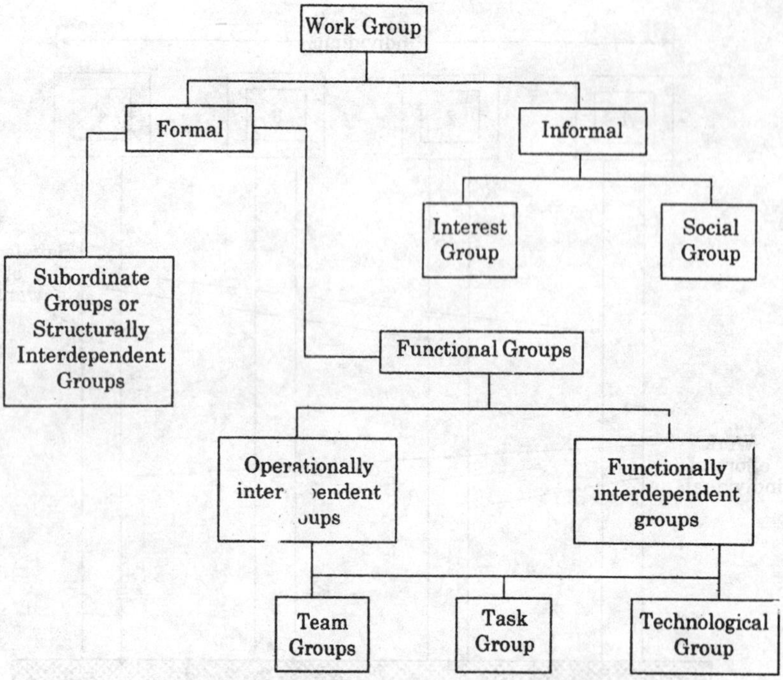

Fig. 39.2.

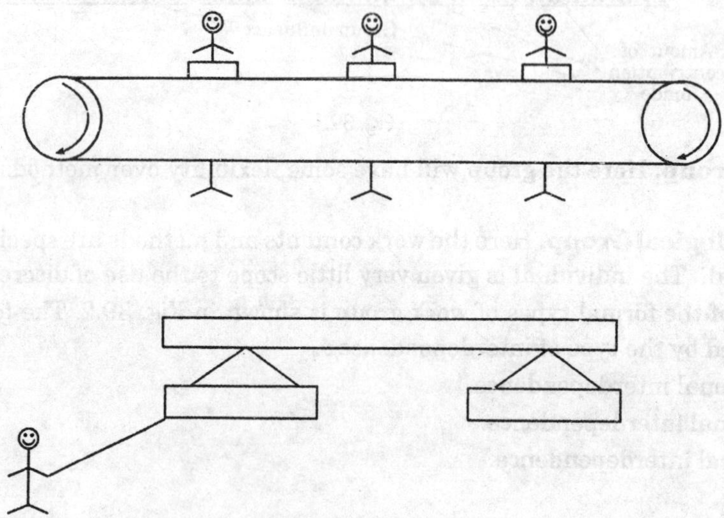

(Parts move between work stations)
Fig. 39.3

Consultative Groups

Groups whose responsibilities are primarily of an intermitent nature are essentially consultative and are used with an object of effective communication encouraging joint management and participative decision-making. Consultation groups usually comprise both management and selected worker representatives. The benefits are often no greater than could be achieved through union representation.

Group Structure

Groups like individuals have structural and negative characteristics and operate in physical and social settings.

As a group develops and achieves some stability it becomes structured. Positions of authority and responsibility emerge, group norms and standards develop and help to regulate the actions of the group members. The structure of the group includes all these relatively stable characteristics of the group's organisation.

Groups develop power hierarchies. We find hierarcies of power in large corporations, governmental agencies. School and college systems and in families. Power refers to the ability to control some aspects of the behaviour of either persons. In other words, power is the ability to deliver rewards to person who comply with demands or expectation and coercive power or punishment is the ability to deliver punishment or withhold rewards for persons who fail to comply. One's position in the power structure will determine what one can do and how autonomous we can be.

Closely related to the power structure but not synonymous with it is the leadership structure of the group. A person with power has actual ability to influence or determine the fate of other. The person in the leadership role is more concerned with mobilising group effort and with planning and coordinating group action and he may have much or little power for doing so. In an highly organised group the leadership usually becomes a mere pervasive characteristic of group structure.

As each one of us belongs to more than one group, we are required to play several different social roles. Some roles need to be followed more rigidly than others. If the organisation of the group is flexible, member may have access to considerably ways of working out roles that are suitable for them. The important elements of social roles are :

Role Expectation	— The behaviour prescribed for an individual occupying a position in the group.
Role Conception	— The way an individual perceives his role.
Role Acceptance	— The way an individual finds his role compatible with his values, needs and self-concept.
Role performance (Behaviour)	— The way an individual performs his role
Role Conflict	— The contradictory role demands resulting from multiple group membership.

Communication is essential for transmitting information and coordinating the activities of individual and sub-groups. In small groups two-way communication gives the group as a whole benefit of each member's ideas, provides members with a sense of involvement and gives group leaders important feed-back. The channels of communication in any group reveal a great deal about its power and leadership structure. Autocratic leaders typically attempt to control the communication system in order to maintain their position of power. Even in democracy there must be continuous vigilance to see that information is not withheld or manipulated by those in power positions.

Groups tend to develop a definite way to do things and a strong feeling that this is the way things should be done. The typical attitudes, behaviour and values not only become the characteristics of a given group but acquire a mandatory character. Similarly, norms of larger social groups are embodied in laws, customs and traditions. In one way or the other, group communicates its norms to the members so that individual is aware of that group norms. *Groups also develop a frame of references and assumptions about themselves and their environment in the same way as an individual does.*

Group Standards of Behaviour

Informal groups create certain standards of behaviour to govern their relations. Probably the most important group standards are those that protect the members of the group against real or imagined outside dangers particularly from top management. Production workers may agree on level of output and exert pressure on those who deviate from it especially on those who produce more than the accepted norms. Group standards of good workmanship and high quality often make management task easier if the group takes trouble makers in hand to reduce the standards there will be need for management to impose discipline.

People are anxious to conform to group standards because, as members of the group, they look at things from the group point of view, they tend to identify with the group and since it helps to meet their needs they accept its goals.

Why Work Groups are Formed

Management decision-making omits many factors that becomes part of group dynamics. Most jobs are under-defined by management and certainly there is little consideration given to differences in personality. But the employees make certain adjustments and from groups. Once the groups are established, a dynamic 'self regulating process' occurs. *Employees interact with one another and build favourable sentiments towards fellow group members. The increased opportunities for interaction build stronger bonds of identification.* The group becomes something more than a mere collection of people. It develops a customary way to doing things and set of stable characteristics that are hard to change. It becomes an organisation in itself.

Every group requires an internal structure. Structure merely means a set of unique characteristics that determine the members relationship to one anather and with the leader. At times, rather than having a commitment to the goals of the larger institution groups evolve their own goals reflecting their own special interests. Group members are more dedicated to group goals. *Group cohesiveness results in the group acting in unified manner. This cohesiveness is a result of the degree to which the group goals help the satisfaction of the individual needs. An important management problem, therefore, is to relate the group's test objectives to the individual needs of the members of the group.* It is, therefore, the job of the good leader to direct the energies of the cohesive group towards, organisational goals for securing maximum organisational productivity. Following factors are responsible for the formation of groups.

Companionship

The need for relationship with other is one of the strongest human drives. One can express his feelings only through companionship. Many research studies have indicated that the employees who have no opportunity for close social contact find their work unsatisfying and this lack of satisfaction often reflects itself in low production and high rate of absenteeism and turnover. Elton Mayo observed the employees in a textile plant who worked at isolated jobs, found to lie highly dissatisfied and consistently failed to meet production standard until staggered rest period helped a little. But when the company permitted these workers to take rest period as a group, production and satisfaction among workers increased.

Identification

Workers get more identified in smaller groups and so smaller groups tend to enjoy higher morale. Employees working in large departments, where everybody does the same job, find it hard to form stable social groupings and so they have low morale.

Understanding from Friends

The daily work routine creates frustration and tension, but one gets a sympathetic ear preferably from someone who has similar experiences. Organisations that lack this outlet sometimes rely on the expensive system or employee counseling in which outsider vent out employee troubles.

Job Satisfaction

The group's solution to a problem may be different from what management expects and it may even be more efficient. Red-tapism is eliminated, short-cuts are evolved, informal channels of communication are established to cut across department boundaries. Many jobs which appear superficially dull and routine are made more interesting by the group.

Protection for Membership

Groups protect their members from outside pressures and authority. Groups often resist management demands for additional output, increased work hours, and higher quality.

Most dynamic organisations have a tendency to introduce changes in work methods and routines at a faster rate than the individual can adjust to them. The speed at which these changes are introduced can be materialised by an effective work groups.

Groups Cohesiveness

It is the degree of unity within the group. All the elements of group behaviour which have been described earlier are influenced in some degree by this factor. The more united the group, the greater is the likelihood that all members will conform strictly to group standard and greater the likelihood that a small core leadership will represent without challenging the feelings of all members.

Factors Determining Group Cohesiveness

(*a*) **Status of the Group.** Other things remaining same, people generally feel loyal towards a high status group than towards a low status group. The are more conscious to conform to the norms of the group from which they want to escape. It should be noted that a high status group receives greater loyalty from its members, which in turns makes the group even stronger and more likely to gain increased status.

(*b*) **Size of the Group.** The effective group is relatively small. Small groups are more close knit than large ones. When the group is small its members have constant face to face contacts. So it is easier to have close relationship with all the members of a small group than with all the members of a large one.

(*c*) **Nature of the Group.** Heterogeneous groups (whose members have different interest and backgrounds) are often less effective in promoting their own interest than groups whose members are more homogenous. Homogeneous groups whose members are alike on such factors as age, education, status, experience, background, etc. do better when the task or goal requires mutual cooperation and conflict, free behaviour.

(*d*) **Communication.** Groups whose members are located together and can interact frequently and easily, are likely to be more cohesive and effective than those at a greater distance. Such groups tend to develop their own language and symbols and codes to communicate with group members. Even scattered groups, like maintenance crews may become tightly knitted if the technology of work requires or permits them to interact frequently with one another. In fact, one of the determinant of group cohesion is the speed with which message can be transmitted through the group.

(*e*) **Location of the Group.** Location of the group plays an important role in enhancing cohensivenss. Particularly, isolation from other groups of workers tends to build high cohesiveness. Where there is no dividing line between one group and anothers cohesion is more difficult to achieve because a chain of interaction develops with little group solidarity. Where members of a group are located close together and are in isolation from other groups, they will develop greater cohesiveness because of constant face to face interaction.

(*f*) **Autonomy.** Like individual, the group of individuals may have dependent or independent functions to other groups and thus will have different structure, when each individual of a group has independent and different activities, then the cohesiveness among members of the group will be less as compared to groups whose members we performing operations which are dependent upon each other.

(*g*) **Leadership Style.** The different styles of leadership influence the group cohesiveness differently. An effective leader keeps the members of the group more close by helping them satisfy their social needs.

(*h*) **Management Behaviour.** The behaviour of manager has a direct influence on the degree of cohesion that exists within a group. By creating competition among employees and by constantly comparing one employee with another, he may make close relations difficult. A manager can also build solidarity by rewarding cooperative behaviour. He can utilise the group cohesiveness for achieving the goals of the enterprise if he can provide them good leadership.

(*i*) **Outside Pressure.** Groups provide security for the individual members from pressure from other groups. This is because group members work together when they are threatened by a common danger. A group of employees may forget their personal differences and may organise against a new supervisor who is regarded as a threat to the group. The various factors contributory to group cohesiveness are shown in Fig. 39.4. Study on the work group cohesiveness revealed the following observations :

1. High group cohesiveness is associated with less anxiety about job related matters.
2. Greater the cohesiveness of the group the greater the influence which the goals of the group have on the performance of the members.
3. Higher the cohesiveness lesser the variation in productivity among the members of the group.

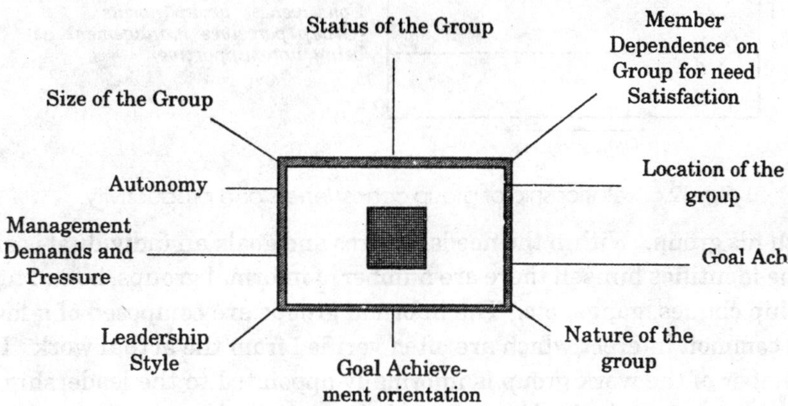

Fig. 39.4.

Fig. 39.5. shows the relationship of group cohesiveness and the anxiety and Fig. 39.6 shows the relationship between conhesiveness and productivity. The Seashore studies indicate that cohesiveness influence behaviour, anxiety and productivity. Once the management fosters a cohesive work group culture the company and the members are rewarded because of the higher level of productivity.

The group of like minded individuals have structural and integrative characteristics and operate in social environments. The groups have power structures, leadership structures, role structures, communication, social structures. Groups have norms, ideologies, systems, cohesiveness and morale.

The same time he is greatly influenced by the powerful forces of his group. The desire for the approval from his colleagues is normally so strong in a man that he will modify his behaviour

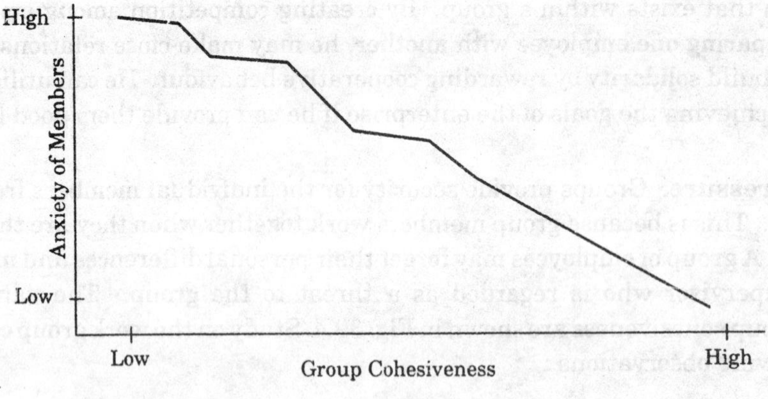

Fig. 39.5. Group Cohesiveness - Anxiety

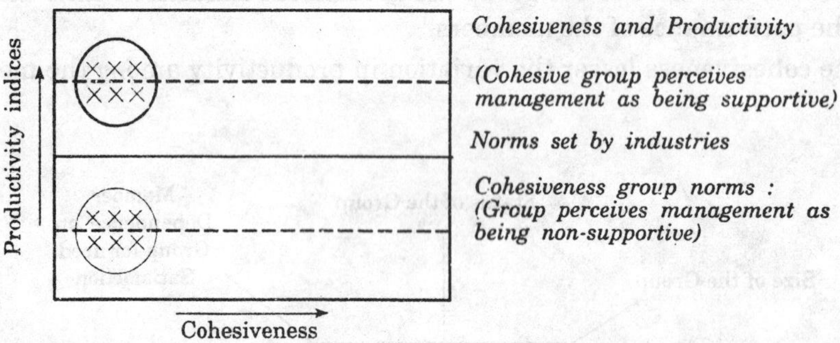

Fig. 39.6. Relationship of group cohesiveness and productivity.

to be in line with his group. Within the needs, desires and goals an individual is similar to that of his group, if he identifies himself there are number of informal groups, bound together by the social relationship cliques, gangs, etc. The informal groups are composed of a few individuals who have some common interest which are often verified from the actual work. In most of the situations a member of the work group is informally appointed to the leadership position. He retains his position as long as he is able to carry the group with him to gain its objectives. Many a time the leaders of informal groups are different from leaders appointed by the orgnisation.

An Effective Group

The nature of the group determines the character and development of its members. The value of the group, the stability of these values, the group atmosphere, and the nature of conformity demanded by the group determine whether a group is likely to have a positive or negative impact upon the growth and behaviour of its members. Loyalty to a group produces pressures to work in conformity. The groups have the capacity to behave in ways other than the behaviour of their member. Nature of a group can vary from one in which there is hostility among the members to one in which the attitudes are warm and friendly. An effective group, as we shall define it, is always conceived as being part of a large organisation. Characteristics of an effective group are as follows :

(*a*) The members are skilled in all the various leadership and membership roles and functions required for interaction between leaders and members and among the members.

(*b*) The group has been in existence sufficiently long to have developed a well established, relaxed working relationship among all its members.

(*c*) The members of the group are cohesive and are loyal to group including the leader.

(*d*) The members and leaders have a high degree of confidence and trust in each other.

(*e*) The values and goals of the group are integrated with the individual goals and values.

Activities of the Group

Background factors determine the group behaviour to a great extent. There is no doubt that any job requires certain set of activities for its being successful.

MANAGING TEAM - ORGANISING PEOPLE FOR MAXIMUM RESULTS

The Single factor responsible for the growth of an organisation and the organisation to the leader in the industry is positive Team Climate where each member experiences growth as a team member as well as an individual. The recognising team work, focusing on specific role as Team builder, developing a team maturity, relevance of process, channalising of team creativity and improving team effectiveness has been discussed in the following text.

TEAM-Together Everyone Achievers More conveys the spirit. If from the term 'Management' we take out TEAM, we are left with term - 'NAGMAN'. In other words 'Management' is nothing but team efforts. Companies of today are more productive and more profitable when the employees are 'On the Team'. The future will belong to those who embrace the potential of wider opportunities but recognise the realities of more constrained resources-and find new solutions that permit doing more with less. New solutions are essential, because business game is being played under more pressure and with a greater international scope than ever before. *Global economy is like a Corporate Olympics - a series of games played all over the world with international as well as domestic competitors.* In this Corporate Olympics, there are many different games to be entered, requiring specialised abilities and with a widely varying competitive conditions. But there are common overall characteristics in those teams that can compete and win again and again-the strength, skill and discipline of the athletes, focused on individual excellence, coupled with the ability to work well within a well organised team.

'Business is like Base Ball - as long as an executive hits the ball well every time, he is at bat. The time is long past when businesses or the people in them can succeed by just hitting the ball themselves and forgetting about the world around them. Individual excellence is not enough; responsibility for the *performance of the whole team* is required. It is getting harder and harder for executives of succeed by traditional corporate methods because of changing technology, customer preferences, employee loyalties, industry regulations, and corporate ownerships. *If game of business is like sports, then winning requires faster action, more creative maneuvering, flexibility and closer ties with employees, suppliers, and customers. There is a strong need for forging closer ties with employees, serving on teams and improving performance to pursue excellence.*

Despite all the reasons for the development of teams in the business environment, the fact is that most people basically prefer to work in Teams, at least for most of the time. Working in a group or a department seems to offer security, indeed to some degree it does, and it can be rewarding at a personal as well as at business level. The need of the Team is because individuals simply cannot do all the jobs alone. It is not just the quantity of manpower needed, it is the variety of skills and disciplines that are beyond one individual to learn or master within one's lifetime. Let us take ideally a Team example - 'Cricket Team' requires the results of combining specialist skills (bowlers, batsman, fielders and sub-dividing each into even more defined roles such as spin bowlers, openers, aggressive players and defensive players etc.). Some of the characteristics of Teams are :

- *A team can demand more authority* to put through its decisions than can an individual.
- *Teams take more risks than individuals.* They have a natural protection - you can sack an individual (as a scapegoat or otherwise) but you can't (usually!) sack the whole team. Risk taking is a necessary and normal part of business. The team structure provides the authority to take the risks, the dare to do so, and the balance of strengths and capabilities that give the wisdom to take reasonable risks, rather than unreasonable ones.
- *Teams have greater access to communications than individuals.* Information both to and from the team is usually more structured, with a consequence that implementation of team decisions is more effective.
- *Team have a more progressive curve than individuals.* -Team learn faster.
- *Team spread a feeling of unity and the sharing of success.* This is generally good for the organisation's morale and creates for many a sense of belonging and increased job satisfaction.

Types of Teams.

In order of understand the dynamics of teams from the point of view of business, following are some of teams normally exist in business viz. Boards of directors, Audit teams, Management groups, Consulting task forces besides specialised teams. Some of the specialised teams are :

Networking Teams

These are less formal associations of managers etc., normally from similar positions of authority within an organisation who communicate (network) with each other across divisional and even corporate boundaries.

Hit Teams

These are formed for a specific purpose, usually for a short duration. They are normally highly mobile, travelling to areas of difficulty whenever needed.

Strategic Teams

These are composed of specialists and people of great experience to whom longer term and strategic issues are continually referred.

Corrective Action Teams

These are one of the tools used in total quality management (TQM). They are problem-solving teams with the authority to implement action on problems referred to them by work groups.

TEAM LEADER

Probably the greatest influence upon the team is the team leader and the role played by him. For this reason, since history was recorded our species has been searching for a set of universal traits that will identify what makes a leader, and throughout history we have seen crude attempts to create a situation or a world that will grow and nurture future leaders. An effective Team leader is one who is able to draw out full potential of his team members. The team leader should be able to give a direction, for investing their potentials. The team leader although vested with the authority but should not become authoritarian but should encourage democratic style of leadership. The team member should have their own individual needs but all the same they have to work together as a team to fulfill the organisational needs. Team leader is supposed to maintain the respect for each member of the team and also recognise their ideas with a spirit to present and defend them. A team leader's job is to do what cannot be delegated. The other functions of leader is communication, motivation, evaluation and organising. *The various types of leader such a 'manipulator', 'glory grabbers', 'status seeker' and 'jokester' are shown in figures.* Team are built around group norms that encourage examination and open discussion of the team members in relationship to task accomplishment. *Team building is a continuing process of diagnosing the effectiveness of a group and their inter-personnel relationships.* The leadership functions to steer the organisation towards long range survival and success. *Team Leadership is a common thread which runs through all levels of the managers and managerial systems. Leadership role is multifaceted and calls for different skills, techniques, aptitude and vision at various levels and in different situations.* Leadership is an ascribed role in group activity in achieving the group objectives. What then are the traits of good leadership, and can we find any universals ? Research shows that people who get to the top where leadership is vital are: -above average intelligence, middle to upper-class background, possessed of higher power needs, often firstborn.

There is not a single set of personality trait from which we are able to predict successful leaders, or conversely from which we can predict non-leaders. The office is more important than the person in it and the office grants power to the office-holder irrespective of his personal qualities. Hence the ideas, which may or may not be true, that the job make the man. Leaders have charisma or gravities, and where the two qualities are combined, or where a charismatic leader gets elected or takes a high gravities position, then you have an unbeatable combination.

The team leader is a figurehead, representing the team both in the organisation and outwardly to customers, suppliers and other organisations. The team leader is a motivator, the team leader is the liaison officer for the team, with outside contacts, the team leader is a monitor of information technology (IT), the team leader has also to be the spokesperson on behalf of the team, the team leader has also to be the spokesperson on behalf of the team, the team leader often has to demonstrate *'entrepreneurial'* abilities, to seek and find opportunities for the team. The team leader is a *'disturbance handler'*, taking corrective action on behalf of the team. The team leader is a *'resource allocator'* for the team. The team leader will also have to be a *'negotiator'* to internal and external contracts. The team leader has to be a good *'Communicator'* both within and outside the team. The team leader must be *'Consistent'* in his or her dealings within and outside the team. The team leader needs to *"be flexible'* to adapt the ever-changing circumstances that modern business demands. The team leader needs to be a *'Student'*, always willing to learn new techniques, systems and new working methods. The team leader needs to be a *'Coach'* to the team, the coach is responsible for the morale, motivation and well being of the team.

To conclude, Team Building is the first step to Fostering an Achievement Climate. Team Building is a philosophy : Not a tool. The ability to build a team is a vital management skill. Managing team requires high level of commitment, performance and effectiveness. Facilitation and support are the two critical elements of positive team climate to be imbibed by the 'Team Leader'.

40

Roles And Roles Ambiguity

Role and Role Ambiguity

'The roles that a person occupies establish what and where that person is in social terms. According to G. Head 'By role taking' we elicit coincidental response from the other. In other words what we feel ourselves to be, is determined and re-asserted by the behaviour of others towards us ans reciprocally by our behaviour to them. In the ideas of role we have a most useful tool to examine people's behaviour in groups. In fact we can use it immediately to pose a fundamental question which faces every group member, and is especially useful at the first point of entry into a group *viz.*, 'who am I in the eyes of the group ? 'It implies that we are studying a group from the point of view of 'I' namely the life of group as 'I' experience it and react to it. It is possible to study a group from the position of 'him' if the person who is not a member of the group and stands beyond it looking in. Then 'I' and the 'him' may to some extent, collaborate as the knowledge of 'him' become available to 'T'. The knowledge is always coloured by the subjective experience of 'I', in the group situation. 'Him' may however have available to him techniques of information gathering which are the objectives or at least, relatively so.

The assumption is made that a great deal of 'I' behaviour is an unware, at unthoughout level and that the process of bringing such behaviour into awareness and making it object of 'I' to study is difficult and often painful. A major instrument for the study of such behaviour is the study of group or 'T' for a training Group. In a study at Tavistock Institute U.S.A. eight or ten trainees assembled with a consultant. They met regularly for about one and a half hours per session for not less than ten sessions. Their task was to study the behaviour of the group, and individual in it. The experimental situation was Intiated by the Tavistock institute of Human Relations and developed by other bodies notably the Group Studies Section of the Association of Psychotherapists. There was no prior rules as to how the study Group should conduct itself, nor how the consultant should behave. His task was to assist the group to understand its own behaviour as best one could. The procedure one usually adopted was, as he thinks fit to draw the group's attention from time to time to behavioural patterns of which one appeared to be unaware. In such a study we find that group members appear to feel considerable anxiety and struggled with the problem of 'What sort of group is this and how shall I behave in it".

It will be seen that the method of exploration used by this Group is to report the current feelings that each member experience. Bearing this approach in mind it is possible here to have a look at the psycho-philosophical system which demands that 'I' should strive to become aware of the moment of experience as it occurs, and in the light of this 'fresh' knowledge, re-interpret the assumption that 'I' is making about the world. In essence that is the Existentialist approach. The threat of potential destruction and chaos is eminent in the group situation, since within it we are locked in the feeling of members to each other, their loves, their hates, their striving for power and their potentialities for destruction. As each individual becomes aware of group situation, and as he discovers that this in turn mirrors his own life, chaos becomes potential not only externally, but internally also. The conflict of personal emotions which surround individual roles and have indicated some of the conditions under which an existing role can be threatened, together with the emotional consequences.

Attention can now be directed to roles in Institutions. Institutions means a complex organisation in which individual have relationships to each other of a semipermananet kind. These relationships enable the institution as a whole to perform in community. The roles are determined to a greater degree by the demands of the work that these institutions do. It can be seen that every Institution must have means whereby new members are introduced to the roles within in and are led to accept them.

Role Ambiguity

In order to perform our jobs well in an Organisation, we have to have a certain amount of information regarding what we are expected to do and what not to do. We need to know our rights, obligations and privileges and essentially our areas of freedom. The role ambiguity is generally stressful for people. There are individual differences in how much ambiguity a person can tolerate. Persons with a high need for structure and a low tolerance for ambiguity are more likely to experience job related tension than person low on their needs when they are faced with ambiguity in their work. Following factors can summarise, role ambiguity :

(*a*) Psychological strains and dissatisfaction

(*b*) Underutilisation of human resources

(*c*) Feeling to cope with the organisational Environment.

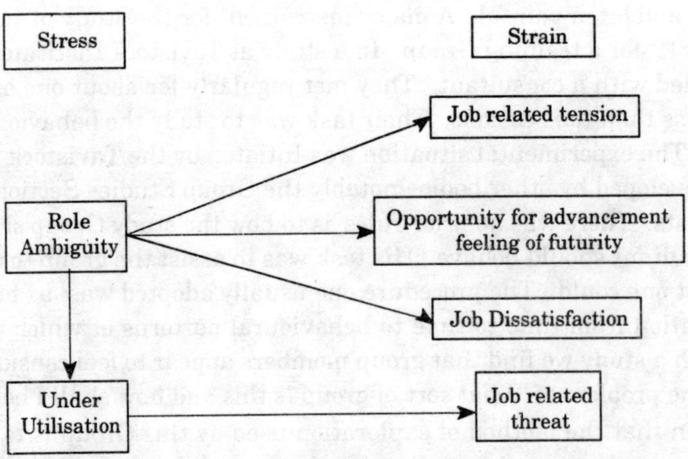

Fig. 40.1.

The role ambiguity reflects a situation where there is a lack of information. Role conflict reflects a situation where the information arouses conflict. The following are items about the conflicts people experience :

(*a*) Being born by conflicting demands.
(*b*) The pressure of having to get along with people.
(*c*) Difficulties in handling subordinates secretaries and others.
(*d*) Difference of opinion between oneself and one's superiors.

We also find that the personality of the individual is an important determinant of how he reacts to role conflict. Specifically, role conflict produces greater job related tension, introverts than in extroverts. The finding show that introverts are less social, that is they enjoy interaction with other persons less than extroverts and they are more independent than extroverts. Thus it may be that the introverts has more difficulty in coping with conflict because it occurs is social situations and threatens his independence. Similar, findings also appear for flexible people who show greater job related tension under conditions of conflict than do rigid individuals. The flexible people are characterised by their tendency to blame themselves when things go wrong while rigid people tend to centeralise blame and assume that the fault lies within the environment.

Although conflicting role pressures have their source in organisational variables such as cunflicting goals of different departments, they have their expression in the demands which are made on a person. When these demands conflict at least one of them must be rejected or ignored. It would not be surprising if such a rejection were resented and taken personally. Studies have revealed that role conflict is related to physiological strain. Finding from the studies of role conflict are summarised in figure.

The figure shows that his form of job stress produces a variety of psychological strains, but these effects of stress on strain vary deepening on the personality of the individual and his relationship with others in the Organisation.

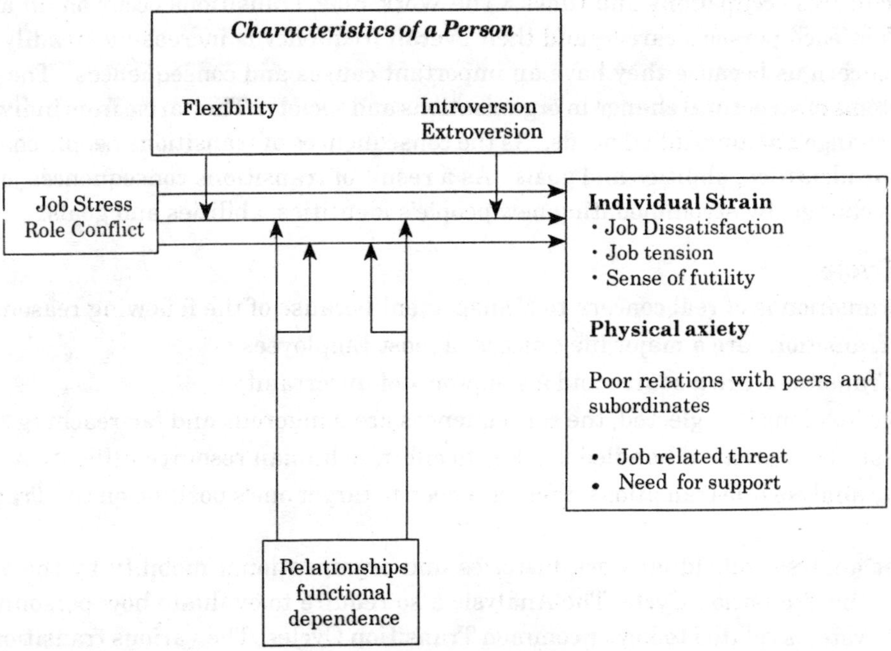

Fig. 40.2. Form of Job Stress.

The several studies on the subject have revealed that the various forms of workload produce at least nine different kinds of psychological and physiological strain in the individual. A summary of the effects of quantitative and qualitative overload in various forms of individual strain is given in Fig. 40.3.

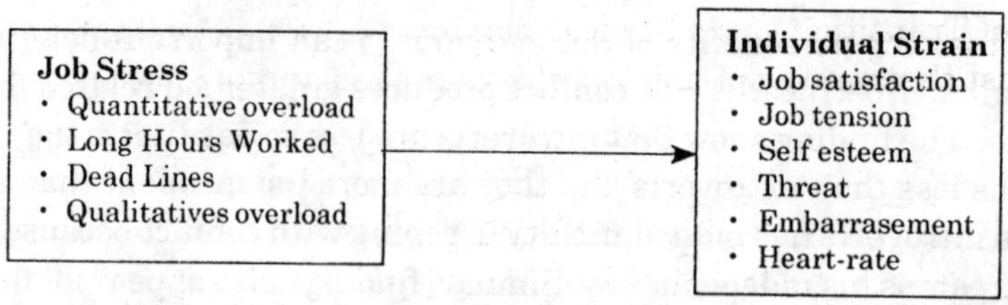

Fig. 40.3.

Poor relations with other members of an organisation may be precipitated by conditions of ambiguity and conditions where adequate information regarding roles and responsibilities and information necessary to carry them out are not provided. The poor interpersonal relations generate dissatisfactions with the job and feelings of threat. Psychologists and social scientists have paid a good deal of attention over the last twenty years to the quality of working relations. Many Organisation theorists have suggested that good relations between organisation members can be a key factor in improving organisational health.

Work Role Transition

Work Role Transition is the movement between jobs, status change, or major alteration in work role requirements. Work Role Transitions are widespread over the number of jobs to be found in all cultures occupations and times. The Work Role Transitions occur on an average several times in each person's career, and their overall frequency is increasing steadily. Such transitions concern us because they have an important causes and consequences. The causes are the symptoms of structural change in organisations and society. They arise from individual's self-directed change and unfulfilled needs. As the consequences of transitions people change by adjusting their identities, abilities and goals. As a result of transitions consequences jobs and organisations change, by accommodating new people's identities, abilities and goals.

Transition Cycle

The job transition is of real concern to Management because of the following reasons :

(*a*) Role Transitions are a major life concern of most Employees

(*b*) Role Transitions are a source and a symptoms of uncertainty

(*c*) Role Transitions if neglected, the consequences are dangerous and far-reaching.

(*d*) The Role Transitions if handled is a key to effective human resource utilization.

In order to analyse role transitions, there is a need to target one's position on the Transition Cycle.

One must analyse individual work histories and organisational mobility by the various dimensions of the Transition Cycle. The Analysis also require to evaluate how personnel and management systems related to key or common Transition Cycles. The various transition cycle can be classified into, tasks and goals transitions, pitfalls and problems of transition cycle and strategies and remedies in the implementation of various transitions. At times, in case of certain individual's job changes are so fast that one is not able to achieve the maximum effectiveness position. The Transition Cycle basically consists of four phases, preparation, encounter, adjustment and stabilisation. Each of these phases have been discussed in the enclosed diagram for tasks and goals, pitfalls and problems and strategies and remedies. Personal development is at each stage of Transition Cycle but it is maximum at the Adjustment stage. At times job changes are so fast that one is not able to achieve the maximum effectiveness position.

The Transition Cycle

Tasks and Goals

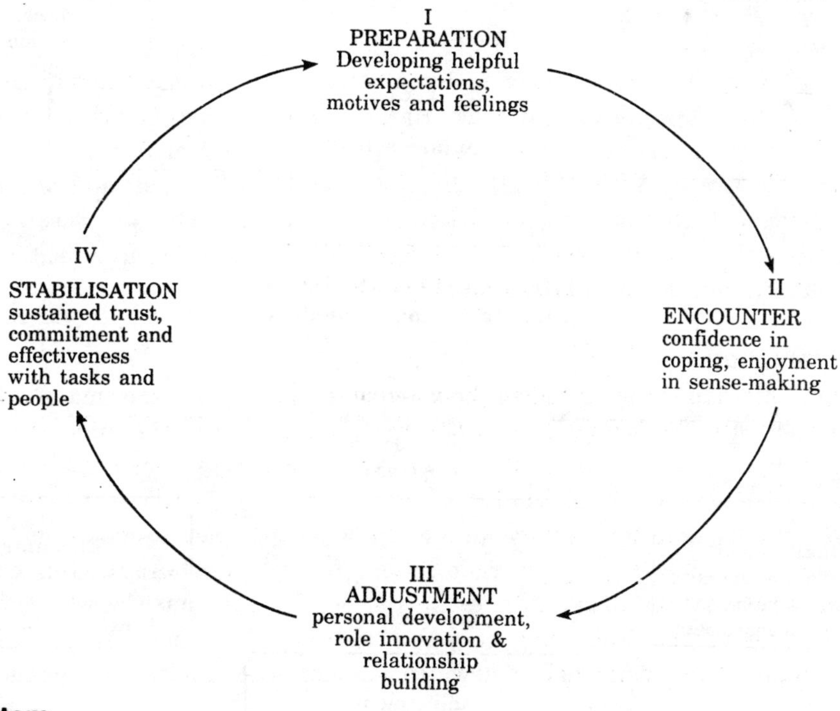

Work System

There are multiple inter-linkages among the work system, the group, the individual, the organisation and the society at large. It is necessary to look into the institution of work and examine the nature of interlinkages between work and some aspects of socio-cultural, psychological and socio-economic areas remain very much in the forefront of workers at least at par with family interests and decidedly more prominent than other segments of their lives. What happens at work tends to determine what can and does happen in the areas of family life education, leisure ?

Work Organisations

Work organisations are open system and do not operate in isolation. Work organisations operate on a high level of interaction through multiple linkages with other systems. Work organisations consist of semi-autonomous groups each of which is engaged in the performance of a total task. Thus, there is a shift from one-man-one-job principle to one-group-one-task where every group enjoys varying degrees of autonomy so that members can be regulated and coordinated in their own activities.

THE TRANSITION CYCLE
Pitfalls and Problems

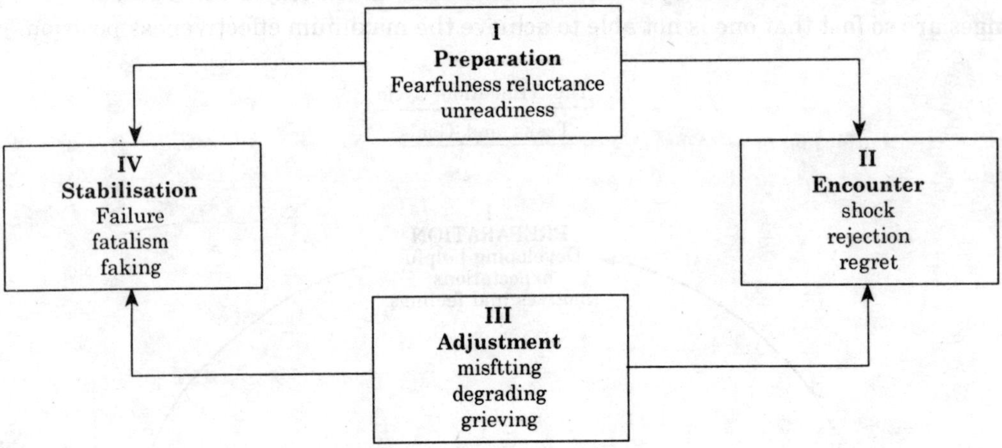

THE TRANSITION CYCLE
Strategies and Remedies

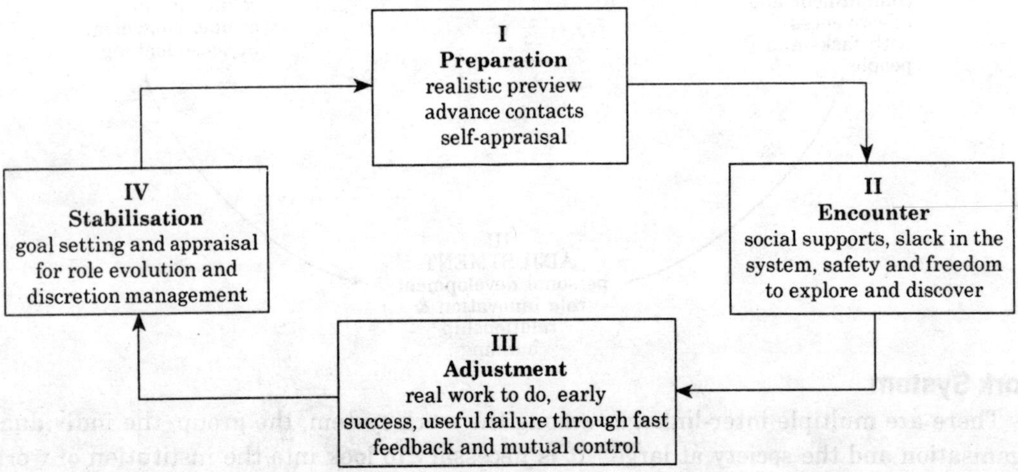

Almost every day, we see a number of advertisement in the local newspapers with dozens of them appearing for various jobs with different specialisations and for various categories of people. Only 5% of these advertisement describe the work required to be done. The managers of today still do not understand the exact meaning of the term work. Managers have not reached the stage where they may talk about work in an objective term. By work they understand nothing more than the description of the people who do the work. Their normal qualifications are managerial work, technical work, financial and accounting work, skilled and unskilled work, commercial and routine work and so on.

The above terms are really more than the description of the person who does the work rather the state of mind while working on the description of the work. The study of management is not merely the study of man involved but understanding of his character, abilities, motivation, objectives, environment and behaviour. The study should involve the structure of roles, the work content of these roles, the relationship among roles and the manner in which the roles are structured. The work content of the roles should be so adopted to match the environment in which a company operates. It is not enough to study the psychological aspects of work but it is important to understand how work is outlined or covered by organisational policies. As we descend in the organisational hierarchy, we find that every individual is responsible for some sort of work connected with the basic functions and the organisational objectives. In other words, work can be objectively, distinguishably described in terms of prescribed and discretionary contents. Thus work can be defined by the occupant's role which he must play to avoid a charge of negligence or in subordination. Discretionary work is composed of all those decisions that we are not only authorised to make but also are held responsible for making.

Role of Work is Life

It is an essential part of man's life. It is that part of his life which gives him status and binds him to society. Each one of us like our work. Whenever we complain of work, it is because of psychological and social conditions of the work rather something in the work. Work is a social activity. Unemployment is a very relative incentive. Unemployment or without work means, man is cut off from the society. To work is to live and, therefore, those who exert their activities of body and mind for the means to live are working. It is difficult to imagine the situation of a man with fortune but without work. Work is a social activity with two main functions of producing the things required by society and binding the individual into a pattern of relationship from which society is built. *The motives of working cannot be assigned only to economic needs. Men continue to work even when they have no need for material goods, even when their economic security and that of their children is assured. It is because the rewards they get from work are social, such as respect and admiration from their followmen. Work is an instrument for satisfying ego by gaining power and exerting it over others. Work provides fellowship and social life.* Work is a source of status both formal and informal. The information material, social rewards which industry has in its power to grant are really valuable. The importance of work can be judged by an example of a man who works hard in his active life and its one or two years after retirement due to sheer misery and lack of things to occupy his mind. It has also been observed that people do not like to be retired and tend to take up jobs of lesser designation and with lesser salary. Money is not that important a factor because it has been observed that workers who have been given a job with higher pay, request at times to return to their old job with much lower wages. We know that if workers are treated as human beings, they will behave like that and if they are treated as unwilling, uninterested and slaves they will act likewise. What work means to a worker can be well understood if we talk to an unemployed father or husband. What job means to a worker can be understood only by an unemployed job seeker. The position in the house and control over the children depends to a greater extent on the job. *The job controls the life of an individual. The greatest evil of an unemployment is that it makes man seem useless, unwanted and a bad citizen.*

Work Environment

The working environment, material and phycological condition of the work have little or no direct relationship to good morale. In London in a slaughter house pigs were killed and there was a small room in which the internal organs were sorted out and washed prior to utilising them for other purposes. The room was below the ground level with very little illumination and high dampness. The room was normally covered with blood, water and the contents of the animal's intestines which smelt collectively and was quite unpleasant to the casual visitor. Under these surroundings six girls were working happily and spending the day. A medical officer who joined this factory was shocked to see the working conditions and recommended that the girls be replaced by men and suggested the transfer of girls to other department as it was not possible to carryout an immediate improvement of working conditions. These recommendations aroused a strong protest from the girls and recommendation had to be withdrawn. It was because these girls had formed a happy working group and were so friendly with each other that they were of the opinion that they were engaged in a skilled job under the control of a good supervisor who allowed them to take their own time and method to work and praised them judiciously.

It was also found that in the same factory in an other department which was well illuminated and was in better conditions and where hundreds of other girls worked and grumbled over their job. *Needless to say that bad working condition is of utmost importance and influence health and happiness but there is no doubt that good physical conditions may co-exist with bad morale and bad conditions with good morale. Good physical conditions of work may increase morale but they will be insufficient in themselves to create it.*

Studies on Work System

There are evidences that workers react negatively to work which is on routine nature and without challenge. Challengeless bureaucratic jobs inhibit the normal development of human personality and leads to poor mental health, apathy and even delusion. It is because of this that workers prefer highly structured work. Workers feeling lack of interest in the job, lack of autonomy and control and lack of challenge in their job, attempt to redirect their potential and energies to other activities of the job. It has been observed that the whole culture may adjust to the job opportunities which calls for little challenge and offers no initiative. Large number of workers have manifested their feelings, attitudes and behaviour that signify unsatisfactory life adjustment in the absence of a meaningful job. Their responses reveal feelings of inadequncy, low self-esteem, anxiety, hostility, dissatisfaction and low personal morale. It has also been observed during the studies that where the technical and social Organisation of work offer more freedom or discretion in methods, pace or schedule or frequent inter-action with fellow-workers, then work attachment will be strong and work will be closely integrated with the rest of life.

Michael Maccoby identified the dissatisfied class of workers and termed them as routine workers. Although these are the workers (men or women) who work in the factory only. Their work in the factories is to supplement their earnings. These routine workers are the most dissatisfied with the factory work. These workers are of independent and democratic character who are to fit into a mechanistic and hierarchial structure where he or she is not respected as an equal. These workers have a general complaint about the factory work, *i.e.* work does not allow them autonomy. They do not have enough time to do a good job and their job does not offer enough to think. They feel the work is too repetitive and fast paced.

We know from the concept of scientific management, that an individual has no choice but to accept the fact that man's specific contribution is always to perform many activities, to integrated, plan, control measure and judge. The individual operations need to be analysed, studied and improved. But human resources will be utilized productively if a job is being performed out of the operations. It is the job only which integrated the workman's specific qualities. Specific management despite all its efforts could not succeed in solving the problem of managing, worker and work. Scientific management have two blind spots-engineering and philosophical. We must analyse work into its simplest constituent motions. We must also organise it as a series of individual motions as carried out by an individual worker.

Scientific management purports to organise human work without an attempt to verify the assumption, that the human being is not a cog in the wheel. There are no two opinions that human beings are not the 'cog in the wheel' rather associated with feelings, emotions, beliefs, attitudes and ideas beside motivation and morale. In other words, we have to see how best to organise people to do their work. Scientific management had a wrong belief their people work best if organised like machines, *i.e.,* when linked in series. It is not only a wrong belief but it is quite dis-integrating to the concept of human relation. People work well when working either as an individual or as a team. The human beings work in groups and form groups to work. No matter how the group is formed the focus is on work only. Group relation influences the work and the work is turn influences the personal relationship within the group. *This means that work must always be organised in such a manner that whatever strength, initiative, responsibility, competence there is in an individual, it becomes a source of strength for the entire group. In other words, group and individual must be brought into harmony in the Organisation of work. In developing countries, it is not only technology that has been borrowed but also the associated Organisation of work which do not necessary fit within the prevailing socio-cultural framework.* During the last one decade or so there had been a qualitative change in the nature of work force particularly in those industries where skill requirements are high. Most workers in these industries are young, educated and have relatively high level of aspiration than their counterparts of older generation. The young workers look for opportunities to utilise and develop their potentialities. They look for opportunities to utilise and develop their potentialities. They look for intrinsic factors in their work. *The near absence of work culture among practically all levels of employed workforce has been yet another important characteristic of the prevailing socio-culture reality. Loss of interest in one's work and consequent apathetic response to diverse situations is not confined to blue collar workforce only but manifestations of these can be seen among all sections and in all sectors including the educational institutions.*

41

Job Evaluation and Job Satisfaction

Introduction

Remuneration to employees is one of the most important aspects of employer-employees relations. It is a pre-requisite to sound industrial relations and for good industrial relations each employee should (*i*) receive sufficient remuneration in the form of wages or salaries and perquisites to sustain himself and his dependents and (*ii*) feel satisfied with the relationship between his wage and the wages of other people performing the same class of the work in some other organisation in the same industry.

The primary objective of wage and salary administration programme is that each employee should be equitably compensated for the services rendered by him to the enterprise because of the nature of the job, type of the job and effectiveness of the job.

These factors are closely related to Job Evaluation and the Performance Appraisal. Generally, wage payments within the organisation are determined by a flow of events including job analysis, job descriptions and specifications, job evaluation, surveys of wages and salaries, analysis of relevant organisational problems, minimum wages law, structuring of wages, establishing rules for administering wages and finally wage payments to individuals. This sequence has been shown in Fig. 41.1.

The most important decision on compensation for a job usually involves comparison of one job to other job, within the organisation or to similar jobs in other organisations. The first comparison is made with the help of job evaluation and the later compression is made through the use of wage and salary surveys to determine the going wages or salary for a position.

JOB EVALUATION

There are different methods used to establish wage rate for a job which range from subjective initiative methods to highly objective quantified methods. Job evaluation is an orderly and systematic technique which aims at determining the worth of job. In other words, it is a formal system of determining the basic compensation of jobs.

The basic object of job evaluation is to ascertain the relative worth of each job through an objective evaluation so that relative remuneration may be fixed for different jobs. Job evaluation may be defined as an attempt to determine and compared the demands which the normal performance of particular jobs make on normal workers, without taking into account the individual abilities or performance of the workers concerned.

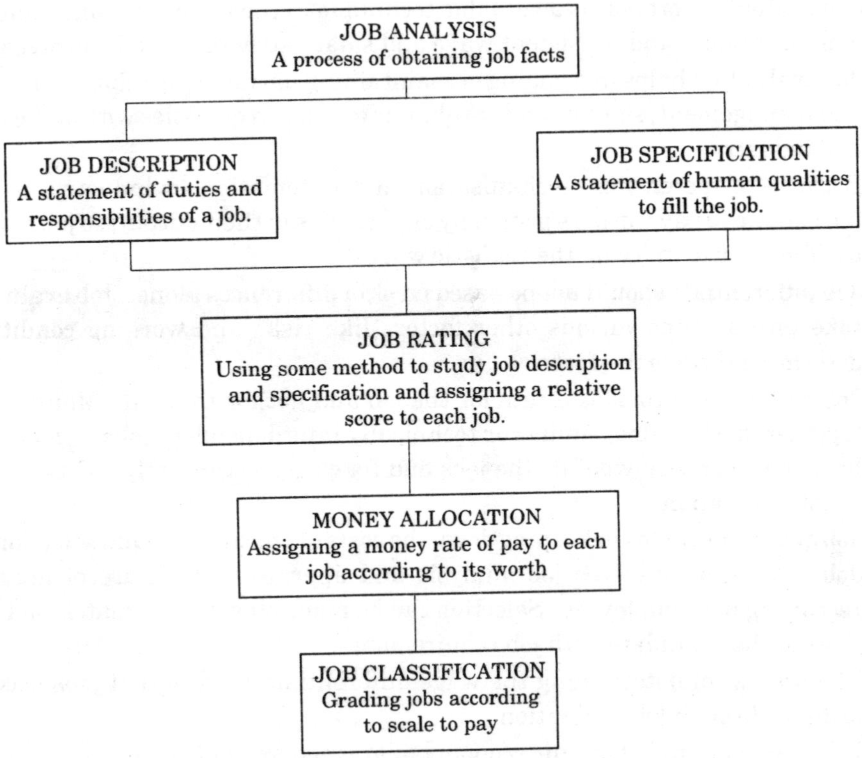

Fig. 41.1. Process of Job Evaluation.

Job evaluation rates the job and not the man. It takes into account the demands of the job in terms of efforts and abilities but it does not take into account the individual abilities and efforts, which may of course be taken into consideration and reflected in the worker's earnings under a system of payment by results or by merit rating.

Job evaluation is a systematic procedure for determining the relative worth of jobs. Thus once the worth of jobs is determined, it becomes easier to fix the wage structure that will be fair and equitable. Thus it is an important tool in fixing the scales of wages for different grades of jobs. Job evaluation is the process of analysis and assessment of jobs to ascertain in a systematic way their relative worth using assessment as the basis for a balanced wage structure. Job evaluation is something more than job analysis, it is in no way concerned with calculation of job's worth. It is only concerned with the collection of data concerning a particular job. Job evaluation follows the job analysis which provides the basic data to be evaluated. Job evaluation aims at measuring the value of job descriptions and job specifications. When the value of job descriptions are determined, they may be translated in terms of money according to some basis to have a balanced wage structure in the organisation. The total wage structure consists of different scales of wages or pay which will lead to classification of wages. Thus the process of job evaluation starts from job analysis and ends with the classification of jobs according to their worth.

WHY JOB EVALUATION

The reasons for growing interest in job evaluation in recent times are discussed below :

(*a*) Job evaluation process is a valuable technique in the hands of management by which a more rational and consistent wage and salary structure can be evolved.

(*b*) Job evaluation helps in bringing or maintaining harmonious relations between labour and management, since it tends to eliminate wage in qualities within the organisation and industry.

(*c*) Because of increasing mechanisation and automation in industry, it has become unrealistic to pay workers primarily on the basis of their output; so job evaluation will be of much use in fixing the realistic wages.

(*d*) Job differentials should not be based on skill differences alone. Job evaluation should take into account various other factors like risks and working conditions also to determine the worth of jobs.

(*e*) Job evaluation provides a rate for the job and not for the man. Many workers work together on the same, similar or technically interdependent jobs. An attempt should be made to precisely define the jobs and fix wages accordingly. This is possible only by job evaluation.

(*f*) Job evaluation helps in keeping down the costs of recruitment and selection of workers. Job evaluation involves job analysis and appraisal which are of great use while recruiting new employees. Selection can be made objective by matching the qualifications of the candidate with job requirements.

(*g*) The process of determining the wage differentials for different jobs becomes standardised through job evaluation.

(*h*) It is necessary in a dynamic economy to arrange for continuous job evaluation.

It must be noted that those who are doing the evaluation must rate the job and not the employee. In deciding how much money a particular job is worth, there is always a temptation to be influenced in one's judgment by the qualifications and caliber of the individual who is present by performing the job. But he may be either over or under-qualified; so the job evaluator should not commit the error of rating the individuals. The clear and accurate job descriptions and specifications must be available to provide data concerning the factors to be measured. Whenever possible, the pooled or combined judgements of several persons should be employed in evaluating jobs. Job evaluation is a systematic, orderly, and logical way of setting the rates of wages within a firm. However, it is not the exact measurement, but it is grading or rating. A decision must be made concerning what group of jobs are to be covered by a evaluation system.

FACTORS RESPONSIBLE FOR JOB EVALUATION

As discussed earlier job evaluation involves the evaluation of various jobs in terms of certain factors. The important factors to be considered under job evaluation may be grouped under the following heads :

(*a*) Skill,

(*b*) Experience,

(*c*) Efforts and initiative,

(*d*) Responsibility to be undertaken,

(*e*) Working environments, and

(*f*) Supervision needed.

In fact, there is no standard classification of factors to be considered under job evaluation. In general, the more difficult the job, the more it is worth. The more scarce the labour supply and higher the demand, the more a job is worth. The more skill, education and responsibility required in a job, the more it is worth. These generalisations usually hold true for most jobs and serve as indicators of what the level of pay should be. Therefore, several systems of job evaluation have been developed which take into account the above mentioned factors either directly or indirectly.

Job Evaluation Methods

There are four types of job evaluation methods. These can be divided into two categories :

(*a*) Non-quantitative methods

- Ranking or job comparison
- Grading or job classification

(*b*) Qualitative methods

- Point
- Factor comparison

The first category covers the sample methods which apparently make no use of detailed job factors. But they remain in the minds of the evaluators and thus affect the results. The job is treated as a whole, and job descriptions rather than job specification are often utilised. But the methods under the second category use a detailed approach. Job factors are selected and measured but job specifications are definitely given consideration. Let us discuss these methods.

Ranking Method

The job ranking method is the simplest of all the methods. A committee of several executives is constituted, which evaluates the job descriptions and ranks them in order of importance beginning with the most important job to the least important job in the organisation. No specific factors are selected for consideration.

The rank order of the job is finally determined by averaging the respective rankings of all committee members. If the committee consists of ten persons and the jobs are ranked on three occasions, the final ranking would be calculated on the basis of thirty estimates.

To establish the rates of pay for these specific jobs, the rates of pay can be associated with those jobs in the rank order. Presumably the jobs already have wage rates attached to them, the ranking system is used to judge whether these are equitable. By arranging the jobs is an array such as given above, necessary adjustments can be made in wage rates to current any apparent discrepancy. Ranking method is suitable for organisations of relatively small size. If the size of the organisation is relatively small the job rates will be in a better position to group up the job descriptions without experiencing much difficulty. This method is very simple and since the raters are fully familiar with the job and worker also understands the process the installation of this system is not a difficult task. However, the ranking method has serious limitations that it limits objective judgement which is required to determine the relation and position of job in the rank order. In addition, judgement is needed in determining what the pay rates should be, since a statistical method of interpolation is not employed. If the job descriptions are not accurate serious errors in ranking can occur. There will be arbitrary ranking which may result in differences in similar jobs which may be resented by the employees.

Grading Method

This method is considered to be an improvement over ranking method in that a predetermined scale of values is provided. This method involves the establishment of job classes or grades. The evaluation committee goes through each job descriptions and carefully weights it in the light of certain factors like skill, experience, etc. In this way, it assignees each job to a particular grade or class. For each grade or class, there is different rate of wage.

The main disadvantage of the grading method is that it requires multiple system, for different types of jobs *e.g.*, description of office jobs differ widely from those of production jobs. Moreover, the installation of this method is not appropriate for big organisations.

Difficulties encountered with the use of this method of job evaluation result in the development of other plans which are based upon the principle of breaking jobs into their components or factors and evaluating them in terms of those components or factors.

Table 41.1
GRADING OF JOB

Unskilled	The jobs in this group are mostly clerical in character, require accuracy and dependability, but no extended training.
Skill	The jobs in this group are mostly clerical in character, require training of hand or mind.
Routine	The jobs in this group call for ability to classify work and apply established procedures to its accomplishment.
Creative	The position of this group are those of a creative character.
Executive	The positions of this group are those of department manager.
Administrative	The positions of this group involve responsibilities of large magnitude or over all character or for mixed functional division.
Policy	The positions of this group are those of the policy makers of the company such as General Managers and Directors, or the Board of Directors.

Point Method

This is the most widely used method of job evaluation. This method, alongwith factor comparison method, involves a more detailed, quantitative and analytical approach to the measurement of job worth. Under this method, a quantitative evaluation of different jobs in terms of various factors is made. Maximum point values are assigned to each of the job factors required to be considered. Then each job is awarded points for each of the factors. The wage level appropriate for each job is fixed on the basis of total points scored by it.

The point system is more analytical in approach and deals with various job factors. A job factor is a specific requirement levied upon the job holder which he must contribute, assume or endure. The major factors are : skill, efforts, responsibility and working conditions. These factors or points are later converted into money value. The procedure for designing of 'Point Method' is discussed below :

(*a*) Determine the type of jobs to be evaluated.

(*b*) Determine the factor to be used in this method, and define them properly.

(*c*) Determine the number of degrees to be allocated to each factor and prepare a suitable definition of each.

(*d*) Assign points to each degree of each factor.

(*e*) Select a certain number of key jobs, say 10-15, and evaluate each applying the previous steps.

(*a*) **Jobs to be Evaluated.** The jobs in any organisation will range from the top executive down to a clerk each involving different skill like -- conceptual, human and technical. There may be some unskilled jobs also. There should be separate evaluation programme for executives, professional, skilled, semi-skilled and unskilled employees. Executives and others on responsible jobs are more liable to be influenced by the ambition, character, personality, dependability and other less tangible traits and this makes it difficult to write adequate job descriptions and specifications. But such qualities are not so important in case of clerical and shop floor jobs. So there is a psychological disadvantage in using this method to evaluate the jobs of both groups since the former group requires a degree of managerial skills and the latter group requires manual skills in greater degree.

(*b*) **Number of Factors to be Used.** It is very difficult to lay down the exact number of factors which should be used for evaluating a job. But there should be sufficient number of factors to evaluate all aspects of the jobs. The number of factors will depend upon the nature of the job. So sufficient number of factors relating to the job under review should be considered according to the need of the organisation and the type of job.

(*c*) **Determination of Degree.** Each factor of job evaluation should further be subdivided into degrees. The point method generally uses four to six degrees for each factor. It is advisable to use even number of degrees in the development of point method and the same number of degree should be used for each factor in order to maintain consistency in the job evaluation plan.

(*d*) **Allocation of Points to Degrees.** For assigning points to the degrees a committee may be appointed to determine the weights of the factors in terms of percentage and estimating what percentage should be allocated to each factor. The committee will determine how 100% can be appointed among the various factors. The percentage that is assigned to each factor will become the number of points for the first degree of each factor. In order to determine the number of points to be allocated to succeeding degrees of each factor, it is necessary to extend the points assigned to the first degree in an arithmetic progression as shown in the table on next page.

(*e*) **Definition of Factors.** After the selection of factors to be used, they should be properly defined and should be put in writing so that the person using these may have the clear idea. Various definitions should be positive statements and should be expressed in simple and unambiguous language.

Education

This factor gives the extent of educational background required by an individual working on the job perform satisfactorily. The various degrees to each factor can be defined as follows :

First Degree. Ability to read, write and follow simple written or oral instructions.

Second Degree. Basic school education or equivalent to do small arithmetical calculations involving adding, subtracting dividing and multiplying of decimals and fractions.

Table 41.2. ALLOCATION OF POINTS OF DEGREES

		Degree of Points					
S.No.	*Factor*	*First*	*Second*	*Third*	*Fourth*	*Fifty*	*Sixth*
1.	Education	25	50	75	100	125	150
2.	Training	10	20	30	40	50	60
3.	Experience	10	20	30	40	50	60
4.	Mental efforts	12	24	36	48	60	72
5.	Physical efforts	12	24	36	48	60	72
6.	Visual attention	8	16	24	32	40	60
7.	Initiative	6	12	18	24	30	36
8.	Responsibility	6	12	18	24	30	36
9.	Working conditions	5	10	15	20	25	30
10.	Physical hazards	5	10	15	20	25	30

Third Degree. High School Intermediate education. Required knowledge of elementary accounting or general knowledge of workshop practice and manufacturing methods.

Fourth Degree. Graduate examination. Required ability to understand and perform work requiring general engineering principles, commercial theory; principles of advanced drafting, knowledge of general accounting, fundamentals and complicated workshop procedures and processes, etc.

Fifth Degree. Post-graduation. Required ability to understand and perform work of a specialised or technical nature. Knowledge of finance, business administration, chemistry, physics, journalism or any other technical or specialised field.

Sixth Degree. Post-graduation. Research experience in any technical or specialised field.

Similarly on the same basis the factors and degree can be well defined. The number of factors and degrees can be determined depending upon the job. Therefore, point method of job evaluation is more effective because even the major factors are sub-divided which ensures accuracy of evaluation. The possibility of in accuracy of job evaluation is likely to arise if the predetermined point values do not exhibit true values. If this is so, this initial determination of points value may lead to further inaccuracies.

Factor Comparison Method

The factor comparison method of job evaluation determine the relative rank of the jobs to be evaluated in relation to monetary scale. This method is often used for evaluating white-collar professional and managerial positions, although it is equally suitable for grading others as well. It is essentially a combination of the ranking and point systems. Like rank order method, it rates job by comparing one job with another and like the point system it is more analytical in the sense of subdividing jobs into comparable factors. Final ratings are expressed in terms of numbers.

In this method five factors are generally evaluated for each job. These are comparatively fewer than the point system but is nevertheless sufficient, because each factor is defined broadly. The five factors which are customarily used are : mental requirements, skill, physical requirements, responsibilities and working conditions. The evaluation of job under this method consists of the following steps.

(*a*) Select the factors and define them clearly.

(*b*) Select the key jobs. Key jobs serves as standard against which all other jobs are compared. A key job is one whose content has become stablized over period of time and whose wage rate is considered to be presently correct by the management and the union.

(*c*) Allocated wage for each key job to different factors.

(*d*) Develop a job comparison scale and insert key jobs in them. When all of the key jobs have been evaluated and wages allocated in this manner, a job comparison scale can be constructed.

(*e*) Evaluate the job in question factor by factor, in relation to key jobs on job comparison scale. Then each job is to be evalulated and compared to other jobs in terms of each factor.

(*f*) Design, adjust and operate the wage structure.

The advocates of factors comparison method point out that it usually results in more accurate job evaluation because it is relatively more objective. It is flexible also and has no upper limit on the rating that job may receive on a factor. The point system does have a ceiling on the factors. Another advantage of this method is that it utilises a few factors and thereby reduces the likelihood of overlap. The procedure of rating new jobs of comparing with other standard or key jobs is logical and not too difficult to accomplish.

The method suffers from certain limitations also. The content and the value of these jobs may change over a period of time and this will lead to future errors. It is very expensive system of job evaluation because experts have to be appointed particularly in selecting weights which are based on actual analysis. Since the method is complicated, an average worker cannot understand this system.

Determining the Factors to be Used

The major compression method of job evaluation requires five critical factors. All these five factors should be explicitly defined to facilitate subsequent evaluation.

(*i*) **Mental Requirements**

(*a*) Inherent mental traits such a intelligence, memory, reasoning, ability to get along with the people and ability to express.

(*b*) Acquired education.

(*c*) Acquired specialisations of education, specialised knowledge.

(*ii*) **Skill Requirements**

(*a*) Acquired facility in muscular co-ordination, assembling, sorting and dexerity of fingers.

(*b*) Acquired job knowledge for the performance of job.

(*iii*) **Physical Requirements**

(*a*) Physical effort such as climbing, walking, pulling, lifting etc.

(*b*) Physical status such as age, height, weight, sex, strength, eyesight, etc.

(*iv*) **Responsibility Towards**

(*a*) Raw materials, processed materials, tools, equipments, and property.

(*b*) Money, securities, raw materials, tools equipments, etc.

(*c*) Profit or loss.

(*d*) Supervision.

(*v*) **Working Conditions**

(*a*) Atmosphere, ventilation, illumination, noise, congestion etc.

(*b*) Hazard from the work and its surroundings.

(*c*) Hours of work.

Selecting the Key Jobs

The first step by means of which jobs are evaluated under the factor comparison method is to select a group of key jobs.

The key jobs so selected should range from the lowest paid to the highest. All key jobs should be exact and well understood and no job should be included in the key position if there is a disagreement about the existing rate. After the key jobs have been selected each member of the committee should be furnished with a complete description of each of the key job.

In order to be familiar with the key jobs, the entire committee might visit and observe the jobs concerned to assure agreement and consistency of interpretation. Each member of the committee will rank each of the jobs in terms of critical factors. For instance, in case of working conditions rank lowest of the job which has the most agreeable and the least hazardous conditions and highest the rank number to that job involving the most disagreeable and the most hazardous conditions. After the members have ranked the key jobs by factors, the chairman of the committee will analyse the returns statistically to determine any misunderstanding regarding the job content, job conditions, job requirements and definitions.

The above process should be repeated until the members of the committee have ranked all the key jobs at three different times before determining the final ranking for the key jobs. Disagreement in ranking is decided by majority vote of the committee. The next step is to apportion the average rate currently being paid to the employees working on each key job among the five factors. The chairman of the committee will then make a statistical analysis of the results and will request the committee members to approtion the average rates by factors for 3 to 4 times at different intervals. The chairman will then average the estimates and report them to the wage administrator.

Applicability

The factor comparison system is frequently applied without change in basic structure to a wide range of jobs including high ranking technical and administrative position while in case of point method, the requirements of more objective definitions of factors weighing make it necessary to restrict the range of job to which that method should be applied. The factor comparison method has decided advantage over the point system because of its adaptability to a wide range of jobs. Both the factor comparison and point methods of job evaluation are limited with respect to the range of jobs that can be effectively evaluated. In spite of the fact that successful results may be achieved through the use of either method the most common question that always comes to mind is, which method should be used. In fact, no definite answer can be given to this question, certainly if it is planned to retain a consultant to install a job evaluation method the wise course of action is to make the choice on the basis of the consultant's reputation and ability to produce results and to use the plane recommended by him. On the other hand, if those contemplating doing work are not experts in job evaluation, it will be found that in most cases a point method will result in the more satisfactory installation because of greater over-all simplicity and objectively.

Appralsal of Job Evaluation

Job evaluation measures the requirements for each job so that a rate can be fixed which is commensurate with job's requirements. In practice, the technique of job evaluation suffers from the following limitations :

(*a*) It lacks scientific precision because there is no standard list of factors to be considered and moreover, all factors cannot be measured accurately.

(*b*) It presumes that jobs of equal worth will be equally attractive to the employees, but it is not true in real life. If a job offers no prospects of a rise, while another job rated equal to it has bright prospects for employees, the latter will attract more people.

(*c*) There is strong feeling among the workers that individuals merit should also be rewarded ; so some kind of merit rating scheme has to be superimposed upon the evaluated rates.

(*d*) Job evaluation tends to be inflexbile. In so far as it does not give right weightage to wage rates prevalent in the industry or region as a whole.

(*e*) It says nothing about the absolute size of wage differentials appropriate to the evaluated job structure.

(*f*) The trade unions often regard job evaluation with suspicion because some of the methods, particularly point method and factor comparison system, are not easy to understand and they fear that job evaluation will go away with collective bargaining.

Though job evaluation has these limitations, it is very useful in certain circumstances. It can remove many complaints about disparities in an existing wage structure by a systematic study and assessment of the jobs. However, in job evaluation we partly guess, and partly learn from the facts that what feature of the jobs tend to raise the supply price of labour and how powerful each feature is ? For instance, the extension of education and training programmes increases the relative supply of technically qualified labour and decreases that of unqualified ; thus varying the supply price of labour. Similarly there may be so many other factors which affect the relative worth of different jobs. In that event, the same process of job evaluation applied to jobs with just the same requirements, will produce the different relative rates if the external factors are taken into account by the evaluators. The working of the local markets may also influence the wage rates. So the job evaluation process must take not only the internal factors like responsibility, skill, initiative etc., but also the external factors like demand and supply of labour, existing wave structure in the industry or the region and so on.

Establishing the Pay Structure

Whatever may be the method of job evaluation used, the ultimate objective is to ascertain the proper rates of pay for all the jobs. In other words, the job structure must be priced. Since both the ranking and job reading methods are non-quantitative and do not arrive at a number for the job rating, the procedure for conversion to emoluments is somewhat more complex and may be handled in a variety of ways. It may be better to decide upon certain key job rates that are fair and correct and then the other rates can be tabulated together with their present rates and then judgements can be made so as to rectify rates for the grades. Here the jobs are already grouped into grades ; therefore, it may be considered good to compute the arithmetic means of the present rates and let that serve as the new grade rate. These means can be adjusted by judgement to make smooth or straight line progression from grade first to the highest grade.

The factor comparison system of conversion to money value is quite simply because the method itself establishes wave directly in the rating process. But it is desirable for administrative convenience to group jobs together into pay trades. In such a situation averages of newly determined rates can be found to give a figure for each grade.

With the points obtained under the point method, a graph may be prepared by plotting difficulty points on the abscissa and existing rates o the ordinate. If the prevailing rates are reasonably fair and if the ratings of the jobs under the point method have been done carefully, the points can be expected to fall along a trend line with very little dispersion. But if the existing structure of pay is loaded with inequalities and errors, considerable dispersion will be found from the trend line. There are a number of methods available to ascertain the best fitting trend line. One is to draw a line in such a way that the same number of points fall below as above the line.

Fig. 41.2 shows a trend line which has been obtained by plotting of present wage rates against job evaluation points for hourly paid jobs. In the figure horizontal lines have been drawn through the mid point of trend line in each grade to arrive at single pay rates as shown in the following table :

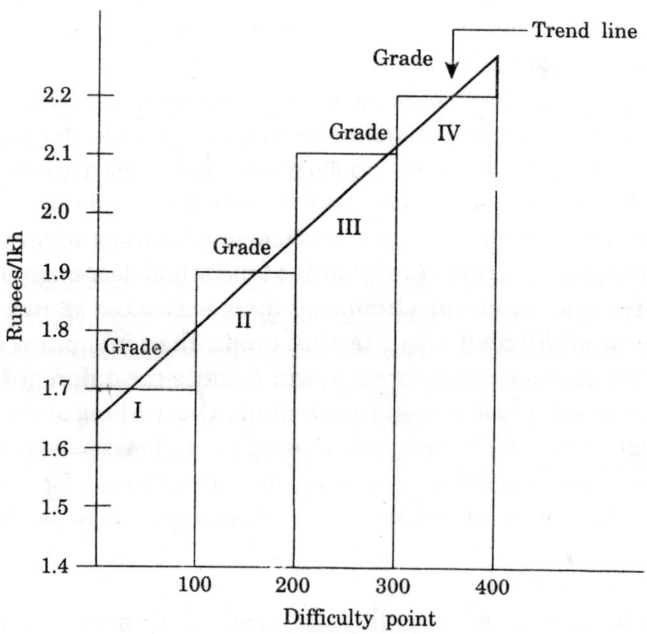

Fig. 41.2. Trend Line.

We have five wage grades and a vertical spread of around 18% from the minimum of each grade to the maximum.

Grade	*Point Range*	*Hourly Wave Rate*
1.	0-100	Rs. 1.62
2.	101-200	Rs. 1.78
3.	201-300	Rs. 1.94
4.	301-400	Rs. 2.10
5.	401-500	Rs. 2.26

The maximum rate for one grade is higher than the minimum rate of the next higher grade. This arrangement is used for white collar professional and administrative types of jobs. The overlapping range are provided to give greater flexibility for management in transferring an employee from a job in one grab to a job in adjacent grade without changing his pay. The overlapping ranges are necessary to compensate employees as they increase in skill and contribution during the years. Various elements of job evaluation have been shown in Fig. 41.2.

Wage Surveys

After the relative worth of jobs has been determined by job evaluation, the actual amounts to be paid must be determined. A major factor in taking such decisions is the survey of waGes and salaries in other enterprises in the same region and in the same industry. The purpose of waGe survey is to determine the extent to which the organisation's pay scales are like those of other enterprises in the region.

The crucial questions to be determined for carrying out a survey are :

1. The jobs to be covered,
2. The employees to be contacted and
3. The method to be used in gathering the data.

All the jobs should not be covered in the job survey because it is not possible to obtain data in regard to each. Only the crucial jobs should be covered by the job survey because these cover all ranges. The second key question concerns the organisation to be surveyed. The organisations to be covered by the survey must be elected with great care. The organiations so chosen must relate to the same industry and as far as possible must be in the same region. Finally, the method of survey must be decided. Personal interview could probably develop the most accurate responses, but this method is the most expensive one. That is why mailed questionnaires are probably the most frequently used method since it is the cheapest method. But the fear in this case is that the response may be very poor. The questionnaires should be designed very carefully so that it may derive maximum information and information so collected can afterwards be processed to determine the average rate of wages for important jobs in the industry.

Job Satisfaction

Job Structuring

Boredom on jobs are usually associated with mass production, particularly assembly lines which are widely used in the manufacture of motor cars, televisions and other consumer goods. The lack of job satisfaction for these workers has been associated with technical problems such as the poor quality of work and behavioural problem such as labour turnover, absenteeism and strikes. These problems are not confined to those working on assembly lines. There are many jobs in industry that are undertaken in poor working conditions, more repetitive and for which rewards are lower. The job designer has an important role to play in the organisation. Job design is concerned with the specification of the contents, methods and relationships of jobs in order to satisfy technological and organisational requirements, as well as the social and personal requirements of the job holder. The physiological and physical environment and also the organisational, social and personal aspects affect the prediction of man's responses to both the physical environment the physiological demands of work have been widely studied and data is available to aid the job designer.

Vroom (1964) concluded that there is a positive, although weak, association between job satisfaction and job performance. He suggests that individuals are satisfied with their jobs so long as the jobs provide what they desire and that they perform effectively to the extent that effective performance satisfies their own goals. Locke 1970, however, takes the view that successful performance is a possible cause of job satisfaction.

Job Satisfaction and Motivation

Workers' attitude and their job performance have not appeared to be strongly associated, their absenteeism, turnover and industrial action does seem to be related to their level of job satisfaction. Labour turnover is likely to be generally lower during periods of economic depression since alternatives may be less attractive than current employment, but during periods of increasing economic activity, when firms expand their labour force, much of the labour turnover occurs among fairly recent employees who fail to settle into the new environment.

Voluntary absenteeism is likely to occur when the individuals perceives the consequences expected from not working to be more attractive than those expected from working. It is possible that prolonged absence from work leads to feelings of isolation which in turn may be the cause of some job dissatisfaction. Workers' attitudes during periods of industrial unrest are considerably different from those expressed during period of normal working where job satisfaction is low there is more likelihood of strike action.

Job Changes

It was suggested that withdrawal from work in the form of high absenteeism, labour turnover and restricted output is more likely to occur where jobs are deficient in certain desired attributes.

Many organisations through redesigning jobs sought improved operating efficiency by reducing costs, improving quality and productivity, reducing specialisation and increasing flexibility. Secondary reasons related to expected behavioural outcomes such as reduced absenteeism and labour turnover as well as improved labour relations.

Some of the techniques which have been used to improve the motivational content of job along with their limitations.

Job Rotation

This rotation may be on either an obligatory or a voluntary basis. As well as increasing job interest due to changes in the environment, skill requirements and job content, it is claimed to have the advantages from the management's point of view, of increasing the operators skills and, therefore, their flexibility.

Work rotation is widely used in industry. It is particularly appropriate where work performed by a group of similar status employees is perceived to vary in difficulty and wave differences do not compensate.

The output of workers who worked on various jobs for varying time periods. They concluded that by rotating the job for assignments of operators and limiting that amount of time spent on any one job, their overall efficiency was higher than if they remained in one job.

Worker resistance may arise where work rotation is compulsory since constant changes in the pattern of social interaction may interfere with group development.

Work rotation has limited value with regard to improving the motivational content of jobs since the object of such changes is generally to increase the variety present in jobs. The number of jobs at which the worker is capable of becoming competent is limited and, therefore, the worker often only rotates between job with one section of a complete process.

Job Enlargement

This is the expansion of the job from a central task to include one or more additional and related tasks which one usually of a similar type to the original. Job enlargemnet usually involves a lengthening of the time cycle required to complete a unit of the operation and, therefore, a reduction in the degree of specialisation. The same effect can result if more frequent changes on introduced in the products being manufactured. Benefits are said to include reduced employee fatigue, reduced feelings of boredom and broadened work skills. Critics of the technique argue that the extended job is usually composed of mutliplies of the original task and that nothing is added that will contribute to increase employee job satisfaction and motivation.

Job enlargement reduces the number of workers involved and, therefore, lowers the task interdependence. The work is also placed, job enlargement by increasing the work cycle will reduce the pacing effect. In many cases where products are simply enlargement of assembly line work has led to either individual or small groups being established to carry out the process. There are limitations in the application of job enlargemnet. In situations where there is considerable task interdependence and the items being assembled are complex. It is difficult to enlarge existing jobs.

In many cases where products are simply enlargement of assembly line, work has led to either individual or small groups being established to carryout the process.

Workers react differently to repetitive work. Individual difference in intelligence, susceptibility to monotony, and age as well as past experiences and future expectations affect the worker's reaction to repetitive work.

Job Enrichment

Technique is generally applied in order to increase the motivation content of jobs by giving employees greater opportunity for achievement and recognition, horizontal job enrichment and vertical job enrichment.

Job Enrichment involves changes to the immediate work to enable the employee to exercise more control over this working speed and use more of his skills. A job enriched horizontal may, therefore, include greater autonomy. Vertical job enrichment is aimed at increasing employee involvement in the organisation providing increased participation in company policy making, increased job responsibility, increased involvment in the process and increased opportunity for training and advancement.

Both horizontal and vertical job enrichment have been applied to white and blue collar jobs. It usually has meant the delegation to the worker of some function generally thought to be managerial. In such cases the union representatives may perceive membership of problem solving teams as one of their union functions since they are elected workers representatives.

Increasing jobs responsibility may diminish job satisfaction unless the worker feels that he is capable of carrying out the duties involved

Job Restructuring

Job designer must consider many inter-connected factors. He should aim for operational efficiency. He should consider the cost of undesired behaviour which may result from extreme task specialisation. In considering the relationship between the individual and his own job, the designer must provide a satisfactory relationship between the individuals and his work group and its total task. There is a cause and effect relationship between these job characteristics and desired attributed.

Job Elements

Job has two main elements :

1. Non discretionary 2. Discretionary

As we go up in the organisational hierarchy the discretionary element increases. Individuals are normally interested to avoid for discretionary element of the job. The ideal method may be 'Time Span Discretion.' The Time Span Discretion for two jobs may be same but the skill invoved may be much more, for example skill involved for a 'Bus driver' is far less as compared to an 'Aircraft Pilot'. All jobs are having three major activities which can be put into a model as shown in the Fig. 41.3.

Role

It is the pillar of the organisation. It is made of job requirement, job expectation, job experience and job performance. When job requirement (including some sanctions) becomes unclear in an organisation. Every individual has problem with the role. The relationship of various elements of role *viz.* Job requirement ; job expectation, job experience and job performance and their inter--relationship is shown in Fig. 41.4.

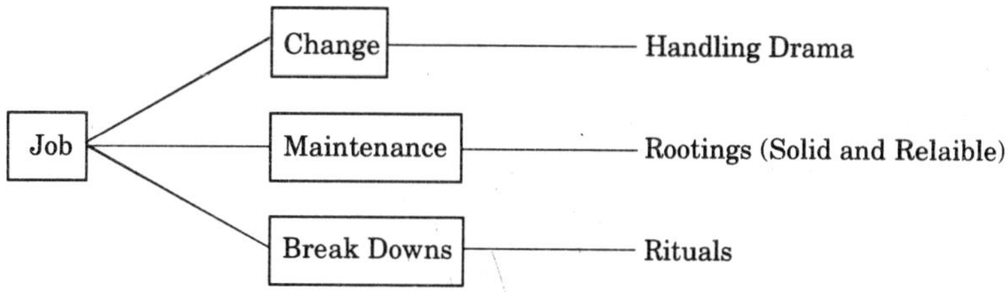

Fig. 41.3. Job Activities

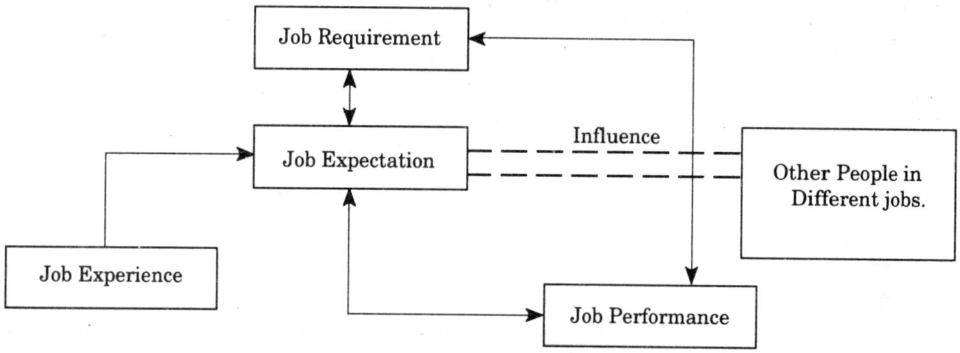

Fig. 41.4. Various Elements of Role

Job Design

Job Design is concerned with specification of the content methods and relationship of jobs. In order to satisfy technological and organisational requirements as well as the social and personal requirements of the job holder. Job design is related with phycological and physical involvement beside organisational, social and personal aspects. According to Vroom, (1964) there is a positive although a weak relationship between job satisfaction and job performance. He suggested that individuals are satisfied with their jobs as long as jobs provides them what they desire. Workers attitudes and their job performance are not strongly associated. Their absenteeism turn over an industrial action do not seem to be related to their level of satisfaction. Workers attitude during period of industrial unrest are considerably different from those expressed during the period of normal working. Voluntary absenteeism is likely to occur when individuals perceive the consequences expected from not working to be more attractive than those expected from the work. It is possible that prolonged absence from work leads to feeling of isolation which in turn may be the cause of some job dis-satisfaction. Job design is highly influencial in increasing production and productivity. An effective job designing has the following advantages :

1. It reduces labour force.
2. Reduces wastage.
3. Save time in change over.
4. It helps in increasing skills, improving methods and making the work more scientific and systematic.
5. It helps in simplification and standardisation.
6. Jobs design helps in increasing skills, decreasing learning time beside reducing time wastage in change over etc.

Job Design

Job design helps to achieve the following :

1. Achieve specialisation and higher skills.
2. Minimise skills, require beside minimising learning time.
3. Maximise human resources utilisation.
4. Making the Job as repetitive as possible.

Approaches used in Job Design

Following are the various approaches used in job design :

(*a*) Job Rotation (*b*) Job enlargment

(*c*) Job enrichment (*d*) Group jobs.

Job rotation helps in providing varied, job identification and skill improvement. Job enlargemnet also provide varieties, identity and the technical aspects are also enlarged. Job enrichment provides identity and responsibility. In group Jobs there is no need of supervision.

Risk vis-a-vis Potential for Improvement

Job design has an element of risk is involved whether individual will share the responsibility or not. In addition to this there is risk of industrialisation also. Since job design provide opportunity for improvement of potential. A group is drawn between the risk and potential and the various approaches are plotted on a graph showing the amount of potential improvement and risk involved.

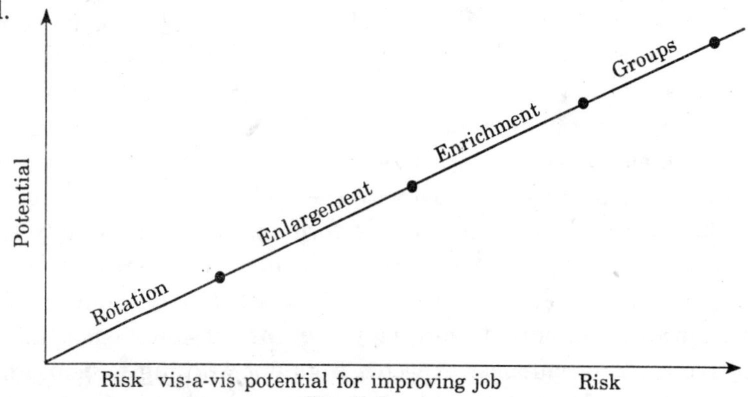

Fig. 41.5.

Risk Factors

Whether individual will acquire skills.

Whether individual will share responsibility.

Whether it will involve industrial relation problems.

The following are the criterias to guide a job designer :

Economic Consideration, Technical Consideration relation to the process requirements, limitations of time and space. Availability of technical manpower, Union management agreements.

It was suggested that withdrawal from work in the form of high absenteeism, labour turnover and restricted output is more likely to occur where jobs are deficient in certain desired attributes. Many organisations through redesigning jobs sought improved operating efficiency by reducing costs, improving quality and productivity, reducing specialisation and increasing flexibility. Secondary reasons related to expected behavioural outcomes such as reduced absenteeism and labour turnover as well as improved labour relations. Some of the techniques which are used to improve the motivational content of job along with their limitations are discussed as under :

Employment Seen

The work-force in India has increased over time but the rate of additions to the person actually engaged in economic activities has been less that the rate of accurals to the labour-force. The number of those who are unable to find work for themselves has thus been increasing. The work-force engaged in the public sector not only exceeds that in the private sector, but is also observed to be increasing more rapidly than in the private sector. Some structural shift in employment in the two sectors is also discernible. There is a decline in the number of workers hired for work in the mining and quarrying, construction, transport, communication and storage activities in the private sector, while an increase in employment in these activities is noticeable in the public sector. Therefore, within the public sector itself services claim the largest share in employment. Steep rise in employment in the quasi-government organisations is partly a reflection of the rapid expansion of public enterprises.

The employment scenario in recent years has shown some encouraging indications. Estimates of employment generated 'in the terminal year of the Sixth Plan showed an axcess over the targets for the year. Likewise, the Seventh Plan also envisages generation of employment for more than 40 million person-years which is estimated to exceed the fresh accurals to the number of job-seekers during the plan period. Some backlog of the unemployment is thus expected to be cleared in the plan period. Unemployment problems in India has the potential of remaining intractable given the rapid increase in population, unless rapid economic growth takes place. The generation of employment opportunities to absorb the existing and growing labour-force calls for an acceleration in the investment programme. The warranted rate as well as the pattern of investment in the country have to absorb the natural growth in labour-force, besides clearing the backlog. Investments, however, need to be so directed as to provide more jobs at higher levels of productivity.

Contract of Employment

The undertaking usually requires labour services in order to achieve its objectives and it is commonly a part of the personnel department's task to ensure that they are acquired in the amounts and of the quality required. But labour is no less a free agent than is capital and there is no compulsion upon workers to take employment in a particular undertaking, just as there is none upon the undertaking to provide work. In effect, therefore, employment is established by agreement between the two parties, employer and employee and this agreement is identified as 'Contract of Employment'. In U.K. Society 'the law' is generally imperative force and a Weber's (1947) terminology, it services as an order to which people are usually willing to orient their behaviour in the sense that they regard it as a duty to obey what it prescribed and proscribes.

Variety of Contractual Element

The worker may be seen to make five distinct demands upon any undertaking in which he might be or become employed, and the undertaking also to make five corresponding offers on these dimensions. The five elements of the contract are :

1. The element of knowledge — The undertaking needs to establish what in the way of knowledge and skill it requires in its employees and which means are to be used to secure them.

2. The element of Motivation — The undertaking needs to determine what psychological contribution it will expect of its employees and what incentive offers it makes to secure it.

3. The element of Efficiency — The undertaking has to set up the performance standards which it will expect of employees and to consider whether award offered forms the basis for an efforts reward bargain.

4. The element of Commitment (Ethics) — The undertaking has to work out how much of the human personality will be required to be committed to the pursuit of the under-taking ends.

5. The element of Interest (Task Structure) — The actual work being offered to the individual such that it meet his expectations.

Dan Gowler has suggested that one way in which the main relationships can be represented is given in Fig. 41.6.

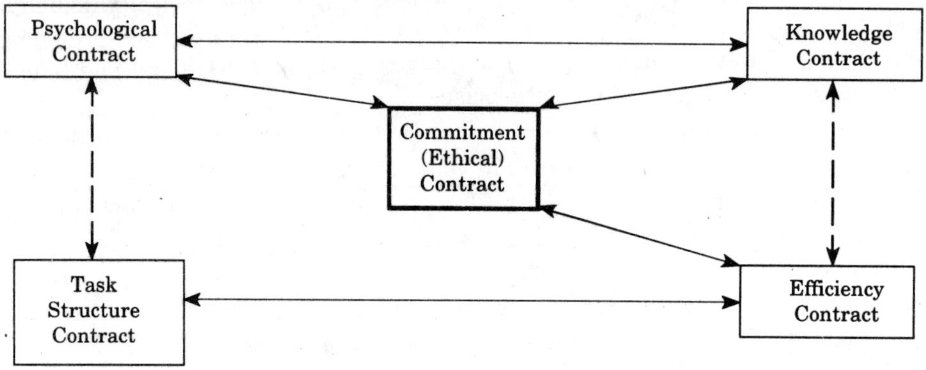

Fig. 41.6.

Source : Dan Gowler. Values, Contracts and Job Satisfaction.

The basic idea of the psychological contract has been further developed by E. Mumford. Mumford has given the concept in the following table.

Table 42.1. The Nature of the Employer-Employee Contracts

Sl. No.		*The Firm*	*The Employee*
1.	Knowledge Contract	Needs certain level of skill and knowledged in its employees if it is to function efficiently	Needs the skill and knowledge he brings with him to be used and developed.
2.	The Psychological Contract	Needs motivated employees.	Needs factors which will motivate employee *e.g.*, Achievement, Recognition, Responsibility Status.
3.	The Efficiency Contract	Needs to achieve set outputs and quality standards.	Needs an equitable effort-reward bargain.
4.	The Ethical (Social value) Contract	Needs employees who will accept the firm's ethos and values.	Needs to work for an employer whose values do not contravene employee.
5.	The Task Structure Contract	Needs employees who will accept any technical, constraints associated with their jobs.	Needs a set of tasks which meets his requirement *e.g.* Variety, Interest, Targets, Feedback, Task identity, Autonomy.

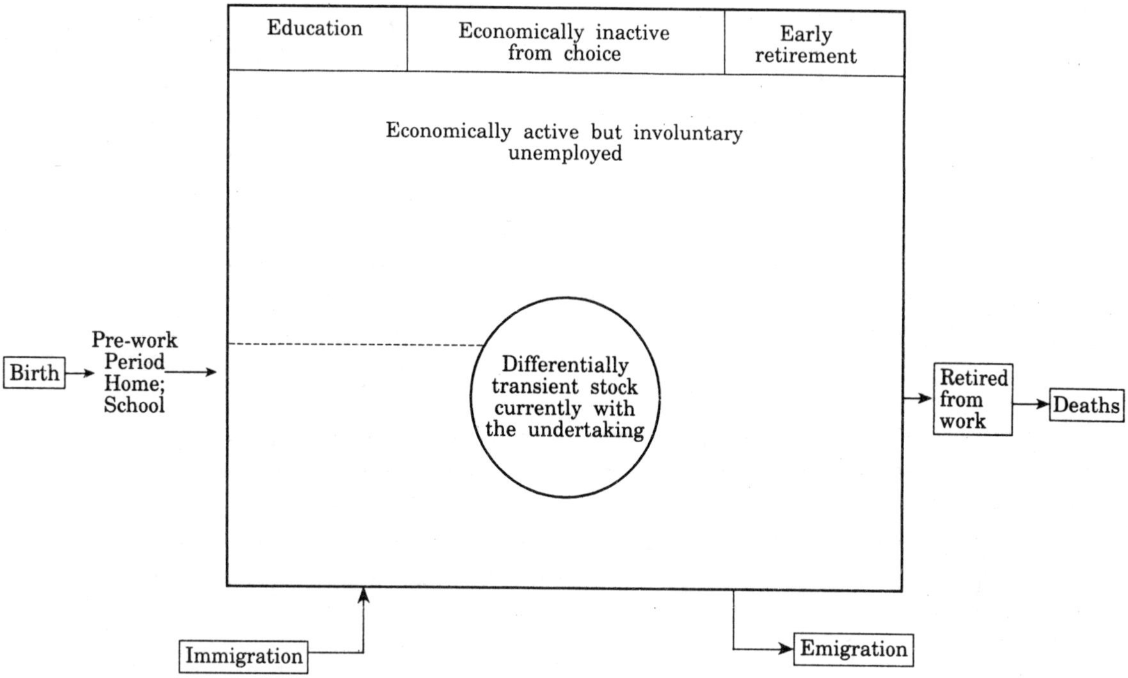

Fig. 42.5. Sources of labour to the Undertaking.

Psychological Aspects of Unemployment

In order to understand psychological aspects of unemployment it is important to study the following factors relating to unemployment.

(*a*) Impact

(*b*) Threat and Stresses.

(*c*) Copying-well and poorly.

(*d*) Support, help.

(*e*) Stigma.

Impact of Unemployment on Social Life

The unemployment has an impact on the individual personality, his family and his social status, and the same can be seen through the process of rejection and failure, loss of confidence and at times a positive, attitude to make a fresh attempt. In order to understand the psychological aspects of unemployment, let us take the case of an individual who is working in an office and is told on his going to office one day that his services are no more required. How he will react ? This will depends on his attitude to the job and his emotional stability. One way is that he may react violently and other is that he may start valuing his own performance and try to find out means and methods to find out an alternative job instead of reacting to the termination of service.

Threat and Stresses

Individual attitude to unemployment due to threat and stresses can be loss of pride, confidence, security and performance. Individual may feel that his pride has been managed or he may feel lack of confidence or alternatively he may develop adequate confidence to face the situation. Hemay start feeling doubt about his confidence or may react with confidence in managing the situation. Similarly, his security and the performance on the role he is doing, will also be affected.

Copying Behaviour

The individual may build up a defensive mechanism by way of his behaviour or may have withdrawal behaviour.

Lonely Affair

In this situation individual is having a feeling of support from friends, colleagues, spouse or children. In fact, friends are concerned for a little while and may forget but members of family may be concerned for a longer period being affected by the unemployment of the individual. The individual may seek the help of spiritual advisor or start depending his time with family members.

Stigma

It is indeed a blamish on the career of the individual. The people tend to pity the individual. There is a break in his pride and self-confidence and thus problem of identity. The individual gets the feeling of second class citizen and get a feeling of helplessness, a feeling of dishonoure. Alternatively individual may get a job at times even more satisfying job and may forget the instance due to a new feeling of success in the new job.

UNEMPLOYMENT IN INDIA

Pace of Generation of Unemployment

In India unemployment has increased over time and it is very large, the Sixth Five Year Plan states 'The pace of generation of employment opportunities seems to have lagged behind the growth of labour-forces. The number of people unemployed and under-employed has risen significantly over the last decade. Since the First Five Year Plan the unemployment has been rising from 53 lakh unemployed at the end of First Five Year Plan to as many as 140 lakh unemployed at the end of the fourth plan. The unemployment position is equally bad both in rural and urban sectors. The number of persons on the roll of employment exchanges increased from 0.7 million in 1966 to 1.6 million in 1960 and as much as 23.6 million in 1984. Therefore, the unemployment situation has gone from bad to worse. As per the National Survey report for 1977-78, the absolute number of unemployed on a typical day was about 21 million (8.2% of the labour force). If we further divide the unemployment to rural and urban employment we find that 7.1% for males and 9.2% for females are unemployed in rural areas and for urban areas it was 9.4% for males and 14.6% for females as unemployed. The unemployment at present is around 20.56 million persons and it is quite alarming as compared to any other country in the world. The major causes can be categorised as :

- Underemployment
- Inadequate employment planning.
- Rapid population growth.

Increasing Unemployment Trends

It is the rapid growth of population which has affected the unemployment the most. It has affected unemployment due to large additions to the labour-force. The rate of job growth could never have been as high as population growth would have required. The new entrants to labour force in the first five year plan were 90 lakhs : 118 lakhs during the second five year plan : 170 lakhs during the third five year plan and 230 lakhs during the fourth plan period. This gives labour force increase of 2.3% to 2.6% per annum. The other cause of rapid population growth is reducing the resources available for capital formation. In India one of the serious problem on unemployment is due to educated unemployed. A survey conducted by Directorate General of Employment and Training, Ministry of Labour, Employment and Rehabilitation (1968) showed that as many as 42.3% persons were unemployed and 50% of the unemployed persons do not register themselves with employment exchanges. In addition 33% of the job seekers on the roll of employment exchanges belong to rural areas. The number of persons registered on the live register in 1984 was as high as 236 lakhs with some of them highly educated. Therefore the scarce resources that go into the education and training are rendered waste because the economy does not make use of them. During 1980-85 (the sixth plan period) it was estimated that on the basis of standard person years the employment would grow at rate of 4.17% per annum. This is indeed higher than the growth of labour--force at 25.4% per annum. The sixth plan period had provided for an employment of 34.3 million standard person plans as against the estimated need for 46.3 million standard person years. Another important factor of unemployment in our country is the disguised unemployment. This refers to unemployment which remain concealed. This is mainly due to agriculture employment where employment is mostly a work sharing device where the existing work is shared. In such a situation even if many workers are drawn from the job the same work will continue to be done with less number of people.

Sociological And Psychological Impacts in Unemployment

According to Raymond Williams on the one hand industry developed from the sense of a general quality of diligent human effort to its modern sense of productive institution. On the other hand *unemployed* and *idle*, which were general terms for being unoccupied with anything, developed their modern senses of being 'out of paid employment', or of being 'in employment but not working'. It represents the specialisation of productive effort to paid employment by another which has been an important part of the history of capitalist production and wage-labour'. This suggests, and it is a very important point, that not only did the rise of capitalism create or understanding of unemployment in its modern sense but that unemployment is an essential part of the capitalist mode of production. The current very high rate of unemployment then should not be understood as qualitatively different--nor as a temporary aberration, but rather as a continuation and growth of a phenomenon always present under capitalism, that is to say that it is only quantitatively different. Does, for instance capitalism need a 'reserve army of labour ? People who can be sucked in as the economy expands and spewed out as it contracts ?

The way social scientists currently 'categorise' unemployment, is now usually understood as a 'flow' — out of work, into unemployment and, hopefully, back into work. The speed of this flow — and whether all move through at similar speed is a matter of much debate. The idea of 'an unemployed flow' is usually contrasted with the idea of an unemployed stock but naturally enough, perhaps, this does lead to accusations that it obscures the presence of a very significant number of long-term unemployed.

Characteristic of Unemployed Flow

What are the characteristic of the unemployed flow ? It is predominantly composed of younger workers. The less skilled and lower paid are substantially over-represented among the 'unemployed flow' relative to the working population. And despite the news-worthiness of large factory closures, small firms and small establishments contribute disproportionately to the 'unemployed flow'. They also usually had relatively very short periods of service in their most recent jobs. It would seem as if about half of those out of employment are family heads. And on of the major consequences of this is that the proportion of *children* affectded by unemployment is higher than the proportion of females. Adrian Sinfield puts it that those worst and longest hit by unemployment have been complelled to pay a harsh tax on behalf of the rest of society in the fight against inflation. By allowing the numbers out of work to rise, and by cutting back benefits and other forms of help, the state, supported by the rest of society.

The consequences for the organisation of the family of the unemployment of the male household head is the subject of a major piece of sociological research that has been conducted from the University of Aston in Birmingham by Lorna McKee founded by the Social Science Research Council. We may well eventually have answers to such questions as to whether or not a husband's unemployment may cause his wife to take up employment or to leave it and how the wife's employment may affect her husband's likelihood of working. Are men with working wives under more pressure to find jobs? Do they have better social contracts and networks through which to find them? Does unemployment lead to any renegotation of the social division of labour between husbands and wives? Does it alter patterns of childrace? As yet we really do not know. These are live areas of current sociological research that will perforce receive a great deal of sociological attention in future. The job of earning one's daily bread brings personal satisfaction when it has been freely chosen; that, is when through sublimation it allows the individual to give rein to his personal learnings, to instinctive impulses previously repressed or particularly intense for reasons of temperament. What is remarkable about the word 'work' is the extent to which, in our kind of society, it has come to apply only to 'paid employment. That means that some activities are seen as 'work' whilst others are not. Why dowe refer to women who are wives, otherwise more than fully occupied with domestic labour. As going 'out to work'? Raymond Williams states that 'the specialization of work to paid employment is the result of the development of capitalist productive relations'. To be *in work or out of work* was to be in a definite relationship with some other who had control of the means of productive effort. Work-then shift from productive efforts to effective social relations.

42

Materials Management & Materials Handling

Introduction

Materials are an important determinant of the total cost of production as it occupies something like 30% to 35% of the total cost of production which in certain cases may be as high as 60% to 70%. Thus materials require a serious, attention in any work of production. Materials mean raw materials, components, sub-assemblies and finished products. Materials can be classified into two main heads.

1. Direct 2. Indirect.

Direct material goes directly into product and forms a part of the end product while indirect material is used in processing or packing the direct materials. Materials management involves number of things like determination of quantity, quality, purchasing, storing, issuing and despatching. Initially purchasing, storekeeping, despatching, material planning and control were considered as separate functions but now these are treated as one function known as Materials Management. It is a specialised systematic and scientific function of a group of people for better procurements/storage and distribution of materials.

In the context of rigid finance and keen competition under which industries are operating at present time, the importance of Materials Management hardly needs any emphasis. The motive of an industry being primarily profit-based, the impact of a sound materials management system on profitability does not call for any assertion.

Materials Management today is distinctive area of Industrial Management and plays a very vital role improving production and productivity. This is a concept, the aim of which is cost reduction as a result of the integrated approach towards the management of materials at all stages *viz.* Planning, Purchasing, Receiving, Stocking and Disposal.

Materials Management covers all aspects of materials, costs, materials supply and utilisation. It covers the whole range of functions involved in covering raw materials and ancillary supplies into finished products. It is concerned with the planning and programming of materials and equipments, market research for purchase; pre-design value analysis, procurement of all materials including capital goods, raw materials, components and assemblies, finishing materials, packaging and packing materials, stores control and inventory control ; transportation of raw material and material handling ; value analysis, disposal of scrap, surplus and salvage and operation research for materials.

Materials Management is basically a most important functional affairs for any organisation or undertaking to achieve the best results is so far as profitability is concerned.

Materials Management covers a much wider field and deals with all aspects of materials supply and utilization as well as costs. It is concerned with the entire range of functions which effect the flow, conservation, utilization, quality and cost of materials. It covers that aspect of

Industrial Management which is concerned with the activities involved in the acquisition, storage and flow of all materials directly and indirectly employed in the production and marketing of finished goods.

The term "Supply Management" used by some governments "Logistic Management" by the Armed Forces aim at representing the same concepts as those underlying materials management but the term "*Materials Management*" has found wider acceptance covering all the inter-related functions mentioned earlier.

Hence small changes in material costs can results in large sums of money saved or lost. Materials Management should therefore, be considered as a function of prime importance for our industrial economy.

In India, a survey was conducted by the Directorate of Industrial Statistics during 1954-57 which showed that in 29 major industries, the average materials cost was 64 paise per sales rupee and the balance 36 paise being accounted for wages and salaries, overhead and profits.

Objectives of Materials Management. Materials management provides tools and techniques, most of which are very simple, to reduce material costs substantially such as inventory control. In addition to reducing material costs, efficient materials management can also bring about :

1. Reduction of foreign exchange requirements by getting the maximum value out of the available foreign exchange or by reducing the value of imports, thus contributing substantially towards narrowing the foreign exchange gap.
2. Reduction of cost finished goods of high quality and maintaining the quality at reduced cost.

Industrial managers have been slow in appreciating the importance of materials management as they have been preoccupied with other matters, such as finding new markets, labour problems and so on. Materials management bring about increased profits, results in increased productivity of capital by preventing large amounts capital being locked up for long periods in inventories.

Increased productivity is the only answer for the peculiar problems of todays' Indian Economy of shortages, stagnation and the threatening recession. Productivity can be increased in a variety of ways such as increased production with fixed quantities of raw materials or same quality of finished goods and services with less use of capital and resources. Modern materials management tries to accomplish increased productivity through optimum use of capital employed.

One of the basic functions of the management is to employ capital resources as efficiently as to yield the maximum results. This can be done in either of two ways or by both :

1. By maximising the margin of profit.
2. By maximising production with a given amount of capital.

This means that the management should try to make its capital work as hard as possible. Much time is devoted to make only labour work harder and in this process the capital turnover and hence the productivity of capital is often neglected.

Definition. "Materials Management is a body of knowledge which helps the manager to improve the productivity of capital by reducing material costs, preventing large amounts of capital being locked up for long periods and improving the capital turnover ratio".

Materials management is a comparatively new concept, in our country. Materials manager must derive its objectives through understanding from the very depth of local environments, at the same time, taking into consideration the human factors, their attitude, sense of responsibilities and their mental make up and approach to new scheme of things. These factors together with the prevalent methods with their good and bad points must be studied in depth before a new procedure is evolved and forced down the throat of the staff concerned.

Function. It may be easy to convince the higher managements about the efficiency of a sophisticated method but down the line with others who are connected with the work, it is not that easy. If the implementations of Materials management is taken up with an open mind it would be easier to achieve the result sooner or later. While the field of Materials management covers all aspects of materials costs, supply and utilization, opinion is divided as to what functions should be included under the unified direction of the Materials manager. Even among undertakings which have accepted Materials management as a distinct management function there exist wide differences regarding its scope.

The *"General Electric Company" U.S.A.* a pioneer in the field of Materials management, have grouped together the following functions under the heading Materials management and these come under the unified control of the Materials manager or vice-president (Materials).

(*i*) Materials Planning and Programming. (*ii*) Purchasing.
(*iii*) Store-keeping. (*iv*) Inventory control.
(*v*) Receiving and warehousing. (*vi*) Value Analysis and Standardization.
(*vii*) Pre-Design Value Analysis. (*viii*) Production control.
(*ix*) Transportation. (*x*) Materials handling.
(*xi*) Disposal of scrap, surplus and salvage.

Objective of Materials Management

The fundamental objectives of an integrated management approach can be viewed as :

(*a*) Procuring Better Value.
(*b*) Obtaining Standard or better yield.
(*c*) Reducing investments in stock through Inventory control and materials flow time broadly discussed as follows :

(*i*) Survival and growth.
(*ii*) Maximum service to customers.
(*iii*) Good working conditions for employees.
(*iv*) Advancement of the employees.
(*v*) Technological lead over competitors.

The objectives of Materials Management as such should be supported in every way by :

(*i*) Maintaining continuity of productive operations by ensuring a uniform flow materials.
(*ii*) Reducing materials costs by systematic use of scientific techniques.
(*iii*) Releasing working capital for productive purposes by efficient control of inventories.
(*iv*) Increasing the competitiveness of end products by ensuring right quality at the right price, especially in foreign markets.
(*v*) Saving foreign exchange through economic use of foreign purchases and import substitution.

(*vi*) Establishing good buyer-seller-relations.

(*vii*) Ensuring low departmental costs and high efficiency.

(*viii*) Setting high ethical standards. In this way, it is clear that Materials management covers all aspects of materials, including flow, cost, quality supply, conservation and utilization.

The prime objective is to supply the user department with the required quantity at a constant rate as well as uniform quality such that production or service rendered is not held up. At the same time materials manager has to ensure the optimum usage of facilities like capital storage space and other aspects of materials management.

Materials management offers a wide scope for reducing costs, saving the foreign exchange, conserving scarce materials, improving productivity and increasing profit.

It will be readily understood that it is much easier to reduce materials costs than to reduce labour costs or overheads, also as mentioned earlier, as material costs predominate in the total cost of a product, the saving is substantial.

Role of Modern Materials Management

By careful financial analysis, it can be shown that a 5% reduction in materials costs will result in increased profits equivalent to a 36% increase in sales. The Break-even chart shown in Fig. 42.1 that a substantial increase in profits can be obtained with a small decrease in material costs which reduce the variable costs appreciably as material costs from the bulk (cover three-fourth of the variable costs).

The chart also shows that profits starts coming of much earlier as the Break-Even point is shifted break-wards with the same total production. Increased production and sales are necessary to bring about the same increase in profits which result by reducing material costs or increasing production and sales to the extent of 30% to 40% which is not easy. Increased production may need increase in fixed assets and increasing sales to that extent, may not always be possible without extra sales efforts like *Additional Advertising* which increase expenses. Further it depends more on external-environments over which the management has little control. The primary task of the modern materials management, with an integrated view is purchasing—

- Right Quality and
- Right Material
- From Right source
- At the Right Time
- Right Quantity of
- At Right Price
- With the Right contractual obligations
- Using Right Mode of Transport.

Storage of Material

Storing the materials in the different warehouses with appropriate methods also forms an important aspect of materials management. As "uncontrolled Inventory is Industries Cancer", the Materials manager is also responsible for the right quantity of inventory norms, *i.e.*, for fixation of safety stock, re-order point, reorder quantity, etc.

Functions of purchases, stores and inventory control primarily fall in the realm of the materials management. There are a large number of techniques and functions which can be applied only with the cooperation of executives in the computer, finance, user, maintenance, traffic departments.

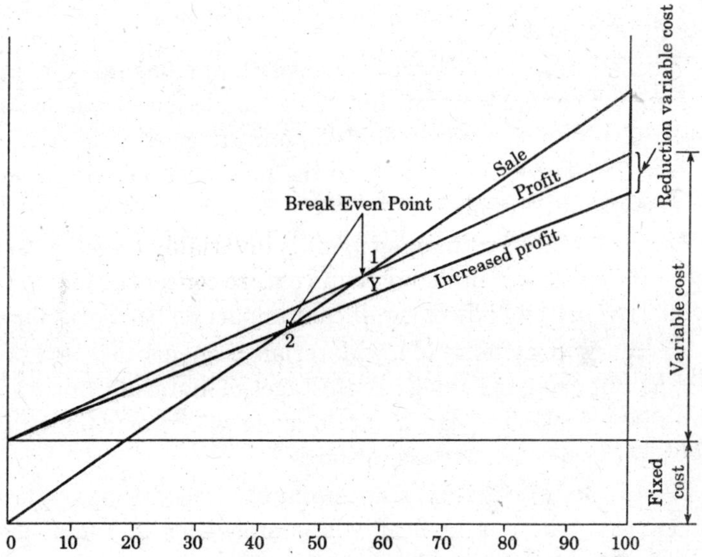

Fig. 42.1

Make or Buy Decisions

"Materials Planning or planning the future requirements is based on the user's needs or forecasts and materials consumption control tends to formulate the broad norms of consumption for individual items of regular use and spare parts.

Important substitution assumes great significance is today's foreign exchange, crisis situation and hence source development becomes very important and prominent. Source Development obviously depends on the ability of an organisation to provide the technical know how and finance as well as to guarantee a minimum off-take etc. The above lead to vendor being 'rated' according to his performance as well as to more meaningful buyer-seller relationships involving ethical principles reflecting in corporate-image of an organization. In this context, one has to decide, whether to *"make"* the item in the workshop or *"Buy"* from outside, after duly considering factors such as economical viability, atmosphere of industrial relation, additional investments and relevant costs, which implies that the other executives are also involved in the *"Decision making process"*.

Value Analysis

The technique of *Codification, 'Standardisation, Variety Reduction, Simplification* and *Incoming Materials Inspection* cannot be fruitfully employed without the whole hearted cooperation of the user *'Value Analysis'*, which aims at reducing the cost of the product without attaching the functional utility by challenging the specification, can be implemented only through the project team-approach. It is desirable to consult colleagues of other departments for savings in costs due to *Materials Handling, Packaging, Transportation and Shipping.*

Analysis of Lead Time

The analysis of *"Lead Time"* assumes great importance particularly in government departments as the fluctuation in Lead-Time affect the inventory. In Government department and Public Sector undertakings, the lead time for available spare parts is over 12 months, whereas in Private sector to produce the same item, it is in the range of six months. The reduction in Lead Time with resultant decrease in the capital looked in Inventory, can be achieved only through proper systems and produces for which the cooperation of the executives in the *Administration, Transportation, Production, Inspection, Maintenance, Finance* and *Audit* are necessary.

Cost Effectiveness

The planning team designs equipment, purchasing team buys and engineers install before it is built into a viable plant. But then production people looks for supply of materials. Many production planners are very fond of aiming at good production, plans, but forget about the time and cost. The time dimension (and the total cost) should in no way be overlooked in effecting good operational design.

The good Materials management is invariably linked with the maintenance and control of materials flow, it will probably require more concentration and effort on those few areas where cost effectiveness will have significant impact on better performance and results.

It is the responsibility of the Materials manager to keep himself aware on the issue of waste and thus can bring in savings at all stages of materials purchasing *e.g.,* the contribution which appropriate packaging can make to avoid waste or damage in materials handling or waste caused by corrosion to metals in stores ?

Trends in Materials Management. Decades ago, when the importance of Materials management was not realized, the storekeeper in India used to report to the production manager, whereas the purchase man was usually a small person in the management hierarchy working in the finance department. Gradually, due to increased size of organization and competition as well as complexity of the business, there was an awakening and in the recent past, the jobs of purchasing and stores were combined and placed under one executive. With the realization that the improved productivity needs streamlining the purchase, stores and related functions as well as application of Modern Material Management techniques, the concept of Integrated Materials Management came into being very recently.

The "Integrated Materials Management" concept is fairly new in the lexicon of Business Management even though 'Materials' constitutes the most important of the M's like Money, Man, Machine, Materials, etc., and Man has been using the materials" since the pre historic days. The concept is hardly two decades old. Even in the developed countries and in India, it is being practised in some progressive undertaking only since last ten years. The result of the integrated approach to materials management, in these organisations is obviously visible now.

Materials Manager

The Materials manager should have sufficient authority to economise purchase and effect cost reduction in all aspects of materials function including optimising inventory holdings. Hence, organisationally, the materials manager, to derive full benefits from the Materials function, should be on par with the other departmental heads, *i.e.,* Finance, Marketing, Personnel and Production and should report to the General Manager or Chairman.

The modern tools and techniques which have been evolved and come to stay must be brought home to the staff concerned in simple language. These being the part and parcel of an approach to an integrated and objective control, essentially the system must fix certain standards or norms.

Thus for the success of this new area, the materials manager has to educate the top management of the crucial and vital role that the department plays in effectively contributing to the corporate growth of any organisation. He has to initiate suitable reporting systems of the results achieved in order to get appreciation of the top management and his colleagues in any organisation.

The degree of success of materials management in any firm obviously depends on the initiative of the materials manager, culture of the organisation as well as inter-relations between different department in the form of cooperation, collaboration and communication as well as machinery for Conflict Resolution.

Non-moving Items

It is defined as particular items which are not requisitioned by the using department over a specific period of items. These items are subject to obsolescence, deterioration, pilferage, inventory carrying cost. Thus material management should resort to study of such items at regular intervals. It has been seen that determining a norm for non-moving item is a difficult task. In some organisations the norms for slow moving and non-moving items are not rightly understood and hence not followed in practice. The non-moving items can always be examined under different categories such as raw materials, bought out components, spare parts and tools and items manufactured for exports. Most of the large projects in India are outcome of collaborations with foreign companies. Regarding technical know-how we have had to depend upon them but for decisions regarding quality and quantity of material to be procure depend upon us. With the result we faced a situation in which on one hand the plant starved of essential spares and on other a large number of parts remained untouched. In certain public sector certain parts or components did not move for more than 15—20 years. The collaborators recommend a certain inventory level depending upon the conditions prevailed in their country.

Vendor Rating

The objective assessment of vendors demands a systematic analysis of their past performance. But re-assessment at regular intervals is a time consuming process and thus did not receive adequate attention. Recently adequate attention has been given to find out the objective standards and procedure to compare and thus evaluate the suppliers. The systematic assessment of suppliers ability to meet the quality, delivery schedules, product price and service giving an appropriate weightage to each factor can help us in designing the vendor rating system. The overall rating could be prepared to evaluate the vendors. Following are the three methods used for rating vendors.

1. The categorical method ; 2. The weighted-point method and 3. The cost-ratio method.

1. The categorical method. This is a functional approach method, giving emphasis on the concept of value analysis. In this method the functional utility is given more importance in vendor selection. We can device a system with three levels namely—High value, Middle value and Low value.

In each of these value system a list of factors is made for the purpose of evaluation. For example, the delivery, price and quality are given high value.

The geographical location, suppliers, reputation are of middle value. The reciprocating and minor services are of low value. This method relies heavily on judgement of the individual carrying out the rating.

2. The weighted point method. The General Electric Company of U.S.A. is responsible for bringing out the weighted point method. In this method the number of factors such as the objectives of the organisation, its products and the economic conditions of the organisation are included. The relative worth of these factors as compared to each other will give a composite performance index. The relative worths of these factors vary from product to product, organisation to organisation. The following are the maximum but average points for the best performance.

	Factors	*Average Points*
1.	Quality	35 Points
2.	Price	30 ,,
3.	Deliver	20 ,,
4.	Service	15 ,,

These points are allocated based on the nature of product. For example, for toys quality is less important but the attraction and price are of main considerations while for aircraft components quality aspect is very important in relation to the price.

Cost Ratio Method

This method attempts to reduce the subjective elements common to other methods. In this method a list of suppliers services is established in relation to the price. In this method the object is to evaluate the suppliers on the basis of proceeding considerations which may not be practical consideration. The small differences in the point score among various suppliers may not be of a great significance to justify their relative merits, for example suppliers X, Y, Z, have scored 60, 62 and 63 points respectively. In such cases place the orders with one of the supplier as long as his performance is satisfactory.

If the first supplier fails to meet the schedule the second supplier is selected and so on. The table 42.1 will indicate the relation of cost factor with the amount spent.

It has been observed that organisational objectives some time limits the free play of the supplier evaluation. The human element is normally a responsible factor in a preventing objectivity in suppliers selection.

Table 42.1

Name of the vendor		
Product to be supplied		
Quantity to be supplied .... say		
Period of Supply		
S. No.	*Cost Factor*	*Amount*
1.	Visit to suppliers plant	—
2.	Sample approval	—
3.	Incoming inspection	—
4.	Value of the projected part	—
5.	Reworking cost (if any)	—
6.	Miscellaneous cost	—
7.	Follow-up cost	—
	Total Cost	X
Total cost of purchases		$= \gamma X$
Hence, quality cost ratio		$- \frac{X}{\gamma X} \times 100$
		$- \frac{1}{100\gamma}$ %

Research in Materials Management

The increasing complexities in the procurement of industrial raw materials and components has given birth to new technique and method for increasing the system effectiveness. It depends to a greater extent on how effectively these techniques are utilised depending upon the availability of their own resources. All over the world large size organisations are spending a considerable amount on research in materials management. The research on availability should be attached more attention and importance. The availability research provides information concerning the availability of raw materials and components in National and International market at a right price.

Availability research should be the direct responsibility of the officer who is reporting to material manager as shown in Fig. 42.2.

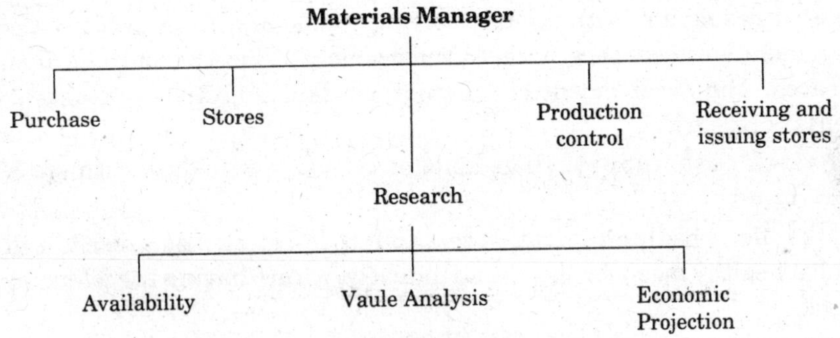

Fig. 42.2.

The executive responsible to availability research should have the following attributes.

1. He should be aware of his organisation's objectives and its products.
2. He must have a logical and analytical thinking.
3. He should be aware of market trends.
4. He must be a creative man.
5. He should not mind his criticism.
6. He should encourage two-way communication.

Development of Information

In addition to this if these activities are to be run in a systematic way then certain amount of autonomy has to be given to the person carrying the availability research. The development of information can be studied as Analysis of Product, its utility and Reliability as given under in Table 42.2.

Table 42.2

Analysis of Products	*Utility*	*Reliability*
Product Information	Value	System
Source	Relations	Forecasts
Availability	Movement Economics	Confidence
Movement Pattern	Variables	Constraints

Data Feeding Loop

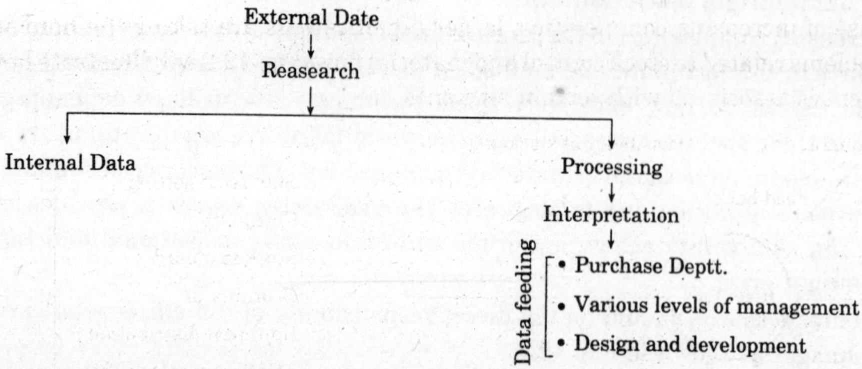

The process of research. With the fast moving technology it has become a problem for material management to keep pace with this movement. This can only be done through continuous research. The development of information, data collection and data feeding are essential elements of research.

Holding of stock costs money. Huge amount of money is tied up with stock on which there is no direct return.

Too high stock reflects badly on operation cost and too low stock may cause loss in business. So we should find a healthy mean for this. In an industry, we are having the following principal categories of stock.

1. Raw materials and components.
2. Work in progress.
3. Goods in transit.
4. Unfinished stock at process stage.
5. Tools.
6. Spares for plant and machinery.
7. Finished product awaiting sales to customers.

Problems in Maintaining Stock Level

Following are the general problems most of the industries are facing in maintaining the budgeted stock level.

1. Due to uncertainty in market condition items are some-time taken into stock to larger quantity than the standard stock policy.
2. Sometime one has to take entire quantity specially the imported components in one go.
3. Uncertainty in getting import licences which has got direct bearing on production and inventory level.
4. Sometime the requirement being very small and it become difficult to procure exactly as per the requirement.
5. Sudden and unwarranted increase in selling by the large scale/medium scale manufacture.
6. Excess of the wrong materials in the wrong place.

Thus to maintain the budgeted level of inventory one needs to review the inventory level and to compare it with budgeted and action should be taken to bring possible improvements. This can be done by inventory board consisting of the following persons :

1. Materials manager,
2. Finance manager,

3. Production manager, and 4. Industrial Engineer.

Because of increasing complexities, larger organisations are taking the help of computive for the problems related to stock control and material flow. Fig. 42.3 will illustrate how inventory management is associated with certain elements.

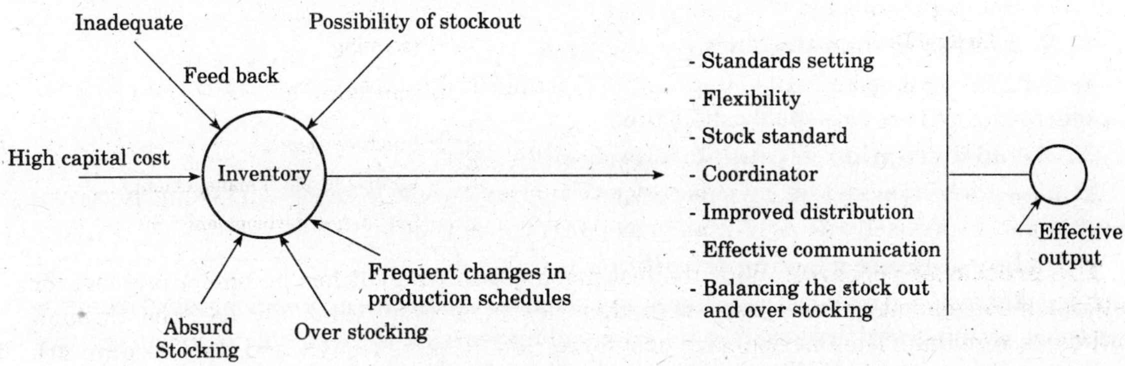

Fig. 42.3. Elements of Inventory Management.

Materials Handling

It is an important area of study with a view to effect cost reduction by suitable materials handling system and devices in a plant. The material handling has became more and more complicated due to the development of new methods and techniques. Materials handling has now become a specialised function. In the pre-scientific management period the material handling was only man handling and handling was done in most uneconomical may be human labour only.

Definition

Materials handling has been rightly defined as an Art and Science involving the moving, packing and storing of substance in any form. Material handling is the preparation placing and positioning of materials to facilitate their movement or storage. The total cost of material handling formed is indicated in the following diagram.

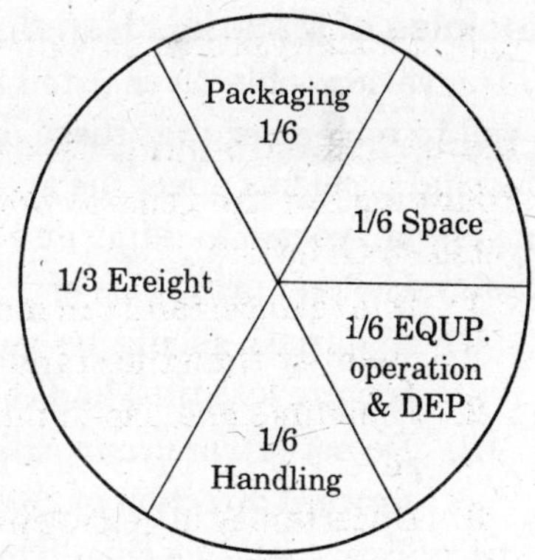

Fig. 42.4.

Briefly materials handling is the moving of material from the raw storage through production to ultimate consumer with the least expenditure of time and effort, so as to produce maximum productive efficiency at the lowest materials handling cost.

Objective of Materials Handling

(*i*) Reduction in wastage of machine time.

(*ii*) Reduction in manufacturing cycle time.

(*iii*) Avoiding disruption in production schedule.

(*iv*) Bring safety to workers and provide for safer working conditions.

(*v*) Bring customer satisfaction.

(*vi*) Enhancing productivity and avoid high costs.

(*i*) **Reduction in wastage of machine time**

Proper materials handling system would ensure regular supply and distribution of raw material and finished product. This will not create the problem of idling of machine and eliminate problem of wastage of machine time.

(*ii*) **Reduction in manufacturing cycle time**

Keeping the loading and unloading time of machine at minimum enables the completion of manufacturing cycle at reasonably short time.

(*iii*) **Avoid disruption in production schedule**

In mass production system, all parts or materials must come in the assembly line in correct quantity and at precisely the right time to avoid risk of shut down.

(*iv*) **Safety and safe working conditions**

Correctly designed material handling system enables utilisation of proper material handling device and training workers in safe material handling practice. It is tangible saving in reduced insurance rates, payment of compensation and boost to worker's moral.

(*v*) **Customer satisfaction**

Regular market supplies by avoiding disruption in production schedule, shortening manufacturing cycle time, timely deliveries lead to customer satisfaction a key to business success.

(*vi*) **Enhances productivity and avoids high cost**

Efficient material handling system results in reduction in cost through various steps discussed above and results in higher productivity.

Principles of Materials Handling

The various objectives listed above can be achieved by following certain principles. It will be well to remember that these are the general principles only and in practice the individual industrial problems affect the evolution of materials handling system. Factors like the production system, types of building and cost of various devices largely effect the system in a particular industry. General principles are :

(*i*) Materials should be moved over the shortest distance possible. Short movements require less time and cost less money than long movements.

(*ii*) Do not retrace your path. The aim of material handling system should be to move in forward direction or clockwise direction.

(*iii*) Terminal time should be kept as short as possible. It is time taken for picking up the finished product.

(*iv*) Loads should be carried both ways on materials handling trips whenever possible.

(*v*) Partial loads and manual handling should be avoided.

(*vi*) Utilise gravity as moving force as far as possible.

(*vii*) Utilise containers and unit loads. The unit load means the product to be moved should be grouped into units of a large and constant size.

(*viii*) Materials should be already marked to help save time in sorting and avoiding mixing up.

Factors Affecting Materials Handling System

The following four factors affect materials handling system :

1. Production system.
2. Product to be handled.
3. Type of building within which material is to be handled.
4. Cost of materials handling device.

1. Production System. There are two basic types of production systems. One is intermittent or job lot production ; the other is continuous production. Intermittent systems are used where a variety of jobs are being done at the same time on a variety of machines and in a variety of places. Since a great deal of flexibility is necessary it is likely that variable path-equipment will be used more than fixed-path equipment. In terms of materials-handling devices lift trucks, pallets, hand trucks and trolleys would be more useful in intermittent production system in continuous production systems. These materials-handling devices would not be so commonly used in continuous-production systems, because fixed-path equipment would be more reliable and more economical in many cases. In mass production or continuous-process systems, one would find extensive use of conveyors, cranes, hoists, pipelines and in modern plants, automatic of transfer machines and tape-controlled indexing machines.

2. Types of Products to be Handled. The type of products being handled greatly affects materials handling decisions. Powders, liquids and gases are well suited to transport by pipelines. Automatic transfer machines should be used in automatic processes where a sufficiently high volume of production is available to offset the high cost of the equipment. Cranes and hoists are best suited to very heavy lifting jobs, where the material to be used cannot be easily lifted from below. Conveyors should be used where high volumes of products move from one fixed point to another. Trucks should be used where flexible destinations are required and where the volume of material to be moved may be low. The characteristics of the products, including weight, size, shape, perishability and whether it is a solid, liquid or gas have significant bearing on the selection of the type of device which should be chosen to move them.

Type of Building

The number of floors has a direct effect on the devices which should be used. Single-storey building, the most common type being built today lend themselves to the use of lift trucks and conveyors. They also eliminate the need for elevators, which often prove to be a bottleneck in materials-handling. Multi-storeyed building, however, find themselves to the use of gravity flow with pipelines and shutters which is the most economical method of materials handling.

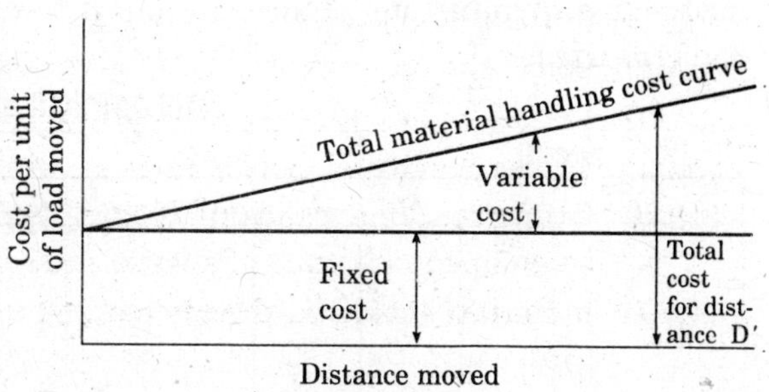

Fig. 42.5.

The last major factor is the cost of various devices which are available for use. Cost comparisons among various alternatives are often difficult to make. The initial costs of alternative devices should be considered. The usual life of equipment will also affect the decision. Resale or scrap value is the other factor. Perhaps most important are operating costs which include fuel maintenance, repair, insurance and labour costs. These costs must be determined for the alternatives before estimates of the value of one device versus another can be determined.

The graphical representation given in Fig. 42.5 shows the relation between cost per unit of load moved and distance moved.

Analysis of Material Handling Problems

Following are the various important factors which need to be studied to analyse the handling problems.

1. Establish the Scope of the Study

(*i*) What is the degree of thoroughness is expected of the study ?

(*ii*) Should the study include related functions such as manufacturing, financing, personal relation etc. ? If not what areas should be included ?

2. Pinpoint the Physical Boundries of the Study

(*i*) What areas in the plant layout should be covered by the study ?

3. Determine Production Forecasts

(*i*) What volume of material is expected to be handled by the equipment ?

(*ii*) What is the expected range of expansion ?

4. Determine the Most-handled Items

(*i*) Which material require the most of the handling work ?

(*ii*) What is the total handling cost of these items in relation of the others ?

5. Compute the Cost of the Present Handling Method

(*i*) What are the functional elements of the system ?

(*ii*) How many man-hours are spent for each element ?

(*iii*) What are the other costs directly related to the handling operations ?

Analysis of Materials Handling

Materials handling problems vary from situation to situation. The gravity of the problem varies according to whether production is continuous or intermittent. This in effect means only that a detailed analysis of various aspects of materials movement is necessary.

1. What to Move

Data is collected on what materials are to be moved. The bill of materials coupled with the production schedule would give this information. Additionally all information regarding weight, size, shape, quantity etc., of the materials to be transported is to be collected. The following form could be used.

ITEM SPECIFICATION LIST

ITEM			*UNIT*					*HOW MOVED*		
Description	*Size*	*Wt.*	*Qty.*	*Qty. per unit*	*Size*	*No. of units reqd.*	*From*	*To*	*Dist.*	*Eqpt.*

2. Where to Move

Once the data is available as to what to move, the details of where to move are to be collected. It is necessary that information is collected in the form of distance × weight since this is the most pertinent information. The information could be collected in the form given below :

To / From	DEPARTMENTS			
	A	B	C	D
A				
B				
C				
D				

3. How to Move

The data required to be collected is (*i*) the equipment used for movement, (*ii*) whether material is moved individually or in units like any, pallets, bundles etc. and (*iii*) the time taken for the movement. Details of equipments used are to be collected, *viz.*, (*i*) capacity, (*ii*) speed, (*iii*) flexibility and (*iv*) manoeurability. Hence the factors affecting materials handling can be summarised as follows :

What to move	:	Materials-form, characteristics, quantity.
In what	:	Containers
Where	:	Routing
How often	:	Frequency and duration
How far	:	Distance
How fast	:	Speed
On what	:	Paved gangway, curves
By whom	:	Type of labour
By what	:	Equipment.

Materials Handling Surveys

These surveys are of mainly three types :

1. Plant-wide survey; 2. Department survey and 3. Area survey.

1. Plant Wide Survey

It is there to provide a materials handling system in the plant. It can be carried out in following steps :

(*i*) Prepare a plant activity drawings

(*ii*) Prepare a plant-layout drawings

(*iii*) Draw the flow of samples of major materials, assemblies and products.

2. Department Survey

After selecting the appropriate department of plant-activity, we should prepare a materials-handling chart showing methods of transportation, quantities, distances moved, times and frequency of movements.

3. Area Survey

In the area survey, we are able to analyse each materials handling situation in the department. In this we use the following techniques.

1. Predetermined times and
2. Activity sampling.

The survey of materials handling reveal—the kind, the type, the volume, the weight and other characteristics during processing, storing and shipping.

In carrying out the survey following information should be available :

1. How often handling occurs.
2. Number of times each type of material is handled.
3. The type of the material to be handled.
4. The form in which the material is received, moved and despatched.
5. The dimension of the material handled.
6. The nature of route the material follows.
7. The probability of plant accident that can be contributed to handling.
8. Cost of material handling at each place.

The material handling equipment will provide three types of services :

1. Material loading and unloading.
2. Inter-departmental movements.
3. Intra-departmental movements.

The choice of the equipment requires a thorough knowledge of all available equipments. The various types of materials handling equipments can be grouped into four major heads as shown in the following diagram.

Types of Materials Handling Equipments

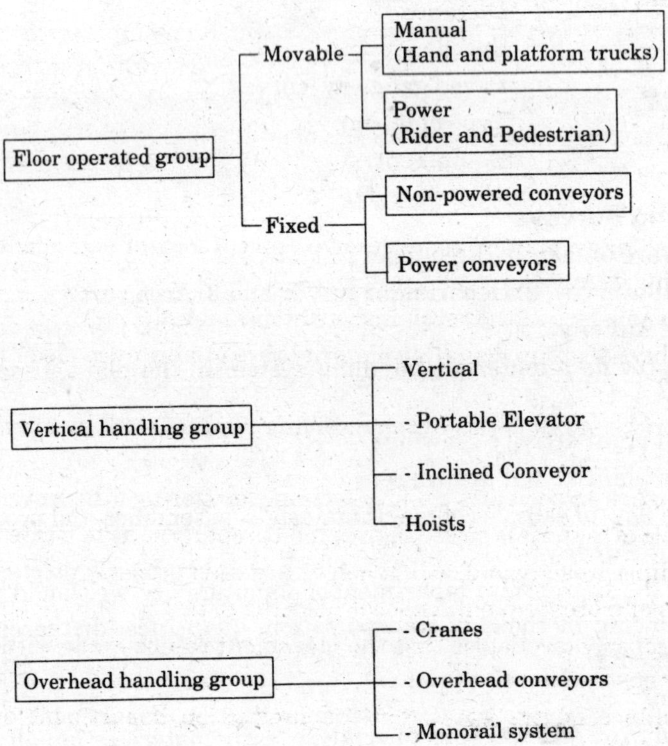

Cost of Materials Handling

Following is the formula which helps us in arriving at economics of a materials handling installation.

The most economical investment = Z

$$Z = \frac{(S + L + U - E)X}{A + B + C + D}$$

where A = Interest on investment

B = Percentage allowance for insurance

C = Percentage allowance for maintenance of materials handling equipment

D = Percentage allowance for depreciation of equipment

E = Annual power cost to operate the equipment

S = Annual saving in direct labour cost

L = Annual saving in fixed and variable overheads

U = Annual saving or increase in earnings

X = Percentage of year the equipment is used

I = Initial cost of equipment

The cost of maintaining the equipment (excluding labour) to operation is :

$$Y = I\,(A + B + C - D)$$

The yearly profit V made from operating the equipments is :

$$(S + L + U - E)\,X - Y$$

Diagnosis of Materials Handling Problems

Normally in a plant there are lot of problems with which an employee is bombarded but, with passage of time he develops a habit to tolerate the inconveniences at that place and accept the problem as inevitable. However, a survey of plant would bring out several facts which need a systematic study. Certain points will show us the need of a study of the Materials Handling Problem.

In Receipts and Stores

(*i*) Does the area where materials are received give a look of bad house keeping ? Are materials being dumped all over the space ?

(*ii*) Are materials piled up in the receiving yard to be moved ?

(*iii*) Are the members of group, handling materials are uniformly loaded ? How many men are engaged ?

(*iv*) Are the materials moved twice in the receiving yard before they are finally sent into the plant ?

(*v*) Has the storage area been divided into sections for storing different materials ?

(*vi*) Are the records of materials stored maintained properly so as to locate them properly?

(*vii*) Are floor loading capacity and ceiling height are used properly displayed ?

(*viii*) Are the items of more frequent use kept near the gate ?

(*ix*) Is the floor properly levelled so that the movement can be made without the danger of accident or obstruction ?

(*x*) Does the distance of the store from the production department ensure shortest distance moved ?

(*xi*) Are the packages ready in time to avoid demberrage of wagons ?
(*xii*) Are there any damages to the materials during handling ?

In Production Areas

(*i*) Do skilled workers handle material or heavy object ?
(*ii*) Are there proper demarcation lines for material movements areas ?
(*iii*) Is the production area clustered with parts and materials for use rejects ?
(*iv*) Are in process material kept on floor ?
(*v*) Has the storage area been divided into sections for storing different materials ?

Diagnosis

If the answers to the above questions are observed to be in affrmative then general diagnosis is that there is need for studying in detail the material handling problems.

Developing Better Methods

After the charts have been prepared, following questions must be answered before selecting a handling system.

Materials

(*i*) What material is handled and why ?
(*ii*) Can it be handled in any other convenient form ?

Location

(*i*) What is existing location of the material ?
(*ii*) Is there a better alternative exists ?

Conveyors are of following variety

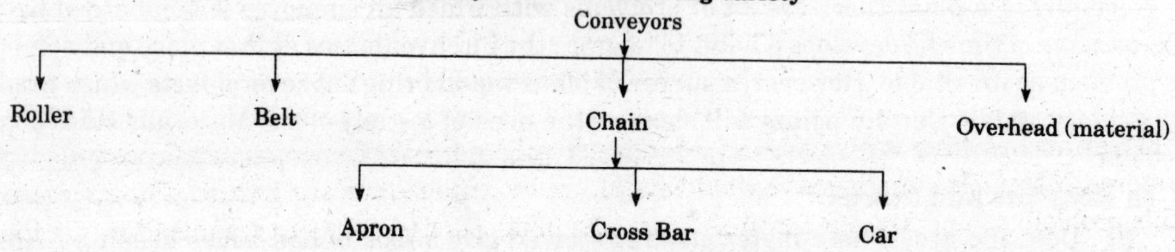

Cranes are of following models

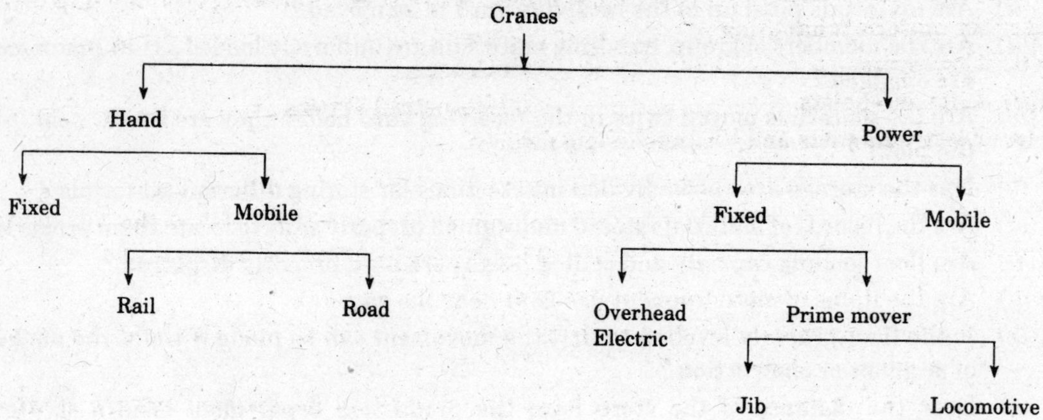

Timing

(*i*) Why must this material be moved now ?

(*ii*) Will other operations be effected if this does not reach in time.

Handling

(*i*) Can the operators be relieved of handling ?

(*ii*) Does material travel effect the pace of operation ?

Selection :

The following comparative table can act as a guide in selecting suitable types of equipment.

Table 42.3
Comparison of Various Types of Materials Handling Equipments

S. No.	*Attributes*	*Conveyors*	*Trucks*	*Cranes*
(*a*)	Flexibility of operation	Move along fixed path	Highest flexibility	Move along fixed path
(*b*)	Economic of conveyance and economic distance	Highest	Medium	Least
(*c*)	Speed of Travel	Least	Fast	Less fast
(*d*)	Cost/Unit work	Cheapest	Less cheap	Costliest
(*e*)	Load Bearing	Least	Medium to high	Highest
(*f*)	Maintenance	Easiest	Not easy	Not easy
(*g*)	Air Pollution	None	Exit Pollutants except battery driver	None for Electric driven

Summary

Materials handling is of major importance not only in production departments, but also in the stores. Materials handling is the main activity in store house and stock yards. The approach to this problem depends on the nature of activities being carried out in an organisation. On the other hand in a large store house which cater for a wide range of products, the mechanical handling is necessary along with manual handling. As discussed, following type of equipments are used for materials handling :

(*i*) Conveyors.
(*ii*) Cranes.
(*iii*) Lifts and hoists.
(*iv*) Industrial Trucks
(*v*) Electromagnets and Vacuum lifting devices.

43

Production Planning, Control and Functions

Concepts

Production Planning and Control embrace all management decisions, policies, plans and actions which have something to do with optimisation or manufacturing objectives.

Production planning must establish the basic relationship, among (*a*) Sales forecasts (*b*) Production capacity (*c*) Inventory levels (*d*) Working capital (*e*) Raw materials requirement (*f*) Production facilities (*g*) Product design and its manufacturing sequence (*h*) Manpower requirement etc. The objection of production planning is to strike the most economic balance between the above factors.

The production planning and control systems are one of the basic activities that determine the effectiveness of a production enterprise. The production planning and control functions and its interaction with other functions is shown below.

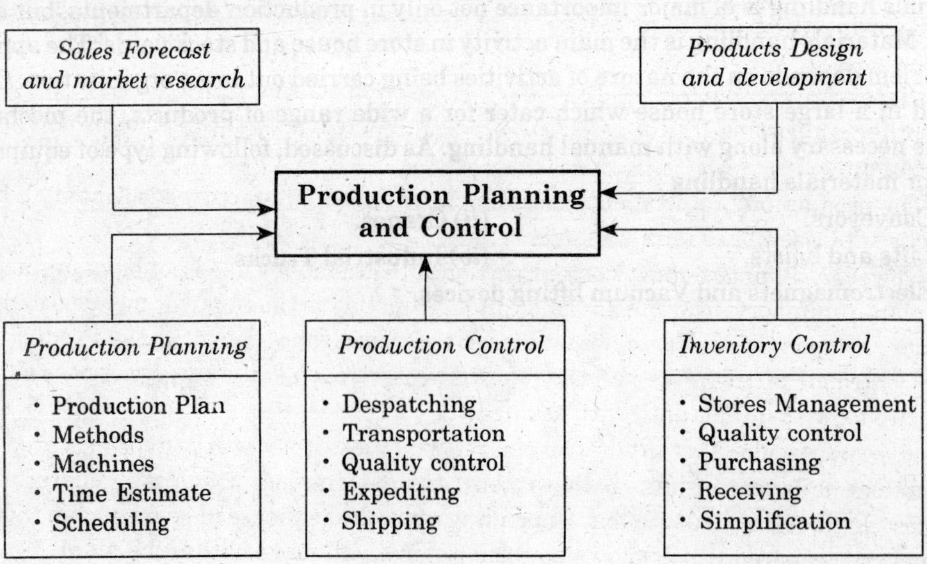

Importance of Profit

Business and Industrial Organisations have grown in size and complexities with the result the operations has also increased and the number of decisions to be made have expanded. Not only the number but also the accurate and timely decisions are expected of every business executive to achieve the objective of an organisation. The prime objective of any business enterprise is to make profit. Profit is the yard stick against which the performance of an organisation can be measured. An organisation which does not make profit becomes "stick" and drag on the economy.

To increase profit one can increase sale revenue by increasing the selling price. However, it may not always be possible to do so because of competition, price control by Government and other factors which are beyond the control of an organisation.

Cost reduction is another way which leads to increased profits. However, cost reduction is also not completely controllable because one has to pay at the existing wage rates in the market to the employees, buy the raw material at the market price and invest in the plant and equipment.

To reduce cost, the only way is to make the best use of resources which include man, machine and materials. Cost consciousness should be there in all the departments of an organisation which include Production, Marketing. Material Finance and Personnel. The material management has to play a very important role in cutting the costs down because it consumes the maximum resources of a company.

Production Requirements

Production activity refers to the conversion of raw materials into finished product of desired quality and shape. In doing so, it must use the resources in such a way so as to produce the desired quantity of goods of desired quality at the right time and at the minimum cost. Production, Planning and Control Department helps in achieving this objective.

Knowing the production requirement, this department plans for the resources, prepares route sheets determines loading and scheduling of machines. Once the production has started, it initiates control action to see that the work is being done according to plan. The type of layout and other supporting facilities like maintenance etc. dictate the type of production schedules one can make.

The production requirement of each product to be manufactured is first of all broken down into its sub-assemblies and component parts.

However, all of the above components or sub-assemblies need not be manufactured within the plan. An important input to the planning function is the make or buy decision with regard to these components and sub-assemblies. Based upon these decisions the Production Planning and Control department known the requirements of each of the components or sub-assemblies that are to be manufactured with the plant.

It is then decided that in what lot sizes each of these items will be manufactured. The various operations to be performed on these items are determined, which are generally specified by process engineering department. Depending upon the sequence of operation an the layout route sheets are prepared which shows how the product will move within the plant.

The time estimates for all of the operations are obtained from the work study department. This helps in loading and scheduling the machines. While scheduling, due attention must be given to the maintenance policy of the company is following. In case of preventive maintenance the machines should not be loaded when they are to be down for maintenance work. Once the detailed production schedules are made, the manufacturing orders are released to all the concerned people. This is known as despatching.

When the production starts, continuous follow up is done with a view to keep control over production and make any modification in plans if the circumstances demand so. For example, because of a rush order the plans might have to be changed. The Quality Control Department is responsible to see that product of the right quality if manufactured. If we are behind the schedule it may be either due to operation or due to faulty material or machines or wrong planning. In any case Production Planning and Control suggests us to pin point and take corrective action.

Managing of Production

Production is the output of a plant or it is the flow of the product through the plan. The primary function of production planning and control is to manage production and inventories skillfully. This requires participation in the sales forecasts coordinating inventory and production levels with the sales forecasts, planning the product controlling production scheduling which included flow up of work improves so meet scheduled delivery promises, controlling production materials and supplies for purchases and delivery on specific data maintaining physical control of all production materials and supplies. The most effective coordination is achieved when it is under one management namely production planning and control. The managing of production can be broken into three major functional areas :

1. Production Planning
2. Production Control
3. Material Control

The three major functional areas can be further subdivided. Production planning can be divided into long range planning and current planning. Production control can be divided into production scheduling, despatching and follow up. The material control is divided into planned control and physical control. The responsibilities assigned to each of these six functions can be further discussed in their logical sequence of occurrence.

In some companies the work of department called production planning and control is limited to the responsibilities shown in production control and material control with perhaps the additional responsibilities of sales order processing and production releases.

Place of Production Planning and Control as a Department

The place of production planning and control as a department in the management of organisation depends upon the scope of its assigned responsibilities.

Production Planning and Control is a joint effort. In production planning and control team every member has some responsibility for developing the programmes and selling it out. Each member should know, understand and accept his responsibility and recognise the way in which it integrates with the responsibilities of others. The planning in many organisations is still left to chance. A successful organisation should think out where it wants to go, why it wants to go, how it can get there and when it should get there and then sets about doing so with minimum of dislocation. In this present era of increased competition and right profit the practices of production. Planning and Control are destined to give a desired progress. No nation can prosper if its industrial companies fall to make adequate profits. The industrial forecasting planning and control enable companies to operate safely and profitably.

Production Planning and Control is the tool that coordinates all manufacturing activities. The management employs this technique to obtain the following targets.

The highest efficiency in production is obtained by manufacturing the required quantity of product of the required quality, at the required time, by the best and cheaper method.

Definition

The understand production, Planning and Control let us define each of these terms :

Production consists of a sequence of operations that transform materials from a given to a desired form. Transformation may be done by disintegration, integration or service.

Planning begins with an analysis of the given data, on the basis of which a scheme of the utilisation of the firm's services can be outlined so that the desirable target may be most efficiently attained.

Control invites and supervises operation with the aid of a control mechanism that feedback information about the progress of work.

Hence, Production Planning and Control may be defined as the direction and coordination of the firm's material and physical facilities towards the attainment of prescribed production goods in the most efficient available way.

PPC-Management Functions

Production planning involves a system to plan production cost, quality and time. In a simple language the production planing and control determines when, where, how and by whom the job is to be done.

Production Planning and Control gas the job of sending a continuous stream of directions given to each of the steps and at all parts of the factory. Its directions are again minute and specific. Production Planning and Control is not essentially a management function which comprise the planning, routing, scheduling, despatching, and follow up function in the productive process, so organized that movements of the material, performance of machines and operations of labour, however subdivided and directed and coordinated as to quantity, quality, time and place.

Comparing Production Planning and Control with Human Body

An industrial plant could be compared with the human body, we could say that the building is similar to the skeleton because both provide a structural frame work. In the industrial body, the productive departments would be similar to the human muscles which do the work. Service departments such as industrial tool and engineering, maintenance, inspection and transport are similar to glands because they make constant adjustment to the physical body that are both corrective and preventive in their nature, sales, product engineering, purchasing personnel and accounting have functions that are similar to the five necessary organs because they react to external and internal events (sensory organs are touch, hearing, smell and taste).

The events which can and do stimulate our sensory departments are infinite in number, some of these events could be arise or decline in the general economy and /or the company's sales, a new product idea or desire to revise a product design, a rise in product cost or overhead, or an anticipated rise in material prices coupled with an opportunity to buy now at lower price.

The nervous system of the plant is its communication system. This is the complex of routes and channels through which ideas, information, and data are transmitted in speech, writing, signs or symbols by human or mechanical means from one person or point to another. Production planning and Control frequently has been compared with the human brain, which is the controlling centre of the nervous system and more particularly with the cerebellum which is that part of the brain which coordinates the muscular activity and movements of the body. Therefore, we can say that production planning and control department is the controlling centre of the communications systems in a plant which coordinates the physical activities of manufacturing and guides their direction.

PPC-Functions

Production Planning and Control functions are much the same as those of the cerebellum of brain. It receives message from the sensory departments, interprets and filters out non-essentials and relays these message to the productive and service departments. In turn, it receives from the productive and service departments, message of reaction to the original stimulates (feedback) it interprets and filters out the essentials in these responses. In this light, the primary function of production planning and control are receiving, interpretations, decisive and communicative.

To perform these functions effectively the people in the production planning and control must have an objective point of view, an intimate knowledge of products and production processes, and most important an understanding of the persons in the Plant who are responsible of responding to their enquiries. The broader their knowledge of products, processes, and people, the keener their ability to listen, the more effective they will be in communicating the ideas information and facts to other people.

For better production planning and control we must fully understand the major forces that influence them. Most prominent among these forces are :

(*a*) Management plans and policies

(*b*) Lead time

(*c*) Usage during lead time

(*d*) Plant capacity and flexibility

Production Control

In is an essential element to ensure that the production is carried as per the plan.

Objectives

If is well-known fact that the survival of any business organisation depends on how it can satisfy its customer. Thus, to satisfy the customer by quality and with regard to delivery date is one of the main objective of any business organisation. This, however, becomes the primary objective of production control.

It is clear from the above discussion that the objective of production control department is very closely linked to the objective of the business enterprise as a whole. Keeping in view the "customer satisfaction," the objectives for production planning and control should be, broadly, as follows :

(*a*) To deliver the product to the customer when he wants it.

(*b*) To promise delivery in the shorter time possible if we cannot deliver our product when the customer wants it.

(*c*) To keep our promises.

(*d*) To maintain flexibility in the manufacturing operations so that we can accept and deliver the occasional rush order for the odd product which gives for us a new customer or additional business from an old customer.

(*e*) To issue coordinated schedules and orders to the production department with complete information to tell them what is expected to meet delivery requirements.

(*f*) To follow up production schedules to assure that delivery promises will be kept.

(*g*) To maintain adequate but not excessive inventories of production materials to support the continuous flow of production.

(*h*) To maintain inventory, production and employment levels that are relatively stable and consistent with the general level of sales.

(*i*) To plan plant capacities that will provide adequate facilities for future production and sales.

Planning and Control

The planning and control is an integral part of the system. This is explained by a control cycle as shown in Fig. 43.1

Whatever be the type of the product to be manufactured the basic production control functions have to be done. The difference lies only in what to do, how to do, how often, where is to be done and who should do it. The difference, in the various kind of production control which are classified as :

1. **Order Control.** This is used for intermittent type of production. Each order is identified separately and all instructions and report form relating to the lot bear this number.

2. **Flow Control.** This is used for continuous production. Instructions and day-to-day directive are reduced to minimum. Nearly all the functions requiring directives like what

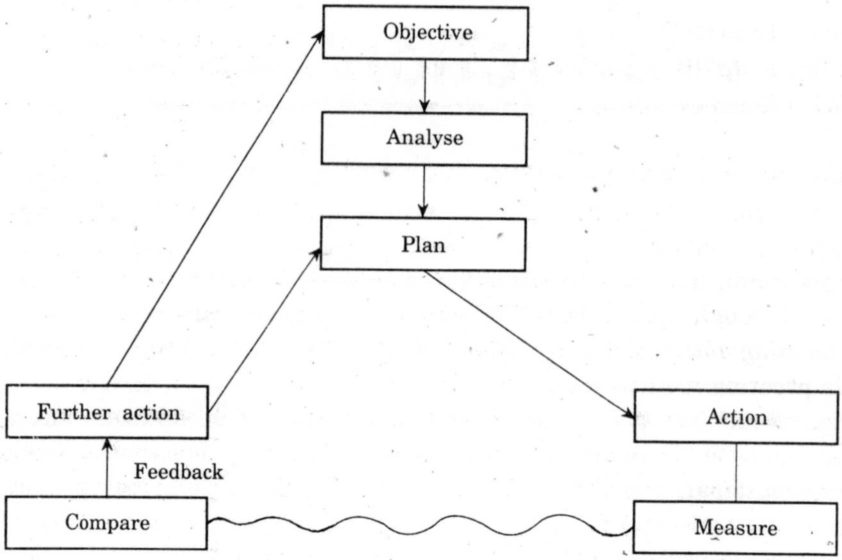

Fig. 43.1

materials to use, how long it will take, what machines to use etc. are very carefully performed during the planning of the production time. Plant layout itself involves a lot of production control functions. Production control instructs the manufacturing department as to the planned rate of production and receives their reports showing their actual rate accomplished.

3. **Load Control.** Similar process industries have their process like continuous industries but their control problem those in intermittent production. The load on the key machines are properly allocated. No separate instruction is issued for every individual lot as all go through the same process.

4. **Block Control.** Where the products are somewhat varied, but all go through the same operations and where the variations have very little effect on processing time, plant loading and progress control can be simplified by using block control. A block is a collection of orders whose work load adds up to a fixed time duration say one half day. The manufacturing department gets orders only in block. Unless block No. 20 is out of the section in full, block 21 cannot go to that section, Garment making industry.

Production Control Organisation

Following are the various forms of production control organisation.

(1) Production Control is through line foreman.

(2) Production Control is through Central Production Control.

(3) Production Control is through expeditors.

(1) **Control Through Forman**

Following are the advantages and disadvantages of introducing production control through a foreman.

Advantages

(*i*) The knowledge and the sequence of operations is best utilised.

(*ii*) Complete control over work assignments.

(*iii*) It builds up the importance of foreman in the eyes of workers.

(*iv*) No overhead expeditors.

Prosuction Control--Machanics

Production control promotes effective shop operation through its direction of activities within the production department. Keeping our production commitment for some period ahead and having assurance that inventory requirements will be cared, we may turn to the details of moving work through the shop itself. There are usually four production control activities *viz. Routing : Loading and Scheduling; Dispatching; and follow up.* **Routing** is necessary where a choice of falircating method exists. Its function is to list the operations should be performed. The decision on just how to manufacture the product and what methods, tools and equipment can be used most effectively may be made by a section of the production control department, by the engineering department, by an independent production engineering, manufacturing engineering, or methods group, or by industrial engineering personal. Many times routing information is an integral part of the manufacturing order which authorises the shop to do the work. The information carried on the route sheet, operation list or shop order may include any of or all such items as : Identification; Operations Involved; Equipment ; Standards ; Scheduling Information and operating results. Infact the heart of the route sheet is the list of required operations. The route sheet if frequently a convenient vehicle for bringing the information to the attention of the dispatcher, foreman; or production supervisor. The route sheet will sometime provide space for a record of operating results, spoilage, actual times and the like.

Date .... Date issued .... Date of shipping ....

Order No. .... Customer ....

Part No. .... Stock .... Amt. ....

Gauge .... Gauge Tolerance ....

Copy of Print and Cutting Design

Fig 43.2. Route Cards.

Loading and Scheduling, are concerned with the flow of work to the shop and the relationship between shop capacity and outstanding orders. The term "loading and scheduling" use grouped together because it is almost impossible to set a realistic schedule without some knowledge of the load on the shop. A schedule is simply a method or relating facilities orders and time. A simple method for handling schedule, load, and progress information graphically. The Chart A and B are drawn giving form of scheduling. In Chart B the margins of free time come after the component schedules rather than before and so serve as safety factors.

The illustration in Fig. 43.4. are simple variations of the Gantt Chart, one of the earliest techniques of graphic scheduling. The graphic type of scheduling is most useful in those applications where :

- There are number of variable which need close control.
- It is desirable to highlight the interrelations of many parts or components.
- Quick comparison of progress with plan are required.
- It is important to spot critical items and incipient delays before they have a chance to become very serious.

S. No.	Operations	Department	Time	Order No. Data
1	Operation A	Deptt X		Sept. 91
2	Operation B	Deptt Y		
3	Operation C	Deptt Z		
4	Operation D			

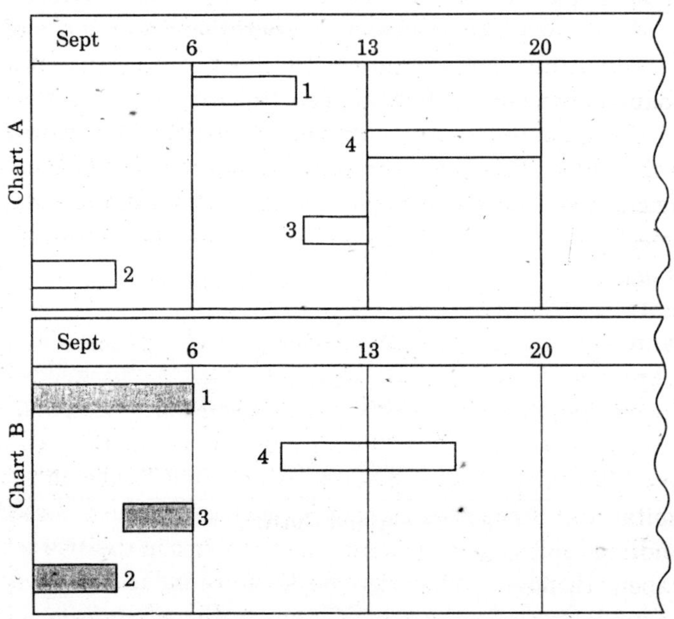

Load summary and order List					Month of ——	
Department						
Machine hours available					Page of pages	
Customer	Order No.	Date	Planned		Actual	Remarks
			Qty.	Date	Qty.	Date

Fig. 43.3. Loading and Scheduling Forms.

B

Weekly schedule for —— Department week ending				
Item	Quantity to make			Remarks
	Packages		Rupees	
	Qty.	Type		

C

Pritorty List	Month of :
—	—
—	—
—	—
—	—
—	—

Fig. 4.4. Loading and Scheduling Forms.

AGGREGATE PLANS AND PROGRAMS

Most of the production managers want to plan and control operations at the broadest level through some kind of aggregate planning that bypasses the details of individual products and the detailed scheduling of facilities and manpower. What is needed first for aggregate plans is to develop some logical overall unit of measuring sales and output for example number of units produced in some mechanical industries. Second management must be able to forecast for some reasonable planning period, perhaps a year, in these aggregate terms. Aggregate planning increase the range of alternatives for capacity use that must be considered by management. The term aggregate planning includes scheduling in the sense of a program; The aggregate planning concept raise such broad basic questions as : To what extent should inventory be used to absorb the fluctions in depend that was occur over the next six to twelve months? Why not maintain a fairly stable work force since and absorb fluctuations by changing production rates through varying work hours ? We know that if inventories are used to absorb reasonable changes in demand, then capital and obsolescence costs, as well as the costs associated with storage, insurance, and handling tend to increase. Similarly changes in the size of the work force affect the total costs of labour turnover. When new workers are inducted, costs arise from selection, training, and lower production effectiveness. The separation of workers may involve unemployment compensation or other separation costs, as were as an intangible effect on public relations and public image. By aggreagate planning and scheduling decisions regarding various costs are difficult to measure and are not segregated in accounting records *viz*. Interest cost on inventory management ; Opportunity costs; cost associated with public relations public image.

Aggregate Planning

Aggregate plans and programmes are of the greatest importance to production and operations management, since through these plans management deploys the major resources at their command. These resources can be deployed effectively or ineffectively. The top management's interest is normally focused on the most important aspects of this development process such as employment levels, production rates, and inventory levels. If basic plans can be based on decisions in these areas which establish operating constraints, then detailed planning and scheduling of operations can go forward. Aggregate planning for non-inventoryable items need not take account of the risk of carrying inventories ; but it also eliminates inventories as one of the managerial degrees of freedom-they cannot be used as a trade--off for the cost of fluctuating production. Forecasting the demand for unique items at first seems impossible but the demand must be related to something in the economy as a whole. Project Planning and scheduling are, in a sense aggregate planning and scheduling. The entire project and all of its activities are planned at one time. Such programmes may call for projecting, load one to two years in a advance. These loads are not forecasts of demand but actual demands for contracted work. The techniques for something loads in net work schedules to be discussed under deployment of Resources and use in fact attempts to reduce the costs effects of load fluctuations or what we have termed the costs of production fluctuations aggregate planning models. As a matter of fact we can view the custom organisation as holding an inventory of capacity and skills to produce in a field, available on demand, rather than holding an inventory of goods. We must recognise that the part of the high cost of turnover is an opportunity cost of maintaining the going concern value of the organisation. Good managers of such organisations are very sensitive to these factors that argue for relative employment stability, even to the extent of altering price policies to maintain the integrity of the organisation in slack times.

Production Line Techniques

The production line is recognised as the way to produce large quantities of standardised items at low costs. Production line is an arrangement of work areas where the subsequent operations are located immediately adjacent to each other, where the material moves continuously and at a uniform rate through a series of balanced operations which permit simultaneous performance throughout, the work moving toward completion along a reasonably direct path.

Principles

Line production takes advantage of the following principles :

(*i*) **The Principles of minimum Distance Moved :** With work areas immediately adjacent, one operation begins where the preceding one finishes.

Control Functions

IMPORTANT FUNCTIONS

The functions of Production Planning and Control can be described as a systematic line diagram as follows :

(1) *Long Range Plans*	(2) *Current Plans*
Sales forecast plant requirement inventory investment.	Sales forecast items, plant capacity,inventory level.
Short term plans, sales forecast, plant capacities, inventory levels, production levels manpower levels.	Sales order processing and inventory interpretation comparison of current orders, forecast historical activity control of financial Goods inventory allocation of production shipping promises, order acknowledgment, order quantity, order timing.
New product introduction sales estimate, plant requirements inventory investment timing and co-ordination.	

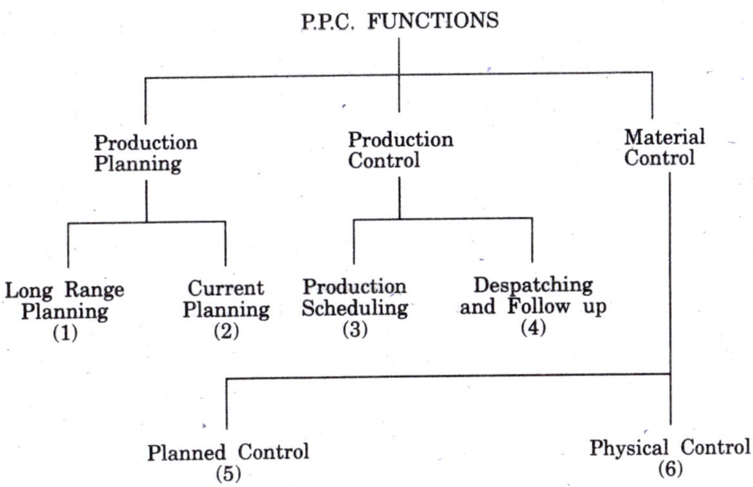

Fig. 43.4.

(*ii*) **The Principles of flow of work.** Flow involves continuous movement at a uniform rate which the production line provides. Flow is measured by the rate of production rather than a specific quantity.

(*iii*) **Principles of Simultaneous Operation.** Up and down the line, workers are continuously performing their operations; the first; last, and middle operations are being performed simultaneously without the completion of one operation at a time on all pieces.

(*iv*) **Principle of Unit Operation :** The line is considered as a single producing unit--One series operations or one group of workers solely assigned to one product. The entire line performs as one producing unit.

(*v*) **Principal of fixed Routing :** The routine is pre--established when the line is set up, and the opportunity for diversion or lost work is minimised.

(*vi*) **Principal of Minimum Material in Process :** Line production achieves a flowing stream of material--a fixed operation sequence with simultaneous operations.

(*vii*) **The principle of Interchangeability :** The interchangeable parts and components are a must-line production takes advantage of this similarity, at the some time being largely dependent on it.

(*viii*) **Priciple of Division Labour :** The most efficient use of labour is to give specific small portion of a job to each of the workers to divide the work and assign one operation of skill to one worker.

HOW TO PLAN A LINE OPERATIONS

Some of the important steps which should be taken to get a line into operation are :

(*i*)Detail Drawings and specifications.

(*ii*)Product Analysis and Suggestion for change.

(*iii*)Rate and volume of production based on sales forecast of contract.

(*iv*)Design freeze and estimate of tooling ; Layout and operating cost ; and Decision to Make or Buy.

(*v*)Based on choice of Processes or production handling of equipment working out the list of Orders and equipment.

(*vi*)To work out the Routing times and Manpower requirement.

Based on Layout approval to work out the New Tools and Equipment Required.

HOW TO PROCEED WITH INSTALLATION AND LINE BALANCE

Based on Vendor analysis; Purchase Authorisation and Material Delivery schedule to bring out the PILOT LOT and thnn to make efforts to IMPROVE AND REBALANCE. The various steps to get a production line is given in following diagram.

From the figure we find that fewer the operations, the shorter the line and the less the investment in expensive assembly fixtures. Lining up the operastions required and the sequence of operations is the next step in planning the line. Many times it is better to supply a line with equipment that is slower then the most efficient machine might be there is little sense in planning over capacity for one operation. It is generally important that adequate operation analysis and methods study go into the job before it start into production. Production lines call for special equipment but it is usually better that the product design be fixed because with line production just one change may upset an entire sequence of highly synchronised operations. *Line Balancing is the balancing of operations in terms of equal times and in terms of the time required to meet the desired rate of production. The line balance is part and parcel of line production.*

Line Speed and Length : Speed of flows bears a direct relation to rate of production and space per work station.

Speed of line (Meter/hr) = Rate of production (pieces/hr) x Station length of space per piece (Meter/piece)

= Station length or space per piece (Meter/piece). Balancing factor or station time (hr/piece)

The station length or space is dependent on the size of the part or unit the size of room, number of equipments and workers and amount of work to be performed.

(3) *Routing*

(4) *Schedule Coordination*

Parts list, Bills of materials, inspection data operation sequence,time allowances set up operation move. Material requistion, tool requistion job instruction, control papers.

Explosion of production orders. Component requirements, sub-assemblies parts, raw materials, planned control work in process inventories. Reporting material used, tools used, progress and delay operations time pieces, utilisation of time operations machines.

*Master Schedules,*detailed scheduled, machine loading.*Physical control* of work in process accountablility of pieces etc.

Physical movement materials to m/cs parts, between operations.

Expediting eliminating and preventing delays and bottlenecks.

(5) *Planned Control*

(6) *Material Control*

Maintaining materials supply inventory records, inventory analysis, purchasing requisitions, expediting deliveries record verification.Storage protection, issuing safeguards physical counts.

FORECASTING

Production control really starts when it is decided how many of each product to make. This requires forecasting. While only manufacturing to order needs less forecasting, manufacturing to stock needs good forecasting, whether recognised or not forecasting is done in every company with varying degree of intensiveness.

Demand forecasting is an important input to the managerial functions. It plays a key role in planning for the future decisions. The business executives need to forecast the future with a view to make certain fundamental decisions for product lines, expansion of plant capacity, location of plants and economic activity, employment and labour policy, advertising expenditure as well as in countless other areas. Without an estimate of the future, the decision making is just like stopping in the dark. The decisions are made keeping in view the developments in the National and International economy, the industry and the particular area in which the firm is more interested. Formal forecasting makes the decisions more rational and it helps to focus the attention of the executives on certain areas which may otherwise get omitted.

Demand forecast has specific significance for the production department. Once the demand forecast for various products is known we can find the total demand for each time period and then the detailed production plans can be made. Demand forecast tells the productaion department what products will be required in what quantity and at what time. Knowing this, the production planning and control department can plan for the resources so as to meet the specified delivery dates. If a forecast is to be of use to production department it must meet the following conditions :

1. The forecast must define expected demand in physical units.

2. The forecast should also include an indication of the probably variation around the expected demand, although admittedly such information is often very difficult to develop.

3. The forecast should be available in time to schedule all tasks required to achieve the necessary output.

4. The forecast must be made repeatedly during future periods to permit the necessary adjustments in materials and production requirements.

5. Finally, the forecast must be reliable because forecasting errors can cost considerable amount of money.

A forecast is essential to plan to production activities. A forecast is necessary to decide when to manufacture each item, how many to manufacture. Similarly a forecast is essential for purchasing new materials, parts or sub-assemblies to find out when to purchase, how much to purchase as item. The forecast is essential even for determining an economic lot size formula.

Sales forecasts are the first approximation in production planning, they provide the base upon which plan may rest and adjustment may be made. For this accurate records sales showing the level and pattern must be known. Sales for each month, quarter and year must be estimated. In case of seasonal sales, analysis may show the need for new products to be sold in other seasons. Annual or monthly figures of production should not be the basis for forecasting sales. The actual sales figure should be employed and adjusted. The sales forecast will not yield accurate result during first few years.

HORIZON OF THE FORECAST

Horizon is determined by the lead time necessary to accomplish the purpose involved. In setting re order points for inventory a probablistic forecasts will be needed.

When the economic lot size is used to determine how much of an item should be purchased, a forecast of demand will be needed which will hold as long as the proceeds of the lot will lost.

FORECAST OVERALL ACTIVITY

Many production control decisions are based on the forecast of the overall level of activity. This include make or buy decisions, production smoothing etc. When one or a few types of end items are being produced in a given plant, the demand for sub-assemblies, parts and raw materials may be derived from the forecast of the end product. The requirements of various parts and components of a compressor can be worked out from the master schedule of an air-conditioning units.

METHODS OF FORECASTING

The forecast may be based on the judgment of the experienced executives. An estimate may be obtained from the field salesman who is the close contact with the customers. The opinion of the traders in the market may also provide an estimate of the future sales. Although these methods are very simple, yet they may not be suitable because these are based on subjective estimates and may be biased. Therefore, it is essential to use some mathematical technique for forecasting.

MOVING AVERAGE

This is a very simple method which project the past into the future, if the forces determining the market demand will remain constant over time. A three month moving average is the average demand during the past three months *e.g.* the demand in the month of April is an arithmetic mean of the demands in the months of January, February and March. Similarly, the demand in May is the average of the demands in February, March and April and so on. This is known as simple moving average.

It may be desirable not to give equal weights to each of the preceding months. The most recent months may be given the highest weight. Then the weighted average may be the correct forecast. There is another way of weighting the demands and it is known as exponential smoothing.

AGGREGATE FORECAST

The average forecast is an important function of the business. It is of an asset to the marketing division as a basis for its planning and to the personnel division for hiring and training programmes. It forms the base for the annual budgets.

The aggregate forecasts is not an activity of the production planning and control.

INDIVIDUAL FORECAST

To implement production planning and control for individual components, it is necessary to forecast these items. Unlike the aggregate forecasts, the individual forecasts have the responsibility of the individuals charged with production planning and control.

DERIVED FORECAST

It is always possible to derive forecasts for material from the overall forecast of demand for the individual end items. A bill of material lists, material required for each of end item produced. The forecast of demand for material on each bill of materials is obtained by multiplying the materials required per end item. The number of the end items to be manufactured.

The bill of materials also lists the specifications and the quantity required for each raw materials needed. The forecasts so obtained should be provided with an appropriate allowance for shrinkage, wastage, during the manufacturing process by applying yield the scrap factors. The final estimate need to be increased by the amount of spare parts required in addition to the number of assembly required. In certain products it is not possible to derive the forecast for individual items form the forecast of overall activities. This problem comes when the forecast of overall activity is not in end product but in monetary units or labour hours. When a series of end items of different specifications are produced it may be different to breakdown an aggregate forecast into end items. The problem of forecasting becomes still more complicated when an item has multiple end item uses. It is true in case of raw materials such as copper or steel bars or angles or sheets of given specifications.

STATISTICAL FORECAST

When a manufacturing company makes a wide variety of end items these statistical techniques may be used to develop forecast only of components but also of end items. Two important techniques of statistical forecasting are :

(1) Opinion forecast

(2) Exponential smoothing

In both these methods the forecasts are based on the record of past demand its level, trend and variation.

OPINION FORECAST

The opinion forecast based on the judgment of the executive and the information obtained from the field salesman who are in direct touch with the customers. The opinion of the traders, distributors are also taken into consideration to estimate the future sales.

These methods are simple yet based on subjective estimate and biases of the various people involved, thus it is essential to envolve mathematical techniques for forecasting. Following are the advantages and disadvantages of opinion forecast :

Advantages

(1) It is less elaborate and requires less technical skill.

(2) It makes use of the knowledge of field personnel, *i.e* gives first hand information.

(3) The process of forecast passes through the review of number of people with various types of specific knowledge who can assess its accuracy.

Disadvantages

(1) It is a subjective approach.

(2) It takes lot of time with the field and office personnel in making up the forecast.

(3) Generally the final results depend for more on the opinions, of a few influential or persuasive individuals.

EXPONENTIAL SMOOTHING

In this case the demand for any period is based on two factors the old demand for this period and the actual demand during the previous period.

REGRESSION OR CORRELATION ANALYSIS

It is likely that the scale of a certain product has some relationship with other products *e.g.* sale of gasoline is related with the sale of automobiles. The sale of a product may also be related with some other indices like material income, income per capita, size of population etc. For example, the time of population and the number of industrial units etc. will affect the demand of electricity in a town. The forecast will be good only if the said indices are coming from reliable sources. The variable which is to be forecasted may be called as the dependent variable and the other one as the independent variable.

In using this technique first of all the relationship between the variables, is defined in the form of a curve. This is known as fitting the regression line, the line is then used to find the correlation between the variables. If the relationship between the two variables is linear then one can use simple linear correlation the simplest form of a Regression line is given by the equation :

$$Y = a \times bX$$

where, Y and X are the dependent and independent variables respectively we know the actual value Y for each value of X. Whereas the value of the dependent variable as obtained from the regress on line is denoted by Y.

The values of coefficients a and b are calculated so that the following conditions are satisfied:

$$Y - y = 0$$

$(Y - y)$ 2 = minimum, *i.e.* the sum of the squares of the deviation by the actual value Y from the value y obtained by regression line is maximum. When we have more than two variables we can use multiple correlation. Thus the information about the independent variables can be used for cost the dependent variables.

COMBINATION METHODS

Generally the combination of various approaches is used for forecasting. Statistical technique and economic methods may be used together with fluctuations about the trend line with a measure of estimated reliability. The trend line is one forecast of demand and the control limits give an estimate of reliability provided the conditions determining the trend do not change.

CONTROL OVER FORECASTS

Setting up of procedures for making the required forecasts and review or control of forecasts are two important aspects of forecasts.

The review of control aspect can be broken into two parts :

(1) Whether forecasts are made as per the procedures established.

(2) Measurement of the accuracy of forecasts and determination of major causes of errors for improving the quality of effectiveness. Control over the use of procedures is very important in case of short term forecasts.

It is very important to keep the record of the actual information versus, forecasted information for the following reasons :

(1) Knowledge of the reliability of forecasts.

(2) Knowledge of the range, forecast errors and examination of the causes of major errors.

(3) Determination of any systematic bias in the forecast.

Planning means getting ready to make the product. Planning is an intellectual process in which creative thinking and imagination is essential. Planning includes setting objectives, policies, decisions and strategies. Planning is deciding in advance what do do ? Where to do it ? How to do it ? When to do it and who is to do it ? Planning bridges the gap from where we were to where we should go, planning makes things to occur which would not occur otherwise. Following are the important concepts about planning :

1. **Objectivity.** Realistic planning is essential conceptualisation of the objectives, the needs, the priorities, the approach and the activities involved. The objectivity requires a long far sight, correct visualsation and practical anticipation.

2. **Futuristic.** The trend in planning is based on the present and future than on the past. It is very similar to vehicle driving where one drives while looking ahead, anticipating, judging and making decisions and rarely peeping into the rear view mirror.

3. **Planning Time.** At all levels of management one has to devote time for planning. The lack of planning or no planning creates increasing work loads piling up of unattended work which deprives him of his planning time and ultimately resulting in a vicious circle. The time spent on forward planning is more and more as one moves up the ladder of organisation. Let us assume the time spent on advance planning as 100% then time spent by different level of management is given the following chart :

TOTAL PLANNING PERIOD 100%

	Advance Planning							
Levels of Management	*Weekly planning, Monthly*	*Six Monthly*	*One Year*	*II Year*	*III Year*	*10 Year*	*Over 10 Years*	
1. Top Managaement (General Manager)	2	5	15	20	25	18	10	5
2. Middle Management - Functional Managers	7	10	15	30	18	12	6	2
- Departmental Heads	12	15	20	35	10	6	2	—
3. Lower Management Foreman	20	20	25	28	6	1	—	—
- Supervisors. 35	40	15	8	2	—	—	—	

Production Planning And Control

Disadvantages

(*i*) No expert knowledge is used in the technique of IPC.

(*ii*) Overburden on foreman.

(*iii*) Very little opportunity for overall planning and coordination among various departments of the factory.

(*iv*) No counter check will be possible.

(*v*) No process inventory will be high.

(*vi*) No accurate picture of machine loading will be available and there will be difficulty in deciding the delivery periods of future orders.

(*vii*) Sequence of jobs may not be as required for meeting the deliveries, but they are more likely as per the availability of machines.

(2) PRODUCTION PLANNING AND CONTROL

Advantages

(*i*) Accurate picture of present, future load on various machines, could be available.

(*ii*) Optimum scheduling *i.e* the expert knowledge would be available.

(*iii*) Proper evaluation of the effect of each new order could be possible.

(*iv*) More accurate delivery commitments can be made.

(*v*) Inter-departmental coordination would be improved.

(*vi*) More realistic evaluation of delays and departmental shortcomings.

(*vii*) Low inventory in process.

(*viii*) Lead time will be reduced because of optimum scheduling.

ADDITIONAL CONTRAINTS IN PPC

(*i*) Increase in overhead costs.

(*ii*) Tendency of central office people to loose contract with shop persons.

(*iii*) Risk of flexibility.

(*iv*) Danger of encroaching the line authority.

(*v*) Possibility of giving more excuses for failures.

(3) CONTROL THROUGH EXPEDITORS

Advantages

1. Important jobs would go through in time.
2. Less overhead cost.
3. More flexibility
4. Opportunity to move some orders through the plant more rapidly.

Disadvantages

(*i*) Very high indirect cost due to increase in set up cost because of frequent settings.

(*ii*) Limited opportunity for overall planning and coordination.

(*iii*) Overall picture of shop load is not available.

(*iv*) Extreme stress on the system when plant operation approach capacity.

INTER-RELATIONSHIP OF PRODUCTION PLANNING AND CONTROL WITH OTHER DEPARTMENTS

The organisations structure of a company is an important factor in determining the nature of production planning and control appropriate to its operations.

Every organisation or a department have a purpose. The purpose must be clearly defined otherwise the functions of a department spread outside the pattern of its framework. So it must have a planned structure suitable to its purpose. The production planning and control department is a service organisation that co-ordinates and secures a smooth, uniform flow of materials into through and out of manufacturing facility — a flow that provides finished products ready for the customer at the right time and place.

FUNCTIONS PPC DEPARTMENT

Production planning and control department can be divided into following sections :

(*i*) The material control section.

(*ii*) Control section.

(*iii*) Planning section.

1. The material control section issues purchase requisition at the right time so that material will be on hand when needed. The object remains that neither the inventories becomes tool small to create production delays nor reduce the net working capital.

2. The control section of production planning and control department follows the planning through. This section maintains a close touch with the sales department so that production plan may be adjusted to maintain inventory within the predetermined limits.

3. The planning section of production planning and control department translates sales forecasts into master schedules that make the best possible use of both equipment and

personnel. The planning section also prepares the load charts, to find out whether delivery dates can be met and to find out whether equipment is being over or under loaded.

Production planning and control are co-operative activities shared by several departments instead of confined within one as shown below.

The production planning and control department should cooperate with accounting department also, in order to establish operational budget, financial planning and production schedules.

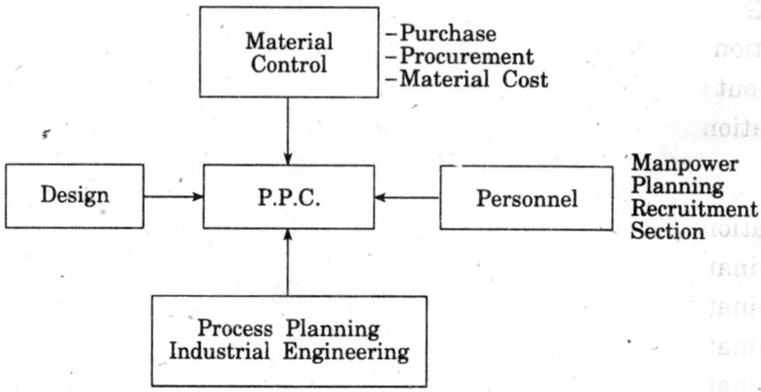

Fig. 43.6.

BENEFITS OF PRODUCTION CONTROL

The advantages of production control may be said to include the following :

(*a*) Help to stablise business by getting more and more customers through better service to them ;

(*b*) Increases the wages to employees as better service to customers results in huge profits;

(*c*) Offers job securities to employees as plans are laid to maintain steady flow of production inspite of the seasonal fluctuations in the market demand ;

(*d*) Increases the value of the goods by way of product development which constantly aims at improving the quality of the product, at the same time tries to bring down the prices ;

(*e*) Increases the productivity through more effective use of men, materials and machines ;

(*f*) Ensures better utilisation of capital, as a result of well balanced inventory control at all levels ; and

(*g*) Assures adequate returns on the capital invested.

FUNCTIONS OF THE PRODUCTION PLANNING AND CONTROL

Functions of Production Planning and Control may be divided as three main phases :

— Planning phase

— Action phase

— Control phase

The phases and functions of productions planning and control are mutually supporting and have very close inter-relationship. Planning is dependent upon the data which is compiled during the action phase. Action in turn, is dependent upon continuous planning of the work to be performed by the activity. Control is the comparison of the work originally planned against the work that was actually accomplished.

PLANNING PHASE

It consists of :

(*a*) Pre-planning and

(*b*) Action planning.

PRE-PLANNING

(*i*) Estimation of future work (forecasting)

(*ii*) To find out the costs of new jobs (estimation)

(*iii*) Preparation of specifications (product design)

ACTION PLANNING

(*i*) Preparation of work details (process planning and routing)

(*ii*) Determination of requirements and control of materials (material control)

(*iii*) Determination of requirements of control of tools (tool control)

(*iv*) Determination of when work is to be done (scheduling)

(*v*) Determination of requirements and control of men and machines (loading).

CONTROL PHASE. It is comparison of :

(*a*) Action phase

(*b*) Progress reporting

(*c*) Corrective action phase

ACTION PHASE

(*i*) Starting the work (dispatching)

PROGRESS REPORTING PHASE

(*i*) Collection of data and interpreting data (Data Processing)

CORRECTIVE ACTION PHASE

(*i*) Making Current Work Corrections (Expediting)

(*ii*) Making Plan Corrections (Replanning)

PRODUCTION PLANNING AND CONTROL - A SYSTEM OF MANAGEMENT

PPC - A SYSTEM OF MANAGEMENT

The planning has become a requisite for enterprise survival. The attribute of planning is to look into the future. Its tool is the forecasting method employed. The results are always accurate but if the tendencies can be clearly recognised, it is a good attempt. The Planning exercise is continuous. Closer approximation are possible as one travels in time. Complete accuracy is possible only when all the parameters are as nearly constant as this dynamic world will allow.

Since planning is an art, it has the capacity to enthuse people to undertake this work. To peep into the unknown area however tenuous, stimulates thinking of the present in the comparison of the future. Risk taking assumes a purpose. The definition of objective has been one of the most important top management activity par excellence.

One way to narrow the gap between estimates and ultimate actual is to plan for a long period on the basis of small interval (six months to one year) on a moving basis. Despite its obvious inaccuracies and the dynamism of situation planning occupies a permanent place in management activity. Plans are usually subdivided as follows :

(*i*) Perspective - for 10 - 20 years at a time divided into yearly based estimates.

(*ii*) Long-term master plans - for 2 - 5 years at a time divided into monthly broad estimates.

(*iii*) Short-term master plans - for one year divided into monthly close estimates.

(*iv*) Monthly plans - divided into weekly or daily plans.

Whenever plans are prepared, assumptions underlying the figures adopted are always indicated in good plans.

Production Planning and Control participates as one of the important systems of management in (1) and (2). It is the spear head and motivating force in (3) and (4) above.

The extent participation of PPC in (1) and (2) depends on the contribution it can make otherwise it is limited to its being the recipient of information on what other systems are contributing. As regards (3) and (4), PPC is one of the basic developers of the plans with the help of all other systems of management.

44

Operational Research

Introduction

The management process essentially involves decision-making relative to finance, production, marketing, distribution etc. The present day science of management helps in the decision-making task by developing and recommending logical basis for choosing from among available operational alternatives. The decisions can, thus, be made on certain accepted quantitative decision rules instead of an institution, experience and subjective judgement alone. Operations research was first applied to military decision-making during world war II, in U.K. Operation research groups, which included mathematicians, engineers, psychologists, physicists and others, were constituted and attached to operational commands at various levels to recommend policies that would improve military effectiveness.

After the war, O.R. found its application in the field of industry and was directed to dead with problems relating to the product development and marketing. In this context O.R. may be considered as an application of scientific methods to problems arising from operations involving integrated systems of men, machines and materials. Operational Research is the application of scientific method to management decision making. It is being used to tackle a wide variety of problems ranging from space exploration to the control of supermarket stocks. Operational Research is concerned with problems which exists in the real words of business, Government, the Armed Forces, etc. One of the features if this reality is the existence of uncertainty. The break-down of machines, the receipt of customers orders at a factory and the arrival of ships at a port are all, to some extent, unpredictable. A company cannot forecast its sales exactly as there is always an element of uncertainty. In dealing with such problems, it is just as essential to obtain a measure of the uncertainty as it evaluate the expected outcomes.

Operations Management

Operations Management can be defined as the management of systems for the provision of goods or services. It is concerned, with the design and operation of systems for the manufacture, transport, supply or service. Since the nature of certain of the problems which face operations management is influenced by system structure, the nature or role of operations management is in part influenced by the structure of the operating system. Similarly the role of operations management is influenced by the objectives which are adopted by or prescribed for operations management. The problem characteristics of the system and objectives together necessitate the use of particular operation management strategies as given in following line diagram. The above diagram outlines the relationships between system structure problems, objectives and strategies and the role of operations management. As indicated earlier the two factors which influence the nature of operations management are :

(*i*) Objectives of operating systems and

(*ii*) Problem areas of operation management.

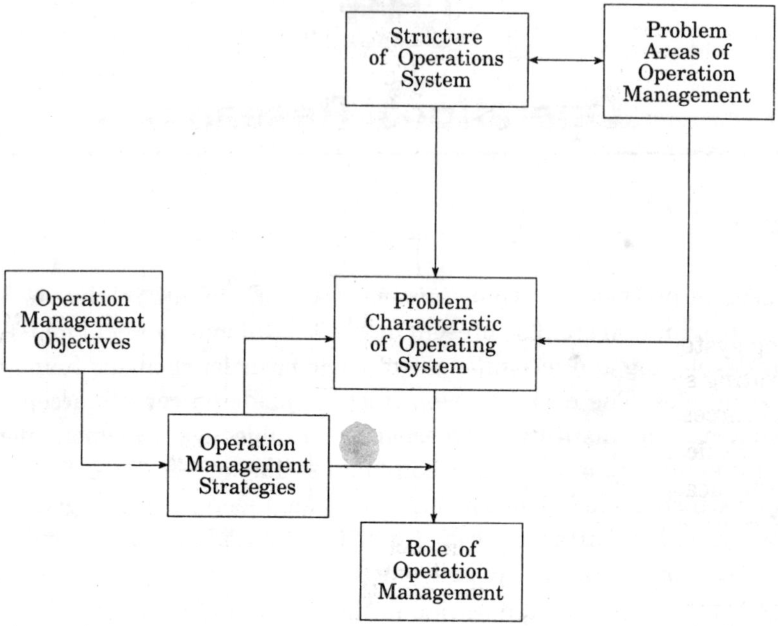

Fig. 44.1.

Operations Management Objectives

The objective of operating systems is the conversion of inputs for the satisfaction of customer wants. Customer satisfaction is therefore a key objective of operations management. The need for operations management arise from the fact that operating system must satisfy multiple objectives customer service must be provided simultaneously with the achievement of efficient operations *i.e.,* effective or efficient utilisation of resources. Either inefficient use of resources or in adequate customer service is sufficient to give rise to the commercial failure of in operating system. Operations management is concerned essentially with the utilisation of resources *i.e.* obtaining maximum effect from resources or minimising their loss, under utilisation or waste. The operations management is concerned with the achievement of both satisfactory customer service and resource productivity. However an improvement in one will often give rise to determination in the other. Often both cannot be maximised hence a satisfactory performance must be achieved to both and sub-optimisation must be avoided. All the activities of operation management must be tackled with these twin objectives in mind. The scope of operations management can be adequately indicated by the following fields of activity :

Operation management will normally be responsible for the management of inventories, quality ; the maintenance and replacement of facilities and the scheduling of activities. Operation managers will normally have some influence on the design or specification of the product or services, processes, manning policies and performance measurement.

Design and Development
- Specification of product
- Location of facilities
- Layout of facilities/resources
- Determination of capacity
- Determination of work standards and determination of remuneration

Design and Control
- Scheduling of activities
- Performance measurements
- Control of maintenance
- Control of quality

Operating Systems

An operating system is a configuration of resources combined for the provision of goods or resources. Operating systems convert physical resources to outputs to satisfy customer wants. The physical resources used by the system are :

Materials. Physical items consumed or converted by the system.

Machine. Physical items utilised by the system.

Labour. Human resource who necessarily provide of contribute to the operation of the system.

The primary function often operating system is a reflection of the purpose it serves for its customer that is the utility of its output to the customer. The various functions of operating systems are categorised as follows in Table I.

Principal function	*Common characteristics*	*Type of organisations*
Manufacture	Change in form utility	Coal Mines, Production Units
Transport	Change in location or place utility	Vehicle or Train Services
Supply	Change in the possession utility of resources	Retail shop, Petrol Station
Service	Change in state utility of resources	Dentist, Hotels

Operational research techniques can be applied to operate 'warning lights' when corrective action is necessary. Prediction of market trends in time for corrective action to be taken is typical of the hard facts which OR can now offer to the busy executive. To put a value on such intangibles as 'One minute's waiting time' of a mechanic or machine is another example of the ability of OR techniques to evaluate the performance of a system.

Methodology of Operation Research

A scientific approach to solve complex operational problems necessarily involves quantification of the factors which control the operations. Further more it also involves quantification of the outcome of these operations to permit comparison of the alternative courses open to achieve the objective. The course adopted by these scientists, working in groups of three or four (called Operational Research Groups) can be summarised in the following steps :

(*i*) Formulation of the problem

(*ii*) Framing a mathematical model to represent the system or problem under the study
(*iii*) Generate alternatives and find an optimal course of action
(*iv*) Test for the optimality
(*v*) Identify the parameters that control the system
(*vi*) Implement of the section found.

Mathematical Models

The most important step in operation and research is constructing the mathematical models of the operations under study. Models are analogies and abstractions and all abstractions and analogies in mathematical model have their limitations. But these models help us to manipulate the various quantifiable factors involved and study and understand the significance of the various factors in relation to the outcome. In any group of operations, which constitutes a sub-system, there are certain factors which can be controlled. An executive incharge of these operations can control these factors within certain limits. The outcome, however, depends on certain factors which are not under the control of the executive. The object of operations research is to understand how the uncontrollable factors affect the outcome and how to assign value to the controllable factors so as to optimize the outcome. Since the outcome depends on certain uncontrollable factors all that an operation researcher can do is to work out the risk involved in adopting a certain course of action and then work out that particular course of action which minimize the risk. In this he uses the well-established theory of probability and statistics.

Areas of Study

One of the advantages which mathematical modelling has led to it is the recognition of similarity of underlying structures of many problems in different fields. The tools which are mostly used in allocation problems are linear programming, transportation and assignment models. The possible areas of study of Operations Research are :

(*i*) *Allocation.* Allocation problems involve the allocation of available resources to job that need to be done. They occur when the available resources are not sufficient to allow each job to be carried out in the most efficient manner. Hence the objective to allot the resources to jobs in such a way as to either minimize the total cost or maximize the total return.

(*ii*) *Inventory Problems.* An inventory consists of usable but idle resources. Inventory problems, we have to find an answer to the two basic questions *viz.* :

(*a*) How much to buy ?
(*b*) When to buy ?

These two questions arise because of certain costs associated. These costs are the cost of ordering, the cost of holding and the cost of shortage. During any planning horizon we have to minimize the sum total of these cost.

(*iii*) *Replacement problems.* Almost all industrial equipment deteriorates with age or usage, unless action is taken to maintain it. At a certain stage it may be more economical to replace the equipment rather than to maintain it. It often happens that items are replaced not because they no longer perform to their designed standards, but because more modern equipment performs to higher standards. Hence a decision has to be made about replacement and maintenance.

(*iv*) *Queueing Problems.* Problems of congestion are common. Very often we have to tolerate such situations. However, occasions arise when undue congestion has to be eliminated. Basically the problems arises when units arrive at a servicing facility. If the facility is unable to cope with the number of units arriving the units have to wait in a queue. If we can reach a cost to the time spent by a unit in the queue and the cost of providing service at a given rate the problem to decide is the size of the service facility in order to minimize the total cost. The types of problems that can be studied are :

(*a*) How many counters to provide in a ship ?

(*b*) How many runways to provide at an air port ?

(*c*) How many berths for ships at a port ?

(*d*) How many maintenance crews in a factory ?

(*e*) How many doctors in a clinic ?

(*f*) How many doctors in a hospital ?

(*g*) How to schedule trains, air lines flights etc.

(*h*) What should be the size of a telephone exchange ?

(*v*) *Sequencing and Co-ordination Problems.* In these problems the object is to determine the sequence in which certain jobs have to be done and the way in which the performance of these jobs can be co-ordinated in order to accomplish a project of which the jobs are its components. There are essentially two basic techniques, *viz.* PERT and CPM, which have now become standard tools in accomplishing all projects.

(*vi*) *Competitive Problems.* All modern business enterprises operate in a competitive environment. The object of each of the competitions is to minimize his profit (or minimize his loss) without being aware of what his competitor is likely to do. Certain types of games of skill provide elements which are typical of competitive situations. The Mathematical Theory of Games attempts to explain what should constitute the rational behaviour of the individual competitors in a given situation. The theory has been used in :

(*a*) Advertising compaigns ;

(*b*) Allocation of search effort in locating minerals and

(*c*) In military operations.

(*vii*) *Search Problems.* In these problems acquisition of information is a part. An audit is a search problem. The design of inspection and quality control procedures are search problems. Information storage and retrieval are also search problems. The object is to gain the maximum information at a minimum cost.

In an operation research study we encounter several of the above prototype problems. An allocation problem is interlinked with an inventory control problem which in turn is interlinked with production schedulling problem.

Definition of Operation Research

There are various definitions of operations research. The earliest definition by Morse and Kimball is :

"Operations Research is a scientific method of providing operations quantitatives basis for executives to take decisions on the under their control".

Miller and Starr defined "OR is applied decimal theory. Operation research uses an scientific, mathematical, or logical means to attempt to cope with the problems that confront the executive when he tries to achieve the objective going rationality in dealing with his decision problems.

The operations Research Society of America defined "Operations research is an experimental and applied science devoted to observing, understanding and predicting to behaviour of purposeful man-machine systems, and operation research workers are actively engaged in applying this knowledge to practical problems in Business, Government and Society."

The common ideas emerged out of all such definitions are :

— the use of the scientific method
— study of the complex relationships
— provision of a basis for decision making.

By combining the above three main attributes it can be defined as "operations research utilises the planned approach (scientific method) and an inter disciplinary term in order to represent complex functional relationships are mathematical models for the purposes of providing a quantitative basis for decision-making and uncovering new problems for quantitative analysis".

Types of Models

A model is defined as a representation of an actual situation. It exhibits relationship between cause and effect. The purpose of developing a model is to find out the variables that affect a given situation significantly so that an executive an exercise control on such variables for the desired level of the result.

Basically there are three types of models *viz.* physical models. Analogies models and symbolic models.

	Type of models	*Main features*	*Examples*
(*i*)	Physical models	1. Describes events at a particular time 2. It cannot accommodate modifications so easily 3. More than three dimensions can not be represented.	Photograph Blue print maps, three dimension models
(*ii*)	Analogies models	1. It represents Dynamic situation 2. It represents quantitative relationships 3. It can be used to study the effect of certain changes in the parameters.	Frequency distribution curves, Demand curves, Flow charts
(*iii*)	Symbolic models (Mathematical models)	It is superior to any of the above models and a full representation of a real situation.	Mathematical equation with rotations or symbols.

The mathematical models can further be classified and are of concern for operations research.

— Quantitative and Quantitative models.
— Tailor made and Standard models.
— Probabilistic and Deterministic models
— Descriptive and Optimizing models
— Static and Dynamic models
— Simulation and non-simulation models.

45

Linear Programming

Introduction

Linear Programming is an extremely useful technique used for the purpose of maximising some objective such as profit or minimising, some objective such as costs in order to achieve the objectives of the organisation.

Linear programming is now used increasingly to solve management problems. Linear programming is used in situations where numerous activities are competing for limited resources. The person responsible for developing linear programming was George B. Dantzig, who in 1947 developed the simplex method of Linear Programming. Since World War II the linear programming models have been used increasingly to solve management problems. The term linear reveals that the techniques is mathematical and involves linear functions and the term programming refers to certain mathematical procedures to get the best solution to a problem involving limited resources. Linear Programming is a technique of numbers and the application of the numbers to arrive at a better decision. It is a tool in the hands of managers to take better decision among the number of alternatives.

Definition

Linear Programming is a technique of selecting the best possible (optimal) strategy among a number of alternatives :

(*i*) Linear Programming is an important tool used by the management, involved in choosing most appropriate (best possible) alternative among a number of alternative action.

(*ii*) Linear Programming helps the management to discover whether the maximum profit or the least production programmes open to it.

(*iii*) It is applied to problems which involve interaction between alternatives.

Uses and Applications of Linear Programming

(*i*) Linear Programming helps in determining the optimum combinations of several variables with given constraints.

(*ii*) It provides additional information for proper planning and control over various operations in the organisation.

(*iii*) It also helps the managers to have better understanding about the phenomenon and various activities of the organisation for the organisation construction of suitable mathematical model visualizing the relationship between variables if any and making improvement over them.

(*iv*) It also contributes the development of executives through the technique of model building and corresponding interpretations.

(*v*) It provides a clear specification of the management problems by defining :

(*a*) the objectives to be pursued by the organisation.

(*b*) the various restrictions imposed by the system.

(*c*) the various alternatives and relationship between various variables.

(*d*) the contribution made by each alternative to the objectives of the organisation.

(*vi*) Linear Programming has found useful avenues in the fields of agricultural, industrial, military, space and research etc.

(*vii*) Specific areas where it can be fruitfully applied are :

(*a*) Production scheduling and inventory control satisfying the demand and minimising the cost of production and inventory cost.

(*b*) Blending operations and problems—where basic components are combined to produce a product that has definite set of specifications and one may be interested in calculating best possible combination of these components which maximises the profit or minimises the cost.

(*viii*) Other important applications of linear programming techniques can be in the area of:

- purchasing and materials management.
- routing and scheduling.
- assignment problems.
- marketing.
- space exploration.

The problem of linear programming can be formulated with the help of the following terms.

Objective Function

An objective function is some sort of mathematical relationship between the variables under consideration. In the case of Linear Programming this relationship is always to be taken as linear. The construction of objective function is a process whereby most important features of a system are considered. Given variables $x_1, x_2, x_3, \ldots, x_n$. An objective function can be of the form

$$Z = A_1x_1 + A_2x_2 + A_3x_3 + \ldots A_{11}x_{11}$$

where A_1, A_2, A_3 are certain constants.

The problem of linear programming is to find out some suitable combination of $x_1, x_2, x_3 \ldots.. x_n$ etc. which optimises (*i.e.* maximises or minimises) the objective function. The objective function is always non-negative.

The objective function is to be optimised under certain restraints imposed on the variables occurring in the objective function. These restraints in most of the cases are never exact, had these been exact the objective function could be easily optimised by the use of differential calculus. These restrictions must be known and should be expressed in algebraic expressions.

A set of values of x_1, x_2 .. which satisfies constraints and the non-negativity restrictions is called a Feasible Solution. A feasible solution which optimises the objective function is known as a *Optimal Solution.*

Methods to Determine Optimal Solution

There are a number of ways to determine optimal solution for a given linear programming problem. Following three methods are generally used :

(*i*) Graphic Method

(*ii*) Simplex Method

(*iii*) Transportation Method.

Graphic Method

The problems involving two variables only can be effectively and easily solved by the method of graphs. The graphical method has only limited applications to industrial problems due to its limitations of handling only two or three variables at a time. In practice it is convenient for two variables only because the geometry of 3 dimensional case becomes so complicated that accurate results are difficult to obtain. The problems containing more than 3 variables are difficult to be solved.

The graphical method consists of following three main steps which are as follows :

(*i*) The constraints of the model are plotted on the graph paper by considering them as equalities.

(*ii*) Lines are drawn in two dimensional plane corresponding to given equations.

(*iii*) These lines refer to the region of permissible values.

(*iv*) The objectives function is also plotted on the same graph.

(*v*) Using the lines in steps (*i*), (*ii*) and (*iii*) the optimal solution that satisfies the constraints and optimises the objective function is determined by trial and error method.

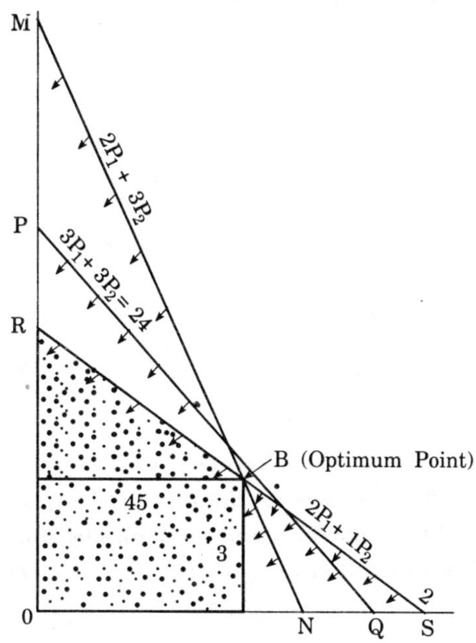

Fig. 45.1.

From the graph we find that point 'B' represents the optimum point in the feasible area ORBN which satisfied the equations (*i*), (*ii*) and (*iii*). Point 'B' gives the optimum value.

PROBLEMS

Problem 1. *Mr. 'X' can purchase his tomatoes of three varieties (A, B and C) from two sources which differ in yields of various sizes and quality. The yield characteristics are given in table with purchase limitations. We find that from source 1, there is 20% yield of product. 'A' 20% yield of product 'B' and 30% yield of product 'C' remaining 30% is waste. From source '2' for product 'C' and 'A' the yield is 30% of product 'B' the yield is 10% and waste 30%.*

From which source the customer should buy tomatoes and how much in order to maximise profit.

Table

Product variety	*Source 1*	*Source 2*	*Purchase limitation tons*
A	0.2	0.3	1.8
B	0.2	0.1	1.2
C	0.3	0.3	2.4
Waste	0.3	0.3	
Relative Profit	Rs. 5	Rs. 6	

Solution (Graphical Method)

Let P_1 be the tomato purchased from source '1' and P_2 be the tomato purchased from source '2'

then
$$Z = 5P_1 + 6P_2$$
$$.2P_1 + .3P_2 \geq 1.8 \quad ...(1)$$
$$\cdot 2P_1 + .1P_2 \geq 1.2 \quad ...(2)$$
$$3P_1 + .3P_2 \geq 2.4 \quad ...(3)$$

Changing the above equations in the form $\frac{x}{a} + \frac{y}{b} = 1$ where $a + b$ are the intercepts in x and y axis respectively.

$$\frac{P_1}{9} + \frac{P_2}{6} = 1 \quad ...(4)$$
$$\frac{P_1}{6} + \frac{P_2}{12} = 1 \quad ...(5)$$
$$\frac{P_1}{8} + \frac{P_2}{8} = 1 \quad ...(6)$$

Problem 2. *A small manufacturing firm produces two types of gadgets, A and B are first processed in the foundry, then sent to machine for finishing. The number of man hours of labour required in each shop for the production of each unit of 'A' and 'B' and the number of man hours the firm has available per week are as follows :*

	Foundry	*Machine Shop*
Gadget *A*	10 hrs.	5 hrs.
Gadget *B*	6 hrs.	4 hrs.
Firm's capacity per week	1000 hrs.	600 hrs.

(*i*) *Construct the objective function and the corresponding restraints for calculating that how many units should be produced per week so that the profit is maximum. The profit on the sale of 'A' is Rs. 30/unit as compared with 'B' Rs. 20/unit.*

(*ii*) *How many units of A and B should be produced to maximise the profit ?*

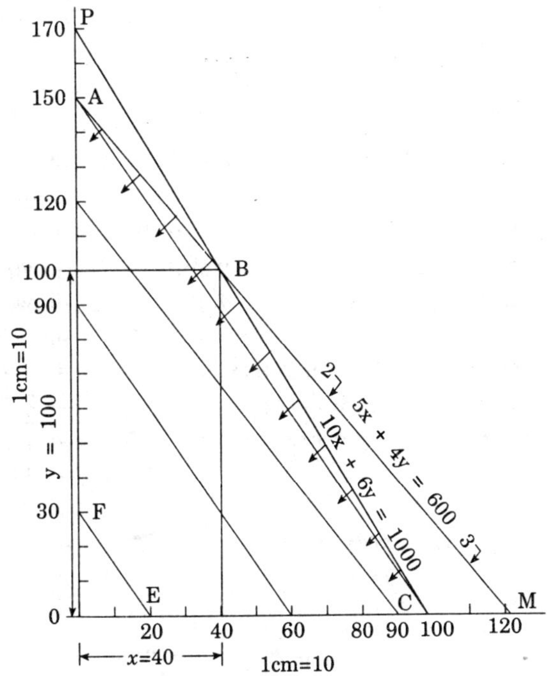

Fig. 45.2.

Solution. Let the firm manufacture x units of A and y units of B then,

The objective function and the constraints for the given problem are :

Max. $$Z = 30x + 20y \qquad ...(1)$$

$$10x + 6y \geq 1000 \qquad ...(2)$$

$$5x + 4y \geq 600 \qquad ...(3)$$

$$x , y \geq 0 \qquad ...(4)$$

the above equations are explained below :

The firm's capacity per week in foundry is 1000 hrs and x units of A will require $10x$ man hours per week in foundry whereas y units of B will require $6y$ hrs. Hence one constraint is

$$10x + 6y \leq 1000$$

Similarly other constraint is

$$5x + 4y \leq 600$$

The last constraint is that both $x + y$ should be positive $x , y \geq 0$.

For graphical solution of the above problem, the inequalities are changed into equations and then the equations thus obtained are plotted on the graph paper. Here equations to be plotted as :

$$10x + 6y = 1000 \quad ...(1)$$
$$5x + 4y = 600 \quad ...(2)$$
$$x = 0 \quad ...(3)$$
$$y = 0 \quad ...(4)$$

Now the line $x = 0$ is y-axis and $y = 0$ is x- axis for plotting the remaining two lines.

Converting the above lines in the form $\frac{x}{a} + \frac{y}{b} = 1$ we get,

$$\frac{x}{100} + \frac{y}{167} = 1$$

$$\frac{x}{120} + \frac{y}{150} = 1$$

Plotting these lines on the graph, we get two lines *PC* and *AM* which intersect at *B*.

Area covered between the two axes and the line *PC* contains at those points which satisfy $10x + 6y \le 100$. Similarly area below the line *AM* and between two axes satisfies the inequality $5x + 4y \le 600$. The area *OABC* satisfies all the constraints of the given problem. It is noted that area below the lines *PC* and *AM* as the constraints for these equations have $\le$ sign. The region *OABC* is the required space for feasible solutions and from this region we want to find *X* and *Y* for which *Z* is maximum. For this we plot the objective function $30x + 20y$ for some numerical value of *Z*, and move this line parallel to itself till it contains a point of the feasible region, say line *EF* is plotted. The line *EF* moves upwards until *EF* cuts most remote corner *i.e.*, the point *B* of the polygon *OABC*. This is the maximum value that *Z* can obtain, *xy* still remaining in the feasible region.

This co-ordinates of the point *B* ($x = 40$, $y = 100$) gives the required solution. The corresponding profit is

$$Z = 30 \times 40 + 20 \times 100$$
$$= 1200 + 2000 = \text{Rs. } 3,200$$

It should be noted that other lines parallel to *EF* will not contain even a single point of the feasible region. The extreme point of the feasible region will be the optimum value. Hence optimum value of *Z* should be tried at the corners of the polygon only.

Problem 3. *A manufacturer can produce two different products A and B, during a given time period. Each of these products requires four different manufacturing operations—grinding, turning, assembly and testing. The manufacturing requirements in hours per unit of product are given below for A and B.*

Operations	*Product*	
	A	B
Grinding	1	2
Turning	3	1
Assembly	6	3
Testing	5	4

The available capacities of these operations in hours for the given time period are grinding 30, turning 60, assembly 200, and testing 200. The contribution to overhead and profit is Rs. 2 for each unit of A and Rs. 3 for each unit of B. They can sell all that can be produced at the prevailing market price. Determine by graphical method the optimum amount of A and B to produce during the given time period.

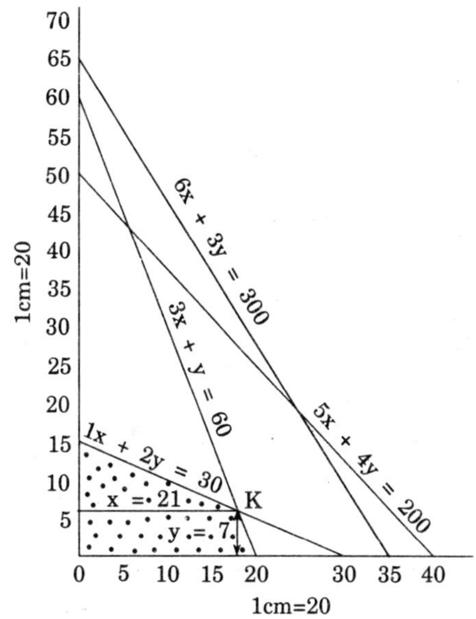

Fig. 45.3.

Solution. Let the manufacturer produce x units of A and y units of B. Then the objective function to be optimised is

$$Z = 2x + 3y$$

The constraints are

$$x + 2y \leq 30 \text{ for grinding}$$
$$-\ 3x + y \leq 200 \text{ for turning}$$
$$6x + 3y \leq 200 \text{ for assembly}$$
$$5x + 4y \leq 200 \text{ for testing}$$

and $$x\ , y \geq 0$$

Considering the constraints as equalities we plot the equations as shown in the graph. We find from the graph that limiting factor is the capacity of the grinding section and the point K determining the maximum profit under the given circumstance.

Problem 4. *Solve the following linear programming problem graphically. Minimize*

$$Z = 3x_1 + 5x_2 \quad x_1 \leq 4$$
$$-3x_1 + 4x_2 << 12\ x_2 \geq 2$$
$$2x_1 - x_2 \leq\ -2\ x_1\ , x_2 \geq 0$$
$$2x_1 + 3x_2 \leq 12$$

The figure of the given constrained equations is drawn in the graph for plotting the objective function for any value of Z, take

$$Z = 15 \text{ , so that}$$
$$Z = 3x_1 + 5x_2 = 15$$

Now draw lines parallel to *PQ*, the line *MN* is the first to touch feasible region at the point *A*. Hence the co-ordinates of *A* give the optimal solution. At the point *A* $x_1 = 3$, $x_2 = 2$ and the value of

$$Z = 3 \times 3 + 5 \times 2$$
$$= 9 + 10 = 19$$

In this case the feasible region lies above the line *MN* as the inequality is ≥0.

Problem 5

Example 1

Deptts.	*Hours Product A*	*Required Product B*	*Available hours in Month*
1	2	3	1500
2	3	2	1500
3	1	1	600

There are 4 basic steps used in the graphical method of linear programming.

Step 1. Initial step is concerned with setting up the firm's objective function and its constraints as mathematical equation or inequalities.

$$\text{Maximize } Z = \text{Rs.}10A + 12B$$

These requirements can be stated as

$$2A + 3B \leq 1500$$
$$3A + 2B \leq 1500$$
$$A + B \leq 600$$

It should be noted that all 3 inequlities represent capacity restrictions regarding output. All elements in the solution of a linear programming problem must be equal to or greater than zero ($A \geq 0$ and $B \geq 0$). These 2 additional constraints mean the solution must lie in the + quadrant of the graph or both *X* and *Y* must be positive.

Step 2. Next we graph the constraints inequalities. If in Deptt. one, units of *B* are produced then

$$2A + [0 \times 3B] = 1500$$

or
$$A = 750$$

The first point (750) units of product *A* and zero unit of product *B*. 2nd point is computed in the same manner, only this time all the hours available are used in making the maximum number of units (500) of product *B* and 0 units of product *A*.

$$2(0) + 3B = 1500$$
$$B = 500$$

Plot this *A, B* line on *X,Y* axis.

The similar calculation is made for other equation, *i.e.*

Deptt. 1 $2A + 3B \leq 1500$

2 $3A + 2B \leq 1500$

3 $A + B \leq 600$

or

1 $B = 750\ ,\ B = 500$

2 $3(0) + 2B = 1500$

$B = 750$

$3A + 2(0) = 500$

3 $A + (0) = 600$

$B = 600.$

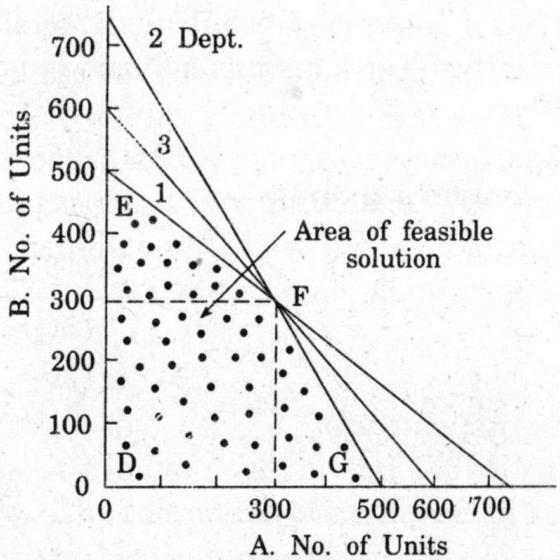

Fig. 45.5

Diagram is given in graph

Step 3. This step is to plot the objective function n, which is given as :

$$Z = \text{Rs.}10A + 12B$$

Step 4. This step is to test the corners, *i.e.*, point D, E, F, G. The stripped area to determine which yields the highest contribution

AB

Point D (0 , 0) = Rs. 0.

Point E (0 , 500) = (10 × 0) + 12(500) = 6000

Point F (300 , 300) = 300 × 10 = Rs. 3000

= 300 × 12 = Rs. 3600

= Rs. 6600

Point G 500 + 0 = Rs. 500 × 10 = Rs. 5000

The maximum profit is yield on F point.

Problem 6. *Demand for circuit boards type 100 and 101 is unlimited. The plant capacity cannot be increased. It is decided to go for second shift for these two products. The capacity of this shift to perform the operations involved is set forth as follows :*

Circuit type	*Assembly*	*Soldering*	*Inspection*
100	8,000	12,000	7,000
101	6,000	5,000	14,000

(*a*) *How should the existing capacity be allocated to the two type of circuit boards ?*

(*b*) *If contribution of type 100 is Rs. 6 per unit and Rs. 4.50 for type 101, what will be total contribution to profit in proposed plan.*

Solution.

Assumptions. Let us say we produce x_1 units of 100 type board x_2 units of 101 type board. Utilization of assembly shop will be :

$$x_2 = (8000 - x) \times \frac{6000}{8000}$$

$$x_2 = (8000 - x_1) \times \frac{3}{4}$$

or $$4x_2 = 8000 \times 3 - 3x_1$$

or $$3x_1 + 4x_2 = 24000 \quad ...(1)$$

Soldering Shop

$$x_2 = (12000 - x_1) \times \frac{5000}{12000}$$

or $$12x_2 = 5 \times 12000 - 5x_1$$

or $$5x_1 + 12x_2 = 60,000 \quad ...(2)$$

Inspection

$$x_2 = (7000 - x_1) \times \frac{14000}{7000}$$

or $$7x_2 = 14 \times 7000 - 14x_1$$

or $$14x_1 + 7x_2 = 98,000$$

or $$2x_1 + x_2 = 14,000 \quad ...(3)$$

$$x_1 \geq 0 \quad ...(4)$$

$$x_2 \geq 0 \quad ...(5)$$

From equation (1)

$$\frac{x_1}{8000} + \frac{x_2}{6000} = 1$$

$$x_1 = 8000 \qquad x_2 = 0$$

$$x_1 = 0 \qquad x_2 = 6000$$

From equation (2)

$$\frac{x_1}{12000} + \frac{x_2}{5000} = 1$$

$$x_1 = 12000 \qquad x_1 = 0$$

$$x_1 = 0 \qquad x_1 = 5000$$

From equation (3)

$$\frac{x_1}{7000} + \frac{x_2}{14000} = 1$$

$$x_1 = 7000 \qquad x_2 = 0$$

$$x_1 = 0 \qquad x_2 = 14000$$

If there is no solution to enforce the capacity of assembly shop to point *F*. The optimum utilization will at points *E, D, C* and *P*.

i.e.

Point	*Type 100* x_1	*Type 101* x_2
E	7000	0
D	6600	13500
C	3000	3900
B	0	5000

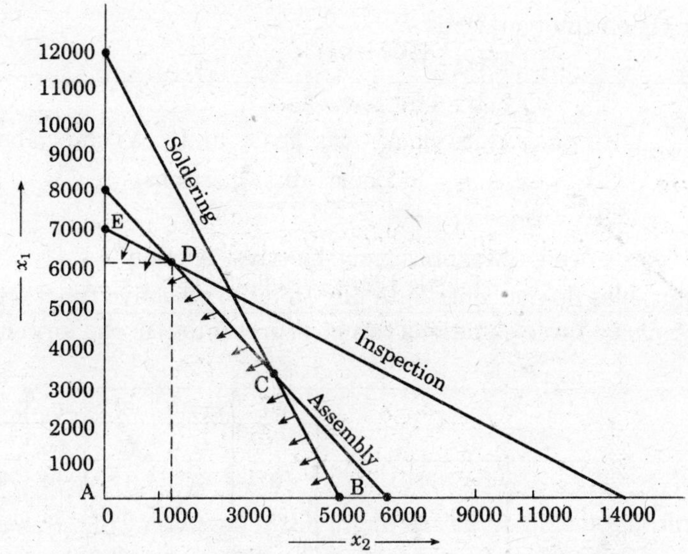

Fig. 45.6.

Optimum utilization of the three shops is possible in the above four situations for these two product lines.

For (*b*) part of the question, we have to optimise the profit.

For the graphical we have to calculate the profit for all the four points.

Point *E*, $P = 6x_1 + 4.5x_2 = 6 \times 7000 + 4.5 \times 0 = 42{,}000$

Point *D*, $P = 6 \times 6600 + 4.5 \times 1350 = 39600 + 6075 = 45{,}675$

Point *C*, $P = 6 \times 3000 + 4.5 \times 3900 = 18000 + 17550 = 35{,}550$

Point *B*, $P = 6 \times 0 + 4.5 \times 5000 = 22{,}500$

Point *D*,

Type 100 $\rightarrow$ 6,600 No.

Type 101 $\rightarrow$ 1,350 No.

is point of maximum profit.

Simplex Method

The simplex method is used generally for large scale problems where it would not be possible to solve them by graphical method. Obviously for problems with three and more variables simplex method is useful. In these complex cases, the simplex method saves time and effort by taking us to the optimal solution in a finite number of steps, thereby each step bringing us closer to the optimum.

To apply the procedure to complex problems it will be useful to reduce it to a set of rigorous rules which can be applied rather mechanically to save time and effort to reduce the computation required to a minimum.

To start with let us try to understand the terminology in simplex method.

Let the objective function be represented by

$$60x_1 + 50x_2 = \text{Maximisation}$$

Subject to the constraint equations

$$2x_1 + 4x_2 \leq 80$$
$$3x_1 + 2x_2 \leq 60$$

To remove inequalities introduce slack variables x_3 and x_4 as shown below

$$\left.\begin{aligned} 2x_1 + 4x_2 + x_3 &= 80 \\ 3x_1 + 2x_2 + x_4 &= 60 \end{aligned}\right] \text{constraint equations}$$

$60x_1 + 50x_2 + (0)x_3 + (0)x_4$ = Maximisation objective function

Since slack variables do not contribute any thing to objective function, their coefficient is taken as zero. The above three equations can be represented in the form of matrix as below :

Solution			60	50	0	0	*Objective Row*
Step			x_1	x_2	x_3	x_4	*Variable Row*
0	x_3	80	2	4	1	0	Constraints equations
0	x_4	60	3	2	0	1	
↑	↑	↑	Body		Identity		
Objective column	Variable column	Constant column					

Procedure Summary

1. Formulate the problem into linear equations with slack variables and the objective function.
2. Develop the initial simplex matrix from the above equations including the initial trivial solution and the index row numbers. The index row numbers in the initial matrix are calculated by the formula.

Index number = $\sum$ [(Numbers in column) × (Corresponding number in objective column)]
– [Number in objective row at head of column]

3. In the above matrix mark the key column, the column with the most negative index number in the body or the identity.
4. Mark the key row, the row with the smallest non-negative quotient obtained by dividing each number of the constant column by the corresponding positive, non-zero number in the key column.
5. The key number is at the intersection of the key row and key column.
6. Develop the main row of the new table.

$$\text{Main row} = \frac{\text{key row of preceding table}}{\text{key number}}$$

The main row appears in the new table in the same relative position as the key row of the preceding table.

7. Develop the balance of the new table.

(*a*) The variable and its objective number at the head of the key column are entered in the stub of the new table to the left of the main row, replacing the variable and objective number from the key row of the preceding table.

(*b*) The remainder of the variable and objective columns are reproduced in the new table exactly as they were in the preceding table.

(*c*) The balance of the coefficients for the new table are calculated by the formula :

$$\text{New number} = (\text{old number}) - \frac{\begin{pmatrix}\text{corresponding number}\\ \text{of key row}\end{pmatrix} \times \begin{pmatrix}\text{Corresponding number}\\ \text{of key column}\end{pmatrix}}{(\text{Key number})}$$

8. Repeat (iterate) step 3 through 7C until all the index numbers (not including the constant column) are positive. An optimal solution then results.
9. The interpretation of the resulting optimum solution is as follows. The solution appears in the stub. The variables shown in the variable column have values shown in the corresponding rows of the constant column. The value of the objective function is shown in the constant column, index row. All variables not shown in the stub are equal to zero :

Example. Maximise the objective function

$$P = 6x_1 + 4.5x_2 \qquad \text{...(1)}$$

Subject to the constraint equations

$$3x_1 + 4x_2 \le 24{,}000 \qquad \text{...(2)}$$

$$5x_1 + 12x_2 \le 60{,}000 \qquad \text{...(3)}$$

$$2x_1 + x_2 \le 14{,}000 \qquad \text{...(4)}$$

Step 1. Formulation of problem. By introducing the slack variables in equations (2), (3) and (4), the inequalities can be removed and written as follows :

$$3x_1 + 4x_2 + x_3 = 24{,}000 \qquad \text{...(5)}$$

$$5x + 12x_2 + x_4 = 60{,}000 \qquad \text{...(6)}$$

$$2x_1 + x_2 + x_5 = 14{,}000 \qquad \text{...(7)}$$

and let the contribution of each x_3 , x_4 and x_5 be zero.

The objective function equation (1) can be written as

$$P = 6x_1 + 4.5x_2 + (0)x_3 + (0)x_4 + (0)x_5 \qquad \text{...(8)}$$

Now these equations (5) to (8) are written in the matrix form and solved by simplex method as per the procedure.

Step 2. Initial Simplex Matrix

Table 1

Solution Step			$6\ x_1$	$4.5\ x_2$	$0\ x_3$	$0\ x_4$	$0\ x_5$	*Coefficient of objective function called Objective Row*
0	x_2	24,000	3	4	1	0	0	
0	x_4	60,000	5	12	0	1	0	Constraint equations
0	x_5	14,000	2	1	0	0	1	
↑ objective column	↑ variable column	↑ constant column	Body		Identity			

Calculate index row number and introduce Index Row in the matrix.

$$\text{Index number} = \sum\left[\left(\begin{matrix}\text{numbers in}\\ \text{column}\end{matrix}\right)\times\left(\begin{matrix}\text{corresponding number}\\ \text{objective column}\end{matrix}\right)\right]-\left[\begin{matrix}\text{Number in objective}\\ \text{row at head column}\end{matrix}\right]$$

1. Index number of constant column

$$= (24000 \times 0 + 60000 \times 0 + 14000 \times 0) - (0) = 0$$

2. Index number of 1st column of body

$$= (3 \times 0 + 5 \times 0 + 2 \times 0) - (6) = -6$$

3. Index number of 2nd column of body

$$= (4 \times 0 + 12 \times 0 + 1 \times 0) - (4.5) = -4.5$$

4. Index number of 1st column of identity

$$= (1 \times 0 + 0 \times 0 + 0 \times 0) - (0) = 0$$

5. Index number of 2nd column of identity

$$= (0 \times 0 + 1 \times 0 + 0 \times 0) - (0) = 0$$

6. Index number of 3rd column of identity

$$= (0 \times 0 + 0 \times 0 + 1 \times 0) - (0) = 0$$

Table 2. Initial Simplex Matrix with Index Row

			6	4.5	0	0	0	
			x_1	x_2	x_3	x_4	x_5	
0	x_3	24000	3	4	1	0	0	
0	x_4	60000	5	12	0	1	0	
0	x_5	14000	2	1	0	0	1	
		0	– 6	– 4.5	0	0	0	Index Row

Step 3. Select Key Column. The column containing – 6 the most negative number in index row is marked as *key column.*

Step 4. Select Key Row. Divide each number of constant column by the corresponding positive non-zero number in key column. The row with the smallest non-negative quotient is called *key row*.

(1)	Number of key column	3	5	2
(2)	Number of constant. column	24000	60000	14000
(3)	quotient = (2) ÷ (1)	8000	12000	7000

Smallest non negative quotient

∴ Key Row is | 0 x_5 14000 2 1 0 0 1 |

Step 5. Select key Number. At the inter section of key columns and key row :

All the above three steps are incorporated in the initial simplex matrix as below.

Table 3. Initial Simplex Matrix with Key column Key Row and Key Number

			6	4.5	0	0	0	
			x_1	x_2	x_3	x_4	x_5	
0	x_3	24000	3	4	1	0	0	
0	x_4	60000	5	12	0	1	0	
0	x_5	14000	2	1	0	0	1	Key Row
		0	–6	–4.5	0	0	0	Index row
			Key column					

Step 6.

$$\text{Main Row} = \frac{\text{Key Row of previous table}}{\text{Key Number}}$$

$$\text{Main Row} = (14000 \quad 25 \quad 1 \quad 0 \quad 0 \quad 2) \div 2$$

$$7000 \quad 1 \quad \frac{1}{2} \quad 0 \quad 0 \quad \frac{1}{2}$$

Write the main row in the new table in the same position as the key row of the preceding table.

Step 7. Develop the balance of the new table 4 :

(*a*) Introduce variable x_1 and objective coefficient 6 in the main row in the stub replacing x_5 and 0 *i.e.*

6	x_1	7000	1	$\frac{1}{2}$	0	0	$\frac{1}{2}$	Main Row

(*b*) The remainder of the variable and objective columns are reproduced in the new table – 4 exactly as they west in Table – 3, *i.e.*

0	x_3						
0	x_4						
6	x_1	7000	1	$\frac{1}{2}$	0	0	$\frac{1}{2}$
↑ Objective column	↑ Variable column						

(*c*) All the remaining rows numbers are calculated by

$$\text{New number} = \frac{\begin{pmatrix}\text{corresponding number}\\ \text{in key row}\end{pmatrix}\begin{pmatrix}\text{Corresponding number}\\ \text{in key column}\end{pmatrix}}{\text{Key number}}$$

First row of Table 3

New number in constant column $= 24000 - \frac{(14000)(3)}{2} = 3000$

New number in 1st column of body $= 3 - \frac{(2)(3)}{2} = 0$

New number in 2nd column of body $= 4 - \frac{(1 \times 3)}{2} = \frac{5}{2}$

New number in 1st column of identity $= 1 - \frac{(0 \times 3)}{2} = 1$

New number in 2nd column identity $= 0 - \frac{(0 \times 3)}{2} = 0$

New number in 3rd column of identity $= 0 - \frac{(1 \times 3)}{2} = -\frac{3}{2}$

Second row of Table 3

New number in constant column $= 60000 - \frac{(14000 \times 3)}{2} = 39000$

New number in 1st column of body $= 5 - \frac{(2 \times 5)}{2} = 0$

New number in 2nd column of body $= 12 - \frac{(1 \times 5)}{2} = \frac{19}{2}$

New number in 1st column of identity $= 0 - \frac{(0 \times 5)}{2} = 0$

New number in 2nd column of identity $= 1 - \frac{(0 \times 5)}{2} = 1$

New number in 3rd column of identity $= 0 - \frac{(1 \times 5)}{2} = -\frac{5}{2}$

Index row of Table 3

New number in 1st column of body $= -6 - \frac{(2 \times -6)}{2} = 0$

New number in 2nd column of body $= -4.5 - \frac{(1 \times -6)}{6} = -1.5$

New number in 1st column of identity $= 0 - \frac{(0 \times -6)}{2} = 0$

New number in 2nd column of identity $= 0 - \frac{(0 \times -6)}{2} = 0$

New number in 3rd column of identity $= 0 - \frac{(1 \times -6)}{2} = 3$

All these above numbers are introduced in the matrix 7(*b*) and written at table 4 as shown below.

Table 4. Simplex Matrix Read- for Second Iteration

			6	4.5	0	0	0
			x_1	x_2	x_3	x_4	x_5
0	x_3	3000	0	5/2	1	0	–3/2
0	x_4	39000	0	19/2	0	1	– 5/2
6	x_1	7000	1	1/2	0	0	1/2 Main Row
			0	– 1.5	0	0	3 Index Row

Step 8 : Repeat steps 3 to 7 *c*

Table 5. 2nd Iteration

			6	4.5	0	0	0	
			x_1	x_2	x_3	x_4	x_5	
0	x_3	3000	0	5/2	1	0	– 3/2	Key row
0	x_4	39000	0	19/2	0	1	– 5/2	
6	x_1	7000	1	1/2	0	0	1/2	
			0	– 1.5	0	0	3	
				↑ Key column				

Since – 1.5 in the most negative number in index row, the corresponding column is the key row

(1) Number of key column	5/2	19/2	1/2
(2) Number of constant column	3000	39000	7000
(3) Quotient = (2) ÷ (1)	1200	4104	14000

(1200 — Smallest running Quotient)

Therefore, 0 x_3 3000 0 5/2 1 0 –3/2 in the key row.

[5/2] the intersection of key row and key column is the key number.

Main row	[3000	0	5/2	1	0	– 3/2] ÷ 5/2
	= 1200	0	1	2/5	0	– 3/5

Introduce variable x_2 and objective coefficient 4.5 in place of x_3 and '0' respectively in the main row and write the main row in place of Key Row of previous table. Remaining rows and numbers are calculated as per the formula of new number and written in Table 6.

Table 6. Simplex Matrix 2nd Interaction Completed

			6	4.5	0	0	0	
			x_1	x_2	x_3	x_4	x_5	
4.5	x_2	1200	0	1	2/5	0	– 3/5	
0	x_4	27600	0	0	– 19/5	1	26	
6	x_1	6400	1	0	– 1/5	0	4/5	
			0	0	– 3/5	0	21/10	Index row

Since all the numbers in the index row are positive, the solution is optimal.

Therefore, $x_1 = 6400$

$x_2 = 1200$

By substituting the values of $x_1 = 6400$ and $x_2 = 1200$ in objective function

$$P = 6.0x_1 + 4.5x_2$$

$$= 6 \times 6400 + 4.5 \times 1200 = 38400 + 5400.0$$

$$P = 43800 \text{ maximum.}$$

Problem 6. *A lock manufacturer can sell all it can produce. It is making two types of locks ; Type 1 fetches a profit 0.30 per lock and Type 2 ; 0.34 per lock and total capacity of the shops are as follows :*

	Lock Type 1	*Lock Type 2*
Forging	1,,000 Nos.	1,000 Nos.
Milling	1,500 Nos.	800 Nos.
Stamping	900 Nos.	700 Nos.
Assembly	1,000 Nos.	1,100 Nos.

Advice the product mix.

Solution.

Let x_1 = Quantity of Lock type 1 produced

x_2 = Quantity of Lock type 2 produced

Forging shop utilisation $x_2 = (1,000 - x_1) \times \dfrac{1000}{1000}$

or $x_1 + x_2 = 1000$ ...(1)

Milling shop utilisation $x_2 = (1500 - x_1) \times \dfrac{800}{1500}$

or $15x_2 = 12,000 - 8x_1$

or $8x_1 + 15x_2 = 12,000$ ...(2)

Stamping shop utilisation $x_2 = (900 - x_1) \times \dfrac{700}{900}$

$9x_2 = 6300 - 7x_1$

or $7x_1 + 9x_2 = 6300$ ...(3)

Assembiy shop utilisation $x_2 = (1000 - x_1) \times \dfrac{1100}{1000}$

or $10x_2 = 11,000 - 11x_1$

or $$11x_1 - 10x_2 = 11{,}000 \quad ...(4)$$

In this case limiting shop is the stamping one, the combination of the mix will fall on stamping line. The optimum mix could be found by taking out the profit. The point which gives maximum profit will be the mix

$$x_2 = 0 \text{ , and } x_1 = 900$$

Putting the value in profit equation, we get

$$P = 0.30 \times 900 + 0.34 \times 0 = \text{Rs. } 270$$

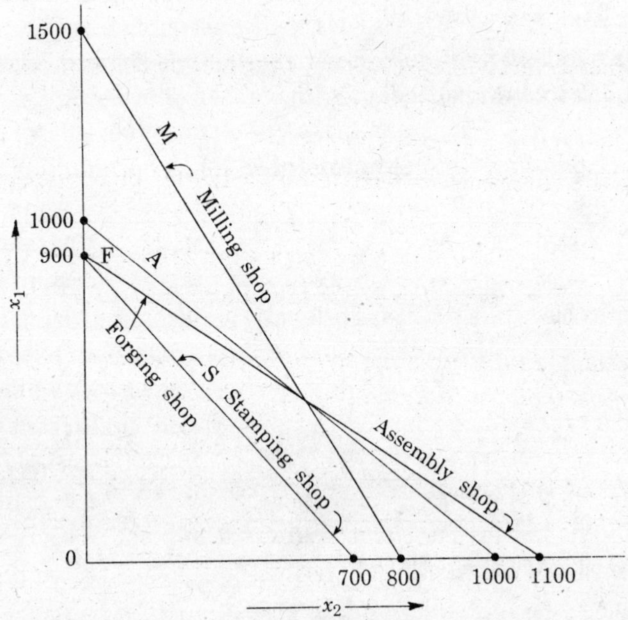

Fig. 45.7.

Problem

Cost reduction. *A company combines factor A and B to form a product which must weigh 50 kg. At least 20 kg of A and no more than 40 kg of B can be used. The cost of A Rs. 10 per kg and that B Rs. 25 per kg.*

Find out quantity of *A* and *B* which should be used.

Solution.

If x_1 is kg of *A* used

x_2 is kg of *B* used

$$x_1 \geq 20$$
$$x_2 \leq 40$$
$$x_1 + x_2 = 50$$
$$C = 10x_1 + 25x_2$$
$$x_1 + x_2 + x_3 = 50$$
$$x_3 - x_4 + x_5 = 20$$
$$x_2 + x_6 = 40$$

The cost function

$$C = 10x_1 + 25x_2 + Mx_3 + 0x_4 + Mx_5 + 0x_6$$

here. $\left.\begin{matrix} x_3 \\ x_5 \end{matrix}\right\}$ are artificial variables

$\left.\begin{matrix} x_4 \\ x_6 \end{matrix}\right\}$ slack variables

By adding variables to all the equations

$$x_1 + x_2 + x_3 + 0x_4 + 0x_5 + 0x_6 = 50$$
$$x_1 + 0x_2 + 0x_3 - x_4 + x_5 + 0x_6 = 20$$
$$0x_1 + x_2 + 0x_3 + 0x_4 + 0x_5 + x_6 = 40$$

Simplex Table 1

	Sol. max	Sol.	M	0	M	0	10	25
C_J	max.	value	x_3	x_4	x_5	x_6	x_1	x_2
M	x_3	50	1	0	0	0	1	1
M	x_5	20	0	–1	1	0	1	0 ←
0	x_6	40	0	0	0	1	0	1
	Z_j	70 M	M	– M	M	0	2 M	M
	$C_j - Z_j$		0	+ M	0	0	10 – 2M ↑	25 – M

Note : We must try to drive out artificial variable first.

Simplex Table 2

	Sol. max.	Sol. value.	M	0	M	0	10	25
C_j			x_3	x_4	x_5	x_6	x_1	x_2
M	x_3	30	1	1	–1	0	0	1
10	x_1	20	0	–1	1	0	1	0
0	x_6	40	0	0	0	1	0	1
	Z_j		M	M – 10	10 – m	0	10	M
	$C_j - Z_j$		0	– m + 10 ↑	– 10 + 2m	0	0	25 – m

Simplex Table 3

	Sol.	Sol.	M	0	M	0	10	25
C_j	max.	value	x_3	x_4	x_5	x_6	x_1	x_2
0	x_4	30	1	1	–1	0	0	1←
10	x_1	50	1	0	0	0	1	1
0	x_6	40	0	0	0	1	0	1
	Z_j	500	10	0	0	0	10	10
			M – 10	0	M	0	0	15 ↑

x_1	x_6
$20 - (-1 \times 30) = 50$	$40 - 0$
$0 - (-1 \times 1) = +1$	$0 - 0$
$-1 - (-1 \times 1) = 0$	$0 - 0$
$1 - (-1 \times -1) = 0$	$0 - 0$
$0 - (-1 \times 0) = 0$	$1 - 0$
$1 - (-1 \times 0) = 1$	$0 - 0$
$0 - (-1 \times 1) = 1$	$1 - 0$

Simplex Table 4

	Sol. max.	*So. value*	*M*	0	*M*	0	10	25
C_f			x_3	x_4	x_5	x_6	x_1	x_2
25	x_2	30	1	1	−1	0	0	1
10	x_1	20	0	−1	1	0	1	0
0	x_6	10	−1	−1	1	1	0	0
	Z_j	950	25	15	−15	0	10	25
	$C_j - Z_j$		$M - 25$	−15	$M - 15$	0	0	0

x_1	x_6
$50 - 1 \times 30 = 20$	$40 - 1 \times 30 = 10$
$1 - 1 \times 1 = 0$	$0 - 1 \times 1 = -1$
$0 - 1 \times 1 = -1$	$1 - 1 \times 1 = -1$
$0 - 1 \times 0 - 1 = 0$	$0 - 1 \times -1 = 1$
$0 - 1 \times 0 = 0$	$1 - 1 \times 0 = 1$
$1 - 1 \times 0 = 1$	$0 - 1 \times 0 = 0$
$1 - 1 \times 1 = 0$	$1 - 1 \times 1 = 0$

$C_j - Z_j$ should be 0 or positive for minimization and 0 is obtained in this case for x_1 and x_2 hence solution is reached

$$x_1 = 20$$
$$x_2 = 30$$
$$C = 950.$$

Problem. *A carpenter has 90, 80 and 50 running feet of plywood, pine and birch respectively. Product A requires 2, 1 and 1 running feet of plywood pine and birch respectively, and product B requires 1, 2 and 1 running feet plywood, pine and brich respectively. If A sells for Rs. 12 and B sells for Rs. 10, how many of each should he make to obtain the maximum gross income ?*

Maximum Gross Income

Solution. To solve this problem first we formulate the problem

(*i*) Let x_1 be the unit of product *A* and x_2 be the product *B*.

So

	Plywood	Pine	Birch
A	2	1	1
B	1	2	1
Maximum quantity available	90	80	50

Selling price per unit Rs. 12 for A and Rs. 10 for B.

So
$$Z = 12x_1 + 10x_2$$
$$2x_1 + x_2 \le 90$$
$$x_1 + 2x_2 \le 80$$
$$x_1 + x_2 \le 50$$

(*ii*) Now next step is the Development of Equation from the inequalities adding the slack variables. Now the new equation will be :

$$2x_1 + x_2 + x_3 + (0)x_4 + (0)x_5 = 90$$
$$x_1 + 2x_2 + (0)x_3 + x_4 + (0)x_5 = 80$$
$$x_1 + x_2 + (0)x_3 + (0)x_4 + x_5 = 50$$
$$Z = 12x_1 + 10x_2 + (0)x_3 + (0)x_4 + x_5$$

(*iii*) Let us now develop the initial Simplex Table 1.

Table 1

			0	0	0	12	10,	
C_j	*Sol. variables*	*Sol. value*	x_3	x_4	x_5	x_1	x_2,	
0	x_3	90	1	0	0	2	1	← key row
0	x_4	80	0	1	0	1	,	
0	x_5	50	0	0	1	1	,	
		$C_j - Z_j$	0	0	0	12	01	
						↑ Key		

Table 2

			0	0	0	12	10 (Key column ↓)	
C_j	*Sol. variables*	*Sol. value*	x_3	x_4	x_5	x_1	x_2	
12	x_1	45	1/2	0	0	1	1/2	
0	x_4	35	– ½	0	–1	0	3/2	
0	x_5	5	– ½	0	1	0	1/2	← KR
		$Z_j =$	6	0	0	12	6	
		$C_j - Z_j =$	– 6	0	0	0	4	

Table 3

			0	0	0	12	10
C_i	*Solution variables*	*Solution values*	x_3	x_4	x_5	x_1	x_2
12	x_1	40	1	1	– 1	1	00
0	x_4	20	1	3	– 4	0	0
10	x_2	10	– 1	0	2	0	1
		$C_j - Z_j =$	– 2	– 12	– 8	0	0

Here the value $C_j - Z_j$ for x_1 and x_2 are zero and for others is in negative so we can't move further. Hence profit maximisation will be at that time when we sell the units of product A and B in the following manner :

$$x_1 = 40 \times 12 = 480$$

$$x_2 = 10 \times 10 = 100$$

Total income would be $= \text{Rs. } 580.$ **Ans.**

Problem. *In a metal shop, two articles are produced, viz. bucket and pressed metal handles. The lids takes 20 sec to stamp, 30 seconds to form and 20 seconds to paint. The handles takes 40 sec to stamp, 10 seconds to form and 16 seconds to paints. The gross profit margins on lids and handles are 6P. and 9P. respectively. The time available per day on each process is 8 hours and 20 minutes, i.e. 30,000 seconds.*

How many lids and buckets should be produced to obtain maximum gross profit ? What will be the maximum gross profit ?

Solution. *First step.* First step is to formulate the linear programming problem.

The objective is to maximise profit. The function will be mathematically stated as under :

$$Z = 6x_1 + 9x_2$$

Capacity retains are $20x_1 + 40x_2 \le 30{,}000$

$$30x_1 + 10x_2 \le 30{,}000$$

$$20x_1 + 16x_2 \le 30{,}000$$

Second Step. Develop equations from inequalities.

$$Z = 6x_1 + 9x_2 + (0)x_3 + (0)x_4 + (0)x_5$$

$$20x_1 + 40x_2 + x_3 + (0)x_4 + (0)x_5 = 30{,}000$$

$$30x_1 + 10x_2 + (0)x_3 + x_4 + (0)x_5 = 30{,}000$$

$$20x_1 + 16x_2 + (0)x_3 + (0)x_4 + x_5 = 30{,}000$$

Table 1

			0	0	0	6	9	
C_j	*Solution variable*	*Solution value*	x_3	x_4	x_2	x_1		
0	x_5	30,000	0	0	1	20	16	
0	x_4	30,000	0	1	0	30	10	
0	x_3	30,000	1	0	0	20	40	← KR
	Z_j		0	0	0	0	0	
	$C_j - Z_j$		0	0	0	6	9	

Table 2

C_j	Solution variable	Solution value	0 x_3	0 x_4	0 x_5	6 x_1	9 x_2
0	x_5	18, 000	– 2/5	0	1	12	0
0	x_4	22, 500	– 1/4	1	0	25	0
9	x_2	750	– 1/40	0	0	1/2	1
	Z_j		0	3	0	9/2	9
	$C_j - Z_j =$		9/40	0	0	3/2	0

Table 3

C_j	Solution variable	Solution value	0 x_3	0 x_4	0 x_5	6 x_1	9 x_2
0	x_5	7200	373/50	– 12/25	1	0	0
6	x_1	900	– 25/4	1/25	0	1	0
9	x_2	300	126/40	1/50	0	0	1
		Z_j	888/4	3/50	0	6	9
		$C_j - Z_j =$	–221	–3/50	0	0	0

Profit Maximisation $= x_1 = 900 \times 6 = 5400$

$x_2 = 300 \times 9 = 2700$

Total profit = 8100

Rs. 81.00 **Ans.**

Problem. Maximise Profit $4x_1 + 3x_2$

$$4x_1 + 2x_2 \le 10$$

$$2x_1 + 8/3\, x_2 \le 8$$

$$x_1 \ge \overline{0}$$

$$x_2 \ge 1.8$$

Removal of inequalities.

$$4x_1 + 2x_2 + x_3 + (0)x_4 + (0)\, x_5 + (0)x_6 = 10$$

$$2x_1 + 8/3x_2 + (0)x_3 + x_4 + (0)x_5 + (0)x_6 = 8$$

$$(0)x_1 + x_2 - x_5 + x_6 + (0)x_3 + (0)x_4 = 1.8$$

$$\text{Profit} = 4x_1 + 3x_2 + (0)x_3 + (0)x_4 + (0)x_5 - Mx_6.$$

Table 1

			$-M$	0	0	0	3	4
C_j	*Solution variable*	*Solution value*	x_6	x_5	x_4	x_3	x_2	x_1
0	x_3	10	0	0	0	1	2	4
0	x_4	8	0	0	1	0	8/3	2
$-M$	x_6	1.8	1	–1	0	0	1	0
			$-M$	$-M$	0	0	$-M$	0
	Z_j		$-M$	M	0	0	$-M$	0
	$C_j - Z_j =$		0	$-M$	0	0	$3 + M$	4

Table 2

			$-M$	0	0	0	3	4
C_j	*Solution variable*	*Solution value*	x_6	x_5	x_4	x_3	x_3	x_2
0	x_3	32/5	–2	2	0	1	0	4
0	x_4	16/5	–8/3	8/3	1	0	1	2
3	x_2	1.8	1	–1	0	0	1	9
		Z_j	3	–3	0	0	3	0
		$C_j - Z_j =$	$-(M + 3) + 3$	0	0	0	0	4

Table 3

			$-M$	0	0	0	3	4
C_j	*Solution variable*	*Solution value*	x_6	x_5	x_4	x_3	x_2	x_1
4	x_1	8/5	–1/2	1/2	0	1/4	0	1
0	x_4	0	–5/3	5/3	1	–1/2	0	0
3	x_2	1.8	–1	–1	0	0	1	0
		C_j	1	–1	0	1	3	4
		$C_j - Z_j$	$-(M + 1)$	+1	0	–1	0	0

Profit maximisation $\quad x_1 = 8/5 \times 4 = 6.4$

$$x_2 = 1.8 \times 3 = 5.4$$

$$\text{Total profit} = 6.4 + 5.4 = 11.8$$

Problem. *Find out the maximum profit, subject to following conditions.*

$$P = 2x_1 + 4x_2$$

$$x_1 + 4x_2 \leq 24$$

$$3x_1 + x_2 \leq 21$$

$$x_2 + x_4 \leq 8$$
$$x_1 \geq 0$$
$$x_2 \geq 0$$

Solution. Removal of Inequalities.

$$P = 2x_1 + 4x_2 + (0)x_3 + (0)x_4 + (0)x_5$$

$$x_1 + 4x_2 + x_3 + (0)x_4 + (0)x_5 = 24$$
$$3x_1 + x_2 + (0)x_3 + x_4 + (0)x_5 = 21$$
$$x_1 + x_2 + (0)x_3 + (0)x_4 + x_5 = 8$$

Table 1

			0	0	0	4	2
C_j	*Solution variable*	*Solution value*	x_5	x_4	x_3	x_2	x_1
0	x_5	24	0	0	1	4	1
0	x_4	21	0	1	0	1	3
0	x_5	8	1	0	0	1	1
	C_j	0	0	0	0	0	0
	$C_j - Z_j =$	0	0	0	0	4	2

Table 2

			0	0	0	4	2
C_j	*Solution variable*	*Solution value*	x_5	x_4	x_3	x_2	x_1
4	x_2	6	0	0	1/4	1	1/4
0	x_4	15	0	1	–1/4	0	1/4
0	x_5	2	1	0	–1/4	0	3/4
	C_j	0	0	0	0	0	1
	$C_j - Z_j =$	0	0	–0	0	0	1

Table 3

			0	0	0	4	2
C_j	*Solution variable*	*Solution value*	x_5	x_4	x_3	x_2	x_1
4	x_2	16/3	–1/3	0	1/3	1	0
0	x_4	23/3	–11/3	1	2/3	0	0
2	x_1	8/3	4/3	0	–1/3	0	1
		Z_j	4/3	0	2/3	4	2
		$C_j - Z_j =$	4/3	0	2/3	0	0

Hence maximum profit will be

$$x_1 = 8/3 \times 2 = 16/3 = 5.33$$

$$x_2 = 16/3 \times 4 = 64/3 = 21.33$$

$$\text{Total Profit} = 26.66 \textbf{ Ans}$$

Problem. *The Meerut Manufacturing Company makes 3 products x_1, x_2, x_3. Their contributions towards profits are Rs. 2, Rs. 4, and Rs. 3 per unit respectively. Each of these products passes through 3 manufacturing centres as a part of the production process. Time required in each to produce one unit of each of the 3 products as well as the total time available at each centre for next week in hours are as follows :*

Product	*Centre 1*	*Centre 2*	*Centre 3*
x_1	3	2	1
x_2	4	1	3
x_3	2	2	2
Total time available	60	40	80

Determine the optimum product plan for the next week's production schedule.

Solution. Objective function

$$z = 2x_1 + 4x_2 + 3x_2$$

Subject to the constraints

$$3x_1 + 4x_2 + 2x_3 \leq 60$$

$$2x_1 + x_2 + 2x_3 \leq 40$$

$$x_1 + 3x_2 + 2x_3 \leq 30$$

Here z is to be maximised.

Introducing slack variables to change the constraints into quality.

$$3x_1 + 4x_2 + 2x_3 + S_1 + 0S_2 + 0S_3 = 60$$

$$2x_1 + x_2 + 2x_3 + 0S_1 + S_2 + 0S_3 = 40$$

$$x_1 + 3x_2 + 2x_3 + 0S_1 + 0S_2 + S_3 = 80$$

and the objective function becomes

$$Z = 2x_1 + 4x_2 + 3x_3 + 0S_1 + 0S_2 + 0S_3$$

Table 1

C_j			0	0	0	2	4	3	
	Sol. variable	*Sol. value*	S_1	S_2	S_3	x_1	x_2	x_3	Ratio
0	S_1	60	1	0	0	3	4	2	15 ←KR
0	S_2	40	0	1	0	2	1	2	60
0	S_3	80	0	0	1	1	3	2	26.6
	Z_j	0	0	0	0	0	0	0	
	$C_j - Z_j$		0	0	0	2	4	3	

↑ Key Column

Replacing S_1 by x_2 in table 2

Table 2

C_j			0	0	0	2	4	3	
	Sol. variable	*Sol. value*	S_1	S_2	S_3	x_1	x_2	x_3	
4	x_2	15	1/4	0	0	3/4	1	1/2	Ratio 30
0	S_2	25	–1/4	1	0	5/4	0	3/2	50/3 ← KR
0	S_3	35	–3/4	0	0	–5/4	0	1/2	70/3
	Z_j	60	1	0	0	3	4	2	
	$C_j - Z_j$		–1	0	0	–1	0	1	
								↑ Key column	

Replacing S_2 by x_3 in table 3

Table 3

C_j			0	0	0	2	4	3
	Sol. variable	*Sol. value*	S_1	S_2	S_3	x_1	x_2	x_3
4	x_2	20/3	1/3	–1/3	0	1/3	1	0
3	x_3	50/3	–1/6	2/3	0	5/6	0	1
0	S_3	80/3	–2/3	–1/2	1	–5/3	0	0
	Z_j	230/3	5/6	2/3	0	23/6	4	3
	$C_j - Z_j$		–5/6	–2/3	0	–11/12	0	3

Since in column $C_j - Z_j$ under, x_2 and x_3 has become negative or zero. Therefore $x_2 = 20/3 = 6.67$, $x_3 = 50/3 = 1666$.

$$\text{Maximum profit} = 230/3 = 76.66$$

or,
$$Z = 4 \times 20/3 \times 3 \times 50/3 = 230/3 = 76.66$$

Problem. *Find the maximum value of*

$$z = 8x_1 + 9x_2$$
$$x_1, x_2 \geq 0$$

Subject to the following conditions

$$5x_1 + 4x_2 \leq 40$$
$$2x_1 + 3x_2 \leq 24$$
$$x_1 + 2x_2 \leq 14.$$

Solution. Introducing the slack variables and changing inequalities into equalities we get the following :

$$5x_1 + 4x_2 + S_1 + 0S_2 + 0S_3 = 40$$
$$2x_1 + 3x_2 + 0S_1 + S_2 + 0S_3 = 24$$
$$x_1 + 2x_2 + 0S_1 + S_2 + S_3 = 14$$

and
$$z = 8x_1 + 9x_2 + 0S_1 + 0S_2 + 0S_3$$

Table 1

C_j		0	0	0	0	8	9		
	Sol. variable	*Sol. value*	S_1	S_2	S_3	x_1	x_2	Ratio	
0	S_1	40	1	0	0	5	4	10	
0	S_2	24	0	1	0	2	3	8	
0	S_3	14	0	0	1	1	2	7	←K.R.
	Z_j	0	0	0	0	0	0		
	$C_j - Z_j$	0	0	0	0	8	9		
							↑ Key column		

S_3 will be replaced by x_2 in table 2.

Table 2

C_j			0	0	0	8	9		
	Sol. variable	*Sol. value*	S_1	S_2	S_3	x_1	x_2	Ratio	
0	S_1	2	1	0	–2	3	0	4	←K.R.
0	S_2	3	0	1	–3/2	+1/2	0	+ 6	
9	x_3	7	0	0	1/2	1/2	$17\frac{1}{2} = 14$		
	Z_j	73	0	0	9/2	9/2	9,		
	$C_j - Z_j$		0	0	9/2	7/2	0,		
						↑ Key Column			

Calculation $S_1 = 40 - 4 \times 7 = 12$

$1 - 4 \times 0 = 1$

$0 - 4 \times 0 = 0$

$0 - 4 \times 1/2 = -2$

$5 - 4 \times 1/2 = 3$

$4 - 4 \times 1 = 0$

$S_2 = 24 - 3 \times 7 = 3$

$0 - 3 \times 0 = 0$

$1 - 3 \times 0 = 1$

$0 - 3 \times 1/2 = -3/2$

$2 - 3 \times 1/2 = 1/2$

$3 - \times 1 = 0$

Table 3.
S_1 to be replaced by x_1

C_j			0	0	0	8	9	
	Sol. variable	*Sol. value*	S_1	S_2	S_3	x_1	x_2	*Ratio*
8	x_1	4	1/3	0	$-\frac{2}{3}$	1	0	
0	S_2	1	$-\frac{1}{6}$	1	−7/6	0	0	
9	x_2	5	$-\frac{1}{6}$	0	5/6	0	1	
	Z_j	77	7/6	0	13/6	8	9	
	$C_j - Z_j$		−7/6	0	−13/6	0	0	

Calculation S_2

$$3 - \frac{1}{2} \times 4 = 1$$

$$0 - \frac{1}{2} \times \frac{1}{3} = -\frac{1}{6}$$

$$1 - \frac{1}{2} \times 0 = 1$$

$$-3/2 - \frac{1}{2} \times \frac{2}{3} = 7/6$$

$$\frac{1}{2} - \frac{1}{2} \times 1 = 0$$

$$0 - \frac{1}{2} \times 0 = 0$$

Calculation x_2

$$7 - \frac{1}{2} \times 4 = 5$$

$$0 - \frac{1}{2} \times \frac{1}{3} = -\frac{1}{6}$$

$$0 - \frac{1}{2} \times 0 = 0$$

$$\frac{1}{2} - \frac{1}{2} \times \frac{-2}{3} = 5/6$$

$$\frac{1}{2} - \frac{1}{2} \times 1 = 0$$

$$1 - \frac{1}{2} \times 0 = 1$$

$$x_1 = 4$$

$$x_2 = 5$$

Therefore, maximum profit $= 8x_1 + 9x_2 = 8 \times 4 + 9 + 5 = 32 + 45 = 77.$

Problem. *A manufacturer of T.V. sets makes following four models* :

1. Monarc 2. Monitor
3. Wintage 4. Koral

Each set requires time to assemble and test. The assembly and testing requirement of four models are :

	I	*II*	*III*	*IV*	*Total available time*
Assembly time (hr.)	8	10	12	15	2000
Testing time (hr.)	2	2	4	5	500
Profit (Rs.)	40	60	80	100	

The supplier of the picture tube indicated that he would not be able to supply more than 180 tubes in the next month of which not more than 100 could be coloured one.

(1) What is the optimum production schedule for Wintage T.V. manufacturer ?

(2) What is the marginal value of an additional hour of assembly time ?

Solution. Let x_1, x_2, x_3, x_4 be the number T.V. sets of 4 types.

Objective function. $Z = 40x_1 + 60x_2 + 80x_3 + 100x_4$

Constrained equations :

$$8x_1 + 10x_2 + 12x_3 + 15x_4 \le 2000 \quad ...(1)$$

$$2x_1 + 2x_2 + 4x_3 + 5x_4 \le 500 \quad ...(2)$$

$$x_1 + x_2 + x_3 + x_4 \le 180 \quad ...(3)$$

$$x_3 + x_4 \le 100 \quad ...(4)$$

Adding slack variables and removing inequalities.

Objective function

$$Z = 40x_1 + 60x_2 + 80x_3 + 100x_4 + 0x_5 + 0x_6 + 0x_7 + 0x_8$$

$8x_1 + 10x_2 + 11x_3 + 15x_4 + 1x_5 + 0x_6 + 0x_7 + 0x_8 = 2000$

$2x_1 + 2x_2 + 4x_3 + 5x_4 + 0x_5 + 1x_6 + 0x_7 + 0x_8 = 500$

$x_1 + x_2 + x_3 + x_4 + 0x_5 + 0x_6 + 1x_7 + 0x_8 = 180$

$0x_1 + 0x_2 + x_3 + x_4 + 0x_5 + 0x_6 + 0x_7 + 1x_8 = 100$

Initial Simplex Table 1

C_j			0	0	0	0	0	40	60	80	100	
		Sol. variable	*Sol. value*	x_5	x_6	x_7	x_8	x_1	x_2	x_3	x_4	Ratio
	0	x_5	2000	1	0	0	0	8	10	12	15	133.3
K.R.	0	x_6	500	0	1	0	0	2	2	4	5	100
	0	x_7	180	0	0	1	0	1	1	1	1	180
	0	x_8	100	0	0	0	1	0	0	1	1	100
		Z_j	0	0	0	0	0	0	0	0	0	
		$C_j - Z_j$	0	0	0	0	0	40	60	80	100	
											↑ Key column	

Replacing x_6 by x_4 in table 2.

Table 2

	C_j		0	0	0	0	40	60	80	100	*Ratio*
	Sol. variable	*Sol. value*	x_5	x_6	x_7	x_8	x_1	x_2	x_3	x_4	
K.R. →	0 x_5	500	1	–3	0	0	2	4	0	0	125
	100 x_4	100	0	1/5	0	0	2/5	2/5	4/5	1	250
	0 x_7	80	0	–1/5	1	0	3/5	3/5	1/5	0	133.5
	0 x_8	0	0	–1/5	0	1	–2/5	2/5	1/5	0	0
	Z_j	10000	0	20	0	0	40	40	80	100	
	$C_j - Z_j$	–100000	0	–20	0	0	0	20	0	0	
								↑ Key column			

x_5 is to be replaced by x_2 in table 3

Table 3

C_j			0	0	0	0	40	6	80	100
	Sol. variable	*Sol. value*	x_5	x_6	x_7	x_8	x_1	x_2	x_3	x_4
60	x_2	125	1/4	–3/4	0	0	1/2	1	0	0
100	x_4	50	–1/10	1/2	0	0	1/5	1	4/5	0
0	x_7	5	–3/20	1/4	1	0	3/10	0	1/5	0
0	x_8	50	1/10	–1/2	0	1	–1/5	0	1/5	0
	Z_j	12500	5	5	0	0	50	60	80	100
	$C_j - Z_j$	–12500	–5	–5	0	0	–10	0	0	0

$$x_2 = 125\ ;\ x_4 = 50$$

Therefore, maximum profit $= 60 \times 125 + 100 \times 50 =$ Rs.12500

Problem. *Maximise* $P = 6x_1 + 7x_2$

with given constraints as $2x_1 + 3x_2 \leq 12$

$$2x_1 + x_2 \leq 8$$

Solution.

Introducing slack variables and changing the inequalities into equalities, we get

$$2x_1 + 3x_2 + S_1 + 0S_2 = 12$$

$$2x_1 + x_2 + 0S_1 + S_2 = 8$$

Also $P = 6x_1 + 7x_2 + 0S_1 + 0S_2$

Initial Simplex Table 1

C_j			6	7	0	0		
	Sol. variable	*Sol. value*	x_1	x_2	S_1	S_2	*Ratio*	
0	S_1	12	2	3	1	0	4	← K.R.
0	S_2	8	2	1	0	1	8	
	Z_j	0	0	0	0	0		
	$C_j - Z_j$		6	7	0	0		
				↑ Key column				

Table 2

C_j			6	7	0	0	
	Sol. variable	Sol. value	x_1	x_2	S_1	S_2	Ratio
7	x_2	4	2/3	1	1/3	0	6
0	S_2	4	4/3	0	-1/3	0	3 ← K.R.
	Z_j	28	14/3	7	7/3	0	
	$C_j - Z_j$		4/3	0	-7/3	0	
			↑ Key column				

S_2 to be replaced by x_1

Table 3

C_j			6	7	0	0
	Sol. variable	Sol. value	x_1	x_2	S_1	S_2
7	x_2	2	0	1	1/2	–1/2
6	x_1	3	1	0	–1/4	3/4
	C_j	32	6	7	2	1
	$C_j - Z_j$		0	0	–2	–1

$$\text{Optimal solution} = x_1 = 3$$
$$x_2 = 2$$
$$\text{Maximum profit} = P = 6x_1 + 7x_2 = 6x3 + 7x2 = 18 + 14 = 32.$$

Problem. *The management of a garment factory hires to recommend the most profitable mix of the three types of garments A, B, C it is desirous to include in its future plans. The processing takes place in three sections x, y, z. The production of one unit in the shops (in minutes) and the total available capacity of the shops is compiled in the table. Table also contains the profit contribution for unit of each product. Recommend the most profitable mix to the management.*

Table

Departments	Types of garment			Available Capacity
	A	B	C	
Cutting (x)	10.7	5.0	2.0	2705
Stitching (y)	5.4	10.0	4.0	2210
Finishing (z)	0.7	1.0	2.0	445
Profit per unit	Rs. 10.00	Rs. 15.00	Rs. 20.00	

Solution. Let x_1, x_2 and x_3 be the number of garments A, B and C respectively.

Framing Problem

$$Z = 10x_1 + 15x_2 + 20x_3 \text{ to be maximised:}$$

Express the constraints

$$10.7x_1 + 5x_2 + 2x_3 \leq 2705$$
$$5.4x_1 + 10x_2 + 4x_3 \leq 2210$$
$$0.7x_1 + 1.0x_2 + 2x_3 \leq 445$$
$$x_1, x_2 \text{ and } x_3 \geq 0$$

Convert the inequalities by adding slack variables :

$$10.7\,x_1 + 5x_2 + 2x_3 + 1S_1 + 0S_2 + 0S_3 = 2705$$
$$5.4x_1 + 10x_2 + 4x_3 + 0S_1 + 1S_1 + 0S_3 = 2210$$
$$0.7x_1 + 1x_2 + 2x_3 + 0S_1 + 0S_2 + 1S_3 = 445$$
$$Z = 10x_1 + 15x_2 + 20x_3 + S_1 + 0S_2 + 0S_0$$

Simplex Table
Table 1

Profit per Unit C_j	$C_j \rightarrow$		0	0	0	10	15	20	
	Solution variables	Solution values	S_1	S_2	S_3	x_1	x_2	x_3	Ratio
0	S_1	2705	1	0	0	10.7	5	2	2705/2=1352.5
0	S_2	2210	0	1	0	5.4	10	4	2210/4=552.5
0	S_3	445	0	0	1	0.7	1	[2]	445/2=222.5
0	Z_j (Contribution lost)		0	0	0	0	0	0	
PTP	$C_j - Z_j$ (Net contribution)		0	0	0	10	15	20	

x_3 enters in place of S_3

Table 2

C_j	C_j		0	0	0	10	15	20	
	Sol. variables	Sol. values	S_1	S_2	S_3	x_1	x_2	x_3	
0	S_1	2260	1	0	–1	10	4	0	2260/4=565
0	S_2	1320	0	1	–2	4	[8]	0	1320/8=165
20	x_3	222.5	0	0	1/2	7/20	1/2	1	$\frac{222.5}{½} = 445$
	Z_j	445	0	0	10	7	10	20	
	$C_j - Z_j$		0	0	–10	3	5	0	
	x_3 enters in place of S_2								

Calculations : S_1

$$2705 - (2 \times 222.5) = 2260$$
$$1 - (2 \times 0) = 1$$
$$0 - (2 \times 1/2) = -1$$
$$10.7 - (2 \times 7/20) = 10$$
$$5 - (2 \times 1/2) = 4$$

$$2 - (0 \times 1) = 0$$

S_2

$$2210 - (4 \times 222.5) = 1320$$
$$0 - (4 \times 0) = 0$$
$$1 - (4 \times 0) = 1$$
$$0 - \left(4 \times \frac{1}{2}\right) = -2$$
$$54 - (4 \times 7/20) = 4$$
$$10 - \left(4 \times \frac{1}{2}\right) = 8$$
$$4 - (4 \times 1) = 0$$

Table 3

C_j ↓	→S		0	0	0	10	15	20,	
	Sol. Variables	*Sol. values*	S_1	S_2	S_3	x_1	x_2	x_3	*Ratio*
0	S_1	1600	1	–1/2	0	[8]	0	0	← 200
15	x_2	165	0	1/8	–1/4	1/2	1	0	330
20	x_3	140	0	–1/6	5/8	1/10	0	1	1400
	Z_j	527.5	0	5/8	70/8	9/2	15	20	
	$C_j - Z_j$		0	–5/8	–70/8	11/2	0	0	
						↑ S_1 is replaced by x_1			

Calculations : S_1

$$2260 - (4 \times 165) = 1600$$
$$1 - (4 \times 0) = 1$$
$$0 - (4 \times 1/8) = 1/2$$
$$-1 - (4 \times -1/4) = 0$$
$$10(-4 \times 1/2) = 8$$
$$4 - (4 \times 1) = 0$$
$$0 - (4 \times 0) = 0$$

Table 4

10	x_1	200	1/8	–1/16	0	1	0	0
15	x_2	65	–1/16	5/32	–1/4	0	1	0
20	x_3	120	–1/80	–9/180	5/8	0	0	1
	Z_j	537.5	1/16	39/32	35/4	10	15	20
	$C_j - Z_j$		–1/6	–39/32	–35/4	0	0	0

x_3

$222.5 - (1/2 \times 165) = 140$

$0 - (1/2 \times 0) = 0$

$0 - (1/2 \times 1/8) = 1/16$

$1/2 - (1/2 \times 1/4) = 5/8$

$7/20 - (1/2 \times 1/2) = 1/10$

$1/2 - (1/2 \times 1) = 0$

$1 - (1/2 \times 0) = 1$

X_2

$165 - (1/2 \times 200) = 65$

$0 - (1/2 \times 1/8) = - 1/16$

$1/8 - (1/2 \times - 1/16) = 5/32$

$- 1/4 - (1/2 \times 1) = 0$

$1/2 - (1/2 \times 0) = 1$

$0 - (1/2 \times 0) = 0$

x_3

$140 - (1/10 \times 200) = 120$

$0 - (1/10 \times 1/8) = - 1/80$

$- 1/6 - (1/10 \times - 1/16) = 9/14$

$5/8 - (1/10 \times 0) = 3/8$

$1/10 - (1/10 \times 1) = 0$

$0 - (1/10 \times 0) = 0$

$1 - (10 \times 0) = 1$

Since all the values of $C_j - Z_j$ are either negative or zero hence optimal result is given by task $4x_1 = 200$, $x_2 = 65$, $x_3 = 120$

$\therefore$ Quantity of product A should be produced = 200

Quantity of product B should be produced = 65

Quantity of product C should be produced = 120

Therefore $Z = 10 \times 200 + 15 + 65 + 20 \times 120$

$= \text{Rs. } 5375$ **Ans.**

Problem. *An animal feed company must produce 200 lb of a mixture containing the ingradients x_1 and x_2, x_1 cost Rs. 3 per lb and x_2 costs Rs. 8 per lb. Not more than 80 lb of x_1 can be used and minimum quantity to be used for x_2 is 60 lb. Find how much of each ingredient should be used, if company wants to minimise the cost.*

Solution. The objective function to be minimised is

$$Z = 3x_1 + 8x_2$$

Subject to the constraints

$$x_1 + x_2 = 200 \quad ...(i)$$

$$x_1 \leq 80 \quad ...(ii)$$

$$x_2 \geq 60 \quad ...(iii)$$

Solution.

We introduce a slack variable S_1 in constraint (*ii*) to get

$$x_1 + S_1 = 80$$

In constraint (*i*) only one artificial variable A_1 is introduced

$$x_1 + x_2 + A_1 = 200$$

and in constraint (*iii*) one slack variable S_2 and an artificial variable A_2 is introduced to get

$$x_2 - S_2 + A_2 = 60$$

The objective function becomes :

$$Z^* = -Z = -3x_1 - 8x_2 + 0.S_1 - 0.S_2 - MA_1 - MA_2$$

Here Z^* is to be maximised, hence the penalty for A_1 and A_2 in the objective function will be $-M$ which has a very large value.

Various simplex tables are now framed as follows :

				0	0	--M	−M	−3	−8
Unit profit, C_j		Sol. variable	*Sol. value*	S_1	S_2	A_1	A_2	X_1	X_2 *Ratio*
0	S_1	80	1	0	0	0	1	0	80
0	S_2	60	0	−1	0	1	0	1	80
−*M*	A_1	200	0	0	1	0	1	1	200
	Z_j	--	0	0	−*M*	0	−*M*	−*M*,	
	$C_j - Z_j$	--	0	0	0	−*M*	*M*–3	*M*–8	

↑ Key column

S_1 is replaced by x_1

Table 2

			0	0	−*M*	−*M*	−3	−8	
C_j	*Sol. variable*	*Sol. value*	S_1	S_2	A_1	A_2	x_1	x_2	*Ratio*
−3	x_1	80	1	0	0	0	1	8	0
0	S_2	60	0	−1	0	1	0	1	60
−*M*	A_1	120	−1	0	1	0	0	1	120
	Z_j		−*M*	0	−*M*	0	−3	−*M*	
	$C_j - Z_j$		3–*M*	0	0	−*M*	0	*M*–8	

↑ Key column

S_2 is replaced by x_2

Table 3

–3	x_1	80	1	0	0	0	1	1	∞
–8	x_2	60	0	–1	0	1	0	1	–60
$-M$	A_1	60	–1	1	1	–1	0	0	60
	Z_j		$-3+M$	$8-M$	$-M$	$M-8$	–3	–8	
	$C_j - Z_j$		$3-M$	$M-8$	0	$8-2M$	0	0	
						↑ Key column			

S_2 replaces A_1

Table 4

–3	x_1	80	1	0	0	0	1	0
–8	x_2	120	–1	0	1	0	0	1
0	S_2	60	–1	1	1	–1	0	0
	Z_j	–1200	5	0	–8	0	–3	–8
	$C_j - Z_j$	–	–5	0	$8-M$	$-M$	0	0

Since all the values of $C_j - Z_j$ are either negative or zero hence table gives the values of $x_1 = \mathbf{80}$ and $x_2 = \mathbf{120}$ lbs.

and $$Z^* = 3 \times 80 + 8 \times 120 = 240 + 960$$

$\therefore$ Minimum value = 1200 **Ans.**

Besides profit maximization problem, the simplex method can be used in cost minimization problems.

Problem. *A cattle feed company must produce 400 quintals of a mixture consisting of ingredients x_1 and x_2. x_1 cost Rs. 6 per quintal and x_2 Rs. 16 per quintal. No more than 160 quintals of x_1 can be employed and a minimum of 120 quintal of x_2 must be used. The problem is to ascertain how much of each ingredient should be employed if the company is to minimise cost.*

The cost function can be written as :

$$\text{Cost} = 6x_1 + 16x_2 \quad \ldots(i)$$

$$x_1 + x_2 = 400 \quad \ldots(ii)$$

$$x_1 \leq 160 \quad \ldots(iii)$$

$$x_2 \geq 120 \quad \ldots(iv)$$

1. Artificial Variables. As case of maximization problems, stock variables are to be introduced, in this case *Artificial variables* are used for the treatment of 2 types of restrictions:

(*i*) for equality

(*ii*) For greater than or equal to type, artificial variable is used.

Now the equation will be

$$x_1 + x_2 + A_1 = 400$$

$$A_1 = \text{[Artificial variable 1]}$$

With stock variable

$$x_1 + x_2 + A_1 + 0S_1 + 0S_2 + 0A_2 = 400 \quad ...(1)$$

$$x_1 + 0x_2 + 10A_1 + 1S_1 + 0S_2 + 0A_2 = 160 \quad ...(2)$$

$$0x_1 + x_2 + 0A_1 + 0S_1 - S_2 + A = 120 \quad ...(3)$$

Cost problem $6x_1 + 16x_2 + MA_1 + 0S_1 + 0S_2 + MA_1$

Table 1

			M	0	0	M	0	16	
C_j	*Solution variable*	*Solution value*	A_1	S_1	S_2	A_2	x_1	x_2	
M	A_1	400	1	0	0	0	1	1	
0	S_1	160	0	1	0	0	1	0	
M	A_2	120	0	0	–1	1	1	1	←K.R.
		400M	M	0	0	0	M	M	
		120M	0	0	–M	M	0	M	
	Z_j	520M	M	0	–M	M	M	2M	
	$i_j - Z_j$		0	0	–M	0	6–M	16–2M	
								↑ Key column	

II. Optimum Column. Which has the largest negative value would be a key column in $C_j - Z_j$.

We have to remember here that the profit maximization, key column is one which has the highest positive value.

Table 2

			M	0	0	M	6	16	
C_j	*Solution variable*	*Solution value*	A_1	S_1	S_2	A_2	x_1	x_2	
16	x_2	120	0	0	–1	1	0	0	
M	A_1	280	1	0	1	–1	1	0	
0	S_2	160	0	1	0	0	1	0	← K.R.
		1920	0	0	–16	16	0	16	
		+ 280M	0	0	M	– M	M	0	
	C_j		M	0	M – 16	16 – M	M	16	
	$C_j - Z_j$		0	0	16 – M	2M – 16	6 – M	0	
							↑ Key column		

Table 3

			M	0	0	M	6	16	
C_j	*Solution variable*	*Solution value*	A_1	S_1	S_2	A_2	x_1	x_2	
6	x_1	160	0	1	0	0	1	0	
16	x_2	120	0	0	−1	1	0	1	
M	A_2	120	1	−1	1	−1	0	0	←K.R.
		720	0	0	6	0	6	0	
		1120	0	0	0	−16	16	16	
		120M		M	$-M$	M	$-M$	0	
	Z_j (Total)			M	$6-M$	$M-16$	$16-M$	16	
	$C_j - Z_j$			0	$M-6$	$16-M$	$2M-16$	0	
						↑ Key column			

Table 4

			M	0	0	M	6	16
C_j	*Solution variable*	*Solution value*	A_1	S_1	S_2	A_2	x_1	x_2
0	S_2	120	1	−1	1	−1	0	0
6	x_1	160	0	1	0	0	1	0
16	x_2	240	0	−1	0	0	0	1
		960	0	6	0	0	6	
		3840	16	−16	0	0	0	16
	Total Z_j		10	−10	0	0	6	16
	$C_j - Z_j$		$M-16$	+10	0	M	0	0

Step III. This is the last step, when in (table 4) $C_j - Z_j$ column, no negative value remain the optimum solution is reached.

Thus we should use 160 quintals of x_1 and 240 quintals of x_2, with this the cost comes to Rs. 4800.

Minimising an Objective Function

In case we have to deal with the costs, the minimisation of costs is often a desired objective. Then it can be expressed as :

Objective function $x_1 + x_2$ = minimum.

The procedure given earlier for maximisation will hold good provided the above objective function $x_1 + x_2$ = minimum is modified. Therefore, multiply the objective function throughout by −1.

$$-x_1 - x_2 = \text{maximum}.$$

Further while selecting the Key Column the largest positive number in the index row is selected instead of the largest negative number (which is done for maximisation procedure). All other steps remain exactly the same. Generally four types of equations are involved *i.e.* restrictions, requirements, equations and approximations. In all these equations the inequalities have to be removed by introducting appropriate slack variables.

Requirement. In same situations the requirement is that same combination of the variables must be greater than or equal to a given number like

$6x_1 + 4x_2 \geq 24$ has the requirement at least 24

To convert this in equality into an equation, a slack variable S_1 is subracted and written as

$$6x_1 + 4x_2 - S_1 = 24$$

Since the coefficient of S_1 is -1 this equation can not be used in simplex method.

To apply simplex method, each equation must have are non zero entry in the identity and this entry must have a coefficient of +1. Therefore by adding in artificial variable A which will appear in identity, the above equation becomes

$$6x_1 + 4x_2 - S_1 + A_1 = 24$$

An arbitrary large negative contribution $-M$ is assigned to the artificial variable A in the objective function so that artificial variables is zero in the optimal solution.

Equations. The combination of certain variables will amount to some exact quantity. By introducing an artificial variable, the equation can be amenable for simplex method as simplex needs one variable for identity.

The equation $10x_1 + 6x_2 = 50$ can be modified to

$$10x_1 + 6x_2 + A_2 = 50.$$

Further a $-M$ contribution is assigned to the artificial variable A_2 in the objective function in order to make the artificial variable zero in the optimal solution.

Approximations. In some problems the combination of some variables will be approximately equal to some number for flexibility like $5x_1 + 3x_2 \cong 40$. This can be modified to use in simplex method, by adding and substracting slack variables say S_2 and S_3.

i.e., $$5x_1 + 3x_3 - S_2 + S_3 = 40$$

These two slack variables make the above equation either slightly smaller or slightly greater than 40. In order to make the above equation as close as possible to 40, the negative coefficient -1 is assigned in the objective function to both slack variables S_2 and S_3.

If the objective function is $20x_1 + 15x_2$ = Maximum.

It can be written as $20x_1 + 15x_2 - S_2 - S_3$ = Maximum.

The slack variable S_2 will appear in the body and slack variable S_3 will appear in the identity of simplex matrix.

Example. Let the objective function be

$$10x_1 + 25x_2 = \text{Maximum}$$

Subject to
$2x_1 + 1x_2 \leq 30$ Restriction relationship
$4x_1 + 6x_2 \geq 50$ Requirement relationship
$3x_1 + 6x_2 = 60$ Equality relationship
$5x_1 + 2x_2 \approx 45$ Approximation relationship.

By applying the above guide lines these can be modified by introducing slack variables and artifical variables.

$$2x_1 + 1x_2 + S_1 = 30$$
$$4x_1 + 6x_2 - S_2 + A_1 = 50$$
$$3x_1 + 6x_2 + A_2 = 60$$
$$5x_1 + 2x_2 - S_3 + S_4 = 45$$

The objective function $10x_1 + 25x_2 =$ maximum is modified to include slack and artificial variables.

$10x_1 + 25x_2$ (0) S_1 – (0) $S_2 - S_3 - S_4 - MA_1 - MA_2$ = Maximum.

By arranging the objective function and problem equations in the matrix form, initial simplex matrix is obtained as below.

Initial Simplex Matrix

			10	25	0	–1	0	$-M$	$-M$	–1	Objective Row
			x_1	x_2	S_2	S_3	S_1	A_1	A_2	S_4	Variable Row
0	S_1	30	2	1	0	0	1	0	0	0	Problem equations
$-M$	A_1	50	4	6	–1	0	0	1	0	0	
$-M$	A_2	60	3	6	0	0	0	0	1	0	
–1	S_4	45	5	2	0	–1	0	0	0	1	

Body (columns x_1 to S_3); Identity (columns S_1 to S_4)

Constant column
Variable column
Objective column

Now the above matrix is ready for its operating. After calculating the Index row as explained earlier. The largest positive number is select (instead of largest negative number) for identifying key column. All other steps are followed as they are given for maximisation by simplex method.

Problem. *The manufacturer of Western Television sets make following four models :*

- *Monarch*
- *Monitor*
- *Wintage and*
- *Koral.*

The assembly and testing requirements of time for four sets is as follows :

Model type	*I*	*II*	*III*	*IV*	*Total Time Available*
Assembly time	8	10	12	15	2000
Testing time	2	2	4	5	500
Marginal profit	40	60	80	100	

The supplier of the picture tube indicated that he would not be able to supply more than 180 picture tubes in the next month of which not more than 100 could be colour tubes. The colour tubes are used in set of Wintage and Koral type only.

Find out :

(i) What is the optimal production schedule for the company ?

(ii) What is the marginal value of the additional hour of assembly time ?

Solution.

Step I. Formulate the problem by defining inequalities and objective function.

Let the company produce x_1 , x_2 , x_3 and x_4 sets of each models respectively.

The corresponding profit is then,

$$Z = 40x_1 + 60x_2 + 80x_3 + 100x_4$$

Subject to the restrictions (constraints) as follows :

$$8x_1 + 10x_2 + 12x_3 + 15x_4 \leq 2000 \text{ For assembly time}$$
$$2x_1 + 2x_2 + 4x_3 + 5x_4 \leq 500 \text{ For testing time}$$
$$x_1 + x_2 + x_3 + x_4 \leq 180 \text{ For total picture tubes}$$
$$x_3 + x_4 \leq 100 \text{ For colour tubes}$$
$$x_1 , x_2 , x_3 , x_4 \geq 0$$

In the problem the objective function Z is to be optimised.

Step II. Convert the inequalities by adding slack variables.

$$Z = 40x_1 + 60x_2 + 80x_3 + 100x_4 + 0x_5 + 0x_6 + 0x_7 + 0x_8$$

$8x_1 + 10x_2 + 12x_3 + 15x_4 + 1x_5 + 0x_6 + x_7 + 0x_8 = 2000$

$2x_1 + 2x_2 + 4x_3 + 5x_4 + 0x_5 + 1x_6 + 0x_7 + 0x_8 = 500$

$1x_1 + 1x_2 + 1x_3 + 1x_4 + 0x_5 + 0x_6 + 1x_7 + 1x_8 = 180$

$0x_1 + 0x_2 + 1x_3 + 1x_4 + 0x_5 + 3x_6 + 0x_7 + 1x_8 = 100$

Step III. Prepare various Simple Tables to get the optimum solution.

Table 1

Unit profit C_j	*Solution variable*	*Solution values*	0	0	0	0	40	60	80	100	
			x_5	x_6	x_7	x_8	x_1	x_2	x_3	x_4	*Ratio*
0	x_5	2000	1	0	0	0	8	10	12	15	$\frac{2000}{15} = 133.3$
			0	0	0	0	0	0	0	0	
0	x_6	5000	0	1	0	0	2	2	4	–5	$\frac{500}{5} = 100$
			0	0	0	0	0	0	0	0	
0	x_7	180	0	0	1	0	1	1	1	1	$\frac{180}{1} = 180$
			0	0	0	0	0	0	0	0	
0	x_8	100	0	0	0	1	0	0	1	1	$\frac{100}{1} = 100$
			0	0	0	0	0	0	0	0	
		$Z_j = 0$		0	0	0	0	0	0	0	
		$C_j - Z_j = 0$		0	0	0	40	60	80	100	

Explanations to table 1. Determination of key column, key row and key number.

Z_j is worked out by multiplying the figures of each column with the unit profit of respective row as shown small type. This is zero in each case. Adding all these values, we get Z_j. We now work out $C_j - Z_j$ as shown in the last row.

The key column is the one which falls in the largest $C_j - Z_j$ value. Decide the solution values from the corresponding figures in key column to get the ratio column. The smallest value in the key ratio column locates the key row and the value lying in the cell at the intersection of key row and column is the key number. If the minimum value in the ratio column are more than one (as in the present case), we may select any one (case of degeneracy). Key column, row and number are shown in black rule. Here 5 is the key number and x_4 is the entering variable in place of x_6.

C_j	*Solution variable*	*Solution values*	0	0	0	0	40	60	80	100	*Ratio*
			x_5	x_6	x_7	x_8	x_1	x_2	x_3	x_4	
0	x_5	500	1	–3	0	0	2	4	0	0	$\frac{500}{4}$ = 125
			0	0	0	0	0	0	0	0	
0	x_4	100	0	1/5	0	0	2/5	2/5	4/5	1	$\frac{100}{2}$ = 250
			0	20	0	0	40	40	80	100	– 5
0	x_7	80	0	–1/5	1	0	3/5	3/5	1/5	0	$\frac{80}{31}$ = 1333
			0	0	0	0	0	0	0	0	5
0	x_8	0	0	–1/5	0	1	–2/5	–2/5	1/5	0	$\frac{0}{-2/5}$ = (– 0)
			0	0	0	0	0	0	0	0	(Negative values are not considered)
		Z_j	0	20	0	0	40	40	80	100	
		$C_j - Z_j$	0	20	0	0	0	20	0	0	

Explanations to table 2

Key row in table 1 is transformed by dividing its elements by the key number. This gives the corresponding row of table 2.

The other rows are also transformed by substracting the product of the corresponding key column number and corresponding value determined in the above para, from the old row number of the non key row as worked out below :

$2000 - (15 \times 100) = 500$
$1 - (15 \times 0) = 1$
$0 - (15 \times 1/5) = -3$
$0 - (15 \times 0) = 0$
$0 - (15 \times 0) = 0$
$8 - (15 \times 2/5) = 2$
$10 - (15 \times 2/5) = 2$
$12 - (15 \times 4/5) = 0$
$15 - (15 \times 1) = 0$

$180 - (1 \times 100) = 80$
$0 - (1 \times 0) = 0$
$0 - (1 \times 1/5) = -1/5$
$1 - (1 \times 0) = 1$
$0 - (1 \times 0) = 0$
$1 - (1 \times 2/5) = 3/5$
$1 - (1 \times 2/5) = 3/5$
$1 - (1 \times 4/5) = 1/5$
$1 - (1 \times 1) = 0$

$100 - (1 \times 100) = 0$
$0 - (1 \times 0) = 0$
$0 - (1 \times 1/5) = -1/5$
$0 - (1 \times 0) = 0$
$1 - (1 \times 0) = 1$
$0 - (1 \times 2/5) = -2/5$
$0 - (1 \times 2/5) = -2/5$
$1 - (1 \times 4/5) = 1/5$
$1 - (1 \times 1) = 0$

Key column, key row and key number are worked out as in case of table 1. Since all the values of $C_j - Z_j$ are not 0 or negative, hence, proceed for Table 3 for optimal solution values. 4 is the key number and x_2 is the entering variable in place of x_5.

Explanation to table 3

Table 3 is formed exactly the same way. Table 1 and 9 values of x_4, x_7 and x_8 are worked out as follows :

Table 3

C_j	*Solution variable*	*Solution values*	0	0	0	0	40	60	80	100	*Ratio*
			x_5	x_6	x_7	x_8	x_1	x_2	x_3	x_4	
60	x_2	125	1/4	–3/4	0	0	1/2	1	0	0	
			15	–45	0	0	–30	60	0	0	
100	x_4	50	–1/10	1/2	0	0	1/5	0	4/5	1	
			–10	50	0	0	20	0	80	100	
0	x_7	5	–3/20	1/4	1	0	3/10	0	1/5	0	
			0	0	0	0	0	0	0	0	
0	x_8	50	1/10	–1/2	0	1	–1/5	0	–1/5	0	
			0	0	0	0	0	0	0	0	
		Z_j	5	5	0	0	50	60	80	100	
		$C_j - Z_j$	–5	–5	0	0	–10	0	0	0	

x_4	x_7	x_8
$100 - (2/5 \times 125) = 50$	$80 - (3/5 \times 125) = 5$	$0 - (-2/5 \times 125) = 50$
$0 - (2/5 \times 1/4) = 1/10$	$0 - (3/5 \times 1/4) = 3/20$	$0 - (-2/5 \times 1/4) = 1/0$
$1/5 - (2/5 \times 3/4) = ½$	$-1/5 - (3/5 \times 3/4) = 1/4$	$-1/5 - (2/5 \times 3/4 = -1/3$
$3 - (2/5 \times 0) = 0$	$1 - (3/5 \times 0) = 1$	$0 - (-2/5 \times 0) = 0$
$0 - (2/5 \times 0) = 0$	$0 - (3/5 \times 0) = 0$	$1 - (-2/5 \times 0) = 1$
$2/5 - (2/5 \times 1/2) = 1/5$	$3/5 - (3/5 \times 1/2) = 3/10$	$-2/5 - (-2/5 \times 1/2) = -1/5$
$2/5 - (2/5 \times 1) = 0$	$3/5 - (3/5 \times 1) = 0$	$-2/5 - (-2/5 \times 1) = 0$
$4/5 - (2/5 - 1) = 4/5$	$1/5 - (3/5 \times 0) = 1/5$	$-1/5 - (-2/5 \times 0) = -1/5$
$1 - (2/5 \times 0) = 1$	$0 - (3/5 \times 0) = 0$	$0 - (-2/5 \times 0) = 0$

$C_j - Z_j$ values indicate that all of them are either zero or negative hence the optimal values are available from this table 3, *e.g.* $x_2 = 125$ and $x_4 = 50$.

Substituting values of x_2 and x_4

$$
\begin{aligned}
Z &= 60x_2 + 100x_4 \\
&= 60 \times 125 + 100 \times 50 \\
&= 7500 + 5000 \\
&= 12{,}500 \text{ Profit}
\end{aligned}
$$

and 125 sets of Monitor and 50 sets of Koral should be produced for optimisation.

The term. With "Transportation method" the Machine assignment, plant location and product mix problems can be solved. Transportation method is limited to problems with resources and requirements given in terms of only one kind of unit.

Problem 20

Plant	Warehouses				*Output (Weekly production in plants A & B)*
	1	*2*	*3*	*4*	
A	3	4	9	2	23
B	6	5	8	8	27
Demand (Customer demand at each warehouse)	12	13	15	10	50 \ 0

3, 4, 9, 2 and 6, 5, 8, 8 are the costs in Rupees per tone of distributing product from plant *A* and *B* to respective warehouses 1, 2, 3, 4.

Solution. The first step in the transportation method is to load the basic matrix without bothering whether the solution formed is optional or not. There are various methods to do it but we shall be considering only two common methods :

(1) Northwest Corner Rule

(2) Vogel's Approximate Method.

(1) **Northwest Corner Rule**

In this method the initial assignment starts by loading the cell located in the upper left hand corner of the matrix and filling the non-requirements to the right and downward until all the requirements of the problem have been satisfied.

1st Solution

Plant	*1*	*Ware house 2*	*3*	*4*	*Output*
A	(12) [3]	(11) [4]	[9]	[2]	23
8	[6]	(2) [5]	(15) [8]	(10) [8]	27
Demand	12	13	15	10	50 \ 50

The transportation cost involved in the first solution can be evaluated as

$$= 3 \times 12 + 11 \times 4 + 2 \times 5 + 15 \times 8 + 10 \times 8$$

$$= 36 + 44 + 10 + 120 + 80 = 290 \text{ (rupees)}$$

In order to ascertain whether the solution I is optimal or not the empty cells in the solution must be evaluated. Following is the procedure to evaluate the empty cell :

1. Shifting 1 unit from loaded cell into the empty cell.
2. Comparing the cost of original schedule with the cost of new schedule involving the empty cell.
3. The loaded cell which is selected must have following two characteristics :

(*i*) Loaded cell must be situated in the same row or column of the empty cell.

(*ii*) The route used for evaluation would not require more than one empty cell during same evaluation.

The effect of shifting 1 unit form plant B to warehouse 1 would be

$$+6-3+4+5=\text{Rs. } 12$$

The plus sign indicates that the total costs cannot be reduced by adding one unit to B_1 combination.

Evaluation of empty cell B-1

Plant	*1*	*2*	*3*	*4*	*Output*
A	3 (11)	4 (12)	9	2	23
B	6 (1) +	5 (1) −	8	8	27
Demand	12	13	15	10	50

Further Evaluation
Evaluation of cell A-4

Plant	*1*	*2*	*3*	*4*	*Output*
A	3	4 (10)	9	2 (1)	23
B	6	5 (3)	8 (15)	8 (9)	27
Demand	12	13	15	10	50

Evaluation of cell A_4 follow the route

$$-4+2-8+5=\text{Rs. } -5.$$

(Assigning positive signs to the cost of those cells which gained one unit and negative signs of those cells which lose one unit.

Evaluation of A_3 Cell

Plant	*1*	*2*	*3*	*4*	*Output*
A	3 (12)	4 (10)	9 (1)	2	23
B	6	5 (3)	8 (14)	8 (10)	27
Demand	12	13	15	10	50 / 50

Moving one unit to A_3, we remove one unit from A_2. In order to restore one unit to warehouse 2, we shift one unit from B_3 to B_2.

The cost associated with these moves are :

$$-4+9-8+5 = +2$$

Thus adding one unit to cell A_3 would not reduce the total costs. Thus evaluation of empty cells give the following inference :

(*i*) If the evaluation is positive, then the cost of new solution would be greater than the cost of present schedule.

(*ii*) If the evaluation is negative than the cost of new solution would be less than the cost of present schedule of the evaluation result into zero value than the cost will not change by using these empty cells.

The second feasible solution and optimum solution after analysing empty cells is given below. Now the evaluation for all empty cells involve costs greater than zero. So any change in the solution would result into increase of total costs.

Plant	1	2	3	4	Output
A	3 (12)	4 (1)	9	2 (10)	
B	6	5 (12)	8 (15)	8	
Demand	12	13	15	10	50 / 50

If the evaluation revealed negative costs then another feasible solution could have been constructed. The evaluation process is complete when all evaluations are positive. Thus an optimal schedule has been obtained.

(2) Vogel's Approximate Method

This method was developed first by W.R. Vogel. This method gives a good approximation and provides an optimum solution to most of the simple problems. Following are the various steps used for Vogel's approximate method :

1. Construct the basic matrix.
2. Find out the difference in each column and row between the minimum and the next higher to minimum.
3. Select a row or column containing the largest difference.
4. Select maximum unit in that square or column which carries the lowest cost.
5. The steps (2), (3) and (4) are repeated till all units are distributed satisfying the capacity and requirement constraint.

Vogel's Method

Let us find with the help of Vogel's Method.

1st step

Plant	*1*	*2*	*3*	*4*	*Output (Weeky production of the products A & B) difference*	
A	3	4	9	2 (10)	23 23 − 10 = 13	4 − 3 = 1
B	6	5	8	8	27	6 − 5 = 1
Demand	12	13	15	10	50 \ 50	

Difference 6 − 3 = 3 5 − 4 = 1 9 − 8 = 1 8 − 2 = 6
↑

IInd step

Plant	*1*	*2*	*3*	*Output*	*Difference*
A	3 (2)	4	9	13 13 − 12 = 1	4 − 3 = 1
B	6	5	8	27	6 − 5 = 1
Demand	12	13	15		40 \ 40

Difference 6 − 3 = 3 5 − 4 = 1 9 − 8 = 1
↑

IIIrd step

Plant	*2*	*3*	*Output*	*Difference*
A	4 (1)	9	1 1 − 1 = 0	9 − 4 = 5
B	5	8	27	8 − 5 = 3
Demand	13	15	28 \ 28	
Difference	13 − 1 = 12 5 − 4 = 1	9 − 8 = 1		

Difference 13 − 1 = 12
5 − 4 = 1 9 − 8 = 1

IVth step

Plant	2	3	*Output*	*Difference*
B	[5] (12)	[8] (15)	27	8 – 5 = 3
Demand	12	15	27 / 27	

Let us combine step I, II, III and IV to get initial solution.

Plant	*Ware house*				*Output*
	1	2	3	4	
A	[3] (12)	[4] (1)	[9]	[2] 10	23
B	[6]	[5] (12)	[8] (15)	[8]	27
Demand	12	13	15	10	50 / 50

Let us evaluate the empty cells, B_1, B_3 and B_4. Evaluating square B_1.

Plant	*Ware house*				*Output*
	1	2	3	4	
A	[3] (12) →	[4] (1) + ↓	[9]	[2] 10	23
B	[6] + ↑	[5] ← (12)	[8] (15)	[8]	27
Demand	12	13	15	10	50 / 50

If we transfer 1 unit from square B_2 to B_1.

The change in the cost of transportation will be

$$+6 - 3 + 4 - 5 = +2$$

Thus transferring one unit to cell B_1 is not economical.

Evaluating empty sq. A_3

Plant	*Ware house*				*Output*
	1	2	3	4	
A	[3] (12)	[4] (1) + →	[9]	[2] (10) ↓	23
B	[6]	[5] (12) – ↑	[8] (15) ←	[8] +	27
Demand	12	13	15	10	

Transferring one unit from square A_2 to square A_3. The new cost of transportation will be :

$$9 - 4 - 8 + 5 = +2$$

Thus the new set of assignment is not economical.

Evaluating empty sq. B-4

Plant	*Ware house*				*Output*
	1	2	3	4	
A	3 (12)	4 (1) +	9	2 − (10)	23
B	6	5 (12) −	8 (15)	8 +	27
Demand	12	13	15	10	

We are not considering the occupied cell B_3.

Transferring one unit from square A_4 to square B_4, the new cost of transportation will be

$$8 - 5 + 4 - 2 = +5.$$

Thus transferring one unit from square A_4 to square B_4 is not economical. The evaluation for all empty cells involves cost greater than zero. So any change in the solution would result into increase of total costs. We can also conclude that Vogel's approximate method gives a good approximation and provides an optimum solution to most of the simple problems.

Problem 21. *Find out the best solution given the following table. Keeping in mind the optimisation of Transportation cost.*

Solution. Let us find out the initial solution *using Vogel's Approximation method.*

Find out the difference between each column and row between minimum and next higher to minimum.

Source / *Destination*	F_1	F_2	F_3	*Units demanded*
W_1	1.0	1.0	1.0	5
W_2	1.0	1.4	0.8	20
W_3	1.3	1.0	0.8	20
Units available	20	15	10	45 / 45

Source / *Destination*	F_1	F_2	F_3	*Units demanded*	Differences
W_1	0.09	1.0	1.0	5	1.0 – 0.9 = 0.1
W_2	1.0	1.4	0.8	20	1.0 – 0.8 = 0.2
W_3	1.3	1.0	0.8 (10)	20 20 – 10 = 10	(1.0 – 0.8) = 0.2 ft.
Units available	20	15	10	45 / 45	
Differences	1.0 – 0.9 = 0.1	1.0 – 1.0 = 0	0.8 – 0.8 = 0		

Either row W_2 or W_3 will get the distribution. Let us take the row W_3. Now the cost of transportation is minimum for square W_3 F_3. Let us allot 10 unit square W_3 F_3. This satisfies the requirement for column F_3. The new matrix will be

Source / *Destination*	F_1	F_2		*Units demanded*	*Differences*
W_1	0.9	1.0 (5)		5	1.0 – 0.9 = 0.1
W_2	1.0 (20)	1.4		20	1.4 – 1.0 = 0.4
W_3	1.3	1.0 (10)		10	1.3 – 1.0 = 0.3
Units available	20	15		35 / 35	
Differences	1.0 – 0.9 = 0.1	1.0 – 1.0 = 0			

Now the initial allocation with the help of Vogel's Approximation. Method will be

Source / *Destination*	F_1	F_2	F_3	*Units demanded*
W_1	0.9	1.0	1.0	5
W_2	1.0 (20)	1.4	0.8	20
W_3	1.3	1.0 (10)	0.8 (10)	20
Units available	20	15	10	45 / 45

A firm has three units in three leading cities of the country and operate through three dealers to sell goods in three regions. The cost transporting each unit from each manufacturing unit to a dealer as shown in the Table 1.

Original Matrix

Dealers / *Factories*	D_1	D_2	D_3	*Factory capacities*	*Differences*
1	3	6	4	10	(4 – 3) = 1
2	2	5	7	5	(5 – 2) = 3
3	4	6	8	7	(6 – 4) = 2
Dealers requirements	6	8	8	22 / 22	
Differences	3 – 2 = 1	6 – 5 = 1	7 – 4 = 3		

1st alternative

Dealers / *Factories*	D_1	D_2	D_3	*Factory capacities*
1	3	6	4	10
2	2 (5)	5	7	5
3	4	6	8	7
Dealers requirements	6	8	8	22 / 22
	(6 – 5) = 1			

The row 2 has been assigned to its capacity.

Dealers / *Factories*	D_1	D_2	D_3	*Capacities*	*Difference*
1	3	6	4 (8)	10 10 – 8 = 2	4 – 3 = 1
3	4	6	8	7	6 – 4 = 2
Requirements	1	8	8	17 / 17	
	4 – 3 = 1	6 – 6 = 0	8 – 4 = 4		

Now in column D_3, assign the value to the cell which has lowest cost of transporting for example, *i.e.* D_3 cell.

Factories \ Dealers	D_1	D_2	Capacities	Difference
1	3 (1)	6	2 2 – 1 = 1	6 – 3 = 3
3	4	6	7	6 – 4 = 2
Requirement	1	8	9 \ 9	
Differences	4 – 3 = 1	6 – 6 = 0		

Assign the value of 1 to 1 D_1 cell because the requirement there is for one unit only.

So we are left only one column with equal cost of transportation. The cell 1 D_2 require 1 rent and cell 3 D_2 require 7 units and thus satisfying the total requirements of D_2 column. Two final values in each cells are :

Factories \ Dealers	D_1	D_2	D_3	Capacities
1	3 (1)	6 (1)	4 (8)	10
2	2 (5)	5	7	5
3	4	6 (7)	8	7
Requirements	6	8	8	22 \ 22

The solution obtained above may not be an optimum solution. This has to be checked by evaluating the empty cells. The evaluating process will be complete when all evaluation are positive.

In fact after evaluating the costs as it was done in earlier problem, it was found that solution obtained by Vogel's method have optimised the transportation cost. The total cost of transportation will be

$$= 1 \times 3 + 1 \times 6 + 5 \times 2 + 7 \times 6 + 8 \times 4$$
$$= 3 + 6 + 10 + 42 + 32 = \text{Rs. } 93$$

The following table shows the problem of material handling. Find out the optimum solution.

From \ To	4	5	6	7	Available equipments
1	10	22	10	20	8
2	15	20	12	8	13
3	20	12	10	15	11
Required	7	10	6	9	

Here 1, 2, 3 and 4, 5, 6, 7 are the departments. Departments 1, 2 and 3 have extra equipments and departments 4, 5, 6 and 7 need equipments. The values in the cells refers to amount required in the transportation. Find the optimum combinations.

Solution. Let us find out the initial solution by the help of North West method.

From \ To	4	5	6	7	Available
1	10 (7)	22 (1)	10	20	8
2	15	20 (9)	12 (4)	8	13
3	20	12	10 (2)	15 (9)	11
Required	7	10	6	9	32 / 32

Total amount required in the process of transportation

$$= \text{Rs. } 7 \times 10 + 1 \times 22 + 9 \times 20 + 4 \times 12 + 2 \times 10 + 9 \times 15$$
$$= \text{Rs. } 475$$

Improving the initial solution

Evaluating the empty square 2-4 *i.e.,* moving one unit from 2-5 to 2-4 departments. Change of cost is

$$15 - 10 + 22 - 20 = +7$$

(So there is no change in cost.)

To From	*4*	*5*	*6*	*7*	*Available equipments*
1	10 (7) − →	22 (1) ↓	10	20	8
2	15 (1) + ↑	20 (9) −	12 (4)	8	13
3	20	12	10 (2)	15	11
Required	7	10	6	9	32

Let us evaluate the square 3-4. Moving one unit from square 3-6 to square 3-4. Change in cost is

$$-10 + 20 - 10 + 22 - 20 + 12 = 14$$

So there is no change in the cost.

From \ To	4	5	6	7	Available equipments
1	10 (7)	22 (1)	10	20	
2	15	20 (9)	12 (9) +	8	
3	20 +	12	10 (2) −	15	

Now let us evaluate the square 3-5 *i.e.,* moving on unit 3-6 to 3-5. Total cost is

$$= +12 - 20 + 12 - 10 = -6$$

From \ To	4	5	6	7	Available
1	10 (7)	22 (1)	10	20	8
2	15	20 (9)	12 (4)	8	13
3	20	12 +	10 (2)	15 (9)	11
Required	7	10	6	9	32 / 32

This shows that there is a scope for reducing the cost of transportation by shifting one unit from 3-6 to 3-5. The maximum shift can be of two units, so maximum improvement possible is

$$2(-6) = -12$$

The new allocation matrix can be as follows.

From \ To	4	5	6	7	Available equipments
1	10 (7)	22 (1)	10	20	8
2	15	20 (7)	12 (6)	8	13
3	20	12 (2)	10	15 (9)	11
Required equipment	7	10	6	9	32

The total cost of transportation will be

$$= (22 \times 1) + (7 \times 20) + (2 \times 12) + (7 \times 15) + (6 \times 12) + (7 \times 10)$$
$$= 22 + 140 + 24 + 135 + 72 + 70 = \text{Rs. } 463$$

Now we will again evaluate the various open squares till no further improvement is possible. It should be borne in mind that squares which indicated no improvement may yield an improvement after the subsequent changes in the loading. The evaluation of all fall empty square and subsequent assignment will result into following optimum solution :

From \ To	4	5	6	7	*Available*
1	(7) [10]	[22]	(1) [10]	[20]	8
2	[15]	[20]	(4) [12]	(9) [8]	13
3	[20]	(10) [12]	(1) [10]	[15]	11
Required	7	10	6	9	32 \ 32

The total cost of transportation for an optimum solution will be
$(7 \times 10) + (1 \times 10) + 4 \times 12 + 9 \times 8 + 1 \times 10 + 10 \times 12 = \text{Rs. } 330.$

46

Waiting Lines and Waiting Lines Models

Queuing Theory or Waiting Lines

A Danish telephone Engineer A.K. Erbeng stated developing the Queuing theory which is also called waiting lines, in 1905. After World War II the theory was applied in various other areas. The Queuing theory deals with problems of congestion and delay which occurs in many situations like :

- Dock yard where ships arrive for loading or unloading.
- Clinics where the patients arrive and are attended by the doctors.
- Manual assembly lines where parts are assembled by a number of different people.
- Booking office where the customers come either for the purchase of a ticket or for booking reservation.
- Bank counter where the public comes for withdrawal or depositing of money.

Common Phenomena

In all such areas the common phenomena, one observes in that

(*i*) Customer arrive to avail a facility.

(*ii*) The customers are attended by a service facility.

(*iii*) Either the customer will be waiting for availing service or the service facility will be waiting for the arrival of the customers.

Minimising the idle time or waiting time of the customer is the most desirable situation. For this purpose the parameters such as service rate, arrival rate of customers, idle time of service facility, idle time of customers, queue length of the customer etc. are found out. Based on this information and cost data, an optimal solution is worked out in order to minmize the idle time of customer.

Types of Waiting Lines

Generally two types of waiting lines situations are found.

(*i*) Single Queue and single service (channel)

(*ii*) Single Queue multi channel.

Again based on the rate of arrival and rate of service, four types of problems are encountered.

(*i*) Constant service time and random arrival of customers.

(*ii*) Random service time and constant arrivals.

(*iii*) Random service time and random arrivals.

(*iv*) Constant service time and constant arrivals.

In a real life situation, random service time and random arrivals are more prevalent. The other three are very rare and generally considered as hypothetical. The arrivals are independent of service facilities. Therefore, normally constant arrivals are not expected. Similarly service time differs with the nature of the job that is attended. Jobs do differ and hence service time also differs and very rarely it can be observed as constant unless a uniform job is attended with automatic devices.

Example 1. *Following are the arrival and service times at a tool room where tools are issued to the fitters who arrive at the tool room. Here the service time is taken as constant and arrival is at random to explain the waiting situation given in Table 46.1.*

The calculations of idle time, waiting time, length of queue etc. are given in the table.

No. of fitters arrived tool room = 20

Average rate of arrival per hour, 11.15 – 9.30 = 105 mts.

$$\frac{60}{105} \times 20 = \frac{80}{7} = 11.4 \approx 12$$

The rate of arrival of fitters to the tool room

= 12 per hour

The rate of service is issuing the tools to the fitters $= \frac{60}{3} = 20$ per hour

Per hour 12 fitters will arrive and the tool keeper will be capable of issuing tools to 20 fitters per hour.

Since the arrival of fitters is at random, there is bound to be idle time on the part of the fitters (not being attended having reached the tool room) as well as on the part of the tool-keeper.

The waiting time of the fitters = 30 mts.

Table 46.1

S. No.	*Time of arrival of fitter*	*Issue of tools begins at*	*Issue of tools completes at*	*Elapsed time between arrivals in minutes*	*Issue time of tools in Mts (4)–(3)*	*Idle time of tools keeper in mts* $(3)_n - 4_{n-1}$	*Waiting time of fitters in mts (3)–(2)*	*Length of queue excluding fitter receiving tools (3)–(2)*
1.	09.30	09.30	09.33	--	3	--	0	0
2.	09.39	09.39	09.42	9	3	6	0	0
3.	09.43	09.43	09.46	4	3	1	0	0
4.	09.49	09.49	09.52	6	3	3	0	0
5.	10.04	10.04	10.07	15	3	12	0	0
6.	10.06	10.07	10.10	2	3	0	1	1
7.	10.07	10.10	10.13	1	3	0	3	1
8.	10.08	10.13	10.16	1	3	0	5	2

9.	10.09	10.16	10.19	1	3	0	7	3
10.	10.12	10.19	10.22	3	3	0	7	3
11.	10.32	10.32	10.35	20	3	10	0	0
12.	10.33	10.35	10.38	1	3	0	2	1
13.	10.35	10.38	10.41	2	3	0	3	1
14.	10.41	10.41	10.44	6	3	0	0	0
15.	10.45	10.45	10.48	4	3	1	0	0
16.	10.55	10.55	10.58	10	3	7	0	0
17.	10.59	10.59	11.02	4	3	1	0	0
18.	11.10	11.10	11.13	11	3	8	0	0
19.	11.12	11.13	11.16	2	3	0	1	1
20.	11.15	11.16	11.19	3	3	0	1	1

Idle time of the tool–keeper = 49 mts.

$$\text{Average waiting time} = \frac{30}{15} = 2 \text{ mts. per fitter.}$$

The idle time has been calculated based on the sample study of 105 minutes of working hours per day the idle time of

$$\text{the fitters} = 137 \text{ minutes a day} \left(\frac{480}{105} \times 30\right)$$

$$\text{tool keeper} = 224 \text{ minutes a day} \left(\frac{480}{105} \times 49\right)$$

If the idle time of the fitters is to be reduced one more tool keeper has to be added. But by adding the tool keeper the second tool keeper will not have sufficient work and the idle time of the tool-keeper will increase.

Poisson Arrival Rates

In real situation, the rate of arrivals follows Poisson distribution. The frequency of arrival of job. Orders at machines if measured for a long period, it exhibits Poisson distribution. Orders received at stores for material issue, receipts of orders for rectification of broken down machine etc. all follow Poisson distribution because the arrivals in all such cases are random and Possion distribution corresponds to completely random arrivals since it is assumed that an arrival is completely independent of other arrivals.

The Poisson distribution is a single parameter distribution. It can be completely described by one parameter the MEAN. For Poisson distribution the standard deviation in the square root of the mean. This is the mathematical characteristics of Poisson distribution.

In waiting line models the average arrival rate is represented by a Greek letter lambda (λ) representing number of arrivals per unit time.

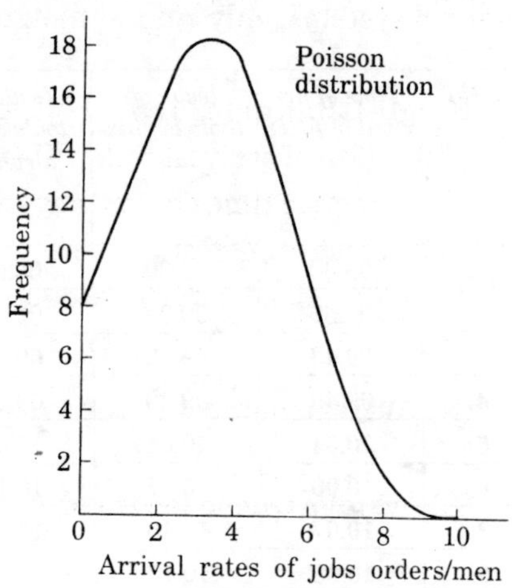

Fig. 46.1.

When the arrival rates follows a Poisson distribution (with mean arrival rate of λ), the time between arrivals follows a negative exponential distribution, with mean time between arrivals of $1/\lambda$. This relationship between mean arrival rate (λ) and meantime between arrivals does not necessarily hold for other distributions. Therefore the negative exponential distribution is also representative of a Poisson distribution.

Exponential Service Times

The distribution service times follow the negative exponential distribution. The negative exponential distribution also is a single parameter distribution and it can be completely described by the mean which is also equal to standard deviation.

Normally Greek letter mu (μ) is used for representing the service rate in waiting line models. (μ) = number of services completed per unit time.

Service rates follow a Poisson distribution with mean service rate (μ) while the distribution of service times follow the negative exponential distribution with mean service time $1/\mu$.

Thus the rates of arrivals and service follow Poisson distribution while arrival times and service times follow the negative exponential distribution.

With the largest mean processing time or service time, the service time in case of number of machines, issue of materials, etc. follow the negative exponential distribution.

It is based on these distributions that the waiting time mathematical models have been developed.

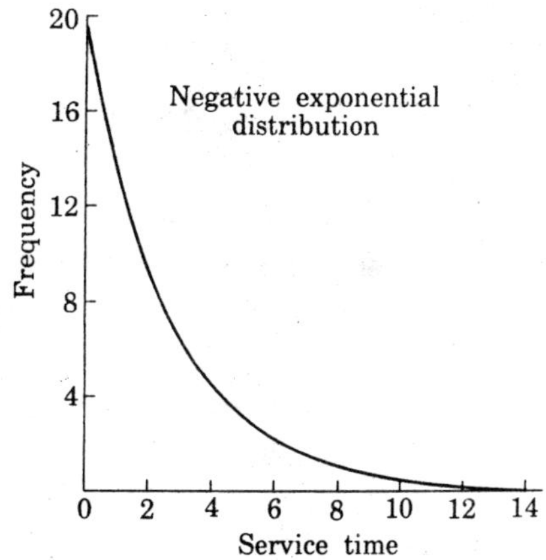

Fig. 46.2.

Waiting Lines Models

Because of the mathematical properties of Poisson and negative exponential distribution which represent the arrival rates and service times respectively, it has been possible to develop waiting line models. Though the waiting line models have been developed for single as well multi channel systems, only single channel system is dealt here.

Single Channel Queue. Following are the various assumptions in Single Channel Queue.

(*i*) Rate of arrivals follow Poisson distribution.

(*ii*) Service times follow negative exponential distribution.

(*iii*) First come-first served.

(*iv*) The mean service rate (μ) is greater than mean arrival rate (τ).

The waiting line models for single channel Queue are given below.

(N) Average number in the system including the one being served $= \dfrac{\tau}{\mu - \tau}$

(L) Average Queue length or Average number in waiting line $= \dfrac{\tau^2}{\mu(\mu - \tau)}$

(T) Average time in the system including service $= \dfrac{1}{(\mu - \tau)}$

(W) Average waiting time for service $= \dfrac{\tau}{\mu(\mu - \tau)}$

(P) Probability of n units in the system $= \left(1 - \dfrac{\tau}{\mu}\right)\left(\dfrac{\tau}{\mu}\right)^n$

(ρ) Utilisation of service facility $= \left(\dfrac{\tau}{\mu}\right)$

Utilisation of service facility. The ratio of mean arrival rate to mean service rate is simply called utilisation factor.

From the model $L = \dfrac{\tau^2}{\mu(\mu - \tau)}$, if a graph is drawn between L the average number in the waiting line and (τ/μ) utilisation factor, L approaches to infinity as the utilisation factor (τ/μ) approaches to unity *i.e.* $(\tau/\mu) = 1$.

Generally such a situation will not happen since

— new arrivals (men) are not expected by seeing long Queue
— working hours will restrict the people coming into the waiting line
— If a long Queue is there, people at service counter will react to it and speed up the work.

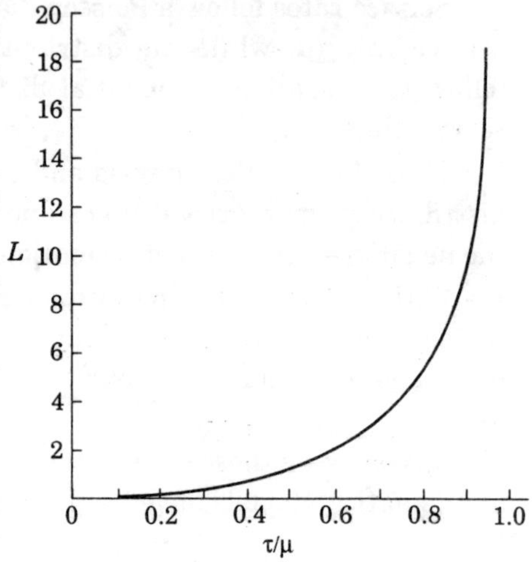

Fig. 46.3.

Limitations of waiting line

If actual distributions of arrival rates and service times do not follow standard Poisson and negative exponential distributions, the formula will not hold good correctly.

Where the arrivals service rates do not follow the standard distributions, SIMULATION by MONTE CARLO method is the only solution.

Example 2. *The customers arrive in a single Queue to booking office at random. The average arrival rate of the customer is one for every 5 minutes. The booking clerk takes on an average 3 minutes to dispose the customer. Find out the following :*

(*i*) The average number of people in the system
(*ii*) Average Que length
(*iii*) Average time in the system including service
(*iv*) Average waiting time for service
(*v*) Probability of zero units in the system
(*vi*) Utilisation of service facility

$$\tau = \text{Arrival rate} = \frac{60}{5} = 12 \text{ customers per hour}$$

$$\mu = \text{Service rate} = \frac{60}{3} = 20 \text{ customers per hour}$$

Based on τ and μ values all the values can be calculated by using the *f* models

$$\tau = 12\ ,\ \mu = 20$$

(*i*) Average number of people in the system

$$N = \frac{\tau}{\mu - \tau} = \frac{12}{20 - 12} = \frac{12}{8} = \frac{3}{2} = 1.5$$

(*ii*) Average Queue length $\quad L = \dfrac{\tau^2}{\mu(\mu - \tau)} = \dfrac{12^2}{20(20 - 12)} = \dfrac{144}{20(8)} = \dfrac{144}{160} = 0.9$

(*iii*) Average time that is taken in the system including service

$$T = \frac{1}{(\mu - \tau)} = \frac{1}{(20 - 12)} = 0.125 \text{ hrs.} = 7.5 \text{ mts.}$$

(*iv*) Average waiting time for the service

$$W = \frac{\tau}{\mu(\mu - \tau)} = \frac{12}{20(20 - 12)} = \frac{12}{20 \times 6}$$

$$= \frac{12}{160} = 0.075 \text{ hrs} = 4.5 \text{ mts.}$$

$$T - W = 7.5 - 4.5 = 3 \text{ mts. service time confirms.}$$

(*v*) Probability of 'zero' units in the system

$$P_0 = \left(1 - \frac{\tau}{\mu}\right)\left(\frac{\tau}{\mu}\right)^0 = \left(1 - \frac{12}{20}\right)\left(\frac{12}{20}\right)^0$$

$$= \left(1 - \frac{12}{20}\right)$$

$$P_0 = (1 - 0.6) = 0.4$$

(*vi*) Utilisation of service $\quad = \dfrac{\tau}{\mu} = \dfrac{12}{20} = 0.6$

Example 3. *Application of Monte Carlo Simulation. This method utilises random numbers for originating the data itself. The random numbers are used in creating a hypothetical data for a problem whose behaviour is known from the past experience (frequency distributions). If no past data is available, the individual must decide whether the variables in the situation under study can be assumed to act at random. The use of cumulative probability distribution for arrival and service time should closely resemble to the real world.*

The frequency distribution of arrivals and service times are given below based on the past record from a tool room wherein the fitters come to take tools from tool keeper. The Queue starts from 10 to 12 o'clock.

Frequency distributions of :

Arrivals *Service times*

S. No.	*Arrival time in mts.*	*Frequency*
1.	3.5-4.5	5%
2.	4.5-5.5	20%
3.	5.5-6.5	35%
4.	6.5-7.5	25%
5.	7.5-8.5	10%
6.	8.5-9.5	5%

S. No.	Service time in mts.	Frequency
1.	3.5-4.5	10%
2.	4.5-5.5	20%
3.	5.5-6.5	40%
4.	6.5-7.5	20%
5.	7.5-8.5	10%

Only from these distribution and random numbers the entire process can be treated.

From the frequency distributions, the cumulative frequency, mid point are calculated and random numbers are indicated as shown below :

Frequency Distribution of Arrivals

S. No.	Mid point of arrival time (mts.)	Frequency	Cumulative frequency	Random Numbers Range
1.	4	5%	5%	1-4
2.	5	20%	25%	5-24
3.	6	35%	60%	25-59
4.	7	25%	85%	60-84
5.	8	10%	95%	85-94
6.	9	5%	100%	95-99

Frequency Distributions of Service Times

S. No.	Mid point of time in mts.	Frequency	Cumulative frequency	Random Numbers Range
1.	4	10%	10%	1-9
2.	5	20%	30%	10-29
3.	6	40%	70%	30-69
4.	7	20%	90%	70-89
5.	8	10%	100%	90-99

Simulation by Monte Carlo Method

S. No.	Random Number for arrival	Time interval between arrivals mts.	Time of arrival	Service begins	Random Number for service	Service time in mts.	Service cards at	Waiting time of		Length of waiting line
								Fitters mts.	Tool mts	
1.	15	5	10.05	10.05	20	5	10.10	0	0	0
2.	09	5	10.10	10.10	72	7	10.17	0	0	0
3.	41	6	10.16	10.17	34	6	10.23	1	0	1
4.	74	7	10.23	10.23	54	6	10.29	0	0	0
5.	72	7	10.30	10.30	30	6	10.36	0	1	0
6.	67	7	10.37	10.37	22	5	10.42	0	1	0
7.	55	6	10.43	10.43	48	6	10.49	0	1	0
8.	71	7	10.50	10.50	74	7	10.57	0	1	0

S. No.	Random Number for arrival	Time interval between arrivals mts.	Time of arrival	Service begins	Random Number for service	Service time in mts.	Service cards at	Waiting time of		Length of waiting line
								Fitters mts.	*Tool mts*	
9.	35	6	10.56	10.57	76	7	11.04	1	0	1
10.	41	6	11.02	11.04	02	4	11.08	2	0	1
11.	96	9	11.11	11.11	07	4	11.15	0	3	0
12.	20	5	11.16	11.16	64	6	11.22	0	1	0
13.	45	6	11.22	11.22	95	8	11.30	0	0	0
14.	38	6	11.28	11.30	23	5	11.35	2	0	0
15.	01	4	11.32	11.35	91	8	11.43	3	0	0
16.	67	7	11.39	11.43	48	6	11.49	4	0	0
17.	63	7	11.46	11.49	55	6	11.55	3	0	0
18.	39	6	11.52	11.55	91	8	12.03	3	0	0
19.	55	6								
						110		19	8	3

Monte Carlo Method

Take the random number from random table and put them at column 2 in the table for arrivals. The first random number is 15. From frequency distribution of arrivals, read the next arrival time in minutes against the range of random from 15. The next arrival time is 5 minutes. Write this 5 minutes at column number 3 in the table. Since, the process starts at 10.0 clock, the fitters arrive at tool room by 10.05. Therefore, time 10.05 will be written at column 4 *i.e.,* time of arrival. Since the issue of tools begins immediately at column No. 5 in the table, 10.05 will be written as service begins.

Pick up random numbers from random table and put them at column 6. Provide for random number frequency distribution of service times read-service time in minutes against random number 20. The service time is 5 minutes and note this time at column 7. Since 10.05 was the beginning of the service time, 10.05 + 5 = 10.10 is the completion of the service time and it is written at column 8.

Waiting time of the fitter is the difference between the time of arrival and time of the service begins *i.e.* column number 4 and 5. This is zero in this case, which is written at column number 9. Similarly, waiting time for tool keeper is the difference between the column 5 and 4 which is zero and written at column 10. This entire process is repeated till 10th arrival when it completes two hours.

Once the events are simulated for a period of 2 hours, the following type of questions of waiting line can be answered.

(*i*) What is the length of the waiting line (L = ?).

(*ii*) What is the average time a customer waits before he is served (W = ?).

(*iii*) What is the average time a customer spends in the system (T = ?).

$$(i)\ L = \frac{\text{Number of customers in Queue for 2 hours}}{\text{Number of arrivals}}$$

$$= \frac{3}{18} = 0.16 \text{ people (Length of waiting Line)}$$

(*ii*) $W = \frac{19}{18} = 1.05$ Mts. (Average time a customer waits)

(*iii*) T = Average waiting time + Average service time

$$= 1.05 \text{ Mts.} + \frac{110}{18} = 1.05 + 6.10$$

$T = 7.15$ Mts. (Average Time Customer Spends in system).

Example 4. Find out the average number of customers in the system. Average number of customers in the Queue (including occasions when Queue length is zero) if the utilisation factor of the service system is 0.5, 0.7, 0.9 and 0.95.

Utilisation factor $\rho = \frac{\tau}{\mu}$

Since the value of ρ only is given, formula for the above questions be converted in the form of ρ.

Average number of customers in the system

$$N = \frac{\tau}{\mu - \tau}$$

where τ is the arrival rate and μ is the service rate

$$N = \frac{\tau}{\mu - \tau} = \frac{1}{\frac{\mu - \tau}{\tau}} = \frac{1}{\frac{\mu}{\tau} - \frac{\tau}{\tau}}$$

Since $\frac{\tau}{\mu} = \rho$

and $\frac{\mu}{\tau} = \frac{1}{\rho}$

$$N = \frac{1}{\left(\frac{1}{\rho}\right) - 1} = \frac{1}{\left(\frac{1 - \rho}{\rho}\right)} = \frac{\rho}{1 - \rho}$$

Similarly average number of customers in Queue or Average Queue length (L)

$$= \frac{\tau^2}{\mu(\mu - \tau)}$$

$$L = \frac{\tau^2}{\mu(\mu - \tau)} = \frac{\tau}{\mu}\left[\frac{\tau}{(\mu - \tau)}\right]$$

Since $\frac{\tau}{\mu - \tau} = \frac{\rho}{1 - \rho}$

as has been already shown

and $\rho = \frac{\tau}{\mu}$

$$L = \frac{\tau}{\mu}\left[\frac{\tau}{(\mu - \tau)}\right] = \rho\left[\frac{\rho}{1 - \rho}\right] = \left[\frac{\rho^2}{1 - \rho}\right]$$

Now N and L both are available in terms of P

S. No.	ρ	ρ^2	$(1-\rho)$	$L = \frac{\rho^2}{1-\rho}$	$N = \frac{\rho}{1-\rho}$
1.	0.50	0.25	0.50	0.50	1.00
2.	0.70	0.49	0.30	1.63	2.33
3.	0.90	0.81	0.10	8.10	9.00
4.	0.95	0.9025	0.0500	18.05	19.00

Thus the average number of customers in the queue including the one being serviced and the queue length both will increase as the utilisation of service facility increases. Therefore in order to keep the queue length low, it is essential that utilisation of service facility be low since the customer service is more precious.

Example 5. *If the average service rate is 5 per hour, what is the average time of a customer in the queue for the utilisation of service facilities at 0.5, 0.7, 0.9 and 0.95 in the service system.*

Average time of a customer in queue

= Average waiting time of the customer for service in queue

$$W = \frac{\tau}{\mu/\mu - \tau} = \frac{1}{\mu} = \left[\frac{\tau}{(\mu - \tau)}\right]$$

$$W = \frac{1}{\mu}\left[\frac{\rho}{1-\rho}\right] = \frac{\rho}{\mu(1-\rho)}$$

Now values of ρ and μ are available

$$\rho = 0.5 , 0.7 , 0.9 \text{ and } 0.95$$

whereas μ = Service rate = 5. The waiting time is calculated as below :

S. No.	ρ	$(1-\rho)$	$\left(\frac{\rho}{1+\rho}\right)$	μ	$W = \frac{\rho}{\mu(1-\rho)}$ *hours*
1.	0.50	0.50	1.00	5	0.20 hour
2.	0.70	0.30	2.33	5	0.47 hours
3.	0.90	0.10	9.00	5	1.80 hours
4.	0.95	0.05	19.00	5	3.80 hours

Rate of service is constant at 5 per hour. Therefore value of ρ increases as the value of arrival rate increases since $\rho = \frac{\tau}{\mu}$.

Let us see, what is the rate of arrival of the customers for

$$\rho = 0.5 , 0.7 , 0.9 \text{ and } 0.95.$$

S. No.	ρ	μ *service per hour*	$\tau = \rho\ (\mu)$ *Arrivals per hour*	$W = (\rho)/\mu\ (1-\rho)$ *are waiting time*
1.	0.50	5	2.50	0.20 hour
2.	0.70	5	3.50	0.47 hours
3.	0.90	5	4.50	1.80 hours
4.	0.95	5	4.75	3.80 hours

Since the service rate is 5 per hour and as the arrival rate of customers increases are waiting time of the customers increases.

47

Simulation and its Applications

Simulation

Simulation utilises a method of finding the successive situations in a problem by repeatedly applying the rules under which the system operates. This successive linkage of one particular situation to previous situation is the main characteristics of simulation. Simulation is resorted to when :

(*i*) Many vales of variables of a problem are not known.

(*ii*) There is no other way to find out the values of variables.

(*iii*) No formula can be established for the event.

(*iv*) Only a logical sequence can be established based on the past experience/event.

In a real business situation, the under lying principles are so complicated that it is difficult to predict the outcome of a situation. Simulation model illustrates the situations on the simple input data rather than on the entire population as the experimentation on population too much time consuming and costly.

Definition

Exact definition of the simulation is difficult, but to cover the main characteristics of simulation, it can be defined as a quantitative technique that ultilizes a computerised mathematical model in order to represent actual decision-making under conditions of uncertainty for evaluating alternative courses of action based upon facts and assumptions.

Methods of Simulation

Basically there are three methods of simulation.

— Gaming method

— Monte Carlo method

— System simulation method.

Gaming Method

These come under the category of competitive models. These models take into account conflicts external to the organisation basically, the competition. The efficiency of the decision by one party is dependent on decisions by another party. The participants of the business games decide based on the past data. The decisions thus made by the participants influence the subsequent situation under which further subsequent decisions be made.

Management game or business game was first developed in 1957 and subsequently with the advent of digital computer, the growth of business games has been tremendous, due to the increased capabilities of the computers.

The main use of business game is :

— to help the participants to evaluate their decisions.

— to help the Managers to learn to decide in the conflicting situations.

— to help the managers with a high degree of participation.

— to help the Managers to acquire higher skills in decision making.

— to train Managers in constructing the business models and translate them into a real situation.

Since the theory of games is dealt separately in a chapter it is not discussed here in details.

Monte Carlo Methods

Monte Carlo is simulation in a narrow sense. Though it is actually only one kind of simulation by common use, the word "simulation" usually means Monte Carlo simulation. Monte Carlo method does not use formula. It uses random numbers for generating the values of variables, to see what will happen, if certain events were to occur. Monto Carlo method is actually the study of laws of chance. This method is used to solve probability dependent problems when physical experimentation is impracticable and the creation of an accurate formula is not possible. The Monte Carlo method is also explained as simulation by sampling techniques. Instead of taking samples from a real unvierse, they are taken from a theoretical counter part of the real population. The Monte Carlo method has been discussed in the previous chapter also. It's applications are discussed here.

Monte Carlo simulation is used in deciding :

— the size of a maintenance crew

— the number of counters/service booths required

— the number of airport run ways.

It is better to show how Monte Carlo helps by way of examples rather than explaining the theory.

Example 1. The aim of the material manger in an organisation is to minimise the total operating costs. The total cost of operation is the sum of the :

— ordering costs

— carrying costs

— stock out costs.

This problem can be visualised by applying a Monte Carlo simulation for 24 weeks of operation with following parameters.

- The reordering level is set at 15 units.
- The ordering quantity is 20 units.
- Inventory carrying costs is Rs. 10 per unit per week.

- Cost of placing an order is Rs. 25.
- The cost of stock out is Rs. 100 per unit per week.

Table 1. The Probability Distribution of Demand.

S. No.	*Demand (units)*	*Frequency*	*Cumulative Probability distribution as percentage*	*Distribution of random numbers*
(1)	*(2)*	*(3)*	*(4)*	*(5)*
1.	0	2	2	00-01
2.	1	8	10	02-09
3.	2	20	30	10-29
4.	3	35	65	30-64
5.	4	16	81	65-80
6.	5	10	91	81-90
7.	6	9	100	91-99
	Total	100		

Table 2. The Probability Distribution of Delivery Time

S. No.	*Delivery time in weeks*	*Frequency*	*Cumulative probability distribution as percentage*	*Distribution of random numbers*
(1)	*(2)*	*(3)*	*(4)*	*(5)*
1.	1	22	22	00-21
2.	2	46	68	22-67
3.	3	18	86	68-85
4.	4	8	94	86-93
5.	5	6	100	94-99
	Total	100		

Table 3. Twenty Four Weeks Simulation of Demand, Delivery and Total Costs

	Demand		*Delivery*		*Inventory*					
Week	*Random Number*	*Demand in units*	*Random Number*	*Delivery (weeks)*	*Units received*	*Balance in the beginning units*	*Inventory carrying costs Rs.*	*Ordering cost Rs.*	*Cost of stock out Rs.*	*Total cost Rs.*
(1)	*(2)*	*(3)*	*(4)*	*(5)*	*(6)*	*(7)*	*(8)*	*(9)*	*(10)*	*(11)*
(0)						22				
1.	9	1				21	210			210
2.	54	3				18	180			180
3.	42	3				15	150			150
			34	2				25		175
4.	1	0				15	150			150

(1)	(2)	(3)	(4)	(5)	(6)	(7)	(8)	(9)	(10)	(11)
5.	80	4			20	31	310			310
6.	6	1				30	300			300
7	6	1				29	290			290
8.	26	2				27	270			270
9.	57	3				24	240			240
10.	79	4				20	200			200
11.	52	3				17	170			170
12.	80	4				13	130			
			24	2				25		155
13.	45	3				10	100			100
14.	68	4			20	20	260			260
15.	59	3				23	230			230
16.	48	3				20	200			200
17.	12	2				18	180			180
18.	35	3				15	150			
			95	5				25		175
19.	91	6				11	110			110
20.	89	5				6	60			60
21.	49	3				3	30			30
22.	33	3				0	0		100	100
23.	10	1			20	19	190			190
24.	55	3				16	160			160
	Total Average		Average 185							4445

Usually the demand of the materials revised per week and the delivery time of the materials from the time of ordering, vary. From the past data the above frequencies have been arrived and in the last column the distribution of random number is given so that by selecting a random number from the random table, it can be referred to this is last column and read the demand or delivery time that may occur as the case may be. By making use of these two tables the figures at Table-3 are worked out.

To start with balance is assumed as 20 units. First pick up a random number which is 9 and write demand column at Table-3. Read the demand against random number 9 in Table-1. The demand is 1 which is written in the column at Table 3 and the balance is arrived as 21 which works out to Rs. 210 as carrying cost when the balance at Table 3 touches 15 or less take another random number and read the delivery time from Table 2 and write in Table 3.

Thus by generating successive steps for 24 weeks we can summarise the conclusions that the designed or envisaged reordering level and ordering policy reveals that :

(*i*) Average inventory cost per week is Rs. 185.

(*ii*) About 4% of the time the stock out can occur.

Computer Simulation

With computer simulation the impact of variations in costs can be studied like :

(*i*) By increase of ordering cost by 10% or 20%.

(*ii*) By varying the inventory carrying cost.

(*iii*) By varying the cost of stock outs or by changing the level of stock outs.

Thus the Management can easily obtain the sensitivity analysis of the various factors on the cost of inventory and can exercise control on the factors which are too sensitive. The same methodology is applied in simulation of various problems in different areas of operations. Monte Carlo simulation has wider applications like :

(*i*) Determination of size of Mechanics groups for maintenance purpose.

(*ii*) Integrating production scheduling models and inventory control models.

(*iii*) For Budget preparation *viz.* sales budget, manufacturing budget, cash budget can be obtained from various alternatives under different varying input conditions with the aid of complex simulation.

System Simulation Method

This is the third method. System simulation is a method where the real or actual data is processed through a mathematical model. The model is simulated in operating environment. The responses are obtained by simulating the model with alternative management actions and thereby the best response or desired response is selected for the quality of decisions to be implemented.

System simulation is different from Monte Carlo simulation. In system simulation :

— The samples are taken from a real population.

— Theoretical counter part of actual population is not used.

— Mathematical model is also used and it can be analytically solved in arriving at a decision.

— The response can be obtained for any set of factors.

Design of Simulation Experiments

After constructing a simulation model one will face the difficulty in deciding the set of factors and their values for processing the model. If one is not careful in determining the variables and their values an enormous amount of computer time is used. Even after collecting a vast amount of data, one may not have sufficiently accurate information to guide a managerial decision. Here statistical design of experiments will greatly help.

For example, let a production system be represented by a quadratic model.

$$y = a + b_1x_1 + b_2x_2 + b_3x_3 + b_4x_1^2 + b_5x_2^2 + b_6x_3^2 - b_7x_1x_2 + b_8x_2x_3 + b_9x_1x_3.$$

If the manger would like to know the best or highest value of y and the corresponding parameters, he has to resort to the trial and error method since there are number of positive and negative effects and interactions. Even then one will not be sure of the highest value. As per the factorial design of experiments, with all permutations and combinations, the number of runs revised can be calculated as follows :

$$N = (L)^V$$

where N = No. of runs revised

V = No. of variables consideration

L = No. of levels of variables.

With this the number of runs revised can be calculated as follows :

V	2	3	4	5	6	7	8	9	10
L	2	2	2	2	2	2	2	2	2
N	4	8	16	32	64	128	256	512	1024

If three variables with 2 levels are to be studied the runs need to be conducted as below :

Run No.	Levels of variables			*Value of y*
	1	*2*	*3*	
1.	–	–	–	τ_1
2.	+	–	–	τ_2
3.	–	+	–	τ_3
4.	+	+	–	τ_4
5.	–	–	+	τ_5
6.	+	–	+	τ_6
7.	–	+	+	τ_7
8.	+	+	+	τ_8

Where + represents higher level of variables and – represents lower level of variables.

If more than two levels are to be studied same formula can be used. However much more higher level of statistical knowledge is required if the levels and variables go on increasing. But certainly simulation under design of experiments will reveal lot of information and aid for better decision making.

Simulation Languages

The reason for several simulation languages is that they can be applied to different types of problems which make their simulation procedures more automatic for the user. It furnishes a generalised structure for designing simulation models and to speed the conversion of a simulation model to a computer progarmme.

DYNAMO and SIMULATE were designed for simulating economic system on econometric models. GPSS, SIMSCRIPT and GASP are well suited for scheduling and waiting line problems.

Specific Application of Simulation

(*i*) Many chemical reactions can be described by a set of different equations and their solution is some times referred to as continuous simulation ; this may involve the use of Analogue computers.

(*ii*) The complex systems involving queuing problems like, Systems for batch-chemical production, Vehicle unloading, Aircraft landing, Telephone traffic etc.

(*iii*) Blending of the powders. How many batches will be in queue at a time and number of extra containers required for the given plan of action.

(*iv*) *Total Service requirements.* A chemical plant often consists of several units each requiring supplies of services such as steam, water, ice etc. Suppose it is known that there is a peak demand of 2000 gallons/hr. of water on a particular unit and that this peak will last for 2 hours. Other units have different peak usages for different durations. It would be wasteful to build a water main which would cope with the aggregate of all the peak demands, since the probability of all the peaks occurring together is usually very small.

A simulation model can be constructed where the 'activity' of each unit at any instant in time is given by its rate of water consumption at that time. By summing over all the units a measure of the total water usage is obtained. The activity of a unit is changed when the demand for water on that unit alters, and this may be at fixed intervals or at some randomly generated times based an actual observed data. By following the activities of the units over a long length of simulated time a distribution of total demand can be compiled. This is then used to estimate the optimum size of water main.

(*v*) *Stock holding policy.* An important problem for any manufacturing is to determine how much finished product should be held stock ready to meet sales demands. This may invlove the use of ware houses for some materials, or storage tanks for bulk liquids. Increasing the stock holding improves the chance of selling more material. The value of the extra sales has to be balanced against the extra costs incurred in providing the storage facilities, in running the material in stock, having capital tied up in stock and so on.

Simulation can be used to determine the optimum size, and strategy to be used for stock holding and is especially valuable in the more complex cases. Here it is necessary to generate sequences representing the demands from customers and the supply of material into storage. The model can be run with different sizes of storage and account can be taken of any special features such as limitations on the storage life of the product.

(*vi*) *Plant Extensions.* In multistage chemical plants where demand exceeds capacity it is usually fairly easy to spot the bottleneck in the system. This may be a particular unit that has been constantly over loaded. It would be useful if we could measure the benefit of replacing or duplicating this unit without going in for actual modificate to the plant.

The solution is to build a simulation model of the plant which allows investigations to be carried out on the effects of possible extensions to the plant. The model describes the flow of materials through the plants and takes into account of charging, processing and discharging times for each unit. Rules regarding the operating procedure of the plant can be built into the model and incidence and duration of plant break downs can also be minimised.

48

Replacement Models

Introduction

Replacement of an equipment, item or machine is resorted to whenever the machine or item deteriorates in its function or fails to work. Therefore the replacement is considered in two cases.

(*i*) Replacement of items that deteriorate

(*ii*) Replacement of items that fail.

Various types of costs are associated in both the cases. The replacement of the item with new item is considered based on the cost criteria.

Replacement of Capital Equipment

When the efficiency of the equipment and machines declines over a period of a time, in addition to the obsolescence the following things happen in a system :

— Forced idle time is caused with loss of production

— Scrap in the process increases

— Rate of rejections increases

— The frequency of repairs increase

— Causes accidents or rate of accidents increase.

Therefore finally the operating costs of the equipment increases as the life of the equipment reduces or as the age increases. It is necessary to predict the time when the cost of maintenance and operation of the old equipment is higher than the cost of replacing old equipment with new one so that the old equipment can be replaced with new one. Some of the examples are :

Example 1. *The owner of a taxi car maintained the record of the costs/year incurred in maintaining and running the car. The purchase price of the car is Rs. 60,000. The sale value of the car and the operating costs at the end of each year are given below. We can find out when the car should be replaced ?*

Year	*Operating costs (Rs.)*	*Sales price (Rs.)*
1	12000	30000
2	14000	15000
3	16000	7500
4	20000	3750
5	25000	2000
6	30000	2000
7	36000	2000
8	42000	2000

Average cost per year is worked out as below.

Year No.	*Cumulative operating costs*	*Cumulative sales price=capital cost*	*Total cost = op. costs+capital cost*	*Average cost per year*
1	12,000	30,000	42,000	42,000
2	26,000	45,000	71,000	35,500
3	40,000	52,500	92,500	30,833
4	60,000	56,250	116,250	29,062
5	85,000	58,250	143,250	28,650
6	115,000	58,000	173,000	28,833
7	151,000	58,000	209,000	29,857
8	193,000	58,000	251,000	31,375

It can be seen from the above table that the average cost per year goes on reducing in the last column upto 5th year and from there inwards again it starts increasing. At the end of 5th year the average cost/year is the lowest. Therefore, after 5 years the car needs to be replaced with a new car.

Discounted Costs

To know whether a replacement proposal is worthwhile or not, one should know the following :

- Amount and timing of investment.
- Amount and timing of savings.
- Life of the investment.
- The criteria for acceptability of the proposal.
- Proper techniques to relate all the costs and benefit factors in a meaningful way.

Just like all gases can be either additive or comparable only at N.T.P. (Normal temperature and pressure), all the existing equipment and new equipment must be brought on common dantom line for meaningful comparison purpose.

Two such techniques used in the analysis are :

(*i*) D.C.F. (Discounted Cash Flow) techniques.

(*ii*) Present value technique.

Concepts of Discounted Cash Flow and present value techniques are essentially the same. The principle is that A rupee in hand today is worth more than a rupee a year hence. The only difference between these two techniques is that, under the present value method, the interest rate at which the future cash inflows are to be discounted is pre-determined. The merit of these techniques is to bring down all the costs as well as benefit factors which are to be incurred at different time points to the same time point by taking into account the worth of money and then to make them comparable. These techniques are eminently suitable to a situation where a number of investment opportunities exist with a total objective of utilizing the limited financial resources in an optimal fashion.

Worth of Money

If the worth of the money is considered as 10% per year, spare money available now can be invested to yield 10% in a year. Spending Rs. 100 today would be equivalent spending Rs. 110 in one year time. Similarly one rupee a year from now is equivalent $(1.1)^{-1}$ rupees today and one rupee γ years from now is equivalent to $(1.1)^{-\gamma}$ rupees to day. This quantity $(1.1)^{-\gamma}$ is called the Present Value or Present Worth of one rupee spent "γ" years from now.

Example 2. *The value of the money 10% per year machine 1 is to be replaced every 3 years and machine 2 is to be replaced for every 6 years with yearly outlay (expenditure) as given below:*

Year	*Yearly Outlay in Rupees*	
	Machine 1	*Machine 2*
1	2000	3400
2	400	200
3	800	400
4		600
5		800
6		1000

Which machine costs less ?

Total discounted cost of machine 1 for the 3 years is

$$= \text{Rs. } 200 + \frac{\text{Rs. } 400}{1.1} + \frac{\text{Rs. } 800}{(1.1)^2}$$

$$= 2000 + 363.6 + 661.1 = 3024.7$$

$$\text{Average per year} = \frac{3024.7}{3} = \textbf{Rs. 1008 per year}$$

Total discounted cost of machine 2 for 6 years is

$$= \frac{\text{Rs. } 3400}{1} + \frac{\text{Rs. } 200}{1.10} + \frac{\text{Rs. } 400}{(1.1)^2} + \frac{\text{Rs. } 600}{(1.1)^3} + \frac{\text{Rs. } 800}{(1.1)^4} + \frac{\text{Rs. } 1000}{(1.1)^5}$$

$$= \frac{3400}{1} + 181.8 + 330.6 + \frac{600}{1.331} + \frac{800}{1.4641} + \frac{1000}{1.6105}$$

$$= 3400 + 181.8 + 330.6 + 450.8 + 546.4 + 620.92$$

$$= 5530.5$$

Average per year $= \frac{5530.5}{6}$

$= \textbf{Rs. 921.8}$ per year.

Machine-2 costs Less

If machine 1 also is discounted for 6 years on par with machine 2.

The discounted cost for machine 1 in 6 years.

$$= \frac{2000}{1} + \frac{400}{1.1} + \frac{800}{(1.1)^2} + \frac{2000}{(1.1)^3} + \frac{400}{(1.1)^4} + \frac{800}{(1.1)^5}$$

$= 2000 + 363.6 + 661.1 + 1502.6 + 273.2 + 496.7$

$= 5297.2$

Average cost per year

$= \frac{5297.2}{6}$

$= \textbf{Rs. 882.9}$

Now machine-1 works out to be cheaper.

Calculation of Present Worth

An algebraic formula as well can be developed for the calculation of the present worth of the expenditure denoted by W

$$W(n) = P + C_1 + wC_2 + w^2C_3 + w^3C_4 + ... + \; + w^{n-1}C_n$$

where $W(n)$ = present worth of the machine expenditure after n years.

P = Purchase price of the machine

C = Running cost or operating costs in a year

w = is the present worth of a unit to be spent a year hence

w = Discounted rate

$w = 1 \div (1 + i)$

i = rate of interest

n = Number of years after which the machine is to be replaced.

It is assumed that expenditure (running cost) is incurred at the beginning of each year.

Example 3. *Let the purchase price of a machine be Rs. 6000, the cost of the money be 10%. The estimated running cost of the machine is given below year-wise.*

Year	1	2	3	4	5	6	7	8	9	10
Running cost	500	500	500	500	500	1000	1200	1400	1600	1800

When the machine should be replaced ?

P = Rs. 6000

$i = 0.1$

n = 1 to 10.

Year	Running cost per year C_n Rs.	Discounted rate $(w)^{n-1} = \frac{1}{(1+i)^{n-1}}$	Present worth for the year $(w)^{n-1} C_n$	Cumulative cost of present worth	Average present worth per year
1.	500	1.0000	500	500	500
2.	500	0.9091	455	955	478
3.	500	0.8264	413	1368	456
4.	500	0.7513	376	1744	436
5.	500	0.6830	342	2086	417
6.	1000	0.6209	621	2707	451
7.	1200	05645	677	3384	483
8.	1400	0.5132	719	4103	512
9.	1600	0.4665	746	4849	539
10.	1800	0.4241	764	5613	561

Since the minimum average present worth of total running cost is 5th year, the machine be replaced at 5th year end.

Example 4. *As new automobile vehicle costs of Rs. 10,000 and it can be sold at the end of any year with the selling price as shown below. The operating and maintenance cost also are given year-wise.*

1. End of year	1	2	3	4	5	6
2. Selling price	7000	5000	3000	2000	1000	500
3. Annual operating and maintenance cost in Rs.	1000	1600	1800	2500	3000	3500

When the automobile vehicle needs to be replaced because of wear and tear.

S. No.	Year end	Selling price year end Rs.	Capital cost 10,000 – col (3)	Cumulative operating and maintenance costs Rs.	Total cost	Average cost / year
1.	1	7000	3000	1000	4000	4000
2.	2	5000	5000	2600	7600	3800
3.	3	3000	7000	4400	11400	3800
4.	4	2000	8000	6900	14900	**3725**
5.	5	1000	9000	12000	21000	4200
6.	6	500	9500	13000	22500	3750

Since the average cost is minimum at the end of 4th year the vehicle can be replaced at the end of 4th year.

Replacement of Items on Failures

The second type of replacement is concerned with the items that either work or fail completely. Such type of items do no deteriorate markedly with age yet they suddenly fail after some age. The life span of such items is not constant but will follow certain frequency distribution. Different life spans have different probabilities. The probability of mortality or failures increases as the age of the machine or item increases. The failures or deaths caused as a result of external factors like natural calamities are not accountable under the probability distribution of life. Replacement of a failed items has to be done and understandable by any one. The problem is to plan replacement of items that have not failed. Replacement of an usable item which is still functioning, will be justified if the cost of replacement is higher after failure than the cost of replacement before failure. There are a number of reasons why replacing failure may be more costly than replacing live items. The cost of replacing failures include

— Cost of the item itself
— Cost of labour
— Cost of loss of production that can occur due to delay
— Cost of damage to the material
— Cost of damage to the machinery/equipment
— Cost of a possible accident.

In view of the above costs, the cost of replacement per unit of item in group replacement is constant and is less than the cost per unit of item for replacement of failed item.

Example. *The rate of failure of bulbs is given below.*

Months	1	2	3	4	5
% failure by end of month	5	15	20	40	20

In a factory premises there are 10,000 bulbs which are in use. To replace one bulb at a time (incase of failure of one bulb at a time) it costs Rs. 2.00. If all bulbs of 10,000 are replaced simultaneously, the cost of replacement works out to Rs. 0.5 per bulb.

If the maintenance incharge decides to replace all bulbs at fixed intervals (whether the bulbs have failed for not) and to replace the bulbs as and when they burnt or fail, what is the periodicity of replacement of all bulbs. Let P_i denote the probability that a bulb after it is installed fails during the ith month of its age. Then the probability distribution represented as shown below.

Month (i)	1	2	3	4	5
Probability of a new bulb that fails during ith month	0.05	0.15	0.20	0.40	0.20

Let R_0 denote the number of all new bulbs which were initially installed = 10,000.

R_i be the number of bulbs replaced at the end of ith month. The number of bulbs replaced at the end of each month can be iterated based on the above probability distribution.

Initially $R_0 = 10{,}000$ bulbs

At the end of 1st month $R_1 = R_0 \times P_1 = 10{,}000 \times 0.05 = 500$ bulbs will be replaced

At the end of 2nd month *i.e.* $R_2 = R_0 \times P + R_1 \times P_1$

So out of 10,000 bulbs, 15% of bulbs fail at the end of second month and out of $R_1 = 500$ bulbs at the end of second month becomes end of 1st month. Therefore out of $R_1 = 500$ bulbs, 5% of bulbs will fail and need to replaced.

Hence total number of bulbs that would be replaced as a result of failures at the end of second month is

$$R_2 = R_0P_2 + R_1P_1 = 10000 \times 0.15 + 500 \times 0.05$$
$$R_2 = 1500 + 25 = 1525.$$

Similarly R_3, R_4 etc. are calculated and shown below.

$$R_0 = R_0 = 10,000$$
$$R_1 = R_0 \times P_1 = 1000 \times 0.05 = 500$$
$$R_2 = R_0 \times P_2 + R_1 \times P_1 = 1000 \times 0.15 + 500 \times 0.05 = 1525$$
$$R_3 = R_0 + P_3 + R_1 \times P_2 + R_2 \times P_1$$
$$= 10000 \times 0.2 + 500 \times 0.15 + 1525 \times 0.05 = 2151$$
$$R_4 = R_0P_4 + R_1P_3 + R_2P_2 + R_3P_1$$
$$= 10000 \times 0.4 + 500 \times 0.2 + 1525 \times 0.15 + 2151 \times 0.05 = 4436$$
$$R_5 = R_0P_5 + R_1P_4 + R_2P_3 + R_3P_2 + R_4P_1$$
$$= 10000 \times 0.2 + 500 \times 0.4 + 1525 \times 0.2 + 2151 \times 0.15 + 4436 \times 0.05 = 3049$$
$$R_6 = R_1P_5 + R_2P_4 + R_3P_3 + R_4P_2 + R_5P_1$$
$$= 500 \times 0.2 + 1525 \times 0.4 + 2151 \times 0.2 + 4436 \times 0.15 + 3049 \times 0.5 = 1958$$
$$R_7 = R_2P_5 + R_3P_4 + R_4P_3 + R_5P_2 + R_6P_1$$
$$= 1525 \times 0.2 + 2151 \times 0.4 + 4436 \times 0.2 + 3049 \times 0.15 + 1958 \times 0.5 = 2608$$
$$R_8 = R_3P_5 + R_4 P_4 + R_5P_3 + R_6P_2 + R_7P_1 = 3239$$
$$R_9 = R_4P_5 + R_5P_4 + R_6P_3 + R_7P_2 + R_8P_1 = 3052$$
$$R_{10} = R_5P_5 + R_6P_4 + R_7P_3 + R_8P_2 + R_9P_1 = 2553$$

It can be seen from the 10 iterations that the number of bulbs failed and replaced every month increased till 5th month. Subsequently the number is increasing and reducing. If these iterations are continued for large number of cycles, the system will reach a steady state and there will not be a marked decrease or increase in the number of failures and replacements once the system stabilises, the *proportion of bulbs failing each month is reciprocal of their average life*. For example the average life of the bulbs based on the probability distribution.

$$= 1 \text{ month} \times 0.05 + 2 \text{ months} \times 0.15 + 3 \text{ months} \times 0.2 + 4 \text{ months} \times 0.4 + 5 \text{ months} \times 0.2$$
$$= 3.55 \text{ months.}$$

The proportion of bulbs that fail in each month in the steady state

$$= \frac{1}{3.55} = 0.28$$

For 10,000 bulbs, the number of bulbs that fail every month

$$= 10000 \times 0.28 = 2800.$$

(*a*) If the maintenance in-charge decides only to replace the bulbs as and when they fail, the cost of replacement

= Rs. 2 per bulb × 2800 bulbs
= Rs. 5600 per month on an average.

(*b*) On the contrary if the maintenance incharge desires to know the fixed periodicity of replacement of all bulbs while replacing the bulbs as and when they fail, the following costs will reveal the fixed periodicity :

(*i*) If all bulbs are replaced at the end of 1st month, the cost of replacement is Rs. $0.5 \times 10{,}000$ = Rs. 5000. In addition the cost of the replacing the bulbs during the 1st month = $500 \times$ Rs. 2 = 1000 rupees also has to be added *i.e.* Rs. 5000 + Rs. 1000 = Rs. 6000 at the end of 1st month.

(*ii*) If all bulbs are replaced for every month, the cost of all bulbs replacement plus the cost of bulbs replaced during 2 months will be total cost

$$= \text{Rs. } 5000 + \text{Rs. } 500 \times 2 + 1525 \times 2 = 5000 + 1000 + 3050 = 9050$$

The average cost of replacement per month works out to (9050) ÷ 2 = Rs. 4525.

(*iii*) If all bulbs are to be replaced every 3 months

$$\text{Rs. } 5000 + 500 \times 2 + 1525 \times 2 + 2151 \times 2 = 5000 + 1000 + 3050 + 4302 = 13352$$

$$\text{Average cost/month} = \frac{13352}{3} = \text{Rs. } 4450.$$

(*iv*) If all bulbs are to be replaced after every 4 months.

$$\text{Rs. } 5000 + 500 \times 2 + 1525 \times 2 + 2151 \times 2 + 4436 \times 2 = 5000 + 1000 + 3050 + 4302 + 8872$$

$$= 22{,}224.$$

$$\text{Average cost/month} = \frac{22{,}224}{4} = \text{Rs. } 5556.$$

Similarly it can be calculated for all 10 months and shown below.

Month	*Average cost of replacement / month (Rs.)*
1	6000
2	4525
3	**4450**
4	5556
5	5664
6	5373
7	5350
8	5491
9	5559
10	5514

Under the second policy all bulbs need to be replaced for at the end of every 3 months while continuing to replace the bulbs as and when they fail as average cost per month is Rs. 4450 lowest of all. If the maintenance incharge desires to know which of the above two policies are better, the operating costs in the above two policies can be compared for arriving at the decision.

As per 1st policy to replace the bulbs as and when they fail, the cost/month=Rs. 5600.

As per 2nd policy to replace all the bulbs (10,000) at the end of every 3 months and continue to replace the bulbs as and when they fail, the average cost per month=Rs. 4450.

Thus the above approach can be applied for a wide variety of situations under this category without resorting to much of the mathematical models only a logical approach is required.

49

The Theory of Games

Introduction

The term games relates to conditions of business conflict over time. The participants are competitors who make use of mathematical techniques and logical thinking in order to arrive at the best possible strategy for winning their competitor. Every game has a goal for which the competitors strive by selecting appropriate courses of action. Even though the game may favour one over the other, each will do his best to maximise his profit or minimise his loss. In many games the attainment of goal is accompanied by a payment of some kind of money. Vou Novmann perceived the Theory of Games in 1928 and it came to light only when Morgenstern published as a co-author the "Theory and Practice of Games and Economic Behaviour" in 1944.

Many of the OR models have dealt with conflicting interests internal to the organisation. The production department wants large order with less in variety and wants the materials, men, machines in as much as possible to avoid any short fall in production. Marketing department would like to have greater variety and more number of orders and more sales irrespective of the profitability. Finance department would try to see that unnecessary money is not locked up in various assets and try to avoid the extra costs. Here are all conflicts with in the organisation. The models under games theory deal with the conflict external to the organisation.

The effectiveness of decisions by one party is dependent on decisions by another party. The games theory is directed towards yielding better understanding of competitive economic behaviour. The theory has a value which is independent of the mathematics. It brings awareness of the possibility of internal choice of policy in competitive situations.

Role of Statistics in Games of Chance

Frequency Distribution. It is possible, however, to express much of the information contained in a frequency distribution in just two quantities or parameters on which contains information on the size of the variables - a measure of location, and one which contains information on how scattered the variables are - a measure of dispersion. These two quantities are the mean and the standard deviation.

Mean. The mean of a frequency distribution is simply the arithmetic average value of the variables, *i.e.* the sum of the variables divided by the number of them.

If the value x_1 occurs with frequency f_1

If the value x_2 occurs with frequency f_2

If the value x_3 occurs with frequency f_3 etc.

then the sum of the variables is $f_1x_1 + f_2x_2 + f_3x_3$ etc.
and the total number of variables are $f_1 + f_2 + f_3$ etc.

These expressions may be simplified by using the mathematical summation sign (sigma). Thus

$$f_1x_1 + f_2x_2 + f_3x_3 \text{.... etc.}$$

may be abbreviated to Σfx and $f_1 + f_2 + f_3$ etc. to Σf. Using this notation the mean is defined as follows :

$$\text{Mean } x = \frac{\Sigma fx}{\Sigma f}$$

Standard Deviation. The standard deviation is a measure of variability about the mean. It is not such an obvious measure as the mean is of location, but it has important applications in statistical theory.

It is defined as follows : $\sqrt{\frac{\Sigma f(x-\bar{x})^2}{\Sigma f}}$

This method of calculating the standard deviation is less straight-forward if the mean $\bar{x}$ is not a whole number, because then, the quantities $(x - \bar{x})$ become fractional. There is an equivalent formula which is generally more convenient from the point of view of calculation. It can be shown as :

$$\frac{f(x-x)^2}{f} = \frac{fx^2}{f} - x^2$$

and it is this latter formula which is used in practice for the calculation of the standard deviation. To illustrate the equivalence of the two formulae the calculation of the standard deviation of the number of accidents is repeated in the subsequent discussions.

The standard deviation is a measure of the degree of scatter of the variables. Subtracting a constant value from every variable does not affect this scatter and therefore does not alter the standard deviation.

Probability

We all have some understanding of probability. The purpose of this short introduction to the subject is to show how to express events as being improbable, more probable than not, or highly probable, we can express the degree of probability in quantitative terms.

Definition

If there is evidence for believing that a particular outcome would occur on a fraction *'p'* of occasions in a large number of similar situations, then the particular outcome is said to occur with probability *'p'*. If a particular outcome would never occur, $p = 0$, and this corresponds to one end of the probability scale-impossibility. If an outcome would always occur, $p = 1$, and this corresponds to the opposite end of the probability scale-certainly. For any outcome which may or may not occur, the probability must lie between these two extremes of 0 and 1. There are certain events whose very nature enables the probabilities of certain outcomes to be predicted. What is probability, for example, that if a penny is tossed it will come down heads? If an event can occur in *'n'* mutually exclusive time then the probability of this outcome is m/n. For example, what is the probability that on being dealt a card from a well shuffled pack it turns out to be a spade? 'A well-shuffled pack' implies that the card being dealt is equally likely to be one of the 52 cards contained in the pack; than $n = 52$. Only 13 of these cards are spades, therefore, $m = 13$. The probability of a spade is, therefore $\frac{13}{52} = \frac{1}{4}$. The law of probability were originally developed to understand and predict the relative frequencies of various events in games of chance. There are two important laws of probability; the "Addition Law" and the "Multiplication Law".

Meaning of Probability

The concept of probability plays an important role in many problems of everyday life, in business, in science, and particularly in statistics. In statistics, probabilities are defined as relative frequencies, or to be more exact, as limits of relative frequencies. For example the percentage probability that the shipment will arrive on time is "0.15", this means that in the long run 15 percent of all similar shipments will arrive in time; if we say, "the probability that it will rain in Delhi on the 6th of June is 0.26" this means that it rains there on the 6th of June about 26 percent of the time. If we say that the probability of getting heads with a balanced coin is $\frac{1}{2}$, this means that in the long run we will get 50% heads and 50% tails. It does not mean that we must necessarily get 5 heads and 5 tails in 10 flips of a coin or 10 heads and 10 tails in 20 flips. No, we will not always get equal numbers of heads and tails, but if we flip a balanced coin a large number of times, we will usually get close to 50% heads and 50% tails.

Some Rules of Probability

In the study of probability there are essentially three kinds of problems. First, there is the question of what we mean when we say that a probability is ? Then there is the problem of obtaining numerical probabilities and, finally, there is the problem of using known probabilities to calculate others. Having resolved the first question by defining probabilities in terms of relative frequencies, the problem of obtaining numerical probabilities becomes a problem of estimation. For example, if we want to determine the probability that a shipment from a given firm will arrive on time we refer to past experience and check what proportion of the time shipments from this firm have arrived on time. If we write the probability of the occurrence of event (A) as P (A) the first fundamental rule of probability may be given as

...(*i*)

This merely expresses the fact that a relative frequency cannot be negative or exceed 1. After all, the proportion of the time that an event takes place cannot be negative and it cannot exceed 1, that is, an event cannot occur more than 100 percent of the time. Although the distinction is rather fine $P(A) = 0$ does not mean that the occurrence of event A is beyond the realm of possibility and $P(A) = 1$ does not mean that the occurrence of event A is absolutely certain. A second rule of probability, which follows directly from the frequency definition, states that if the probability of the occurrence of event A is P (A), the probability that it will not occur is

...(*ii*)

For instance, if the probability that it will rain on a certain day is 0.24, then the probability that it will not rain is $1 - 0.24 = 0.76$; if the probability that the value of a stock will go up is 0.63, then the probability that it will not go up is $1 - 0.63 = 0.37$; and if the probability that a certain train will arrive late is 0.60, then the probability that it will not rate is 1 – 0.6 = 0.40. Clearly, if the train is late 60% of the time it must be on time (or early) the remaining 40% of the time. The rule of probability refers to events that are mutually exclusive. Two events are said to be mutually exclusive if the occurrence of either precludes the occurrence of the other. If we toss a coin, heads and tails are mutually exclusive events; we can get one or the other but never the both. The occurrence of the one event renders the occurrence of the other impossible.

Events are Mutually Exclusive

If A and B are mutually exclusive, then

$$P(A \text{ or } B) = P(A) + P(B).$$

This formula tells us that if A and B are mutually exclusive the probability of the occurrence of A or B is equal to the sum of the individual probabilities of A and B.

Formula (1) can easily be generalised to apply to more than two mutually exclusive events. A number of events are said to be mutually exclusive if the occurrence of any one precludes the occurrence of all of the others. Given a mutually exclusive events A_1, A_2 ....and A_n, the probability that one of them will occur is $P(A)$ or A_2 or ...... or $An)$

$$= P(A) + P(A_2) + \ldots\ldots P(An) \qquad \ldots(2)$$

If the probability that an executive will spend his summer vacation in Bombay, Calcutta, Simla, Mossourie or Nanital is 0.12, 0.19, 0.27, 0.20 and 0.06, respectively, then the probability that he will spend his summer vacation in one of these 5 places is

$$= 0.12 + 0.19 + 0.27 + 0.20 + 0.06 = 0.84$$

To formulate a general rule of addition for events which need not be mutually exclusive, we shall first have to explain what is meant by two events being independent or dependent. Two events are said to be independent if the occurrence or non-occurrence of either in no way affects the occurrence of the other. If A and B stand for getting heads in two successive flips of a coin, then A and B are independent ; the second flip is in no way affected by what happened in the first.

Events which are Independent

If two events A and B are independent, the probability that A and B will both occur is given by the equation (3).

If A and B are independent, then;

$$P(A \text{ and } B) = P(A)\, P(B) \qquad \ldots(3)$$

This formula tells us that if A and B are independent, the probability that they will both occur is equal to the product of their individual probabilities.

Events not Independent

To consider two events that are not independent, let A stand for a firm's spending a large amount of money on advertisement and B for its showing an increase in sales. Of course, advertising does not gurantee higher sales, but the probability that the firm will show an increase in sales will be higher if A has taken place. The probability that event B will take place provided that A has taken place is called the conditional probability of B relative to A and it will be written symbolically as as $P(B/A)$. In terms of conditional probability we can now formulate a more general rule for the probability that two events A and B will both occur.

General Rule of Multiplication

$$P(A \text{ and } B) = P(B)\, P\,(B/A)$$

or $$P(A \text{ and } B) = P(B)\, P\,(A/B) \qquad ...(4)$$

To return to the problem of finding a rule of addition for events that need not be mutually exclusive. Let us suppose that $P(A)$ is the probability that there will be sunshine and that $P(B)$ is the probability that there will rain. If $P(A) = 0.70$ and $P(B) = 0.50$.

By using the equation (1) the formula for mutually exclusive events we made the error of counting twice all days on which there was both sunshine and rain. To compensate for this we can subtract the days which are counted twice and use the following rule.

$$P\,(A \text{ or } B) = P(A) \times P(B) - P(A \text{ and } B) \qquad ...(5)$$

If in the previous example it is known that there is both sunshine and rain 40% of the time we get

$$P(A \text{ or } B) = 0.70 + 0.50 - 0.40 = 0.80$$

If in the example given on the previous page, we are interested in the probability that the student will pass either in accounting or in business law, that is in at least one of the two subjects, we obtain.

$$P(A \text{ or } B) = 0.80 + 0.75 - 0.72 = 0.83$$

Zero Sum Game

A Zero Sum Game is one in which the payments, upon completion of the game are equal to zero. Thus if X pay Y Rs. 10.00 then Y pays—Rs. 10 to X. The sum of these payments is zero.

A strategy is a player's predetermined method for making his choices during the game. Hence strategy is a set of decision rules. A Pay Off Matrix is a table which specifies how payments should be made at the completion of the game.

Finally games theory is a clear theory applicable to competitive situation.

Two-Person Zero Sum Games

In a two person zero sum game, the interest of the two competitors are opposed in that the sum of the gains for one exactly equals the sum of tosses for the other or the sum of the game adds upto zero.

			Player B	Minimum of Row
	Plan	3	4	
Player A	1	10	14	10
	2	8	12	8
Maximum of column		10	14	

Both the players A and B are equal in ability. A has the plan 1 and 2 while B has the plan of action 3 and 4. Both know the pay offs for every possible strategy. The possible plans for both competitions are.

1. A wins the highest game value if he plays the plan 1 all the time.
2. B realises this situation and plays plan 3 in order to minimise his losses.
3. The game value must be 10 since, A wins 10 and B looses 10 each time a game is played.

4. The game value is the average winnings per player over a long number of plays.

Rectangular Games (Two person zero sum)

Let the player X has three possible plans P, Q, R the player Y has two possible plans S, T payments are made according to the choice of plan as shown below:

Choice of Plan		*Payment*	
P	S	X pays Y	Rs. 4.00
P	T	Y pays X	Rs. 4.00
Q	S	X pays Y	Rs. 2.00
Q	T	Y pays X	Rs. 6.00
R	S	Y pays X	Rs. 2.00
R	T	Y pays X	Rs. 4.00

Find out the best strategies for player X and Y in this two person zero sum game.

For better understanding, the rules of payments be arranged in the matrix form. Let the positive number indicate a payment of Y to X and a negative number a payment of X to Y. Then the following "pay off" matrix can be had.

← +		Player Y		Minimum of row
→ −	Plan	S	T	
Player X	P	− 4	4	− 4
	Q	− 2	6	− 2
	R	2	4	2
Maximum of column		2	6	

References

(1) When Y chooses plan T he always looses since he has to pay X only. Therefore Y prefers to choose plan 5 so that Y can loose least *i.e.* Rs. 2 *i.e.* when X chooses plan R. This is the worst come worst Y can loose otherwise he gains in case X chooses P or Q plans. *Therefore plan S is the best strategy for Y.*

(2) X will gain highest Rs. 6 choosing plan Q provided Y chooses plan T. Since Y can not choose plan T because of maximum loss, and always prefers only plan S, *the best plan X can choose is R in* which case he can gain at least Rs. 2.

(3) Thus the best strategy for X in R and for Y is S *i.e.* X gains Rs. 2 maximum and Y looses Rs. 2 minimum. Rs. 2 is the value of the Game.

(4) *Thus the solution is to find out best strategies for two players and the value of the game.*

Mini Max and Maxi Mini Rule

Player X

With plan P, X gains least	– Rs. 4
With Plan Q, X gains least	– Rs. 2
With plan R, X gains least	+ Rs. 2

The maximum of the least gain for P is Rs. 2 *i.e.* RS. Therefore to find out the minimum value of each row write as shown in table and circle it, which ever is the *maximum of these minimum* values.

Player Y

With plan S, Y looses highest Rs. 2

With plan T, Y looses highest Rs. 6

He wishes to loose least. Therefore the minimum of the highest loss is Rs. 2 *i.e.* RS. Therefore find out the maximum the each column and write as shown in Table and square it whichever is the *minimum of the maximum values.* Gains for which maximum of X= minimum of maximum of Y are called games with Saddle Point and the Saddle point is represented with a circle inside the square.

		Player Y				*Minimum of row*
	Plan	A	B	C	D	
Player X	E	6	–10	0	12	–10
	F	–8	–4	2	4	–8
	G	10	8	4	6	4 max. of min.
Maximum of column		10	8	4	12	
				Min. of max		

Thus the easiest technique in searching a Saddle point is to find a number that is "*lowest in its row and highest in its column*" when one such a number exists it is a Saddle point. The corresponding strategies are the best strategies and the number itself is the value of the game. If there are more than one such saddle points, there are more than one solutions. Each solution corresponds to one saddle points.

C is the best strategy for Y

G is the best strategy for X

Value of the Game is Rs. 4 as it is the saddle point

X wins and Y looses.

Rectangular Games (without saddle point)

It is a 2 persons with no zero sum game. Let us examine the pay off matrix shown in the following table which has no saddle point.

		Player Y	
	Plan	A	B
Player X	C	-9	21
	D	18	3

Since there is no saddle point, player X and Y do not have one single best strategy as their best plans. Therefore each player has to work out some mixed strategy so that his gain is maximised or his loss is minimised.

The possibilities of playing the game by X and Y are:

(*a*) X plays C and D strategies with different frequencies when Y plays only A strategy.

(*b*) X plays C and D strategies with different frequencies when Y plays only B strategy.

(*c*) X plays C and D strategies with different frequencies when Y plays A and B strategies with different frequencies.

Similarly there are three possibilities for Y.

Let X play C half of the time and D half of the time whereas Y chooses to play only A all the time. Then the gains of A are

$$\frac{1}{2}(-9)+\frac{1}{2}(18)=\frac{1}{2}\times 9=4.5$$

If X plays C and D half the time when Y chooses to play only B all the time, the gains of X are

$$=\frac{1}{2}(21)+\frac{1}{2}(3)=\frac{1}{2}\times 24=12$$

If Y also choose mixed strategy say half the time A and half the time B are played and X plays C and D half the time each, the gains of X are

$$=\frac{1}{2}\left[\frac{1}{2}(-9)+\frac{1}{2}(18)\right]+\frac{1}{2}\left[\frac{1}{2}(21)+\frac{1}{2}(3)\right]$$

$$=\frac{1}{2}\left(\frac{1}{2}\times 9\right)+\frac{1}{2}\left(\frac{1}{2}\times 24\right)=\frac{1}{2}(4.5+12)=8.25$$

Evaluating Best-strategy

How to find the best strategies for X and Y so that the loss is minimised and gain is maximised and the value of the game is ascertained.

Let X play C with frequency α and D with a frequencies of $(1-\alpha)$.

Then if Y plays always only A strategy the gain of X

$$= G(X, A) = \alpha(-9) + (1-\alpha)(18) = 18 - 27\alpha$$

If Y plays always only B strategy, the gain of X

$$= G(X, B) = \alpha(21) + (1-\alpha)(3) = 3 + 18\alpha$$

Let the value of α is so chosen that

$G(X, A) = G(X, B)$ which will lead to the best strategy.

Therefore $18 - 27\alpha = 3 + 18\alpha$

$$\alpha=\frac{1}{3} \text{ and } (1-\alpha)=\frac{2}{3}$$

in the above problem the gain of X will be

$$G(X)=\frac{1}{3}(-9)+\frac{2}{3}(18)=\text{Rs. } 9.00$$

Thus irrespective of the frequency with which Y plays either A or B, the gain of x is Rs. 9.00.

Similarly let Y play A with a frequency of γ and B with a frequency of $(1-\gamma)$.

If X plays all the time only C, the gain of Y will be

$$G(Y, C) = \gamma\,(-9) + (1-\gamma)\,21$$

If X plays all the time only D, the gain of Y is

$$G(Y, D) = \gamma\,(18) + (1-\gamma)\,(3)$$

Since $\quad G(Y, C) = G(Y, D)$

$$\gamma(-9) + (1-\gamma)(21) = \gamma\,(18) + (1-\gamma)\,(3)\ \gamma = \frac{2}{5} \text{ and } 1-\gamma = \frac{3}{5}$$

The gain of $Y = G(Y) = \frac{2}{5}(-9) + \frac{3}{5}(21) =$ Rs. 9.00

Even in the non zero sum game

$G(X) = G(Y) =$ Rs. 9.00 for the best strategies of X and Y.

Thus the best strategies are :

I. X should play C and D with frequency of 1/3 and 2/3 repectively.

II. Y should play A and B with frequencies of 2/5 and 3/5 respectively.

III. The value of the game is Rs. 9.00.

50

Maintenance Models

Introduction

Machines and equipment wear out all the time. Greater the number of parts in a machine, greater the possibility of wear, tear and hence the break downs. When the machines break down they can be repaired and put back to work but that becomes too costly. The costs that occur due to beak down are :

(*i*) Down time of machines resulting into loss of production and sales.

(*ii*) Idle time of direct and indirect man power.

(*iii*) Increase in the scrap and rejections.

(*iv*) Dis-satisfaction of the customer due to delay in delivering the commitments.

(*v*) Actual cost of the repairs.

If the reliability of the system is improved, the frequency of break downs time can come down and hence the costs too will come down. The total down time of a mahcine is the summation of down time multiplied by its frequency. For increasing the reliability of the system, either the size of the repair facilities (services) have to be increased (to reduce the machine down time) to attend it quickly as and when break downs occurs or the system of preventive maintenance, needs to be followed (to reduce the frequency of break downs).

This Maintenance Models deal with both the methods. To reduce the down time of a machine. Queuing models based on cost considerations will help, whereas to reduce the frequency of break downs, preventive maintenance models based on cost factors are to be employed.

Before we deal with either one knowing the frequency distribution of break down and their interpretation is a prerequisite.

Frequency Distribution

Break down time distributions indicate the frequency with which machines have maintenance free performance. Depending upon the nature of the equipment, the frequency distribution curves takes different shapes.

(*i*) A simple machine, breaks down nearly at regular intervals of time with least variation in time distributions. This type of distribution resembles to normal distribution in the sense major portion of the break downs happen near about an average value of break down time T_a.

(*ii*) In a complex machine, will have a number of sub assemblies or parts. Each part of the machine will have its own frequency distribution of break down time. Therefore even after the repair of one part, the machine can break down at any time due to the wear out of any other part of the machine. The variability in the time of break down is much more when compared to the 1st case. Such mahcine break down will follow Skewed distribution, Beta distribution or gama distribution. Therefore for the same average break down T_a, more wider variability of break down time is noticed.

(*iii*) In few machines like electronic equipment or very precise and sophisticated instruments etc. they have a long free of trouble time after the repair. Even after the machine is repaired they need a little bit adjustments here and there, then and now but they run for long time trouble free. These three types of curves are shown in the Fig. 50.1.

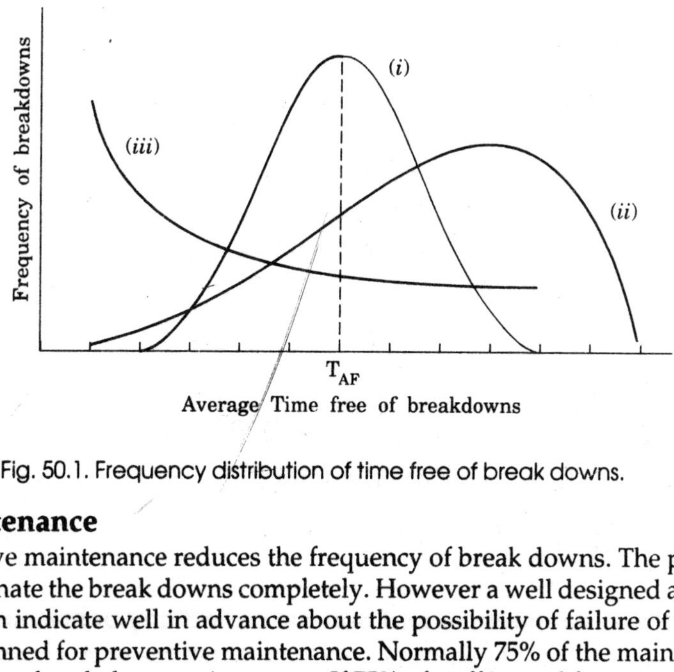

Fig. 50.1. Frequency distribution of time free of break downs.

Preventive Maintenance

A good preventive maintenance reduces the frequency of break downs. The preventive maintenance can not eliminate the break downs completely. However a well designed and implimented inspection system can indicate well in advance about the possibility of failure of a particular part and hence can be planned for preventive maintenance. Normally 75% of the maintenance strength is used on emergency or break down maintenance. If 75% of staff is used for preventive and 25% of maintenance staff is spent on break down maintenance, then preventive maintenance will pay rich dividends.

Example 1. *A mahcine shop has 100 machines, to be kept in service. Over-haul of the machines periodically will greatly reduce the break down frequency, but it costs Rs. 200 per over-haul. As and when the machines break down, they can be repaired by the repair crew who have to wait for the break down to happen or broken down machines will have to wait since the repair crew might be busy in attendting the other machines. The break down machine costs Rs.3000 if they are repaired. The machine shop has been keeping record from which the probability of break down is given below, calculate the periodicity of over-haul on economic basis and see whether over haul is better than break down repair ?*

Months after Over-haul	*Probability of break down*	*Cumulative probability of break downs*
1	5.00%	5.00%
2	2.00%	7.00%
3	1.00%	8.00%
4	6.00%	14.00%
5	5.00%	19.00%
6	4.00%	23.00%
7	7.01%	30.00%
8	12.00%	42.00%
9	13.00%	55.00%
10	14.00%	69.00%
11	15.00%	84.00%
12	16.00%	100.00%

Break Down Repair Costs

Let average elapsed time between break downs be T_a

$$T_a = T_1P_1 + T_2P_2 + T_3P_3 + T_4P_4 + ... + T_{12}P_{12}$$

where T_1, T_2, T_3 etc. are months after over-haul

P_1, P_2, P_3 etc. are the corresponding probabilities

$$T_a = 1 \times 0.05 + 2 \times 0.02 + 3 \times 0.01 + 4 \times 0.06 + 5 \times 0.0 + 6 \times 0.04 + 7 \times 0.07 + 8 \times 0.012$$
$$+ 9 \times 0.13 + 10 \times 0.14 + 11 \times 0.15 + 12 \times 0.16 = 8.44 \text{ months.}$$

or an "average every machine is to be repaired after every 8.44 months.

Total costs of repair = No. of machines × cost of repair per machine

= 100 × 3000 = Rs. 300,000

Average cost per month for break down repairs.

$$\frac{300,000}{8.44} = \text{Rs. } 35,545$$

Costs of preventive maintenance and optimal periodicity of preventive maintenance

The distribution does not follow any standard distribution. A number of iterations are required to find out the number of break downs that can occur for different periods of overhaul.

Let the machine be over-hauled once every month. In that case the only break downs need to be attended are within one month. If the machines are over-hauled once every two months, the break down will increase. First in two months whatever break down occur they need to be repaired. In addition few of the machines repaired in the first month will break down again before the scheduled over-haul.

No. of break downs if scheduled over-haul for every month then

$$D_1 = n\,P_1$$

D_1 = No. of break downs in one month

n = No. of machines

P_1 = Probability of break downs after one month

$$D_1 = 100 \times 0.05 = 5.00$$

No. of break downs if scheduled over-haul is for every 2 months.

$$D_2 = N(P_1 + P_2) + D_1P_1$$
$$= 100(0.05 + 0.02) + 5(0.05)$$
$$D_2 = 7 + 0.25 = 7.25$$

Like this for the entire period of 12 months it can be calculated.

Scheduled over-haul for every 3 months

$$D_3 = N(P_1 + P_2 + P_3) + D_2P_1 + D_1P_2$$
$$= 100(0.05 + 0.02 + 0.01) + 7.25 \times 0.05 + 5 \times 0.02$$
$$= 8 + 3.625 + 0.1 = 11.725$$

No. of break down for Scheduled over-haul every 4 months

$$D_4 = N(P_1 + P_2 + P_3 + P_4) + D_3P_1 + D_2P_2 + D_1P_3$$
$$= 100(0.14) + 11.725 \times 0.05 + 7.25 \times 0.02 + 5 \times 0.01$$
$$D_4 = 14 + 0.58625 + 0.1450 + 0.05 = 14.79$$

No. of break downs for scheduled over-haul every 5 months

$$D_5 = N(P_1 + P_2 + P_3 + P_4 + P_5) + D_4 + P_1 + D_3P_2 + D_2P_3 + D_1P_4$$
$$= 100(0.19) + 14.79 \times 0.05 + 11.725 \times 0.02 + 7.25 \times 0.01 + 5 \times 0.06$$
$$D_5 = 19 + 0.74 + 0.24 + 0.07 + 0.3 = 20.35$$

No. of break down for scheduled over-haul every 6 months

$$D_6 = N(P_1 + P_2 + P_3 + P_4 + P_5 + P_6) + D_5P_1 + D_4P_2 + D_3 P_3 + D_2P_4 + D_1 P_5$$
$$= 100(0.23) + 20.35 \times 0.05 + 14.79 \times 0.02 + 11.725 \times 0.01 + 7.25 \times 0.06 + 0.5 \times 0.05$$
$$D_6 = 23 + 1.02 + 0.3 + 0.12 + 0.44 + 0.25 = 25.12$$

Similarly the number of break downs that can occur for every 7, 8, 9, 10, 11 and 12 months have been calculated and will be as under.

$$D_7 = 33.08$$
$$D_8 = 46.47$$
$$D_9 = 61.177$$
$$D_{10} = 78.81$$
$$D_{11} = 97.78$$
$$D_{12} = 119$$

	Probability		0.05	0.02	0.01	0.06	0.05	0.04	0.07	0.12	0.13	0.14	0.15	0.16,	
	Cumulative probability		0.05	0.07	0.08	0.14	0.19	0.23	0.30	0.42	0.55	0.69	0.84	1.00,	
D	*N*	*Cumulative probability*	*Probabilities of*												
			D_1	D_2	D_3	D_4	D_5	D_6	D_7	D_8	D_9	D_{10}	D_{11}	D_{12}	*Total value of D*
D_1	100	0.05													5
D_2	100	0.07	0.05												7.25
D_3	100	0.08	0.02	0.05											11.725
D_4	100	0.14	0.01	0.02	0.05										14.79
D_5	100	0.19	0.06	0.01	0.02	0.05									20.35
D_6	100	0.23	0.05	0.06	0.01	0.02	0.05								25.12
D_7	100	0.30	0.04	0.05	0.06	0.01	0.02	0.05							33.08
D_8	100	0.42	0.07	0.04	0.05	0.06	0.01	0.02	0.05						46.47
D_9	100	0.55	0.12	0.07	0.04	0.05	0.06	0.01	0.02	0.05					61.77
D_{10}	100	0.69	0.13	0.12	0.07	0.04	0.05	0.06	0.01	0.02	0.05				78.81
D_{11}	100	0.84	0.14	0.13	0.12	0.07	0.04	0.05	0.06	0.01	0.02	0.05			97.78
D_{12}	100	1.00	0.15	0.14	0.13	0.12	0.07	0.04	0.05	0.06	0.01	0.02	0.05		119.00

Since the expected break downs for each policy have been calculated, the economics of each policy is worked out as shown below.

Preventive maintenance for every N number of months (1)	*No. of break downs in N number of months (2)*	*Average number of break downs per month* (3) = (2) ÷ (1)	*Cost of break downs per month Rs.* (4) = *Rs.* 300 × *column* (3)	*Total cost of break downs over hauls per month Rs.(5)=Rs. 200+column (4)*
1	5	5.00	1500	1700
2	7.25	3.63	1089	1289
3	11.725	3.91	1173	1373
4	14.79	3.70	1110	**1310**
5	20.35	4.07	1221	1421
6	25.12	4.19	1257	1457
7	33.08	4.73	1419	1619
8	46.47	5.81	1743	1943
9	61.77	6.86	2058	2258
10	78.81	7.88	2364	2564
11	97.78	8.89	2667	2867
12	119.00	9.92	2976	3176

Cost of break downs overhaul per month when plotted against months. The minimum cost occurs at 4th month. Therefore for every 4th month overhaul can be done and this preventive maintenance policy is the best.

51

Management Information System

Concept of Information

We perceive information as paper work, which means nuisance. This feeling is not correct. Information at present is one of the ingredient of industrial operations. In a simple organisation, the amount of information needed to provide efficient utilisation of men-materials and machinery is not very significant, but in a larger size production unit efficient production depends considerably on systematic flow of information regarding the sales forecasts, materials planning, production scheduling, costs and profitability at various production levels. Information is an action concept. What you want somebody to work, you must tell him what to do and how to do it. Modification for creative and intelligent work come only from job satisfaction and job satisfaction cannot be achieved without understanding the objectives of the job to be achieved which in turn can not be understood without information.

Executives in industries normally complain of :

(*i*) Increasing amount of paper work.

(*ii*) Paucity of information available for decision-making.

The two are contradictory. On one hand, information is pouring in through papers, submerging the executives and on the other hand, there is not enough information for rational decision-making.

The information system is based on 'the analysis of each aspect of information with respect to different utility for decision making and the cost of getting the information.

The information system reflects the style of management. In many concerns, the management exists only at the top. All the decisions are taken by the top man himself. With this unity style of management, there is a possibility of inefficiency in decision making due to overwork rather than to share power and depend on the loyalty of others. Management normally has two options :

(*i*) Fire Brigrade management and

(*ii*) Look ahead management.

The Fire Brigrade Management can ask for information when required. But look ahead management, believes in formulating carefully its needs for information ahead of time. The information is closely tied to the possible action to eliminating superfluous information. Thus there is a need to devise a system which provides symbolisation and information to substitute for seeing actual work.

The importance of professional managers has considerably increased during last 30 years. Many factors are responsible for this importance such as rapid change of technology increasing size of business, changing socio-political environment in which business have to operate. According to Peter Drucker managing of business goes a way beyond passive reaction and adoption. It implies the responsibility for attempting to shape the economic environment for planning initiating and carrying through changes in the economic environment for constantly pushing back the limitations of economic circumstances and enterprise's freedom of action.

In order to provide this kind of creative leadership in a complex environment, the management needs information. Manager needs the information in order to perform following tasks :

- Setting of objectives.
- To establish the plan for achieving the objectives.
- To execute the plans.
- To evaluate the performance of the organisation.
- To have the feedback of the plans.

Thus management's number one task is to get the right information in the right form, at the right place and at the right time. The right information is that information which is necessary for the effective functioning of the management. Thus the increased complexity of business has forced management to rely heavily on information system.

Following are the parallel developments which have increased the availability of quantitative and qualitative information.

- Standard costing.
- Marginal contribution and break-even analysis.
- Flexible budgeting.
- Electronic data processing.

We know that as a business grow in size and becomes complex it becomes impossible to pay attention to all the aspects of the business. At this stage we need the advice of functional specialists in the area of production planning, production control, accounting, work study, marketing, quantitative techniques etc. In addition to this the changes in the organisational structure had to be made to meet the various changes. The term management information can be defined as an efficient and purposeful system which have the capability to provide all levels of management, a timely, prompt, accurate and reliable information M.I.S. is a nervous system of the organisation and any deficiency in this system is very likely to reflect of the functional and administrative efficiency of the organisation. To understand the concept of management information system. Let us understand each of the following terms :

A—Management
B—Information
C—System.

A. Management

It is essential part of any group activity. An organisation cannot survive without management. It is the management which makes people realise the objectives of the organisation and directs the efforts towards their achievement. Management is a multi-purpose organ of an organisation that manages the work and personnel at work. It is a creative and innovative force striving to secure the maximum result by the use of available resources. Management provides new ideas and vision to the work group and integrates its efforts in such a manner as to account for better results. The word Management refers to top, middle and lower level as well as different functional area of management such as production, operations, marketing, finance, accounts, management services, personnel etc.

B. Information

It is something which management expects to know at a given time. Information is not data, the data comprises of a host of information, which may be of little or no consequence to management. The information is needed to plan, organise, direct and control the business and suitably designed information pays for itself. The effectiveness of any information is dependent on the timing and content of the information presented and the management action. The need for management information is felt when the managers have to make decisions. The manager will have to rely on his judgment but he must have information on the basis of which he arrives at the decisions. The three important uses of information are :

(*i*) Process of management planning (decision making).

(*ii*) Execution.

(*iii*) Control.

Once the objective of the business are decided than it is necessary to plan the course of action to be followed inorder to achieve these. Such a plan need reliable information so as to obtain best results. The next step is to communicate the plan or decisions to lower levels for execution. This requires information from those higher up as to what action is to be taken all along the line to the lowest levels. The next is the control functions of management. After the plan has been made and executed one must have the information of the results and standards to evaluate whether objectives have been achieved or not. This calls for a regular flow of feedback information which will indicate in what way the result vary from planned targets. By examining these variances management can decide the corrective actions to be taken. Thus planning, executing and controlling the affairs of a business will require information. Information is required by all levels of management free but the same information will not be useful at all levels. At the top management level what is required is a very broad survey relating to areas where results have varied from plans. This is known as management by exceptions. Lower down the organisation structure the same principles will be followed by each executive and will be given more detailed reports directly bearing the responsibility.

Information can be presented by means of graphs, charts, (pie, charts, Bar charts, Histograms, Ideographs and Flow charts). The timing and frequency of reports depend on the nature of the report whether routine or special. In considering the timing and frequency of reports, the financial cost of preparation must be weighed and balanced against the anticipated benefits expected from the use of the reports. Reports normally present information regarding a period of time. Reporting is the physical aspects of manufacturing on its technological aspects and economics aspects. Reporting is a matter of planning and creation of record.

Following are the types of records which are usually created.

(*a*) Records of basic information.

(*b*) Records showing what is available.

(*c*) Historical Records.

(*a*) **Records of basic information**

(*i*) Blue prints. (*ii*) Bills of materials.

(*iii*) Production routing.

(*b*) **Records showing what is available**

(*i*) Raw materials. (*ii*) Work in process.

(*iii*) Semi-processed stock. (*iv*) Machinery and equipments.

(*v*) Finished stock. (*vi*) Tools, jigs, fixtures and gauges.

(*c*) **Historical Records**

(*i*) Records of production. (*ii*) Records of waste and rejects.

(*iii*) Records of machine performance. (*iv*) Records of sales.

(*v*) Records of absenteeism.

The records exhibit information about actual production, about actual input as compared to pre-conceived standards. In a small organisation the reports are prepared on the shop floor and the management evaluates the daily report and takes prompt action. In a large plant the same course is followed by the production planning and control on an adequate scale relevant to the operational requirements. Following are the various type of reports normally used in a large plant.

(*i*) Daily production reports, (*ii*) Weekly raw material position,

(*iii*) Monthly cost statements, (*iv*) Monthly Maintenance Plan,

(*v*) Monthly Quality Control Report.

Various forms are used for evaluation and considering the reports. Management information need not always generate from within the company. It has been realised by now that the top management should have a continuous flow of information. Following are the areas on which routine information is given importance.

(*i*) Customers. (*iii*) Competitors.

(*ii*) New areas of Investment. (*iv*) Government Policies.

(*d*) **Types of Management Information**

The various types of management information which are commonly required by the general management in most of the business organisation are :

(*a*) Budgets. (*b*) Revenue Statements.

(*c*) Cost Reports. (*d*) Statistical Information.

(*e*) Capital Expenditure.

(*a*) Budgets

Budgets are normally prepared annually and submitted in advance to the management.

A consolidated budget comprising of detailed budgets is prepared to show the broad aims and plans of the organisation as a whole and give a forecast of the financial effects.

(*b*) Revenue Statements

The revenue statements are prepared on monthly or quarterly basis. Statistical information is given wherever possible and correlated with the financial information. The revenue statements will give the comparative figures of corresponding and previous periods.

(*c*) Cost Reports

Costing information is essential for production and service oriented companies in view of its impact on project margins.

(*d*) Statistical Information

The volume of business is perhaps the most critical single factor having repercussion on net project arising from the burden of fixed overhead expenses. Statistical information deal separately with each activity usually started in quantitative unit.

(*e*) Cash Flow

Every good information system have cash under control, amounts locked up in sundry debtors are drawn and so are losses from bad debts.

Every business organisation uses the concept of cash flow. The cash flow statements are the projection for a future period of time. The opening and closing cash balances will give us the surplus or shortfall in cash resources. As borrowed money command high interest rates, it is essential that a proper scheduling of cash resource is achieved.

(*f*) Capital Expenditure

Capital expenditure statements are used as part of annual budget. This gives us the estimates of expenditure to be incurred during the forthcoming period on capital project to be taken up. The capital expenditure plan are part of the long term forecast.

(*c*) System

System refers to a group of components which interact to provide management with the information it seeks. The system would have its components as :

1. Inputs.
2. Outputs.
3. Processing devices.

Nature and Design of M.I.S.

Nature. The unique information requirements of different management levels and the functional areas is outlined in Fig. 51.1. The diagram clearly describe the information systems in the corporate hierarchy. Table 51.1 shows the various management areas and the kind of information that might be needed.

Design

It is indeed a difficult task to design a suitable and efficient information system for the management. This demands a through knowledge of the organisational structure working and system. It requires experience, skill and vision of the Information System. Designer who must understand, assimilate and foresee the information needs of the management. A few of the important steps involved in the design of M.I.S. are :

1. Analysis Phase → –Problem Recognition
   –Problem Identification
   –Problem definition

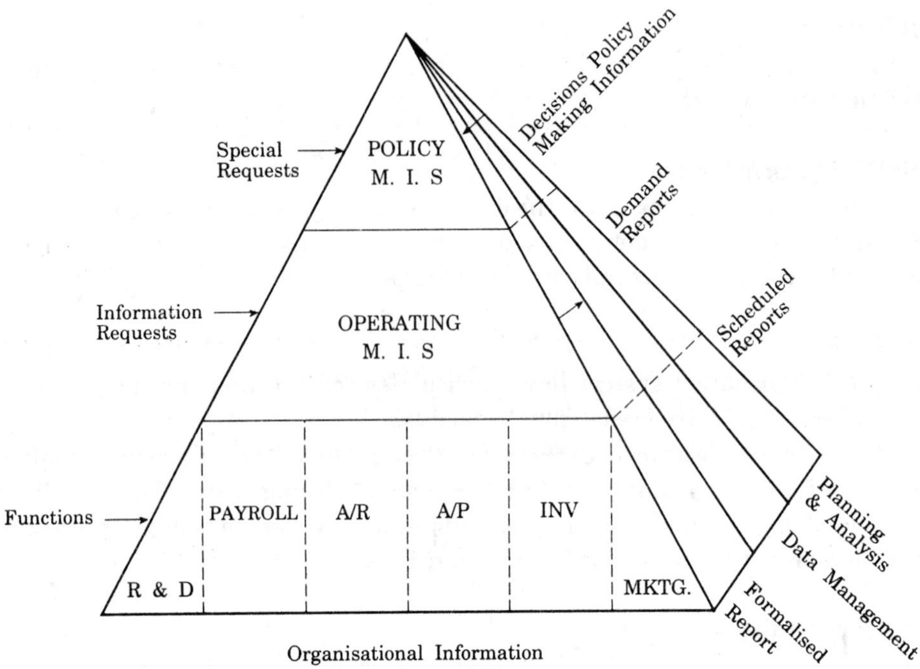

Fig. 51.1.

2. Synthesis —
- –Problem of Flow Chart
- –Examination of the document flow
- –Working out quantities
- –Hardware and software considerations
- –Establishing inputs and outputs
- –Fixing user responsibility
- –Running in Parallel.

Table 51.1. An Information System and Corporate Hierarchy

Level	*Organisation Identity*	*Activities*	*Information System*	*Outputs*
Strategic Planning	Top Management	Set objectives	Special "one-time reports"	Goals and Policies
Management Control	Departments heads	Allocate assigned resources	Many regular reports and Formats	Decisions "personal" leadership
Operational Control	Supervisors, Foremen, Clerks	Use resources to carry out tasks	Formal	Actions

Analysis Phase

(*i*) *Problem recognition.* The designer must recognise the potential areas which need to be served better and supplied with information which is better, prompt and acurate. This has to be accomplished by frequent and free discussion with the various levels of management. Enough time should be spent in the recognition of the problem, because it is preferable to have wrong solution for the right problem rather than the right solution for wrong problem.

(*ii*) *Problem identification.* This involves a further study into the areas which have been broadly recognised in the problem recognition phase and a closer scrutiny of the selected areas already identified a deficient areas.

(*iii*) *Problem definition.* This phase is a further detailed study of the problem identification phase. For instance, it will point out the exact discrepancy.

Synthesis

(*i*) *Preparation of a document flow chart.* The purpose of the flow chart is to present the flow of different documents relating to the discrepancies of the different areas.

(*ii*) *A close examination of the document flow chart.* This is an exercise involving a careful examination of the several deficiencies thrown in by the document flow chart.

(*iii*) *Working out quantities.* This involves the computation of the record size and the data elements involved in the systems design. The total volume of data to be processed and maintained have to be determined. This will, in turn constitute the basis for indentifying the type of information system that may be necessary and the kind, of organisation, hierarchy equipment and procedures which will be required to support such as information system.

(*iv*) *Hardware and software considerations.* Now it is the time for identifying the exact computer configuration, input output terminals, data storage devices, on-line terminals and other peripherals. It is the time when exact software support that will be necessary needs to be analysed, planned for training personnel as an integral part of this phase.

(*v*) *Establishing inputs and outputs.* This calls for the identification of the areas of entry of raw information into the information system including the exact contents of that information. This also involves determination of the kind of outputs which will be required out of the M.I.S.

(*vi*) *Fixing user responsibilities.* It is important to state precisely and clearly the user responsibilities in the matter of data entry including instructions on such vital matters as the formats, the input output times, the devices, the equipment and the location in which the entry will take place. It will also have to be explained to the user the importance of feedback from him to the reporting output in order that discrepancies in the reporting could be rectified without loss of time.

(*vii*) *Running in parallel.* Any newly designed M.I.S. has to be observed through a period before it is finally accepted. It is important that the new system should run in parallel with the existing system. This is referred to as 'running in parallel '. This phase of new system development and testing could last from a few weeks to several months depending upon the feedback received from the user with respect to the report reliability offered by the new system.

Impact of Management Information System on Management

Following points give the impact of M.I.S. on management :

(1) Information is power and a kind of *information or computer man* has grown in the organisation. Information man is consulted by the top management as well as heads of functional groups, in connection with the fulfilment of information needs of the organisation.

(2) M.I.S. growth has resulted in centralisation. The availability of prompt, accurate and timely information about the various activities of the organisation to the management has enhanced their capacity to perform the control function.

(3) M.I.S. one growth of computers has changed the entire philosophy of the management. Certain problems which is used to be considered very complicated and almost impossible to solve are now a matter of fact. Production scheduling, Linear Programming, Transportation and assignment models problems are now solved in no time by the help of computers.

Accounting Information System

One of the most essential part of a good management information system is the accounting information system. The principles underlying a good accounting information are :

(*i*) Consistency
(*ii*) Flexibility
(*iii*) Comprehensiveness
(*iv*) Applicability.

A clear assignment of responsibility is essential to an effective information system. A good information system gathers data on costs, revenues and profits. The effectivness of management information is ultimately determined by the quality of its reports. A common defect of most management reports it that they give too detailed information, which may often lose sight of even by the skilled manager. The reports are useful to management if they are designed towards performance measurement. The reports should be confined to exceptions. The reports should be designed to highlight the areas where action is necessary. The reports should be designed to match the organisational structure of the organisation.

Objective of Management Information System

The object is to provide timely and effective information for the management. The management information system can be divided into following 4-sub systems.

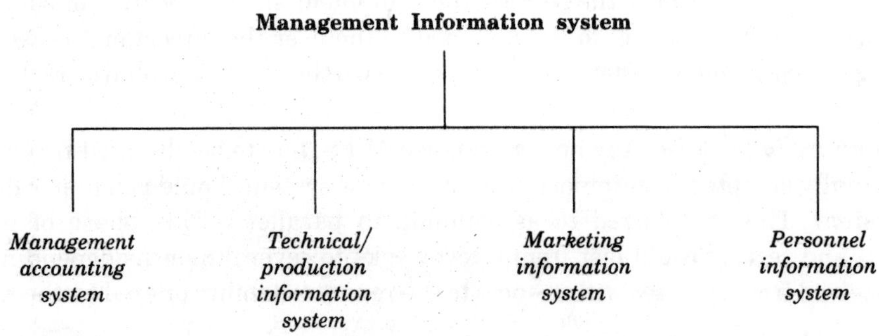

Let us see the line diagram for Marketing Personnel and Production Information Systems.

COMPUTER BASED INFORMATION SYSTEM

Computer Based Information System (C.B.I.S.) is an invaluable aid to the various levels of Management. The computer enables all management philosophy system such as :

(1) Management by direction.
(2) Management by results.
(3) Management by objectives.

MARKETING INFORMATION SYSTEM

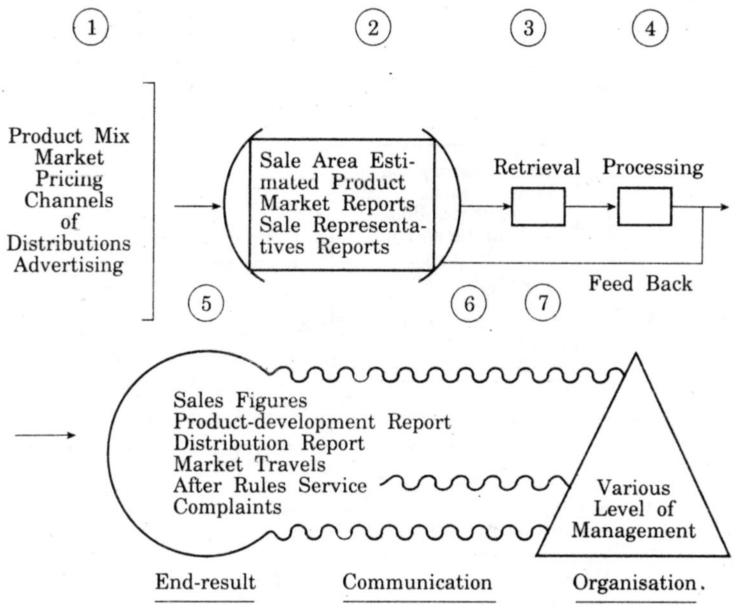

Fig. 51.2.

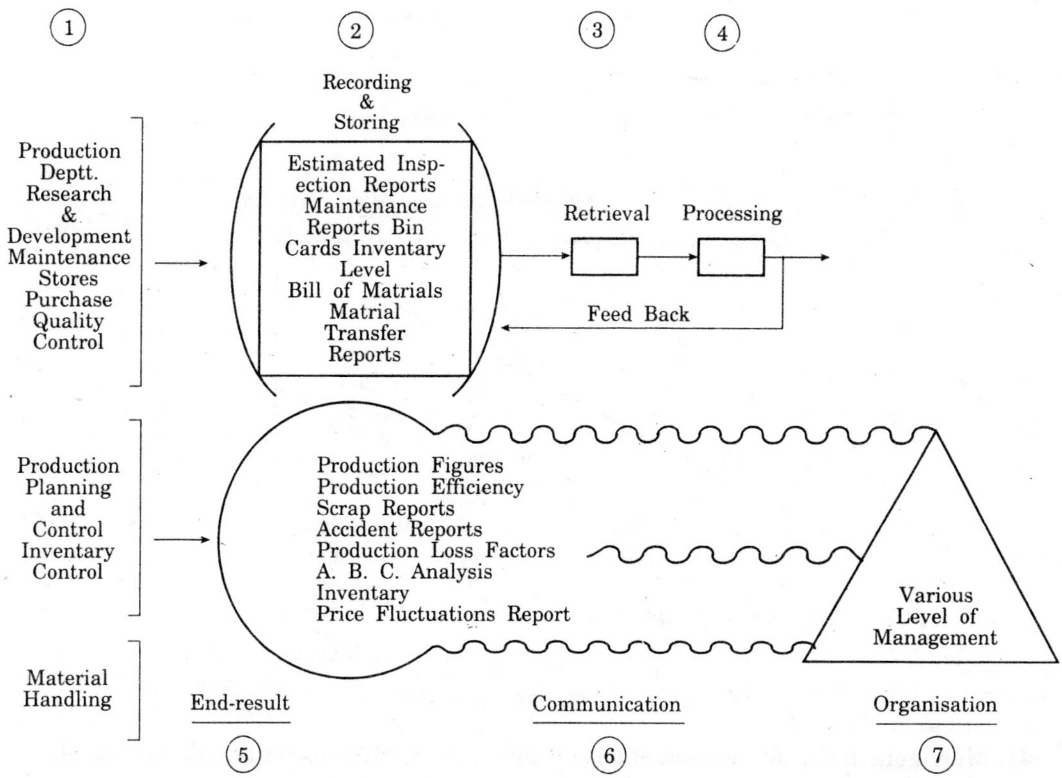

Fig. 51.3.

PERSONNEL INFORMATION SYSTEM

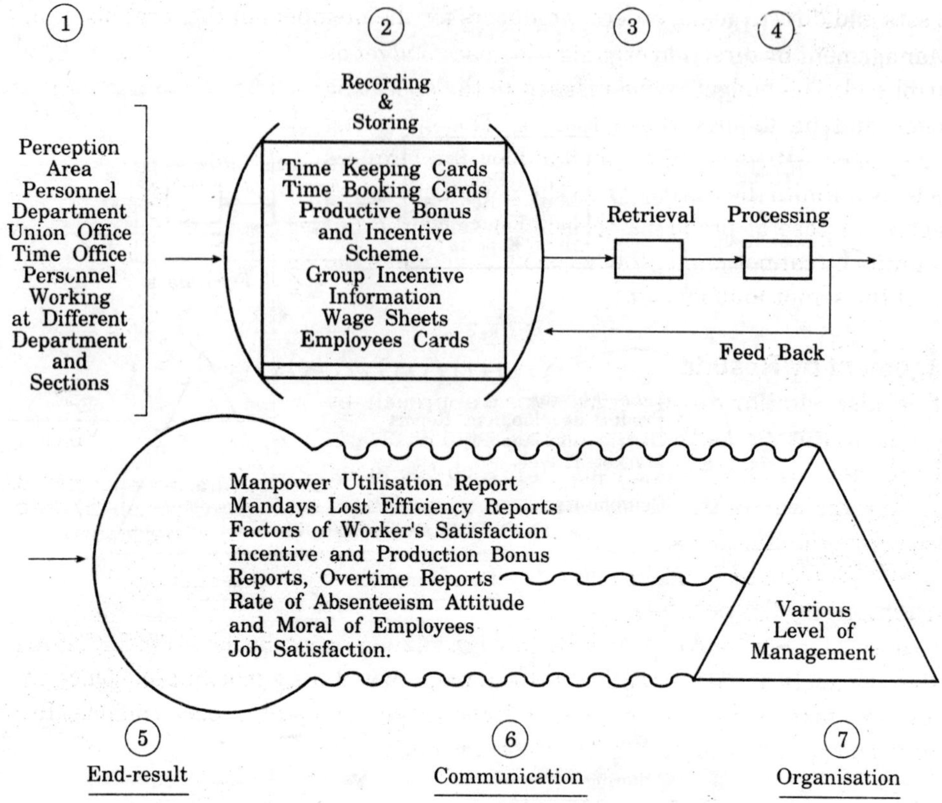

Fig. 51.4

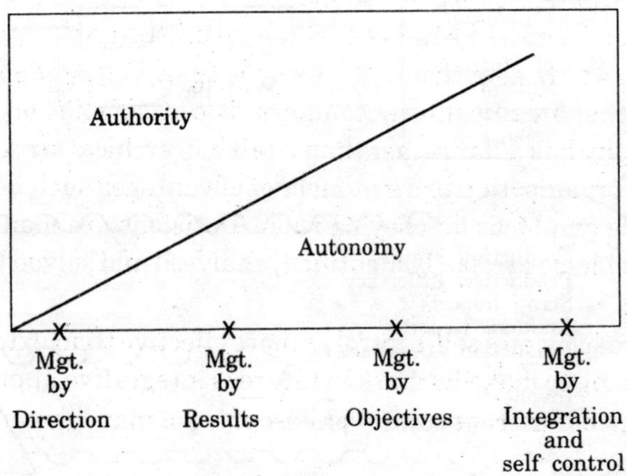

Fig. 51.5

(4) Management by integration and self control to operate efficiently and effectively.

Let us see each of these four types of control philosophies of management before studying the impact of (C.B.I.S.) on each of these philosophy.

Management by Direction

It is the autoritative and directive form of management. In this approach the top management sets and directs goals, orders, producers for the members of the organisation.

Management by direction organisation uses budget as a control tool. The budget is then issued to the operating manager and he follows these budget. The operating managers operate between the upper and lower tolerances limits thus it limits the creativity on the part of operating managers. In case of problems occuring outside the imposed limits he cannot make, the decision as he seeks the advice of the senior management.

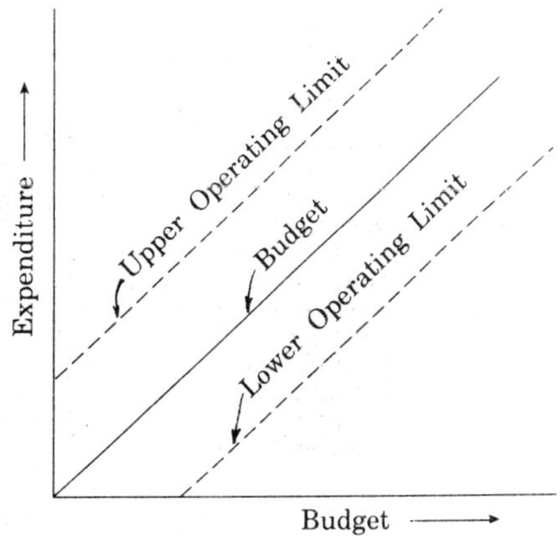

Fig. 51.6. Influence of C.B.I.S. on Management by direction organisation

Management by Results

It is also similar to directive types approach by management. But the controls are not that rigid as in case of Management by Direction. In this approach the members have same way in the implementation of operations and devising procedures.

Management by Objectives

It relies more on participation style than Management by Results. In Management by objective the goals are set fourthly by the managers and his subordinates. Once the goals are accepted by both parties it becomes a standard for acceptable performance. In an M.B.O. organisation the subordinate has an important role to play.

Management by Integration and Self-control

It is the most participative style. In this approach although the top management is responsible for the achievement of organisational objectives but the management shares the commitment with the work force. To achieve this the organisation through it policy must have enough flexibility to permit, its adoption to the everchanging requirement of its members and changing environments that organisation encounters. The integrative organisation by virtue of its management philosophy has a flat rather than a tall hierarchical structure. The elimination of many layers from the organisation has a number of advantages such as loss of delay, passing the buck and undesirable emphasis on obeying rules. Decisions are made at lower echelons of the organisation. The problems are easily identified, analysed and solved by work groups rather than middle managers.

The integrative approach views self-control as more effective than external imposed control. The approach which is going to make its mark in future is integrative approach to management.

The relative approach of different control philosophies of management is shown in the Fig. 51.7.

In case of management by integration and self control the senior management has delegated a broad range of authority to the operating managers to make budgetary decisions.

C.B.I.S. suggest that no one type of management philosophy is superior to other but C.B.I.S. can improve the effectiveness of highly centralised directive organisations.

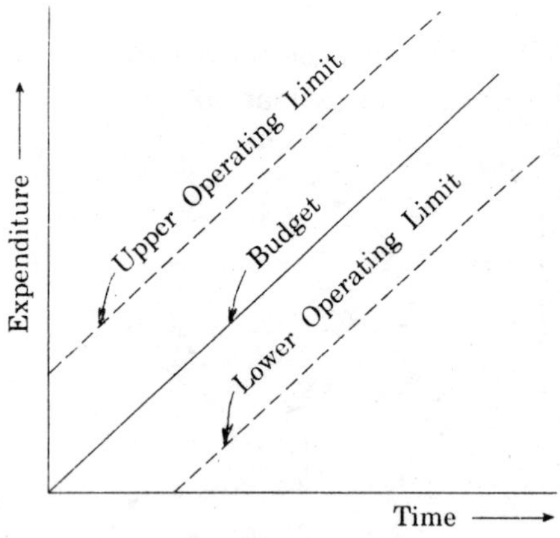

Fig. 51.7.

We know that control is both a philosophy and a techniques used to guide the organisation in the achievement of its objective by the use of various skills. The control function emphasises the importance of communications in the achievement of the objectives of the organisation. Control can be viewed as the extension of planning process. The first step in a planning process is the determination of the objectives of the organisation. Management control is the measurement of actual performance *versus* desired results. A properly controlled system enables any manager to quickly spot out the areas of deviation from planned results as shown in Fig. 51.8.

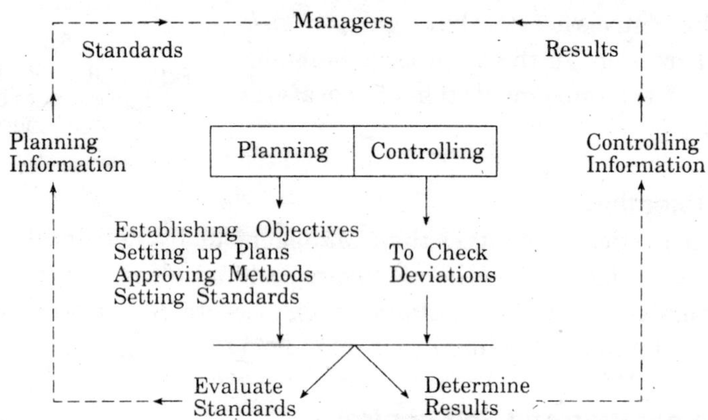

Fig. 51.8.

Organisation Control System

The ineffectiveness of many management control system is attributed to the cybernetic philosophy on which are they based. Anthony and Vancil define Management Control as "The process by which managers assure that resources are obtained and used effectively and efficiently in the accomplishement of the Organisation's objectives". Management control is the domain par excellence of formalised systems in organisations, and these systems tend to be designed according to a cybernetic philosophy.

Cebernetics

By "cybernetic" is meant is process which use the negative feedback loop represented by : setting goals, feeding back information about unwanted variances into the process to be controlled, and correcting the process. This is a much narrower use of the terms "cybernetic" than that advocated by Wiener who coined it to deal with the transfer of messages in the widest sense. In the cybernetic view, a management control process in its most simplified form is similar to a technical control process, for example control of the heat of a room by a thermostat. The model in Fig. 51.9 uses only first order feedback.

All cybernetic models of control have to assume that :

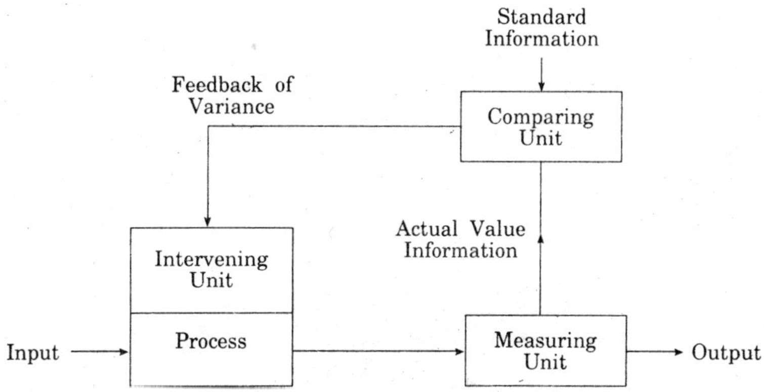

Fig. 51.9.

1. There is a standard, corresponding to effective and efficient accomplishment of the organisation's objectives.
2. Actual accomplishment can be measured. The "Measuring Unit" is connected to the output as the process but the measuring may include data about the input, or about the ratio between output and input.
3. When standard and measurement are compared and variance information is fed back, this information can be used to invervene in the process so as to eliminate unwanted difference between measurement and standard for the next round.

Cybernetic Model of Control

There is no doubt that the cybernetic model of control has been eminently successful in the design of machine's electronic circuits, or similar technical systems, but management control in an organisation is a special process in a social or may be socio-technical system. The 'units' in this case are people, or even groups of people. This subjects the use of cybernetic model to severe limitations. The three assumptions of the presence of a standard, the measurability of accomplishment, and the usability of feedback are most justified for routine, industrial-type processes. One remarkable fact about control process in organisations which has become associated with the cybernetic paradigm is that they are usually tied to a division of labour-different units in the model correspond to different people who are specialised in their tasks. Proper functioning of the control process presupposes communication : the necessary messages should be sent and correctly received between the various specialised factors ; it also presupposes that all will feel motivated to act according to the model. A difference in value between people in controllers 'department and line managements' is evident to anyone familiar with organisational folklore. Studies suggest that people in control department would end to stress form where those in line roles would rather stress content. In most cases, the controller's department is responsible not only for measuring and comparing but also for design and the entire controlls system. People at the interface between the classical and the re-structured part of the organisation, such as supervisors found their roles extremely difficult. The case shows that under favourable circumstances, semi-autonomous groups were created and took over most of the management control roles previously fulfilled by superiors and specialists. All tasks within the classical cybernetic control loop-measuring, comparing feedback, intervening--were carried out within the group itself. Its links to the organisation's needs were mainly established through the standards set by others in the organisation for the group's tasks. Like the word "cybernetic", "homeostatic" can be used to mean different things ; the term is used here because of its predominantly biological connotation. Homeostatic processes are composed of cybernetic elements, but without the deviation of labour between controlling and controlled units ; control is exercised within the system itself. We could also call these processes "self-regulating".

The transfer from cybernetic to homeostatic management control systems will demand a drastically changed control philosophy, especially with regard to the traditional division of labour tied to the cybernetic model. The homeostatic approach needs a new types of controllers. It may also need a new type of information systems.

Non Cybernetic Processes

If we consider the full range of human organisations in which control processes occur, those that satisfy the conditions for the cybernetic model tend to be the more structured ones. What we notice in practice when we try to follow a cybernetic approach is : (*a*) Objectives : may be missing, unclear or shifting ; (*b*) Accomplishment may not be measurable ; and /or (*c*) Feedback information may not be usable. Each of these three conditions is illustrated below :

1. **Objectives are missing, unclear, or shifting.** If there is to be a standard, there should be objectives from which this standard is derived. Setting of standards presupposes clarity about the organisation's objectives. In such cases, decisions, if they are consciously taken at all, are based on processes of negotiation and struggle and cannot be derived from any prior organisational objectives. Objectives may forever remain unclear. This may even be true if someone in the organisation publishes eloquent espoused objectives.

2. **Accomplishment is not measurable.** Even in cases, where objectives are clear to all involved, it is often not possible to translate them into unambiguous, quantitative output standards against which performance can be measured. How should we measure the output of a police department ? One of its final objectives is definitely to prevent crime, so we might consider the decrease of crime rates as on output measure. In such cases, organisations often resort to surrogate measures of performance, measures which are less directly tied to the organisation's objectives but which are more easily measurable. In the case of the police department, the number of people arrested or the amount of fines levied could be such surrogate measures.

For many organisations or activities within organisations, outputs can only be defined in qualitative and vague terms, the only thing really measurable about such activities is their input–how much money and other resources will be allotted to them. These include most management and indirect activities in industrial organisations, like advertising, personnel departments, control activities in headquarters, research, government services, universities, hospitals and voluntary associations. In all these cases, the sole control of management exists at the time of resource allocation but the criteria for resource allocation to this and not to that activity are judgemental.

Feedback Information is not usable. The cybernetic model presupposes a recurring cycle of events ; variance information is used to correct the present state of affairs to eliminate unwanted variances for the future. A few organisations do sue regular evaluation studies of past investments reviews and claims as one of their potential effects a "Symbolic use". The

Planning/Programming/Budgeting System which became widely known as PPBS a number of objectives, but among these is control which it tries to execute by enforcing the cybernetic model, and in its most ambitious form it claims to apply to any organisation.

MBO is also based on a cybernetic philosophy of objective setting (jointly between the employee, who is often himself a manager, and his superior), performance review and corrective action. However, MBO is also advocated, and applied for indirect jobs, in medical institutions, school systems and government agencies. In these cases, accomplishment is much less measurable, and it is rare to find surrogates acceptable to both parties. If a commonly agreed measurement of accomplishment is lacking, the cybernetic model again does not apply and MBO is simply bound to fail. A second reason why MBO may fail, even if the cybernetic model does not apply, is that MBO is based on simplistic and mechanistic assumption about the relationships among the people involved ; it uses a reward--punishment psychology. There is more going on between people than cybernetic objective setting and feedback alone.

The essence of the non-cybernetic situations if that they are political. The decisions are based on negotiation and judgement. Decisions often deal with policies. There is a well-known slogan, "there is no reason for it is just our policy. What this means is that policy is not merely composed of rational elements, its main ingredients are values, which may differ from person to person, group to group and norms which are shared within groups in society but vary over time and form groups to group. It makes little sense to speak of control processes here, at least in the formal sense of which such processes described in cybernetic situations. It does make sense to speak of control structure, taking into account the power positions of the various parties in the negotiations. Within this structure, we may study the control games played by the various actors. Once resources are allocated there is no automatic feedback on the effectiveness of their use, the only controls possible are whether the resources were really spent and if no funds were embezled. Beyond that, it is a matter of trust in those in charge of carrying out the programs, the real control takes place through the appointing of a person to task. Activities once decided upon will tend to perpetuate themselves, corrective action in the case of ineffective or inefficient activities are not automatically produced by the control system but ask for a specific evaluation study, deciding upon such a study is in itself a political act which may upset an established balance of power.

52

Work Study

Introduction

Work study is mainly concerned with the examination of human work. In fact planning cannot be done unless one knows how long it will take to do a particular job. It is important in modern time that our lives take cognizance of time. Time is very important to the manufacturer who must keep to promise, to estimate quantities, and to other industrial and business arrangements. The need for this managerial tool arose in the middle of nineteenth century, when the greater use of machinery and increasing size of manufacturing units necessitated a more efficient means of controlling production schedules. It was F.W. Taylor who argued that greater, attention should be paid to the method of timing tasks Taylor advocated the breaking down of a task into what he termed. Elements of work and the timing of these elements separately with the aid of a stop watch. He also emphasised the use of a differential piece rate system. In this system a strong incentive was offered to those who reached or surpassed the standard established by Taylor's time study methods.

A contemporary of F.W. Taylor was Gilbreth; he and his wife, Dr. Lilian Gilbreth were sure that the way in which work was done was far more important than trying to devise timing systems of how long it took to do a set task. Gilbreth often found it necessary to take motion pictures and examine them frame by frame to examine the smallest elements of movement.

Definition of Various Terms

Time Study—means the straight timing of work elements. Work measurement–it implies that human effort is somehow measured and one of its objective is the installation of financial incentive systems of payment. The object of motion study, method study, micro motion study is to devise new and improved working methods. H.B. Maynard suggested that to obtain the maximum effectiveness from the study of work it was necessary to use all the known techniques. He named his co-ordinated and systematic approach to the development of improved methods "*methods engneering*".

WORK STUDY

Method Study: It is the study of methods of work for a job to achieve process improvements, improved layout, improved design, better working environments and reduced fatigue.

Work Measurement: It is the measure of the work for a job to arrive at the best method of work, improved planning and control.

Work study is term used to embrace techniques of Method study and work measurement which are used to ensure the best possible use of human and material resources in carrying out a specified activity.

Importance and Scope

Work study is not a theoretical concept but essentially a practical one dealing with human beings who have their own style and attitude. So the success of work study depends upon the existence of good relations between management and workers. Work study involves lot of changes of various kinds of working methods. Since people in general do not like changes but prefer to carry on as they are already doing. There will always be a tendency to resist any new methods suggested by work study officers. But if relations are good and the workers have confidence in the ability, integrity and fair mindedness of work study man, there is a good chance that sound proposals will be accepted willingly by the workers.

Work Study as a Science

Work study have been criticised on the grounds that many of its techniques depend upon human judgement and therefore the result have only limited application. Let us see how far this criticisms hold true. It is true that some of the techniques such as rating as used in work measurement depend upon the estimates of work study man. Thus properly trained and qualified man with correct judgement should be acceptable for all practical purposes. As we know that many times the predictions of weather forecasters are wide of the truth but this by no means that we should ignore a weather forecasts. In any area new concepts and knowledge keep emerging similarly in work study new and more accurate technique will emerge.

Uses :

Following are the important uses of work study :

(*a*) Direct means of raising productivity.

(*b*) It is systematic, no factor is overlooked.

(*c*) Most accurate method and yet provide a sound basis for production planning and control incentives.

(*d*) It is most important tool of analysis.

(*e*) Every one concerned with industry benefit from it such as customer, worker and management.

Work Study and Productivity

Productivity increase is the key factor in raising the standard of living. Work study indicates how resources can be effectively utilised and study would help in realising this aim.

Selecting the Work to be Studied

We should select for study the work that is likely to have the longest production run, offers the greatest scope for improvement, and which promises the greatest financial saving for a given outlay.

Recording Facts

The techniques used in recording the facts may be divided into three categories :

(*a*) Process and time,

(*b*) Diagram and models,

(*c*) Charts.

Process Charts

It is useful diagrammatic means of presenting information on the major activities associated with particular investigation.

The advantages of process chart are :

(*a*) It is convenient means of presenting information.

(*b*) It shows clearly the relationship between several sets of data.

(*c*) It permits quick analysis of the problem.

(*d*) It provides a record for future reference.

Charts are like machines which requires the fuels on which it runs. Chart is a means to an end. It cannot solve the problems by itself but it shows up inefficiencies and the way to speedy solution.

Outline Process Charts

It is graphic presentations of the points at which materials are introduced into the process, the sequences of operations and inspections carried out. Charts include information as the time required the grade of labour, type and location machine employed. Outline process chart records the following two type of activities :

(1) An operation represented by the symbol O. An operation occurs when information is given or received or when planning or calculation takes place.

(2) An inspection represented by the symbol □. It occurs when an object is examined for identification.

Process Charts Symbols

A chart is a diagram or picture or a graph which gives an overall view of process.

Process charts are denoted by symbols. The symbols give a better understanding of the facts. Following are the various symbols to recover various events.

Event	*Symbol*	*Description*
Operation		It represents an action.
Storage	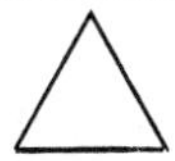	It represents a stage when material (raw or finished) awaits an action.
Delay	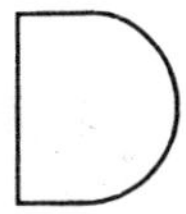	It represents a temporary halt in the process.
Transport	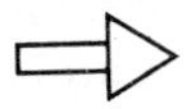	It represents movement of an item.
Inspection	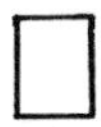	It represents an act of checking.
Combined Activities		
Operation-cum-Transportation	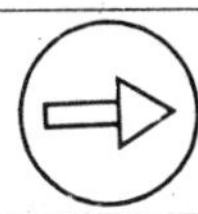	First activity represents outer part and second activity the inner part.
Inspection-cum-Operation	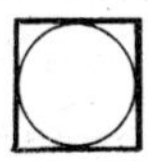	

Thus a chart indicates the process with the help of symbols and aids for better understanding with a purpose of improvement for indentification.

Flow Process Chart

It is a graphic representation of the sequence of all operations, transportation, inspections, delays, storage etc. occurring during a process or procedure. This will include in greater details all relevant information for analysis such as time of each activity distance moved, frequency of movement.

The Flow Process Chart will assist in drawing a complete sequence of events occurring in process and keeps us in finding the delays, improper handling frequency of movement and keeps us in finding the tracking etc.

It is a means of recording information and is an extension of outline process chart. In addition to two activities—operation and inspection of outline process chart, it has three further activities:

(*a*) Transportations—It is represented by the symbol ⇒

(*b*) Delays—It is represented by the symbol D

(*c*) Storages—It is represented by the Symbol Δ

Flow process charts can relate to material or individuals.

Multiple Activity Charts

These charts are the pictorial representative of relationship between man-time and machine time. These charts show the relation between two or more separate but selected operation cycles and may also be used to study the work of several operators on a group of operation. Multiple activity charts help us considerable to visualise the sequence and relationship of events.

Travel Charts

This is drawn in conjunction with a flow diagram. In the case of multiproducts and non standardised products this chart helps us to indicate flow between processes, departments of shop areas as shown in Fig. 52.1.

VARIOUS MODELS

The Layout Diagram

It is a floor plant upon which the arrangement of all equipment is marked to scale. Such a diagram help an investigator to record his findings in a form which is simple to visualise.

Flow diagram

This is a sketch or model to scale of the layout of work places, machines, equipments, floor areas and building particularly showing the location of all activities in a flow process charts. This also indicates the paths and movements followed by men, materials, equipments in executing the activities.

	To →						
F	Departments - A	B	C	D	E	F	Total
O	A		—	4	1	2	10
R							
M	B		3	2	—	3	9
	C			3	2	3	8
	D	3	3		1	2	9
	E			1		1	2
↓	F	3	2				5
	Total	9	8	10	4	11	

Fig. 52.1

String Diagram

It is essentially the same scale plan of the layout as used in the flow diagram with the only difference that movements are shown by continuous threads. This diagram will help us in finding out the points of congestion and back tracking. Better routes could be chosen by following different routing of the thread and comparing it with the previous routing.

Micromotion Films

In many cases the high speed movements made by operators cannot be seen by the eye or with stop watch. The techniques of micromotion is used to record rapid movements. It consists essentially of a cine camera which takes a film of the operator's movements. Micro-motion study besides giving a more accurate recording of both movements also provides a permanent record which can be studied at a latter date also. The equipment for micro motion study is a 16 mm cine camera, a tripod and exposure meter and a timing a clock known as microchronometer.

Microchronometer is provided with a self-starting motor with geared movement designed to read 1/2000th of a minute.

The Memotion Technique

It is technique named after its inventor Marvin E. Mundel who developed this particular use of the cine camera for recording industrial activities and subsequent analysis of the film. It is mainly used to study the work dentist, a pharmacist and a group of men in a foundry. This technique is mainly used for long and irregular activities and work of a group of people. The equipment required for memotion is a cine camera capable of carrying a film magazine of at least 30 meters. Memotion is a kin to activity sampling. Activity sampling is quicker and more economical method, but memotion provides a permanent record.

Memotion consists of three stages:

(*a*) **Filming.** Two pictures are taken at usually slow speeds.

(*b*) **Analysis.** The investigator has first to determine the activities under which he wishes to sub-divide the entire task.

(*c*) **Presentation.** The presentation is to present the information by analysis as detailed sino chart, simple bar chart or even tabulation of results.

Work Measurement

It is the application of techniques designed to establish the time for a qualified worker to carry out a specified job at a defined level of performance. Work measurement or time study is the technique for determining the standard time to perform a specific task. In other words motion study and time study is the systematic study of work system with the purpose of :

(*i*) Developing the desired system and method usually the one with the lowest cost.

(*ii*) Standardising the system and method.

(*iii*) Determining the time required by a qualified and properly trained person working at a normal pace to do a specific operation.

WORK MEASUREMENT

Work measurement, as the name suggests, provides management, with a means of measuring the time taken in the performance of an application for series of operation in such a way that ineffective time is shown up and can be separated from effective time. In this way, its existence, nature and extent become known where previously they were concealed within the total. One of the surprising thing about factories where work measurement has never been employed is the amount of ineffective time where every existence is unsuspected or which is accepted as the "usual thing" and something inevitable that no one can do much about built into the process. Once the existence of ineffective time has been revealed and the reasons for it was traced down, steps can usually be taken to deduce it. Here work measurement has another role to play. Not only can it reveal the existence of ineffective time; it can also be used to set standard time for carrying the work, so that if an ineffective time does creep latter on it will immediately be shown up as an excess over the standard time will thus be brought to the attention of the management.

Work measurement may start a chain reaction throughout the organisation.

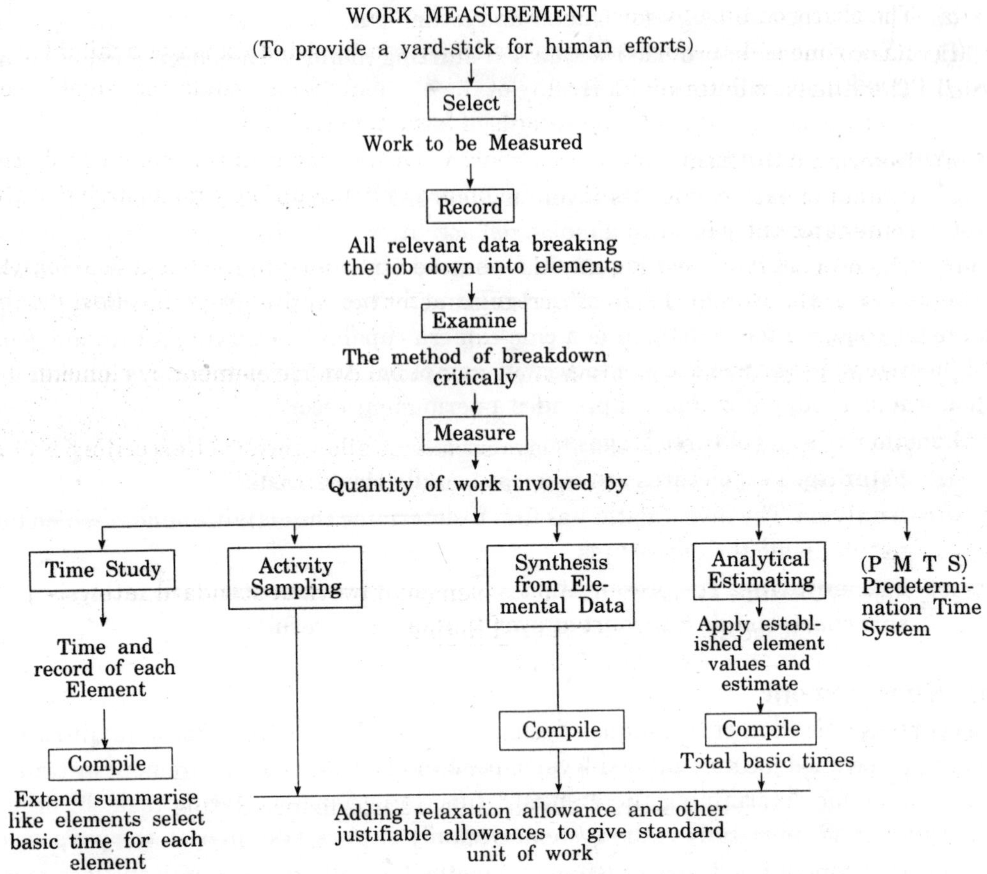

Fig. 52.2.

Objectives of Work Measurement

Using as a target the times established for jobs at the defined level of performance, work measurement will be found to have the following uses.

(*a*) To compare the efficiency if alternative methods other conditions being equal, the method which takes the least time will be best method.

(*b*) To enable realistic schedule of work to be prepared by relating reasonably accurate assessment of human work to plant capacity.

(*c*) As the basis of realistic and fair incentive schemes.

(*d*) To assist in the organisation of labour by enabling a daily comparison to be made between actual times and target times.

(*e*) As a basis for labour budgeting and bugeting control systems.

(*f*) To enable estimates to be prepared of future labour requirements and costs.

Procedure of Work Measurement

The general procedure followed in Work Measurement is as follows :

(*a*) The job is broken down into its elements.

(*b*) The observed time for each element is recorded.

(*c*) Basic time is determined for those elements for which data is not available.

(*d*) The values so determined for any of the elements which could conceivably secure in another job are added to the records of basic times.

(*e*) Determine the frequency of occurrence of each element in the job, multiply the work content of each element with its frequency and add up the time to arrive at the work content for the job.

(*f*) The proportion of rest required is assessed and added to the basic time for doing the work at the standard rate of working and for recovering from the effort *i.e.* the work content.

(*g*) The addition of the relaxation allowance may be made element by element.

(*h*) If there are any contingent delays a blanket allowance (not exceeding 5%) may be added since they are not economical to measure.

Basic Time

Basic time is the time for carrying out an element of work at standard rating *i.e.*,

$$\frac{\text{Observed Time} \times \text{Observed Rating}}{\text{Standard Rating}}$$

Normal Time

This can be computed by the following formula :

$$\text{Normal Time} = \frac{\text{Average observed actual time} \times \text{Performance Rating}}{100}$$

Standard Time

Standard time is the total time in which a job should be computed at standard performance *i.e.* work contact, contingency allowance for delay, unoccppied time and interference allowance considered.

Observed time + Rating = Process Time (Normal Time) Normal time + R.A.% of Normal Time + Contingency allowance for work as % of Work content = work continue (in minutes).

Work content + Continuing Allowance for delay (minute) + unoccupied time (minute) + Interference allowance (minute) = Standard Time (minute)

Performance Rating

Performance rating will be calculated as follows:

$$\text{Performance Rating} = \frac{\text{Normal time}}{\text{Actual time}} \times 100$$

Unit of Work

The Human Work Content of different types of job can be expressed quantitatively in terms of common unit. Allowance for rest, which varies according to mental and physical efforts involved in each job is included in human work, after addition of the relaxation allowance (RA) appropriate to the work, the resultant values are totalled to give a value for complete job in composite units. These composite inits are referred to as unit of work.

WORK	RA

← UNIT OF WORK →

Fig. 52.3.

The following are the *principal techniques* by which work measurement is carried out :

Techniques of Work Measurement

(*i*) Time study.

(*ii*) Synthesis from elemental datas.

(*iii*) Predetermined motion-time system.

(*iv*) Analytical estimating.

(*v*) Activity sampling.

Time Study

It is a work measurement technique for recording the times and rates of working for the elements of a specified job carried under specified condition and for analysing the data so as to obtain the time necessary for the carrying out of the job at a defined level of performance.

Usefulness of Time Measurement

It is indeed useful to the management to know how long it should take to carry out various kinds of work in a plant. Let us discuss various uses :

(*a*) It reveals the capacity of each machine and enables the planning department to apportion work correctly.

(*b*) It increases accuracy in forecasting delivery dates.

(*c*) It is useful in costing.

(*d*) It enables reliable forecasts to be made of machine when a new department or factory is planned.

(*e*) It helps in choosing the best method.

(*f*) It helps to prevent misuse of manpower in each department.

(*g*) It fosters the development of equitable incentive payments system.

It is the oldest work measurement technique. It is regarded as the fundamental technique. A systematic method study should be carried out before the time study because it is no good carrying out a time study on any work until the simplest way of carrying out that work has been determined by a systematic method study.

Object of Time Study

Production cost of any commodity is made of three components :

(*a*) Raw Material Cost.
(*b*) Overheads.
(*c*) Labour Cost.

A production manager can easily predict the cost of raw material and with some past experience and judgement overheads can be estimated pretty accurately. To estimate labour cost, we need to know the labour time. The practical experience of production specialists helps them exercise considerable judgement in estimating direct labour time. However, costly errors can occur if personal judgment is used exclusively. Time studies are conducted to make precise evaluation of direct labour time.

These time standards, in addition to establishing standard labour costs, also establish capacity of productive equipment. The standards are thus used for scheduling production orders.

Another use of time study is that as a result of time study, a time-study engineer inevitably discovers constructive refinements in operation methods, tooling, plant lay-out and materials handling. Thus he is in a position to compare the various alternatives and recommend the best possible method.

Also time standards are used for setting pay incentives. Anybody who can do better than standards by his extra skill or extra labour should be given the suitable award. Thus the time standards are also used for determining pay incentives.

Last but not the least, time standards help in evaluating the productivity of individual employees. Thus line standards help the supervisor in determining fair days work for the individual employees.

To sum up, the objects of time study are :

(*a*) For cost allocation.
(*b*) For determining production.
(*c*) For determining alternatives.
(*d*) For determining pay incentives.
(*e*) For determining fair days work for individual employees.

Method of Time Study

Any work measurement system must perform the following two tasks :

(*i*) Measurement of actual observed time, and
(*ii*) Adjustment of observed time to obtain normal time.

Measurement of actual observed time can be done by the following methods :

(*a*) Stop Watch Method

(*i*) Decimal-minute stop watch.
(*ii*) Decimal-hour stop watch.

(*b*) Motion Picture Camera

(*i*) Slow speed 50/1000 frames/minute
(*ii*) Normal speed 960 frames/minute.
(*iii*) Modified normal speed 1000 frames/minute.
(*iv*) Sound speed 1440 frames/minutes.

(*v*) High speed 64--128 frames/minute.
(*vi*) Very high speed 1000--3000 frames.

(*c*) **Machi·ıe using moving Tape and Disk**
(*i*) Time Study machine-Marsto-Chron.
(*ii*) Kynograph *e.g.* Esterline-Angers Operation recorder.
(*iii*) Series recorder.
(*iv*) Electronic timer. Information and time, date punched on tape-IBM Machines.

Conducting Time Study

The time study is not carried out unless the request for the same comes from the right man. The plant manager, chief engineer, production control supervisor, cost accountant, foreman or other members of the organisation may make such requests.

After the request for time study has been received the Industrial Engineering Department will assign the job to a trained and experienced analyst. The analyst should go over the job with the foreman of the department. The time study standard established for a job will not be correct if there is :

(1) Change in the job
(2) Material is not as per specification
(3) Machine speed has changed
(4) Conditions of work are changed.

To have a systematic time study the analyst must ask the following questions :

(*a*) Can the speed of the machine be increased without affecting the tool or equipment life or the quality of the product ?
(*b*) Can we bring changes in the tooling made to reduce the cycle time ?
(*c*) Can we bring the material closer to the work area to reduce the Material Handling time ?
(*d*) Is the equipment rightly operated ?
(*e*) Is the operation being safely performed ?

Equipments For Work Measurement

Stop Watch

There are many types of stop watches. One type is controlled by pressure on the winding knob. The second kind is the flying back type which is started and stopped by a slide at the side of the winding knob. Another stop watch may be decimal-minute type. It may be divided into one hundred division called centiminutes. Another type could be decimal-hour. In this the dial is divided into 100 divisions. The larger one makes one revolution in 1/100 of an hour (0.6 min) instead of one minute.

A CENTIMINUTE STOP WATCH

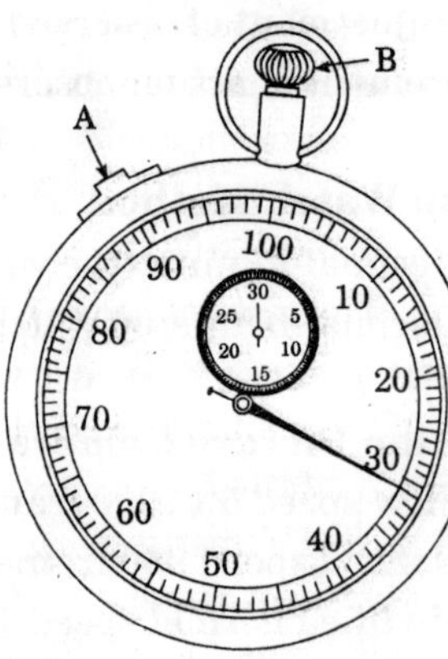

Fig. 52.4.

Study Board

This is a sheet, usually of wood slightly larger than the record form to be used. It has a clip to hold the form in place and another clip to hold the stop watch in a convenient position for operation by the left hand.

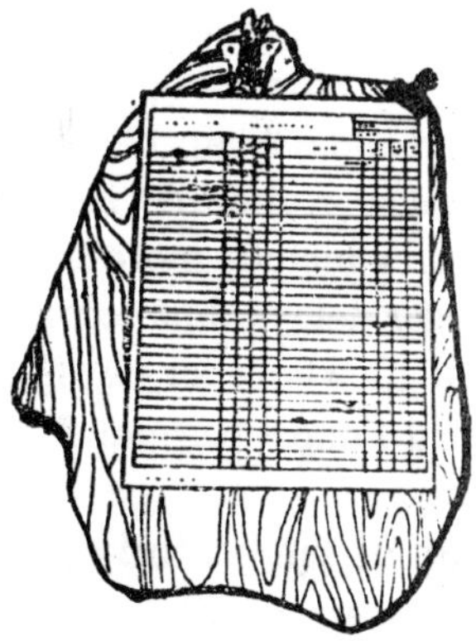

Fig. 52.5.

Study Sheet

It varies with the type of the job under study. In the study sheet brief particulars of the job are entered on the form including the elements which it has been decided are most suitable for study.

(TIME STUDY)

Particulars of job and operator :

Element	*Rating*	*Watch Reading*	*Observed time*	*Ineffective or check time*	*Normal time*

Methods of Timing

Following are the various methods of timing:

— Flyback Timing

— Selective Timing

— Comulative Timing

— Differential Timing

Flyback Timing. In this method as soon as the first element starts the winding knob is pressed and the large hand returns to zero. The time elapsed between the check time and the start of first element is noted. Before the start of the next element the hand is returned to zero and the duration of the previous element is entered on the form.

Comulative Timing. In this method the watch is started as the check time and the hand runs without being returned to zero. In the beginning of each element the watch reading is noted on the form. The time of each element is obtained by subtraction.

Selective Timing. It is used to time an isolated element. The watch is started at the beginning of the element till the end and the element is timed as often as necessary. This is the most accurate method.

Differential Timing. In this the element is observed and timed with an adjacent longer one, when sufficient times for the combined elements have been taken, the longer element is timed by itself. Time for the short element is then obtained by subtraction.

Production Standards

These are computed and set to answer questions like 'what is a fair day's work' ? These standards state how many parts, assemblies should be provided per minute, hour or day. Thus production standard can be expressed in terms of pieces per unit of time or time per piece. Although these standards are designed to determine how much output is expected of an employee, they include more than just work. Actually, production standards include standard allowances for delays that occurs as a part of the job, time for personal needs and where work is heavy, an allowance for physical fatigue.

Standard Time = Normal Time + Delay Allowance + Fatigue Allowance.

Application of Time Study in Setting of Production Standards

The first step in setting standards is the determination of normal time for performing a specific task. The actual observed time, however, is not the normal time. In order to arrive at normal time from observed time, rating method is used. Rating is that process during which the time study analyst compares the performance of the operator under observation with the observers own concept of normal performance. The time study analyst must judge the operators' speed while he is making the study, and award the performance rating.

$$\text{Performance Rating} = \frac{\text{Normal Time}}{\text{Actual Time}} \times 100.$$

Determination of Standard Time

The actual observed time and hence the standard time can be measured by the following two methods :

1. Stop Watch Method. The following steps are undertaken in work measurement by stop watch method:

(*i*) Standardisations of methods for the operations-standard method for the operation is determined, specifying work place lay-out, tools, sequence of elements. The resulting standard practice is recorded.

(*ii*) An operator who is trained and experienced in standard methods is selected for study.

(*iii*) For timing purposes, elemental structure of operation is determined. Operation is broken down into elements and elements are separated on the basis of their occurrence (in each cycle, periodically or randomly).

(*iv*) Actual time required for the elements is observed and recorded, making simultaneous performance rating.

(*v*) The number of observations required to yield the desired precision of the result based on the sample data obtained in step (*iv*) is calculated (this step is explained later). More data is collected if necessary.

(*vi*) Normal time is computed now by the formula :

$$\text{Normal time} = \frac{\text{Average observed Actual Time} \times \text{Performance rating}}{100}$$

(*vii*) Allowance of personal time, delays and fastigu are determined by the formula.

Standard Time = Normal Time + Allowances.

Number of Cycles to be Timed

Variations in time may result from such things as a difference in the exact position of parts and tools used by the operator, from variations in reading the stop watch, and from possible differences in determining the exact end point at which the watch reading is made. Time study is a sampling process. Consequently the greater the number of cycles timed, more nearly the results will be representive of the activity being measured.

The standard error of the average for each element is given by :

$$\sigma \overline{X} = \frac{\sigma'}{\sqrt{N}} \quad \text{...(A)}$$

$\sigma \overline{X}$ = Standard deviation of the distribution of averages.

σ' = Standard deviation of the universe.

N = Actual number of observations of the element.

A 95% confidence level and ± 5% precision are commonly used in the study.

Let N' is the required number of observation to predict the true value within ± 5% precision and 95% confidence level.

This means there is atleast 95 out of the 100 that the sample mean or average value for element will not be in error more than ± 5%.

Then, $$0.05\, X = 2\, \sigma \overline{X}$$

$$0.05 \frac{\Sigma X}{\sqrt{N}} = 2\, \sigma \overline{X}$$

$$0.05 \frac{\sigma X}{N} = 2 \times \frac{1}{N} \sqrt{\frac{N \Sigma x^2 - (\Sigma x\ 12)}{\sqrt{N'}}}$$

$$N' = \left(\frac{40 \sqrt{N \Sigma \bar{x}^2 - (\Sigma \bar{x}\ 12)^2}}{\Sigma \overline{X}} \right)$$

Rating

It is defined as worker's rate of working relative to the observer's concept of rate corresponding to standard rating. It is infact the assessment of the speed and effectiveness of a given worker and in order to rate reliably the work study man must be thoroughly familiar with the correct way of carrying out the job, he is studying. It is really an important part of time study.

Rating Standards

The work studying man must have a standard to which he can relate his observation of a particular worker. In other words the rating is that process during which time study analyst compares the actual performance of the operator with the observer's own concept of normal performance. It is a matter of judgment on the part of analyst.

Systems of Ratings

Bedaux introduced a system of rating based on time study. His time standard were expressed in points. Under this system the amount of work one does per minute is known as standard work unit of minute. Thus the basis of Bedaux plan is energy and time. Bedaux point or unit for a work may contain 75% effort and 25% rest or other proportions.

Westing House System of Rating

It is a four factor system for rating operator's performance. The four factors are :

(1) Skill, (2) Effort,

(3) Conditions, (4) Consistency.

Synthetic Rating

It is the method of evaluating an operator's speed from predetermined motion time values. The ratio between the predetermined motion-time standard for the element and the average actual time volume in minutes for the same element is called performance rating factor.

$R = P/A$.

R = Performance rating factor.

P = Predetermined motion time standard for the element.

A = Average actual time value for the same element in minutes.

Standard Performance

Standard Performance is the rate of output which a qualified worker will naturally achieve without over-exertion as an average over the working day or shift provided they know and adhere to the specified method and provided they are motivated to apply themselves to their work.

This performance is denoted as 100 on the standard rating and performance scales.

Scales of Rating

In order that a comparison between the observed rate of working and the standard rate may be made effectively, it is necessary to have numerical of scale against which we make the assessment.

The rating can then be used as a factor by which observed time can be multiplied to give the basic time which is the time, it would make the qualified worker, motivated to apply himself to carry out the element at standard rating.

There are several scales of rating where the most common of which are those designated the 100-133 scale, the 60-80 the 75-100 and the British Standard Scale which is 0.100 scale.

Allowances

Various types of allowances may be applied depending upon the type of job. Following are the various allowances :

— Relaxation Allowances.

— Contingency Allowances.

— Interference Allowances.

— Periodic activity Allowances.

— Introductory Allowances.

— Learner Allowances.

— Unusual condition Allowances.

— Unoccupied time Allowances.

Relaxation Allowance. It is the time that an operator is allowed for his personal needs and for fatigue. The personal need allowance is constant for the various operations carried out in a factory. The fatigue allowance will vary with the nature of the job.

Contingency Allowance. Certain elements may occur so in frequently that it would not pay to study enough work cycles to evaluate them accurately. The elements for which the contingency allowance should be made are following :

— Consultation with supervisors
— Sharpening of tools
— Obtaining special materials from stores.

If for a job the total time taken is 50 hours and the time taken for eight odd elements are 15 minutes then contingency allowance would be,

$$\frac{0.25}{50} \times 100 = 0.5 \text{ per cent}$$

Interference Allowance. This allowance is given when two or more elements occur simultaneously. If more than one machine requires attention at the same time and the cycle time of these machines differ, interference will occur more frequently.

The accurate assessment of this allowance requires a thorough studies. The allowance is added as percentage.

Periodic Activity Allowance. This is the allowance for activities to be carried out once only for example setting up of a lathe machine before production starts. The time for these activities can be noted and the cycle time can be proportionally adjusted.

Introductory Allowance. This is the allowance at times given at the introduction of an incentive scheme. The allowance is strictly temporary and decreases week by week until it disappears say after 4-5 weeks.

Learner Allowance. The introduction of new man into the system may show down the working of the whole team until he became proficient. If no allowance is given, the training of the apprentice or leanrer will be neglected.

Unusual Conditions Allowance. This allowance covers the additional time required for special case of some specific type of raw material or equipment in handling at loading or unloading points.

Unoccupied-Time Allowance. It is the other name to process allowance. It is the time, the operator has to wait till his machine or his work group is free. The idle time of this nature is undesirable but some allowance is necessary to help the operator to reach his standard performance.

Policy Allowance

It is an allowance given at the discretion of the management due to inherent features of the work. This allowance is not genuine part of time study and should not interfere with calculation of standard as shown in Fig. 52.6.

The examples of policy allowances are the one discussed above that is:

(*a*) Introductory Allowance
(*b*) Learner Allowance
(*c*) Unusual Conditions Allowance.

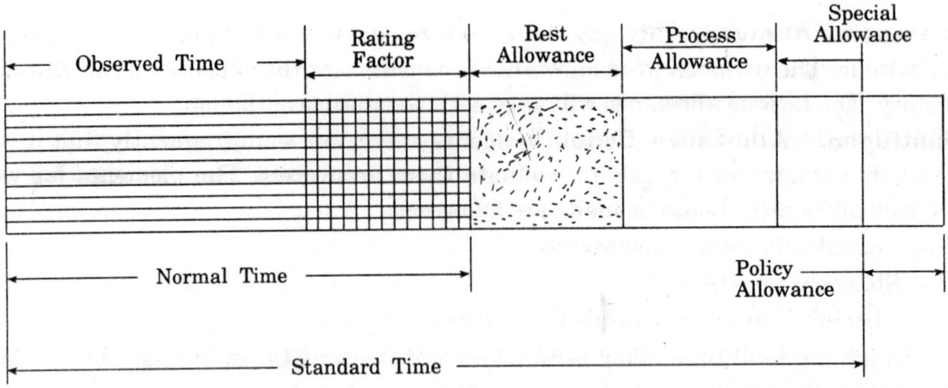

Fig. 52.6.

If the policy allowance is also added then it is termed as "allowed time". Standard time is expressed as standard man/machine hour or standard man/machine minutes. Symbolically they are represented by (S.M.H.) and (S.M.M.) respectively.

Production Studies

It does not constitute a new technique but it is specialised form of time study. It is carried out over a specified period of time say for half a day or one shift for the purpose of ascertaining the frequency and duration of activities.

Production study is relatively a continuous study designed to check an existing standard time to obtain additional information affecting the rate of output. The object of this study is to account for everything that occurs during a working period.

The main uses of production studies are:

(*a*) To check the ouput of a particular worker or machine.

(*b*) To find out the idle time and factors affecting further delays.

(*c*) To secure information to find relaxation, contingency and interference allowance.

(*d*) To check the accuracy of time arrived at.

Production study is a lengthy and costly business so the activity sampling is used as a substitute.

Synthesis from Elemental Data

It is a work measurement techniques for building up the time for a job at a defined level of performance by totalling element times obtained previously from time studies in other jobs containing the elements concerned. It is seen that many of the timed elements reoccurred in the similar forms in various jobs. This realisation led to the recording and filing of times so that when elements reoccurred the existing records could be utilised in order to save time and energy. This recording would save work and make job times much quicker and cheaper to produce.

Limitation of Synthetic Data

F.W. Taylor suggested that after a detailed time studies had once been made, it would be possible to lift them in handbook but it could not be done because methods vary from plant to plant, industry to industry. However, Gilbreth stated that each therblig should be performed within a certain time range. He could foresee the development of predetermined motion-times. So far no manual of synthetic data is obtained so far because of some particular difficulties.

Predetermined Motion Time Systems (P.M.T.S.)

It is work measurement technique whereby times established for basic human motions are used to build up time for a job at a defined level of performance. This technique is used for finding the times for basic motions of the therblig. To obtain these times various operations are filmed and then the film is analysed very carefully. The advantage of films is that each element can be observed many times merely by projecting the film repeatedly.

The following diagram gives a quick understanding of the nature of the methods time measurement procedure

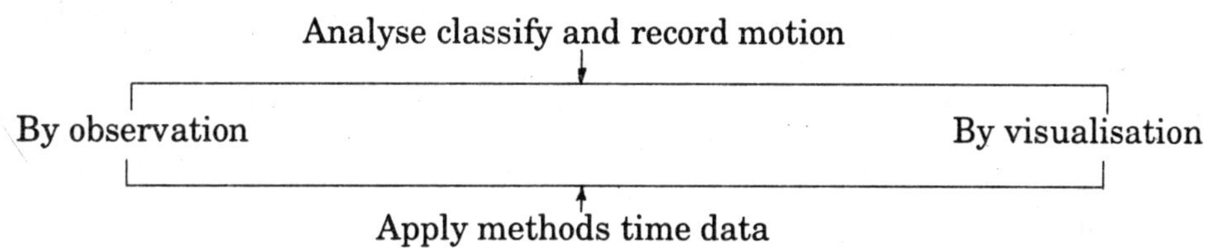

Analytical Estimating

It is a work measurement technique whereby time required to carry out element of a job at a defined level of performance is estimated from knowledge and practical experience of the elements concerned. Analytical estimation is widely used to estimate times in engineering, maintenance and construction work. In this method the estimator should be fully conversant with all the details of work being studied. Analytical estimating can give satisfactory results although these are less accurate than those obtained by time study or by synthesis from elemental data. In this method time is not estimated for the job as a whole but the task is first broken into elements as in time study, but elements are longer. Time for longer elements are worked out by the trained estimator only.

Activity Sampling

It is a work measurement techniques in which a large number of instantaneous observation are made over a period of time of a group of machines, processes or workers.

Such observations indicates:

What is happening at that instant. The concept is that random observations can produce results whose accuracy depends upon the number of observations made. This technique is also known by Random observation, Work Sampling and Ratio delay.

Work sampling is used in:

(*a*) Measuring the working and non-working time of man and of machines (for delay allowances or utilization time of M/cs.)

(*b*) To estimate the percentage of time devoted to each duties included in the jobs performed by such people as maintenance personnel, office workers, managers etc.

(*c*) To establish time standards.

The work sampling method consists of taking a number of random observations of the activity being studied and from this determining the percent of time devoted to each aspect of the operation.

As it is obvious the procedure is simple. However, the key to the accuracy of the technique is in number of observations. A greater number of observations provides a higher degree accuracy. The question of how many observations are necessary to ensure a certain level of accuracy may be calculated through the use of standard formulas based on the binomial dist. Suppose we want a confidence level of 95% and an accuracy of 5 per cent.

We know that standard deviation of a binomial distribution mean is

$$= \sqrt{\frac{P(I-P)}{N}}$$

Since we want 95% confidence level and since we know that 95% area under a normal curve includes two standard deviation, then

$$SP = 2\sqrt{\frac{P(I-P)}{N}}$$

S = desired relative accuracy.

P = %age expressed as a decimal.

(idle or working activity)

Example. *Suppose we want to determine the % of the idle time of a certain machine. Assume a confidence level of 95% and accuracy of 5%. We want to determine the number of observations to give us the desired results.*

Now before we can use the formula

$$SP = \sqrt{\frac{2P(1-P)}{N}}$$

It is necessary to estimate the value of P. What we do is to conduct a trial study to get a first estimate of the % of idle time (P). Suppose 100 observations were made and in this preliminary study 25 observations showed the machine to be idle.

So $P = 0.25$

$S = 0.05$

$$SP = 2\sqrt{\frac{P(1-P)}{N}}$$

$$0.05P^2 = 2\sqrt{\frac{P(1-P)}{N}}$$

$$0.0025P^2 = 4P\frac{(1-P)}{N}$$

$$N = \frac{4P(1-P)^2}{0.0025P} = \frac{4(1-P)}{0.0025P} = \frac{1600(1-P)}{P} = \frac{1600(1-0.25)}{0.25} = 4800$$

This is only the Ist estimate. As the work sampling study is underway and 500 observations have been made, a new calculation might be made.

Now suppose machine working = 350 times.

Idle = 150 times

$$P = \frac{150}{500} = 0.30$$

$$\text{Now } 0.05\,(0.30) = 2\,\frac{0.30\,(1-0.30)}{N}$$

$$N = 3633.$$

Actually it is advisable to recalculate N at regular intervals, perhaps at the end of each day.

Advantages of Work Sampling Over Work-study

(*a*) Eliminates stop watch study.
(*b*) It is economical in bigger set ups.
(*c*) Applicable to activities that are impractical to measure by Time Study.
(*d*) No trained work-measurement analyst required.
(*e*) Measure can be made with pre-assigned degree of reliability.
(*f*) Time study evens out the results of day-to-day variations.
(*g*) A work sampling study may be interpreted any time without affecting the results.
(*h*) It is easier for the studied people.
(*i*) It is less resented by workers as no stop watch or other timing device is needed.
(*j*) A simultaneous work sampling study of several operators or machines can be done by a single observers.

Limitations

(*i*) Non-economical for work at single location.
(*ii*) Not much scope for improving work methods.
(*iii*) Harder to explain to union and management.
(*iv*) Non-random sampling may bias results.

Example. *An operator works for eight-hours a day. A work sampling study shows that he was idle 15% of the day and that he worked the remainder of the day at an average performance index of 110%. The record shows that he turned out 420 pieces of acceptable quality during the day. Find the standard per peice. Assume 15% allowances.*

Solution. Total time expended by worker = 8 × 60 = 480 min
No. of parts produced = 420
Working time = 85%
Idle time = 15%
Average Rating = 110%
Allowance = 15%
Standard time per piece

$$= \frac{(\text{Total time}) \times \%\text{working time} \times \text{Rating}}{\text{Total No. of pieces produced}} + \text{Allowances}$$

$$= \frac{480 \times 0.85 \times 1.10}{420} \times \frac{100}{100-15} = 1.26 \text{ min.}$$

Example. *A furniture making factory contained a group of 13 machines. The management of the factory decided to find the percentage of time spent on the following activities.*

1. Working (Processing on timber).
2. Running (Running time of machines without processing).
3. Set up (Being prepared for the next job).

The observations were recorded between 9 A.M. to 12.30 P.M. and from 1.30 P.M. to 5.00 P.M. The total observation of four activities were :

	M/c working	*M/c Running*	*M/c being set-up*	*M/c idle*
Total observation	288	475	83	530
Percentage	20.9%	34.5	6.1	38.5

To determine the limits between which it would be reasonable to assume the true values to lie.

Solution. We know that dispersion of the curve is expressed in terms of the standard deviation represented by the σ (Sigma)

$$\sigma = \pm\sqrt{\frac{p(100-p)}{n}}$$

p = It is the percentage of an observed activity

n = Total number of observations

$$\sigma = \pm\sqrt{\frac{p(100-p)}{n}}$$

For 68 per cent of chance tolerance when the machine is working the standard deviation is

$$\sigma = \pm\sqrt{\frac{20.9\ (100-20.9)}{1376}} = \sqrt{1.204} = 1.1$$

Total No. of observations

288
475
83
530
———
1376 Nos.

So limits are (20.9 + 2.2) and (20.9 – 2.2)

That is 23.1% and 18.7%.

The results show that machine is under utilised and something seriously wrong with either production planning or production control mechanism.

Determining time standards by work sampling.

Example. *A work sampling study might show that a worker on a drilling machine was idle 15% of the day or 72 minutes in eight hours shift. If he has produced 240 acceptable pieces in the day, standard time can be computed as follows :*

Information	*Source of data*	*Data of one day*
Total time spent by operator	Time card	480 mts
No. of parts produced	Inspection Deptt.	240
Idle time in %	Work sampling	15%
Working time in %	—do—	85%
Average performance idex	--do—	110%
Total allowances	Company time study manual.	15%

Standard time per piece,

$$= \frac{\text{(Total time in mts.)} \times \text{(Working time in \%)} \times \text{(Performance index \%)}}{\text{Total No. of pieces produced + Allowances}}$$

$$= \frac{480 \times 8.5 \times 1.10}{240} \times \frac{100}{100 - 15} = 2.2 \text{ minutes.}$$

Human Side and Work Study

To make the concept of work study successful the human relations must be considered. An organisation can apply work study successfully only if it maintains a continuous watch over the human issues. Thus work study is 10 per cent technical and 90 per cent psychological. In an organised organisation the trade union exist. The union is concerned with employees hours of work and other working conditions such as financial conditions governing the employees. Thus any change brought about in the working conditions of the employees the union must be involved.

Following are likely to be the points in particular upon which the Union will wish to be satisfied.

(1) There should be adequate consultation before introduction of any change which affects their member.

(2) There should be definite policy in respect of those people which may be affected as a result of work study and incentive schemes.

Management Reaction

(*i*) One possible source of difficulty is general conservatism of human being, any change in the existing method and practices is considered as an interruption of a comfortable situation.

(*ii*) Work study team is likely to get resistance from department managers.

(*iii*) It is necessary to get the support of top management without which any efforts the initiate work study is meaningless.

(*iv*) Supervisors, Engineer, Foremen, Chargemen should be given fullest information. This group is closest to the workers and it is from where the work study group need a day-to-day cooperation.

Hence any cause or conference intended to introduce work study to supervision should concentrate on the following points :

(*a*) Economic necessity of reducing manufacturing cost.

(*b*) The advantage of systematic method study over occasional and haphazard attempts made to improve methods.

(*c*) The advantages of measuring work.

(*d*) The fairness and advantage to the workers of additional payments for additional work.

(*e*) The basis of incentive scheme and the way in which incentives are calculated.

WORK STUDY AS A SERVICE TO MANAGEMENT AND SOCIETY

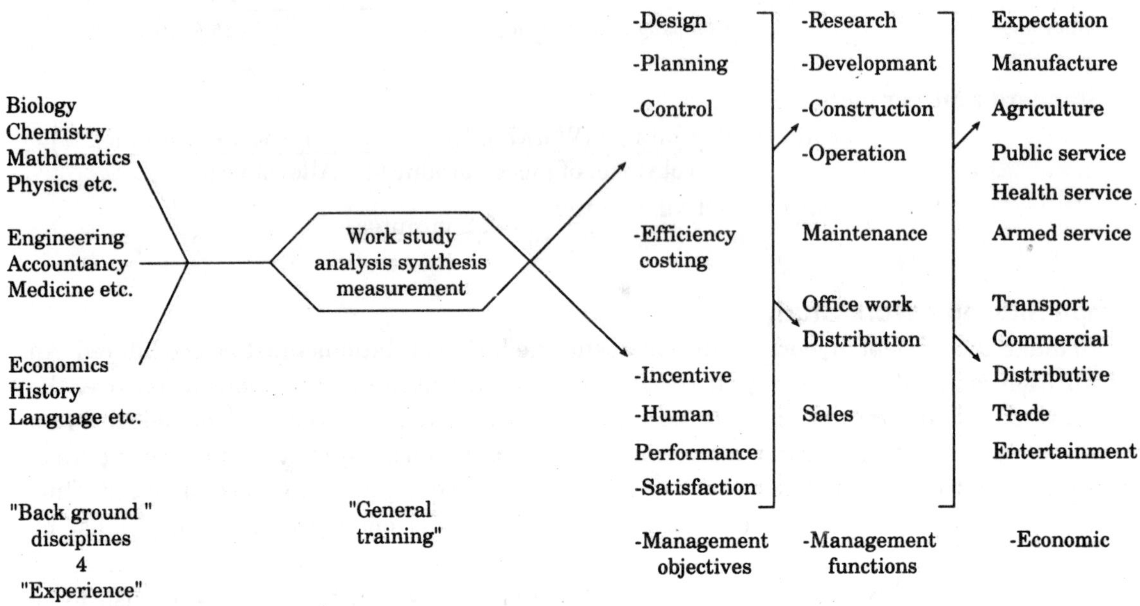

Fig. 52.7.

Individual Reaction to Work Study

"What are the goals to which a man works and the fulfilment of which he may regard as successful living" ? Professor Bakke summarised the following points:

(*a*) **Society and respect of other people.** One of the bases of mutual repeat in a working group is that there should be some balance of favourness in the distribution of work and responsibility and that each member should feel that others should attach some meaning and value to his job. This is one of the objective of work study also.

(*b*) **Degree of creature comforts and economic security.** This scheme is based on work study, demonstrate a clear link between extra efforts and extra award, hence a man may feel that creature comforts within his reach. As it decides, the number of people to be employed once there is "build in" security also.

Independence in and Control Over his Own Affair

Complete independence is not enjoyed by any body at work and perhaps independence for the man at the bench is difficult to visualized. In practice it may be taken as training him to do a job, telling him exactly and what is expected of him and then letting him get on with it. Knowledge of results has been proved to be a great spur to better performance.

Understanding of the Forces and Factors at Work in his World

A worker need to know about the effort of environment to his job and the factors affecting him, the answers is best provided by a work study team.

Integrity

Work study enables a man to do.

"A fair days work for a fair days pay". He feels wholeness in his job.

The figure gives an idea about the application of work study in the service of management and society at large.

Method Study

It is a systematic recording and critical examination of the factors and resources involved in existing and proposed ways of doing work as a means of developing and applying easier and more effective methods and reducing costs.

This technique is very useful in the following cases :

(*a*) More valuable in case of repeated operations.

(*b*) More applicable to people working on incentive system.

(*c*) More useful in case of automatic machine tools turning out large number of machined parts.

(*d*) More applicable in case of parts to be machined which require high degree of accuracy.

(*e*) More applicable where there is a need to simplify the movements and sequence of operations.

In fact the principles of motion economy are important in all types of operations. It may not be possible to analyse highly skilled man's movements and teach him to improve them but it is almost possible to alter the design of equipment and improve tools layouts to effect economies in production.

Method Study in Relation to Time Study

Motion or method study is necessarily an integral part of time study. Since it would be wasteful and in-effective to carry out an expansive time study on an operation in which the methods had not been previously simplified and improved. Thus time study alone is not enough, because it may only serve to correct inaccuracies in standardized operation times. If the management and the worker and the organisation are to profit in the long run there is a need of economy of motion in all productive operations. To standardise existing production methods may be merely a standardise inefficiency.

Procedure for Method Study

The basic procedure in method study can be classified into following components :

(*a*) Select—The work to be studied.

(*b*) Record—The relevant facts of all present methods.

(*c*) Examine—Facts in sequence.

(*d*) Develop—Economical, practical and effective methods.

(*e*) Install—Method as standard practice.

(*f*) Maintain—Standard practice.

(*g*) Feed Back—To get back the information.

53

Decision-Making

Introduction

Decision-making lies deeply embedded in the process of management. Decision-making spreads over all the managerial functions and covers all the areas of the enterprise. Management and decision-making are bound to go side by side. Whether knowingly or unknowingly the manager makes decisions constantly. The principle of decision-making requires that the task of decision-making should always be pushed down as far as practicable. On the other hand, the top manager can concentrate on important problems in order to give an effective judgement over the issues leading to decision-making.

Most outstanding characteristic of a successful manager is his ability to make sound decisions. Decision-making involves choosing a course of action from several alternative courses of action. Decision making-the actual selection from among alternatives, course of action, is at the core of planning. Decision making is a matter of planning organisational objectives and the methods that will be used to achieve them. Managers consider it as their job, because they must constantly choose what is to be done, who is to do it and when is to be done. Decision making must be regarded as a step in planning, even when done quickly and with little thought or when it influences action only for a few minutes. Planning imposes organisational responsibilities on subordinates (managerial and nonmanagerial personnel). Decision making is also concerned with the problem of motivating subordinates.

Right from the day when the size of business use to be very small to the present day size of the business when ownership is corporate, the importance of decision making has been there. The only difference is that in today's complex business structure, the decision making is getting more and more complex and important. Whatever a manager does, he does through making decisions. Some of the decisions are of routine nature and it might be that the manager does not realise that he is taking decisions. Other decisions are of a special nature that may require years of systematic and scientific analysis. The fact remains that management is always a decision making process.

What is Decision-Making

A manager's effectiveness is related directly to the quality of his decisions. His work in planning, organising, leading and controlling is based on decisions. The action he takes is implemented through decisions. The efforts of his subordinates are predetermined and guided by the decisions he makes. Decision-making in the work a Manager performs to arrive at conclusions and judgements. Decision making is often considered an inborn amptitude largely based on intuition and luck. However, while both good judgement and intuition enter into decision-making, it is a skill made up of separate elements that can be learned.

PRINCIPLES

Principles of Decision-Making

Three basic principles will help provide a sound basis for management decisions.

(*a*) **Principle of Definition.** A logical decision can be reached only if the problem is first defined. To solve a problem effectively, you must first know what the problem is. Time spent in developing a solution to a problem is often wasted because we are treating only the symptoms—we have not come to grips with the problem itself.

(*b*) **Principle of Adequate Evidence.** A logical decision must be valid in terms of the evidence upon which it is based. It should be possible to support the decision you reach with sufficient verifiable evidence to establish that your decision is both reasonable and logical.

Principle of Indentity

Facts may appear to differ depending upon the point of view and the point in time from which they are observed. The real value of money varies with time. The relative importance of the same facts may differ from year to year.

For these reasons, it is important to identify facts clearly and, in this identification, to make sure that we have taken into consideration differences that may exist because of point of view and point in time. The relative importance of the same facts may differ from year to year.

Logical Thinking Process

A management decision should be the end product of a series of logically related steps. The logical thought process is made up of five steps.

(*a*) **What is the Apparent Problem.** When we first see a problem situation, the problem may seem quite apparent. Most often we plunge ahead eager to come to grips with the problem and to get action underway. In solving problems, also, we tend to observe symptoms arising from underlying causes. Often we jump to conclusions based on the superficial view. When this is the case, the probabilities are that our solution will be a treatment for the symptoms, and not for the basic problem. We can avoid this by taking systematic steps to identify the key issues and the central problem. Writing it down at this point will help to clarify our thinking.

(*b*) **What are the Facts ?** If we are to identify the problem precisely, we must first examine the circumstances surrounding it. This calls for collection and analysis of available facts, determining what the facts means and consideration of assumptions based on these facts.

Data-gathering should be a sharply-focused effort. It is rarely advisable to collect all of the facts bearing on the problem. Some information may be more difficult or costly to secure than the situation warrants. Since the time available for fact gathering is limited, it is wise to determine in advance what information we really need and in what priority we require it. Other wise, we may find ourselves arriving at conclusions on the basis of large amounts of detail while we have virtually no information on the most significant aspect of the problem. Facts by themselves are not enough. We must determine what the facts mean, what special significance they have in the problem we are considering. Facts are past history. We need to make assumptions of the basis of the facts if we want to develop creative solutions. In fact-gathering, we can focus on the most essential information by investigating systematically each of the decision factors outlined below.

(*i*) **The Situation Factor.** What happened and precisely how did it happen ? Here we establish a clear-cut picture of the situation as it now exists. So far as possible, we rely upon first hand evidence. The information we gather at this early stage is historical. This should be acceptable to all who are concerned with solving the problem.

(*ii*) **The People Factor.** Who is involved ? In what way do the people affect the situation? Consider the point of each person who is important to the problem and determine what special significance this may have.

(*iii*) **The Place Factor.** Where did the problem occur ? Does the location have any significance ? Are future changes expected which will affect the place factor ?

(*iv*) **The Time Factor.** When did the situation occurs ? Has the time factor particular significance ? How will the time factor affect the decision you reach and the action you will carry out ?

(*v*) **The Causative Factor.** Why did the situation come about ? Why did the problem occur? Will the factors that caused the present situation remain constant or will they change in the future ?

Information be gathered from many sources. This is one aspect of decision-making that a manager can most easily delegate. The more different sources are considered in securing data, the more varied the viewpoints consulted, the more accurate and objective the information is likely to be.

(*c*) **The Real Problem.** After we have thoroughly digested the facts and the inferences, we are in a position to review the problem as we first identified it. We may find, in view of the facts, that we had only identified symptoms of a deeper, more fundamental problem.

As much time and effort as necessary should be invested in identifying the basic underlying problem. Our solution will probably not be better than our identification of the problem. Finding the real problem is often difficult because we generally find a number of related problems in the situation. One or more of these may be immediate or emergency problems which require prompt action. Other aspects of the problem may have longer range implications. They require management action, that is, renewed planning, organizing, leading and controlling. In terms of the Principle of Operating Priority, we know that our natural tendency is to ignore the basic management problem and to take operating action without probing deeper. Two factors must be given proper consideration in coming to grips with the basic problem : scope and timing.

Regarding scope much wasted effort may occur if we try to solve problems for other people, or to extent our solutions beyond our own area of accountability. At the same time, we may little our own potential results if we do not take into account in our problem solving the needs and capabilities of other units.

A professional manager considers his problems and solutions in terms of their implications for other units and for the company as a whole. Executive times, unifies and integrates his own actions with those of his superior and with other units. Timing is important. The right solution at the wrong time is better than wrong solution at the right time. We can give full consideration to the time element if we make sure the problem we state encompasses the two aspects : What is the problem now, and what will it be over the long term. Once we have identified the difference, we can begin to look systematically for both short and long term solutions. An important skill of the professional manager is the ability to recognise the difference and to provide for it. The decision as to what really is the problem in matters involving two or more subordinate units, or who own group and other groups work is the area where the manager cannot safely delegate.

(*d*) **Possible Solutions.** The ready answer will become obvious once the problem is clearly defined. Develop other possible solutions, and carefully analyze those which have promise. Discuss the pros and cons, or advantages and disadvantages of each with subordinates. Consider in each case what will happen if you carry the proposed solution through to its logical conclusion. If need to be analysed after asking questions : Will it give you the results you want ? Has it provided for long range requirements as well as putting out the immediate fire ? This is an excellent stage to secure participation of subordinates perhaps it is not possible to ask your subordinates to help identify the real problem because they did not have sufficient background or an alround viewpoint. But now explain the problem fully to them. Ask for their suggestions. Make sure they back up their proposals with proper study and analysis. They will probably think of some ideas that would never have come to your mind. And remember that the more they know about the problem, the more they recognize its complexities and implications, the more effectively they will carry out the solution you develop with their help.

(*e*) **Best Solution.** The professional manager decides, not by pulling an idea out of the air, nor on the basis of hung but by rational selection of what promises to be the best of the various possible solutions he has analyzed and considered. Selecting the best solution requires objectivity. Try to get your emotions and feelings out of the picture. At this point let your head guide your heart. Where the decision involves two or more subordinates, or the interests of his unit overall, or other units, the manager himself must make the decision. Because he has been organizationally placed to have best all around perspective for his own unit, the accountability for final decision is his. Once you have made the decision, let people know about it. Tell them why you made it. Some will be disappointed, perhaps, that you did not follow their ideas more closely. But you can incorporate their suggestions more fully as you take the final step, developing a course of action.

(*f*) **Course of Action.** Now you decide how to implement the decision. Establish a fully-detailed course of action by planning the necessary activities. Determine :

(*i*) *Objectives.* What are you trying to accomplish ? Get full participation of those who are to carry out the action.

(*ii*) *Policies.* What policies apply ? Make sure that you identify these and explain why and how they apply.

(*iii*) *Programs.* Precisely what action steps are to be taken, and in what priority ?

(*iv*) *Schedules.* Participation is most important in programming and scheduling. So far as it fits within your overall course of action, let each individual determine for himself what he will do and how he will do it, to reach the goals you have agreed upon.

(*v*) *Procedures.* If certain work has to be accomplished in a standardized and uniform manner, specify what procedures are to be followed or make provisions for developing the necessary procedures.

(*vi*) *Budgets.* Are these expense limitations ? Specify what can be spent in terms of the time of people, material and tools and facilities.

Types of Decisions

There are two basic types of decisions—spontaneous and reasoned.

Spontaneous Decisions

These are intuitive decisions. They are conclusions arrived at without conscious thought or analysis. A spontaneous decision is often a hunch-an intuitive reaction to memories or previous conditioning. Spontaneous decisions are, to a large extent, unthinking decisions. Even if they are made after observation of a situation or following review of facts, there is little attempt to determine what the facts mean or to reason logically to a judgement based upon the facts. Often we decide in term of precedent because it requires least effort. Also it is easiest to rationalize.

But situations are rarely identical. All things tend to change with time. So do people. Yesterday's decision may seem best because it is familiar and was successful. But now conditions may call for a revised estimate and fresh conclusions. Spontaneous decisions are useful when dealing with routine. They may be necessary in handling emergencies. But since they do not provide for logical analysis and the development of alternatives. They harness us to the past and offer little opportunity for developing innovations or improving established methods.

Reasoned Decisions

These are based on systematic study and analysis of a problem. The facts are assessed, the alternatives weighed and a decision reached in terms of what is best in the light of all the pertinent factors. Reasoned decision making should be followed wherever possible. It brings into play our full mental resources. It emphasizes the creative aspects of problem-solving and enables us to bring to bear upon our problems a consistent approach to thinking which will minimize the probability of error and give us greater assurance of productive results.

Similarly the types of decisions can be further classified as (*i*) Tactical routine and (*ii*) Strategic.

Tactical routine decisions are those which one makes over and over again following the established rules, policies and procedures. These decisions do not require collecting new data nor conferring with people, nor passing judgment and nor for any originality. Tactical decisions can be taken from the view point of finding a correct answer because here the tactical decisions are one dimensional and at times manager does not realise that he is taking decision. The only action which has to be taken is to accomplish the goals with the minimum of effort and disturbance.

The second type is the strategic decisions. These are the really important ones. They either involve finding out what the situation is, what the resources are and what they should do. A manager is, in fact, concerned with these types of decisions and the higher his level the more of these he is required to make. In this type of decisions, effort should not be towards finding a correct answer only but also towards finding a correct question. Secondly, more finding out a correct answer to a correct question is also not sufficient unless the answer/decision can be implemented. Decisions are not made because they are important or they should be the show pieces of filing cabinets, but the managers are concerned with their performances. Really, this means that the decision must be compatible with each other and also consonant with the goals of the whole business. Therefore, the decisions cannot be taken in isolation of the prevailing situations. For the purpose of making a good decision, limitations must also be kept in view.

Importance of Decision Making

The importance of decision making is very much realised, but the problem is that there is a tendency more towards finding a correct answer rather than a correct question. It is here that the crux of the problem lies. The crux of the problem implies that answer has no importance, but what is of importance is that the manager should find a correct answer to a correct question. Merely finding an answer would be very much misleading and may jeopardise the total objectives since right answer to a wrong question is more harmful than wrong answer to a correct question.

An executive is a man who has to make up his mind quickly and who should always make good decisions. It is also not correct that executives have to make spur-of-the moment decisions all the time. For most of the decisions they get enough time for careful fact finding, consultations, analysis and mulling things over before they have to decide. Deciding is a human process. When one decides he chooses the course which he thinks is the best. It may or may not be the one that is truly the best. Decision making is a blend of thinking, deciding and acting. An important executive decision is only one event in a process which requires a succession of activities and less decisions all alone the way. Decisions also have a time dimensions and a time lag. It takes time to collect facts and to weigh an intelligent decision. Moreover, after one decides it takes still more time to carry out a decision and often it takes longer before one can judge whether the decision was good or bad. Also, it is difficult to isolate the effects of any single decision.

Process of Decision Making

The process of decision making has shown in Fig. 53.1. It has the following phases :

(*i*) Defining the problem ;
(*ii*) Analysing the problem and gathering information ;
(*iii*) Developing alternative solutions ;
(*iv*) Deciding upon the best solution ; and
(*v*) Converting the decision into effective action.

Depending upon how the decisions are made, they can either be complete waste of time or best guide to solve the problem. A word of caution here is that sufficient time should be spent on defining the problem, analysing the problem and developing the alternatives. Good time is also necessary to make the solutions effective, but much less time should be spent on finding the right solution because if the preceding steps are taken carefully, finding the right solution will not be much of a problem. Decision making is a cooperative activity performed by executives who occupy positions in a organizational structure. The positions and persons in such a structure are inter-related by a communication system. Therefore, for an effective decision making, importance of a good communication is not ruled out.

(*i*) **Defining the Problem.** Every problem has two aspects. First there is a situation and second there is your dissatisfaction with a situation. When you become dissatisfied with a situation and decide that you ought to do something about it, you recognize that you have a problem. This is the start of decision making.

After recognize that you have a problem, you may try to define and clarify it and to pin-point it. It is not always easy to define the problem, to see the fundamental thing that is causing the trouble and that needs correcting. Yet the manager has to try to find it out and to decide what the core problem is, otherwise he will ask and answer the wrong questions, make wrong decisions and may not solve the real problem. He stays in trouble because he gets answers to the wrong questions. Here again a decision involved and he has to decide what the problem is.

Generally what is experienced is that a problem never presents itself as a case for solution. What at the most can be observed are certain elements or certain symptoms. The first task in decision making is, therefore, to find out what the problem is. To pin point the problem simply by symptomatic diagnosis is not the right answer. In business, we are not dealing with physical sciences that the response to a particular situation will always be the same. A manager has to analyse and find out the critical factors of the problem, what are the elements of particular situation which lead to and constitute the problem. Symptomatic treatment of diagnosing the problem is wrong because first the symptoms may not be dependable and even if they are, there is no guarantee that those symptoms will always lead to one particular problem. Therefore, the best way is to analyse the problem rather than diagnose the problem.

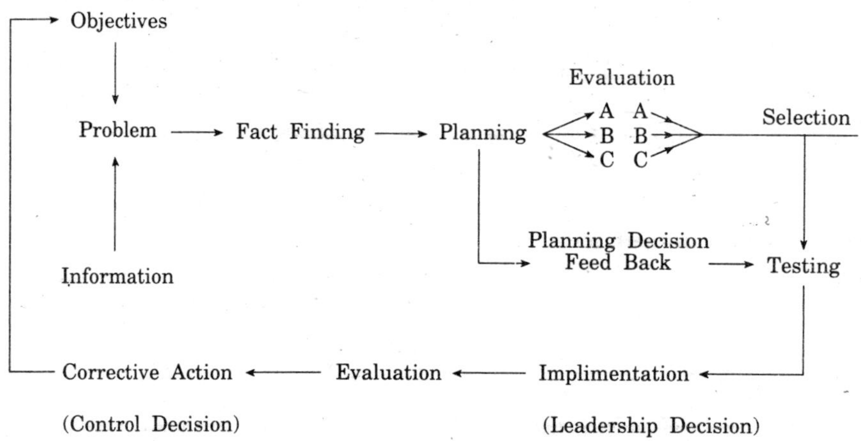

Fig. 53.1. Decision Making Process.

The second step in the definition of the problem is to determine the conditions for its solution. In defining any problem, it is of utmost importance that the objectives of the business, both immediate and the long range are kept in view. Side by side, the principle of limiting factor must also be borne in mind. What are the principles, policies and rules of conduct that have to be followed ? To spell out the rules is necessary because in many cases, the right decision will require changing accepted policies or practices. Unless the manager thinks through clearly what he wants to change and why, he is in danger of trying at one and the same time both to alter and to preserve established practice.

(*ii*) **Analysing the Problem.** Finding right the question, setting the objectives and determining the rules together constitute the first phase in decision-making, that is to define the problem. The next phase is to analyse the problem ; classifying it and finding facts. It is necessary to classify the problem in order to know who should take the decision, who should be consulted in making it and who are the persons to be informed. Without prior classification,

the effciency of the decision may be jeopardised. By classification we can know how to convert the decision into practice.

There are four principles of classifcation :-

(*i*) the futurity of the decision ;

(*ii*) the impact of the decision on other areas and functions ;
(*iii*) the number of qulitative consideration that enter into it ; and
(*iv*) the uniqueness or periodicity of the decisions.

The classification alone can ensure that decision really contributes to the whole business rather than solving the immediate problem at the expense of the whole business.

In order to classify the problems, the facts relevant to the case are essential. Until this information is forthcoming, any classification would be misleading. The manager has to determine what information he needs and how he should get it. The more facts he has about different courses of action the more he cuts down the crisis. Trying to decide without facts is like guessing directions at a cross road instead of reading the highway signs. Gathering facts also takes skill and requires decisions. So a part of any problem is deciding what facts one wants to find out relating to it. Another part of the problem is to decide how to get the desired facts. Finding out facts may be expensive and even difficult. Before one can decide any big problem, he must decide how much time and money he is willing to spend to get the information he needs. It is better to have incomplete information on time than to wait for more complete information that arrives too late to be of use. Since gathering facts costs money, the readily available sources may be used whenever possible. One should use easily tapped files of current information, statistical data, controlled experiments, and the like whenever these are available at low cost getting facts which bear on a problem does not always require doing a research project. A good many people seem to think that no fact exists unless a survey unearths it and proves that it exists. They seem to forget that facts are there all the time and that a survey does not make them, it just unearths them. Men working on almost any job are actually engaged in informal research all the time. One can use their knowledge, if one can and it may save him from going into an expensive research. When one collects the facts to help solving problems, he wants facts that relate to alternative courses of action. The facts gathering must be solution oriented. One must decide what the several alternatives are and then collect facts which will allow him to compare them. Getting the information is not sufficient, the manager should also know how to use this.

Another aspect of analysing the problem is that it is not always possible to get all the information which is needed for defining the problem. Here the job of a manager is to judge how much the risk the decision involves, as well as degree of precision and rigidity that the proposed course of action can afford. In other words, the decision making process involves precisely judging the unknown factors.

(*iii*) **Developing Alternative Solutions.** Assuming known goals and clear planning premises, the next step in the decision making process is the development of alternative-solutions for every problem. Without this, one is likely to be caught in a wrong solution. Without resorting to the process of finding alternative solutions, the manager is likely to be guided by his limited imagination. It is rare for alternatives to be lacking for many courses of action. But it times the manager assumes that there is only one way of doing a thing. What the manager has probably not done is force himself to consider other ways, open his eyes and develop alternatives. Unless he does so, he cannot know whether his decision is the best possible. From the above it appears a key planning principle, which might be referred to as the principle of alternatives. In every course of action alternatives exist, and effective planning involves a search for the alternatives representing the best path to a desired goal. Once the manager has decided upon a particular course of action, he thinks that this is the only and the right way of acting. On the other hand, once the manager starts developing alternatives, various assumptions come to his mind which can be a force to compel him to bring those assumptions to the conscious level. A word of caution here may also be added. Alternatives solutions are not a guarantee of the righteousness, but these help the manager to weigh one alternative against another and thus minimise the uncertainties.

Nevertheless, development of alternatives cannot provide a person with an imagination he lacks. But most of us have definitely more imagination than we ever use. The mind's viscous can be trained, desciplined and developed.

It is not always necessary that the alternative solutions will necessitate taking some action. To take no action is also a decision fully as much as to take a specific action. Only few people realise this. It is of imperative nature that in all organizational problems, the alternative of taking no action is considered. For example, if there is an unnecessary post in the organisation, the solution not to fill the post will be the best one. The ability to develop alternatives is often an important as making a right decision among alternatives. The development of alternatives, if thorough, will often unearth so many choices that the manager cannot possibly consider them all. Even with latest mathematical techniques and electronic computers, the analysis of alternatives and their comparison with one another is almost impossible without some preliminary selection.

(*iv*) **Finding the Best Solution.** Once alternative solutions have been thought of, the next step is to analyse each solution and weight one against the other. Decision making implies freedom to choose from among alternative courses of action. If the steps preceding to finding out the best solution have been dealt with adequately, the manager will have several alternatives from which he can make the choice. It is rare situation where there are no alternatives. In fact, if one is faced with such a situation, it will only imply that the preceding steps have not been taken systematically.

There are four criteria for finding the best from among the possible solutions. These are :

(*a*) *Risk :* The manager has to weigh the risks of each course of action against the expected gains. There will not be any situation where risk is not involved. What matters is the intensity of one risk against another and the expected gains.

(*b*) *Economy of Effort :* The best manager is one who can mobilise the resources for the achievement of results with the minimum of efforts and the least of disturbance in the organization.

(*c*) *Timing :* Another important aspect in the process of choosing the best course of action will depend upon the particular situation. If the situation has great urgency, the preferable course of action is one that alarms the organization that something important is happening. If, a long, consistent effort is needed, a 'slow start gathers momentum' may be preferable.

Decisions concerning timing the extremely difficult to systematize. They elude analysis and depend on perception. Here, there is one guiding principle whereby managers must change their vision to accomplish something new. It is preferable to present to them the big view, the completed programme and the ultimate aim. Wherever they have to change their habits it may be best to take one step at one time, to start slowly and modesty, to do no more than is absolutely necessary.

(*d*) *Limitation of Resources* : One of the most helpful principles of planning and decision making may be called principle of the limiting or strategic factor. In choosing from among alternatives, primary attention must be given to those factors that are limiting or strategic to the decision involved. In every area of decision certain factors are strategic in determining whether goals will be attained.

In decision-making the discovery of the limiting factors may not be so easy, since economic factors are often obscure and people and their reactions complex, but the principle is the same. The search for and recognition of limiting factor in planning and decision making nevers ends. Discovery of the limiting factor lies at the basis of selection from alternatives and hence of planning and decision making. It is generally not possible to explore thoroughly every problem and the solution of every limiting factor, so the business manager must exercise judgement in determining where and how research in this area can best be used. In selecting from among alternative three basis for decision are open to the manager—experience, experimentation and research. The most important resource whose limitations have to be considered, are the human beings who will carry out the decision. The competence, skill, working conditions, abilities and understanding have to be kept in view. A course of action may require the line of competence etc. of the people which is not available in the organisation. Then the obvious preceding step will be to train the people in the organisation or to hire trained people.

Another consideration which is important is that a wrong decision must never be adopted because the resources for implementing the right decisions are lacking. The decision should always be among the alternatives which are genuinely directed towards the solution of the problem. It is no use deciding upon the solution for which the appropriate resources are not present. Such a decision will only be the show piece of the filing cabinet rather than directed towards any better course of action.

(*v*) **Making the Decision Effective.** The decision will have no meaning unless it can be implemented. The managers are not concerned with the decisions in remoteness, but with their performance. The manager's decision is always concerning what other people should do. For this purpose, it is imperative that people should feel attached towards the performance of the decisions. Any idea of the decisions being sold will be a futile exercise. If this has to be the case, it might also sometimes be that the good decisions have to be subordinated because these cannot be sold to the persons concerned. What is right has to be decided by the nature of the problem rather than by wishes, desires and receptivity of the people in the organisation.

In order to make the decision effective, it is necessary that the concerned people understand what the decision involves, what is expected of them and what reasonably they should expect of others. In order to accomplish this, it is desirable that in matters of bringing about change in the behaviour, the principle of slow and steady should be followed. It will be poor decision making which expects the overnight transformation. Another principle which is important is that there should be effective communication. This principle involves that concerned people should be informed only of significant deviation, but this should be in very clear and unambiguous form.

In order to make the people attached to the decision, it will be necessary that there is participation by the people in the decision making process. People accept more willingly decisions that they have helped to make. Superiors who discuss problems with their subordinates and who give them a chance to ask questions and make suggestions and more support for their actions than the superiors who decide everything themselves. Of course, subordinates participation is not desirable in every step. For example, they should not participate in the definition of the problem. At this stage, the manager does not know who should participate and who should not because it is not clear whom the decision is going to effect. Their participation is also not desirable at the information gathering stage. The area where the concerned people can participate is in the development of alternatives. If this can be achieved, the people will feel attached to and responsible for taking the definite course of action. Secondly, certain alternatives might come to surface which the manager may not have though of. Participation by subordinates has established itself as one of the most effective methods of decision making. The research in this area shows that participation is helpful in overcoming resistance to the decision of change from one job to another and increases motivation for work. The practice of participation however a complex problem. It is dependent on the nature of decision, the organizational climate and attitude of employees towards participation.

Though the participative decision making in the manner as detailed above is considered an effective approach but opinions also exist in its favour and against. There is some evidence that group decisions are likely to be poorer decision than one man decisions. Group participation does not necessarily improve the quality of the decisions and, in fact, sometimes imairs it. Group decision making is like a train in which every passenger has a brake. People however often seem to feel strongly about the group participation in decision making. They are strongly for it or strongly against the idea. *Harold Smiddy,* former Vice-President of General Electric Company says that there is too widespread drift toward group responsibility 'togetherness', 'other directedness' and a flight from 'apartness'. He thinks that this weakens responsibility and dilutes managerial functions too much. One loses time, encourages managers to evade responsibilities and becomes indecisive and makes it hard to fix responsibility. There is another argument against too much group participation in decision. Not every one wants to participate. Furthermore it is discouraging to participate and suggest and be overruled again and again, whether by equals or superiors. Participative decision making has had good points as well which have been discussed above.

Psychologist *Rober McMurray* says that you can have a considerable degree of authoritarian decision making without upsetting people. He says that employees tend to be contented with what they are used to. Firm decisive and authoritarian leadership does not upset most employees who are used to it. In fact, says *McMurray,* it is preferable unless employees are interested in more participation, or are ready to assume responsibility for it, and have sufficient experience and knowledge, to deal with the problems at hand. He says that most employees are unable or unworthy to participate in management decisions.

Tools of Decision Making

So far we have talked about the importance, types and the steps for taking the decisions. However, much of this process will become cumbersome unless the manager is adequately equipped with certain tools for sorting out many complexities at every stage. Above all, it is essential that the manager understands the process. Firstly a number of mathematical tools have become available which are very useful and powerful. Secondly, with the rapid development in technology, the balance between tactical and strategic decisions is rapidly shifting. Most decisions that have always been tactical, if not routine, are rapidly becoming strategic decisions containing a high degree of futurity.

Management and Non-Management Decisions

Management decisions are concerned with organizational objectives, and managers are the persons who accept the responsibility for making such decisions. The leader of an informal group within the organisation, though he may make decisions that govern the behaviour of others, is not a manager. The same conclusion can be made about a labour leader who participates in the negotiations of a collective bargaining agreement. The decisions made by informal group leaders and labour leaders involve the personal goals of organizational participants.

Top level decisions are series of inter-related and continuing activities. Also the environment at the top level of management hierarchy is a complex relationship. It is at this level where the managers must be a specialist and at the same time a journalist. At this level the job specifications are very broad, overlap of responsibilities is common practice and communication is of vital importance and is frequently carried out on an informal basis. But with in the same managerial hierarchy there are functional identifications that may stand in the way of smooth operation of the decision making process. In situations where an executive identifies strongly with a department, the tendency is for the manager to make decisions that consider the interest of the department first and the total organisation afterwards. At all levels of management the managers must make decisions on the basis of overall organisation objectives as well as departmental goals. It is in such an amorphous environment that the members of top management must make decisions, maintain, control and should carry out their responsibilities to society. There is a tendency among the managers at the top of management pyramid to view objectives, policies, strategies etc. differently than those on the lower levels. This is an indication of organisation weakness. If the lower levels of management do not comprehend the significance of decision made by top management as related to objectives, policies etc., then inefficiency may occur at all levels. This lack of understanding is not only due to mis-communication but also due to not knowing that different points of view exist. In general, managers should view the problems from its many sides to have a greater understanding of the situation.

Analysis of Decision-Making

The analysis of any problem for decision-making requires a step by step evaluation of the facts and ideas presented before plans or strategies may be developed. It is difficult to set-up a procedure of analysis that would be suitable for every problem.

Several Centres may be critical in the diagnosis of a case. All but one of this diagnostic centres pertain to internal factors which are illustrated in Fig. 53.2. The external environment of the firm is an additional diagnostic centre. In a very complex problem all of the critical factors are involved so that it would be necessary to include them when making the diagnosis. In Fig. 53.2 the analysis starts with sizing up and continues on to objectives, policy, control, organisation, industrial relations and finally decision making. Whether a centre is critical or not depends upon the scope of the problem and its relationship to other diagnostic centres. Such relationships will be indicated by the connections or paths between them. It should be considered as an analytical frame work, a way of thinking about the retationships between the various factors that bear upon the success of an organisation.

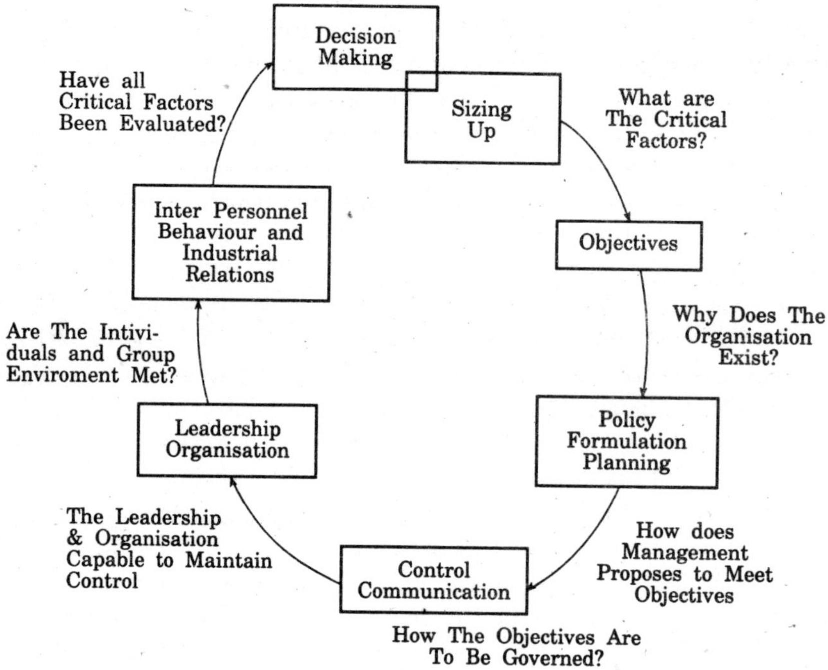

Fig. 53.2. Critical diagnostic centres and paths in decision making.

Sizing Up

It is best to size up the situation first by deciding what areas are to be analysed in what order. In analysing, the critical centres should be identified at the beginning. Some of the problems or cases require a complete examination of every factor and going through the complete diagnostic cycle while other problem or cases require only a part of diagnostic scheme. As shown in Fig. 53.3 (*a*), it requires an analysis of leadership, organisation and inter-personal behaviour; and policies, planning and strategy are not critical to decisions. Sizing up also means an examination of the evidence, determining the relationship of facts, making some pre-judgements dealing with possible causes and effect.

Objectives

The objectives of organisation must be defined in workable or useful terms so that they can be related to the executive decisions. Keeping an eye on the profit is of course a very suitable activity for a manager but just as important is the continuous re-evaluation of the product or service objectives. It is of no good for any organization to watch only the profit if the next year it will be out of business because of poor service to the customers. Therefore, a manager must not consider objectives sacred and unchangeable but rather is being flexible to meet the dynamics of the business environment.

Policy Formulation—Planning Strategy

Not all cases are concerned with policy planning and strategy. This means that a determination must be made as to whether the present policy of the organisation is adequate or appropriate.

Policy establishes the general ground rules for meeting the objectives and policy must be matched with objectives and it should not be formulated in a vacuum. The inter-relationships between objectives and policy are direct and critical as shown in Fig. 53.3 (*b*). Combined with policy are planning and strategy. Once objectives are confirmed and compatible policies established, the organisation is in a position to examine the planning and strategy used to carry-out the policies. Strategy is dependent on the resources available and controlled by the executives. Planning is the determination of how best to carry out the strategy.

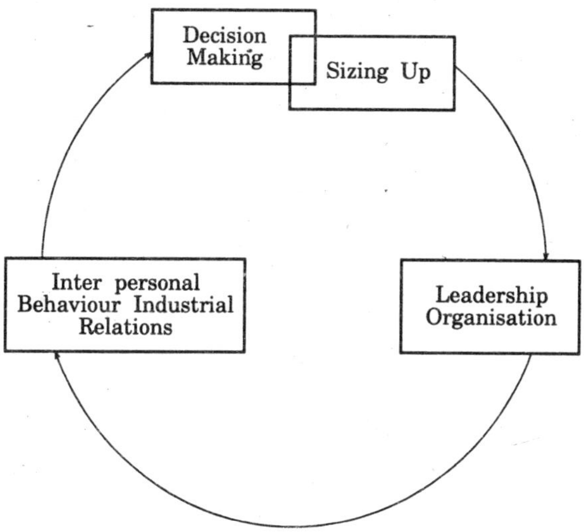

(a)

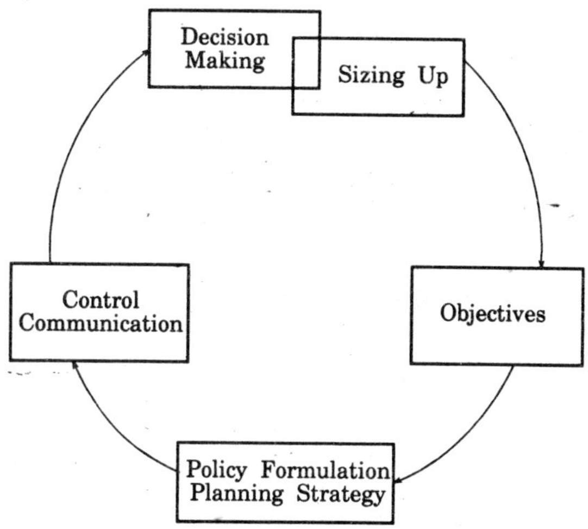

(b)

Fig. 53.3.

Control and Communication

As nerves are necessary to the human body, in the same way control and communication net works are necessary to an organisation. It is really important to evaluate the communication aspect because it is an integral part of the control system within an organisation. Reports, memoranda and official notices are part of communication and are also an integral part of the control system with in an organisation. Wordless actions feed-back and lack of communication are also part of communication net work. In diagnosing a problem or a case the manager should examine the controls and communication involved to determine their adequacy and indeed see if the appropriate controls exist. Appropriateness is determined by whether the controls aid in carrying out the plans and strategy and whether they are suitable for the existing organisation and leadership.

Leadership and Organisation

This part of the analysis is related very closely with the control and communication factors. There is such a close integration that it is not always clear as to which center should be diagnosed first, it may be that an investigation of the communication or controls is meaningless without relating them to the organisation and leadership patterns.

Inter-Personal Behaviour and Industrial Relations

There are the other analysis factors where diagnosis of the human element is carried out. The organisation is established by people and is operated by people. It is only in the area of human behaviour where one finds that the logical decisions may not be the correct decisions. It is difficult to relate profits to human activity but as the companies are profit making organisations, human element decisions should be oriented in that direction.

Social and Economic Setting Influencing Decision-Making

The external environment is an integral and important part of the problem analysis. The environment may include legal requirements as established by laws, social moves of society and economic conditions. The external environments surround the organisation and since the company is dependent entirely on the society it must continuously refer to the outside world. The social and economic setting constitute the eight critical diagnostic centres as shown in Fig. 53.4. It is no doubt a difficult task for the manager to balance his responsibilities to the individual employees and to the company. If management by itself does not take the initiative in discovering its responsibilities, society will impose the responsibilities upon the company and the managers through legal channels and social pressure.

In carrying out an analysis one should keep in mind that the end result should be a recommendation for action. A decision is to be reached and implemented. The process of analysis should examine the related factors such as :

(*i*) Assessing the risks involved in various courses of action.

(*ii*) Predicting the obstacles of making the various plans of action operational.

(*iii*) Evaluating the financial resources and cost.

(*iv*) Considering the human factor when recommending changes.

The decision making process is described at times in terms of models that contain inputs, variables and outputs. It is simply illustrated in Fig. 53.5.

One of the jobs of the manager is to decide what information is to be available for decision making. Sales, cash inventory, accounts payable and receivables are the obvious facts that most companies maintain. Other informations which need to be available are customers preference, employees morale, competitor's position, market trends, changing manpower needs, evaluation of employees performance, changing social norms, etc.

Once the decision has been made, it is important to size up the situation again to be sure that vital information has not been overlooked. It is manager's job to make decisions based on his own evaluation of the facts and upon the judgement concerning the probability of the success of decision in the light of his analysis of critical areas.

Managerial Functions and Decision Making

In analysing the various functions of management ; namely, planning, organising, staffing, coordinating and controlling, we find that each one of them involves decision making. Planning for example, is in itself a decision making process. In planning, we choose between alternatives and in selecting one particular course of action we decide to eliminate other proposals. Similarly, in organising, we 'decide' which activities should be grouped, who should be incharge, and what type of authority should be employed. In the same fashion, when employees are recruited and their efforts directed, the decision making process comes at work. A manager must decide whom to employ or to promote or how best to direct them and lastly, the "controlling function" becomes meaningless without decision. Control implies a "decision" must be made as to what action needs to be taken.

Some Tools to Effective Decision-Making

The reason why many people are indecisive is fear of having to assume responsibility for the choices they make. The following rules could help overcome the common fears that enter into decision-making.

(*i*) An executive is bound to make a wrong decision occasionally. So what ? As the British statemen Gladstone remarked, "No man ever became great or good except through many and great mistakes. Therefore forget your mistakes, but never 'what they teach you'. They are your best instructors".

(*ii*) Whenever you find yourself hesitating unduly in arriving at a decision ask yourself, "How important to me or other people is this matter ?" Take an objective and impersonal view point as far as possible. If the matter is really an important one, take time to think it over and consult others if you think they can help. But if the problem is minor one, take a decision and then forget it.

(*iii*) Comfort yourself with the thought that you have added to your stature mentally and emotionally by taking action yourself instead of avoiding the issue or procrastinating or passing the buck.

(*iv*) Never forget that others will judge you by the long range overall accuracy of your decision, and not by each isolated instance.

The only intelligent attitude to overcome indecision is to develop determination. It may not be possible to overcome it completely because it does not take much strength to do things, but it requires great strength to decide on what to do. It is only by putting forth constant and continued effort and conforming to the process of decision making that any manager can make up his mind as to when and what he should do. Making business refers to a variety of needs and goals. It requires judgement, making it possible by narrowing the range and the available alternatives, giving it clear focus, and providing reliable measurements of effects and validity of actions and decisions.

Need for Creativity in Decision-Making

Planning that adds some new and useful element is 'creative'. Every invention of a product, process or machine contains some creative element. Advertisers strain to make their display and slogans new and original ; and sales executives think of new markets, shopping certres, or new packages or merchandise, creativity is need in all socio economic activities *viz*. medical, science, development of atomic energy and in the discovery of new forms of arts such as literature, music, painting etc.

Because of such a widespread need for creative thinking it is important for a manager to decide whether this quality can be developed by him and encouraged in his subordinates. Some individuals have a greater element of creativeness than their colleagues. It is therefore less imaginative or conservative individual who looks on change as something reasonable. Creative ability are by no means rare. Much of the work in decision making involves creativity. A manager who is full of creative ideas will take better decisions.

From the discussion, we reach to the conclusion that good decisions do not just happen. They must be developed by good analysis, study, understanding and evaluation. In decision making, the first essential is to define the problem. This requires a thorough and careful diagnosis. If we do not know what we are trying to solve, we cannot render a rational solution. Once the problem is defined, the next logical step is the assessment of the situation. We must gather and analyse the related facts. However, one thing we must not overlook is that we should be aware of our personal bias. When a manager fully realises these aspects it will not be difficult for him to measure the situation. This will help him to take objective decisions. Lastly, the decision maker, to find out the effectiveness of his decisions, must answer the question whether or not his alternatives are adequate both in number and in magnitude considering the situation.

Judgement and Decision-Making

Judgement is an important element in decision making. When values are clear, information is adequate and risks are reasonably predictable, the decision making may not appear to involve so much of judgement. But this is not always true because in selecting the alternative, comparison of values and relations of things must be mentally formulated and asserted. Let us take a situation where value comparisons are difficult, information spotty and risks are unknown. Here the presence and need for judgement is more evident. Actually, under such conditions, judgement becomes the medium by which conflicting values are resolved, risks assessed and alternatives evaluated.

Decision-Making Environment

Our decision-making environment, is increasingly becoming more complex and highly interacting and interwoven. Therefore, it is essential to utilise the modelling approaches which can identify the controllable and uncontrollable situational variables, and can develop appropriate strategic plans which are technically feasible and economically viable. In the initial stages of application of the modelling approaches, we may fail because of 'our inadequacies but no doubt is there that such approaches can lead us to pragmatic decision frontiers where we shall be able to coordinate both technocratic and bureaucratic patterns of behaviour. Its primary role should be of process-change-agent to diffuse power, to divide authority and distribute influence for a successful adoption of the approach or revision of the existing approaches. The analytical findings of the technocratic methods and discretionary judgements of the bureaucratic methods should be amalgamated depending on the environmental requirements. The modelling approach requires that the technocrats, for their part, have an obligation to use more direct, concise terminology, to phrase their findings in terms relevant and understandable to the bureaucrats, and try to understand all elements of the problem facing the bureaucrats. On the other hand, bureaucrats must try to learn more of the languages of technocracies atleast enough to understand the general working of the modelling techniques, if not the details of methodology.

Decision Making :-Use of Modelling Approaches

Management science models are potential tools within that design and implementation process. These scientific tools provide only the methodological insights into the problems to recognise the relevant factors and their systematic interrelationships. But primarily the design process requires the art component of management, *i.e.*, it requires an intuitional amalgam of observation, experience and judgement.

Formalisation of Decision Problem

The decision process is as old as human civilization. It has been recognised progressively that the public policy decision process is a complex one. The complexity assumes different facets; largeness, multidimentionality and hierarchy, etc. A public policy decision problem, in the formal sense, can be categorised by the following characteristics :

(*a*) one or a group of decision makers.

(*b*) a set of possible actions.

(*c*) a set of outcomes resulting from the choice of a particular possible action or actions.

(*d*) a set of value dimensions or objectives which enables the value of a particular outcome to be measurable in some sense.

(*e*) a set of utilities representing the utility of the outcome with respect to its measured value by the decision maker and using the given action.

Behavioural Aspects

In the real life situations we observe the various behavioural truths. Behaviourally, people as customers or users of the utilities or outcomes, are the sole causes of any public activity. In this context, they believe in maximum welfare. They judge the welfare by value of growth criteria in terms of use, quality, reliability, service and other benefits.

Behaviourally, people as planners or who take the responsibility of the final users either in the constitutional manner or in the obligatory manner, identify the needs of the users, create environmental conditions for possible actions and outcomes, and make recommendations. In an open democratic society, the behaviour of these three different groups overlap, because the role playing or functional boundaries are not specifically marked. In this paper, our focuss is towards the role of decision makers, and purpose is to elaborate how public decision models are constructed and what are their limitations and potentialities.

Nature of Decision-Making

The primary role of decision maker is to make right decisions, which may be defined as decisions made on the basis of perfect information. Perfect information in this context signifies that the decision maker knows exactly the probabilities of outcomes as well as their values to him. Under no circumstances, perfect information can be available for a decision problem solution. The best one can do is to seek for some rational solution under the information constraints. In a democratic pluralistic social framework, the decision maker selects a specific course of action over a series of plausible alternatives put forth by planners. He uses some compromise criteria to judge the best alternative. The compromise criterion, may not be always an optimal criterion, but recognises many side effects of the decision problem for its acceptance by the users.

There are two different types of decision making models, in practice. They may be considered as two different approaches for the solution of decision problems. They are : the technocratic approach and the bureaucratic approach.

In the technocratic approach, one starts from the recognition and analysis of the problem in question. The analysis is carried on in sequential steps and finally feasible alternatives are developed and selection is made by some criterion of optimality.

In the bureaucratic approach, the problem is solved in an incremental fasion, *i.e.*, the advances in the solution are made in small steps. In such an approach, there is no absolutely right solution, but a continuous stream of minor decisions on the problem. This is purely a trial and error approach and can be described as a process of muddling through. There are no standard procedures of practices for this type of approach, except being guided by a few traditional and established guidelines.

Strength and Weaknesses of Decision-Making Approach

The technocratic approach can either be quantitative or semiquantitative. It very often disregards irrationalities of socio-political processes and preferences of individual decision makers in view of lack of pragmatism, the solutions although obtained in a systematic fashion are often unacceptable to the policy makers, and if acceptable sometime become very difficult to implement, apart from the problem of convincing the end users about their utilities. On the other hand, bureaucratic approach which is very much linked to our present democratic framework takes into account all those irrationalities and becomes very much appealing to policy makers. In reality, we can observe that in the bureaucratic approach, hardly any attempt is made to incorporate long-term objectives of public policy systems in the analytical framework. Probably, in a country like ours where the political system is more interested in retaining power at least for a period of five years, and where there is no cohesion in political ideologies, a short-term solution of the decision making problem is considered safer, because, a short-term approach can be treated as a satisfactory means in contrast to the process of optimising in the long range.

There are, however, some significant advantages in the incremental method of decision making. In practice, the technocratic approaches are basically target or optimisation apporaches where feasible alternatives are generated, evaluated according to some predetermined set of objective values. Such an approach is reasonably accurate and even justifiable if the informations that are necessary as inputs are complete, timely exact. Whereas, in actual practice, such situations never occur, and hence incremental decision approach is sought for to obtain a compromise instead of optimisation, to involve a trade-off between several issues instead of incorporating assumptions, to revise views from time to time instead of waiting for a long time to monitor the solution. In the technocratic approach, ambiguity in solution results are never tolerated and also one cannot incorporate interests and conflicts of pressure groups of public systems managers in the analysis.

Appropriateness of an Approach

In a country like ours, the management policy is bound to be dynamic in nature. A dynamic management policy as either a long term, predetermined equilibrium policy aimed attaining a stable target state subject only to short-term fluctuations ; of a quasi-equilibrium management policy aimed at attaining, after transients, a target state that requires deliberates and continuous corrective interventions to keep the system in quasi-equilibrium with its surroundings and to prevent run-away conditions ; or a non-equilibrium final state while ensuring for a specific period, our ability to utilise the publicly mobilised resources under such conditions.

Decisions making in our country, and also in many developing countries, is at present being done by bureaucratic apporach, probably due to historical reasons. However, we feel here that such an approach is not purely irrational. The complexities and inter-connections of decision problems make the attainment of rationality a difficult job. Rationality is bounded by many constraints both internal and external. However, the present mode of decision making can be improved.

We believe that decisions, within the existing organisational framework, can be made on the basis of thorough and systematic analysis. We do not see any reason why a model for every situation cannot be developed to that the current decisions can be linked to the long range objectives. What is necessary is a change of styles of reorientation of strategies or reordering of the problems or restructuring of priorities. What we simply require, is to develop a thinking little more for the future.

Modelling of Situations

In the context of present discussion, let us assume that successful managers are the managers of situations. Situations, we should perceive from the interaction viewpoint of the public policy system. The intensity and diversity of demands on our limited resources have increased considerably during these days. Furthermore, the recognition and acceptance of public policy systems in the fabrics of economic development, increasing social awareness, quality of working life emergence of articulate and diversified special interest groups due to our political systems, and rapidly changing public perceptions of an attitude to the fundamental principles of management, need a different kind of manager altogether.

Recent developments and contributions by the management scientists in the arena of systems analysis have made it possible to provide the managers with a selected range of alternatives within which decisions may be made. Systems analysis is basically a modelling process, which consists of several tools and techniques to analyse a decision problem. The modelling should be carried out by technical experts and the results of it should be used as an input to the recommendations by the policy makers. We suggest some of the basic rules of modelling as follows :

(*a*) A model should be judged from its utility viewpoint, *i.e.*, how one can implement the model in the real world situations. Therefore, a simple model construction is always desirable which can facilitate easy implementation. A simple model is again very much deceptive, because, it cannot incorporate all the relevant parameters and variables. Therefore, it is always necessary to develop some simple models first, and keep the framework flexible to make it sensitive to the changes. A quantitative model may not always satisfy such requirements. Wherever possible, qualitative structuring can be made.

(*b*) There should be some initial commitment from the decision makers to use a model, and this support should come from the upper echelon of management hierarchy.

(*c*) Before constructing a model, three important but basic considerations are necessary. They are : technical commitment, which will answer whether a model construction is at all necessary ; if necessary, is it possible to construct or not, economical commitment, which will answer about the costs and benefits of modelling work ; and finally the organisational commitment, which will answer, if the other two commitments are justified, and whether the model will be accepted and used.

(*d*) Modelling and data collection process should be considered as a simultaneous affair. Modelling very often offers a clear insight to the type and quantity of data that should be collected.

(*e*) Model development should not be judged as one-shot affair, rather attempts should be made to continually up-date the models as and when more information and data become available. Updating should be considered as a regular process. otherwise models will be out-of-date, and they will loose their usefulness and credibility.

(*f*) Models should be so structured that current decisions can be linked to the long-term plans and programmes. Flexible models are more adaptive than models constructed under rigid boundary conditions without taking into consideration the long-run consequences of the present decisions.

There are some positive and negative factors to consider about the possible use of the modelling process in decision making. Developments in computer technology in recent years and their capability have become so much encouraging that most of the complex problems which require evaluation of a large number of alternatives can be solved without any difficulty. Further more, in our country, we do not find lack of expertise in mathematical modelling. Young engineers, economists and scientists as well as graduates in business management are now entering in large numbers to our labour market, and also are familiar with the new modelling technologies. What our requirements are to develop their abilities by training them to handle real life problems using the modelling approaches. In spite of all these potentialities, we have several other limitations.

Both top management and operating management must recognise their respective roles in the evolution of a modelling approach. Active participation of both the groups in the formulation, administration, and evaluation of the system can bring success to the approach. It is both difficult and foolish to impose an approach on the operating management that has not been a party to its introduction. Anyone who has got experience knows that the best of plans can be so cleverly sabotaged by a group of unwilling personnel that the promulgators will look like fools. One should first clearly realise what sort of managerial judgement will be required before making a move. The data requirements must be ascertained early, and the information collection should avoid long delays. Transitional difficulties must be anticipated and problem boundaries should therefore be made flexible to incorporate the transitional difficulties.

54

Network Analysis

Network analysis is synthesis of two techniques namely programme Evaluation and Review Technique and Critical Path Method evolved independently during 1956-57. The two methods have many features in common and are now combined and called Network Analysis. For large non-repetitive operations or projects CPM-PERT and other related network techniques are usefully aids for project managers. A few of the features making the techniques powerful are :

A logical and disciplined basis for planning. CPM and PERT are useful at several stages of project management starting from early planning stages, when various alternative programmes or procedure are being considered, to the scheduling phase, when time and resources schedules are laid out to final stage *i.e.* in the operational phase, when used as control device to measure actual versus planned progress.

Simplicity. They are straight forward in concept and easily explainable to the layman with no background in network theory. Data calculations, is tedious for large projects, are not difficult. Basic critical path data may be hand calculated with reasonable speed for projects with 500 or 600 activities. Computer programs are readily variable for large projects.

Improves co-ordination and communication. The network graph displays a simple and direct way the complex manager of various sub-divisions of project may quickly perceive from the graph.

Pinpoints trouble spots and responsibility. Network calculations pinpoint attention to the relatively small subset of activities in a project which are critical to its completion. Managerial action is thus focused on exceptional problems, contributing to more reliable planning and more effective control.

Better management of resources. CPM enables the manager to reasonably estimate total costs for various completion dates. These various trade of possibilities along with other decision criteria, enable him to select an optimum or near optimum schedule.

Versatile and application. CPM and PERT are applicable to many type of projects: from jobs, from new product introduction programme to missile procedures. Moreover, they may be applied at several levels within a given project from a single department working on a sub-system to multi-plant operations within a large corporation.

Scope for unseen changes. As simulation tools, they enable the manager to project into the future effects of planned or unanticipated changes and to take appropriate action when such projections indicate the need for it. Thus for example the manager can quickly study the effects of crash programmes and can anticipate in advance potential resource battle. When wisely used by a project manager who understands their strengths and limitations, CPM and PERT can be effective amplifiers of his managerial skills.

Utility

1. It aids the manager in planning, scheduling, controlling the activities.
2. In guiding and directing team efforts more effectively.
3. It permits advance planning indicates current progress warns of potential future trouble spots when there may still be time to avoid them.
4. It aids in handling uncertainties regarding time schedules, co-ordination of many activities and control of cost involved.
5. It shows its values most strikingly when a special projects of new kind is undertaken.

The Concept of "Planning" and "Control"

Work comprises everything carried out to change the state or position of materials. Simple work may consist of one activity or two and complex work of millions of activities. Program is any work attuned to a target or an objective. Space craft building of which more than 6 million components are required, it is impossible to imagine that such a programme could be executed with speed and efficiency without having a plan of action. The considerations of efficiency make planning necessary for all programmes. *Planning is a comprehensive term which embraces definition of objectives, forecasting and sequencing of resources requirements and marrying them with the resources potential into an action plan.*

Every planning process, howsoever scientific, has to reckon with imponderables. It is necessary to continuously review the plan as work necessary. This is briefly the concept of the term "Control" a function complementary to "Planning". In fact, without effective "Control" "planning" in reduced to a simple academic exercise only. "Control" requires feedback information on Progress Status. If managers resist feedback then it often leads to non-acceptance of "planning and control" function. Line managers should instead look to this function as staff assistance and take advantages of the modern management tools and techniques.

What is a Project ?

Project is a term which covers once-through and small-batch programmes. When attempting to determine the completion data for any task/project. Where it is

(1) Construction projects, building of a bridge etc.
(2) Research and development projects.
(3) Designing of a new pieces of equipment.
(4) Erection and commission of Industrial Plants.
(5) Preventive maintenance.
(6) Trial manufacture.
(7) Heavy Engineering.
(8) Custom engineered products.
(9) Market launching of new products.
(10) Finalisation of annual accounts.
(11) An inaugural.

(12) A banquet.

(13) A marriage programme.

(14) Preparation for a dinner party.

(15) A picnic party.

(16) A picnic outing etc.

Or any other project it is necessary to time-table all the activities which make up the task or the project, that is to say, a plan must be prepared. The need for planning has always been present,.but the complexity and competitiveness of modern undertakings now requires that this need should be met rather than just recognized.

Network Techniques of Program Management

The need for management direction on a program or job depends upon two factors--its repetitiveness and complexity. Simple job that occur infrequently do not require any involved direction. The techniques for direction of project type jobs are rather new. However, there has recently been an explosive growth in the family of these technique a number of network techniques have been developed which are named below:

(1) P.E.R.T.	:	Programme Evaluation and Review Technique.
(2) C.P.M.	:	Critical Path Method.
(3) R.A.M.P.	:	Resource Allocation and Multiproject Scheduling.
(4) P.E.P.	:	Programme Evaluation Procedure.
(5) C.O.P.A.C.	:	Critical Operating Production Allocation Control.
(6) M.A.P.	:	Manpower Allocation Procedure.
(7) R.P.S.M.	:	Resource Planning and Scheduling Method.
(8) L.C.S.	:	Least Cost Scheduling.
(9) M.O.S.S.	:	Multi-Operation Scheduling System.
(10) P.C.S.	:	Project Control System.
(11) G.E.R.T.	:	Graphical Evaluation Review Technique.
(12) L.O.B.	:	Line of Balance Technology.

The most commonly known and used Network Techniques are PERT and CPM and most of the other techniques are the variations or developments of these techniques only.

Nature of the Techniques

In any project there are usually three types of problems:

(*a*) *Technical*

(*b*) *Executive Type*

(*c*) *Human.*

More complex the project, more difficult the executive type problems--say co-ordination to name one. An example of vastness of this problems in complex projects is given by the polaris weapon system which involve 250 prime contractors and at least 9000 job-contractors. In such projects it is possible that delay in the delivery of as small component might hold up the progress of the entire project. These techniques help to co-ordinate efforts of different agencies :

(*i*) *To plan resources*

(*ii*) *To anticipate the occurrence of bottlenecks*

(iii) *To guide corrective action*

(iv) *To forecast the likelihood of meeting target dates.*

The basic functions of management are to make decisions and enforce their implementation. The function still remains, not withstanding the new techniques. The techniques are merely tools in the hand of management--the tools that make the decision process more rational and less painful.

Historical Background to "CPA" "CPM"

(1) *Critical Path Analysis : CPA*

(2) *Critical Path Method : CPM*

(3) *Critical Path Planning : CPP*

History of Net-Work Analysis

Before CPA coming on the scene probably the best-known method of trying to plan was by means of a bar or Gantt chart. There were certain drawbacks and problems in it. *In Great Britain* the *Operational Research Section of the Central Electricity Generating Board investigated* the Problems concerned with the overhaul of Generating Plant—an area of considerably complexity which was increasing in importance as new higher Performance Plant was being brought into service. By 1957 the O.R. section had devised a technique which consisted essentially of identifying the *"Longest irreducible sequence of events"*, and using this technique they carried out in 1958 an experimental overhaul at a Power Station which reduced to overall time to 42% of the previous average time for the same work. Continuing to work upon these times the overhaul time was further reduced by 1960 to 32% of the previous average time. The name, "Longest irreducible squence of events" was soon replaced by the name, *"Major Sequence*, and it was pointed out for example, that delays in the "major sequence," would delay completion times, but the difficulties elsewhere need out necessarily involve extensions in total time. This work of the O.R. groups was not made public, although comprehensive reports were circulated internally elsewhere.

Similar development work was being undertaken elsewhere—for example in the U.S. Air force under the code name P.E.P. *Also in 1958, the E I. du Pont de Nemours Company used a technique called the "Critical Path Method" "CPM"* to schedule and control a very large project, and during the first complete year's use of CPM it was credited with saving the company $ 1 million. Subsequent use underlined the basic simplicity and extra-ordinary usefulness of this method, and by 1959 Dr. Mauchly, who had worked on the Du Pont Project, set up an organisation to solve industrial problems using the Critical Path Method.

Since 1958 considerable work has been carried out. Mainly in the United States of America, in consolidating and improving these techniques. Much of the effort has been expanded by the Computer companies, who have devised special names to distinguish their own work.

"CPM" and its advantages

Critical Path Method is a technique employed to schedule and control project. CPM is applicable to both large and small projects. It is widely recognized, most versatile and important management planning.

Some of the important advantages are given below :

(1) It helps in ascertaining time schedule.

(2) With its help control by the Management becomes easy.
(3) It makes better and detailed planning possible.
(4) It encourages discipline.
(5) It provides a standard method for communicating project plans, schedules, time and cost performance.
(6) It identifies most critical elements and thus more attention can be paid on these activities.

Those techniques require a greater planning than required otherwise. Thus these methods increase the Planning cost, but this Cost is easily justified by concentrating attention Critical Paths only and avoiding unnecessary expenses on the strict supervision over whole programme.

Steps in "CPM" Technique

CPM employs the following steps for accomplishing a project planning.

1. Break down the project into various activities systematically.
2. Label all activities.
3. Arrange all the activities in Logical sequence.
4. Construct the arrow diagram.
5. Number all the nodes and activities.
6. Find the time for each activity.
7. Mark the activity times on the arrow diagram.
8. Calculate early a[illegible]ate, start and finishing times.
9. Tabulate various times and mark EST and LFT on the arrow diagram.
10. Calculate the total float for each activity.
11. Identify the critical activities and mark the Critical path on the arrow diagram.
12. Calculate the total project duration.
13. If it is intended to reduce the total Project duration, crash the critical activities of the network.
14. Optimise the cost.
15. Up-date the netwrok.
16. Smooth the network.

Difference between "PERT and "CPM"

CPM is a technique used for the Planning and Controlling the most logical and economic sequence of operations for accomplishing a project. The project is analysed into different activities whose relationships, as in PERT, are shown on the network diagram. The network is then utilized for optimising the use of reources, progress and control. PERT is a technique used for scheduling and controlling the projects, whose activities are subject to considerable degree of uncertainty in the performance time. The method of start finish critical path and project time of P.E.R.T, and C.P.M. are similar. CPM is an activity oriented technique, while PERT is the event oriented technique.

Event means the beginning or exceeding of one or more activities. CPM has one time estimate, while PERT has three time estimates.

The fundamental network of PERT and CPM are though identical, yet there are certain differences in details as mentioned below :

PERT	*CPM*
1. A probabilistic model with uncertainty in activity duration. Expected time is calculated from to t_m and t_p.	1. A deterministic model with well-known activity (single time based upon past experience. It assumes that, the expected time is actually the time taken.
2. An event oriented approach.	2. An activity-oriented system.
3. PERT terminology uses words like network diagram event and slack.	3. CPM terminology employs words like arrow diagram, nodes and float.
4. The use of dummy activities is required for representing proper sequencing.	4. The use of dummy activities is not necessary. The arrow diagram thus becomes slightly simpler.
5. PERT basically does not demarcate between critical activities.	5. CPM marks critical activities.
6. PERT find applications in projects where resources (man, materials and specially money) are always made available and when required.	6. CPM is employed to those projects where overall costs is of primary importance. There is better utilization of resources.
7. Especially suitable in defence projects and R and D where activity times cannot be reliably predicted.	7. Suitable for problems in Industrial setting, plant maintenance, civil consturction projects : expansions schemes etc.
8 PERT has three-times estimates.	8. CPM has one-time estimate.

Thus PERT should be explicit intengible, capable of accepting changes and capable of being monitored.

PERT

Program Evaluation Review Technique

P Program
1. *Job Analysis.*
2. *Management by Objective.*
3. *Determination of Events and Activities--their relationship.*
4. *Network Representation.*

E Evaluation
1. *Time*
2. *Cost*
3. *Feasibility*
4. *Probability*

R Review
1. *Progress*
2. *Resources Allocation.*
3. *Time schedule*
4. *Expenditure*

T Techniques
1. *To attain objectives*
2. *So foretell Hurdles*
3. *To avoid failures*
4. *To attain maximum benefit from efforts put in*

PERT Defined as

1. A Manager's Tool : for defining and co-ordinating what must be done to successfully accomplish the objectives of a project on time.
2. A Technique : that aids the decision maker but does not make decisions for him.
3. A Technique : that presents statistical information regarding the uncertainties faced in completing its many activities associated with a project.
4. A Method : for focussing managerial attention on; latest problems that require decisions and/or solutions.
5. A Method : requiring managerial attention procedures and adjustments, regarding time, resources or performance which may improve the capability of meeting target dates.

Distinguishing Features of PERT

These techniques have several distinguishing characteristics :

(1) They give management the ability to plan best possible use of resources to achieve a given goal within overall time and cost limitations.

(2) They enable executives to manage "one of a kind" programs, as opposed to respective situations.

(3) They help management handle the uncertainties involved in programs where no standard time data of the Taylor--Gantt variety are available.

(4) They utilize a so-called " time network analysis" as a basic method of approval to determine Man-power, interests and capital requirements.

Advantages of PERT

1. It provides clear objectives.
2. It provides an analytical approach to the achievement of an objective.
3. It enumerates detailed plans and important programmes events.
4. It establishes sequence of activities and their inter relationship.
5. It focuses attention on important and critical activities and events.
6. It provides a logical plan for formulating a realistic schedule of activities.
7. It provides up-to-date status information of the project and enables quick review of the progress at all stages.
8. It can point out improbabilities and may even predict before their occurrence, and they help remedy the situation.
9. It can foretell the feasibility of a plan and can help in formulating new schedules if the one under consideration be found impracticable or wanting.
10. It avoids slippage of plan and waste of time, energy and money.
11. It is an aid for allocating the available resources for optimum results.
12. It brings about time and cost consciousness at all levels of management.

Introducing PERT into an Organization

As with any other new managerial tool, PERT will require to be introduced into an organisation with care. It is suggested that the following points should be observed.

1. PERT is not a universal tool--there are situations where it cannot be usefully employed. These situations are, in general those where activity is continuous, for example, flow production. A PERT type situation is characteristically on which has a definable start and a definable finish.

2. PERT is not a life saving drug, it does not cure all ills. Indeed, PERT in itself does not solve any problems, but it does expose situations in a way which will pursuit effective examinations both of the problems and of the effect of possible solutions. However ,the formulating and implementing of any solution will remain the responsibility of the appropriate manager.

3. PERT must not be made a mystery, known only to a chosen few. All levels require to appreciate the method and its limitations, and an extensive educational programme will be necessary to ensure that knowledge is spread as widely as possible.

4. The person initiating PERT into an organisation must be of sufficient stature and maturity to be able to influence both senior and junior personnel.

5. Whenever possible, the early applications for PERT should be to simple situations. If PERT is first employed on a very difficult task, it may fail, not because of the difficulty of PERT but because of the difficulty of the task itself. However, the failure is likely to be attributed to PERT and the technique will be discredited.

6. PERT will involve committal to, and the acceptance of responsibilities expressed in qualitative terms. Many supervisors find this difficult to accept, and will often try to escape by creating unreal problems. It is vital to make it quite clear that PERT is not a punitive device ; it is a tool to assist, not a weapon to assult.

7. Difficulties in using PERT are almost always symptoms of same Managerial Weakness.

Steps in the Technique of PERT Planning

1. Define clearly the end objectives.
2. Determine the major events that must be completed prior to reaching the end objectives.
3. Analyse and record the work to be done in between events.
4. The project is broken down into different activities systematically.
5. Arrange the events and activities in the order of sequence of their occurrence.
6. The network diagram is drawn. Events and activities are numbered and make sure no activity is left over.
7. Layout and finalize the network in a neat form. May be more than one attempt is needed.
8. Event numbers should be given with the starting event as 1, and progressing successively to the right in the order in which they occur.
9. Any dummy activity should by shown by dotted arrow times on the network.
10. Check your network it should not have loose ends. Network is always closed and all activities lead to the objective.
11. Each activity should have a single location.

12. Using three times estimates, the expected times for each activity are calculated.
13. Standard deviation and variance for each activity are computed.
14. Earliest starting times and latest finishing times are calculated.
15. Expected time earliest starting time and latest finishing times are marked on the network diagram.
16. Slack is calculated.
17. Critical path is identified and marked on the network diagram.
18. Subcritical Path are also identified.
19. Length of critical path or total project duration is found out.
20. Lastly, the probability that project will finish at due date is calculated.

Development of PERT

Project Managers increasingly noted that the techniques of Frederick, Taylor and Henery L. Gantt introduced during the early part of the century for large scale productions, were inapplicable for a large portion of the industrial effort. The work was being undertaken in the U.S.A., and in early 1958 the U.S. Navy Special Project. Office concerned with performance tends on large military development programs set up team of the management consulting firm of Booz, Allen and Hamilton ; to devise a means of dealing with the planning and subsequent control of complex work. This investigation was known as the Programme Evaluation Research Task, which gave rise to (or possible derived from) the code name PERT. By February 1958, Dr. C.E. Clark, mathematician in the PERT team presented the early notions of arrow-diagramming, military drawing from his study of graphics. This early work of Dr. Clark was rapidly published and by July 1958, the first report, PERT Summary Report, phase I, was published. By this time the full title of the work had become "Programme Evaluation and Review Technique", and the value of the technique seemed well established. By October, 1958, it was decided to apply PERT to the Fleet Ballistic Missiles Programme, where it was credited with saving two years in the development of Polaris Missile. Since that time PERT has spread rapidly through out the U.S. Defence and Space Industry. Currently almost every major Government and military agency concerned with space Age Programs is utilising the technique as large industrial contractor in this field. Small business wishing to participate in national defence programs have found it increasingly necessary to develop PERT capability.

Terminologies

Activity. A time consuming element occurring between two events and represented by an activity.

Activity
Start ————→ finish

1. The arrow is not to be drawn to the scale.
2. It may be curved, bent, horizontal or vertical.
3. Time values can be assigned to activities.
4. An activity may have zero time value.

Event. A meaningful accomplishment or 'mile stone' usually represented by small, circle or box in network.

— Activity start and finish points are events.

— Events have no time values.

Critical path. In network the path with smallest amount of positive slack or largest amount of negative slack. The most rigorous time constraint for this path $T_e = T_l$.

Slak or Float. Difference between last event time and early event time *i.e.* $Tl - Te$ = Float.

Negative slack. The amount of time which is not available to perform the series of activities in a particular slack path and still meet the required completion date.

Positive slack. The amount of additional time which is available to perform the series of activities in a particular slack path and still meet the required completion date.

Network. A flow plan containing the pertinent activities and events.

Dummy activity. An activity with no time value constraining the succeeding activity.

Estimation of activity duration

It is not always possible to estimate the duration of each activity accurately specially when a new project is undertaken. Since to start a network the determination of these durations is necessary, the following method is used—From the people who will be responsible for those activities or from the persons who have undertaken similar works in past, we obtain the following estimates for each activity—

(*i*) Pessimistic estimated time = b

(*ii*) Most likely estimate time = m

(*iii*) Optimistic estimate time = a

The early expected time for completion of activity is

$$Te = \frac{a + 4m + b}{6}$$

If we draw a histogram for frequencies, various estimates of activities against duration it will lead to a bell shape curve which is normal distribution curve.

Variance $= \left(\dfrac{b-a}{6}\right)^2$

$$Vt = \sigma 2$$

Deviation $\sigma = \dfrac{b-a}{6}$

$$= \sqrt{V}.$$

Te, Vt can be added up for variou activities to find out total early expected time *TE* and total variance *VT* for a Project, while standard deviation *σt* for activities cannot be added up to give total deviation.

TE = Early expected time for completion.

TL = Latest expected time for completion.

TS = Schedule time for completion.

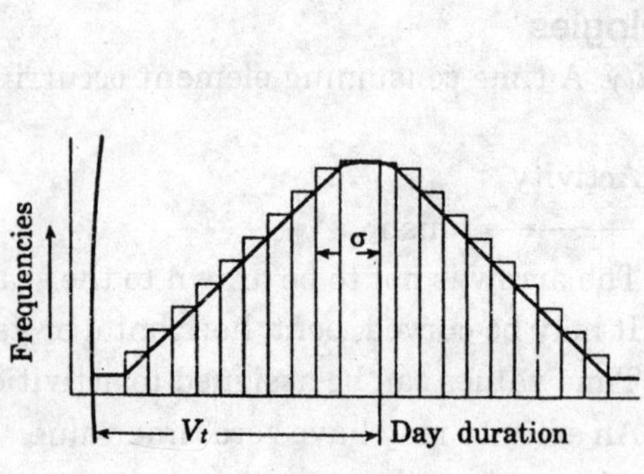

Fig. 54.1.

$$Z = \frac{T_S - T_e}{\sigma}$$

When $T_S = T_e + 3\sigma$ probability of completion is 99.7%

$T_S = T_e + 2\sigma$,, ,, ,, ,, ,, 95%

$T_S = T_e + \sigma$,, ,, ,, ,, 68%

$T_S = T_e$,, ,, ,, ,, 50%

Network Logic

To organise the activities into network, the following questions are asked concerning each activity :

(i) What activity must produce this one ?
(ii) What activity can be concurrent with this one ?
(iii) What activity must follow this one ?

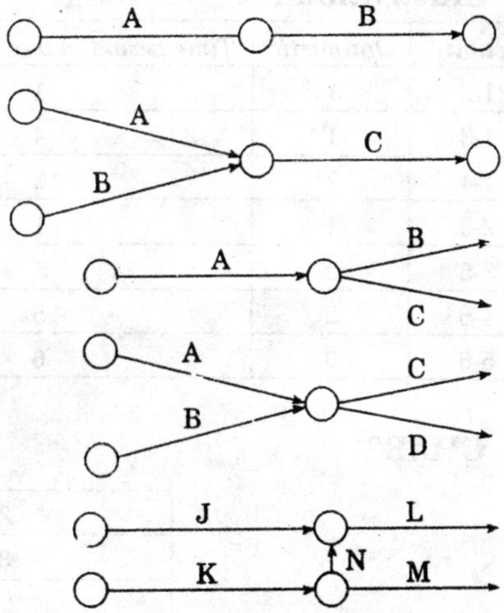

Examples

Activity *B* cannot start until activity *A* is completed.

Activity *C* can not start until both activities *A* and *B* are completed.

Activity *A* must be completed before either B or *C* started.

Both *A* and *B* must be completed before *C* or *D* or both can start.

Both *J* and *K* must be completed before *M* can start, *L* can start only on completion of *J* and is independent of *K*.

Fig. 54.2.

Dummy Activity

In network the activity *N* is dummy activity and always represented by broken arrow it always has zero time value and used only to describe logical connections.

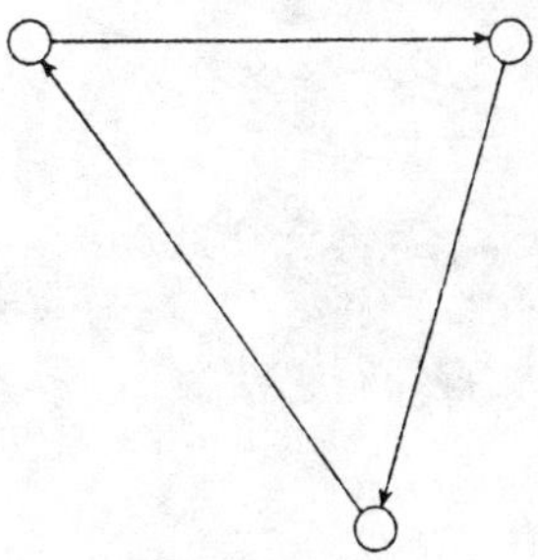

Fig. 54.3.

A loop should never occur in a network as shown in Fig. 54.3.

Float or Slack

The term slack is used with an event *i.e.* in case of PERT and float is used with reference to an activity *i.e.* in case of CPM. But still these terms are interchangeable. Float or slack means spare time, a margin of extra time over and above its duration which a non-critical activity can consume without delaying the project.

Let us find Earliest Start Time—The time at which an activity can start and worked out by moving from first to last event in the network. The earliest finished time is the earliest possible time at which an activity ends.

EFT = *EST*+Duration of the activity.

Latest Finish Time

It is worked out by moving backward from event 2 to event I.

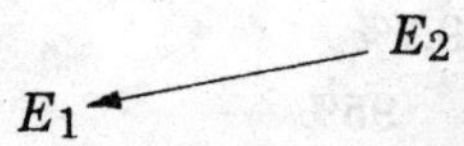

Similarly latest start time is the possible time by which an activity start

LST = *LFT*–Duration of an activity

Free Float = *(EST)* Tail Event– *(EST)* Head even– Activity time

Total Float = *(LFT–EET)*

or *(LST–EST)*

Procedure PERT Analysis

It can be understood in best way by solving illustration given below :

Illustration-I

Activity	*Optimistic*	*Time period in weeks most likely*	*Pessimistic*
1-2	1	1	7
1-3	1	4	7
1-4	2	2	8
2-5	1	1	1
3-5	2	5	14
4-6	2	5	8
5-6	3	6	15

CHART

Z	*Probability*
3	0.999
2.8	0.997
2.6	0.995
2.4	0.992
2.2	0.986
2.0	0.997
1.8	0.964
1.6	0.945
1.4	0.919
1.2	0.885
1.0	0.841
0.8	0.788
0.6	0.728
0.4	0.655
0.2	0.572
0.0	0.500
–0.2	0.421
–0.4	0.345
–1.0	0.159

Find the probability of its completion in 14 weeks

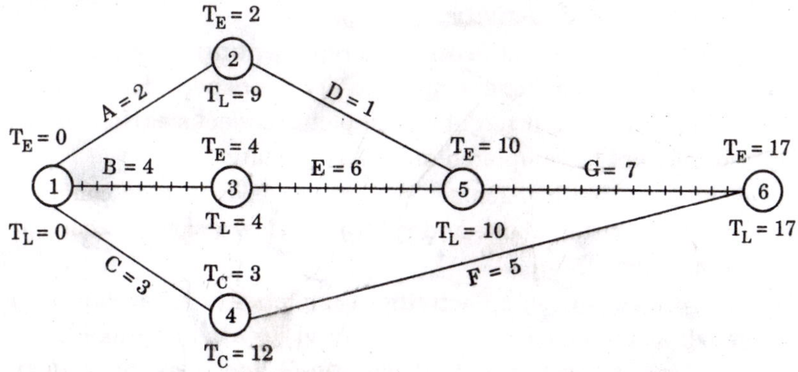

Fig. 54.4.

PERT Analysis of Product Development

Time data in weeks	*ACTIVITIES (Arrows)*						
	A	*B*	*C*	*D*	*E*	*F*	*G*
1. Activity time (*t*)	$\frac{1+4\times1+7}{6}$ $= 2$	$\frac{1+4\times4+7}{6}$ $= 4$	$\frac{2+4\times2+8}{6}$ $= 3$	$\frac{1+4\times1+1}{6}$ $= 1$	$\frac{2+4\times5+14}{6}$ $= 6$	$\frac{2+4\times5+8}{6}$ $= 5$	$\frac{3+4\times6+15}{6}$ = 7 *Total*
2. Expected variance (*U*)	$\left(\frac{7-1}{6}\right)^2$ $= 1$	$\left(\frac{7-1}{6}\right)$ $= 1$	$\left(\frac{8-2}{6}\right)^2$ $= 1$	$\left(\frac{1-1}{6}\right)^2$ $= 0$	$\left(\frac{14-2}{6}\right)^2$ $= 4$	$\left(\frac{8-2}{6}\right)^2$ $= 1$	$\left(\frac{15-3}{6}\right)^2$ $= 4$
3. Event (circled) shown by arrow	2	3	4	5	5	6	6
4. Shortest feasible route to the event	*A*	*B*	*C*	*B+E*	*B+E*	*B+E+G*	*B+E+G*
5. Earliest expected time *TE* (Based on shortest route)	2	4	3	10 (4+6)	10 (4+6)	17 (4+6+7)	17 (4+6+7)
6. Latest expected time *TL*	9	4	12	10	10	17	17
7. Slack time *(TL-TE)*	7	0	9	0	0	0	0
8. Critical path (zeroes)		*B*			*E*	*G*,	
9. Time of critical path		4			(4+6 = 10)	(4+6+7 = 17)	
10. Total variance of critical path *(TV)*		1			4	9	
11. Standard deviation (*TS*)						3	
12. Time schedule (*TS*)							14
13. Ratio : *(TS – TE)/σ* = (14 – 17)/3							1
14. Probability *P* of fulfilling schedule from chart							16

(1) Enter the estimated time *i.e.* optimistic time, pessimistic time and most likely times, required to complete each of the activities *A, B, C, D, E, F* and *G* as evaluated by the supervisor and managers concerned with each activity.

(2) Enter the expected variance in the estimate representing the most optimistic and most pessimistic possibilities envisioned. For example activity *B* is expected normally to be completed in 4 weeks, but with unusual 'luck' it might be completed 3 weeks earlier. Also by an unusual amount of bad luck it may not be completed until 3 weeks later.

(3) Show the event indicated by each activity arrow depending on constraints if any, the name of activity generally written above and its value below arrow or above arrow infront of Activity with equal mark. (See figure I).

(4) Find earliest expected time of an activities completion write it, above the event where that activity-completed. At the event where many activities are merging it is the longest path which is taken as *TE*. For example at event (5) activities *A* and *E* are merging giving two paths to event *i.e.*, A + D = 2 + 1 = 3 weeks and B + E = 4 + 6 = 10 weeks. As value of *B*+*E* is more it is the longest path and is taken as *Te* for event (5).

(5) Find the longest path for final event or adjective of the Project.

(6) The longest route for completion of a project is known as Earliest expected time *TE*. As we cannot delay this the earliest expected time for completion of the project and also the latest expected time *(TL)* in which the objective should be completed.

(7) Do the backward calculation to find out *TL* of various even starting from last event where *TE* = *TL* by subtracting the time of preceding activity or activities. When two or more activities are bursting out from an event the shortest route is taken as *TL*.

(8) Slack time is the difference between latest expected time (*TL*) and the earliest time (*TE*). For example for event (4) slack is 12 – 3 = 9 weeks. An activity with slack time is one that has extra resources, need not to meet the schedule of the program from over all view point. Sometimes these extra resources are revised or rescheduled to assist in shortening some of the more critical activities.

(9) Slack time value of zero for various events or activities leader or speaks of critical path which represent by activities *B, E, G.*

(10) Duration of critical path is 17 weeks represents the amount of time to be expected to complete the program if shortest route is used for latest expected time or longest route for earliest expected time.

(11) As a computational step, add individual variance associated with critical path only. Since this is the path that governs the expected time to complete the program.

$$VT = V_{B_t} + V_{E_t} + V_{G_t} = 1 + 4 + 4 = 9$$

(12) The standard deviation = $\sqrt{V_T} = \sqrt{9} = 3$

(13) Hence $$Z = \frac{T_S - T_E}{\sigma} = \frac{14 - 17}{3} = -1$$

Finding the value of probability from chart as 0.159 or 0.16 (Approx.) find the probability of completion of the project in 14 weeks is 16%.

Illustration-II

TABLE I

		Days		
S. No.	*Activity*	*to*	t_m	t_p
1	1—2	2	5	14
2	1—6	2	5	8
3	2—3	5	11	29
4	3—4	1	4	7
5	3—5	5	11	17
6	4—5	2	5	14
7	6—7	3	9	27
8	5—8	2	2	8
9	7—8	7	13	31

It is given that the scheduled date of completion of project is 38 days.

(1) Find out the probability that project can be completed at scheduled time.

(2) Find out the scheduled time for 94.5% probability of completion of the project.

(3) Find out the probability of completion of path 1-6, 7-8.

Solution. T_e = Expected time for each activity

$$= \left(\frac{t_o + 4t_m + t_p}{6}\right) \quad ...(1)$$

$$\text{Standard Deviation} = S_t = \left(\frac{t_p - t_o}{6}\right) \quad ...(2)$$

$$\text{Variance} = V_t = \left(\frac{t_p - t_o}{6}\right)^2 = (S_t)^2 \quad ...(3)$$

$$Z = \left(\frac{D - T_e}{S_t}\right) \quad ...(4)$$

Z = Probability that project will meet the schedule or due date.

T_E = Total project duration

D = Scheduled date = 38 (days) given.

Using formulae (1), (2) and (3) let us find out the value of t_e, S_t and V_t for various activities.

TABLE II

S. No.	*Activity*	t_e	S_t	V_t	*Critical Path*	*Total Variance on critical path*
1	1—2	6	2	4	—	4
2	1—6	5	1	1		
3	2—3	13	4	16	—	16
4	2—4	4	1	1		
5	3—5	11	2	4		4
6	4—5	6	2	4	—	
7	6—7	11	4	16		
8	5—8	3	1	1	—	1
9	7—8	15	4	16		25

Let us draw network diagram.

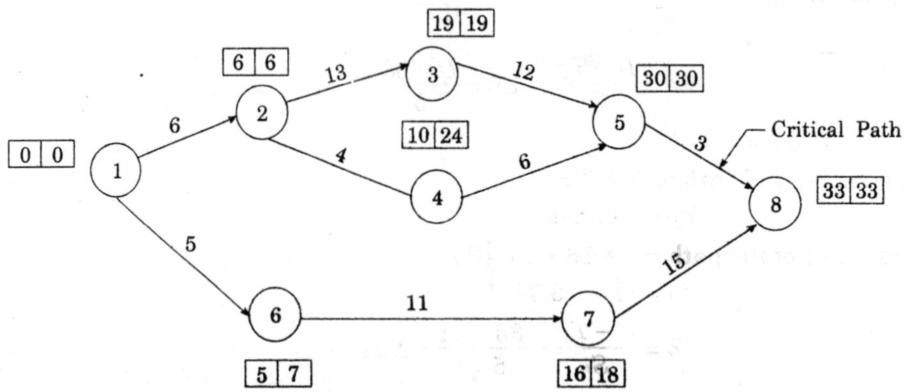

Fig. 54.5. On the Critical Path Total Stock is Zero.

Working out of *EST* and *LST* for the various activities as given in *Table I*.

TABLE III

S. No.	*Activity*	***EST***	***LST***	***Total Slack LST—EST***	***Activity on critical path***
1	1—2	0	0	0	—
2	1—6	0	2	2	
3	2—3	6	6	0	—
4	2—4	6	20	14	
5	3—5	19	19	0	
6	4—5	10	24	14	
7	6—7	5	7	2	—
8	5—8	30	30	0	
9	7—8	16	19	2	—

So critical path is 1-2–3-5-8

Project duration on critical path, we get

$$T_E = 6 + 13 + 11 + 3 = 33 \text{ days}$$

Total variance of critical path = 4 + 16 + 4 + 1 = 25

Total project duration = 33 days

D **= Scheduled date = 38 days**

$$Z = \frac{D - T_E}{S_t} \qquad ...(4)$$

$$t = \sqrt{variance\ of\ critical\ path} = \sqrt{25} = 5$$

Substituting the value of *D*, T_E and S_t, in equation.

$$Z = \frac{38 - 33}{4} = 1$$

After finding the value of Z, let us read table III we find that probability is 0.841. In other words there is a probability that project shall be completed in 38 days is 84.1%.

For the 94.5% probability of project being completed. Let us look at the value of Z for 0.945 value of probability.

So $$Z = 1.6$$

$$Z = \frac{D - T_E}{S_s} = 1.6 = \frac{D - 33}{5}$$

Thus $D = 41$ days

Assuming critical path as 1-6-7-8

$$T_E = 31 \text{ days}$$

Variance of the path = 1 + 16 + 16 = 33

$$S_t = \sqrt{33} = 5.74$$

$$Z = \frac{D - T_E}{S_t} = \frac{38 - 31}{5.74} = 1.22$$

Now given the value of $Z = 1.22$ and read table I, the probability of meeting the due date is 0.888 or 89.88%.

PROJECT SCHEDULING

The project management calls for a clean pronunciation of the end objectives. It can be analysed into various activities which must be performed, before the end objective is reached. The time estimates for various activities can be obtained and their status and relationship projected in the form of PERT network. The earliest expected time for the end of a project can be forecasted. If the earliest expected time for a project and latest allowable time is known, we can determine critical path on network, and subsequently the square network can be drawn which can be a guide to lead the activity to completion in a scheduled manner. The earliest expected time and latest allowable time for all events follow the normal distribution for any cause of variation.

The area under the curve of frequency distribution represents the probability of occurrence of the variable. The area of the curve between any two values X and X_1 represents the probability that any observation chosen at random from distribution will fall between the values Y and Y_1 of the variable as shown in Fig. 54.6.

When an event is on critical path, there is no slack. For an event to become critical the condition is,

$$Te = Tl$$

or $$Te - Tl = 0$$

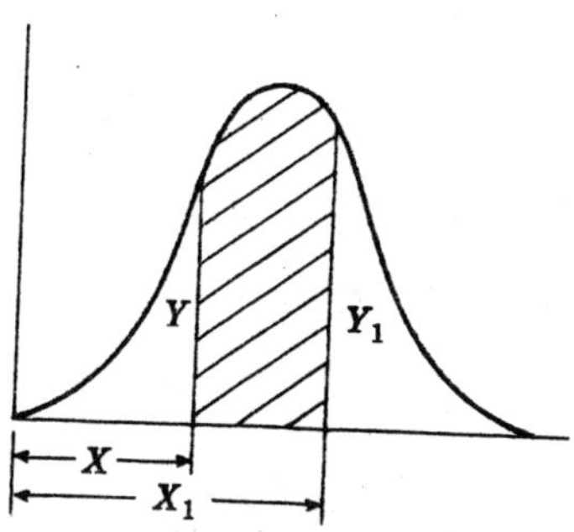

Fig. 54.6

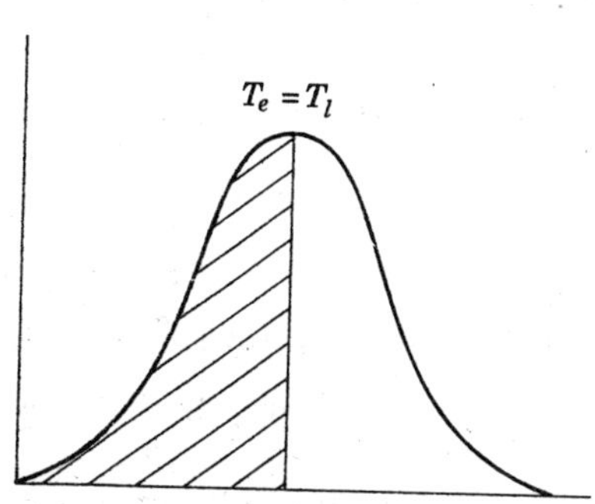

Fig. 54.7.

Probability of no Slack

The probability of no slack or probability of success for a critical event is 50—50 if $Tl = Te$. Te when taken as the peak of normal curve divides it exactly into two equal areas and the probability of no slack—represented by shaded area of the curve shown in Fig. 54.7.

When T_L is greater than T_E there are good reasons to expect that the project will be completed in schedule time, *i.e.* there would be more than 50% chances of its completion—Time T_E or the probability of project completing time in this would be more than 5. It will be how much more depends on how far Tl is located from Te on the distribution curve. The unshaded area of the curve to the right to T_L would indicate the probability of 'no slack' and thus will indicate uncertainties. Therefore, uncertainty in measurable term P is

$$P = \text{Probability of no slack} = \text{Area}$$

It can be physically seen that the programme has got positive slack when T_L is greater than T_E.

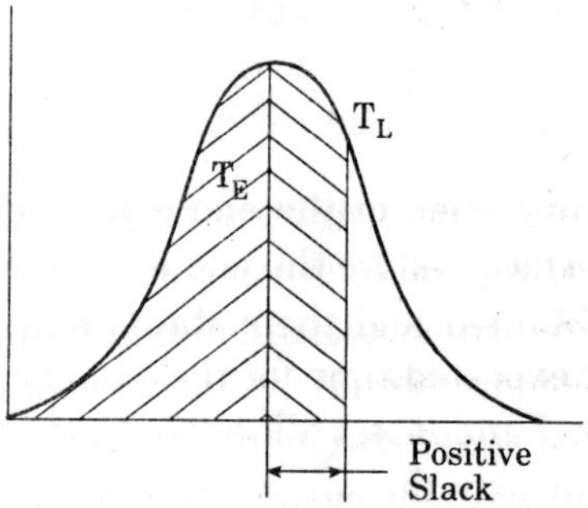

Fig. 54.8

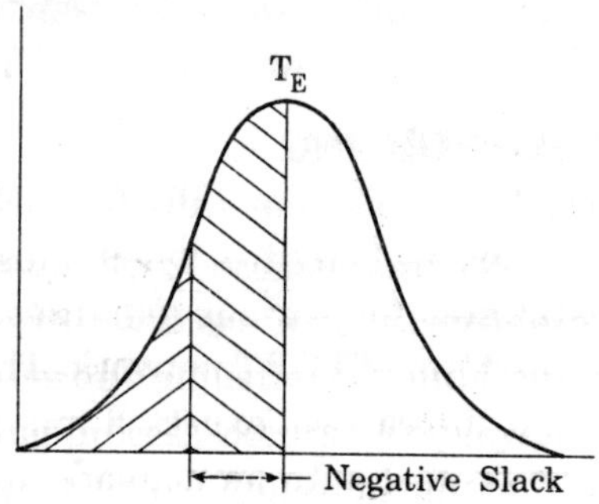

Fig. 54.9

When TL is less than TE, we similarly argue that the programme has negative slack, and probability of slack or uncertainly of reaching the objective in time will be more than 53. Therefore, probability of no slack or uncertainly (P) in this case is

$$P = \text{Area}\,\square + \text{Area} = 50 + \frac{(TL - TE)}{TE}$$

Gantt-Chart

In the Gantt chart horizontal bars are drawn for each activity in proportion to the time required for carrying out the activity drawn to the time scale. These bars represent time schedule and progress can be indicated by additional bars along side.

Thus the status of an activity can be observed by progress bar in comparison to schedule bar.

The Gantt chart indicates :

(*i*) What is to be done ?

(*ii*) What has been done ?

(*iii*) What should have been done ?

Gantt chart can be used for any number of activities.

A typical example of Gantt chart for several activities is shown in Fig. 54.10.

Limitation. It does not show the relationship between activities and their impact on project schedule.

PROGRESS REVIEW

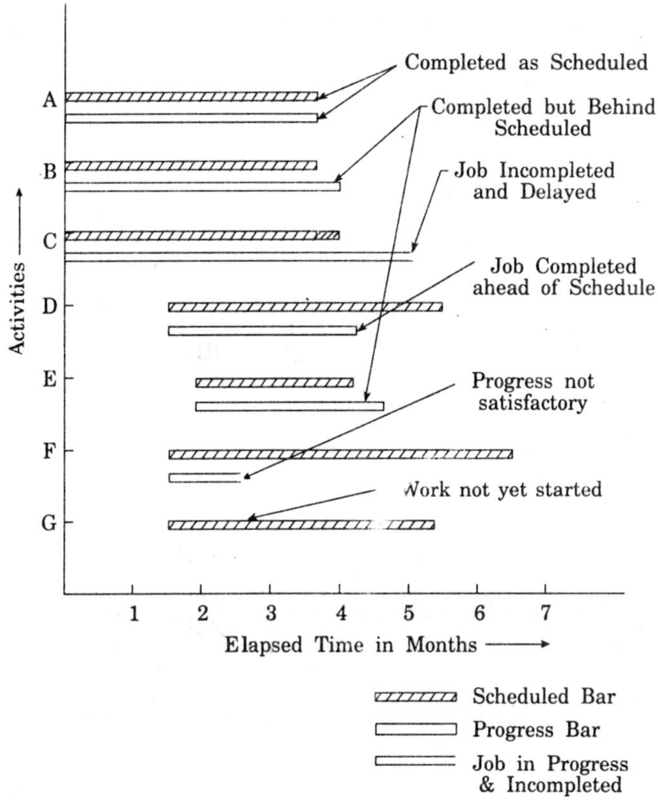

Fig. 54.10.

MATRIX METHOD

For complex projects involving more than two activities it is rather impossible to draw space network. To over come this difficulty the matrix method is used. In the activity oriented matrix

		A	B	C	D	E	F	G	H	I	J	K
	–	3	2	2								
	A				4							
	B					4	7					
	C							4				
	D								2			
	E									5		
	F										6	
	G										6	
	H											3
	I											3
	J											
	K											
(i)	T_E	3	2	2	7	6	9	6	94	11	15	14
(ii)	T_L	6	2	5	10	7	9	9	12	12	15	15
(iii)	S	3	0	3	3	1	0	3	3	1	0	1

Fig. 54.11.

method it is not necessary to space network. The inter-relationship and duration of activities is put directly in the form of a matrix as illustrated by an example.

Illustration III

Interdependency	*Activity*	*Duration*
A—D	A	3
B—E	B	2
B—F	C	2
C—G	D	4
G—J	E	4
F—J	F	7
E—I	G	4
I—K	H	2
D—H	I	5
	J	6
M—K	K	3

All the activities are written in columns as well as in rows in their order as shown in Fig. 54.11. In columns succeeding activities are written while in rows the preceding activities are written.

In column, the succeeding activity duration is written against its constraint indicated in row.

From the inter-relationship table we find that the first constraint is that *D* is dependent on *A*. The duration of *D* is 4. As such 4 is inserted under the column of *D* against row of *A*. This way the body of matrix is filled up. After transforming all relationship into matrix it will be observed that no entry is made under column heads *A, B* and *C*. This is because *A, B* and *C* are independent activities. Thus the values of *A, B* and *C* are inserted under column heads *A, B* and *C* against a blank row which means *A, B* and *C* are preceded by nothing. Similarly there is no insertion against row heads *J* and *K* which means that *J* and *K* are succeeded by nothing.

Under the principle that an activity cannot begin until all activities precedent to it in its sequence have been completed. It is easy enough to calculate *Te* values for each activity as inserted in row (1) at the bottom of matrix. Activities *A, B* and *C* are preceded by nothing (they are initial activities). So their *TE* values are equal to their respective durations assuming of course they start at zero time. Since *D* is precedent by *A, TE* of *D* is equal to *TE* of *A* plus duration of *D* in row (*O*). The procedure is followed column headwise from 1st to last activity. One point has to be kept in mind, when a certain activity is precedent by more than one activity the *TE* value for all the path have to be calculated and larger value retained. As in this matrix, activity *J* is preceded by *F* and *G, TE* for *F* and *G* are 9 and 6 respectively. The larger value 9 is retained and hence *TE* for *J* is 9 + 6 = 15.

The largest value obtained in the forward pass computation is 15 which is project duration. Hence project can be planned for completion is not less than 15 units time. If the objective is to allow no slippage in project duration from its early finish time, then the maximum value as obtained in row (*I*) in the matrix is also the latest finish time for final activity.

Whereas the *TE* is calculated and forward path starting from *A* to *K* column headwise. The *TL* is calculated as backward path from bottom to top row headwise. This is because only *TL* known for at the moment of calculation is of activity *J* which is 15. It is necessary to obtain the remaining *TL* of other activities by considering preceding activities. For example activity *I* preceds *K*. *K* being last activity, precedes nothing must have *TL* = 15. Therefore, *TL* for *I* must be equal to *TL* for *K* minus its duration, *i.e.* 15 – 3 = 12. Hence *TL* = 12 for *I* activity the process is continued until all the values are inserted in row (*II*) below matrix. As in case of forward path in backward pass also we have to be careful when we come across a situation where more than one activities are successors to a single activity *e.g.* activity *B* is succeeded by *E* and *F*. We have to calculate both the values of *TL* for *B* and take the lower value.

Finally in row (*III*) the slack *S* is completed as under :

$$S = TL - TE \text{ for each activity.}$$

Advantages

(*i*) Drawing a network for bigger project by trial and error method is quite laborious and time consuming. The matrix method obviates all these troubles and gives relevant data of basic scheduling computations mechanically.

(*ii*) It is a better trial for implementation of changes in activities duration and effective project control and review.

However, the value of having a well drawn network of a project in understanding the relationship and dependency of activities should not be under-estimated.

Squared-Network

Gantt chart represents activities in time scale but do not establish inter-relationship between various activities while space network establishes inter-relationship between activities but do not take time scale into consideration. A combination of these two is developed into the form of a Square Network.

Square Network indicates the inter-relationship of activities of space network and also mark event to the time scale.

Preparation of Square Network

(*i*) Determine the project duration from space network.

(*ii*) Layout the critical path in straight line against time scale on chart.

(*iii*) Develop secondary paths above and below critical path, showing constraints as vertical broken lines show direction of dummies.

(*iv*) Make all bars equivalent in length to their activity duration and indicate slack by broken line.

(*v*) Schedule all activities for their earliest start time or latest completion time as the need may be.

Advantages

(*i*) It facilitates the review of progress of various activities from time to time.

(*ii*) It is a better tool for reporting progress against schedule to the management.

(*iii*) It affords for suitable adjustments of activity bar with the slack duration to meet schedule and manpower loading considerations.

(*iv*) It helps in resources levelling.

Illustration II is drawn here on square network as given in Fig. 54.12.

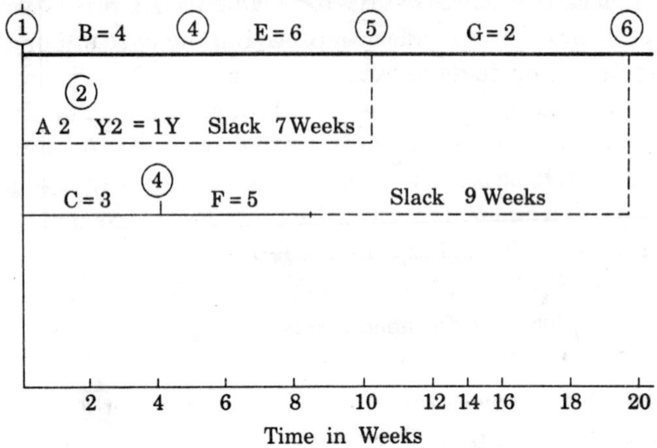

Fig. 54.12.

Cost Concept of PERT

PERT tells us to achieve the committed objectives in best possible manner and also in the least possible cost and time. To effect this, the management must know that :

(*i*) What is required to be done ?

(*ii*) Schedule time required.

(*iii*) The estimated cost.

PERT provides a dynamic total for the execution of a programme and for developing a technique to control time and cost of achievement. The following functions are required to be carried out :

1. To make a budget of expenditure for given time schedule.
2. To assess the increase or decrease of cost in relation to decrease or increase in time.
3. To arrive at optimum cost.
4. To draw expenditure plan against time.
5. To review the progress in terms of expenditure incurred and time spent.

The cost or expenses to be incurred in the performance of an activity is divided into two sub-heads :

1. **Direct Cost.** The cost incurred in compressing the activity completion time. Each of the activity in network can be performed in a shorter time than early expected time by providing additional resources. The resources can be evaluated in terms of money or cost. Direct cost has the tendency to increase with decrease in time.

2. **Indirect Cost.** All overheads such as interest on capital, rent for various equipments, cost of supervision cost of storing materials etc. comes under indirect cost. It has the tendency to reduce with the reduction in time of an activity. Direct cost of indirect cost cannot be zero at any time.

Total Cost. It is the sum of direct and indirect costs and it can also be plotted against activity time. From graph shown in Fig. 54.14.

The project duration time X, both direct and indirect costs are equal to Y and, therefore, the total cost of project is $2Y$ which may or may not be minimum cost. If an activity span is reduced, the direct cost increases. If we plot cost vursus duration on a graph we will find a point where the further crushing of activity is not possible irrespective of the amount of resources applied. This cost is known as crash cost and denoted by C_c.

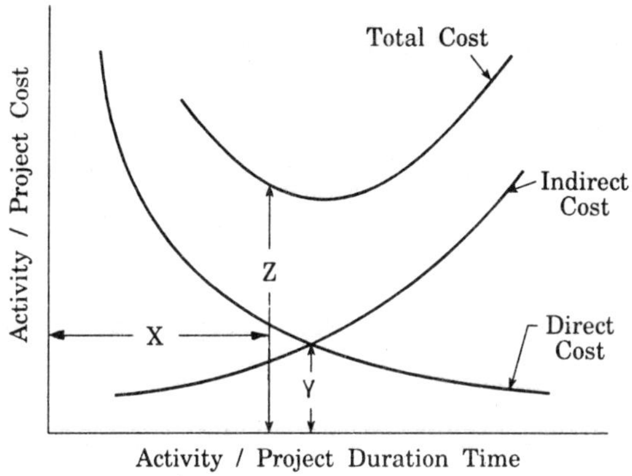

Fig. 54.14.

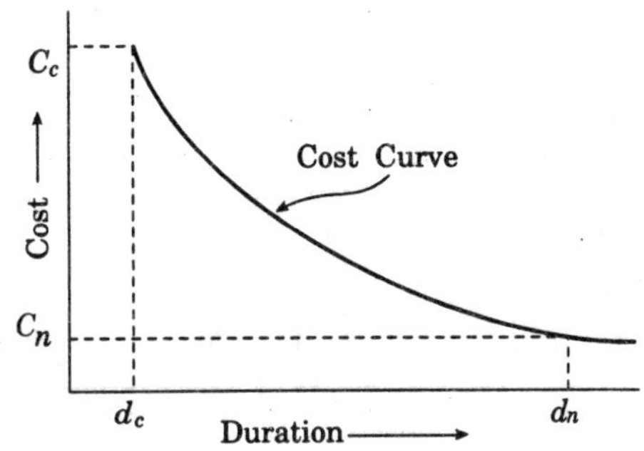

Fig. 54.15.

Crash duration

It is the minimum possible duration of an activity which cannot be reduced any more irrespective of resources applied.

Crash Cost

The minimum cost incurred for crash duration.

Cost Slope

$$\text{Cost slope} = \frac{C_c - C_n}{d_n - d_c}$$

where C_c = Crash cost

C_n = Normal cost

d_n = Normal duration

d_c = Crash duration.

Illustration IV

Activity	*Normal time*	*Crash time*	*Normal cost*	*Crash cost*	*Cost slope*
1-2	10	7	400	640	80
1-3	19	11	600	1160	70
2-3	10	8	500	600	50
2-4	19	15	700	1000	75
3-4	10	4	300	810	85
Total			2500	4210	

Analyse the feasibility of cost reduction for 22 days.

1. Find out critical path for the project which comes as (1-2), (2-3) and (3-4) the cost slope for these are Rs. 80, 50, 85 respectively.

From cost slope are find that activity (3-3) is having minimum cost slope of Rs. 50/- on critical path. It is also evident from the graph that in order to crash activity (2-3) by one day we have to crash either of the activities (1-3) or (2-4) along this activity. The cost of crashing two activities will definitely be more than activity (1-2) alone which is higher only two activity (2-3).

Hence minimum crashing cost for 1 day crashing the activity (1-2)

= Rs. 80.00

Hence crash cost for 29 days = Normal cost + cost slope

= 2500 + 80

= 2580 ...(*i*)

Redraw the square network again for 29 days it is clear that activity (3-4) is most economical to crash.

Hence crashing cost for one more day it is clear that activity (3-4) by a day is

= 85

Hence crash cost for 28 days = 2500 + 85 = 2665 ...(*ii*)

Again redraw new square network basis on 28 days duration.

It is clear that for further crashing of critical path means crashing of more than one activity at a time. The possible ways of further crashing are—

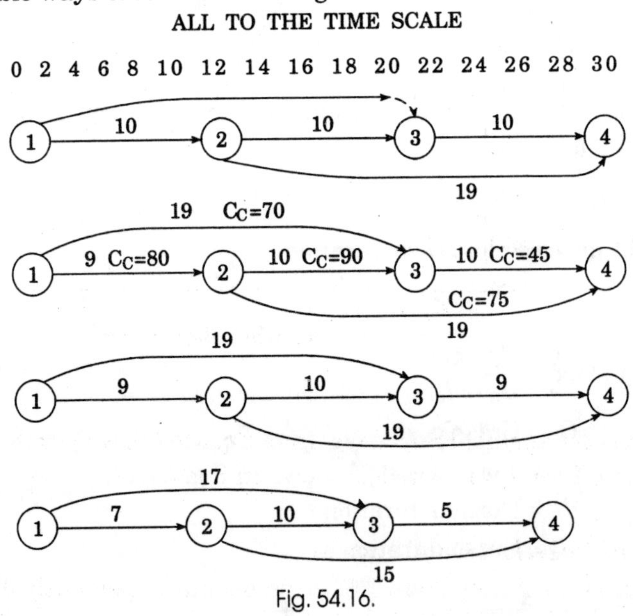

Fig. 54.16.

Crashing activity	*Total crash cost per day*
(1-2) and (1-3)	80 + 70 = 150 ...(*i*)
(1-3) and (2-3) and (2-4)	70 + 50 + 75 = 195 ...(*ii*)
(3-4) and (2-4)	85 + 75 = 160 ...(*iii*)

Proposal (*i*) is most economical. Activity (1-2) can be crashed further only by 2 more days. Hence combination (*i*) can be crashed maximum for 2 days.

Crashing cost for 2 more days = 2 × 150 = 300

Crash cost for 28 days = 2665 + 300 = 2965 ...(*iii*)

Further 4 days crashing can be done by adopting proposal (*ii*) which is 2nd most economical.

Hence crashing cost for 4 more days = 4 × 160 = 640

Crash cost for 22 days = 2965 + 640 = 3605 ...(*iv*)

We also know that for 30 days normal schedule the normal cost is 2500.

COST SLOPE

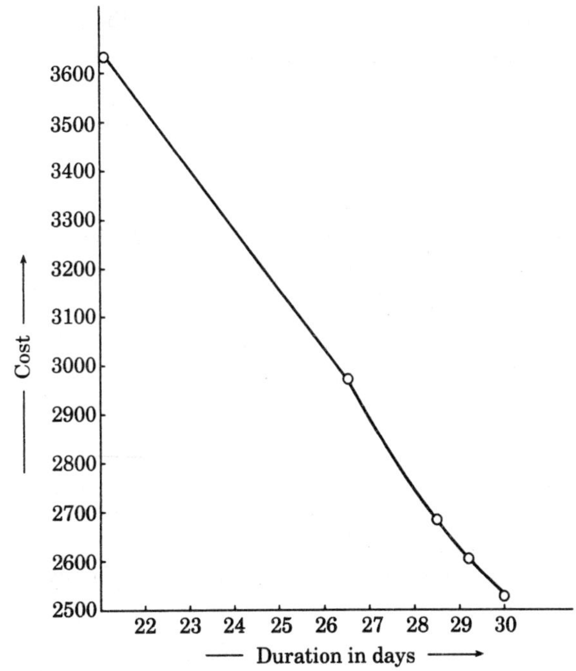

Fig. 54.17.

Plotting the crash cost against crash days (from Eq. *i* to *iv*), we get the feasibility curve for cost reduction in most efficient way which is shown in Fig. 54.17.

Basic Concept of Network Cost System

The basic concept of the PERT and CPM is simple but importantly different from that of most accounting systems. In PERT/ Cost, individual activities or groups of activities from the micro cost centres for accounting (and therefore management control) purpose, rather than organisational units (Divisions, departments, sections and so forth). Under PERT or CPM management system, project manager, sub-managers or ordinarily are chosen for supervising individual activities or group activities. Since they are responsible for seeing that activities are completed on schedule, it is argued that they should be responsible for controllable costs associated with activities.

Costs under PERT/Cost system are more easily detected and corrective active are taken more readily.

Analysis and Control of Project Cost

Basic to most cost control systems is a procedure for comparing actual costs with budgeted costs. The PERT/Cost system not only permit such comparison but because of its integration with project scheduling procedures, also provides a mean of comparing work scheduled with work accomplished. The resulting cost and scheduled information allows project managers at both top and intermediate organisational levels to detect problem area and pin point their sources much readily than would be possible with conventional methods of costing.

The costs should be coded according to the net work activities. The cost data should be collected in such a way as to be useful for pay roll and other accounting purpose.

At the same time as costs are reported, an estimate should be made of the percentage of work accomplished. The percentage of cost incurred should match with the percentage of work accomplished.

Human Relations and PERT

It is clear that it is not necessary to be a mathematician to know PERT. The concept of part is to outline the various activities required to be formed, and make an analytical approach to objective achievement. Every activity is done by a group of people. Therefore if every person to whatever group he may belong forms an important parts of the plan. The link relationship of various activities and their effect on final objective, once understood by the participants, will ensure their active participants. Participation will and enthusiasm in plan ensure success.

PERT and Top Management

PERT is management by objective, and is a top management oriented scheme, with help of PERT/GPM top management combining the projects completion time as early as possible with maximum economy. It can do everything for them, starting from making schedules, and forecasting success to cost control and even can pretell failure and can reason out where it has failed, why it has failed, or how it has failed. It can pin point responsibilities. It can be used for any project.

Even when projects are less complete, and technological break through less frequent it is difficult to look fair enough into future to determine whether the progress to date is sufficient to meet the schedule and carry all details of the project always in mind. The management would seek knowledge of some method by which they can assess probabilities, delays and failures. Problems must be recognised advance and either eliminated or planned for. PERT/CPM would need care and attention and patronage to keep it trim and effective. PERT/CPM without top management understanding and support is not worth the attempts.

Management at other levels of control

PERT at best is a mean to an end and not an end itself. It is the person applying it who would get the maximum benefit by way of reducing his efforts to minimum, and he should be enthusiastic in its application. It is not meant to be imposed. Top management, middle management and direct supervisors all have to be assigned clear responsibilities, and can have a separate net work for themselves to follow. This net work, of course, is a part of the entire plan.

PERT planner and PERT Cell

The PERT cell should be created for future planning. Assessment of activities required to be performed should be entrusted to members of PERT cell. The drawing of network, keeping various combinations of circumstances in view, their calculation part should be left to PERT planner. He should high light important activities in the plan. It is his responsibility to keep PERT dynamic and uptodate.

Progress Review

As the work on project progresses, the PERT planner must keep the programme in constant review. Data should be collected by him directly from those who are responsible for executing the activities. Any activity no longer required should be deleted, and any activity that may become necessary should be added to the plan without hesitation. The plan is evolutionary. It is an argumentative and logical approach, and never originally low. By accepting flexibility of your plan you can lead to success and always adjust to circumstances to resources and to unseeing without giving any chance for failure. PERT should be dynamic in nature.

Replanning

Review and replanning are the corner stones of PERT programming. No labour saving should be thought of when any replanning is to be made. A PERT planner should not hesitate to replan the whole thin if require, and it is then that it becomes an assistance to the executive staff. Many a failure to achieve desired results from PERT are due to PERT planner at times being led away to dictate the plan and avoid labour required for any necessary modification. Any activity requiring re-estimating or rescheduling to care for any programme delays should be readily undertaken.

Data Processing

The effect of various combinations of circumstances should be studied and analysed and their impact on the project to produce optimum results within the stipulated time. The PERT planner can help the management in decision-making, by providing the pros and cons of various combinations. The data regarding progress, resources consumed, on unforeseens to be used in most effective way. They should be reflected in a net work in a simple and facts representative way. If the solutions with increased number of activities and more data to be processed, electronic data processing machines are to be used.

Personal Touch

Though PERT is a management oriented scheme the PERT planner should keep himself personal touch with first level supervisors and should always be keen to learn their difficulties, if any. This contact should not be for finding the faults and pinpointing the failures and shortcomings, but it should be aimed at finding how these could be avoided, by passed, eliminated, solved or faced.

Project Scheduling without Limited Resources

Until now we assumed that the only constraints for an activity to start and finish are of technological nature. The second equally important assumption made is that of unlimited resources. But in practice most of the managers are faced with the problem of relatively fixed manpower availability, a certain number of machines, or places of equipments and considering money as resource—a limited budget. Jobs which occur on parallel path may complete for the same resources, and even through procedure constraints would not prevent their being scheduled simultaneously, a limited supply of resources might force them to be scheduled sequentially. Heuristic, programs for resources scheduling usually take following two forms :

1. **Resource levelling program.** These attempt to reduce peak resource requirements and smooth out period to period assignments, within a constraint on project duration.

2. **Resource allocation program.** These allocate available resources to project activities in an attempt to find out the shortest project schedule consistent with fixed resource limits.

Resource Levelling Program

In some project situations resources can be acquired or released in practically any desired amounts if one is willing to pay the expenses involved in changing resource levels, such as cost of hiring, training, and so on. It is usually prudant, however to maintain relatively stable employment levels and to utilize resources at a more constant rate. In such situation resources levelling program are of most appropriate nature.

In this method the activity slack is used as a means of smoothening peack resource requirements. Start with calculating early start schedule for project and then plotting a resource loading chart for the schedule. In Fig. 54.18 (*a*) the projects early start schedule graph gives rise to the resource loading chart shown in Fig. 54.18 (*b*) (The number above each arrow represents its resources requirement in number of man, and since each activity has a different requirement, this number can be used to identify the activity as well).

The peak requirement of 24 men comes on 3rd day when job, 7, 8 and 9 all are activated in early start time. Both 7 and 8 are having slack of 2 and 7 days respectively so these jobs can be delayed upto that slack period without effecting the project schedule. Job 7 is on critical path so it seems reasonable to examine the possibility of moving the other jobs. Since job has the most slack, and could be easily postponed beyond the peak beriod of 3 days and it will be of use to full up the low point on loading cart from 8th day to 11th day. Such a move will result Fig. 54.18 (*b*).

The man power loading chart has been smoothened considerably and for further improvement days 3 and 4 are peak days now and of the two jobs active on these days only job 8 has slack if we delay job 8 by its full amount of slack, we obtain the result in graph Fig. 54.18 (*c*).

The peak period now occur days 1 and 2, spannal by job 3, 4 and 6. Job 6 is critical but both 3 and 4 are having slack of 2 days each. The best results are obtained by delaying job 3 as shown in Fig. 54.18 (*d*).

In the example given above it is ideal giving completely flat manpower loading chart. But in real practice it is difficult to achieve, the approach taken in this example can be used in real projects.

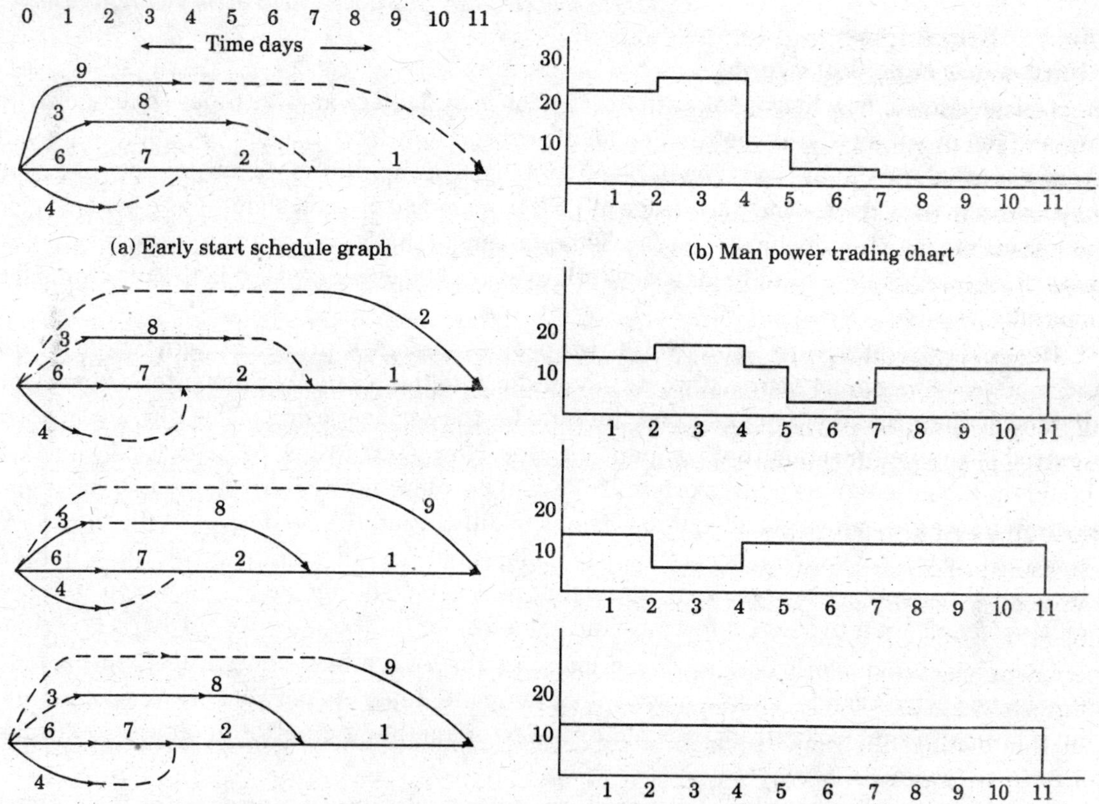

Fig. 54.18

GUIDELINES FOR THE USE OF PERT

As every new technique for area of human endeavour makes its appearance, there always arises a certain amount of specialised technology. This generally comes about because it is easier to generate new works than to use old ones and perhaps because it enable those who first came on the scene to make others think something magical of difficult.

PERT is no exception to this phenomenon. Enough PERT jargon can be developed to confuse and score many people. However, PERT especially basic PERT is really an easy concept to understand. Knowledge about PERT is picked up quite rapidly, but of course, real skill in Perting comes only with experience. One cannot know how to PERT a job well with all the necessary trade off and replanning that are involved—unless one has had actual practice in the application of this technique.

Normally the question comes in mind, where PERT can be used whether it is better on small jobs or big jobs. The answer is that there is no restriction on the size of the project. The greatest benefit from PERT when you have kept the networks simple that in no case should net works be linked, unless they are needed for reproduction purpose in a proposal. It is possible to do some of the calculations in PERT by hand. One may have monography to use on some occasions. As experience in PERT grows, it is possible to make these calculations rapidly. However, it does get to be being part of the job. In general, hand calculations are not used unless there is an emergency or the network is so small that it is wasteful to get to the machine.

Network can Hold 300 Events

The question of how long it takes to PERT a job is difficult to answer unless one knows the depth of the planning that is required on an average, it may be two hours per 100 events with about one of the two, hours spent on decision making. This applies to the initial network when those participating have some knowledge of PERT. A perting session should, as a general rule, not last over three or four hours in one day. This is about all that a group can do without becoming slopy. Besides, this time-limit holds a network to about 300 events, which is the recommended size when possible.

It is best to get back with an analysis to the people making plan on more than two days later and preferably within 24 hours. If we do not get back to them rapidly their interest generally diminishes their confidence wanes, and the time for the decision passes. The amount of detail required is another question that frequently arises. How shall a work content, or short a time should the activities on the networks have ? We can consider that we have planned to the proper depth when we are able to get adequate warning of difficulties that will occur in the future. We should go into whatever detail is necessary to understand the full significance of the activity. If the detail is excessive, however, we will find that we are not getting a true prediction. The only real way to find out it to PERT a few jobs and get a feel for it. There are no hard and fast rules.

One point often overlooked by those learning the PERT technique is that the activity between two events can be broken down into a complete, separate network. If we spot an area that is critical or that looks strange for some reasons or another it is better to separate networks for it.

As far as the minimum time is concerned, it is better to use weeks than days ; but sometimes, when trouble is really at hand using days may be necessary. We must remember that a number of people working a short time get paid as much as few people working for a long time.

Factors should be Considered before Implementing PERT

Engineering department often gets committed to release job on a specific date and must release it regardless of the need for total release by the manufacturing groups. PERT planning has greatly increased understanding between engineering and manufacturing. As long as the manufacturing people understand the overall sequence of release, it does not bother them. They no longer scream for engineering to release unless we are really at fault. Better understanding and better relations with manufacturer save money and keep the inventory low.

1. **Top Management Support.** Following factors should be taken into consideration before impementation of PERT. In the implementation of a PERT system the top management support is in use. However, by support we mean encouragement and not comments. Arbitrary imposition of PERT will hinder its eventual acceptance. This is true even though resistance to PERT is now weaker that is used to be. In fact, PERT is coming into such widespread use that people are becoming afraid not to use it.

2. **Adopt PERT to local requirements.** Requirement of every plant is different, and each has its own peculiar organization. The people are different, the business are different, and the PERT needs are also different.

3. **Replan when necessary.** The basic feature of the PERT technique is that replanning is inherent. We first plan the project ideally and then make the necessary changes to get within the prescribed schedule limitations. There have been instances in which PERT systems have been set up where the plans required formal alteration, notices and formal meetings to get them changed. Such procedures are considered to be too rigid and time-consuming and are generally bad practice. If at any time new difficulties arise which call for a change in the PERT planning, we should make the change and start from the new position.

With PERT we are taking advantage of the law of probability. Even though one event might be missed, we can very well pick up the another one, and if we do not, we can replan later event.

On the other hand, it is something overlooked that replanning in PERT inherently increases the risk of not meeting a schedule. The first plan and the first time estimates for a job usually are found to be best. West should not change the estimates once they are made unless the plane are changed. However, in planning alternative, we must be sure to consider the increase in risk that follows.

4. **Leave room for expansion.** When we set up a PERT system, we must be sure to set it up so that it can grow and expand as time processes. We cannot install a PERT system with high calibre people and then leave it for lower-level people to operate. We should always have some knowledgeable individual working with PERT and adapting it to newer requirements. Moreover, the system should not be frozen after it gets working properly. When installing it, we should indicate to the users that it will change from time to time. Like all systems, PERT should be flexible and changed to meet too needs of the users when this is desirable and necessary.

5. **Establish PERT on a permanent basis.** To use PERT just to keep the customer happy is like keeping the front parlor locked up for use only when visitors come.

6. **Do not force formal reporting.** We have for a long time steadily maintained that PERT is basically a planning tool which will report what we want it to. In implementing a PERT operation, some may find that only way the work to be planned and do not want any formal reporting back to management. This as it should (not force formal reporting into) be. We should not force formal reporting to a PERT system unless there is a real need for it. When reports are necessary, they should be geared to the information requirements of each level involved.

Much of the successes of PERT has been attributed to the fact that it just does not take the information, chew it up, and send it back and pretend and as if it were something new. PERT adds new information.

7. **Don't use Inaccurate Estimates.** We can depend to PERT as easily as we can to any other system. But if we will only be wasting time and money. There have been cases where PERT groups should not be fed superfluous data for part of a job. This is obvious when the whole job is analysed. Excessively long estimates will show up on the critical path. There is nothing wrong about being on the critical path, somebody has to be there. However, if we show up there all the time, there is usually something wrong. The effect of safe estimate is to force management to take increased risks in other areas. Being accurate with PERT estimates pays off.

8. **Don't add estimates first.** In planning a project with PERT we should first plan the network and then add time estimates. These should be made at random. If we start estimating at one end of the network and workout our way through, we will probably pick up the possible critical paths and shorten the estimates on these paths. The randomizing of the time estimates eliminates this difficulty.

9. **Don't demand commitments.** One point which cannot be ever-stressed is that we must be sure to separate or estimates from our commitments. An estimate is an estimate and not a commitment. We should use commitments only when absolutely necessary. We must realise that a man is exercising his best judgment, then he gives us estimates, and we should not force him to a commitment. If we, do we will get longer estimate the next time.

10. **Don't plan with overtime.** When planning with PERT the first time through, estimates should be based on a normal work week, and overtime should be saved for schedule completion when needed. Otherwise the method of shortening the schedule is lost later on when it is needed for handling trouble spots.

11. **Don't standardize event titles.** One other pitfall to avoid is standardizing event titles. We all agree that standradization is necessary for many facts of our work. In PERT, however, standardization of event titles tends to slow planning and cause confusion. We found that the people doing the planning spent more time deciding on which event title should be used than they did not plan. While doing the work call the events what they wished. This works out very well because then it was part of their work.

12. **Resource Allocation Program.** The resources scheduling problem is not only one of smoothing requirements but it is also one of allocating resources that are available only in fixed or relatively fixed amounts, the manager may have a limited staff of skilled design Engineers or other difficult to replace, skilled personnel of there may be some fixed number of certain machinery or pieces of equipments or perhaps some construction material can be obtained only at a limited rate. Frequently too, there are budget restrictions. Even if resources could readily be purchased in unlimited quantities the funds to do so may be limited to certain monthly allowances. As a result, activities can be scheduled only as necessary resources become available, even if the effect is to delay the project completion date.

To achieve it, we have to remove the constraint of a fixed due date and push down. If the limits are rather confirming, it is likely that many jobs will be squeezed to the right on schedule chart, delaying the project due date. In resource allocation we cannot have constraints both on resources limits and on project due date.

Problems in Critical Path Analysis

Ordinarily critical path scheduling techniques do not take explicit account of job resources requirements or of possible limitations on resource availability. Implicitly, it is assumed that only constraints on the start time of a job are technological, *i.e.* a job can be started as soon as its predecessors have been completed. The schedules for early start time and latest start time are established and any job on non-critical path can be delayed upto its total slack period without delaying finish date of project.

Slack in a Limited Resource Schedule

1. The slack concept, though modified, may still be used and retain its utility as a measure of flexibility in a project schedule.
2. Slack is dependent upon both procedure orderings and resource availability.
3. In general resource limitations reduce the amount of slack in a schedule.
4. Since, in general, the early and late start schedules are not unique, so the set of slack valves for a project is not unique. Slack is conditional upon the scheduling rules for creating early start and late start schedules.
5. While a critical parts of technologically connected jobs does not always exist in a limited resource schedule, under certain conditions a critical sequence of slackless jobs which span the length of the project can be identified. The jobs are continuous in time, if not in predecessor successor relationship.

55

Marketing and Channels of Distribution

Introduction

The word market has been derived from Latin word 'Marcatus' which refers to place of trade or a place where business is carried out. Marketing has two fold meaning, *i.e.*, in the traditional sense and in modern sense. Traditionally, "*marketing consists of those efforts which effect transfers in ownership of goods and care for their physical distribution.*"

In the modern times of large scale production and cut-throat competition, the concept of marketing has altogether changed. It has occupied wide proportions. Markets are no longer local, but have become national and international in character. The field of marketing is being rapidly transformed into a much broader and more significant field in recent years. In the past marketing was often referred to simply as "selling." Today the nature and scope of marketing have widened. Marketing is no longer considered to be the same thing as selling or advertising. It is viewed in a broader context comprising several other elements besides 'selling' and 'advertising.'

Marketing involves all efforts to create customers for the product and to maintain them permanently. According to this concept the main aim of marketing is to provide maximum satisfaction to consumers. Consumer is the focal point in modern concept of marketing. *"If marketing is at all important, it is because it is directed towards the satisfaction of consumer and in this context, the consumer is the attraction for which marketing is carried out".* The decision of the consumer makes and unmakes the manufacturers, jobbers and retailers, whoever wins the confidence of the consumer wins the day; and whoever loses it, is lost." It can be said that modern concept of marketing clusters around the consumer. The firm's main objective then becomes to satisfy its customers through the constant study of their changing needs and wants.

Concept

In common usage the word 'market' refers to a place where goods are purchased and sold. In simple words, it refers to a place where actual buyers and sellers meet to effect purchases and sales. The term 'market' does not only mean a particular place where goods are bought and sold but the whole of any region in which buyers and sellers purchase and sell. It should be clearly understood here that the word 'market' does not refer to any particular geographical meeting place of buyers and sellers but as the getting together of buyers and sellers in person, by mail, telephone or other means of communication. 'Market' is not essentially concentrated at one particular point, it can scatter throughout the region. In order to understand the term clearly, a few definitions are given below :

Marketing is a centre about which or are area in which, the forces leading to exchanges of title to a particular product operate towards which and from which actual goods tend to travel."

"Market means any body of persons who are in intimate business relations and carry on extensive transactions in any commodity."

The 'market' does not necessarily mean a place. It is the sum total of the situation or environment in which the resources, activities and attitudes of buyers and sellers affect the demand for products in a given area. In simple words, marketing is a process which carries goods from producer to ultimate consumer. Marketing bridges the gap between consumer and producer. It is in this sense that marketing has been defined as "all the activities involved in the creation of place, time and possession utilities'. Marketing is thus concerned with handling and transportation of goods from the point of production to the point of consumption. In this process of carrying the goods from the place of production to the place of consumption, many hindrances have to be removed. Marketing involves three types of utilities' *viz.*

(A) **Place utility.** Goods are to be taken from the place of their origin or production to the place where they are needed.

(B) **Time utility.** Goods are to be made available at the time when they are needed by the consumers. It means that they are to be stored and protected against the risks of fire, rain, pests etc.

(C) **Possession utility.** The ownerships and possession of these goods are to be transferred from the producer to the ultimate consumer.

Definitions. There are innumerable definitions available on marketing. Some of the definitions are given below :

"Marketing includes all those activities having to do with effecting changes in the ownership and possession of goods and services. It is that part of economics which deals with the creation of time, place and possession utilities and that place of business activity through which human wants are satisfied by the exchange of goods and services for some valuable consideration."

"Marketing is that phase of business activity through which human wants are satisfied by the exchange of goods and services".

"Marketing is the business process by which products are matched with market and through which transfers of ownership are effected".

- Market is a total system of interacting business activities designed to plan, price, promote and distribute want satisfying products and services, to present and potential customers.
- Marketing includes every activity that has to do with the movement of goods from the point where they are produced to the point where they are consumed. It includes advertising policies, pricing, product planning and the analysis of market in terms of its present and potential customers.
- Marketing includes all the activities involved in the creation of place, time and possession utilities.
- Marketing consists of those efforts which affect transfer in the ownership of goods and services and which provide for their physical distribution.
- Marketing is the process of discovering and translating consumer wants into product and service specifications and then in turn helping make it possible for more and more consumers to enjoy more of these products and services.
- *Marketing is the creation and delivery of a standard of living.*

• Marketing includes the performance of those business activities that direct the flow of goods and services from producer to consumer or user.

• Marketing is concerned with all the resources and activities involved in the flow of goods and services from producer to consumer.

• Marketing is the process of getting the right goods to the right consumers at the right place and time and at the right price.

From the above mentioned definitions, it is clear that marketing is primarily concerned with carrying the goods and services from the producer to the ultimate consumer.

Marketing and Selling. Marketing and selling are synonymous in nature, as such there is not much difference between the two. Still we can draw a line of demarcation between marketing and selling. Marketing is a wider term including selling. Selling is one of the activities (functions) performed in marketing. Selling is concerned with the plans to get the customer to exchange his money for the goods or services. Marketing is concerned with trying to have what the customer wants while selling is concerned with passing on what the seller has got. Selling focuses attention on the needs of the seller, marketing on the needs of the buyer. In other words, marketing is essentially consumer oriented and conforms to the new concept of marketing, where as selling is basically production oriented conforming to old concept of marketing. Selling involves physical transfer of goods from seller to buyer, whereas marketing aims at the fullest satisfaction of the customer. From the above it is clear that the scope of marketing is wider as compared to selling.

Importance of Marketing

The success of an organisation depends largely on its successful marketing. Peter F. Drucker has rightly pointed out. "It is in marketing that we satisfy individuals and social values, needs and works, be it through producing goods, supplying services, postering innovation for creating satisfaction." Marketing occupies vital place in the economy. If marketing is scientifically organised, it makes the economy strong and stable. Importance of marketing can be studied as follows :

— **Helps in transfer, exchange and movement of goods.** Marketing is very helpful in transfer, exchange and movement of goods. Goods and services are made available to customers through various intermediaries *viz.*, wholesalers and retailers etc. Marketing is helpful to both producers and consumers. To the former, it tells about the specific needs and preferences of consumers and to the latter about the products that manufacturers can offer.

— **Helpful in raising and maintaining the standard of living of the community.** "Marketing is the delivery of standard of living." Professor Malcolm McNair has further added that "Marketing is the creation and delivery of standard of living to the society." By making available the uninterrupted supply of goods and services to consumers at a reasonable price, marketing has played an important role in raising and maintaining living standards of the community.

— **Creates employment.** The major marketing functions are buying, selling, financing, transport, warehousing, risk bearing and standardisation etc. In each such function different activities are to be performed by a large number of individuals and bodies. Thus marketing gives employment to many people. It is estimated that about 40% of total population is directly or indirectly dependent upon marketing. In the modern era of large scale production and industrialisation, role of marketing has widened. This enlarged role of marketing has created many employment opportunities for people.

— **A source of income and revenue.** The performance of marketing function is all important, because it is the only way through which the concern could generate revenue or income and bring in profits. Marketing should be given the greatest importance, since the very survival of the firm depends on the effectiveness of the marketing function.

A basis for making decisions. A business man is confronted with many problems in the form of what, how, when, how much and for whom to produce? In the past problems were less on account of local markets. There was a direct link between producer and consumer.

—**A source of new ideas.** The concept of marketing is a dynamic concept. It has changed altogether with the passage of time. Such changes have far reaching effects on production and distribution. With the rapid change in tastes and preference of people, marketing has to cope up with the same. Marketing as an instrument of measurement, gives scope in understanding this new demand pattern and thereby produce and make available the goods accordingly.

Helpful in development of an economy. Marketing is the kingpin that sets the economy revolving. The marketing organisation, more scientifically organised, makes the economy strong and stable, the lesser the stress on the marketing function, the weaker will be the economy.

Marketing Process

The end objective of marketing is to take the goods from the place of their origin (producer) to the place of destination (consumer). Various marketing functions are performed in taking the goods from producer to the ultimate consumer. These activities or functions are performed within a broad (frame work) of marketing mechanism which involves three distinct marketing processes. Three major marketing processes are :

- Concentration.
- Equalisation.
- Dispersion.

• **Concentration.** The word concentration refers to assembling the goods at central points. Goods are brought from small producers and are collected and concentrated in markets. These goods generally include raw materials, agricultural products and manufactured goods. After concentrating these goods at specific points, they are then made available to many retailers so that they could possess adequate stock of goods for final disbursement to customers.

Equalisation. Equalisation is a process in - between concentration and dispersion. According to Clark and Clark "It consists of adjustment of supply to demand on the basis of time, quantity and quality." In simple words, it refers to the adjustment of supply at the centres of marketing to the prevailing demand for goods through storage and transporting goods in required quantities to different places.

Dispersion. Dispersion means the distribution of goods from the central locations to the ultimate consumers. This is done through various channels of distribution or marketing intermediaries or middlemen *viz.*, wholesalers and retailers.

MARKETING FUNCTIONS

Marketing is made up of a number of activities known as marketing functions. These activities and operations are primarily concerned with taking the goods from producer to ultimate consumer. Having decided upon the marketing system to be followed, producer has to consider the question of journey that his product has to follow. In completing this journey the product has to pass through many operations and activities. All these various activities and operations are usually termed as marketing functions.

Classification of functions. The classification makes it easier to analyse specific marketing situations. This has been explained by various authors as under :

Pyle has given two fold classification of marketing functions *viz.*,

(A) Concentration process of marketing.

(B) Dispersion process of marketing.

Diagram showing classification of functions as given by Pyle

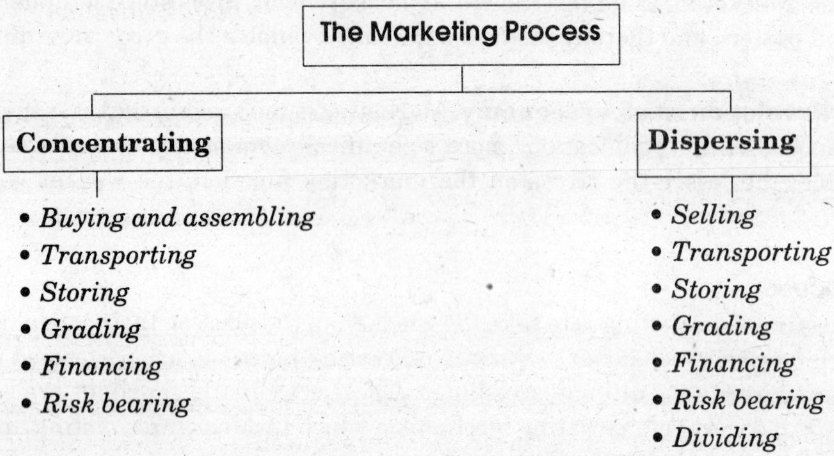

Cundiff, Still and Govoni have given the following classification of these functions :

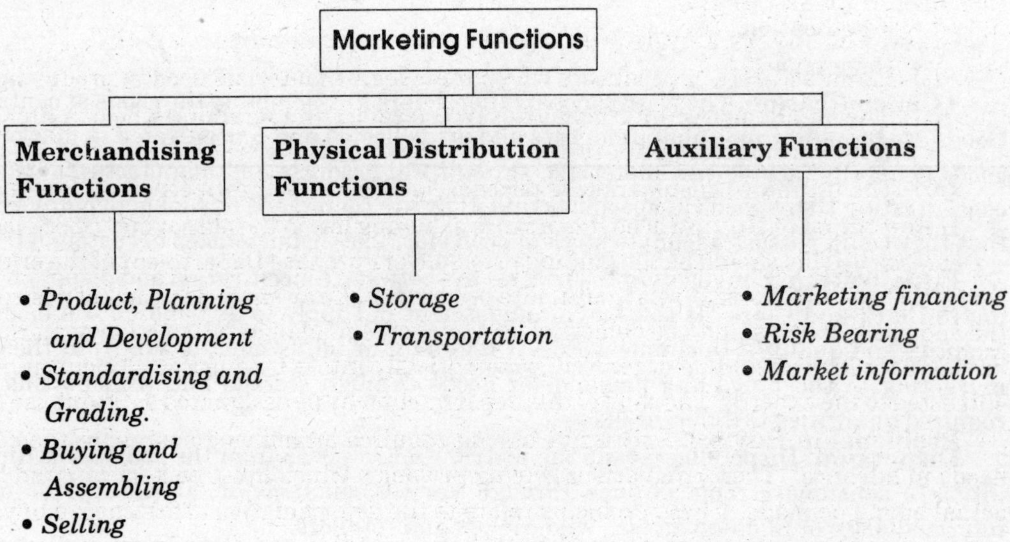

Following diagram explains other classification. This classification has been followed in explaining marketing functions in subsequent pages

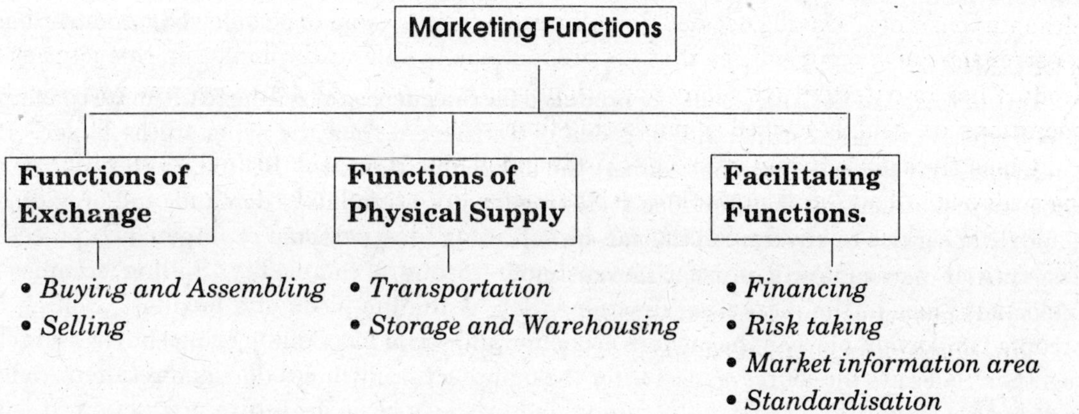

Functions of Exchange

Exchange implies the transfer of goods and services for money or money's worth. It involves change in the ownership of goods. Two important functions are explained under this head :

- Buying and Assembling
- Selling

• Buying and Assembling

Meaning of buying. Buying is the first step in the ladder of marketing functions. Buying refers to all such activities involved in the assembling of goods, under a single ownership and control. Buying is a wider function including the determination of one's needs, seeking out of sources of supply, the determination of prices and transfer of title from seller to buyer. Buying is concerned with the procurement of goods or services for eventual resale of goods to the consumer or industrial user.

Classes of buyers. Buyers are classified into three categories :

(*i*) Manufacturers or producers who purchase raw materials used in producing góods.

(*ii*) The middlemen or intermediaries (wholesalers and retailers) who buy finished goods from manufacturers for resale.

(*iii*) The ultimate consumers who purchase goods for their own consumption and use.

Importance of Buying. The importance of buying lies in the old saying *"Goods well bought are half sold."* This should be the guiding principle of Purchase Department of the organisation. Buying plays an important role in ultimate production. If raw material is not of desired quality, the end product is bound to be defective. Buying is the fundamental function of marketing. All buying activities should be organised systematically into a buying department and are to be entrusted to the experts. The chief of this department may be designated as 'Purchase Manager.'

Problems in Buying. Successful buying requires an ability to estimate the consumer's needs in advance. There are various buying problems which must be kept in mind before the actual buying is made. These problems relate to the determination of (*a*) what to buy; (*b*) when and how much to buy; (*c*) where and how to buy; and (*d*) to negotiate prices and terms. These problems can be solved, if buying department operates properly in the organisation. Problems of overstocking and understocking must be properly checked with the help of sound inventory control system.

• SELLING

Importance of Selling Goods are produced for the purpose of selling to ultimate consumer. It is a process whereby ownership of goods is transferred from the seller to the buyer. It is concerned with the activities that convert the desire into **demand**. Selling, in its broad sense, aims not just at making sales but also at finding buyers, stimulating demand, and providing of advice and service to buyers. Selling can be defined as the personal or impersonal process of assisting or persuading a prospective customer to buy a commodity. Selling occupies an important place in the marketing functions. Sale is the life blood of a business. Selling has occupied important place in the modern economic and social life. Selling brings buyer and seller together. Sales are the source of income for the manufacturer, wholesalers and retailers. Selling is of utmost importance in future planning and provides basis for future production. It is the only function on which hinges the future of the company and which brings in the income that will pay for all other activities.

Functions of Selling. Following are the five functions of selling :

- Product, Planning and Development
- The Contact with Buyers
- Demand Creation
- Negotiation
- The Contractual.

A brief explanation of these functions is given below :

• **Product, Planning and Development.** Product is the central point around which all the marketing activities revolve. According to Prof. Stanton, "Product is a complex of tangible and intangible attributes, including packing, colour, price, manufacturers, prestige, retailer's prestige, their services which the buyer may accept as offering satisfaction of wants or needs." Utmost care should be taken in deciding the product to be produced and marketed. Product should be such as to provide maximum satisfaction to the customer. Product planning means deciding in advance what sort of product is to be produced. Various considerations and factors are kept in mind while planning the product to be produced.

The product development is concerned with giving practical shape to product planning. Its aim is to provide the products or goods as per the plan in terms of quality, quantity, price, packaging, time etc. In a nutshell, product planning '*plans the work* and Product development *works the plan.*' Product Planning and Development has been discussed separately in a separate chapter.

• **Contact with Buyers.** After deciding the product to be produced and marketed, next step in the process of selling is to establish contacts with ultimate buyers of the product. Under this function a choice between 'limited' and 'wider' markets and 'small' and 'large' buyers has to be made.

• **Demand Creation.** As already pointed out demand creation means the conversion of desire into demand. It is a process whereby demand for the product is created.

• **Personal selling.** This is a direct method of creating demand. It is the oldest method and still quite prevalent in modern times.

• **Advertising.** This is referred as impersonal approach of selling as there is no direct link with the customer like personal selling. According to American Marketing Association, Advertisement has been defined as "any paid form of non-personal presentation and promotion of idea, goods or services, by an identified sponser." There are various advertisement media available for carrying out this function *viz.*, newspapers, magazines and periodicals, radio, television, cinema slides, audio-visuals etc. Advertisement has become indispensable in modern business.

• **Demand creation.** This includes' displaying the goods in show windows, organising trade fairs and exhibitions, free samples and gifts etc.

• **Negotiation function.** This is concerned with the bargaining over a deal between the buyers and the sellers. Ideas are exchanged between the parties pertaining to price, quality, quantity, date of delivery, discount allowed and mode of payment, etc. The period of negotiation varies from commodity to commodity.

• **The contractual function.** This is the last but not the least function of selling. This function legally binds the parties concerned. The parties enter into a contract. For example, it is the seller's duty to supply the goods within stipulated time and buyer's, duty to pay the price in accordance with agreed terms and conditions. If any one *i.e.* either seller or buyer, breaches the contract, he shall be liable for damages under the Sales of Goods Act.

Functions of Physical Supply

Two important functions are performed under this classification *viz.*, transportation, storage warehousing. These functions create time and place utilities. This is attained through the function of transport. Similarly goods are retained by the producers and wholesalers and released when they are needed. This is achieved through the function of storage.

Pricing Policies. Policies are the broader guidelines for achieving the end objectives of an organisation. Determination of a proper price policy is of utmost importance for a business undertaking. There are various factors to be taken into consideration before deciding a suitable price policy. These factors are :

Cost factor or cost of the goods. This is the most important factor in the determining a proper policy. The price should not be less than the cost of goods. The selling price of the goods should cover the cost of goods produced including the expenses as materials, labour and other direct and indirect overhead, administrating and selling expenses. Besides, this a sufficient provision should be made for certain expenses like depreciation, taxes, wages and salaries, interest etc. and sufficient margin for profits. This is also referred as cost plus pricing. The basic idea is that the sales price of a product should cover both the cost and a reasonable margin of profit.

• **Nature of the market**. While fixing the price of a product, a sales manager should carefully study the nature and conditions of demand. He should properly analyse the composition of the market. He should see whether the product is needed by industrial users, commercial undertakings or individual consumers or householders ? A further classification of customers can be made by classifying them into rich and poor, males and females, young or old etc. Price of the product can be fixed by taking into consideration the elasticity of demand. If demand is inelastic higher price can be fixed for the product.

• **Price charged by rival producers.** Another important factor to be kept in mind is the competitor's price for the same product. If our price is higher than the price charged by competitors, he will be able to win our customers. On the other hand, if our price is very much lower then it may create doubts in the mind of customers about our product, that the quality of our product is inferior to the quality of product of rival manufacturer.

• **The sales method.** The marketing policies or distribution methods followed affects the pricing of a product. If the channel of distribution is long *i.e.* the goods are distributed with the help of wholesalers and retailers the price of the commodity will be more as compared to if mill's own shops.

• **Government policy and regulations.** Sometimes the price policy is not determined by the concern itself, but a general policy about price is declared by the Govt. to control the increase in the prices of goods. Control prices of goods are fixed by the Govt. in case of certain necessities of life.

Different methods of Pricing. There are various methods or techniques available for price fixation. The basic methods are :

(*i*) Cost plus pricing.
(*ii*) Marginal cost pricing.
(*iii*) Break-even Analysis.

(*i*) **Cost Plus Pricing.** This method has already been discussed while discussing various factors to be taken into consideration before deciding a proper price policy. A brief reference of this method can be made here. According to this method price of the product includes cost plus a reasonable margin of profit. This method of pricing is extensively used. A cost sheet is prepared in order to ascertain the cost of production, total cost and selling price. Results shown by this method sometimes differ from industry to industry. This is because the basis adopted for the allocation of overheads may differ. For example, in one concern overheads may be allocated as 20% of prime cost (cost of materials and direct labour) and in other it may be 10%. Sometimes direct labour is also allocated on the basis of direct material. The main advantage of this method is that it is easier and safest to apply. It discourages the manufacturers from facing cut-throat competition. The results given by this method are reliable and accurate. There are certain limitations of this method, which are given as follows :

• Under this method there are certain cases where price bears no relation with the cost of the product. For example, products sold to rich people. The price charged is not based on the cost.

• In certain products it is not possible to ascertain the cost of the product produced and in that case cost plus method cannot be used.

• Another limitation of this method is that cost and price are both variables reacting upon each other. Cost and price effect each other through the volume of sale. For example, if the prices are low, the sales will increase and reduction in cost takes place.

• This method does not tell about the competition prevalent in the market.

• This method cannot predict the willingness of the customer to pay for the product *i.e* how much customer is ready to pay for the product.

(*ii*) **Marginal Cost Pricing.** Marginal cost pricing is another important method of price determination. Marginal cost is the cost which includes direct material, direct labour, direct expenses and variable overheads *i.e.* prime cost plus variable overhead is known as marginal cost. This is also referred to as direct costing. Marginal cost is the cost by which the total cost rises or falls by increasing or decreasing one unit to the existing volume of production in a factory.

In other words, the cost of a marginal unit of production is known as the marginal cost. Under this method the production cost is divided into two parts: (*a*) fixed and (*b*) variable. The increase or decrease in the volume of production upto a certain extent influences only the variable overheads, whereas the fixed overheads remain unaffected. The theory of Marginal costing maintains that in relation to a given volume of production additional output can normally be obtained at less than proportionate cost, because, with in certain limits, certain expenses remain fixed while certain aggregate expenses only vary with production and in the same way if production decreases the aggregate cost falls by less than proportionate fall in output.

Break-even analysis. Under this method demand of the product and cost of production are taken into consideration in the process of price determination of the product. Management is interested in determining the volume of sale at which costs are fully recovered, and beyond which profits emerge. The analysis of cost behaviour in relation to changing volume of sale and its impact on profit is known as Break even analysis. Out put at any stage below the break even point will result in a loss to the seller. This is clearly indicated in the break even chart. Break even chart shows the profitability or otherwise of an undertaking at various levels of activity and as a result indicates the point at which there will be neither a profit nor loss. The break even chart is a graphic chart which presents the varying costs along with the changing sales revenue, indicates the sales volume at which costs are fully covered by revenue, and reveals the estimated profit or loss which will be realised at different levels of activity. Break even point refers to the point on the break even chart at which cost is equal to the sales revenue. It is also known as the point of 'no profit no loss'. This is clearly illustrated in the diagram. In the above diagram sales volume are shown on x-axis and cost and revenue are shown on y-axis. The fixed costs are represented by horizontal line. The total cost of sales is represented by the fixed cost line. It moves upward proportionately with the volume. The sales revenue is represented by the line moving upward uniformaly from the origin of the axes. The point of interaction of the total cost line with the revenue line is the break even point. The main advantage of break even analysis is that it tells about probable levels of profits at different levels of output. It clearly indicates the interrelationship between revenue, cost and profit in graphic form which is easily understood. It also reflects the comparative significance of fixed and variable cost.

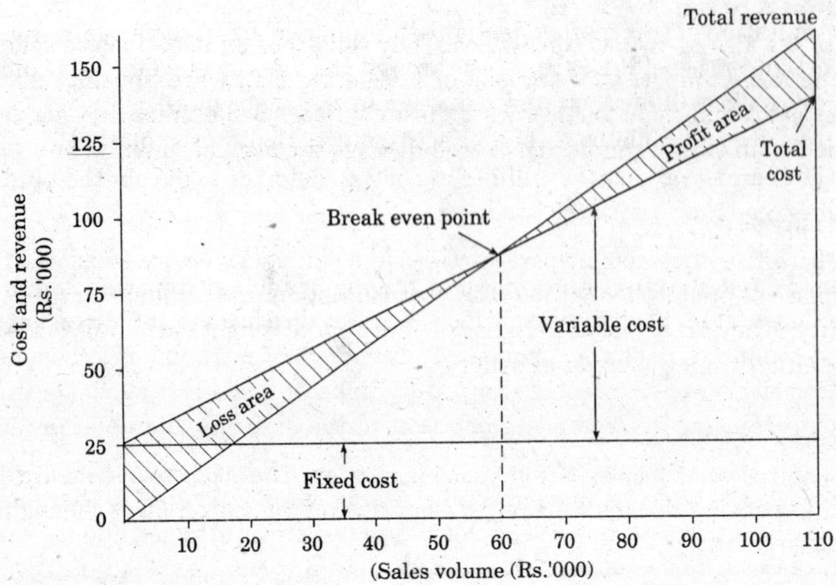

Fig. 55.1.

Channels of Distribution

In the production, a product is delivered to the ultimate consumer. This is done through marketing intermediaries or channels of distribution. The word 'Channel' has been derived from French word *canal* and refers to the path or route which a product follows from the point of production to the point of consumption. It is a trade link between producers and ultimate consumers and acts as bridge which connects both the parties. *"A channel of distribution may be defined as the vehicle for viewing marketing organisation in its external aspect and for bridging the-physical and non physical gaps that exist in moving goods from producers to consumers through the exchange process including the determination of price".* A channel of *distribution may be defined as a path traced in the direct or indirect transfer of the title to a product as it moves from a producer to ultimate consumers or industrial users.* The channels of distribution include various marketing intermediaries or middlemen like retailers and wholesalers but it does not include banks, insurance companies, warehouses transport agencies and Railways etc. which render valuable marketing services but are not direct marketing intermediaries.

Types of Distribution Channels

There are two main categories of marketing intermediaries *viz*., (*a*) Functional Middlemen or Mercantile Agents, and (*b*) Merchant Middlemen.

Mercantile Agents

The mercantile agents perform important marketing services or in other words facilitate the process of distribution of goods. The following are the various kinds of functional middlemen:

- **Brokers**

They do not possess the goods themselves, their main function is to bring buyer and seller together. They charge brokerage or commission from both the buyer and the seller of the goods.

• **Commission Agents.**

These agents are also known as consignees. They sell goods on behalf of the sellers. They sell goods and performs important functions of marketing *viz.*, ware housing, packing and grading etc. They get commission for rendering these services. Some times they get del credere commission which is an extra commission over and above the normal commission.

• **Common Carriers**

These include railways, road transport, airways and shippers who are engaged in carrying goods from the place of production to the place of consumption. In this manner these agencies create place utility. They are not paid commission, but charge freight for taking goods from one place to another either from the buyer or seller.

• **Auctioneers**

They are appointed when goods are to be sold on auction. The goods to be sold are displayed before the intending buyer and bids are invited from them. Who so ever gives the highest bid is delivered the goods.

• **Insurance Companies, Banks**

These agencies render valuable services in the form of facilitating functions in the process of purchase and sale of goods. Most of the business transactions are carried through banks. Payments are received and made through banks. Banks provide credit facilities against hypothecation of goods. The insurance companies perform the important marketing function of risk bearing while goods are in the warehouse of the seller or in transit.

• **Merchant Middlemen**

These primarily include wholesalers, retailers and direct consumer selling etc. These are explained in detail in subsequent pages. Usually any of the under-mentioned processes is undertaken to distribute goods to the ultimate consumers :

• **Manufacturer to Consumer**

This is the direct channel of distribution which involves direct sale of goods from the producer to the consumer. This process can be carried by appointing certain salesmen, sending goods to the consumers by mail. This refers to direct consumer selling. The manufacturer can open his own retail shop within the premises of the factory to sell good directly to consumers.

• **Manufacturer to Retailer**

This method is undertaken in order to cover wider markets. Retailers connect the manufacturers and the consumers. This channel is suitable in case the products are perishable and quick delivery is needed. This method is acquiring immense popularity these days. Big departmental stores and super markets are covered under this category.

• **Manufacturer to Wholesaler**

This is the traditional and widely used channel of distribution. This method is suitable in case of scattered and wider markets. The most important advantage of this method is that the manufacturer can concentrate on production activities and distribution of goods is transferred to wholesalers and retailers. Wholesalers and retailers provide specialised and valuable services in the process of distribution of goods.

• **Manufacturer to Agent**

This is a long chain of distribution. Some manufacturers appoint sole selling agents for the delivery of goods to the wholesalers who in turn sell to the retailers. Most of the textile mills and big business houses in India have sales agents for the distribution of goods. These selling agents sell goods on commission basis directly to wholesalers or large retailers.

• **Manufacturer to Institutional Buyers**

This method is usually adopted in case of large and institutional buyers *e.g.*, government, consumer cooperatives, hospitals, educational institutions, military supplies and business houses etc.

Selecting a Channel of Distribution

Distribution of goods is as important as production. Existence of an organisation largely depends upon a proper and well organised system of distribution. It is, therefore, necessary that utmost attention should be paid in selecting a channel of distribution. Various constituents of the marketing mix like price promotion etc., are closely related to the channels of distribution. A wrong choice of distribution channel ultimately increases the price of the product.

Factors Responsible For Channel of Distribution

Deciding a proper channel of distribution is not an easy task. It involves a careful study and consideration of many factors stated below :

• **The nature of the product.** These factors include physical characteristics of a product and their impact on the selection of a particular channel of distribution. Various factors under this category are :

• Perishability

Products which are perishable in nature are distributed by employing a shorter channel of distribution so that goods could be delivered to the consumers without delays.

• Size and weight of product

Bulky and heavy products like coal and foodgrains etc., directly distributed to the users involve heavy transportation costs.

• Unit value of a product

Products with lesser unit value and high turnover are distributed by employing longer channels of distribution. Household products like utensils, cloth, cosmetics etc., take longer time in reaching the consumers. On the other hand, products like jewellery having high products value are directly sold to the consumers by the jewellers.

• Technical Product

Industrial products which are highly technical in nature are usually distributed directly to the industrial users and take lesser time and adopt shorter channel of distribution. In this case after sales service and technical advice is provided by the manufacturer to the consumers. On the other hand, consumer products of technical nature are usually sold through wholesalers and retailers. In this manner a longer channel of distribution is employed for their sales. After sales services are provided by the wholesalers and retailers. Examples of such products are televisions, scooters, refrigerators, etc.

Product Lines

A manufacturer producing different products in the same line sells directly or through retailers and lesser time is consumed in their distribution.

- **The Nature of the Market.** This is the most important factor influencing the choice of a proper channel of distribution. *Marketing managements* select channels on the basis of *customer wants how, where and under what circumstances.* The number of buyers of the product affects the choice of a channel of distribution. Following factors are considered in this regard.
- **Consumer of Industrial Market.** In case of industrial markets, number of buyers is less, a shorter channel of distribution can be adopted. These buyers usually directly purchase from the manufacturers. Marketing intermediaries are not needed in this case. But in case of consumer markets, when there are a large number of buyers, a longer channel of distribution is employed. Distribution process can not be effectively carried out without the services of wholesalers and retailers.
- **Size of the order.** If the size of the order placed by the customers is big, direct selling can be undertaken by the manufacturer as in case of industrial goods.
- **Geographic concentration of market.** Where the customers are concentrated at one particular place or market, distribution channel will be short and the manufacturer can directly supply the goods in that area by opening his own retail shops or sales depot.
- **Buying habits of customers.** This includes tastes, preferences, likes and dislikes of customers. Customers also expect certain services like credit and personal attention and after sales services etc. All these factors greatly influence the choice of distribution channel.

56

Marketing Research-Creating Customer Value

Introduction

Beginning and end of marketing management is marketing research. With the expansion of business, marketing management becomes more complex. It has to rely more heavily on marketing research as a management tool for solving problems in the field of marketing. Various definitions of marketing research are given below :

— *The systematic gathering, recording and analysing of data about problems relating to the marketing of goods and services. The systematic objective, and exhaustive research for and study of the facts relevant to any problem in the field of marketing".*

— *Marketing research is the careful and objective study of product design, markets, and such transfer activities as physical distribution and warehousing, advertising sales management".*

— *Marketing research is the inclusive term which embraces all research activities carried on for the management of Marketing work, the gathering, recording and analysing of all facts about problems relating to the transfer and sale of goods and services from producer to consumer.*

From the above mentioned definitions, it is clear that marketing research is concerned with tackling the problems emerging from initial to the final stage of total marketing process.

Marketing research techniques and methods are being increasingly adopted by every country of the world whether developed, developing or underdeveloped. Marketing research is a broader term including market research in it. Marketing research is concerned with all the major functions of marketing and how they should be carried out. Market research is primarily concerned with the capacity of the market to absorb a particular product. Scope of marketing research is wider as compared to market research. Marketing research is not only concerned with the jurisdiction of the market but also includes, nature of the market, product analysis, sales analysis, time, place and media of advertising, personal selling and marketing intermediaries and their relationships etc.

Objectives

Marketing research is undertaken for attaining the following objectives :

- **To provide basis for proper planning :** Marketing and sales forecast research provides sound basis for the formulation of all marketing plans, policies, programes and procedures.
- **Reduction in marketing costs:** Marketing research provides ways and means to reduce marketing costs like selling, advertisement, and distribution costs etc.

- **To find out new markets :** Marketing research aims at exploring new markets for the product and maintaining the existing ones.
- **Determination of proper pricing policy :** Marketing research is considerable helpful in the formulation of proper price policy with regard to the products.
- **To study likes and dislikes of the consumers :** Marketing research tries to find out what the consumers, the men and women who constitute the market, think and want. It keeps us in touch with the consumers minds and to study their likes and dislikes.
- **To know the market competition :** Marketing research also aims at knowing the quantum of competition prevalent in the market about the product in question. The company may need reliable information about competitor's moves and strategies which are of immense significance for further planning.
- **To study the external forces and their impact :** Marketing research provides valuable information by studying the impact of external forces on the organisation. External forces may include, conditions developing in foreign markets, govt. policies and regulations, consumer incomes and spending habits, new products and substitutes entering in the market and their impact on the company's products.

For successful implementation of marketing process, marketing research is of utmost necessity. Consumer oriented and competitive markets have further increased the importance of marketing research. Marketing research provides valuable information which provides basis for sound and accurate decisions. In other words, top management is greatly facilitated in the process of decision making with the help of marketing research.

Marketing research has brought producer and the ultimate consumer very close to each other by crossing the walls raised by marketing intermediaries in between. It has greatly filled the communication gap between the producer and the consumer. It studies in detail the buying habits of consumers, their tastes and preferences, needs, opinions and reaction etc. According to S.H. Turner *Marketing research involves a study of consumer preferences, habits and attitudes.* Marketing research provides valuable information with regard to new developments and innovations brought about by rapid growth of science and technology. On account of these developments, prompt adjustments and changes in various policies *viz.,* advertising, sales, pricing and distribution etc. have got to be made so that a business concern can keep itself up-to-date in the dynamic market place. Marketing management has accepted the real challenge of finding new customers, new products and new markets with the help of vital instrument of marketing research.

Marketing research has greatly reduced the possibility of error and has provided right goods at right place, at right time and at right price. According to Small bone "Marketing research then is the haudmaiden of good management but can never be a substitute for it".

Advantages : Following benefits can be derived from a well organised system of marketing research:

- Marketing research keeps informing the organisation about the changes in tastes and preferences of consumers from time to time. This is very helpful for the producers to adjust the production accordingly.
- Marketing research is helpful in discovering new markets for the products and maintaining the existing markets.

• Marketing research provides valuable information to the sales manager whether marketing policies of the organisation are being applied properly or not, on the basis of this research right type of marketing policies can be initiated.

• Marketing research is greatly helpful in the improvements of the quality of the products produced as it keeps informing the organisation about likes and dislikes of consumers. If the product is not of desired quality, improvements can be made in its quality on the basis of information revealed by marketing research.

• Marketing research discloses invaluable information which is not only helpful for marketing or sales department but affects the working of production and purchase departments also.

• Marketing research is greatly beneficial in minimising marketing cost and removal of wastage and inefficiency.

• Marketing research equips the organisation with the strength to face the cut-throat competition prevalent in the market by informing about the strategies and *modus operandi* of the competitors.

• Marketing research discovers the new lines of production in addition to the existing ones.

• Marketing research acts as a sales booster as it establishes direct relation with consumers thereby knowing their requirements.

Limitations

The following are the limitations of marketing research:

• It requires large finances on account of its costly techniques.

• It provides only probable, complex and abstract solutions where as traditional management expects 'definite, simple and concrete' solutions.

• It can't be carried out successfully when some executives prefer to rely more on their own judgement and decisions.

It can be profitably and effectively carried out by experts possessing sound knowledge of statistics, data processing and operational research etc. These competent and expert personnel may not be available.

Methodology of Marketing Research

Marketing research involves the systematic and scientific methodology in collection, processing and interpretation of marketing data. The logical steps undertaken in conducting proper marketing research process are enumerated as under:-

• **Define the problem :** The researcher should clearly understand the nature and scope of the problem being undertaken by him. If he clearly defines and understands the problem, it will make his task easier. For example, there may be a problem relating to decline in sales.

• **Establishing the specific objectives :** After understanding the problem, the next step is to develop certain objectives to be achieved by the researcher by conducting the research. The objectives to be laid down should be self explanatory and clearly understandable.

• **Formulation of research plan :** After the determination of objectives, overall planning of research project is of utmost necessity. It relates to determination of plan pertaining to research. Planning may be in relation to (*a*) Problems regarding questionnaire and other forms (*b*) selection and training of staff conducting research (*c*) designing and selection of proper sample for research (*d*) determining cost estimates and preparation of budget for research.

• **Collection of data :** Now the researcher can proceed with the process of collecting information from various sources. The source may be either primary or secondary. The primary sources may relate to original data collected by the researchers through interviews, questionnaire and surveys etc. The information may be directly collected by interviewing customers, marketing intermediaries and dealer etc. The secondary sources of information include Govt. publications, publications of private institutions like trade associations and chambers of commerce etc.

• **Analysing the information collected :** After collecting the information, it should be analysed and processed properly. Data processing equipment for the analysis may be applied. After analysis it is tabulated and arranged in orderly form. The researcher clearly understands the meaning of data by undertaking the process of analysis.

• **Drawing conclusions and making recommendations :** After analysing and interpreting the data, various conclusions and end results are derived and recommendations are made to management to take necessary steps.

• **Preparation of report :** A written report containing finding and recommendations of study should be presented to the management. The report should be precise and written in simple language. The report should highlight the alternative solutions to the marketing problems under study.

Sources of Marketing Research

There are two sources of information where data for marketing research can be obtained. These sources are : (*a*) Internal sources and (*b*)External sources.

• **Internal sources :** These refer to the sources of information within the organisation. In certain cases internal sources are indispensable without which the researcher can not obtain desired results. Internal sources include accounting information (Trading, P & L A/c and Balance Sheets of different years), salesmen's reports, statistics in relation to advertisement expenditure, transportation costs etc. Information from internal sources is easily available and no financial burden is involved in gathering the information.

• **External sources :** In order to study marketing problems in detail the need of external sources of marketing research arises. External sources are of immense importance and utility in case where research needs detailed and thorough investigation. External sources data can be divided with two categories : (*a*) Primary data (*b*) Secondary data.

• **Primary data:** This refers to the information collected by the researcher from original sources. It is not published data, it has to be gathered by the researcher himself by tapping various resources. Primary data is usually collected for specific purposes. The main sources from where primary data can be obtained are *viz.*, (*a*), Salesmen (*b*), Dealers: (*c*) Consumers etc. This is a very slow process of collecting data and involves huge costs.

Secondary Data

Secondary data is already existing which has been collected and published by some individuals or institutions. This data is available at a very low cost and it requires lesser time to collect it. The main sources of secondary data are :

Periodicals and newspapers : Business magazines and journals published periodically contain data which is very useful for marketing research. Newspapers like Economic Times and

Financial Express also contain data regarding business trends and market reports. Important trade journals are Industrial Times, Commerce, Capital, Indian Finance etc.

Govt. Publications and Reports: There are innumerable publication brought about by Central and State govts. which contain valuable data for conducting marketing research. Census reports of the Government of India, publication of planning commission, periodical publication such as Indian Review, various markets bulletins, Reserve Bank of India bulletin publication of the Statistical Departments of various State Govts., supply valuable information extensively used in marketing research.

Trade Associations

Various trade associations like chambers of commerce, export promotion council etc., publish useful data of immense help to the researcher.

Published Surveys of Markets : This is another useful source of supplying secondary data. Market survey and reports are important instruments in the hands of researchers for conducting marketing research. These are published by business houses or independent research organizations. These pertain to specific lines of products.

Methods of Conducting Marketing Research : As far as secondary data is concerned the researcher need not to collect himself as it is readily available data. But for collection of primary data there are certain techniques available. These techniques can be discussed as under:

Survey Method : This is also known as questionnaire method and is most prevalent and easier in application. A Survey consists of gathering data by interviewing a number of persons. This is referred to as census survey. If a survey is conducted in relation to selected people it is called sample survey.

Sample Survey techniques are usually undertaken, for conducting marketing research as it involves lesser expenditure and consumes lesser time. If a concern can afford to undertake census survey, that will provide more reliable and accurate results.

The main instrument with the help of which survey is undertaken is questionnaire. Questionnaire has been referred to as the soul of the survey. Utmost care should be taken in forming a questionnaire. Following are the requisites of a good questionnaire :-

- The questionnaire should be simple and easily understandable by the reader.
- The number of questions should be limited and there should be no ambiguity and doubts about any questions.
- The questions should be in proper sequence and logical order.

  — The process of answering the questions should be simple *i.e.* the answer should be either 'yes' or 'no'.

Personal questions and enquiries should be avoided otherwise the informant might be antagonised.

- The question should be such involving no calculation to be made by the informant.
- The layout of the questionnaire should be properly designed.
- The survey method is very useful as :

• It provides factual information from the informants.

• Personnel opinions and suggestions of respondants can be collected by undertaking opinion surveys with regard to use of the product and other related matters.

• Interpretative survey can be conducted to probe into the personal feeling, motives, attitudes etc., of the respondent.

Methods of conducting surveys : Surveys are conducted with the help of questionnaire. Following are the methods of conducting surveys :—

Personal Interview of Field Survey : It is the direct method of gathering information from the respondant. It involves face to face communication between the researcher and the informant. Detailed and accurate information can be collected by using this method. Personal interview may be conducted with or without questionnaire. This method can be successfully applied only when the interviewer takes proper interest in the respondent. The most significant advantage of this method is that every type of consumer whether educated or illiterate can be covered within the ambit of this method.

Mail Survey : This method involves sending printed questionnaire to respondents by post with a request to send it back within a stipulated time. The questionnaire may be sent to a selected group of individuals or a large number of persons mailing list is prepared. This method is economical and can be extended to a large number of respondents. There is no bias on the art of interviewers under this method.

Telephone survey : Under this method contact is made with respondents on telephones asking them selected questions by the researchers. The scope of this method is narrow as it can cover only those respondents who have telephones.

Observation Method. Observation is the act of recognition and noting facts of occurance. Under this method no questions are asked from the customers rather they are observed by the researcher *i.e.* what they buy and from where they buy. Sometimes mechanical devices are also undertaken to observe the behaviour of consumers, for example hidden cameras may be fixed in a departmental store to have the photograph of customer while purchasing various commodities. This method is definitely more reliable and accurate as compared to interview method.

NEW MARKETING CONCEPTS

Customer Retention

How often the marketer make sure that customer is happy. Have market men made sure that customer will return. If you haven't you have lost the deal. Retention is keeping customer after the sale is made.

Customer retention is the process by which an organisation identifies and maintains a relationship with prime customer group. Such a relationship add value to both producer and consumer.

Relevance of Customer Loyalty Index

Key Drives of loyalty	*Company A*	*Company B*	*Company C*
Product performance	7.8	9.6	6.9
Delivery & service performance	8.2	9.2	5.8
Brand repurchase likelihood	8.8	9.5	6.5
Average score	8.3	9.4	6.4
Loyalty Index	1.0	1.2	0.8
(Company Average/{8.3+9.4+6.4)/3})	(Average loyalty)	(High loyalty)	(Low loyalty)

Why retention marketing ?

The concept of retention marketing is appealing because unlike relation marketing and service quality initiatives, improvements in retention can be correlated to an increase in profitability. Retained customers are much more profitable than new ones because they purchase more and frequently too, often at a price premium, while at the same time requiring low operating costs.

WHAT DOES REFENTION MARKETING ENTAIL ?

Customer recruitment

- Focus resource upon acquiring prime customer groups only
- Develop product/service propostions to appeal to prime customer groups
- Position prices to reflect costs and expected lifetime values

Customer retention

- Half defections from prime customer groups
- Increase customer tenures to recover acquisitions costs and maximise value of income streams

Re-purchase frequencies

- Seek to increase re-purchase frequencies of prime customer groups
- Increase frequencies to recover costs of acquisition more quickly

Selective cross-selling

- Sell incremental products/services to prime customer groups of increase expected lifetime values
- Structure offers to meet needs of prime customer groups

A recent study by the All India Management Association showed that among service firms, reducing customer defections by just five per cent can boost profits by 25 to 85 per cent.

By achieving retention rates that are superior to the competition, an organisation can yield competitive advantage regardless of whether its generic business strategy is built on low cost production marketing strategy.

No company can indefinitely sustain a continuous turnover of dissatisfied customers. However, before anything can be done about it, companies have to learn how to measure their customer turnover and track the specific reason for it. A Customer Loyalty Index (CLI) provides management with an easily understood tool that helps focus the organisation toward improving satisfaction and retention, for a positive impact on the bottom-line.

Further, companies can use the survey data to calculate individual CLIs which would enable them to classify their customer base into the three loyalty segments *viz*., flirtatious, vulnerable and faithful, and thereby focus its retention strategies.

The economics of retention

When valuing a business for the purpose of acquisition, customer retention rates are a significant indicator of an organisation's potential for future earnings. Customer retention economics is built around the idea of lifetime value *i.e.*, the value that a costomer or group of customers has to a business over the expected lifetime of their relationship with an organisation measured in terms of financial contribution.

Competitive advantage from the customer retention strategy is sustainable only when the organisation reprioritises its marketing activities away from above-the-line spending aimed at acquiring new customers, and towards utilising direct marketing channels to retain customers rather than concentrating on the product or services.

Retention marketing is necessarily concerned with every situation in which a customer might interact with the company. This requires consistent attention to details. As Walt Disnley once said: "There is no magic to magic. It's in the details".

The Indian milieu

Marketers in India are finally accepting one truth-marketing strategies of yesterday are no longer effective. Indian marketers need to develop retention marketing strategies to survive in the radically different market to tomorrow and implementing these programmes have become a pre-requisite in the choice-choked buyers' market. This realisation has crept into various sectors, one of them being the airlines industry. Indian Airlines was among the first to initiate retention marketing programmes in India. Their frequent flier schemes enhance customers' loyalty and increase tenure by doling out free miles for every trip they take.

Titan has used the concept of cross selling to existing customers to good effect. By targetting a reward programme to certain categories of current owners, Titan believes it can increase the depth of penetration and lure them into buying thc higher value Titan collections.

The way it works is simple. When a customer buys from a certain category of watches, he is offered membership to the Titan Signet collection. Once a member enrolls in the club, his purchase behaviour is tracked. And the more the number of watches a customer buys, the greater rewards he is entitled to on his purchases. It helps Titan in two ways. One, it allows a direct access to gauge consumer response to its new brand introductions. And two, it helps to retain its customer base before the international majors like Citizen moves in.

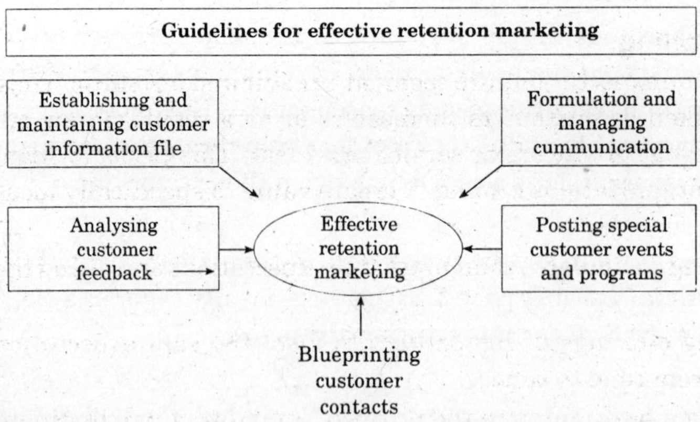

Another case in point is the tie-up between British Airways and the Taj group of Hotels in India. When an Executive Club member checks into any of the 38 Taj hotels in India, all that he has to do is flash his card. That not only entitles him to special privileges like rooms at a special Executive Club preferred rate, but an array of other benefits like late check-outs early check-ins, a complimentary additional miles while staying at the Taj, etc.

In this era of brand parity, retention marketing is just as appropriate for the small business as for large multinationals. Anyone who has customers should practice retention marketing more so because the customer has become the arbiter of corporate destiny.

CREATING CUSTOMER VALUE

A company's competitive advantage rests singularly on following two factors :

(*i*) The manner in which it is able to create customer value to make it unique *vis-a-vis* its competitors.

(*ii*) How does it deliver such value at the least possible cost.

The company if successful in achieving the above it automatically maximise shareholder value. In other words the value of a product or service to a customer is a basket of tangible and intangible benefits which he or she is looking for to satisfy specific needs. If these needs are not met the offer to the customer becomes irrelevant.

What is value? It is the basket of benefits or utilities which a customer gets while consuming a product or a service. His rule is simple: If he does not get the value he expects from the products or services offered by an organisation, he/she is not interested in the offer.

Value expectation reflects a customer's concern for the time, money and effort spent by him to procure the specific product or service and the resulting tangible and intangible benefits he gets out of the same. The range of value expectations for a particular segment of customer can be tracked by understanding the specific demographic and psychographic factors pertaining to the same.

It needs to be kept in mind that value expectations are normally a combination of both tangibles and intangibles. In the case of manufactured products, tangible components are more than intangible parts while in services, the opposite is normally the trend.

Need for positioning

Customer value expectations are segment-specific and not static. These expectations change due to actions taken by customers themselves or as a result of new offerings that are made available by different producers or service providers. This periodic change in customer expectations requires organisations aiming to create value to specifically focus on three key aspects *viz:*

- assessing customers', changing value expectations and sizing the same on a continuing basis
- tracking offerings of competitors to meet the said expectations and changes being made from time to time.
- creating a positioning in the prospect's mind that will distinguish the company from its competitors offering a similar value not only in terms of quality and range of offerings in tangible and intangible terms - but also ensuring that the customers get best price-performance ratio.

These days, products and services of every category are proliferating. And with numerous modes of promotion and distribution, the customer has the option of seeking multiple options before making the choice. In such a scenario, it has become a daunting task for any company to retain and strengthen its positioning on an ongoing basis. Needless to say, if a company does not position its product favourably in its customers' minds,as against the competitors' offerings, the product's long-term viability cannot be ensured.

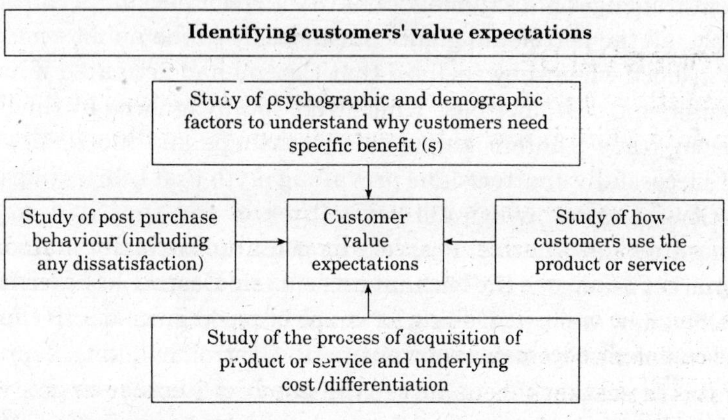

Customer's Value Expectations

In order to understand this, four important areas to examine are :

- Why do target customers need the benefit?
- What is the process by which target customers procure the products/ services being offered?
- What is the process by which customers use or consume the products/services?
- What is the post consumption behaviour of customers, including level of dissatisfaction, if any?

An examination of the above four aspects should reveal the areas where the organisation should concentrate upon to create the benefit or value customers are looking for. Understanding the rationale behind customers' requirements can be obtained by studying the demographic and psychographic factors pertaining to the target customer group. This will clearly indicate what specific product features and "add ons" are to be offered to ensure value acquisition by the customers.

Importantly, the value or benefit which any customer normally expects can be broadly classified into three categories, *viz*:

(*a*) those fulfilling the functional needs that normally accrue from the products or service attributes,

(*b*) those flowing out of the process of acquisition of the product or service giving benefits in such areas as reduced time to purchase, better shopping or procurement experience, hassle-free transaction, etc and

(*c*) those that are made available during the post-purchase phase such as good after-sales service, providing updates on technical information, periodic visit to or contact at customers' place, etc.

Ability of an organisation to categorise value expectations along these three heads will help it identify areas where it should pay attention for creating and delivering value to the customers.

One way to decide what steps should be taken to improve value delivery will be to undertake a study on areas where customers are dissatisfied *via-a-vis* value expected by them. Study of customers dissatisfaction can give important clues to companies about where to improve value proposition to enhance competitive advantage.

The key to innovations is customer dissatisfaction analysis. Most often, there are possibilities of incremental changes but a manager has to watch for paradigm shifts in the structure of the market. In fact, all the petroleum giants (incidentally in the public sector) which market lubricating oil had a shock when they realised that Castrol had activated if not created a new channel for distribution and customer base which were totally ignored by them earlier. This is the now famous bazar trade wherein automobile workshops and mechanics constituted the customers. Castrol successfully shattered the prevailing myth that lubricating oil had to be sold through petrol stations. Castrol, which did not sell petrol and thus had no access to petrol stations, had to innovate a new channel to access its potential customers. About 40 per cent of the lubricating oil market belongs to the bazar at present and Castrol is the leader there. Castrol explored and identified new ways (*e.g.* size and shape of packaging) to offer further value and thus minimise the level of dissatisfaction of customers. Castrol, in addition, provided sufficient advertisement support to sustain this impact in the minds of the customers.

The key to successful customer value management through competitive innovations is not just offering products and services but also talking about it. It is not good enough to love a person, there should be manifestations of such love reflected through actions. We need to keep reminding the customers that "we are here to take care of you always". Customers should feel the comfort and warmth like a spouse.

Post Marketing Experience

Marketing has radically changed in the Indian context-proliferration of brands, product categories positioning strategies and customer satisfaction are some of the areas in marketing which have been applied to practice.

While there are number of strategies to enable a marketer to position of the product, there seems to be little attention paid to consumer experience after the sale of the product.

These experiences include after sales service, and establishing consumer behaviour offers an interesting concept of post - purchase experience on product service.

The various dimensions associated with this post-purchase dissonance are important because these have an impact not only on how the consumers 'feel' about the brand they have bought but also on what they may "advocate" (word-of-mouth) about it. A brand may be offering superior value but if these feeling of dissonance are not addressed by the marketer, the consumer may spread negative publicity. This may have devastating results for the brand (especially given a situation where brand extensions are the order of the day).

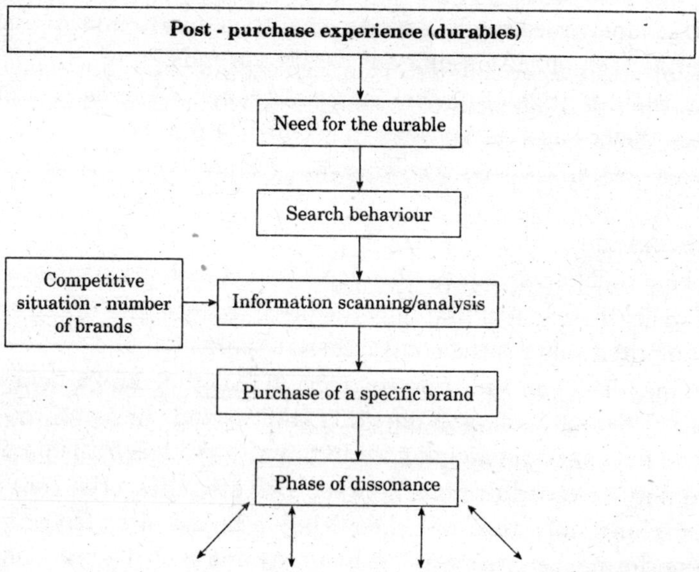

The distinguishing feature of the concept is that the doubts expressed by consumers about the chosen brand, seemed to emerge from the decision-making process in which they were involved. It is to be noted that this study was done just to explore the presence of dissonance among consumers who had recently bought durables.

Dissonance could differ from one product category to another and from one consumer group to another.

The concept of cognitive dissonance was initiated by Leon Festringer in the late 50s. The concept established that dissonance (in simple terms, conflict within a consumer) may occur as a result of contradiction between the decision-making process the consumer undgergoes and the final decision he makes with regard to the selection of a specific brand. The very concept has three basic assumptions:.

- The product category should be crowded with several brands.
- The consumer should have made an effort to screen, analyse and select a specific brand.
- The product should have been very important to the consumer.

Consumer Brand Situation

The concept could be further explained with a specific example. A consumer may buy a brand of watch (for *e.g.*, Titan). He might have been taken in by the symbolic appeal of the brand. After buying this brand, he may start thinking about the economy appeal of a HMT model or the symbolic appeal of Westar and experience cognitive dissonance.

It is to be noted here that the consumer would have gone through a elaborate procedure of decision-making, scanning a number of brands and comparing the attributes which were important to him such as price, symbolic appeal, after-sales service, design, reliability, etc. The consumer experiences dissonance shortly after purchase the time period would depend on the importance of the product to the customer.

One may then attempt to react in any or more of the following ways to reduce the dissonance:

- obtain more information on the brand to strengthen the buying decision.
- look at competitive brands' advertisements in an attempt to find out how the brand which has been bought is superior to other brands.
- attract the attention of his/her informal group of friends in a manner which would exhance his/her association with the chosen brand, or
- become a opinion leader advocating the positive aspects of the brand.

Cognitive Dissonance

There may be a number of causes which result in cognitive dissonance :

- The consumer may feel that only his piece (unit) of the brand is not perfect: he may feel the brand sold to other consumers are perfect.
- There may be a contradiction between an attitude and a behaviour. The consumer may have the habit of complimenting HMT brand, for instance - which is an attitude - and he may end up in buying Titan brand - which is his behaviour.
- There may be contradictions between two attitudes - the consumer may believe in economy and infer that one should buy a brand of watch only on functionality or price-performance attributes but he may want to own a brand of watch which has an aura of prestige.
- The consumer may experience dissonance if there is a "gap" between expectations. He/she may expect a high mileage from a brand of two-wheeler (especially from a brand which makes high claims on this attribute) but may experience dissonance if the actual mileage is not in tune with the claims.

What could marketers do ?

There may be a few factors which may be within the control of the marketer and these factors could be used to reduce cognitive dissonance to a certain extent.

1. Marketers should never "over-promise" either in communication campaigns or in retail outlets. Overpromising is almost a certain way of triggering dissonance.
2. Marketers of durables could have "relationship" programmes which may be effective in reducing dissonance; these may also help the brand to cultivate a loyal base of consumers who could be targeted at a later point in time if the brand enters into several product categories (a brand like BPL has millions of consumers).
3. "Post-buy" services could be established at the dealer level. Consumers are likely to develop confidence about the brand if they are aware that it is genuinely concerned about them especially when a huge investment is made on the brand.

Staying on "top of the mind" among consumers is important for any brand to sustain itself in today's competitive context. Post-purchase dimensions provide an opportunity for the brand to get closer to consumers.

RURAL MARKETING

Eight consecutive good monsoons, a phenomenal increase in plan outlay for rural development programmes from Rs. 14,000 crore in the Seventh Plan to Rs. 30,000 crore in the Eighth Plan and a mind-boggling Rs. 60,000 crore for the Ninth Plan, a 250 per cent increase in the flow of institutional credit for agriculture between 1990 and 1996 and the rural market is looking up. Contrast this with the sluggish growth rates of the urban markets that are getting increasingly competitive and saturated and there's just one way to go-rural.

Indian Market Research Bureau's (IMRB) study 'Rural Market Probe 1990' attempted a development index for villages and found that a large village is likely to be more developed than a small village. In other words there is a correlation between the size of the village and the purchasing power of the people. Corporate marketers would therefore benefit by focussing their distribution and promotion efforts in the larger 2,000+ population villages.

Table 55. I. According to Census of India, 1991, the 6,30,000 villages in the country fall into these population categories.

Village population	*% age of villages*
less than 500	49.0
501 - 999	24.0
1000 - 1999	17.0
2000 - 4999	8.4
5000 - 9999	1.3
10000 and above	0.3

Traditional Marketing Systems refers to *traditional haats* (weekly village markets) and *melas* (fairs) in India. We estimate that 47,000 *haats* and 25,000 *melas* are held in rural India. Most *haats* are held once a week with an average of 314 stalls and a sale exceeding Rs. 2 lakh per *haat* day. Each *haat* caters to the needs of a minimum of 10 to a maximum of 50 villages from where an average of 4,000 persons come to buy a range of daily necessities and services. These periodic markets also act as a conduit for redistributing local products to smaller villages through the bulk buyers with frequent *haats*.

The study found that the larger *haats* are generally held in bigger villages because of better road and transport connections and higher purchasing power available in the host villages - 4,300 are held in the 5,000+ category and another 10,300 in the 2,000-4,999 population villages. By targeting, 14,600 distribution points, a consumer compaign can reach almost 50 per cent of the rural population, as each *haat* caters to an average 25 village.

Unlike *haats* which caters primarily to the essential needs of the local people, *melas* catch a cater much larger population, both rural and urban with more sophisticated factory-made product. In fact, almost half the outlets at *melas* sell manufactured goods, making a *mela* an excellent plan for introducing new products and brands among both durables and non-durables.

Most *melas* held immediately after the harvest season when farmers, flush with funds, frequent them with their families. Women, who ordinarily are restricted from moying out of the village, have universal social sanction to visit the *mela.* Marketers can take advantage of this tradition to establish a face-to-face communication with women which they would otherwise find difficult to accomplish as women seldom visit local markets.

Companies should pick the *melas* closest to the largest villages, where people are relatively more urbanised and exposed to brands. The list of such longer duration, regional and national level commercial melas does not exceed 500 all over India. By using these *melas* to create awareness about brands, a company can hope to reach almost half the population of rural India at a fraction of the cost as compared with TV, video vans or other equally expensive media options.

Right Price

All the three '*P*'s of marketing get translated into this 'P' the price.

Price is the ultimate "transaction border point" between a corporation and its customer. An organisation's myriad costs (and processes) get converted to price and a customer's value perceptions gets reduced to price.

The Value of value

If cost allocation is a business of debate, value judgement is worse. Do women value diamonds because they are expensive or are diamonds expensive because its properties are valued ? Why would some-body pay more for the same Canada Dry in a can than in a bottle or pay ten times its price in a five star hotel ? Did the value of Ceilo go down (or up) when the price was reduced ?

Value determination is the most crucial (and least understood) task of pricing strategy. Careful, well-planned research, sales team workshops, core customer focus groups, international experience only add to the mumbo-jumbo of intuition, experience and judgement. But how can one convert these soft skills into logical algorithms ?

Real value vacuumizer could never figure this out and got sucked into a vacuum.

The exploitation factor

We define the E factor as the ratio of value upon price. If it is 'one', you have little room to use price as strategy. If it is 'less than one', contact BIFR or become The Economic Times headline by being part of the M & A fashion these days.

If it is 'more than one', you are strategically well placed. Hold on, increase the ratio and build market share. If you already have a big share, increase price and build returns. Disney in the late 80s increased its theme parks gate price by one-third and it had no impact on the number of visitors. But its RoE increased from seven per cent to 20 per cent.

Back home Nirma is the perfect example of using the E factor to build share (and on empire). Detergent powder had a certain perceived value and Nirma at a low price had an E factor of two and it quickly gained share. We can recommend an objective for the marketing manager for next year - "Increase E factor by 10 per cent".

We have been often asked this question: Should price be communicated ? We put it on its head and the said price can be a great communication tool. Price can act as a great differentiator and can be wrested to one's advantage.

Communication of price helps to differentiate, to increase usage among non-buyers and to administer prices.

Does low price lead to a dilution of a brand image ? Or does communication of a low price leads to this dilution ? How often has one heard this: "Akai is suicidal, it cannot substain and people will suspect its quality" or "I don't want to be seen a Cambridge shirt, I want the Arrow or a Van Heusen logo". But has not Akai grown six-fold in just a few years and has not Cambridge's growth put all shirt manufactures to shame ?

This is purely a matter of long term business strategies as well as execution. It is difficult for a Nirma to become a luxury soap and may be, they need another brand name. Akai would find the going tough when the economic correction gets over. It needs to be ready to exploit its market share to sell features and image.

It is not a great philosophical statement to say that it starts with the business philosophy. A Titan was great look at reasonable prices but Timex is just affordability and Tanishq is luxury. Each slot needs a different mindset. Pricing is also an interphase of different functions - marketing, sales, finance, accounts, legal and factory processes. All the interplay needs to converge to one number. It needs a well-coordinated organisational process to get to good strategy.

57

Advertising and Branding

INTRODUCTION

The word 'advertising' has been derived from the Latin term *'advertere'* which means 'turn to' or 'turning the attention towards the product'. Advertisement is the art of making yourself and your product known to the world in such a way that a desire for buying that product is created in the hearts of the people.

It is the endeavour of a businessman to increase sales. For achieving higher sales, advertisement is undertaken on extensive scale by a manufacturer. It has been rightly pointed out that *in order to fly the aeroplane of sales, advertisement acts as fuel.* Advertising in fact, is a salesmanship in print. It is inevitable for increasing the volume of sales. Some of the important definitions of advertisement are given as under. *Advertising consists of all the activities involved in presenting to a group, a non-personal, oral or visual, openly sponsored message regarding a product, service or idea; this messages, called an advertisement, is disseminated through one or more media and is paid for by the indentified sponsor. Essentially form of communication through such diverse media as hand bills, newspapers, magazines, bill boards, letters, radio and television broadcasts and motion pictures. Advertisement is any paid form of non-personal presentation and promotion of ideas, goods or services by the identified sponsor. Publicity is any form of commercially significant news about a product, an institution, a service or a person published in space or radio time that is not paid for by the sponsor.*

It is selling in print or presenting a commodity in print to the people in such a way that may be induced to buy it. "Advertising is printed, written, spoken or graphic salesmanship. Advertisement are designed to sell the products of the advertiser and to influence favourably the public mind, individually and collectively with respect to the interest of the advertiser. "Advertising is the art of disseminating marketing information through various media of communication (such as newspapers, magazines, radio etc.) at the expense of the company for the purpose of increasing (or maintaining) effective demand and facilitating the sale of specific goods and services".

Objects of Advertising. The main objective of advertising is to introduce properly a new product in the market and the ultimate goal is to achieve large sales volume thereby increasing profits. The main objectives of advertising are given below to

Apprise people about the new product and to create their interest in the product.

Extend active support to personal selling and to make the process of sale easier.

Increase the volume of sales and to reduce the selling expenses.

Create and maintain permanent demand for the product.

Reduce the number of middlemen and establish a direct link between the producer and the consumer.

Enhance the goodwill of the concern whose products are advertised.

Protect the people against the imitations of the manufacturer's product.

Educate the people about the use and application of the product.

Create confidence in the minds of the people with regard to quality of the product.

Help the manufacturer in meeting the cut-throat competition.

Develop proper and cordial relations among manufacture, dealers and the customers.

Functions of Advertising. Following are the main functions of advertising.

It encourages the prospective buyers to purchase the products.

It is indispensable in the introduction of a new product in the market.

It acts as a potent instrument in the hands of the manufacturer for increasing the sales by creating permanent demand for the product.

It is considerably helpful in decreasing the number of middlemen.

It builds up the reputation of the producer thereby enhancing the goodwill of the concern.

It educates the people in the use of new products and tells about the different uses of the existing products.

It provides an important source of revenue for the publishers of different newspapers and magazines.

It extends many employment opportunities to different type of people like artists, singers, actors, models and painters etc.

It is instrumental in increasing production and sales and considerably reduces per unit cost of production and sales.

It eliminates seasonal fluctuations in the demand of the product.

Advantages of Advertising.

The benefits derived from advertising are manifold. It is one of the most important components of the marketing process. This is beneficial to manufacturers, traders, consumers and society as a whole. Advertising offers the following advantages.

Introduces a new product in the market. Advertising plays significant role in the introduction of a new product in the market. It stimulates the people to purchase the product.

Expansion of the market. It enables the manufacturer to expand his market. It helps in exploring new markets for the product and retaining the existing markets. It plays a sheet-anchor role in widening the markets for the manufacturer's products even by covering the customers living at far flung and remote areas.

Increased sales. Advertisement facilitates mass production of goods and increases the volume of sales. In other words, sales can be increased with additional expenditure on advertising with every increase in sale, selling expenses will decrease.

Fights competition. Advertising is greatly helpful in meeting the forces of competition prevalent in the market. Continuous advertising is very essential in order to save the product from the clutches of the competitors.

Enhances good-will. Advertising is instrumental in increasing goodwill of the concern. It introduces the manufacturer and his product to the people. Repeated advertising and better quality of products brings more reputation for the manufacturer and enhanced goodwill for the concern.

Educates the consumers. Advertising is educational and dynamic in nature. It familiarises the customers with the new products and their diverse uses and also educates them about the new uses of existing products.

Elimination of middlemen. It aims at establishing a direct link between the manufacturer and the consumer, thereby eliminating the marketing intermediaries. This increases the profits of the manufacturer and the consumer gets the products at lower prices.

Better quality products. Different goods are advertised under different brand names. A branded product assures a standard quality to the consumers. The manufacturer provides quality goods to the consumers and tries to win their confidence in his product.

Supports the salesmanship. Advertising greatly facilitates the work of a salesman. The customers are already familiar with the product which the salesman sells. The selling efforts of a salesman are greatly supplemented by advertising. It has been rightly pointed out that "*selling and advertising are cup and saucer, hook and eye, or key and lock words.*"

More employment opportunities. Advertising provides and creates more employment opportunities for many talented people like painters, photographers, singers, cartoonists, musicians, models and people working in different advertising agencies.

Criticism Against Advertising.

Despite of many benefits drawn from the advertising, it suffers from a severe criticism advanced by different segments of society. It is not an unmixed blessing. It has been criticism on the following grounds:

— **Increased price of the product.** Advertising increases the cost of the product as the expenses on it form the part of the total cost of the product. The increased prices are borne by the consumers. But it cannot be denied that advertising leads to large scale production which considerably reduces the total and per unit cost of production. The consumer may pay less rather than higher.

— **Multiplication of needs.** Advertising creates artificial demand for the product and induces people to buy those products which are not needed by them. On account of its repetition, it allures and creates a desire in the minds of the people to possess an article not required by them.

— **Deceptive.** Sometimes advertising is used as an instrument of cheating. In order to impress upon the people false statements are given with regard to different virtues of a product. Fradulent means and deceptive practices are resorted to by various traders in order to sell their products. All these things adversely affect the public confidence in the advertising.

— **It leads to monopoly.** Advertising sometimes leads to monopoly in a particular brand of a product. By investing large sums in advertising of his brand, a big producer eliminates small producers of the same product from the market and creates brand monopoly. This leads to exploitation of consumers.

— **Harmful for the society.** Sometimes advertisements are un-ethical and objectionable. Most often, these carry indecent language and virtually nude photographs in order to attract the customers. This adversely affects the social values.

Advertising Media. The selection of a proper advertising media is not an easy task as it involves careful consideration of many factors by a manufacturer. Following are the important considerations to be taken into account before selecting an advertising medium.

— **Nature of the Product.** This is the first important factor to be considered in selecting an advertisement medium. Products may be either consumer or industrial. For consumer products, newspapers, radio, television and letters etc. will be suitable whereas in case of industrial products various trade and industrial journals can be successfully employed.

— **Nature of the market.** This factor mainly includes size and composition of the market whether the market is local, national or international basis. Vernacular newspapers are suitable for advertising local products, whereas newspapers having wider circulation and magazines are appropriate for the products to be advertised on national basis. In the case of international markets, trade exhibitions and fairs, foreign magazines would be more suitable.

— **Finances required.** The cost of advertising is another important consideration to be taken into account by a manufacturer. A large scale manufacturer having huge funds can undertake extensive advertising campaigns by employing different advertising media.

— **Duration of advertisement.** The duration of the period for which advertisement is undertaken should also be taken into account before selecting a particular medium of advertising. Advertisements given in newspapers, radio and television are normally for shorter period, on the other hand magazines, out door displays and direct mail etc., have longer duration.

— **Media followed by competitors.** As has already been pointed out that advertising is an important instrument in the hands of a manufacturer to fight competition prevalent against his product in the market. Competition can be minimised by adopting the same media in popularising his product as undertaken by the competitors. This method is gaining immense popularity these days.

— **Coverage of media.** An advertising medium having wider circulation and larger coverage will take the message of the manufacturer to a large number of people. Newspapers and magazines have wider coverage. On the other hand, other media have limited coverage.

— **Type of consumer.** Whether the consumers are illiterate or educated will greatly influence the selection of advertising media. In case of illiterate and lesser educated people, films, television and radio can be effective media of communication, whereas in case of educated people, letters, newspapers, magazines and displays can be more successful and appropriate media.

BRANDING

Introduction

In order to distinguish a manufacturer's product from the other, brand names are attached to the products. It is a comprehensive term which includes brand names, designs and symbols. The American Marketing Association has defined a brand as "*a name, term, symbol, or a design, or a combination of them which is intended to identify the goods of one seller or group of sellers and to differentiate them from those of competitors*". Extensive advertisement campaigns and large scale selling cannot be undertaken without the brand name of the product. It is a pre-requisite of advertising and mass selling techniques. Branding can be of three types *viz.*,

(*a*) Symbols and marks are used for different products *e.g.*, Atlas cycle, Rath vanaspati, Anchor brand threads, Cavenders cigarettes and Gulab Ghee etc.

(*b*) Special names are given to different products, *e.g.*, Usha fans, Royal enfield motor cycles and Time star watches etc.

(*c*) Sometimes the manufacturers may use their own names for the product produced by them, *e.g.*, Bata shoes, Godrej Steel furniture, Escort tractors and Kelvinator refrigerators etc.

Advantages of Branding

Branding is indispensable for carrying an effective advertisement campaign.

Branding is greatly helpful in eliminating middlemen, particularly wholesalers. Popular branded goods can be easily sold by the manufacturers by establishing their own retail shops.

Branding widens the market for the product and improves reputation the concern.

Branding establishes the individuality of a product which can be easily distinguished from the products of similar nature. The main objective of branding is to introduce "product differentiation".

Branding ensures constant demand for the product which is further helpful in formulating future production policies properly.

Branded products and their prices are under the direct control of the manufacturer.

Branded articles require lesser time to sell.

Branding helps in introducing a new product in case where a concern is selling one or more lines of products.

Branding simplifies the purchasing of the retailer and saves him from the botheration of choosing and selecting his stock.

Branded products ensure manifold advantages to consumers *viz.*, assuring them better quality, stability in prices and easy availability of the goods.

Packing and Packaging. Packing refers to wrapping and crafting of goods before they are distributed or preserved in stores. Goods are packed in proper containers or packages in order to protect them against breakage, spoilage, leakage and damage of any kind. In fact, packing has become a district and separate function of marketing. Packaging has been defined "*as the general group of activities which involves designing and producing the container or wrapper for a product*" - Stanton. In other words packaging is a process concerned with putting the goods in different type of containers by keeping in view the nature of the commodity to be packed *viz.*, bottles, boxes, containers, cans and bags etc.

COMPARATIVE ADVERTISING

Comparative Advertising and Brand Management

Comparative Advertising can be described as any advertising that explicitly or implicitly compares at least two brands in the same generic product or service.

The comparative advertisement compare the brands on specific product or service attributes.

While the comparison itself might be explicit or implicit, in all cases the brand(s) being compared is fairly obvious to the consumer. If it isn't all of these; then it isn't comparative advertising either.

Comparative, naturally would have the ability to grab the consumer's attention as it works on much the same premise.

The objective of any advertisement (including comparative ads) can be split into three. First, the consumer needs to have noticed the ad and processed information, facts and knowledge. Second, based on this she would prefer or like the brand Finally, this liking should stimulate desire and cause the consumer to buy the brand.

It has been observed that consumers tend to attend comparative ads more than non-comparative ads. Further, consumers recall more messages in comparative ads than in non-comparative ads. This is because two brands are mentioned and that grabs interest. Users of the compared brand (as against the sponsored brand) find the advertising personally relevant because the brand they are currently using is being depicted as inadequate. Greater involvement with a larger target group means more mental activity and information processing which could show the sponsored brand at an advantage.

Captain Cook, when the advertising went comparative against Tata salt, had to establish its superiority on a tangible property - in this case free flowing. Pepsi has often taken potshots at Cola internationally - but the ads were memorable and enhanced Pepsi's image contrasting Pepsi's youth vigour with Coke's grey age associations. (See Pepsi on *Eat Cricket* with the Coke salesman ad aired in America.)

Information processing can be a double edged sword. Greater mental activity could induce consumers to either argue in support or against the main appeal in the message. Supporting reasons can be functional as in Captain Cook or emotional as in Pepsi. But in any case the ad should give the audience permission to believe in the claim.

Creating dissonance is not the same as rubbing the consumer the wrong way. That means the advertisement should still be built around an insight and a big idea—not merely comparision for kicks.

Not forever

No discussion on comparative advertising can be complete without mentioning Avis. Avis did the right comparison with Hertz when the company embarked on its now famous "We' re No 2" campaign.

Comparative advertising cannot be continuing campaigns for a brand. Once the audience has processed your message and acted on it, she moves on. Driving the same message then becomes counter-productive. That's also because comparative ads score rather low on likeability. So audiences do not want to see dissonance creating advertising again and again. Comparative advertisements can at best be tactical and not a long term position.

On the other hand, we had the case of Pepsodent in India. The brand had achieved sufficient mass to take on Colgate, the market leader (so timing was important).

Guidelines for comparative advertising

- Comparative ads attract more attention and processing.
- Comparative ads need factual substantiation to be believed.
- Comparative ads need insights.
- Consumer ads should be only tactical.
- Timing and language are important.
- Market leaders should not resort to comparative ads.

Many brands fail to make the transition from comparison to stand alone and fall by the wayside.

Leaders act, not react

Finally, Comparative ads seem to work best for a challenger brand. When Parachute responded to the entrapping advertising of Clinic Plus Hair Oil, it only managed to increase the Clinic Plus salience. Hertz went about consolidating their position with Avis in mind but did not react to the Avis ads. A leader can be competitive without being comparative.

Advertisers need to use all tricks in the bag to outdo competition. If a brand has genuine news and can exploit it through comparative advertising, it would be foolhardy to not do so. Comparative advertising is here to stay. Twenty years back advertising was considered the last resort for scoundrels. Today, it has been replaced by comparative advertising. Tomorrow will be another day.

The brand makes all the difference

The creation, maintenance and registration of a distinct brand identity among the consumer mindset becomes the biggest challenge for any marketer. The problem is big; the opportunity even bigger. There can be no better news for a marketer than the fact that brands consumed by individuals have become possibly the greatest way in which they can distinguish themselves from each other. Brands are instrumental in the process of self-signification and individuals project themselves through brands. Brands have thus become symbolic extensions of the consumer. Hence, any brand which helps consumers in the process of self-signification is guaranteed tremendous equity and an assured sale. Specifics of the brand are nurtured and expressed in everything that is presented under the brand umbrella.

Integral to the fructification of this philosophy is the selection and development of media vehicles that merge the brand's identity with that of their own such that the medium and the message come across as one single entity for the end consumer.

Such a communication strategy will have three particular implications in terms of the way in which it influences consumers as well as the parameters for measuring advertising effectiveness.

- The strategy is likely to work over the long term rather than the short term.
- The communication objective shifts from boosting immediate sales to nudging consumers up the loyalty scale which if successful, will result in a slower longer term build up in sales. This is most true for mature product categories where there is little opportunity for dramatic rational 'product news' that would result in a short term lift in sales. 'Promotions then become the only way of achieving the above.

  The message is often working more on the emotional rather than the rational plane.

- The key communication is often the implicit take - out rather than the explicit message.

This implies that the communication is working at a deeper level. The more communication strategies converge in this direction, the greater is the ineffectiveness of surrogate measures like top-of - mind awareness and advertising recall. In the information age, where discerning patterns will become increasingly difficult, relying on wrong measures of communication effectiveness, will prove fatal. The surrogate for a communication objective then becomes increasing mind share or rather effective mind share which in the long term, will lead to an increase in sales. This as an objective is truer for media planning.

Currently, the ideal way in which we plan and set media objectives, is in terms of a reach frequency level arrived at after iterating incremental levels in GRPs, awareness, cost and sales. However, because of the above mentioned changes in communication dynamics, a deeper introspection is warranted, specially on the subject of awareness.

We measure awareness, in terms of an absolute base awareness and absolute incremental awareness. However, it, would make greater sense if we break up the set of people constituting awareness into those who recalled, were involved or persuaded.

	High Persuasion	*Low Persuasion*	*Tuned out execution*	*Enterining but not persuasive*
Persuaded	60	10	40	30
Involved	25	30	15	50
Recall only	10	55	40	15
Bypass	5	5	5	5
Total	**100**	**100**	**100**	**100**

For example out of the 100 people who see the ad, five may completely forget and bypass it.

Thus, 95 people are aware of the ad. Out of these, 20 may only recall having seen the ad, 20 may be involved with it (*i.e.* find it entertaining) and 55 people may be persuaded by it *i.e.* among those 55 people, messages, moods and values of the brand having been communicated. These 55 people find the communication relevant and having strengthened the existing brand-consumer relationship. Hence, the effective awareness or effective mind share become 55 and not 95.

There are four possible distributions of these 95 people across recall only, involved and persuaded groups. The pattern of distribution indicates the nature of advertising impact. If we do not measure increments in frequency against increments in effective awareness, we will continue to under-utilise communication budgets. This is because increments in overall awareness resulting out of increases in recall only and involved groups may not result in a tangible, long-term benefit for the brand.

Strategic Brand Management

Since the first product in history was traded. Governments awoke they argued to the ideas that a trade - mark was a tool of evil First World multinationals and therefore must be restricted or even banned.

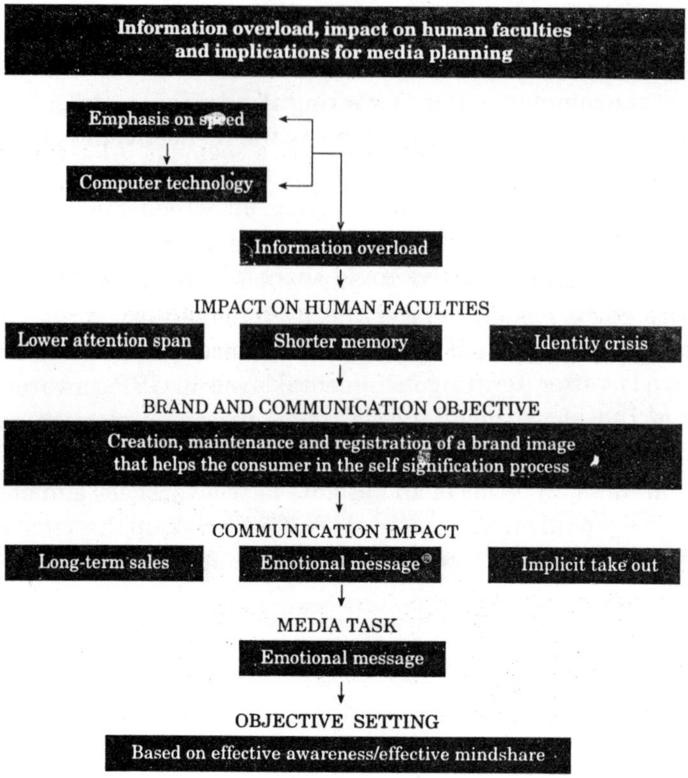

An UNCTAD report in 1974 against use of trade marks by subsidiaries of foreign-owned companies was a manifestation of this approach.

Liberalisation of economies in India and elsewhere in the past 10 years has carried with it the acceptance that brands form part of inward investment into emerging economies and that restrictions inhibit growth and employment. Of course, old attitudes die hard.

The development and maintenance of an international brand demands three things - forward thinking management, ability to supply to products and a legal infrastructure to protect the investment.

What percentage of the Indian economy is involved in exporting unbranded products to foreign-owned companies, who then supply their own brands, mark-up the products to reflect the consumer's perception of the value of the brand and sit back to enjoy the extra profit ?

In 1994, India's total exports were valued at US$ 26,230.6 million - how much higher would that figure have been if all those exports had been Indian-branded. Numbers to give a direct indication of the Indian-branded percentage are not readily available but those involved in the textile, footwear and computer software industries, among others, might recognise themselves..

India's GDP for 1994 was US$ 293.6 billion - world ranking 16 in terms of size or world ranking five in terms of GDP in purchasing power parity. But in Indian-owned branded products?

Position Strategy - Branded Products

It involves the use of retailing mix variables. The retailing mix variables include product price, presentation, promotion, personal selling and customer services.

The blend of the retailing mix variables for a branded retail store's effective positioning strategy is:

Product variable

Quality should be the best within the given price segment. Also the width and depth of products must be sufficiently large to cater to a wide range of consumer buying preferences.

Price variable

The price offered must differ from that of competition in that it should offer moderate prices. This is a consequence of the moderate price sensitivity of the consumers it is targeting. The strategy follows from the need to build up the volumes needed to run the chain profitably.

Presentation and customer service variables

The exercise to 'brand' the retail chain cannot be complete without a unique image of the chain. It is in this aspect that presentation such as in upgraded exteriors and interior design, drive-in window options and late night hours assumes considerable importance. The accent is now more on brand recall through the use of standardised hoardings at the entrance and similar internal layouts.

Promotion variables

A consistent theme emphasising the retail chains core competencies is recommended to facilitate top-of-the-mind recall. This is primarily based on the original theme of elaborating on the unique product attributes of the chains.

Strategy implementation

A sound strategy is no guarantee of success if it cannot be successfully executed. To implement a firm's desired positioning effectively, every aspect of the store must be focused on the target market.

Merchandising must be single-minded; displays must appeal to the target market; advertising must talk; personnel must have empathy for it; and the customer service must be designed with the target customer in mind.

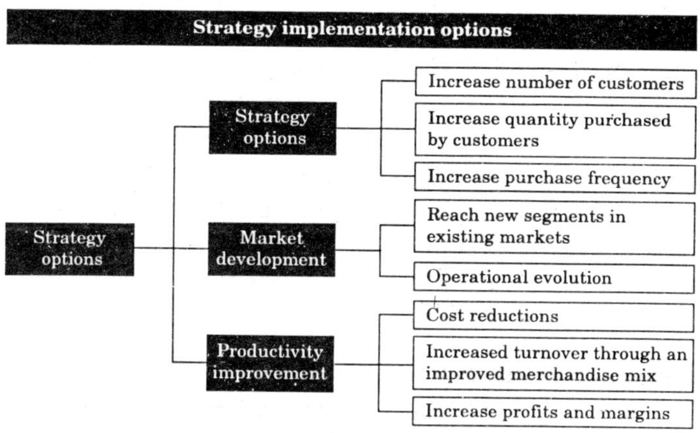

Once a strategy is implemented, managers need feedback on the performance of the new strategy. Some types of information are needed on a routine, ongoing basis to help the management determine whether objectives have been met.

The effectiveness of long term strategy of the branded retail store, however must also be evaluated periodically. Such an evaluation covers all elements of the plan and guarantees that it does not degenerate into fragmented, ad hoc efforts that are not in sync with the overall competitive strategy. Management can also use the process to decide what changes, if any, should be made in the future to ensure that the combination of retailing mix variables supports the firm's strategy.

58

Product Development and Product Planning

Research

Research unlocks nature's secret. Research has to do with learning nature's laws but industry has to put nature's laws to work and this is where development and design comes in. It is as a result of research, development and design the technologies went on fast changing of late, and a number of products have become absololite. Today we find a number of products as substitutes and even with cheaper in price, better in their functional values. Plastics have replaced may metals excepting with one property that they can not withstand temperatures of high ranges. Particularly research in petroleum has opened up a wide range of products which have revolutionised the way of living itself. The technological innovations from low grade technologies to highly sophisticated technologies have started influencing the socio economic conditions at a rapid rate now. Because of lower pay offs, todays research work needs more careful management than it did in the past. New scientific findings come on so fast that scientists and engineers also find themselves obsolete. For every 5 to 10 years the new sciences Technologies have been developing and now it develops at a faster rate.

Purpose of Research

Generally the industrial research is to try to :

(*i*) Search for basic chemical or physical relationships, of products and processes.

(*ii*) Improve their products.

(*iii*) Find new user for their present products.

(*iv*) Develop new products.

(*v*) Reduce the cost of present products.

(*vi*) Develop tests and specifications for products and materials.

(*vii*) Analyze competitors products.

(*viii*) Find profitable uses of by-products.

Types of Research

These are two types of research (*i*) Basic or pure research (*ii*) Applied research. Pure research deals with nature's basic laws, regardless of law that knowledge can be used. This type of research is usually done at universities and the institutes. Applied research is concerned with solving a problem and usually one that now costs money and will make more money if it is solved. Many industries try to do both type of research but only 10 to 20 percent of resources are spent an basic or pure research. The distinction between pure and applied research will fade away as the time advances, since what is pure research to day becomes an applied one once it finds the application.

Development

Product development changes the products' design, the discoveries of the research may have to be incorporated into the product or into the manufacturing process. New ideas need to be tried out. Ideas stem out from day to day back and forth exchange of information between engineering, sales and production.

Product-Policy Decisions

Product-policy decisions are shaped by a multitude of factors, including the basic nature of the firm's business, its objectives, its resources and its opportunities. Product can be defined as a bundle of physical, service and symbolic particulars expected to yield satisfaction or benefits to the buyer. Today most companies are multi-product organisations. Whether large or small, whether in manufacturing, wholesales or retailing, a company generally handles a multitude of products and product varieties. Product policy decisions are made at three different levels of products aggregation (*i*) Product item (*ii*) Product line and (*iii*) Product mix.

Product Item. A specific version of a product that has a separate designation in the seller's list.

Product Line. A group of products that are closely relates either because they satisfy a class of need, are used together, are sold to the same customer groups ; are marketed through the same types of outlets or fall within given price ranges.

Product Mix. The composite of products offered for sale by a firm or a business unit.

Product mix has three concepts (*i*) Width (*ii*) Depth and (*iii*) Consistency.

The width of the product mix refers to how many different product lines are found within the company. Through increasing in the width of the product mix, the company hopes to capitalise on good reputation and skills in present markets.

Through increase in the depth of its product mix, the company hopes to encash the patronage of buyers of widely differing tastes and needs. The depth of the product mix refers to the average number of items offered by the company within each product line. The consistency of the product mix refers to how closely related the various product lines are in end use, production requirements, distribution channels or in some other way. Through increase in the consistency of its product mix, the company hopes to acquire an unparalleled reputation in a particular area of endeavour.

Product Life Cycle

As time elapses the product mix of a company will undoubtedly change, new items and lines will be added and old ones dropped. This is because current company products cannot hold their market positions indefinitely. The life time sales of many branded products reveal a typical pattern of development, known as the product life cycle. The five stages can be distinguished as:

(*a*) *Introduction* : The product is put on the market. Awareness and acceptance are minimal.

(*b*) *Growth* : The product begins to make rapid sales, gains because of the cumulative effects of introductory promotion, distribution and word-of-mouth influence.

(*c*) *Maturity* : Sales growth continues but at a declining rate because of the diminishing number of potential customers who remain unaware of the product or who have taken no action.

(*d*) *Saturation* : Sales reach and remain on a plateau marked by the level of replacement demand.

(*e*) *Decline* : Sales begin to diminish absolutely as the product is gradually edged out by better products or substitutes.

The length of the product life cycle is governed by the rate of technical change, the rate of market acceptance and the case of competitive entry.

Important Phenomena of Product Life Cycle

(*i*) Products have a limited life. They are boring at some point, may or may not pass through a strong growth phase and eventually degenerate or disappear.

(*ii*) Product profits tend to follow a predictable course through the life cycle. Profits are absent in the introductory stage, tend to increase substantially in the growth stage, slow down and then stabilize in the maturity and saturation stages and all but disappear in the decline stage.

(*iii*) Products require a different marketing programme in each stage and management must be prepared to shift the relative levels and emphasis given to price, advertisement. Product improvement and other marketing elements during different stages in the product life cycle.

Product Mix Decisions Stability

Many managements adopt the objective of reasonably stable sales from period to period. High sales variability can be quite costly to the firm. It means that the company has to invest in facilities for peak demand or carry higher inventories to meet peak demand ; hence to pay more interest and greater risk. This increases the number of wrong decisions in forward planning because sales are more difficult to forecast.

Suppose, the company's product mix generates highly variable sales and four different products are under review as possible additions to the product mix. The first product promises highly stable sales. The second product is unrelated to the current products and would produce sales subject to about the same amount of variability as now exists. The third product's sales are expected to show high positive correlation with present total sales. The fourth products sales are likely to show high negative correlation with present total sales. Since the product's sales are highly stable, the addition of this product would not alter the existing level of variability. Since the second product's sales are uncorrelated with current sales the addition of this product would increase slightly the level of sales variability. Since the third product's sales are positively correlated with sales arising from the current product mix, the addition of this product would increase substantially the level of sales variability. Only the fourth product, whose sales are negatively correlated with total current sales, would decrease over all variability. In fact, if a new product were found whose expected sales equaled, in magnitude present total sales and showed perfect negative correlation with them, the addition of this product would produce a new pattern of total sales that would be perfectly stable. The main point is that the objective of sales stability imposes certain constraints on which products might be added or deleted.

Growth

Another objective emphasized by a large number of companies is raising sales through time. The rate of sales growth depends upon where various products in the company's current mix are in their respective life cycles and what plans are made for product additions and deletions. For the company that is committed to a high rate of growth, four basic product market strategies are available :

(*i*) *Market Penetration.* The company seeks increased sales for its present products in its present markets through more aggressive promotion and distribution.

(*ii*) *Market Development.* The company seeks increased sales by taking its present products into new markets.

(*iii*) *Product Development.* The company seeks increased sales by developing improved products for its present markets.

(*iv*) *Diversification.* The company seeks increased sales by developing new products for new markets.

The Optimal Product Mix

The company's current product mix is said to be optimal if no adjustment would enhance the company's chances of achieving its objectives. If the company's objective is primarily profit minimisation then the product mix is optimal if profits could not be improved by deleting, modifying or adding products. If the company's objective is primarily sales growth, then the product mix is optional if it yields a rate of sales growth that could not be profitably enhanced by and product mix changes. Typically there are many objectives, and this complicates the problem of defining an optimal product mix.

Any of the following conditions suggests that a current product mix might be less than optional optimal :

1. Excess productive capacity on a chronic or seasonally recurring basis.
2. Disproportionality high per cent of total profits from a few products.
3. Insufficient product width to exploit sales force contacts efficiently.
4. Steadily declining sales or profits.

We will present a management science perspective on the problem of achieving an optimal product mix. We shall distinguish between the static and dynamic optimal product mix problem.

Static Optimal Product Mix

Given in product possibilities, choose one of them such that profit is maximised subject to certain constraints being satisfied. Under certain conditions the problem may be solved by mathematical progress ; the most important condition being no demand and cost interactions among the various products being considered. This condition is rarely satisfied in practice.

Dynamic Optimal Product Mix

Management is interested in what will happen to profits, and sales growth as the product mix is changed. The computers contribution would consist of making rapid calculations of profit, stability and growth characteristics of many different possible transformations of the product mix through time.

Some products require periodic modification if they are to remain competitive. Some other products pass on the stage where further modification could not help ; they are candidates for elimination. A product modification is any deliberate alteration in the physical attributes of a product or its packing. A number of factors may prompt the manufacturer to alter his product. Since products have such attributes as colour, size, material, functional features, styling and engg. Any one or combination of these attributes would require change. Let us discuss three important and contrasting product modification strategies. Quality improvement, Feature improvement and Styling improvement.

Quality Improvement

A strategy of quality improvement aims at increasing the reliability and durability of the product through better materials of Engg. A premium quality producer often finds it easier to identify potential customers, because income or other customer variables tend to be correlated with an interest in quality.

Feature Improvement

A strategy of feature improvement aims at increasing the number of real or fancied user benefits. It involves redesigning the product so that it offer more convenience, safety, efficiency and versatility. Following are the advantages of feature improvement strategy :

(*i*) The development of new functional features is one of the most effective means of building a company image of progressiveness and leadership.

(*ii*) Functional features are an extremely flexible competitive tool because they can be adapted quickly, dropped quickly.

(*iii*) Functional features allow the company to gain the immense preference of preselected market segments.

(*iv*) Functional features often bring the innovating company free publicity.

(*v*) Functional features generate a great amount of sales force and distributors' enthusiasm.

The chief disadvantage of this strategy is that feature improvements are highly imitable ; unless there is a permanent gain from being first, the investment in original may not be justified.

Style Improvement

A strategy of style improvement aims at increasing the aesthetic appeal of the product in contrast to its functional appeal. In the case of packaged food and house hold products, where the opportunities for product styling and featuring are minimal except for colour, texture variations etc. treating the package as an extension of the product may be used.

Optimal Product Modification

In practice, a firm generally pursues some mixture of all three strategies. Just to maintain its competitive position the firm must incorporate the latest developments in quality, styling and functional feature. At the same time, each firm may specialize in one strategy in order to achieve leadership in that area.

Product Elimination

Many sick or marginal products never die, they are allowed to continue in the company's product mix until they "Fade away". In the mean time, they consume considerable resources which may be more fruitfully employed elsewhere. As a result, these marginal products lessen the firms profitability and reduce its ability to take advantage of new opportunities.

The weak products tend to consume a disproportionate amount of managements time. It often requires frequent price and inventory adjustments. If generally involves short production runs in spite of expensive set up times. It requires both advertising and sales force attention that might better be diverted to make the healthy products more profitable. Its very unfitness can cause customer misgivings and cast a shadow on the company's image. There are in fact many reasons for this aversion, logical as well as sentimental.

(*i*) Sometimes it is expected or hoped that product sales will pick up in the course of time when economic or market factors become more propitious. Here management thinks that poor performance is due to outside factors which will change.

(*ii*) Sometimes the fault is thought to lie in the marketing programme which the company plans to revitalize. It may be felt that the solution lies in reviving dealer enthusiasm, increasing the advertising budget, changing the advertising theme or modifying some - other marketing factor.

(*iii*) Even when the marketing programme is thought to be competent management may feel that the solution lies in product modification. Specially the thinking might be that sales could be stimulated through an upgrading of quality, styling or features.

The foregoing are all logical arguments for retaining weak products in the mix. But there are also situations where the persistence of weak products can be explained only by the presence of vested interests management and consumer sentiments. A lot of people inside and outside an organisation grow to depend on a particular product. Among them are the products manager the employees and certain customers. Eliminating a product from the mix is organisationally disruptive. Personnel may have to be shifted or released.

Process Planning

For the manufacture of a part or product, the exact specifications are required. Based on these specifications the design drawing is prepared. After the release of the design drawing, process planning starts by developing the broad plan of manufacture of the part or product. In fact the selection of materials and process such as casting, forging and die casting etc. are necessiated in the design stage itself.

The relation of process planning to layout and facilities planning. Process planning necessarily blends with the layout of physical facilities. Some process planning takes place during the layout phases of the design of a production system. Subsequently due to limitation in space, or to improve the methods of sequence, the original process plan is modified. The process plan needs the route sheets and operation sheets which summerize the operations required the preferred sequence of operations, auxiliary tools, operation required etc. Therefore process plans are inputs to the development of a layout.

The inputs to the process plan are the drawings or specifications which indicate what is to be made is decided by the orders or forecasts. Then an over all planning is made how many and which of the parts are to be bought from outside and how many are to be manufactured in side.

For the each parts to be made in side, the plant, tooling a detailed routine is developed. Here the technical knowledge of processes; machines and their capabilities and knowledge of production, economics is required. Since the range of processing alternatives is large, the selection of process is influenced by over all volume, and hence the economics of break even volume with respect the alternative process will be a deciding factor.

The distinction between product design, process planning manufacturing is shown in the following diagram:

Functional Design
↓
Form Design
↓
Drawings and Specifications

→ Product design

↓
Product Analysis
↓
Analysis of operations
↓
Make or buy economic analysis
↓
Route sheets operations sheets
↓
Work place and tool design

→ Process planning

↓
Modifications of Process
↓
Plans due to constraints in the space, quality of manufacturing product, availability of machine etc.

→ Manufacturing

59

Product Design

Introduction

Product design consists of mainly two features, form and function. The features of form are like shape of the product, appearance of the product etc. The functional features are concerned with the performance characteristics of the products like time required in washing, spinning and drying in a washing machine or number of pieces that can be washed per hour in a washing machine. For the same functional design, different manufacturers make the same product slightly in a different model or shape or appearance so that the advantage is gained by the customer either in the appearance or shape for the price variance he pays for. Sometimes with little extra additional cost, the functional features are improved to a great extent and it appeals the customers. Here the value analysis and value engineering plays a vital role in product design. Some products are demanded by the customer in different model every year or once in 5 years etc. Sometimes the manufacturer himself changes the modes periodically with additional features inform and functions to boost up the sales to keep in tune with the taste of the customers. This will lead to a number of innovations.

Factors Responsible for Products Design

— Design of products is quite often imitated from other existing products. To have a completely innovative idea in developing a product is quite costly and time consuming. In the long range product planning the innovative design is very much beneficial. Design by imitation pays quick but cannot last for long since the design of products by innovative research can sooner or latter because of its latest technology will throw all the existing designs out of market.

— The decision of a product design is generally based on the team work. The team usually consists the representatives of sales, design engineer, purchase, finance and production. Sales representative will assist in the design features of the product that are required from the customer point of view. Design engineer will link into the extent of possibility of such design required by the customers. Purchase will throw the ideas as to the choice of materials available and the finance will link into the cost aspect of such design. Once the team approves the new product design, as a prospective one, it is taken for the manufacturing and sale.

— After the commercial production, if the costs of the product happened to a more than what the market can absorb, it needs a detailed analysis of costs and remedial measures to arrest the escallation of costs. Finally one needs a value analysis approach towards maximisation of the cost affectiveness so that the product can continue to be in the market.

- When the demand is large compared to the supply, one can think for mass production so that the products can be made at low costs/unit. Every effort is required to study in detail about methods of production and the improvement. Since a minor improvement will result in large savings of resources and enable the manufacturers for better competition in the market.
- The design of the product be such that it is easy to repair. Customers prefer it. Alternatively, the concept of modular design is more advantage in the design of the product. Products are assembled from easily detachable sub-assemblies. Whenever a particular part fails, the whole component of which it is a part, can be taken out and replaced with a new component,where the repair or break down costs are too high this modular design is preferred by the customers.
- As the time advances miniaturization of the product is desirable like electronic products. Make it smaller and lighter in weight. It may not be possible in all products. This miniaturization is done partly by research and partly by design where sufficient knowledge is available. Miniaturization reduces the costs and increased the effectiveness appreciably. Example computer developments from Ist stage to 4th stage or 5th stage.

Standardisation

Standardisation of components is essential for interchanging capability of parts which is of vital significance to mass production on assembly line basis. In its simplest form, modern standardisation has been recognised and used since the advent of mass production techniques to which it is a necessary adjunct.

According to the international standard organisation. Geneva "standardisation is the process of formulating the applying rules for an orderly approach to specific activity for the benefit and with the cooperation of all concerned, and in particular for the promotion of the over all economy, taking due account of functional conditions and safety requirements".

A standard is based on the consolidated results of science, technology, research, development and experience. Normally a standard is established by custom authority or practice as a model to which an action or object can be compared. Hence it should represent the crystallised best thought of the practice of art. Standardisation in its broadest sense permeates almost all fields of human activity.

Standardisation As a Concept

The concepts of standardisation can be traced back to Noah's Ark. We all know that standardisation of components is essential for after changeability of parts which is of vital significance to mass production on assembly line. In other words importance of standardisation was realised since the advent of mass production techniques. Standardisation is defined by the International Standardisation Organisation Geneva as the process of formulating and applying rules for an orderly approach to a specific activity for the benefit and with the co-operation of all concerned and in particular for the promotion of the overall economy taking due account of functional conditions and safety requirements.

A standard is based on the consolidated results of science, technology, research development and experience. A standard is established by custom, authority or practice as a model to which an action or object can be compared. Standardisation in its broadest sense permeates almost in all fields of human activity.

Indian Standard Institute

In order to establish standardisation at National level, the Government of India established (I.S.I.). Indian Standard Institute in 1947 with the help of scientific, technical and industrial organisations. I.S.I. is an autonomous body with Union Minister of Industries as *ex-officio* president. In order to provide the assured quality of industrial goods, the I.S.I. Certificate Market Act was passed by the Parliament. This I.S.I. mark is intended to protect the consumer's interest and to achieve optimum utilisation of material resources by producing the quality and product from the right type of raw materials and processes. At organisational level standards deals with product process, methods, materials, specifications, inspection, tests, procedures or other type of requirements.

Advantages of Standardisation

(*i*) It enables one to have large quantity of few ever items economical buying quantity.

(*ii*) It reduces negotiation burden and results in a reduction in procurement lead time and better vendor relations.

(*iii*) It promotes healthy competition amongst multiple sources avoids shortages, reduces obsolescent items.

(*iv*) It enables one to operate running contracts leading to lower departmental operating costs. It reduces design time and efforts, minimises drafting effort through repetitive use of standard drawings, reduces specification.

(*v*) Writing by repetative use of standard specifications.

(*vi*) It enables to reduce the variety of items and hence results reduction in the inventory of tools and maintenance items.

(*vii*) It results in the improved interchangeability of parts.

(*viii*) It reduces the burden on inspection and quality control departments.

(*ix*) It enables to achieve over all reduction in operating costs and better the efficiency of all departments. For successful application of standardisation in an organisation following aspects should be considered :

(*a*) Dynamic and flexible nature of standardisation.

(*b*) Organisational aspects and responsibility of standardisation.

(*c*) Objectives of company standards.

(*d*) Technique and process of standardisation. In many public and private industries most of the non moving and excess inventory is mostly or account of lack of standardisation. Hence the Govt. gave a serious thought to over come this increasing inventory problem and established Indian Standards Institution (ISI) in 1947, with the active support of scientific, research technical and industrial organisations. The I.S.I. has standardised a number of items covering various sectors like steels, Fertilisers, chemicals, automobiles, Electrical goods. The I.S.I. mark is intended to protect the customers interest and to achieve optimum indisation of material resources by producing goods from quality raw materials.

Standardisation is a dynamic process. It can not remain static at one level. It has to move from one level to another higher level is from company standards to industry standards from industry standards to National standards, from National standards to Internatioal standards.

Disadvantages of Standardisation

Industry wide standardisation programmes are often only partially successful as standardisation tends to favour large business houses. Small or new companies cannot get a sizable business by making the same things and selling at the same price as the big companies. They survive by offering something different at the same time close to the same price as standard products. Such type of companies might be said to specialise on specialities and by doing so, to some extent, under cut or standardisation programme. Often customers do not want the standard items, unless it is priced lower. The salesmen also side this view of the customer sand prof make prepay under that "our product is different." If new products are standardised before they have become stable in design standardisation may become an obstacle to progress. In a product development stage, performance standards rather than form or shape standards should be used.

— Standards once set, resist change, thus retarding progress.

A standard of any given time is more the prevailing style than it is a permanent standard.

60

Total Quality Management

Total Quality Management

Total Quality Management (TQM) is born out of the market driven factors and hence all those organisations which operates in competitive environment do need it most. TQM embodies development of a company-wide culture for quality. TQM is nothing but an understanding and performance of roles by each and every individual in pursuit of quality movement.

Customer satisfaction is important to the success of any business. The quality products/service is expected to yield satisfaction to customer and success to organisation. The quality is a "Value", in which both customer and marketing claim to provide "Value"-for customer's money.

Companies have been giving increasing attention to customer satisfaction. A study has revealed that 49% of the CEO's rated "Customer Satisfaction,"among their three more critical strategic initiative similarly 38% identified customer satisfaction as their first priority. The need of the time is not only to meet customer's expectation only, but to exceed it and delight the customer by exceeding their expectations.

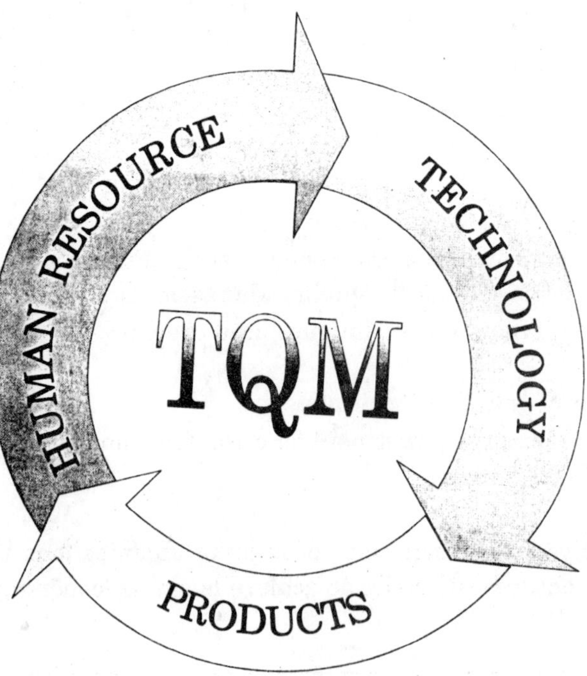

LAUNCHING OF TQM

Launch of TQM can be driven extrinsically but it can be sustained only through intrinsic motivation both organisationally and individually. The greatest difficulty in launching "TQM" is in building awareness and understanding of the same through the organisational hierarchy. The greatest difficulty is "Attitudes," "Skills and knowledge" that can be developed, but attitudes would be difficult to change. The other difficulty is to get the employees to see the linkage between their efforts and the end results. Therefore establishing this connection upfront is very important for the success of "TQM" programme. "TQM" programme requires a change in the mind-set. Rather it would be in order to put up that TQM is not a programme but a process of bearing, which integrates tools and techniques with culture to produce business results.

"TQM" is survival strategy with an objective to institutionalise continuous improvement. TQM is not an independent standard above activity. These concept should clearly be integrated into the business planning process. It would be helpful if cross-functional teams address the essential areas to bring about a visible change in the style of functioning. In fact working should be so transformed that it takes its root and begins to be reflected in the normal working.

To meet the "Total Quality Management," the organisations should glide effortlessly through the data, information, knowledge, wisdom chain at every level in every department and every function. The cycle of TQM involves four phases *viz.* "Plan"; "Do the plan," "Check results" and finally "Act".

INTEGRATION OF "TQM" WITH BUSINESS

In order to ensure that TQM does not become a jargon and is integrated to business necessity, it is important to have documentation, training of personnel, continual internal audits and management reviews to ensure constancy. Making plans for quality as an annual feature, good monitoring, reward and recognition systems to encourage implementation of plans, will further ensure constancy. Visible results will follow if quality objectives, strategies of the Company are clearly defined and identified from the point of view of "Customer Satisfaction."

TOTAL QUALITY MANAGEMENT AND BUSINESS

Integration of TQM with Business involve

— Policy management, Business re-engineering, Strategic Business process and linkage with TQM. The Total Quality Management focus is on

— Customer focus (Tools and Techniques used to achieve planned customer satisfaction).

Empowerment for Team Performance

— Self managed teams, empowerment for cross-functional or quality improvement of the team's effectiveness.

TQM Systems

— Structures, Systems which help in building organisations that are responsive, flexible and continuously strive to achieve business leadership through customer satisfaction.

WIN FOR EVERYONE THROUGH QUALITY

Total Quality Management is the total aspects of quality at all stages of the products service.

Whether we run a business, a project, a programme, an institute or even social organisation, the concept of "Quality" is universal and core of all business activities.

The management of Quality now called **"Total Quality Management," can in brief be summarised as doing small, small things greatly.**

Total Quality Management is carrying out incremental improvements and it is :

- Pay attention to details
- Doing things right the first time
- Practice good human relations

"TQM" is a "Journey, not the Destination". The Journey even to the moon, starts with a single step. But before we go further, let us audit our activities to find out, whether we are "doing small things greatly" and paying attention to details. Some of the activities for Quality audit could be :

- Carry out an audit about the fused tubelight, broken chairs, scratch on the wall, torn carpet, old calendars or charts on the wall, noisy door closers, squeaky door, cleaned venetian blinds.
- Finding about the leaking flush, wet floors, overflowing, or clogged drains, rusty water storage tanks, pedestal fans or desert coolers in winters in offices etc.

Attending these small things are nothing but ensuring "Quality," both in attitude and action. Quality or efforts towards **"TQM" will be effective when we adopt an attitude "Every activity makes a lot of difference towards everything and anything that is quality."**

TQM — IT IS AN ATTITUDE

Overcoming Attitude of Let Us Carry On

Look at this way - The attitude that - "Let us carry on," give a message of being careless and indifferent. It gives a message that management does not care and immediately, the employee gets the message and adopts an attitude of - don't bother. This will result in employees becoming lazy and less interested in doing the right things at the right time. It is like undertaking audit of one's activities, to be able to judge our quality in practice.

Do not give lip services, instead do "small-small things greatly." **Some of TQM activities could be :**-Japanese polish the gears in the gear box, even though they are not seen by the customers. **In good hotels, even the top of the fan blades are cleaned regularly. Ensuring prompt reply,** Quality is when every letter is replied promptly or within a reasonable time. Maki4ng a list of the dates and replies sent out. May be the situation is atrocious, may be it is very good - either way, we can improve it. Quality is Good housekeeping - It calls for spending regularly some time on the EPABX board to get the feel of the "Incoming" and "Outgoing" calls to give dignity to the operator's

WORK IS LIFE
• Work is a social activity. • Work plays a central role in the life of most of the people engaged in productive activities. • Work provides fellw feelings. • Work controls the life of an individual. • Work is a source of status both formal and informal.

jobs. **Housekeeping" is excellent if the operators room is properly lit, there are no naked wires anywhere and also get the equipment professionally cleaned once in a month. Quality is like reputation.** To understand that, it reminds me of the story told to me by one of my friend. He purchased a "Canon Camera" from a shop at Tokyo in 1960, when "Canon" was not very well known. Some months later, it so happened that he was returning to India *via* Japan and happened to visit a Canon Shop again. He showed his camera which had stopped working. In 30 minutes flat, he was given a new camera. There was no paper work, no meetings with battery of managers. The girl at the counter exchanged the camera with a smiling face. This system gives confidence in the product as a few customers (4 per cent) will cheat anyway. Then why punish the balance (96 per cent) of customers. We can build this 'misuse' cost into own price, but after ensuring better "After Sales Service."

• **Quality is prompt Service** - It is quality when every phone is picked up before the "Third" ring. At places, chances are that the phone will be picked up before the first ring itself. Well, how do they do it? **The pay scales of the employees are very reasonable but "Money" is not motivator, it is the "Training" that makes the difference.**

• **Quality starts with each one of us, just like charity begins at home.** Let us look at the things with the eyes of the third party. Let us see our visitor's chairs. Are they in good condition ? If the upholstery changed before it looks dirty or is torn somewhere. The carpet — is it dirty or torn ? And in that way, have a look at everything with a magnifying glass.

Let us make a list of such items and call the list "DIN" - DO IT NOW.' **Make regular intervals say every alternative Saturday. Start giving "Do it now" (DIN) number. It works beautifully.** The important thing is that every unimprovement becomes important and starts whispering, and when many unimportant things whisper - it becomes shouting. **"TQM" is when we "do small, small things greatly." before the things start whispering.** TQM is nothing but doing one's business but in a different way. It is a set of best management practices.

TQM & STRATEGIC TECHNIQUES

Total Quality Management consists of two major elements. The first element is the "Use of Strategic Techniques" such as flowchart, "Cause" and "Effect Diagrams" and Statistical Process Control to help in the decision making process. These tools, help us to eliminate non-value added activities in all functions. Second element is a "Change in Managers Behaviour." Mangers ar of two types. One type is-who directs, rely on roles and organisational hierarchy, makes isolated decisions, view people as costs, encourages secrecy and passivity. The second type of mangers are those who lead, guide and collaborate, focus on the process, use information networks, view people as assess and promote diversity, flexibility, openness, share risks taking and involvement. Both these elements should be implemented with the goal of meeting "Customer's Needs." "TQMs" successful implementation depends on developing a business strategy based on core competencies (doing the right thing) and providing value added customer focused process (doing things right). The overall strategy of "Doing the right thing right" must become a way of life. *In other words, generic road map for introducing TQM involves, working towards customer satisfaction and finally towards customer delight.*

TQM ORGANISATION

Value addition - quantitative or qualitative is the core function of various activities under an organisation structure. Value of a product can be increased by either increasing features (pertaining to "functional" or "esteem") or by decreasing the operation costs, or by both simultaneously.

HUMAN FACTORS AND TQM

Teamwork: Solving a selected problem through quality circle activities results in qualitative improvement in product features or process, thus adding value. *Employee involvem4ent and empowerment* : Tapping employee strengths and facilitating their active participation in the continuous improvement process, through cost reduction exercises and innovative suggestion schemes, is a proven method of improving quality and reducing cost. By empowering the employees, the organisation provides necessary freedom to act upon everyday quality problems, thus promotion them to own responsibility for quality.

Training : Training the employees on problem solving skills, application of statistical techniques and developing core competencies in tune with state-of-the-art knowledge/technology is yet another key facilitator of quality improvement. Thus the sum of economic and human value addition factors prescribed by TQM will upgrade the quality of products / services.

CUSTOMERS VALUE SYSTEM

To understand what value means to a customer, we need to understand first his perceptions and expectation of value. Customer expectation about value is essentially a complex mix of objective and subjective elements. Customer focus through continuous value improvement is what an organisation should aim at.

In the present environment of fierce competition the customer is rightly crowned King, for it is only he who knows best what he wants, thus dictating the terms of market demand accordingly. Today, the customer does not intend to buy just products/services ; he purchases the benefits associated with them. Thus in turn means that the customer is interested in the 'value gains' that accrue to him by having a product/service. And given that under an open market economy the customer now has multifarious options at his demand, he would always prefer the products/ services of those organisations which provide value to him on a continuously improving basis. Hence, providing commensurate value to the customer's money should be instituted as a fundamental commitment by an organisation aiming to achieve customer focus in its true spirit.

To understand what value means to a customer, we need to understand first his perceptions and expectation of value. Customer expectation about value is essentially a complex mix of objective and subjective elements. The objective face of his expectations pertain mainly to the 'use' (functional) value of the product. This is defined as the virtue of a product, such as technology, reliability, serviceability etc., by which it accomplishes a set of functions assigned to it satisfactorily. The subjective face of expectations correspond to 'esteem' (aesthetic) value attached to a product since it fulfils his instinctive desires by satisfying his ego and emotions, by giving him pride, identity and so on. Here the soft aspects of the organisational approach towards the customer such as attitude, communication, deliverance, responsiveness (in sum, 'culture') play a vital role in meeting his expectations.

After having defined and framed quality policy and in order to achieve the customer satisfaction the entire organisation need to be transformed from seller's market into an "environment" of buyer market and re-oriented so that the service rendered by people are aimed at customer satisfaction.

This is possible by up--grading the skills and talent of the people with the latest tools and techniques of management.

BUSINESS PROCESS MANAGEMENT

A process managed organisation is quicker to respond to changes in the market place. They are focused on results rather than tasks and have flatter organisation structures. Employees understand their customer requirements and are effective to value addition.

MANAGEMENT FOR GROWTH

A workshop can be organised to discuss how to more towards a horizontal, prices managed organisation and reasons why this critical to build a versatile and responsive organisation. This will help in building a link between strategic vision and efficiency.

CORE PROCESS IDENTIFICATION

Process Improvement starts top down starting with identification of the organisation's core processes and core competencies required. The workshop will help in executive to identify strategically critical processes, identify process owners and develop a mandate for change.

BUSINESS PROCESS IMPROVEMENT

Object is to detect and eliminate in the organisation's processes resulting in short ended cycle time, improved productivity and core competencies required reduced cost and increased

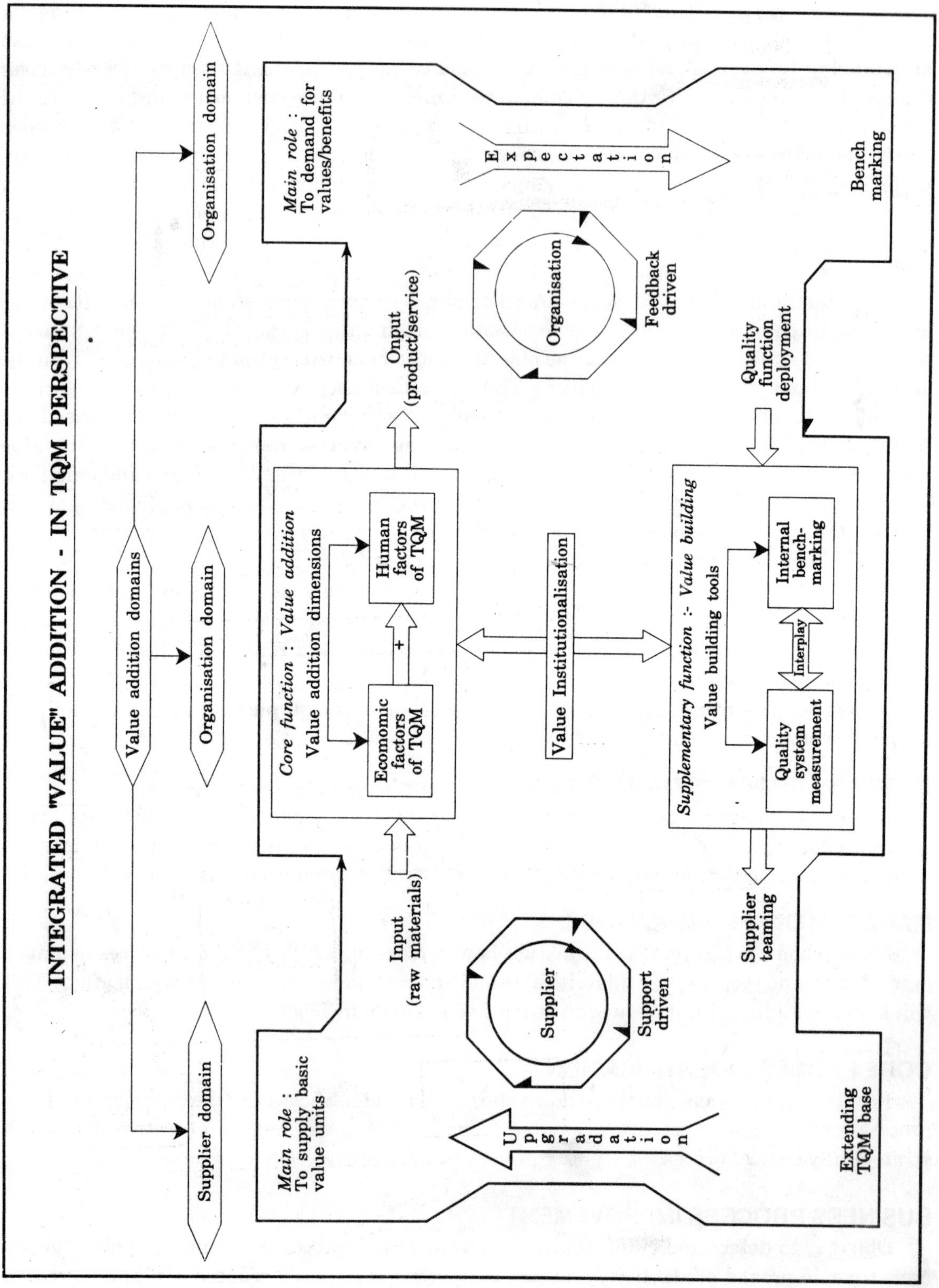

INTEGRATED "VALUE" ADDITION - IN TQM PERSPECTIVE

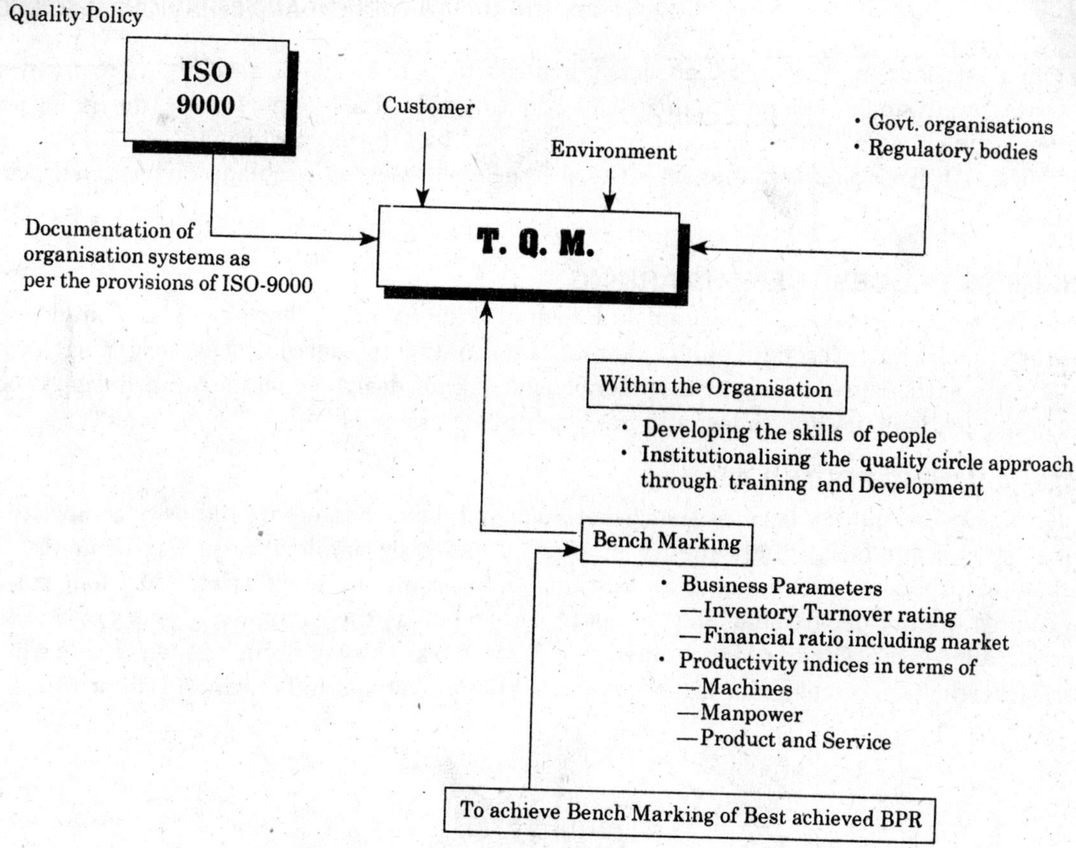
Quality Policy
ISO 9000
Customer
Environment
• Govt. organisations
• Regulatory bodies
Documentation of organisation systems as per the provisions of ISO-9000
T. Q. M.
Within the Organisation
• Developing the skills of people
• Institutionalising the quality circle approach through training and Development
Bench Marking
• Business Parameters
—Inventory Turnover rating
—Financial ratio including market
• Productivity indices in terms of
—Machines
—Manpower
—Product and Service
To achieve Bench Marking of Best achieved BPR

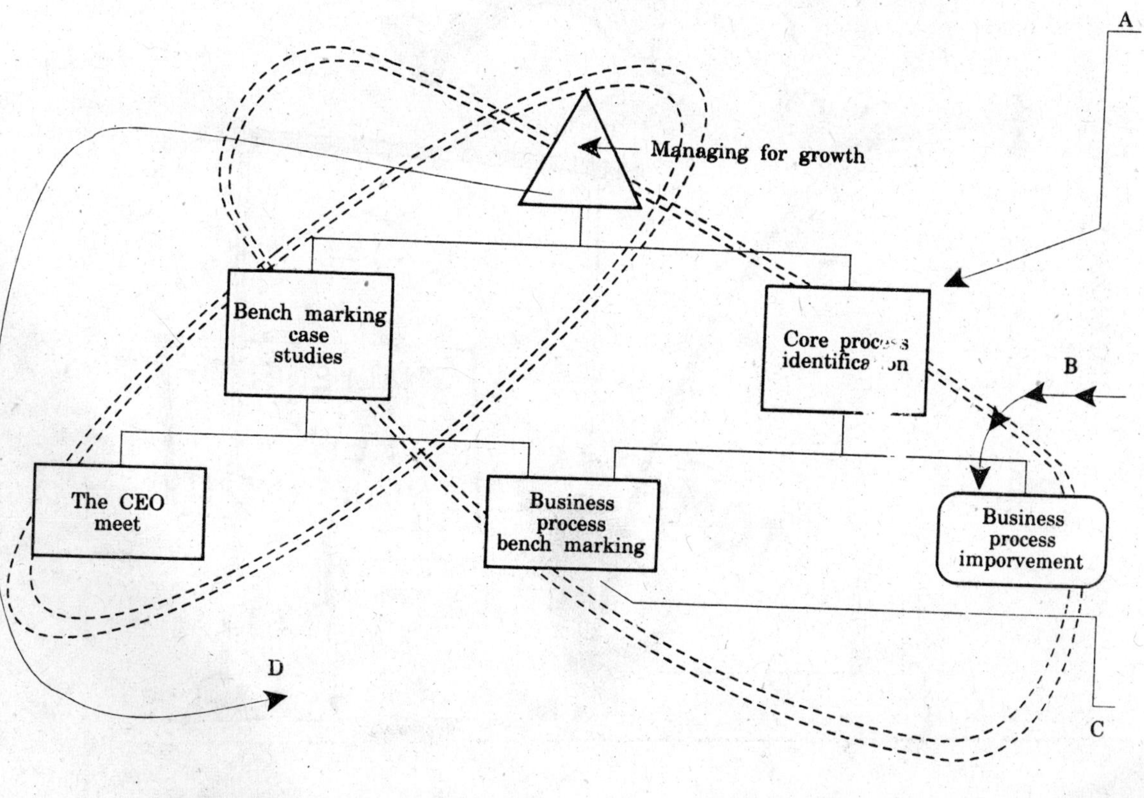
A
Managing for growth
Bench marking case studies
Core process identification
B
The CEO meet
Business process bench marking
Business process imporvement
D
C

customer satisfaction. The workshop will give the participant hands in training in documenting processes, analysing practioners, deficiencies, identifying business opportunities designing and implementing changes, standardising procedures and monitoring performance. Linkages established with other quality management-tools like Benchmarking, problem solving and Process ________.

BUSINESS PROCESS BENCHMARKING

To equip senior executive to complete Benchmarking exercise. The object is to build skills on how to navigate through public domain information resources locate organisation to benchmark with, approach organisation for benchmarking, design benchmarking, design bench marking questionnaire and collect and implement best practical.

TQM - A WINING FORMULA

In the 1970s, quality became the cornerstone of Japan, to make its industry competitive, and it started producing high quality products. Later, by employing quality principles in controlling process waste, it was realised that quality could not be restricted any longer to a designated quality department, but it was to spread across the company, giving birth to the concept called "Total Quality Management," or TQM marks the beginning of a new era in which managers will focus on customer values cross--functional systems and continuous improvement.

Quality is never an accident. It is always the result of high intentions, sincere efforts, intelligent direction and skillful execution. It is an attribute or characteristic whose dictionary meaning is the degree of goodness or worth of a person, place or thing. In determining the quality of a product the customer's expectations about the product should be given the topmost priority.

According to the product-based approach, quality is an attribute which can be measured quantitatively. The manufacturing-based approach, on the other hand, uses the universal definition of conformance to requirements. The value-based approach says that the consumer purchase decision is based on quality at an acceptable price. In this age of liberalisation, the quality of products has become a major concern for all industries. To be competitive, an industry needs to provide a provide a product /service into which quality is designed, built, marketed and maintained at the most economical cost; which allows full customer satisfaction. This competitive edge made the Industries think of approaching quality management efforts in their total forms, known as Total Quality Management. Quality management is a companywide activity involving the combined efforts of various departments such as design, engineering, purchase, production Inspection, etc. in different phases, with a view to achieving the desired quality of the product.

The Job of quality management is not just advising a sampling plan for the acceptance/rejection of the incoming materials and controlling conditions. It is, in fact, Job at every stage of the company's activities.

Quality management is a companywide activity involving the combined efforts of various departments such as design, engineering, purchase, production Inspection, etc. in different phases, with a view to achieving the desired quality of the product.

A better-managed corporation like General Electric believes that about 15 cent of its sales is attributable to waste of the cost of poor quality. Unlocking that potential, itself can be a good enough reason for many organisations try embark on the rigours of TQM (Bagchi 1996).

THE TQM VISION

The quality cycle begins and ends with the user. It starts when the user's need is analysed to design a product. During the development and manufacture of that product, various departments and sections of the company make their contribution in building quality into it.

Quality management, like any management process, has three main components :

(*a*) Quality Planning-designing desired and deliverable quality standards

(*b*) Quality Implementation and

(*c*) Quality monitoring and control

It is imperative that TQM affords should be properly organised to co-ordinate the various contributing aspects of quality. As such we need to know the basic ideas behind TQM. Organisations are made up of a complex system of customers and suppliers. People pay attention to who supplies them, with what they need to do their job and who the customer is for what they produce. When everybody becomes concerned about meeting their customers, requirements, quality will be there,without doubt.

In meeting customer expectations, the focus must be on the process; not just on the results. To improve a process, it is important to look at the socio-cultural issues of organisation; to create a healthy, open atmosphere if which people are willing to open up and do some introspection on their processes. And this is something the management must be able to facility.

In contrast to traditionally managed organisations, TQM managed organisations believe that though there is no complaint from the customers, there is always room for improvement. Everybody in the organisation is trained to plan and participate in groups. Meetings and brainstorming sessions become primary vehicles for planning and creative problem solving. Each member in the team is recognised and rewarded. Errors and problems are viewed as opportunities for learning rather than blunders to be punished.

The Indian context: In the recent past, TQM got its formal recognition by way of ISO 9000.In Order that Indian organisations may successfully compete with worldclass leaders, it is imperative to look at and be prepared for quality way beyond the popular ISO 9000.

In the context of the Indian organisation, the common perception held is that quality improvement is uneconomical since it increases cost and investment, thereby decreasing productivity. Traditional Indian managers are not prepared for intense global competition, where quality, cost sticking to the deadlines and customer satisfaction are of paramount 2importance. They are not prepared to shed the belief that they can get business by cornering licences; influencing the bureaucrats.

Indian companies should wake up to the realities and try to build up an organisation where information flown freely; employees are empowered with decision making and problem solving; and where teamwork is awarded and encouraged. Our executives have to learn how to becomes successful quality managers, so that they can become global managers, and this primarily means a change in there mind set.

The key word here is "professionalism". It is not surprising that many new managers want to keep control firmly in their own hands, but TQ manages see their employees as a work group and believe that their team to do a good job,

The manager must learn skills of collaboration. He is to make certain his team has had the correct training in the use of data and statistical tools. Management by fact is the main characteristic of the TQ manager.

He should also reward the deserving team of individuals for their support of the TQM philosophy. Recognition and reward are his key tools, and he has to know how to use them in order to support TQM. He should help employees to gain insights from their personal experiences, and how to improve on them thereupon. Many companies in India are realising this and are now focusing their efforts on team building and teamwork. Companies like Daewoo, Samsung, Ford, have brought in certain skills worthy of emulation. Indian companies like TVS and Tata Steel are implementing TQM--Tata steel has announced that, through TQM, it was able to cut down rejection of its steel from 18 per cent to 3 per cent in just 24 months!

Hindustan Lever Limited, a Unilever Group company operating in India, started implementing Quality assurance in place of quality control. Looking at the success of quality assurance, the company has started TQM in 1990, mainly to focus intensified broad--based training at all levels, institutionalising quality improvement programmes, vendor development and certification

TQM TECHNIQUES

Benchmarking: In this book Managerial Breaktbrough, Joseph Juran asked the question "what is that organisations do which gets results so much better than ours? The answer to this question opened the door to new techniques like Benchmarking, and for many companies Benchmarking has become component of their TQM programme.

In most developing countries, like India, untial recently, almost all the industries had a few number of products and services which differed markedly in their utilitarian characteristics. However, such a situation is hardly sustainable with increasing competition from foreign goods and services. In such a situation, competing firms have to continuously improve. The Benchmarking approach not only provides a comparative profile, but also helps the management to identify innovative products and services. Benchmarking is a continuous process of measuring one's products, services and practices against toughest competitors. It will search for the best practices in industry,which will lead to superior quality goods. With the growing emphasis on quality, it has got great significance in the present competitive world.

If best practice are followed, customer requirements can easily be met, leading to increasing profitability of the company. But the employees resist change at the beginning because they are habituated to old processes (Rama Mohan 1996).

BUSINESS PROCESS REENGINEERING

Business process reengineering generally redesigns processes and the organisation that performs them in order to reduce the number of boundaries crossed. Each time a process crosses an organisational boundary, opportunities for error aries. Business process reengineering is the fundamental rethinking and radical redesigns of business processes to achieve dramatic improvements in critical contemporary measures of performance, such as cost quality, service and speed. As the traditional organisations are unable to meet the present challenges, there is every need for new techniques and philosophies with which organisations can survive and thrive under gruelling competition. To retain their competitive edge, companies should change their traditional ways of working, to read their customers'minds. No organisation can offered to overlook customer, competition and change, the three vital force of today's competitive environment. TQM is an important milestone in the ongoing evolution of the field of management.

KAIZEN

Kaizen is the overriding concept behind good management. It is the unifying thread running through the philosophy, the systems, and the problem solving tools developed in Japan over the last 30 years. The essence of most of the Japanese management practices viz : " Quality circles" "Quality control", "Life long employment", "Total quality control", or "Productivity improvement" can be reduced to one word : KAIZEN

KAIZEN promotes process-oriented way of thinking Leading to the development of strategies that ensure continuous improvement involving people at all leaves of the organisation. The key elements of KAIZEN are as under:

- Customer Orientation, TQC (Total Quality Control)
- QC Circles
- Suggestion System
- Automation
- Discipline at the workplace
- TPM (Total Productive Maintenance)
- Quality Improvement

- Just-in time
- Zero Defects
- Small-group activities
- Co-operative labour-management relations
- Productivity Improvement and New-product development.

Historical Perspective

The emergence of quality consciousness in Japan dates back to the fifties. Dr. W.E. Deming was quick to notice the interest of the Japanese in quality and predicted during one of his visits- that Japan would soon become a world leader in quality products . Deming introduced the famous PDCA cycle -also called 'Deming cycle"which meant continuous improvement. He taught his cycle in all his training courses and emphasised that this unique process would enable organisations to win customer confidence.

KAIZEN AND TQC

In the Japanese approach TQC movement is considered as part of the Kaizen movement.

But, the first and foredmost concern in Kaizen is with the quality of people. Building quality into people means helping them become kaizen-conscious.

KAIZEN REDEFINED

Kaizen means improvement. It means continuing improvement in working life, home life, social life and working life. When applied to the personel life, kaizen means continuing improvement involving everyone — managers and workers alike.

KAIZEN SUGGESTIONS SYSTEMS

Kaizen suggestion systems are currently in operation in most of the large manufacturing companies and about half of the small and medium-size companies in Japan.

The Kaizen suggestion systems :

— Improvement in one's own work

— Savings in energy, material and other resources

— Improvements in the working environment

— Improvements in machines and processes

— Improvemants in office work

— Improvements in product quality.

— Ideas for new products.

— Customer services and customer relations.

Japan Human Relations Association conducted a **Survey on kaizen suggestion system** in 1987. The survey involved 620 companies and more than 2 million persons.

Findings of Kaizen Suggestions :

— Average number of suggestions submitted per person per year stands at 24 number.

— Participation ratio -67%

— Suggestions Implemented-80 %
— Average amount of award per person every year amounts to Yen 8000
— Cost savings per person per year amounts to Yen 360,000
— Cost savings per suggestion accepted amounts to Yen 18,000

The average number of suggestions per employee per year hovered around five per year until mid-1950s. Since then, the number of suggestions has gradually increased. Today the average in the private sector has risen to 24 suggestions per employee per year.

To day, most of the suggests that have economic impact come from groups, while individual based suggestions serve as morale boosters and educational experiences.

The Japanese system has evolved into two segments : individual suggestions and group suggestions, including those generated by QC circles and other group based activities.

Traditionally, suggestions systems are introduced with the installation of a suggestion box and the announcement of a cash reward for an adopted idea. This formula is out of data today in Japan. Because it does not work well. We find no organisations successfully implementing such styles of suggestions system today.

WALKING SUGGESTION BOX

It is a new suggestion system without a suggestion box. The new system requires everybody to look for problems, solve them, and write suggestions after they are implemented in the workplace. Under this new system. Each manager should also be more involved . He extends help to his colleagues in finding and solving problems.

A SUCCESSFUL IMPLEMENTATION

The Kaizen suggestion system should go through three stages.

- In the first stage, management should make every effort to help the employees provide suggestions, no matter how promitive, for the betterment of the employee's own work and his work place. This will help the employees to analyse the way they are doing their own jobs.
- In the second stage, management should stress on employees' education to promote awareness about the problems in the work environment so that employees can provide better suggestions.
- In the third stage, after the employees are both interested and educated, should the management be concerned with the economic impact of the suggestions.

This means that the *management must think of the KAIZEN suggestion system in terms of a five to ten-year span.* The difficulties most Indian companies encounter stem from the fact that they usually try to skip stages one and two and move straight to the third stage.

Various Kaizen Programmes that can be introduced at the work place are :

KAIZEN PROGRAMMES

— 5s
— Kaizen Suggestion System
— Quality Circle

— Employee Award Scheme
— Information Sharing Meeting
— Company Newsletters
— Total Quality Control — TQC
— Total productive maintenance — TPM
— Just-In Time Production System — JIT
— Awareness Promotion Month.

61

Quality Systems Installation of ISO - 9000

The ISO-9000 standards play the role on a global scale. Companies are increasingly using the standards as effective tools for improving the quality of their products/services. ISO - 9000 standards reflect, the most current state of the art for building Total Quality Management.

The business relationship are extending beyond national boundaries and across cultural barriers with the result, the importance of accepted quality standards - ISO - 9000 has become the need of the time. Since associated with the installation of ISO-9000, would like to share my experience with other members of Dalmia Parivar.

WHAT IS ISO-9000

ISO-9000 is a major quality phenomenon which has taken the world by storm. The ISO-9000 standards have been adopted as national standards in more than 50 countries.

ISO-9000 is a series of five international standards on Total Quality Management (TQM). These standards come from the International Organisation for Standardisation.

WHY IS ISO-9000 SO IMPORTANT

— Provides good platform for continuous improvement to ensure implementation of TQM.
— Vehicle to hold quality improvement gains.
— Enables consistency in quality of products and services.
— Provides methods for involving non-manufacturing areas in quality and quality improvement.
— EC has adopted ISO-9000 is its Quality system standard.
— Meet quality competition—Domestic and International

ISO - 9000 — A JOURNEY NOT A DESTINATION

The Quality journey can be initiated when we decide as an Organisation to go in for ISO-9000 certification. Obtaining ISO-9000 certification does not mean "arriving" at the destination, rather this could at best be the first step in "Total Quality Management" journey. *A journey with a shifting finish line.*

ISO-9000 AND TOTAL MANAGEMENT

The ISO standards tell us "WHAT IS REQUIRED" and not "HOW TO DO"- What is required. ISO-9000 does to guarantee Product Quality itself, it will not ensure "sustainable competitive advantage". It means going beyond improving our processes to implement "TGM" which cover delivering Quality at competitive price while enhancing organisational health. There is no doubt that "Quality" require extreme hard work but more than that it requires a lot of persistence and patience. It is not just hard work but a systematic work.

The expected results are a competitive position in the market, improvement in productivity, reduction in waste, quicker response to the needs of the customers and market and eventually, these get reflected in the bottomline of every organisation.

ISO-9000 PROVIDES THE PLATFORM

ISO-9000 provides good platform for continuous improvement to ensure implementation of "TQM". The ISO-9000 is a vehicle to hold quality improvement gains. ISO-9000 enables consistency in quality of products and services. There is a strong feeling among executives that once we have obtained ISO-9000, we have quality system in place, it is not so as it is less than one seventh of the "Total Quality Management System".

ISO-9000- A STEPPING STONE FOR SUCCESS OF TQM

Since majority of people seem to operate from the value frame of compliance to authority it would be faster to implement ISO-9000 to move towards TQM as a vehicle. ISO-9000 is more structured, more immediate and convincing vehicle. Guided by discipline to ISO-9000, organisation propels itself towards TQM process. ISO-9000 covers the various aspects of TQM. It is an intermediatory goal.

Some Organisations have started their "Quality" movement by moving in the direction of ISO-9000 and others have begun the TQM journey as a system concept. The road map of the two may be different but an ideal organisation may use different methods of linking them, depending on the purposes and direction of business.

ISO-9000-LEAD TO TOTAL QUALITY MANAGEMENT

- ISO-9000 standards complement TQM emphasis on the human element.
- ISO-9000 helps us to assess our company's quality requirements.
- ISO-9000 translates quality concepts into achievable targets.
- ISO-9000 provide an opportunity to create and improve quality systems.
- ISO-9000 helps to spread the message of quality across the organisations.

WHY ISN'T ISO-9000-TOTAL QUALITY MANAGEMENT

- ISO-9000 is based on standards and ignores the human element/cost element.
- ISO-9000 lays down only systems, it says nothing about implementation.
- ISO-9000 certification is unsustainable and prone to the day-after effect.
- ISO-9000 makes no demands on or assurances about final product quality.
- ISO-9000 transfers the ones of ensuring quality to the certifier.

QUALITY POLICY

The quality policy is formulated before the start of installation process. It reveals the over all intentions and directions of an organisation towards quality as expressed by the Management. The quality policy is akin to Mission statement and objectives of the organisation. Communication of Quality Policy is to assure that "Quality Policy" is accepted as the responsibility of every employee. The Quality Policy of some of the organisations are given as under:

COMPANY(A) — It is their vision to nurture and cherish to the position of a leader in the industry, in India, and also be recognised and respected as a manufacturer of world-class products.

A company of people who enjoy working together as a team, to create superior and distinct products and services for their customers.

Focused, fast and flexible, they seek neverending improvements, in order to create an enterprise that is dynamic, ever-expanding profitable and in constant pursuit of customer satisfaction.

COMPANY(B) — Total customer satisfaction through "TQM" is the basic policy. This is achieved by :

- Maintaining a global business focus. The Company is dedicated to supplying quality products and services at optimum value, for total customer satisfaction.
- Appreciating national need for generation of optimum surpluses, to optimise ROI.

COMPANY(C) — QUEST

QU= QUALITY

E = EXCELLENCE

S = SERVICE

T = TRUST

COMMUNICATION OF QUALITY POLICY

- Communication of policy be during employees get together.
- Laminated card giving quality policy, Mission statements and Quality objectives be given to all employees.
- Quality policy be highlighted on company's letter heads, visiting cards and posters etc.

INSTALLATION OF ISO-9000

The installation of ISO-9000 starts with Chief Executive of the Company taking a decision to go for ISO-9000 certification. The "CEO" should also take the following decisions :

- Appointment of Consultant — Consulting Organisation *viz.* Confederation of Indian Industry.
- Finalisation of Certifying Agency- Bureau Veritas Quality International (BVQI), (RVC) Holland, or some other agency holding accredation from National Accredation of Certification Bodies (NACB) U.K.

The various activities of ISO-9000 can be classified into seven phases. The phase I & II and phase V. These phases helps in establishing a Training Plan, understand, develop and implement Quality Systems.

THE PHASE I & II STARTS

It covers the mandatory requirements of ISO-9000, awareness and documentation programme, Review of existing Quality System, Action Plan for developing, implementing and maintaining Quality Systems.

- Quality Policy is formulated and communicated.
- Awareness and documentation workshop should be conducted at all levels on ISO-9000.
- The Management representative appointed.
- Core quality assurance group should be formed.
- The ISO-9000 posters are designed and put up at all prominent places in the organisation
- Personal letters sent by the Chief Executive to all the employees highlighting what is ISO-9000, its benefits and how each employee can contribute for installation ?
- "PERT" (Programme Evaluation Review Technique) Chart for ISO-9000 installation is finalised by the Management representative with core group members.
- Assignment of tasks for writing of documentation/procedures is given to concerned executives.
- Procedure for Management Review is finalised.

PHASE III & IV

It covers the following :

- Preparation of Matrix Organisation for deciding requirements of procedures of Company.
- Methodology for writing the procedure is finalised. After reviewing the existing procedures, then comparing with ISO-9000 standards and writing of procedure is undertaken.
- Writing of Apex Manual.
- The help of consultancy organisation like CII etc., is taken, if required. The steps for preparation of quality manual undertaken.
- Issue of procedures for implementation.

PHASE V & VI

It covers Training of Internal Auditors and Lead Assessors to develop self assessment capability Review of Standards, comparing with Management of auditing, Auditing skills and non-conformance reporting.

- Internal audit programme is conducted by the consultancy organisation or by Core Group of the Company trained as Lead Assessor.
- This gives an opportunity to the organisation to look into it own systems. The internal audit has a regular activity while management review (higher level review) contains the analysis of the internal audit. To conduct internal audit, audit plan is prepared alongwith audit schedule and checklist.
- The Consultancy Organisation is involved, in counseling preparation of documentations

- The audit of Quality System and establishing linkages among procedures to find out how well the organisation has prepared its documents viz-a-vis the procedures.
- Conducting adequacy audit for certification by CII.

PHASE VII

- Certification by 3rd party comes at this stage.
- Normally 3rd party carries out "Adequacy Audit" or "System Audit" of quality manual and based on that they decide for the assessment audit before giving the certification. Surveillance audit is conducted regularly.

QUALITY AUDIT

Quality Audit forms a basis for improving the quality of company operations to ensure that the procedures to maintain quality are amended if non-compliance with them is due to their wording and to take corrective action to improve the product.

OBJECTIVES

The primary objectives of an external quality audit is to examine a quality system, to determine the degree with which it complies with a given set of requirements (Quality standard, Quality Manual etc.). Quality Audit should not result in transfer of the responsibility to achieve quality from operating personnel to the auditing organisation.

AUDIT OBJECTIVES

The audit objectives are :

(*a*) COMPANY QUALITY SYSTEM'S/ EFFECTIVENESS

To determine the conformity or non-conformity of the quality system element with specified requirement

(*b*) REGULAR SURVEILLANCE. To provide the audit with an opportunity to improve the quality system.

(*c*) TO IDENTIFY IMPROVEMENT AREAS. To determine the effectiveness of the implemented quality system in specified Quality objectives.

(*d*) CERTIFICATION. To meet regulatory requirement.

FEATURES OF AUDITS

All Audits are formalised, regular, systematic documented checks on a quality system and all have following characteristics in common :

(1) Audit should always be carried only by personnel outside the product/Division/Department.

(2) Audits are random checks of the system. They are designed to uncover non-conformances or non-compliance faults *viz*. Poor documentation control, lack of understanding of the system; Inadequate Training and qualification.

Audits are carried out in an objective manner *viz*. demonstratable factual evidence and not subjective impressions is the basis for assessmen. The features of Audit are :

- INDEPENDENCE
- OBJECTIVITY
- RANDOMNESS
- GRADUATION OF NON--CONFORMANCES

TYPE OF AUDITS

Quality Audits should not lead to an increase in the scope of Quality functions over and above the necessity to meet Quality objectives. The various types of Audit are :

Adequacy Audit

This is also known as a system audit, a documentation audit or management audit and is normally an exercise which determines the extent to which the documented system represented by the Quality Manual and the associated procedures adequately meets the requirements of applicable standards. An adequacy audit should also seek to have clarified any ambiguous, unclear or conflicting statements on the ground that if the auditor cannot understand them the workforce probably can't either!

TYPES OF AUDIT

- ADEQUACY AUDIT
- A COMPLIANCE AUDIT
- AN EXTERNAL AUDIT
- AN INTERNAL AUDIT
- A PRODUCT/PROCESS/PROJECT AUDIT

Compliance Audit

This is the audit which seeks to establish the extent to which the documented system is implemented and observed by the workforce *i.e.* the people complying with the system?

Internal Audit

This is the most important of all audits which require a company to look in on its own systems, procedures and activities in order to ascertain whether they are adequate and being complied with.

Product/Process/Project Audit

This is a vertical audit looking at all the systems that went into the marketing of a specific end product or service. They are applicable to auditing specific projects or contracts.

Importance of Checklist in Auditing

It is often helpful when conducting an audit, to use checklists. It helps the auditor to overcome the mental stoop which he may face during an audit. The aim of a checklist is to give the auditor a list of items which he needs to cover during the audit. It helps to ensure that auditor do not get side tracked. The ideal checklist is one that is drawn up by the auditor prior to actual audit itself.

Non-Conformance

Major

(*a*) The complete absence of a statement or procedure to meet a requirement of the standard.

(*b*) The break down or Non observance of a specified procedure or requirement.

MINOR

A single observation lapse in the use of a defined procedure or requirement.

A number of minors against one procedure or requirement around the organisation or in a single department proving a breakdown can become a "Major".

NON-CONFORMANCE REPORT

It is the requirement of ISO-9000 standard that the results of the audits shall be documented and brought to the attention of personnel having responsibility in the area audited as per Annexture-V. The non-conformance report should comprise following three elements :

Observation

Fully and accurately describes what was seen by the auditor.

Attribution

To the clause of standard and or organisations quality standard.

Explanation

Paraphrasing of the exact requirement of the clause quoted as the attribution.

NON-CONFORMANCE REPORT

AUDIT OF : NO.

Date :

		QUALITY	
PRODUCT	PROCESS	DEPT.	OFFICE

Auditor : Auditee :

Auditor's Report :

Signed : Date :

Proposed Corrective Action :

Signed : Date :

Review of Corrective Action :

Signed : Date :

Management Comments!

Signed : Date :

INTERNAL AUDIT SCHEDULE

Auditee	*Auditee Responsible*	*Audit Scope*	*Dates of Audit*	*Team Leader Responsible*	*Team members*	*Report Number*
Contract Review						
Document Control						
Design Control						

CHECKLIST IN AUDITING

AIDE MEMOIRE

PURCHASING

	COMMENTS TIME
1. Completion of previously Identified corrective sections.	
2. Provision of effective procedures for procurement.	
3. Assessment of sub-contractors performance.	
4. Addition and removal of sub-contractors.	
Auditor...................... Date............................. Report No........................	

62

Total Quality Management--Applied Concept

Application of TQM

In order to understand the concept of total Quality Management as applied in an organisation. We must be clear also the business philosophy of the organisation which could be :

— Organisation commitment to Quality
— Organisation vision to the world's preferred organisation
— Organisation guide is the Quality Policy
— The path is the organisation way to customer satisfaction
— Organisation pledge is the Responsible care
— Organisation catalyst is business People.

The organisation must have five foundation documents to capture its commitment to quality are :

— Strategic Intent
— The Quality Policy
— Team
— The organisation way

and

— Responsible care.

The following are some of the diagrams which explain the introduction of Total Quality Management in an organisation :

— Total Quality Model
— Process Control
— Total Quality Management Strategy
— Quality Policy
— Value Thrusts-Goals
— Team Development-plan
— Teaming
— Team organised for Quality Management
— Interlocking Team concept
— The organisation way
— Responsible care

TOTAL QUALITY MODEL

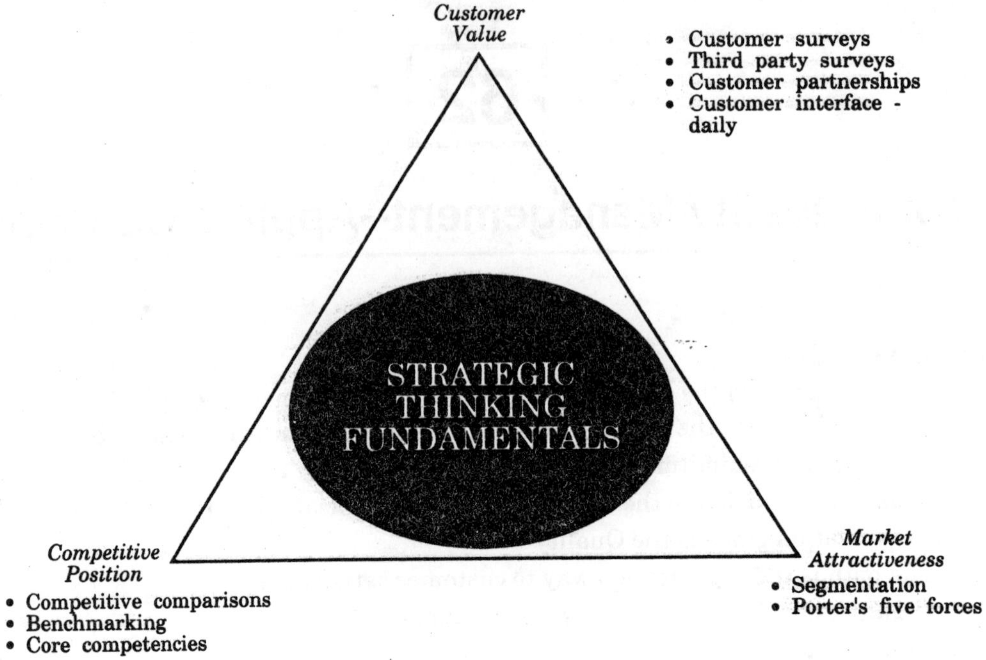

Fig. 62.1.

QUALITY POLICY

QUALITY GOAL

To be the leader in quality and value of products and services

QUALITY MANAGEMENT PROCESS

Focus on customers

Establish mission, vision and indicators of performance

Understand, standardize, stabilize and maintain processes

Plan, do, check, act for continual improvement and innovation

OPERATIONAL POLICY

Achieve process stability and reliability

Control every process to the desired target

Improve process capability

PRINCIPLES

Customer Satisfaction Anticipate, understand and excel at meeting customer needs.

PROCESS CONTROL

Quality Management Process

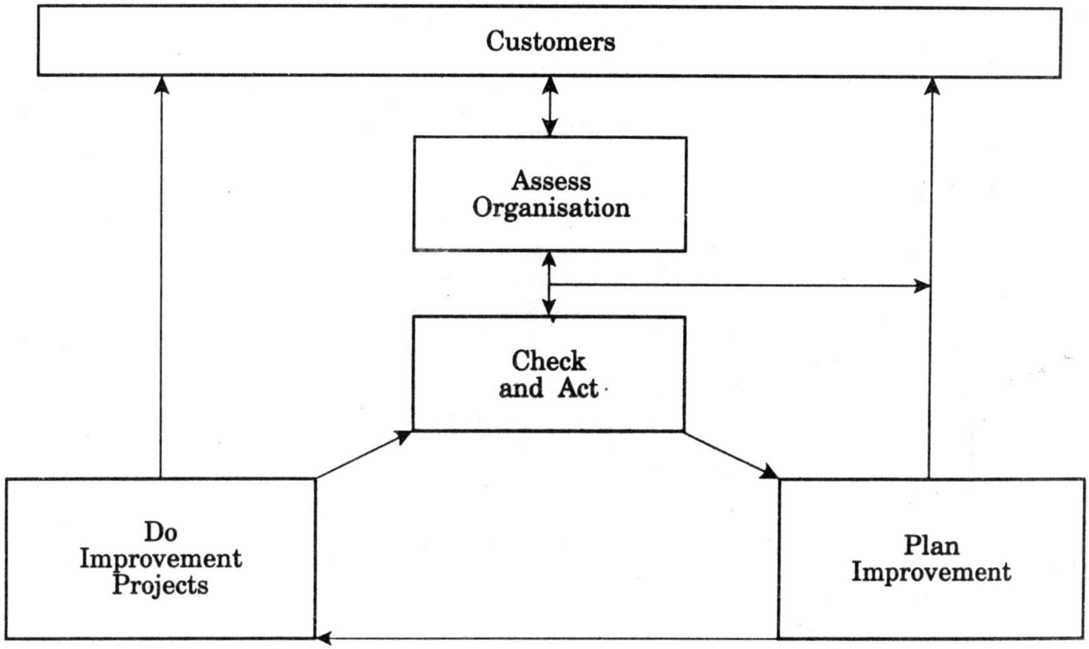

Process Control

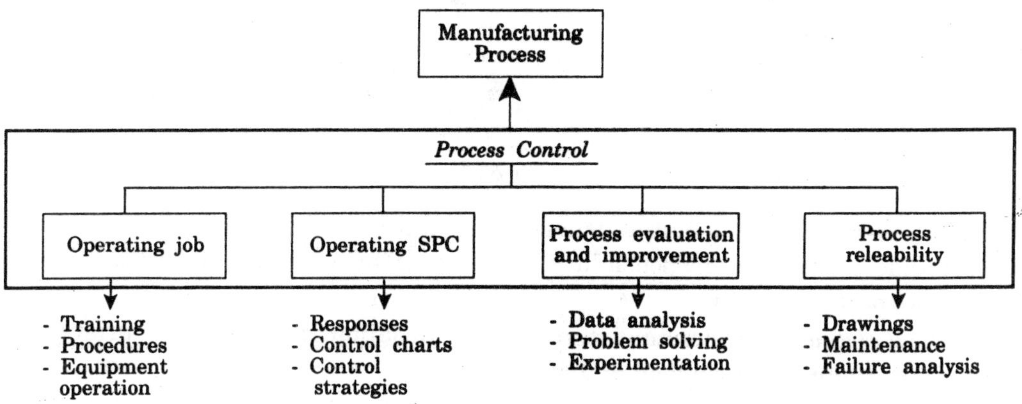

Fig. 62.2.

Continual Improvement. Improve the current level of performance of processes products and services

Innovation. Search for and implement creative processes, products and services

Process Emphasis. Focus on process as the means to improve results

Management Leadership. Create and maintain a shared vision consistancy of purpose and supportive environment that includes appropriate recognition and reinforcement.

Total Quality Management Strategy

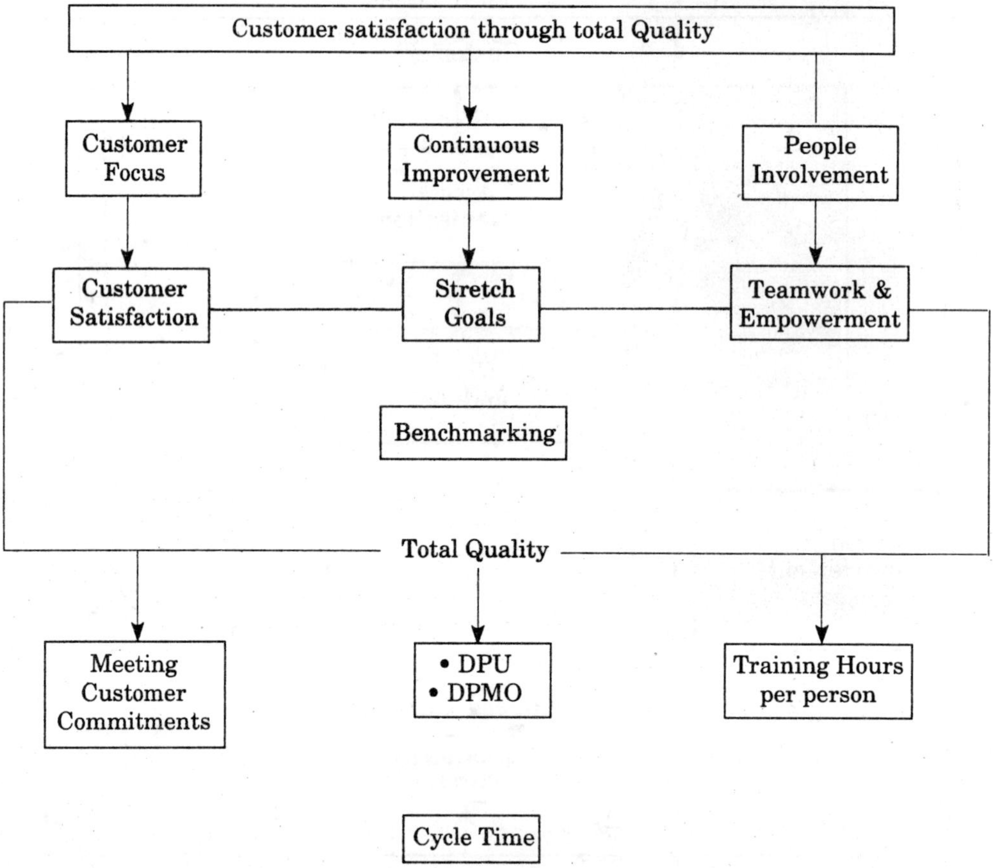

Fig. 62.3.

Empowerment. - Create a culture where people have the knowledge. skills, authority and desire to decide, act and take responsibility for results of their actions and for their contribution to the success of the company.

Statistical Methods. - Understand the concept of variation and apply appropriate statistical methods for continual improvement and innovation.

Employee Development. - Encourage and support life long earning and personal growth

Partnerships. - Build long term relationships with customers and suppliers

Assessment. - Assess performance and benchmark against world's best

THE ORGANISATION WAY

In an Organisation people are the key to success organisation have recognized throughout its history the importance of treating each other fairly and with respect. Organisation will enhance these beliefs by building upon the following values and principles.

Values-Thrusts-Goals

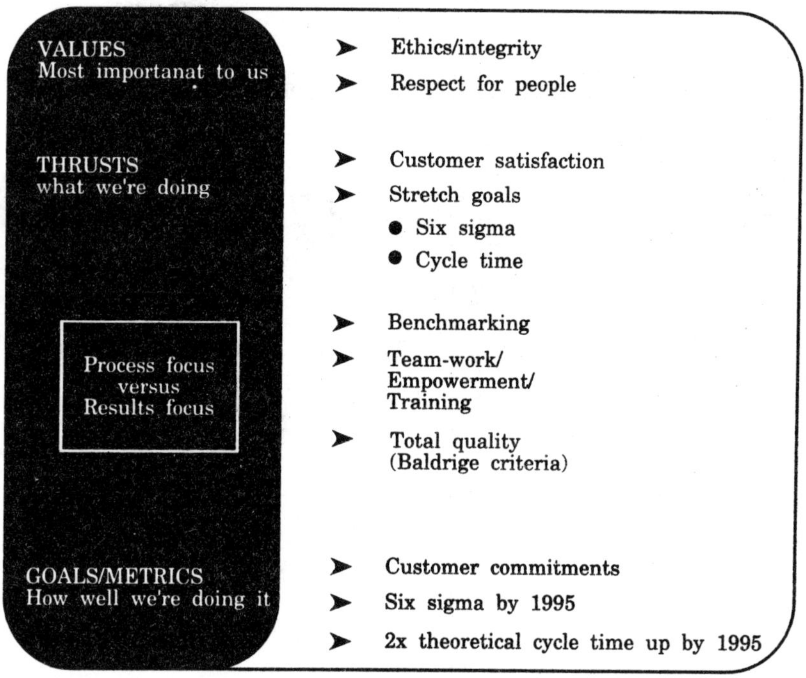

Fig. 62.4

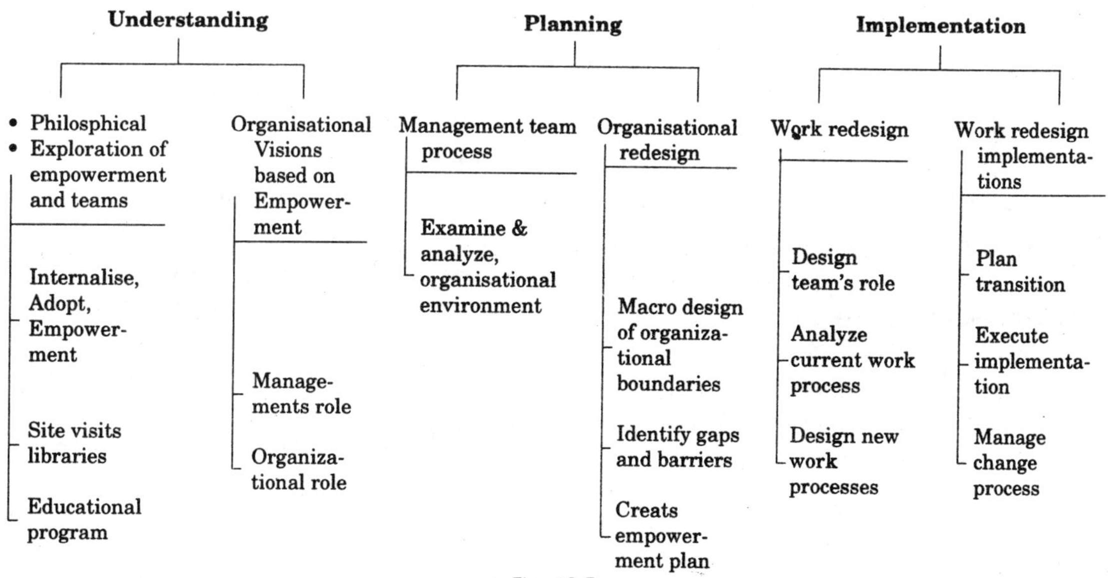

Fig. 62.5.

*Honesty and Integrity*We are honest with ourselves and others. Our integrity is exhibited through relationships with co-workers, customers, supplies and neighbours. Our goal is truth in all relationships.

TEAMING

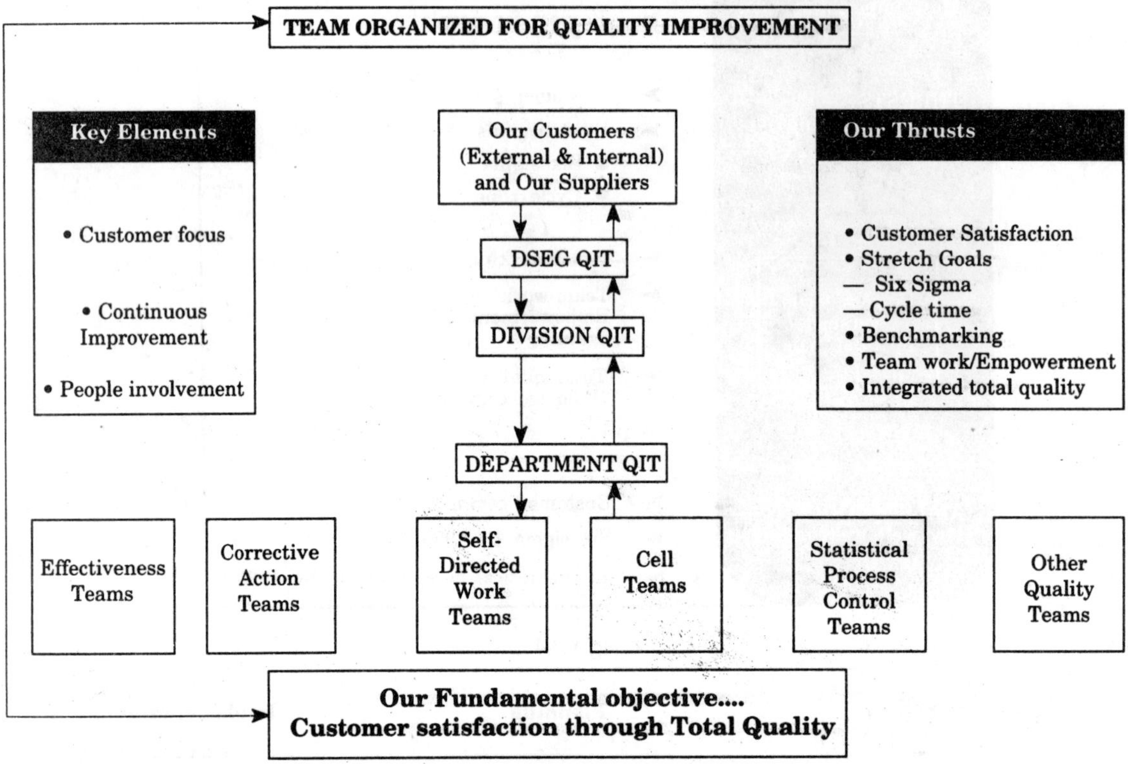

Fig. 62.6.

Fairness. - We treat each other as we expect to be treated.

Trust. - We respect and rely on each other. Fair treatment, honesty in our relationship and confidence in each other create trust.

Teamwork. - We are empowered to manage our areas of responsibility. We work together to achieve common goals for business success. Full participation, cooperation and open communication lead to superior results.

Diversity. - We value different points of view. Men and women from different cultures an backgrounds enrich the generation and usefulness of these different points of view. We create an environment that enables all employees to reach their full potential in pursuit of company objectives.

Employee Well-being. - We have a safe, healthy and desirable work-place. Stability of employment is given high priority. Growth in employee skills is essential. Recognition for contributions and full utilization of employees capabilities promote job satisfaction.

Winning Attitude. - Our can-do attitude and desire for excellence drive continual improvement, making us winners in everything we do.

Interlocking Team Concept

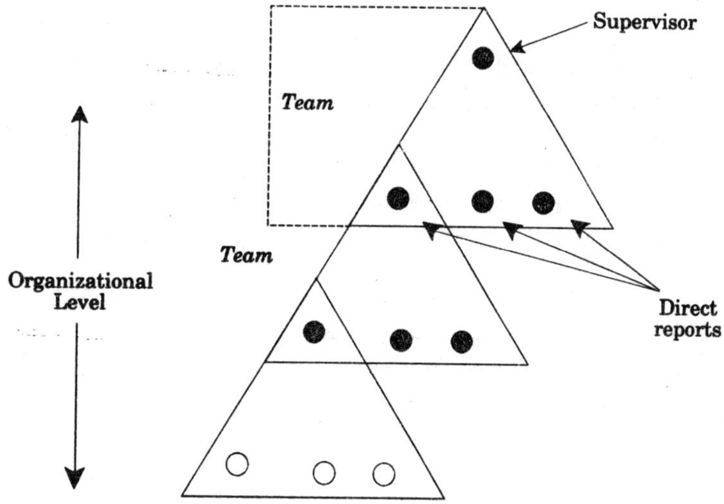

Fig. 62.7.

PRINCIPLES : The principles committed to protect health, safety and environment and continuously improving performance

- To recognize and respond to community concerns about chemicals and our operations
- To develop and produce chemicals that can be manufactured, transported, used and disposed of safely.
- To make health safety and environmental considerations a priority in our planning for all existing and new products and processes.
- To report promptly to officials, employees, customers and the public information on chemical-related health or environmental hazards and to recommend protective measures.
- To counsel customers on the use transportation and disposal of chemical products
- To operate plants and facilities in a manner that protects the environment and the health and safety of our employees and the public.
- To extend knowledge by conducting or supporting research on the health, safety and environmental effects of our products, processes and waste materials.
- To work with others to resolve problems created by past handling and disposal of hazardous substances.
- To participate with government and others in creating responsible laws, regulations and standards to safeguard the community work-place and environment.
- To promote the principles and practices of Responsible Care by sharing experiences and offering assistance to others who produce, handle use, transport or dispose of chemicals.

Business Process Re-engineering

In the new liberalised environment, the competitive edge will go to the organisations that are innovative and knowledgeable and continuously rethink the way they operate and realise that employees are assets to be nurtured and developed. Most of the present successful organisations, are thinking about restructuring in order to cope with the opportunities and challenges posed by liberalisation. Since, an organisation is a dynamic system composed of many interdependent elements ushering in an organisational culture conductive to a professional order is imperative. The old ways of managing no longer work. The organisation charts, the compensation schemes, the hierarchies, the vertical organisation, the whole tool kit of command and control management techniques no longer work. The change will go deeper than techniques. It touches not merely what managers do, but who they are, not only their sense of the task, but their sense of themselves not just what they know but how they think.

WHAT IS RE-ENGINEERING

Re-engineering is the fundamental rethinking and radical redesign of business processes, top achieve dramatic improvements in critical contemporary measures of performance, such as cost quality service and speed." Hammer and champy emphasised that re-engineering should be resorted to only when the organisation perceives a need for "heavy blasting" Re-engineering has important implications because of liberalisation.

Those orgainsations will truly excel in the future who will discover how to tap people's commitment and capacity at all levels. Promoting the right people into leadership positions, to ensure shaping positions, organisation's strategies and organisational climate for years.

The key challenge facing us in the 90's is the same one that faces us every day; to keep taking the risk of change. Sometimes when you're trying to improve, you break sometimes that's already fixed. But unless you change and take the risk of failure, you limit your opportunities for success. That's why questioning, probing and reinventing are so important.

MOBILIZATION OF ORGANISATION

Because markets and customers are always changing,customers ratchet up their demands on every front;price quality, service, novelty and timeliness. At the same time, we must also respond to and take advantage of changes in our industries, changes driven both by technology and by political and social reform. But to do all this requires the mobilization of the entire enterprise, and it is this mobilization that begins radical change within the organisation.

People work for a paycheck, sure. But if that's the only reason they can find for going to work every day, they won't work every day with the imagination, the resourcefulness, the steady willingness, and the sensitivity to the marketplace that we've got to promote all the way, through the organisation if we want to prevail in today's environment.

But the job for management is two fold: First our times' require us to re-examine and restate our business purpose ; and second we must use this restatement to fully mobilize our companies for change. In prior times, we referred to these jobs as the "hard" work of strategy, and the "soft" work of changing behaviour. To bring about change today managers must do both, the "hard" and the "soft" and treat them as equally important. For re-engineering to succeed there are broad issues which have been discussed as under :

Issues of Purpose

Insistently persistently, relentlessly, the new manager must ask "What for ?" What is it that we're in business for ? What is this process for ? This product ? This task ? This team ? This job? What aer we doing here, anyway ?

Issues of Culture

If successful re-engineering requires a change in a company's whole culture, as seems to be the case in many instances, how is it to be accomplished by the same management that did so well in the old culture? It is true that re-engineering is unlikely to succeed where the corporate atmosphere is charged with fear, we must generate better environment of willingness and mutual confidence to succeed.

Issues of Process and performance. How do we get the kind of the processes we want ? How do we get the performances we need from our people? How do we set norms and standards, or measure results - for worker performance, management performance, and the performance of the whole enterprise ? Re-engineering usually demands radical objectives, leadership, and political and social skills to realise the potential and performance.

Issues of people. Whom do we want to work with ? How can we find them from both inside and outside the company ? How do we get them to want to work with us ? How do we know, whether they're the kind of people we want ?

Fig. 62.7.

Although these are hard questions to pose, they are harder to answer - and learning to live with the answer is far harder still.

In the wholeheartedly re-engineered corporation, responsibility and authority are so widely distributed throughout the organisation, that virtually everyone becomes a manager, of one's own work. It should be well understood that if management doesn't change, re-engineering will be stopped in its tracks, and we can't afford to let that happen.

If a great business can't be human, what can it be? Our whole sense of a business depends on it, as does our image of the people who work there, of what we can ask of them, of ourselves as managers, and of our work.

DEMANDS OF REENGINEERING

The best sign of intelligence is the ability to hold two good, but contradictory ideas in one's head at the same time. More is required of management today than intelligence. Character is required, and the best sign of it--the reengineering character anyway -- is not only to hold two good, contradictory ideas, but to act on them.

In order to understand the demands of Re-engineering, we must ask ourselves the following questions :

(*a*) What is the business for ?

(*b*) What kind of culture do we want ?

(*c*) How do we do our work ?

(*d*) What kind of people do we want to work with ?

(*a*) What is the Business for :

What business results do we want in the market ? What changes in our core work and management processes must we make to effect those results? The need and task of leadership. It was a belief that only top managers needed to know a corporation's business purposes, which is not so. Now everyone wants and needs to know, what they're in business for.

(*b*) What kind of Culture do we want?

A company's culture cannot be proclaimed or easily manipulated. It consists of the deeply shared values and beliefs of its people, what shows up in how the company and its people behave.

(*c*) How do we do our Work

We must also focus on our managerial processes--the processes through which we manage that value-adding work.

(*d*) What kind of people do we want to work with ?

Hiring and promotion, development and deployment, are all now far too important to be left to Human Resources. Managers unilaterally deploy team-members only at the risk of destroying team morale--that is, at the risk of doing harm to the business. On the other hand, there are large issues of process and procedure surrounding the "people question", that can only be defined and tentatively resolved by managers of the enterprise.

It's our purpose and processes that will suggest on optimum structure. It's our processes and culture, that will dictate how we want to design our systems. Purpose, culture, process, and people replace strategy, structure and systems. Our constancy of purpose and our continuous discontent with the "immediate present" helps us to tea innovative, creative and helps in implementation of Re-engineering.

CULTURE

Everything we've learned about re--engineering drives towards one solid conclusion-effective business enterprises today, are being determined by their culture and not by their organisational structure. In short, reducing hierarchy, bureaucracy, and the rest of it is not enough to face our customers and markets. It is a matter of rearranging the quality of people's attachments--to their work and to each other which are the basic cultural issues. The "living question" for managers today: how to change our business's culture and in what way.

Every organisation has to specifically determine their own values and the culture. Values take their shape and substance from many sources--from many sources--from the "real" business, from the political and social ideals, from the individual beliefs of the people in the company. These courses are so different, and mix so differently in different corporations, that it is difficult to expect a single statement of values that could fit all companies.

Following are some of the key values which if introduced in the organisation will help us to have the desired culture for reengineering the organisation.

- Customer satisfaction as the top priority of every employee and the purpose of every job. Cost effective, on-going achievement of customer satisfaction as the foundation of business.
- Strategies, goals and objectives established to ensure consistent customer satisfaction, corporate financial health and employee development and support.
- Management believes in, promotes and pursues excellence throughout the organisation.
- Initiative and ingenuity applied to the conduct of business and the resolution of problems, are encouraged and supported throughout the organisation.
- The roles and responsibilities of every employee are clearly defined.
- Reward structures recognise contributions to and achievement of results, which enhance customer satisfaction, improve cost effectiveness and strengthen profitability.

The concept of re-engineering has become an active principle 'in advance economies.' In India, mind-sets have to change as we globalise our economy. We must remember that the concept of re-engineering is not a fad 'but a radical process which keeps the company ahead and competitive domestically and internationally.

Gaining Competitive Advantage through Benchmarking

Let us not fight against nature's law, 'Survival of the fittest!' Let us Benchmark! According to Robert Camp, Benchmarking is nothing but "Finding and implementing best practices in high performing work process that fully satisfy customer requirements." The Xerox Corporation believed that "It is better to copy well rather than do it yourself poorly."

American Productivity Centre have provided the following definition: Benchmarking is the practice of being humble enough to admit that someone else is better at something and being wise enough to learn how to match and even surpass them at it." In essence, it is a continuous systematic process for evaluating organisations recognised as industry leaders and to develop processes that incorporate 'best practices' and establish rational goals. One key to effective benchmarking is to look beyond one's own industry.

It must be appreciated that Benchmarking works though concept and it does not bring in novelty. When some of the studies on TQM implementation revealed that an attempt to drift towards 'non-strategic' process proved detrimental in the long run, through Benchmarking it is ensured that developing strategic goals and the process of acceleration of business change is not underestimated. While continuous improvement need not be sacrificed, but breakthrough thinking and generation of urgency is emphasised. An enabling climate is a must. The comparison of business strategies by identifying key factors in terms of long term decisions held in market place success. In our country, companies like Modi Xerox, BPL, Hindustan Lever, Arvind Mills, to name a few have achieved competitive advantage. Benchmarking ensures substantial value addition to its process. It is like being a seeded player in each competition. It is an institutionalisation of efforts to increase effectiveness constantly and selectively.

63

Competitiveness of an Enterprise

Factors Responsible for Competitiveness

The word competitive can be achieved by an enterprise if the enterprise take care of the following factors:

1. Quality of Management
2. Domestic Economy
3. People managing the organisation
(Labour laws of the land)
4. Sensline to change in technology and Research and Development
5. Infrastructure
6. Financial structure and financial management
7. Government guidelines
8. Internationalisation

These factors are not only important for the organisation with a vision of going global but also holds true for work competitiveness. In addition the above factors which influence in achieving "value added creation" are :

(*a*) Aggressiveness (Exporting to other countries)
(*b*) Attractiveness (Foreign Investment)
(*c*) Globality (Business on Global scale)
(*d*) Proximity (Neighbouring Countries primarily)
(*e*) Managing Assets (Oil and Natural Resources, various minerals viz Bauxite)
(*f*) Processed Management (Process which add value to the Assets)
(*g*) Social Cohensiveness(Social Welfare of the citizens)
(*h*) Risk taking Ability

The above factors helps in achieving subtainality and competitiveness. Based on the above factors Peter Lorange Professor Maucher Nestle' Switzerland has ranked the various countries on the World Competitiveness as an May 97. The figure gives the ranking during the year 1990 and during the 1997. It has been observed that quite a large number countries viz United Kingdom, Sweden, Malaysia, Iceland, Taiwan, Belgium has shown tremendous growth in their economy.

The total ranking based on factors viz. Infrastructure Quality of Management, Science and Technology and the people is given in figure (3). Based on the ranking we find that we quite behind in the relative ranking on Infrastructure. However our progress on Telecommunication Purchasing Power; Domestic Market is good but we lack on Road and Transport and Power generation.

On the overall performance India was on 41st position. The country is an Right Direction with Recovery in Foreign Investment. The rating on Domestic Economy was (24) out of the (97) countries. On thė "Economic Sectors Performance" the rating is (12). The rating of India on Labour Costs is (1).

Factors of Competitiveness

Infrastructure		*Management*		*Science & Technology*		*People*		
97	96	97	96	97	96	97	96	
30	27	35	44	37	42	28	31	ARGENTINA
8	6	19	25	24	21	14	18	AUSTRALIA
14	13	21	17	19	11	9	5	AUSTRIA
18	18	22	12	15	9	15	14	BELGIUM
41	38	29	36	36	45	36	37	BRAZIL
6	4	10	16	9	10	2	6	CANADA
25	16	15	9	33	27	34	23	CHILE
40	40	34	30	20	28	31	35	CHINA
43	37	33	27	39	32	43	36	COLOMBIA
29	35	42	39	44	43	24	28	CZECH REPUBLIC
5	8	5	5	23	18	3	1	DENMARK
3	5	8	6	6	8	1	3	FINLAND
15	17	20	19	4	5	25	20	FRANCE
7	12	25	20	3	3	19	12	GERMANY
37	41	32	43	34	39	30	29	GREECE
19	9	2	14	18	20	13	22	HONGKONG
23	24	40	38	28	36	29	33	HUNGARY
10	10	23	24	31	23	7	7	ICELAND
45	43	39	32	30	33	45	44	INDIA
39	36	41	42	41	40	44	45	INDONESIA
22	21	12	21	7	14	20	24	IRELAND
24	20	24	22	13	15	16	17	ISRAEL
32	29	27	26	35	24	27	25	ITALY
20	26	7	2	2	2	11	4	JAPAN
34	34	26	28	22	25	22	21	KOREA
17	19	16	11	17	19	18	19	LUXEMBOURG
27	22	17	15	25	29	33	34	MALAYSIA
26	31	38	35	46	46	40	39	MEXICO
12	15	4	3	12	7	10	11	NETHERLANDS
13	7	11	7	16	22	8	13	NEW ZEALAND
2	2	13	8	11	13	4		

44	44	30	29	29	26	38	38	PHILIPPINES
36	45	44	37	42	37	35	30	POLAND
35	39	43	41	43	35	32	32	PORTUGAL
46	46	46	46	26	31	41	41	RUSSIA
11	33	1	4	8	12	5	8	SINGAPORE
33	32	37	40	40	34	46	46	SOUTH AFRICA
21	23	28	33	27	30	26	26	SPAIN
4	3	6	1	21	6	17	9	SWEDEN
9	11	9	13	5	4	6	10	SWITZERLAND
28	30	18	18	10	17	21	16	TAIWAN
42	42	31	31	32	44	37	40	THAILAND
38	28	36	34	38	41	39	42	TURKEY
16	14	14	23	14	16	23	27	UNITED KINGDOM
1	1	3	10	1	1	12	15	USA
31	25	45	45	45	38	42	43	VENEZUELA

DOMESTIC ECONOMY INTERANATIONALIZATION GOVERNMENT FINANCE

	97	96	97	96	97	96	97	96
ARGENTINA	37	30	20	28	17	24	31	41
AUSTRALIA	22	18	28	29	14	13	18	15
AUSTRIA	27	24	18	20	26	27	21	14
BELGIUM	28	27	8	6	43	39	17	12
BRAZIL	25	35	41	46	16	18	41	34
CANADA	21	26	19	17	9	10	10	13
CHILE	10	9	16	13	10	5	24	17
CHINA	14	2	29	23	6	9	40	37
COLOMBIA	43	31	40	38	37	26	44	38
CZECH REPUBLIC	36	34	24	34	41	34	35	33
DENMARK	18	15	9	11	23	22	4	5
FINLAND	23	38	13	15	15	30	13	18
FRANCE	29	23	10	7	35	36	16	22
GERMANY	26	19	7	9	25	19	9	8

GREECE	38	39	33	35	40	42	33	39
HONG KONG	9	8	3	4	2	2	12	7
HUNGARY	44	43	21	30	39	40	38	43
ICELAND	7	1739	36	19	20	26	32	
INDIA	24	32	43	41	31	14	37	30
INDONESIA	11	25	35	37	27	25	39	36
IRELAND	5	16	12	10	12	23	20	23
ISRAEL	15	14	34	18	36	31	30	24
ITALY	30	28	27	21	44	45	34	27
JAPAN	6	5	32	14	28	21	5	2
KOREA	13	4	45	43	32	33	43	40
LUXEMBOURG	4	6	5	3	24	17	7	10
MALAYSIA	2	7	17	16	4	4	19	19
MEXICO	41	41	38	40	29	38	42	42
NETHERLANDS	16	22	6	5	22	28	2	4
NEWZEALAND	34	10	22	22	3	3	15	16
NORWAY	8	13	23	24	13	15	11	11
PHILIPPINES	20	29	31	31	11	12	28	35
POLAND, 39	40	44	42	45	43	45	44	
PORTUGAL	40	42	15	32	30	32	27	29
RUSSIA	45	46	37	45	46	46	46	46
SINGAPORE	3	3	2	1	1	1	6	3
SOUTH AFRICA	42	44	46	39	34	37	36	31
SPAIN	33	33	14	25	21	35	22	25
SWEDEN	31	37	11	12	3[illegible]	41	14	20

SWITZERLAND	32	20	26	19	5	11	3	6
TAIWAN	17	11	30	26	20	6	23	21
THAILAND	12	12	25	33	18	8	29	26
TURKEY	35	36	36	27	33	29	25	28
UNITED KINGDOM	19	21	4	8	8	16	8	9
USA	1	1	1	2	7	7	1	1
VENEZUELA	46	45	42	44	42	44	32	45

Domestic Economy

Value Added	36
Investments	5
Savings	35
Final Consumption	42
Economic Sectors Performance	12
Cost of Living	25
Forecasts	10

Internationalization

	97
Current Account Balance	29
Exports of Goods and Services	41
Imports of Goods and services	41
Exchange Rate	9
Portfolio Investment	18
Foreign Direct Investment	23
National Protectionism	42
Openness	46

Government

	97
National Debt	36
Government Expenditure	8
Fiscal Policies	9
State Efficiency	39
State Involvement	43
Justice and Security	22

Finance

	97
Cost of Capital	41
Availability of Capital	42
stock Markets Dynamism	15
Banking Sector Efficiency	38

Infrastructure

	97
Basic Infrastructure	45
Technological Infrastructure	45
Energy Self-Sufficiency	45
Environment	10

Management

	97
Productivity	33
Labor Performance	44
Management Efficiency	36

Science and Technology

	97
R&D Expenditures	30
R&D Personal	7
Technology Management	37
Scientific Environment	23
Intellectual Property	40

People

	97
Population Characteristics	32
Labour Force Characteristics	44
Employment	5
Unemployment	26
Education Structures	46
Quality of life	45
Attitudes and values	41

SUCCESSFUL ENTRENEURSHIP

Motivation, whether individually or collectively is the result of equilibrium between "satisfaction" and "expectation". The need for searching for new ways of improving performance arises when satisfaction falls below the previously set expectation level, or the present expectation rises above the previous level of satisfaction.

It should be clearly understood that technical progress and Human factors are two sides of the same coin,affecting the persons who are involved in these processes-they are also their victims.

FLEX MANAGEMENT

A new paradigm for managing the workforce in year 2001. is a new mind set- a distinct philosophy of management -with a set of intrinsic values (core values), providing a framework for action. It goes far beyond the principle of "equality" to bring out individualised policies. The new workforce is treated as highly diverse, and is managed not as a set of groups, but as a collection of individuals, each with unique needs and preferences.

Flex management, *inter alia,*grants greater autonomy for employees ; empowerment; options that people can exercise to reach *self management. For example, an individual can work at home through a network computer instead of commuting to office everyday.*

The four decided strategies of workforce management based on flex management are as:

1. Matching people and jobs to ensure compatibility between an employee's capacity and the demands of the job.

2. Managing and rewarding performance with a view to compensate and provide incentives for meritous services rendered by employees.

3. Informing and involving people with the object of bringing home to employees corporate objectives, business policies and other plans, and totally involving them in the corporate goals set forth for achievement.

4. Supporting lifestyles and life needs by providing full latitude to social and environment needs.

PIVOTAL ROLE OF R&D

In view of the fact that technological progress has assumed added significance, and considering the fact that the urge for innovation places great demand on R&D, it is of crucial importance that the industry earmarks a seizable portion of its bottom line for reinvestment in R&D areas as a *sine qua non*not only for meeting stiffening competition the world over, but, at times, to ensure its own survival.

R&D strategies needed not only at a manufacturing but at each and every technological interface?

(*a*) It is a matter of common knowledge that R&D groups is expensive and has been constantly on the increase.

(*b*) It must be ascertained that R&D groups are working on the right track, to avoid any mismatches. It is essential that they keep the top management informed of the costs being incurred and the progress made periodically.

(*c*) A road map has to be drawn up to determine probable performance, with present time and resource parameters.

NEED FOR AND THE IMPORTANCE OF SURVIVAL

As the survival of the individual firm becomes a significant criterion of economic activity, the closer the approximation to monopolistic conditions. When we assume that time is the function of profit maximisation, one has to come to the inevitable conclusion that almost every other consideration is subordinate to survival. For the individual entrepreneur, the random sector of circumstances affecting his strategies increases enormously with time. As it were, he makes hay when the sun shines.

The World Competitiveness Model

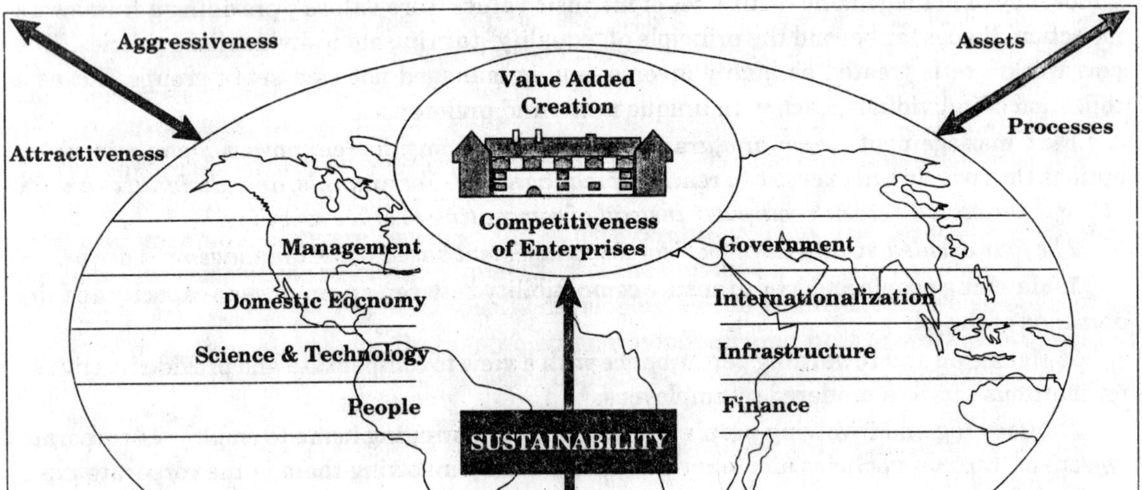

64

Organisational Climate Analysis

Introduction

The organisational climate forms a significant determinant of human behaviour in organisation. It connects the objective aspects of the organisation, such as technology, leadership etc. with the motivation and behaviour of the human resources.

It is the perception which people have of the organisation and their feel for it from the stand point of such variables as autonomy, structure, reward consideration, warmth and support and openness. The objective of various organisational climate studies is to diagnose the prevailing climate in the company with a view to improve it through modification of structure leadership styles, production lived incentive systems, HRD policies, practice, procedure and programs of the company.

The approach followed for organisational climate study in a leading organisation was to give a multi Dimensional Assessment. Personality test *i.e* its very executives which determined their Personality on 20 personality Dimension their total personality Score, Strength and weaknesses, Training Inputs required, addition training input for their future growth in the organisation. Now the above data for key executive was given for analysis to an organisational psychologist for analysis. The data was analysed to determine organisation climate, group training needs of executives *viz* vice president group; General Manager Group and Manager Group. The data so obtained was discussed with each group separately to involve the problem areas. As a concept following could be the area of concern :

(*a*) Lack of Growth Culture from top to bottom
- CEO must be out in front
- He should listen to his organisation and

(*b*) Too much organisational complexity for customers.

(*c*) Story Kingdom
- Lack of co-operation
- Lack of maturty

(*d*) Lack of speed-urgency
- Speed is key
- Not market driven
- Winner takes all.

(*e*) Lack of Benchmarking
- Do something new
- Break mold

(*f*) Lack of cost competitiveness
- A basic condition for growth

MIND SET FOR GROWTH

The forward looking management which is committed to rapid growth address the following.

- Do we "see" potential business opportunities that others do not see.
- Do we have the competences needed to go after the opportunities. The ability to mobilise what will be needed to serve the customer. The management must look for new alternative ways of doing it viz :
- The Team
- Key to put the best talents at work.
- Today for today and today for tomorrow.

RE-SHAPING GROWTH AGENDA

Due to the shifting paradigms regarding organisation growth following waye are available for reshaping organisation growth agenda ;

(*a*) Nature of growth
- Is product demand drivers
- Is product supply drivers
- Less willingness to consume
- True value to the consumer--the latest
- Focus on probability of transaction is key--avoiding wasting energy.

(*b*) Underlying shifts
- Ageing Executives, succession planning
- Competencies Analysis
- Training need analysis
- Slowing spending on Training and Developments
- Increased spending on health case.

(*c*) Global Revolution
- News/Information travel
- Globalised Consumers—faster new trends
- Traditional barriers to entry are vanishing—economy opening up.

(*d*) The way we do business
- Technology shifts
- Alternative channels
- Consolidation/Expansion of Industries

MANAGING RAPID INTERNAL GROWTH

From the following models we find that company must align itself to Human Resource Plan. Organisation must continuously think how can the "ORGANISATION" built on strength.

The senior executives who guide the future of the company and create and manage "Rapid Internal Growth" adopt various models to create the business of tomorrow.

The various models are :—

(*a*) *A focused multi-lens approach*

- To see something promising
- See potential business opportunities that others do not see.
- To have the competence needed to go after the opportunities.

(*b*) *Growth Driver*

- Encourage Innovation
- Customer Intimacy
- Productivity

(*c*) *Team Task Focus*

- Create new business concepts
- Mobilise expansion
- Fulfill needs through process innovation

(*d*) *Team composition and Focus*

- Creative
- Diverse representation
- Entrepreneurial mind
- Cost and Quality focus

(*e*) *Dominant Learning modes*

- Holistic childlike
- Path finder
- Incremental

(*f*) *Strategic Implementation Team*

- Team Management's Strategy Review Focus
- Longer term focus
- Risk taking
- Clear competition focus
- Multi expansion scenaries

(*g*) *Strategic Central modes*

- Management Control Mode
- Contigent Control

• Steering Control

(*h*) *Creating And Managing Rapid Internal Growth*
• Volume of Business
• Winning Wars in Mature Markets
Capturing and keeping increased market share
Growth at the expense of your competitors

(*i*) *Riding the Tiger :*
Keeping up with exploding markets
Grow or die

(*j*) *Creating the Business of Tomorrow*
Entrepreneurship to build on today's success
How to Identify and Anticipate Strategies Tasks

TEAM TASK FOCUS

	Pioneer	Rapid Expansion	Dominate
Team Task Focus	— Identify opportunities	Mobilize for expansion to pre-empty competitors	Make good even better
	— Create new business concepts with visionary customer	Make interactive changes to find the right strategic path	Fulfill needs through process innovation
	Value-driven approach	More D than R in R&D! incremental relaunches	Value to customer
			Price aggressively

FOCUSED MULTI - LENS APPROACH

Yes - we see something promising
Do we "see" potential business opportunities that others do not see?
No-we all see the opportunities more or less the same way
No we need to assemble/build our team
Yes- we do have our team in place

Do we have the competences needed to go after the opportunities
Pioneer
Rapid Expansion
Restructure
Dominate

COMPOSITION OF THE MANAGEMENT TEAM

Team Composition and Focus, Creative, Doers-finding workable path, Classical discipline-based teams

Diverse representation, complementary strengths and skills, "Experiments", Cost and quality focus

One team with specialists Brainstormers, Temporary assignments modified as necessary, Deliver bottomline results aggressively

Growth Drivers, Innovation, Customer Intimacy, Productivity

Benefits to customer that he does not know what he needs !, Cooperate with customer, Restructure

Dominant learning Modes

TEAM DOMINANT LEARNING MODE

Pioneer, Rapid Expansion, Dominate

Team Dominant Learning Mode, Holistic-"childlike" approach to conceptualizing a business - **Piaget**, Path-finder - how to realistically scale up the business - **Leavitt**, Incremental provide ongoing improvements and more value to customer -

TEAM MANAGEMENTS STRATEGY REVIEW FOCUS

Team Management's Strategy Review Focus, Allow for experimentation, Multiple-expansion scenarios, Clear competitive focus

"Sit down and thing together", Which path is best?, "Bottom line to be defended"

Stimulate curiosity, Modify until the best team is in place, "Good can be done better

Longer term focus, , Shorter term focus

Risk-taking

MANAGEMENT CONTROL MODE

Pioneer, Rapid Expansion, Dominate

Management Control Mode, Go/no go, Contingent Control, Steering Control

"Either we take the business or not", Either we stick to the projected scenario or we change path", "Budget deviations must lead to incremental corrective actions"

65

Industrial Relations

INTRODUCTION

Industrial Relations fall in two heads *viz.* Personnel Relations and Labour Relations. *The term 'Personnel' refers to individual workers while labour refers to the collectivity of workers. The relationship between the organised labour and employer is known as labour relations. The first phase of industrial relations is the personnel relations which are essential on the individual level. The second phase of industrial relations are the labour relation.*

Developing and maintaining harmonious relation is a two-way process. It depends not only on the responsiveness of labour but equally on the responsiveness of management. If the relations are not cordial the reason may be found either with the management or with the labour or with both. Once an unhappy situation was developed, the blame could be apportioned to both the parties. However, it is responsibility of the management to create such conditions in which relations may be improved and harmonised. The responsibilities for breaking the vicious circle is exclusively that of the management even to serve their own ends. If the labour or the unions ar not responsive the relations are not cordial, therefore, the efforts of interaction from the management side becomes all the more important and necessary.

Industry Relations are eventually human relations, therefore, the same basis of human psychology prevails in the field of industrial relations as well. Dr. Van D. Kennedy has observed that Indian unionism and labour relations are not the product only of their environment and internal forces.

Labour management Relation is the sum total of relationship that exist at every level in the organisation structure. The relationship between the organised labour and the employer is known as Labour Relations.

CONCEPT

Generally, by Industrial Relations we mean relationship between Management and Workers or the relationship between the Employers and Employees. This dichotomy has been so strongly nurtured and maintained that often there has been a clash between the interests of so called Managers and so called Workers. Such clash of interests is quite frequent and its impact on the Industrial Relations mean only relationship between Workers and Mangers or the Employers.

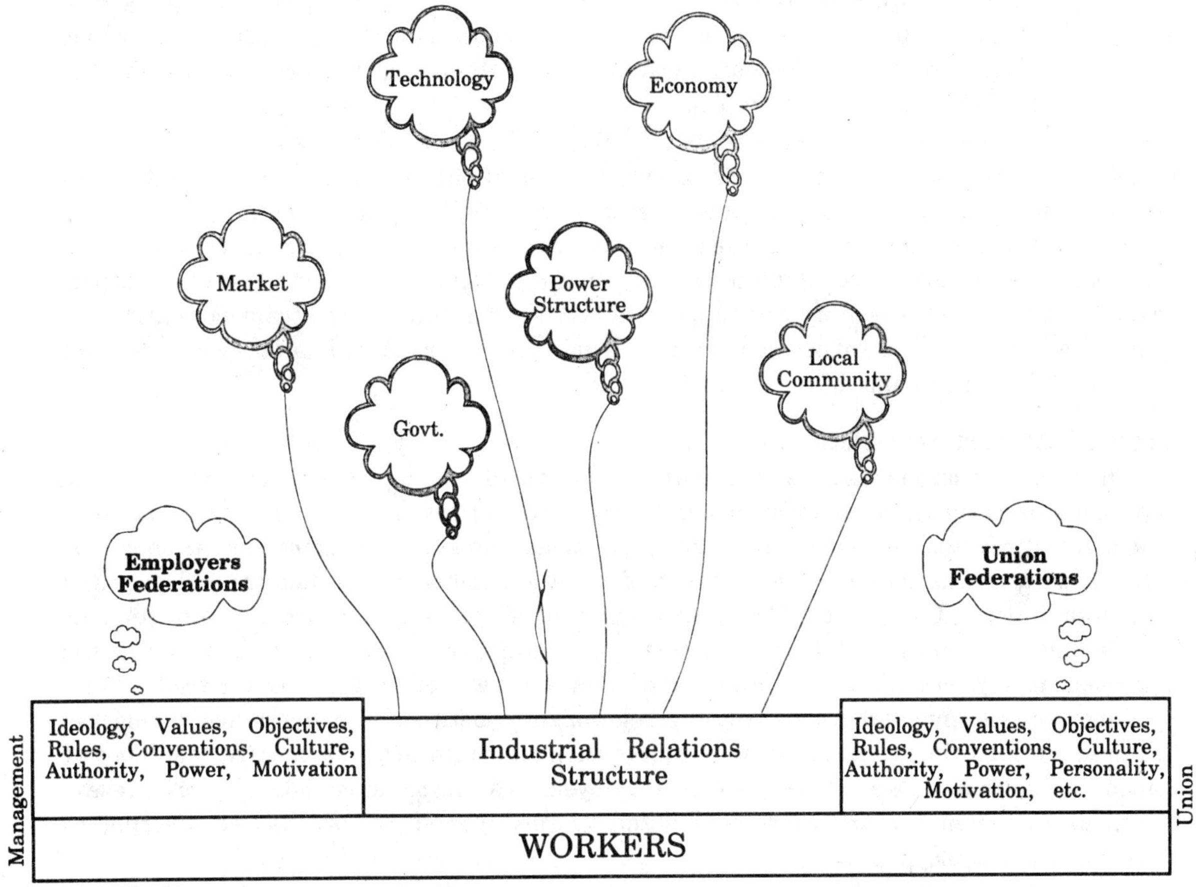

Conceptual Model for Understanding Industrial Relations

Fig. 53.1

Industrial Relation Process

In an industrial relation process there is a multiplicity of relationship and all of them are very important if the industrial relations process has to operate effectively. As a matter of fact, industrial relation process is basically relationship building exercise in which we try to convert natural, financial, human and environmental resources into end products for improving human welfare. It will be a narrow approach if we define industrial relations as relationship between workers and managers alone. There has been a significant change in the structure of industries *viz.* in Public Sector Enterprises all the employees have equal stake in the Organisation. The only difference in the so called workers and so called managers is the difference in the Wage Structure which is diminishing very fast. Thus, the problem of relationships within the industry which is commonly known as Industrial Relations is more complex and multidimensional than it appears on the surface. It may be emphasised that in the context of modern industries which are characterized by growing sizes, fast technological changes, mounting competitions, changing environments etc., the problem of industrial relations has assumed a special significance. The efficiency of an industry is directly related with the quality of relationship which is being built up amongst the individuals who work together. It is not uncommon to see Organisations which are having all the resources and favourable situations but their performance is highly unsatisfactory due to industrial relations problems.

One can find examples where there is no strike, no lock-out or go-slow tactics and yet the Industrial Relation performance is much below the expectations. Therefore, when we talk about the industrial relations it is not merely the external symptoms like strikes, lock-out which should concern us but we should be concerned with real symptoms of healthy relationships in an organisation which are reflected in the morale, commitment, sense of duty, sense of belongingness amongst the employees. Another important factor in the industry is a team work and team spirit. We may see a group of people having high individual merits but when they have to work in a group, the performance of the group is very low.

Labour Management Relations

The writing is on the wall that "without healthy labour - management relation, there is no hope of our overcoming the multifarious problems to which the country is confronted." Labour-Management relations are eventually human relations. Labour-management relation can be defined as the relationship between the management and employees or among employees and their organisation. The concept of labour-management relations have undergone a tremendous change and undergoing a continuous change. Originally, labour management relation was employer-employee relationship in an industry, but when workers organised into trade union, the labour-management relations was the relationships between employers and employees acquired the public importance, the state intervention came into picture to modify, regulate and control the relations between employers and employees as a part of industrialisation. At present labour-management relation has come to stand for employers, trade unions and government relationship in employment.

Good labour - management relations are all the more important in a public undertaking because of the role which have been assigned to them. The public undertakings are around 250 in number with an investment of over 45,000 crores. The spectrum of activities of these enterprises cover the basic and infrastructure industries, *e.g.mining, metallurgical engineering, chemical fertilizers, drugs and even wide range of consumer-oriented goods and services.*

The public enterprises have become the instruments of national development and their economic and social objectives are derived from those of national plans with emphasis on removal of poverty attainment to self-- reliance, better distribution of income, reduction of disparity, expansion of employment opportunity, prevention of concentration of economic power, development of professional personnel in technical, managerial and administrative fields. The public enterprises are accountable to the Parliament and the Government. The Parliament looks into the performance of the enterprises through its committee of public undertakings with specialists in the area of Materials Management, Financial Management, Personnel Management, Industrial Relation and Production Management.

AREAS OF LABOUR - MANAGEMENT RELATIONS

Co-operation

The two important areas of labour-management relations are conflict and co-operation. The industrial production is based on cooperation between Labour and Capital. Co-operation between the two if one of the basic requirement for the growth of industrialisation. Co-operation is the formal feature of Labour-Management Relations. The co-operation between the two is nothing more than the mere coming together of labour and capital or union and management and regarding each other as partners. Co-operation is out of necessity of some sort of working relationship' to be reached for the co-operation in the factory on which both are depending and may continue to depend. Lack of cooperation are barriers of industrial relation such as mistrust, craze for authority and power, dissatisfaction without rewards do not exist only at the inter-face of management and labour alone. The various other constituents of industrial relations are consumers, buyers, the society and the government. It is the interaction of two or more of these constituents which will have a direct bearing on the labour-management relation in the near future.

In public enterprises, the intervention of government, bureau of public enterprises, central body of various labour-management relation is there to a greater extent. The table on page 571 gives the information regarding industrial disputes, number of workers involved and number of mandays lost. The table on page 572 gives the information regarding industrial disputes, number of workers involved and number of mandays lost as classified under two categories -- Public and Private Sectors. The table may not give an exact comparison because we have nearly 250 public undertakings while the number of private undertakings are too large. The industrial unrest in public undertakings is on the higher side due to the following reasons :

PRESENT TRENDS IN INDUSTRIAL RELATIONS

Industrial Relations Climate

The industrial relations climate in the country is witnessing the emergence of new forces, duly supported and motivated by the political ideologies of the erstwhile constituents of the ruling party and the Government. The disruption of industrial harmony is some-how being understood, by and large, as an act of 'letting off of steam by the industrial worker.' The country has been waiting for overhaul of the industrial relations machinery that was set up under the Industrial Disputes Act, 1947. For nearly 9 years now there have been reports that a Bill had been drafted and it was being discussed at various forums -- the Indian Labour Conference, the State Labour Minister Conference and the other concerned Ministers but nothing appears to be in sight.

Following the report of National Commission on Labour in 1969, the National Commission on Labour constituted a 30-member Committee in July, 1977 to 'discuss and study in depth' all problems relating to a comprehensive industrial relations law. It was proclaimed that it would be panacea for all the industrial relations problems in the country. Earlier in May, 1977, the Government had also set up a tripartite committee on workers participation and equity in Management. Several such committees having been appointed in the past with a view to rationalise the wage payment, dearness allowance and other issues of industrial relations. A study group on wage, income and price policy was appointed in October, 1977 headed by Shri S. Bhoothlingam. Bhoothlingam Committee's task was gigantic not only in its terms of reference but extremely wide in scope. It had to deal with very complex and involved issues. The wage structure in India is a jungle of complex systems and practices grown out of lack of a coherent and consistent socio-economic policy. The capacity to pay concept has led to serious intra-industry, wage differentials and set up a vicious circle of demands of wage increase in industrial units within the industry. Diverse dearness allowance systems in different regions or even in the same region linked with diverse cost of living index have destroyed all wage norms.

Industrial life revolves round the job content, and the job compensation. The industrial workers and their unions are totally involved in the job compensation and the job content becomes secondary for them. The basic objectives of two cooperatives *viz.* The management and the unions tend to disagree beyond manageable limits. The former is basically interested in efficiency and productivity ; whereas the later tends to confine itself with protection and welfare.

Lack of mutual interest between the management and the unions, poor and weak organisations of workers, absence of mutual recognition and the lack of responsibilities on the part of both necessitates State regulation of Industrial Relations.

The mutuality of interest would increase through forums of participative management, which are to be designed, as so to be more effective and meaningful in the process of organisational decision making. These may considerably cut down the clash of 'Interest' through an effective system of 'self-management.' The mere sense of belonging in the industry and the organisation, which may be achieved through the process of participative management is bound to bring about a big change in the Industrial Relations in the country in the years to come.

Labour Relations System

The labour relations system in an enterprise is influenced by combination of factors and circumstances which may broadly be divided those relating to the internal environment within an organisation and those external to it. The parameters of labour Relations and their interface so shown in Fig. 53.1. As figure shows there are many factors influence organisational practices, policies, procedure,etc., and therefore, their effectiveness. Organisational environment includes the nature of employees; their attitudes and preferences, the nature of the task to be performed, the leadership style of management etc. The work organisation is also restricted in the way it arranges the forces if its environment, such as the labour union, labour market etc. The factors in the external and internal environments influence the organisational arrangements, policies and procedures which, in turn, determine the effectiveness in maintaining harmony in industrial relations. The environmental factors at the national level and the socio--cultural economic and political factors at the regional level have a direct bearing on the industrial relations climate as well as labour relations policy of an organisation.

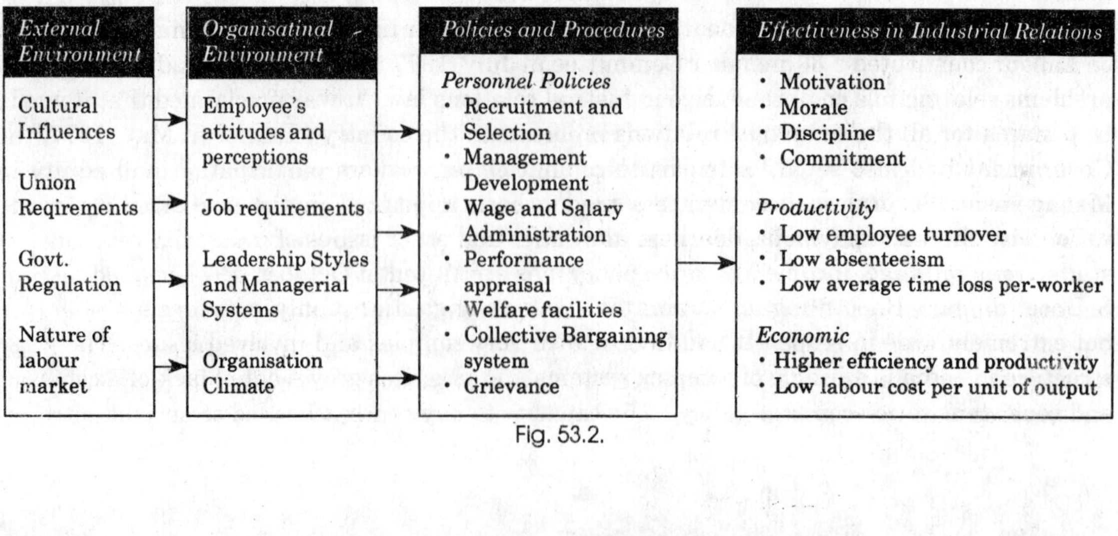

Fig. 53.2.

Industrial Relations in India

Industrial Relations in our country are governed mainly by three central laws--the Industrial Employment (Standing Orders) Act of 1946, the Industrial Disputes Act of 1947 and the trade Union Act of 1926. Three laws are still found to be in their basic from and contents though some changes have been made recently in the industries Disputes Act. The Industrial Employment Act lays down the conditions of employment and provides the framework and certification of standing orders which govern the terms and conditions of workers employment including hours of work, holidays, disciplinary actions etc. The Industrial Disputes Act provides for a machinery for the settlement of conflict, disputes by conciliation, arbitration and adjudication. The workmen have the right to raise an industrial dispute with the conciliation machinery but in case it fails the appropriate government is empowered to refer the dispute to the Labour Court or the Industrial Tribunal for adjudication.

The Industrial Disputes Act also provides for conditions and remedies in case of strikes and lockouts, lay -off and retrenchment. The courts,

of course, have placed certain restrictions on the employer's right to hire and fire cases of unwanted termination of service leading to victimization or unfair labour practice.

In view of the directions laid down in the Constitution due importance is attached to the concept of social justice, human dignity and a decent standard of life for the working class. All efforts are made for proper education to workers, proper insurance schemes and good working conditions with proper wage structure. The object of the directive principles is to build a welfare society in which social, economic and political justice will prevail in all institutions of our national life. There is a direction under article 41 of constitution that the State shall make affective provisions for securing the right to work, to education and to public assistance in case of unemployment, old age, sickness and disablement and there is a provision for just and humane conditions at the work place and for maternity relief under Article 42. The State shall see that the workers get a living wage and a decent standard of life under Article 43. There is also a provision of worker's participation in Management under Article 43 A. Keeping these objectives in view we have formulated employment generation plans, intensive workers education and training centres, provisions for workers health, safety and comfort, minimum wage and social security. India, today is determined to keep up the object of making its labour policy humanitarian, economic as well as civic Humanitarian--because it aims to provide certain facilities and amenities of life to the workers, economic--because it improves the efficiency of workers and thereby boosts up productivity besides maintaining a harmonious relationship in Industry.

An Integrated Approach to Industrial Relations

It is the management of human resource that plays a key role in opening up new opportunities for increasing productivity and a need for redefining the role objectives and structure of the Personnel and industrial relations functions.

Personnel Management and Industrial Relations cannot isolate itself from the growth of the total organisation. There is a need for more emphasis of planning and developing the company's human resources as opposed to more pre-occupation with regard to record keeping and negotiations. This would also mean a more direct involvement in deploying and developing human resources.

There is a need for an integrated systems approach which would emphasis direct relationship between the personnel management and industrial relations systems and objective of the company. The day--to--day individual and collective grievances and negotiations at shop level with unions is like effective preventive maintenance system which is the principal ingredient of an industrial relation policy. This determines in turn, the ability to handle periodic and non-recurring crisis be they in the shape of stoppages of works and strikes or wage disputes. Most of us talk of industrial peace but what need to be talked about should be industrial balance. In a democracy, there are and there have to be situations involving friction and even conflict but an enlightened manager and a responsible union will work out systems to resolve such situations and conflicts.

It has been found that during negotiation, worker's representatives are much more in problem than the management's representatives because the management is by and large a captive leadership. On the management side the chairman of the negotiation team is appointed by the top management with certain security or tenure. He has a few top people to convince and that too in the confidential confines of the office. Even if the discussions are wise, there is a lacuna in the final agreement and he is not sacked. The workers, representative, on the other hand, has to be a natural leader and the task of maintaining the leadership is far more difficult than a tight rope walking. The management tries to trip occasionally. His esteemed colleagues within his unions make several angular transactions at him and above all the general body workers have a chance at least once a year if not more to throw him out. He has political bosses who also need to be kept in a good humour. In addition to the above when he sits of the bargaining table, he faces a long list of doubts and fears such as : Would I be fool to believe management?Should I compromise at this proposal? What will happen to my Job ? Will I be able to convince my union executive, workers,etc.

The most successful agreement is one which is accepted as reasonable by management as well as the workers, because it balances the returns to the employers and the workers. Such agreement will give workers a suitable satisfaction in their achievement which would spur them on to greater efforts for giving adequate returns in production and productivity. A good agreement will result in increase of production, productivity and goodwill and understanding between the management and the workers.

Wage negotiations these days are not restricted to workers and the union alone. Supervisor have also Organised themselves into organisation conducting militant action against the management as regard wage negotiations. The reasons for formation of Supervision and Officers Association can be traced back to 1970's when the management made handsome assurances and tributes to supervisors and officers that supervisors and officers were part of management and would be given all consideration without even asking for it. In actual practice, they were the last to get any benefit, they were the last to know, that too from the workers only about any agreement arrived at between management and the union. On the other hand they were the first on the firing line doing manual jobs almost round the clocks during the stoppage of work of strike of breakdown of law and order situations.

In most of the industries, the supervisors found that their interest were not fully safeguarded because of their inability to organise as a force to bargain. It is therefore, required that we now accept the facts that management must sit and bargain with officers association on all matters connected with wages. Most of us talk of workers participation but if we search our heart, we find that even there is no management participation in management.

FUTURE TRENDS IN INDUSTRIAL RELATIONS

To understand the future trends in personnel management industrial relations, it will not be adequate to review the present practices alone but there is a need to understand the studies on causes of industrial imbalances or industrial peace. The major developments in the area of personnel management industrial relations are : (*a*) Increased application of the system approach to personnel management-industrial relations.(*b*) Planning of more emphasis on human resource polymerisation and development. Personnel management -industrial relations should play an important role in managing of change in the organisation. The scope of personnel management-industrial relations function is to be broadened to cover inter--relationship and environment.

The increased challenge demand that professional Manager in the area of personal management should acquire advanced level education and training,contributing towards innovation, broad understanding, insight and interpersonal skill. This calls for broad studies as also covering the working knowledge of various quantitative techniques as also inputs from behavioral sciences like industrial psychology, sociology and anthropology. Employees selection, testing and interviews are becoming more and more sophisticated. This also requires to keep abreast of the developments using electronic data processing in the matching of applicant profiles, skills, aptitudes and interest with actual job requirement. This is important because wrong induction of today will cause industrial problems for tomorrow. Behavioural science have also given new techniques in the area of job satisfaction, motivation and leadership which had an important impact on personnel philosophy and practice.

All those who are concerned with the industrial relations will have not only to bear in mind all these trends but also to apply them in the development of new techniques for the benefit of the organisation and those who serve it. Industrial relations play a vital part in the establishment and maintenance of industrial democracy. The problem of industrial relations is inextricably interlinked with freedom of association, collective bargaining and conciliation and arbitration. Industrial democracy cannot succeed unless all concerned--workers employers, Government and public--fully realise its importance and its due place in the national life.

Industrial Relation in Public Enterprises

Stable industrial relations are the vital pre-requisite for industrial progress. Stable relations means situation when the problems of management and the workforce are discussed between them in a spirit of mutual trust and confidence without unnecessary delay and friction. Without healthy management relations, there is no hope of overcoming the multifarious problems to which the country is confronted today.

Industrial relations in a public undertaking will obviously be different from that of a private enterprise. Profit being a major motive for a private enterprise, the management is looked upon as a part and parcel of ownership and traditional labour-management conflict is inevitable because of their divergent interests. But in the case of public sector, the objectives of management are more often not in conflict with the objectives of the workforce. In fact, as part of their social objectives, public sector enterprise endeavour to create maximum employment opportunities and also to provide enough welfare for its workforce in the form of township, schools, colleges, hospitals, free transport and recreational facilities etc. in addition to their normal wages and salaries. Sometimes this expenditure is incurred much before the investment into the productive facilities undertaken. The Government considers this, as a developmental expenditure in the area rather than as additional burden on the company's resources. Industrial relation problems of the public sector are connected more with the relative emphasis assigned by each party, i.e. management and the trade unions to various objectives. For example, the management may give more emphasis to increasing the sales turnover and contributing to the national income whereas a trade union may be considered mainly with the issues of wage settlement or bonus. Neither the management considers the question of wage settlement or bonus as less important, nor the unions are against increasing increasing the level of output. It is more an exercise in understanding each other's position rather than sorting out any basic differences. The major role of negotiating machinery for settlement of such disputes is to improve communications and mutual understanding rather than bargaining.

Another characteristic of the public enterprises which set them apart from the private organisation is their own relative size. Most of the private sector enterprises are small in size, communication is much faster and the chief executive of the enterprise carries enough authority to take independent decisions. The public sector undertakings, on the other hand, are generally large in size and some of them are having workforce exceeding 10,000 employees. Naturally with such a large workforce, the problems of industrial relations will be more complex and the machinery to resolve them should also be more sophisticated. Moreover, the decisions taken in one public sector enterprise cannot be independent of others. If certain benefits in one of the public enterprises is given,it becomes precedence for negotiation on other public undertakings. This inter-dependence stresses the need for having appropriate norms as well as a corporate machinery for creating this uniformity. This role is being played by the Bureau of public Enterprises. Most of the strategic decisions concerned with the wages are not taken independently by the chief executives of the Organisations. The guidelines available from the Bureau of public Enterprise are to be followed by all the undertakings irrespective of their financial positions.

The third factor, characterising the public enterprises is the influence of political and bureaucratic set up and various committees and government bodies who are involved in the prices of industrial relations. Most of the trade unions have their political affiliations and in many public sectors they have their linkages with the ruling party. They are in a position to have direct access to the politicians who are at the helm of affairs. Some of the decisions which are beyond the control of the chief executives of the organisations are taken at the level of Ministry or Union Cabinet. Although with the liberalisation of economy the ministrial interference has reduced considerably still it is one of the key factor for industrial relations.

With this perspective in view, we will now analyse the industrial relation framework and their special problems in public undertakings. One major problem of industrial relations in the public sector is the poor appreciation for setting norms to regulate the industrial relations with their relatively large size and mutual interdependence. The importance of setting norms therefore becomes all the more important. But unfortunately till now, only half hearted measures have been taken to establish norms which underline the need for exercising control on the part of the both the parties. The major psychological barrier in the establishment of norms is the lack of awareness. It is generally not appreciated that this norm setting is important in view of the large objective of economic upliftment of the country. Similarly management, trade unions and staff associations are by and large obsessed by the immediate issues rather than such problem as have long term implications. When a specific issue becomes emotional in character, it is hardly possible to take overall reality into account. For example, marginal adjustment of wages. D.A. or house subsidy is an enterprise is no solution to the persistent effect of inflation on the value of money. Benefit based industrial disputes are totally fruitless unless they are considered in long term perspective.

Another factor responsible for the short term approach is the limited tenure of the chief executives. This leads to a tendency of leniency error and an approach of avoiding the industrial conflict and of achieving good relations at the cost of overall objectives.

Lack of efficient management system is a constraint both on the management side as well as trade unions. It is possible to work out good communication systems in public sector organisations which will avoid most of the problems arising out of mis- communication. Even trade unions should have a scientific and information based control system.

Another problem of industrial relations is a lack of consistency in maintaining relations at a collective level. Good industrial relations are nothing but good public relations and if there is a swing of behaviour depending of the political situation or changes in the power structure, this will certainly be noticed by either of the parties which will not be a good reflection on the seriousness and sincerity of purpose.

Improving Industrial Relations

Some of the broad guidelines which can improve the effectiveness of industrial relations in a public sector :*(i) change should come in the attitude of management and and trade union leaders since their roles are complementary in nature. We have all learnt about theory 'X' and theory 'Y' in our study on Organisational Behaviour and we have also learnt that the assumptions of theory'Y'are more effective in an environment of maturity. So, there is a need to bring about maturity in the attitude and behaviour of management as well as trade union leaders. This can be done through systematic training and education of the trade unions. Such training programme will enable the trade union leaders to appreciate their role vis-a vis the role of the organisation, the external constraints to which the organisation is exposed and the objectives to which the organisation has been committed and their contribution will thus be in line with the overall organisational objectives. This will be able to appreciate rather the long term perspectives of industrial relations than a short-term view of getting immediate gains . The importance of such training and development programmes should be recognised by all the public sector undertakings and massive drive should be started to achieve awareness and maturity at all levels.*

Even the management of public sector enterprises should realise that the old policies of divide and rule which emerged from capitalistic set up industry, is not effective in the modern industrial set up. We have experienced in our own organisation that it is easier to deal with a few strong unions headed by strong and matured trade unions leaders. They are in a position to appreciate the problems of management and also enjoy the full confidence of workers so that the process job communication becomes much easier. Strong trade union can play an effective role of communication with the workforce and it is easier to resolved even long standing conflicts and issues through the process of negotiations.

It has already been studied that efforts should be made to improve the management systems in the organisation. Effective communication system is very essential for management as well as trade unions.

Public sector enterprises should also appreciate role of corporate bodies like Bureau ofPpublic Enterprises in establishing uniformity in procedures and policies. They should give up their myopic view of the environment which is standing in the way of establishing appropriate norms and procedures. In the absence of appropriate norms, it will not be easy to settle various issues in the public sector organisations because of their inter dependency and large size.

Recently the management and the trade unions have realised the importance of bilateral negotiations rather than taking the issues of adjudication process. It may be observed that the legal set up for settlement of industrial disputes has not proved to be so effective as a method of negotiation. Such negotiations may be at the unit level or corporate level or sometimes even at the level of ministry. The Trade Union Movement in our country is process of mutation of politics and the trade unions have been close associations with the ruling party and national leaders. So political framework for settlement of disputes is generally more effective than the legal framework. Instead of advocating a divorce between trade unions and politics, why not to frame a system for effective negotiation at the political level.

The problems of labour management relations are going to be more difficult and complex in the times to come because of greater barriers between organisations, political surrounding and social environment. The organisational policy and practices are open to question by the government, consumers, workers and other social groups. The workers are bringing their own aspirations, attitudes, value systems to the work place . There is going to be a greater change to the industrial managers of future.

In the coming two decades, there is going to be a serious concern for unemployment and under employment. The unemployment is increasing at a faster rate and we are unable to generate new jobs. Our efforts will be necessary not only in finding employment but also in learning to live with unemployment. If we do not accommodate ourselves with these social factors, we may have to pay the price in terms of wasted manhours, intolerance, conflict and even in violence.

Economy has experienced a rapid growth in the last 15 years and is showing a slackening of growth now. The slow rate of growth will impose an inhibiting factor on the growth of the organisation and even pose a threat to their survival causing anxiety and lack of job security.

Changes due to technology will take place even more rapidly and will quicken the total change in the last 30 to 35 years. With these fast changes, the new opportunities, products and markets will be created. The changes will also widen the channels of communication within the organisations and this will require unprecedented flow of information through which the management and workforce will have an easy access to each other. The changes will create scope for use in more constructive way and there will be more effort to assist in environment protection and resource consumption.

Social progress does not occur automatically. It has to be brought about by various means including legislation, education, negotiation and persuasion. Pre-occupation with human welfare and social betterment introduced through a vast array of social services such as pension plans, health care, educational benefits carry with them an economic cost which in good measure is changed to the enterprise. There is a limit to the social cost, if a good measure of it is passed on to the consumers in the form of rise in the prices of various commodities.

The family ties are also becoming less strong with the passage of time. It is believed that more permissiveness will govern the relations between family members rather than traditional parental authority. These changing life styles will pose new problems in managing industrial relations. The people will have to change their living habits to fit in with the place and time of work. The issue of participation, job satisfaction and career development will become the milestone of our future personnel policies.

Recently the labour has acquired considerable organisational power in the industrial set up. The organised labour force can now bring to a stand still, the productive machinery of the society. In many cases, the organised unions, force the employers to concede to their demands which are beyond the capacity of the industry. In this way, they can render the industry sick or push up the prices to the detriment of social interests. These restrictive and wasteful practices of work under utilisation of the productive capacity of the industries and render social investments ineffective. The situation can be tackled only by bringing about maturity in the attitudes and values of unions as well as management, improving the systems of management and communication and adopting a practical and positive approach in resolving the issues.

66

Labour Welfare

Aim of Welfare Activities

Labour welfare work aims at providing such service facilities and amenities which enable the workers employed in industries factories to perform their work in healthy, congenial surrounding conductive to good health and high moral. The aims or objectives of welfare activities is partly humanistic, to enable the workers to enjoy a fuller and richer life. The relevance and necessity of welfare work in India can be easily realised if one observes the pitiable working conditions of workers in this country. A stable and efficient labour force, therefore, cannot be built up without an improvement in the conditions of their life and work in industrial centres. The development of community and society depends only on the development of labours. The importance of labour welfare work is beyond the stage of debate and is recognised as an integral part of industrial tradition in all industrially advanced countries. Labour welfare is a vital part of business organisation and management now-a-days attaches more importance to human angle. It increases the productivity, as well as productive efficiency of the workers and induces in them a new spirit of self realisation and consciousness. Welfare activities can go a long way in keeping the workers contented. The importance of labour welfare measures was accepted as early as 1931, when the Royal Commission on Labour stated, "the benefits, which go under this nomenclature are of great important to the worker and which he is unable to secure by himself. The labour welfare scheme may be regarded as a wise investment. The worker should at least have the means and facilities to keep himself in a state of health and efficiency. The working condition should be such as to safeguard his health and protect him against occupational hazard.

What is Welfare

The work place should provide reasonable amenities for its essential needs. The betterment of worker's conditions must proceed more from the employers down rather than be forced by demands from below. It is so important because if the labour is contented, well housed, well fed, well looked after it is not only an asset to the employer but serves to raise the standards of industry and labour in the country. Labour welfare activities are the useful adjunct to motivational approach and help in maintaining positive attitude towards the job and the organisation. Therefore welfare is also fundamentally in the interest of larger society as the health, happiness and efficiency of each individual connotes the general well being of all. The concept of welfare is dynamic in nature and vary from country to country and from time to time and even in the same country depending upon its value system, social institution, degree of industrialisation and general level of social and economic development. Welfare activities are partly humanitarian, partly economic and partly civic. It is humanitarian, as its aims are providing certain facilities and amenities of life to the workers which they themselves cannot provide. It is economic because it approves the efficiency of the workers. It is civic, because it promotes a sense of responsibilities and dignity among workers and to make them better citizens. According to Frederic Engels, "Labour is the source of all wealth. It is next to nature, which supplies it with the material that it converts into wealth. But it is even definitely more than this."

Welfare is the basic condition for all human existence and this to such an extent that, in a sense we have to say that labour created man himself.

Definition

Labour welfare is one of the major determinants of industrial relations. Encyclopedia of Social Science defines welfare work as "Voluntary efforts of the employer to establish, within the existing industrial system working and sometimes living and cultural condition of the employers beyond what is required by law, the customs of the country and conditions of the market." Royal Commission on labour defined 'Welfare' as one "which must necessarily be flexible, elastic and differs widely with times, region, industry and bearing a somewhat different interpretation in one country from another, according to different social customs the degree of industrialisation and the educational development of the worker. Labour welfare is, therefore, one of the major aspects of national programmes towards improving the lot of labour and creating a life and work environment of decent comfort for this class of society. The object of welfare is one in which much can be done to combat the sense of frustration of the industrial worker to relieve him of personnel and family worries to improve his health, to afford him a means of self expression, to offer him some sphere in which he can excel all others, to help him a wider perception on life."

In May 1944 the International Labour Organisation laid down the grand Charter of Labour, popularly known as the Declaration of Philadelphia. The declaration emphasised the aims and objectives of International Labour Organisation. One of the objective is that "The war against want requires to be carried on what unrelenting vigour within each nation, and by continuous concerted international effort in which the representative of workers and employers enjoying equal status with those of Government representatives."

Indian National Congress in its Karachi resolution stated that States shall safeguard the interest of industrial workers and shall secure them by suitable legislation, the living wage, healthy working conditions of work, limited hours of work, suitable machinery for settlement of disputes between employers and workmen and protection against old age, sickness and unemployment. Anything done for intellectual, physical, moral and economic betterment of the workers, whether by employers, by government or by other agencies over and above what is laid down by laws of the land is labour welfare.

International Labour Organisation Report refers with regard to labour welfare as "such services facilities and amenities which may be established in or in the vacinity of undertaking to enable the persons employed in them to perform their work in healthy, congenial surroundings and provided with amenities conductive to good health and high morale."

Labour welfare is a very broad term governing from social security to such activities as medical aid, creches, canteens, recreation, housing, adult education, arrangement for transport of labour to and from work place to residence etc.

Need For Labour Welfare

Labour welfare work has its beneficial efforts on the workers. The welfare measure influence the sentiment of the worker and contribute to Industrial peace. The aim of labour welfare work are to provide facilities and amenities which enable the workers employed in industries to perform their work in healthy, congenial surrounding conducive to good health and high morale beside other factors such as.

(*i*) *Humanistic - to enable the worker to enjoy fuller and richer life.*

(*ii*) *Economic - To improve the efficiency of the worker.*

(*iii*)*Civic - To develop a sense of responsibility and dignity among the workers.*

The need for labour welfare was strongly felt by Royal Commission on labour as far back as 1931. The need was emphasised in free India by the Constitution which laid down the following Articles in this regard :

Articles 41, 42 and 43 of the Constitution relating to the concept of welfare highlight the concern of the State for Labour Welfare.

Article 41 states that the State shall within limits of its economic capacity and development make effective provision for securing the right to work, to education, old age, sickness and disablement."

Article 42 of the Constitution states that the State shall make provision for securing just and human conditions of work and for maternity relief.

Article 43 of the Constitution states that the State shall endeavour to secure by suitable legislation to all workers, agricultural, industrial or otherwise. The living wage and condition of work of ensure the decent standard of life leisure, social and cultural opportunities.

Committee On Labour Welfare

Government of India in 1959 set up a committee on labour welfare. The Committee observed that the trade unionist asserted that welfare must not mean philanthropic or gratuitous help to the working class. It should not be treated as matter of right obtainable under Constitution but all social security measures should be treated as essential part of labour welfare. The Committee on Labour Welfare emphasised that the welfare amenities relating to work should conform to sociological and environmental changes which have been taking place in the country.

The Committee indicated that the trade unionist insisted on for labour welfare to include all that is necessary for physical and mental development of a worker. Labour Unions wanted that labour welfare should include provisions for housing, medical, educational facilities, nutrition facilities, rest and recreation, cooperative societies, creches, social insurance measures undertaken voluntarily by employers alone or jointly with workers.

The object of any welfare work is to create congenial and healthy atmosphere to enable the workers to enjoy their leisure. According to the Encyclopedia of Social Science "Industrial welfare work has taken numerous forms such as":

(*i*) The dealing with immediate working conditions such as adequate light, heat, ventilation, toilet facilities, accident and occupational disease prevention, lunch room, recreation room etc.

(*ii*) Concerned with less immediate working condition such as : club room, playground, gardens, disability and unemployment funds, pensions, saving banks, provision for conciliation and arbitration shop committees and works councils.

(*iii*) Improved community conditions such as housing, retail-stores, arrangement of picnics, summer camps, day nurseries and dispensaries.

The test of welfare activity is that it removes directly or indirectly any hindrance, physical or mental of the worker and restore to him the peace of living. Labour welfare is one of the major determinants of industrial relations. Prof. Kirkaldy has rightly observed that the whole field of welfare is one in which much can be done to combat the sense of frustration of industrial worker, to relieve him of personnel worries and to help him to wider conception of life.

Statutory Welfare Fund

The coal mines labour funds, mica mines labour funds and such other statutory welfare funds which have been in operation for more than two decades. Statutory requirements should be considered as minimum standard laid down by law for the welfare of million of workers engaged in trade and industry. Under voluntary welfare work the progressive and forward looking employer should take steps to provide not only the basic human needs but should also enlist support of the working force and reduce labour unrest. Progressive employer should realise that organised labour and social welfare activities and other such measures help to create the working climate and held the industry at least to reduce sickness and accident if not absenteeism.

Following are some of the voluntary welfare work undertaken in India :

(*a*) Adult and Social Education Centres

(*b*) Educational scholarship granted to the deserving poor children.

(*c*) Movie shows, indoor and outdoor games and sports.

(*d*) Library and reading room in the Industrial Undertakings.

(*e*) Publishing of quarterly journals and purchase of periodicals newspapers and magazines for the workmen.

(*f*) Fair price shops, cooperative consumer societies, cooperative credit societies etc.

SOCIAL SECURITY

The quest for social security and freedom from want and distress has been the consistent urge of man through the ages. It is a device provided by society against insecurities arising out of natural, social and economic causes. Social security which the society furnishes in an organised way against certain risks to which workmen are exposed such as sickness,maternity, invalidity, old age and death. The doctrine of social security is an outcome of careful reflection on the practical realities of social assistance and social insurance which is endeavoured to adopt and reconcile within a totally new framework. There is no doubt that the need for security has become a fundamental concern in modern societies. But too many and too much diversified social security schemes also lead to confusion rather than benefitting the employees. Coherence in such schemes is not only desirable, but is an absolute necessity.

Social Security As a Concept

The vast industrialisation has shattered the fabric of traditional society which has provided some in built security measures for their members. Therefore industrialised society had to provide its own measures for the security of the workmen against contingencies of modern industrial life like unemployment, disease, accident, death maternity etc. Government, therefore, had to interfere through legislation and other measures to protect the interest of the workmen. The definite schemes for Social Security and Labour Welfare have been made out not only law but also through convention, agreement etc. signed by Union/Associations and Managements/Societies interested in the upliftment of the working class. In India providing help to the poor and the destitutes has been regarded as a religious duty. Joint families, Panchayats and other Religious and Charitable institutes have provided assistance to the needy persons including orphans and widows. On the other hand, for the management of modern industries it has become legally obligatory that Social Security and Labour Welfare schemes are made the integral part of modern industrial life.

Social Security is one of the dynamic concepts of the modern age which had deeply influenced the social and economic policy of many countries in the world. Social Security is a very comprehensive term. There is no such definition of Social Security which may be accepted universally. Its meaning and scope differs from country to country according to the prevailing social legislations, traditions, and ideals. The approach of Social Security towards these human hazards is mainly three-fold *viz.*, the Compensation,Restoration and Prevention. Compensation means income security during spell of risks because the individual and his family should not be subjected to a double calamity, involving both destitution and loss of life, health, work. Restoration means cure for the sick, invalid, re-employment and rehabilitation. Prevention goes to avoid the loss of productive capacity due to sickness, unemployment or invalidity.

Social Security includes the creation of family responsibility of the state. Through the social security methods State tries to cover.

- Medical care in times of illness.
- Maternity facilities and cash allowances before and after the birth of the child in case of female.
- Pension during inability.
- Pension in old age after retirement.
- Payment of funeral expenses.
- Allowance during the period of unemployment etc.

The object of providing above social security is to ensure that the workmen get at least the minimum requirement of life during the period of contingencies in life. The object is to ensure that workmen who are dependent upon their income and when they are in need of assistance either in the form of medical assistance, money etc., the same are provided to them by the society so that the individuals in community can live with dignity and self-expression.

Realising the importance of social security and assistance, the Universal Declaration of Human Right proclaims; Everyone, as a member of Society, has the right to social security and is entitled to realisation, through national efforts and international co-operation and in accordance with the organisation and resources of each State of the economic, social and cultural rights indispensable for his dignity and the free development of his personality. The Constitution of India has affirmed to all people of the country inter alia, social and economic justice, but this has yet to be secured by peaceful social and legislative steps. The underlying idea behind social security measures is that a citizen who has contributed or is likely to contribute to his country's welfare should be given protection against certain hazards. Social security covers through an appropriate organisation, certain risks to which a person is exposed. These risks are such that an individual of small means cannot effectively provide for them by his own ability or foresight alone or even in private combination with his colleagues. The concept of social security is based on ideals of human dignity and social justice.

History Of Social Security

The concept of social security is as old as society. The individual had been provided security by the society and joint family system, caste system and many religious institutions against death, sickness, incapacity in employment, inadequate etc. The timeless quest for security has created a number of social devices to afford protection to the needy individuals and these devices took different forms in different countries such as joint family, caste system, mutual aid societies, religious institutions, the state philanthropic institutes etc.

Institutions of Social Security

With the growth of factory system and industialisation, the older institutions of social security became inadequate due to certain factors such as :

(*i*) Workers dependence only on money wage.

(*ii*) Workers retaining links with villages had to manage two houses.

(*iii*) Stoppage of child labour as a source of income.

(*iv*) Chronic unemployment due to the growth of industries under capitalism.

(*v*) Industrialisation gave rise to individuality.

(*vi*) Increase in number of accidents due to increase of labour multiplication of plant and inadequate working conditions.

Industrial workers being exposed to employment injuries, occupational diseases, unemployment, loss of income etc. necessitated the estate to play very active and importance role. The term 'Social Security' has gained immense popularity in recent years having originated in U.S.A. in 1933. Soon after it spread in almost all countries of the world and its importance being recognised greater and greater. State is a social organisation within a certain territory and ever since it came into existence people have accepted it to perform certain function for the good of the company as a whole. State, in fact, should provide support to poor, pregnant women, their new born off-spring, orphans, aged and to the helpless. In the past, state only touched the life of a citizen superficially. Even in European countries the position was not only very much different in the ancient and medieval periods when the state assistance was no more than irregular charity. During the last century, joint family had been the most effective institution for social security. The family used to pool together all their resources and give each member a share in the product which was regulated to his needs and not proportionals to his individual contribution. In India, joint family system is till working and providing support to the members of the family. But it is not as strong a bond as it used to be. Even the caste systems also provide certain measures of economic security though not so direct as that of the family to help its needy members. The social customs and conventions also help the family systems in meeting unforeseen contingencies and economical occasions.

Social security has now gone around the world and has caught the imagination of the Government and the people alike. The first Inter-America conference of Social Security was held in 1942 which appealed to the people that :

"Each country must create, conserve and build up the intellectual, moral and physical vigour of its active generation. prepare the way for its future generation and support the generation that has been discharged from productive life. This is the concept of social security, a genuine and rational economy of human resources and values". In 1944, I.L.O. stated that poverty anywhere constitutes a danger to prosperity everywhere. On December 10, 1948, the General Assembly of the United Nations adopted and proclaimed the Universal Declaration of Human Rights as a common standard of achievement for all Nations, the Declaration says that :

"Everyone has the right to a standard of living, adequate for the health and well being of himself and of his family including food, clothing, housing and medical care and the right to security in the event of unemployment, sickness, disability, widow-hood, old age or other lack of livelihood in circumstances beyond his control".

International Labour Organisation also defined "Social Security as the security that the society furnishes through proper and appropriate organisation against certain risks such as contingencies against which the individual of small means cannot effectively provide by his own ability or foresight or even in private combination of his fellow".

As social security system means a set of legal provision entitled to define benefits for defined categories of persons, such as contingencies, including maternity, child maintenance, conditions requiring medical care, maintenance of community health (when combined with provisions for other contingencies in-capacity for work, unemployment, old age, etc.).

Social Society

It is based on the ideals of human dignity and social justice. According to Lord Beveridge, "Social Society" is a fight against want, disease, ignorance, inequality and idleness. It is the protection which the society gives to its members against calamities over which members does not have any control. The Industrial workforce which is responsible to the country's prosperity should be provided with adequate protections against certain risks or hazards to which their life is exposed. The risks can be transferred from the individual to the community in either of the following two ways :

(*i*) *Social assistance*

(*ii*) *Social insurance*

Both of these *viz.* social assistant and social insurance from integral parts of the system social security.

(*i*) **Social Assistance**. It is an assistance provided by the Government to the poor and needy individuals. All such benefits are paid out of public revenue. In this, the beneficiaries are not required to contribute to the fund. Social assistance schemes are adopted in societies where workers are too poor to contribute or illiterate.

(*ii*) **Social Insurance.** It is a scheme wherein members of community pool their resources to secure one another against the risks which each one of them cannot face individually. In France, social security received adequate attention of the social reformers. Japan has adopted some novel schemes of social security. Japan while maintaining its traditional social system also introduced modern systems. In Japan beside other schemes there is child and mother protection schemes also. In U.S.S.R. the labour code of 1922 introduced the provisions for social security. In U.S.S.R., it covers all risks, insure all workers and does not enjoin on them to pay any contribution. A citizen of U.S.S.R. can, therefore, claim social security as matter of right.

A worker gets 50% to 60% of his salary after retirement depending upon the industry to which he belongs. Total disablement benefit varies between 60 to 100% of the wage. In Norway the system of social security is most established in the world. The social security scheme in Norway provides too much of economic protection to all its people.

Thus, the social insurance is a co-operative device resulting in the creation of collective fund to meet contingencies such as unemployment, maternity, sickness, injury, disability, old age, death of breadearner involving loss of total or partial earnings. The social security is now the aim of social welfare activities of all countries irrespective of their ideologies, social and political structure and economic policies. However, the emphasis on various aspects of social security varies with problems of the country in that country. The emphasis may be on family allowances and in another it may be on unemployment. At present there is emphasis on a comprehensive social security schemes so as to cover manifold contingencies such as employment, injury, disablement, sickness and medical care, maternity, old age, retirement and survivor's pension, contributory provident fund etc.

The basic difference between the two approaches lies in the fact that in the former the individual concerned gets the benefit as a matter of right, in the later he gets the benefit after proving the need. India has been far behind in this sphere as compared to other countries of the world. In U.S.S.R. the Social Security measures were introduced even when her industrialisation was in its infancy. In Germany, New-Zealand, Australia, etc. Social Security measures were introduced at a fairly early stage of industrial development.

International Labour Conference Session

The International Labour Conference in the course of its 32 sessions held since 1919 till 1950 adopted '87 recommendations out of which 19 related to social security, India had travelled too slowly on this path; out of only 12 conventions ratified by India; 2 relates to social security.

Article 32 of the Indian Constitution embodies the concept of social security *viz.*, the right to work, to education and public assistance in the case of unemployment, old age, sickness, disablement etc. The working class in India had also been demanding the above. The Government has not been able to do much in this respect, as is evident from the growing unemployment under-employment, both among educated and uneducated even in professions with specialisation like engineers, doctors etc. The attitude of the Business houses towards Social Security Schemes in India is lukewarm as can be seen from large number of cases of violations of the provisions of the various Social Security Acts specially on the part of small employees who exhibit the ignorance of the illiterate workers in utter disregard of their own social responsibilities. To meet the needs of the Industrial workers, the Government of India enacted various acts, mainly of two types. The first group constitutes the Acts like Minimum Wages Act, Payment of Wages Act, Mines Act. The Indian Railways Act, the Plantation Act. The Second group encompasses the important pieces of legislation towards protection against old age, occupational diseases etc. Employees Insurance Act provides (for sickness, cash-benefit, disablement benefit, medical benefit, maternity benefit etc.) The Workmen's Compensation Act (for injuries arising out of and in the course of employment). Employees P.F. Act, Bonus Act, The Coal Mines P.F. Act, Maternity Benefit Act etc.

However, considering the magnitude of the problem in Indian conditions, in just touches the fringe of the problems. In India, while some measures have been taken in respect of the Industrial Workers, nothing worthwhile has been done for the remaining class of people specially agricultural workers who are comprising of 65% of the population. The Government has to pay special attention towards the legislation like Health Schemes and old age pension for non-working class specially rural, social, insurance and national assistances. Such schemes ar prevalent in many countries of the world. At present only a few classes of the population are covered and are eligible to get certain class of benefits. The agriculture class has been completely neglected in this regard.

Unemployment Insurance

Unemployment Insurance is very common in many advanced countries as a part of the social security with the objective of helping the employees to overcome the difficulties of unemployment thereby indirectly helping the society also. In India, for industrial workers, there exists provisions in the I.D. Act for Lay Off and Retrenchment Benefit which is not considered adequate and which does not apply to non-industrial workers. To overcome the above short comings, the State is to evolve a comprehensive Security Plan, having the following two main features :

(*a*) Coverage of the whole population regarding income security and medical services.

(*b*) Coverage of all principal contingencies such as sickness, maternity, employment injury, invalidity, old age, death of bread earner, unemployment and childhood.

Agriculture Sector

The problem of social security for agricultural population will have to be taken separately because of the following reasons :

(*a*) Over 70% of the population directly dependent on agriculture.

(*b*) Rural population is scattered all over the country and social security authorities must take village as the unit.

(*c*) The agriculturist class consists not only of landless agricultural wage earner but also of the tenant farmers and peasant proprietors. The economic needs of each of these groups are different from these of the either two.

(*d*) The various insurance risks such as sickness, accident, invalidity, old age and even death do not have the same meaning for the cultivator, as for the urban wage earner. The most beneficial system of insurance to cultivator would be the crop and cattle insurance.

Problems in the Implementation

On analysing the existing Social Security and Welfare facilities is some of the industrial units following complaints were noted :

— There is no proper communication system between the management and workmen in connection with Social Security and the manner in which it is implemented.

— There is no active participation of workmen in the administration of Social Security and Welfare facilities.

— Multiplicity of unions and lack of strong representation union.

— Sometimes management find excuses in providing some Social Security and Welfare measures on the ground that it will have repercussion on other units of the company.

Recommendations

To translate the National Objectives, as enshrined in the Preamble of the Constitution of Indian Republic, a part of which reads as "To secure to all the citizen, justice, social, economic and political liberty of thoughts, expression, belief, faith and worship into action, it is incumbent upon the State to constantly endeavour to better the lot of the citizens : Industry has a vital role to play in the national economy, so that Social Security and Labour Welfare needs of the workers require added attention. The following are the recommendations for effective implementation of Social Security and Labour Welfare measures.

(*i*) A proper communication system should be maintained to make the employees understand the Social Security and Labour Welfare measures in right perspectives.

(*ii*) Induction programme should be conducted through which employees will come to know of the amenities and facilities for which most of the workmen are not aware.

(*iii*) Posting of Welfare Officer is essential for implementation of welfare measures. Factory Act, 1948 provides employment of welfare officer where 500 or more workers are employed. Management should appoint Welfare Officer for the benefit of employees.

(*iv*) Management should issue strict instructions to be concerned department to pay the dues of the retired/resigned employees so that there may not be any difficulty in getting the payment in time.

67

Discipline In Industrial Employment

Disciplines

Good human relation is not a cult to be blindly followed, rather it is a way of thinking and working together to achieve the best results. It is the force of discipline which enables a manager to reach the hearts of his subordinates.

Discipline has to be learnt, studied and applied by every manager every day in all walks of his life. It is always best to keep people under discipline. Human relations to be good must not be all sweets, but should contain some spice and iron too. It has been proved beyond doubt that the employees will feel absolutely secure even under the iron claws of discipline. Discipline and indiscipline in an industry are like two sides of the same coin. Disciplined behaviour brings harmony and is conducive to the interest of school group. Indiscipline, on the other hand, leads to disharmony and chaos and is disruptive to social needs. The real causes of indiscipline emanate from the experiences of an employee from his organisational culture, ideology and environment.

Since discipline has to come from within, the organisation has simply to provide environment, formulate policies, programmes and procedures in such a way that the employees behaviour are conditioned to discipline. Enthusiasm of discipline is not a mechanical process, it requires proper study of human being and their inter-personnel relationship with other employees. The concept of discipline in industry varies from maintenance of proper subordination to willing acceptance of norms of conduct of the organisation.

Discipline is the key note of civilisation and is the pivot of modern society. Discipline indicates a mode of conduct and is essential for the orderly conduct of any organisation and effective utilisation of time and energy of workers and the economic use of the resources. It is the responsibility of the employer to maintain and infuse discipline and therefore employer has the inherent right to punish suitably delinquent employees. The I.D. Act does not lay down any procedure for taking disciplinary action. The section 33 of the Act only restrains the employer from discharging or punishing a worker during pendency of a dispute. Section 2A of the Act gives jurisdiction to Labour Courts and Tribunals over industrial disputes relating to dismissal and discharge of individual worker even if their cases are not taken up by any union. A Labour Court and an Industrial Tribunal set up under the I.D. Act can order reinstatement, if the order of discharge is considered unreasonable or malafide.

Principles of equity and justice require that in case of misconduct proper enquiry is conducted before taking any action and the worker concerned is given an opportunity to explain his act or omission. The Industrial Employment (Standing Order Act) 1946 list out certain acts and omission which could be treated as misconduct. The Act requires the workers to be given an opportunity to explain the misconduct alleged against him.

Code of Discipline

The importance of Code lies in its educative values. It has helped in creating a positive climate for industrial peace. Labour unrest, as reflected in loss of Mondays through work stoppages, has been steadily declining since the adoption of the code of discipline.

The importance of code has been accepted by most establishment in the public sector. The indifferent working of the code in some states has also been a cause of frequent complaints. The rank and file of workers and middle management are yet to acquire full awareness of their responsibility under the code. More vigorous efforts are required from the employers and workers to educate their members in their responsibilities toward code of discipline.

This code binds employers and employees to settle all future disputes by mutual negotiations, conciliation and voluntary arbitration. It lays down that both labours and employers would avoid go-slow tactics, lock-outs, strikes without notice, intimidation and other terms of discipline, which are usually the causes of industrial disputes. The code itself symbolises Government's current policy to promote, on a voluntary basis, industrial peace with the cooperation of employees and employers.

In 1957, the Standing Labour Committee of the Indian Labour Conference adopted a 'Code of Industrial Discipline' which was ratified by the Employees' and Employers' Association.

Discipline and disciple are the two words derived from the same source. Discipline means to induce among employees a sense of discipline. Professor McGregor's Hot Stove Rule gives characteristics essentials of discipline. According to McGregor a good disciplinary system should have the following characteristics :

(*a*) Advance Warning,

(*b*) Impartiality,

(*c*) Consistency,and

(*d*) Impersonality.

(*a*) **Advance Warning.** When Hot Stove is really hot, the heat and glow are an amount of warning so that no one touches the stove. If any one touches it, the fingers are burnt and there can be no argument about it. Therefore, if the rules and penalties are clear and well understood a violation produces some natural consequences. Therefore, standing orders or rules of the company should be made known and communicated down the line. There should be better induction of the worker in the organisation wherein they should be explained the standing orders of the company in details. The should be explained about their responsibility and duties.

(*b*) **Impartiality.** The Hot Stove does not have any kind of subjective or personal feeling in inflicting pain and suffering on any one who touches it. The disciplinary authority should not feel a sense of pride or be apologetic while inflicting any penalty in the interest of the organisation.

(*c*) **Consistency.** The disciplinary procedure should be so maintained that there should be consistency of inflicting the punishment on different individuals or groups, of course past performance of a worker, his record of service or valid considerations in determining the penalty to be imposed. But the principles of consistency should be observed in the sense that under identical situation, there should not be marked difference in the action taken, as the Hot Stove burns the fingers or any other limb that touch it, in the same manner whether it is a child or an old man.

(*d*) **Impersonality.** Hot Stove has no personal feeling and likewise should have no personal feeling while dealing with discipline.

Disciplinary Action

The management can use either of the following possible approaches to any act of indiscipline :

(*a*) **Judicial Approach;**

(*b*) **Human Relations Approach;**

(*c*) **Human Resource Approach.**

(*a*) **Judicial Approach.** Under judicial approach, the degree of offence in a particular situation is determined by carefully weighing the evidence and taking all the steps prescribed for disciplinary procedure. However, this is a time consuming process and leads to delays and there is also a reluctance on the part of disciplinary authority to get involved in it. However, depending upon the situation, management may have to follow strategic leniency when it is feared that any disciplinary action might provoke excessive direction from the powerful trade union, leading to stoppage of work. However, the decisions in such matters have to be left to the discretion of the top management only which has to think of overall interest of the organisation.

(*b*) **Human Relations Approach.** The idea is to treat the offending employee as human being and to consider the totality of his personality and behaviour. Human relations approach would prove him the cause of violation of rules. Under this approach, attempt should be made to help the worker to get over his personal difficulty or to shift him to a new job to handle him rather than to take an extreme view and punish him consequently.

(*c*) **Human Resource Approach.** The starting point here in this approach is that every employee is a resource to the employer and the human resource is the most important factor of production. In this approach the extreme form of penalty like discharge or dismissal will be rarely resorted to as the human resource even trained and motivated to work with the requirement of the organisation's norms or behaviour. This approach does not have sympathy for misfit, the sub-standard worker or the budli

An employee shall devote his whole time and energy exclusively to the work and interest of the company. An employee shall not even while on leave, directly or indirectly engage in any other profession or business or enter into the services of or employed himself in any capacity or fraud for any purpose whatsoever and for any part of his time. Government department, firm of company etc. shall not have any financial dealings with persons or firm etc. having business relations with the company for sale or purchase of materials, equipments or supply of labour if any or for any other purpose. An employee shall at all times conduct himself soberly while on works premises and shall show proper respect to all concerned and shall use his best endeavour to promote the interests of the company and to maintain and promote the good reputation thereof.

Industrial Employment

The underlying idea of the industrial adjudication is to bring about settlement of disputes between employer and employees so that there should be peace in industry and the production should not suffer. Although the Labour Court have been given very wide powers but the Supreme Court has held in Rohtas Industry's case that every case has to be decided on it own merits.

Under the common law, an employer is entitled to terminate the services of any of his employees on giving him the customary notice or wages in lieu of notice. This right has been practically denied under the Industrial Disputes Act. Similarly, he cannot discharge or dismiss an employee during the pendency of any industrial dispute before the Conciliation Officer, Conciliation Board and Labour Courts without the express permission in writing or approval as the case may be, of the authority before whom the said industrial dispute is pending. A dispute about employment as well as non-employment is an industrial dispute. In the case of wrongful termination of service by any means, the situation tantamounts to denial or refusal on the part of the employers to employ the employee. The demand for employment, therefore, in fact is a demand for reinstatement. According to the definition of the workman, the relationship of master and servant does not cease with the termination of employment by the employer de-facto because in the event of an industrial dispute being raised such an employee is deemed by legal binding to be the workman capable of raising an industrial dispute.

The dispute which finds its way to tribunal for adjudication regarding termination of employment may be such as has been subject matter of a domestic enquiry or where the services have been terminated without any charge-sheet or enquiry or where the employee has been removed after charge-sheet and explanation of the employee but without holding any enquiry or where the termination is sudden and instantaneous.

It is also to pertinent to note that a wrongful dismissal in the field of industrial employment is not merely a breach of the contract to be compensated by award of damages alone. An Industrial Tribunal is competent to direct reinstatement with relief which cannot be awarded by the Civil Courts.

It is also to be noted very carefully that an industrial employee cannot be discharged from his employment simply in exercise of the power of discharge vested in an employer. This stand has consistently been accepted by Labour Courts and the Supreme Court has also held that there is no such inherent right in an employer. If he takes recourse to this power, he must disclose the reasons for the termination of service and prove his bonafides.

There is no hard and fast rule that every discharge without charge-sheet and enquiry is bad and is invalid. It all depends on the peculiar facts of each case. The enquiry is ordinarily

necessary because otherwise it is not possible to know whether the action of the management is bonafide or not. People have a wrong notion that dismissal without issuing a charge-sheet or holding an enquiry is bad and in such cases the concerned workman is entitled to reinstatement. The Supreme Court has set at rest this controversy that non-holding of enquiry does not necessarily invalidate the order of dismissal. They have further held that in case where the enquiry has not been held by the employer that Tribunal can conduct that enquiry and come to his own conclusions on the evidence produced before him. In Punjab National Bank Limited case, it has been held, 'where, no enquiry has been held by the management the issue about the merits of the order of dismissal is at large before the Tribunal. The Tribunal has to decide for itself whether the misconduct alleged is proved, and if yes, what would be the proper order to make. Therefore, the fact that the management failed to hold a proper enquiry before making its order would not by itself be a ground of reinstatement."

Discipline is a management function, and therefore,ordinarily no interference should be there from any quarter. But then there is other side of the picture also where an exercise of such function can be unduly harsh, vindictive and malafides so as to affect security of employment, situation which can disrupt the industrial peace.

There may be cases where the instantaneous dismissal has to be resorted to in the interest of internal administration. It has been held by the Labour Courts that in certain justifiable cases the action of the management was proper. Such cases belong to the realm of insubordination to the Managing Director or the employer himself was convinced that there is no point hold any enquiry.

Punishment

The Management's decision is only to be revised if the Tribunal is of opinion that the punishment is so unjust and harsh that it affects the conscience of man. But this interference should be subject to the rule and the matter should not be viewed altogether subjectively from the point of view of the employer or the employee alone but should also be viewed objectively in the interest of industry for bringing about harmony in the relationship between the two. It has been held by the highest judicial pronouncements that once the misconduct has been held to be proved, the Tribunal ordinarily should not substitute his own punishment for that awarded by the management.

Reinstatement

An employee who has been unjustifiably dismissed can be awarded relief or reinstatement. Reinstatement means to be restored to or to be reestablished in a former post having the same service conditions. In other words, this would need restoring the employee to the same occupation in which he lost employment and on terms and conditions not less favourable than those to which he would have been entitled had his services not been terminated by the employer.

If the Tribunal finds the termination of employment to be unjustified, the question of relief is the next question to be considered. The relief which can be awarded is either (a) reinstatement or (b) compensation in lieu of reinstatement or (c) both. It is not possible to lay down rules which could be regarded as exhaustive on the subject and none such have been valid down. Industrial Tribunals has the right to order the reinstatement of a workman who has been wrongfully dismissed, and the normal rule is that a workman wrongfully dismissed should be reinstated, the tribunal should also take into consideration the question of discipline in the concern. The past record of the employee, the nature of his alleged lapse and the ground on which the order of the management is set aside are factors which should be considered. Each case has to be considered on its merits.

Retrenchment

Retrenchment is another form of termination of service of an employee which means discharge of surplus labour or staff otherwise than the punishment inflicted by way of disciplinary action. Industrial Disputes Act,1947 has recognised retrenchment as a statutory right but there are certain mandatory conditions precedent which have to be fulfilled under Section 25F of this Act. It provides that no workman who has been in continuous service for not less than one year under an employer shall be retrenched by that employer until (*a*) the workman has been given one month's notice in writing indicating the reasons for retrenchment, or the workman has been given one month's wages in lieu of notice; (*b*) the workman has been paid at the time of retrechment, compensation which shall be equivalent to fifteen days average pay for every completed year of service or any part thereof in excess of six month's; (*c*) notice in the prescribed manner is served on the Appropriate Government.

The employer can exercise this power only in the cases of bonafide retrenchment. If the dispute is raised it is for the employer to prove that the retrechment was bonafide. Non-compliance of these provisions will render the retrenchment null and void. If the termination of service is by way of discharge or dismissal as a punishment for any misconduct, then the employer has not to pay any compensation in the terms laid down in S. 25 F.

If a case of retrenchment is made out it would be normally for the employer to decide which of the employees should be retrenched, but there is no doubt that ordinarily industrial rule of retrenchment is "last come first out" and when other things are equal, this rule has to be followed by the employer.

Procedure For Employee's Discharge

The discharge of an employee can be linked to sentencing him to "economic death." Nothing seems to evoke stronger personal feeling than the discharge of an employee. Nothing provokes industrial unrest more quickly or contributes more damagingly to poor employees relations than a mishandled discharge. At times it becomes a great problem for the management specially where the union is strong, to discharge a troublesome and inefficient worker. Experience shows that one undesirable employee can demoralise and reduce the efficiency of a department of even of entire establishment.

Employee's Misbehaviour

There are two categories of employee's misbehaviour that lead to discharge.

(*a*) The first involves a series of minor infractions, the cumulative effect of which justifies permanent dismissal.

(*b*) The second involves the single employee's act which on its merit is so serious to justify immediate dismissal without regard to the employees' past service record or other facts.

Under the first category comes to minor misconducts such as minor acts of indiscipline of late coming, smoking or absenteeism. In the Standing Order under the Industrial Employment Act provision is generally made for minor misconducts and major misconducts. For minor misconducts the punishments such as censure, warning etc. is provided while for the major misconduct the discharge or dismissal is provided.

Misconduct

The managers or the departmental heads frequently commit the error of issuing verbal warnings for minor infractions. Verbal warnings are too often taken lightly by the employees and are subject to challenge by the union representatives when the accumulation of minor offences has brought about a discharge. They, however, must justify their positions as representatives of the workmen in the eyes of the members.

PROCEDURE FOR DEALING MISCONDUCT

When an act of misconduct is alleged against an employee for which the penalty or fine or censure is proposed to be inflicted, the employee shall be given an opportunity to show cause before the penalty is imposed. In case of misconduct for which any of the other penalties are proposed to be imposed, a charge sheet stating the allegations and charges shall be given to the employee concerned and after receipt of this written explanation within the period to be specified in the charge sheet, an enquiry, if the allegations are denied by him will be held by an Officer or Officer nominated by the Management, into the alleged act of misconduct. At the enquiry, the employee concerned will be accorded reasonable opportunity of explaining and defending allegation. Any such enquiry, may relate to the alleged misconduct of several employee together, in which case the enquiry may be held for all the employees together.

When an employee is charged with misconduct for which there is a prima facie case for imposing the penalty of removal or dismissal from service, he will be suspended forthwith from duty. The order of suspension shall be given in writing and shall set out in general terms, as far as possible, the misconduct alleged against the employee and shall take effect immediately on communication thereof to him. The suspended employee shall not, during the period of suspension, enter the works premises except with the special permission of the management or when he is specially called by the management in connection with the enquiry. He shall also not leave the station without the written permission of the Management.

An employee under suspension shall be entitled to a subsistence allowance at an amount equal to the leave salary admissible to him during half pay leave provided the suspending authority is satisfied that the employee is not engaged in any other employment, business, profession or vocation. In addition he shall be entitled to Dearness Allowance admissible on such leave salary and any other compensatory allowance of which he was in receipt on the day of suspension provided the suspending authority is satisfied that the employee continues to meet the expenditure for which the allowances were granted.

If, after enquiry, an employee is adjudged guilty of mis-conduct and punishment is awarded the employee shall not be entitled to any remuneration for such period other than what is admissible understanding orders. If, however, he is found not guilty of the alleged misconduct or any other act of misconduct, he shall be reinstated in his post and shall be paid the difference between the emoluments which he would have received had he not been suspended and the subsistence allowance already paid to him, and the period of suspension being treated as duty.

If, during the enquiry it is found that the employee is guilty of misconduct, other than that stated in the order of suspension, the employee shall not be liable for punishment but before any punishment is awarded to him, he shall be afforded reasonable opportunity in writing of explaining and defending his action in respect of such act of misconduct.

The management reserves to itself the right to suspend the employee accused in a Court of Law of any criminal offence involving moral turpitude until the disposal of the trial.

The rule for the supervisory personnel is that where a warning is worth marking, never issue it verbally, rather put it in writing. Duplicate copies of the warning notice should state in a few words, the nature of facts of the offence and the date of its occurrence. A copy of the warning notes should be presented to the employee with one copy retained for the file.

Each copy should be signed at the time of issuing to the employee by the departmental head if there is any.

By following this procedure, the management has reduced, if not eliminated, the context of memory and has also placed the employee and the union official on notice that discharge is in the offing, if the employee's conduct is not corrected. Additionally, should the matter find its way to the labour authorities, the management has the benefit of documented case attested to by the employee involved. Generally issuing of three warning notices during a period of 3 to 6 months justifies discharge. Such system should also be clearly brought to the knowledge of the employee either in the letter of appointment or the service conditions. Secondly, it greatly reduces the adverse effect to the other employees because the element of surprise has been minimised.

Minor Misconduct

The following have been held to be minor misconducts :

(*i*) Late attendance and absence without leave or without sufficient cause.

(*ii*) Neglect of work, negligence in performing duties.

(*iii*) Distribution or exhibition within the premises of any establishment, any newspapers, handbills, pamphlets, or posters without the previous sanction of the Management.

(*iv*) Carrying on trade union activities during working hours.

(*v*) Wrongful use of the property of the company not involving the company in any financial loss.

(*vi*) Unauthorised use of company's quarters.

(*vii*) Indecent behaviour while on duty.

(*viii*) Absence from place of work after reporting for a period not exceeding 15 minutes.

(*ix*) Causing damage to work in process or to any property of the company involving small financial loss.

(*x*) Refusal to accept any communication or charge-sheet.

The workman found guilty of minor misconduct may be punished as under :

(*a*) Be warned censured.

(*b*) An adverse remark entered against him.

(*c*) Fine.

Procedure

No order imposing any of the penalties in respect of minor misconducts should be passed unless :

(*a*) The workman is informed in writing of the allegations against him,

(*b*) Given an opportunity to make any representation he may wish to make in respect thereof,

(*c*) Such representation, is taken into consideration by the Management, and

(*d*) Personal hearing given to him if he so desires at the time of his representation.

GRIEVANCE HANDLING MACHINERY

Grievance

'Grievance' implies dissatisfaction, or distress, or suffering or grief caused unnecessarily or illegally. In labour-management relations it is a complaint or representation made in writing as regard to a company related matter arising from employment or service conditions, or from conditions involving unfair treatment by the employers, or from violation of any agreement or standing instructions. Grievance is defined as real or imaginary feeling of personal injustice which an employee has concerning his employment relation.

Prompt redressal of grievances is a must for creating good labour-management relations and promoting efficiency at the plant level. Grievances must not be allowed to accumulate because grievances breed grievances. Piling up of grievances may create a sense of frustration, disloyalty and non-cooperation among workers who may lose interest in work and must may affect the quality and quantity of output. This may also lead to indiscipline taking the form of increased absenteeism, go slow, work to rule, demonstrations, gherao, violence and strikes. Proper disposal of grievance needs a serious consideration for harmonious industrial relations and maintenance of industrial peace.

Employees sometimes do not know precisely what is making them dissatisfied. Their own feeling may set-up mental blocks which prevent them from interpreting correctly what is happening. They may not have sufficient knowledge of human nature or of the many social forces impinging on them. Not knowing their actual grievance but still feeling dissatisfied they tend to file grievances about something else.

A grievance rate is usually stated in terms of, number of written grievances presented for 100 employees in one year. A typical grievance rate is 10 to 20 and any rate above or below that range might indicate a labour relations situation meriting further investigation. Method of handling grievances will affect the rate of grievance.

Employees of all types and at all levels develop grievance. Grievances are not some headache, brought about by union but may complicate the situation and cause more grievances either temporarily or permanently. Other factors affecting grievance are management job conditions, governments rules, general social conditions and the home environment.

The principal object of any grievance system is to encourage human problems to be brought to the surface. Management can learn about them and may try corrective action. The social organisation of a plant is very much like a complicated machine. Both need constant attention and frequent adjustments. Grievances which are expressed, whether they are presented formally or informally, are symptoms which should be carefully studied by management to determine the real causes of this "human machine" breakdown. Almost everyone agrees that it is better to prevent fire than trying to stop them after that have started and the same philosophy applies to grievances.

Grievance System

Grievance system helps to solve problems before they become serious. If problems are allowed to accumulate unsolved, their quantity may get so great that they may have adequate pressure" to blow off the lid of the whole section or department". A good grievance system can prevent the developments of unwanted system and keep social pressures within bounds.

A grievance system like counseling is a process of employees emotional release of their dissatisfaction. It provides a means by which a frustrated and aggrieved employee can become aggressive and strike back at the various controls which any group impose on him. Emotional release often plays an important role in individual grievance cases. Grievance procedures help to establish and maintain a work culture or way of life. Each group has its own particular way of living together, and the grievance procedure helps to develop this group culture.

A manager tends to give more care to the human aspects of his job when he knows that some of these actions are subject to challenge and review in a grievance system. He is encouraged to develop effective compromises and working relationship with his group. However, that the pendulum can swing too far, a supervisor may become so aware of the grievance system that he is afraid to make decisions and hesitates to direct and discipline his men.

Grievances are human problems and are to be handled in a human way. Every worker has the right to present his grievances to his employer and obtain their redressal. The management has to see that grievances are so received and settled that the worker gets the necessary sense of satisfaction. The following are important steps that should be taken in handling grievances.

1. Define, express and describe the nature of grievance at the heart of the employee's complaint as early as possible, so that the wrong complaint may not be handled and the real grievance may not turn up again to plague management.

2. After locating the real issue, the next step is to gather all relevant facts, about the issue, *i.e.* how and where it took place and the circumstances under which it transpired. Such fact gathering requires interviewing and listening to employees. This will, however, convince the employees that the management was sincere in seeing that justice is done.

3. After getting the real picture of the grievance the management must make a list of alternate solutions. If possible the suitability of this decision may be checked before taking and announcing the final decision.

4. Gather additional information for checking tentative solution for finding out the best possible one. For this, or the past experience of the executive in similar cases may be helpful. Company's own record of grievances, if maintained can also be helpful in this respect.

5. The decision having finally being reached, should then be passed in clear unequivocal terms to the employees concerned. The ultimate decision is the tool of action.

6. Follow up the case so that it is handled satisfactorily and the trouble eliminated. It is essential to see the attitude of the workers after the decision is given whether he is satisfied with that or not.

Successful Handling Of Grievances

In handling grievances, adequate time must be spent on talking to employees, gathering data from them and passing various types of information. During the interview of the employees the attitude of the executive concerned should be such as may enable him to gain the confidence of the employees concerned. Firstly, the executive should not think that his subordinates are ignorant. Secondly, he should feel that the employees are fair in presenting their grievances, unless it is proved otherwise. Thirdly, in handling grievances, management should display a sincere interest in the problems of employees and a constructive willingness to be of help. All executives must have confidence in themselves and should be fully aware of their responsibilities and be willing to carry these burdens. Such a positive attitude must be apparent to employees in order to gain their respect and cooperation. The manager should consider the grievance seriously and should not show a casual attitude. Grievances should be handled in terms of their total effects upon the organisation and not merely their immediate or individual effects.

Organisational Responsibility

Organisational responsibility for handling grievances should be divided and shared by all levels of management and representative of labour unions. As a good practice or procedure the employees should be required to present their grievances to their immediate superior, even if the final decision in the matter rests with the higher authority. The will save the supervisor from losing his importance and respect with his subordinates. After examining and investigating the matter at his level he can pass it on to the higher level with his findings and recommendation. Similarly, action can be taken by the executives at the middle level, if the matter is beyond their jurisdiction. The top level management has the responsibility to decide cases which are having company wide implication. In this they may be even assisted by personnel or labour officers with their advice and the information collected and maintained. The top level management must establish the broad policies and rules which may form the basis for handing grievances. In some companies labour union assume the responsibility of getting the grievances redressed, particularly at the middle and top level management.

Grievance Procedure

For the guidance of the employees and the unions the management should lay down a procedure for getting the grievances redressed. The procedure should be simple, expeditious, preferably time bound, which may be understood by the employees. At the Indian Labour Conference held in 1950 a voluntary code of discipline was evolved for employers and workers and their unions and this code required the management and unions to establish a mutually agreed grievance procedure which may ensure speedy investigation of grievances leading to settlement. This model grievance procedure has been adopted by a number of concerns but still many firms have to design it. Grievance procedure should be such that it may give a sense of satisfaction to the individual workers, reasonable authority to the management and participation to the unions. It should not comprise more than three steps, *i.e.*, immediate supervisor, departmental head and grievance committee. Arbitration should be the last resort. Unions may be associated at the level of departmental head for discussing the grievance. In case of large size organisations formal procedure should be a constructive and not a destructive force as it is the people who deal with each other every day. National Commissions of labour suggested that grievance procedure should be simple and should give relief to the workers rather than keep the in suspense.Thus the grievance procedure is the method by which a grievance is filed carried through different "Steps" to an ultimate decision. Most is the grievance procedures have four or more steps, as given below :

(*i*) Employee discusses grievance with foreman.

(*ii*) If grievance is unsettled, employee presents to foreman in writing.

(*iii*) If still not settled, foreman present grievance to department head.

(*iv*) If still unsettled, union committee presents it to factory manager who is advised by the personnel manager.

(*v*) If still unsettled, it is taken to an outside arbitrator for final and binding decision.

Most labour and management people agree that a grievance procedure should begin with the foreman. He is the person in direct contact with workers, and in many cases it is his action which caused the grievance.

68

Collective Bargaining

Definition

Collective bargaining is a made of fixing the terms of employment by means of bargaining between an organised body of employs or an employer or an employees or an association of employees, usually acting through duly authorised agents.

Collective bargaining is fundamentally, a method of joint regulation as it necessarily involves both the parities directly interested in the industrial relation. The essence of collective bargaining is a bargain between interested parties and the readiness of both the parties to regualte Industrial relation. Collective bargaining aims at reaching some settlement. Although both the parties involved in the bargaining process attempt to get their own terms accepted by the other party, Yet by its nature it implies, some awareness of necessity. Collective bargaining is "the process of employs -union negotiation for the purpose of reaching a agreement as to the terms and conditions of employment for a specific period."

Collective bargaining has been defined as negotiations about working conditions and terms of employment between as employer, a group of employers or one or more employers organisations on one hand and one or more representative organisations workmen on the other hand with a view to reach agreement.

Collective bargaining has been defined in the Encyclopedia of social sciences as "a process of discussion and negotiation between two parties, one or both of whom is a group of persons acting in concert. More specifically, collective bargaining is the procedure by which an employer and a group of employees agree upon the conditions of work.

Characteristics

Collective bargaining has been characterised as a form of industrial democracy and industrial government . The management and union representatives sit down at the bargaining table, where they deliberately,persuade, try to influence, argue and reach an agreement, which they recording the form of a labour management contract. This is legislative phase in which the two parties s2et up a type of company wide set of laws and regulations, for the right and responsibilities of the company the union,the union and the employees. Ordinarily management takes on the authority, and responsibility to administer and operate an agreement.

Levels Of Collective Bargaining

To a layman collective bargaining process may appear to be similar to both negotiation of a commercial contact and the bargaining of a labour agreement. But this point of view is somewhat naive. The employment of human beings cannot be handled in same manner as the purchase of physical goods . If one businessman contracts with another for the purchase of commodity and the seller delivers inferior commodity the buyer can terminate the relationship at that point. But this cannot be done in the relations between management and labour. Generally speaking the union and the management must learn to live with one another whether they like it or not. They must accommodate each other the labour law of the land. Once bargaining relationship have been commenced both sides must honestly seek an agreement .They must bargain in good faith. Dealings cannot arbitrarily be roken off. Further the negotiation of a labour agreement is quite different from the handling of commercial contract of human relation and political aspect of labour management relationship. A union is a political economic organisation. Union leader being elected must represent the interested of these caonstituents. They are often placed in a position where they must cater to the pressure of a strong position within the unoin. Union leaders are interested in being re-elected. They cannot always negotiate a contract with management according to cold logics.

Collective bargaining can be conducted at three levels, plant, industry and national. In United states it takes place at all these levels. Industry wide bargaining both at regional and national and national level is common is Scandinavian countries, like France, Germany, Italy, Switzerland and United Kingdom and other European countries.

As collective bargaining is in the process of maturing as a concept in India. It is hard to say what would be the most appropriate level for bargaining here. It depends on many factors, such as the pace of industrialisation,the means of communication, the scope of industry, and the development of the trade union movement.

If the scope of industry is limited to small units for local consumption plant level bargaining would normally be most fruitful. Eighty--five per cent of the agreements signed in India through 1961 were negotiated at the plant level. If many enterprises in the same industry are situated in one city industry--wide bargaining would be economic and useful. If the Industry is spread over a region and the union is quite strong, the bargaining may be conducted for the whole of the region. In plant level bargaining the union is responsive to the rank and file and to their problems . The union makes every efforts to resolve them as quickly and effectively as the leaders have to alive with the workers. But in most of the small industries the union are weak and the industry--wide bargaining has the advantage of getting uniform terms for the entire industry. It benefits the workers in the smaller firms, as they often can get better wages and working conditions which a strong union can obtain.

Nation--wide bargaining has the same advantage as industry--wide bargaining in addition it leads to better economic integration and higher living standards. It also may mitigate divisive tendencies of caste, community, language and religion which exit at regional levels. The disadvantages are that nation--wide strikes sometimes may be their chain reactions paralyse all industries and at critical movements may jeopardise the security of the nation. Nation--wide bargaining may also aggravate the evils of labour monopolies

Pre-requisites

1. Freedom of associations and independence of unions.

2. Stability of organisations of workers and employers.

3. Favourable political climate - the Government should not only be sympathetic but also encourage collective bargaining and agreements.

4. Mutual trust and respect and also willingness on the part of the parties concerned to settle all matters by collective bargaining or negotiations.

5. Bargaining power of each party depends on the (*a*) strength of its organisations (*b*) knowledge and skill of negotiation of its representatives (*c*) trade recession, or boom and shortages and (*d*) surplus of labour, particularly in regard to semi-skilled and un--skilled workers.

History Of Collective Bargaining

The collective bargaining principals has been applied in India for a long time in various situations. However,voluntary collective bargaining has developed in India only after independence.

Gandhiji as the leader of the Ahmedabad Textile Workers, advocated the resolution of conflict by mutual negotiation and discussion between employers and labour in 1918. He put forward a three step system of negotiation, conciliation and arbitration for settlement of labour disputes. In fact, the wage dispute in 1918was settled, at Gandhiji's instigation, by an arbitration board representing mutual interests. Voluntary arbitration cannot be called collective bargaining . At the time of the formation of the permanent Arbitration Board in 1931, there was still no general trade union in Ahmedabad . The arbitration mechanism was subjected to severe strains in the years immediately before and after the Second World War, and compulsory adjudication under the Bombay Industrial disputes Act was resorted to in 1940.

The Ahmedabad pattern of industrial relations was not successful for the major reasons, that both the employees lacked a progressive and far sighted leadership. The Ahmedabad pattern of collective bargaining spearheaded but Gandhiji has influenced Government legislation in India. Collective negotiation was not encouraged by the institution of works committees. They did not develop as as instrument for the voluntary settlement of disputes and the whole emphasis on industrial relations swung away from voluntary settlement to compulsory adjudication through the machinery set up under the Industrial Disputes Act, 1947.

Industrial Disputes Act And Collective Bargaining

With the passing of the Industrial Disputes Act in 1947 and the growth of trade unions, management of companies found it increasingly difficult to deal with the demands of the workman, These demands used to be presented as charter, and the unions also addressed a copy to the appropriate labour commissioner. The intervention of outside machinery, both managements and unions found it unconducive to industrial peace. Conciliation efforts on the part of the labour commissioner rarely succeeded, because both parties attended the conciliation meeting with their minds made up and anticipating reference to adjudication.

The sum up the collective to bargaining in India has not made that of much headway as in some other countries because of the following factors :

(i) Absence of enlightened management. A few managements of employers are still allergic to trade unions.
(ii) Weakness of trade unions due to their multiplicity, intra and inter-union rivalries, poor financial conditions, lack of leadership.
(iii) Easy availability of Govt. intervention for conciliation and compulsory manpower.
(iv) Surplus manpower.
(v) Restricted rights of workers and employers to strike and lockout.
(vi) Different political affiliation of unions and consequent political rivalry make difficult to settle the disputes amicably by mutual negotiations.
(vii) Lack of mutual trust, respect and the spirit of gone and take.
(viii) Unfavourable political and economic climate since the government though want to encourage collective bargaining, is not prepared to allow endless trials of strength for fear of the planned economy of the country being disrupted.

Nature Of Collective Bargaining

Collective bargaining has existed in United States since the early 1800's. However, it did not develop to its present form until recently. In the early days the general practice was that either the employer or unions, depending upon their relative economic strengths, would notify the other party of wage rates and other conditions of employment which it intended to put into effect. There was very little negotiation and discussion between the parties. If one party refused to accept the terms imposed by the other then either a strike or lockout was ensured.

The nature, scope and methodology of collective bargaining continues to evolve even today. Collective bargaining is dynamic, and requires concrete understanding of concerned parties. The bargaining is collective in the sense that the chosen representative of employees acts as bargaining agent for all the employees in carrying out negotiations and dealing with management. The process may also be considered collective in the cases of the corporation where the paid professional manager represents the interest of the stock holders and the board of directors in bargaining with union leaders. On the employer side it is also collective on those common situations when companies have joined together as an employer association for purpose of bargaining with a union.

Subject Matter Of Collective Bargaining

(a) Union recognition and scope of bargaining unit.
(b) Management Rights.
(c) Union Security.
(d) Strikes and Lockouts.
(e) Union activities and responsibilities.
(f) Wages.
(g) Working hours and working conditions.
(h) Job Rights and Seniority.
(i) Discipline, Suspension and Discharge.
(j) Grievance Handling and Arbitration.

(*k*) Health and Safety.

(*l*) Insurance and Benefit Programmes.

Objective And Scope

The objective of collective bargaining is a labour-management agreement. Collective bargaining is generally referred to as a contract. In early days, agreements were merely lists of wages to be paid to the various occupational groups covered. Today there is a tremendous variation in labour management agreements. The negotiation of wages is a very complicated matter. Different arguments are put forward. The criteria put forward by unions used in wage negotiations are :

(*i*) Changes in the cost of living.

(*ii*) Wage uniformity.

(*iii*) Changes in productivity.

(*iv*) The ability of the employer to pay.

Several of the criteria used by unions in seeking wage increases are also used by management in resisting such demands. It is often argued by management that increases in productivity are not the result of greater labour effort but stem from improved products and production processes. If these gains are to be sustained, management feel that a seizable part of the earnings need to be ploughed back into new equipments. Management, in most cases is willing to concede that workers should have a share in gains resulting from productivity. But the issue is the proportion that should go to the workers of a particular company. It is frequent claimed by management that if higher wages are granted the increase in cost will lead to a drop in employment. While unions press for wage uniformity, management generally objects to this criterion serve as a code defining the rights and obligations of each party in their employment relations with one another.

The signing of the contract makes a great impression on the rank and file of the union. It strengthens the position of the union in the eyes of its members and it provides the basis for a continuing and signified relationship between the management and the employees. Below is a list of topics commonly appearing in union-management agreement.

Success Of Collective Bargaining

Lester and Sister outline factors which determine the success of collective bargaining. They have been grouped into :

(*i*) Economic environment factors.

(*ii*) Psychological factors and structure of power relation.

(*iii*) Nature and characters of the product market.

(*iv*) Nature of the labour market.

(*v*) Capital requirement and cost conditions.

(*vi*) State of business conditions.

(*vii*) Types of industrial relationship.

(*a*) Employers' attitude.

(*b*) Worker's attitude.

(*c*) Government policy.

Importance Of Collective Bargaining

Collective bargaining is very important as it places the union at par with the management in status and at the same time it is one of the most effective instruments in the hands of the workers to better their conditions. For this reason in the recent times when aspiration of the workers to gain a better social status has been articulate the importance of collective bargaining has increased a good deal.

The importance of the collective bargaining can be summarised as follows :

(*a*) It is best suited to the concept of industrial democracy.

(*b*) It ensures an important status for workers.

(*c*) It ensures lasting industrial peace.

(*d*) Collective bargaining is not a method of setting disputes only but also its prevention. It can dispel conflicts and ensure lasting industrial peace.

(*e*) Collective bargaining fosters responsibility on the part of both workers and employers. People who have reached an agreement have responsible ibehaviour than is imposed by the decision of third party.

(*f*) Collective bargaining presupposes workers' right to strike and employers' right to lockout. Both parties are conscious that if collective bargaining fails then there will be a loss to employer and workers both.

(*g*) Collective bargaining is the result of give and take. The parties to the agreements are likely to consider it more binding than statutory regulations.

Collective Bargaining Generate Success

The collective Bargaining is superior to statutory regulation as it adds to confidence trust and understanding.

Misconduct can be defined as bad management, mismanagement, culpable neglect of an official in regard to his office. It can also be defined as "improper or wrong behaviour or unlawful behaviour or conduct. The word mosconduct is a generic term while the specific misconducts are like insubordination, neglect of work, etc. Misconduct is a specific word with a specific connotation and it cannot be mere inefficiency or slackness. To understand misconduct some cases are given below :

(*a*) Misconduct is not established by provoking even culpable negligence. It is doing of something which the doer knows to be wrong or which he does recklessly not caring what results will be (M.S.H. Railway Co. *vs.* Sunderji Kalidas ILR 60 Cal. 996 : AIR 1933).

(*b*) Misconduct is distinguished from accident and is not far from negligence. It is incorrect that misconduct only refers acts of gross or culpable negligence and not by mere negligence. (Bengal Nagpur Railway Co. Ltd. *vs.* Moolji Sieka Co. AIR 19[illegible] : Cal. 815).

(*c*) Micconduct does not ordinarily cover acts of negligence. It means that an employee is guilty of something which was inconsistent with the conduct expected of him by the rules of the company. (B.B.C.I. Railway *vs.* Rajnagar Spinning Co. Ltd. AIR 1930 : Bom. 129).

(*d*) Thus misconduct is an acta or omission which, is violative of the express or implied obligations of employer and, therefore, if tahe negligence is so persistent or is of such a mature that it is inconsistent with any express or implied obligation of an employee, then it is misconduct. Misconduct is something in the nature of improper behaviour and is not merely wrongful commission or wrongful omission. Misconduct involves some degree of moral obliquity (Secretary of State *vs.* Allahditta AIR 1930)

(*e*) Misconduct under Section 11 of the Arbitration Act refers to legal misconduct and not to moral turpitude, dishonesty of any unethical or immoral act (Mohinder Singh and Co. *vs.* Union of India, AIR 1972 : J & K 63).

69

Plant Location

Introduction

A new business is always faced with the problem of where to locate. The organizer of a new business seldom consider sites outside of his own community. This is probably because of the more pressing problems involved in establishing a new business. The problem of plant location in established industry receives more attention. A number of conditions can lead to the consideration of the plant location problem. These conditions are : (1) expansion, (2) decentralization, and (3) economic factors, such as a shift of the markets or an inadequate labour supply.

Expansion is the most frequent cause for considering the problem of plant location. Established industries often expand when (1) their facilities become obsolete, (2) market demand grows beyond a capacity of the plant site and facilities, or (3) inadequate services are available to the customer.

The decentralization of industry in this country is increasing at a rapid pace. Many of the industrial giants that historically grew in one location have found that decentralization pays off in a number of respects. The company benefits by the availability of new sources of labour supply, the improved labour relations of smaller plant, a lower absentee rate, and the greater interest in their work shown by citizens of small communities. The worker benefits from the lower cost of living in uncongested town, the elimination of expensive and annoying buying off. The increased opportunities for advancement and better opportunities to utilize his spare time is available in bigger towns. A decentralized marker is a cause for decentralization of the industry servicing it. The Coca Cola plant, which are spread or decentralized from coast to coast are good examples of locating in the concentrated market areas (mostly urban).

In the final analysis, the objective of any location is to able to deliver the products to the customer at a cost equal to or less than the competition within the product field. The cost of goods delivered to the customer depends upon

(*a*) The cost of gathering the material ;

(*b*) The cost of fabricating the material ;

(*c*) The cost of distributing the finished product to the consumer.

Keeping the above cost breakdown in mind it is possible for any manufacturing facility to make a list of those location factors which will tend to effect one or all of the above three costs. The list will vary depending upon the product and production characteristics, the objective and the sizes of the particular installation. There are a number of factors, however, which tend to have an effect in cost plant and location studies *e.g.* nearness to market and raw material ;

availability of power and water ; climate, availability of capital, labour ; transportation facilities; site availability. There are more factors which will interact with each other.

Definition

Plant location can be defined as the determination of that location which when considering all factors will provide minimum cost delivered to the customer. Amongst the different problems relating to the management of the production system is that of location of industrial plant. The plant must be located in a place which influences the cost of production. It can be imagined that manufacturing and distribution costs may vary to an extent of 10 per cent simply by virtue of the choice of plant location.

Location Problem

Two levels of problems must be considered when considering plant location. They are : (1) the selection of the general territory, and (2) the selection of the community and plant site. Although some location factors, discussed later, may be applicable at both levels, there are certain unique considerations when selecting both a general territory and the community with its plant site.

In Western countries much attention is given now to the problem of dispersal on account of nuclear attacks. This may become a real problem, even in this country. Apart from the dispersal needs for unclear attack, there would be a problem of strategic location of plants connected with defence production either as sub-suppliers or main producers. The continuous treat of disruption of trade along the borders automatically prevent any concentration of industry near these areas. Such major factors are generally considered to eliminate (or alternatively, narrow down) the choice of the general territory after which the selection of the community and plant site follows.

Territory Selection

When making the selection of a general territory, obtaining specific information about a given community can be a waste of time. Territory selection calls for information of a more general nature. Location information of a general nature may be obtained from the following sources :

- Ministry of Industrial Development and Internal Trade.
- Institute of Public Opinion.
- Techno-economic surveys conducted by State Governments.
- National Control of Applied Economic Research.
- Indian Federation of Chambers of Commerce.
- State Chambers of Commerce.
- Department of Industry in State Governments.
- Survey of India Maps.

Community and Site Selection

Once the general territory for location has been selected, it becomes necessary to choose community and a site. This choice is based upon consideration of the factors discussion in the next section. It should be noted that some to these location factors must be considered at the community and site level as well as when making the selection of the general territory. An early decision must be made regarding the size of the community in which the plant is to be located. The alternative choices can be classified as : (1) city, (2) sub-urban, and (3) country locations.

City *versus* **Sub-urban** *versus* **Country**

The advent of the automobile (and State Road Transport) has brought new mobility to our working force. This is one of the reason for present day industrial rush to the country. Wide open spaces and freedom to expand are probably two of the biggest inducements. The type of manufacturing process may decide the site selection. for example, a country location is desirable for a plant producing explosives. Some of the general conditions leading to the selection of an appropriate type of community might be listed as follows :

1. Conditions suggesting urban location

(*a*) Large skilled labour force required.
(*b*) Processes heavily dependent upon availability of city utilities.
(*c*) Multifloor building desirable.
(*d*) Close contact with suppliers demanded.
(*e*) Rapid public transportation available.
(*f*) Technical and Research requirement.

2. Condition suggesting rural location

(*a*) Semi-skilled or female labour force required.
(*b*) Avoidance of heavy city taxes and insurance desired.
(*c*) Labour force residing close to plan.
(*d*) Plant expansion easier than in city.
(*e*) Community close to but not in large population centre.

3. Conditions suggesting a country location

(*a*) Large site required for either present demands or expansion.
(*b*) Lowest property taxes available desired.
(*c*) Unskilled labour force required.
(*d*) Low wages required to meet competition.
(*e*) Morale of working force improved by country location.
(*f*) Manufacturing process is dangerous or objectionable.
(*g*) Processes causing environmental pollution.

One rule of thumb regarding the size of a site is that it should not be less than five times the actual size of the plant itself. This is considered a minimum in order to allow for loading platforms, siding, tractor tailer access, parking facilities, and storage area. Wherever possible, open land is desirable on two or more sides to allow for future expansion.

Unfortunately tempting offers of a fine site or attractive tax promises frequently influence plant location decisions. Objective data is essential to good plant location. Tempting proposal from those with an axe to grind should be considered with caution.

In order to properly select a site, a list of general specification should be prepared as follows:

1. Description of building to be constructed (including sketch).
2. Size of plot.
3. Necessary railways, highway and waterway facilities.
4. Minimum size of water mains, gas line, and power line.

5. Volume of ground water to be utilized.
6. Sewerage and effluent disposal requirements.
7. Safety area for offensive odours, noise, smoke etc.
8. Provisions for spinkler pressure (gravity tank or local waterman).

The maps published by the Geological Survey of India are very useful in selecting a good plant site. These maps show land elevations, water features and works such as roads, dams, buildings, railways, but not power lines.

Influence of Location on Plant Layout

Plant location will determine the proximity of a plant to its source of raw materials and its market area, the distance from the plant to these two areas tends to determine the method of transportation to be used. The type of transportation will in turn, determine whether the layout should provide for railway; truck or water loading and unloading facilities. The arrangement of the shipping and receiving department will vary in the layout according to the type of transportation utilized. A plant location may be determined in part by the fuel requirements of the concern. The plant layout must provide for storage of this fuel, whether it be coal, oil, or gas. Also, the layout must consider the requirements for power generation.

The demands of future expansion on the plant layout are influenced by the location of the plant. When plant expansion in a city location must take place by adding stores to a presently constructed building, the plant layout problems are somewhat different than they would be in a country location, where plant expansion might take place horizontally by adding a wing to a single storey building.

Factors Influencing the Plant Location

Following factors must be kept in mind before final selection of plant location is made :

1. Market. Proximity to market is one of the important factors affecting the choice of plant location because both promptness and cost of service to customers depends upon proximity to the market.

Depending upon the product, market may be concentrated or widely dispersed. When a market is concentrated, the market factor would tend to influence the enterpreneure to choose close to this concentration.

For example, a manufacturer of textiles would opt to locate near Bombay and Ahmedabad or a manufacturer of automobile parts would be opt to locate near Madras or Bombay.

2. Labour. The business can never bring fruits unless it can obtain and maintain a productive labour force. Not only must the labour force be available in adequate number but also it must contain the skill required in a given manufacturing process.

There may be any development in modern machinery, which in many instances reduces the importance of skilled labour, the key to success in any business or organisation is the human factor ; worker can make or mar any organisation. Wage levels must of course be considered. In general wage and skill are lower in south than in the west or east. Therefore industries requiring many unskilled workers, which traditionally pay low wages are attractive to the south. Lower wages in south are partially explained by the fact that area standards are also low in that area.

3. Transportation Facilities. The problem of transportation is of great importance specially when raw materials are bulky and of low value. The more rent of material can consume a very high percentage of the final cost to the customer. An industry tends to be localized at places which have developed means of transport. Faridabad in Haryana is an excellent example. It is well served both by railway and road transport. It lies on the mainline between Bombay and Delhi.

Transportation Media

The following are the transportation media with particular advantages of each.

Rail (all classes of traffic).

Water carries (all classes of traffic).

Highway vehicles (all classes of traffic).

Pipelines (bulk liquids and gases).

Aircrafts (where speed is essential and where access by surface agencies is specially difficult as in Assam).

Pack animals (in difficult terrain).

Belt, cable or rail conveyors of various types (short distances).

Human carriers (short distances and small quantities for example, purchases of compact, finished consumer goods and delivery of letter mailed to final destination).

Self delivery (livestock and self propelled vehicles).

Electric cable (electric energy).

Telecommunication (information, commercial negotiations).

Railways

Indian Railways have very large net work of traffic system. According to the type of the product, Railway carriages are designed for better transportation. This is one of the cheapest mode of transport also.

Roadways

Many transport organisations are existing in India. For hill station and to carry heavy machinery, Road transportation quite good and Rail transportation may not be suitable for this purpose.

Waterways

This mode of transportation is mainly for international transits. Bulk and non perishable materials can be transported to far of places with low charges. But the transportation time is very high. Port Trust of India, and some Shipping Corporations of India are playing very vital role in this method of transport.

Special Methods

(*i*) **Pipe lines.** To transport bulk liquids and gases to short distances. This is the economical method, for example the supply of cooking gas to houses near to a Refinery city. Similarly transport of crude oil from a well to a Refinery.

(*ii*) **Belt and cable convertors.** For internal transport, or from a mine to shipping area, for example Coal after quarrying will be transported to Rail or Truck looking places by only bucket conveyors.

As you can see, each of these transportation media has its advantages and limitations. In order to select the proper transportation media, the shipper should consider the following :

1. Type of extent of materials handling facilities at origin and destination.
2. The relative costs for the various media.
3. The urgency of the shipment.
4. The demand for special services, *e.g.*, refrigeration.

Transportation costs vary with the type of route used and the type of media selected as well as the length of haul. In general, the cost of moving materials per mile tapers off as the length of haul increases.

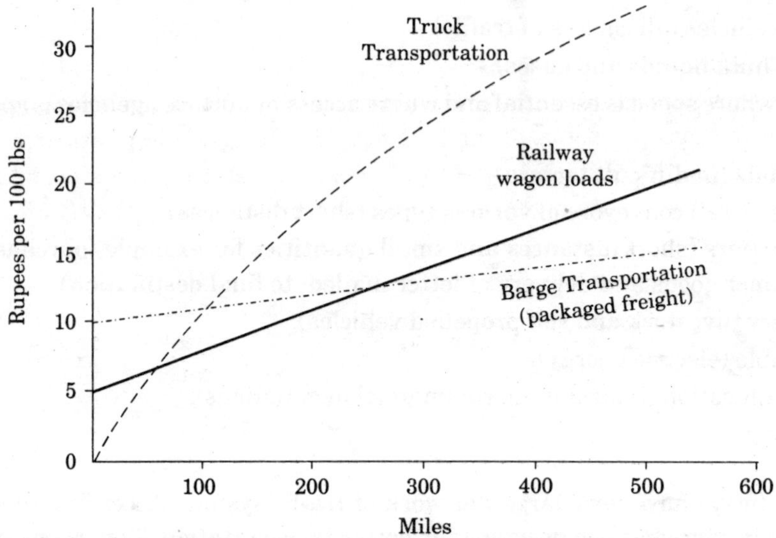

Fig. 69.1. Hypothetical Cost Comparison of Various Transportation Methods.

We can use as analysis involving the break-even point to select a transportation media (Fig. 69.1). In this case truck transportation appears to be the most economical up to a distance of approximately 40 miles. Transportation by large appear as to be the most economical for long-distance hauling, that is for distances greater than about 280 miles. For hauling between 40 to 280 miles the railway appears to be the most efficient carrier.

The transportation method of linear programming has established itself as a useful tool for considering the transportation problems in locating a plant. The linear assumptions required by this technique are usually quite realistic in this type of problem.

Availability of Power and Fuel

In the last century the industries were located near the coal mines or the locations where coal could be taken cheaply and conveniently. But today all industries require electric power of some sort. There are certain process, that require usually large amounts of electric power. For example heavy water plants or chemical processes of hydrolysis nature are all located in areas where large sources of cheap power are available. In India we have three types of power sources: (*i*) Thermal power, (*ii*) Hydro electric power (*iii*) Nuclear power.

For any industry the availability of power should be cheap, continuous and regular. Technologists are exploring the possibility of obtaining power from wind and sea waves.

Availability of Raw Materials

The location of raw materials is influential in the location problem. Some industries by nature of their manufacturing process are forced to locate near raw material sources. The iron and steel industries have been located close to coal fields since it uses coal in large quantities.

Climate and Atmospheric Conditions

Climate greatly influences the process in several industrial such as textile industry where atmosphere high humidity is essential. Clean and dust free atmosphere for pharmaceutical industry. In modern days, air conditioning has helped to a great extent in solving the climate and atmospheric conditions.

Availability of Water

This is another important factor for the selection of plant location. Chemical process plants especially require huge quantities of soft and pure water. The temperature of water may also be a influencing factor for plant to location. For example selecting the site of Antibiotics Plant at Virbhadra is due to low temperature of Ganges water and less bacteria logical load to reduce the refrigeration loads.

Laws and Taxation

State and local laws should be studied when considering various locations. Labour laws and employment regulations vary widely from one location to another. Some of the aspects of industrial operations regulated by laws are hours of work, minimum wage and fringe benefits to workers and working conditions for woman employees.

Special and Recreational Facilities

As social and recreational facilities are the necessities of one's life after the plant hours and on holidays, the employees need the same. Therefore it is essential that Government should provide suitable parks, cooperative stores, community halls, cinemas and education facilities for the employees. All the above facilities shall be for the good health and will therefore create much interest in the work. In certain factories it is seen that the employees are given very cheap subsidised meals.

Waste Disposal

Pollution control act is in force now. The effluents and sewage disposal of a plant should not harm the public. So proper effluents treatment and waste disposal methods should be available. It must be examined that drainage may accumulate water around the plant and create unhygienic conditions. Similarly, if the load bearing capacity of the land is low, a company may not be able to establish sound building foundation or build a heavy building. The installation of heavy machinery may also be difficult.

Technology Know How

The know how techniques should be available near sources ; so that delay in consultation will be reduced if any break down or troubles occur in the plant. Thus a plant should also be near to a consultation organisation so that for future expansion problems and present difficulties can be discussed oftenly for smooth running of the plant.

70

Plant Layout

Introduction

Production results from the working of men, materials and machinery. One or more pieces of materials are taken and their form, nature or chemical characteristics are changed by using machinery including tools and equipments to give a product. The product has a greater value than the sum total of all the inputs that goes into the making of it as it serves a need and is functional. The value is created by incurring the cost in the process of production and using of varieties of production facilities. While physical arrangement of production and other facilities have a bearing on the cost due to maintenance, quality control etc. They have also a direct effect on the cost due to the handling of material and movement of men and other facilities. It is estimated that in the cost of production about 30% is the cost of material handling at various stages in various steps. The chapter deals with the study the effect of systematic and good plant layout and material handling system.

Definition

The layout of a factory, workshop or working area means the position of the departments or shops in the factory and of the machines, work places and storage points in the working areas, including officers and staff facilities relative to one another.

A bad layout can add a good deal of time to the total work. Contents of a process which causes unnecessary movement of material and consumes time and energy of the worker without any value addition in completion of a job.

Many establishments have never thought of any change in the layout ever since they were established. Machine, pieces of plant and even whole departments have been added from time to time wherever space could be found. The result has been that material takes often long time and charters a round about journey in the course of process.

The importance of layout to the production of process varies from industry to industry. Equally important variable is the extent to which it is possible to alter the layout once it has been established. These two factors must be borne in mind while studying the flow of materials or movement of workers about the plant.

Objectives of Layout

If a finished layout is to present an effective arrangement of related work areas in which goods can be economically produced, it must be planned with objectives of plant layout well placed in mind.

The major objectives are :

(*i*) Facilitate the manufacturing process.

(*ii*) Minimise the materials handling.

(*iii*) Maintain flexibility of arrangement of operations.

(*iv*) Maintain high turn over of works in process.

(*v*) Hold down investment in equipment.

(*vi*) Make economical use of floor area.

(*vii*) Promote effective utilisation of labour.

(*viii*) Provide employee convenience and comfort in doing the work.

Manufacturing Process Facilitation

Arrange machines, equipment and work so that material is caused to move as smoothly in a straight line as possible. This does not mean that flow line must be straight, there should be minimum of back tracking and

(*a*) Eliminating all delays possible.

(*b*) Planning the work so that work can be identified and came with little possibility of mixing with other parts.

Plant maintenance of machines which will maintain quality of work. This may involve capital expenditure. Such air-conditioning of areas or good house keeping to prevent damage of parts.

Minimizing Materials Handling

The material should travel from the machine to the other as little as possible, specially the heavy components should flow in line only because excess flow of material require man power as well as equipment for lifting and carrying the material.

Flexibility

The layout should be flexible for the following causes :

(*a*) Design change.

(*b*) Increased production.

(*c*) Adding a new product.

(*d*) Maintaining high turn over *i.e.* the storage time of the material inside the line should be minimum. Because extra storage of material require more storage areas as well hinders the flow of material.

Economical use of Area

Each square feet area costs money. Unaccepted waste or idle floor is burden on rest of the plant spacing between machines after necessary spacing required for movement of men and material.

Effective use of Labour

Labour may be wasted through poor layout. Following factors should be considered for effective use of labour utilisation :

I. Reduce manual handling.
II. Minimize walking.
III. Balance machine cycles so that man and machine are not idle.
IV. Laying the machine in such a way that supervision is simplified.

Employees Comfort

The layout should be such that the worker is not effected by heat, moisture or dirt. Direction of light should also be considered for laying the machines. Equipment causing more noise should be isolated as far as it is possible. Equipment which vibrates should be cushined or specially mounted to prevent transmission of vibrations to floor or surrounding area.

Plant Layout Problems

Ordinarily when one thinks of plant layout, then comes the problem of planning a complete layout for a new product, that is planning a new plant, starting from scratch. This is usually not the case more frequently problem involves the re-layout of existing plant or alteration of some sort of arrangement. Following are the main problems of plant layout.

Changes of Design

Frequently change in design of a part calls for change in process of operations to be performed. This change may require only alterations of existing layout, or it may cause extensive re-layout programme depending upon nature of change.

Enlargement of a Department

If for one reason or the other it becomes necessary to increase the production of certain part of product, a change in the layout may be called for. This involves the addition of a few machines which call for entirely new layout so that, part need not to travel long.

Reduction of a Department

This problem is a reverse of the Enlargement of a Department. If products demand are reduced drastically and permanently then few machines have to be removed and rest of the machines have to be rearranged.

Adding a new Product

If a new product is to be added to a line then it is similar to the product already being done, the problem is similar to enlarging a department. However, if the new product differs considerably from those in production, a different problem presents itself. The present equipment may be used by adding a few machine or completely a new department may be desired.

Moving a Department

Moving a department may or may not present a new problem. If present layout is satisfactory it is only necessary to shift to another alternative position. If, the present layout is not satisfactory, an opportunity presents itself for correction of past mistakes.

Planning a New Plant

This presents a largest problem in plant layout. Building can even be designed to suit the layout. The additional area has already been provided by removing the receiving department from its present position.

Types of Layout

As already noted production results from men, material and machinery together with management. The characteristics are changed to make a product. An analysis of the above gives the various types of layouts. There are three types of layout :

1. **Layout by fixed position or by fixed material location**

Here the material or major component remains stationary. The complete job is done herewith material, men and machinery brought to the location, *e.g.* ship building.

2. **Layout by Process or Layout by Function**

In this case, all operations of the same process or type of process are grouped together, like all welding in one area, all drilling in one area.

3. **Layout by product or line production**

This layout places one operation adjacent to the previous operations. The equipments regardless of process are arranged as per the sequence of operations.

In ideal conditions, the raw material comes in at one end of the factory, travels through it in a straight line and comes out at the other as a finished product ready for dispatch.

Ideal conditions are not often possible in real life situation. There is no harm in the work travelling around the factory, provided that it follows a fixed path, that the distances between successive operations are kept as short as possible and that the work moves steadily forward.

In factories where many products are made, or where the products are made up of many different parts, a good layout is much more difficult, especially where batch quantities are small and there is a choice of processes. This situation is generally found at its worst in the engineering industry. A decision may have to be taken between having a *process* layout and a *product* layout.

A process layout is one which all machines or processes of the same type are grouped together.

A product layout is one which all machines or processes concerned in the manufacture of the same product or range of product are grouped together.

Most workshops today are a mixture of the two types. The following is a short list of the advantages and disadvantages of both.

Process Layout : Advantages and Disadvantages

1. The sequence of manufacturing is flexible and a minimum investment in machines is involved. More floor space is usually occupied than in a product layout.
2. Machines can be kept busy most of the time, low and medium-volume production costs can be kept down.
3. There are no definite physical channels along which work must flow. The results of this are more handling of materials, larger bank of works in process and a more complicated system of production control than with a product layout.

4. Workers and supervisors become skilled in the operation of a single type of machine but require longer training to be able to deal with varied jobs. Thus specialisation can be achieved.
5. Machine breakdowns do not help up a succession of operations ; work can be transferred to other similar machines.

Product Layout : Advantages and Disadvantages

1. The flow of work over direct physical routes cuts out delays ; there is less materials handling, and the definite sequence of operations over adjacent machines simplifies production control and cuts out forms and records.
2. The total time of production is kept low, less floor space is occupied and the capital tied up in work in process can be kept down. The capital investment in machines may, however, be raised by duplication of the same machine on several lines.
3. Manufacturing costs are low at high volume production but rise steeply as it drops. If one or more lines are running light there is considerable machine idleness.
4. It is easier to train workers inexperienced in industry upto a certain level of skill.
5. A single machine break down may shut down a whole production line.

Which of the layout types of be used

1. Layout by fixed position—this type of layout is suitable where :

(*a*) Operations required hand tools or simple portable machines.

(*b*) Making only one or few pieces

(*c*) Cost of moving the major pieces is high

(*d*) Skill of workmanship lies in the ability of workers or where we wish to fix responsibility for product quality to one workman.

2. Layout process—this layout is used where :

(*a*) Expensive machinery is involved.

(*b*) Variety of products are made.

(*c*) Operations are unbalanced or in other words wide variation in time required in different operations are encountered.

(*d*) The demand for the product is small or intermittent.

3. Layout by-product or line production—this type of layout is used when :

(*a*) There is a large quantity of pieces of products to make.

(*b*) Design of the product is more or less standardised.

(*c*) Demand for the product is fairly steady.

The Fig. 70.1 shows on the cost comparison between product ar d Process type Layouts.

Factors affecting layout

Whatever be the type of layout being contemplated, the following factors influence the selection in every case.

(*i*) Material ;	(*ii*) Machinery
(*iii*) Man ;	(*iv*) Movement
(*v*) Waiting ;	(*vi*) Service ;
(*vii*) Building ;	(*viii*) Flexibility.

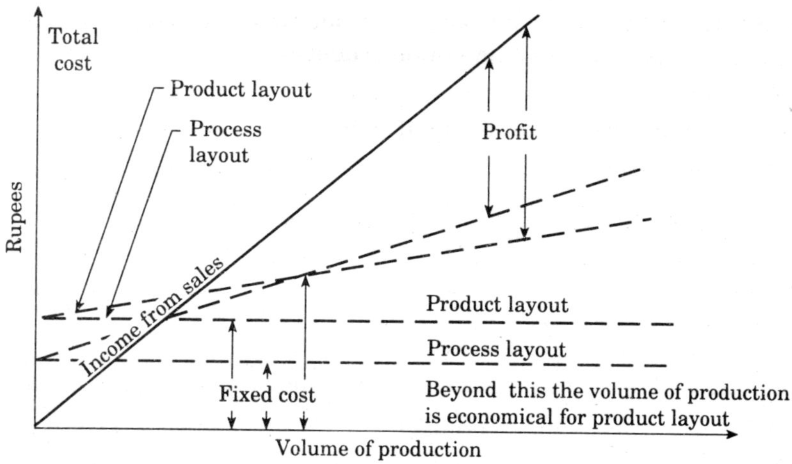

Fig. 70.1

1. **Material factor.** This include the design, variety, quantity, necessary operation and their consequence. These are affected by : (*a*) Design and specification, (*b*) Physical and chemical characteristic, (*c*), Quantity and variety of products and material and (*d*) Component parts or material and how they go together.

2. **Machinery factor.** This include process or method, machinery, tools and equipment, machine utilisation and requirement of machinery and power.

3. **Man factor.** This include safety and working condition, manpower requirement, man utilisation etc.

4. **Movement factor.** This include the flow pattern reduction of unnecessary handling, space for movement and analysis of handling methods and equipment.

5. **Waiting factor.** This include location of storage or delay points space for waiting, method of storing; safeguard equipment for storing and delay.

6. **Service factor.** This include services for personnel such as fire protection, lighting, heating and ventilation etc., services for material such as quality control, production control and services for machinery such as maintenance and utilities like, gas steam, water supply etc.

7. **Building factor.** This includes features like Railway siding, yard areas for parking and storing, shape of building, numbers of floors, facilities of elevation stairs etc.

8. **Flexibility factor.** This includes consideration due to changes in material, machinery and process, man, supporting activities and installation limitations etc. It means easy changing to new arrangement and is facilitated by mobile or mounting or movable machinery, self-contained equipment, readily acceptable service lines, standardised equipments.

Planning a Layout

1. **Systematic Approach.** Whether a new layout is being contemplated or an existing layout is to be changed, there is a systematic approach in doing so. Dis-coordinated thinking and hanches for movement do not pay in the long run. A systematic approach ensures to the layout engineer that due consideration has been given to all factors affecting the layout.

The procedure for layout project will entail the following steps :

Step 1 : Study the 'make' and 'buy' items in the material list.

Step 2 : Study the current and future output target for each product. Determine the component quantities to be stocked and manufactured.

Step 3 : Prepare operation planning sheet. Obtain production routine equipment requirements and process times from other departments.

Step 4 : Determine number of equipments of each category required and direct man power requirement.

Step 5 : Determine space requirement at each work spot and make tentative work place layout.

Step 6 : Study the stock policy and find out the storage requirements for raw materials, work in process, 'Buy' items and finished goods.

Step 7 : Obtain packaging informations to determine the quality of packaging materials and the final shape of material for shipment, obtain also the shipping schedule.

Step 8 : Prepare operation process chart, flow process chart and an overall and detailed diagram of the flow.

Step 9 : Make tentative layout by trial and error.

Step 10 : Choose handling procedure. Determine the size of the unit load number of units to be moved and the distance. Also calculate the indirect man power required.

Step 11 : provide adequate gangways for movement.

Step 12 : Discuss with line management and incorporate their suggestions.

Step 13 : Prepare detailed layout drawings with as much visual aid as possible. Locate all services facilities like gas, compressed air, water etc.

Step 14 : Explain to line management.

Step 15 : Prepare a detailed cost analysis sheet for all equipment additions movements installations etc.

Step 16 : Draw up a work schedule for your course of action for the installation.

Any layout problem requires that these steps are properly taken care of. At some stage or the other, whether scientifically or by guess work and by approximation all the data entailed in the steps have to be collected before a change or a new layout is brought into effect. The various steps are discussed in detail below.

Techniques of Plant Layout

One of the mathematical techniques used for making a layout is known as Travel Chart method. This method can quantitatively compare various layouts by finding the total weighted distance for each layout.

The method consists of making three matrices known as Volume matrix. Distance matrix and Volume-Distance matrix. Volume matrix gives the total flow of material from one department to another. This is an input data to the problem and remains unchanged throughout the solution procedure. It is independent of the layout. Distance matrix gives the distance to be travelled in moving the product from one department to another. It is dependent on layout. Volume Distance matrix is calculated from the above two matrices and is used for finding the total weighted distance.

The method of Travel Charting may be explained with the help of an example.

Example. *Suppose we have four product groups I, II, III and IV requiring the services of some or all the five departments A, B, C, D and E. The problem is to determine the location of these five departments. The five departments are required in different sequences for each product group as given on next page.*

Group	*Sequence*	*% Volume of the Product*
I	A B C D E	30
II	A C B E D	35
III	A C D B C	20
IV	A E D C	15

The volume matrix for this problem is given below :

Volume Matrix

From/To	A	B	C	D	E
A	—	30	55	—	15
B	—	—	50	—	35
C	—	35	—	50	—
D	—	20	15	—	30
E	—	—	—	50	—

Now a tentative layout may be made and inter-department distances calculated. Suppose we obtain the following distance matrix, which shows the distances in feet between various departments. Distances between two departments, where there is no flow of material between them are not needed hence they are not shown in the Distance matrix

Distance Matrix

From/To	*A*	*B*	*C*	*D*	*E*
A	—	20	15	—	40
B	—	—	10	—	25
C	—	10	—	30	—
D	—	25	30	—	15
E	—	—	—	15	—

Distance Volume matrix is determined by multiplying the corresponding all of the above two matrices.

Distance-Volume Matrix

From/To	*A*	*B*	*C*	*D*	*E*	*Total*
A	—	600	825	—	600	2025
B	—	—	500	—	875	1375
C	—	350	—	1500	—	1850
D	—	500	450	—	450	1400
E	—	—	—	750	—	750
					Grand Total	7400

Total weighted distance in this case is 7400. A number of layouts are developed and the weighted-distance for each one of them is calculated. The layout with minimum weighted distance is then selected. The layouts are also compared on the basis of qualitative factors like safety and aesthetic aspects etc. if there is no significant difference between them on the basis of weighted distance.

Conclusion

Layout and Materials handling should be considered as an integrated system since there is a lot of inter-dependence between the two, which necessitate the planning of layout and materials handling as an unitary problem. A good plant layout and materials handling system improves the economics of production by reducing wastage in material and improving utilisation of man and material. It also results in reduced accidents, good house keeping and increased employee morale.

71

Ergonomics

Human Engineering or Ergonomics

The main objective of human engineering or ergonomics is to assist in design and operation of man-machine environment system which will ensure physical and mental ease to the human beings. It is really surprising that equipment designers often overlook the requirements. The details of equipments are most often determined by the engineering requirements rather than the workers' convenience. It is here that need of the study of human engineering arises. The attempt should always be made to design the machines and equipments in such a manner that not only the users but also those in the vicinity should be protected against dangers of accidents. Guards for the moving parts, barriers for dangers of spots are some examples of safety measures that need to be installed in all factories.

What is Human Engineering ?

Human Engineering means engineering for human use. It can be described as an attitude by which an engineer approaches the problems of designing machines and equipments to be used by human beings. The human engineer implements scientific experiments and other research methodology to study 'human factor' areas as they pertain to the operation of the man-machine systems and concepts. Human engineering group generally includes engineers, psychologists, mathematicians, anthropologists, physicians and specialists from various related fields. Some of the techniques commonly used in engineering include experiments design, mathematical tools, games theory and statistical sampling. The methodology of human engineering research and design relates in many ways to operational research, industrial engineering, and systems development engineering.

Human engineering in the study of people at work and of work methods. It includes the study of equipments design, hours of work and environmental conditions of work. Its purpose is to improve productivity and job satisfaction. Beginning in 1940, the term 'human engineering' was associated with equipment design. By the mid of fifties, several aircraft companies began, to utilise human engineering in equipment design and training programmes.

Functions and Responsibilities of Human Engineering

The functions and responsibilities human engineering have continuously broadened in scope and participation by 'human factors' specialists has also increased. In feature also, human engineering will have a wide spread utilisation in civil systems, architecture, heavy equipments, agricultural machinery, etc.

To understand the idea of human engineering work clearly for equipment design, let us study the following problems forced by one aircraft company.

(*i*) What should be comfortable finger's pressure for knobs ?
(*ii*) How much force should be required for a wheel control ?
(*iii*) What should be the volume occupied by a man ?
(*iv*) What should be the angle of vision from a prone position ?
(*v*) What should be the height of "no smoking" sign ?
(*vi*) What are the effects of drugs on the human body in fight ?

Human engineering should be able to increase the usefulness of many machines and tools. There seems to be enough room for improvements in control indicators and work space arrangement. To have the insight of the concept of Human Engineering let us understand the concept of 'work study'. Work study is comprised of Motion Study and Time Study. In motion study all manual work can be analysed into various elements and consequently studied and rearranged as desired. Motion study and time study were essential parts of the scientific management movement. Time study originated by Frederic W. Taylor is mainly used for establishing time standards and piece rates. Motion study developed by Frank and Gilbreth is employed for the analysis and improvement of work methods. Motion and time study provides a means for performing work and a means for measuring work. In other words, time and motion study help to determine a standard day's work and to determine the standard time required to perform a specific task. The various elements of motion study are shown in Table 71.1.

Elements of Motion

The elements of motion can be used to break down any job to show the details of hand work. The various principles of effective motion can be stated as follows :

1. Successive movements should be so related that one movement passes easily into that which follows.
2. The order movements should be so arranged that the mind can attend to the final aim.
3. The sequence of movements is to be so framed that an easy rhythm can be established.

Table 71.1 : Elements of Motion Study

Physical Elements	*Semi mental elements*
	— Search
Transport empty	— Final
Load	— Selects
Transport loaded	— Position
Unload	— *Mental element*
	Plan
Change direction	Inspect
Hold	Remember
Assemble	
Disassemble	*Delay elements*
Use	Avoidable delay
	Unavoidable delay
	Normal delay
	Rest for fatigue

4. The continuous movements are preferable to angular movements involving sudden changes in the direction of movements.
5. The number of movements should be reduced as far as possible.
6. Simultaneous use of both hands should be encouraged.
7. Fixed positions should be provided for tools, materials, etc.

Motion Study Techniques

The tools and techniques of motion study may be divided into three classes :

(*a*) Process Analysis.

(*b*) Equipment Utilisation.

(*c*) Operation Analysis.

Process Analysis. It is the process of making a component or performing an activity before undertaking a thorough investigation of specific operations in the process. The device to record a process in a compacts manner is the process chart. The chart represents graphically the separate events that occur during the performance of a task. The chart begins with the raw material entering the factory and follows it through every step such as transportation to storage inspection, machining operations and assembly till it becomes a finished unit. At times a better picture of the process can be obtained by putting flow lines. Both a process chart and flow diagram are sometimes needed to show clearly the steps in a manufacturing process.

Equipment Utilisation. In order to have a complete breakdown of the process, the series of operations are plotted against time scale. This diagram is called as activity chart. In order to eliminate unnecessary waiting time for the operator and the machine it is important to perform the following three steps : (*i*) Get Ready ; (*ii*) Do ; and (*iii*) Put Away.

Operation Analysis. The overall study of the process should result in a reduction in amount of travel of the operator, materials and tools and should bring about orderly and systematic procedures.

Micromotion Analysis

Most work is done with two hands and all manual work consists of a relatively few fundamental motions which are performed over and over again. Motion pictures are made of the operations. A special clock is placed in the picture to indicate time on the film. After the film has been processed it can be placed in a special analysis projector and the motion for the hands, arms or other body parts can be determined and the time for each motion can be measured and recorded.

The main objective of motion and time study and other changes in work methods has been to increase production and therefore, profits. Demonstration has the spectacular example of loading pig iron. Through a study of this operation, production was raised and fatigue reduced. Procedure at the Bethlechem Strel Company installed by the Taylor, the originator of scientific management, increased the amount of pig iron loaded from 12.5 tons to 47 tons per man day.

Providing good working conditions is often thought to increase production. This is frequently justified on the grounds that it leads to improved morale, which in turn is believed by many businessmen to cause higher productivity and profits.

Time Study

In case the time study principle and applications are perfect, we should arrive at the same time for a job regardless of each worker and the final time should entitle normal amount of effort and which would be same amount of effort for all kinds of jobs studied and result in average earnings each job studied at equitable pay levels determined in advance. In other words, if it decided in advance that turret lathe operator should be paid more than capstin lathe operator, the earnings would average out that way and there would be none of the upsets that occasionally occur.

In an experiment, it was shown that all the time study men used the same division into elements of motions and an unlimited length of time for each study. It was found that the average deviation or each time study export from the average of the whole group was 21 per cent, the average deviation for men from the same organisation was 9 per cent, an indication that training and similar procedures reduce differences. The time study engineer at times overestimated considerably the speed of some operators and underestimated the speed of others.

Standard Data

Barnes thought that mechanical errors the measurement in time study have been reduced by the use of standard data. Standard data are results of previous studies of the time it takes to make frequently. The reliability of using standard data has been carried out in various studies.

Acceptance of Time Study

Time studies in industry have shown that the attitudes of the group was a more powerful motive. Management is now aware that workers are not motivated primarily by the pay cheque. Determination of group attitudes would give management a better ground for understanding the worker.

The Western Electric Company found that group attitudes also go against the objectives of management. The management and particularly the industrial engineers at Western Electric had found that when the task is one that depends on the efforts of the group, the group will exert pressure on each individual to put out as much work as possible so that each member will make the maximum amount of money.

Group Attitude

The group considers a certain amount of work, a proper day's work, and the motive of the social group is stronger than is the pay incentive. Group pressure was exerted on fellow employees not to exceed the pump standard and to maintain output at a regular rate. On occasions when output actually exceeded the group standard, the additional output would not be reported but would be held back and reported later. These group attitudes regulated the workers' reactions to all outsiders the particularly supervisors. Workers did not confine in supervisors, who were looked upon as outsiders. The group attitudes decreed that workers would have to do a certain amount of work but that they should not do too much, even though a group bonus plan was in effect that would have resulted in addition pay for more work. The workers could have done much more than they did without physical damage.

Most efficiency experts, especially a recent years have sincerely applied motion and time study principles which these sincere men have failed to obtain acceptance, it has probably been because of a failure on their part to be sensitive to the human relations problems which are inevitable. In the past the details of motion and time studies have been kept secret from the employees.

The Best Way of Work

The experts have stressed that the purpose of motion study is to find the one best way of doing work for each job and to train every employee so that he may perform in that one best way. Psychologists have raised the objection that, because of individual differences, the best way of work for one worker is not necessarily the best for others. In fact, the employees should be taught the best way to work, and should be allowed to express their individual initiative after that.

Work Curves

A graph showing the level of performance against time spent at work is called a work curve. Since practices to alleviate fatigue depend to a large measure on the nature of the work curve, its discovery and use are important. No difficulty exits in obtaining such a curve where work is uniform and successive in terms of units produced. However, where work changes are frequent, as in ordinary varied office work, work curves are most frequently obtained by the use of laboratory task tests. The results of these tests are then plotted and used as index of fatigue for such jobs. Motivation might be higher in the laboratory tests then on the jobs. The degree of transfer depends on the similarity of task, environment, attitudes, and neuromuscular processes.

The work curves can be typed according to the nature of the task involved, namely, simple muscular, complex muscular and mental, as shown in Figs. 71.1, 71.2 and 71.3.

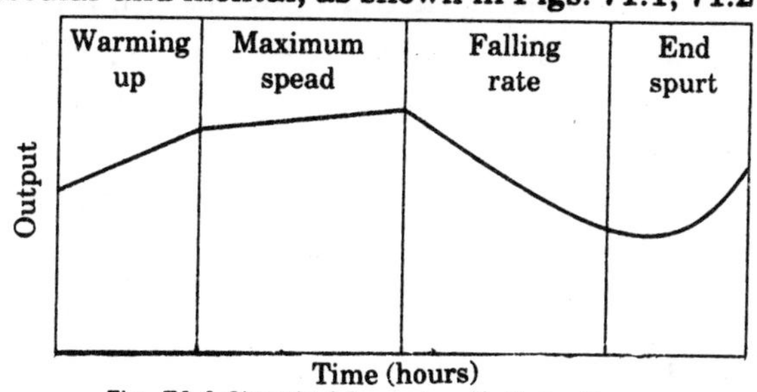

Fig. 71.1 Simple Muscular Activity Curve.

Simple Muscular Work

The first curve is a simple muscular activity curve. It is derived by recording the units and output of a group of muscles against the force of some weight or spring. It can be seen from the drawing that the curve for simple tasks shows a short warm up period followed by a high level of performance. A gradual tapering off then appears. Subsequently, a sudden drop occurs to a point of complete exhaustion. Such work curves have a general resemblance to motor curves, but they involve simpler coordination and fewer muscles. One can generally conclude from a study of such curve that the more complex and rapid the task the faster fatigue sets in. Moderate task permits a greater total amount of work before complete exhaustion occurs than doing heavier tasks.

Complex Muscular Work

The second curve depicts the amount of work done per unit of time in analytical industrial situation at a complex muscular task. This job is assumed to be motor in nature and not monotonous. As interpreted, the initial upward slope of the curve indicates, a warm up period. This is followed by a gradual rise in production until mid-day when a drop occurs. The afternoon curve taken after the mid-day rest is similar in appearance to the morning curve but it does not rise to a high production peak and it falls more rapidly near the end of the day.

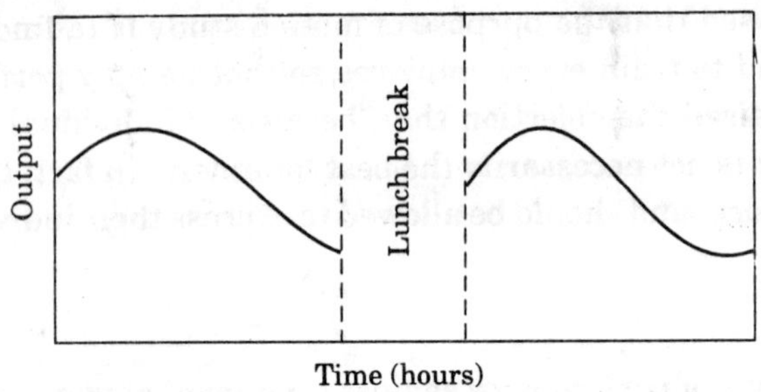

Fig. 71.2 Complex Muscular Activity Curve.

Mental Work

The third graph shows a typical mental work curve. As in muscular work, mental work decrement occurs in quantity, speed and accuracy of output. Again large individual differences and the nature of work tend to determine the timing of extent of such declines. The work decrement in mental tasks requiring continuous attention has been attributed to interferences known as "blocks".

Psychological Aspects

There are three main types of psychological contributions to human engineering :

1. Principle and practice of human relations to obtain co-operation in changes.
2. Research on methods to ensure that adequate experimental and statistical controls is there to make findings accurate.
3. Recognition of psychological characteristics of workers such as perceptions, speed and tendency to boredom under certain conditions.

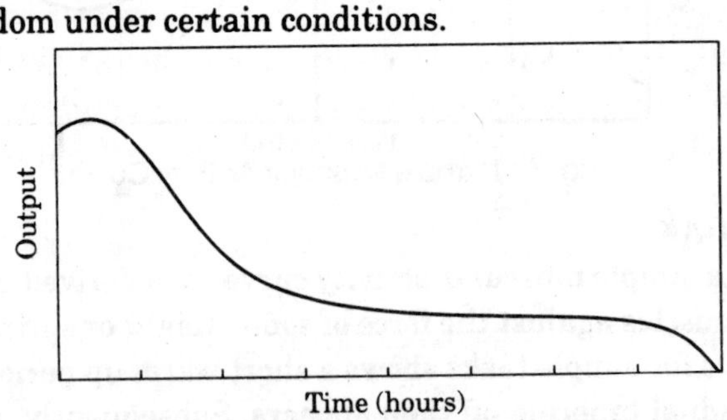

Fig. 71.3. Mental Work Curve.

One Best Way to Work

The use of time study as well as of motion study, generally implies that there is one best way of work. The influence of the work group on employee morale is a powerful force. The resistance to the idea of the introduction of improved work method is largely avoided if workers are afforded greater participation in the origin of these improvements. The advantage of workers' participation is that people are much more willing to do what is forced upon them.

Morale of employees needs to be recognised as a factor in the introduction of new methods. Generally there is resistance to change unless people are changed. It is important to recognise the attitude of employees toward the new methods, toward their job, toward their company and immediate supervisor for promoting a change in methods. Plans for increasing production by improving working conditions and introducing rest pauses have been made mainly by engineers, although these developments involve psychological problems, such as the determination of the cause and effect under sufficiently controlled conditions.

Job Methods

In fact, the decisions should be jointly made by engineers and psychologists to have deep insight of the problem.

Equipment Design

Human engineering equipment design involves the knowledge of not only the motion and time study analysis but many other areas to fit man over machine.

Motion and studies attempt of adopt the man to the machine, whereas human engineering places more stress on changing the machine, if necessary.

The design of any tool and equipment should be based on the capabilities of prospective operators. For example, sledge hammers should be light enough to be within the lifting capabilities of an ordinary man. Machines are becoming substitutes for people on the more routine jobs, but people must design, build and maintain the machines.

Duties of a Human Factor Engineer

The system development corporation of America which is probably the largest single group of human factor engineers in that country lists typical duties as follows :

1. The human factor engineer designs and implements scientific experiments and other research methodology to study human factor areas as they pertain to the operation of man, machine, weapons and other complex systems and concepts.
2. Evaluates existing or proposed man machine systems and sub-systems in terms of human physiological and psychological requirements so that optimum suitability and durability from a human input stand points are established.
3. Consults with design engineers and other professionals prior to, during and after design and development of systems to ensure optimum operation in terms of human capabilities, limitations and variables.
4. Provides the most current stage of the art information in his particular field of specialisation.

The functions and responsibilities of this discipline have continually broadened the scope and participation of human factor specialists. The future of human engineering will see a wide spread utilization in civil systems, architecture, heavy equipments, agricultural machinery etc.

Approaches, Techniques and Usefulness

Some of the well-known tools and techniques now used in human engineering include the following :

1. Experimental Design.
2. Mathematical Modelling.
3. Game Theory.
4. Linear Programming.
5. Information Theory.
6. Decision and Testing.
7. Simulation and Testing.
8. Field Testing.
9. Statistical sampling.
10. Direct cast history studies.

The methodology of human factor engineering research and design relates in many ways to associated technical fields such as operations research ; industrial engineering, weapons systems analysis, industrial design ; life support engineering and system development engineering.

Human engineering should be able to increase the usefulness of many machine and tools. There seems to be enough room for improvements in control indicators and work-space arrangement. Human engineering is the outgrowth of motion study originally developed by Gilbreths. It is broader in concept than motion study and accepts a broader set of criteria such as frequency of error and psychological and physiological costs as well as the older criteria of economy of motion and labour cost. To have the insight of the concept of human engineering we have to understand the concept of work study. The work study is comprised of motion study and time study. In motion study, all manual work can be analysed into various elements and consequently studied and rearranged as desired.

Fatigue

Fatigue is one of the most significant problems before industrial engineers. Fatigue can be defined as negative appetite for an activity. Industrial fatigue affects the worker's muscle, nerves and mind. In nervous fatigue, the nerve fibres terminate at the muscles and the plate stops transmission of the nerve impulses to the muscles which initiate muscular activity. The initiation of nerve impluses in the brain also stops questioning if the organism continues to work for a long period. This stopping of sending the impulses from the brain saves the organism and its muscles from damages. Thus the fatigue is defined as a reduction in the activity because of previous work. Different authors have given different definitions to the term fatigue.

— It can be a decrease in the capacity to do work or loss of efficiency.
— A decrease in interest in or willingness to work-a feeling of weakness.
— A more or less complete loss of irritability and responsiveness of a tissue.
— A condition of mind resulting from prolonged mental activity.
— A failure to maintain physiological or organic equilibrium.
— Not an entity but convenient word to describe a variety of phenomena.

Nature of Fatigue

The complexity of the fatigue phenomenon can be understood by an interesting experiment carried out at the University of Zagreb in Yugoslavia. In this a group of 25 college students was confined in a lecture room all night without sleep and was kept active by reading, music, dancing etc. At 6 O'clock in the next morning the students went on a six mile quick walk, after which they were tested for two hours. Another control group of 25 students was given the same tests after a normal night's sleep. Experiment as showed that, 87.5% of the experimental group rated their condition as "very tired" or exhausted and none reported "no fatigue". Only 12 per cent of the second group rated their condition as "very tired" and none rated it "exhausted", while 28 per cent reported "no fatigue" or "slight fatigue".

However, with respect to performance on 12 psychological tests requiring reasoning, spatial judgements, verbal tests, and locating printing errors there were no significant difference between the groups. It is found that changes in the integration of processes account for some of the difficulties in isolating the effects of fatigue in the organism as a whole. The body seems able to compensate for fatigue effects by spreading the work, in the same way a man shifts a suitcase from right to left arms. One doctor has written a book entitled, 'The wisdom of the body' in which he points out how certain organs of the body can take over the functions of a diseased organ and serve as second and third lines of defence against loss of life.

Fatigue can be known by studying the feelings of the fatigued person. An individual may 'feel' completely rested, but his work record may show a rapid decline. Under conditions of strong motivation, men may continue to work for long period of time without being aware of fatigue whereas, under other conditions they may feel fatigued before they go to work. The various signs of fatigue include inefficient eye movements, closing the eyes, looking about, and periods of skimming alternates with serious reading. If in an individual motivation is present, the same individual will feel no decrement in reading ability even after six hours of continuous reading.

Individual's Attitude of Work

An individual's attitude is an important factor in the ability to do work, but the presence of the attitude cannot be detected by any physiological measure. The study of fatigue must control not only the actual physical activity but also the indefinite environmental factors which influence a man's outlook and attitude toward the work. It has now become very apparent that emotional stability and mental hygiene cannot be closely related to fatigue. To the extent the fatigue involves the organism as a whole, it is a psychological problem. The work produces chemical and psychological changes in muscles nerve tissue, and the blood. The problem is the concern of both biological chemists and physiologists.

Studies of Fatigue

Angelo Masso, the Italian Scientist was the first to develop an instrument known as the "ergograph" which made it possible to investigate the relation between fatigue and work in a relatively isolated part of the body. He was able to induce fatigue in a muscle group and he could study the phenomenon without complicating it greatly with such psychological effects as monotony and boredom which are likely to accompany longer periods of work.

The principle of the ergograph is simple. All fingers except middle are similarly immobilized. A string is then fastened to the free finger, which is to be put to work. By placing a load on the other end of the setting, the free finger can be made to pull against the load. In Masso's apparatus, the string led over a pulley or the finger pulls against a known spring tension. The work of the finger is done by contracting and relaxing the muscles, which, in turn, lifts and lowers the weight.

In order to obtain a graph of the work output, a recording device is fastened to the moving string. Each contraction carries a needle over a revolving drum which records the magnitude of successive contractions by a series of straight lines.

The use of the ergograph has established a number of important relationships, each of which has a definite application to the relationships, each of which has a definite application to the industry and are discussed as follows :

1. If the contraction with a given load are spaced one every two seconds, there is a gradual decrease in the amplitude of the contractions until finally no further contractions can be made.
2. If the contractions with a given load are spaced 10 seconds there is no apparent evidence of fatigue.
3. If the load is lifted in a fast rhythm, it produces more fatigue for lift than the same load lifted at a slower rhythm.
4. The time for complete recovery increases rapidly as the period of work is increased.
5. The activity of other sets of muscles reduces the ability of the finger to do work.
6. The ability of the muscles to do work is decreased by loss of sleep, mental activity, hunger and failure of the muscles.
7. The ability of the muscle to do work is increased by messaging the muscle, injecting sugar into the blood stream and by good health and nourished body.
8. The rate of fatigue differs greatly in different people.

Signs of Fatigue

Mental fatigue expresses in many different ways the phenomena of monotony and boredom. Monotony is a state of mind caused by forming repetitive tasks. Boredom means lack of interest and is generally characterised by depression and a desire for change of activity. Boredom is affected by personality, attitude and interest patterns. The boredom and monotony can be differentiated from fatigue because it is a desire of a change in activity rather than for a rest or relief from work altogether.

Prolonged mental work result in an incapacity to evaluate what is being read. Common characteristics of prolonged mental work are increased errors and an increase in the amount of time necessary to assimilate written material or to sole perlexing problems towards the end of the period. In addition this the physical state of the body is no indication of its mentally satisfied state, although there is a state of tension which expresses itself in both muscular and neutral form during the mental work. The change in the nerve centres that result in prolonged metal activity are uncertain. Consequences of mental overwork in children are disturbances of vision, headache, bleeding from nose, loss of appetite and indigestion, ceretral disorders and nervousness.

Physical Phenomena

The effects of prolonged work on the body result in excessive muscular activity. These can be grouped as :

(*i*) overt results

(*ii*) internal changes.

Over Results. If the muscles are stained then the following phenomena occur :

(*i*) The amount of work that the muscles can do depends upon the speed with which successive contractions are made.

(*ii*) Decreased capacity on the part of one set of muscles is accompanied by a increased capacity on the part of other muscles of the body.

(*iii*) The interference with the removal of waste products or with the supply of blood to the area lessons the working capacity of the muscle, loss of sleep, anemia, hunger, or dissipation reduces the number and amount of contractions that the muscle can make.

(*iv*) The rate and extent of contractions diminish rapidly at first, then maintain a constant pace and finally speed up a little just before exhaustion sets in.

Internal Changes. Any muscular activity is accompanied by following changes :

(*i*) Waste products are constantly being formed and thrown into the blood stream consisting of lactric acid, potassium phosphate and carbon dioxide. With any accumulation in the active muscles, they exert a poisonous and paralyzing effect on the whole organism.

(*ii*) The muscles are provided with a store of carbohydrates and are constantly being supplied with other carbohydrates and with a steady supply of oxygen. Normally these serve to balance the effect on the waste products but if constant strain is put on any muscular set, there is a gradual accumulation of lactric acid and carbonic acid, and a steady decrease in the supply of oxygen acidity which expresses itself in the form of the experience of the general fatigue.

(*iii*) The supply of oxygen is dependent upon the capacity of the organism for transporting oxygen from the lungs to the tissues.

(*iv*) The carbohydrates supply consists mostly of a simple blood sugar called as glycogen which is manufactured in the liver. During the contraction of muscle activity, the glycogen changes to lactric acid and during the relaxation phase, part of the lactric acid is converted back into glycogen and part is united with oxygen producing carbon dioxide, when that is combined with the water in the tissues, carbonic acid is formed. A great deal of the carbonic acid passes out of the muscles through the cell walls, whereas the lactric acid is removed only by oxygen. There is concentration of sugar in the blood of 0.1 per cent, and in the normal activity of the work the percentage remains fairly constant. In fact, the excess of lactric acid is the sign of fatigue.

Psychological Fatigue

Psychological fatigue is here used to designate those factors which cause work decrement. It includes the falling off in efficiency of work commonly referred to as mental fatigue, also known as monotony and boredom.

Monotony and boredom are influenced by the way a person views his ask from time to time. Causing the output to fluctuate rather than to fall of progressively. The way in which a job is perceived is an individual matter, but certain kinds of tasks and work atmosphere are more likely to induce monotony and boredom than are others.

Motivation is important factor in all forms of fatigue and the rate of fatigue for almost any type of task varies with the intensity of the motivation. When motivation is low, fatigue effects appear very costly, but when motivation is high, fatigue may not be apparent until physical exhaustion is manifested. Mental conflicts and frustrations are so commonly associated with man's work that it is to be industrialists' interest to determine methods for reducing their incidence.

Motivation Theory of Fatigue

Motivation influences a man's will to work. The amount of energy a man may have available for a task seems to depend upon the motivating conditions he finds in the situations. It appears that the influence of motivation on work is one of determining the amount of energy which will become available for the task.

The energy is generally rationed and a particular job must have certain priorities if it is to get a good share of the energy. After the office work the man may be too tired to work overtime or so but if cards playing is suggested, plenty of energy becomes available. The man's basic supply of energy is not depleted by his work, but the portion allocated to a given task is expanded. If many allotments are made, the total supply is reduced. Rationing then becomes more strict, higher priorities are needed and smaller allocations are made.

FATIGUE-MONOTONY-BOREDOM

Fatigue

It is inactiveness to work or negative attitude to work. It can be defined as reduction in the ability to do work because of previous work.

Monotony

Monotony can be defined as a desire to have changed due to similar job. Monotony is the state of mind caused by performing repetitive tasks.

Boredom

It is mental fatigue due to routine job. Attitude and personality are related with boredom or lack of interest is generally characterised by depression and a desire for change of activity.

Monotony and boredom can be differentiated from fatigue because the former are desired for change in the activity rather than for a rest or relief from work altogether.

Prolonged mental work results in a capacity to evaluate what is being read. A common characteristic of prolonged mental work are increased errors and increase in the time to assimilate written material or to solve perplexing problem towards the end of the work. In addition to this, physical state of the body is no indication of its mentally tension which expresses itself in both muscular and neutral form during the mental work. The changes in the nerve centres that result from prolonged mental activity are uncertain-consequences of mental overwork in the children are disturbances of vision, headache, bleeding from nose, loss of appetite and indigestion, cerebral disorders and nerveousness.

Reduction of Monotony and Boredom in Industry

The following steps should be taken by the management in order to reduce monotony and boredom :

1. When a supervisor gives an unusual job to a worker, he should explain the background and purpose of the special job.
2. Most people work better, and are more willing when they have a good understanding of the end results of their work.
3. The increased verbal communication between supervisor and employees is likely to produce a better personal relationship and give the supervisor a more dependable "size up" of the individual members of his group.

4. It gives lower level jobs a "fourth dimension" to the dimensions of what to do, how to do it, and when to do it. It adds why it is done and what is accomplishes.

Monotony and boredom are the specific areas under the heading of fatigue. The mental state of monotony is associated with definite fluctuations in the rate of working and with a fall in production.

In one of the most exhaustive studies this relationship was demonstrated by showing (1) that production was low and variable during periods when boredom was experienced and (2) that the production of individuals felt very bored was lower.

Monotony effects were most pronounced during the middle of the work period and disappeared in anticipation of the end of the worked period, causing the end spurt in the production curve. The individual feels restless and under the strain time seemed to pass slowly. The extent of the monotony is dependent not only upon the repetitive nature of the task, but also upon the degree of attention required. There is general agreement, however, that workers tend to slow down, talk, become restless and show variable production when bored. In other words, both productivity and the mental state are influenced by a variety of factors, and although some of these may be common to both, each is influenced by special ones. Letting the mind wander seems to be one way of escaping monotony. If day dreaming does not interfere with the ability to do good work, it is probably a useful adjustment, but if constant alertness is imperative, it may cause errors and accidents. That a good deal of the loss in production in repetitive work is due to the specific condition of boredom rather than a muscular fatigue as indicated by the following facts :

1. Afternoon monotony effects do not exceed those of the morning as could be expected from accumulated fatigue.
2. Application of the end of the work period tends to abolish signs of monotony, and
3. Intelligent workers are more subject to monotony effects that are less intelligent ones. These facts indicate that a knowledge of the mental effects of respective work is highly important since such information might suggest methods for eliminating this mental condition.

Fatigue Versus Boredom

Mayo and Lovekin have suggested that what is commonly called "fatigue" had better been called by its right name, 'Boredom'. It is difficult to eliminate the term "fatigue" from the scientific discussion. The distinction between the two terms is discussed below :

1. Fatigue is usually associated with psychological depletion while boredom is a concomitant of mental dullness.
2. Fatigue is a decreased capacity for work. Boredom is a decreased interest in work.
3. Fatigue is conscious inability. Boredom is a feeling of incapacity with or without there being a psychology basis for the feeling.
4. Fatigue expresses itself in the form of a gradual decrement in the work curve with a final end spurt indicative of the functioning of second wind. Boredom expresses itself in the form of irregularities in the work curve with intermittent spurts of short duration, a sharp drop in the work curve during each work spell and a rapid rise toward the end.

5. Fatigue is due to the work task being temporarily beyond the capacity of the worker while boredom is due to the consciousness of the uniformity of the work task and a temperamental incapacity to subject oneself to that particular type of routine work. Fatigue is the result of too long continued physical or mental work. Boredom is due to the absence of work challenges.
6. Fatigue is, to some extent, measurable. Boredom is a subjective attitude that defines objective evaluation.
7. Fatigue has physiological accompaniments which are fairly definite. Boredom has mental and emotional accompaniments that do not lend themselves to ready calculation.
8. Fatigue express itself in the desire for rest. Boredom expresses itself in the desire for change.

Monotony and Boredom

The repetitive work destroys such human values as pride in workmanship and individuality. In fact, boredom and dissatisfaction are common in our present methods of production.

The monotony and boredom are described as the undesirable effects of repetitive work. The monotony is described as the state of mind caused by repetitive work. The term boredom is referred as a more inclusive term, talking in the person's unfavourable outlook and feeling tone for the task he is performing. The boredom will be affected more than monotony by the following factors :

(1) The personality of the person (2) the attitude and mood of the person ; and (3) the perception of the task performed. This means that the individual may not agree on the task that is most boring ; individual persons may shown more boredom one day that another.

Work which requires constant alertness and attention is subject to interferences known as Blocking. The phenomenon of mental blocking becomes objectively apparent when we measure the continuous result of mental work. If a person is asked to name a series of colours, give the opposites of a list of words, or add a series of sums, and if his responses are recorded on a revolving drum so that each response makes a mark ; it will be found that these marks are irregularly grouped. A few responses occur rapidly, then there is a delay, followed by another set of responses. Such records show that the responses are either very close together or fairly far apart.

The blocks or lapses in performance are associated with the making of errors. There are wide differences among people in the length of their mental blocks, as well as in the frequency with which these occur. These number of blocks range from two to six per minute in different people. Individuals who tend to perform slowly in experimental tests are likely to be the ones who have long or frequent blocks. Blocking probably functions as an automatic method of resting.

Measurement of Fatigue

Fatigue can be measured, if the muscle is taken out from a living organism and put into the laboratory experiment. This is done in the physiological laboratory by taking a muscle from the living organism and giving electrical impulses ryhthemically to the nerve attached to the muscle. The muscle contracts with the electrical impulses and the contraction of the muscle is recorded graphically on a recording drum by means of a stylus. If the electrical impulse continues to stimulate muscle for certain period, the muscle gradually diminishes its contraction and finally stops contracting. It will not be possible to experiment this in case of an industrial worker. It is a fact that if a muscle remains attached to the living organism, it cannot be made fatigued. The central nerve system of the organism, will stop the muscle long before it becomes fatigued in order to save it from damages. So muscular fatigue cannot be measured so long as the muscle is attached to a living organism.

When a muscle works, it undergoes electrical changes. It is possible to amplify the electrical activity of the muscle, so that even the slightest contraction can be detected.

This respiration undergoes changes during mental or physical work. The rate of respiration increases in muscular activity, but there is no definite change of the rate of respiration during mental activity. If the individual feels happy, the rate of respiration decreases significantly. The human organism acts as a machine and its activity transforms energy, then a work that it performs can be measured directly in terms of such energy transformation which is technically known as metabolism. In metabolic activity there are two processes going on in any living organism. Metabolism is a destructive process by means of which energy is consumed. Anabolism is a constructive process which assimilates food and converts it into energy for consumption during activity.

Fatigue Tests

Fatigue tests are classified as psychological, physiological, and workshop records. The psychological and work-shop tests are valuable indicators of small bodily changes and the physiological tests of gross bodily changes. Until fatigue has reached the stage in which there is a disturbance of physiological equilibrium, the physiological tests do not show any change. The tests that have been used may be divided into three clauses, tests of motor power and reaction time, of skin sensitivity, and of efficiency of mental functions. Psychological tests are most valid for determining fatigue.

Tests of Motor Power and Reaction Time

In this method, the usual practice is to isolate as far as possible the activity of one group or pattern of muscles and infer that it is made up of activity representative of the muscles patterns of the whole organism. The following are representative tests :

1. *Tests of Physical endurance.* In an ergograph, the isolated finger is attached to a set of weights, which the finger repeatedly pulls back and forth, the exhaustion sets in, and the extent of the finger movements is recorded.

The findings of the results from the ergography are :

(*a*) the speed with which exhaustion takes place if the palter is constantly stimulated.

(*b*) the ergograph that characterizes one muscle pattern is typical of that form any other pattern, and seems to represent the individual's form of energy expenditure.

(*c*) the regularity of the work curve seems to depend on the maintenance of a condition of physiological and emotional balance. Characteristics differ between different subjects in their resistance to work. Ergographic curves seem to fall into the following three clauses:

(*i*) Those maintaining a high and consistent level for some time, followed by a sudden drop to the exhaustion point.

(*ii*) Those starting with a high level, but quickly falling to a low average.

(*iii*) Those with a maximal start but with a gradual decrease in activity until the exhaustion point is reached.

2. *Tests of Strength.* Various types of strength tests have been used, and in most of the dynamometer tests, norms are provided for the different groups. The tests can be administered in very short time, and in these tests, the strength of the hand, the leg, the back, and the shoulders can be determined.

3. *Tests of motor speed.* Sapping board is an instrument to measure the endurance for such types of work as typing and fitting small mechanical parts together.

4. *Tests of muscular precision and muscular steadiness.* Steadiness tester is used to measure muscular steadiness. It consists of a mental casting with one face at an angle of 45 degrees and pierced with nine holes of different diameters. To one end of the casting is attached a binding post so that it may be put in circuit with a battery and a sounder. A stylus with a connection card is provided, and the task given the subject is to insert the stylus into the holes without making contact. The accuracy with which this can be done is indicative of muscular control, the degree of control ; which the subject exercises can be estimated after varying spells of work.

5. *Reaction time tests.* Many varieties of these tests have been used. The purpose of reaction time test is to form an estimate of the speed and accuracy with which a person can make adjustments under different types of situations.

One of the most commonly used tests is McDong three hole dotting test, which consists of revolving band with holes which the subject thrust pierce as they revolve past a certain point. In fact reactivitive means the time taken by a given individual after presentation of stimulus and his subsequent response to the stimulus. The apparatus used is known as chronoscope.

6. *Tapping test.* The rate of tapping is calculated by recording the number of tappings and correlating it with time taken in tapping. If an individual continues to tap, his rate of tapping is fast in the beginning and gradually slows down with the lapse of time.

7. *Body sway.* Stylus is fitted on the head or on the shoulder of an individual. The individual is asked to stand without moving for a considerable period. The stylus records his body sway on a paper attached to it. It has been observed that the rate of body sway increases alongwith the time.

8. *Steadiness of hands.* The subject places an electric stylus inside the bigger hole first for 2 minutes without touching the plate. If he touches the plate, an electric bulb or a dazzer indicates the touch. Then he puts the next hole which is smaller than the first and continues the experiment till he reaches the smallest hole, the steadiness of hand suffers by continuous activity.

9. *Flicker.* In the flicker test a disc which is partly black and partly white is rotated. As a certain speed, it is seen as a solid grey. At lower speed, it flickers. A fatigued man sees the flicker more. This test is mainly used for the selection of drivers.

Test of Efficiency of Mental Functions

As measures of fatigue, they have a very little value, supposedly one or more of them may be responsible for changes in the quantity and quality of production, especially in the frequency of errors or accidents at different times of the day.

Physiological Tests (Skin Tests)

Tests of physiological nature have usually been limited to changes that occur in the blood and in metabolism as a result of the expenditure of energy.

1. *Blood changes.* These can be measured in a number of ways like tests of blood pressure, pulse rate, pulse pressure and pulse product.

2. *The pulse rate.* Normal pulse rate varies in different people. For man the usual estimate is from 68 to 76 beats per minute, and for woman from 74 to 80, some people, however, may have normal rate as low as 50 or as high as 90. During severe activity the increase in pulse rate is very rapid.

As an indication of a so called fatigued condition, pulse rate is of value only for the heavier types of activity, in lighter continuous work *e.g.* type-writing, no change is noticed after 8 hours practice.

The pulse rate change may indicative an increased expenditure of energy, it cannot be taken as indicative of the feeling of fatigue.

3. *Blood pressure.* Maximum pressure occurs at the time of contraction of the left verticle, and it termed diastolic blood pressure. Measurements are taken with a sphyamomanometer, an instrument consisting of a rubber sleeve with a graph inflated to the point where the flow of blood is cut off, gives scale measurement of blood pressure. Normal systolic blood pressure ranges between 100 and 130 and diastolic between 50 and 65. When the body is under exertion, the systolic pressure usually increases and the diastolic decreases. When the body is in an exhausted state the increase may be as high as 50 to 70 per cent and the decrease from 0 to 50 per cent.

4. *Metabolic Changes.* Metabolic changes indicate the rate at which body energy is being used. Several devices are in use for the measure of the rate of respiratory exchange *i.e.,* the ratio of oxygen consumption to carbon dioxide production. Under experimental conditions and in hospitals, measurement is made by breathing oxygen from a container through a mouth piece or a gas mask.

During moderate work, the metabolic rate is usually from two to four times the normal rate, but is unusual for a person to maintain a level of work that demands more than eight times the based metabolic rate.

Metabolic rate can be measured as :

(*i*) Changes in sl.in temperatures.

(*ii*) Insensible weight loss, due to evaporation of water from the skin and lungs.

(*iii*) Decreased skin resistance as a consequence of increased neuromuscular activity.

The Value of Tests of Fatigue

There is no such test, and there is not likely to be one which can give a definite proof of the depleted organic state of worker. The interpolation of a test inevitably introduces a change of attitude and a change of interest and introduction of some other feeling. This individual may be annoyed, apathetic, at being called away from his daily work to the test. The individual may become bored with the test to which he is repeatedly submitted.

No doubt, there is no one test that is possible. Tests are needed, not so much to indicate the fatigued condition of a worker as to point out the time spans between rests and the places in the work period when rest pauses or other devices are introduced that will serve to maintain the worker's physiological equilibrium and keep the quality and quantity of production at a standard place.

Indirect Measures of Fatigue

Psychologists measure industrial fatigue in terms of production, rate of absenteeism, rate of accident, job satisfaction, wastage, etc.

Environmental Conditions Affecting Fatigue

The environmental conditions such as noise, improper lighting and extreme heat, cold and dust, have all shown an increase in fatigue.

The improvement in these conditions contribute the fatigue alleviation which results into higher morale, lower accident rate and less absenteeism.

The conditions which affect fatigue are :

(*i*) Noise and Industrial Music.

(*ii*) Illumination.

(*iii*) Temperature and humidity.

(*iv*) Ventilation.

Noise. Noise is unwanted sound and it increases fatigue. If the noise is to much and continues for a long time it might cause deafness, for example, boiler maker deafness, sheet iron worker and blacksmith deafness. The effect of noise depends on the kind of noise and kind of work. Mental work is affected more than manual work by noise. The effect of noise is greater when it is irregular. Sounds of either very high or low tone qualities are more irritating than those in middle zone. In a study of mental arithmetic metabolism was much higher during the first noisy period but reduces with adjustment.

The noise of moderate intensity serves as a psychological inducement to work. One study of the reduction of noise concludes that it is an investment which under ordinary conditions will increase productivity by 10 to 15 per cent.

Meaningful noise, however, has a great intellectual work. It is very difficult to adopt to a meaningful noise and as such this has a continuous effect on the efficiency of the workers. Meaningful noise with moderate intensity in the form of music increases the output. This is more true in case of monotonous and repetitive work. Some industries such as Glaxo Laboratories, Bata Shoe Company, DCM Chemicals, and Telco are using music in packing sections which is giving good results. The effect of noise on learning has been observed more clearly than its effect on fatigue. It is commonly believed that workers produce a great deal more under conditions of quiet. The available evidence suggests that noise has an effect but only slight one on production.

But if the individuals who are exposed to very high pitch noise such as boiler makers and aeroplane pilots, they suffer permanent deafness.

Industrial Music. Music in factories has become faily common and therefore, requires an evaluation. Some of the first studies were made in England where researches found the initial interest for dealing with monotony. The effects of musical programmes on simple assembly operations showed production increases upto 6 per cent, when production on days with music was compared to that on days without music. In a radio tube assembly factory in which music was customarily played, the effectiveness of fact, slow and mixed programmes was studied. The scrap rate was found to be less when either fast or slow music was played than when there was no music or when fast and slow musical programmes were alternated. Musical programmes also had a beneficial effect on employee morale.

The increase in production varies considerably with the job and the shift. Simple repetitive jobs that can be performed well while talking seem to benefit most by music. The research findings indicate that music seems to encourage young, inexperienced workers to increase production on routine jobs. No significant effects were found for older skilled workers.

The general finding is that employees like music. At least 75 per cent strongly favour it and only 1 to 2 per cent oppose it. Slow music seems more desirable than fast music, variety is essential to keep young and older employees satisfied with the programmes. Vocal music may be distracting for some employees, and music with strong beats may disturb or help depending on how it fits into the movement rhythms of a job. Spaced programmes seem to be favoured. At present, it appears that the music should be on about 12 per cent of time for the day shift and as much as 50 per cent of the time for the night shift.

Most favourable effect of music is its influence on boredom. It takes the mind from the work as well as frees the brain of the obligation of initiating the activity.

Illumination. Many industrial undertakings take this advantage of natural light during the day time. But it should be remembered that the illumination of the work place by means of artificial modern lights is far better than taking the natural day light in carrying out any work efficiently. Any natural light which the industry uses should be carefully utilized in the working conditions. North light is commonly used in industries because the variation of light is not much during the day time in a factory.

Engineers are utilizing modern techniques in the plant layout to avoid such changes of illumination during the day in the work shop either by putting the transparent shades on the top of the factory or cutting down lights from all directions except from the north.

Some jobs need special light which needs more illumination. Because of the uniform light in the work pace, the workers do not find any visual difficulty while coming out from a specific work situation which is illuminated brightly.

The entire work area should be uniformally illuminated. Areas outside the immediate focus of observation, wall surfaces, for example, if unevenly illuminated cause continual adjustment changes and consequently higher visual fatigue. Since the pupil of the eye must adjust itself when focusing on a bright spot and then on a dark spot, expansion and contraction of the pupil sets up an increased strain and fatigue in the worker.

Indirect lighting in the best method of producing uniformity. Eye muscles tend to pull toward areas of high illumination. Where the high point of light is not in the work area, a tug-of-war exists between the muscles that are concentrated on the work area and those that veer to the higher illumination.

The human eye adjusts so readily to changes in illumination that the effects of poor lighting are usually not immediately observable to the untrained eye. Errors in judgement are often found when people's reports on brightness are checked against readings on light meters.

Poor illumination causes fatigue and irritability and is a source of errors and industrial accidents. Money spent to current improper lighting will be more than rapid in higher output per worker, lower production costs, and a generally happier, healthier and probably safest work force.

The colour of surrounding objects and surfaces is related to lighting. The use of white or light pastes improves illumination by reflecting high percentage of light, while deeper tones have a considerably lower reflective value. The occurrence of glare should however, be avoided. Several studies made on the use of coloured light show that people prefer the light of daylight colour. The use of this so-called white light is said to assit materially in visual efficiency.

(*i*) Various jobs requires different intensity of light above 50 foot candles.

(*ii*) The severe and prolonged visual tasks, such as fine engraving, and discrimination or inspection of time details of two contrast requires 50 to 60 foot candles.

(*iii*) The prolonged critical visual task such as drawing, fine assembling, fine machine work, and proof reading, require 50 to 60 foot candles.

(*iv*) The visual tasks such as skilled bench work, require 19 to 20 foot candles.

Temperature. Indian are accustomed to working in a temperature which will be considered as high. At several places like Calcutta, Madras, Bombay etc. where the employees work in a moderate climate throughout the year, there the temperature does not rise or drop to the extremes. The efficiency goes down during the extreme temperature conditions.

Humidity. Variation in humidity play very important role in industry.

Rise of humidity in low temperature to a moderate extent gives relief to workers from severe dry cold, whereas, rise in humidity adds further discomfort to the rise of temperature. It is more discomfortable to withstand wet heat and dry cold.

On the other hand, in-textile industry high humidity is required. The shipping and weaving departments require as high as 80 to 85% of relative humidity.

Prolonged discomfort from heat will no doubt affect efficiency.

The effect of temperature on worker's productivity is encountered at much lower temperature levels in physical work.

Low temperatures can also affect productivity. Ability to make precise movements with the hands and fingers decreases.

Discomfort has been reported where sizable temperature differences existed within a room, that is, cool air at floor level and warm air at head level. Furthermore where sizable temperature differences existed within a building and the nature of the work required worker's movement from are a to area, discomfort was noted.

Individual differences make it impossible to set exact temperature and humidity limits within which all workers will be satisfied.

Ventilation

Temperature and humidity can be controlled to a great extent if adequate ventilation by the circulation of fresh air is arranged in the factories. The circulation of fresh air is generally done by fans, ventilators, and blowers. Artificial arrangements are also made in chemical industries to avoid pollution of air, through gases and fumes. In cement factory where the stances are crushed the operation creates lot of dust. Similarly, in the spray shop the spray particles pollute the air. In such cases, exhaust fans are not adequate enough to supply fresh air and so gas marks are provided to workers to avoid fumes and dust during work. Dust and fumes are constant health hazards in the Indian industries.

1. During winter the temperature for light work should be 65°F, for active yet light work, 60 to 65°F. For work involving more muscular exertion, 55°F to 60°F.
2. During summer the temperature should be kept below 60°F.
3. The introduction of fresh air should not be less than 1,000 cubic feet per person per hour.
4. In summer adequate air circulation should be arranged. The efficiency increases if the air movement is moderately high.
5. During summer the relative humidity should be 70 per cent atleast.

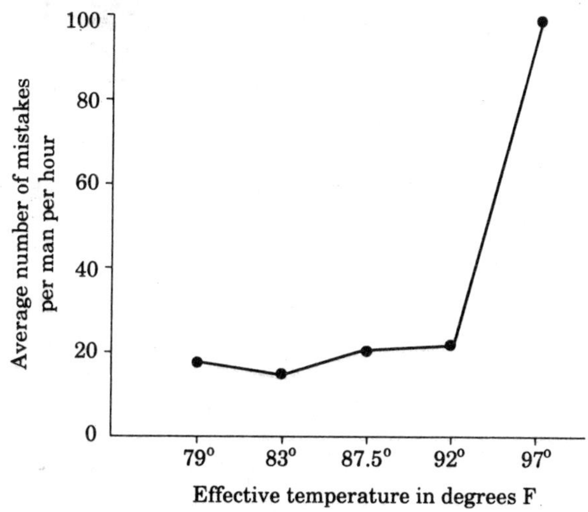

Means of Eliminating or Reducing Fatigue

The factors which remove fatigue are many, some of them are peculiar to the environment, some are peculiar to the individual worker, and some are peculiar to the particular type of work.

Number and length of Rest Pauses. A major change in the number, duration and location of the rest pauses owes its origin to the famous experiment of F.W. Taylor on the pig-iron handler.

Mayo reports that in one department of a mill in Philadelphic the best results were secured when the rest pauses were kept at 10 minutes.

A brief pause from activity may cause considerable loss of swing and only a slight recovery from the effects of fatigue. Too long a pause may be equally unfavorable. It may be more than enough to dispel the factors which have been impeding working capacity.

It is difficult to tell what the proper length of a work and rest pauses should be, unless considerable experimental work has preceded the judgement. The length of the pause should vary for different jobs in the same organisation, a general rest pause for all employees will not have the same effects.

The fatigue in general is natural. If activity of one set of muscles reduces the ability of other to do work, then recovery must proceed most effectively when the person is completely relaxed. This suggests that work pauses for heavy muscular activity should not only be work stoppages but periods of complete relaxation. Unfortunately, workers who have the most strenuous occupations too often have the last accessible facilities for relaxation.

Best pauses and production. Various studies have indicated that different amount of rest pauses have a definite effect on production. In one of the study, rest pauses of seven minutes, introduced in both morning and afternoon work periods, favourable changed the entire shape of the hourly production curves. Favourable results have been found with a five minute rest after each hour of work and even when a two minute rest is alternated with three minutes of work.

The distribution of rest pauses has not been determined for industry but it may be expected to vary considerably with the type of work, length of the work day, length of the work week, individual differences, sex of the worker and the level of motivation. It has been seen that whether or not employees have rest pauses is not entirely under the control of the company. Employees can pace their work so that short rest pauses are continuously taken. Management can control only the rest pauses that are officially given, and these result in decreased unofficial rest pauses.

Unofficial rest pauses actually reflect the employee's way of budgeting his energy. When men work long days they pace their work differently and work more slowly than when they work short days.

The problem for management is one of finding efficient work rest distributions and motivating employees to accept them. Official rest pauses may be regarded as one of the ways in which management can influence the work rest distributions.

The official rest pause should be introduced just before production being to fall off. If an individual is engaged in finishing a unit of work, an externally imposed pause may serve as an irritant because it disrupts the work pattern. Jobs should be carefully studied and the rest pauses adjusted properly. Training individuals to space their rest properly may be the best solution of the problem of distributing rest periods in accordance with variations in jobs and differences in people.

The need for rest pauses varies in different types of work. In many positions, there are frequent pauses due to delays of various kinds, and to superimpose additional rest pauses on an already crowded series of undesired rest pauses would be quite illogical. Rest pauses are necessary for the worker under the following conditions :

(*a*) When the work is repetitive and monotonous.

(*b*) When work involves continuous sitting or standing.

(*c*) When workers are exposed to extreme heat and unfavourable ventilating conditions.

Now the rest pauses are proclaimed almost in every organism. Before the use of rest pauses the workers were victims of postural fatigue, pessimistic reverses, and frequent clashes with the supervisor and with co-workers.

From a production stand point, the introduction of rest pauses has almost invariably resulted in an increase in production rate. A study reports an average increase of 6.2 percent in 10 different types of work as a result of two rest periods daily, and an increase of 2.8 per cent in five other types of work as a result of 5 to 10 minutes rest per hour or per work spell.

Myers reports an increase of 44 per cent in production among workers in a shoe factory when work and rest periods were out a 40 minutes to 20 minutes basis, and a 13 percent increase in work on labelling when the 50 to 10 minutes ratio was used.

Difficulties of rest periods. The universal adoption of rest periods in both impossible and unwise. The nature of the work in some organisations makes rest periods unnecessary. Even in places where rest periods are desirable, they are often difficult because of objection on the part of management and because of opposition on the part of piecewage workers. Sometimes objections are raised because of the greater experience of boredom during the rest than during the work periods. If an operator stands by a machine waiting for the 10 minutes to expire is to abuse the common meaning of the term. Rest periods can be effective only when preparation has been made for introducing them, when adequate study has been made of representative jobs, in order to find the most effective time for and length of the rest.

Optimum work weeks. Let us consider the effects of reducing hours below those of the eight hours day. Studies have shown that production for a six hours day was approximately the same as for an eight hours day.

In a more detailed study, work weeks of 36, 40, 44 and 48 hours were compared. The hourly output for the 40 hours week was found to be the most efficient, the production being 868 units. With the 44 hours week hourly production fell to 839 units and with the 48 hours week, it dropped to 793.5. For the 36 hours week, production was 734 units which made the work pattern less efficient (per-hour) than the 40 hours week but more efficient than the 44 and 48 hours weeks. The inefficiency of the shortest work week may have been due to less in practice and improper work attitude or to any number of other factors.

Apparently, the 45 to 50 hours week is approximately the work pattern which yields the greatest weekly output, only when the work period exceeds these hours there is the decrease in hourly output sufficiently great to make the longer week productive than the shorter week.

The studies have shown that the work of one day may seriously hamper that of the next. The fact that Monday's production was found to be below that of Tuesday suggests a phenomena analogous to warming-up. The rate of production falls off during the week and is highest on Tuesday and lowest on Saturday. The persisting fatigue phenomenon is due to incomplete recovery from one day to the next or to a need for recreation without which man is deprived of a necessary stimulus to life.

The work shift. The industries are required to operate three shifts in order to give 24 hours of service, to increase the productive capacity of the plant. As capital investment or fixed cost per employee increases, it becomes more and necessary to operate more than one shift to reduce overhead.

The psychological problems created by the shifts are perhaps to most striking. Most employees prefer the day shift, the expressed reasons being health, output and social life. The investigators found general agreement among the workers that the feeling of fatigue was greater for the night than for the day shift. Failure to get enough sleep at home while working on the night shift is the serious problem.

Many problems were revealed in the production records. The production records of the fortnightly changes revealed that production was better on the second week than on the first week of the day shift. For the monthly changes there was a slight but continued improvement for each successive week of the day shift. However, the night shift schedules showed no such improvement.

Shift rotation is an attempt to distribute the inconvenience to all employees. Although the changes introduce an additional problem of adjustment, it does permit each family to live a normal life for a part of the year.

Persons who live out of phase with other people also have problems with shoping, recreation and a social as well as of community life. When a large number of persons work on a night shift, the possibilities of developing more nearly normal patterns of life should be explored.

Automation. With automation the pace of the work is controlled by the machinery and heavy work is largely eliminated. It has already been pointed out that lack of sleep and fatigue affects vigilance. Automation increases the cost of errors and the need for vigilance and the difficulty of maintaining attention. Automated plants often are confronted with a similar problem of reducing fatigue without promoting sleep. Anticipation of automation also introduces job insecurity, and a good deal of preparation is needed to make an organisation ready for change. Loss in the use of developed skills, boredom, loneliness and reduced job satisfaction are problems created by automation and these states of twin affect fatigue as well as motivation.

72

Break Even Analysis

Introduction

A business is said to break even when its income equals its expenditure. The break even point means the level of output or sales at which no profit or loss is made. It represents the position at which marginal profit or contribution is just sufficient to cover fixed overheads when production exceeds the break even the business makes a profit and when production is below the volume of production at break even point, the business makes a loss. The following problems are solved with the help of break even analysis.

— the total profit of business is ascertained at various levels of activity and different patterns of production and sales.

— reporting the top management the affect on net profits of introducing a new line or discontinuing the existing line.

— where severe competition is being met and it is desired to reduce the selling price, the affect of any reduction on profits can be easily ascertained.

— where the reduction in selling price is intended to increase sales, the increase necessary to allow to earn the previous profit can be calculated.

— the controlability and postponability of expenditure can be worked out from the break even point.

— it helps in planning and managerial control.

— break-even point can be helpful in detecting the effect of gradual changes that may have crept into the operation of budget planning and evaluating new proposals and alternative courses of action.

Thus the utility of Break-even analysis to the management lies in the fact that it represents a cross-sectional view of the profit structure. It highlight the areas of economic strength and weaknesses in the firm.

Assumptions Underlying Break Even Analysis

Following are the assumptions which are taken into consideration before drawing the Break Even Analysis.

1. All costs are perfectly variable over the entire range of volume of production.
2. All costs are absolutely fixed over the entire range of volume of production.
3. All revenue is perfectly variable with the physical volume of production.
4. The volume of sales and volume of production are equal.
5. For multi-products firms the product mix should be stable.

Following are a few terms which are commonly used in Break Even Analysis. These are :

1. Margin of safety. 2. Angle of incidence. 3. Contribution.

Margin of Safety

Margin of safety is the output at full capacity—the output at break even point (it is the difference between output at full capacity— output at break even point) which may be expressed as percentage of output at full capacity. If the margin of safety is small, a small drop in production capacity will reduce the profits considerably.

Angle of incidence

It is the angle at which income line or sales line cuts the total cost line. If the angle is large, it is an indication that profits are being made at a high rate. On the other hand, if the angle is, small, it indicates that profits are being made and are achieved under less favourable conditions.

Contribution

Contribution is the difference between sales and marginal cost. It is also called as marginal profits or gross margins.

The marginal profit provides the contribution towards fixed cost and profit. If contribution is less than the fixed cost the loss is incurred. If the selling price is reduced, contribution will also be reduced assuming variable cost remains unchanged.

Break Even chart is an aid to management in decision making. It is a graphical representation of sale and cost informations. It shows the manager the profitability of an undertaking at various levels of activity.

The break even chart is needed where the business is new or a new product is introduced. In fact, the concept of break even assist the management to appreciate the significance of quantity in relation to price. The objective of the chart is to indicate what happens to total costs and total revenues as output and sales change from one level to another. The genuine structure of the break even chart shows on horizontal axis the measure of output such as physical volume of production, percentage of full capacity output or sales volume. The sales lines relates total revenue on the vertical axis to total output on horizontal axis and is always drawn as straight line. There are usually two components variable costs (assumed to vary with output) and constant costs (assumed in independent of output) the vertical distance between total sales and cost is total profit at output greater than break even point and at the output less than this represents losses. The break even chart is shown in Fig. 72.1.

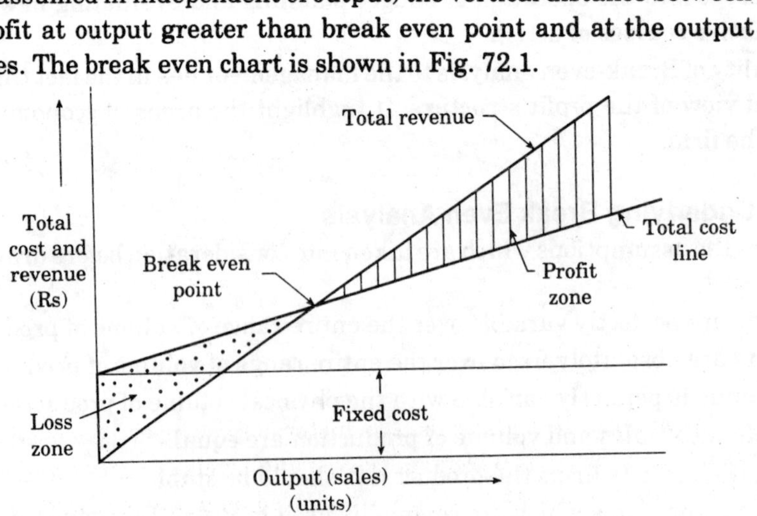

Fig. 72.1

Contribution to Overhead and Profit

Fig. 72.2 readily gives us at a glance the contribution to overhead and profits. The short term decision making is more concerned with contribution to both overhead and profits than it is to the profit figure alone.

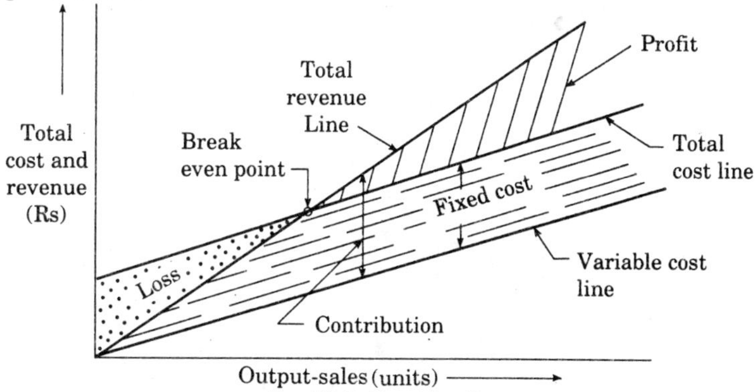

Fig. 72.2. Contribution.

Construction of Break Even Chart

The plotting of Break even chart is normally in the following two ways :

1. **Analytical Approach.** In this approach we take one single income statement for the firm. The manager confines himself with the concept that if output is increased it will increase the expense also and he estimates the amount of increased spending. This process may have to abandon the linearity assumptions upon which the break even chart are constructed as shown in Fig. 72.3.

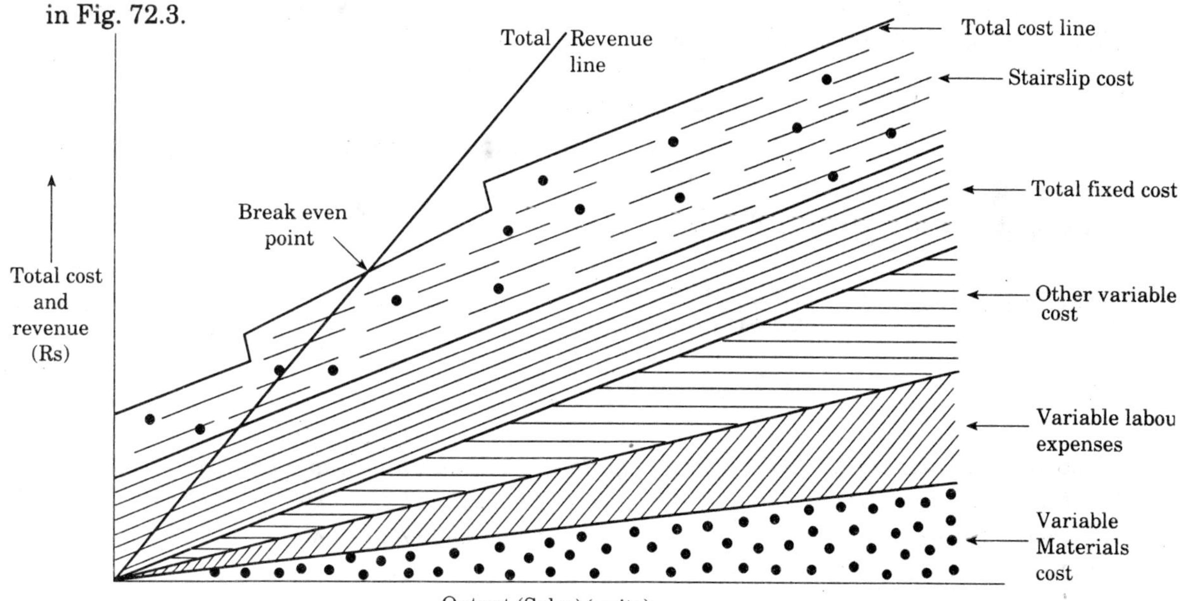

Fig. 72.3. Non-Linear Cost Break Even Chart.

2. **Statistical Approach.** It is also called as historical approach because in this approach series of income statements periods which reflect varying levels of output and costs are taken. In this approach the output and cost relations are plotted on a scatter diagram and if the cost output relation is linear we can draw back the total cost line back to the vertical axis.

Calculations of Break Even

Let S = Sales price

V = Variable or marginal cost

F = Fixed cost

P = Profit

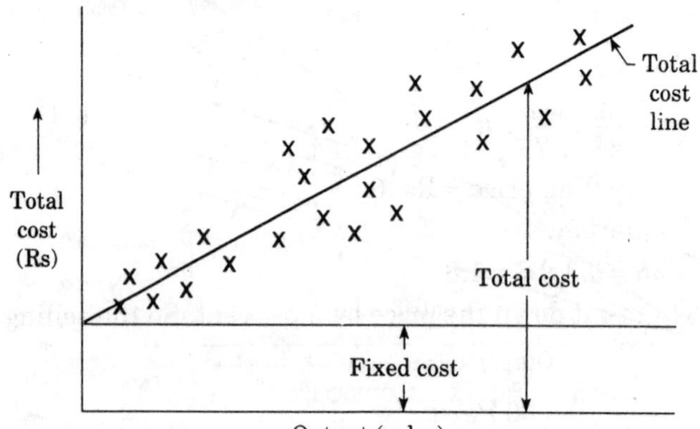

Fig. 72.4 Finding Total Cost from a Scatter Diagram.

Let $S - V = P + F$ ... (*i*)

At break even $P = 0$

Equation (*i*) reduces to

$$S - V = F \quad \text{...}(ii)$$

Let us multiply both sides of Equation (*ii*) by S

$$S(S - V) = F \times S$$

$$S = \frac{F \times S}{S - V} = \frac{F \times S}{\frac{S - V}{S}} = \frac{\text{Fixed Cost}}{\text{Contribution per unit}}$$

Sales at B.E.P (Rupee-Value) $\frac{F \times S}{S - V}$

Sales at B.E.P. unit $= \frac{\text{Fixed Cost}}{\text{Contribution per unit}}$

$= \frac{\text{Fixed Cost}}{\text{Marginal profit per unit}}$

Example. *A company "A" sold 2,50,000 gallons paints with variable cost of Rs. 4.20 per gallon. Each gallon contribute 30% of its revenue to fixed costs and profits.*

This year the company is contemplating a price reduction of 5 per cent.

(i) How many more gallons will the company have to sell at years 5 per cent price reduction in order to earn the same profit this the as lost ?

Solution. Total Revenue = Fixed cost + Profit + Variable cost.

Divide both sides by numbers of units.

Sales price = Fixed cost/units × Variable cost/unit + Profit/unit ...(*i*)

Let us assume that sales price be = Rs. x

It is also given that 30% of contribution goes to the fixed cost and profits per gallon of paint

(Fixed cost + Profit) = 0.3 x ...(*ii*)

Putting the value in equation

$$x = 0.3x + 4.20 \qquad ...(i)$$

$$(x - 0.3)x = 4.20$$

$$0.7x = 4.2$$

$$x = \frac{4.2}{0.7} = \frac{42}{7} = 6$$

$$x = \text{Selling price} = \text{Rs. } 6$$

So putting the value in equation

(Fixed cost + Profit)/gallon = 0.3 × 6 = 1.8 ...(*ii*)

It is given in the problem to cut down the price by 5 per cent. So the selling (New) price per unit

$$= \frac{6 \times 5}{100} = 30 \text{ Paise}$$

New selling price = 5.70 Paise

We know that $Q = \dfrac{(F \times P)}{S - V}$ ...(*iii*)

With change in the selling price

$$Q_n = \frac{(F + P)}{S_n - V}$$

$$Q_n = \frac{1.8}{5.70 - 4.20} \times Q = Q \times \frac{1.8}{1.5} = 1.2$$

$$= 2{,}50{,}000 \times 1.2 = 3{,}00{,}000$$

$$Q_n - Q = 3{,}00{,}000 - 2{,}50{,}000 = 50{,}000$$

In order to reduce the price from Rs. 6 to Rs. 5.70, we are to produce 50,000 additional units.

Principles of Break Even Analysis

The break even analysis involves following principles :

1. To find the safety margin with proposed volume.
2. To find the quality needed to have desired profit.
3. To find the effect of change in price.
4. To find the effect of change in costs.
5. To find whether to accept an order or not.
6. To find whether to add or drop a product line.
7. To find whether to make or buy.

1. Finding safety margin. The safety margin refers to the extent to which the company can afford to decline in sales before it starts incurring losses. The safety margin can be represented by the percentage ratio of sales over break even volume to volume of sales.

$$\text{Safety Margin} = \frac{(\text{Sales} - \text{B.E.P.})}{\text{Sales}} \times 100$$

2. Quality needed to have desired profit.. This is one of the most common application of break even analysis.

The formula used to find the desired quantity is :

$$\text{Target quantity} = \frac{\text{Fixed cost + Target profit}}{\text{Contribution per unit}}$$

3. Effect of change in price. This problem with which the management is most often faced whether to reduce prices or not. To take this decision the management will have to consider the following points.

Reduction in price leads to reduction in contribution margin and thereby increasing the sales volume. But at times reduction in price may not always lead to proportional increase in the volume of sales which depends on the elasticity of demand of the product. The information about elasticity of demand may not be easily available. The change in the break even point due to change of price is drawn below.

A different price levels, total revenue lines can be drawn as shown in Fig. 72.5. From the chart one can then estimate the volume that will be sold and produced at each price and thus profit at each price value.

$$Q \text{ (B.E.P. in units)} = \frac{F + P}{S - V} \qquad ...(iii)$$

S = Sales price

V = Variable cost

F = Fixed cost

P = Profit

As price changes equation (*iii*) changes

$$Q_1 \text{ (New B.E.P. in units)} = \frac{F + X}{S_n - V}$$

S_n = New sales price

R_1 = New B.E.P. in units

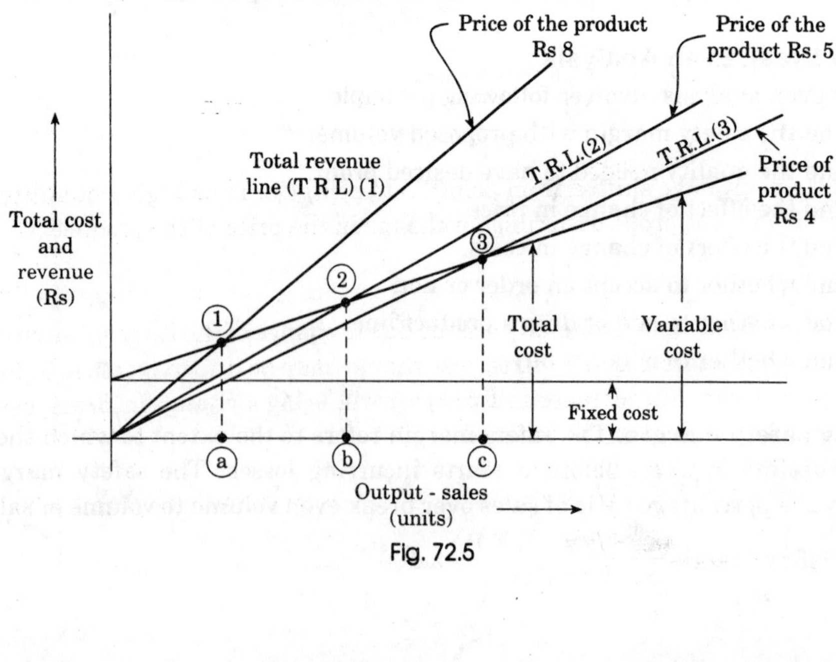

Fig. 72.5

4. Effect of change in costs. The change in costs can be grouped as change in the variable costs and change in the fixed costs.

Variable Cost Change

An increase in variable cost leads to reduction in the contribution margin. Now immediate question in mind is what should be the sales volume to maintain our present profit without change in the price or what should be the new price to maintain the present profit without any change in the sales volume.

$$Q = \frac{F + T}{S - V};$$

$$Q_1 = \frac{F + T}{S - V_n}$$

Q_1 = New break even points

V_n = New variable cost

The new selling price will be $S_n = S + (V_n - V)$

These relations can be graphically shown as follows :

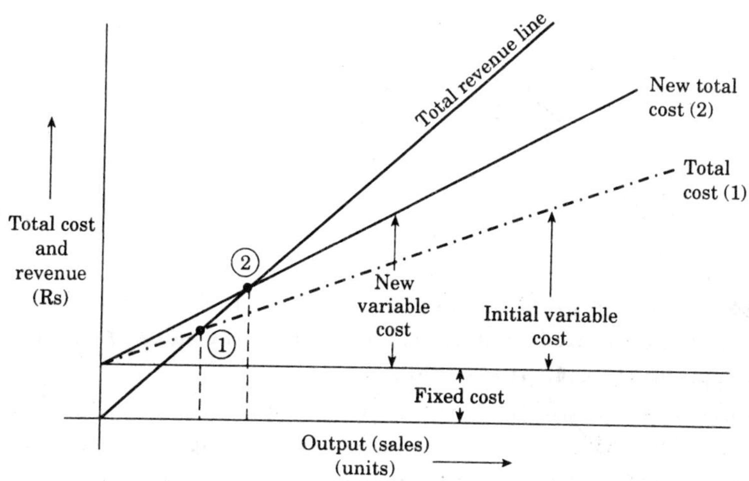

Fig. 72.6. Units

The break even point have shifted from point (1) to point (2). Thus higher quantity is to be sold to maintain the present profit assuming no change in the price of the product.

Fixed Cost Change

An increase in the fixed costs a company may be due to change of the external environments in which the company is operating. The fixed cost change may be due to increase in executive salaries, property taxes etc. An increase in fixed cost will bring a change in Break even point assuming no change in the price of the product.

$$Q = \frac{F + P}{S - V} \qquad ...(iv)$$

$$Q_n = \frac{F_n - P}{S - V} \qquad ...(v)$$

Solving (*iv*) and (*v*)

$$Q_n - Q = \frac{F_n - P}{S - V} \quad ...(vi)$$

$$S_n = S + \frac{F_n - F}{Q} \quad ...(vii)$$

Q_n = New Break Even Point.

F_n —New Fixed Cost.

S_n —New Selling Price.

This can be represented graphically as shown below :

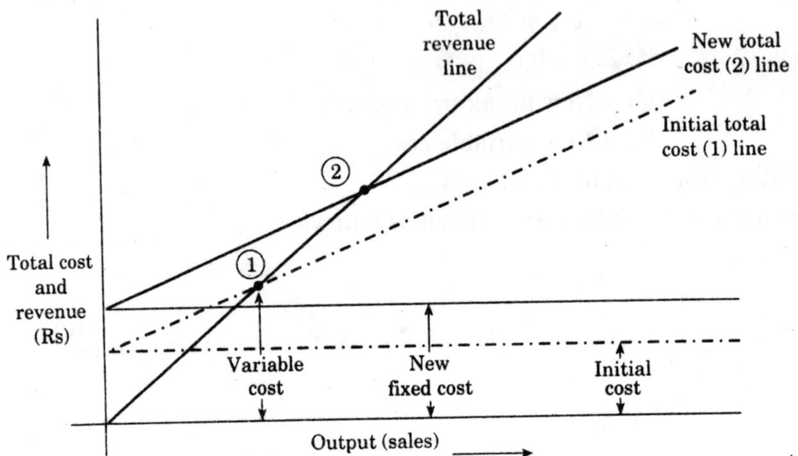

Fig. 72.7

The Break even point has shifted from point (1) to point (2) if there is no change in price and volume of profit is maintained or there will be a rise in the sales price if there is no change in the sales volume provided profit is maintained.

5. **To accept an order or not.** Quite often the management is faced with an alternative to accept an order at a price with less than the selling price if extra capacity to produce a product is available. Company can accept an order which meets not only the direct cost but also contribute towards common cost.

A company manufacturing a certain component was operating at 50 per cent of the capacity. A foreign importer offerred to purchase 5,000 units of the component at Rs. 5 per unit (The average cost of the product is Rs. 6.00). The question was whether the order should be accepted. The cost data were as follows :

Total capacity	20,000 components
Actual output	10,000 ,,
Direct material	Rs. 10,000
Direct labour	Rs. 10,000
Fixed expenses	Rs. 40,000
Total cost	Rs. 60,000
Average cost	Rs. 6 per unit.

If we look into the problem deeply, we find that the additional cost of producing 5,000 units would be only Rs. 10,000 (Rs. 5,000 for materials and Rs. 5,000 for labour). The incremental revenue would be Rs. 25,000 and the firm would gain Rs. 15,000 by accepting this order. In fact, it would be profitable for the firm to accept anything more than Rs. 2.00 which is the direct cost per unit. Thus for highly competitive situation, what is more important is that at least the direct costs must be covered. But if the customers learn that the component is being sold at a lower price, they may also demand a similar price cut or else threaten to cancel their orders. So what is necessary is that the acceptance of this order should be kept a secret.

In the long run, the aggregate revenues from all products must cover not only the direct costs but also contribute towards common cost. Ideally, each product should make a significant contribution to common costs, but it is not possible to state any general rule for determining satisfactory or unsatisfactory contributions. If factors of competition prevent a firm from setting a price of one of its products that will cover direct costs, there may be no alternative but to discontinue that product.

If a competitive price does cover direct costs and yields some contribution to common costs, the question arises 'how high must that contribution to be justify long-run continuance of that product in a company's line'? The question can be answered in the light of availability. But if the product is discontinued, there are others which must be substituted for it so that there is a higher contribution to common costs. The elimination of one product from the line may cause the loss of sale of other complementary products. Product pricing decisions should be made with a view to maximise company profits in the long-run.

6. **Whether to add or drop a product line.** Any executive in a business organisation will be confronted with following problems when he decides among the two alternatives of add or drop a product line :

1. Should a new product be added in view of the estimated revenue and cost ?
2. If the product is dropped from the product line, what would be the consequent effects on revenues and costs. The break even analysis is quite helpful in deciding the question of product planning.

In a medium size industry, the following datas are given :

Product	*Price Rs.*	*Variable Cost Rs.*	*% Sales Units*
A	6	4	30
B	10	6	20
C	20	12	50

Fixed cost per year = Rs. 7,500

Total sales of the three products = 2,50,000 units

It was decided by the management to drop the Product *B* and introduce the product *D*. To find out whether it is worth while to drop product *B* and introduce product *D*.

Product	*Price (Rs).*	*Variable Cost per unit Rs.*	*% Sales Units*
A	6	4	50
D	16	6	10
C	20	12	40

Total fixed cost per year = Rs. 7,500

Sales for the current year = Rs. 26,000

Solution. Product A contribution is Rs. (6 – 4) = Rs. 2. We have the sales price of Rs. 6 or in other words for the selling price of Rs. 6, we get a contribution of Rs. 2. The contribution for 33% sales of product A shall be

$$\frac{6-4}{6} \times 30\% = 1/3 \times 30\% = 0.10$$

Similarly for Product B,

$$\frac{10-6}{10} \times 20\% = 0.08$$

For Product C,

$$\frac{20-12}{20} \times 50\% = 0.20$$

Thus the contribution ratio for product A, B and C is 0.38

$$= (0.10 + 0.08 + 0.20) = 0.38.$$

Total sales in Rs. 25,000

$$= 25{,}000 \times 0.38 = 9{,}500$$

Profit $= 9{,}500 - 7{,}500 = 2{,}000$ profit

Similarly the profit or contribution on new product line of products A, B and C,

$$= \frac{6-4}{6} \times 50\% = 0.17 = \frac{16-6}{16} \times 10\% = 0.06$$

$$= \frac{20-12}{20} - 40\% = 0.16$$

Thus contribution ratio is 0.39

Total sales $= 26{,}000 = 0.39 = 10{,}140$

Profit $= 10{,}140 - 7{,}500 =$ Rs. 2,640

Hence the proposed change is worth taking.

7. Make or Buy. Break even analysis helps us to a greater extent in resolving the decision on Make or Buy. Make or Buy decisions are vertical integration decisions. Make or buy is specific. It is used to decide whether to utilise the production facilities or not.

Example. *A car manufacturer buys a component at Rs. 10 each. If he decides to make it himself his fixed and variable cost will be Rs. 10,000 and Rs. 5 per component respectively. To decide whether to make or buy the component.*

$$\underset{\text{(Quantity)}}{\text{B.E.P.}} = \frac{\text{Fixed Cost}}{\text{Purchase Price} - \text{Variable Cost}}$$

$$= \frac{10{,}000}{10-5} = 2000 \text{ components.}$$

Now interpretation is that if the car manufacturer wants more than 2,000 components it should be manufactured in the plant and for more than 2,000 components should buy from the same supplier.

Scope

Break even analysis can be most helpful in detecting the effect of gradual changes that may have crept into the operating relationship, checking the proposals, soundness, budget planning and evaluating new alternatives.

Budget Planning

The detection of creep can be accelerated by applying break even analysis in budget planning, and the overall soundness of a new budget can be tested as well. The approach under these circumstances would be through a break even chart, comparing the break even point determined from flexible budget figures with the break even point of past operations, and comparing budgeted profit with the profit that should be earned at the budgeted volume according to the break even chart.

Evaluating New Proposals and Alternatives

Proposals to add or drop a product line, changes in selling prices, changes in a manufacturing process, makes a part instead of purchasing it, or take similar courses of action should first be evaluated in terms of the effect on profits at expected operating levels. A secondary consideration however, should be effected on the "cushion" between expected operating levels and the break even point. Knowledge that a change will drastically reduce the cushion should receive careful consideration in determining whether such reduction is too great a price to pay for anticipated benefits.

The Break even analysis is useful in the area of managerial planning and review, including detection of unplanned change, overall review of budget planning, and evaluation of new proposals and alternative actions. The technical problems of break-even analysis, we know that no consideration has been given to such matters as changes in production mix, price level changes, allocation of fixed costs between plants or products, or non-linear cost factors. These factors are, however, of major importance and must be given due consideration in break even point determinations.

Limitations

The static break even has serious limitations which we normally ignore. The limitations are:

1. Errors of estimating the true static cost-function.
2. Over simplification of static revenue function. The dynamic forces shift and modify the static functioning and managerial adoption to altered environment.
3. Profits are residuals, the profit function gets the full impact of these inaccuracies.
4. The correlation between output and selling does not mean a stable relation. Because the salesmen's commissions may be function of sales. Similarly advertising appropriation is determined by certain percentage of expected sales. Thus correlation between output and selling is not a true functional relationship. The output may depart from forecasts which are causing changes in advertising plan.
5. Plotting Company's past cost and revenue, is plotting its migration path, this has little validity for current profit forecasting.
6. The other drawback of break even chart is the wage and materials price increase causing trouble because they are nonreversible.

7. The lines drawn between cost and income are straight lines but these lines should be wary line. We know that if production goes beyond a certain point, we have to give overtime, may have to put second shift and add more supervisors and resulting much higher cost at once. The straight line assumption may also be fallacious on the extreme right side of our charts because of our capacity limitations.
8. The lines on break even chart should be bands or zones extending across the chart and not these lines only.
9. Output indices used in most break even analysis are not very satisfactory.
10. The break even chart is based on the past data and information which are not adjusted for changes in wages, changes in price of raw materials. These adjustments are quite cumbersome. We should use analytical techniques to avoid these adjustments.
11. The chart assume that the price of the output are given. This assumption of horizontal demand curve holds true only for a perfect competition only.
12. Break even charts are based on arbitrary assumptions as to the relative importance of different products in multiproduct firms.
13. The simple break even chart makes no provision for corporate income tax. If company cause profit and suffers loss every alternative year then the adjustment for taxes is quite difficult.
14. The break even chart concentrate mainly on short run cost functions and thus neglecting the other cost elements of the enterprise cost structure which in turn effect the accuracy of short run cost-function.
15. The break even chart is an over simplification of expected profits at various levels of output. The assumption that profit is a single valued function of output is wrong. The profit indeed varies with output, but it also changes with changes in production plants, the intensity of selling efforts.

According to Elwood Buffa, the break even point is really a bolt on the chart and not a point.

Break even analysis may be useless for certain companies because of the wide fluctuation in price and predominant cost. When product mix varies greatly, profit margins differ among products, advertising or sales promotion are highly shifting, product design and technology change cautiously over short periods then it is very difficult to use break even analysis.

73

Inventory Control

Introduction

Inventory constitute one of the most important elements of any system dealing with the supply, manufacture and distribution of goods and services. The concept of inventory control is very old by it came in light when Harris F.W. published his work on classical order size model.

This work was extended by Raymond F.E. (1931) and Wilson R.M. (1934). But only after the second world war with the development of operational research and computer technology that the theoretical concepts got a practical application. The basic purpose of inventory holding stocks in a material flow system is to decouple successive stages of system. Following are important purposes of inventory :

1. Existence of time lags between manufacturing, and transport operations.
2. The need to schedule various stages of the system independently.
3. The need to meet the fluctuation in demand and production rates.
4. The need to maintain control over the quality of the finished product.
5. The need to exercise influence over changes of materials prices particularly basic raw materials.

All the above factors involve costs. The inventory control mainly concerned with making optimum decision with respect to the variables which are subject to control. Inventory control is a multi-item, and multi-stage in nature. Inventory is an idle resource which is useable and have value. The idle resource may be men, money, materials, plant acquisition. Many man-power, capital and plant acquisition problems are essentially inventory control problems.

The scientific inventory management helps the purchase department to determine when to buy and how much to buy. The problem before the management is to balance the following opposing costs.

S. No.	*Cost to have Inventory*	*Cost not to have Inventory*
1.	Return on Investment	Stock out costs.
2.	Storage cost	(Demand × Profitability × Future)
3.	Handling cost (Labour and Industry)	Loss of customers.
4.	Handling Equipment	Down time cost.
5.	Obsolescence	Idle Labour and idle Production.
6.	Spoilage and Shelf life	Capacity and other cost.

The inventory control can also be defined as a system of internal check to control. We know that inventory tie up a sizable part of working capital and also cost a good deal to carry them. Money resources are scarce and efforts should be directed to conserve it by all means.

Inventory is money but it is not at all like money in the bank but it is the money in which we pay interest instead of earning interest. Arriving at a level between too much and too little stock is a real challenge to the management. The uncontrolled inventories are dangerous and at times it is called as graveyard of business.

The inventory control exist in some form in every plant. The system in a particular company may be formal or informal, cheap or expensive. In one case control may depend upon the efforts of a large central staff while in another the responsibility may rest with the plant manager and the foreman. Even systems used in similar plants, differ in outward appearance at least.

Production planning coordinates the production department with other department of the business. Production control promotes effective shop operation through its control of activities within the production department itself.

Inventory control determines the levels of composition of inventories of parts, materials and products which will protect most effectively the production, sales, and financial requirements of the business.

A system of production planning and control is not an end in itself. It can only be justified because it :

1. Provides the means for effective coordination of the Production department with other departments of the business ; and
2. Promotes effective shop operation through its control of activities within the production department itself.

In any given company a good system of planning will strike the best balance possible between the required amount of control and the overhead cost entailed in achieving it. If tight control cost not more than loose control management would of course try to attain the maximum control possible in a particular situation. This is not the case. The tighter the control a system produces, the more overheads is required to operate it.

Every businessman must have faced the problem of either being out of stock or a large amount of money tied up in the form of inventories., Inventory is an civil which cannot be eliminated. On the other hand large level of inventories hamper the growth of the company. Inventory control is to determine the optimum level of inventory which is essential to carry out the various operations of the organisation efficiently and effectively.

Inventory control is essential for effective plant operations. The inventory carrying charges from 12% to 22% of inventory value with the average near 18%. A company with restricted working capital is always in a dangerous position and there is no easier way to dissipate working capital than to build up excessive inventory.

Definition of Inventory

1.Inventory in wider sense is defined as any idle resource of an enterprise. It is commonly used to indicate materials-raw, in process, finished, packaging, spares and others—stocked in order to meet an expected demand or distribution in the future. Even though inventory of materials is an idle resource in the sense it is not meant for immediate use, it is almost a necessity to maintain some inventories for the smooth functioning of an organisation.

2. Inventory is made of all those items ready for sale or of items which keep the process running.

Why Inventories are Essential

In some circles inventories are thought of as a sign of wealth, even excess inventories in relation to the magnitude of production and distribution function are considered advantageous. On the other hand, the wise businessman place more emphasis on having working capital in the form of cash and securities. In recent years a greater emphasis has been placed on having the means of purchasing materials than having the materials themselves. Excessive inventories have been the death of many a business and very high inventory levels have tipped the scale in our economy.

The finished product after packaging are first stored and sent to the market as the need arises or orders are received. Also the raw materials needed for the finished product cannot be directly fed to the production department from the market. These have to be stored first after procurement. These things put together give an idea of stored these items. This process of storing is called inventory.

Necessity and Advantages of Inventory Control

There are various reasons why organisations should maintain inventories of goods. The fundamental reason for doing so is that it is either physically impossible or economically unsound to have goods arrive in a given system precisely when demands for them arises. Without inventories customers would have to wait until their orders were filled from a source or were manufactured. In general, however, customers will not or cannot be allowed to wait for long periods of time. For this reason alone the carrying of inventories is necessary for almost all organisation that supply physical goods to customers.

There are, nevertheless, other reasons for holding inventories. For example, the price of some raw materials used by manufacturers may exhibit considerable seasonal fluctuations. When the price is low, it is profitable for him to procure a sufficient quantity of it to last through the high price seasons and to keep it in inventory to be used as need in production. Another reason for maintaining inventories, a reason particularly important to retail establishments, is that sales and profits can be increased if one has an inventory of goods to display to customer. Furthermore to even out the work loads on the shops in the event of fluctuating loads and a protective buffer against transportation delays and production rate changes.

Advantages :

1. Introduction of a proper inventory control system helps in keeping the investment in the inventories as low as feasible.
2. Ensures availability of material by providing adequate protection against uncertainties of supplies and consumption of materials.
3. Allows full advantage of economics of bulk purchases and transportation.
4. Reduces changes of going out of stock.
5. Leads to reduction in inventory levels.
6. Releases more of capital for other operations.
7. Increases profitability of an organisation.

8. Adequate customer service.
9. Advantage of price discounts by bulk purchasing.
10. Providing flexibility to allow changes in production plans due to changes in demands or any other reason ; and
11. Even out the work loads on the shops in the face fluctuating demands.

Evils of Excess Inventory

1. Essential though they are, inventories also mean lock up capital of an inventories which could be invested in more profitable operations.
2. Excess inventory adds to the cost of carrying the inventory more store space, equipment and personnel, insurances, taxes, pilferage etc.
3. Excess inventory invites risk or deterioration and obsolescence.
4. Changes in the prices of inventory materials sometime go unfavourable.
5. Maintenance of cost money.

Control Aspect of Inventory

A company which finds that different portions of its inventory present different problems will have three general methods of control to choose from . These are :

1. Elimination of certain inventories.
2. Semi automatic routines.
3. Periodic review.

Eliminations

At first glance, elimination inventory may seem a strange form of control. In some instances it is the most sensible form possible. It is more feasible to eliminate the inventories entirely if little advance information is available on exact specifications and quantities. Steel plate is one item required in the manufacture of every unit, if the firm did carry inventory, this would be one material it would have to stock, however, where one customer specifies 1″ plate, another calls for $1\frac{1}{2}$″. In the view of these facts the company does not order steel plates until the actual specifications for each order area at hand., This solution is possible because the manufacturing interval is very long and vendors can provide the required plate in a reasonable period.

Semi-automatic

The semi-automatic types of control are usually variations of the maximum minimum system. They are most applicable for standard items with fairly stable prices and steady usage. For materials which do not possess these characteristics, maximum-minimum control offers few advantages. This system is usually established by considering the minimum balance desirable, the re-order point, the standard order quantity, and the maximum allowable the minimum balance is the point below which the minimum represents is determined by the rate at which an item is used, its size and cost its similar factors, importance in the process, whether substitutes are available and by ideally, a new shipment should arrive just as stock reaches this minimum. Slight variation in usage or delivery intervals will prevent such exact operation in practice. The order point is located somewhere above the minimum. Its exact location will depend upon the delivery or manufacturing intervals required after an order is placed and upon the usage rate of a particular item. When the available balances reaches the order point, a clerk will note this fact and place an order. The standard quantity is that amount of material which will be requisitioned each time available balances drop to the order point. This quantity is determined by considering such things as vendors' discounts, economic lot sizes, storage and handling costs, order processing costs, the danger of obsolescence and desired rates of turnover. The maximum minimum type of systems offer semi-automatic control over inventories which have the characteristics mentioned in the first paragraph of this section. The phrase semi-automatic should be emphasised because it is the key to successful operation of the system. The precise amounts established as minimum order points and adhering to them, given the system an appearance of exactness and automaticity which it does not always possess.

Periodic Review

The third type of inventory control might be called 'periodic review' for want of a better term. All the factors considered under the maximum-minimum system are applicable here. But definite points are established in advance. The interval will be shortest where :

1. price of usage fluctuates widely.
2. cost is high.
3. shortages are apt to be critical.
4. there is considerable risk of obsolescence.
5. materials are bulky.
6. delivery or manufacturing cycles are long.

These three methods of control are not mutually exclusive. One company may use any or all of them to control different categories of inventory. Some commodities, such as special motors, may not be ordered until their use and specifications can be established exactly.

The inventory control system is a composite of many routine operations.

Types of Inventory

1. Transaction inventory
2. Speculative inventory
3. Precautionary inventory.

1. **Transaction inventory.** It is formed basically of those items which are basically needed for transaction for example transaction of finished saleable products or transaction of raw materials.

(*a*) *Delinking production with purchasing Department* is one of the function of this for example receipt of raw material is stored in the form of inventory and whenever production department needs raw material it put indent to inventory organisation rather than to purchase department.

(*b*) *Delinking production with sales organisation.* Similarly it delinks sales and production departments.

2. **Speculative Inventory.** It is basically kept as a measure of speculation of increase in the price of raw material or increase the sale price of finished goods. It is generally resorted to before the budget proposals.

3. **Precautionary Inventory.** The machines are to be kept running. There may be breakdown of machines at any time due to damage of any part due to wear and tear. At that time it cannot be purchased immediately. Therefore, such items, which are essential to keep the process running are to be stored like machine parts tools etc. It is also called maintenance repair and operation inventory.

There are another way of classifying various types of industrial inventories such as :

1. **Production Inventories.** Raw materials parts, and components which go into the manufacturing process of the company products.

2. **M.R.O. Inventories.** Maintenance, Repair and Operating supplies which are consumed in the production process but which do not form a part of the product (often known as Consumables).

3. **In-process Inventories.** Semi-finished products at various stages in the production operation.

4. **Finished Goods Inventories.** Completed products ready for shipment.

Different Technique of Inventory Analysis

Altogether the company deals with stocks of thousands of items raising a serious problem or how one can keep control or track of all items ; also, whether is it necessary to have the same extent of control on each and every item. Different types of analysis each having its own specific advantages and purpose, help in bringing a practical solution to the control of inventory. The most important of all such analysis is *ABC* analysis. The others are :

V.E.D. — (Vital, Essential, Desirable) Analysis.

S.D.E. — (Scarce, Difficult, Easily Available) Analysis.

H.M.L. — (High, Medium, Low cost) Analysis.

F.S.N. — (Fast, Slow, Non Moving items) Analysis.

ABC Analysis

Any average medium size organisation consumes a few thousand tons of stores. An organisation choosing high degree of control of each item would, therefore, neither be practical considering the work involved, nor worthwhile since not all items are of equal importance. Hence it desirable to classify or group of items depending upon their importance and subject each class or group of items to control, commensurate with importance. This is the principle of selective control as applied to inventories and the technique of grouping is termed as A.B.C. analysis or classification which it said to be "Always Better Control". The basis of analysing the annual consumption cost goes after the principal "Vital Few"—"Trival Many" and criterion used here is the money spent and not the quantity consumed. The following Fig. 73.1 brings out clearly the concept of ABC Analysis.

'A' Items

From the graph and analysis it may be found that about 8% of items cost more than 75% of the cost on inventory. This is classified as *'A'* items. These are the most important items from the control point of view. These should be ordered and scheduled for receipt on a monthly, weekly or even daily basis in order to keep the investment on them as low as possible. Their movement through the shop should have high priority and the movement time kept at a minimum. Safety

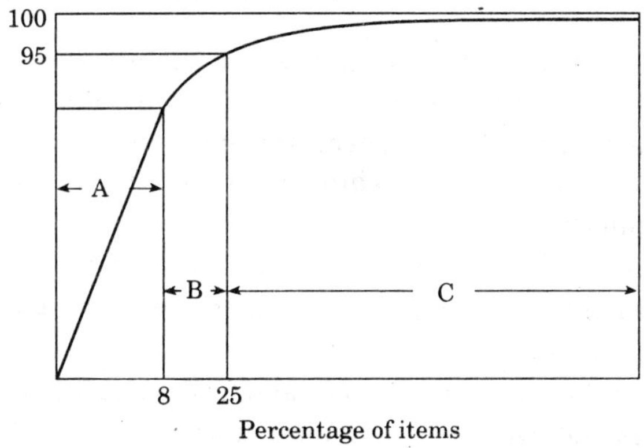

Fig. 73.1

stock or reserve stock on such items should be kept to an absolute minimum. A close watch on the ordering, follow up stocking and issue of these items are a must for economy on Inventory.

Control on Policies for A Items

The measure to taken on *'A'* items can be briefly put down as follows :

1. Annual or half yearly contracts for supplies with as frequent staggered deliveries as is economical.
2. Develop and revise more often ordering quantities, reorder points and safety stocks for items not covered by long terms contracts as indicated in item 1.
3. Frequently reviewing of stock position and consumption patterns and maintenance of records of issues and stock to enable to get the up-to-date position of stocks at any time.
4. Precise quality specifications or material standard.
5. As far as possible, two or more suppliers should be sought for each item so that the dependency on one supplier is not there. Due to any contingencies the other supplier could be approached.
6. The control of *'A'* items should be directly under the charge of Purchasing Manager himself.
7. As these items are to be stocked to a minimum level, the purchase department should pay maximum attention to expedite the delivery of the items.
8. Waste control measures to reduce the scrap, rejection, rework and substandards.
9. Continuous development work or research carried out wherever possible.

'B' Items

These are of secondary importance and in between *'A'* and *'C'* items. Even though, they do not require as detailed and close control as *'A'* items, they need more attention and control than *C* items. The minimum stock and economic order quantity of these items should be calculated based on the average consumption lead time for prominent, cost of inventory holding etc.

"C" Items

"C" items are the numerous in expensive items *i.e.* about 70% of the items contributing to only 50% or near about of the total cost on material. However, these items may be critical items which may hold up production in case of their non-availability. These items are to be purchased

in large quantities in order to secure purchase discounts and minimise time and effort required by order clerks, store keepers and accountants, the company should carry say six months to one year stock of these items taking into consideration storage facilities available and storage costs.

Advantages of ABC Analysis

1. Preference for keeping inventory can be placed properly after ABC analysis.
2. Stores personnel are placed better with this analysis *i.e.* their time can be utilized better.
3. Storing, handling and delivery of material to production department become better.
4. We know *'C'* items take more time in review as they are more in number. Review can be decided accordingly.

VED-Analysis

This analysis specially pertains to the classification of maintenance spare denoting the essentiality of stocking spares.

V—Stands for vital-items when go out of stock or when not readily available, completely bring the production to a halt.

E—Stands for Essential-items without which temporary losses of production or dislocation of production or work occurs.

D—Stands or Desirable-all other items which are necessary but do not cause any immediate effect on production.

SDE-Analysis

For developing countries and especially where certain items are in scarce supply, this analysis is very useful.

S—Stands for Scarce items, especially imported items and also those which are very much in short supply.

D—Stands for Difficult items which are available in the market but not easily available. For example, items which have to come far off cities.

E—Items which are easily available ; mostly local items.

HML-Analysis

The cost per item (per piece) is considered for this analysis. High cost terms (*H*) Medium cost terms (*M*) and low cost items (*L*) help in bringing controls over consumption at all departments level.

FSN-Analysis

Here the quantity and rate of consumption is analysed to be classified as Fast-moving (*F*), Slow Moving (*S*) and Non-Moving (*N*) items.

Techniques of Inventory Control Ordering System

With the discussion on general inventory policies for the different groups of items *A, B* and *C*, there are two basic problems of inventory control :

1. What quantity of an item should be ordered each time.
2. When should an order be placed.

There are four cost factors in the picture when we try to seek a solution to these problems. These are :

(a) The cost of materials itself.
(b) The costs associated with keeping the materials in stock (*Inventory carrying charges.*)
(c) The cost associated with the placement of a purchase order (*ordering costs.*)
(d) Carrying Inventory.

The price of material is by far the most important and for items with frequent unexpected price variations (speculative item) 1, and 2 are totally dictated by price and no set rules are possible. However, most of the items have more or less steady prices over substantial periods of time and for these items the price has less influence on how much and when to order.

The inventory carrying cost and ordering cost are considered here.

The Inventory Carrying Cost

These arise out of the following factors :

1. Interest charges (4 to 5%).
2. Insurance cost (1 to 3%)—protection against fire, theft, etc.
3. Property taxes (1 to 3%).
4. Storage Cost (Rent) (0 to 3%)
5. Obsolescence and deterioration cost (4 to 10%)
6. Stationary and other consumable used by the stores.
7. Depreciation and repairs cost for the stores facilities and handling equipment.

These costs come nearly 20 to 25%. These costs are arbitrary and vary from industry to industry and from item to item even in the same industry.

Ordering Cost or Acquisition Cost of Items

Placement of a purchase order for a material is associated with certain obvious cost due to advertising, consumption of stationary and postage, telephone charges, telegrams etc. In fact all the annual expenditure of the purchasing department of a company can be considered to be on the purchase orders it places during the year. The cost associated with ordering would, therefore consist of

1. Salaries of the staff in administration and purchase department.
2. Rent for the space used by the purchasing department.
3. The postage, telegram and telephone bills.
4. The stationary and other consumable required by the purchasing department.
5. Entertainment charges on vendors.
6. Travelling expenses.
7. Lawyers and court fees due to any legal matters arising out of purchase.

These all usually come to 20—25% as ordering cost. Obviously more the number of orders placed in a period, the more would be the stationary and postage consumed, more staff and officers will be required for handling the work, the more will be the space required for accommodating them and so on. Thus the total expenditure on purchasing or ordering would depend on the numbers of orders placed. It is assumed that the expenditure on ordering of material is directly proportional to the number of orders placed.

The ordering cost is expressed as the cost/order and is calculated by dividing the total ordering cost during a year (or a period). These are about 20-25%.

Following are the components or elements of Inventory carrying cost and Procurement cost which are the most important costs in inventory management.

Components of Inventory Carrying Cost

The components are :

(*a*) The salaries and wages of storing, receiving and issue of the material personnel.

(*b*) The loss by way of interests in the capital invested in the stocks of materials.

(*c*) The rent of the stores premises.

(*d*) Taxes on inventories.

(*e*) The depreciation and repairs cost for the stores facilities and handling equipments.

(*f*) Loss of materials through pilferage and deterioration, obsolescence.

(*g*) Stores insurance cost.

(*h*) Stationery and other consumables used by the stores.

The cost generally varies from 10 to 20%.

Procurement Cost

This includes :

(*a*) The salaries and wages of the purchase staff purchasing the materials.

(*b*) The expenditure on travelling etc.

(*c*) The expenditure on the use of Post and Telegraph services such as postage, telegrams and telephones.

(*d*) The expenditure on stationery and other consumables.

(*e*) Entertainment expenditure on receiving of suppliers.

(*f*) Rent for the premises used by the purchase department.

Certainly it can be said that more the number of orders are placed the more shall be the above expenditures.

The ordering cost is generally dependent on the purchasing procedures of the individual organisation. The procurement or ordering cost generally have no relation with the value of an order.

Carrying Inventory

Cost of carrying is not the same as carrying inventory. Carrying inventory results where there is stock left on hand after the demand for the item has terminated. This cost is called the overstock cost. This inventory problem can be static or dynamic. Static inventory problem is with retailer who wishes to sell greeting cards. His sale season is very limited and few cards left over at the end of season will have a very little or no salvage value. Thus if he has too much stock, he will have a cost due to the loss he will suffer for each greeting card he overstocks. The dynamic inventory problem could be for household items such as towels etc. There is always a demand for towels so any towel left over after one time period can be sold in the subsequent periods thus there is no overstock cost to a greater extent. The similar examples holds true for high fashion items, woman clothes. If only one order can be placed we have the static inventory problem if several orders can be placed during a season then we have dynamic problem. There will be no overstock cost involved until last order period of the season.

Procurement and Consumption Cycle

A simplified procurement and consumption cycle for an item having a steady consumption all through the year and which is available immediately on placing an order is shown below :

At time *A* the stock is zero and hence an order would be placed and the delivery being immediate, the stocks would be brought upto a level say *Q*. These would be steady issued upto time *B* and another order would be placed at *B* to bring up the stock to *Q* and so on. The inventory at the beginning of the period *A-B* would be *Q* and at the end of the period zero or the average inventory would be *Q*/2 and orders would have to be placed of *A*, *B* and *C* etc.

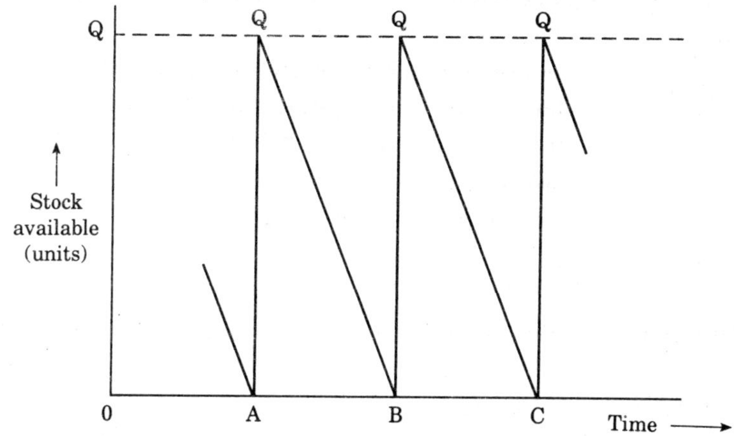

Fig. 73.2

Economic Order Quantity (E.O.Q.)

It is discussed here as to what should be the quantity *Q* ordered each time to keep down both the inventory carrying cost and ordering cost in this consumption and procurement cycle.

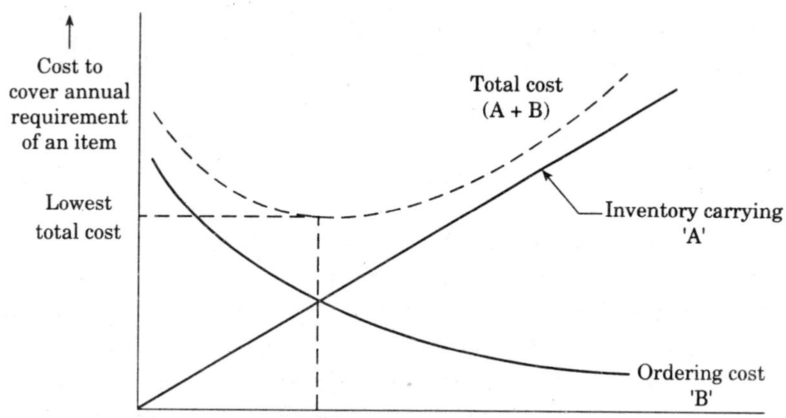

Fig. 73.3

Consider the procurement of the entire annual requirement of an item under the procurement and consumption cycle. For keeping the inventories and inventory carrying costs low it would be better to procure the item in as small consignment as possible. But this would mean larger number of orders and so more ordering cost. This has been graphically shown below. The requirements are thus conflicting and there is a particular quantity at which the sum of both the ordering and inventory carrying costs is minimum and this quantity is called EOQ (Economic Ordering Quantity).

Let us now derive the formula :

Let A = Ordering cost/order

Q = Quantity/order

λ = Total quantity ordered in the period under consideration

IC = Inventory carrying cost per unit

TIC = Total procurement and inventory cost or total inventory cost or No. of orders in the period under consideration would be = λ/Q.

TIC = Ordering cost + inventory carrying cost

= Cost per order × No. of orders + (average inventory × inventory carrying cost per unit)

$$TIC = A \times \frac{\lambda}{Q} + \frac{1}{2} Q.I.C. \quad ...(1)$$

Differentiating (1) with respect to Q, for the total cost to be minimum and then equating to zero.

$$\frac{d\,(TIC)}{dQ} = -\frac{\lambda A}{Q^2} + \frac{1}{2} IC = 0$$

or
$$\frac{\lambda A}{Q^2} = \frac{1}{2} IC$$

or
$$Q^2 = \frac{2\lambda A}{IC} \quad : or \quad Q = \sqrt{\frac{2\lambda A}{IC}} = EOQ$$

$$EOQ = Q^* \times \sqrt{\frac{2 \times \text{Annual consumption} \times \text{ordering cost}}{\text{Inventory carrying cost as a fraction}}}$$

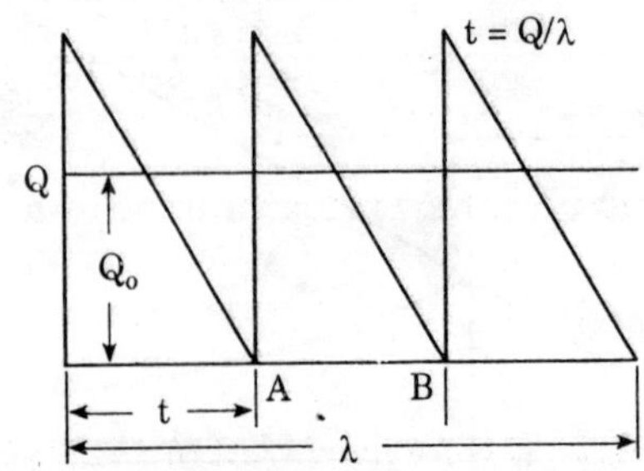

Fig. 73.4

It can be proved that at EOQ the ordering cost and inventory carrying cost are equal.

$$Q = \sqrt{\frac{2A\lambda}{IC}}; \quad or \quad Q^2 = \frac{2A\lambda}{IC}$$

or $$\frac{QIC}{2} = \frac{\lambda A}{Q} \text{ at } EOQ \quad ...(2)$$

Equation 2 indicates that at *EOQ*, inventory carrying cost and ordering cost are equals.

It may be noted here that shape of the total cost curve is fairly flat near $Q = EOQ$ in other words if little more or little less is ordered than *EOQ*, the total cost only increase slightly. In practice 25^0 less or more than *EOQ* makes very little difference in the total costs. Also the formula is quite general and '*A*' need not necessary be annual consumption. '*A*' could be very well for 6 months consumption cost. When simultaneous consumption is there and the rate of which is *X* then the formula for *E.O.Q.* becomes,

$$= Q\ \sqrt{2A\lambda/IC}\ (1 - \lambda)$$

Problem I. Given :

Annual consumption (λ) = *36,000 units*

Inventory carrying cost (I) = 20% per annum

Ordering cost (A) = Rs. 25

Cost/unit (C) = Re. 1

Find Q at EOQ and total cost of Inventory.

Solution. $$Q = \sqrt{\frac{2\lambda A}{IC}}$$

Here $\lambda = 36{,}000$

$A = 25$; $C = 1$; $I = 0.2$;

Putting the values of λ, *A*, *I*, *C*,

we get, $$Q = \sqrt{\frac{2 \times 36{,}000 \times 25}{0.2 \times 1}}$$

$$= \sqrt{36{,}000 \times 25} = 600 \times 5 = 3000$$

This means that for the order quantity 3000 units company will incur the minimum total cost on ordering and carrying inventory. This is explained below :

Qty. per Order (Q)	*No. of Orders*	*Inventory levels (Rs.) (Q/2)*	*Ordering cost (Rupees) (A)*	*Inventory Carrying cost (Rs.) (B)*	*Total cost (A × B)*
3000	12	1500	12 × 25 = 300	1500 × 0.2 = 300	600
2400	15	1200	15 × 25 = 375	1200 × 0.2 = 240	615
3600	10	1800	10 × 25 = 250	1800 × 0.2 = 360	610

When 12 orders are placed and inventory is maintained at an average of Rupees 1500, the total cost is the minimum is

(300 + 300) = Rs. 600

Problem 2. *In the above example, it is forecast that the next year consumption will increase to 144,000 units i.e. 4 times. On this basis calculate EOQ and TIC.*

Solution. Given : $\lambda = 144{,}000$

$$A = 25$$
$$Q = 6000$$
$$I = 0.2$$
$$C = 1$$

$$EOQ \text{ (for new consumption)} = \sqrt{\frac{2A\lambda}{IC}} = \sqrt{\frac{2 \times 25 \times 144{,}000}{0.2 \times 1}}$$
$$= 5 \times 1200 = 6000 \text{ units.}$$

Note. Sometimes deviations from economic order quantity have to be made for variety of reasons. In such cases some believe that deviations towards a quantity less than the economic order quantity is more desirable than deviations towards a quantity greater than EOQ. This however is not correct. In our example, if the deviation is greater than the EOQ by 20% total cost of ordering and carrying inventory increases by Rs. 10. If the deviation is less than EOQ by 20%, the increase in total cost is Rs. 15. Thus we have noted that deviation towards a greater quantity than EOQ increases total cost of ordering and carrying inventory by lesser amount than what the same % deviation of 20% towards the lower side would increase the total cost of ordering and carrying inventory.

$$TIC = \frac{A\lambda}{Q} + \frac{1}{2} QIC$$
$$= \frac{1{,}44{,}000 \times 25}{6000} + \frac{1}{2} 6000 \times 0.2 \times 1$$
$$= 24 \times 25 + 600 = 600 + 600 = 1200.$$

Problem 3. *A sewing machine manufacturer buys from a nearby foundry the body casting in which the machine is assembled. The foundry provides usually good service and always makes delivery on 8th day of the receipt of the order. The normal consumption of casting is at an average rate of 100 / day. The consumption varies from 80-120 casting / day. The management decides to set an order point and safety stock so that under the present operating conditions they do not run out of stock.*

Solution. Average number of casting needed $= 8 \times 100 = 800$

Maximum number of casting needed $= 8 \times 120 = 960$

Buffer stock or safety stock $= 960 - 800 = 160$

The management has concluded here that they should not run out of stock by establishing this order point at the level of 960 units. The safety level stock is 160 unit.

Lead Time — 6 — 10 days.

Average No. of casting used during the lead time $= 8 \times 100 = 800$

Minimum No. of casting used during the lead time $= 6 \times 80 = 480$

Maximum No. of casting used during the lead time $= 10 \times 120 = 1200$

Safety Stock $= 1200 - 800 = 400$

Order pt—minimum use $= 1200 - 480 = 720$

Order pt—maximum use $= 1200 - 1200 = 0$

Problem 4. *An oil engine manufacturer purchases lubricators at Rs. 42 / piece from a vendor. The requirement of these lubricators is 1800 per year. What should be the order quantity per order (A = Rs. 16 and I = 0.2).*

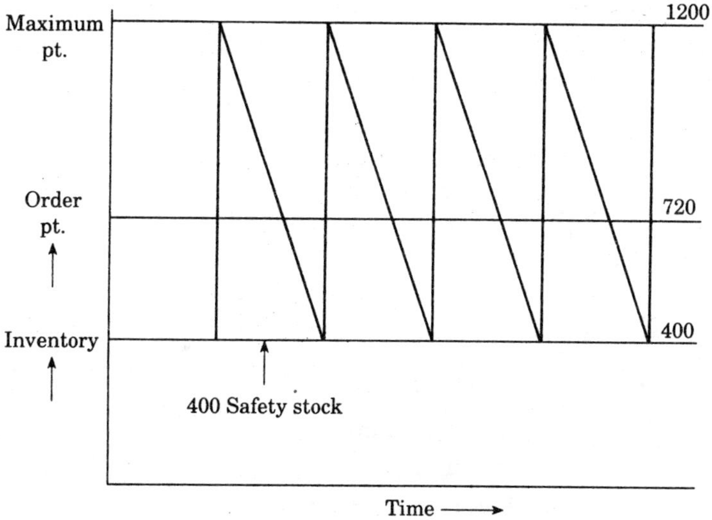

Fig. 73.5

Solution. Annual requirement is

$$= \text{Rs. } 1800 \times 42 = 75600$$

$$A = \text{Rs. } 16$$

$$I = 0.2$$

$$EOQ = \sqrt{\frac{2A\lambda}{IC}}$$

$$Q^* = \sqrt{\frac{2 \times 1800 \times 16}{0.2 \times 42}}$$

$$= 82.8 \text{ or } 83 \text{ lubricators.}$$

Problem 5. *Calculate the value of Economic Order Quantity. Given the following :*

Annual usages = *50 units*
Procurement Cost = *Rs. 15 per order*
Cost per price = *Rs. 100 per item*
Inventory Carrying Cost = *10%.*

Solution. We know that

$$Q^* = \sqrt{\frac{2A\lambda}{IC}}$$

A = Procurement Cost = Rs. 15 /order

λ = Annual Usage = 50 units

I = Inventory Carrying Cost = 0.1

C = Cost per unit = Rs. 100

Q^* = Economic Order Quantity

$$= \sqrt{\frac{2 \times 15 \times 50}{0.1 \times 100}} = \sqrt{\frac{2 \times 10 \times 15 \times 50}{100}} = \sqrt{2 \times 15 \times 5} = \sqrt{150}$$

$$Q^* = 12.21$$

Taking the whole number. The most Economic Order quantity where the inventory carrying cost and inventory procurement cost are minimum are 12 Nos. per order.

Problem 6. *The annual consumption of an item is 12000 per year. The procurement cost is Rs. 15 per order and inventory carrying cost per unit per year is Re. 1.*

Find out the most economic order quantity and the total cost of inventory also.

Solution. We know that

$$Q^* = \sqrt{\frac{2A\lambda}{IC}} \qquad \text{...}(a)$$

A = ordering cost per order.

Q^* = Economic order quantity.

λ = Annual consumption.

I = % of inventory carrying cost.

C = Cost of item.

If we substitute the value in (A) we find that economic order quantity is

$$Q^* = 600.$$

So everytime order is placed the number of units to be ordered are 600. Since the total requirement is 12000 per year, 20 orders at an interval of 18 days are to be placed assuming 360 days in one year. The total cost of inventory consists of two parts :

1. Total procurement cost.
2. Total inventory carrying cost.

Total ordering cost = Rs. 20 × 15 = 300.

Similarly total Inventory carrying cost = 300.

Total inventory cost is = Rs. 600.

Any other policy will increase the total cost. If e..ch item cost Rs. 10 then total usage value per year is Rs. 120,000 inventory carrying cost I is 0.10 and Q^* can be calculated with the formula given before.

In calculating the economic order quantity on the cost of ordering and stock holding have been taken into account. In certain cases the ordering quantity might have to be adjusted taking into consideration :

(*a*) Bulk

(*b*) Available space

(*c*) Package size

(*d*) Shipment size.

The economic order quantity is suited in a static equilibrium or when there is no uncertainties.

To deal with economic order Quantity in the real situation following terms should be discussed.

1. Lead time 2. Re-order point or level ; 3. Safety stock.

Lead Time

The procurement and consumption cycle has got two elements in it—(1) Lead Time and (2) Safety Stock.

In the earlier simplified cycle the supplies of material were assumed to be immediate on order but in practice this is not so. *From the time the requisition for an item is raised, it may take several weeks or months before the supplies are received, inspected and taken into stock. This time is called as lead time,* and involves the time for the completion of all or some of the following activities :

1. Raising of a purchase requisition.
2. Inquiries, quotations, scrutiny, and approval, (Import license procedure for imported item).
3. Placement of an order on supplier/suppliers.
4. Suppliers time to make the goods ready (may have to be manufactured or supplied ex-stock).
5. Transportation or clearing.
6. Receipt of goods at the company.
7. Receiving inspection.
8. Taking into stocks.

Obviously, in order to receive supplies before the stock reaches zero level, it is necessary to order the materials much in advance *i.e.* when the stock available is sufficient to last during the lead time. This is shown graphically in Fig. 72.6.

Suppose an item has a lead time of 15 days and the monthly consumption of the item is 600 units, then a recorder must be placed when the stock available is sufficient to last 15 days is 300 units.

In graph Q = Order quantity.

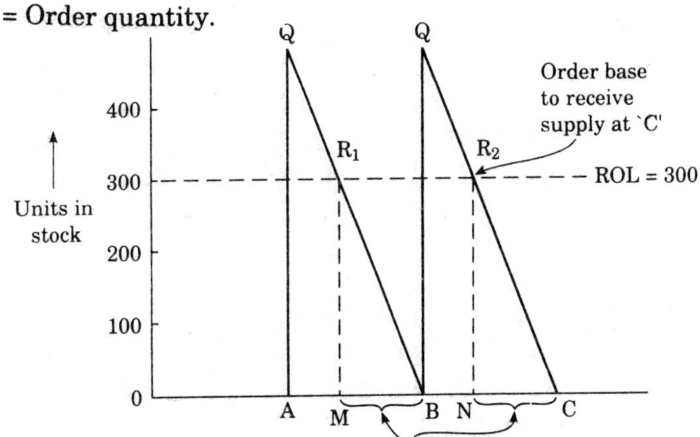

Fig. 73.6

$NC = MB$ = 15 days is lead time Recorder level

(ROL) = stock sufficient to last during the lead time is 300 units.

Safety Stock (Buffer or Reserve)

It is well known that neither the consumption rate of a material is constant throughout the year nor is the lead time. Hence in the earlier example though recorder is placed at a stock level of 300 units, the consumption rate may rise subsequently and the stocks may well be exhausted in 7 days instead of 15 days or it may be that the supplier fails to supply after 15 days as expected. In either case a stock out would be experienced resulting into hampering of production to guard mainly against these uncertainties in consumption rate and lead time, an extra stock is maintained all along and this is called as buffer stock or safety stock or reserve. This stock also comes in use when :

1. Any excesses in process rejections.
2. Rejection at the time or receipt or goods due to damages or substandard quality.

Since safety stock is a part of inventory, it should be maintained just sufficient to guard against the uncertainties and not too excessive (especially for *A* items).

Before deciding how much the safety stock should be analysis of the following aspect is essential :

1. If the variation in consumption more predominant in the lead time :
2. If the variation in consumption is more predominant way, it is so and can it be forecasted in advance.
3. If the variation in lead time is more predominant is it restricted to a particular period (say monsoon) or spread all over the year ?

In most cases it is found that the variations in consumptions can be predicted fairly in advance accurately by good production and maintenance planning and does not present much of a problem. But in the present Indian conditions, it is the lead time variation that is more erratic and unpredictable.

Uncertainty

The safety stock is needed because of uncertainty. The uncertainty can consist of :

(*a*) Uncertainty of demand, *i.e.*, how much the actual demand differs from what you expected.

(*b*) Uncertainty of delivery, *i.e.*, how long the lead time is going to be.

(*c*) Uncertain quantity, *i.e.* how many scrap or imperfect items the ordered quantity is going to contain. Uncertain quantity is usually small and will be neglected in the discussion.

Determining Safety Stock

One simple method of determining safety stock in such cases is to approximately estimate the maximum lead time and the normal lead time for an item in consultation with the purchasing personnel and from the past records. The safety stock should then be sufficient to last the periodic difference between maximum and normal lead time period.

Suppose for an item monthly consumption is 100 units, the normal lead time is 14 days and maximum lead time is estimated as one month. The safety stock would be,

(Maximum lead time in a month — Normal lead time in a month) — (monthly consumption)

$$= \left(1 - \frac{1}{2}\right)100 = 50 \text{ or say 50 to be on safe side.}$$

Or for an imported item with a normal lead time of 1 year and maximum estimated lead time 15 months, the safety stock would be

(15 — 12) = 3 months or say 4 months for additional safety.

It should be well understand that safety stock is meant only to provide for above normal lead time and above normal consumption rate. The normal lead time and consumption rate is already taken care of in setting Re-Order Level (ROL). If normal lead time consumption is 300 and safety stock is 100, the reorder level is set at 400 units (*i.e.* safety stock = lead time = ROL).

Optimum Safety Stock

If the safety stock maintained is inadequately low, the inventory carrying cost would be low on the safety stock but stock-outs will be very frequently experienced and the stock out cost would be very high. As against this, if safety stock maintained is rather large stock-outs would be rather rare but the inventory cost would be high. An optimum stock is better. Stock outs may give rise to following cost :

1. Customer loss or customer dissatisfaction.
2. Loss of production.
3. Idling of machines or man.
4. Emergency purchases at high prices.
5. Extra transportation changes for speedier modes of transportation.

In fact the cost of holding high levels of stock must be weighted against the cost of having stock out. The problem is of calculating the two costs. The cost of running out of stock is often difficult to assess. If the management decides it could not run out of stock on more than 2% of the orders. In other words, management policy is that 98% of orders must be met from stock, *i.e.*, the defined service level is 98%. We must know what service level is defined before one can workout what safety stock should be hold.

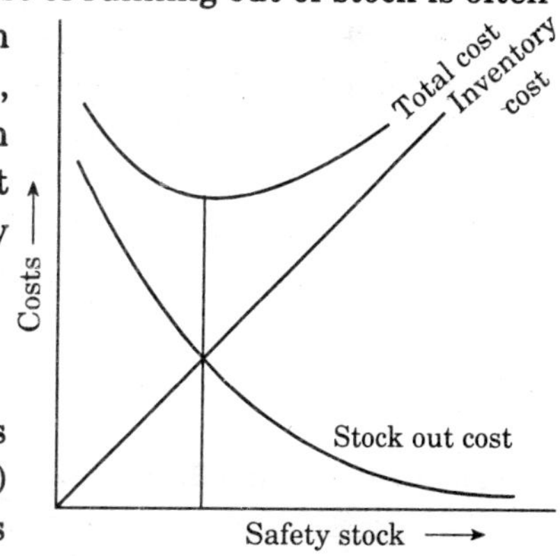

Forecast

The expected demand is a forecast of demand. In this difference between the actual demand the expected (forecast) demand is known as the forecast error. To compensate for this forecast errors we hold safety stocks and so the level of safety stocks is, to a large extent, based on the extent of the forecast errors.

Service Level

We hold safety stock to make sure that we can satisfy the demand but because of the uncertainty we won't be able to satisfy all the demand all the time. So we must decide what proportion of the demand we want to satisfy, *i.e.*, how often we will allow stockouts to occur. In other words, we must decide on the service level we desire.

Forecast Errors

Since the safety stock depends on forecast errors and the desired service level, we would like to find forecast error. For this we study the past data on forecast errors and try to see what pattern they fall into. In statistical terms, we want to find out the distribution of the forecast errors. Once we have found how the forecast errors are distributed, we can go on to draw conclusions about the probability of getting errors of any size.

Suppose we have a record of the last 30 forecasts of the demand made for an item. We can group the errors and draw up a table given below :

Forecast Error	*Frequency*	*%age frequency*	*Cumulative*
– 100 to – 50	12	40	40
– 50 to – 0	6	20	60
0 to 50	5	16	76
50 to 100	2	7	83
100 to 150	1	3	86
150 to 200	0	0	86
200 to 250	1	3	89
250 to 300	0	0	89
300 to 350	1	3	92
350 to 400	0	0	92
Over 400	2	7	99
	30	100 (Approximate)	

From the table we can see that 18 times the actual demand was less than the forecast. It means that more than half the time the actual demand was less than the forecast demand. We are not much worried about the occasion when demand turns out to be less than what had been the forecast, since the safety stock is not affected.

The table also shows that 89% of the errors were less than 250. Hence, if we had safety stock of 250 units we would have been able to satisfy the demand 89% of the time *i.e.* the service level would be 89%.

If the distribution of forecast error is one of several well known statistical distributions or can be approximated, then we can calculate the safety stock for any required service level quite easily from statistical tables.

Techniques of Inventory Control (Ordering System)

Having discussed all the basic elements of a procurement and consumption cycle we can now depend on various ordering systems.

1. **The fixed internal System/cyclical review System/Replenishment System.** The basic type of state control is known as the fixed internal system. In this system, the stock level is reviewed on a regular cycle say once a month. The interval between review is known as the review period. From the cycle shown in the figure below can be explained how the system is determined.

Suppose 4 months is fixed as the review period for an item and lead time for the item is 30 days. Then the order would be placed every 2 months *i.e.*, at ordinates R_1, R_2, R_3 etc. and the respective supplies would be received at ordinates S_1, S_2, S_3 etc. (30 days after R_1, R_2, R_3 etc.). At R_1, the stock available to be Y_1 then this stock together with the quantity ordered at R_1 (supplies received at S_1) should be sufficient to last till the next supplies are received at S_2 *i.e.* to last for a period of 5 months (1 Review + 1 lead time). In addition some buffer/safety stock would also be necessary to take care of any increased consumption or increase in lead time.

To find out how much to order, we calculate a figure called stock required. The stock which we have in hand and an order immediately after a review date must be good enough to last until the order which we place at the next review date is available. This order would not arrive till one lead time after the next review date.

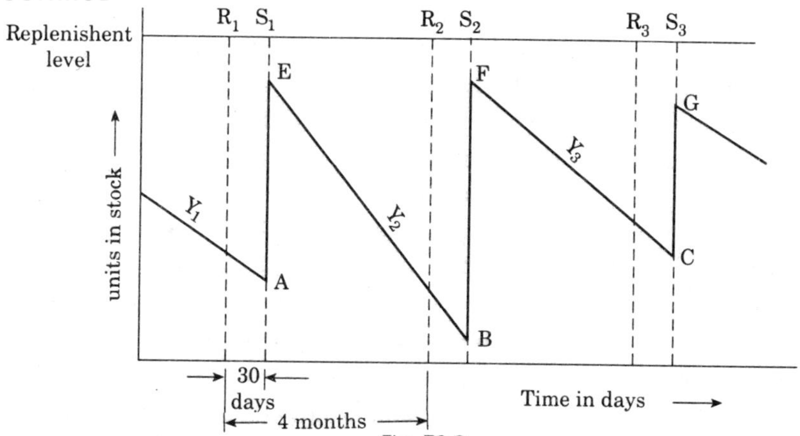

Fig. 73.8

So stock required = (Lead time + review period) × usage + safety stock on each review date the stock in hand plus that an order is compared with "Stock Required" and an order is placed to bring to stock upto "Stock Required" level.

In a fixed internal system the combined cost of stock holding and placing orders will always be higher than a fixed order quantity system because the stocks have to last not only over the lead time but also over the review period.

2. **The Fixed Order Quantity System.** The following diagram, in a simplified form should show the stock level of an item fluctuates.

The amount used over a period is the usage in that period. As the stock used up over the period, the stock level falls until it reaches a level at which an order is placed. If × is the reorder level. When the stock falls to re-order level, an order is placed for a certain amount. This is known as the order quantity and is shown as *OQ* in the diagram.

To take a couple of extreme examples. Suppose an item whose consumption is 10 number per month and its lead time is one month and perhaps it might be possible that 150 units are left over from a construction job. After 6 months the store keeper orders whatever the *EOQ* tells him which might be 20. But in 6 months he has used only 60, so he is reordering at 90. With usage of 10 per month and 1 month lead time store keeper will still have 80 on hand when the ones he ordered arrives. That is 8 months supply.

The order extreme : if the store keeper waited until he got down to 10 before reordering he would run out of stock just about the time the newly ordered ones arrive. No protection against variation in lead or in usage. If these were never any variation in usage or lead time he would reorder when stock was depleted to 11 units. Which is a best set up ; minimum inventory and never a stock out. But there are bound to be fluctuation in lead time and in usage so there is a need to set the Reorder point high enough to provide protection against those fluctuations.

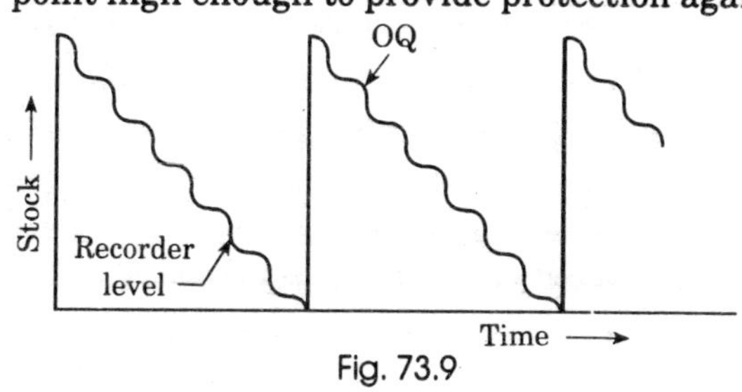

Fig. 73.9

If the reorder point were 15, for instance, still 5 are on hand in the normal course of events (10 per month usage 1 month lead time). The inventory would vary between 25 and 5 averaging 15 of which 10 is "working stock's". The 5 is called safety stock ? A normal 2 week's supply in the example which might be adequate if there were very little variation in lead time or usage, but might not be nearly enough with wide variations.

Reorder Point should be whatever one determines one should have as a safety-stock for each item, plus the number of that item which normally be used during the lead time.

($RP = SS$ + Usage during lead time) obviously the more uniform these factors are the fewer pieces needed as Safety stock protection, and wider the fluctuation the more is needed for comparable protection.

In the example given suppose once every 5 years, the monthly usage would exceed 15 units. By setting the Reorder point at 15 protection have been provided equivalent to one stock out in 5 years.

The complications are compounded, however, by the other variable : Lead Time. Not only the usage vary, but lead time might also. The usage might be high one month but a short Lead time, so the two variables would tend to offset each other. But the usage might be high one month but a short lead time during the same period, in which case the effect is cumulative, and should be taken into consideration.

In order quantity does not arrive immediately after it has been ordered. The time which elapses between the stock reaching the reorder level and the arrival of order quantity is known as the lead time.

Stocks go on falling during the lead time until the order quantity arrives and is in the stores. In an ideal situation, the stock should reach zero just as the new stocks arrived. Then when an order quantity come in the stock level would rise to a maximum.

From the diagram we can set that the maximum stock level is equal to the order quantity and the minimum stock level is equal to zero. The stock we have been talking about, is called the working stock. The average working stock is equal to half the order quantity.

Organisation of Inventory Control

Production, planning and control, inventory control and purchasing are independent. None can operate effectively without support of the others. Their importance varies widely from company to company. In a sense, inventory control is the link between production, planning and purchasing.

The relation between production, planning and control, inventory control, and purchasing depends on the relative importance of material availability or material value. Both inventory availability and inventory value are always important. A plant cannot manufacture its products without the necessary materials not can it operate successfully for very long if its working capital is dissipated through unwise accumulation of inventory. Purchasing, Production, Planning and Inventory Control Relationship for one shoe company is an under. Purchasing, production planning and inventory control

Purchasing — Production, Planning and Control

Inventory control

Relationship for one manufacturer of industrial machinery is indicated as under :

Purchasing	Production, Planning and Control	Inventory Control

Inventory Control System

The inventory control system can be subdivided into following six headings :

1. Identification
2. Classification
3. Demand
4. Replenishment
5. Costs
6. Constraint.

Identification

The item to be stocked by a description and number. After this it is necessary to obtain other information from existing records for purpose of classification and this may include usage rate, nature of usage, item value, physical nature rule as size, shape, weight, storage method.

Classification

It is necessary to classify items in order to satisfy the problem of control. The classification has a basic aim to concentrate control effort where it is really needed.

Demand

The inventory control assumes that demand continues at a certain rate or having a certain frequency and size.

Demand often does not emanate from a single source but it is to aggregate demand which deplets stocks.

Demand generally have a co-relation between the various demand source and between time periods for a single source.

Demand may be even negative when a customer return his supply.

Replacement

The inventory control deals with "when to order and how much" ? The time between consecutive decisions of replenish is called the replenishment period and may be variable. The time elapsed before the replenishment arrived and this is termed the lead time.

Costs

Following three costs are associated with inventory control system—carrying costs, shortage costs and replenishment costs. In addition to this other costs much be considered include purchase, or acquisition costs and review costs.

Constraint

The inventory control systems are subject to various types of constraint. The constraints are maximum investment in stock, storage space, number of orders placed. The important of all the constraints is that inventory control system do not remain static. Cost structures are also subject to change but constraints such as management directive to cut stocks by a certain percentage can be imposed very fast.

74

Maintenance Management

It is not very late when maintenance used to be considered as a necessary evil and attracted least attention of the management. Frequent failures were put-down to old age or to bad machines or sometimes to bad operators. The entire maintenance department use to consist of a skilled foreman with 10 to 12 gangmen and they were mostly left to their derives and operated more or less on "firebrigade" concept, and preventive maintenance was a new word. The situation has, no doubt, undergone a big change since then and management have really started giving much more importance to planned maintenance of the equipment and machinery.

The purpose of maintenance is to make available for production purposes, machinery and equipment to fulfil their technological functions as specified and economically which means that the output quality and quantity from each machine or equipment will conform to specified purposes. For instance, a properly maintained machine tools much produce components to the desired accuracy and quality of surface finish. The purpose of the entire maintenance organisation is to fulfil this function satisfactorily with the machine and equipment utilization factor as high as possible.

Although all machines are thoroughly tested under strict quality control methods at the manufactures works before supply to the user and user also tests these before finally putting them into operation. After some use, the machines are subjected to wear and to reduce wear proper care to lubrication, cleaning, timely inspection and systematic and scheduled maintenance is to be given. The machines even repaired when not in use so that any defect or damage to the part is taken care so that machine starts behaving as new. In this way the maintenance is responsible for the smooth and efficient working of any plant or industry and helps in improving its productivity.

Different System of Maintenance

Maintenance systems can be grouped into five major groups :

(*i*) Operator Maintenance.

(*ii*) Breakdown Maintenance.

(*iii*) Scheduled Maintenance.

(*iv*) Planned Maintenance.

(*v*) Preventive Maintenance.

(*i*) **Operator Maintenance.** This type of maintenance system is largely confined to a small engineering industries where supervisors and employees possess the qualifications necessary to control and perform maintenance of their own machines. This system of maintenance is obviously the most elementary one and is perhaps not applicable to anything other than very small factories. Even there the lack of separate control of maintenance records and costs would not reveal the real size of the maintenance problem year after year.

(*ii*) **Breakdown Maintenance.** This is intended to imply that an independently organised maintenance section acts only as an emergency repair service summoned by the production staff when interruption or restriction of production has actually occurred. It is obvious that in the world of modern industry even this system can be satisfactorily operated in very special conditions and for a limited period. This method will generally be found over the long term to reduce machine availability and give a lower overall mechanical efficiency for production machinery.

(*iii*) **Scheduled Maintenance.** This is the first stage in the approach to a modern maintenance system. This involves joint discussions in advance by production and maintenance programme so that items considered of use by maintenance staff to need attention can have scheduled periods of availability for repairs. In this way the "where" and "when" of the maintenance programme can be approximately fixed and the most efficient use made of any idle time.

(*iv*) **Planned Maintenance.** The development is one step ahead of schedule maintenance which decides not only the "when" and the "where" of maintenance but also answers the question" "what" and "by whom". Experience in schedule maintenance can be further used to make more detailed analysis of programmed work so that more precise planning of work and allocation of labour is it are possible. At the stage some method of estimating the work content of the jobs to be done is necessary. This system of maintenance is perhaps the better on which should be adopted by a manufacturing plant of modern complexities.

(*v*) **Preventive Maintenance.** This system is a further improvement over planned maintenance and answers the "why" for the maintenance work. It involves the policy of upkeep, replacement and modification rather than repair and has invariably to incorporate periodical inspections of the plant in order to diagnose the trouble, if any, and to plan the requirements of maintenance. Many times the work of inspection, maintenance, replacement or modification (by way of accuracy checks, periodic overhand and major overhands) are analysed for a considerably long time, for each important unit of production equipment and is broken down into elements to be further analysed to improve the methods and determine the standard work contents. The techniques of works Study can be applied with advantage under this system.

It is, however, necessary to bear in mind that irrespective of any amount of sophisticated maintenance system being enforced, the breakdown maintenance cannot be avoided altogether. The ultimate goal is therefore to introduce more and more sophistication in the preventive maintenance techniques to minimise the breakdown maintenance in the plant and machinery, since no piece of equipment or machine will have a breakdown without having shown certain signs of malfunctioning earlier.

The preventive maintenance programme cannot be introduced overnight, and has to be based on a detailed study of the earlier maintenance schedule, breakdown hours etc. A detailed study is required to be carried out to cover every important component of the equipment with respect to its condition of working, the past maintenance history, downtime etc. Sometimes inherent design weaknesses can also be identified.

The equipment history card for each equipment and entity so prepared can be analysed to locate the types of repairs calling for extensive maintenance work *i.e.* in terms of men hours and spare parts. This would guide with respect to the planning for stocking the spare parts, their quantities, and nature of the work to be executed and can be recast and planned on work study principles. The manufacturers of the equipment generally recommend certain norms, or maintenance frequencies, pre-supposing, a certain working environment. This should be treated as a guide or a cross check, and the maintenance history of an equipment only should show up actual need of equipment in the given environment with respect to the preventive maintenance programme. The higher frequencies of inspection in the beginning can be justified to minimise to breakdown maintenance, but cost over a period would show that such inspections could be reduced to stabilise the preventive maintenance programme, as a maintenance discipline. To object of preventive maintenance is to attain overall lower costs, and hence the need to constantly review its costs *vis-a-vis* the cost of lost production, in order to achieve the optimum maintenance.

Objectives of the Preventive Maintenance

Broadly, the objectives of a systematic maintenance scheme are :

(*a*) To prolong the working life of the equipment and assure optimum availability.

(*b*) By minimising the wear and tear, preserve the value of the plant.

(*c*) To safe guard the investment.

(*d*) To ensure safety of the equipment and the personnel.

(*e*) Keep the productive assets in good working conditions.

Maintenance Functions

The necessity to have a maintenance engineering organisation in a factory is not any more questioned by today's managements but the proper importance of the maintenance functions and the rightful place of importance which the maintenance function should occupy in an organisation is not recognised by all. With the growing complexity of processes and equipment and with the growing magnitude of potential losses suffered in production due to breakdowns, modern managements can no longer look upon the maintenance function as a subsidiary of production but as one of the main tool of plant productivity which must be effectively used to obtain the highest availability of the production equipment commensurate with total maintenance cost. This concept has extended the role of maintenance to include close and active contact during the design stage, full involvement in process selection and continuous coordination with operation of the plant. Maintenance engineer has been responsible for a number of modern techniques being developed to improve the performance of the maintenance function itself.

Top management, should, therefore, realise that even though maintenance engineering is not a primary function, it is a very important support of the primary function of production and on it depends successful production.

The maintenance function would embrace to following activities.

Primary Tasks

1. Inspection, lubrication, repair and maintenance of all equipments.
2. Maintenance of existing buildings and structures.
3. Operation and maintenance of utilities, operation and distribution.

4. Alternation to existing equipments and buildings.
5. Installations of new equipments and new construction.

In order to fulfil these primary functions there are a number of secondary function which the maintenance department is called upon to perform.

1. Store keeping.
2. Plant protection including fire protection.
3. Waste disposal.
4. Salvage.
5. Pollution and noise control.
6. House keeping in the plant.

Elements of Preventive Maintenance

Following are some of the elements which are to be taken care in Preventive Maintenance.

1. **Inspection/Check ups.** This is again split up into two categories :

(*i*) External Inspection, and
(*ii*) Internal Inspection.

External Inspection means to check the equipments or machines for external defects such as vibrations and abnormal sound in the machines and checking up of the bearing and bushings for heating up. These defects are felt during the operation of the machine.

Internal Inspection means inspection of internal parts such as gears, cams bearing and other moving parts. It is done when the machine is under shutdown.

Under this heading, let us have an idea of planned maintenance which the countries like Russia and Czechoslovakia are following on National basis. In India as well many plants which have come up with the collaboration of above countries following the same procedure with little adjustment here and there according to local plant environments.

The planned Preventive Maintenance consists of :

(*i*) Minor Repairs
(*ii*) Medium/Intermediate Repairs
(*iii*) Major/Capital Repairs.

The maintenance system must fit the pattern of maintenance cycle *i.e.* the number of planned overhauls and the order in which they are to be carried out between capital repairs. Both the Russian and Czechoslovakia patterns have adopted repairs or overhauls between 2 major overhauls and they have been adopted at National levels. They are more or less in conformity with each other and pattern is in the following order :

I—I—II—I—I—II—I—I—III (IV—V)

This is the pattern in the Engineering Industry particularly for machine tools and it is the same for all types of models of metal cutting lathes and all operating conditions. The period between any of these repairs is known as the inter-overhaul time and the period between the major overhauls is known as the maintenance cycle. The manpower and machines utilised for a given type of overhaul have also been standardised in these two countries and approved at the National levels. The machine tools are designated into different categories according to their complexity. Each category is assigned a conventional coefficient and the tool taken for the base standard is a general purpose turning lathe of average complexity coefficient '*R*' has a value of

10. A cylindrical grinding machine has a complexity coefficient of 15 which means 1.5 times more than a lathe.

The average complexity coefficients for certain types of machine tools as given in the Russian Publication is given below.

S. No.	*Types of machine tool*	*Complexity coefficient*
1.	Lathes medium size	9—13
2.	Heavy lathes	17—19
3.	Vertical drilling machine	3—8
4.	Radial drilling machine	6—12
5.	Open-side Jig borers	20—35
6.	Horizontal bores (medium)	16—18
7.	Cylindrical grinding machines	10—15
8.	Gear Cutting machines, medium size	10—12
9.	General purpose horizontal milling machines	8—14
10.	Planning machines, medium size	12—15

After establishing the complexity coefficients of these machine tools, the number of man and machine hours required for these preventive maintenance operations are also standardised as follows :

Type of Repair	*Man hours*	*Machine hours*
Minor Repairs (*I*)	4.0	2.0
Intermediate Repairs (*II*)	10.0	7.0
Major Repairs (*III*)	26.0	10.0

Thus, the ratio of man and machine hour utilisation for planned overhauls is :

$$I : II : III = 1 : 4 : 6$$

From the knowledge of the complexity coefficient of a machine tool and the man and machine hours utilisation requirement for any type of repair, the time required for any type of rapair can easily be found out of shown below.

For a cylindrical grinding machine with a complexity coefficient of 15 time required for major handling would be 15 (26 × 10) = 540 hours and 360 hours for intermediate repairs.

Such patterns as for engineering industry, can also be worked out for other industries as well.

2. **Planning and Scheduling.** Every preventive maintenance work should be preplanned in details on the basis of the analysis done on the past records. In order to have effective maintenance planning, certain prerequirements are necessary. Below shows the various maintenance management area and suggested outline of the relationships of basic and defined controls. The failure of defined maintenance systems, such as critical path scheduling or material delivery, can usually be traced to an inadequate base.

Certainly a solid foundation should be established before complicated preventive maintenance or date-processing systems are instituted. There are number of basic requirements.

Areas of Maintenance Management

Work order system

|

Time Keeping

|

Materials control

|

Planning and scheduling system

|

1. Backlog
2. Job costs
3. Performance
4. Budget

|

Defined controls

1. Preventive Maintenance
2. Cost control
3. Spare parts
4. Stores
5. Materials delivery
6. Maintenance engineering
7. Training
8. Maintenance evaluation
9. Critical path scheduling
10. Data processing
11. Facilities evaluation
12. Others

The production and maintenance department must useful formal work order to specify the work that is to be done and execute the work order before the work is undertaken. Planning and control cannot be applied unless the job itself is controlled through a work order system which provides the basic paper work for preplanning and for individual cost identification of each job

A typical work order form is shown below :

Work Order

Class of work	*Code*	*Acctt. No.*
Repair	—	Labour
Alterations	—	Material
Renewal	—	Issued to Date
New-work	—	Equipment No.; Work order No.

Description of Work

Requested By	*Data wanted*	*Completed*	
		By	*Date*
Posted to Equipment Record	—	—	—
By Date	—	—	—
Reasons			
Budget Item No.	*Checked By*	*Estimated By*	
Cost	Labour	Material	Total
Budgeted Estimate			
Project Approved By (Initials)		*Date*	
Maintenance Engg.		—	
Operation. Asstt. Supdt.		—	
Plant Engineer		—	
Chief Engineer		—	
General Manager		—	—

A second requirement is for a timekeeping system which identifies the actual labour hours against each work order. The time keeping system should be simple and the basic requirements are only work order number and the actual hours spent against that number, any additional information can be obtained from the work order. The hourly machine should keep his own time and foreman participation should be limited to an approval of the time ticket at the end of the day.

Lastly, materials control is necessary, maintenance stores and spare-parts control must be effective and maintenance planning is also to be effective. A listing of terms carried in stores must be available in a stores and spares catalogue so that materials must be purchased can be ordered before the job is under way. Location of stores items, inventory control, obsolescence problem, and other stores control will seriously effect maintenance performance.

The practical maintenance planning also involves delivery of materials to the job site before the job is started. Since planning includes materials and a good materials-delivery system requires materials availability.

Net work analysis for scheduling and a controlling maintenance work is a powerful tool to economise on the man-hours spent in shut down maintenance and progressive top management should take it obligatory on the part of the managers in charge of Preventive Maintenance or Scheduled Maintenance to involve, net works for each major scheduled maintenance job.

To give an example, let us solve one example to understand how PERT/CPM is applied for capital maintenance.

The example is overhauling of huge Reciprocating Pump.

For getting optimum performance out of any individual, activity or group of staff, it is advisable to streamline the actions in such a way that all the activities may be completed in the shortest possible time with maximum results and minimum of wastage. This is possible by making a PERT (Programme Evaluation and Review Technique) chart of the activity.

First the various activities and events were made out as per requirement. The time is calculated as per the general experience and datas available. It was found that by making a

PERT chart not only a complete direction of sequence could be given to the staff concerned but the job could be done within the shortest possible time with minimum staff. With a complete picture of the process available it was also possible to make put the needs of spares and machining activities and plan ahead before taking up the job.

The following assumptions were made while drawing the PERT/CPM of capital Maintenance of reciprocating pump in a factory.

1. Three groups of fitters with the following strength are to be employed :
   (*i*) Group "A" with 4 fitters, 4 helpers.
   (*ii*) Group "B" with 2 fitters, 2 helpers.
   (*iii*) Group "C" with 2 fitters, 2 helpers.
2. Three riggers are to be employed to work with the above mentioned three group of fitters.
3. Civil works have not taken into consideration while drawing the PERT and have assumed that the base of Pump is misaligned and that needs rectification by realignment and minor civil work on the foundation bolts.
4. All the materials, spares and manpower would be available at site as and when required to avoid wastage of man hours.

Conclusions

The minimum possible manhours required to complete the capital maintenance of the pump are = 293 manhours.

$$\text{Minimum mandays} = \frac{293}{8} = 36.6 \text{ or } 37.$$

While working out above mandays it has been assumed that work will be done on 8 hours single shift basis allowance for fatigue etc., may be added locally.

3. **Lubrication.** In lubrication, the first and foremost thing is lubrication survey. A complete survey of the plant equipment should be made to ascertain the proper requirement of lubricants. The oil companies render such services which would be well-worth availing of. It is better to rationalise these lubrication requirements by reducing the variety of lubricating oils to the absolute minimum after considering the suitability of alternative brands.

Design of colour scheme or a codification system to indicate all spots which need lubrication, the type of lubricant and the frequency lubrication.

Lubrication should not be left to the lowest paid helpers or untrained illiterate operators. The system of codification, the various types of oils and greases and administering correctly measured quantities of lubricant should be explained at length to mean and should be well understood by them.

Storage and handling of lubricants are of utmost importance and this itself can cover full chapter. But the method of storage and handling of lubricants leaves much room for improvement in many enterprises. The lids of containers are found missing and exposed to dirt, grit and moisture. Workers pick up the grease with their hands which under workshop conditions are not free from dirt and grit.

In addition to the colour coding scheme it is preferable to develop and display on each equipment a lubrication chart. This chart should indicate all the lubrication points, the brand lubricant for each point the method of lubrication the quantity and application frequency. This is because colour marking are apt to become indistinct after a period before they are renewed.

The results of a lubrication system can be studied through the correlation between expenditure on lubrication and the loss of machine hours through breakdowns. Such a study can make the advantages of a planned lubrication system assignable in monetary term.

4. **Training of Maintenance Personnel.** Proper training of maintenance staff is an aspect which can never be over emphasised. Apart from the initial training of maintenance craftmen, it is necessary to organise refresher courses for craftmen and maintenance supervisors. The advantage of refresher course is that they enable pooling of experience gained by the participants during their years of working. A regular programme for refresher courses in maintenance for the craftmen and supervisors should be drawn up and implemented faithfully by every enterprise. Advantage of specialised agencies can be taken in organising and addressing these refresher course.

Organised instructions are necessary, however, to import knowledge about the function of the equipment, its operation and sequence of assembly of the components. Wherever possible working models preferable sectionised, can be of great help to in such instructions and demonstrations. Defects or defective system may or may not always follow the same pattern nor any textbook solution available to problems. An effective maintenance manager is, therefore, who had developed an analytical mind and flaire for improvisation.

5. **Motivation Techniques.** Job motivation involves the following fragments that impinge on job selection and performance :

1. Salary and other tangibles.
2. Titles (includes extension of responsibilities)
3. Worksite location.
4. Element of competition.
5. Opinion of others.
6. Freedom of decision and movement.

Motivation to work is very much an individual and environmental factor. Some of the factors which go in for this aspect are as follows :

(*a*) Much faith is put in various works entrusted to individuals.

(*b*) Extreme share of consideration is shown by supervisors in case some mistakes or errors in work come to light and remedial training measures are initiated.

(*c*) Proficient planning and scheduling is exercised and most of the work is required to be done at a normal pace in the most suitable atmosphere.

(*d*) Suggestions for alteration and improving methods, working tools, equipment, etc., are taken in the correct spirit by all supervisors and implemented whenever possible. Reward are also given whenever justifiable.

(*e*) Good salary and fringe benefits.

(*f*) Good production incentives scheme.

(*g*) A reasonable good performance rating system.

6. **Maintenance of Records.** Good record keeping is essential for good preventive maintenance. Management information system for maintenance is to be designed for timely collection of data, its processing to information to appropriate levels of management with required

frequency and details so that each manager may plan and control and totality of all efforts is coordinated to have best maintenance at minimum cost.

The following maintenance information system is desirable.

(A) **Registers and Codes :**

(*i*) Equipment classification (cost centre).

(*ii*) Card (description/identification/Quarterly consumption/equipment identification).

(*iii*) Machine part Register.

(*iv*) Drawing Register.

(*v*) Equipment classification and numbering of drawing.

(B) **Organisation and Personnel :**

(*i*) Departments under Engineering Services (Functional distribution).

(*ii*) Department organisation chart.

(*iii*) Service cards (Personal/family details of employees).

(*iv*) Approval and character roll (Officers).

(C) **Planning :**

(*i*) Monthly shut down planning (Equipment/purpose/effect or product/date and hours of shut down).

(*ii*) Long term planning (capital and major repairs).

(*iii*) Job planning for Maintenance and repair (day/description/type of work/workers allotement details.).

(*iv*) Operational Estimates-Consumables stores for financial year (Quantity/Value)

(*v*) Revenue Budget-Spare parts for financial year.

(D) **Operational Reports and Control :**

(*i*) Daily Breakdown Reports. (Delay hours/nature of break down/causes/steps to avoid reoccurrence.

(*ii*) Daily Delay Report (delay hours/nature and causes of break down/steps/agency responsible).

(*iii*) *Shift attendance of working Report.*

Strength

Absentee-Reason By categories.

Utilisation analysis

Working Report showing nature of engagements.

(*iv*) Analysis of capital investment, spares stock, spare consumption value, maintenance cost, wages and salaries.

(*v*) Work order for spares/Repairs.

(*vi*) Inspection Reports (for spare parts). (*vii*) Indents to stores/Purchase.

7. **Material Management for Maintenance.** Maintenance inventory costs are known to contribute a large proportion of the total inventory costs of plants. Effective control of spares parts inventory is of great importance for good maintenance management and the timely execution of maintenance schedules. Many times a large portion of the downtime towards maintenance is spent is due to the problem of spare parts. The problem could be due to any of the following.

(*a*) Due to uncertainty about the time when required and quantity required.

(*b*) Due to difficulties in physical procurement.

(*c*) Due to difficulties of distribution, storage and control identification.

(*d*) Due to indifferent quality of supplied spares.

However, the importance of having ready inventory cannot therefore be over-emphasized. Here again, the spare parts for vital and non-vital machines could be treated on different footings as also imported spares. A distinction is also to be made between fast moving spares needed periodically at regular intervals and insurance spares. The spares should be properly codified for identification and standardised to the most possible extent. Attempts should be made for finding better materials for spare parts.

It is advantageous to undertake manufacture of certain simple spare parts like pins, bushes, cams, gears etc., in a centralised maintenance workshop (within the enterprise or in ancillary industry developed by the present enterprise) and maintain small but ready inventories.

Economic Aspects of Maintenance

1. Systematic maintenance procedure offers tremendous possibility for savings in money, materials and manpower. These savings come through :

(*i*) Reduction in down time.

(*ii*) Reduced loss of materials in process.

(*iii*) Increased life of the equipment.

(*iv*) Reduction in overtime.

(*v*) Timely replacement of spares and machinery.

(*vi*) Optimum spares inventory.

(*vii*) Maintenance of product quality.

(*viii*) Proper running of equipment.

(*ix*) Optimum operated cost of the machine.

2. It is necessary to decide the degree of maintenance effort needed, since over maintenance increases the maintenance with increases downtime and other losses.

3. The costs involved in a systematic maintenance procedure is more than off set by the advantages gained thereon. However, it is essential to categories the equipment and decide the type of maintenance of each piece of equipment needed based on their criticality.

4. Replacement of machinery is an important aspect of maintenance while availability of equipment and the resources are great limitation, an efficient cost accountings system and the collection of relevant data for decisions regarding repairs and renewals are important. Thus a proper costing system and adequate records are of extreme importance for the efficient and economic performance of maintenance activity. Allocation of adequate resources for replacement of equipment and for providing maintenance facilities need attention.

5. The capital blocked in inventory of spares is considerable in Indian industries. A proper system storing and control of spares would facilities release of much wanted capital and also ensure their availability when needed. Preventive maintenance is extremely helpful in streamlining the consumption and storage of spares.

6. In this connection standardisation of spares and equipment, warrants attention of the management and the government, which will help in reducing the variety of spares and

standardise the same to the extent possible. In finding better and cheaper substitutes, modifications for better performance and import substitution, value engineering will prove to be a useful technique.

Engineering Aspects

The cost of maintenance accessibility for repairs and maintenance lubrication etc. all need to be thought of. In developing countries most of the equipment is still being imported. Even with in the country climatic and other conditions may differ from place to place. Hence it is necessary to ensure the suitability of the equipment to local conditions before buying the same. At the same time availability of spares and after sales service are important points and for consideration.

Managerial Aspects

Collection and analysis of data and proper planning and control and the causes of efficient maintenance management.

Planning of maintenance work due to the inherent nature of the jobs involved, is far more difficult than production planning. With a system of break-down maintenance, it is almost impossible to plan maintenance activities. However, establishment of a preventive maintenance system greatly facilities planning, by reducing the incidence of breakdowns. Schedules can be prepared for inspection and lubrication and the other activities can be reasonably well planned. After the system is in operation for sometime ; data can be built up and the system can be redefined.

Although accurate measurement of maintenance work is difficult, there are tools and techniques available to get a good estimate of the time required which is necessary for a proper development of labour and control.

Application of network techniques for scheduling of maintenance work has become popular and is being increasingly practised by maintenance managers.

Proper staffing of the maintenance department is another factor which is important. This will have to be based on anticipated workloads, on routine as well as non-routine jobs. While it is necessary to have the right amount of staff, maintenance jobs, being such that a certain amount of wastage is inevitable. It is, however, necessary to get the right type and amount of skills.

Training of maintenance personnel is a subject which should receive some attention of the management. Technical training to improve their skills and also productivity and attitude oriented training are both necessary.

There cannot be any hard and fast rule about the organisation of the maintenance department in an industry. It depends on various factors and varies from company to company depending upon the type, size and other factors. What is important in proper coordination and control among the various functions of maintenance and with other departments.

The maintenance should be independent entity apart from production, with sufficient authority and responsibility with due status, reporting to a fairly level higher level of management.

Maintenance Management will be really effective in an organisation only when there is understanding co-operation and co-ordination between production and maintenance. It is necessary that the production personnel appreciate the importance of maintenance of their equipment. At the same time maintenance should up-to-date its plans in consultation with production.

The performance of maintenance function need to be evaluated from time to time with a view to improve the same. The evaluation may be done through an analysis of costs, downtime hours or losses as compared to the available hours or through frequency of breakdowns.

It is needless to emphasise the priority to be accorded to plant maintenance by the Industrial Management in India. Proper and perspective planning at the National as well as the unit level will pay rich dividends.

Organisation for Maintenance

The success of a maintenance department is largely dependent on its organisation. Each enterprise has to adopt an organisation best suited to its purpose but the following guidelines can be indicated for adopting a particular set up for specific enterprise.

(*i*) **Centralised Maintenance Organisation.** It can be adopted with advantage in a small and compact factory when interunit communication is speedy. The Chief Maintenance Engineer heads the organisation and should report to the General Manager, who is responsible for overall functioning of the factory.

(*ii*) **Decentralised Maintenance Organisation.** If the factory is large and its various units are situated far apart with difficulties of inter-unit communication, a decentralised maintenance organisation is generally favoured. A separate maintenance group for each unit functions under the administrative control of the Production Superintendent.

(*iii*) **Partially Decentralised Maintenance Organisation.** This set up is an improvement over the second category. Here the running maintenance of the equipment is day-to-day attention to equipment is entrusted to a group of maintenance workers, who are administratively responsible to the Production Superintendent. Other important maintenance functions *i.e.* planning of scheduled maintenance works, procurement of spares for maintenance, and major over-hauling, operations are kept centralised under the Chief Maintenance Engineer. Such a set up serves the need of Production Superintendent for their day-to-day flexibility of work, and also enables a centralised maintenance policy to be adopted and implemented. Here also the Chief Maintenance Engineer is placed at the same level of authority as that of Production Superintendent, under the General Manager.

75

Production Management, Process and System

Introduction

The term production quite often means the same as manufacture. To carryout the process of manufacturing we need the following things : Man to do the job, Equipment, Material.

Man to do the Job.
Equipment.
Material.

However, if we have a lathe machine, a skilled operator, a metal bar for turning. Will we be equipped for production ? Although we have now all the ingredients to start manufacturing but still we are not ready to manufacture. We do not know what is to make ? When it is to be made ? Do we have customer to buy the product ? What will happen if the lathe machine breakdown ? Are we making the right type and quality of the product ? These questions show us that we need more than just the technical ability to manufacture. We also need : Service activities, control and functions.

Control and Functions

The service abilities are those which make sure that the manufacturing process can go on and control makes sure that it goes in the right direction. Economics defines production as utility creation. An activity which imparts form utility, time utility, space utility. Economists also define production as the act of making something with the object of satisfying human wants thus production is not only confined to goods and commodities but also include services. Consequently the economists definition of production is not restricted to the process of creation of physical items, but the transportation system, banking system, library and hospital can also be considered as a production process. Present views of production are that it is a sequence of operations that transform materials from a given state to a desired state.

Objective of Production. The main object of production is to ensure that it makes a product which can satisfy the needs of the customer by giving the right quality of the product at right place at the right time at right price. To achieve the above objective it is essential that production organisation is well managed.

What is Production Process

Production is a sequence of operations that transforms material from a given to a direct form. The transformation may be done in one or in combination of the following ways :

Transformation by disintegration

Transformation by integration, and

Transformation by service.

Transformation by Disintegration

It has one ingredient as input and producing several outputs. This transformation is accompanied by changes in the physical shape of the input, for example, making of steel bars from cast ingot, making components from standardised materials on machine tool.

Transformation by Integration

In this we have several components as input and one product as output for example producing of household appliances, automobile, TV set computers etc.

Transformation by Service

In this no change in object under consideration is perceptible, only certain operations are carried on the job, to change on of the parameter which define the object for example heat treatment of various jobs to increase tensile strength or other mechanical properties of the object, servicing and repairs of automobiles, loading and unloading of trucks etc. Many service operations are not considered as part of industry, but for the planning and control of these industrial operations. The objective of production management is the same as any other area of management that is to realise the overall objectives of the organisation.

Production Management Concepts

Production management is the process of designing, manning operating, servicing, and centralising the activities of a manufacturing organisation, responsible for the actual transformation of material inputs into marketable finished goods. Production planning and control which is an integral and important part of the Production Management has to play a vital role. Production management is to decide the objectives of production. This will involve all the functions of planning, organising, directing and controlling the production activities from the short term and long term aspect. The area which help us in setting up our production facilities are :

— Method study,

— Plant lay out

— Work measurement

— Production planning and control,

— Stock control

— Quality control and

— Maintenance.

Production management is a sub-system of the business organisation. Production management is what a production-manager does. The production manager's role is that of a decision maker. After he has planned allocation of inputs, the creation of value through production process can be. Once the production processes are started, it must be controlled. The control involves observing results and checking that they confirm to the original plans. The checking is possible by feed-back mechanism. Thus production management is to plan, organise, direct and control the production activities of a business concern. Now we know that production is an art of making something with the object of satisfying human wants which include service in addition to goods an commodities. But the wants of the customers are not satisfied until the right quality of the products are in their hands with the result the marketing process may also be considered as part of the process of production. In certain organisations marketing of products is a major task in comparison to creation of product while in other organisations marketing process may be of greater importance and may dominate even the creating process. Clearly, the production and marketing are separate but still interdependent functions in a business.

Any business organisation performs functions of production and marketing. Marketing system discovers the need and transmit need to business while production system supply the needs. Fig. 75.1. gives us an idea about the flow of activities in production.

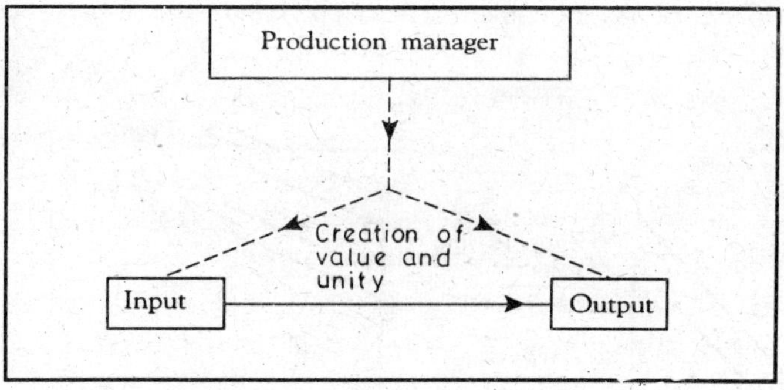

Fig. 75.1. Flow of Activities in Production Management

Production and its Integration with other Areas of the Firm

The interaction of production with various areas of Business Organisation as are shown in Fig. 75.2. The basic functions of Business Organisation are Production, Marketing and Finance.

Finance provide the necessary funds for the maintenance of Production and Marketing activities. Funds not only comes from the sale of goods and services but also acquired through loans—from banks and other financial institutions, sale of stock investment and income. These three functions—Production, Marketing and Finance are to be performed by all the Business Organisations.

The object of production activity is to provide inputs which include raw materials, men, machine, operating supplies, semi finished products, water, power and plant etc. The inputs are assembled and changed to finished goods thereby creating value. The finished products and services are available so that the marketing functions can be utilised to provide, sell and distribute them. Thus production and marketing are separate yet inter-dependent functions in business. The relationship between production management and accounting system is shown in Fig. 75.3.

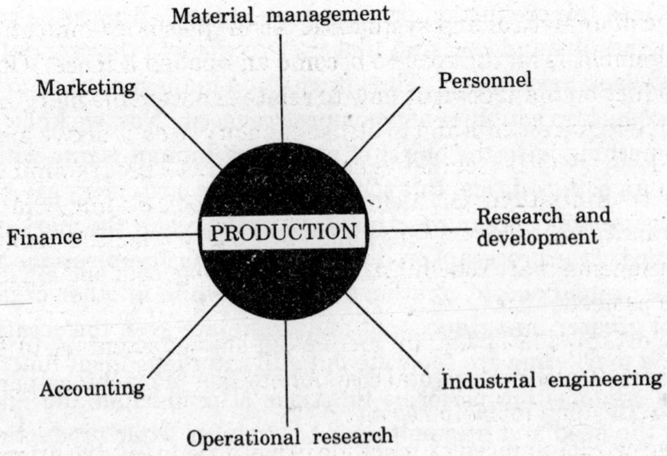

Fig. 75.2. Quantitative Techniques, Interaction of Production with other Areas of Business Organisation.

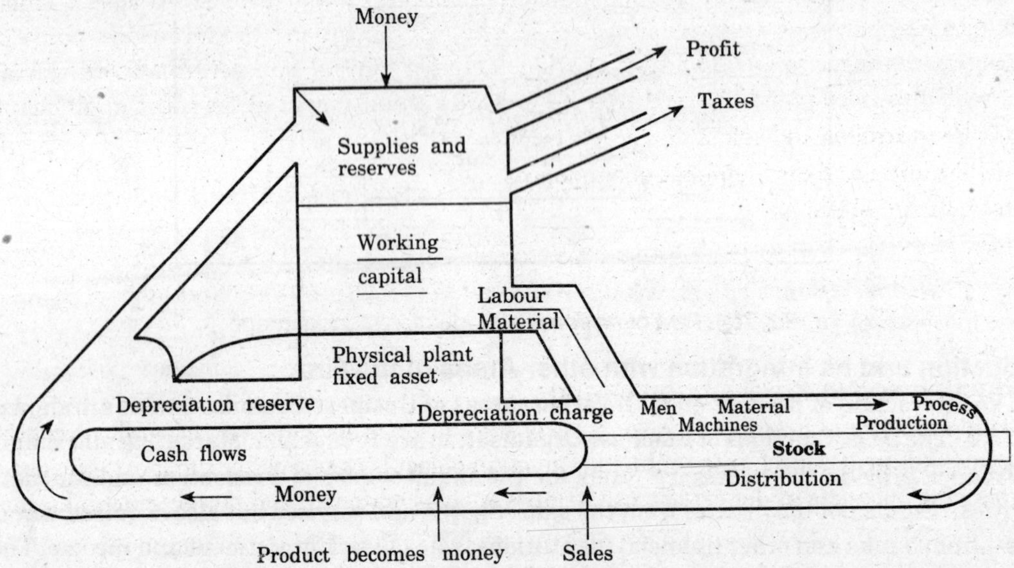

Fig. 75.3. Relationship between Production Management and Financial and Accounting System.

Fig. 75.3 show that money flows from money block to labour, material, taxes and finally dividends to the stock holders. The labour and material enter the production process and the output is obtained.

This output is kept in the form of finished goods inventory until it is distributed and sold. After the money from the sale is realised it goes into the money block and the whole cycle is repeated. The production management significantly influence the control of inventories and process flow.

Production and Quantitative Techniques

The more use of analytical and systematic techniques is an indication that production and operation management is on the road to become an applied science. Operation Research (OR) provides the production management how to relate the variable margin to each product model against productive requirements and to utilise capacity so as to arrive at an optimum marketing goal. The well known (OR) techniques is mathematical programming which has its use in production sales co-ordination. OR techniques helps us in finding what inventory policies and corresponding quality decisions will minimise inventory cost. The common applications of OR is production management are scheduling, transportation, sequencing, forecasting and network analysis of large projects.

Another important use of OR in production management is to find out the optimum machine-per-operator to minimise total cost. As number of machines-per-operator in any group of machines depends upon following costs :

(*a*) Cost of bad-work produced by machine in the absence of operator attending the machine.

(*b*) Cost of having too many operators in waiting for breakdown.

Personnel and Production

The personnel function in any business organisation is mainly concerned with all matters related to manpower as an input system of business organisation. From the view point of the production manager following are the various areas of mutual interest. Each of these areas have been discussed in detail in the area of Personnel Management in the subsequent chapters:

(*a*) Recruitment and selection

(*b*) Training and development of employees.

(*c*) Labour relations

(*d*) Safety.

(*e*) Wage and salary administration including various incentive programmes.

(*f*) Motivating employees to give their best.

Production and Industrial Engineering

This department is responsible for translating the ideas developed in research and development, marketing research into realities. The main object is to search for the most efficient way of producing products under certain constraints such as material, manpower, machines, money etc.

Types of Production

There are three types of production which represent their basic approaches to production. The three types are :

(*a*) Job production

(*b*) Batch production

(*c*) Flow production.

Job Production

In job production the whole product is looked as one job which is to be completed before going on to next. The most common examples are building a ship or a large civil engineering construction job. Job production is hot confined to large projects, it could be the making of a special piece of equipment or a tool.

Batch Production

If qualities of more than one are being made, it is sometimes convenient to split the production into a series of manufacturing stages or operations. Each operation is completed as one of the single items being made, before the next operation is started. In this way a group of identical products, or a batch are made, which move through the production process together.

If more than one types of product is being made, then batches of different products may be moving around the shop floor sometimes requiring operations from the same machine. This leads to problems of how long a machine should be processing a batch of one type of product before going on to the next process, a different one, or which batch should be worked on first. This type of problem tends to make the planning and control of batch production a difficult task.

Continuous Production

When there is a continuous demand for a product, it is sometimes worthwhile setting-up facilities to make that product and no other product. In these circumstances flow production may be the best way of operating. Here the manufacturing is broken down into operations, but each unit moves, or flows, from one operation to the next individually, and not as one of a batch examples are motor manufacturing fertiliser, pharmaceutical and urea manufacturing. Since only one product is being made there are no problems about priorities, but it is necessary to balance the work load at all stages of manufacture.

Production Process

MANUFACTURING

Production Process is a process of producing goods and services by combining and utilising the services of factors of production. Production process is a continuous process which has been going on since the dawn of economic history and will continue till this world lasts. If a man has to live and prosper, he must get goods and services to satisfy his multiplying wants. Since goods and services are produced through production process, the latter becomes very essential for human existence. Production process is a continuous process of economic activity which enables the flow of goods and services and their use for satisfaction of human wants. Human wants are unlimited and go on multiplying and are recurring in nature. The urge to satisfy wants keep the wheels of production process going. Similarly the nature of production process has always been changing with the change in the civilisation of human race because of change in the different aspects of production process. The Production Process has different concept in Traditional Economy and Modern Economy. The main features of production process in traditional economy and modern economy are discussed below :

Table 75.1

S. No.	Traditional Economy	Modern Economy
1.	Production of goods and services is primarily for self consumption	Production of goods and services is for sale in the market.
2.	Use of capital and machinery is nominal as labour intensive methods are used.	Use of capital and machinery is at a large scale and capital intensive methods are used.
3.	There is lack of specialisation and division of labour	Specialisation is at tremendous scale in all lines of production.
4.	There is no uniformity and standardisation of products	Products are uniform and standardised.
5.	Technology is simple and not much change in technology	Technology is latest and continuously changing and complex.
6.	The role of Government is limited as Government does not interfere in the economic activities.	Government participation in production and economic development is increasing continuously.
7.	Production Process is simple and carried out independently	Production process is complex and interdependent.
8.	Organisation of labour and technology is simple	Organisation of labour and technology is complex.

Modern economy is believed to have come into existence after the industrial revolution in European countries in the middle of 18th century. The technological discoveries in the field of transport and communication ; electricity and industrial chemicals has revolutionised the techniques of industrial production. All these led to the emergence of the modern economy in which tremendous changes like production for market, growing specialisation, increasing use of capital technology, large scale production, greater use of money etc. were noticed. The system of production in the modern economy is increasingly capitalistic where capital goods like tools, machinery raw materials, plants, buildings, railways, trucks, chemicals etc. form the basis of large scales production. Thus modern economy where production is for the market and at a large scale, makes extensive use of capital.

What is Manufacturing

Production is a sequence of manufacturing operations that transforms materials into finished products. Manufacturing includes in all the actions and processes which result in the production of finished articles. The production process consists of several stages *viz.*

- Preparing for production
- Receiving materials
- Making and machining billets and blanks
- Making components
- Assembling units
- Separate articles
- Checking the quality of the parts and assemblies
- Testing the finished articles
- Painting
- Packing
- Shipment etc.

The success of each step depends on type if the organisation and also on an uninterrupted supply of materials, the proper tools, efficient maintenance and accurate stock taking. Due to the great variety of types of production, there is no uniform structure of machine building plants. The most efficient structure for the plant is adopted in each case depending on the specific conditions and preserve only the basic common principles of organisation. The shops, which are the basic production sections of any plant, are subdivided into main and auxiliary shops. In the main shops the parts are manufactured and the units and complete articles assembled. The auxiliary shops (tool repair shops etc.) and services keep the main shops functioning normally.

The division into shops can be made either on the 'object' principle, each shop producing a certain variety of parts or units, or on the 'technological' principles, each shop being assigned certain operations. The shops are sub-divided into sections organised either on the principle of similar equipment or the production of one type of article. The sections in turn are sub-divided into work places each for one work man or for a team. In addition, the plant comprises of a number of departments ; planning, supply, preparation, design engineering, labour and wages, accounts etc.

Types of Production

There are three types of production depending on the quantity of articles produced and the nature of their manufacture the types of production can be classified into three categories *viz.* piece meal system lot system and mass production system.

(*i*) **Piece meal production system.** It is characterized by the output of small quantities of articles of diverse nomenclature. On the piece production system each article is made by consecutive operations specified in the flow process charts.

(*ii*) **Lot Production System.** It is characterised by the output of recurrent batches of articles. It is sub-divided into small lot and large lot production. The lot production process is based on the principles of parallel - consecutive operations, sub-divided into separate elements. Lot production is recorded in operating process charts.

(*iii*) **Mass Production System.** It is characterised by manufacturing one type of article in large numbers. The mass production process is based on the principle of 'parallel operations'. In mass production greater efficiency of labour is achieved due to high specialisation.

Similarly Types of Production can also be classified as under :

(*a*) **Line Production.** The main characteristics of line production are the use of line layout, and the minimization of the transfer quality. Line production can be used for machining - in all industries - and also for assembly. Although the term line production can be used in a general sense to cover several of variants described below, it is reserved in a particular sense for cases where lines are used for one particular established product. Because the work centres in this case are left permanently set-up, run and set-up frequencies are low. Because the machines are adjacent and in the transfer quantities of one can be used, and transfer frequencies are therefore very high.

(*b*) **Line batch production.** Line layout can also be used for families of similar items of established design which are all tooled to use the same machines or assembly line in the same sequence. In this case, batches of the different components follow each other down the line, each machine being reset as it completes the last item in a run. The transfer quantity is again minimised but cannot achieve the high transfer frequencies obtained with pure line production.

In this instance the capacities of the different station on the line are balanced to the total requirements of different components at different stations on the line, there is generally some ebb and flow of work in progress stock between the machines.

(*c*) **Group batch production.** Group batch production is characterised mainly by the use of group layout. Because in this case all machining operations for each components in the group family are controlled by one supervisor, it is possible to start some operations before the previous operations are completed, but it is generally impossible to achieve the high transfer frequencies attainable with line production.

(*d*) **Functional batch production.** Functional batch production is characterized mainly by the use of functional layout. Due to the administrative complication with this type of layout. It is generally essential to fix the same values for order, run, set-up, and transfer quantity for each component processed. This type of production is therefore generally accompanied by very low rates of stock turnover.

(*e*) **Line jobbing production.** Jobbing production is a type in which the product design is not established, but is only known with the customer's order is received. Where there is specialisation in the type of product for which orders are accepted, line production can still be used. It is much more difficult to achieve a balanced line, and such devices as variable overtime for different parts of the line may have to be used to maintain balance and minimise the stock between stations.

(*f*) **Group jobbing production.** In this instance group layout is used, each group being equipped to produce a general type of product.

(*g*) **Functional jobbing production.** Functional jobbing production finally is jobbing production with functional layout. Because production is infinitely variable, it is probably impossible to design a classification system which will cover all possible differences, even in simple production systems. In most companies there is a wide variety of flow types, and the type varies according to the level which is being examined and from one process to the next. In spite of these difficulties the above classification has been found in practice to give a useful indication of the general type of material flow in use.

Foundation of Production Management

During the last two to three decades, the focus of attention has moved from traditional techniques such as time study, wave incentive determination, production control, plant layout, work methods design job evaluation, equipment selection, tooling etc. to systems techniques including or techniques and the use of EDP. Further, it can be noticed that a change of interest from the efficiency of individual, manual work, the use of individual technical resources and the interaction between the man and machine to methods and techniques related to the process of planning and control of materials flow through a system of man machine components. As a result of this change various disciplines such as production control operations management logicsticks, materials management and systems analysis concepts have been developed.

Approaches to Production Management

Three main approaches in modern production management are :

1. The decision theory approach
2. The systems approach
3. The contigency approach

1. **The decision theory approach.** It has adopted elements from decision theory. The approach is based upon the assumption that there is a general decision and problem hierarchy which provides a logical structure to describe the subject.

Problems which fall outside the hierarchical structure tend to be looked as non-production management problems. The approach is oriented towards the decision maker and the ambition is to provide the decision maker with a set of techniques that makes rational decision possible for example, the *first* decision is the decision as to which process orientation is the best. The process can be continuous, intermitted or project. After this major choice is made other process design decisions must follow. This includes selection of equipment, detailed design of the process, make or buy decisions facility location and the way in which the process facilities are laid out or decisions that follow subsequently. Then the focus is shifted to the work station. Once the process has been designed it must be scheduled operate land control. A forecast is required to draw the schedule. Routine inventory planning and control system must be employed. Finally the quality of product must be periodically sampled to ensure that actual output complies with process objectives

2. **Systems approach.** The systems approach is characterised by the use of the general systems theory framework. Systems theory helps us to get in sides into the over all structure of production management problems. It tends to be a strong instrument for description and it has some sort of analytical appeal. It emphasis a total few rather than isolated problems.

It has been demonstrated that the most common approach includes the idea that we are dealing with two separate systems : a production system and a decision and information system. The decisions can be categorised into two groups -- those related to the design of the system and those related to the control of the system. The design of the system includes problem areas such as the selection and design of products, selection of equipment and process, job design, location of the system and facility layout. The control of the system includes inventory control, production control, maintenance, quality control, labour control and so on.

Type	*Flow System*	Batch Frequency			*Order Cycles*	Order-ing Phase	*Remarks*
		Run	*Transfer*	*Set-up*			
Line production	Line	Low	V. high	Low	Single	Single	On line per component
Line batch production	Line	12-100 p.a.	High	Same as run	Single	Single	On line per family
Group batch production	Group	12-26 p.a.	High	Same as run	Single	Single	One group per family
Functional batch	Functional	1-12 p.a.	Same as run	Same as run	Multi	Multi	—
Line jobbing production	Line	Same as order	High	Same as order	—	—	One line per family
Group jobbing production	Group	Same as order	High	Same as order	—	—	One group per family
Functional job-bing production	Functional	Same as order	Same as order	Same as order	—	—	—

The above table is highly comprehensive as it integrates the various type of production with Batch frequency, orders cycle and ordering phase.

A more co- sistent systems approach can be classified as follows :

(*a*) the formation of objectives for the system and its components.

(*b*) the design of a system containing human and fiscal resources to achieve the objectives.

(*c*) the allocation of resources to organisational units.

(*d*) the design of planning and control system.

(*e*) the evaluation of components and systems performance.

3. **The contingency approach.** This approach is characterised by the assumption that there are some important contingencies determining the relevance of different problems and therefore determining the problem structure in a given situation. The contingency approach seems to offer a significantly better instrument for description as well as better framework for explanation and prediction concerning management problems. However, it is not based on imperical dates.

Major Production Management Problems Vis-a-vis Major Production System

1. **Distribution Systems**

(*a*) Determination of the distribution of demand.

(*b*) Forecasting demand.

(*c*) Determination of how much to order at one time.

(*d*) Determination of when to reorder.

(*e*) Determination of service levels and the size of buffer stocks.

(*f*) Design of data-processing systems.

2. **High-Volume Production Distribution Systems**

(*a*) Forecasting demand and the behaviour of multi-stage inventory systems.

(*b*) Long-range aggregate planning for facilities - plant capability, sizes and location, and warehouse sizes and location.

(*c*) Production facility design.

(*d*) Aggregate planning and scheduling for facilities and manpower.

(*e*) Raw materials procurement

(*f*) Day-to-day scheduling and adjustment of production levels as demand become known.

(*g*) Design of data-processing systems.

3. **Intermittent Systems**

(*a*) Design and layout of a system to minimize aggregate handling cost.

(*b*) Forecasting demand.

(*c*) Aggregate planning for the use of facilities.

(*d*) Scheduling orders to meet promised delivery dates.

(*e*) Scheduling labour and equipment to minimised combined costs of machine set-up, machine down time, labour over time and under time and in-process inventories.

(*f*) Scheduling equipment to utilize most efficient process.

(*g*) Procuring materials in economical quantities to mesh with the production schedule.

(*h*) Developing bidding policy and procedure to obtain orders at margins that will achieve a balance between the use of labour and facilities and the desire for profit.

4. **Large Scale Projects**

(*a*) Planning a network of operations to accomplish the desired result.

(*b*) Developing schedules of the network of operations such that the critical patch schedule of the network meets promised delivery dates.

(*c*) Allocating the use of limited resources of equipment and/or labour in ways that will not interfere with the critical path schedule.

(*d*) Procuring materials by a schedule that minimises total inventory costs but meets the needs of the critical path schedule.

(*e*) Developing bidding policy and procedures to obtain contracts at margins that will achieve a balance between the use and maintenance of the stockpile of critical resources (engineers, scientists, skilled labour, key facilities and so on) and the desire for profit.

Trade off Decisions

The various important trade off decision indicating Decision Areas ; Decisions and various alternatives are given in Table 75.1. Similarly Table 75.2 indicates the various constraints which should be studied to understand the Economics of the Industry and Technology of the Industry.

Table 75.1. Trade off Decisions in Manufacturing

Decision Areas	*Decision*	*Alternatives*
Plant and Equipment	Span of process plant size plant location	Make or buy one being plant or several smaller locate near markets or locate near materials
	Investment decisions	Invest mainly in buildings or equipment or inventories or research.
	Choice of equipment Kind of tooling	General purpose of special purpose equipment. Temporary minimum tooling or production tooling.
Production Planning and Control	Frequency of inventory taking	Few or many breaks in production for buffer stocks.
	Inventory size	High inventory or a lower inventory.
	Degree of inventory	Control is great detailor in lesser detail
	What to control	Controls designed to minimize machine down time or labour cost or time in process or to maximise output of particular products or usage.
	Quality Control	High reliability and quality or low costs.
	Use of standards	Formal or informal or none at all.
Labour and Staffing	Job Specialisation	Highly specialized or not highly, specialized.
	Supervision	Technically trained first line supervisory or non technically trained supervisors.
	Wave system	Many jobs grade or few job grades, incentives wage or hourty wages.
	Supervision	Close supervision or loss supervision
	Industrial Engineers	Many or few such men.
Product Design/Engineering	Size of product line	Many customer specials or new specials or none at all.
	Design stability	Frozen design or many engineering change orders
	Technological risk	Use of new processes unapproved by competitors or follow-the-leader policy
	Engineering	Complete packaged design or design as you go approach.
	Use of manufacturing engineering	Few or many manufacturing engineers.

Organisation and Management	Kinds of organisation	Functional or product focus or geographical or other
	Executive use of time	High involvement in investment or production planning or cost control or quality control or other activities.
	Degree of risk assumed	Decision based on much or little information
	Use of staff Executive style	Large or small staff group much or little involvement in detail ; authoritarian or nondirective style ; Much or little contact with organisation.

Table 75.2. Various Constraints to Production

A. Economics of the Industry

-- Labour, burden material depreciation costs
-- Flexibility of production to meet change in volume
-- Return on investment, prices, margins
-- Number and location of plants
-- Critical control variables
-- Critical functions (*e.g.* maintenance, production control, personnel)
-- Typical financial structures
-- Typical costs and cost relationship
-- Typical operating problems
-- Barriers to entry
-- Pricing practices
-- 'Maturity' of industry products, markets, production practices, and so on.
-- Importance of economics of scale
-- Importance of integrated capacities of corporations
-- Importance of having a certain balance of different types of equipment
-- Ideal balances of equipment capacities
-- Nature and type of production control
-- Government influences

B. Technology of the Industry

-- Rate of technological change
-- Scale of processes
-- Span of processes
-- Degree of Mechanisation
-- Timber requirements for making change.

Production System

Introduction

It would be difficult to over emphasize the crucial role the effective productive systems play in modern society and in our life style. *Webster* defines a system as a regularly interacting or interdependent group of items forming unified whole. Thus a system may have many components and objects, but they are united in the pursuit of some goal. The components of a system contribute to the production of a set of outputs from given inputs which may or may not be optimal or best with respect to some appropriate measure of effectiveness. Systems are often complex although the definition does not specify that they need to be. Invariably, every system is affected by its environment and every system can be thought of as a part of an even larger system. A broad definition of systems runs the risk of leaving out important details involving in the functioning of the system. It is true that some of the most interesting systems for study are complex and that a change in one variable within the system will affect many other variables of the system. Thus in productive system a change in production system may effect inventory, hours of work, overtime hours, facility layout, and so on.

In a given production system, successful management depends on information system concerning what is actually happening, and how we react to changes in demand, inventory position schedules, quality level and product and equipment innovation. It is a known fact that the high out per man hour economy is thought of as being efficient while its opposite is thought of as being inefficient. But production efficiency is a relative term meaning, essentially, how effectively we employ the appropriate available resources for a given unit of output.

In order to meet the objective of a company all the subsystems must also be streamlined in the overall production system. In order to meet the production system. In order to meet the production plan, certain realities interfere such as equipment failure, human error, discrepancies in the timing of order flow quality variation, and so on. Therefore, systems for scheduling maintenance, quality control, and cost control are invented to help retain order where otherwise the system would naturally tend toward chaos.

History of Production System

A formal attention to production economics was paid by the great scottish economist *Adam Smith* in his book "The wealth of the Nations" in which he emphasised the importance of division of labour. The book was a milestone in the development of production economics because Smith observed that there existed a rational for production. After Adam Smith, an Englishman, *Charles Babbage,* augmented Smith's observations about production organisation and economics. Charles Babbage, crystalised his views in the book, "On the Economy of Machinery and manufactures" concerning the economic advantages resulting from the division of labour. In the years after Adam Smith's and Charles Babbage's observations, the division of labour continued and then accelerated during the first half of the twentieth century.

Frederick W. Taylor was undoubtedly the outstanding historical figure in the development of the production management field. Smith and Babbage were observers and writers, but Taylor was both a thinker and a doer. He was an authoritarian with indomitable will, a fact that caused him to be greatly criticised but, at the same time, may have been a source of his great contributions. Taylor listed four new duties of management which may be summerised as under:

(*i*) The development of a science for each element of a man's work to replace old rule-of-thumb methods.

(*ii*) The scientific selection, training and development of workers instead of allowing the workman to choose his own tasks and to train himself as he could.

(*iii*) To develop the spirit of co-operation between the work-man and management to ensure that work could be carried out in accordance with scientifically devised procedure.

(*iv*) The division of work between the workers and the management in almost equal share for which they are best suited.

Taylor's work developed in the field of methods engineering, work measurement and human engineering. Taylor's uncomprising attitude in developing and installing his ideas caused much controversy, and he was strongly opposed in many quarters. Taylor's followers were numerous. *Cart Barth; Henry L. Gantt ; Harrington Emerson, Frank and Lillian Gilbreth and others worked within Taylor's general framework and philosophy.* Some of the products of Taylor's thinking are *viz*; Wagė Payment plans; Time study methods; and Charts and Mechanical control boards.

System

System is a very popular word with different meaning to different levels of executives. In a business organisation which is composed of formal and informal groups which function both within themselves and as part of the total organisation. Man is a system yet he has sub-systems such as reciprocatory digestive and nervous system. Each system receives stimuli and reacts. The sub-system operating within itself and it receives information from and sends information to other sub-systems. Each sub-system operates in a logical way both internally and as a part of the larger system. The idea of system in a business is the flow of information. Information flows into sub-system and causes certain actions. In a system the information flow is man made. System analysis is the study of the information flow and the development of systems is best serve the whole organisation. The term system can also be referred to as a methodical way of planning, coordinating the work to produce complex project.

The PERT is a system of this type. A system can also means a mathematic model. The system can also be defined as a means of maintaining existing routines work or it is a means of bringing a clear vision of the business to those who operate it. Let us discuss here that part of system which is basically concerned with the transmitting of information to the right place in the right form with right content for taking right action. We spend a lot of money to transmit information, part of the information is really pertinent and part of it is really redundant. Certain types of information do not change for long periods such as engineering design, costing and planning information.

Designing a System

One should know the following steps to design a system.

1. A system is merely for the purpose of mechanising highly routine tasks such as preparation of pay rolls, bills, divident for the shareholders etc.

2. One should work on the system of thought before working on the system modernisation.

3. The systems are known as control systems and are presumably designed for the purpose of providing information to certain key executives so that through them centralised location may exercise broader control of operations.

4. One must know to design an efficient system--the purpose, time span, inherent stability and keeping in view of potential changes.

Challenges to System Approach Risks

The danger and opportunity to system approach stem from the ability to handle large amount of information quickly. The new tools of data handling and computation which can centralise authority and power in small groups of people. The risk of inflexibility, problem of adequate information, recentralisation, challenges of the near future are the limitations.

Challenges

The growth and the progress of an organisation depends to a considerable extent on simplifying processes to move forward with the complicating and complex processes.

These can be accomplished with executives ability to go forward indefinitely without becoming the causalities of their own complexities. We should devise our systems so that business managers and individual contributors become part of the system, rather than the servant of these managers.

System Staff

The integrated system cover the flow of information throughout the company, therefore there is a need to have a staff department to develop and see the operations of the system. The system staff improves business management by applying creative thinking to problems of business communication. The medium of communication is written. Its products are policies and procedures. Systems studies recommend management action, form and flow charts are designed to picture the sequence of staff in a procedure. In a real sense the system staff is responsible for the network of company communication, (written and verbal) between groups and departments, between management and employees linking the operations of the organisation to its future plans. System approach work out the problems from management's point of view but to accomplish this it must be close to companies activities.

Organisation

In system staff there are two types of men :

1. The practitioner--responsible for all efforts of certain departments.

2. The specialist-who goes in certain fields in depth such as production equipment, tabulating systems, special requirements of electronic data processing and so forth.

Definition

A system can be defined as a inter connected complex of functional related components designed to achieve pre-determined goals of the organisation. A system can be considered as a structure of sub-systems each having the following characteristics as shown in Fig. 75.4.

Characteristics are :

- Inputs
- Transformation Process
- Output and
- Feedback.

A production system on the other hand is defined as the frame work of activities within which the creation of value can occur. To understand the economics of production the concept of production system should be clearly understood. If we look up a manufacturing plans in normal operation we find that it groups of related activities which frequently cut cross the functional or departmental subdivision of the plant. Such group of related tasks are known as system. They reflect a particular objective and are combined in a manner which permits its economic achievement. Thus a system of periodic maintenance and over-haul of production plant interacts with production schedules, maintenance budgets, spare parts inventory, equity control etc. A system can be a simple and local or complex with a number of sub-systems integrated within an overall structure.

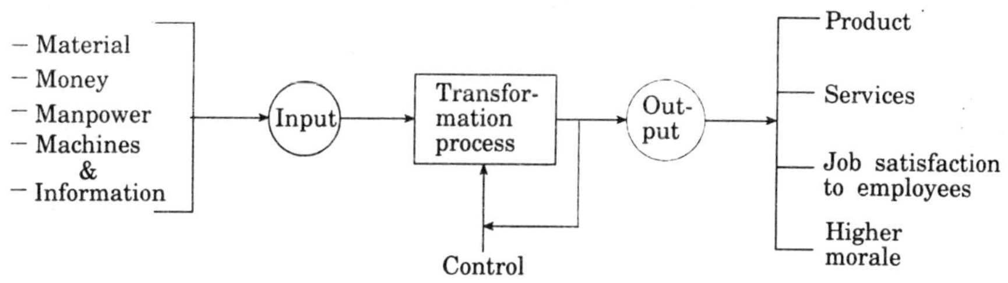

Fig. 75.4 Characteristics of a System

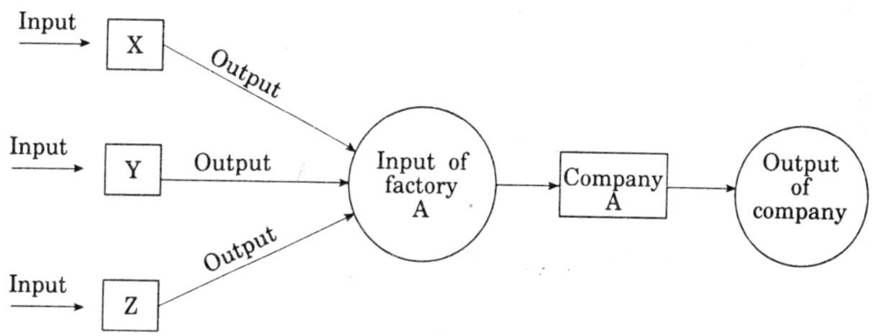

Fig. 75.5. Represent a Production System

A system can be an open system or a closed system. In a closed system we assume that the outside events influence takes to long to make an impact that they can be neglected. It is although unrealistic to assume this in case of companies which have developed a separate to analyse and evaluate changes and trends in the outside work as a management-services function.

Fig. 75.5 in an example of a production system approach. It shows a parallel configuration where the output from three sub-systems X, Y, and Z are bought together to form the input to the sub-system A.

The output of factory A is the input of company A and similarly the output of Company A is the final output of the Company.

A broader view of system approach treats a business organisation a system with various departments as sub-system. The organisation is further surrounded by a bigger system, that is Industry of which the organisation is the part. The Industry is also surrounded by a still bigger system that is society. So each system becomes a sub-system when it is compared with a still larger system. Similarly a smaller sub-system when studied in isolation becomes a system in itself if Marketing department when studied it becomes a Marketing system as shown in the Fig. 75.7.

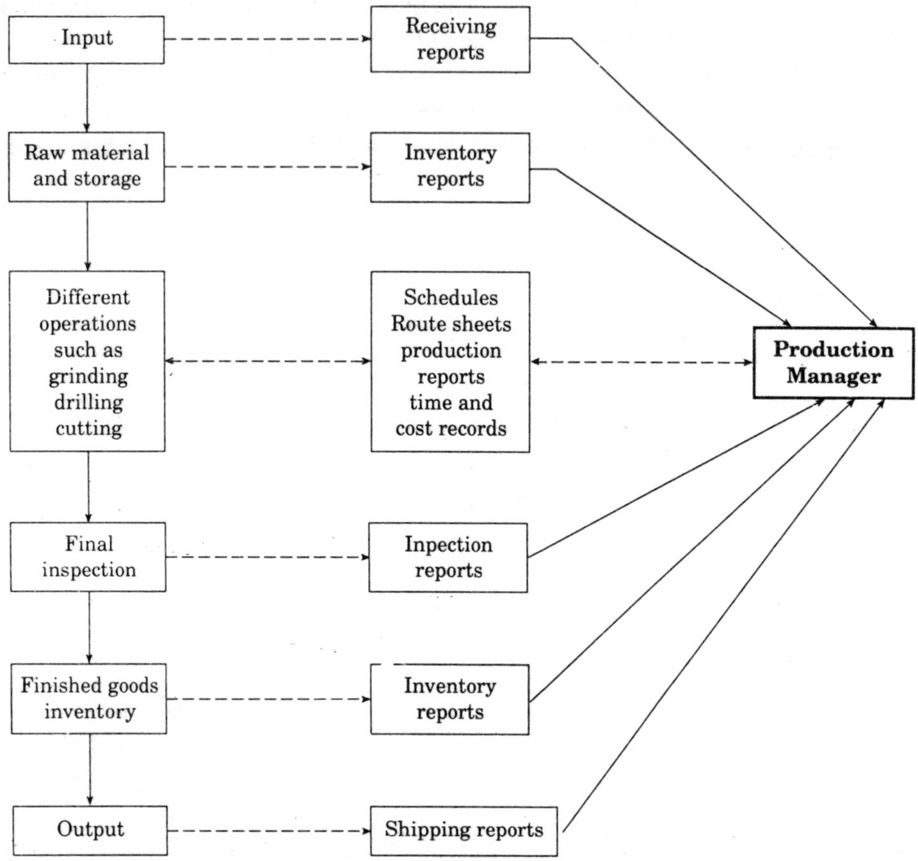

Fig. 75.6. Production System.

System Man Coordinates Activities

1. Reduction in the operating time cycles.
2. Lowering of inventories.
3. Reductions of errors in predicting cost and delivery dates.
4. Elimination of unnecessary functions and activities.
5. Faster working capital turnover and reduction of working capital requirements.
6. Greater operating flexibility-Faster transfer of top management decisions into action.
7. Elimination of the conflicting systems and operations which work at cross purposes.
8. Increase in the effectiveness of supervision.

MARKETING SYSTEMS

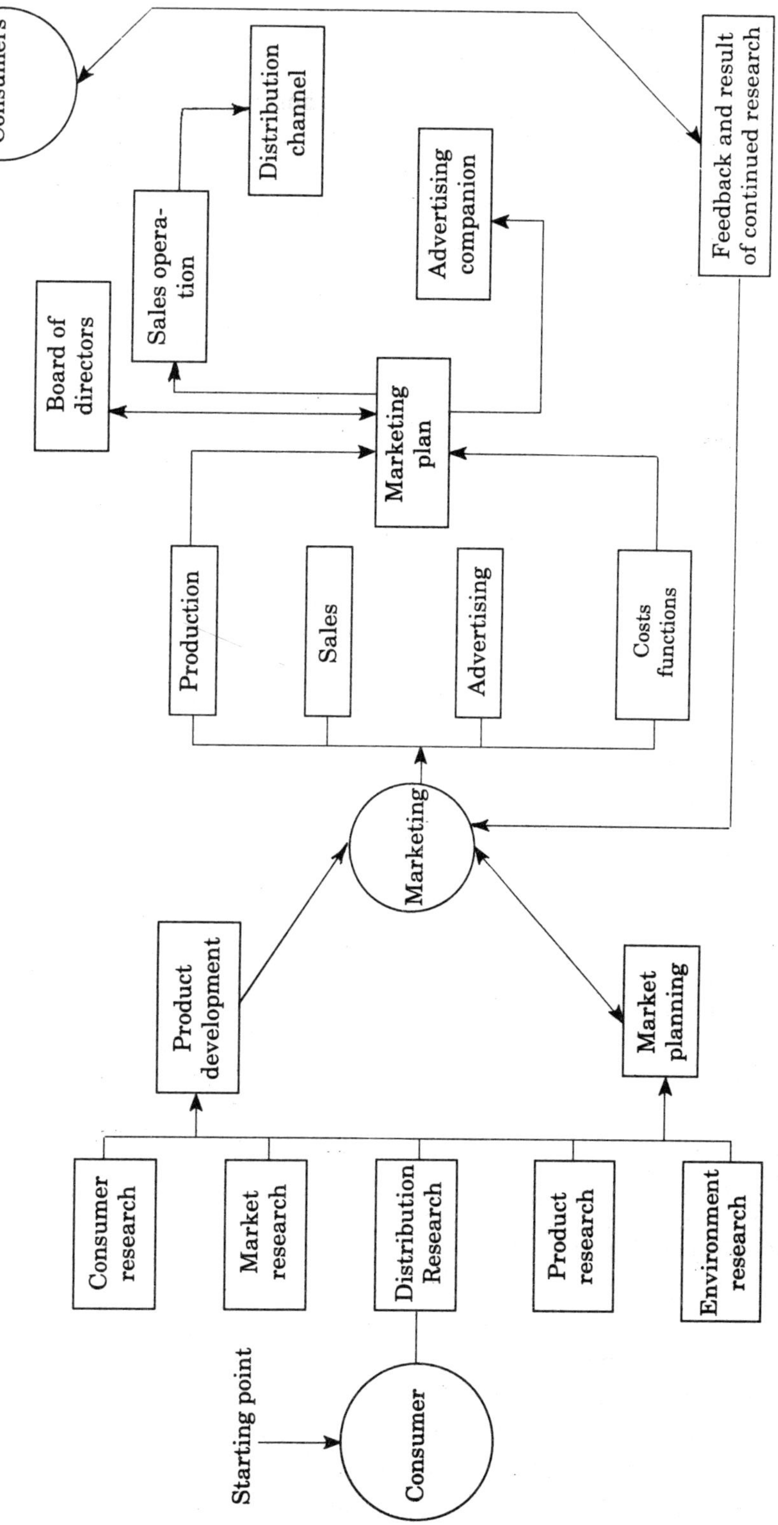

Fig. 75.7.

9. Strengthening of the organization structure of the enterprise through the disclosure and elimination of practices which violate sound organizational principles.

10. Reducing of the routine cost of performing the planning organizing, controlling and service functions required in the enterprise.

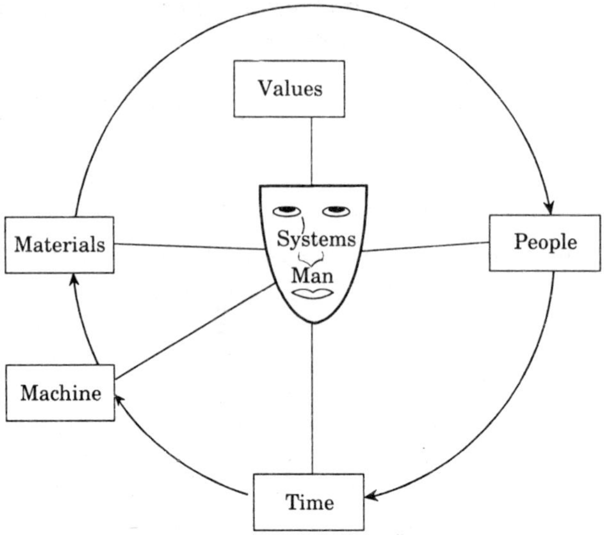

Fig. 75.8. Activities coordinated by system man.

The narrow view of the system approach we treat the system only as a flow of information in the organisation. The information flows into the sub-systems and causes certain action. This generates results and so resultant information flows out. Each sub-system operates in a logical way both internally and as part of the whole. If this is the concept of the system then Organisation and system can be compared as follows :

Organisation *Vs*	*System*
1. It refers to individual and group.	It refers what and how things are done.
2. It emphasises designs of organisation structure.	It emphasises communication structure-than of organisation needs.
3. It stresses chain of command authority and responsibility.	It stresses channels of communication - information flow and decisions.
4. It provides compartments of authority and responsibility	It provides network of questions and answers.

Types of Production Systems

There are two types of Production Systems (1) Intermittent Production (2) Continuous Production.

The intermittent production system examples are machine shop production, building contractor. The continuous production examples are chemical plants, automobile industry etc. Most of the companies cannot be classified straight as intermittent or continuous production, rather in one department of the company continuous production is there while in other departments intermittent production exists. The time required for a continuous production system is always less than the intermittent production systems. The assembly line production of cars or scooters where the product is coming off every few minutes is considered as continuous production. On the other hand in intermittent production systems the products are in a state of partial completion for several weeks or days.

In continuous production systems the most common material handling equipments are belt conveyers, roller conveyers, chutes, rails etc. It is because in continuous production systems one or a few standard products are manufactured with pre-determined sequence of operations with inflexible material handling devices. In intermittent production system portable materials handling equipments are used and various products are produced with greater flexibility in the system.

Continuous production system require a larger investment than intermittent production system because of fixed path material handling equipments, costly control mechanism and special purpose machines for various operations. Even the marketing techniques also differ for continuous production system and intermittents production system.

Intermittent production system the marketing efforts are directed towards meeting individual orders for various products while in continuous production the marketing efforts are directed towards developing distribution channels for the large volume of output. The design of a production system starts with the firm and re-occurs intermittently when redesign is necessary. The major decision in the design of production system is the location of plant. Once the location has been decided the next decision relates to layout of facilities. Another problems which concerns the decision of production system is how products are designed and manufactured.

Man-Machine System

The man-machine-system basically consists of three typical systems; Manual, Semi-automatic ; or Mechanical and Automatic System.

Manual System involve man with only mechanical aids or hand tools. Man supplies the power required and acts as controller or the process; the tools and mechanical aids help multiply his efforts. *Semiautomatic system* involve "man" mainly as controller of the process. He interacts with the machine by sensing information about the process, interpreting it and using a set of controls which may start and stop the machine and possibly make intermediate adjustments. Power is normally supplied by the machine. These are combinations of the manual and semiautomatic systems where the man is also supplying some of the system power. The Man-Machine system is given as in (Fig. 75.9*a*) and (Fig. 75.9*b*). The figures show the general cycle of activity of "man-machine." system of the semiautomatic type imbedded in the working environment. The 'Man' is supplying some of the system power ; in loading the machine or in some activity in which the man may be involved while machine goes through its cycle in the combinations of manual an semiautomatic systems. *Automatic systems* presumably do not need a man since all of the functions of sensing information processing and decision, and action are performed by the machine Automation at such a level is not economically justified even if the machines could be designed. In this role the man periodically or continuously maintain surveillance over the process through displays which indicate the state of the crucial parameters of the process. Man-Machine system analysis study the information input focussing on visual displays, human control of man-machine systems including human motor activities, human control of systems, man-machinery relationships, analysis of hand motions, and the analysis of man and man-machine cycles; and working environment and its impact on output. The manipulative activity is representative of the dominant features of manual systems; the information input, sensing, and controlling activities are representative of both semiautomatic and automatic system, and the information input and general monitoring or surveillance activities and representative of automatic systems. The impact of environment and the physical relationships of the man to work flow and workplace arrangements are of course, applicable to all "man-machine" systems.

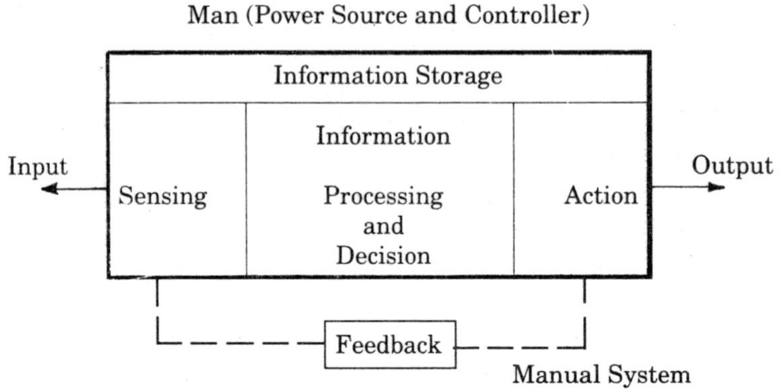

Fig. 75.9a. Man as Controller

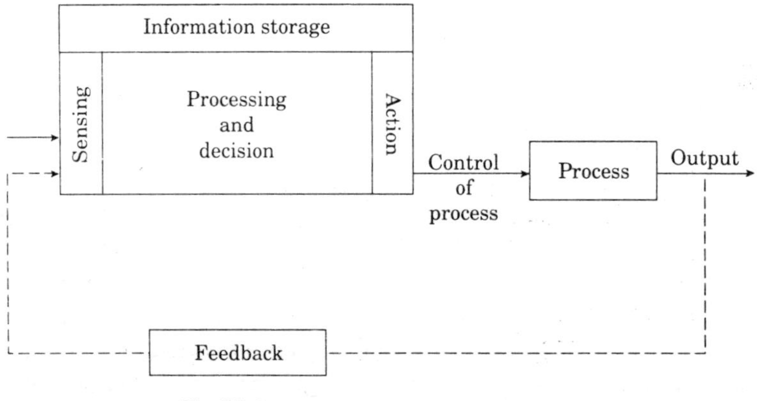

Fig. 75.9b. Semiautomatic System

Functions Performed by Man-Machine Systems

The functions performed by man man-machine systems are represented in Fig. 75.10. The functions are generally comparable to these of the closed loop feed back diagram. The four basic classes of functions are sensing, information allage, information processing, and action. The information storage interacts with three of the other functions. Information is received by the sensing function. The machine sensing is usually much more special or single purpose in nature than the broadly capable human sense. Information storage for man is in the human memory or by access to records. Machine information storage can be magnetic drum; magnetic tape; punched cards, discs; etc. Input and Output is related to the raw material or the thing being processed. The output represents some transformation of the input. The process themselves may be of any type, that is chemical, processes to change shape or form, assembly, transport, clerical, and so on. Information feedback concerning the output rates is an essential ingredient for it provides the basis for control.

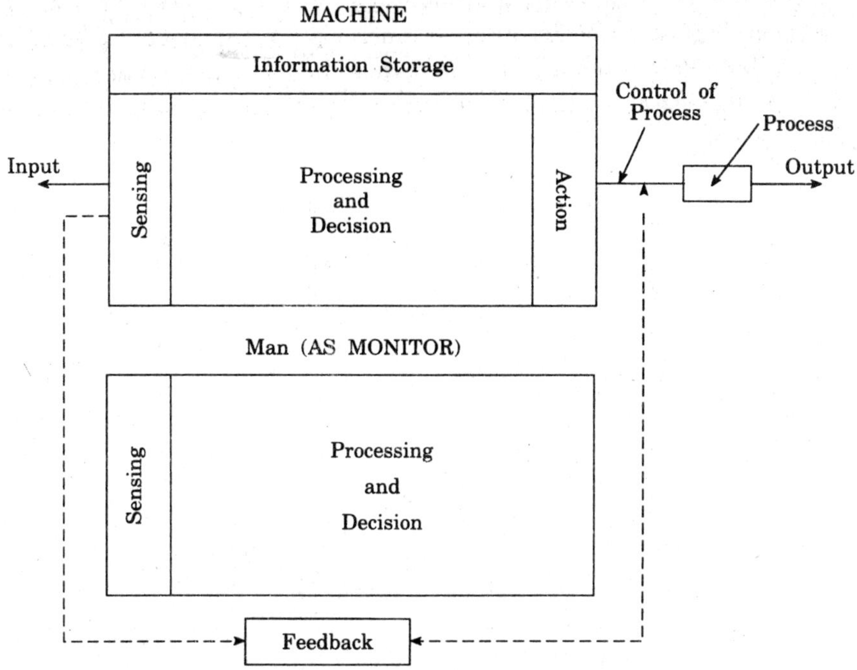

Fig. 75.10. Automatic System.

Man Versus Machines

The man has certain physiological ; psychological and sociological characteristics which define both his capabilities and his limitations in the work situations. These characteristics are not static but vary form individual to individual. In performing work, man's functions fall into three general classifications *viz* ; Receiving information thorough various sense organs ; making decisions based on information received ; Taking action based on decisions ; Machines on other hand perform tasks as faithful servants reacting mainly to physical factors. But man reacts to his psychological and sociological environment as well as physical environment. Human beings appear to surpass existing machines in their ability to ; Delect small amounts of light and sound;

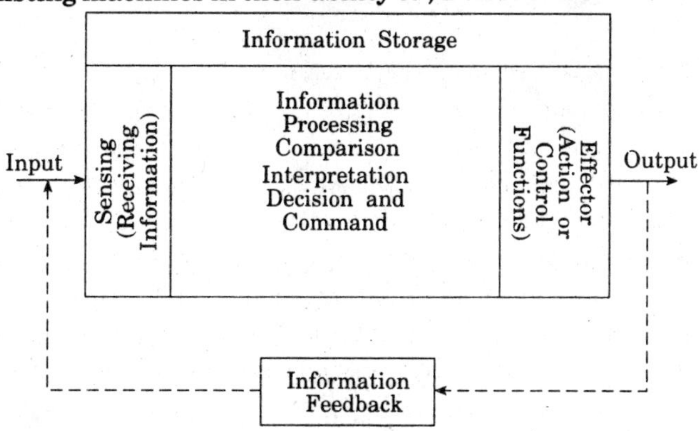

Fig. 75.11.

store large amounts of information for long periods and recall the relevant facts at the appropriate time; Exercise Judgment ; develop concepts and create methods. The existing machines however appear to surpass humans in their ability to ; Respond quickly to control signals ; Apply great force smoothly and precisely ; Perform repetitive and routine tasks ; Perform rapid computation ; Perform different functions simultaneously. Where low cost labour is available as in India it is economical to use manual labour even in many tasks in which man is not well suited. Because of relatively high wages in developed country the machines are used much more extensively.

76

Productivity and System Concepts

What is a System

According to Mason Richardson, a system is a set of coordinated components. These components can be considered as subsystems. These sub-systems interact with each other to produce an output in relation to the inputs utilised. A system, therefore, has basic objectives to be achieved. The performance or output of a system has to be compared against the objectives. A system approach stipulates to look at performance in totality ; the performance as a result of interaction of components (sub-systems) comprising the system. An organisation can be considered to encompass systems of Production, Marketing, Financial Management, etc.

Productivity of a System

It represents the overall efficiency of the system. It signifies so to how well a system is performing against the objectives or goals. Essentially, therefore, in systems approach, the performance objectives of the system under evaluation form an important aspect in an exercise of productivity measurement. The performance objectives become the pivotal point to start the exercise. These must be laid down and qualified. The performance objectives also help one to know the resources (as inputs) for development for improvement in productivity.

Good Productivity Measurement under Systems Concept

The following essential attributes of Productivity Measurement Model are needed :

(*a*) Productivity measures should reflect as to how well a system is doing with reference to its performance objectives.

(*b*) It should take into account all outputs of the system. Outputs are not only the products manufactured or products sold. Outputs are the achieved objectives.

(*c*) It should take into account all the resources consumed in the process to achieve the output (achieved objectives).

(*d*) The model should provide information as the deployment or reallocation of sources to obtain better productivity.

(*e*) If the system has multi-performance objectives, the model should reorganise the relative importance of each of the objectives.

(*f*) The data, which the model proposes to use should be easily available and comprehensible. It should be management oriented.

What comprises a Production System

A Production System basically is meant to produce marketable goods in right quantity, right quality, at minimum cost and in right time. In the process the production system uses several, resources, including men machinery, materials and capital, and through conversion known as manufacturing process converts raw materials or semi-finished goods or components to finished saleable products. The production system, therefore, essentially is an organised entity which uses facilities of man power, machine or plant capacity, materials and capital in a controlled manner to achieve the desired objectives decided well in advance. In manufacturing saleable goods it also takes into account requirements of the customers existing or potential, to meet their demands of quality, quantity and timely supplies. The production system organises (itself essentially in these directions. Besides, product on system as considered above does not vary widely in different types of production operations like the mass production, the batch-size production or the flow production. Only the extent of utilization of different resources vary. The production system to comprise of a number of manufacturing facilities alongwith man-power, direct as well indirect, to convert raw materials to finished goods. The process of conversion calls for expenses on tools, consumables, utilities, maintenance, etc. and it is presumed that the expenditure falls under the perview of the production system. In line with known organizational practices, it is presumed that materials procurement storage, design and development of products do not forms a part of the production system under review.

Performance objectives of a Production System

A Production System can have several objectives. These will vary in consonance with the corporate objectives of the company. However, it is essential that these objectives are known in concrete quantitative terms. A proper modification of objectives helps in planning, organising activities and monitoring of the performance. As a matter of fact, an exercise of productivity measurement is meaningful only if performance objectives are identified and qualitified. For the production function the following task can be considered as important ones for a satisfactory performance :

— Control of Labour Costs.
— Control of Material Costs.
— Optimum use of Plant and Machine capacities.
— Fulfilment of Production Programme on time.
— Improvement of Profitability.
— Achievement of Quality Standards.
— Training of Workmen.
— Control of through-put cycle.
— Control of the use of capital.
— Protecting Company Assets.
— Good House Keeping.
— Reduction of Costs.
— Improvement in Technology.
— Maintenance Expenditure.

In brief the following can be considered as performance objectives of a Production function:

(*i*) Labour Utilization.
(*ii*) Capacity Utilization.
(*iii*) Material Utilization.
(*iv*) Completion of Schedules.
(*v*) Capital Utilization.
(*vi*) Control or Indirect Expenditure.
(*vii*) Cost Control.

Labour Utilization

The most important function in any production set-up is that the budgeted quantity of work over a period must be achieved. Labour utilization is essentially an objective in that direction. Labour utilization measures as to how work has been planned to go through at various machines/departments or work centres and as to what has been the achievement against the plan. The labour utilization can be higher or lower depending upon several factors or outside the control of the management. Some of the factors can be the availability of work loads, materials, work tools break-downs of machines availability of power, worker efficiency, the quality of basic raw-materials for conversion etc. Performance objectives against labour utilization can be considered as :

— Standard hours equivalent to a minimum of 70% attendance hours of all direct workmen are produced. This objectivated output can be expressed as performance ratio as :

$$= \frac{\text{Standard Hours (Budgeted)}}{\text{Attendance Hours (Budgeted)}}$$

Capacity Utilization

Capacity has been defined in many terms. It can mean almost anything and also virtually nothing. It is, however, safe to define it as the maximum output which can be delivered during a period of time under given conditions. Maximum manufacturing capacity (or simple capacity) is not a constant deterministic quality as it is a function of use and technical design of product manufactured. This can be improved upon through introduction of better manufacturing technology in the form of better cooling, selection of appropriate machine tools, manufacturing processes, automation, etc. To an extent, this measure also reflects on the steps taken by the production system to improve upon the manufacturing technology. Capacity of a facility is also inter-related to other facilities. Measurement of capacity, in case of a production system having multi-product and multi-facility dimensions, is a difficult exercise as a number of constraints have to be taken into account to arrive at the figure. One way to define this performance objective is :

— A minimum of 70% of maximum capacity is utilized. Translated in terms of a ratio, it would amount to :

$$= \frac{\text{Standard Hours (Budgeted)}}{\text{Capacity Hours (Budgeted)}}.$$

Materials Utilization

In the context of the present case study, procurement, purchase, storage, and the inter-related issues of inventory control, failures in supply, loss of production due to delays in supplies, vendor development, etc. are not considered to form a part of the production system. Production system converts materials to finished goods. The material utilization in this context is the utilization or conversion of purchased items in the form of raw or semi-finished stages to finished goods against a budgeted norm. Utilization varies depending upon the percentage of rejection, creation of scrap, spoilage an obsolescence, work wastages, etc. The performance objectives against material utilization is the yield of materials used and can be expressed as :

$$= \frac{\text{Useful conversion of material (Budgeted)}}{\text{Total expenditure on material (Budgeted)}}$$

Completion of Schedules

A customer looks forward to the receipt of goods in time. Delay can result in a bad image of the Company, and consequently there can be a loss in sales, decrease in goodwill etc. For a production system, therefore, keeping to the delivery schedules, *i.e.* manufacturing the goods as per the programme is equally an important performance objective. In the case of a production system manufacturing a single product, it should have been possible to arrive at an acceptable throughout cycle time and co-relate the delay in completion to the same to establish some norms.

Capital Utilization

For any production set up, facilities, machine tools and processing assets of capital nature are essential. Capital utilisation, in this context refers to the use of capital for use of capital assets. Decisions are also required as to when to replace fixed assets. Decision to replace early will bring down maintenance costs but will call for capital expenses. On the other hand decisions to replace late will no doubt give a better ratio of production to capital expenditure but simultaneously increase maintenance costs. Somewhere a balance is desirable. The performance objective is to obtain a high ratio of standard hour produced to per unit of capital spent on production assets. Although there are many accounting methods of valuing fixed assets, one such method is written down value. The performance objective to be considered here then becomes :

$$= \frac{\text{Standard Hours (Budgeted)}}{\text{Capitalised Cost (Budgeted)}}.$$

A production system incurs a lot of indirect expenditure, which helps the production process. This may comprise of manpower employed in planning, store keeping, record keeping, inspection as well as in the form of labour employed in any indirect operations covering maintenance tool room, tool issue etc. Indirect labour is also employed in materials movement, good house keeping, cleaning operations and all other sundry jobs. Indirect expenditure is also incurred in the form of use of indirect materials like tools, oils, lubricants and other consumable items required in the production of goods.

Performance objective for the control of Indirect expenditure can be considered as :

$$= \frac{\text{Total Expenses (Budgeted)}}{\text{Indirect Expenses (Budgeted)}}$$

Direct expenditure is incurred in utilities as well. In many an organisation a total of indirect expenditure form a formidable percentage of total expenditure.

Cost Reduction

"What does it Cost" and how to control cost are two important questions in every day transaction of business and the latter one is most important. If costs are not controlled at the point of occurrence, the spiral up and lead to lower productivity. From national angle cost reduction is a vital factor in increasing productivity and standard of living. Lower costs make for lower prices and can facilitate improved quality through value engineering and analysis ; which in turn stimulates consumer demands. These reasons support the view point that cost reduction must be practised much more strongly and on a much wider scale. Cost reduction is the prime concern of today but it should not be at the cost of product quality. Other values like use value, exchange value and esteem value of the product must be given equal importance. Every economy and consequently every business industry must try to continuously increase its productivity through cost reduction and quality improvement. The industry around the world and in India is in many different stages of development ; so action oriented cost reduction approach will go a long way in improving national economy and productivity.

Direct Costs

Certain costs, which can be easily identified with specific products or processes are direct costs. Direct cost of materials is an important element in the total cost of product. It varies from 50-80% of the total unit cost. In the control of this material cost, Designers, Method Engineers, Material Planners, who determine and deal with Direct Material in various capacities, can play a significant role. They determine standard cost of the product.

Labour Cost, both direct the indirect, is an other important element of this cost. Performance standards may be set up through Time and Motion Study. Actual performance should be compared with standard performance and in case of various steps should be taken. Money cost of labour is not the only thing.

Indirect Costs

Overhead expenses such as Indirect labour, Indirect material, Administrative and Selling Expenses are controlled by means of budget. For the control of Indirect Materials, norms of consumption must be set up.

Works Costs and Works Overhead

This includes expenses on Indirect labour, indirect material, power, rent, repair, depreciation etc. They are all indirect expenses right from the receipt of order to the despatch of finished goods.

Administrative Overheads

Direction, control and administration of an undertaking, rents and rates of offices, premises and furnishing, if any, office lighting, salaries of office staff, stationary, postage and other miscellaneous expenses are covered under Administrative overheads.

Selling and Distributive Overheads

Cost of soliciting and securing orders for the articles of products and of efforts to find and retain customers, publicity and advertising, catelogues, leaflets, and price list, packing and forwarding charges, godown rent etc. includes all the expenditure incurred from the time a product is manufactured until it reaches its destination.

Costing

Costing means classifying, recording and allocating the appropriate expenditure for determining the cost of products or services and the presentation of suitable arranged data for the purpose of control and guidance of management.

Factors Contributing Cost Reduction

- Optimum utilisation.
- Select right person with right skill.
- Training in the desired field to meet the challenges of fastly changing techno-economic environment.
- Recognition of work and proper motivation for best performance and reduced absenteeism.
- Ensure availability of all input at right time.
- Better working environments.
- Job re-design.
- Re-deployment possibilities instead of fresh induction.
- Career Planning.
- Scientific manpower assessment and planning in case of fresh induction.

Machines and Equipment

- Proper maintenance of machines and equipment so that (*i*) Downtime is minimum, (*ii*) Full capacity is available.
- Proper machine loading to ensure optimum utilisation and reduced cycle time.
- Proper job on right machines.
- Use of special purpose machines rather than conventional machines *e.g.* using Numerical Control Machines (Gas Cutting) instead of manual Gas cutting.
- Replacement at proper time.
- Use of proper Jigs and fixtures to reduce setting time and operating time.

Materials

- Use proper size and type of material.
- Make use of Tailoring Charts to ensure optimum utilisation of plates.
- Vendor evaluation.
- *ABC* Analysis.
- Reduction in lead time as far as possible.
- Proper storage to avoid damage and ensure quick availability when required.
- Minimum use of indirect material.

Energy Conservation

In short term good house-keeping in industry gets priority. This involves improving fuel-consumption in boilers, furnaces and engines, effective plant maintenance, adoption of heat recovery systems, re-using waste materials to produce energy etc. The appointment of an energy officer responsible for day-to-day supervision in each large industrial unit to check machine, idle time, frequent start ups and stops, leaks and spillage and ensure compliance with energy conservation norms would be particularly worthwhile.

Lands and Buildings

— Scientific layout to optimise area utilisation.
— Better vertical space utilisation whenever possible.
— Multistorey buildings for expansion of office areas.
— Design of buildings to make use of natural light and ventilation.
— Make use of gravity flow/feeding of materials and equipment wherever possible.
— Plant for least material transportation to avoid spillage and damage.

Time Management

Management Effectiveness. A check list for the top management is as under :

— Are responsibilities clearly defined and assigned ?
— Is a full organisational analysis made periodically to evaluate competence and redundancy ?
— Is there an established executive development programmes ?
— Are vendors rated for services and quality ?

Tools of Cost Reduction

Some of the following tools may overlap somewhat, but each may have its purpose in a comprehensive programme.

Cost Accounting and Analysis

Cost Control takes the established cost standards and endeavours to keep operation cost in line with those standards. Cost reduction challenges all cost standards and endeavours to reduce these continuously. Standards are targets in cost control procedures but are suspect in the case of cost reduction.

Cost reduction should be applied in every section of business. It is not dependent upon standards, though target amounts may be set. Cost control seeks to get the best results at the lowest possible cost under existing conditions. Cost reduction recognises no condition as permanent, where a change will secure a lower cost figure. Cost accounting and analysis are most valuable tools for analysing potentialities and possibilities of reducing cost of the product; the process and operating procedure or the general factory expenses. Cost accounting reports are necessary to give an appraisal of the effectiveness of cost reduction and control.

Budgets and Budgetory Control

Budget plan and Budgetory control figures provide a store-house of cost reduction possibilities. The operation of Budgetory control shows where operations are not going according to plan. Budgets are often the best source of information. Cost reduction agencies use budgetory control by setting up targets for savings.

Analysis

(*a*) No organisation is too small or too large to rule out the attractive possibilities of saving through cost reduction.

(*b*) Cost reduction is a state of mind and should be promoted as such.
(*c*) Involve as many employees as possible in cost reduction programme.
(*d*) It should be a continuing programme, for it is never finished. Cost reduction should, therefore, be a permanent, alive and vital part of company's organisation.
(*e*) Saving can be made in all directions, but priorities must be fixed.
(*f*) Cost reduction is the real key to national prosperity under a rising standard of living.
(*g*) No concern can afford to ignore cost reduction.
(*h*) Cost reduction requires resourcefulness imagination and enthusiasm. Success in effecting savings today merely reduces extra affort tomorrow.
(*i*) Cost reduction leadership flows from top. It will rarely climb up from the bottom.

Performance Objectives of a Production System

Performance Objectives of a Production System are examined and measurement of productivity demonstrated through the use of Performance Objective Productivity (P-O-P) Approach. The concept lays emphasis on Performance Objectives and corresponding inputs to arrive at an integrated Productivity Index. The emphasis is on production function to be considered as a system.

Conventional Productivity concepts and hence measures relate output to inputs, such as Labour, Materials and Capital. As a variation, some of the productivity measures consider input as an aggregate of all factorial inputs. These measures suffer from several drawbacks as they fail to recognise interactions of various inputs within themselves as well as influences of other factors such as managerial practices, environment, changes in technology and organisational skills. Productivity measurement models have been presented as if the inputs of Labour, Capital, Materials, etc. can be fully identified in isolation to each other without any inter-relationship. The models also suffer from inadequacies of Units of measuring both the outputs and inputs.

Labour Productivity as an Index of Productivity

Often labour productivity is considered as synonym to productivity of a Production system. As a matter of fact, it is generally perceived that a level of productivity achieved is what is produced by the labour on machines and work benches. An effort to reach higher productivity is interpreted as an action to achieve more output from labour force. Labour on the other hand is only one of the input resources responsible for output. In many products labour may form only a small percentage of input resources ; the materials may constitute the bulk of the proportion of the inputs. In other cases, technology may play a major role.

Labour Productivity is generally perceived and interpreted as a measure of labour efforts or effectiveness. Higher the labour productivity, it is recognised, higher are the labour efforts having been put in. Labour productivity is a function of many variables and is dependent on factors, such as technology, environment of the plant, the management practices, policies and other organisational characteristics of the plant. These affect production from a workman considerably. It is well known that output per labour hour can be increased through use of better quality of raw materials. Components, with a high degree of fabrication in the form of castings, forgings etc. require less machining hours. In a similar context better manufacturing technology in the form of advanced tooling, jigs, fixtures, tool control systems, machine tools with multiple work and tool stations and higher work parameters, or a high degree of automation and production engineering systems increases the output with perhaps lesser efforts from a workman. Managerial decision to replace manual operations with electronically controlled machine tools and machining centres can result in higher output, and hence a higher labour productivity. In all these instances, labour productivity, as it can be seen, has been determined by factors beyond the reach of a workman. Labour productivity cannot, therefore, be viewed as solely representing the efforts or effectiveness of a worker.

Factorial Productivity as Index of Productivity

Even output cannot be considered as resultant of one output. Several input factors join hands and interact to provide an output. There are trade-offs in between. Savings over one input can correspondingly result in an increase in another input with possible overall result of productivity having been lowered. For example, use of better quality raw-materials of a higher degree of fabricated components would show an increase in labour productivity measured, say in a number of units produced per labour hour, but simultaneously it would also result in increased costs of materials seen as another input and thereby decrease overall productivity measures, say as a number of units produced per unit of money spent together on labour and materials. Similarly, an advanced technology might yield a higher labour productivity, but perhaps in the process lower capital productivity. Besides, output is equally affected by factors, such as environment which might be beyond the controls of the organisation. A factorial productivity, such as capital productivity or Materials productivity measures as ratio of output to factorial inputs of Capital or Material cannot be a representative index of productivity of an organisation. On the other hand, a factorial productivity can lead to wrong perception of performance of the organisation.

Production, Productivity and Quality

The difference between production and productivity is well understood and requires no elaboration. Whereas production is output or performance measures in absolute terms with no reference to its relationships with resources spent. Productivity essentially represents the relationship between the performance (or output) and input. Production, Productivity and Quality cannot be considered in isolation. Both production and productivity have a common dimension in the form of output. It is a fallacy to pressure that production as well as productivity can be increased through simplistic means of diluting quality does not carry same economic or use value as foreseen without lowering of specifications. As a safeguard against the tendency of aiming at highest output, and hence productivity, in a product on system at the cost of quality of output, a good productivity measures, should preferably have a built-in provision for accountability of rejection rate defective, workmanship, scrap generation, spoilage, costs of rework, yield of materials used as inputs or similar other characteristics which reflect on the quality of output. As a first step in an exercise of productivity measurement, acceptable quality characteristics of the output must be specified and quantified as performance objectives. Any deviation form the same should have a bearing in the productivity measure.

Productivity and Profitability

It is generally presumed that higher productivity results in higher profits. This is again a fallacy. Profits are essentially related to market conditions, the quality of the product and the marketing strategy. There are instances of increased profits although productivity went down. This happens in cases of monopoly manufacturing when the customer is asked to pay for low productivity of the suppliers. Similarly, increased productivity need not necessarily bring better profitability because of other matching steps having been taken to meet the competition.

Productivity and Good House Keeping

Many an organization spend a lot of money on house-keeping, cleanliness, landscaping etc. as to present the plant as a showpiece to a visitor. Very often colourful progress reports, charts, graphs, are prominently displayed on notice boards as well as in departments. These might be aids to contribute to a good morale or a project a systematic work to a client. To a small extent in this context good house-keeping can influence productivity. But this cannot be considered as an end objective and cannot be a part of the output of a plant. A plant with an extreme good house-keeping outlook cannot be an alternative to an efficient operation. However, it is not a significant input factor to increase output.

77

Chief Executives

Successfully run business, today, are people with chief executive officers and managers who demonstrate a flair for breaking out of the mould. Peter Drucker, once said "You can tell right away whether a company is well-run, because the well-run factory is a bore. It runs like clockwork. The poorly managed factory is a drama of crisis.

The tradition or convention-bound manager swears by the theory of the "divine right of kings", and exercises his prerogative over the freedom of his business. Often, he exhibits more feelings of confidence in his plans than he deserves. After a while, he begins to think he's something special". That he can handle every problem. While in fact, he cannot. This is especially true to executives who have acquired "celebrity" status. Perhaps one of the most difficult hurdles for any corporation to overcome is the attitude of its managers-especially to "change". The traditional, "we've never done it that way before", attitude has often hindered progress in many companies. In large industrial corporations, it is not uncommon to come across managers who sitting on the laurels of past glories, grow complacent. Such men refuse to see the need for scrapping old ways and responding to new challenges.

Sheer size poses a formidable obstacle to change at General Motors the biggest American car maker. General Motor has more than 130,000 white-coller workers in its North American automotive operations alone. "All of these folks are busy" says a consultant, who is helping to cut General Motor down to size. "But so much of what they do has nothing to do with making better cars. Traditionally, this has not been a stick-your-neck out kind of place", "confides a General Motor Chief executive "People follow procedure. Whether it produces any effect on the final product, the car, gets to be almost besides the point".

Today, General Motor is aware that technology has its limits. As a result, one major change underway is a "healthy loss of faith in technology" coupled with a "get tough" attitude is cracking this culture of complacency. To get General Motors moving again, Ross Perot director is reported to have said that the company must first admit that it was slipping. Most General Motor executives, he had talked to, were even unwilling to admit that problems existed.

To support this belief, Perot/asserted that General Motor had a cumbersome bureaucracy, which had "turned away from the needs of customers. According to him the company must start listening to customers again, if it is to regain its momentum. Another Chief Executive who has put distinctive stamp on management style is John F. Welch. According to him under previous Chairman the General Electric was a place where going through channels was a hallowed tradition. The degree to which Welch had transformed the existing bureaucratic culture at General Electric was astonishing. To assist managers, he moved decision-making downwards to divisional levels, promoted a feeling of ownership"—urging managers to act like entrepreneurs, instead of hired help. In pursuit of this policy, he encouraged free communications, believing that "If people are treated with honesty and dignity, and are allowed to participate in a process of constant communication, they respond with commitment." As Welch puts it : "We are out to get a feeling and a spirit of total openness. It is natural that Welch has not been able to convert all people to his beliefs and practices as to how a corporation should be run. In fact, his style of sometimes getting the information directly from those involved, rather than their supervisors-plus his technique of putting executives "in the box", has rankled some upper-level managers. Some critics point out that the approach could drive away some key subordinates. Welch's observations : "If there are occasional human sacrifices on the alter of change, so be it.

Role of Chief Executives

The successful chief executives are managers or idea men are the leaders who set the policy and establish the direction for the organization—without devoting larger chunks of their time to peripheral issues. They operate on the principle that : "There is no limit to what a man can do, or where he can go, if he does not mind who gets the credit." They also believe that delegating authority is not an admission that "there's something they can't do".

Such Chief Executive also demonstrate a high tolerance for hearing competing views argued very intensely. A Chief Executive doesn't have to be popular", according to Harry Levinson, psychologist and management consultant. He has to take charge, of the situation and give direction. If people see the logic of what executive doing, and believe he's doing it for the good of the organisation, they will buckle down and face the hardships. For Chief Executive credibility is very fragile. It is built day by day and a corporate leader can lose it in an instant by covering up. Corporate executives establish their authority by sticking with their decisions. When they have made a decision, they live with them. A successful corporate executive knowns that success tends to go not to the person who is error free because he also tends to be risk averse. Rather, it goes to the person who recognises that life is pretty much a percentage of business. It is not making mistakes that is critical it is correcting them and getting on with the principal task.

Chairman and Directors

*The bottleneck is at the head of the bottle goes an old saying. No business is likely to be better than its top management, have broader vision than its top people or perform better than they do.

Top Management plays a vital role in promoting productivity consciousness and accelerating economic growth. It is universally recognised that the process of economic development is positively dependent upon dynamic top management, and top management in its turn depend on the ability of the production capacity of the senior managers as agent of development at all levels in the economic structure. The role of top management is that of an agent of development in the process of growth of the country. Top management has a responsibility to society as a whole, to its employees, to the consumers and to the owners of the enterprise. Therefore dynamic top management is very essential for the organisation and mobilisation of the country's resources. A dynamic manager can be defined as an organisor, mobilisor and utilizer of capital, technology, human and natural resources in a way best suited to the attainment of his individual goals, organisational goal and the country's goal. Without a dynamic top management and without managerial ability much of the country's wealth and resources would undoubtedly be wasted, mis-allocated or left un-touched. Dynamic management in all types of business activity have made immeasurable contribution towards the economic development of the organisation and the countries.

Top management as a non-conventional factor of input has set aside and has become the most important factor in the economic development. Top management have played an important role if not a decisive role in enhancing the economic welfare of the society, in providing more and better goods and services at lower price or raising the people's per capita income. The economic world in which we live today require almost a total re-orientation of management philosophy and practices. The traditional characteristics of management which usually characterised by :

(*a*) Strong reluctance to delegate authority, to adopt new technology and innovation, to co-operate with others, to exchange and undertake new ideas, to train or develop subordinates.

(*b*) A lack of competence in making business analysis and evaluation based on facts rather than instincts or fancies.

(*c*) Lack of vision in thinking of economic activities and business leading towards broader scope and co-operation has become serious limitation without contemplating new and bigger jobs in the framework of the country's economic development.

The top dynamic managers in the country have the following main functions for the economic development of the nation :

- To participate in the intensive and extensive mobilisation of country's available resources.
- To improve existing allocation of capital, human and natural resources.
- To offer more and better quality products at lower prices to the consumer.
- To develop and enlarge the trans-national trade.
- To train and develop managers.
- To provide trained management inventory to the country.
- To ensure and increase in Government revenue.

Chairman and Board

Board is a Committee which has a value and use in management, provided they do not cut across a manager's personnel accountability. Chairman—the public image and voice of the Company. Chairman can speak for the company as a whole. He is the one who is clear of what he is doing and why ? He seeks decisions from the Board. He does not mis his own opinions. He guides the board but does not dominate. Chairman and Managing Director must know to get along together. Chairman provides suggestions, guidelines and consultation to Managing Director. Normally Chairman should not take over the process of decision making. For the successful top management, board and the senior management should operate without any interference.

Executive Directors

Executive Directors have a dual role to play with the Chief Executive. They are the directors to carry out the corporate responsibility but are subordinate to the chief executive. Executive Directors are the heads of the key managerial functions.

Directors, as described in the literature, represent the shareholders. Yet, typically, they are actually selected by the management and not by the shareholders. Accordingly, the directors are on the Board because of the fact that they represent the management.

After the second world war, the nature of business has grown more complex than it used to be before. The running of business has become comparatively more intricate as a result of cataclysmic changes in the internal composition of the companies and in the pressures placed on them from outside. The size and complexity of modern companies and progressive extension of their spheres of activity have dominated trade and industry all over the world. To cope with this greater complexity of business and also to compete successfully against increased competition requires higher levels of professionals performance from both managers and directors. The company director in conjunction with others on the Board has the job of efficiently conducting the business of the company. They carry a heavy responsibility on their shoulders in planning coordinating and controlling the utilisation of available resources. They are accountable not only to the shareholders but also to the employees, consumers, their bankers, governments and in fact to society in general. The increasingly complex nature of director's task and his key role in making the decisions upon which the creation of both wealth and jobs largely depend make it imperative that he should be a professional at his job. The professional director is required to make himself acquainted with the company's activities and products and with its key managers, and bring to bear on the business of the company such personal skills and experiences as he may possess. He should be able to identify management problems, evaluate business and economic situations and consider alternative problem solution; be a wise judge of people.

This would be possible only when he possesses a reasonable understanding of the skills and tools of some management disciplines like Strategic planning, forecasting organisation, Motivation and Personal Relations, and other functional skills like Marketing, R&D and Finance.

In a sense, a professional director is the corporate anchorman who tries to keep pace with the rapid change in today's business world. As the problems of companies keep on changing with the times. Therefore the professionalisation of the company director would appear to be the "possible strength" for the present shortcomings in the corporate management. In India the supermacy of board of directors in company management has been established by the section 291 of the Companies Act 1956. The Board of Directors of the company shall be entitled to exercise all the men powers and to do all such things as the company is authorised to exercise and do. Although the board of directors occupy the pivotal position in the management of companies, there is no provision yet for compulsory appointment of any specific number of directors from the promoters group. Attendence of directors in periodic board meeting is not compulsory and by availing of the leave of absence from the Board Meetings a person can continue to be director of as many as twenty companies for any length of time. Recently the companies (Amendment) Act 1988 has made an upward revision of the amount of remuneration for attending board meeting from Rs. 250 to Rs. 1000 per meeting depending on the paid up share capital of the company.

The survival and growth of a company depends on the quality of its board of directors and dynamism of its chairman. What counts in the long run in the vision, vigour, ingenity ; commitment, intellectual calibre, integrity and effectiveness of directors as individuals and the dynamic leadership of the chairman. In this context, the law and practice of company management in France deserve special consideration. The French law provide for two alternative systems of management for "societe anonyme" which are fully limited companies.

Two Tier System of Management

The two tier system of management of companies provide for the executive board and the supervisory board. The executive board is responsible collectively for the management of the company's affairs. The executive board are appointed by the supervisory board. The supervisory Board members collectively supervise the management of the company. The supervisory board consists of atleast 3 and not more than 12 members. No member of the supervisory board may be a member of the Executive Board. The members of the supervisory board are elected from among the shareholders by the constitutive general meeting. The general powers of the supervisory board includes exercising a permanent oversight of the management of the company by Executive Board.

The Directors may be removed at any time by an ordinary general meeting, it is not necessary that reasons should be assigned or notice of dismissal given or compensation paid.

The management of the company's business is entrusted to the President who may be assisted by one or more general managers Chairman and President of the company has the widest powers to act on behalf of the company in all circumstances subject to the limitations that he must not encroach upon the functions of the general meeting and the board of directors laid down by law and that he can not validly mortgage company assets or give a guarantee in the name without the express or general authorisation of the board and that he must exercise his powers within the limits of company objects.

Types of Managers

A business must innovate the excell. *Mary Parkot Follett,* an early advocate of scientific management expressed that the fundamental responsibility of management is to recognise the moment of passing that increment of time just before old products become obsolete and new ones must be moved out of the development labs.

There are five principles that management must master and if one is to recognize the "moment of passing".

Give a free hand to those responsible for long range strategic planning.

Spell out a well defined organisational plan with clear statement of duties and responsibilities.

State precise objective and establish disciplined measurement systems to check performance.

Review programme for the introduction of new products constantly. New products take time. They must be re-examined and if necessary, their objectives redefined in other to keep in step with the volatile demands of the market.

Innovative Managers

There is nothing more difficult than to take the lead in the introduction of a new order of things, because the innovator has enemies all those who have done well.

The innovator in market research and product strategy, industrial research, design and development, manufacturing, technology, organisation and personnel relations, sales and finance are aided by innovators' integrated systems variously known as work study, industrial engineering, operations research, standard costing and budgetary control, etc.

The managers in all the above fields are aided by routine maintainers of management services. Thus we come across two groups of personnel who are distinct in their long-term relation to the organisation employing them. The innovators can give their best only when they dare to be different from the set of organisational modes and can freely express their independent professional judgement without blind hierarchical loyalty.

The innovators in industry should be consultants in practice atleast like the best of doctors, lawyers and auditors. But even when under employment obligation in an organisation, the true-innovator can always contribute and can continue innovating towards real gains for the organisation.

Care Taker and Builder Managers

Peter Drucker divides the managers into two categories namely caretaker and builder. The caretaker manager keeps the organisation alive while builder manager is one who takes the organisation into newer heights and newer places. The caretaker will sink with the organisation while the builder will grow with the organisation. The manager's burden as an innovator is perhaps the most exciting assignment. It confers on him great responsibility and demands of him a level of seriousness and sense of responsibility in order to determine what changes are needed, how they are to be introduced and at what pace. The manager has to be innovator in altogether different sense and pursue a different but purposeful path of trial and error to arrive at work rate solutions which are viable in the changing context.

A builder manager, therefore, should possess the following characteristics.

— Inner drive, spirit to achieve and dashing personality.

— Flexibility in his approach.

— Excellent group relations.

— Integrity.

A builder manager has a desire to achieve. It has an urge in him to go in ahead and reach the goal. He has an ambition, the fire is always burning in him to do something new. He initiates action in the right direction. He becomes effective in his approach. He is always restless to come out with his new ideas to achieve the objectives of the organisation. While normal desires of a builder manager are compounded on a variety of needs—he may want more money, prestige or status or achievement.

An innovative manager's moto is to succeed in the organisation and in association with the people with whom he is working. Flexibility in approach on the part of an innovative manager is an essential requirement. If he is rigid in his approach, goes into wrong direction and does not change himself according to the circumstances and situations, he cannot be a builder. He should be able to change the direction and correct himself.

How intelligent a man may be unless he has the capacity of adjustment in the group he cannot be a builder. What is required is that the group should accept him as a manager in order to achieve common objectives. At the same time the group should realise his contributions and this is possible when he has the ability to get along with the people with whom he is working. In endeavouring to achieve the corporate objectives an innovative manager knows that the objectives can be achieved only through cooperation of employees and therefore is always willing to understand them, listen them and meet them and when he says 'NO' he adds a reasonable reason.

It is only with an integrity that one succeeds in the organisation. In fact this is one of the essential characteristics of an innovative manager to have integrity.

Business Strategies

Every business should have some kind of informal and formal corporate strategies. Corporate planning of deciding what the company is to be and defining the major steps to reach and maintain that goal. In order to achieve the organisational objectives, specifically in the corporate planning, innovation plays an important part by bringing about the technological changes and improve existing methods. The innovation can be divided into two categories :

(*a*) Technical innovation ; and

(*b*) Social Innovation.

(*a*) **Technical Innovation.** Research and development is the factor responsible for further growth of the organisation which clearly gives an idea of innovation. Thus it is very necessary to develop the research techniques for the betterment of the organization by establishing well equipped research and development section within the organisation.

(*b*) **Social Innovation.** Social innovation is the primary requirement of management. The management is to produce social wealth and output of goods and services that must add to the well-being of the society. The management's decision on society is not just public responsibility but these are inextricably intermixed with the management's responsibility. The organisation is an organ of society and its actions have an impact on social scene. There has to be a correlation between management's social responsibility and management's social power. An innovative manager will take the social needs of an organisation into consideration when he takes effective and dynamic steps to achieve the corporate goals.

The innovative goals of the management may be of the following nature :

— news products which are required to meet future demands because of technological advances.

— improvement in the existing methods and anticipate expected changes in the technology.

— innovation in all areas of accounting, training, office management, labour relations and so on.

— innovation in locating new sources of raw materials, processes and equipments in order to keep pace with the technological advancements.

Difference between Innovative and Non-Innovative Managers

An innovative managers gives importance to the new idea to be introduced while non-innovative manager gives no importance to the new ideas.

Creativity is a must for an innovative manager while in the case of non-innovative manager creativity is ignored.

An innovative manager takes steps to ensure that the company's philosophy and objectives are properly developed and clearly stated. But this is not the case with the non-innovative manager.

An innovative manager ensures that all employees known that what, when, where, who, how and above all, why of their-jobs and the organisation. He knows that the people are more efficient and happy when they understand clearly what results are expected of them. An innovative manager knows that all personnel will contribute and receive more if they are helped to develop a clear feeling of purpose, direction and dignity. He believes in utilising all the modern management tools fully. He cultivates a curiosity for new dimensions of knowledge and resists efforts to predicate plans on and present knowledge only.

An innovative manager has a major role in educating, training and developing to accomplish the objective of the organisation. He strives to develop in all people an awareness of the value of work to them.

Contraints before Innovative Manager

There are certain barriers in the way of an innovative manager which are to be overcome for the success of the organisation. They are summarised briefly as under.

Habit. As is evident an individual has varied interests. In this way one interest overtakes the other interest and he thus spends his maximum time in other non-productive work. He is in the habit of it and is happy where he is. He may not be aware that habit has taken his whole thinking process and thus everything goes wrong.

On the contrary, a builder manager might be spending days and nights to find out something new which may change the whole pattern of organisation as well as increase the productivity by innovating new ideas in the existing methods which are possible only by sacrificing other interests.

Contentment. This is one of the important barrier in the way of an innovative manager. When an individual is contended, his further development or progress comes to a standstill. He becomes satisfied where he is and thus further progress is hampered. In this way, he is a deal wood to the organisation. On the other hand, because of dynamic approach and far-sightedness a pushing achiever has certain enemies who might criticise him on some pretext or the other. This price every successful/innovative manager has to pay. He should not therefore be moved by these empty slogans but should go ahead with the task set-forth. With the passage of time he would find that people who oppose him follow his policies and ideas and give their whole-hearted support to accomplish the organisational goals.

Lack of Courage. The man who has no courage and positive action and is opposed innovation of any kind cannot become an innovative manager. His usual reaction to new ideas is "come on let us be realistic".

Bringing Innovation in Management

Overall innovation strategy involves the setting of objectives for innovation. Since innovation offers one of the best prospects for a company's growth and for achieving and expanding its activities, top management should take an action and aggressive attitudes towards it. Most essential activities in this area should include :

(*a*) Providing research with a clear understanding of company goals and strategies and defining specific objectives for research within the context of these Plans.

(*b*) Seeing that appropriate organisation structure is developed.

(c) Developing a project evaluation procedure which results in a balanced package of projects to meet company objectives.

From this point of view management must continuously evaluate its programme innovation to see that both research and operating units carry out their functions in developing and utilising technology to support company goals.

The need for innovation in social areas is just as important need for such innovation is in marketing and distribution.

78

Skills for Success

To be a successful executive of tomorrow we have to make ourselves more effective by developing and importing the skills, abilities and even character traits that lead to success :

The immediate question what comes in mind is "What exactly is Success" ? The definition of success is "Work Smart not Hard". This divide the executives in two categories.

Successful Executives and
Unsuccessful Executives

Successful Executive

The successful executive is one whose response is authentical, being credible, praiseworthy, responsive and genuine both as an individual or as the member of the organisation.

Unsuccessful Executive

The unsuccessful executive on the other hand fails to respond authentically. Executive's much of the potential remains dormant, unrealised and unrecognised. A lack of response in childhood, unhappy dependency relationship, continuing dependence, inadequate physical care resulting in lack of normal progress ; the autonomy and self realisation result in unsuccessful executive career.

The characteristics of successful and unsuccessful executive are :

Successful Executives

Specific Traits

— Enjoy work, interact freely and appreciate the world of nature, take pride in the work;
— Possess winning attitude ;
— Knows what success means to his life ;
— Believes that time is precious and lives in here and now situation ;
— Response appropriately to situation and assumes responsibility ;
— Separate facts from opinions ;
— Do not leave success to chance ;
— Possess critical skills.

Personality Traits

— Persistence in the accomplishment of objectives ;
— Integration toward goals ;
— Self confidence ;
— Freedom from inferiority complex.

Unsuccessful Executives

Specific Traits

— Lives in the past ;
— Dwells on good old days or part performance ;
— Feels sorry for himself ;
— Shift the responsibility for his unsatisfactory life on to others ;
— Live constantly under dread of future failures ;
— Distorted or incomplete perception ;
— Pretends, manipulates and perpetuates old roles from childhood.

Personality Traits

— Inferiority complex ;
— Lack of confidence in self and other (I' M NOT OK— YOU'RE NOT OK)

You can also be Successful

The traits of successful executives give us a clear picture that you can achieve success by acquiring the skills of successful executives.

Therefore, Managerial success is not the prerogative or privilege of only a selected few executives but all those executives who have the grit and determination, can achieve, success.

The managerial domain is full of extraordinary success stories as well as those of disappointing failures. A close scrutiny of these successes and failure reveals an interesting phenomenon. A person with no formal management education turns out to be a most successful manager while a bright management graduate with an impressive track records proves to be a fiasco.

The successful managers are "Men on the Move", who know how to take effective action and how to change with the times. What distinguishes between successful men from the rest is not only their understanding of how others work, think and react, but also their knowledge of what motivates them to work to their full potential.

The managerial success of a person is basically attributed to his 'down to earth' approach in responding to and handling business realities. In today's environment, management of a business entreprise is no doubt a complex affair. If the people who are entrusted with the responsibility or task of handling the business do not respond and perform at the opportune moment the enterprise will suffer on the long run viability. Certainly, both these activities of response and to performance involve a lot of other functions like planning, organising, staffing, decision-making and controlling. The greatness of successful managers lies in their judicious use and application of these management functions, so that every relevant business opportunity is responded to.

The second trait of successful managers is their "Indepth understanding of human resource". The life-line of any organisation is its human-resources. It is only through and with them that an organisation can attain any semblance of success. This is easier said than done, as the behaviour of human beings is not only unpredictable but also difficult to gauge. However, these successful managers, have an immense ability to understand the needs of human resource and make them give their best to the organisation.

The third quality of a successful manager is "To create a Team". It is said that we Indians are good individual performers, but poor team players even in the organisational set up.

The fourth characteristic of successful managers is their "Tactfulness in handling people in high places", namely the Government, the bureaucracy, etc. In today's context, it is an accepted fact that the Government and the bureaucracy has a vital role to play not only in the existence of an enterprise but also in its management and viability.

The last, and the most important attribute which is responsible for managerial success is nothing but "High achievement motivation". The successful managers are a band of people who are self-motivators and have a strong desire to achieve, the impossible.

Understanding Executive's Job Profile

Executive determines what is going to be run ; managers do the running, dreaming to become a manager is worthwhile effort that provides a great deal of professional satisfaction. Executive must keep their eyes on the real objective, while being up-to-date on what is really going on "out-there".

What is the Job of an Executive

If we ask an executive what he does, he will most probably tell us that he "plans", "organises", "coordinates" and "control". If we watch what he really does ; we should not be surprised if manager can't relate what he does and what he has told.

The fact is that these four words, which have dominated management vocabulary since Henri Fayol first introduced them in 1916, tells us very little about what managers actually do.

Is it not surprising that the field of management, so devoted progress and change, has for more than half a century not seriously addressed the basic question : What do managers do ? The synthesis of the findings of some of the discoveries of systematic research paints an interesting picture about how managers spend their time. Considering the facts about managerial work, we can see that the manager's job is enormously complicated and difficult. The manager is over burdened with obligations, yet he cannot easily delegate his tasks. As a result he is driven to over work and is forced to do many tasks superficially.

Let us try to put up the various components of the Job together. A manager by virtue of his interpersonal contact emerge as nerve centre of his organisational unit.

A managers job can be described in terms of various roles or organised behaviours identified with a position.

Interpersonal Role

Role by virtue of executive's position as head of an organisational unit. Interpersonal roles may include routine functions, responsible for the work of other people of the unit ; various aspects related to motivation of sub-ordinates and the leadership role.

Informational Role

A manager by virtue of his interpersonal contacts, both with his sub-ordinates and with his network of contacts, the manager emerges as the nerve centre of his organisational units. The Chief Executive spent 40% of their contact time on activities devoted exclusively to transmission of information, 20% of their incoming mail purely informational. The manager perpetually scans his environment for information, interrogates his liaison contacts and his subordinates and receive unsolicited information as a result of contacts.

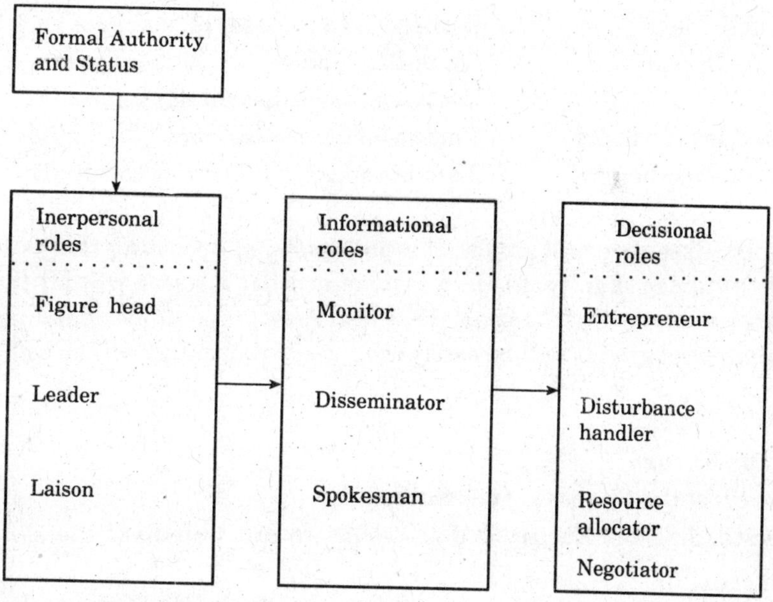

Decisional Role

Complete Manager—A Perceived Role

The Executive Job for the future can be studied if we perceive what will be a Complete Manager.

Everything is different as we approach the 21st Century. The 21st century will offer the greatest opportunity for planned success ever-seen. The essential management characteristics will be to run an organisation that gives to customers exactly what they have been led to expect and does it what pleasant efficiency. The principles of completeness should implement.

1. Cause employees to be successful
2. Cause suppliers to be successful
3. Cause customers to be successful.

The Centurion executive will be an "Adult"— yet urge for "Innovation" and adventure of child and will be required to do the following :

Implement the Principles of Completeness

Cause employees.... Suppliers and Customers to be successful.

Adopt a 21st Century Management Style

Plan and create something so well that it immediately becomes effective.

Make Employees Successful

Realise that people are the most critical asset to success.

Centurion Executives will be required to increase earnings and revenues, have the best quality ; develop people ; create and market new products or services.

The Centurion Executive will be able to manage with the foundation of "Zero Defects" with a perceived System Grid for 21st Century which is as under :

MANAGEMENT SYSTEMS GRID

Organisation's Characteristics	Management System Grid 21st Century
	Completeness
Organisational Policy	Consent of the Governed.
Requirements Definition	Clear Description.
Education	Everyone Keeps Learning.
Performance Measurement	Climate of Consideration.
Purpose of Organisation	To make employees/customers/suppliers successful

The Centurion Executive will establish a philosophy of operating that is consistent with completeness and human dignity. Modern communication systems will let the management know and understand the will of the people. For that reasons, misunderstandings will be easily avoided, special interest groups will be easily identified, and things will be well through out.

SKILLS

Skills for the Future

How can we boost the Chances of our Success ?

After understanding the Executive Job Profile we can visualised the skills required for "effectiveness".

The skills and abilities can make us more effective and efficient, "On the job and off the job". The skills and abilities are critical to success and mustering them will give we more satisfaction and confidence.

We take for granted many of our vital skills and abilities not realising they can be developed and improved. We as an executive can boost our chances of success by developing the traits and life styles we need to make it in today's competitive world. We need to develop in the areas such as "Communicating", "Decision-Making" and "Time Management".

Successful managers of the future will be those who master Six independent "New Age Skills".

New Age Skills

Creating Insight. *This requires concentration and broad prospective and knowledge base to get to the heart of a problem-* not just to visible symptoms. Creative skills enables us to discover all facets of an issue—the hidden opportunities, advantages, and strengths opening the door to the best strategies.

Sensitivity. *Sensitive to needs and motivation of others. To understand people's moods and expectations and act on that understanding.* To bind people together so they feel motivated to achieve high goals. We have to look inside each individual to gain knowledge of that person's expectations and needs.

Vision. *Vision is a mental journey from the known to unknown. It is a process of creating the future from facts, figures, dreams, threats and opportunity.* It is through vision that we position ourself and our organisation to create and take advantage of opportunities. Vision helps to chart a course that creates change and helps us to respond to external changes. It joins strategy and culture to achieve corporate excellence.

Versatility. *Change is inevitable and there is no point in resisting it.* So stay alert to anything in our environment that might signal a trend or change in customer or competitor behaviour. "Versatility" helps us how to welcome change as an opportunity, not a threat, and learn to control it to out advantage.

Focus. *To exploit changes effectively so that we as an executive should determine what specific people and operational changes would be required.* Based on this we should develop a plan and time table for shifting focus, then begin implementation ; monitoring and adjusting.

Patience. The executive should live in the long term. *We can have immediate goals, but we need a long-term view that evaluates those goals* in terms of a more distant future. We should rise above the thoughts and actions of others and have the patience to see our vision through. Patience helps us to use our other five "New Age Skills" at the right time and in right combination and proportion.

UNDERSTANDING AND DEVELOPING AN EXECUTIVE

Understanding of an Executive

There are two basic approaches to buildings an accurate understanding of an executive and developing a profile (*a*) working from the outside In" (*b*) "Working from the "Inside Out".

Method—I : Working from the "Outside In" means you observe the person's actual habits or behaviour and attempt to identify meaningful patterns. We do this most of the time with existing colleagues, superiors and subordinates. Then we flesh out the profile with knowledge of the value system that we gain through social interaction.

Method—II : Working from the outside means that we discover the subject's life history and values, formulate a model of his psyche, and use this to predict his behaviour patterns.

HOW TO SIZE UP THE EXISTING COLLEAGUE

Executive suffer a loss of mental skills with the passage of time, becoming rigid, unable to deal with new concepts, frightened of change, resentful of younger executives, defensive, and in brief incompetent to act in a changing world.

Challenge before each of us as an executive is how to evaluate oneself ; discover and revise our "psychic contract" and invest our life and our work not just with effectiveness but with the kind of meaning from which the true success springs.

Understanding Danger of Incompetence

How to go up

Competent executive show good results and incompetent executives shows poor result. The results are a good index of competence. No matter how great an executive may look if he consistently fail to achieve reasonable goals he is likely to be incompetent. From the management point of view, it is extremely important to spot competence and the potential for promotion. It is better to adopt the practice of making negative selections *i.e.* spotting and discarding last competent people until finally we are left with a person who is least likely to foul up.

Management is often puzzled when considering incompetent executives, for such people are usually long time employees, who know the industry, work hard and look good but fail to achieve the results. Why is this ?

The incompetence spring, not from technical or intellectual short-comings, but from emotional factors. The incompetent executive just has not got his head straight. Following are some of the basic problems of incompetence.

Understanding fear of failure. The fear of failure often reduce and otherwise very ambitious executive incompetent because (*a*) the fear of failure is stress—provoking in itself (*b*) it renders working towards success more difficult.

Incapacitating fear of success. Many Parents/Friends install a fear of success among their children/friends. They accomplish this by warning that success may entail a loss of friends, suggesting that it is not right to "risk too far" and implementing the ideas that "the higher one climbs, the more unpleasant will be the inevitable fall". The executives who suffers a fear of success suffer by an inability to seize opportunity, or on becoming successful by suffering self doubt and guilt that provokes unconscious acts of self sabotage.

SIGNS/SYMPTOMS OF INCOMPETENCE

— Delegate the problems of committee, then wait and wait and wait for it to make recommendations.

— Practice an extreme version of democrative participative management and delegate the problems to subordinates.

— Initiate a research study, install a computer system, send for the consultants on each time.

— Looking for an Answer in the Book. If the contingency is not covered in the book no action can be taken.

— Dissolving the problem in Alcohol. The world seems a far less threatening place, when viewed through a prism.

— Falling Ill. Coming down on the job with a stress—related ailment such as migrain, headache or ulcer.

IMPROVING YOUR SKILLS FOR SUCCESS

Getting Most from Yourself

Is there a secret of success ? Does one concept or strategy enable you to develop and improve skills, abilities and character traits that Lead to Success ?* The answer is a qualified "NO". Following are some of the thought provoking perspectives on what it means and what it takes to succeed.

MAKE THE MOST OF YOUR CAREER

— Set Goals for Oneself.

— Creativity—Open Your Mind

— Listen and Learn

— Make the Best Decisions

— Avoid Burnout

— Get Organised

— Get the best from the people

— Leadership

SET GOALS FOR ONESELF

Goals must be specific and they must cover many areas. The goals could be set in following categories :

— Career —To reach a professional level.
— Financial —To earn a certain amount.
— Educational —Acquite additional skills.
— Physical fitness —Diet control, health club, etc.
— Community/Charity —To undertake voluntary work.
— Personal—Work to become less anxious, hostile, jealous, or insecure.

Write each of the goals at the top of a sheet of paper and think of the ways to reach them. It is important to keep goals specific and measurable. Putting goals in writing is important. Make your goals a part of your daily life and plan to achieve them.

CREATIVITY

Once you know where you want to go, there are several abilities one can develop to speed you on your way. Individual creativity is SPIRITED. It's based on key strengths in at least some of the following characteristics :

Spontaneous	:	Willing to take risk.
Persistent	:	Courageous, assertive, independent.
Incentive	:	Looks at problem in new ways.
Rewarding	:	Willing to share credit.
Inner Openness	:	Intuitive ; open to emotions, think/act/create innovate in different modes.
Transcendent	:	Sees situations realistically chooses growth over fear.
Evaluative	:	Discerning, discriminating, judgemental at times.
Democratic	:	Values and respect for people.

Courage to take risks are very characteristics of the creative person. Start with a vision of who you are and want to be rather than what you want to do or have. Creativity is a matter of unlocking the ideas that are within each one of us. Open yourself up to new and more ideas where ever and however you can. Creativity is more than act or a skill or a style of working. It's a way of being and of benefitting organisation.

LISTEN AND LEARN

If we want to foster involvement in the team concept in management, one has to listen constantly, share ideas and information, recognise achievement. But listening is not that simple- and it's a skill few people think of developing. Listening is getting meaning from situations involving the spoken word. Listening help us to know the motivation of the people we can deal with. We learn by listening. Listening can be more tiring than talking as it demands intellectual, perhaps even emotional efforts. It is draining and tiring because it demands total concentration.

Focus on listening. Words spoken to you come at the rate of 90 to 200 a minute. The differential between the speech and speed of thought explain why we are so easily distracted. Words have definitions but meaning comes from the people you are listening to Feeling and emotions are part of that meaning. Maintaining eye contact and an appropriate nod or two also help to let the speaker know you are listening. In order to power listening following are the Tips :

TIPS TO EFFECTIVE LISTENING

— Don't Interrupt
— Take Brief notes
— With hold judgement
— Read the feelings between the lines
— Concentrate on substance, nor style.
— Listen for Main Ideas
— Let others talk first
— React to the message
— Ask questions

Make the Best Decisions

Most of us wait for things to happen instead of making them happen. The first essential of the successful decision is to make that decision. The act of making a decision is always more important than the substance of the decision itself.

Steps of Decision Making

— List Options
— Observe feelings
— Designate our Choice
— Commit to the Decision
— Think about choices
— Relate choices to priorities
— Register the decision
— Make our decision work.

Decision-making is just one stage in a mental process. But decision thinking is a well managed regrous and imaginative process. It is a process that begins with Identifying problem and ends with taking a decision. Following are the check points which should be kept in mind before taking a decision.

Check Points

— Has the right questions formulated and been asked in the complete way ?
— Have all credible alternatives been considered.
— Have all possible consequences of each alternative been imagined and thought through.
— Have all foreseeable contingencies been provided for, as far as possible ?

Decision thinking, however well it is practiced, does not guarantee in fallibility. But if it is executed professionally, it can tip and odds, in favour making a good decision.

Avoid Burnout

In this world of cut throat competitions every job has become stressful but perhaps it is this stress that makes jobs more interesting and motivates people to strive for professionalism. However, stress without an outlet, a buffer or support mechanism can lead to "burnout". What is unique about burnout as opposed to job stress arises from social interaction. So when a young executive who is otherwise pleasant comes home and screams over trivial matters it indicates not only his job is stressful but he is burning out.

The major symptom of "burnout" is change in attitude—from positive, caring considerate to uncaring, not bothered negativism. Executives who suffer burn-out exhibit an array of symptoms. :

— Physical depletion and feeling of helplessness and disillusion.
— They develop a negative concept of themselves and negative attitudes toward their work.

Normally there are four stages of burnout :

1. **Idealistic enthusiasm.** This is the first stage. In this phase individual develops unrealistically high enthusiasm and expectations in a job which is difficult to accomplish.

2. **Stagnation.** After initial outburst of enthusiasm the individual stalls. There is a slow realization that the goals are too ambitious and the strategies need to be revamped.

3. **Frustration.** The realization that goals are far away leads to frustration. Depending on the social upbringing and psychological make up of the individual an attempt to give a vent to the frustration would be made sometimes successfully but more often through the application of defence mechanisms which increase the frustration.

4. **Apathy.** The long periods of frustration lead to detachment and often cynicism. This is not a linear process but often cyclical. The process can repeat itself.

Some of the ways of dealing with/preventing burnout are :

1. **Vacations.** Make sure after every six months of stressful work one gets away for a holiday. The break should be planned in such a way that the problems of work are not carried to the holidays.

2. **Do not think that one is indispensable.** There are others who could and would do the jobs that one is so possessive of more effectively. At an individual level one has got to be careful not to take all the problems of the world.

3. **Time Management.** This is an important element if one wants to slow down the burnout process. Set a limit to how much one works. It is important to ensure that working hours do not stretch.

4. **Life style.** One needs to develop non-work interests. Ensure amply time for family, friends and socializing.

A. Corporate Mechanisms

1. **Team work.** Increasingly people are realizing effective corporate management lies in the participation of people in the affairs of the organisation. Studies have revealed that there is an inverse relationship between Team work and Burnout rate.

2. **Staff Development Policies.** Staff development Policies should become mandatory. There should be opportunities for individuals to take sabbaticals. Sabbaticals would provide individuals with necessary break which increase efficiency and ultimately benefit the organisation.

3. **Human Resource Management.** Corporate Managers should ensure that their staff are not overworked.

B. Social Support Mechanisms

At the social support level it is important to encourage formation of groups/clubs of people with common interests at work place. The increase opportunities of interaction and emotional support. Often these forums pose a challenge to the individual. Boredom and lack of challenge can be as much a problem as overwork.

Avoid Burnout

Take time—to smell the roses. Set goals for both your work and your private life. These goals should be to give purpose and meaning to life. Place your job in perspective and keep it there. Appraise the value of other facets of your life including your spouse, children, friends and hobbies.

Get Organised

A disorganised approach to our work and size can leave us wondering at the end of each day what we accomplished—and knowing it wasn't much. We won't get anywhere until we gain control of our time and tasks. We have to get organised and learn to manage our time, our paper work and even the telephone.

Time Management

The place to start is with time management. Following are some of the areas where we should concentrate to improve our management of time.

— Draw up a plan each day of what we want to accomplish.
— Develop daily, weekly, monthly and yearly list of goals.
— Don't passively accept a deadline you can't meet.
— Never handle a piece of paper more than twice. Once is much better. Aim for that.
— Use technology—computers, calculators, phones.
— Cut down on business reading. Learn to skim.
— Do business during coffee breaks and lunches.
— Delegate. Use one's time and effort for those tasks that require special skills to handle.
— Attend only the most important meetings.

Remember Priorities

Take a few minutes to analyse one's workday. Do you find yourself, at the end of the day, unable to think of any true accomplishment ? If the answer is "yes"—you are creating tremendous stress and anxiety for yourself, because you are feeling vulnerables and out of control.

Daily "To Do" List

Make a daily "To Do" list with items listed in order of importance. Check them off as you complete them. You will know at the end of each day, what you accomplished and what you wasted time in doing.

Learn to Say "No"

Interruption can be one of the biggest problem you face in managing time. Adopt a "screen-door policy" instead of "open-door-policy". Help your staff to become independent by asking them, before they bring a problem, suggest three possible solutions and identify the best solutions of the three.

Make List

Planning your work day requires you to make the basic lists, a comprehensive master list and a specific daily list.

Delegate

Refer all tasks that can be delegated to staff and cross them off, using your calendar or tickler file for follow ups. To work with the Daily List, late each afternoon draw it up for the following day. A Daily List should not include more than ten tasks. Limiting the list to ten items prevents the paralysis that can arise when your work load seems unmanageable.

LEADERSHIP

It is not limited to the person at the top of the pyramid. It is a mix of trait that skill that you can develop at any time and that will help move you up the ladder. Leadership is the ability to inspire other people to work together as a team following your load, in order to attain common objective.

Leader has the power to shape and mould an organisation through group co-operation. This calls for many abilities some of them are :

A Leader's Abilities—Recognise weaknesses and strengths in yourself and others.

— Set goals and meet them.
— Pass on credit to others for personal contributions.
— Turn every situation into a learning experience.
— Understand the use of power. Accept it in your position.
— Discriminate between truth, wishful thinking, and hard facts.
— Awaken those around you to have understanding of the full potential.
— Set an example as a leader, as people take in information more through the eyes than through the ear.

79

Social Welfare

Introduction

The concept of social security is as old as society is. The individual has been provided security against death, sickness, incapacity in employment, inadequate income etc. by the society and joint family system, caste system and many religious institutions. The timeless quest for security has created a number of social devices to afford protection to the needy individuals and these devices took different forms in different countries such as joint family, caste system and customs, mutual aid societies, religious percepts and institutions, the state philanthropic institutes and poor reliefs.

With the growth of factory system and industrialisation, the older institutions of social security became inadequate due to certain factors such as :

(*i*) Workers dependence on money, wage thereby alienation from agriculture.

(*ii*) Workers retaining links with villages had to manage two houses.

(*iii*) Stoppage of child labour as a source of income due to labour loss.

(*iv*) Chronic unemployment due to the growth of industries under capitalism.

(*v*) Industrialisation gave rise to individuality.

(*vi*) Increase in number of accidents due to increase of labour, multiplication of plant and inadequate working conditions.

Industrial workers having exposed to employment injuries, occupational diseases, unemployment, loss of income etc. necessitated the state to play very active and important role. The term Social Security has gained immense popularity in recent years having originated in U.S.A. in 1933. Soon after it spread in almost all countries of the world and the importance being recognised greater and greater. State is a social organisation within a certain territory and ever since it came into existence people have accepted it to perform certain functions for the good of the company as a whole. People accept state leaders to behave like a father towards all men. State in fact should provide support to poor, pregnant women, their new born off-spring, orphans, aged and to the helpless. In the past, state only touch the life of a citizen superficially. Even in European countries the position was not very much different in th ancient and medieval periods when the state assistance was no more than irregular charity. During the last century, joint family had been the most effective institution for social security. The family used to pool together all their resources and give each number a share in the product which was regulated to his needs and not proportional to his individual contribution.

In India, joint family system is still working and providing support to the members of the family. But it is not as strong a bond as it used to be. Even the caste systems also provide certain measures of economic security through not so direct as that of the family to help its needy members, social customs and conventions help the family systems in meeting unforeseen contingencies and ceremonial occasions.

Social security has now gone around the world and has caught the imagination of the Government and the people alike. The first Inter-America Conference of Social Security was held in 1942 which appealed to the people that :

"Each country must create, conserve and build up the intellectual, moral and physical vigour of its active generation, prepare the way for its future generation and support the generation that has been discharged from productive life. This is the concept of social security, a genuine and rational economy of human resources and values."

In 1944, I.L.O. stated that poverty anywhere constitutes a danger to prosperity everywhere. On December 10, 1948, the General Assembly of the United Nations adopted and proclaimed the Universal Declaration of Human Rights as a common standard of achievement for all Nations, Art. 25 of the Declaration says that :

"Everyone has the right to a standard of living, adequate for the health and well being of himself and of his family including food, clothing, housing and medical care and necessary social services and the right to security in the event of unemployment, sickness, disability, widowhood, old age or other lack of livelihood in circumstances beyond his control."

I.L.O. also defined "Social Security as the security that the society furnishes through proper and appropriate organisations against certain risks such as contingencies against which the individual of small means cannot effectively provide by his own ability or foresight or even in private combination of his fellow".

A Social Security system means a set of legal provisions entitled to define benefits for defined categories of persons, including maternity, (cost benefits) child maintenance, conditions requiring medical care, maintenance of community health when combined with provisions for other contingencies in-capacity for work, unemployment, old age, funeral and death of bread earner.

Social Security

It is based on the ideals of human dignity and social justice. According to Lord Beveridge, "Social Security" is a fight against want, disease, ignorance inequality and idleness. It is the protection which the society gives to its members against calamities over which members does not have any country. This industrial work-force which is responsible to the country's prosperity should be provided with adequate protections against certain risks or hazards to which their life is exposed. The risks can be transferred from the individual to the community in either of the following two ways :

— Social assistance — Social insurance

Both of these social assistance and social insurance from integral parts of the system social security.

Social Assistance

It is an assistance provided by the security or the Government to the poor and needy individuals. All such benefits are paid out of public revenue. In this the beneficiaries are not required to contribute to the fund. Social assistance schemes are adopted in societies where workers are too poor to contribute or illiterate.

Social Insurance

It is a scheme wherein members of community pool their resources to secure one another against risks which each one of them cannot face individuality. In France, social security received adequate attention of the social reformers. They stressed the need of income security with freedom to individuals and families. Japan has adopted some novel schemes of social security. Japan while maintaining its traditional social system also introduced modern systems of western industrialisation. In Japan beside other schemes there is child and mother protection schemes also. In U.S.S.R., the labour code of 1922 introduced the provisions for social security. The significant feature of social scheme. In U.S.S.R. it covers all risks, insure all workers and does not enjoin on them to pay any contribution. A citizen of U.S.S.R. can, therefore, claim social security as a matter of right. A worker get 50% to 60% of his salary after retirement depending upon the industry to which he belongs. Total disablement benefit varies between 60 to 100% of the wage. In Norway the system of social security is most established in the world. The social security scheme in Norway provide too much of economic protection to all its people.

The main features of social insurance scheme are :

—Benefits given up at the subsistence level.

—The benefits provided under the scheme are not in proportion to the amount of contribution made by the members.

Thus, the social insurance is a co-operative device resulting in the creation of collective fund to meet contingencies such as unemployment, maternity, sickness, injury, disability, oldage, death of breadwinner, involving loss of total or partial earnings.

The social security is now the aim to social welfare activities of all countries irrespective of their ideologies, social and political structure and economic policies. However, the emphasis on various aspects of social security varies with problems of the country in one country. The emphasis may be on family allowances and in another it may be on unemployment.

At present there is emphasis on a comprehensive social security scheme so as to cover manifold contingencies such as employment, injury, disablement, sickness and medical care, maternity, old age, retirement and survivor's pension, contributory provident fund etc.

Social Insurance and Social Assistance

The methods commonly employed for securing the objective of Social Security can be broadly grouped under two categories *viz.* Social Insurance and Social Assistance. The basic difference between the two approaches lies in the fact that in the former the individual concerned gets the benefit as a matter of right, in the later he gets the benefit after providing the need. India has been far behind in this sphere as compared to other countries of the world. In U.S.S.R., the social security measures were introduced even when her industrialisation was in its infancy. In Germany, New-Zealand, Australia, etc. social security measures were introduced at a fairly early stage of industrial development.

The International Labour Conference in the course of its 32 sessions held since 1919 till 1950 adapted 87 recommendations out of which 19 related to social security. India had travelled too slowly on this path ; out of only 12 conventions ratified by India, 2 relate to social security.

Article 32 of the Indian Constitution embodies the security, the right to work, to education and public assistance in the case of unemployment, old age, sickness, disablement etc. and the working class in India has also been demanding the above. The Government has not been able to do much in this respect, as is evident from the growing unemployment, under-employment, both among educated and uneducated even in professions specialised like engineers, doctors etc. The attitude of the business houses towards Social Security Schemes in India is lukewarm as can be discussed from large number of cases of violations of the provisions of the various Social Security Acts specially on the part of small employees who exhibit the ignorance of the illiterate workers in utter disregard of their own social responsibilities. To meet the needs of the industrial workers, the Government of India passed various acts, mainly of two kinds. The first group constitute the acts like Minimum Wages Act, Payment of Wages Act, Mines Act. The Indian Railways Act, The Plantation Labour Act. The Second Group encompasses the important pieces of legislation towards protection against old age, occupational diseases etc. Employees Insurance Act provide for sickness, cash, benefit, disablement benefit, medical benefit, maternity benefit etc. The Workmen's Compensation Act (for injuries arising out of and in the course of employment). Employees P.F. Act, Bonus Act, The Coal Mines P.F. Act, Maternity Benefit Act etc.

However, considering the magnitude of the problem in Indian conditions, it just touches the fringe of the problems. It will be a far to attempt reaching the levels of advanced countries in the foreseeable future. In India, while some measures have been taken in respect of the Industrial Workers, nothing worthwhile has been done for the remaining class of people specially agricultural workers who are comprising of 65% of the population. Government has to pay special attention towards the legislation like Health Schemes and old age pension for non-working class specially rural, social, insurance and national assistances. Such schemes are prevalent in many countries of the world. At present only a few classes of the population are covered and are eligible to get certain class of benefits. The agriculture class has been completely neglected in this regards. The E.S.I. covers only factories employees.

Unemployment Insurance

Unemployment Insurance is very common in many countries as a part of the social security scheme with the objective of helping the employees to overcome the difficulties of unemployment thereby indirectly helping the society also. In India, for industrial workers, there is a provision in the I.D. Act that in case of "Lay Off" upto 45 days, payment @ 50% and Retrenchment Benefit @ 15 days for each year of service exists which is not considered adequate and which does not apply to non-industrial workers.

To overcome the above short-comings, the State is to evolve a comprehensive Security Plan, having the following main features :

(*a*) Coverage of the whole population regarding income, security and medical services.

(*b*) Coverage of all principal contingencies such as sickness, maternity, employment injury, invalidity, old age, death of breadearner, unemployment and childhood.

The population of the country may be classified into two groups :

Persons who are gainfully occupied in the various areas of economic activity which will include :

(*a*) Agriculture

(*b*) Industries

(*c*) Transport and Communication

(*d*) Commerce, Personnel and Professional Services etc.

The class of non-gainfully occupied persons consist of children, old persons and other dependents—males and females.

The problem of social security of agricultural population will have to be taken separately because of the following reasons :

(i) Over 70% of the population directly dependant on agriculture.

(ii) Rural population is scattered all over the country and social security authorities must take village as the unit.

(iii) The agriculturist class consists not only of landless agricultural wage earner but also of the talent farmers and peasant proprietors. The economic needs of each of these groups are different from these of the other two.

(iv) The various insurance risks such as sickness, accident, invalidity, old age and even death do not have the same meaning for the cultivator, as for the urban wage earner. The most beneficial system of insurance to cultivator would be the crop and cattle insurance.

Social security is one of the pillars of which the structure of a welfare state rests. Social assistance is a method according to which benefits are given to the needy persons fulfilling the prescribed conditions. The social assistance benefits are paid out of public revenue, and the recipient cannot claim such benefit as a matter of right. Social insurance is a method of giving in return for contribution, benefits upon subsistance level. It is a method under which the members of the community, pool the resources to secure one another against risks which each one of them cannot face individually.

Number of steps have been taken by the Government of India to introduce various types of social insurance schemes for the workforce, more so for the industrially employed persons. The important social insurance legislations for workers in India are as follows :

(a) Workmens' Compensation Act, 1923.

(b) Employee's State Insurance Act, 1948.

(c) Maternity Benefits Acts.

(d) Provident Fund Acts.

(e) Dock Workers Act, 1948.

(f) Employees State Insurance Act, 1948.

Employees State Insurance Act 1948

This act is applicable to the whole of India except the State of Jammu and Kaskmir. The act covers all perennial factors employing 20 or more workers and using power. Indian Army, Naval and Airforce establishments of local body undertaking are excluded from the scope of this act. The act include sickness, employment, injury including fatal accidents and maternity in case of women employees. The statutory body is the Employees' State Insurance Corporation created under the act to administer and execute the various provisions of the act. It is a body having 31 members including representatives of employers employees equal principles of representatives from State and Central Government, medical profession and parliament. Ministers of Labour and Employment is the Chairman of this body. Under the control of the corporation the Standing Committee has been instituted, Standing Committee consist of members of the corporation and includes two representatives each of employers and employees. The act provides for appointment of tripartite regional boards, local committees. The act provides for the appointment of Director General to act as the Chief Executive Officer of the scheme who is assisted by 4 other principal officers and necessary staff. In order to pay benefits to the insured persons, the act creates a fund called E.S.I. fund. The fund is constituted all the employers' contribution, the employees' contribution, grants from the Government, donations etc. The fund can be used for the payment of benefits to the insured persons, cost of administration and making provisions thereof. THE ESI (AMENDMENT) Act. 1951 envisages that contributions are payable by employers in covered factories all over India, irrespective of whether their employees receive benefits or not. The rate of employees' contribution in respect of an employee depends on his average daily wage. Employees have been divided into 8 wage groups and the contribution are related to their wages. Employees' earning less than Re. 1 a day are not to make any contribution, but are entitled to all benefits. The act provides the following five benefits to the insured persons :

(*i*) Medical Benefit. (*ii*) Sickness Benefit.
(*iii*) Disablement Benefit. (*iv*) Maternity Benefit.
(*v*) Dependence Benefit.

(*i*) Medical Benefit

All insured persons are entitled to free and complete medical care which includes consultation, dispensation, diagnostic and investigational service, hospitalisation and domiciliary visits.

(*a*) Medical benefits are organised either under panel or the service system. The State Governments creates a panel of Insured Medical Practitioners in a particular city. Medical practitioners are allowed to have a specified number of insured persons in their panel and are paid a fixed amount of annual capitation fee according to the number of insured persons registered with them.

(*b*) Under the service system, corporation opens its own dispensary staffed by full time medical officers and other necessary personnel. The arrangement are also made to reserve certain beds for insured persons in civic hospitals.

(*ii*) Sickness Benefits

Sickness benefit is available to the insured person at the rate of ½ of the daily wage for a period of 56 days in any continuous period of 365 days, provided he fulfils the other qualifying conditions. ESI follows the principle of social insurance and an insured person must pay contribution according to his earning atleast for 26 weeks before he shall be entitled to receive sickness benefit duly certified by the Insurance Medical Officers. Sickness benefit has been extended to 309 days in certain qualifying conditions for patients suffering from T.B., leprosy, mental disorder etc.

(*iii*) Maternity Benefit

These benefits are paid to an insured women for a period of 12 weeks. The insured woman should be eligible for sickness benefit and have made atleast one contribution during 35 to 40th weeks preceding the week of expected confinement. The insured woman should have atleast a pregnancy for a period of 26 weeks, mis-carries after that period of 26 weeks or delivery of a dead child will be considered as conditions of maternity. The weeks of pregnancy and also the date of expected confinement should be certified by the Insurance Medical Officer.

(*iv*) **Disablement Benefit**

It is a employment injury sustained by an employee resulting in either temporary disablement or permanent disablement or death. The permanent disablement may be classified as total or partial. The temporary disablement means a condition which required medical treatment and refers an employee, incapable, work for a temporary period. The disabled worker is entitled to receive cash benefit. If incapacity due to injury exceeds 3 days, the payment of benefit will be from the first day of incapacity and will be paid as long as it continues. In case of permanent partial disablement, the rate of benefit will be in proportion to the degree of such disability. Its benefits shall be payable for life unless they are reviewed. Any occupational disease will be considered as an employment injury as per the act. The disablement benefit shall be an amount equivalent to 1/52 of the monthly wage calculated in accordance with the section 5 of the Workmen Compensation Act 1923.

(*v*) **Dependence Benefit**

If an employment injury results in the death of insured person, the benefits shall be payable as follows :

A. Widow

Period—Life or until re-marriage.

Share—3/5 of the full rate.

Remarks—If there are two or more widows, the amount shall be divided equally between the widows.

B. Son

Period—until he attains 15 years of age.

Share—2/5 of full rate to each legitimate.

C. Daughter

Period—Until she attains 15 years of age, or marriage whichever is earlier.

Amount—2/5 of full rate to each legitimate unmarried daughter.

If the share of all the above dependence is more than the total of depedance benefit, then the share of each of the dependence shall be proportional rates so that total amount payable to them does not exceed the amount of disablement benefit at full rate. If the individual does not leave widow or legitimate children, dependence benefits shall be payable to parents or grand parents or other dependents as such rates as may be decided by the Commissioner appointed under the Workmen's Compensation Act.

The benefit provisions of the act were first introduced in Kanpur and then in Delhi in the year 1952 and further extended to other parts of the country. Organisationally, the headquarters of the corporation is located at New Delhi with regional offices headed by regional directors in every state to implement, administer and to superwise the working of the scheme. The state governments have appointed medical officers to administer and supervise the medical benefits.

The employers of industrial undertakings in general are of the opinion that Social Security Scheme have diminished production and hampered the national economic growth. The All India Manufacturers Organisation feel that labour policy has let to the appeasement of labour through concessions, undermining their efficiency and causing steady rise, important militant attitude and high headedness among labours and it decline in the authority of management and bitterness in management relations. The leave benefits available to the employees for accident and sickness has considerably reduced the production. Most of the industrial undertaking reported during one of the study that the leave benefits are being misused by the employees by pretending sickness or minor accidents. Then the Employees State Insurance Doctors have similar feelings that at the times, they had been very liberal in granting sickness certificates and workers often resorted to false certification to avail the sickness benefits. Similarly, Doctors also complaint that administration set up of E.S.I.C. and Employee's Provident Fund Schemes are over administered.

Employees feel that their contribution to the Social Security Scheme is quite heavy. This complaint that women workers are costly as they receive in addition to statutory benefits, they also get maternity benefits in the form of leave sickness and cash benefits. Because of statutory Social Security Schemes, the cost of production has increased thereby adversely affecting, industrial production and reduction the competitiveness of industrial products in overseas markets. It is also important to note that the entire expenditure of social security even if incurred by an employer and appearing in his account as an expenditure of social security, it is actually not borne by the employers. In real terms the impact to social security expenditure as the incidence of the expenditure up to 60% is on the Government. For the remaining 40% of the expenditure, it is also not born by the employer, 60% of this 40% that is 24% of the aggregate is allocable surplus within the payment of Bonus Act, 1965 and 1978. Therefore, 24% of the expenditure on Social Security initially borne by the employer is on the employees themselves. Because of this money would have gone to the bonus of an employee. The Social Security Schemes render to balancing benefits to the employees. Firstly—they attract better workers and secondly—it prevents employees from raising their voice for increase in wages. The attack on Social Security Schemes is that they breed absenteeism of workers on the basis of false certification by medical practitioners. The employers also alleged that the government does not make any monetary contribution but the administrative machinery is over-loaded than the government representatives. This is important to observe that entrepreneure though covered by various social security laws have been trying to evade implementation of social scheme measures by disputing the coverage of their establishment. Has pointed out by employers that female worker is costly and, therefore, their reluctant to employment women. According to annual report of ESIC the rate of confinement per thousand insured women employees was 58. The probable number of confinement per woman employee would not be more than 2 for 33 years of service and the maternity confinement benefit, according to the report is 536. Therefore, the total expenditure per woman worker for the entire service of 33 years works is to be approximately Rs. 1100 that is Rs. 2.80 per month. As we have earlier 16% of the expenditure is borne by the employers and thus the expenditure per woman worker works out to be 55 paise per month. Therefore the social security measures in any case enhance the cost of production rather it helps in increasing industrial development.

80

The Trade Unions Act, 1926

Introduction

The enactment of Indian Trade Unions Act 1926 was expedited by a popular feelings against a court decision injecting a union in Madras in 1920 for inciting and organising the workers to violate the contract of service and thereby interfering with the business of employer. After this criminal suit filed by Messers Minny & Co. against Madras Labour Union, it was felt that legal protection against civil and criminal liabilities was essential if workers interest was to be protected. The Act recognised the existence of trade unions in the industrial relations system. The fundamental object of the Act is to make the trade union legal and provide an infrastructure where unions can operate and continue their activities. The Act extends to the whole of India including the state of Jammu and Kashmir. It came into force on the first day of June 1927.

Trade Dispute

A trade dispute means any dispute :

(*a*) between employers and workmen

(*b*) between workmen and workmen

(*c*) between employers and employers.

Any such dispute as mentioned to be a Trade Dispute must also be associated with :

(*a*) the employment

(*b*) non-employment

(*c*) the terms of employment

(*d*) the conditions of labour of any person.

The definition of Trade Dispute in this Act is almost similar to the definition of Industrial Dispute given in the Industrial Disputes Act, 1947. In Trade Dispute, it is necessary that there must be a demand from one party and refusal to accept that demand by other party. There can be no dispute by the unilateral action of one party and similarly disputes must be real and substantial between the parties to such dispute.

Trade Union. The term trade union can be expressed both in an ordinary sense and in broad sense. In ordinary sense it is a combination of workmen and in a broader sense it includes combination of employers and federation of two or more such combinations. The trade union means :

Any combination whether temporary or permanent formed for the purpose of regulating relations between :

(*a*) Workmen and employers

(b) Workmen and workmen

(c) Employers and employers. Or

combination for imposing restrictive conditions the conduct of any trade or business and includes any federation of two or more trade unions, but certain agreements given below have been excluded from the scope of the term trade union :

(a) Agreement between partners in a business.

(b) Agreement in consideration of the sale of the good-will of business or of instruction in any profession, trade of handicraft.

Similarly an association whose main object was to acquire patent right was held not to be a trade union. Similarly federation of teachers cannot be referred as association of trade union for teachers not being in the employment of industry.

Trade union should send an application for registration to the Registrar and shall be accompanied by the following :

— Name and addresses of members making the application.
— The name of the Trade Union and address of its head office.
— The titles, names, ages, addresses and office bearers of the Trade Union.
— General statement of the assets and liabilities of the Trade Union, if the union is in existence for over one year.

The Trade Union can be registered only under the Trade Unions Act, 1926 and the registration of Trade Unions under any other Act such as the following shall be void :

— The Societies Registration Act, 1860.
— The Cooperative Societies Act, 1912.
— The Companies Act, 1956.

The registration of Trade Union is not legally necessary but it brings certain advantages which are :

— It becomes a corporate body by name.
— It can enter into a contract.
— It attains a legal entity.
— It can sue and be sued in its registered name.

The registrar can cancel or withdraw the registration and can exercise power on Trade Unions for the following issues where :

— Certificate of registration has been obtained by fraud or mistake.
— Trade Union has ceased to exit.
— Trade Union has violated any provision of this Act.
— The primary objects of the Union are no longer statutory objects.

The Trade Union can request the registrar to cancel their registration after the approval of the general meeting of Trade Unions or majority of the members of Trade Union. The Registrar must give atleast two month's notice in writing giving the grounds on which he propose to cancel the certificate of registration. Registration confers on the Trade Unions certain rights and privileges which are as follows :

(a) Body corporate.

(b) Separate fund for political purposes.

(c) Immunity from criminal conspiracy.

(*d*) Immunity from civil suit.

(*e*) Enforceability or agreements.

(*f*) Right to amalgamate.

(*g*) Right to inspect books of Trade Union.

Registration of Trade Unions

Appointment of Registrars (Section 3)

As regards registration of a trade union, the Act empowers the appropriate Government to appoint a person to be the Registrar of Trade Unions for each state. The appropriate Government may appoint as many additional and deputy registrars of trade unions as it thinks fit. They shall work under the superintendent and direction of the Registrar.

The appropriate Government shall specify and define the local limits within which any additional and Deputy Registrar shall exercise and discharge his powers and functions.

Mode of Registration

A Trade Union can be registered only under the Trade Unions Act, 1926. The Societies Registration Act, 1860, the Co-operative Societies Act, 1912, and the Companies Act, 1956, shall not apply to any registered Trade Union, and the registration of a Trade Union under any such Act shall be void (Section 14).

Any seven or more members of a Trade Union may apply for registration of the Trade Union. All the members applying for registration must subscribe their names to the rules of the Trade Union and also comply with the provisions of the Act relating to registration.

Application for Registration (Section 5)

Every application for registration of a Trade Union shall be made to Registrar. It shall be accompanied by a copy of the rules containing matters as given in Section 6. It also contain a statement of the following particulars :

(*a*) the names, occupations and addresses of members making the application ;

(*b*) the name of the Trade Union and the address of its head office ; and

(*c*) the titles, names, ages, addresses, and occupations of the office-bearers of the Trade Union.

Where a Trade Union has been in existence for more than one year before its registration, a general statement of the assets and liabilities of the Trade Union in the prescribed form must be submitted along with the application.

Registration (Section 8)

The Registrar will register Trade Union, if he is satisfied that the trade union has complied with all the requirements of this Act in regard to registration. The Registrar shall register the Trade Union by making necessary entries in the register, to be maintained in such form as may be prescribed. The particulars relating to the Trade Union contained in the statement accompanying the application for registration shall be entered in the register.

Where the Registrar takes no action on an application for more than three months, writ petition under Article 226 can be issued commanding the Registrar to deal with the application.

Certificate of Registration (Section 9)

The Registrar, on registering a Trade Union shall issue a certificate of registration which shall be conclusive evidence that the Trade Union has been duly registered under the Act.

It is obligatory on the part of the Registrar to register a Trade Union provided the provisions of the Act are complied with. He is not entitled to question whether the Union is lawful or unlawful.

Advantages of Registration

Although it is not legally necessary for a Union to be registered, registration does bring with its certain advantages. Some of the advantages gained by registration as given in Section 13 are as under :

- (*a*) A Trade Union becomes a body corporate by name under which it is registered and it is a legal entity distinct from its members of which it is composed.
- (*b*) It gets perpetual succession and common seal.
- (*c*) It can acquire and hold both movable and immovable property.
- (*d*) It can enter into a contract.
- (*e*) It can sue and be sued in its registered name.

Cancellation of Registration (Section 10)

Power to withdraw or cancel registration of a Trade Union is given to the Registrar. The Registrar on exercise the power in the following cases namely:

- (*a*) On the application of the Trade Union for such a course.
- (*b*) Where the certificate of registration has been obtained by fraud or mistake :
- (*c*) Where the Trade Union ceased to exist ;
- (*d*) Where the Trade Union has wilfully and after notice from the Registrar allowed any rule to continue in force which is inconsistent with the provision of this Act ;
- (*e*) Where the Trade Union has wilfully and after notice from the registrar violated any provisions of this Act ;
- (*f*) Where the primary objects of the Union are no longer statutory objects.

Where the Union desires to have its certificate of registration withdrawn or cancelled, the registrar on receiving such application, must, before granting the application satisfy himself that the withdrawal or cancellation was approved by a general meeting of the Trade Union or if it was not so approved, it had the approval of the majority of the members of the Trade Union.

The Registrar is not competent to cancel registration of a Trade Union without-giving requisite notice and giving an opportunity to the Trade Union to show cause against the proposed action.

The Registrar must be given not less than two month's previous notice in writing giving the grounds on which it is proposed to withdraw or cancel the certificate of registration. No such notice is required where such application is made by the Trade Union itself.

Appeal (Section 11)

Section 11 of the Act gives a limited right of appeal from the decisions of the Registrar. Any person who is aggrieved by the refusal of the Registrar to register a Trade Union or the withdrawal or cancellation of certificate of registration is given the right of appeal. The appeal must be within 60 days of the date on which Registrar passed the order against which appeal is made.

Trade Union can be restrained by injection from applying its funds for an unauthorized object or for an unlawful purpose, because such as expenditure shall be ultra vires the Act. Thus it would be illegal to devote Union funds in support of any illegal strike or lock out.

Constitution of a separate fund for political purposes (Section 16)

In addition to primary objects, a trade union may have certain other political objects which are not inconsistent with the primary objects. Under section 16, a registered Trade Union may raise a separate political fund from contributions separately levied or made to that fund.

Rights and Privileges

Registration confers on the Trade Unions certain rights and privileges. Similarly some rights are granted to the members of a registered Trade Union both collectively and individually. These are as under.

Body Corporate (Section 13)

Every registered Trade Union is a body corporate by the name under which it is registered. A registered Trade Union is an artificial persons in the eyes of law capable of enjoying rights like a natural person. It has a perpetual succession and a common seal. It has the right to acquire and hold both movable and immovable property. It can enter into a contract and can sue and be sued in its registered name.

Separate fund for political purposes (Section 16)

Every registered Trade Union constitute and raise a separate fund for political purposes from contributions separately levied for or made to that fund.

Immunity from Criminal Conspiracy (Section 17)

The Act provides that no office bearer or member of a registered Trade Union will be liable to punishment under section 120-B of the Indian Penal Code in respect of any agreement made between the members unless the agreement is an agreement to commit an offence. This section provides immunity to members and office bearers of a registered Trade Union from punishment for criminal conspiracy. Criminal conspiracy is an agreement of two or more persons to do an unlawful act or to do a lawful act by unlawful means.

Immunity from Civil Suit (Section 18)

Section 18 of the Trade Union Act deals with immunity from civil proceeding afforded to a registered Trade Union and to its members, or office-bearers. No suit or legal proceeding is maintainable in any civil court against registered Trade Union.

A registered Trade Union is also not liable in any suit or other legal proceeding in any civil court in respect of any tortuous act done in contemplation or furtherance of trade dispute by an agent of the Trade Union if it is proved that such agent acted without the knowledge of or contrary to express instructions given by the executive of the Trade Union.

Proportion of office-bearers to be connected with the industry (Section 22)

Section 22 provides that not less than one half of the total number of the office-bearers of every registered Trade Union shall be persons actually engaged or employed in any industry with which the Trade Union is connected. But the appropriate Government may by special or general order declare that the provisions of the section shall not apply to any Trade Union or class of Trade Unions specified in the order.

Amalgamation of Trade Unions

Section 24 of the Act provides a method for amalgamation of two or more registered Trade Unions. Amalgamation may take place with or without any dissolution or division of the funds of the amalgamating unions. Before any amalgamation take place, at least one-half of the members of each or every such Trade Union entitled to vote must record their votes, and those in favour of the proposed amalgamation should be at least sixty percent.

According to Section 25, notice in writing of the amalgamation must be given to the Registrar. Notice must be signed by the Secretary and seven members of each and every Trade Union that is a party to the amalgamation.

An amalgamation of two or more Trade Union does not prejudice any right of any of the Trade Union or any right to a creditor of any one of them.

Returns

Every registered Trade Union is required by Section 28 to send annually to the Registrar on before a prescribed date, a general audited statement of all receipts and expenditure during the year ending 31st day of December. A general statement of the assets and liabilities of the Trade Union existing on 31st day of December shall also be sent on the prescribed date to the Registrar.

The general statement shall be accompanied by :

(*i*) a statement showing all changes of office-bearers made by the Trade Union during the year.

(*ii*) a copy of the rules of the Trade Union corrected up to the date of the despatch of the statement.

A copy of the every alteration made in the rules of a registered Trade Union must be sent to the Registrar within fifteen days of the making of the alteration. The Registrar is empowered to inspect all the original documents included in the general statement or connected with the general statements at all reasonable times at the registered office of the trade union. Alternatively, he may require production of these documents at such place as they may specify. But in no case shall this specified place be at a distance of more than 10 miles from the registered office of a Trade Union.

Any person who wilfully makes or causes to be made any false entry or any omission from the general statement or any other document, required to be submitted under section 28, shall be punishable with fine which may extend to five hundred rupees.

Under Section 29 of the Trade Unions Act, 1926, the appropriate Government is empowered to make regulations for the purpose of carrying into effect the provisions of the Act. All such regulations made by the appropriate Government shall be published in the Official Gazette.

81

The Factories Act, 1948

Introduction

The Factories Act, 1948 is a comprehensive piece of legislation covering all aspects regarding the factories namely :

(*a*) Approval (*b*) Licensing (*c*) Registration of factories (*d*) the inspecting authorities (*e*) health (*f*) safety (*g*) welfare (*h*) working hours (*i*) employment of adults and young children (*j*) annual leave and penalties.

The Act extends to the whole of India including State of Jammu and Kashmir. It came into force on 1st April 1949. Under the Act the State Government is empowered to make rules for the purpose of approval, licensing and registration of factories. The liability to apply for registration and obtaining a licence is on the occupier. Failure to apply for the registration of the factory and a licence under section 6 amounts to an offence punishable under section 92. Once the application for permission accompanied by plans is sent to the appropriate authority by registered post and further no communication is received to the applicant for three months from the date of despatch of the application, it will be presumed that permission of the Government is granted. The occupier is required to serve a notice atleast 15 days before he begins to occupy any premise as a factory to the Chief Inspector with following particulars :

—Name and situation of the factory.

—Name and address of the occupier.

—Name and address of the owner.

—Address to which communication relating to factory may be sent.

—Nature of manufacturing process carried on and to be carried out.

Whether following facilities are available ;

(*k*) Drinking water (*l*) Latrines and urinals.

(*m*) Spittoons.

Safety

Whether it contains the provisions relating to the safety of the workers. The various provisions have been grouped as under :

(*a*) Fencing of machinery.

(*b*) Working near a moving machinery.

(*c*) Employment of young persons on dangerous machines.

(*d*) Striking gear and devices for cutting off power.

(*e*) Self-acting machines.

(*f*) Casing of new machines.
(*g*) Prohibition of employment of women and children near cotton openers.
(*h*) Hoists and lifts, lifting machines, chains, ropes and lifting tackles.
(*i*) Revolving machinery.
(*j*) Pressure plant.
(*k*) Floor, stairs and means of assess.
(*l*) Pits, sumps, openings in floor.
(*m*) Excessive weights.
(*n*) Protection of eyes.
(*o*) Precaution against dangerous fumes.
(*p*) Explosive or inflamable dust gas.
(*q*) Precaution in case of fire.
(*r*) Safety and maintenance of building.

Safety Officer

There is a need to appoint safety officer in each factory where one thousand or more workers are ordinarily employed or where operations are carried out which involves any risk of bodily injuries or any other hazard to health to the persons employed in the factory.

—Total rated horse power installed.

—Name of the manager of the factory.

—Number of workers are being employed.

The failure of an occupier of the factory to give a written notice of occupation as required under section 7 (*i*) is an offence.

Inspecting Staff

The State Government has the power under the Factories Act to appoint the following persons as inspecting staff :

—Chief Inspector.

—Additional Chief Inspector.

—Joint Chief Inspector.

—Inspector.

—Certifying surgeons.

According to the Factories (Amendment) Act 1976, the State Government is authorised to appoint as many Additional Chief Inspectors as it thinks fit. Their appointment must be notified in the official gazette.

Let us see in little more details some of the important provisions of Factories Act :

Health

Chapter 3 of the Factories Act 1948 deal with the health of workers in a factory. Following provisions have been incorporated to protect the health of workers :

(*a*) Cleanliness.
(*b*) Disposal of wastes and effluents.
(*c*) Ventilation and temperature.

(*d*) Artificial humidification.
(*e*) Dust and fumes.
(*f*) Artificial humidification.
(*g*) Overcrowding.
(*h*) Lighting.

Health

Sections 11 to 20 contained in Chapter 3 of the Factories Act, 1948, deal with the health of workers in a factory. These provisions have been incorporated to protect the health of workers. Following are the provisions under the Act.

Cleanliness (Section 11)

Every factory must be kept clean and free from effluent arising from any drain, or other nuisance. In particular the following measures must be adopted :

(*a*) Accumulation of dirt and refuse shall be removed daily from the floors and benches of work rooms passages and staircases ;
(*b*) The floor of every work room shall be cleaned at least once in every week by washing, using disinfectants etc. ;
(*c*) Where the floor is liable to become wet, means of draining shall be provided and maintained :
(*d*) All inside walls, partitions, and ceilings etc. should be painted otherwise than with washable water paints and should be repainted or revarnished at least once in fourteen months. In any other case they shall be white washed or colour washed at least once in fourteen months;
(*e*) Where they are painted with washable water paints, be repainted with at least one coat of such paint at least once in every period of three years and washed at least once in every period of six months ;
(*f*) All doors and window-frames and other wooden or metallic framework and shutters shall be kept painted or varnished and the painting or varnishing shall be carried out at least once in every period of five years.

Disposal of wastes and effluents (Section 12)

Effective arrangements shall be made in every factory for the treatment of wastes and effluents due to the manufacturing process carried on therein so as to render them innocuous, and for their disposal.

Such an arrangement must be approved by the authority prescribed under the rules.

Ventilation and Temperature (Section 13)

Effective and suitable provision shall be made in every factory for securing and maintaining in every work-room.

(*a*) adequate ventilation by the circulation of fresh air ; and
(*b*) such a temperature as will secure to workers therein reasonable condition of comfort and prevent injury to health.

The walls and roofs of work-rooms must be of such material and of such design as to keep the temperature low. Where the maintenance of high temperature is necessary for the process carried on in the factory, the work-room should be separated from the process either by insulating the hot parts or by some effective devices. The State Government may prescribe a standard of adequate ventilation and reasonable temperature and may also provide for the adoption of methods which will keep the temperature low. It may also make rules providing for the keeping of thermometers in specified places.

Dust and Fume (Section 14)

In any factory where dust or fume is given off in any manufacturing process which is likely to be injurious or offensive to the workers, effective measures must be taken to prevent the inhalation of the dust or fume. Any exhaust appliance which may be necessary shall be applied as near as possible to the point of origin of the dust or fume, and such point shall be enclosed so far as possible. The exhaust fumes of stationary internal combustion engines must be conducted into the open or outside the factory.

Artificial Humidification (Section 15)

The State Government is empowered to make rules for all factories in which the humidity of the air is artificially increased. The rules should relate to :

(*a*) prescribing standard of humidification ;

(*b*) regulating the methods for artificially increasing the humidity of the air ;

(*c*) directing prescribed tests for determining the humidity of the air ;

(*d*) methods to be adopted for securing adequate ventilation and cooling of the air in the work-rooms.

The water used for humidification shall be taken from a public supply or other source of drinking water or shall be effectively purified before it is so used.

Overcrowding (Section 16)

This section provides that there must not be over-crowding in any room of a factory so as to cause injury to the health of the workers. In order to prevent overcrowding the section requires a minimum of 500 cubic feet of space per worker for factories built after the commencement of the Act and 350 cubic feet for factories built before the commencement of the Act. In calculating the amount of space available, no more than 14 feet above the level of the floor is to be counted. The Chief Inspector may past a notice in the workroom indicating the maximum number of workers who may be employed in the room.

Lighting (Section 17)

Every part of the factory must be provided with sufficient and suitable lighting, natural or artificial or both. Effective provision must be made for the prevention of glare and the formation of shadows likely to cause eye-strain or the risk of accident to any worker. The State Government may prescribe standards of sufficient and suitable lighting.

Drinking Water (Section 18)

Arrangements shall be made to provide and maintain at suitable points a sufficient supply of wholesome drinking water. All such points shall be clearly marked 'drinking water' in a language understood by a majority of the workers and every such point shall not be situated within 20 feet of any washing place, urinal or latrine. Factories employing over 250 workers are required to provide cool drinking water during hot weather.

Latrines and Urinals (Section 19)

The section requires sufficient latrine and urinal accommodation and there must be separate closed accommodation for male and female workers. Such accommodation must be adequately lighted, ventilated and maintained in a clean and sanitary condition. These should be situated at suitable place accessible to the workers. Sufficient number of sweepers should be employed to keep urinals latrines, and washing places clean. Where more than 250 workers are ordinarily employed, all latrines and urinals accommodation shall be prescribed sanitary types. The State Government may prescribe the number of latrines and urinals to be provided in any factory in proportion to the number of male and female workers.

Spittoons (Section 20)

There shall be provided a sufficient number of spittoons at convenient places and they shall be maintained in a clean and hygienic condition. No person shall spit anywhere except in the spittoons. If a person violates this provision he may be fined up to Rs. 5.

Safety

Sections 21 to 41 of the Act contain the provisions relating to the safety of the workers. These provisions are absolute in character and it is the duty of the occupier of every factory to comply with them. They are summarised as under.

Fencing of machinery

Compulsory fencing of all sorts of machinery is provided for by this section. In every factory, every dangerous part of any machinery shall be securely fenced by safeguards of substantial construction which shall be constantly maintained and kept in position while the parts of machinery they are fencing are in motion or in use. A machine is said to be securely fenced if fenced against dangers which may be reasonably foreseen. The liability to fence is absolute and the employers cannot evade his liability on commercial or mechanical reasons. The State Government may also prescribe by rules such further precautions in respect of any particular machinery or its part for securing the safety of the workers.

Work on or near machinery in motion

With a view to secure the safety of the workers, this section requires that examination, lubrication, etc. of the machinery while it is in motion should be carried out only by a specially trained adult male worker wearing tight fitting clothing (which shall be supplied by the occupier). The name of such a male worker should have been recorded in the register prescribed in this behalf.

Such worker shall not handle a belt at a moving pulley unless :

(*i*) the belt is not more than fifteen centimetres in width ;

(*ii*) the pulley is normally for the purpose of drive and not merely a try-wheel or balance wheel (in which case a belt is not permissible) ;

(*iii*) the belt point is either laced or flush with the belt ;

(*iv*) the belt, including the joint and pulley rim are in good repair ;
(*v*) there is reasonable clearance between the pulley and any fixed plant or structure ;
(*vi*) any ladder in use of for carrying out any examination or operation aforesaid is securely fixed or lashed or is firmly held by a second person.

No woman or young person shall be allowed to clean, lubricant or adjust any part of the machinery while it is in motion if it is likely to expose her or him to risk or injury from any moving part.

Employment of young persons on dangerous machines (Section 23)

No young person shall work at any dangerous machines unless :

(*a*) he has been fully instructed as the dangers arising in connection with the machines and precautions to be observed ; and
(*b*) he has received sufficient training in work at the machine or is under adequate supervision by a person who has a thorough knowledge and experience of the machine.

This section only applies to young persons and not to women.

Striking gear and devices for cutting off power (Section 24)

In every factory, suitable striking gear or other efficient mechanical appliance shall be provided and maintained. Driving belts when not in use shall not be allowed to rest or ride upon shafting in motion. Suitable devices for cutting off power in emergencies from running machinery shall be provided and maintained in every work-room.

When a device, which can inadvertently shift from 'off' to 'on' positions, is provided in a factory to cut off power, arrangement shall be provided for locking the device in safe position to prevent accidental starting of the transmission machinery or other machines to which the device is fitted.

Self-acting machines (Section 25)

No traversing part of a self-acting machines in any factory and no material carried there on shall be allowed to run on its outward or inward traverse within a distance of 18 inches from any fixed structure which is not part of the machine. This restriction would apply if the space over which it runs in a space over which any person is liable to pass, whether in the course of employment or otherwise.

The Chief Inspector may permit the continued use of a machines installed before the commencement of the Act which does not comply with these requirements. He may impose such conditions for ensuring safety as he may think fit to impose.

Casing of new machinery (Section 26)

All machinery driven by power and installed in any factory after 1st April 1949 must be encased or otherwise effectively guarded as to prevent danger. It is a punishable offence to sell or let out on fire any machine which does not comply with the above provision. The offender may be punished with imprisonment up to three months or fine up to Rs. 500 or both.

Prohibition of employment of women and children near cotton openers (Section 27).

No woman or child shall be employed in any part of a factory for pressing cotton in which a cotton-opener is at work. But when the feed end of a cotton-opener is in a room separated from the delivery end by partition extending to the roof or to such height as the inspector may specify in writing, women and children may be employed on the side of the partition where the feed-end is situated.

Hoists and Lifts (Section 28)

In every factory every hoist and lift shall be of good mechanical construction, sound material and adequate strength. They should by properly maintained and thoroughly examined by a competent person at least once in every period of six months. A register containing the prescribed particulars of every such examination shall also be kept. Every hoistway and liftway must be sufficiently protected by a proper enclosure fitted with gates. The maximum safe working load must be clearly marked on every hoist or lift and a larger load should not be carried thereon.

Lifting machines, chains, ropes and lifting tackles (Section 29)

In every factory, lifting machines, chains, ropes and lifting tackles must be of good construction sound material and adequate strength and free from defects. These shall be properly maintained and thoroughly examined by a competent person at least once in every period of twelve months. A register shall be kept containing the prescribed particulars of every such examination. No lifting machine and no chain, rope or lifting tackle shall be loaded beyond the safe working load which shall be plainly marked thereon.

Revolving machinery (Section 30)

In every room in a factory in which the process of grinding is carried on, there shall be permanently affixed or placed near each machine a notice indicating the maximum, safe working speed. Effective measures must be taken to ensure that the safe working speed is not exceeded.

Pressure plant (Section 31)

If in any factory any operation is carried on at a pressure above atmospheric pressure, effective measure shall be taken to ensure that the safe working pressure is not exceeded. However, the State Government can exempt any part of any plant or machinery from the provisions of this section.

Floors, stairs and means of access (Section 32)

In every factory all floors, steps, stairs, passages and gangways shall be of sound construction and properly kept and maintained and shall be kept free from obstructions and substances likely to cause persons to slip.

Where any person has to work at a place from where he is likely to fall, a distance exceeding two metres, then, unless the place is one which provides secure foothold and, where necessary secure handhold, provision shall be made, so far as it reasonably practicable, by fencing or otherwise, to ensure the safety of the person so working. Safe means of access must be provided and maintained to every place at which any person in at any time required to work. The obligation under this section is absolute.

Pits, sumps, openings in floor, etc. (Section 33)

In every factory, every fixed vessel, sump, tank, pit or opening in the ground or in a floor, which may be a source of danger, shall be either securely covered or securely fenced. The covering or fencing of a pit securely means covering or fencing it is such a way that it ceases to be a source of danger to those who have occasion to go near it. An omission to securely fence is a continuing offence.

Excessive weights (Section 34)

No person shall be employed in any factory to lift, carry or move any load so heavy as is cause him injury. State Government may make rules prescribing the maximum weights which may be lifted, carried or moved by adult men, adult women, adolescents and children employed in factories.

Protection of eyes (Section 35)

In respect of any manufacturing process carried on in any factory involving risk of injury to the eyes from particles or fragments thrown off in the course of process or by reason of exposure to excessive light, the State Government is given the power to make rules requiring that such factories must provide effective screens or suitable goggles to protect the employed persons.

Precautions against dangerous fumes (Section 36)

In any factory, no person shall enter or be permitted to enter any chamber, tank, vat, pit; pipe, flue, or other confined space in which dangerous fumes are likely to be present to such an extent as to involve risk of persons being overcome thereby unless it is provided with a manhole of adequate size or other effective means of egress.

A—Precautions regarding the use of probable electric lights (Section 36 A)

In any factory :

(*a*) no portable electric light or any other electric appliance of voltage exceeding twenty-four volts shall be permitted for use inside any chamber, tank, vat, pit, flue or other confined space ; and

(*b*) if any inflammable gas fume or dust is likely to be present in such chamber, tank, vat, pipe, flue or other confined space, no lamp or light other than that of flame proof construction shall be permitted to be used therein.

Explosive or inflammable dust, gas, etc. (Section 37)

When in any factory any manufacturing process products dust, gas, fume or vapour of such character and to such extent as to be likely to explode on ignition all practicable measures shall be taken to prevent any such explosion by :

(*a*) effective enclosure of the plant or machinery used in the process ;

(*b*) removal or prevention of the accumulation of dust, gas, fume or vapour ;

(*c*) exclusion or effective enclosure of all possible sources of ignition.

Where any part of the plant or machinery in a factory contains any explosive or inflammable gas or vapour under pressure greater than atmospheric pressure, that part shall not be opened except in accordance with the provisions contained in this section.

The State Government is empowered to make rules to exempt any factory from the compliance of this section.

Precautions in case of fire (Section 38)

Precautions must be taken in every factory for escape in case of fire. Section 38 lays down the following rules in this connection :

(*i*) In every factory there shall be provided such means of escape in case of fire as may be prescribed.

(*ii*) In every factory, the doors affording exits should not be locked or fastened and should be capable of being opened immediately and all such doors, unless they are of the sliding type, shall be constructed to open outwards.

(*iii*) Every window, door or other exit affording a means of escape in case of fire, other than the means of exit in ordinary use shall be distinctly marked in a language understood by the majority of the workers and in red letters of adequate size.

(*iv*) In every factory effective arrangements should be made for giving audible warning to the workers in case of fire.

(*v*) There shall be maintained a free access to the means of escape in case of fire for the use of all workers in every room of the factory.

(*vi*) Effective measures shall be taken to ensure that in every factory :

(*a*) wherein more than 20 workers are ordinarily employed at any place above the ground floor, or

(*b*) Wherein explosive or highly inflammable materials are used or stored.

All the workers are familiar with the means of escape in case of fire and have been adequately trained in the routine to be followed in each case.

(*vii*) The State Government may make rules prescribing, in respect of any factory the means of escape, to be provided in case of fire and the nature and amount of fire-fighting apparatus to be provided and maintained.

(*viii*) Where the inspector, having regard to the nature of work carried on in the factory are not adequate to permit safe, easy or quick exist of the workers in case of fire, may be by order in writing require that such additional means of escape of other measures as he may consider reasonable and necessary be provided in the factory before such date as is specified in the order.

Power to require specifications of defective parts or test of stability (Section 39)

This section empowers the inspector to serve on the manager or occupier or both of a factory an order in writing requiring him to furnish specifications of defective parts such as those of building machinery or plant or he may order the manager, occupier or both to carry out tests as he may specify and to inform him of the result.

Safety of building and machinery (Section 40)

This section also empowers the Inspector to serve on the manager or occupier or both of a factory an order in writing specifying the measures which should be adopted before a specified date for safety of building and machinery. In case of imminent danger the Inspector is empowered to prohibit the use of such buildings, machinery etc. Until properly repaired or altered.

Maintenance of buildings (Section 40-A)

Where it appears to the inspector that any building or part of a building in a factory is in such a state of disrepair as a likely to lead to conditions detrimental to the health and welfare of the workers, he may serve on the occupier or manager or both of the factory an order in writing specifying the measures which in his opinion should be taken and requiring the same to be carried out before such date as is specified in the order.

Safety officers (Section 40-B)

This section requires the appointment of safety officers in every factory :

(*i*) wherein one thousand or more workers are ordinarily ever employed, or

(*ii*) wherein, in the opinion of the State Government any manufacturing process or operation is carried on which involves any risk of bodily injury or any other hazard to health to the persons employed in the factory, the occupier shall if so required by the State Government by notification in Official Gazette, employ such number of safety officers as may be specified in that notification.

Power to make rules to supplement this chapter (Section 41)

The State Government has the power to make rules to supplement the provisions relating to safety contained in chapter IV of the Act. The rules will tend to provide further devices and measures for securing the safety of persons employed in any factory.

82

Industrial Security

Introduction

Functions. The main functions of Industrial Security are as under :

1. To protect the personnel and property of the organisation against theft, sabotage, pilferage, vandalism etc.
2. To protect the personnel of the organisation against violence and gheraos.
3. To arrange fire-fighting and maintenance of fire-fighting appliances.
4. To control the movement of workers and visitors.
5. To check all incoming and outgoing goods and vehicles.
6. To assist the management in case of strikes and labour unrest.
7. To investigate accidents and thefts.
8. To bring the irregularities to the notice of the management and suggesting remedial measures.
9. To assist management in case of threats, intimidation etc.
10. Assisting managements to implement civil defence schemes.
11. To give timely information to the management about the negative plans of certain misguiding elements in the organisation.
12. To conduct search of the personnel of the organisation while getting out of the factory.
13. To control the movements of company's vehicles.
14. To register the theft cases etc. with police station and pursue such cases at the court levels.
15. Industrial security should work well for the success of the team work in the organisation.
16. The industrial security should set an example of good behaviour and on their part should maintain their own characters and dignity of their organisation.
17. They should see that fire-fighting equipment is always maintained trim and ready. A system of fire-alarms should be installed. More over security personnel should be well trained in fire-fighting.
18. Industrial security men should be properly alert and armed. They should not allow unauthorised persons entry into the premises of the establishment. They should organise a fool proof system of entry passes for all kinds of visitors.
19. They should introduce, if necessary, a system of checking the person of visitors. Trespassing should be scrupulously checked.

20. They should be adequately armed add equipped.
21. They should be well trained in fire-fighting and false refresher courses off and on.
22. They should be in proper uniforms for easy differentiation from other workers.
23. They should be careful while handing and taking over charge of their duties.
24. The industrial security men must be regular, punctual and possess integrity, loyalty and honesty.
25. They should be ready to do their duty at all times on their organisation comes under essential category of services.
26. They should be gentle and tactful in all their dealings with others.
27. They should bring the negative elements and saboteurs to work.
28. They should keep contracts with pro-management and right thinking persons in all parts of the organisation so that they could get information of any negative action well in time and timely remedial steps could be taken.
29. Industrial security should have good relations with police and other officers of government machinery.
30. Industrial security should have good relations with neighbouring industries as labour trouble in neighbourhood affects industrial relations in other industries.
31. Industrial security should educate the workmen about the good policies and programmes of their management and hollówness of the slogans and speeches etc. of negative thinking groups.
32. They should provide timely help to the workmen when he is in trouble, *i.e.* providing conveyance to hospital when injured, medicines etc. when sick, right opinion when he is compelled to go into litigation etc.

Provisions for Safety Contained in the Factories Act 1948 and the Coal Mines Regulations 1957

The Factories Act 1948 provides for the following safety measures :

1. That adequate fencing of machinery shall be secured in case of all types of dangerous machinery and its moving parts.
2. The moving machinery shall be kept in a position which provides sufficient safeguard against any accident.
3. That works on or near machinery in motion, *i.e.* examination, lubrication or mounting the belts etc., shall be carried on by a male adult worker wearing tight-fitting clothes and the one who is specially trained for the purpose. Moreover he shall not handle the belt at a moving pulley unless the belt is less than 15 cm in width.
4. All types of floors, stain, and means of access shall be of sound construction and shall be properly maintained.
5. All pits and openings in floor etc. shall be security covered and fenced.
6. All parts of a machine with which a worker is likely to come in contact shall be security fenced.
7. No woman or child shall be allowed in any factory to clean, lubricate or adjust a moving machine or work between moving parts of machine in motion.

8. No young person shall work on dangerous machines unless he has received sufficient training and is under adequate supervision.
9. Devices are provided to cut off power from running machines in emergency.
10. Mechanical appliances are to be provided for driving belts.
11. Safeguards have also been provided against contact with self-acting machines.
12. All new machinery shall be ceased for which the responsibility lies with the manufacturing/selling agents and also on owner.
13. Employment of women and children near cotton openers has been prohibited.
14. No worker shall be required to lift or carry loads which are likely to cause injury to him.
15. Every factory is required to provide fire-extinguishers and various means of escape in case of fire.
16. Every factory is required to provide safe means of access to places of work.
17. Every factory is required to test, examine and maintain in good condition appliances such as hoists, lifts, cranes, chains and pressure plants.
18. Every factory is required to false adequate precautions against dangerous fumes and explosives.
19. Every factory is required to maintain buildings properly against their being detrimental to the health, safety and welfare of the workers.
20. Every factory employing 1000 or more workers is required to appoint safety officer.
21. Every factory is required to report every accident to the Inspector of factories within 24 hours of its occurrence.

83

Industrial Dispute Act, 1947

Introduction

The Industrial Dispute Act has no doubt made a great impact on industrial dispute regulation in the country. The Act provides a comprehensive machinery for settlement of disputes.

The Industrial Dispute Act, 1947 extends to the whole of India and came into force on the first day of April 1947. The act is a progressive piece of legislation and designed to settle dispute on a new pattern, different from the judicial machinery set in the country. The object of Industrial Disputes Act is to provide machinery for just and equitable settlement by adjudication and it substitutes arbitration and negotiation to trial of strength by strikes and lockouts. Industrial Disputes Act provide the machinery and procedure for investigation and settlement of industrial disputes.

After having the experience of working with Trade Disputes Act, 1929 which restrained the rights of strikes and lockout in public utility services but with no provision made to render the proceedings institutable under the Act for the settlement of an industrial dispute. This defect was overcome during the war by introducing number of emergency legislations under the Defence of India Rules for restraining strikes and lockouts. The Central Government empowered Rule 81-A of the Defence of India Rules to refer industrial disputes to adjudication and to enforce their awards. Rule 81-A which was to lapse on 1st October 1946 was being kept in force by the Emergency Power Ordinance 1946 for a further period of six months. After this the Government decided to incorporate most of these emergency labour legislation into a permanent labour laws.

The Industrial Dispute Act provided two important institutions for the prevention and settlement of industrial disputes :

— Works Committees and — Adjudication.

The Act emphasises that industrial peace will be most enduring where it is founded on voluntary settlement such as Works Committees which can render recourse to the remaining machinery for settlement of disputes. Similarly the reference of dispute to an Industrial Tribunal will be where both the parties to the industrial disputes apply for such reference and also where the appropriate Government considers it expedient to do so.

The act also seeks to re-orient the administration of the conciliation machinery provided in the Trade Disputes Act. Conciliation is compulsory in all disputes in public utility services and optional in the case of other industrial establishments.

The industrial disputes may start between an individual worker and the management but when it is sponsored and espoused by Worker's Union, it ceases to be an individual dispute and assumes the character of industrial dispute. But if the cause of the workmen is espoused by a union which has absolutely nothing to do with the establishment from which the workman comes, then it is not an industrial dispute.

Industrial Dispute includes a claim of an employee who has ceased to be a workman. Such a claim can be referred by the Government to an Industrial Tribunal under the Act. The question of reinstatement of workman has been held by the Federal Court of India to be an Industrial dispute. There cannot be a dispute between an employer and an employee as regards the continuance of the business and any reference of the question to an industrial tribunal will be invalid. However, the state has the right to regulate any business and may impose condition in the interest of the general public but state cannot compel an employer to carry on his business. The act does not touch an employer's right to close down his business and therefore it does not deal with the consequences arising out or it. But whether the lockout is justified relates to employment or non-employment of the workmen and therefore, is the subject matter of an industrial dispute. Individual dispute, not supported by the evidence to have been taken by the Union does not come under section (2k) and the reference for adjudication is bad. Where the demand for reinstatement of employees dismissed in service, the reference of such dispute must be competent and valid. Under section 10 of the Act, it is necessary that the disputes referred to a tribunal must have actually arisen between the employer and employees. The reference of industrial disputes covered by prior award between the same parties must be held to be bad in law. The appropriate Government is at liberty under Section 10 to refer the dispute to Industrial Tribunal or other persons. The reference once made by the appropriate government to the Industrial Tribunal for adjudication cannot be amended, modified or cancelled. Under section 10-A of the Act, the State Government may, by order, in writing and for reasons to be stated therein, at any stage transfer any industrial dispute pending before a tribunal constituted by the state government to any other tribunal constituted by the state government for adjudication. The emphasis of the Act has been on the following :

(*i*) To use adjudication machinery only when condition has failed.

(*ii*) To minimise litigation by laying down some provisions for cases of lay off and retrenchment and change in service conditions.

(*iii*) To define legal and illegal strikes.

There has been wide spread criticism of the act on the following grounds :

(*a*) It has hampered the growth of collective bargaining.

(*b*) No provision has been made in the act to discourage the union, to raise the dispute on the same issue on which the employer and recognised union has already entered into an agreement.

(*c*) Compulsory adjudication has encouraged multiplicity of unions.

(*d*) Compulsory adjudication has encouraged outside leaders and political leaders into the unions. Industrial Disputes Act, 1947 replaced the Trade Dispute Act of 1929. An institution of conciliation was created by Government under the Act to provide a standing panel of officers with requisite qualifications and experience in the field of Labour Management Relations so that their free and impartial services could be availed by the employers and employees as and when necessary for prevention and settlement of disputes and for preservation and promotion of healthy relations so essential for maintenance of industrial peace.

Some of the important terms used in the Act are :

Industry

"Industry" means any business, trade, undertaking, manufacturing or calling of employers and includes any calling, service, employment, handicraft or industrial occupation or vocation of workmen.

Industry as defined in Sec. 2(J) of I. Dispute Act and can be explained in D.N. Banerjee *vs.* P.R. Mukherjee as a wide import.

(*a*) Where

(*i*) Systematic activity.

(*ii*) Organised by Co-operation between employer and employee the direct and substantive element is commercial.

(*iii*) for the production and/or distribution of goods and services calculated to satisfy human wants and wishes (not spiritual or religious) but inclusive of material things or services geared to celestial bliss that is making on a large scale, or prasad, there is an industry in that enterprise.

(*b*) Absence of profit motive or gainful objective is irrelevant, be the venture in public, joint, private or other sector.

(*c*) The true focus is functional and the decisive test is the nature of the activity with special emphasis on the employer-employee relations.

(*d*) If the organisation is in a trade or business, it does not cease to be one because of philanthropy animating the undertaking.

Sovereign functions. Sovereign functions strictly understood alone qualify for exemption, not the welfare activities or economic adventures undertaken by Government or statutory bodies. Even in departments discharging sovereign functions, if there are units which are industries and they are substantially severable then they can be considered to come within Sec. 2 (J).*

Charitable Institutions

Charitable institutions fall into three categories :

(*a*) those that yield profit, but profits are siphoned off for pious purposes ;

(*b*) those that make no profit but hire the services of employees as in any other business but the goods and services which are the output are made available at a low cost or no cost to the poor ; and

(*c*) those that are oriented on an human mission fulfilled by men who work not because they are paid wages, but because they share the passion for the cause and desire of job satisfaction.

Among the three charitable institutions mentioned above, first two are industries but not the third on the assumption that they all involve co-operation between employers and employees.

Following institutions are held industry :

(*i*) State Hospital.

State of Bombay *vs.* Hospital Mazdoor Sabha, AIR 1960 SC 610.

---

*Bangalore Water Supply and Sewerage Board *vs.* A. Rajappa (1978) S.C.C. (L & S) 215.

(*ii*) Ayurvedic Pharmacy and Hospital-Lalit Hari Ayurvedic College Pharmacy *vs.* Workers Union, AIR 1960 SC 1261.

(*iii*) Indian Standard Institute, Workmen *vs.* ISI 1976 SCC (L & S) 16.

(*iv*) Co-operative Societies.

(*v*) University and Research Institutions are industries. Bangalore Water Supply and Sewerage Board *vs.* A Rajappa (1978) SCC (L & S) 215.

(*vi*) Federation of Indian Chamber of Commerce. Federation of Indian Chamber of Commerce and Industry *vs.* Workmen (1972) AIR 1972 S.C.763.

(*vii*) Visakhapatnam Dock Labour Board *vs.* Stevedor's Association (1969) 2 S.C.C. 801.

Industry is the partnership of labour and capital. A professional man like a solicitor or a lawyer does an individual work, so a firm of solicitors is not an industry.

Dunderdale *vs.* Mukherjee AIR 1956 Cal. 465.

University is not an industry (University of Delhi *vs.* Ram Nath, etc. 1963 ILLJ 335).

Where a society established for the purpose to satisfy purely spiritual needs and subsequently enlarge its scope and start making profits held that the society is an industry (Madras Pinjrapole *vs.* Workmen).

Hospital run by Government is not an industry (Management of Orissa *vs.* Workmen, AIR 1971 SC 1259).

Industrial Disputes

"Industrial Disputes" means any dispute or difference between employers and employers or between employers and workmen or between workmen and workmen which is connected with the employment or non-employment or their terms of employment or with the conditions of labour of any person.

The definition of Industrial Dispute in Sec. 2(k) of the Act could be divided in three parts :

(*i*) There must be a dispute or difference.

(*ii*) The dispute or difference must between workmen and workmen.

(*iii*) The dispute or difference must be connected with the employment or non-employment or the terms of employment or with the conditions of labour of any person.

The first part deals to the facture of a substantial dispute : the second part to the parties to the dispute and their to the subject matter of that dispute.

The term industrial dispute as defined in Sec. 2(k) of the Industrial Dispute Act, 1947 includes to claim of an employee who has eased to be a workman.

The term individual disputes includes a dispute between a single workman and his employer. Individual disputes espoused by the union becomes an industrial dispute. The only condition for an individual disputes turning into an industrial dispute is the necessity of community of interest and not whether workman was or was not a member of the union at the time of dismissal. Following, held, as industrial disputes :

(*i*) Dispute regarding contract labour. Express Newspapers (P) Ltd. *vs.* Workmen, AIR 1963 SC 569.

(*ii*) Demand for modification of standing orders Shahadra Delhi Shahranpur. Light Railway Co. Ltd. *vs.* S.S. Rly. Workers.

(*iii*) A question of re-instatement of a workman has been held to be an industrial dispute Western India Automobile Association *vs.* The Industrial Tribunal Bombay, FJR 97, Union AIR 1969 SC 513.

(*iv*) Alteration of condition of service of employees of a Cooperative Society.

(*v*) Claim of an employee who has ceased to be a workman. Triangular Motors Ltd., *vs.* Bombay Automobiles Union, 2 FJR 179.

Following, held, did not amount to industrial disputes :

(*i*) Employer's failure to keep his verbal assurance. Express Newspapers (P) Ltd. *vs.* Workmen AIR 1963 SC 569.

(*ii*) Claim for compensation for loss of business, Rohtas Industries Ltd. *vs.* Staff Union (1976), 2 SCC 82.

In the case of Bangalore Water Supply and Sewage Board *vs.* A Rajappa (1978) I. LLJ 349) the Supreme Court Bench has over-rules all its past decisions on the issue. It emphasised that wherever there is an employer-employee relationship, the activity it will be an industry. The true focus is functional and the decisive test according to the court, is the nature of the activity with special emphasis on the employer-employee relation irrespective of any gainful objective.

In the case of Budge Municipality *vs.* P.R. Mukherjee when Mr. Justice Chandrasekhera Aiyar of the Supreme Court was asked to decide whether a municipality was an industry within the meaning of Industrial Dispute Act. In this case two employees of the Municipality who were the Members of the Municipal Workers Union were suspended on the charges of negligence, insubordination and indiscipline. On receiving their explanation which was unsatisfactory, they were dismissed from the service. The Union questioned their dismissed and the matter was referred to Industrial Tribunal for adjudication. The Tribunal awarded that the suspension and punishment of two employees were cases of victimisation and directed their reinstatement in their respective offices. The Management moved to High Court under article 226 of the Constitution of India. The petition was dismissed but leave was granted to appeal to Supreme Court. The Court in this case analysed that Municipality's normal functions include water supply, lighting, maintenance of roads, running educational institutions, maintaining charitable dispensaries etc. A dispute will be an Industrial Dispute if it is between the municipality and its employees engaged in branches of work that can be said to be trade or business. The Court upheld the judgement of the High Court and that of the Industrial Tribunal saying that the dismissed workmen be reinstated because the municipality was an industry.

Workman

"Workman" means any person (including an apprentice) employed in any industry to do any skilled or unskilled manual, supervisory, technical clerical work for hire or reward whether the terms of employment be expressed or implied, and for the purpose of any proceedings under this Act in relation to an Industrial dispute includes any such person who has been dismissed, discharged or whose dismissal, discharge, retrenchment has led to that dispute but does not include any such person :

(*i*) Who is subject to the Army Act XLVI of 1950, Air-Force Act XLV of 1950, Navy Act of 1954.

(*ii*) Who is employed in Police Service.

(*iii*) Who is employed in a managerial or administrative capacity, or who, being employed in supervisory capacity, draws wages exceeding five hundred rupees per mensem or exercised either by the nature of duties attached to the office or by the reasons of power vested in him, functions mainly of managerial in nature.

Test of "WORKMAN" is what the main work assigned to an employee. The designation given to an employee is not conclusive to hiring him within the definition of workman nor he becomes workman, if he does some manual or clerical work as ancillary or incidental to such an employment. The main feature and substance of his employment must be manual or clerical before the definition is attracted under Section 2 (s) of the Act.

Medical Representatives, held are not workman.

May & Baker India Ltd. *vs.* Workman, AIR 1967 SC 678 (1961).

A person employed to play any musical instrument must be held to be a workman.

Barat Brass Band *vs.* the Workman (1959), ILLJ 78.

The designation of employee could not be but what duties he carried be the basis whether he is workman or not, following were held to be workmen.

(*i*) Ex-employees.

(*ii*) Malis employed by mill for looking after the garden attached with officers bungalows in the mill colony. J.K. Cotton Spg. and Wvg. Mills *vs.* Badri Mali, AIR 1964 SC 737 (1963).

(*iii*) Dismissed or discharged workers.

(*iv*) Retrenched workmen, Employees of municipalities.

(*v*) Transport engineers, Sales engineer or representatives, District Sales Representatives.

(*vi*) Manager of a hotel who had to write ledgers, enter cash book etc., Indian Iron and Steel Co. *vs.* Workmen (AIR 1958) SC 130 (1958) ILLJ 260.

(*vii*) Accountants who are merely senior clerks with supervisor ; duties. South India Bank Ltd. *vs.* A.R. Chacko AIR 1964 SC 1522 λ (1964).

(*viii*) Salesmen doing work on fixed pay, not on commission, selling goods, giving cash memos, preparing accounts and writing reports.

(*ix*) A foreman though designated as such, with no power of control or direction.

Conciliation Machinery : Function

The Industrial Relations Machinery was set up under the charge of a Chief Labour Commissioner with head-quarters located in New Delhi. Similar organisations were also set up in different states under the charge of Labour Commissioners. Besides the enforcement of Industrial Disputes Act, 1947 the officers of the Central Industrial Relations Machinery were also made responsible for the enforcement of various other Labour Laws and offer them services to arbitrate in Industrial disputes under the Code of Discipline in Industry. The Field Officers of the Central Industrial Relation Machinery consist of Junior Labour Inspectors, Labour Enforcement Officers, Assistant Labour Commissioners and Regional Labour Commissioner. Our country at present has been divided into seven regions and each region is under the charge of a Regional Labour Commissioner under whom the other officers work. All these officers are under the control of the Chief Labour Commissioner who is assisted in his work at the headquarter by Deputy Chief Labour Commissioner and Assistant Labour Commissioners etc. The set up of the Industrial Relations Machinery in the states is more or less on similar lines. The State Labour Department being in the charge of a Labour Commissioner who is assisted in his work at the Headquarters by Deputy Labour Commissioners and Assistant Labour Commissioner and in the field by Labour Inspectors, Labour Officers, Assistant Labour Commissioners/Conciliation Officers etc.

Conciliation

Conciliation in Industrial Disputes in a process by which the representatives workers and employers are brought together before a third person or body of persons with a view to persuade the parties to come to an agreement, to the satisfaction of both and in the larger interest of industry and community as a whole. It may be regarded as one of the phases of collective bargaining and extensions of the process of mutual negotiations. For this purpose, Conciliation Officers have been appointed by the appropriate Government under the Industrial Dispute Act, 1947 for specified areas or for specified industries in specified areas either permanently or for a limited periods. Their duty is to mediate in and promote settlement of Industrial Disputes. Therefore, conciliation is meditation in an Industrial dispute.

Duties of Conciliation Officers

The Conciliation Officers has a vide discretion and may do all such things as he deems fit in order to bring about an amicable settlement of dispute. In the case of public utility services, wherein a notice of strike or lockout has been given and received by a conciliation Officer he is required to interview immediately the parties concerned. In fact in all such disputes relating to public utility services, the conciliation proceedings are deemed to have commenced from the date on which the notice of strike or lockout is received by him. In other cases of intervention ; he is required to give formal intimation, in writing, to the parties declaring his intention to commence conciliation proceedings with effect from such date as he may specify therein. He may hold a meeting with the representatives of both the parties jointly or with each party separately. A joint meeting saves time and also afford parties an opportunity to face each other and put forward their respective view points and comments about a dispute. Conciliation proceedings are conducted expeditiously and in a manner considered fit by the Conciliation Officer for the discharge of duties imposed on him under the Act. If a settlement of disputes or any of the matters in dispute is arrived at in the course of conciliation proceedings, a report of it is sent by the Conciliation Officer to the appropriate government together with a copy of the memorandum of settlement signed by the parties to the dispute in the form prescribed under the rules. Both, in the case of a settlement and failure to arrive at a settlement, a Conciliation Officer has to submit his report to the Government within 14 days of the commencement of conciliation proceedings or within such shorter period as may be fixed by the Government. This time limit may be extended subject to the approval of the Conciliation Officer if the parties to the dispute agree in writing.

Powers of the Conciliation Officer under the Industrial Act, 1947

To enable the Conciliation Officer to discharge the duties cast upon him under the Act, he has been empowered to enter the premises occupied by any establishment to which the disputes relates, after giving reasonable notice for inspecting the same or any of its works, machinery, appliances or articles. He is also empowered to interrogate any person there in respect of anything situated therein or any matter relevant to the subject matter of conciliation. He can also call for and inspect any document which he has ground for considering relevant in the dispute or to be necessary for the purpose of verifying the implementation of any award of carrying out any other duty imposed on him under the Act.

Board of Conciliation

The Industrial Disputes Act has also provided a Board of Conciliation for promoting settlement of an industrial dispute. The appropriate Government is empowered to constitute a Conciliation Board which consists of a Chairman and two or four other members, in equal number, to represent the parties to the dispute.

Duties of the Board

As soon as a dispute is referred to a Board, it has to endeavour to bring about a settlement of the same and for this purpose, it has to investigate the dispute and all matters affecting the merits and right settlement thereof, for the purpose of inducing the parties to come to a fair and amicable settlement. The procedure followed by the Board in this regard is almost the same as adopted by the Conciliation Officers. The Board is, however, required to submit its report within two months of the date on with the dispute was referred to it or within such shorter period as the appropriate Government may fix in this behalf. The proceedings before Board are to be held in public but the Board may at any stage direct that any witness shall be examined or proceeding shall be held by it in camera.

Failure of Conciliation Proceedings

If no settlement is arrived at in the course of conciliation proceedings, the Conciliation Officer submits a report to the appropriate government together with a copy of the statement of demands submitted by the union. Conciliation Officers in the Central Government endorse a copy of the report also to the parties concerned. Receipt of this report is acknowledged by the parties to the Central Government which marks the end of conciliation proceedings. A conciliation proceeding shall be deemed to have concluded :

(*i*) when a memorandum of settlement is signed by the parties ;

(*ii*) when failure report of the conciliation officer is received by the appropriate Government ;

(*iii*) when a reference is made to an adjudicating authority under Sec. 10.

Proceeding before adjudicating authority and an arbitrator shall be deemed to have commenced on the date of reference of such dispute and shall deemed to have been concluded on the date on which the award becomes enforceable under section 17A.

Voluntary Adjudication

If the parties to an industrial dispute apply in the prescribed manner, whether jointly or separately for a reference of the dispute to adjudication by a Labour Court, Tribunal or National Tribunal, it is obligatory for the appropriate Government to order adjudication accordingly if it is satisfied that the persons applying represent the majority of each party.

Adjudication

Adjudication means settlement of industrial dispute through judicial procedure. The appropriate Government is also empowered to refer any industrial dispute, existing or apprehended, for adjudication to a Labour Court of Industrial Tribunal. The Labour Courts and Industrial Tribunal can be constituted by both the Central and State Government but the National Tribunal can be constituted only by the Central Government. Matters within the jurisdiction of the Labour Court can also be referred by the appropriate Government to an Industrial Tribunal for adjudication. If a dispute is referred to a National Tribunal, no Labour Court or Tribunal will have jurisdiction to adjudicate upon any matter which is under adjudication before the National Tribunal, and any reference is so far as it relates to such a matter pending before a Labour Court or an Industrial Tribunal will be void.

The Labour Courts are to deal with day-to-day matter like the legality of an order passed by an employer under the Standing Orders ; application and interpretation thereof ; discharge/dismissal of workmen including relief for wrongful dismissal or discharge ; withdrawal of any customary concession or privilege ; illegality or otherwise of a strike/lockout etc. as specified in the Second Schedule. Third Schedule covers matters relating to wages, allowances, bonus, gratuity, provident fund, shift working other than, in accordance with standing orders, discipline, rationalisation, retrenchment, closure etc. All these matters are within the jurisdiction of Industrial Tribunals. If a dispute is referred to a National Tribunal, all references to other tribunals become void. The Industrial Tribunal has the power to confer new rights and privileges and create new obligations essential in the interest of Industrial peace.

Labour Court shall deal with following matters in the Second Schedule to Act :

(*i*) The legality of an order passed by an employer under the Standing Orders.
(*ii*) The application and interpretation of Standing Orders.
(*iii*) Discharge or dismissal of workmen including reinstatement.
(*iv*) Withdrawal of any customary concession or privileges.
(*v*) Illegality of a Strike or Lockout.
(*vi*) All matters other than Third Schedule.

Tribunal deals with matter listed in the Third Schedule to the Act. These are :

(*i*) Wages, their mode of payment.
(*ii*) Compensatory allowances.
(*iii*) Hours of work.
(*iv*) Leave with wages and holidays.
(*v*) Bonus, profit sharing, provident fund and gratuity.
(*vi*) Shift working.
(*vii*) Classification of grades.
(*viii*) Rules of discipline.
(*ix*) Rationalisation.
(*x*) Retrenchment of workmen and closure of establishment.
(*xi*) Any other matter that may be prescribed.

National Tribunal shall deal with any subject if the dispute involves any question of national importance or are of such a nature that industrial establishment situated in more than one States are interested in by such disputes. The adjudicatory authorities, shall have the same powers as are vested in a Civil Court under the Code of Civil Procedure 1908, in respect of the following matters, namely :

(*a*) Enforcing the attendance.

(*b*) Compelling the production of documents.

(*c*) Issuing commission for the examination of witness. Every enquiry by Labour Court.

Industrial Tribunals

It consists of one or more members possessing the qualifications required for appointment as a judge of a high court. A dispute can be referred to the Industrial Tribunal when both parties to a dispute and the government agree to it. The Industrial Disputes Act 1947 was amended during the year 1971 with a view to give powers to tribunal to go into the merits of dismissal, discharges and retrenchment. The Industrial Disputes Act aims at regulating industrial relations with a view to promote industrial peace, provide measures for prevention and settlement of industrial disputes. The various provisions of the Act can be classified as :

(*i*) Measures for prevention of industrial disputes.

(*ii*) Machinery for settlement of disputes.

(*iii*) Prohibitions of strikes and lockouts.

The Industrial Disputes Act has been in operation for over 21 years. The act has benefited workmen by providing some reliefs in the form of compensations such as lay off and retrenchment etc. The Act looks more like a social security measures providing protection to workmen against temporary involuntary unemployment. Beside these benefits the Act has not been able to promote industrial peace and harmony by controlling the industrial disputes and mandays lost. Recently National Commission on Labour reviewed the working of this legislation and its machinery for the settlement of disputes. It was observed by the commission that neither employers nor workers were happy with the working of the Act. Commission recommended the following issues :

(*i*) Compulsory registration of trade unions.

(*ii*) Constitution of Industrial Relations Commissions to replace Labour Courts and National Tribunals.

The Central Government in consultation with the State Governments, employees and employer reported that a comprehensive industrial relations legislation will soon be undertaken to remedy the situation.

Compulsory arbitration as a method of settling disputes is resorted to only when all other methods have been tried.

Awards and Settlement

Award means an interim or a final determination of any industrial disputes or of any question relating thereto any Labour Court, Industrial Tribunal or National Tribunal and includes an arbitration award made under section 10-A (2A). A court shall inquire into the matters referred to it and report thereon to the appropriate government ordinarily within a period of six months from the commencement of its inquiry (S. 16), and submit its award to the appropriate Government. An award becomes enforceable on the expiry of 30 days from the date of its publication unless otherwise decided by the appropriate government in relation to an industrial dispute on public grounds affecting national economy or social justice. It is also empowered to reject or modify the award within 90 days from its publication and lay the award with a copy of its order on the very first available opportunity before the appropriate legislature. The award so modified becomes enforceable on the expiry of 15 days from the date on which it is so laid.

An award including an arbitration award under Sec. 10-A shall be binding on ;

(*i*) all parties to the dispute :

(*ii*) all other parties summoned to appear in the proceeding with proper cause ;

(*iii*) employer, his heirs, successors or assignees ; and

(*iv*) all persons employed in the establishment or all persons who subsequently become employed in that establishment.

After the expiry of the award it shall continue to bind the parties until either party bound by the award serves notice and two months passed from the date of notice.

Settlement

As per definition in Sec. 2 (*b*) there are two types of settlement under the Industrial Disputes Act. First settlement arrived at in the course of conciliation proceeding which is commonly known as tripartite settlement. Secondly any written agreement between employer and workmen which has been signed by both the parties and a copy thereof has been sent to the appropriate Government is known as tripartite settlement. Unless this has been sent to the Appropriate Government and signed there it does not get the legal status. Thus all settlement are agreements but all agreements are not settlement.

Settlement arrived at the course of conciliation proceedings under the act shall be binding on all the parties to the industrial dispute. In case of an employer it will bind his heirs, successors or assigns in respect of the establishment to the dispute relates. In case of workmen, it will bind all persons who were employed in the establishment and all persons who are subsequently employed therein. Settlement arrived at in the course of conciliation proceeding has greater force and more extensive coverage than settlement arrived bilaterally.